ORGANIZATIONAL BEHAVIOR

Fifth Edition

A Diagnostic Approach

JUDITH R. GORDON

Carroll School of Management
Boston College

Prentice Hall International, Inc.

Acquisitions Editor: Natalie Anderson
Marketing Manager: Jo-Ann DeLuca
Production Editor: Lynne Breitfeller
Associate Managing Editor: Carol Burgett
Manufacturing Buyer: Vinnie Scelta
Interior Design: Lorraine Castellano
Design Director: Pat Wosczyk
Copy Editor: David George
Proofreader: Maine Proofreading Services
Associate Editor: Lisamarie Brassini
Development Editor: Steve Deitmer
Editorial Assistant: Crissy Statuto
Production Coordinator: David Cotugno

©1996 by Prentice Hall, Inc.
A Simon and Schuster Company
Upper Saddle River, New Jersey 07458

Printed in the United States of America

10 9 8 7 6 5 4 3 2 1

ISBN 0-13-242827-X

Prentice-Hall International (UK) Limited, *London*
Prentice-Hall of Australia Pty. Limited, *Sydney*
Prentice-Hall Canada Inc., *Toronto*
Prentice-Hall Hispanoamericana, S. A., *Mexico*
Prentice-Hall of India Private Limited, *New Delhi*
Prentice-Hall of Japan, Inc., *Tokyo*
Simon & Schuster Asia Pte. Ltd., *Singapore*
Editora Prentice-Hall do Brazil, Ltda., *Rio de Janeiro*
Prentice-Hall, *Upper Saddle River, New Jersey*

*To Steve
and Brian, Laurie, and Michael
With All My Love*

Brief Contents

Part 4 — DIAGNOSING BEHAVIOR AT THE ORGANIZATION LEVEL

CONTENTS

Chapter 3–Managing Work–Force Diversity 70

Chapter 4–Motivating and Rewarding Individuals 112

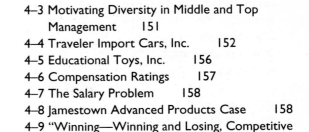

Part 3   DIAGNOSING GROUP BEHAVIOR

Chapter 7–Improving Communication   258

*P*art 4 — DIAGNOSING BEHAVIOR AT THE ORGANIZATIONAL LEVEL

Chapter 13—Structuring Adaptable and Responsive Organizations   562

Chapter 14—Creating Effective Organizational Designs   616

Chapter 15—Changing Organizations for Increased Performance and Competitiveness   662

Preface

All around the world, organizations are remaking themselves as they respond to the challenges presented by the global economy. These exciting changes are reflected throughout this revision, beginning with its title. This edition offers a new face to *A Diagnostic Approach to Organizational Behavior.* Retitled, *Organizational Behavior: A Diagnostic Approach,* the fifth edition has been significantly rewritten to present a fresh appearance, with a strong emphasis on theory, research, and practical applications in organizational behavior. The book includes extensive real-world examples and is intended to help students meet the challenges created by the increasing complexity and globalization of management.

IMPORTANT CONTENT AREAS

The fifth edition incorporates the most current thinking in each area of organizational behavior. Note particularly the inclusion of the following topics:

- total quality management
- learning organizations
- impact of information technology
- reengineering
- horizontal, modular, and virtual organizations
- global competitiveness
- social cognition
- the diverse work force
- family-friendly organizations
- state-of-the-art reward systems
- cognitive biases in decision making
- self-managing teams
- electronic media and communication
- gender-based leadership styles
- the negotiation process
- innovation in organizations

The book offers extensive examples of real-world organizations that have applied the theories and principles presented. Thus, the book attempts to help students understand current organizational practices within the context of organizational theory and empirical research. The book draws from both the current and historical organizational behavior literature. The endnotes document primarily the research and thinking of the last decade but also include classics of organizational behavior.

Besides traditional text materials, this book includes cases and hands-on exercises. This format allows students to apply the theory they learn to real-world and simulated organizational situations. The book is designed for students of organizational behavior at all levels. Undergraduate students, graduate students, and practitioners all can study it to enrich their understanding of human behavior and improve their effectiveness as organizational members.

THE DIAGNOSTIC APPROACH

The fifth edition retains the dual emphasis of previous editions. It focuses on *diagnosis:* describing, understanding, and explaining behavior in organizations. And it considers *action:* controlling, managing, or influencing behavior.

The book continues the fourth edition's emphasis on a strong integration of issues associated with managing in a global economy and leading a multicultural work force. It also considers the ethical responsibilities of organizational members and leaders.

The diagnostic approach encourages the application of diverse conceptual and theoretical frameworks to analyzing an organizational situation. The complexity of organizations and their environments makes it unlikely that any one theory will provide a definitive answer to all questions about how people in organizations act. The equity theory of motivation differs from reinforcement theory. The trait theory of leadership differs from situational theories. Numerous ways of classifying organizational structure—by means of coordination, type of specialization, or sets of alliances, for example—exist. Yet, the various theories can complement each other. Each can provide insight into individual, group, and organizational functioning and lead to more effective managerial behavior. Understanding theories of communication, group development, individual needs, conflict, leadership, and power, among others, improves the understanding of group problem solving. Knowing theories of motivation, learning, and communication helps managers identify issues of work design. Focusing on diverse facets of behavior improves diagnosis and ultimately action. Students are also encouraged to carefully consider the implications of organizations functioning in a multinational and multicultural environment.

The viewpoint of this book assumes that more than one perspective can be right. Thus, understanding an organizational situation requires the ability to analyze it in a number of ways, rather than to assume that any one explanation is adequate. The use of *triangulation,* the taking of a multiperspective viewpoint, to more completely understand a situation and to reinforce the accuracy of the diagnosis is a significant feature of the diagnostic approach. Students are encouraged to utilize triangulation by viewing a situation from a variety of theoretical perspectives as a way of increasing their understanding of behavior and using this enriched understanding to improve action.

The thorough internalization of new theories and concepts for regular use in observing and understanding behavior follows as a result of practice in diagnosis. More effective action can then occur, since more effective action follows more accurate diagnosis. Of course, experienced managers do not try all approaches in each situation. They choose the tools that fit and are helpful. As students become more practiced in using the diagnostic approach, they too become more adept at immediately selecting the appropriate frameworks to apply.

This book presents several processes for practicing diagnosis and action. First, students are asked to analyze a situation using various theoretical perspectives one at a time. Second, they are presented with a complex case study and asked to identify diverse perspectives that help understand the events in the case. They analyze the situation from the various perspectives and ultimately suggest action on the basis of the perspectives. Finally, students are asked to observe their own and others' behavior in organizational simulations, analyze it from diverse perspectives, and consider the implications for action. The book encourages the use of a multifaceted pedagogy, where materials presented in text and activities provide mutual reinforcement and practice in using the diagnostic approach.

ORGANIZATION OF THE BOOK

The book begins with an introductory chapter that describes the diagnostic approach and illustrates it using numerous historical perspectives on organizational behavior. The book next discusses, in Part II, individual behavior. It then moves, in Part III, to an examination of interactions among individuals in group behavior and teamwork, which builds on knowledge of individual behavior and individual interactions. Finally, in Part IV, the book presents organizational issues. This discussion incorporates our knowledge of individuals and groups. Thus the organization of the book reflects a key feature of the diagnostic approach: viewing behavior from an increasing number of different but complementary, more complex but elaborating perspectives.

More specifically, in Part I, Chapter 1 sets the stage by defining the diagnostic approach. The first chapter also details various historical perspectives on behavior in organizations, concluding with a discussion of the contingency perspective that is the foundation of the diagnostic approach.

Chapter 2 begins Part II, which focuses on individual behavior, by describing perception, attribution, and learning. Chapter 3 introduces perspectives related to the diverse work force, including individual personality and career development. Chapter 4 presents various theories of motivation.

Chapter 5, which begins Part III, discusses self-managing teams and group dynamics. Chapter 6 examines decision making. Chapter 7 looks at communication. Chapter 8 explores the impact of leadership on organizational behavior. Chapter 9 considers power and conflict in organizations. Chapter 10 concludes the discussion of group behavior by looking at the process of negotiation and intergroup behavior, thus providing a transition to organizational issues.

In Part IV, large-scale organizational issues are discussed and prescriptions for changing organizations are emphasized. Chapter 11 discusses an organization's culture, and presents Total Quality Management and learning organizations as examples. Chapter 12 investigates work design, technology, and innovation. Chapter 13 describes options for structuring organizations. Chapter 14 examines the factors that influence the choice of design option. Chapter 15 concludes the book with a discussion of organizational change and organizational effectiveness.

The book is designed to be versatile in its use. Each chapter includes a presentation of key theories or concepts regarding a particular topic, and cases and exercises that allow the application of the theoretical perspectives to diverse situations. Each chapter includes a summary of the textual material as well as concluding comments intended to integrate the text with the outcomes of the case discussions and exercises.

SPECIAL FEATURES OF THE FIFTH EDITION

Real-World Examples. Each chapter includes numerous organizational examples in an array of companies, such as IBM, General Motors, Ben & Jerry's Ice Cream, United Parcel Service, and so on. These are highlighted with a special design feature in the text. Reviewing the examples allow students to better understand the application of course theories in real organizations.

Opening Cases. Each chapter begins with a real-world situation that illustrates the major topics presented. The case is integrated into the text and provides a real-world backdrop for discussing theories and concepts.

Cases. These offer the unique advantage of allowing students to experience a real-life situation without leaving the classroom. As in real-life situations, the complexity of the human actions provides a significant challenge to the students' diagnostic skills. We can analyze the behavior that occurs and offer solutions for improving individual, group, and/or organizational effectiveness without suffering the consequences of inaccurate diagnosis or inappropriate recommendations. Students are encouraged first to list the facts of the case. They then identify the key managerial and behavioral issues in the situation. In problem situations they next specify the symptoms that indicate problems exist, as well as describe and show other evidence of the problems in the case. In all situations they then apply relevant theoretical models to diagnose the situation more thoroughly. They conclude by offering a prescription or plan for managerial action, directed at acting effectively or remedying a problem situation.

Video Cases. This edition includes a series of video clips drawn from ABC News programs. The instructor can use these as the basis of class discussion. The text includes an exercise based on each video case.

Exercises. Students can practice responding to situations similar to those they might experience as a member of an organization. The exercises may call for students to make certain decisions, redesign jobs, or plan ways to correct a dysfunctional situation. Students may be asked to participate in roleplays, where they act the part of a character in a work situation. Or they may be asked to complete self-assessment questionnaires or interviews. Also, students may be asked to participate in other activities that encourage the description and diagnosis of their own and others' behavior followed by the prescription and implementation of effective action.

Diagnostic Questions. Each chapter includes a set of diagnostic questions drawn from the theories and concepts presented. These questions can guide students, in their future roles as managers and employees, in applying the material presented to real-world situations.

ACKNOWLEDGMENTS

The development of this book has been influenced by the contributions of many individuals. I would like to thank adopters and reviewers of previous editions of *A Diagnostic Approach to Organizational Behavior.* In addition, I would like to thank the reviewers of this book:

Peggy Anderson–University of Wisconsin–Whitewater, Whitewater, WI

Chandler Atkins–Adirondack Community College, Queensbury, NY

Sharon Clinebell–University of Northern Colorado, Greeley, CO

Barbara Hassell–University of North Texas, Denton, TX

Gary Kustis–Kent State University, Kent, OH

Helen Linkey–Marshall University, Huntington, WV

James McElroy–Iowa State University, Ames, IA

Dale Rude–University of Houston, Houston, TX

Many people at Prentice-Hall have contributed to this revision. I particularly want to thank Natalie Anderson, the acquisitions editor for the book, Lynne Breitfeller, who oversaw the book's production, Nancy Proyect and Lisamarie Brassini, who handled many administrative details. My special thanks go to Developmental Editor, Linda Muterspaugh, for her guidance, support, encouragement, and good spirits during the revision process.

My colleagues at the Carroll School of Management at Boston College have always offered their friendship and their enthusiastic support for my writing efforts: Jean Bartunek, Judith Clair, W.E. Douglas Creed, Dalmar Fisher, Candace Jones, John W. Lewis III, Richard Nielsen, Joseph Raelin, William Stevenson, and William Torbert. I also wish to thank the Dean of the Carroll School of Management, John J. Neuhauser III, for his support.

My deepest thanks go to my family, who cheerfully tolerated the long hours required to write a book with a rapidly approaching deadline. I dedicate this book to them.

Judith R. Gordon

Organizational Behavior

Chapter 1

Chapter Outline

- **Organizational Behavior at General Motors**
- **Organizational Behavior Defined and Studied**
    - **Methods of Data Collection**
    - **Research Methods**
- **An Historical Perspective on Organizational Behavior**
    - **Structural Perspectives**
    - **Behavioral Perspectives**
    - **Integrative Perspectives**
- **Organizational Issues for the Twenty-First Century**
    - **The Global Arena**
    - **Total Quality Management**
    - **Advances in Information Technology**
    - **Ethical Action in Organizations**
    - **Managing a Diverse Work Force**
- **The Diagnostic Approach**
    - **Description**
    - **Diagnosis**
    - **Prescription**
    - **Action**
- **Organization of This Book**
- **Summary**
- **Diagnostic Questions**

Setting the Stage

Organizational Behavior at General Motors

John F. (Jack) Smith, who assumed the chairmanship of General Motors Corporation (GM) in 1992, faced some significant challenges in returning the company to its status as an industrial giant. On assuming his position, Smith was charged with making the company profitable again. He promised to strengthen GM's deteriorating credit rating. To do this, he undertook significant cost-cutting measures.

Smith faced strained labor relations. Continuing plant closings and worker layoffs contributed to tense relationships between the United Automobile Workers (UAW) and GM. Smith tried to improve labor–management relations by developing a positive relationship with Steve Yokich, the head of the UAW at GM, although a strike remained a strong possibility. Although he did not appear to take a tough stance in labor relations, Smith received in exchange for pledging $3.9 billion in jobless benefits the ability to cut 65,000 blue-collar jobs within three years. He spearheaded an early retirement option that removed 16,500 hourly workers from GM's payroll.

Poor productivity also plagued many GM plants. Although Smith accelerated plant closings, he also streamlined decision making by reducing GM's bureaucracy and eliminating committee meetings and reports; instead he created the North American Strategy Board to create policy and make rapid decisions to allow GM to respond quickly to environmental changes. He simplified the company's structure, reduced the corporate-level staff, increased their accessibility, and eliminated the pampering of executives. He created simple goals for workers and management, widened participation, and shared credit for successes.

Smith continued to use the low-key, unobtrusive style that worked well for him in restoring profitability to GM Europe. Although some believed that he should be more visible throughout the organization, Smith continued to steadily make changes that would increase GM's ability to compete in the cutthroat automobile industry. He focused on improving the product development process and pared product offerings. He introduced a team concept in both design and purchasing.

In his first year as CEO, GM had two profitable quarters, but missed production targets in a third. GM also began to experience financial integrity.[1]

How did Jack Smith determine what problems existed at General Motors? How did he decide which changes to make to correct these problems? How did he know that these changes would be effective? Like all managers, Jack Smith faced the traditional challenges—effectiveness versus efficiency, cost versus quality, satisfaction versus productivity. But he also faced some new challenges and opportunities: how to manage in a global environment, how to meet customer needs in a rapidly changing environment, how to deal with an increasingly educated work force, and how to ensure ethical action in organizations, among others.

In this book, we will show you how the study of organizational behavior can help you deal with both types of management challenges. In the first chapter, we begin by looking at how organizational behavior is defined and studied. Then we examine the historical perspectives on organizational behavior. Next we look at organizational issues for the twenty-first century. We then show how the diagnostic approach will help you handle these issues and manage more effectively in the twenty-first century. We conclude the chapter with a presentation of the plan of this book.

ORGANIZATIONAL BEHAVIOR DEFINED AND STUDIED

Knowledge from the field of *organizational behavior (OB),* among others, helped Jack Smith identify problems, determine ways of correcting them, and know whether the changes would work. Such knowledge can help members of organizations to better understand situations they face in the workplace and to find ways to change their behaviors to improve performance and increase the organization's effectiveness.

We can define *organizational behavior* as the actions and attitudes of people in organizations. The *field of organizational behavior* is the body of knowledge derived from the study of these actions and attitudes. It has its roots in the social science disciplines of psychology, sociology, anthropology, economics, and political science.

As a field of study, organizational behavior includes a collection of separate theories and models, ways of thinking about particular phenomena. These diverse perspectives together contribute to the understanding of specific, concrete events such as those faced by Jack Smith at GM and others in organizations. Organizational behavior offers the chance to understand some of the *complexity* of organizations and of organizational dilemmas and situations; it supports an understanding that most organizational problems have several causes.

The study of organizational behavior once focused on local events, and then extended to regional and national concerns. Now, it considers the factors that contribute to or hinder effective performance in the global arena. Recognizing that significant differences exist between national and multinational organizations, as well as those organizations that function totally outside the United States, is important for diagnosing the causes of functional and dysfunctional behaviors. The more fully we understand all the reasons for specific organizational events or problems, the more we can respond appropriately to them. The better Jack Smith understands the reasons for General Motors' performance problems, the more easily he can determine appropriate action for improving the situation. Organizational behavior principles play an essential role in assessing and increasing organizational effectiveness, which is a central responsibility and focus for all managers.

METHODS OF DATA COLLECTION

Managers and other organizational members begin to understand organizational behavior by describing events, behaviors, and attitudes. How can they obtain high-quality information for use in such descriptions? Managers and organizational researchers primarily use four methods for collecting data about situations they face or analyze: direct observation, questionnaires, interviews, and written documents. Each of these methods helps us to report events, not to diagnose their causes or effects. Together these methods help us validate our perceptions of the events, behaviors, and attitudes, as described in greater detail in Chapter 2.

Direct Observation When as managers or organizational researchers we use direct observation, we describe concrete events that we see. We might, for example, spend some time attending meetings between Jack Smith and his managers and then describe what we saw happening, such as who talks most often, what topics they discuss, or how frequently Jack asks for the managers' views on a subject. We can construct formal instruments to use in collecting and tabulating our observations or we can rely on more informal commentaries. For example, we can watch the actions of company employees as they wait for an elevator, sit in the company lounge, or meet in the hallways. We can listen to their conversations and thereby learn their expressed attitudes toward their supervisor, job, or organization.

Questionnaires Rather than relying on our view of events, we can write questions designed to elicit organization members' opinions. We might develop a questionnaire that we distribute to all employees of General Motors to help determine their attitudes toward their job and their supervisor. Analyzing the responses to such a questionnaire might help explain their dissatisfaction or low morale. Repeated administration of such a questionnaire might indicate changes over time in their attitude toward the organization. Note that the administration of questionnaires is quite common in the United States, but is less frequently used in other countries.

Interviews We could also ask organization members a series of questions in person to explore in depth their attitudes and opinions. Managers often *interview* employees informally, chatting with them about their views of a particular situation. We might, for example, interview several department heads at GM to discuss their experiences since the change in leadership. We might interview Jack Smith to learn his rationale for changing the organization's structure. We would then describe their experiences and attitudes as part of the first step in the Diagnostic Approach.

Written Documents Finally, we could gather data about past performance, work team behavior, or other aspects of individual, group, and organizational functioning from the firm's records, including annual reports, departmental evaluations, memoranda, or nonconfidential personnel files. Then we could analyze the content of these documents. A review of records, such as all internal memoranda or performance reviews, might further specify the nature of communication, the quality of supervision, or other possible reasons for the situation at General Motors.

RESEARCH METHODS

Organizational researchers and occasionally other organizational members use systematic research methods to determine the *causes* of events, behaviors, or attitudes.[2] Laboratory experiments, field studies, or even simulations (often computerized) of organizational situations can assist in the diagnosis of the causes of certain behaviors and attitudes.

Researchers select a research design that helps them determine the relationship between two variables as conclusively as possible. A *variable* is the representation of a behavior, attitude, or event under study; for example, a leader's style might be a variable studied. A variable may be measurable and observable, such as turnover, absenteeism, or sales, or inferred by measuring it indirectly, such as by examining indicators of morale, commitment, or motivation. The researcher may offer a *hypothesis,* or a proposed explanation of the relationship between a *dependent variable*—the event, behavior, or attitude the researcher is trying to explain—and an *independent variable*—the event, behavior, or attitude that the researcher believes affects the dependent variable. For example, a researcher may hypothesize that giving workers more responsibility and autonomy in their jobs (the independent variable) increases worker satisfaction (the dependent variable). Researchers may hypothesize either an association (or correlation) between variables or a cause-and-effect relationship, although causality is generally more difficult to prove.

Laboratory Experiments In laboratory experiments, researchers choose a phenomenon to study, such as obedience to authority, risk-taking in decision making, or conflict in negotiations. They attempt to control all extraneous stimuli so that they can pinpoint the cause of certain behaviors. Although such studies do not capture the complexity of organizational life, a set of these studies about a particular topic considered together may explain behavior outside the laboratory. No single laboratory study could show, for example, that risk behavior is caused by the interaction of an individual's personality, characteristics of the organization, and pressures exerted by group membership. Considering the results of all laboratory studies about risk behavior together, however, might provide a more complete explanation of the phenomenon. In addition, the rigorous controls imposed to identify the "real cause" of the observed phenomenon often result in laboratory behavior that differs from the behavior obtained in real organizational situations. The type of risk individuals take in spending money in a laboratory may differ significantly from the risk they take when their own or their employer's resources are at stake.

Field Studies To study behavior in more realistic settings and as it occurs naturally, researchers conduct field studies.[3] This approach differs from laboratory studies in the amount of control exerted over the behavior and the circumstances in which the behavior occurs. Here many factors can explain an observed phenomenon. Lowered performance might be attributed to changes in incentives, the personality of the subject, new organizational policies, or merely the weather. Thus, researchers can be more certain that they are obtaining "true" behavior but less certain of the correct explanations of the behavior or attitudes observed. Because field studies acknowledge the complexity of real-life situations, organizational researchers are increasingly relying on this approach, rather than on more controlled laboratory testing.

Simulations Organizational simulations attempt to combine the advantages of laboratory and field studies. An organizational simulation is a computerized or noncomputerized facsimile of an organization that allows researchers to simultaneously study and control complex behavior. It prescribes the rules and regulations of the organization, specifies the actions and interactions of organization members, and defines the impact of various inputs and processes on the organization's functioning. Researchers manipulate the behavior or attitudes being studied as well as the circumstances in which they occur by providing diverse inputs and examining their effects. The challenge is modeling affective and behavioral responses, such as worker satisfaction and productivity, as accurately as organizational outcomes such as return on investment or market share. Because of the artificiality involved in manipulating the factors being studied, some argue that this research approach lacks realism and thus yields results of limited use. Using this method in conjunction with the other two may overcome some of its limitations. You will have the opportunity to participate in numerous organizational simulations, in which you experience real-life organizational behavior in a classroom setting, when you perform the activities in this book.

AN HISTORICAL PERSPECTIVE ON ORGANIZATIONAL BEHAVIOR

Although the challenge of management has remained the same over time in many regards, the field of OB has looked at it in many different ways. These earlier viewpoints and schools of thought still have some relevance for managers today. Tracing the history of organizational behavior provides a context for understanding the evolution of organizational behavior and effective management. By using these historical perspectives concurrently we can enrich our understanding of organizational situations since they both provide a backdrop for the development of current organizational thought and remain current and relevant to organizational diagnosis today. In the next section we briefly recount the history of organizational theory by presenting selected representative perspectives, as shown in the time line of Table 1–1.

STRUCTURAL PERSPECTIVES

The earliest theorists focused on the structuring and design of work and organizations. Organizational theory prior to 1900, scientific management, classical theory, bureaucracy, and decision theory each addressed issues of structure in the organization.

Organizational Theory Prior to 1900 Very little formal management or organizational theorizing occurred prior to 1900. The military, the Catholic Church, and European governments acted as the basic models of effective organizations because few industrial organizations of the types we know today existed. As the factory system developed in the late nineteenth century it created strong demands for theories of management.

Early economists such as Adam Smith provided the underpinnings of management theory and laid the foundation for later theories about the structure of organizations and work. Smith included a chapter on the division of labor in his eighteenth-century book, *An Inquiry into the Nature and Cause of the Wealth of Nations,* which laid the groundwork for the later introduction of assembly-line processes.[4] In this chapter Smith spoke approvingly of a pin manufacturer that divided the work into a number of "branches," causing the separation of pin making into eighteen different operations. His book assumed that most workers held relatively low-skilled jobs, rather than being artisans who could complete an entire project. The separation of operations radically increased the quantity of pins manufactured in a day, since this separation required the workers to concentrate on a single task. Smith also emphasized the importance of proper machinery to facilitate labor.

Scientific Management The theorizing of Frederick W. Taylor, a foreman at the Bethlehem Steel Works in Bethlehem, Pennsylvania, helped management emerge as a field of study in the early twentieth century. Taylor's observations about industrial efficiency and *scientific management* offered prescriptions for the effective structure of organizations and design of management activities in manufacturing organizations, which had become more common after 1900. He described management as a *science,* with managers and employees having clearly specified yet different responsibilities, and characterized them as follows:

TABLE 1–1 *Historical schools of thought and their components (by decade)*

SCHOOL	DECADE	PERSPECTIVE	DESCRIPTION
Organizational theory prior to 1900	Before 1900	Structural	Emphasized the division of labor and the importance of machinery to facilitate labor
Scientific management	1910s	Structural	Described management as a science, with employees having specific but different responsibilities; encouraged the scientific selection, training, and development of workers and the equal division of work between workers and management
Classical school	1920s	Structural	Listed the duties of a manager as planning, organizing, commanding employees, coordinating activities, and controlling performance; basic principles called for specialization of work, unity of command, scalar chain of command, and coordination of activities
Bureaucracy	1920s	Structural	Emphasized order, system, rationality, uniformity, and consistency in management; these attributes led to equitable treatment for all employees by management
Human relations	1920s	Behavioral	Focused on the importance of the attitudes and feelings of workers; informal roles and norms influenced performance
Classical school revisited	1930s	Structural	Reemphasis on the classical principles described above
Group dynamics	1940s	Behavioral	Encouraged individual participation in decision making; noted the impact of the work group on performance
Leadership	1950s	Behavioral	Stressed the importance of groups having both social and task leaders; differentiated between Theory X and Theory Y management
Decision making	1950s	Behavioral	Suggested that individuals "satisfice" when they make decisions
Sociotechnical school	1960s	Integrative	Called for considering technology and work groups when understanding a work system
Systems theory	1960s	Integrative	Represented an organization as an open system with inputs, transformations, output, and feedback; systems strive for equilibrium and experience equifinality
Contingency theory	1980s	Integrative	Emphasized the fit between organizational processes and characteristics of the situation; called for fitting the organization's structure to various contingencies

- Managers develop a science for each element of a man's work, which replaces the old rule of thumb method.

- Managers scientifically select and then train, teach, and develop the worker, whereas in the past he chose his own work and trained himself as best he could.

- Managers heartily cooperate with the men so as to insure all of the work being done in accordance with the principles of the science which has been developed.

■ There is almost equal division of the work and the responsibility between the management and the workers. The management takes over all the work for which they are better fitted than the workers, while in the past almost all of the work and the greater part of the responsibility were thrown upon the men.[5]

Taylor's principles applied best to increasing productivity on a relatively simple task. He showed that a pig-iron handler, who formerly loaded 12½ tons per day, loaded 47½ tons after application of the principles of scientific management.[6] Imagine, if you can, someone shoveling iron ore into a furnace. An observer, the equivalent of a modern-day industrial engineer, times how long it takes a worker to pick up a shovel, move it and the ore into a car; drop off the ore, and then prime the shovel for the next load. At the same time another observer records the precise physical movements the worker made, such as whether he picked up the shovel with his right hand or his left (no women handled iron ore at the Bethlehem Steel Works), whether he switched hands before moving it, how far apart he placed his feet, and so on. Taylor used these data to help determine the physical positions that led to the fastest time for shoveling ore, and developed the *science* of shoveling.

Classical School Henri Fayol, a French manager who wrote at about the same time as Taylor but did not have his works translated into English until 1949, influenced organizational behavior, but from outside the country. Fayol's comments, which listed the duties of a manager as planning, organizing, commanding employees, coordinating activities, and controlling performance, typified the *classical* view of administration, as specified in the fourteen principles of management shown in Figure 1–1.[7]

Organizational theories used these structural elements and principles to identify four features of organizations.[8]

1. *Specialization.* Organizations arrange workers according to logical groupings, such as client, place of work, product, expertise, or functional area. General Motors, for example, groups workers for the same make of car (e.g., Pontiac, Chevrolet, Cadillac) into a single division.

2. *Unity of command.* Each organizational member has exactly one direct supervisor; Jack Smith supervises the presidents of the five car divisions and the regional General Motors operations. These presidents in turn supervise vice presidents in their division.

3. *Scalar chain of command.* The formal organizational structure begins with the chief executive and extends to the least skilled employee and delineates the reporting relationships in the organization. The scalar chain of command at General Motors begins with Jack Smith, continues through the heads of the various product divisions, to managers, and ultimately to nonmanagerial employees.

4. *Coordination of activities.* Managers use mechanisms that ensure communication among specialized groups. This seems to occur formally through written directives and other corporate policies at General Motors.

Bureaucracy Max Weber, a German sociologist, illustrated the international influence on management in his discussion of organizational administration.[9] Although his principles were well known in the United States through spokespersons and interpreters, his writings were not translated into English until the 1940s.[10] Weber studied European organizations in the first part of the twentieth century and de-

FIGURE 1–1

Fayol's fourteen principles of management

1. Division of work—the specialization of work

2. Authority—"the right to give orders, and power to exact obedience"

3. Discipline—"obedience, application, energy, behavior, and outward marks of respect"

4. Unity of command—"an employee should receive orders from one superior only"

5. Unity of direction—"one head and one plan for a group of activities having the same objective"

6. Subordination of individual interests to the general interest—the interest of an individual or group should not supersede the organization's concerns

7. Remuneration—fair payment for services

8. Centralization—degree of consolidation of management functions

9. Scalar chain (line of authority)—"the chain of superiors ranging from the ultimate authority to the lower ranks"

10. Order—all materials and people should be in an appointed place

11. Equity—equality of (although not necessarily identical) treatment

12. Stability of tenure of personnel—limited turnover of personnel

13. Initiative—"thinking out a plan and ensuring its success"

14. *Esprit de corps*—"harmony, union among the personnel of a concern"

SOURCE: Adapted and excerpted from H. Fayol, *General and Industrial Management*, trans. C. Storrs (London: Pitman, 1949).

scribed a **bureaucracy,** which he considered to be a prototype form of organization. Although bureaucracy conjures up an image of massive red tape and endless unneeded details for many people, Weber, in contrast, saw its emphasis on order, system, rationality, uniformity, and consistency as the major asset of bureaucracy. He believed that these attributes resulted in equitable treatment for all employees by management, rather than whimsical or arbitrary application of rules to benefit favorites, with the resulting loss of motivation among nonfavorites.

Figure 1–2 summarizes Weber's principles of bureaucracy, which offered prescriptions for the best structure of an organization. Each employee in a bureaucracy has specified and official areas of responsibility that are assigned on the basis of competence and expertise. Not only do rules and regulations exist, but these are translated into detailed employment manuals; hence managers use written documents extensively in managing employees. Managers of offices, departments, or other groups of workers receive extensive training in their job requirements. They are expected to use rules that are consistent and complete and that can be learned.

BEHAVIORAL PERSPECTIVES

Whereas the scientific management, classical, and bureaucratic perspectives emphasize issues with the structure and design of organizations, they do not consider worker dissatisfaction, dysfunctional leadership, or ineffective interpersonal com-

FIGURE 1–2   *Weber's principles of bureaucracy*

■ Specified and official areas of responsibility based on knowledge

■ Orderly system of supervision and subordination

■ Unity of command

■ Extensive use of written documents

■ Extensive training in job requirements

■ Application of consistent and complete rules

SOURCE: Based on M. Weber, *Essays on Sociology*, trans. and ed. H.H. Gerth and C.W. Mills (New York: Oxford University Press, 1946).

munication, among other behaviors of workers and managers. The human relations, group dynamics, decision theory, and leadership schools explicitly considered this *human* side of organizations.

Human Relations School The Western Electric Company, in conjunction with the National Academy of Sciences, performed five studies of various work groups at Western Electric's Hawthorne plant beginning in 1924.[11] The first study looked at the effects of lighting on the productivity of workers in different departments of the company. In the tradition of scientific management, it considered whether certain illumination levels affected output positively or adversely. Essentially, the researchers first increased the lighting to an extreme brightness and then decreased the light until the work area was so dim that assembly material could hardly be seen. Do you think employee output increased, decreased, or remained at normal levels? Surprising to the researchers, the workers maintained or even exceeded their normal output whether researchers increased or decreased illumination.

Subsequent studies attempted to explain these results by introducing a variety of changes in the workplace.[12] The researchers examined the impact of rest pauses, shorter working days and weeks, wage incentives, and the nature of supervision on output. They also suggested that something other than the physical work environment (which scientific management would have suggested) or the organizational structure (which classical principles would have suggested) resulted in improved productivity among workers. In observing and interviewing the employees, the researchers discovered that during the experiments the employees felt that someone paid attention to them, so their morale improved and they produced more. This so-called *Hawthorne effect* offered the first dramatic indication that the attitudes and feelings of workers could significantly influence productivity.

Consequently, Western Electric instituted a program where interviewers questioned workers regarding their feelings about work. The interviewing program suggested even more strongly the close relationship between morale and the quality of supervision, and resulted in the creation of a new training program for supervisors. In the final experiments of the Hawthorne series, the researchers identified one other human feature of organizations: the informal groups that workers develop among themselves, as discussed in detail in Chapter 5.

Group Dynamics Later in the century—during World War II— Kurt Lewin, a social psychologist at the University of Iowa, studied methods of changing housewives' food habits away from meat consumption, since there was a shortage of meat.[13] He believed families, parents, and other housewives expected the housewives not to serve other kinds of food, which created a significant barrier to change. He and his associates conducted experiments that showed that participation in decision making broke down these barriers: housewives who joined in group discussions were ten times more likely to change their food habits than were housewives who received lectures on the subject.[14]

Lewin's associates later extended these experiments to industrial settings. For example, Lester Coch and John R.P. French found that employees at the Harwood pajama plant in Marion, Virginia, were much more likely to learn new work methods if they had the opportunity to discuss the methods and have some influence on how to apply them in their jobs.[15] Studies such as these led to a greatly expanded awareness of the impact of the work group and spawned research on the relationship between organizational effectiveness and group formation, development, behavior, and attitudes.[16]

Decision Theory Herbert Simon and James March introduced a different decision-making framework for understanding organizational behavior in the 1950s.[17] They elaborated on the bureaucratic model by emphasizing that individuals work in rational organizations and thus behave rationally. But they also added a new dimension to their model (which eventually won Simon the Nobel Prize for economics): they proposed that a human being's rationality is limited. Unlike the more rigid classical assumptions of rationality in decision making, this model suggested that individuals examine a limited set of possible alternatives rather than all available options when making decisions. Individuals *satisfice;* that is, they accept satisfactory or "good enough" choices, rather than insist on optimal choices.

Leadership The 1950s saw the beginning of concentrated research in the area of leadership. One series of studies described groups as having both task and social leaders.[18] The task leader helped the group achieve its goals by clarifying and summarizing member comments and focusing on the group's tasks. The social leader maintained the group and helped it develop cohesiveness and collaboration by encouraging group members' involvement.

A second classification distinguished between Theory X and Theory Y managers.[19] Those who believe Theory X assume that workers have an inherent dislike of work, that they must be controlled and threatened with punishment if they are to put forth adequate effort, and that they prefer to avoid responsibility. Managers who believe Theory Y, on the other hand, assume that people feel work is as natural as play or rest, that people will exercise self-direction toward the objectives to which they are committed (so they do not need strict control), and that the average human being can learn to seek responsibility. These assumptions that managers hold, then, affect the way they treat their employees and also affect the employees' productivity.

INTEGRATIVE PERSPECTIVES

Rather than focusing primarily on either structure or the human side of organizations, organizational thought in the past few decades has emphasized the integration of these two perspectives, along with more specific consideration of environmental and other external influences. More recently, contingency theory has accented the fit between managerial and organizational features of a specific work situation. The contingency perspective provides the foundation of the diagnostic approach presented in this book: effective diagnosis is situational in nature.

Sociotechnical School Several theorists in the 1950s studied technology, rather than either structure or behavior. They viewed technology as influencing structure and interacting with work groups, thereby incorporating both the structural and human perspectives into their theorizing. Trist and Bamforth, two members of the sociotechnical school, described the impact of a change in technology in a British coal mine.[20] Workers in the British mine functioned independently in small self-contained units, in which they organized the work themselves. Improvements in the technology for mining coal, however, required management to increase job specialization and decrease the workers' participation in job assignments. This greater job specialization, which followed from the scientific management and classical management traditions, was expected to increase productivity. But the coal miners hated the specialization. They much preferred working with each other and performing a variety of tasks.

Trist and Bamforth compared the performance of work groups with specialized jobs to work groups that retained the same pattern of social interactions when the new technology was introduced. They found that absenteeism in the specialized groups was several times greater and productivity much lower than in the groups that had maintained their original interrelationships. After a number of studies such as these, the sociotechnical systems researchers concluded that technological changes must be made in conjunction with a strong social system: that both social and technical/structural aspects of jobs must be considered simultaneously.

Systems Theory The general systems model, with roots in both the behavioral and natural sciences, represents an organization as an open system, one that interacts with environmental forces and factors, akin to physical systems such as the human body, a microscopic organism, or a cell.[21] According to this view, the organization as a system has these characteristics:

- **Every system is made up of a number of interrelated, interdependent, and interacting subsystems.** General Motors is an organizational system, as is each department, individual worker, and manager. Each subsystem can be considered a system, also composed of other subsystems. Consider, for example, the way a work team writing new computer software and the team who will provide customer support for the product are interdependent and interrelated. Interactions between such subsystems contribute to the complexity of organizations and make effective diagnosis and action more challenging.

- **Every system is open and dynamic.** The system continually interacts with the surrounding environment. It constantly receives new energy, called *inputs,* in the form of new resources (people, materials, and money), goals, or information from the environment.

- **Every system transforms inputs into outputs.** For example, in manufacturing a CD player, metal pieces (inputs) are combined (transformed) in a way to produce a functioning unit (outputs). Less tangible inputs, such as worker knowledge or information, are similarly transformed through processes such as decision making, leadership, or motivation, into outputs such as performance, satisfaction, turnover, or absenteeism.

- **Every system seeks to maintain equilibrium.** Organizations that receive new inputs or experience transformations seek stability. When they become unbalanced, such as when changes in the environment or organizational practices make current resources inadequate, the organizations attempt to return to the original or a different steady state. They use information about their outputs, called *feedback,* to modify their inputs or transformations to result in more desirable outcomes and equilibrium, as shown in Figure 1–3. Jack Smith might use feedback from dissatisfied customers to call for modifications in GM's product design.

- **Every system has multiple purposes, objectives, and functions, some of which are in conflict.** Various parts of an organization, for example, different departments, work groups, or even managers, may have different and even conflicting purposes, functions, and objectives. The marketing department might willingly make changes in product specifications to satisfy the customer, whereas production might want more stable specifications so it can ensure high-quality products at an acceptable cost.

- **Every system demonstrates equifinality.** Organizations may employ a variety of means to achieve their desired objectives. No single structure or other transformation processes results in a predetermined set of inputs, outputs, and transformations. For example, Burger King Restaurants achieves its objectives of growth and profitability by employing a highly specialized system for producing its product. A small, neighborhood restaurant, on the other hand, might employ a more flexible and adaptive operation to achieve the same objective.

- **If a system does not adapt to changing circumstances, it will experience entropy.** Failing to make appropriate changes in a system in response to new inputs will eventually result in the system's decay and demise.

Contingency Theory Like systems theory, contingency theory provides a more comprehensive view of behavior. It also calls for a *fit* between organizational processes and characteristics of the situation. Early contingency research looked at the fit between an organization's structure and its environment. One early study prescribed a mechanistic structure—a machinelike, bureaucratic structure with an emphasis on a rigid hierarchy and chain of command, as the best structure for organizations functioning in a stable environment. The same study prescribed an organic structure—a more flexible, less bureaucratic, less hierarchical structure—for organizations operating in a dynamic environment.[22]

FIGURE 1–3   *The systems model of feedback*

Other research found that the type of structure the organization develops (and should develop) is influenced by the organization's technology: whether the technology focuses on producing a single unit in its entirety, mass producing products using an assembly line, or creating products from a continuous process, such as oil from a refinery.[23] A mechanistic type of organization fits best with a mass production technology (for example, manufacturing heavy equipment or processing insurance claims); a more organic form of organization responds best to a unit technology (manufacturing *objets d'art* or writing novels) or continuous-process technology (e.g., producing chemicals).

Recent thinking in organization design has reemphasized the importance for organizational effectiveness of fitting organizational structure to various contingencies.[24] Contingency theory has also extended to leadership, group dynamics, power relations, and work design, as described later in this book. Its basic premise of fitting behavior to the situation underlies the diagnostic approach described in this book.

ORGANIZATIONAL ISSUES FOR THE TWENTY-FIRST CENTURY

Will organizational theorists and practitioners continue to focus on the integration of structure and behavior in thinking about organizational functioning? More particularly, what issues will managers face in the twenty-first century? Increasingly, managers function in a dynamic and unpredictable environment; even well-managed companies can fail as a result of unexpected events or a few bad decisions. Although managing effectively involves risk-taking, meeting significant challenges, and even professional dangers, good managers can increase the likelihood of their company's success. Excellent managers can attain major breakthroughs in their group's, department's, division's, or organization's performance. Increasingly, managers and other workers are seeking new and innovative ways of working together to respond to the issues they face:

- Managers operate in a global arena and must meet the challenges of global competitiveness.

- Total quality management has combined concerns for quality, productivity, and meeting customer needs.

- Advances in information technology have significant consequences for organizing and managing.

- Concern for ethics in business dealings has received renewed attention.

- Access to the most skilled of the diverse work force allows organizations to better meet competitive pressures.

THE GLOBAL ARENA

Managers now and in the future will function in a global marketplace, where organizations deal within and across national boundaries. Continuous change in economic circumstances, rapidly accelerating technological advances, and dramatic upheavals in the political arena present hurdles to conducting business globally.

The automobile industry illustrates the extent to which global competitiveness has affected organizations in the United States. In the 1980s, while American automobile manufacturers assumed that Americans still wanted large, gas-guzzling, luxury cars, Japanese auto manufacturers made significant inroads into the U.S. market by offering small, highly efficient, well-designed compact cars, their introduction timed serendipitously with a major oil shortage.

Managers require more open thinking about where operations will be located and who will staff those operations to take greatest advantage of lower labor costs outside the United States. The availability of lower-cost labor outside the United States has caused organizations to close manufacturing facilities here and seek low-cost choices abroad.

REEBOK, INC. AND NIKE. Reebok, Inc. and Nike, for example, major manufacturers of footwear, subcontract all manufacturing, primarily to companies in Asia.[25]

Companies also need to question their old assumptions about how individuals in different geographical locations work together, or how customers' preferences may vary in different countries.

OKIDATA. John Ring, a manager with Okidata, was innovative in getting people to work together in new ways. He motivated six divisions on three different continents over whom he had no formal authority to pool their technologies and resources on a common product; he even overcame resistance to reducing the product size by creating a prototype in a neighborhood garage. Doc-it, which combines a desktop printer, fax, scanner, and copier, was named product of the month in September, 1992 by an industry consulting group.[26]

TOTAL QUALITY MANAGEMENT

Increased competition from abroad required U.S. companies to reexamine the quality of their goods and services. Large numbers of defects, complaints from customers about outdated products, and declining productivity caused U.S. manufacturers to seek new solutions to the competitiveness problem. The 1980s saw the development of a comprehensive approach to improving quality and increasing productivity known as *total quality management (TQM).* Companies such as Xerox, Motorola, Inc., E.I. DuPont de Nemours, Aluminum Company of America, and NRC introduced broad-based, system-wide programs to address these concerns.[27] TQM programs often involved giving workers more responsibility for making decisions, changing the way work was performed, and introducing statistical techniques for monitoring the cost of quality. Managers introduced changes in the manufacturing process or delivery of services that encouraged continuous improvement. Using teams of workers, flexible organization structures, and management control and management information systems helped increase quality.

MOTOROLA. The company's yearly quality competition, called the Total Customer Satisfaction Team Competition, calls for employee teams to share their experiences and present their successes in improving the quality of the company's activities and products. For example, one team's modifications of robotic equipment and product testing procedures for manufacturing Bravo pagers increased production by 50 percent and saved $4.2 million in new equipment costs and $100,000 a month in operating expenses.[28]

ADVANCES IN INFORMATION TECHNOLOGY

Significant advances in information technology, including both computer software and hardware, have reshaped the work place. Now, for example, individuals can do their work from remote locations, allowing them more flexibility in meeting work versus nonwork demands. The ability of organizations to share large quantities of information electronically has resulted in significant restructurings that likely will continue into the next century. Organizations have **reengineered** their work processes, beginning virtually at ground zero and reconstructing tasks and their interactions in an optimal fashion. The **virtual corporation,** in which individuals or even subsidiaries are connected only through computer terminals, has become a reality.

Companies that have downsized as a response to the availability of information technology for performing tasks previously done by individual workers may find that they will need to deal with insufficient staff, employee burnout, and lowered productivity in the next decade. The challenge remains for managers to be well informed about technological advances so they can choose appropriate information technology for performing work and accomplishing organizational goals.

CALYX AND COROLLA. This mail order flower business promises to deliver fresh flowers the day after cutting because they are shipped directly from the grower. When a customer places an order with Calyx and Corolla, its information system transmits the order directly to one of its 25 suppliers. These flower growers are electronically tied into Calyx and Corolla's order and delivery system, which automatically prints the order, including a card and message, shipping label, and Federal Express airbill. Suppliers can even reduce the price of overstocked flowers by entering a new price into the system, which immediately displays it for the customer service representatives at Calyx and Corolla.[29]

ETHICAL ACTION IN ORGANIZATIONS

Legal requirements mandate certain types of ethical behavior. More importantly, citizens generally agree that organizations have a social responsibility to help sustain a high quality of life.

UNION CARBIDE. In 1984, a chemical explosion at a Union Carbide plant outside Bhopal, India, killed 3,800.[30]

EXXON. In 1989, the oil tanker Exxon Valdez ran aground off Prince William Sound, Alaska, spoiling pristine beaches and killing thousands of plants and wildlife.[31]

DREXEL. In 1990, Michael Milken was indicted for insider trading.[32]

Each instance served to remind us that organizations need to consider ethics, since their actions can affect so many people and have significant costs for society.

The challenge of doing business internationally complicates the notion of ethical action. Cultural differences in the meaning of "bribery," for example, highlight problems in setting ethical standards. The variety of standards espoused by international law further reflects the complexity of the ethical arena.

MANAGING A DIVERSE WORK FORCE

The Civil Rights movement in the United States and equal employment laws passed in the 1960s and 1970s have contributed to changing the composition of the work force. Recent predictions suggest that by the turn of the century, 33 percent of Americans will be nonwhite and more than 33 percent will be 65 or older; 85 percent of new entrants into the work force will not be white males.[33] The fact that a diverse work force creates a larger pool of talent is a bonus, well respected by progressive executives. The practical fact, however, is that managers often experience difficulty in getting members of a diverse work force to work together in a way that guarantees that "minorities" feel comfortable and respected on the job. By law, managers have to offer equal opportunities to all individuals. Yet these legal protections have not been sufficient because people bring prejudices to the workplace, need to be made aware of differences, and taught to respect them.

CORNING GLASS. As early as 1983, Corning Glass, one of the most progressive companies in dealing with diversity, made the diverse work force one of its top three priorities. The CEO saw this focus on diversity as a way of reducing the costs attached to a higher attrition among women and minorities. He believed that the company could obtain a competitive advantage if the work force mirrored Corning's customer base. The company established quality improvement teams for African-American workers' and women's progress, introduced mandatory racial and gender awareness training, improved communication about promotion and career development, established a scholarship program for minority workers, expanded its summer internship program to focus on women and minorities, and improved recruiting contacts with campus groups that represented women and minorities.[34]

Even if a company hires a diverse work force, managing diversity requires managers to develop a greater awareness of and sensitivity to differences because unseen forces, such as prejudice or ignorance, can impair the effectiveness of the workers. Managers and nonmanagerial employees may need special training to prepare for the challenges of the multicultural and multinational work force. Addressing the relationship between individual supervisors and subordinates and creating a culture that supports diversity are essential ingredients of such preparation.[35] Organizations may also need to introduce reward systems that show that they value diversity and can use it to successfully accomplish organizational goals.

AVON. In 1984, Avon, a cosmetics company, first changed its affirmative action policies to focus more on moving minorities into the decision-making process.[36] Since that time they have introduced awareness training, formed a Multicultural Participation Council that oversees the management of diversity, developed a diversity training program, and helped African-Americans, Hispanics, and Asians to form networks across the country.

Effective managers and employees will need five key characteristics to function effectively in the twenty-first century. The diagnostic approach, described in the next section, provides a systematic framework for practicing these skills and addressing the issues managers will face in the twenty-first century.

■ *Adaptability.* Organizational members must be able to recognize and respond to ongoing and unexpected changes, to alter plans and activities in a timely fashion to respond to new pressures and demands.

- **Knowledgeability about State-of-the-Art Practice.** Managers and other organizational members need a repertoire of techniques for handling organizational situations or addressing problems.

- **Critical-thinking.** Not only do managers need a repertoire of techniques, they must understand when to apply them. The diagnostic approach fosters the development of critical-thinking skills.

- **Creativity.** Managers need to demonstrate creativity in inventing new options or reconfiguring previously-used approaches. Recognizing problems also calls for creativity in looking at a situation as "half full" rather than "half empty." Managerial creativity involves bringing workers together in new ways to perform their jobs and accomplish their organization's goals.

- **Interpersonal Effectiveness.** The increasing emphasis on team work and collaboration in organizations heightens the importance of managers possessing strong interpersonal skills. They need the ability to diagnose human problems, offer humane solutions to them, empathize with workers' situations, and recognize the complexity of workers' lives.

THE DIAGNOSTIC APPROACH

How can a manager use these skills to meet the challenges of the twenty-first century? Consider, for example, the challenges facing Jack Smith when he took over as CEO at General Motors. What did he need to do to improve the company's performance? The primary objective of this book is to make use of the field of organizational behavior to develop your ability to **understand** organizational events as fully as possible and then to **act effectively** on the basis of this understanding. We are defining the application of knowledge and skill to a real situation as **diagnosis**. **Accurate diagnosis forms the basis for effective action.**

Although some managers and other organizational members rely on a more ad hoc, less controlled approach to diagnosis, applying the diagnostic approach enriches their diagnoses and ultimately improves their action. In this book, we take a specific approach to diagnosis: we assume that events, behaviors, and attitudes that occur in organizations typically have more than one cause, and that it is important to try to understand the causes as fully as possible. The more completely we understand the causes, the more appropriately we will act in organizational situations.

In this book, then, we will use a four-step diagnostic approach that will help you meet the many managerial challenges awaiting you. The approach involves four phases: (1) description, (2) diagnosis, (3) prescription, and (4) action (see Figure 1–4). Although you may find using this approach slow or cumbersome at first, over time you will begin to use it easily and automatically.

DESCRIPTION

Phase 1, **description,** is simply that: a reporting of concrete aspects of or events in a specific situation without any attempt to explain the reasons for the events, or to make inferences about a person's motives or purposes.

FIGURE 1–4   *The diagnostic approach*

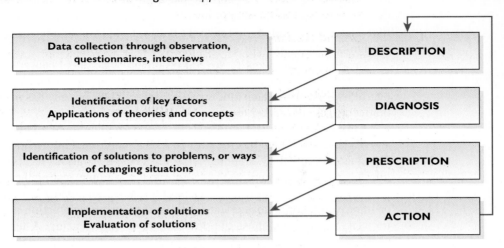

We can describe a number of concrete and observable occurrences at General Motors. Jack Smith eliminated committee meetings and decreased the company's bureaucracy. He restructured the company and established a good relationship with the head of the union. He reduced the work force through early retirement. In analyzing any situation, then, you can begin by listing the facts. In analyzing this or other situations you might also specify any assumptions you are making about the events: for example, you might assume that the workers have a legitimate right to influence the way they are managed, that complaints signal the existence of a problem situation, or that effective managers respond to employees' complaints. As much as possible you should test these assumptions to identify any that can be added to the list of facts.

The process of simple description is much more difficult than it looks: sometimes it is not easy to separate facts from assumptions. Most of us have little practice in making such a separation. Yet, effective diagnosis and understanding of the situation depend on a valid and factual description of it. The better we can describe situations, the better we will understand them. So, throughout this book you will be given opportunities to describe what you have read or seen.

In the case of General Motors, we base our description primarily on the summary of the situation presented in the introduction to this chapter. This description is probably not complete; nuances of attitudes and seemingly insignificant behaviors may be excluded. Nor does description completely recount the views of the company's managers or employees.

DIAGNOSIS

The next phase, *diagnosis,* attempts to explain the reasons for, or causes of, the behaviors and attitudes described. We diagnose when we first describe a situation, behavior, or attitude, and then identify its components and causes. In examining the case of General Motors, for example, we must first identify the key elements of the situation. Jack Smith inherited a poorly performing company with a low credit rating, excessive labor force, and poor labor–management relations. We also know that several *symptoms* exist; symptoms are indicators that there is a problem situation. Here, for example, productivity is low, GM cannot compete effectively with foreign car manufacturers, and the possibility of a strike exists.

Second, we can identify several problems or potential causes of these behaviors and attitudes. Strained relations exist between union and management. An overblown, highly bureaucratic structure exists. The company has made limited and ineffective use of worker teams.

Complete diagnosis would involve a full specification of all relevant aspects of a given situation. Often this requires collecting additional information or describing the situation more fully. Hypothesizing links between various facets of the situation may be required to complete the diagnosis; for example, testing the implications of leadership style for employees' behavior, organizational structure for productivity, or improved labor–management relations for worker satisfaction may be essential for Jack Smith to diagnose the problems he is experiencing. After identifying all possible causes of the situation, we can determine the likelihood that each of these potential causes affects the situation we have described. We can use the various theories presented in this book to help us evaluate the relevance of each potential cause to the situation.

This book will offer and describe a number of theories that people studying organizational behavior have developed to explain why events such as these occur. You can then use these theories to diagnose the situations or problems that exist. You can apply them in sequence and test whether they help you understand the situation better. Once you know and understand the theories you can choose the most appropriate ones to use in diagnosis. In the case of General Motors, we might believe that union and management lack two-way communication; or we might argue that more decision-making responsibility should be given to the workers. Focusing on Jack Smith's leadership style, we might explore whether it fits with the requirements of the situation or whether Jack demonstrates transformational leadership. Applying leadership and communication theories such as these, among others, helps us gain greater understanding of the reasons people such as Jack Smith act as they do, and the reasons our behavior is more effective in some circumstances than in others.

Formally speaking, the diagnostic stage involves four steps:

1. **Study a number of theories by themselves, without applying them to concrete situations.**

2. **Explain the situation with each theory in turn.** You might use, for example, leadership and organizational structure theory to explain the situation faced by Jack Smith at General Motors.

3. **Develop connections between the different theoretical perspectives.** You will see, for example, how motivation, leadership, and organizational design theories complement each other and provide a richer explanation of organizational events.

4. **Check to ensure that all relevant theoretical models have been applied.** This step increases the completeness and accuracy of your diagnosis. As you grow in experience and competence you will learn better which theories to use.

Keep in mind that not all organizational problems and events can be understood by *all* organizational behavior models and theories. At best they only facilitate and enhance understanding—they do not produce it. Lack of two-way communication, described in Chapter 7, may help explain the situation at GM, but lack of assertiveness may not. Looking at group norms may offer new insights into the situation, but looking at Jack Smith's cognitive style may not. The ability to diagnose includes the ability to critically evaluate different perspectives and theories, and to determine whether they apply to each specific case. By examining the degree of fit between the theories and the key aspects of each situation, you will identify the most likely causes of specific behaviors and attitudes. You will also determine how well different perspectives apply. And, throughout the process of diagnosis, you will continually be encouraged to develop your own explanations for the events you describe.

PRESCRIPTION

Phase 3, *prescription,* is the first part of translating diagnosis—or your understanding of a situation—into action. It involves identifying, reviewing, evaluating, and then deciding on a desired course of action for particular circumstances based on the foregoing diagnosis. The manager or other organizational member proposes one or more ways of correcting each problem identified in the diagnosis phase. Managers and other organization members do not have the luxury of simply understanding problem and other organizational situations; they must act to correct them. A course of action based on a strong diagnosis should be more effective than action based on very little understanding of the problem. Correcting defective communication calls for different strategies than improving inefficient job design; changing individual perceptions calls for different approaches than improving negotiating processes.

In the prescription phase, Jack Smith, for example, would propose ways of improving the poor relations between union and management. He might also look for ways to improve the ineffective decision-making process. Prescriptions might include using a third party to facilitate union–management interactions. Training or organizational redesign may improve a faulty decision-making process. Because most problem situations have no single correct response, in part because the problems are complex, we should begin the prescription phase by proposing multiple solutions to diagnosed problems.

In the Activities of this book you will be asked to suggest solutions to problems, to develop specific courses of action for different situations. You will then have the opportunity to evaluate the solutions proposed in terms of the models and theories discussed, and to test whether the recommended changes should result in the desired consequences. In the case of General Motors, you might prescribe more autonomous decision making by its workers. By comparing this prescription to the nature of decision making described by various organizational behavior theories, you can predict the effectiveness of your prescription before it is implemented.

You should consider as many reasonable, feasible, and practical alternative solutions to each problem or behavioral concern diagnosed as possible. Evaluate these alternatives and their effectiveness by using the relevant theoretical models to predict outcomes of various actions. Determine the costs and benefits of each alternative. Then select the alternative with the relatively lowest costs and highest benefits.

ACTION

The final phase, *action,* is the implementation of the solutions you propose. It involves testing the feasibility and practicality of the solutions. Often we know the correct solution, but cannot apply it. We might agree, for example, that Jack Smith should reorganize General Motors. But how does he actually do that? What pitfalls will he encounter in trying to translate prescriptions into reality?

Action might involve testing the prescription in a limited part of the organization. Or we might simulate the action we propose using facsimiles of the organization. Pilot programs are frequently used to implement change in organizations in measured, observable ways. Top management might introduce a bonus program or a new performance evaluation instrument. They might provide extensive training throughout the organization. Experimentation often precedes a plan of effective action.

The action phase also includes a careful scrutiny of all individuals and other systems in the organization to plan for the impact of the changes. It means assessing potential resistances to change and planning ways to overcome them. Implementing staffing or policy changes might require the introduction of new education programs; new resources might be necessary to support the new programs. The effects of action may cascade through the organization.

And so, the cycle may start again: as part of the evaluation you will describe your own and others' behavior and attitudes. Then you can diagnose the reasons the behavior succeeded or failed, offer new prescriptions, and once more act.

ORGANIZATION OF THIS BOOK

This book directs students to apply the diagnostic approach by looking at three types of behavior: individual, group, and organizational. Chapter 1 in Part I has set the stage.

Part II examines individual behavior by addressing questions such as the following:

- What factors contribute to accurate perception and attribution?

- What influences individual learning?

- How do a multicultural work force and individual differences affect individuals' behaviors and attitudes?

- What motivates people to perform and what role does the reward system play?

More specifically, Chapter 2 looks at perception, attribution, and learning. Chapter 3 examines diversity and individual differences. Chapter 4 considers theories of motivation and reward systems.

Part III focuses on group behavior and answers questions that include:

- How do managers build effective work groups?

- What factors contribute to an effective decision-making process?

- What facilitates and what hinders effective communication?

- What characterizes effective leadership?

- How can power be secured and used productively?

- How can conflict be resolved or managed?

- How can relationships between groups be managed effectively?

- What factors contribute to effective negotiations?

Chapter 5 describes the functioning of a variety of work groups. Chapter 6 looks at decision making. Chapter 7 considers communication. Chapter 8 examines leadership. Chapter 9 describes issues of power and conflict. Chapter 10 examines intergroup relations and negotiations.

Part IV discusses organizational behavior and addresses questions such as:

- How can organizations create the culture they desire?

- How can quality be ensured in organizations?

- What factors characterize a learning organization?

- How can jobs and organizations be effectively designed?

- How can innovation be encouraged in organizations?

- How can an organization be structured to accomplish its goals and strategy and respond to its environment and technology to compete effectively?

- How can managers help workers deal effectively with change?

Chapter 11 looks at organizational culture, quality management, and learning organizations. Chapter 12 considers technology, innovation, and the design of work. Chapter 13 identifies a variety of organizational structures. Chapter 14 delineates the factors that influence selection of specific organizational designs. Chapter 15 concludes the book with a discussion of organizational change and effectiveness.

SUMMARY

Organizational behavior refers to the actions and attitudes of people in organizations. The field of organizational behavior is the study of these actions and attitudes and includes a collection of separate theories and models. Managers study organizational behavior by collecting data using direct observation, questionnaires, interviews, and written documents. They may conduct laboratory experiments, field studies, or simulations to evaluate the relationship between various phenomenon.

Historical viewpoints and earlier schools of thought help set the stage for understanding organizational behavior. Structural perspectives, including organizational theory prior to 1900, scientific management, classical theory, bureaucracy, and decision theory focused on the structuring and design of work and organizations. Behavioral perspectives, including human relations, group dynamics, decision theory, and leadership schools focused instead on worker satisfaction, leadership, and interpersonal relations. Integrative perspectives, including the sociotechnical school, systems theory, and contingency theory, focused on both structure and interpersonal interactions.

Managers will face an array of challenges in the twenty-first century. They operate in a global arena and must meet the challenges of global competitiveness. Total quality management has combined concerns for quality, productivity, and meeting customer needs. Advances in information technology have significant consequences for organizing and managing. Concern for ethics in business dealings has received renewed attention. Access to the most skilled of the diverse work force allows organizations to better meet competitive pressures.

The diagnostic approach, which includes the phases of description, diagnosis, prescription, and action, should help managers meet these challenges by encouraging them to systematically diagnose the causes of events before acting. Description involves specifying the major aspects or events in a specific situation. Diagnosis attempts to explain the reasons for the behaviors and attitudes described. Prescription involves identifying, reviewing, evaluating, and then deciding on a course of action. Action is the implementation of the solutions proposed.

DIAGNOSTIC QUESTIONS

The diagnostic questions that follow offer a way of beginning to describe and diagnose an organizational situation.

- Does the organization have effective mechanisms for collecting data about its functioning?

- Is there an appropriate division of labor, is work done efficiently, and are workers sufficiently trained to do their jobs?

- Do employees have specified areas of responsibility and is there work well defined?

- Do work groups operate effectively?

- Do managers perform organizing roles and have an appropriate span of control?

- Does the group have effective task and social leadership?

- Does management work with the correct assumptions about employees?

- Is decision making effective?

- Is the interface of technology and individual workers effective?

- How does the organization function as a system?

- Does the organization's structure respond to environmental contingencies?

Chapter 2

Chapter Outline

Perception, Attribution, and Learning in Organizations

The Problem Order at Elegant Interiors

Julie Sykes, president and owner of Elegant Interiors, angrily slammed down the telephone. She had just placed her twentieth call in the past two weeks to Westlake Wallpaper Company to track a customer's order and still did not know when it would be delivered. A large wallpaper order she placed for a customer should have arrived two weeks after it was ordered. Now it was eight weeks after Julie had placed the order for the customer and she was still trying to determine its status. The customer service representative at Westlake kept giving her contradictory information: one day the order was being shipped that day; the next day it was on back order until Friday; then it was being shipped in two days, and so on. She knew that her customer did not believe that she could not get good information from Westlake about the status of the order. Julie was also quite perplexed because she had dealt with Westlake quite successfully for the past ten years. She had heard rumors that Westlake was experiencing some management problems since a change in ownership almost two years before, but until now she had not encountered any difficulties. Unfortunately, Westlake was the only source of the wallpaper selected by her client.

The customer service representative at Westlake, Elizabeth Dawson, claimed that she was not getting responses to the faxes she sent to the mill to request the status of the order. Julie felt particularly frustrated because Elizabeth did not keep her informed about the situation. Each morning Elizabeth promised that the material had been shipped but could not check whether Westlake had received it until the afternoon, generally after the mill closed for the day. Julie found Elizabeth to be infuriatingly polite but not at all helpful. She did not believe that Elizabeth had followed procedures that normally result in timely delivery of wallpaper from the mill.

Julie had even tried to contact the president of Westlake. Originally, Elizabeth refused to connect her with the president, but eventually told her that the president and his special assistant were on vacation. Julie felt caught in a vicious cycle: both she and her customer had invested too much time to simply cancel the order. She also knew that the customer was not satisfied with the service that Julie was providing. The customer had repeatedly asked Julie whether she could "speak to someone in the company's management." Julie's real dilemma was that she had no idea when or whether the wallpaper would arrive. She needed to advise her client whether to cancel the wallpaper hanger she had booked three months previously because the paper hanger's schedule was so filled.

What caused the delay in the wallpaper order placed by Elegant Interiors? Do Julie, Elizabeth, and the customer agree about its cause? What did each person perceive as the cause of the delay? Why did the perceptions of these women differ? How did their experiences—their learned behaviors—influence the events described here? Questions such as these are fundamental to the diagnostic approach, since they deal with the description of events and the reasons given for them. As the case suggests, different observers of an incident may describe and diagnose it very differently. They, in turn, would act based on their different understandings of the situation.

In this chapter we explore three areas of organizational behavior. *Perception* deals with the way we perceive and thus describe events or other people. *Attribution* focuses on the way we understand and thus analyze or diagnose the events and people we perceive. *Learning* refers to the way our past experiences and acquisition of knowledge and information influence this description and diagnosis.

While these processes remain fairly constant, the context in which they occur may influence the outcome. For example, the *process* of perception is the same in the United States or in Japan, but people living in different cultures may draw different conclusions from observations of identical situations. Work force diversity also will affect the outcomes of the perception, attribution, and learning processes. Thus, the chapter's final section will discuss these global influences.

THE PERCEPTION PROCESS

We begin our discussion by considering the wallpaper order situation. We can view the problem from several different perspectives. First, think of yourself as Julie Sykes. What do you notice about the situation relating to the wallpaper order? Which features of the situation stand out for you? You might notice the contradictory information you receive from Elizabeth Dawson. You might focus on your customer's repeated calls to you about the delivery date for the wallpaper. You might recognize your increasing frustration with your inability to speak with someone with authority at Westlake Wallpaper. Now think of yourself as Elizabeth Dawson. What features of the situation do you notice? You might experience Julie's repeated calling as annoying. You might feel frustrated because Julie does not believe that you have tried to give her accurate information about a delivery date. You might feel disempowered because you cannot control the actions of the mill—they refuse to respond to your faxes. Now put yourself in the place of the Elegant Interior's customer. How would you feel about this situation? You might echo Julie's or Elizabeth's views or feel instead that Julie is ineptly handling the situation and not providing the customer with accurate, helpful information.

When you put yourself in these different positions, you probably notice different features of the situation and think about the wallpaper order in different ways. Even though objectively this situation was a single event, your experience of it—your perception—varies when you put yourself in the position of different observers of the event. You then act based on your perception.

Perception refers to the active process of sensing reality and organizing it into meaningful views or understandings.[1] Perception typically results in different people having somewhat different, even contradictory, views or understandings of the same event or person. Linda Wachner, the CEO of Warnaco, sees herself as "effective and good, with an excellent record. You don't achieve that without focus, strategy, and having people do it your way." Others see her as "smart, impatient . . . rewards employees but demands absolute fealty . . . a screamer who's not above swearing like a trooper."[2] Often managers and their subordinates, coworkers, or supervisors see and describe the same situation differently.

FIGURE 2–1

The perceptual process

Sensations →

Attend to sensations based on	Organize sensations by
• characteristics of stimuli • internal states and cultural experiences	• grouping them into patterns against backgrounds • comparing them to schemas and scripts

→ Perceptions

NEWTON, MASSACHUSETTS, TEACHERS' WORK SLOWDOWN. A work slowdown by teachers in a Boston suburb illustrates such differences.[3] Teachers perceived the work-to-rule action, in which they perform only the duties specified in their contract, as appropriate and reflecting their right to a fair contract. Many parents viewed the action as inappropriate, frustrating, and harmful to their children because teachers no longer provided academic assistance outside regular school hours or acted as advisors for after-school extracurricular activities.

Presenting a clear, well-documented, agreed-upon description of a situation—the first step in the diagnostic approach—is paramount. Understanding the perceptual process and the factors that affect it also allows us to improve our diagnoses of events and the resulting prescription and subsequent action.

In this chapter we present two alternative but complementary views of the perceptual process. The first, which emphasizes both the physiological processes and the social context in which they occur, describes perception as having two parts, as shown in Figure 2–1: (1) *attention* and (2) *organization*.[4]

ATTEND TO SENSATIONS

So many stimuli bombard us that we have difficulty taking full account of all of the sensations they cause. Different observers often select different sensations to which they pay attention. The individuals dealing with the delinquent wallpaper order *attend* to certain features of the situation. For example, Julie Sykes might focus on Elizabeth Dawson's failure to keep Julie apprised of the situation, whereas Elizabeth Dawson might emphasize Julie's repeated telephone calls. We tend to focus on only selected features in any situation. We may pay attention to certain workers' actions and conversations. For example, we might focus particularly on the behaviors of a worker who has received a poor performance evaluation and ignore those of a top performer. We also attend to selected characteristics of the people we meet: we might be alert to a worker's experience with a particular piece of equipment or the worker's age or sex. This selection process helps us avoid information overload by focusing on the most relevant information in a particular situation. It also helps us avoid dealing with information that seems to be irrelevant to us.

Characteristics of the Stimuli Certain characteristics of the stimuli themselves influence that to which we attend. We tend to select stimuli that are larger, more intense, in motion, repetitive, either novel or very familiar, or in contrast to their background.[5] We tend to overlook stimuli that are small, less intense, stationary, or blend with their background.

Consider, for example, a bank teller's error: in reconciling accounts the teller may more likely see a large than a small error. Consider next a salesperson's response to a ringing telephone, a relatively intense stimulus. A salesperson frequently answers a telephone before helping a customer waiting in person because the customer in the store—unless he or she is very vocal or demanding—offers a less intense stimulus. In another work situation, a manager may not hear (or select) the voice of a particular employee who offers suggestions for improving workflow in the department: the voice may lack sufficient intensity, novelty, or contrast. Which sensations in Elizabeth's response attracted Julie's attention? Julie attended to Elizabeth's failure to give a precise delivery date, perhaps because the response was particularly frequent or contrasted with Julie's previous experience with Westlake.

Internal States and Cultural Experiences We also attend to sensations according to our internal state and cultural experiences. Such states evolve from an individual's experiences, motivation, and personality. For example, we are more likely to attend to food commercials before a meal than after one. In business situations, we in the United States tend to pay more attention to comments by men and women wearing business suits than to the ideas of those wearing blue jeans.

Consider the situation of Mark Reston. Four months into the new year, Mark had used his allotted sick days. When you think of Mark, do you focus on the person, his work performance, or his absenteeism? The answer will depend, to a large extent, on cultural expectations, which differ among companies and countries. If you are a manager or coworker you might perceive his absenteeism in terms of your own motivation or personality. The more diverse the work force, the more likely individuals see events differently. Eastern Europeans, for example, might have different expectations about work attendance than those who are Japanese or South Americans. In addition, as organizations become more global, the number of different views of the same situation increase.

Think of the situation that opened this chapter. Which stimuli in the situation did Julie Sykes select? Which ones did Elizabeth Dawson select? Which ones did the customer select? Why did each person select the particular stimuli? Why, for example, did Julie Sykes overlook Elizabeth Dawson's attempt to contact the mill and focus on her inability to secure a precise date? Why might she have overlooked Westlake Wallpaper's previous good delivery record? Why did the customer similarly focus on Julie's lack of success in securing this order, when Julie had delivered five other orders to the customer as promised? Both Julie and her customer, for example, probably hold certain cultural expectations about "the customer is always right" and what constitutes "good" service. Not surprisingly, based on their own experiences, they were outraged at Elizabeth's seemingly shoddy service. Different experiences, needs, or personalities might have resulted in different perceptions of the situation. These different perceptions, in turn, result in different actions by various organizational members.

ORGANIZE SENSATIONS

Once we have selected stimuli, we categorize and organize them so that the new material makes sense to us.

Patterns and Background First, our brains follow certain laws in seeking patterns in the stimuli. Some of the more common laws are shown in Figure 2–2. These laws also affect the way we perceive situations at work.

■ *Figure-Ground.* At a business lunch, for example, uniformed wait staff fade into the background so that we focus mainly on our companions.

FIGURE 2–2   *Common patterns used in organizing sensations*

Figure-Ground. We tend to organize sensations into figures and backgrounds.

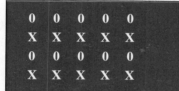

Similarity. We tend to group similar items. Do you see alternating rows of O's and X's or columns of alternating O's and X's?

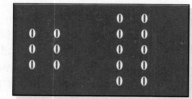

Proximity. We tend to group elements that are close together. How many groupings do you see at the left?

Closure. We tend to fill in the gaps in incomplete stimuli. Do you see a rectangle or four lines?

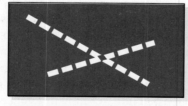

Continuation. We tend to organize stimuli into continuous lines or patterns. Do you see two intersecting lines or four lines?

Simplicity. We tend to reduce stimuli to their simplest shapes or patterns. Do you see an overlapping rectangle and triangle or an unnameable polygon?

- **Similarity.** At work, people in business attire usually belong to managerial or professional ranks, whereas those in casual clothes are generally assembly-line workers or clerks.

- **Proximity.** A manager might evaluate an employee's attitude by looking at the people with whom the employee associates; if the employee spends free time with malcontents, the manager will assume the employee shares those attitudes.

- **Closure.** When we buy a product, we assume that a warranty and service accompany the purchase.

- **Continuation.** A manager assumes, based on past performance, that an employee will continue to accept certain work conditions (long hours, low pay) or demonstrate qualities such as loyalty or leadership.

- **Simplicity.** Managers sometimes try to reduce complex work problems to their simplest components, such as tardiness, as the root of an employee's performance problem rather than also considering poor supervision, equipment failures, and inappropriate organizational policies.

Inaccurate organizing of sensations can become particularly problematic in organizations that have a multicultural work force or that operate internationally. Faulty organizing contributes to the distortions of perceptions discussed later in this chapter.

SCHEMAS AND SCRIPTS

More recent research about the structure and acquisition of knowledge links cognitive theory and perception.[6] Cognitive psychologists suggest that we store in our memories *schemas,* or descriptions of the characteristic features of people, situations, or objects. These schemas help people group objects, individuals, and situations into clusters in their thought processes.[7] Individuals may form schemas about persons, known as categories. For example, managers build ***prototypes*** (person schemas) about the characteristics of good and poor workers. A prototype of a new faculty member might be an individual with a doctoral degree from an accredited university, a strong research record, some classroom teaching experience, and so on. Or they may form a schema based on a role, such as working mother. Self-schemas present generalizations about an individual abstracted from present situations and past experiences. For example, individuals may demonstrate self-schemas of self-efficacy, showing that they feel competent to accomplish a particular goal or perform a particular task. We also match new sensations to *exemplars,* which represent concrete examples or a sampling of circumstances.[8] An exemplar might be the faculty member hired most recently in your school or university.

We can also develop schemas about a sequence of events, known as ***scripts.***[9] Scripts provide a mental representation of the events that guide our behavior. For example, managers develop scripts about the process for hiring new employees, evaluating existing employees, and even conducting staff meetings.[10] Scripts can be used in both the diagnostic and action stages of the diagnostic approach. Consider this example.

Ford Motor Company. In 1970, Ford Motor Company introduced the Pinto, a subcompact car designed to compete with European and Japanese automobiles. Routine crash testing indicated that the Pinto's fuel tank ruptured when struck from the rear at speeds as low as 31 miles per hour. Subsequently, individuals died in real-life crashes that involved the rupturing of the Pinto's gas tank. Ford had decided it was not cost-effective to recall the popular cars or modify their design. A researcher involved in the incident used scripts to show how he could have better analyzed and changed the sequence of events that led to the fateful decision.[11]

PERCEPTUAL DISTORTIONS

Truly objective perceptions rarely occur; rather, most perception is subjective and hence suffers from inaccuracies or distortions. Look, for example, at the picture in Figure 2–3; do you see an old woman or a young woman? Although such biases are normal and human, they can have significant consequences when managers or other organizational members act upon them. Although an array of distortions can affect perceptions, we discuss four distortions—stereotyping, the halo effect, projection, and the self-fulfilling prophecy—in greater detail here.

STEREOTYPING

Stereotyping occurs whenever we assume others have certain characteristics or attitudes simply because they belong to a certain group or category. "Blondes have more fun" and "all managers are smart" illustrate stereotyping. We frequently stereotype members of ethnic groups, women, managers, white-collar workers, and blue-collar workers. While some stereotypes may be accurate, they often are not and result in uninformed action. Sex-role stereotyping is particularly common. Recent court decisions in the United States require that companies avoid the appearance of sexual stereotyping and develop strategies to avoid it.[12] When you think of

FIGURE 2–3   *The old woman/young woman illusion*

female managers, what images and characteristics come to your mind? Are the images and characteristics the same for male managers?

STEIN & COMPANY. Julia M. Stasch, president of Stein & Company, a large Chicago real estate developer and builder, probably contradicts most stereotypes of the leader of a large construction and development company. Her career in construction began in 1976, when she took a secretarial job at Stein & Company. Today, as one of the top-ranking female builders in the United States, she insists that her company's contractors meet stiff affirmative action goals. In building Chicago's Metcalfe Federal Building, for example, women worked 7 percent of the total number of hours worked. This is in sharp contrast to the traditional hiring practices of large construction companies, where women comprise only 2 percent of the work force.[13]

Why does stereotyping occur? Often, individuals do not gather sufficient data about others to describe their behaviors or attitudes accurately. They may be pressed for time, for example, and eager to find shortcuts for categorizing people or phenomena. For example, male management students in the United States, Great Britain, and Germany were more likely to see managers in their countries as having "male" characteristics; the female students in Great Britain and Germany also tended to see managers as having "male" characteristics, but female students in the United States did not.[14] Alternatively, some individuals have personal biases against certain groups of individuals. Historical attitudes toward certain cultural groups may result in stereotypes. Americans may have certain views of Europeans and different views of Asians, based on their historical experiences with the two regions.

HALO EFFECT

The *halo effect* occurs when an individual lets one salient feature or trait of a person dominate his or her evaluation of that individual. Working overtime, for example, can cause a supervisor to evaluate an employee as highly cooperative and productive. A sloppy personal appearance can cause a person to be judged as imprecise in his or her work, unreliable, and a poor employee.

The halo effect frequently occurs in assessments of employee performance. In one study, for example, a supervisor who had information suggesting identical performance from two female subordinates gave them different evaluations according to their personal attractiveness. Attractiveness increased the performance evaluations, pay raises, and promotions of women in nonmanagerial positions but decreased these same outcomes for women in managerial positions.[15] Another study indicated that expanding the wording in an audit report in the United Kingdom to more closely resemble recent changes in its United States counterpart created a more positive feeling for the auditors about matters not directly described in the report.[16]

PROJECTION

Projection occurs when an individual attributes his or her own attitudes or feelings to another person. Individuals use projection as a defense mechanism, to transfer blame to another person, or to provide protection from their own unacceptable feelings. Individuals frequently attribute their own prejudices against minorities, managers, or employees, for example, to the other party. Hence, projection and its dysfunctional consequences can increase as the work force becomes more diverse.

Individuals who lack understanding or mistrust people who are different from themselves may project these insecurities onto others.

Projection involves an emotional biasing of perceptions. Fear, hatred, uncertainty, anger, love, deceit, or distrust may influence an individual's perceptions. In union–management relations, for example, each side attributes feelings of mistrust (often its own) to the other side. Management might state that the union mistrusts them, when, in fact, it is management that mistrusts the union. They project their own feelings onto the other group, representing them as that group's feelings.

SELF-FULFILLING PROPHECY

In many situations, the participants expect certain behaviors from other participants and then see these behaviors as occurring whether or not they actually do. Their expectations become *self-fulfilling prophecies.* Managers, for example, may expect workers to be lazy, bossy, or tardy, and then perceive them as actually being lazy, bossy, or tardy. Employees, in turn, may expect managers to be authoritarian, uncaring, and inflexible, and then perceive them as authoritarian, uncaring, and inflexible. Sometimes these expectations accompany stereotyping, the halo effect, or projection, or they can occur independently of other biases.

Assume you are a senior accountant with two subordinates. The first subordinate has demonstrated initiative and high productivity in the audits she has conducted. The second subordinate precisely follows the directions you give her, but has demonstrated neither initiative nor enthusiasm for her work. You have just found a high-quality, unexpected audit report on your desk that you have not requested from either employee. Which employee do you congratulate for the excellent work? If the self-fulfilling prophecy is operating, you would approach the first subordinate; based on past performance you expect her to demonstrate initiative and productivity. Could you be in error? Of course. Studies show that these self-fulfilling prophecies also influence the performance of others. The second subordinate, for example, might never demonstrate initiative because she knows you will attribute the excellent or unexpected performance to her coworker.

The use of the self-fulfilling prophecy is particularly common in cross-cultural situations. We often have expectations about how individuals in other cultures will act. These expectations generally result from similar experiences in our own culture. Cultural differences, however, often change seemingly identical situations. In the United States, for example, we commonly accept the price on an item as nonnegotiable; in many other countries, such as in the Middle East, residents know that the price is never the final price. But we act on the basis of our own experiences and create a self-fulfilling prophecy that the price is fixed and thus too high for goods sold abroad. Similarly, we may see individuals in other countries as "strange" because their behavior differs from our experiences; the self-fulfilling prophecy then results in their acting in a "strange" or unusual manner, which is in fact quite appropriate to their culture.

DEALING WITH DISTORTIONS

How can we reduce dysfunctional perceptual distortions in organizations? Here we offer five steps to increase perceptual accuracy, as shown in Figure 2–4. To see how this works, let us take another look at the conflict between Elegant Interiors and Westlake Wallpaper.

FIGURE 2–4   *Dealing with perceptual distortions*

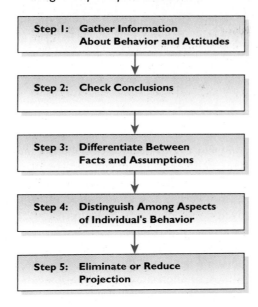

First, gather sufficient information about other people's behavior and attitudes to encourage more realistic perceptions. Managers, for example, should judge an individual's performance based on his or her observed behavior, rather than on the behavior of a group to which the person belongs or the manager's expectations about the employee's performance. Julie Sykes needs to document her own and Elizabeth Dawson's behavior regarding the wallpaper order.

Second, check conclusions to ensure their validity. To the extent possible, Julie Sykes should determine the true reasons for the delay in delivering the order. She should also make sure that she communicates with the customer so that the customer's perceptions are valid and accurate.

Third, differentiate between facts and assumptions in determining the basis of perceptions. Julie Sykes may assume that Elizabeth Dawson has not actually contacted the mill; in fact, Elizabeth may not have only called the mill five times each day, but also informed her boss about the mill's lack of responsiveness.

Fourth, distinguish among various aspects of an individual's behavior, rather than grouping even superficially related aspects. Separate appearance from performance, productivity from attendance, personality from creativity. Julie does not appear to have difficulty in focusing on Elizabeth's specific behavior, but she may need to be careful in future dealings with Westlake Wallpaper. This advice becomes particularly important when dealing with a cross-cultural work force whose appearance or personal demeanor may vary from that typically seen by a corporate manager. Using stereotypes reduces the accuracy of our perceptions about these multicultural and multinational groups. The danger in some training in managing diversity is that understanding different cultures better might enhance stereotyping, rather than encourage managers to recognize individual differences *within* a cultural context.[17] Because diversity training often highlights differences between workers based on the group to which they belong, e.g., women, Hispanics, African-

Americans, physically challenged, organizational members need to carefully analyze the specific and unique characteristics of individuals with whom they interact.

Fifth, identify true feelings as a way of eliminating or reducing projections: does Julie feel frustration, distrust, or fear? Does she lack confidence in her judgments or feel inexperienced in the situation she faces? After recognizing these feelings, repeatedly assess whether and how these feelings influence perceptions of others.

THE ATTRIBUTION PROCESS

Determining **why** events occur is essential for individual, group, and organizational effectiveness and key to the diagnostic approach. Many of us, consciously or unconsciously, try to determine why events occur: we attribute causes to the events. We move from **description** to **diagnosis**. **Attribution** refers to our specification of the perceived causes of events. Not surprisingly, different people often attribute different causes to the same event.

Research suggests that when people try to understand reasons for their own or another person's behavior, they focus on either **personal** factors, such as habits, needs, abilities, or interests, or **situational** factors, such as increases in competition, poor supervision, shortages of resources, or the nature of the work itself. They may or may not correctly attribute the reasons for the behavior to these two types of factors. For example, a recent study indicated that the performance of women was less likely to be attributed to ability than the performance of men; similarly, comparisons of the performance of black and white managers indicated that black managers' performance was less likely to be attributed to effort and ability and more likely to be attributed to the help of others.[18]

Theorists and researchers suggest that the attribution process occurs in three stages, as shown in Figure 2–5.[19] Consider Julie Sykes's attribution of the cause of the delay in the wallpaper's delivery. First, she observes or is told about Elizabeth Dawson's action—the failure to deliver the wallpaper as expected. Second, having identified the action, Julie determines if the observed behavior was intended or accidental. If Julie assumes that the delay occurred accidentally, she would attribute its cause to fate, luck, accident, or a similar uncontrollable phenomenon. If, however, she assumes that the delay was intended or controllable, she would then move to stage 3. In the case of the wallpaper delivery, do you think Julie assesses the de-

FIGURE 2–5   *The attribution process*

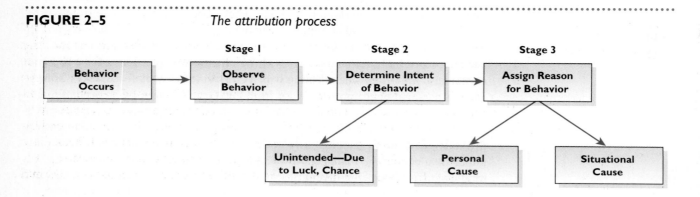

lay as intended or accidental? Perhaps she initially viewed it as accidental, but after receiving repeated misinformation, she likely now views the delay as intended.

In the third and final stage she questions whether situational causes or personal characteristics explain the behavior. She might consider, for example, whether an equipment failure in the mill or lack of appropriate paper on which to print the design explains the delay; if so, she will attribute the decline to situational factors. If, on the other hand, she feels that Elizabeth's handling of the order—personal factors such as her laziness or ineptitude—influenced its delay, then she likely concludes that personal causes explain the problem. While both situational and personal factors may have influenced the delivery delay, those involved in the situation often simplify their understanding and attend primarily to only one cause. At this point, Julie likely attributes the cause to personal factors. To what does Elizabeth likely attribute the delay? Would Julie's customer likely have the same attribution for the delay as Julie or Elizabeth?

ATTRIBUTIONAL BIASES

Attributions and attributional errors occur in predictable ways. The original research about attribution identified three factors that influence attributions about the cause of behavior:

- ◼ *consensus*—how many others behaved in the same way as the individual; we tend to assign personal causes to unique behaviors and situational causes to behaviors performed by many others;

- ◼ *distinctiveness*—how consistent (or unusual) an individual's behavior is across situations; we tend to assign personal causes to consistent behavior and situational causes to unusual behavior;

- ◼ *consistency*—how consistent an individual's behavior is over time and situations; we tend to attribute consistent behavior by an individual to personal causes and situational causes to behaviors that represent isolated instances.[20]

Attributing the cause of a situation to personal or situational factors also depends on the individual's point of view, the appropriateness and impact of the behavior, the nature of the outcomes, the individual's response tendency, and the individual's self-concept.

THE INDIVIDUAL'S POINT OF VIEW

An individual can participate in a situation as an *actor* or an *observer.* In looking at the situation regarding the late wallpaper delivery, we can view Julie Sykes, the owner of Elegant Interiors, as the observer in the situation and Elizabeth Dawson from Westlake Wallpaper as the actor, or the reverse. Whom we designate as the actor and observer depends on the behavior to which we are attributing causes.

Research about such attributions indicates that an actor in a situation emphasizes the situational causes of a behavior and deemphasizes personal factors as a way of protecting his or her self-image and ego; the observer does the reverse.[21] For example, Elizabeth Dawson, as actor, would emphasize conditions at the mill (situational factors). Julie Sykes, as observer, would emphasize Elizabeth's ineptness (personal factors).

LESLIE FAY COMPANIES. John H. Pomerantz, the CEO of Leslie Fay Companies, the second-largest women's apparel maker in the United States, was called from a meeting to learn that reported profits for the company's previous five quarters had never existed, and the company books had been doctored.[22] Who was responsible? Not surprisingly, individuals involved in the situation offered different attributions. Pomerantz, as the actor in the situation, attributed the cause to the actions of the controller, who Pomerantz said overstated profits. Financial analysts, as observers of the events, attributed them to personal causes, in this case to Pomerantz's lack of financial knowledge and his emphasis on socializing rather than careful control of company operations.

In addition, actors are less likely to assume moral responsibility for an action because they attribute it to external causes.[23] If a mid-level manager engages in financial fraud, for example, he or she most likely attributes this behavior to external circumstances, such as top management's directive or changes in relevant laws. These biases may extend to ethical judgments through the moral evaluation of one's own or another's behavior.[24]

APPROPRIATENESS AND IMPACT OF THE BEHAVIOR

If an individual acts in inappropriate ways, an observer will usually attribute the actor's behavior to personal characteristics.[25] If an advertising copy writer (the individual) was observed making false claims about a product (acting in an inappropriate way), for example, top management (the observer) would attribute this action to the employee's personal characteristics because the behavior violates agreed-upon standards of behavior. Similarly, an observer who believes that a person has acted to specifically influence the observer will attribute the observer's behavior to his or her personality traits. If a manager (the observer) felt that an employee "blew the whistle" on questionable business practices to "get back at management," she likely would attribute the cause of that worker's behavior to his or her personality.

THE NATURE OF THE OUTCOMES

The perceived success or failure of a behavior may also complicate the attribution of its cause, as shown in Figure 2–6. Successful behaviors, such as increases in performance, efficiency, or following work rules, are actions that are viewed as effective and as fitting with the organization's goals. Failures include increased turnover or absenteeism, declining productivity or morale, or more specific performance of unacceptable behaviors. Although the research results are somewhat mixed, the weight of evidence suggests that actors tend to attribute successes to personal factors and failures to situational factors, and observers do the reverse.[26]

BIG SIX ACCOUNTING FIRMS. The behavior of Big Six accounting firms, frequently observers in situations of fraudulent executive behavior, is often the attributed situational cause of performance problems. These accounting firms spent nearly $480 million in 1991 in defending and settling lawsuits that blamed them for low-quality audit work, in particular, their failure to detect phony financial records.[27]

A research study of 65 managers in a large municipal government indicated that providing the managers training in feedback skills resulted in a decrease in their tendency to attribute subordinates' problem behaviors to personal factors.[28]

FIGURE 2–6   *An example of attributions*

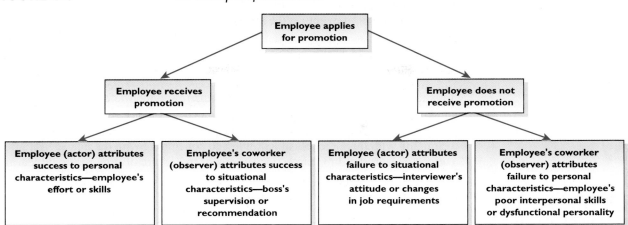

A manager's tendency to make the easiest response can also affect his or her attributions.[29] A manager more easily assumes that a worker, rather than the situation, is responsible for a problem. To identify a situational cause, the manager typically must spend time investigating the situation in great detail. Correcting the situation is also more difficult than dealing with or removing the "responsible" individual, since the manager may have little or no control over the organizational factors. The more expedient approach is to attribute the cause to the individual.

INDIVIDUAL'S SELF-CONCEPT

Our effort to maintain a positive self-concept also can modify our perceptions and attributions. Managers, for example, may view their employees' behavior as a reflection of their own. Maintaining their own self-esteem causes the managers to more likely attribute employees' successes to the manager's contributions (part of the situation) and failures to the employees' personalities. Successes then become a reflection of the manager's behavior and attitudes; failures become disassociated with the manager.

CORRECTING ATTRIBUTIONAL PROBLEMS

Testing the nature of attributions in a problem situation should be an early and recurring step of diagnosis. As much as possible, individuals should be involved in *actively* processing information about the situation.[30] Individuals who know the typical attributional biases can recognize these biases in their own attributions and verify the accuracy of the causes they identify. They can then act on the basis of correct causal attributions. A manager who has an employee who is regularly tardy can query the worker about the reasons for the lateness, rather than assuming that personal characteristics cause it.

In this book, we present a wide range of explanations for various phenomena so that individuals can attribute causes as *accurately* and *completely* as possible and then act on the basis of correct attributions. The diagnostic approach encourages us to first describe the situation completely. Then, as part of the diagnosis stage, we attribute the causes of events in the situations we describe.

LEARNING IN ORGANIZATIONS

In addition to perception and attribution, *learning,* which refers to the acquisition of skills, knowledge, ability, or attitudes, influences both description and diagnosis of organizational behavior. In this chapter we focus on the way individuals learn, beginning with three models of learning and concluding with the managerial implications of learning. In Chapter 11 we look at the nature of organizational learning and its contribution to an organization's culture.

BEHAVIORIST APPROACH

Behaviorists emphasize external influences and the power of rewards in learning. They emphasize the link between a given stimulus and response. Recall Pavlov's groundbreaking work with dogs, as presented in Figure 2–7.[31] He noted that, upon presentation of powdered meat blown through a tube (unconditioned stimulus) to a dog, the dog salivated (unconditioned response). The ringing of a bell (neutral stimulus) yielded no salivation responses. After pairing the ringing bell with the meat several times, Pavlov then rang the bell without the meat, and the dog salivated (conditioned response). In classical conditioning, as illustrated by Pavlov's experiment, after repeated pairing of neutral and unconditioned stimuli, solitary presentation of the neutral stimulus led to a conditioned response.

Operant conditioning extends classical conditioning to focus on the consequences of a behavior, as shown in Figure 2–8.[32] While a stimulus can still cue a response behavior, the desired or undesired consequence that follows the behavior

FIGURE 2–7 *Pavlov's conditioning experiments*

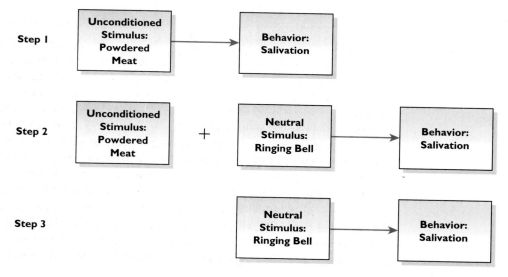

FIGURE 2–8   *Two examples of operant conditioning*

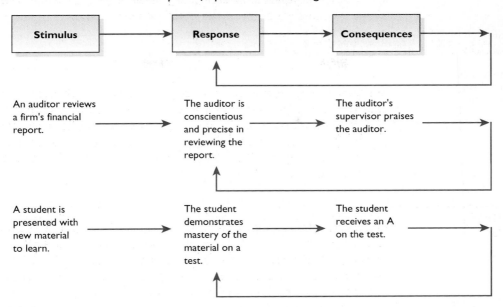

determines whether the behavior will recur. For example, an individual who receives a bonus (a positive consequence) after creative performance (behavior) on a work assignment (stimulus) is more likely to repeat the creative behavior than if his or her performance is ignored (a negative consequence). Continuation of Elizabeth Dawson's giving inaccurate information at Westlake Wallpaper may depend on the consequences associated with it. If she continues to receive pay increases and praise from her supervisor she is more likely to continue her poor performance than if she receives reprimands for giving inaccurate information because she has learned that her current behavior results in desirable outcomes. Chapter 4 examines the significance of operant conditioning for motivation in organizations.

COGNITIVE APPROACH

In contrast to the behavior-reinforcement links that are central to behaviorist theories, cognitive theorists emphasize the internal mental processes involved in learning. They view learning as occurring when various cues in the environment form a mental map. In early cognitive experiments, for example, rats learned to run through a maze to reach a goal of food.[33] Repeated trials cause the rat to develop and strengthen cognitive connections that identified the correct path to the goal.

Employees, too, can develop cognitive maps that show the path to a specific goal, as illustrated in Figure 2–9. Here, the cognitive processes join (and act on) the stimulus to result in a given behavior. On-the-job training in new work processes should result in a new cognitive map of job performance for the employees. More specifically, individuals should develop and sustain new links between the tasks that comprise their job and optimal ways of linking and performing them.

ALLSTATE INSURANCE COMPANY. Agents employed by Allstate Insurance Company participated in a teaching system called Landamatics that addressed the problem of

FIGURE 2–9

An example of a cognitive map

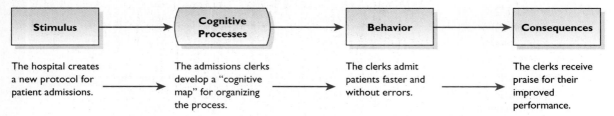

Stimulus	Cognitive Processes	Behavior	Consequences
The hospital creates a new protocol for patient admissions.	The admissions clerks develop a "cognitive map" for organizing the process.	The clerks admit patients faster and without errors.	The clerks receive praise for their improved performance.

determining whether a driver qualifies for a discount on car insurance.[34] Workers are presented with a step-by-step diagram of the decision-making process. Initially they make "yes/no" decisions which they eventually internalize—that is, develop into a cognitive map—so that they can automatically apply the principles learned. Agents who used the Landamatics approach improved the percentage of correctly determined discounts and downpayments from 56 to 97 percent and reduced the average time required from 2.1 minutes to 1 minute.

Cognitive learning theories have also been integrated into expectancy and goal-setting theories as described in Chapter 4.

SOCIAL LEARNING APPROACH

Social learning theory extends beyond both behavioral and cognitive learning theories and integrates these approaches with the idea of modeling or imitating behaviors.[35] Learners first watch others who act as models. Next, they develop a mental picture of the behavior and its consequences. Finally, they try the behavior themselves.[36] If positive consequences result, the learner repeats the behavior; if negative consequences occur, no repetition occurs. Figure 2–10 illustrates the cognitive approach.

This model can describe both on-the-job and off-the-job training. Trainees are presented with models of effective behaviors, such as serving customers or performing managerial analyses, as well as the relationship between these desirable behaviors and consequences, such as praise, promotions, or customer satisfaction.

FIGURE 2–10

Social learning approach to learning

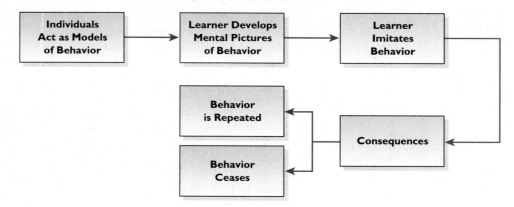

Trainees then rehearse the behaviors and consequences, building cognitive maps that intensify the links and set the stage for future behavior. The learning impact occurs when the subject tries the behavior and experiences a favorable result, as in the behaviorist approach. At the same time, the learner's development of a cognitive image of the situation incorporates a basic aspect of cognitive learning. The learner then has a *gestalt* for viewing the learning situation and thinking about the steps in acquiring new skills, knowledge, or even attitudes.

MANAGERIAL IMPLICATIONS OF LEARNING

How can managers encourage their own and others' learning in the workplace? They can ensure that appropriate conditions for learning exist. Providing appropriate stimuli, including complete and understandable information or material, should facilitate acquisition of skills, knowledge, or attitudes. Managers should also reinforce desired learned behaviors. For example, they should praise employees' behaviors that result in customer satisfaction. They should also provide environmental cues that encourage learning. Structuring a context (e.g., a physical and emotional climate) that supports learning is essential. Increasingly, organizations create off-site opportunities for employees to acquire new skills; these situations eliminate the distractions of the normal work environment that interfere with learning.

To improve training and other forms of individual learning, managers can use the modeling strategy shown in Figure 2–11. The manager can begin by identifying the goal or target behavior(s) that will lead to improved performance. Elizabeth Dawson, for example, needs to find a way to provide accurate information to interior decorators such as Julie Sykes. Next, the manager should select an individual to model the appropriate behavior and determine how to present the model—through a live demonstration, training film, videotape, or other media. Elizabeth might look to her own boss as such a model or view relevant training videos. The manager should also ascertain whether the employee can meet the technical skill requirements of the target behaviors: does Elizabeth have the skills to respond to the customer's requests in an accurate and timely fashion? The manager next should structure a favorable and positive learning environment to increase the likelihood that workers will learn the new behaviors and act in the desired way.

Managers, too, should model the target behavior and carry out supporting activities such as role playing—practicing behaviors through simulating real organizational situations and roles. They must clearly demonstrate the positive consequences of engaging in the modeled target behaviors. They should then positively reinforce the reproduction of the target behaviors both in training and back on the job. For example, Elizabeth's boss should reward her when she meets the cus-

FIGURE 2–11 *A modeling strategy for managers*

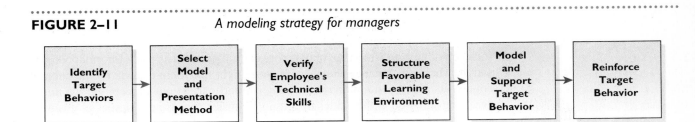

tomer's needs, but not reward inadequate performance. Once the target behaviors are reproduced, management should maintain and strengthen them through the continued use of appropriate rewards. Finally, managers should continue to provide individuals who can model desired behaviors, as well as encourage and reinforce desired behaviors and attitudes.

The application of learning theories applies most directly to training in organizations. Training is a set of activities designed to increase an individual's skills, knowledge, or experiences, or change an individual's attitudes.

THE BIG THREE AUTOMOBILE MANUFACTURERS. General Motors, Ford Motor, and Chrysler, for example, conduct training programs to teach workers basic literacy and mathematics skills; General Motors, for example, has invested $30 million in basic education.[37]

In analyzing the process and outcomes of training programs, we can use either the behaviorist, cognitive, or social learning approaches to describe the learning process. How, for example, does an individual acquire the skills to use a new computer system or develop improved managerial skills? We can also use these approaches to diagnose deficiencies in training. Does sufficient modeling of behavior occur? Are positive consequences, such as increased job responsibilities, greater job autonomy, increased pay, or simply praise tied to the performance of learned behaviors (or skills)?

PERCEPTION, ATTRIBUTION, AND LEARNING IN A GLOBAL ENVIRONMENT

Cultural differences exist in the way individuals process information. They affect the cognitive map, or the content and structure of schemas used to understand the environment and influence behavior.[38] They affect the stimuli we select to perceive, the way we organize them, and the way we interpret them. Our cultural background may cause us to distort our perceptions and attributions in predictable or unpredictable ways. Cultural differences can also affect our approach to and style of learning. These differences are increasingly important in a global economy.

CROSS-CULTURAL PERCEPTIONS

Consider how the crisis at Elegant Interiors might be perceived differently if it occurred in China, in Bulgaria, in Brazil, or in the United States (where it actually occurred). Certainly the interaction between Julie and Elizabeth might be perceived differently by both parties, as well as by outside observers. The customer might also have different perceptions about the women's behavior.

Cultural biases exist and affect perceptions and ultimately behavior and attitudes. Our cultural heritage, for example, may cause us to ignore certain stimuli and focus on others: an American may ignore certain gestures as part of normal conversation, whereas a Japanese business person might find them offensive. The cultural context in which a situation occurs may similarly affect our perception; we might "see" legs crossed at the ankles in certain countries because of the special meaning of crossed legs and not perceive them in others because crossed legs lack meaning in that culture.

Cross-cultural misperceptions occur for four reasons.[39] First, we have subconscious cultural blinders that cause us to interpret events in other countries as if they were occurring in our own. Second, we lack a complete understanding of our own culture and its influence on our behavior. Third, we assume people are more similar to us than they are. Finally, and in general, our parochialism and general lack of knowledge about other cultures contribute to our misperceptions. An awareness of these differences can help us consider and represent the perspectives of several different observers when we describe events or people. If we can incorporate many people's perceptions into an account of a person or event, our description should be more accurate than if we attend only to our own perceptions.

CROSS-CULTURAL ATTRIBUTIONS

In theory, attributions in cross-cultural situations may follow the patterns described earlier in this chapter: either the behavior is attributed to the situation or to the personal characteristics of the individual. To date, however, little research has been done about attributional biases in a multicultural environment. As a result, these attributions may follow unique patterns.

As a practical matter, making accurate attributions in such situations calls for a familiarity with the culture in which the situation occurs. For example, managers of a multicultural work force should not equate poor grammar or mispronunciation with lack of ability, since these errors may instead reflect the use of a second language.[40] Managers should also recognize that multicultural employees may reflect their cultures' assumptions about personal and situational responsibility.

LEARNING BY A MULTICULTURAL WORK FORCE

Although the basic processes of learning remain the same regardless of the type of worker or his or her cultural origins, the context in which learning occurs can significantly influence the outcomes. We know, for example, that on-the-job training may have different outcomes than off-the-job training. Consider the implications of conducting the training in an array of different countries, which typically have significantly different approaches to learning. British universities, for example, emphasize tutorials, whereas schools in the United States more commonly use larger group learning experiences. Different personal learning styles also may be fostered by these various educational experiences. Japanese reasoning has been characterized as analytical, where the whole is broken into parts, and Western reasoning as comprehensive, where the parts are combined into the whole.[41]

Diversity or cross-cultural training often incorporates a social learning approach.[42] Trainees view examples of cross-cultural interactions, then rehearse the same types of behaviors, building cognitive maps of actions that when reinforced serve as the basis of future effective action. Diagnosing the nature of learning and constructing experiences that maximize it are essential for functioning in a global environment.

SUMMARY

Perception, or the selection and organization of stimuli, influences the way we describe organizational situations. Because organizational phenomena are not totally objective, characteristics of the object being perceived and the perceiver influence what aspects become important and are incorporated into a description. Organization of stimuli occurs by setting them against a background or grouping them into patterns. We also store sensations in schemas, as well as act out scripts of sequences of behavior. Often, we distort perceptions through stereotyping, the halo effect, projection, self-fulfilling prophecy, and other mechanisms, resulting in inaccurate descriptions or diagnoses.

Just as we attend to and organize stimuli in predictable ways, we also attribute reasons for behavior in predictable ways. We determine whether an event was intended or accidental; if intended we then attribute its cause to either personal or situational factors. Individuals assign reasons according to the individual's point of view, the appropriateness and impact of the behavior, the nature of the outcomes, the individual's response tendency, and the individual's self-concept. Recognizing the biases is essential for accurate diagnosis.

Learning, which refers to the acquisition of skills, knowledge, ability, or attitudes, influences both description and diagnosis of organizational behavior. The behaviorists emphasize the links between behaviors and their consequences. Cognitive theories focus on attempts to understand and predict the functioning of the human mind. Social learning theorists encourage the development of a mental map of the situation and then build on it with the use of imitation in learning. Managers can develop protocols for learning that incorporate the principles of these approaches. Training in organizations best illustrates the application of these learning principles.

Cultural differences exist in perception, attribution, and learning. Individuals need to recognize cultural biases, such as lack of understanding, a parochialism about culture, differences in language, time, social custom, and a cultural ethnocentrism that affect these processes.

DIAGNOSTIC QUESTIONS

The following diagnostic questions focus on the basic individual processes of perception, attribution, and learning.

- What factors influence the selection of stimuli?

- How are sensations organized?

- What schemas and scripts do individuals use?

- What perceptual distortions occur?

- What factors influence individuals' attributions?

- What biases exist in their attributions?

- What behaviors are reinforced as part of the learning process?

- What cues encourage learning?

- What modeling strategies exist and how are they supported in the organization?

- How accurate are cross-cultural perceptions, attributions, and learning?

- How can individuals improve their perceptions, attributions, and learning in the organization?

$\mathscr{A}$ctivity 2–1 | LORA GREY CASE

STEP 1: Read the Lora Grey Case.

In August 1986 things were progressing well for Lora Grey in the Corporate Planning Department at Frontier Life Insurance Company in Montreal, Quebec, until she unexpectedly came up against her former boss, Hadar Rashad, Information Centre Manager. Rashad had been openly critical of Lora's proposed solution to an information systems problem in Corporate Planning. His criticism not only caused Lora considerable stress, she was worried it could jeopardize her working relationships with her new bosses. Lora knew that the upcoming meeting with Rashad would likely be stormy.

FRONTIER LIFE INSURANCE

Frontier Life Insurance was one of Canada's largest life insurance companies. Frontier was organized around five core areas. (1) The Actuarial Group managed the complex task of developing and costing a full range of life insurance and related products. (2) The Investments Group managed Frontier's portfolio of assets, in excess of $14 billion. (3) The Administration Group was responsible for the extensive internal coordination system required to support 7,000 employees. (4) The Customer Service Group managed premium collection, claims, and renewals for all policyholders. (5) The Marketing/Sales Group was responsible for individual and group insurance sales through a company sales force, as well as developing the promotional and materials strategies for Frontier and its products. Each major area had an executive vice president who reported to the president. Each area was subdivided into organizational units that were led by senior vice presidents, vice presidents, assistant vice presidents, or managers depending on the size and relative importance of the units. The Information

FIGURE 2–12   *Lora Grey: partial organization chart*

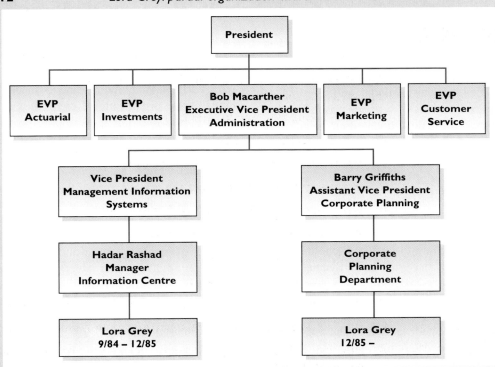

Centre and the Corporate Planning Department were under the broad responsibility of the executive vice president of Administration. The Information Centre was led by a manager. The Corporate Planning Department was led by an assistant vice president (see Figure 2–12).

THE INFORMATION CENTRE

Shortly after its start-up in late 1983, the Information Centre was still a relatively small department with only one consultant, a clerk, and Rashad. Its main function was to support and develop end-user computing in Frontier. End-user computing had not always been possible because computers (either mainframe or mini-computers) were not "user friendly"—that is, computers were sufficiently complex that they were only useful to technical specialists who had a specific use for, and a thorough understanding of, computers. Microcomputers and versatile software programs created a new generation of computer users. The Information Centre was established to support end-users in several ways:

- a "PC literacy" program was available to make senior executives aware of the benefits of end-user computing and to help overcome their apprehension;
- training on various hardware and software programs was provided;
- feasibility studies were conducted to evaluate requests for hardware and software;
- advice on special applications, such as computer graphics, was available; and
- design and technical support was offered to end-users who developed their own software applications.

LORA'S EXPERIENCE IN THE INFORMATION CENTRE

Lora Grey graduated with an MBA at the age of 32 in the spring of 1984. She had six years of information systems experience before returning to business school and decided to stay in systems after graduation. Because Hadar Rashad was looking for an MBA graduate with an information systems background, he actively recruited Lora. Lora concluded that there was a good fit between herself and Frontier and that Rashad was keen on having her join his department. She agreed to join Frontier's Information Centre as its second consultant in the fall of 1984.

Lora described her first eight months in the Information Centre as a "honeymoon." The work was exciting, the Centre was growing, and Hadar Rashad treated her with kid gloves. Hadar Rashad was a 32-year-old East Indian who had been with Frontier for ten years. He had spent the first six years of his career in the Planning and Information Services Department and was promoted in 1983 to the manager of the Information Centre when it was created as a separate department. Rashad was known for hiring very capable women, giving his employees plenty of support early on, having high expectations for quality performance, as well as his dictatorial management style and his vague directions. True to form, Rashad gave Lora considerable support during her first several months in the Information Centre. His support complemented Lora's talents and she quickly earned a reputation for doing creative and innovative work.

Lora was certain that Rashad was on her side. He was keen on her from the first time they had interviewed through his offer to have Lora join the Information Centre. Rashad was just as keen after she had joined Frontier. He treated her well and gave her considerable responsibility and latitude to complete her assignments. Rashad not only had a good professional relationship with Lora, he seemed to enjoy her as a person. When he hosted an office Christmas party at his home, Rashad lavished attention on Lora the whole time. In fact, he spent so much time with her she began to feel embarrassed. Lora left the party early because Rashad was being so excessive.

The Information Centre had a new role in Frontier. It was important for the Information Centre to do good work early and to communicate its success stories to establish some organizational credibility. Rashad thought that the Information Centre should produce a monthly publication to establish a better profile. In December of 1984, he approached Lora to do the publication as a special project. Lora agreed that a publication was a good idea, but she was concerned that it might be premature. She reasoned that a monthly publication would draw considerably on the Centre's already limited resources and the Information Centre did not have a backlog of success stories yet. Lora wondered if a publication at that time might have an adverse effect on the Centre's credibility and whether the limited resources could be spent on higher payback projects. Rashad insisted on the project and Lora reluctantly went ahead. She worked hard on the publication, which was an extra responsibility for her. Despite the constraints she worked under, the first issue of *The First Byte* was a tremendous success. Positive feedback poured into the Information Centre that praised Lora and *The First Byte*. Circulation for *The First Byte* grew by five times within only six months. Rashad also thought *The First Byte* was successful and praised Lora. Lora had a nagging suspicion that Rashad was somewhat envious of the attention she was receiving.

Lora also demonstrated her talents through the development of end-user training programs. It was common in end-user training to rely on material and teaching aids provided by the software and hardware vendors. Lora tailored her programs to the unique needs of Frontier end-users by developing all of her materials and courses from scratch. In addition, Lora's personality and skills were well suited to the training role. Lora ended up enjoying as much success with her training programs as she had with *The First Byte*. In fact, word travelled so quickly about Lora's programs that Jim Oattes, the Manager of the Corporate Training Department, wondered whether Lora was encroaching on his territory. Lora remembered that "Jim literally poked his head into my seminars to find out what I was doing. I thought that the Corporate Training people felt threatened by my programs, but the response from the users was so positive." In the end, Corporate Training recognized Lora as a complement to their efforts—not a threat. In fact, Oattes eventually approached Lora about transferring from the Information Centre to Corporate Training. "He said he was so impressed with my programs and my training skills that he wanted me to work in his department. We also got along extremely well together—he used to call me cookie." Oattes communicated his interest in Lora to Rashad. Lora recalled that Oattes kibitzed with Rashad on several occasions: "If you don't watch out, Hadar, I'm going to steal her—you know she's damn good."

"THE HONEYMOON ENDS"

Lora had been warned by some of her colleagues that Rashad had a habit of drastically changing his management style. She had also been warned of and had observed his tendency to hire capable women, treat them well initially, "end the honeymoon," and then block their progress. Lora recalled an example:

Sheila was hired into the Information Centre as a clerk even though her skill level was consistent with an M&A (Managers & Administrators) classi-fication. He (Rashad) was really good to her up front—until she demonstrated that she was overqualified as a clerk. She tried to get promoted to consultant, but he wouldn't think of it. In fact, he hired three new consultants from outside the company, claiming that consultants should have a university degree (which Sheila did not have). Everyone else in the Centre knew that she was more than qualified. It was perfect irony that one of his new hires turned out to be a terrible flop and Sheila took over *The First Byte* and continued its tremendous success.

Not long after Lora had been approached by Jim Oattes, she developed a new training program for end-users of computer graphics packages. She thought that the program should also cover overall presentation skills, since a graphics package was only one of the tools used in good presentations. She asked for Rashad's input on the graphics program. He was negative and strongly resisted the program. He thought that the presentation skills segment of the program was redundant because he had run a similar program two years earlier. He also did not think that there would be enough interest in the course to justify offering it. Lora thought that two years was a sufficient space between programs and further noted that many new employees who could benefit from the program had joined the company in that time. Rashad reluctantly let Lora offer the program to 15 subscribers on a trial basis. However, he was so opposed to her new program that "he went around the Centre and openly denounced it as being doomed for failure." To Rashad's surprise, 48 people (including vice presidents and assistant vice presidents) enrolled in the course within two days of its being announced. Rashad took the success of Lora's program as a slap in the face. At that point, Lora knew that the honeymoon was over and that her situation would only get worse.

Several things combined to put considerable pressure on Lora. The change in Rashad's attitude towards her alone was difficult to deal with. She had trouble reconciling his criticism with the praise she was receiving from *The First Byte* readers and the participants in her training programs. Lora remembered "having difficulty being comfortable with her success" because of the way Rashad treated her. To complicate matters, Lora's eldest daughter was going through a very troubling phase that pressured Lora even more.

By the summer of 1985 things between Lora and Rashad had reached the intolerable stage. Rashad directed Lora to attend a conference in Nashville, Tennessee, in the third week of July; Lora thought this was Rashad's way of getting her out of his hair. Lora did not mind, she needed a break from him as well. Rashad pointed out that Frontier would reimburse her travel expenses, either mileage or airfare. He encouraged Lora to take advantage of the mileage allowance by taking her children with her and tack on a vacation after the conference. Lora was a single mother, so she took the opportunity to be with her children and minimize vacation costs.

Lora did not feel rested when she returned from Nashville. The conference turned out to be very demanding. Combined with the lengthy drive, Lora's vacation ended up taking a great deal out of her. The final straw came when Rashad approved $1,500 of the conference expenses but disallowed a $30 meal voucher because Lora had included her children. Rashad lit into Lora as if she had committed a crime. The cumulative pressure of the past several months combined with Rashad's antagonistic behavior and his pettiness: Lora broke down into tears in front of him. Rather than back off, Rashad pushed Lora harder and raised the issue of her declining performance. Lora acknowledged that her most recent performance was not as good as before, but pointed out that she had been affected by pressures at home, her workload over the summer had been too heavy, and she had not had a vacation until the Nashville conference—which turned out to be exhausting. She did not admit how much he frustrated her. Rashad reminded Lora that her annual performance appraisal was due and told her that, based on her most recent performance, he could only give her a low-D rating. Lora estimated that 80 percent of Frontier's employees received a low B, 3 percent received a medium B, 3 percent received a high B, less than 1 percent received an A and the balance received C's and D's. Lora thought that her performance over the past year had been well above a low-D rating and was therefore shocked at the possibility of a D rating. Rashad then told Lora to take a few days off and "put things back together." Lora took the time to regroup.

While she was home, Lora resolved that Rashad would not beat her. She returned to work after three days with a more positive frame of mind and a renewed sense of determination. A few days later, Lora found out, to her surprise, that Rashad had deducted the days she took off from her vacation entitlement.

Although Lora was totally exasperated with Rashad, she was happy with Frontier. She had built a strong reputation beyond the Information Centre and was pleased with the benefits and long-term career opportunities in Frontier. She decided to leave the Information Centre, but did not want to consider alternatives outside the company. She knew she still had the standing offer from Jim Oattes to join the Corporate Training Department. In the fall of 1985, Lora went to the Human Resources Department for career planning guidance and advice on Oattes' offer. She simply told Human Resources that it was time for her to tackle a new challenge. She did not mention the difficulties she was having with Rashad.

Frontier had a policy of rotating its employees to broaden its overall staff capability. Human Resources was receptive to Lora's request for a transfer. However, they felt strongly that her talents would not be fully utilized in Corporate Training. They suggested that Lora should consider a position in the Corporate Planning Department. It was common knowledge in Frontier that Corporate Planning was the fast track for ambitious and capable employees. A planning trainee could often springboard to senior management. Several planning trainees had gone on to become Frontier's youngest vice presidents. The planning position would be a significant promotion for Lora and a recognition of her senior management potential. In December of 1985, Lora was offered the Corporate Planning trainee position, a first for women in Frontier. She gladly accepted the position and was shocked by Hadar Rashad's reaction.

Rashad could not have been happier for Lora. When he heard the news he congratulated her, hugged her, and organized a dinner party to celebrate. At the dinner, Rashad led a champagne toast. In addition, Rashad conducted a performance appraisal of Lora just prior to her leaving the Information Centre. He gave her a low-B rating and a generous raise. Because she had left the Information Centre on such seemingly good terms, Lora assumed that her differences with Hadar Rashad had been resolved.

CORPORATE PLANNING

Corporate Planning was a staff function that supported the overall planning process in Frontier. Frontier's planning system was driven by an annual corporate direction statement. The president and the executive vice presidents issued the direction statement and the Corporate Planning Department worked with all other departments to filter the statement through the organization. Corporate Planning's key role within Frontier was to negotiate the annual direction statement with various managers on behalf of senior management. Therefore, negotiation skills were critical to all members of the Corporate Planning Department. Because Corporate Planning was a cross-functional group that worked with employees from the entire organization, Corporate Planning staff tended to have a wide network of internal contacts.

Corporate Planning was headed by Barry Griffiths, Assistant Vice President. Griffiths reported directly to Bob Macarthur, Executive Vice President of Administration. Macarthur was 57, had been with Frontier for 35 years, and had worked in most areas of the company. He had risen to become one of the most powerful people in Frontier through his excellent leadership and his ability to delegate responsibility to capable people. His management style was supportive, positive, and loyal. He was always very clear with his directions and took the blame if there was a problem or a misunderstanding. Griffiths was 32 and had been with Frontier for four years, all in Corporate Planning. Griffiths was personable and supportive, but he was nit-picky and very detail oriented. He didn't always give clear direction and was critical of small mistakes. He was not a very powerful assistant vice president, but he had a strong network of contacts, many of whom were very senior.

Although Griffiths did not normally deal with Hadar Rashad, an extremely antagonistic relationship between them had developed two years earlier because of an odd incident. Consistent with his "last minute" approach, Griffiths had not left enough time to prepare a graphics presentation for a meeting. When his secretary went to the Information Centre to use some graphics equipment, she discovered that Rashad had double-booked the equipment. Griffiths was caught in a real bind. Griffiths then blamed Rashad. Rashad then blamed Griffiths' secretary and the feud started. From then on, Griffiths and Rashad seemed to look for opportunities to get back at each other.

As a planning trainee, Lora reported directly to Griffiths. Her responsibilities were varied, the work was project oriented, and she typically worked under the supervision of senior people in the department. The objective of the training program was to expose the trainees to all facets of Frontier's planning system and to make them comfortable working with senior management. After several months in Corporate Planning, Lora realized that Ingrid Schrieber was having problems with her information workstation. Schrieber was Bob Macarthur's executive secretary and she used her workstation for word processing, printing electronically stored documents, and transmitting memos through an electronic mail system. Although it was not Lora's responsibility to deal with workstation problems, it made sense for her to investigate the problem because of her extensive systems background and her proximity to Schrieber. Lora sat within earshot of Schrieber and they had become good friends within the office, so they spoke candidly about many things, including Schrieber's workstation problem. Figure 2–13 shows the office layout in Corporate Planning.

FIGURE 2–13 *Lora Grey: corporate planning—office layout*

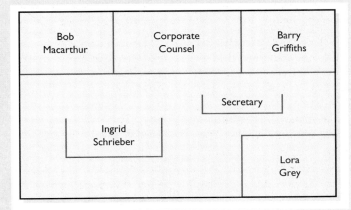

ADDRESSING THE WORKSTATION PROBLEM

Schrieber's workstation was made up of a dedicated word processor, a superior letter-quality printer and a terminal for Frontier's ExecNet system. The ExecNet system was an electronic network that linked all senior managers in Frontier. It allowed executives to communicate internal memos, letters, and documents instantly. ExecNet was a useful system but it was fairly old and "went down" 30 to 40 percent of the time. This was not a big problem for electronic mail users. However, Schrieber's dedicated word processor was linked to ExecNet and her word processor also went down when ExecNet did. This situation was intolerable for the secretary to one of Frontier's most senior executives. Lora figured that if Schrieber had her own personal computer with a word processing package, she could bypass ExecNet and eliminate a considerable amount of her downtime. Lora thought the solution was technically feasible and called Jason Detlor, one of her former colleagues in the Information Centre, for confirmation.

Detlor examined Schrieber's workstation and agreed that a PC would solve the problem. The process for acquiring a PC required a senior manager to send a formal request to the Information Centre. The Information Centre then conducted a feasibility study. A

FIGURE 2–14   *Lora Grey: Lora's first memo to Macarthur*

Date: August 7, 1986

To: Bob Macarthur, Executive Vice President--
    Administration

From: Lora Grey, Trainee--Corporate Planning

RE: <u>Problems with Ingrid Schrieber's Workstation</u>

Over the past couple of months, it has come to my attention that Ingrid is having considerable technical difficulty with her workstation, particularly with the downtime caused by the ExecNet system. I estimate that Ingrid is unable to use her word processor 30%-40% of the time because of problems with ExecNet. ExecNet is an excellent system, but it has not been updated recently and several technological advances have been made that could improve Ingrid's efficiency. Specifically, there are several excellent word processing packages that can be used in conjunction with a Personal Computer (PC). A PC could probably be linked to ExecNet so that Ingrid could continue to transmit all of her documents internally. The only change would be that Ingrid would have to use a letter-quality printer instead of the superior letter-quality printer that she currently uses. Overall, a PC word processing system would increase Ingrid's productivity and provide you with increased turnaround time and suitable quality printing.

Given my background in the Information Centre, I would be happy to contact them and put the wheels in motion. Please let me know if you agree. Thanks.

PC could only be acquired with the approval of the Information Centre. Detlor temporarily routed Schrieber's word processor through Lora's PC to eliminate the downtime that was plaguing Schrieber. The temporary solution required Schrieber to use Lora's letter-quality printer instead of her own superior letter-quality printer.

Lora was satisfied that a PC would solve Schrieber's problem, that it was technically feasible, and that the financial benefit of significantly improving Schrieber's productivity would outweigh the cost of a PC. She drafted a memo to Bob Macarthur outlining the situation and her proposed solution. She sent the memo to him directly via ExecNet (see Figure 2–14). If Macarthur agreed with her, Lora assumed he would follow up with a formal request to the Information Centre or ask her to do one. If he disagreed, Lora assumed he would either do nothing or talk further with her about it.

Based on the scores of memos she had seen in the Information Centre, Lora thought that her memo was straightforward.

LORA'S CONFRONTATION WITH HADAR RASHAD

One week after she had sent the memo to Macarthur, Lora received a copy of a new memo on ExecNet. The new memo was written from Hadar Rashad to Bob Macarthur. Rashad had not copied Lora on the memo; Macarthur had sent the copy to Lora (see Figure 2–15).

Lora was surprised and shocked by Rashad's memo. She reacted first to the content. Although she was still confident that her solution was sound, she was concerned about how Macarthur may have reacted to Rashad's assertion that she was wrong. She also reacted to the process. Until she received Rashad's

FIGURE 2–15   *Lora Grey: Rashad's memo to Macarthur*

```
Date: August 13, 1986

To: Bob Macarthur

From: Hadar Rashad

RE: Lora Grey's Memo of August 7, 1986

Thank you for sending the above letter to me and asking
for my comments. It is a good thing you asked for my input
because Lora has obviously not done her homework on Mrs.
Schrieber's situation. Firstly, there is no card available
that would allow a PC interface with ExecNet. Secondly,
the system Lora proposed would not give you a sufficiently
high quality of printing. I suggest that I discuss the is-
sue with the ExecNet people to get better support for Mrs.
Schrieber and possibly get some new equipment if her sta-
tion is going down that frequently.

I was very disappointed to learn that Lora had not ap-
proached me first on this issue. She still does not have a
good grasp of how to get things done in Frontier. Clearly,
this falls within my area of responsibility and there was
no need for her to get you involved at this stage. Unless
you advise me otherwise, I will follow up.
```

memo, Lora had not realized that Macarthur had communicated with the Information Centre. Lora drafted a new memo to Macarthur (see Figure 2–16). This time she copied both Barry Griffiths and Hadar Rashad. Lora assumed that Barry Griffiths would back her on this because she was well aware of Griffiths' strong dislike for Rashad. She was not sure how Macarthur would react, though.

Griffiths called Lora into his office on Wednesday August 20, 1986, to ask for more details and learn Lora's side of the story. Griffiths told Lora that Macarthur had spoken to him and asked him to look into the workstation situation. Then he called Rashad on the telephone while Lora was still in his office. Lora described the conversation as "aggressive." Griffiths basically defended Lora and eventually told Rashad that his position was "hogwash." He suggested that Rashad should meet on the following Monday with Schrieber and Lora to discuss and resolve the entire situation. After Griffiths hung up, he reassured Lora that he supported her. However, he didn't think he should get involved any further because he did not want to be seen as having to fight Lora's battles.

Lora knew that Rashad would probably be angry and maybe even irrational. She had seen him lose his cool before and she anticipated that Rashad could be particularly incensed because Lora had made him look bad in front of Macarthur. The situation had

FIGURE 2–16   *Lora Grey: Lora's second memo to Macarthur*

```
Date: August 19, 1986

To: Bob Macarthur, Executive Vice President--
    Administration

From: Lora Grey, Trainee--Corporate Planning

Re: Hadar Rashad's Memo of August 13, 1986

In response to Hadar's above memo, I disagree with him
that I did not do my homework. In fact, Jason Detlor from
the Information Centre was up here two weeks ago and he
successfully demonstrated the ExecNet interface that I had
suggested. I think Hadar should check the technical speci-
fications of my recommendation with his people.

In addition, I think Hadar has overestimated Ingrid's
needs for superior letter-quality printing. She advises me
that she does external documents only 3-4 times per week.
For those cases, she could use Central Word Processing or
Norma's equipment if the document is confidential.

I suggest that Hadar might wish to confer with Ingrid on
her exact needs before any decision is reached.




cc: B. Griffiths
    H. Rashad
```

also given Griffiths a reason to jump on Rashad's back. As Lora thought ahead to Monday's meeting, she reflected on what had already happened and what could happen.

STEP 2: Prepare the case for class discussion.

STEP 3: Answer each of the following questions, individually or in small groups, as directed by your instructor.

DESCRIPTION

1. What was Lora's perception of her performance in the Information Centre?
2. How did Lora's perceptions change during the case?
3. What was Hadar's perceptions of Lora's performance?
4. How did his perceptions change during the case?
5. How do Lora's and Hadar's perceptions of Mrs. Schrieber's situation differ?

DIAGNOSIS

6. What factors affected their perceptions?
7. What were Lora's and Hadar's attributions for their actions regarding Mrs. Schrieber's situation?
8. What attributional biases existed?

PRESCRIPTION

9. How could the situation have been improved?

STEP 4: Discussion. In small groups, with the class as a whole, or in written form, share your answers to the questions above. Then answer the following questions:

1. What symptoms suggest a problem exists?
2. What problems exist in the case?
3. What theories and concepts help explain those problems?
4. How can the problems be corrected?
5. Are the actions likely to be effective?

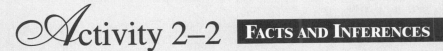

Activity 2–2   FACTS AND INFERENCES

STEP 1: Carefully read the following report and the observations based on it. Indicate whether you think the observations are true, false, or doubtful on the basis of the information presented in the report. Circle **T** if the observation is definitely true, circle **F** if the observation is definitely false, and circle **?** if the observation may be either true or false. Judge each observation in order. Do not reread the observations after you have indicated your judgment, and do not change any of your answers.

A well-liked college teacher had just completed making up the final examinations and had turned off the lights in the office. Just then a tall, broad figure appeared and demanded the examination. The professor opened the drawer. Everything in the drawer was picked up and the individual ran down the corridor. The dean was notified immediately.

1. The thief was tall and broad.   **T F ?**
2. The professor turned off the lights.   **T F ?**
3. A tall figure demanded the examination.   **T F ?**
4. The examination was picked up by someone.   **T F ?**
5. The examination was picked up by the professor.   **T F ?**
6. A tall figure appeared after the professor turned off the lights in the office.   **T F ?**

7. The man who opened the drawer was the professor. **T F ?**
8. The professor ran down the corridor. **T F ?**
9. The drawer was never actually opened. **T F ?**
10. In this report three persons are referred to. **T F ?**

STEP 2: In small groups, discuss your answers and then reach consensus about the answers. Write these answers in a separate place.

STEP 3: The instructor will read the correct answers. Score the questions, once for you as an individual and again for your group.

STEP 4: Discussion. Did your scores change? Why? Why do people answer these questions incorrectly?

This exercise is taken from Joseph A. Devito, *General Semantics: Guide and Workbook*, rev. ed. Deland, Fla: Everett/Edwards, 1974, p. 55, and is reprinted with permission.

*A*ctivity 2–3   A-PLUS AERONAUTICS

STEP 1: Read the following case. (Your instructor will distribute the performance charts to you.)

A-Plus Aeronautics is an electronics firm that manufactures components for instrument control panels used in commercial jets. The company operates as a large job shop, routing custom-ordered products through the work centers in three major shop areas: Fabrication, Assembly, and Testing. There are several work centers in each shop. The custom-ordered products are manufactured in lots of approximately 100 to 1,000, with each item flowing through at least thirty work centers on its way to completion.

Subcomponents such as circuit boards are assembled in the Assembly Shop, where there are fifteen different work centers dedicated to particular kinds of technologies and tasks. The 100 employees in this shop are highly skilled and most of them have been with the company for five or more years.

Hanna Yates is a first-line supervisor for the employees in Work Center 7 of the Assembly Shop. She was transferred to this position from Testing and has not previously held a strictly supervisory position. There are fifteen people reporting to her, ten of whom are on the day shift, and five of whom are on the night shift. The performance of day-shift employees is the easiest to monitor because it is possible for Hanna to observe them. Performance of night-shift employees is more difficult to monitor, however, and she relies heavily on daily performance charts generated by the company computer as a source of information about this group. Hanna has learned through informal channels that there may be a performance problem, having to do with declining output, during the night shift. She refers to her performance charts to see what the problem might be.

STEP 2: Answer the following questions as if you were Hanna, using only the information available to you. Respond to each one by circling the number that best represents your assessment of the situation.

1. How would you rate the seriousness of Employee C's output decline?

1	2	3	4	5	6	7
not serious			moderately serious			extremely serious

2. What is the likelihood that the problem has something to do with Employee C him/herself (e.g., effort, ability, attitude)?

1	2	3	4	5	6	7
not likely			moderate likelihood			extremely likely

3. What is the likelihood that the problem has something to do with the work environment (e.g., task difficulty, materials, equipment, available information)?

1	2	3	4	5	6	7
not likely			moderate likelihood			extremely likely

STEP 3: Your instructor will direct you in tallying the questionnaire results and displaying them.

STEP 4: Discussion. In small groups, with the entire class, or in writing, as directed by your instructor, answer the following questions:

DESCRIPTION
1. How did the ratings of Group A and Group B differ?

DIAGNOSIS
2. Would attribution theory have predicted these differences?

3. How do attributional biases influence supervisors' diagnostic judgments?

PRESCRIPTION
4. How could we improve their judgments?

This exercise was drawn from Karen Brown and Terence Mitchell, Teaching attribution theory with graphical displays of performance comparisons, *Organizational Behavior Teaching Journal* 8(3) (1983): 23–28.

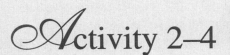 **THE CASE OF BRIAN McCARTHY AND BEACON HILL PUBLISHING**

STEP 1: Read the case of Brian McCarthy and Beacon Hill Publishing.

> As I walked to my car, I felt as though a dream had just ended, before it had begun. All of the expectations, the hopes, were crushed. How could it not have worked? Did I fail? Why has it ended, so soon? As I left Beacon Hill Publishing, for the last time, I was, at once, shattered and liberated.

THE MATCH

Brian McCarthy, a bright, energetic full-time MBA student at the Carroll Graduate School of Management of Boston College was in his second and last year of studies. At 23, he was young and his work experience was limited, having immediately entered the MBA program from undergraduate studies. Yet he exuded self-confidence and maturity. He excelled in academics, and was active in a number of extracurricular activities, among them, the editorship of the *Graduate Gazette*. It was in this capacity, he first met Roger Goldberg, President of Beacon Hill Publishing, the printer of the *Gazette*.

BEACON HILL PUBLISHING

Beacon Hill Publishing had been in existence for over 14 years. The company's niche was primarily college publications. With annual sales of 12 million, and about 90 full-time employees, Beacon Hill was very much a family company. Sales had plateaued during the last three years, after impressive growth during most of the 1980s. Beacon Hill prided itself on the quality of its work and the neatness of its operations. Yet, the industry had undergone change during the early 1990s. Competition had increased and profit margins had been squeezed. Internally, Beacon Hill was somewhat insulated from recent market changes—in particular, the consumer move from "premium priced quality" to "value orientation." Additionally, for the past few years, the sales department was considered quite weak.

Roger Goldberg, 42, was the founder, majority stockholder (the company was privately held), and president. Charismatic and diplomatic, Goldberg's life was devoted to his work. At the age of 15, he began working for his father's small printing company in Vermont. After various jobs in the industry, he, at 28, started Beacon Hill in 1978. According to company veterans, Goldberg *was* Beacon Hill, and Beacon Hill *was* Goldberg.

Louise Goldberg, 44, was the controller, as well as Roger's wife of 16 years. She had been with Roger from the start, and held a minority interest of the stock. While her accounting procedures were generally primitive—literally performed out of notebooks, she had tremendous influence on the course of the company. Her power was pervasive at Beacon Hill.

Paul Olivetti, a friend and business partner of Roger well before the inception of Beacon Hill, was vice president who oversaw computer information systems and technical printing issues. At 63, Paul, the only other shareholder, was perhaps past his prime, but like Roger, printing was his life. Filled with nervous energy, Paul saw himself as somewhat of a father figure to Roger Goldberg, as well as to the company in general.

Cindy Williams, 38, customer service manager and assistant to the president, had been with Roger for over ten years and she was married to the production manager, Ron Williams.

Many of the others in the company were either relatives, people who had been with the company since the beginning, or close friends of these individuals.

THE BEGINNINGS: COMING TOGETHER

The initial phone conversation between *Graduate Gazette* Editor McCarthy and Goldberg was professional and cordial. McCarthy was impressed with the fact that the president of the company was to be his primary contact, as well as with Goldberg's warm and personable tone. During September, they spoke a number of times, mainly to iron out any production or technical details. Roger invited Brian to tour the plant, and once actually offered to go to the campus to help with the preparation of the *Gazette.* Brian was immediately struck by Roger's openness and generosity. Later, in satisfying a course requirement, he contacted Roger for "An Interview with an Entrepreneur." Roger eagerly accommodated.

The interview went extraordinarily well. For nearly two hours on a Sunday morning in his posh suburban home, over coffee and doughnuts, Goldberg discussed the personal and professional dimensions of his venture, as well as entrepreneurship in general. Brian recalled his fascination as Roger proudly discussed the excitement and satisfaction of creating and building a successful organization. But later in the interview, he also pointed with sadness to the fact that he and his wife Louise had forgone having children—that the company was their life.

"You might say that we truly hit it off," Brian recalled excitedly to a classmate. "I am impressed with this guy. As a businessman, he seems wise and progressive, and as a person, charismatic, and candid. I sensed that he has a genuine interest in me and my future. He asked about my background and education—he loves the idea of the MBA."

Brian continued almost giddily to his classmate: "He mentioned in passing something about a position as director of sales at Beacon Hill that he had been trying to fill for some time. We grinned and suggested that that topic might be more appropriate for a future discussion. I might have accomplished more than simply satisfying the entrepreneurship requirement."

Over the next three months, the relationship between McCarthy and Goldberg continued to grow. Often Brian would drive the *Gazette* to Roger's house early in the evening for Roger to take to the press. On some of these occasions, the two would discuss school, business, pleasure, and the Red Sox at Roger's kitchen table until 11:00 at night. A few months later, Roger relayed to Brian, "I remarked to Louise that you are becoming our adopted son." Brian was flattered.

"He's a sharp kid," Roger said to Louise over dinner one night. "I like him a lot. Can you see him in sales? Maybe helping get the department on track, taking some pressure off me?" he asked Louise.

"Well, I don't know him. I mean, what does he know about printing?"

"He's got a lot on the ball. He's young, aggressive. He'll have his MBA."

"Yeah . . ."

"Well, it's just a thought," he ended.

In January, Brian began his job search. He was targeting management consulting firms in the Boston area. Due largely to the effects of a deepening recession, early results were discouraging. But as the number of rejection letters increased, so too did Goldberg's probings of Brian's career intentions. "What is your 'wish list'? What are you trying to accomplish in the job search?" Brian sensed there was more than a casual interest in the questions and remembered the director of sales position that Roger mentioned at the initial meeting. In April, at Roger's invitation, Brian visited the Beacon Hill plant. He reflected:

It was a great afternoon. The plant was very impressive—large, clean, it looked like an exciting place to work. And Roger was an awesome sight, strutting briskly and confidently from the production area through to the offices. He introduced me to various managers, "This is the guy from BC. He's graduating with his MBA next month." I can easily see myself working there.

Soon after the visit to Beacon Hill, with graduation imminent, McCarthy was not surprised when Goldberg invited him to talk more directly about the job. McCarthy recalled the occasion:

Meeting for dinner and drinks at Roger's favorite restaurant, we engaged in deep discussion of what Beacon Hill faces in an increasingly competitive market, the kind of company that Beacon Hill is, and we talked about the role of sales director. We conversed personally about the kind of people we are and shared some of our expectations. We discussed employment terms briefly, then returned to our dreams. We talked about taking over the publications printing industry. We went from "a serious discussion," to Roger offering me the job and my accepting during this one evening. It seemed to be a perfect match.

Louise Goldberg happened to be in the same restaurant with some friends that night and stopped by their table. Roger announced, "Louise, we just hired our first MBA." She responded somewhat favorably, then, turning to McCarthy, she launched into a colorful and emphatic instruction portraying the culture of Beacon Hill. She stressed that Beacon Hill was a tightly knit, familial environment, that was a "down to earth" operation. She cautioned him to understand his role as an outsider coming into such a company and to go slowly, particularly in the beginning. Because she spoke most earnestly, Brian listened attentively.

It was near midnight when Goldberg and McCarthy toasted their agreement and parted. Though weary, McCarthy drove to his parents' house to celebrate the good news. He mused during the ride "graduation will be all the sweeter now."

He was to start on June 1st.

THE FIRST WEEK

The first week was a whirlwind introduction and orientation to Beacon Hill, its people, as well as the industry. As Brian began to learn the technical nature of the printing industry and to sort out the issues confronting the Sales Division he now headed, Roger spent an extraordinary amount of time with him. Both were excited with the arrangement. They met each morning for an hour or so, a few brief times during the day, and then again in the late afternoon. During the week, Brian had formal meetings with each of the dozen or so key people in the organization. His initial orientation appeared to be going well. Friday evening, Brian wrote in his journal:

The first week has been terrific. Where has it gone! I am listening and learning as much as I can. I feel each of my meetings with the managers went quite well. People appear to be open and welcoming, except for Louise, that is. In my meeting with her, she conveyed a similar tone as her acerbic remarks at the restaurant the evening I accepted the offer. She lectured me about the company and her expectations of me. I think this relationship is going to take some work.

McCarthy was very sensitive to the organizational issues associated with his entrance as "an outsider," and tried not to wear the MBA on his sleeve. He suppressed any natural inclinations of brashness and self-assuredness in an effort to facilitate the process of achieving organizational acceptance.

At the end of the first week, Goldberg commented to McCarthy, "You are not the neophyte I thought you might be. Your reception here is going much better than I expected. I think that your energy has been contagious in a very positive way. And my bringing someone in to run sales shows the company that we are serious about turning things around there." Brian was very pleased and smiled to himself that he *was* gaining acceptance.

THE SECOND WEEK

The second week went much the same. Some of his fellow employees were friendlier than others. As Louise had said, communication within the organization was rather informal. An informal lunch group that included Paul, Cindy, Ron, and some others gathered daily. Brian had not yet been invited to these. And being so new to the organization, he was excluded from the informal discussions he noticed throughout the plant each day. Yet he was glad for the end of the day meetings with Roger, by whom he felt fully accepted.

McCarthy worked hard to learn about the industry, the printing process, Beacon Hill Publishing, as well as to understand the condition of the Sales Department. He devoured trade journals; observed the operations and meetings at Beacon Hill; discussed internal and external challenges with individuals from sales as well as others in the company. He became aware that the Sales Department had some serious problems. There were only four salesmen and their productivity was modest at best, as Brian saw it. As far as he could determine, no mission, strategy or supporting structures had ever existed in the Sales Department. In the words of one salesman, "Roger simply watches over our every move and regularly intervenes to help out when he senses a problem. In fact, if the truth be known, Roger himself is the leading salesman in the company." Morale in the Sales Department appeared to be quite low.

During a midweek visit to his alma mater to meet with his successor at the *Gazette*, McCarthy encountered one of his professors and related what he had found in the Sales Department.

> This company is entirely production driven, not at all sales oriented. I'm picking up an inferiority complex among the salespeople and there are also some disturbing signs that those outside of sales have little respect for us. In fact, I heard a story from someone in production that two salesmen in the past had allegedly left the firm with customer lists and other sensitive information. That certainly doesn't help any. There is lots of work to be done.

McCarthy told Goldberg at the beginning of the second week that he was determined to turn Sales around. Goldberg beamed. McCarthy reported on the status of his efforts—including his perception that people in sales seemed cooperative. McCarthy had begun to formulate and implement some basic measures. First, two regularly scheduled sales meetings were to be conducted each week. Second, a central database for prospect tracking purposes was to be created. Roger nodded in the affirmative. Both steps, in fact, were accomplished in conjunction with the salesman, Roger, and Cindy, the Customer Service Manager (and assistant to the president). Initial results appeared to be favorable.

During the second week, Brian was invited to a managers meeting. This was a great moment for him. It was all coming together, he thought to himself. He bragged to a classmate over drinks one evening.

I introduced the notion of a value oriented market versus a premium demand. You should have seen the looks on their faces! They thought it was brilliant! You would not believe how backward this company is. All the accounting and control systems are obsolete, if they exist at all. They don't even have a spreadsheet on-line. It's amazing. Wait until I unleash my secret weapon, the Mac. At least I'll take Sales into the twentieth century.

Before leaving on Friday of the second week, Brian noted on his calendar, "Things are going very well!"

THE THIRD WEEK

In the third week, a critical situation developed. In a discussion with Goldberg early in June when he arrived at Beacon Hill Publishing, McCarthy had broached the subject of bringing in his own Macintosh personal computer into the office to assist in his duties as director of sales. After two weeks of direct observation, McCarthy delicately suggested that Beacon Hill was somewhat behind in terms of computerization and that his personal computer could help close the gap. Roger seemed hesitant at first, then approved Brian's introduction of the computer. Assuming the president's pause related to doubts about the utility of the Mac, Brian identified a number of sales activities that would be made infinitely easier using it. Though Roger approved, he did not appear entirely convinced. The subject was dropped as the two moved on to discuss another matter.

On Wednesday, Brian happily carried his Mac into Beacon Hill, declaring with a smile to a couple of managers he passed, "Now I can call this place home." A number of events occurred in the following hours. During lunch with his fiance, Brian recalled a bewildering morning.

> Shortly after I had set up the Mac in my office on the second floor, I walked downstairs to photocopy some document. Roger, with a somewhat frantic look, called me into his office. "You've caused quite a firestorm by bringing in your Mac," he said in a raspy voice I'd never heard before. I was shocked—I asked the reason. Roger said that he was not sure exactly why the computer had caused this disruption, but it had. He told me he had to run out to see a customer, and instructed me to keep the issue quiet until he returned. I nodded in

agreement but stood for a moment trying to digest what had happened. I went back to my desk. I couldn't imagine what was going on.

Within 10 minutes, Paul Olivetti walked into Brian's office and paced uncomfortably. He indicated to McCarthy that he was concerned about who would pay for a printer (an issue still unresolved), and the integration (or lack thereof) of the Mac to the company's DOS network. McCarthy avoided entering further into a discussion, or defense, recalling Roger's caveat of a few minutes earlier. McCarthy told Paul that Roger intended to have a meeting to address the questions and concerns of people in the organization later that afternoon. Brian remembered, "As Paul left, I sat back with a sinking feeling." He continued to his fiance:

> Would you believe, about five minutes later, Louise marched toward my desk. She began, "About the computer . . ." With a smile of disbelief and almost resignation, I tried to acknowledge the impact of this computer: "Louise, I realize this has caused quite a commotion . . ." Pointing her finger at me, as I sat and she stood, she fired, "This is not one bit funny."
>
> I sat motionlessly as she excoriated: "Bringing this computer in looks like you really don't want to be part of the team . . . that you're separate from the rest of us, and doing your own thing up here. People in this company look at you and say 'Who does this punk think he is, coming in here with his own computer?' You're still a stranger. You have to earn respect, you just don't get it because you have an MBA or title or something."
>
> Gee, I can't tell you how insulted and infuriated I felt. But I bit my tongue and tried to explain that Roger said that I could bring it in.
>
> She fired right back, "So what? Who is Roger? He is one person. Did you think to check with me? Did you check with Paul? Or anyone else to see if it is OK? No, obviously you did not."
>
> By this time, she was getting to me, so I said "Certainly, it is not my intention *not* to be part of the team. Precisely the opposite, in fact. I feel I have done everything in my power to become part of the team, and to earn respect over the past three weeks."
>
> I tried to allay her fears and give insight as to my motivations: "The computer will help me be a

better sales director. If I am a better sales director then I can be a better part of the team."

> As if she hadn't heard a word I had just said, she fired the same argument again. It was clear she would have the last word and so I didn't contest. I remembered Roger's advice to avoid the issue until later. She left the room with the same unbelievable view with which she entered. The computer is in trouble, and so am I.

During the afternoon, Brian, though still angry and confused about the furor over his Mac, worked on some sales projects manually with the computer conspicuously unplugged in the corner of the office.

Goldberg did not return until six that evening. Louise had left, and only Paul and Brian were still in the building. At Roger's request, the three met to discuss the computer issue. Though the atmosphere was tense, the tone was civil and constructive. Once again, Brian tried to present a convincing case for how the Mac would enhance his own effectiveness as well as that of the Sales Department. He stressed the point that his computer would not be on-line,[1] so any concerns of confidentiality were unwarranted. The three agreed that incorporating the Mac could be a sound solution to some of the problems in sales. But, the sensitivity of the issue, i.e., Louise's reaction and public position, was a serious consideration. Roger and Paul were emphatic that it would be best to table the issue for the time being, to defer using the Mac, and that the issue would be reopened soon.

Before turning in for the night, McCarthy entered in his journal:

> Tonight as Paul and I walked to our cars, he chided me for moving too quickly with the computer and said that Roger is not necessarily the one to consult on that sort of issue. He suggested, with a smile and a nod, that I "speak to Uncle Paul" in the future for advice on such matters.

THE FOURTH WEEK

During the end of the third week, and into the fourth, Brian noticed a sharp drop off in the amount of time Roger was spending with him. When Brian mentioned this, Roger explained that the desperate need for sales was pulling him away. Indeed, talk around the company had focused on deteriorating sales and profit margins in a cyclical market exacerbated by a persistent general recession. Even though McCarthy recognized the critical business situation, he still felt Roger's increasing inaccessibility had other causes and that began to disturb him. In an evening out with his father, Brian struggled with these recent developments:

I get the sense that he is less pleased spending time with me. Certainly the demands on him as the chief company breadwinner are important, but somehow he sees me a bit differently now than before. Maybe the computer issue revealed that I could be a thorn in his side with others in the company. The honeymoon sure is over, Dad.

McCarthy spent the end of the third and most of the fourth week working largely on his own. He was creating the Central Database and conducting Sales meetings. Other than that, his orientation and training, which had primarily relied on Roger's tutoring, had broken down. He was patient, but troubled. He tried to pin Roger down but was leery of pushing too hard. Most of their meetings during this period were conducted at the end of the day. And the days were long, so they met usually at 6:30 or 7:00 P.M. when both of them were tired, especially Roger. They were both unhappy, but McCarthy was waiting for things to turn around.

Brian was not invited to any more of the managers' meetings during this period, a fact that displeased him. Goldberg explained that they were discussing pressroom layoffs and he wanted the other managers to feel completely comfortable and to express their feelings frankly, undistracted by the presence of a newcomer.

Brian also gingerly raised the computer issue again because, as he told Roger, "It is an increasing handicap as I try to develop in my position." Roger and Paul both persisted that he wait longer, cautioning him not too be too aggressive.

On Wednesday of the fourth week, at about 9:30 A.M., Goldberg summoned Brian to his office. Roger appeared very serious.

Looking Brian straight in the eye, he snapped, "What have you been using the copier for?"

Caught off guard and puzzled, Brian answered, "Ah, business stuff . . . business purposes."

"What business purposes?"

"All sorts. Copies of quotes. Copies of memos. Ah, copies of articles from trade journals. That sort of things. Why do you ask?" Brian was off balance.

Never breaking eye contact and leaning forward, Roger elaborated, "The reason I ask, Brian, is that someone has seen you coming into the plant first thing in the morning, photocopying documents, going to your car, and then not returning with them."

Dumbfounded, and deeply offended by the charge, Brian reddened and blurted, "What? Definitely not! Absolutely not. Are you serious? Where is this coming from? It simply is not true."

"Okay. That is what I hoped you would say," Roger responded slowly, sounding somewhat rehearsed. "I don't know exactly who said it. It came to me secondhand. But I believe you."

His eyes now glistening with rage, Brian angrily continued, "This is unbelievable. I never, not once, ever copied a document, any document, then deposited it in my car. Not once. Not ever. Roger, over the last month I might have gone to my car three or four times. My sunroof was open once. I left my lunch in there once or twice. But that is it."

"Okay. Okay. I believe you. I do," Goldberg said seemingly trying to convince himself.

As if he did not hear Roger, Brian fired back, "The implication is insulting. It is untrue. At least let me know who said this so I can confront the person and explain the situation."

With a shrug of his shoulders, Roger said, "I don't know who. What matters is that you have *me* on your side. I believe you." He sighed. "Well, enough of this. Now on that publication for the University of Massachusetts . . ."

Brian did not hear anything else. Flabbergasted, and deeply offended, he proceeded mechanically. The rest of the day was a near total loss.

Brian could not put this searing encounter out of his mind. The more he thought, the more bothered by these events he became. The computer episode and now this accusation of stealing company documents utterly confused him. His character had been challenged and he was hurt and angered. He questioned himself. He wrote in his journal that night:

This is gnawing away at me. I am beginning to see a pattern and I wonder if perhaps I've had a role in provoking these situations and reactions. Did I instigate these problems? Have I predisposed the company to look upon me with suspicion through my attitude or my actions or comments, however subtly? Was it me? Is this a normal part of my introduction to the proverbial "real world?" Or not? Why are they suspicious? Why are they resisting me? Should I fight or should I acquiesce?

On Thursday, an eerie mood pervaded the plant. The unwelcome sight of "the accountants" heading to the conference room, made everyone uncomfortable. Roger and the rest of the managers were in meetings for hours. When not in conference, Roger was out of the office. Brian spoke with him only briefly late in the day, and the talk was of no consequence.

On Friday, the last day of his first month, Brian was on the road for most of the day, at bid openings and some other activities. As he entered the plant, returning from an appointment at about 4:00 in the afternoon, Cindy, Roger's assistant, was summoning everyone in the company to the back lunchroom—the only place in the plant large enough to accommodate all the employees. Noticing Brian's quizzical look, a salesman whispered that Roger would be addressing the company shortly, and then added that there had been a 15 percent layoff that afternoon.

As Roger made his way to the lunchroom, he directed Brian to the director of Human Resources, Whit, who asked Brian to join him in Roger's office. "What is going on?" Brian asked impatiently.

"There has been a major layoff today and . . ."

"Am I part of the layoff?"

"This is something that Roger should . . ."

"Whit, am I part of the layoff?"

"Yes." The word almost stuck in his throat. Brian slumped in the chair.

Whit hastened, "This decision is solely an economic one. It has nothing to do with anything you have done or not done. You weren't here long enough to fail."

Struggling to keep his composure, "All I can say is that this doesn't square with the commitment Roger and I made to one another. It is totally, totally inconsistent." Brian shook his head in disbelief.

Roger entered after about 15 minutes or so. He had difficulty looking Brian in the eye. He expressed regret in having to lay him off. He stressed that the decision was solely financial and that the "things that had been going on" were completely irrelevant. He said that laying Brian off was the most difficult part of the decision.

Crestfallen, Brian concluded to his father on the phone that night, "I wished Roger 'good luck' as I left. Louise avoided me on my way out of the building. I made my way over to her office and wished her luck as well. She smiled and said, 'You too.'"

STEP 2: Prepare the case for class discussion.

STEP 3: Answer each of the following questions, individually or in small groups, as directed by your instructor.

DESCRIPTION

1. What was Brian's perception of his performance?
2. How did Brian's perceptions change during the case?
3. What were Roger Goldberg's and Louise Goldberg's perceptions of Brian?
4. How did their perceptions change during the case?
5. How did the perceptions of Brian, Roger, and Louise differ?

DIAGNOSIS

6. What factors affected the perceptions of Brian, Roger, and Louise?
7. What were Brian's attributions of the reasons for Louise's behavior toward him?
8. What attributional biases existed?
9. What learning occurred during the case?

PRESCRIPTION

10. How could the situation have been improved?

STEP 4: Discussion. In small groups, with the class as a whole, or in written form, share your answers to the questions above. Then answer the following questions:

1. What symptoms suggest a problem exists?
2. What problems exist in the case?
3. What theories and concepts help explain those problems?
4. How can the problems be corrected?
5. Are the actions likely to be effective?

Reprinted with permission of the authors, Professor John W. Lewis, III and Robert McGrath.

[1]The MAC was not compatible with Beacon Hill's DOS system, so no client files or financial information on Beacon Hill were accessible to McCarthy. The MAC was simply to serve him as a personal tool for word processing and basic spreadsheet operations.

Activity 2–5 THE LEARNING-MODEL INSTRUMENT

STEP 1: For each statement choose the response that is more nearly true for you. Place an X on the blank that corresponds to that response.

1. When meeting people, I prefer
   _____ a. to think and speculate on what they are like.
   _____ b. to interact directly and to ask them questions.

2. When presented with a problem, I prefer
   _____ a. to jump right in and work on a solution.
   _____ b. to think through and evaluate possible ways to solve the problem.

3. I enjoy sports more when
   _____ a. I am watching a good game.
   _____ b. I am actively participating.

4. Before taking a vacation, I prefer
   _____ a. to rush at the last minute and give little thought beforehand to what I will do while on vacation.
   _____ b. to plan early and daydream about how I will spend my vacation.

5. When enrolled in courses, I prefer
   _____ a. to plan how to do my homework before actually attacking the assignment.
   _____ b. to immediately become involved in doing the assignment.

6. When I receive information that requires action, I prefer
   _____ a. to take action immediately.
   _____ b. to organize the information and determine what type of action would be most appropriate.

7. When presented with a number of alternatives for action, I prefer
   _____ a. to determine how the alternatives relate to one another and analyze the consequences of each.
   _____ b. to select the one that looks best and implement it.

8. When I awake every morning, I prefer
   _____ a. to expect to accomplish some worth-while work without considering what the individual tasks may entail.
   _____ b. to plan a schedule for the tasks I expect to do that day.

9. After a full day's work, I prefer
   _____ a. to reflect back on what I accomplished and think of how to make time the next day for unfinished tasks.
   _____ b. to relax with some type of recreation and not think about my job.

10. After choosing the above responses, I
    _____ a. prefer to continue and complete this instrument.
    _____ b. am curious about how my responses will be interpreted and prefer some feedback before continuing with the instrument.

11. When I learn something, I am usually
    _____ a. thinking about it.
    _____ b. right in the middle of doing it.

12. I learn best when
    _____ a. I am dealing with real-world issues.
    _____ b. concepts are clear and well organized.

13. In order to retain something I have learned, I must
    _____ a. periodically review it in my mind.
    _____ b. practice it or try to use the information.

14. In teaching others how to do something, I first
    _____ a. demonstrate the task.
    _____ b. explain the task.

15. My favorite way to learn to do something is
    _____ a. reading a book or instructions or enrolling in a class.
    _____ b. trying to do it and learning from my mistakes.

16. When I become emotionally involved with something, I usually
    _____ a. let my feelings take the lead and then decide what to do.
    _____ b. control my feelings and try to analyze the situation.

17. If I were meeting jointly with several experts on a subject, I would prefer

_____ a. to ask each of them for his or her opinion.

_____ b. to interact with them and share our ideas and feelings.

18. When I am asked to relate information to a group of people, I prefer

    _____ a. not to have an outline, but to interact with them and become involved in an extemporaneous conversation.

_____ b. to prepare notes and know exactly what I am going to say.

19. Experience is

    _____ a. a guide for building theories.

    _____ b. the best teacher.

20. People learn easier when they are

    _____ a. doing work on the job.

    _____ b. in a class taught by an expert.

	ABSTRACT/CONCRETE		COGNITIVE/AFFECTIVE	
	COLUMN 1	**COLUMN 2**	**COLUMN 3**	**COLUMN 4**
	1. ___	2. ___	11. ___	12. ___
	3. ___	4. ___	13. ___	14. ___
	5. ___	6. ___	15. ___	16. ___
	7. ___	8. ___	17. ___	18. ___
	9. ___	10. ___	19. ___	20. ___
Total Circles	___	___	___	___
Grand Totals	_____		_____	

FIGURE 2–17 *The learning model for managers*

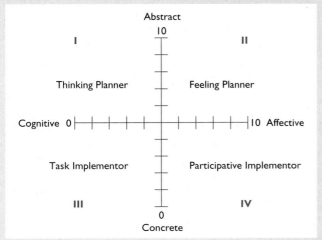

Now circle every *a* in Column 1 and Column 4. Then circle every *b* in Column 2 and in Column 3. Next, total the circles in each of the four columns. Then add the totals of Columns 1 and 2; plot this grand total on the vertical axis of the Learning Model for Managers (Figure 2–17) and draw a horizontal line through the point. Now add the totals of Columns 3 and 4; plot that grand total on the horizontal axis of the model and draw a vertical line through the point. The intersection of these two lines indicates the domain of your preferred learning style.

STEP 2: Discussion. In small groups or with the class as a whole, answer the following questions:

DESCRIPTION

1. What was your score?
2. What type of learning style did it represent?
3. How does this result compare with the styles of others in the class?

DIAGNOSIS

4. What are the implications of your style for learning in an organizational setting?

Activity 2–6   LEARNING BY MODELING

STEP 1: Select a (target) behavior you wish a fellow student, friend, or coworker to acquire.

STEP 2: Develop a social modeling strategy to use to help the other person acquire this behavior.

STEP 3: Implement the strategy.

STEP 4: Discussion. In small groups or with the entire class, answer the following questions:

1. What target behavior did you specify?
2. What strategies did you implement?
3. Which strategies were effective?
4. What are the characteristics of an effective social learning strategy?
5. How could your strategy or other strategies be improved?

Activity 2-7   "THE PRIMA DONNA—TEMPERAMENTAL OPERA STARS"

STEP 1: View the ABC segment entitled "The Prima Donna—Temperamental Opera Stars."

STEP 2: Answer each of the following questions, individually or in small groups, as directed by your instructor.

DESCRIPTION

1. Describe the critics' views of the behavior of the opera stars' presented in the video.

2. Describe the opera stars' own views of their behaviors.

DIAGNOSIS

3. How do the perceptions of the critics and the stars differ?
4. How do the attributions of the critics and the stars differ?
5. What explains these differences?

PRESCRIPTION

6. What changes are necessary to ensure accurate perceptions and attributions by both critics and opera stars?

Chapter 3

Chapter Outline

- **Managing Diversity at Allstar Hotels**
- **Tracing the Rise of Work-Force Diversity**
- **Understanding Personality Differences**
    - **Measuring Personality**
    - **Classifying Personality Types**
- **Understanding the Impact of Values and Attitudes**
    - **The Influence of Values**
    - **The Impact of Attitudes**
- **Understanding the Effects of Personal and Career Development**
    - **Personal Development**
    - **Career Development**
    - **Family Issues**
- **Understanding the Impact of Demographics**
    - **Race in the Workplace**
    - **Gender in the Workplace**
    - **Older Workers**
    - **Two-Career Families**
    - **Physically Challenged Employees**
- **Making Cross-Cultural Comparisons**
- **Prescriptions for Managing Work-Force Diversity**
- **Summary**
- **Diagnostic Questions**
- **Activities**

Managing Work-Force Diversity

LEARNING OBJECTIVES

After completing the reading and activities of Chapter 3, students will be able to

1. Trace the rise of diversity in the workplace.

2. Define the dimensions of personality and other individual differences and show how they influence behavior in organizations.

3. Illustrate the impact of values and attitudes on organizational behavior.

4. Trace the stages of personal, family, and career development and show their significance for organizational behavior.

5. Describe the impact of demographics (race, gender, age, and physical limitations) on organizational behavior.

6. Show how cross-cultural differences can influence behavior and attitudes in the workplace.

7. Offer two primary strategies for managing a diverse work force.

Anthony Sebastian has recently joined the Allstar New Yorker Hotel as general manager. The New Yorker is a moderately sized, European-style hotel that caters to international travelers from an array of countries.

Sebastian had worked at hotels throughout the world and had managed multinational staffs at most properties. Now he had been hired to solve a serious problem at the New Yorker, which has always had a diverse work force. Even before landmark civil rights legislation of the 1960s, upper management had adopted a formal policy of fairness that "treated all employees alike," ignoring their differences.

In recent years, though, employee dissatisfaction had grown. They no longer were satisfied to "melt into" the dominant culture, losing their racial and ethnic identities. Rather, they believed that they should be proud of and show their identity in their language and dress. In addition, promised opportunities for the advancement of minorities never materialized. Because top management believed that the minorities were not interested in nor qualified for advancement, minority employees soon found their opportunities for advancement were limited. Labor unrest and threats of strikes had occurred repeatedly during the past five years. Turnover had been higher at the New Yorker than at the other Allstar Hotel properties.

The former manager had been totally confused by the charges. Pointing to the formal policy that stated the hotel's support for equal opportunity, the manager became first defensive and then antagonistic. In time, the growing worker unrest and the threat of strikes began to affect customer service. The hotel's reputation and its profits both began to suffer. In desperation, Allstar's top management fired the ineffective manager and hired Sebastian, giving him one year to solve the hotel's problems.

What should Anthony Sebastian do to solve the problems at the Allstar New Yorker? The diagnostic approach can help Sebastian solve these problems by using organizational behavior theories first to better understand individual differences among the workers and their impact in the workplace and second to prescribe ways of responding to these differences.

We begin this chapter by describing the rise of workplace diversity. Next we look at personality differences among workers. We then consider the impact of values and attitudes. The chapter continues with an examination of personal and career development and related family issues. Then we discuss the impact of demographics. Next we look at cross-cultural comparisons to diversity in the workplace. The chapter concludes with prescriptions for managing workplace diversity.

TRACING THE RISE OF WORK-FORCE DIVERSITY

Demographics, competition for talent, marketplace demands, and the changing environment are among the factors calling for a *diverse work force,* one that includes (and treats equally) men and women, employees with differing ethnic backgrounds, younger and older workers, disabled employees, and other workers who differ from the dominant group of white, male employees in the United States.[1] Diversity brings a greater pool of talent to the workplace, which often results in better decision making, an increased understanding of customers' needs, and greater flexibility in staffing when a shortfall of traditional workers occurs.

Changes in the workplace have made *cultural ethnocentrism,* the belief in the preeminence of one's own culture, dysfunctional in a global economy. Three factors have contributed to a rejection of cultural ethnocentrism in the United States:

- Moral convictions that individuals should be treated with respect for individual and cultural differences.

- Legal requirements that attempt to codify values and attitudes regarding equal opportunity and nondiscrimination in the workplace.

- Practical requirements of the global economy, where companies are trying to market goods and services to diverse cultures and hire and manage employees from them as well as deal with the already changing composition of the work force.

LEVI STRAUSS. This company had a long-standing reputation as a socially responsible employer. Yet, the reality was that before 1985 corporate executives talked about workplace diversity but failed to implement it. Now the company follows a vision of "responsible commercial success," which means acting ethically, including creating real opportunities for minority workers. The company has doubled the percentage of minority managers to 36 percent since 1984. The company values a diverse work force at all levels of the organization, seeking and respecting differing points of view.[2]

Diversity in the work force requires that managers understand the uniqueness of each employee so that they can create collaborative relationships among individuals with different skills, abilities, experiences, aspirations, and expectations. Managers may be challenged to develop positive attitudes about individuals different from themselves and to recognize the unique contribution and potential of each employee. Managers begin by using their knowledge of organizational behavior to diagnose the nature and impact of individual differences in the workplace and then prescribing ways of ensuring that these differences result in effective outcomes.

UNDERSTANDING PERSONALITY DIFFERENCES

A diverse work force typically includes individuals with a variety of personality types. *Personality* here refers to a set of distinctive personal characteristics, including motives, emotions, values, interests, attitudes, and competencies. These characteristics frequently are organized into patterns that are influenced by an individual's heredity and social, cultural, and family environments.

MEASURING PERSONALITY

Personality is generally assessed by trained and certified professionals in three ways. Individuals can complete *inventories,* which are lists of questions that describe the respondent's personality. Second, individuals can complete *projective tests,* in which the respondent describes to the test administrator what he or she sees in a picture or relatively ambiguous stimulus, such as an inkblot. After using a detailed protocol to score the descriptions, individuals are placed along a variety of personality dimensions that are reflected on a series of items that comprise the scale measuring a specific dimension. In the third assessment approach, an individual's behavior in simulations, role playing exercises, and stress interviews is observed and scored along a variety of dimensions, such as adaptability, assertiveness, or dominance.

Managers might use information collected from instruments such as these to first describe and then diagnose the behavior of their employees. Once they understand the impact of personality on an employee's behavior, they can reshape elements of the work situation to result in a better fit and better outcomes.

CLASSIFYING PERSONALITY TYPES

Psychological research has identified a wide range of psychological characteristics that compose an individual's personality. No single classification best describes an individual's personality. Different theorists have studied different aspects of personality and demonstrated their impact on behavior in the workplace. Thus, in this section we look at a number of personality dimensions considered significant for organizational behavior.

Internalizers–Externalizers Rotter described the extent to which individuals believe that their behaviors influence what happens to them.[3] *Internalizers* feel that they control their own life and actions. *Externalizers* believe others control their lives. Figure 3–1 shows some questions from a test used to assess these two dimensions.

FIGURE 3–1   *Questions for diagnosing internalizer–externalizer personalities*

An *Internalizer* would answer *Yes* to the following questions:

1. Do you believe that if somebody studies hard he or she can pass any subject?

2. Do you feel that you have a lot of choice in deciding who your friends are?

3. Do you believe that whether or not people like you depends on how you act?

4. Do you feel that when good things happen they happen because of hard work?

5. Do you think it's better to be smart than to be lucky?

An *Externalizer* would answer *Yes* to the following questions:

1. Do you believe that most problems will solve themselves if you just don't fool with them?

2. Are some people just born lucky?

3. Are you most often blamed for things that just aren't your fault?

4. Do you feel that most of the time it doesn't pay to try hard because things never turn out right anyway?

5. Do you believe that wishing can make good things happen?

SOURCE: These questions are excerpted from R. Aero and E. Weiner, *The Mind Test* (New York: William Morrow, 1981), pp. 20–23.

Assume that a manager has two subordinates. Kristen O'Leary is an internalizer and Susan Jamieson is an externalizer. How might these two women differ in their views of the best way to advance in an organization? The first might view advancement as being within her control, the second would view it as being out of her control. What implications would these differences have for managing these two employees? The first might develop specific strategies for career advancement and want assistance in implementing them, while the second would not. The description and analysis of an individual's personality or personal style can help us understand the way that individual behaves in organizations and then suggest some issues to consider in managing or interacting with that person.

Type A–Type B Type A or Type B characteristics reflect an individual's desire for achievement, perfectionism, competitiveness, and ability to relax, as reflected in the scale in Figure 3–2. *Type A* people tend to feel very competitive, be prompt for

FIGURE 3–2   *Excerpt from type A–type B scale*

Circle the number of the continuum (the verbal descriptions represent endpoints) that best represents your behavior for each dimension.

Am casual about appointments	1 2 3 4 5 6 7 8	Am never late
Am not competitive	1 2 3 4 5 6 7 8	Am very competitive
Never feel rushed, even under pressure	1 2 3 4 5 6 7 8	Always feel rushed
Take things one at a time	1 2 3 4 5 6 7 8	Try to do many things at once; think about what I am going to do next
Do things slowly	1 2 3 4 5 6 7 8	Do things fast (eating, walking, etc.)
Express feelings	1 2 3 4 5 6 7 8	"Sit on" feelings
Have many interests	1 2 3 4 5 6 7 8	Have few interests outside work

Now score your responses by totaling the numbers circled. Then multiply the total by 3. The interpretation of your score is as follows:

Number of Points	Type of Personality
less than 90	B
90 to 99	B+
100 to 105	A−
106 to 119	A
120 or more	A+

SOURCE: Adapted from R.W. Bortner, A short rating scale as a potential measure of pattern A behavior, *Journal of Chronic Diseases* 22 (1966): 87–91 with kind permission from Elsevier Science Ltd, the Boulevard, Langford Lane, Kidlington OX5 16B, UK.

appointments, do things quickly, and always feel rushed, whereas *Type B* individuals tend to be more relaxed, take one thing at a time, and express their feelings.[4] The Type A–Type B distinction has been related to cardiovascular fitness and stress-proneness.[5] In a study of Canadian nurses, for example, Type A nurses showed greater job stress and role pressures, but also higher job involvement, effort, and attendance, than Type B nurses.[6]

Myers–Briggs Dimensions The Myers–Briggs Type Indicator (MBTI), based in Jungian psychology, uses an individual's preferences to indicate his or her overall personality type.[7] Individuals demonstrate one of two basic personality types: introverted and extroverted.[8] The *introverted* person is shy and withdrawn, likes a quiet environment for concentration, dislikes interruptions, and is content to work alone. The *extroverted* person is outgoing, often aggressive, likes variety, likes to function in a social environment, often acts quickly without thinking, and may dominate situations or people. These two basic personality patterns affect the way people gather information, make decisions, and evaluate alternatives during problem solving (see Figure 3–3).

Individuals acquire information by sensing or intuition. *Sensing* types like action and focus on getting things done; they work steadily and reach a conclusion step by step. *Intuitive* types dislike doing the same thing repeatedly, enjoy learning new skills, may leap to a conclusion quickly, and often follow their inspirations and hunches.

Individuals make decisions by thinking or feeling. *Thinking* types excel at putting things in logical order, respond more to people's ideas than feelings, need to be treated fairly, and tend to be firm and tough-minded. *Feeling* types like harmony, respond to individual's values and feelings, as well as their thoughts, tend to be sympathetic, and enjoy pleasing people.

Individuals also differ in the way they evaluate information about the world. *Judgment* types like to get things finished and work best with a plan; they dislike interrupting their projects and tasks and use lists as agendas. *Perception* types adapt well to changing situations and do not mind last-minute changes; they may begin

FIGURE 3–3   *Problem-solving orientations*

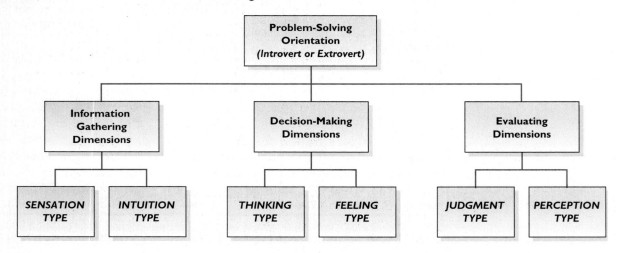

many projects but experience difficulty in finishing them or may postpone unpleasant tasks.

We can characterize individuals along combinations of two or more of the four dimensions: for example, introverted-sensing-thinking-judging. One study identified four types of writers and classified them along two dimensions: (1) correspondents—sensing/feeling types; (2) technical writers—sensing/thinking types; (3) creative writers—intuitive/feeling types; and (4) analytical writers—intuitive/thinking types.[9] Another study found that the most common types among employees in a Canadian metal- and uranium-mining firm were ISTJ (introverted, sensing, thinking, and judging) and ESTJ (extroverted, sensing, thinking, and judging).[10]

The diagnosis of such patterns in organizations can facilitate manager–employee interactions by helping managers match employees to jobs, explain differences in perceptions of various situations, understand the reasons different employees demonstrate different styles in performing their work, and then respond to the unique aspects of each worker's style.

In addition, the manager might respond differently to work situations depending on his or her own style. Consider a manager with a thinking-type personal style. How would the manager begin to deal with a poorly performing employee? He or she likely would perform a logical, systematic inquiry into the situation that focuses on behaviors. Compare this behavior to that of a feeling-type manager in the same situation. He or she might begin by conducting an assessment that focuses first on the employee's feelings. The effectiveness of the manager's interaction with the employee will depend on both the manager's and the employee's personalities and the resulting behaviors.

In addition, recent research has suggested that the personalities of top executives can help explain dysfunctional organizations.[11] For example, an executive who believes that no one can be trusted often creates an organization in which secrecy and guardedness characterize the culture. Or a manager whose personality reflects a need for control more often will create an organization that relies too much on formal controls and direct supervision to accomplish the organizational goals.

Of course, we need to take care not to stereotype individuals by using these personality types. However, diagnosing the possible impact of an individual's personality on an organizational situation can help us anticipate the possible consequences and make provisional plans for responding. This is particularly important when dealing with a diverse work force, so that racial, ethnic, general, or personality stereotyping is minimized.

Machiavellianism An individual with a Machiavellian personality demonstrates manipulative and unethical behavior and attitudes.[12] (The term can be traced back to the principles for government analyzed in a treatise titled **The Prince,** written by the Italian political philosopher Niccolo di Bernardo Machiavelli around 1500.) Typically measured using the 20-question Mach IV scale, the Machiavellianism (Mach) scale indicates the degree to which the respondent believes others can be manipulated in interpersonal situations.[13] High scorers tend to manipulate and persuade others, win, and regard persons as objects more than low scorers.[14] One study of the Machiavellianism of department store executives indicated that Machiavellianism predicted success, as measured by job title and income, for the male executives, but not for female executives; a negative association existed between Machiavellianism and job satisfaction for both sexes.[15] The presence of

Machiavellianism may increase behavior that focuses on gaining control or power in an organization.[16]

Self-Efficacy *Self-efficacy* refers to an individual's perception about whether they can successfully perform a task. It influences an individual's motivation; for example, it influences goal level and goal commitment as well as an individual's selection of tasks.[17] Analysis of task requirements, an individual's judgments about the reasons for particular levels of performance, and his or her assessment of both personal and situational resources and constraints likely influence an individual's estimate of self-efficacy.[18] The following can also increase an individual's self-efficacy: giving a job holder a more complete understanding of a task's attributes, complexity, and environment; providing training to improve understanding of how a person can use his or her ability to perform a task; and providing information to give a better understanding of performance strategies and effort required for effective task performance.[19]

UNDERSTANDING THE IMPACT OF VALUES AND ATTITUDES

An individual's values and attitudes develop over time, beginning in early childhood, often are linked to personality, and can influence his or her behavior. Understanding the nature and impact of values and attitudes in the workplace can help both managers and employees diagnose the causes of particular organizational situations and offer prescriptions for maintaining or improving them to ensure organizational effectiveness.

THE INFLUENCE OF VALUES

An individual's values refer to the basic principles and tenets that guide his or her beliefs, attitudes, and behaviors. Values tend to be relatively stable characteristics, often developed throughout childhood and manifested in work and nonwork settings throughout adulthood. An individual's values can influence his or her beliefs about money, social interactions, the importance of work, and other aspects of his or her work and nonwork lives. An individual who demonstrates a **work ethic,** for example, a set of values that emphasize working hard, "doing a good day's work for a good day's pay," and living a simple life, might demonstrate different work-related behaviors than an individual who has a different set of values.

Values can be described as ***peripheral values,*** which are more susceptible to change, and ***core values,*** which are less susceptible. A research study of Israeli workers indicated that organizational influences affect peripheral values and nonwork influences affect core values.[20] It is unlikely, for example, that a manager could change a worker's basic values through training or other interventions, but a parent, spouse, or friend, or even a powerful religious experience, might alter an individual's core values. Although changing core values is difficult, diagnosing their impact on work situations is a first step in helping managers place workers in situations that fit well with their values and result in productive outcomes.

THE BODY SHOP. Anita Roddick, founder and CEO of The Body Shop International, which sells natural lotions and cosmetics, instilled her core values into her company, which grew from a small shop funded by a $6,400 bank loan to a multimillion dollar enterprise. Known for its environmentalism, the company has set a standard by campaigning for environmental causes and offering only biodegradable products.[21]

THE IMPACT OF ATTITUDES

An *attitude* is a consistent predisposition to respond to various aspects of people, situations, or objects. We infer an individual's attitude from his or her verbal expressions of beliefs, feelings, or behavioral intentions toward an object or situation; from perceptual and physiological reactions; or from overt behaviors.[22] We might, for example, determine an individual's job satisfaction by inferring it from his or her general demeanor on the job or by asking the person to describe this attitude. We can also use attitude surveys or other collections of attitude scales to assess individuals' attitudes toward their job, coworkers, supervisor, or the organization at large.[23]

The more diverse the work force the more likely individuals will have an array of attitudes. Their beliefs, formed largely from their socioeconomic background and other experiences, could vary significantly and hence result in different attitudes. Recent research suggests significant changes in attitudes toward various national and racial groups as well as various gender roles.[24] These divergent attitudes likely have significant consequences for the effective management of diversity in organizations such as the Allstar New Yorker Hotel.

Research about the relationship between attitudes and behaviors, for example, has been done primarily in the United States at work sites that function solely in this country. Would the same attitudes occur in France, Germany, or Japan? Would the same behaviors result from the same attitudes? Because we can only conjecture the specific correlation, we must be sure to describe and diagnose situations as accurately as possible. Once we understand particular attitudes and their impact on specific work situations, we can prescribe ways of changing attitudes or the situations to result in more productive outcomes.

Components of Attitudes Research has suggested that attitudes have cognitive, affective, and behavioral components.[25]

- ◼ *Cognitive.* This component includes the *beliefs*—tenets accepted as true based on an individual's values and experiences—an individual has about a certain person, object, or situation. These learned beliefs, such as "you need to work long hours to get ahead in this job," lead to specific attitudes. Although we have many beliefs, only some lead to attitudes that have an impact on behavior in the workplace.

- ◼ *Affective.* This component refers to the person's *feelings* that result from his or her beliefs about a person, object, or situation. A person who believes hard work earns promotions may feel anger or frustration when he or she works hard but is not promoted. The affective component becomes stronger as an individual has more frequent and direct experience with a focal object, person, or situation and as an individual's feelings about the object, person, or situation are expressed more frequently.[26]

- ◼ *Behavioral.* This component refers to the individual's behavior that occurs as a result of his or her feeling about the focal person, object, or situation. An individual may complain, request a transfer, or be less productive because he or she feels dissatisfied with work. Employees of the Allstar New Yorker have a series of beliefs and values about their job performance. For some, these result in negative feelings of job dissatisfaction. These attitudes, in turn, result in the behavior of turnover.

Organizational behavior also describes the development and manifestation of attitudes as a representation of an individual's interaction with his or her social environment.[27] The object of an attitude is represented as a prototype in a person's memory. Then an individual uses an attitude as a schema for evaluating an object. The person may assess the object as good or bad, positive or negative, favored or not; then the person determines the strategy to take toward it. The accessibility of an attitude, or ease with which it is activated, affects its implementation.[28] Personal experience with the object and the repeated expression of the attitude increases its accessibility.[29] In this way, attitude-related information helps process complex information. Applying this way of thinking about attitudes to the customer services department in the Allstar New Yorker Hotel would suggest that staff members develop attitudinal strategies that may or may not be appropriate for objects in the work situation. For example, they may have negative attitudes about coworkers or bosses that result in their refusing to cooperate with specific individuals.

Individuals may also experience *cognitive dissonance,* which describes the situation where items of knowledge, information, attitudes, or beliefs held by an individual are contradictory.[30] Cognitive dissonance will affect the relationship between an individual's attitudes and behaviors. For example, an employee at the Allstar New Yorker Hotel might assess her own performance as excellent. This attitude might conflict with her supervisor's written appraisals of her performance. To reduce the dissonance, the employee might not "hear" her supervisor's assessments, or might hear them but devalue the supervisor and hence the importance of her comments.

Job Satisfaction Satisfaction results when a job fulfills or facilitates the attainment of individual values and standards and dissatisfaction occurs when the job is seen as blocking such attainment.[31] This attitude has received extensive attention by researchers and practitioners because it was at one time believed to be the cause of improved job performance. Recent research questions or negates such a relationship and suggests instead a more complicated interaction between satisfaction, commitment, turnover, and productivity.[32]

Now, because of managers' concern for creating both a humane and high-performance workplace, researchers continue to search for definite answers about the causes and consequences of job satisfaction. For example, recent research suggests that employee involvement in information processing, decision making, and problem solving has only a small, although statistically significant, effect on job satisfaction.[33] A study of Australian telecommunications employees showed that both participation and task variety were positively related to job satisfaction.[34]

UNDERSTANDING THE EFFECTS OF PERSONAL AND CAREER DEVELOPMENT

Research has suggested that adults have clearly defined stages of biological, social, family, and career growth and development. Individuals at a particular stage often have common needs or similar ways of coping with and responding to situations they encounter. These ways may be modified by an individual's personality, causing variations within stages. We describe a typical progression in this section that is common in the United States but not universal here or abroad. Little cross-cultural research has been done regarding personal or career development. We might hypothesize that patterns vary in different cultures. Expectations about women and older persons, the financial supports provided for medical care, childcare, and other personal needs and the opportunities for individuals of various social and economic classes may influence the patterns.

PERSONAL DEVELOPMENT

Consider, for example, the customer services department at the Allstar New Yorker Hotel. Do you think its managers and employees respond to their work the same way? Although different job responsibilities as well as ethnic, racial, or gender differences might explain their different reactions, so too might differences in their respective stages of personal development, as shown in Figure 3–4.

FIGURE 3–4   *Stages of personal development*

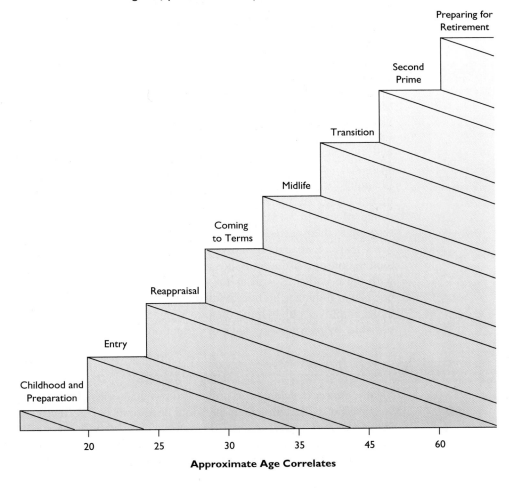

Approximate Age Correlates

Most staff members who have just completed their professional training or who are holding their first job after high school or college are primarily concerned with getting into the adult world, developing their sense of identity, and building a life that reflects their personality and personal style. They can experiment with various combinations of work and nonwork in their lives. At times they may spend 60 or 70 hours at work and at other times they may work only the minimum time required.

An administrative assistant such as Josh Stapleton, who is in his late twenties, has probably spent much of his twenties establishing his own identity and lifestyle. Now, approaching the age of thirty, Josh and others like him review all past commitments and reappraise their personal and career progress to date. Some workers try to make themselves indispensable to their organizations as one way of encouraging employers to provide greater flexibility. Individuals in their thirties typically must come to terms with both career and family concerns. Some staff members may feel pressure to have children if they have not already done so. If they already have children, they might experience a dilemma about how much time and energy to devote to family versus career. Other staff members may choose alternate lifestyles and seek to gain their acceptance in the workplace. Managers of a diverse work force must develop and implement strategies for easing these dilemmas as a way of retaining productive employees.

The customer services department may also have some staff members like Eleanor Wright. Eleanor reentered the work force when her children reached school age. Now she encounters the difficulties of midlife, of being part of the *sandwich generation,* where she has responsibility for both her children and for aging parents. Or, the department may have individuals on the staff like Fred Talenor, who like some men in their early forties, has experienced a *midcareer crisis,* where he questions the fundamental value, appropriateness, and real accomplishments in his life so far.[35] Individuals at this stage must manage the transition between the two chronological parts of their lives to ensure their personal satisfaction and well-being.

Productivity remains a key issue for men and women in their late fifties, sixties, and even seventies or eighties. They can continue devoting significant energy to work and careers, or they can refocus their energies on related aspects of their lives. Planning for a reduced status and work role requires significant thought and investment of time. As we noted earlier, older workers will continue to be a significant source of staff in the next century, and managers must understand their abilities and respond to their needs.[36]

Clearly, managers of a diverse work force need to understand that individuals tend to confront different issues at each decade of their lives. Their abilities to deal with these issues as well as the organization's success in responding to different needs will influence both individual and organizational performance. Managers can assist employees by helping them recognize their developmental needs and, where possible, by restructuring the work situation to meet those needs.

CAREER DEVELOPMENT

Ideally, *career development,* progress through a series of jobs over a forty- to fifty-year period, will complement personal development.[37] Effective managers recognize and attempt to respond to the issues associated with specific career stages as a way of creating motivated, satisfied, and productive employees. Note that the career development described here reflects typical patterns in the United States and is only one prototype for career development. In Israel and other countries with mandatory military service for all men (and women in some cases) the sequence of career stages presented here may be delayed or altered. Countries such as Sweden with liberal maternity and paternity leave policies may also have workers with different career patterns from the one described here. Increasingly in the United States, too, individuals pursue serial careers, a set of unrelated, sequential careers over an individual's life span; for example, teacher–banker–bed-and-breakfast owner; homemaker–social worker. Managers need to recognize such variations in patterns in diagnosing individual development.

Career Stages Figure 3–5 presents one prototypical time line of career development. Think of managers of various departments (for example, sales and marketing, housekeeping, reservations, human resources) at the Allstar New Yorker. Are they likely at the same career stage? What do they expect from their jobs in relation to their careers? Will they react in the same way to the requirements of their job and their organization?

Individuals in the *entry stage* try to become effective and accepted members of their organizations as quickly as possible while they learn the job's ropes and routines. Newcomers seek information about role demands, feedback about their performance, and technical information from supervisors. They seek information about organizational norms and social relations from peers.[38] Research has shown that the quality of their information seeking influences their mastery of their job, definition of their role, acquisition of knowledge about the organization's culture, and their extent of social integration.[39] They must spend time learning to get along with their boss and coworkers, as well as trying to become effective members quickly. The nature of the workers' experiences on entering the organization significantly affects their longer-term commitment to it.[40]

At the next stage, often known as *early career,* individuals become more concerned with advancement and establishing a career path. In multinational companies, rapid advancement may require taking overseas assignments.
GERBER PRODUCTS. With an expanding presence in Latin America and Central and Eastern Europe, Gerber emphasizes foreign assignment as part of the career development of its executives.[41]

FIGURE 3–5   *Stages of career development*

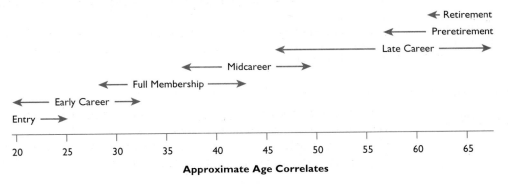

Increasingly, the work in organizations is changing. Some academicians and practitioners argue that jobs as we know them will soon cease to exist. Rather, individuals will engage in a series of short-term projects, which may or may not be within the same organization. In particular, the predictions suggest that the percentage of classic factory workers and agricultural workers will shrink dramatically.[42]

Regardless of the particular work configuration, employees in this early stage can benefit by finding a *mentor,* usually a more senior executive who helps influence their movement through the organization and affects their career success. A mentor typically provides the career and psychosocial functions shown in Table 3–1.[43] Alternatively, individuals can seek developmental support from peers by becoming part of a *relationship constellation,* a group of individuals from various departments in the organization who provide mutual support, friendship, and sponsorship.[44]

Mentoring for women has not occurred to a sufficient degree in the workplace, in part because women do not seek mentors or mentors may not select females.[45] Similar problems likely exist for other minority groups in the workplace. The barriers for women result for numerous reasons.[46] Women lack access to networks within organizations. They also may be viewed as tokens who cannot reach top management. Stereotypes and misattributions about women's abilities to manage lower evaluations of their performance. Women may be seen as having been social-

TABLE 3–1 *Examples of mentoring activities*

CAREER FUNCTIONS	PSYCHOSOCIAL FUNCTIONS
Sponsorship Opening doors. Having connections that will support the junior's career advancement.	**Role modeling** Demonstrating valued behavior, attitudes and/or skills that aid the junior in achieving competence, confidence, and a clear professional identity.
Coaching Teaching "the ropes." Giving relevant positive and negative feedback to improve the junior's performance and potential.	**Counseling** Providing a helpful and confidential forum for exploring personal and professional dilemmas. Excellent listening, trust, and rapport that enable both individuals to address central developmental concerns.
Protection Providing support in different situations. Taking responsibility for mistakes that were outside the junior's control. Acting as a buffer when necessary.	**Acceptance and confirmation** Providing ongoing support, respect, and admiration, which strengthens self-confidence and self-image. Regularly reinforcing both as highly valued people and contributors to the organization.
Exposure Creating opportunities for the junior to demonstrate competence where it counts. Taking the junior to important meetings that will enhance his or her visibility.	**Friendship** Mutual caring and intimacy that extends beyond the requirements of daily work tasks. Sharing of experience outside the immediate work setting.
Challenging work Delegating assignments that stretch the junior's knowledge and skills in order to stimulate growth and preparation to move ahead.	

SOURCE: Reprinted with permission from K.E. Kram, Mentoring in the workplace. In D.T. Hall and Associates, eds., *Career Development in Organizations* (San Francisco: Jossey-Bass, 1986), p. 162. © 1986 by Jossey-Bass Inc., Publishers.

ized to develop personalities alien to management success. Cross-gender relationships may be viewed as taboo. Finally, women may rely on ineffective sources of power, reducing their success.[46]

Mentoring becomes particularly important in a multicultural environment where nonperformance-related factors can block career progress. In one study of cross-race mentoring, a supportive mentor–protégé relationship only occurred when both parties preferred to deny or to openly discuss their racial difference.[47] Individuals who have experienced extensive mentoring reported receiving more promotions, having higher incomes, and being more satisfied with pay and benefits.[48] Organizations also benefit from mentoring because mentors help perpetuate or change the organization's culture. Mentors improve worker motivation, performance, and retention or act as a less formal, less costly monitoring and control system.[49] The establishment of formal mentoring programs, the conduct of educational programs about mentoring and career development, and the implementation of more significant changes in organizational structure, norms, and processes are three strategies that have been used to support the mentoring process.[50]

AVON. At Avon Products, all minority employees belong to in-house race-based advocacy groups.[51] The Black Professionals Association, Avon Hispanic Network, and Avon Asian Network began as social groups and evolved into self-help groups that focus on minority recruiting and career development.

Workers who are typically in their late twenties or early thirties strive for *full membership in an early career.* The primary emphasis of such individuals must be on performing effectively, accepting responsibility, managing subordinates, discharging duties, and developing special skills. Early research about this stage suggested that young professionals may experience conflicting expectations from their coworkers and bosses, incompetent supervisors, insensitivity to the internal political environment, personal passivity and ignorance of real performance criteria, and dilemmas about loyalty, integrity, commitment, and dependence.[52]

Workers with a somewhat longer employment history at the same stage also have *full membership,* assume additional responsibilities, and become increasingly autonomous. These employees must also assess to what extent they wish to remain as technical experts or advance into a managerial position. If they choose to remain technical, they must ensure that they maintain up-to-date knowledge in their career field. Today, employees at this stage increasingly find teams replacing middle managers, requiring them to develop new skills and potentially new ways of advancing in organizations.

CLAIROL. Michael K. Lorelli, while employed at Clairol, accepted a special assignment. His task was to head a project that would respond to the Federal Drug Administration's plan to ban key ingredients from Clairol's hair-dye products. This type of high-profile assignment in a crisis situation increased his visibility and reputation and helped propel him into management assignments that expedited rapid career advancement. He learned that the study was flawed and successfully launched a media campaign to highlight the safety of the product.[53] Now he is president of the Pizza Hut International Division of PepsiCo.

Workers with full membership should also ensure that they do not become *plateaued performers,* executives and workers who cannot advance because of limited advancement opportunities and whose job responsibilities never change.[54] Professional employees who bring specialized expertise to organizations, such as scientists, engineers, teachers, and accountants, face unique career and organizational issues. Managers who do not share the same professional background may have difficulty motivating or supervising these employees and in understanding the autonomy they expect.[55] Managers may also have difficulty acknowledging the technical quality of their employees' work because of their own lack of technical knowledge. Because these experts often have a high commitment to their profession, they may appear less committed to their organizations. Scientists and engineers also face obsolescence issues, where their expertise does not keep pace with technical advancements in their field.

FEDERAL EXPRESS. This company requires each of its 40,000 customer service agents and couriers to complete a computer-based examination once every six months to make certain they have up-to-date knowledge about government regulations, company policies, and other related subjects. The computer identifies weaknesses and prescribes remedial action. This practice helps ensure that employees remain current in their field.[56]

Individuals may not be able to advance in their organizations without assuming managerial responsibility.[57] *Dual ladders,* as shown in Figure 3–6, where individuals can assume increasingly higher positions in the organization (with greater pay, status, and responsibility) without assuming such managerial or supervisory responsibility, are uncommon in organizations. More recent research suggests a third option may exist and become more popular as workers get older. In the *treble ladder* individuals can progress through a series of interesting projects over time rather than through either traditional career path.[58] To ensure the productivity of professionals, top executives must use these and other accommodative mechanisms, including changing the way jobs are performed, offering professional reward systems, and providing mentorship for managers.

FIGURE 3–6   *Example of a dual ladder*

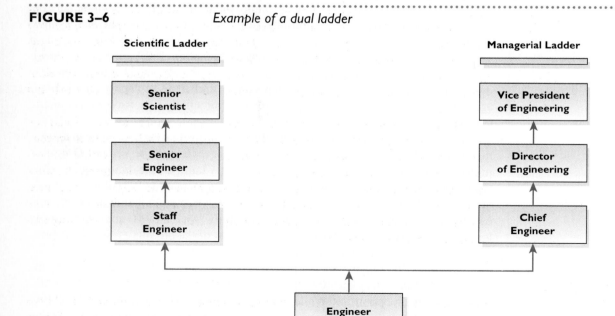

Midcareer refers to the period that follows establishment and perceived mastery and precedes career disengagement.[59] Those individuals who are between the ages of thirty-five and fifty may face a challenging midlife transition in their careers as well as their personal life as they reappraise their life's accomplishments to date. Some men at midcareer experience a need to disrupt their habitual behavior and initiate career exploration, whereas women become concerned with balancing the various aspects of their lives and ensuring that they have not sacrificed too much time with their family in favor of career activities and advancement.[60] Resolving these dilemmas may result in new choices about career and family or an acceptance of old choices as appropriate.

Once past midcareer, individuals in organizations must find a way to continue to contribute. Depending on the person's skills, interests, and motivation and the organization's culture and goals, such employees might help shape the direction of the organization by *sponsoring* career advancement of younger workers. One study of such professionals considered this role a prerequisite for continued career performance.[61] For executives this might mean *payback*—frequent job changes with final grooming or competition for the top executive position—or *payoff*—attainment of the CEO position.[62]

Would the same model hold for both men and women? Recent research suggests that the same model of career development may not apply to both men and women since they differ in career preparation, job opportunities, their role in marriage and childbearing, and the likely interruption of their careers.[63]

Implications for Managing Careers Career effectiveness and the individual job effectiveness that accompanies it often arise from the organization's ability to integrate the employee into the organization and to help that employee make career transitions effectively. Both employees and their managers should assume some career development responsibilities. Employees should know and understand the implications of their own stage of career development for satisfaction and job performance. Managers should provide opportunities to discuss career development issues, give feedback about reasonable expectations for employees, identify employee potential, provide relevant growth opportunities, and link employees to appropriate resources.[64] A lack of such information in addition to the dilemmas experienced at various stages of biosocial, family, and career development may contribute to confusion and conflict in the performance of work and nonwork roles.

Managing career development in an environment in which the work force and hence career opportunities are shrinking poses significant challenges to managers. Long-term workers have lost their jobs, suffered a decline in quality of life, and often had to take less-skilled, significantly lower paying positions to reenter the work force. *Downsizing* poses significant career development challenges for organizations. Organizations that once valued low turnover may no longer foster it and may implement voluntary severance programs, early retirement options, mandatory employee relocations, or layoffs.

FAMILY ISSUES

Responding to issues associated with the interaction between work and family has become particularly important in managing a diverse work force in the United States. The family issues individuals face vary significantly depending on their age, marital, parental, and economic status. In this section we illustrate one set of typical issues an individual might face, as shown in Figure 3–7.

Single Adult A single adult new to the work force focuses on developing his or her sense of self, and increasing his or her independence from parents and extended family. This person must decide where to live and how to divide time and energy between parents and friends, work and nonwork.

Married Adult Marriage adds the challenge of learning to live with a spouse. Balancing personal needs with the needs of another may create performance dilemmas. For example, work demands of one spouse, a manager at the Allstar New Yorker Hotel, may require a geographical relocation that could affect the other spouse's career. A recent study of employees of Fortune 500 companies suggests that a spouse's willingness to relocate was the single most important predictor of a worker's willingness to relocate.[65] Conflicting work schedules may also limit the amount of time spouses and friends can spend together.

Parents of Young Children These employees often face very real conflicts between their work and home responsibilities. Finding quality child care becomes a major issue that remains in the forefront for ten to fifteen years of their work life. In addition to dealing with parenthood emotionally, they must determine a workable division of responsibility, since work demands may limit the amount of time either spouse can devote to home responsibilities. Many women at this stage experience so much tension between work and family demands that they seek more flexible working arrangements. Some leave the work force entirely, often resulting in a significant personnel loss for their organization.[66]

Parents of Adolescents A midcareer crisis at work may be compounded by the emerging independence and possible rebellion of children, reinforcing parental feelings of inadequacy or dissatisfaction. Increasingly, individuals at midlife face issues relating to the care and well-being of their own parents. The financial strains of day care, college tuition, or elder care may contribute to stress and cause performance problems. Sometimes a greater career security at midlife will free more energy for dealing with family issues. Of course, divorce and its attendant financial requirements may further intensify the stress.

Empty Nest and Later Stages After midlife, building enduring relationships may create new challenges. The challenges of later life include caring for a sick

FIGURE 3–7 *Examples of family issues*

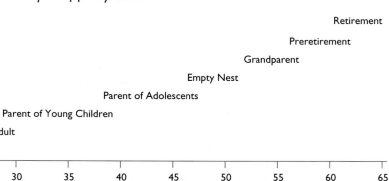

spouse, helping adult children with child care responsibilities, or even beginning new families. Making decisions about retirement has emotional, financial, and social implications for both women and men. The increasing life span and elimination of mandatory retirement for most workers complicate this decision making.

Organizational Responses Organizations have begun to respond to workers' needs and benefit from the results. Flexible and innovative managers, for example,

- seek equitable, not uniform treatment for workers
- recognize that individuals perform better free from personal pressures
- realize flexibility is a competitive issue and management tool
- measure performance based on value added, not hours worked
- meet business objectives by helping employees meet personal needs
- willingly take risks
- focus on results, rather than rules and procedures
- respect individuals but acknowledge and respond to differences
- gain top-level support and backing from peers
- produce change within the organization that outlives themselves.[67]

JOHNSON & JOHNSON. A survey of 2,000 employees of Johnson & Johnson indicated that employees who rated their supervisors more supportive of personal and family needs said they experienced less stress, more company loyalty, and more job satisfaction.[68]

UNDERSTANDING THE IMPACT OF DEMOGRAPHICS

The United States has witnessed several demographic trends that have increased diversity in the workplace. The representation of racial and ethnic minorities, women, and older workers in the workplace has increased. The number of two-career families has also grown. Legislation has granted broader employment rights to physically challenged employees. In this section we briefly comment about the issues related to these groups of workers.

RACE IN THE WORKPLACE

The percentage of African-Americans in the workplace has increased significantly in the past twenty-five years, prompted largely by affirmative action requirements.[69] Hiring preferences still appear to put African-Americans at a disadvantage in the workplace. African-Americans in the executive ranks often feel isolated because of their small numbers. Too often they are treated as tokens rather than as individual performers. Researchers have described the ***whitewashing*** of management as the barriers that prevent women of color from advancing into executive positions.[70] In addition to barriers experienced by individuals, minority-owned companies have experienced a ***lucite ceiling,*** an unbreakable glass ceiling, that prevents breaking into areas such as corporate finance.[71]

BLACK ENTERPRISE MAGAZINE. The African-American business community attempts to support minority-owned businesses. For example, the publisher of *Black Enterprise* magazine helped return Motown Record Company to profitability.[72]

Other African-American executives feel the responsibility for mentoring young African-Americans. The effort to help and retain minorities was initiated by the creation of an informal network of African-American employees initiated in 1971 and known as the *Corporate Few.*[73]

Racial incidents continue to occur in the workplace.

MILLER BREWING COMPANY. Through 1992, for example, racial harassment of workers at the Miller Brewing Company plant in Fulton, New York, was common.

FORD MOTOR COMPANY. Workers at the Ford Motor Company filed a class action suit against the auto manufacturer in 1993 charging lack of equal opportunities for African-American employees.[74]

The Allstar New Yorker Hotel, if typical of other major hotels, likely employs more African-Americans in lower-skilled than in more highly skilled jobs in the organization. Diagnosis of the impact of race on organizational behavior must also include the posing of unasked questions about race such as: "How are societal race relations reproduced in the workplace?" "To what extent is race built into the definition of a 'manager?'" and "What are the patterns of relationships among different racial minorities in organizations?"[75] Reducing stereotypes and promoting workers on the basis of ability and demonstrated competence presents a major challenge for managers.

GENDER IN THE WORKPLACE

Equal employment and affirmative action legislation of the 1960s and 1970s, the feminist movement of the 1970s and 1980s, and the economic realities faced by women who are single, heads of their families, or members of two-career families have motivated a dramatic increase in the numbers and percentage of women in the workplace.

SERVICE EMPLOYEES INTERNATIONAL UNION. Rachel Brickman represents a new breed of union organizer. A young, well-educated woman, she assumed a position previously held mainly by men. Recruited by the Organizing Institute, an arm of the A.F.L.–C.I.O., her job was to recruit health-care workers in Ohio to the Service Employees International Union District 1199.[76]

Even as their representation has increased, women continue to experience unique concerns and problems. The lives of women are qualitatively and structurally different from those of men.[77] For example, they have responsibility for childbearing and often assume primary responsibility for childrearing. Women more often than men choose to reduce their work commitment to part-time or conduct their careers in a serial fashion, spending time as a full-time wife and mother followed by reentry into the workplace. Socialized to value relationships, they can experience difficulty in organizations that promote competition.[78] The women employees at Allstar Hotels may experience barriers that hinder their performance. For women, the *glass ceiling* may impede advancements. This invisible barrier to movement into top management results from discrimination in the workplace, the inability of women and minorities to penetrate the *old boys' network,* and the tendency of executives to promote others like themselves.[79] Still, the number of top women business leaders is increasing.

MATTEL USA. Jill Barad, president of Mattel USA since 1990, typifies these leaders. With a career path in sales, she has a reputation for developing new ideas and has been credited with the remarkable success of Barbie dolls, more than doubling sales between 1988 and 1992.[80]

Women expatriates hold only 3 percent of international management assignments, primarily because companies have been unwilling to send them on overseas assignments.[81] Myths that women do not want to be international managers and that foreigners may be prejudiced against women expatriate managers have been shown to be untrue.[82]

OLDER WORKERS

By the year 2001 the baby boomers will begin to reach the age of 55. At that point, the U.S. Bureau of Labor will count them as older workers. By the age of 50, they can join the American Association for Retired Persons (AARP).[83] Managers can diagnose problems in the hiring and advancement of older workers by recognizing stereotypes about their skills, energy, and interests. Doubts about their ability to learn, speed of response, creativity, adaptability, and manageability have been disproved by research on older workers. The Japanese, for example, value older workers and show the advantage of using their skills and wisdom.

HOME SHOPPING NETWORK. The Home Shopping Network instituted the HSN Prime Timer Program, in which it hired and trained 400 older workers (of 2,200 employed) for positions as sales representatives in St. Petersburg, Florida. Members of this program have demonstrated lower turnover and at least comparable performance to the younger members of the work force.[84]

B&Q PLC. The B&Q PLC in the United Kingdom opened a new store near Manchester in October 1989 and staffed it entirely with workers over the age of 50. (Age discrimination laws in the United States would prohibit such an experiment.) The store was 18 percent more profitable than the average of five comparison stores. Employee turnover was six times lower and absenteeism was 39 percent less. Unwanted losses of inventory were less and no extra training was required.[85]

TWO-CAREER FAMILIES

Workplace issues seem to be most critical for adults with child-care responsibilities. The increasing commonality of two-career families as well as the rise of such nontraditional family styles as single parents, stepfamilies, divorced parents alternating childrearing responsibilities, and increasing numbers of adult couples with no children call for greater attention to the work–family interaction. Women are increasingly relocating their families because of workplace promotions. For example, more than 25 percent of the married executives who changed jobs in Richmond, Virginia, were women whose husbands followed. In addition, increasing numbers of women are accepting foreign assignments.[86]

The passage of the *Family Leave Act* in 1993 provides up to 12 weeks of unpaid leave to all workers employed by companies with 50 or more employees for the birth of a child, placement of a child for adoption, or caring for a seriously ill child, spouse, or family member with a guarantee of the worker's old job or equivalent job upon return. Still, the United States lags significantly behind other industrialized countries in dealing with these issues. Many European countries, for example, have liberal parental leave policies and provide convenient, affordable day-care options for workers. Japan, in contrast, lags behind the United States; there are no provisions for maternity leaves, company-sponsored day care, or sexual harassment.[87]

Increasingly, organizations have become more *family friendly,* that is, they have introduced programs that help employees balance the various aspects of their lives by easing the interface between work and family. Companies such as Johnson & Johnson, IBM, Aetna, Corning, and AT&T have introduced family-friendly, flexible work arrangements such as part-time work, job sharing, and flexible hours, parental leaves such as maternity or paternity leaves, family-care leaves, personal days, dependent-care services, and work–family stress management, among others.[88]

US WEST. This regional telephone company provides an array of family-friendly programs for employees. These include information and counseling, such as employee assistance, resource and referral, workshops, and learning centers; time off and flexible schedules, including personal days, family-care and new-born child-care leaves, and flexible work; and financial assistance for ongoing dependent-care and child-care expenses incurred for working outside of ordinary hours. Increasing numbers of employees work at home, reachable by telephone or beeper.[89]

STRIDE RITE. This shoe manufacturer was a pioneer in the introduction of family-friendly benefits. It opened the first child-care center in 1971 and more recently opened an intergenerational day-care center.[90]

Even when U.S. companies have family-friendly policies, only a fraction of workers take advantage of the options available to them because they fear working fewer hours or following other flexible work schedules will hinder their advancement.[91] This trend seems to occur in spite of the espoused benefits of work–family policies.

PHYSICALLY CHALLENGED EMPLOYEES

The Vocational Rehabilitation Act of 1978 and the Americans with Disabilities Act of 1990 have made the workplace in the United States more accessible to individuals with physical disabilities. While certain disabilities may prevent a person from performing certain jobs, employers must ensure that no discrimination in the hiring, advancement, evaluation, and compensation of physically challenged workers occurs. For example, blind or deaf individuals cannot be prevented from holding jobs for which they meet the basic qualifications. In some situations companies make special provisions, such as providing specialized reading equipment for blind employees, to allow them to perform their jobs. Organizations must also remove any physical barriers that prevent access to job locations for physically impaired employees; for example, they might install special ramps or elevators for wheelchair bound workers.

Although legal regulations caused many companies initially to hire physically challenged workers, now they find that such workers are equally productive and loyal as those without physical impairments. Companies also employ mentally handicapped workers in jobs particularly appropriate for their abilities and temperaments.

BANK OF MONTREAL. The bank's manager of recruitment and employment equity attempted to increase the number of job applicants with disabilities. He published the company's recruiting booklet in English and Braille. He also hired a woman who had mental disabilities due to a brain injury. He asked department managers not to exclude candidates with disabilities from jobs such as bank teller.[92]

MAKING CROSS-CULTURAL COMPARISONS

As organizations have become more multinational, the importance of integrating home country and foreign workers has increased. Managers and employees of organizations that operate in more than one country must deal with the diverse cultures of the global marketplace. In companies located solely in the United States, the ethnic and cultural backgrounds of employees influence their behaviors and attitudes. Immigrants have had a significant and positive impact on American industry.

AT&T. Almost two-fifths of 200 engineers and scientists employed by the Communications Sciences Research division of AT&T were born outside the United States.[93]

Cultural differences affect the way individuals perceive each other in the workplace and these different perceptions affect behavior. Language differences reflect unspoken attitudes, assumptions, and even attributions and can shape workers' views of the world and actions in the workplace. Workers at the Allstar New Yorker Hotel who speak limited English may have difficulty communicating with other employees who are fluent only in English. Rituals and customs can also influence individual perceptions and attributions. Americans, for example, value efficiency and speed, while the Japanese place a higher value on ceremonies and practices that reflect an awareness of social standing and mutual respect.

Workers from different cultures may also lack knowledge about the ethical appropriateness of various practices and hence act in unacceptable or unexpected ways. For example, paying an official to sanction a business act may be standard operating practice in some South American and Middle Eastern countries, but not in the United States. Political and economic differences among nations also create significantly different cultural patterns that may affect the level of education, experience, and expertise of various workers. The United States, for example, emphasizes equality whereas British culture honors class differences. Diagnosing cultural differences, understanding their impact on perceptions and attributions, and then prescribing ways to ensure effective behavior help improve individual functioning in the workplace.

EXXON CHEMICAL. A highly skilled female Asian engineer employed in the Baytown plant had been taught by her family to wait for silence and to "roll her words seven times on her tongue" before speaking to make certain that she did not say anything offensive. This approach was the direct opposite of the general approach to communication in the plant, which prevented her from making any contributions to team meetings. Other team members eventually recognized her way of communicating and introduced a more polite communication style in the plant to facilitate her participation.[94]

PRESCRIPTIONS FOR MANAGING WORK-FORCE DIVERSITY

Companies promote diversity in the workplace in several ways. Top management of these organizations typically develops corporate policies fostering diversity. Managers receive rewards for hiring, developing, and promoting women, minorities, and older workers. Programs to support the diverse work force are instituted.

HONEYWELL. At Honeywell, for example, diversity training focuses on various types of development. Management development increases the visibility, understanding, and commitment to diversity throughout the company. Organizational development promotes an equitable work environment that values diversity. Talent development encourages diversity throughout all functions. Individual development empowers individuals and helps reduce barriers to reaching their full potential.[95]

Managers and other workers must learn how to deal with employees other than themselves. Increasingly, companies have introduced diversity training, which highlights differences among workers and offers strategies for handling them. Companies with diversity efforts have learned a number of lessons, as shown in Table 3–2.

AT&T. AT&T introduced a training program that helps workers value diversity. Its Chief Financial Office has a network of diversity coordinators, publishes a newsletter about diversity, and has written and distributed a booklet entitled "Valuing Diversity."[96]

Managing a diverse work force calls for strong diagnostic skills. A manager must understand the unique needs of the workers and find ways to meet and mesh them. Managing diversity begins with valuing individual differences. Managers and nonmanagerial employees need to develop a sensitivity to, as well as understanding and acceptance of individuals with different ethnic and cultural backgrounds, races, genders, and ages.

In all countries, effective managers recognize the links between values, attitudes, and behavior. Influencing an attitude requires recognizing the underlying value and then altering both resulting beliefs and their related feelings. At the All-star New Yorker, for example, changing attitudes toward new work procedures would require first altering the beliefs of the workers, often through training and education. Dissemination of factual information may also eventually change some beliefs, but more emotion-oriented persuasive techniques and longer-term educational efforts may be needed to alter them. In the United States, for example, training in managing a culturally diverse work force begins with awareness training, which focuses on changing attitudes toward various ethnic, racial, and national groups.[97] Changing behavior then follows.

Managers can overcome racial, gender, and age stereotypes through effective education and communication about the issue, participation in task forces to discuss

TABLE 3–2   *Lessons about instituting diversity programs*

> Obtain the CEO's commitment
> Include diversity among the organization's business objectives
> Recognize and address the concerns of white males
> Evaluate the fairness of compensation and career tracking
> Offer top executives an experience of what minorities experience
> Use diversity training carefully
> Celebrate differences
> Increase the supply of diverse employees
> Continue to focus on diversity during downsizing

SOURCE: Based on F. Rice, How to make diversity pay, *Fortune* (August 8, 1994): 79–86.

career concerns of these workers, and receipt of rewards for developing and utilizing them. Offering scientific and technical training, management development opportunities, cross-training for production and administrative positions, Total Quality Management training, and other informal training can help ensure the competence and value of employees. Tailoring jobs to the requirements of older workers, for example, who may wish to reduce their time commitment while still remaining actively engaged in organizational life and recognizing their individual competencies is a major challenge of managing the diverse work force.

DAYS INNS. Days Inns of America began a program for hiring older workers as reservations agents in 1986. Days Inns provided older workers with only one-half day more training than they gave younger workers. Older workers remained on the job longer and booked more reservations, although took longer to handle a call than younger workers.[98]

Helping workers set and meet priorities, providing flexibility in working arrangements, and judging workers in terms of output instead of time or effort should facilitate the interaction between work and family. Changing the way jobs are performed to give workers more autonomy and control over their work and transforming the organizational culture to one that supports the needs of individuals with families are also significant organizational responses. At middle and late career, offering opportunities for respite and reflection, such as through learning sabbaticals or paid leaves, would also rejuvenate a worker stressed from coping with multiple demands. In the short term, however, the feasibility of such programs may appear less frequently as organizations continue to downsize by offering early retirement opportunities.

In addition, many organizations have international training programs to help build both a culturally diverse and a global management team.

GILLETTE. Gillette uses the firm's International Trainee Program for building its worldwide management corps.[99] Although it uses both U.S. and foreign nationals to staff operations worldwide, it prefers to hire foreign nationals to staff management positions outside the United States. These managers, too, become part of the cadre of employees with international experience who hold staffing positions throughout the world in their own and other countries.

Structural supports also facilitate diversity in organizations. In particular, two-career couples benefit from flexible work arrangements and flexible benefits, where the ability to select from among an array of benefits prevents, for example, duplication of medical benefits and the possibility of selecting child-care reimbursement.[100] Older workers may also want part-time employment or greater flexibility in their work schedules. The organizational culture should reflect the diverse cultural and social groups that compose the organization, attempt to eliminate discrimination in the organization, and distribute power and influence throughout the organization.[101]

SUMMARY

Organizational leaders have increasingly recognized the value of a more diverse work force. Diversity brings a greater pool of talent to the workplace, which often results in improved decision making, better understanding of customers' needs, and increased flexibility in staffing.

A diverse work force typically includes individuals with a variety of personality types: internalizers and externalizers, Type A and Type B, introverted and extroverted, sensing and intuitive, thinking and feeling, judging and perceiving, high and low Machiavellianism, and high and low self-efficacy describe some of these personality types.

An individual's values and attitudes also influence his or her behavior in the workplace. Values describe the underlying beliefs of an individual. Attitudes include cognitive, affective, and behavioral components.

Personal and career development also poses significant challenges for effective organizations. Individuals proceed through a series of stages that each have a different set of concerns and issues. An individual's stage of personal and career development has implications for appropriate organizational responses. Top management needs to recognize and respond to the family issues faced by employees.

Recent demographic trends significantly influence the diversity of the work force in the United States. The number of women, minorities, and older workers will continue to increase. Members of two-career families face special problems in managing their careers and home lives; family-friendly organizations attempt to address these problems. Organizations also now employ more physically challenged workers and face special challenges in ensuring the workplace does not provide hurdles to their performance.

Multinational corporations also experience a diverse work force, but more often along cultural dimensions. These differences are reflected in the ethnic origins of American citizens working in the United States and abroad and in foreign citizens working in U.S. companies here and abroad.

Managing diversity in organizations calls for a manager to have quality diagnostic skills. The manager should understand the unique needs of workers and find ways to meet them. Educational programs and structural supports characterize two major types of organizational responses to diversity issues.

DIAGNOSTIC QUESTIONS

The following diagnostic questions highlight issues relating to work–force diversity.

- How diverse is the organization's work force?

- What are the personalities of organizational members?

- Do the personalities of participants fit with the situation?

- What beliefs and values do individuals hold?

- How do these beliefs and values influence the individuals' attitudes?

- How would you characterize the stage of personal or career development of organizational members?

- Do organizational members experience problems in personal or career development?

- What family issues do workers face and how well does the organization assist them in meeting family needs?

- What are the cultural, ethnic, and demographic characteristics of workers?

- What cross-cultural issues does the organization face?

- What programs exist for managing diversity?

$\mathscr{A}$ctivity 3–1   LOCUS OF CONTROL TEST

STEP 1: Answer the following questions the way you feel. In the column, mark a Y for yes and an N for no next to each question.

_____ 1. Do you believe that most problems will solve themselves if you just don't fool with them?

_____ 2. Do you believe that you can stop yourself from catching a cold?

_____ 3. Are some people just born lucky?

_____ 4. Most of the time do you feel that getting good grades meant a great deal to you?

_____ 5. Are you often blamed for things that just aren't your fault?

_____ 6. Do you believe that if somebody studies hard he or she can pass any subject?

_____ 7. Do you feel that most of the time it doesn't pay to try hard because things never turn out right anyway?

_____ 8. Do you feel that if things start out well in the morning it's going to be a good day no matter what you do?

_____ 9. Do you feel that most of the time parents listen to what their children have to say?

_____ 10. Do you believe that wishing can make good things happen?

_____ 11. When you get punished does it usually seem it's for no good reason at all?

_____ 12. Most of the time do you find it hard to change a friend's opinion?

_____ 13. Do you think that cheering more than luck helps a team to win?

_____ 14. Did you feel that it was nearly impossible to change your parent's minds about anything?

_____ 15. Do you believe that parents should allow children to make most of their own decisions?

_____ 16. Do you feel that when you do something wrong there's very little you can do to make it right?

_____ 17. Do you believe that most people are just born good at sports?

_____ 18. Are most of the other people your age stronger than you are?

_____ 19. Do you feel that one of the best ways to handle most problems is just not to think about them?

_____ 20. Do you feel that you have a lot of choice in deciding who your friends are?

_____ 21. If you find a four-leaf clover, do you believe that it might bring you good luck?

_____ 22. Did you often feel that whether or not you did your homework had much to do with what kind of grades you got?

_____ 23. Do you feel that when a person your age is angry at you, there's little you can do to stop him or her?

_____ 24. Have you ever had a good-luck charm?

_____ 25. Do you believe that whether or not people like you depends on how you act?

_____ 26. Did your parents usually help you if you asked them to?

_____ 27. Have you felt that when people were angry with you it was usually for no reason at all?

_____ 28. Most of the time, do you feel that you can change what might happen tomorrow by what you do today?

_____ 29. Do you believe that when bad things are going to happen they just are going to happen no matter what you try to do to stop them?

_____ 30. Do you think that people can get their own way if they just keep trying?

_____ 31. Most of the time do you find it useless to try to get your own way at home?

_____ 32. Do you feel that when good things happen they happen because of hard work?

_____ 33. Do you feel that when somebody your age wants to be your enemy there's little you can do to change matters?

_____ 34. Do you feel that it's easy to get friends to do what you want them to do?

_____ 35. Do you usually feel that you have little to say about what you get to eat at home?

_____ 36. Do you feel that when someone doesn't like you there's little you can do about it?

_____ 37. Do you usually feel that it was almost useless to try in school because most other children were just plain smarter that you were?

_____ **38.** Are you the kind of person who believes that planning ahead makes things turn out better?

_____ **39.** Most of the time, do you feel that you have little to say about what your family decides to do?

_____ **40.** Do you think its better to be smart than to be lucky?

....

STEP 2: Scoring the Scale. Using the scoring key below, compare your answers on the previous page to the ones on the key. Give yourself one point each time your answer agrees with the keyed answer. Your score is the total number of agreements between your answers and the ones on the key.

Scoring Key

1. Yes _____	**21.** Yes _____
2. No _____	**22.** No _____
3. Yes _____	**23.** Yes _____
4. No _____	**24.** Yes _____
5. Yes _____	**25.** No _____
6. No _____	**26.** No _____
7. Yes _____	**27.** Yes _____
8. Yes _____	**28.** No _____
9. No _____	**29.** Yes _____
10. Yes _____	**30.** No _____
11. Yes _____	**31.** Yes _____
12. Yes _____	**32.** No _____
13. No _____	**33.** Yes _____
14. Yes _____	**34.** No _____
15. No _____	**35.** Yes _____
16. Yes _____	**36.** Yes _____
17. Yes _____	**37.** Yes _____
18. Yes _____	**38.** No _____
19. Yes _____	**39.** Yes _____
20. No _____	**40.** No _____

Total score

Interpreting Your Score

Low Scorers (0–8)—Scores from zero to eight represent the range for about one-third of the people taking the test. As a low scorer, you probably see life as a game of skill rather than chance. You most likely believe that you have a lot of control over what happens to you, both good and bad. With that view, internal-locus-of-control people tend to take the initiative in everything from job-related activities to relationships and sex. You are probably described by others as vigilant in getting things done, aware of what's going on around you, and willing to spend energy in working for specific goals. You would probably find it quite frustrating to sit back and let others take care of you, since you stressed on the test that you like to have your life in your own hands.

Although taking control of your life is seen as the "best way to be," psychologists caution that it has its own set of difficulties. Someone who is responsible for his or her own successes is also responsible for failures. So if you scored high in this direction, be prepared for the downs as well as the ups.

Average Scorers (9–16)—Since you've answered some of the questions in each direction, internal and external control beliefs for you may be situation specific. You may look at one situation—work, for example—and believe that your rewards are externally determined, that no matter what you do you can't get ahead. In another situation, love perhaps, you may see your fate as resting entirely in your own hands. You will find it helpful to review the questions and group them into those you answered in the internal direction and those you answered in the external direction. Any similarities in the kinds of situations within one of those groups? If so, some time spent thinking about what it is in those situations that makes you feel as though the control is or is not in your hands can help you better understand yourself.

High Scorers (17–40)—Scores in this range represent the external control end of the scale. Only about 15 percent of the people taking the test score 17 or higher. As a high scorer, you're saying that you see life generally more as a game of chance than as one where your skills make a difference.

....

STEP 3: Discussion. In small groups or with the class as a whole, answer the following questions.

DESCRIPTION

1. What was your score?
2. What type of personality does this represent?
3. How does this compare to scores of others in the class?

DIAGNOSIS

4. What behaviors and attitudes is each personality type likely to demonstrate?
5. What are the implications for encouraging organizational effectiveness.

By Stephen Nowicki, Jr., and B. Strickland in *The Mind Test* by Rita Aero and Elliot Weiner (New York: William Morrow, 1981), pp. 20–23. Reprinted with permission.

*A*ctivity 3–2 · LIFE LINE EXERCISE

STEP 1: Draw a time line that represents the major events in your life (your life line). Represent it in any way you choose, but be sure to identify all key events.

STEP 2: Now draw separate life lines for (1) your career, (2) your family, and (3) your biological development.

1. How do they interface?
2. Identify the times of stress.
3. Identify key transitions.
4. What effect did these transitions have on your motivation and perceptions at work at the time?

STEP 3: Discussion. In small groups or with the entire class, answer the following questions:

DESCRIPTION

1. What elements do the life lines share?
2. How do the life lines differ?

DIAGNOSIS

3. Can you delineate common phases or stages in your careers? in your lives?
4. For each stage identified, specify the key issues members of the group had to confront.
5. Identify the times of greatest stress.
6. What factors contributed to stress at these times?

PRESCRIPTION

7. For each stage, specify ways stress at that time could be reduced.

*A*ctivity 3–3 · THE DUAL-CAREER COUPLE DILEMMA

STEP 1: Read the Dual-Career Couple Dilemma case.

"Well, Fred, I think that about covers the major points of our proposal," said Jim Franklin, "If you accept, we will be pleased to have you in the department." Jim was head of the Management Department at Lawrence State University (LSU).[1] He was speaking by telephone with Fred Johnston, an applicant for a faculty position in business policy at LSU. Fred had published several articles, had presented good student evaluations of teaching, and had received high marks for service activities at his present school. He had also made a positive impression on the LSU management and faculty during his recent campus visit. His wife, Alice, was just completing a Ph.D. in English at Warner University, where Fred was employed.

She had applied for a teaching position in LSU's English Department. Fred responded, "I'm really excited to get your offer, Jim. Lawrence State is on the way up, and I'd like to be part of its success."

Jim was anxious to get a firm answer from Fred. "How do you think your wife will feel about this?" asked Jim. Fred replied, "Alice told me this morning that she thought she'd prefer Lawrence State over any of the other schools we're looking at. She's not heard anything about a campus interview from Dr. Allen yet, but expects to soon." Dr. Jordan Allen was head of LSU's English department.

Fred continued, "You know, of course, that timing is becoming critical for us. Alice and I are both going to interview at Evergreen College in Wisconsin next week, as I told you." He added that Evergreen seemed to be "really interested" in hiring both of them. Jim knew Evergreen did not have an accredited program in business and felt going there would not be a good career move for a person with Fred's credentials. Fred confirmed this, saying, "The business faculty at Evergreen is very small, and I'd have to teach in both management and marketing. The little town is okay, but there'd be few opportunities for my research and consulting in that setting. Also, they have only an undergraduate program. They're talking about trying to add an MBA. But that seems a long way off."

Still, Fred had made it clear he considered Alice's career fully as important as his own. He explained, "As you know, Alice will have fewer job opportunities than I, given the abundance of English Ph.D's relative to the available jobs. So we have to be interested in Evergreen at this point, even though we would rather come to LSU." Fred continued, "Jim, I can't say for sure, of course, but if we both get offers from Evergreen, we'll probably go there."

Jim replied, "I know that you and Alice have a lot to consider in this move. I have stayed in touch with Jordan Allen. He knows we are making you an offer. Hopefully, he'll get on the stick."

"OK, Jim," said Fred, "I'll get back to you after we return from Evergreen next week. Then we'll know if Alice and I have that option—at least I think we will know. But I hope Dr. Allen can at least schedule an interview for Alice soon."

"Fred, I'll call you next Friday. In the meantime, be thinking about our offer. You could have a fine future here at Lawrence," said Jim.

"You know we're seriously considering it, Jim," Fred replied.

"Okay. Goodbye Fred," said Jim.

Early the next week, Jordan Allen called Jim to discuss the Johnstons and the status of Alice's application. Another candidate for the position had recently visited the campus and the interview was "almost a disaster." Also, one of the other finalists had withdrawn his application. Indeed, Jordan said he was planning to call Alice that afternoon since "her position on the list had advanced," and she had now become a probable candidate. Jim was pleased to hear this. Filling the business policy slot would really reduce his recruiting woes, and placing Alice seemed to be the only roadblock.

But Jim knew the Johnstons would be leaving the next morning for Wisconsin. It was March 14, late in the recruiting season, and Jim feared Evergreen College might be as anxious as he to close a deal with Fred and Alice. Jim felt he had already violated academic protocol in trying so hard to get Alice placed in the English Department. Yet, he thought all his work with Fred would be for naught unless Jordan gave Alice some affirmation immediately.

BACKGROUND

The Management Department at LSU, like the College of Business generally, had experienced rapid enrollment growth over the preceding five years. A new faculty position in business policy had been approved for the coming year. There were two other management vacancies (due to a retirement and a transfer) that also had to be filled.

Although recruiting consumed a tremendous amount of his time, Jim realized that probably nothing was more important to the department. He knew that a strong faculty was a key element in maintaining accreditation and competing with other schools for good students. Performance and potential in teaching, research, and service were the main selection criteria, but it was also important that new hires be congenial and fit in well with existing faculty.[2]

At LSU, as at many other schools, the faculty hiring process was lengthy and elaborate. It involved a sequence of steps that included securing approval for the position, listing the position with the professional associations, advertising the vacancy in professional journals and newsletters, reviewing and responding to applications, having applicants evaluated by a faculty committee, selecting candidates for campus interviews, arranging and administering campus visits, negotiating with the chosen candidate, and processing the appointment package through the university administrative hierarchy.

The three openings in Jim's department were in human resource management, organizational behavior, and business policy. There were more qualified candidates for jobs in the first two fields, so Jim thought he would be able to fill those jobs. On the other hand, business policy was a rapidly developing field, and demand for qualified policy teachers far exceeded the supply. A position listing in the Academy of Management Placement Roster had resulted in many inquiries about the policy slot, but very few promising applications.[3] Jim had contacted three persons listed in the applicants section of the roster and found no desirable candidate among them. The several unsolicited inquiries he had received were equally unsatisfying. Calls to colleagues at other universities provided several good leads, but only one seemingly qualified person applied. Like most academic department heads, Jim attended several national and regional academic conferences each year and filled out the usual placement forms at the meetings. He could have advertised the policy position in such publications as the *Chronicle of Higher Education* (a newspaper) and the American Assembly of Collegiate Schools of Business *Newsline* (a newsletter), but had not found those media to be very effective in the past.

EARLY CONVERSATIONS

Fred Johnston first called Jim in early October, after seeing the policy job listed at a September meeting. Fred said he had been on the faculty at Warner University for two years and was planning to make a job change. He explained that although his experience at Warner had been generally favorable and that he felt he could have a good future there, his wife, Alice had to move because Warner had a firm policy of not hiring its own graduates. He and Alice had agreed to consider only places where there were employment opportunities for both.

After describing his general background, qualifications, and professional interests, Fred asked Jim if he felt there might possibly be a "match" of his qualifications and Lawrence State's needs. Jim responded that, indeed, there seemed to be and suggested that Fred send his résumé for review by the faculty recruiting committee. He further suggested the two meet at the Allied Southern Business Association (ASBA) meeting in New Orleans in November.

In the meantime, Alice scheduled an appointment with a recruiting representative of Lawrence State's English Department at an upcoming language arts meeting in San Francisco. The opening in the English Department was in technical writing. Alice's minor field of study; her major was Shakespearian studies.

From Jim's point of view, Fred Johnston had several appealing qualifications. He had completed his doctoral degree at a respected school, had significant teaching experience, and had worked several years in industrial management. Jim much preferred to hire a candidate who had completed the degree, rather than an "ABD" (all but dissertation), since it could take several

years to complete the dissertation project and there was always the risk that it would never be finished.[4] Also, because of the work involved in the dissertation, the ABD seldom assumes a full share of departmental duties such as teaching, advising, committee work, and so forth. In addition, an ABD does not formally start any other research projects that might accrue to the credit of the college while involved with the dissertation. Faculty publications had become an important measure of a school's relative stature, and Fred Johnston had already written several professional papers and articles.

CONTINUING DISCUSSIONS

Jim soon received a glowing evaluation of Fred's résumé from the faculty recruiting committee. And calls to Fred's references evoked expressions of admiration and respect. The recruitment process continued over the next few months, with admission of recommendation letters and other documentation. It became increasingly clear that Fred Johnston was an exceptional candidate.

Alice was the problem. Jim was concerned about the English Department in their handling of Alice's application, so he checked about faculty vacancies in English at three other colleges in the Lawrence area. But each either anticipated no openings or already filled those that had existed.

At the November ASBA meeting, Jim and Fred talked for more than an hour. Fred seemed to be as good as he appeared on paper. And Fred seemed impressed with Lawrence State, which Jim considered just as important.

After Jim returned to the campus, he called Jordan Allen to check on Alice's application. Jordan said that the person who interviewed her at the meeting was favorably impressed, that Alice "certainly hadn't eliminated herself," and that she did seem to have "good potential." However, he said, the recruiting committee ranked four or five applicants ahead of her overall. Jordan noted that Alice was just completing the doctorate, had little teaching experience, and had not published.

Although Jim did not want to try to pressure Jordan to give Alice special consideration, he did emphasize that the Johnston's were looking first at schools that would hire them both. He pointed out that Fred's interest in Lawrence State would surely facilitate the recruiting of his wife, perhaps on favorable terms for the university. Jordan acknowledged this, but said he was relying on his committee. He said they were not ready to invite Alice Johnston in for a campus interview—at least not at that time.

About two weeks later, early in December, Jim called Jordan, "Hello, Jordan," he began, "I wanted you to know that we're inviting Fred Johnston in for a campus interview. Any chance that you are ready to move on Alice's candidacy? We could surely sell them better on Lawrence if we had them both here."

Jordan replied, "No, sorry Jim. We've got two others we're going to look at first, although our list is getting shorter. You're going to bring Dr. Johnston in anyway, right?"

"Yes, we think he'd fit in well here," Jim answered, "And who knows, maybe the Johnstons will decide they can't get exactly what they want. Fred said if he finds something really attractive and the chances look good for his wife they might go ahead and make the decision. So we're going to take the risk and have him in."

"Well, thanks for keeping me posted, Jim," Jordan said, "Let me know how the interview goes with Fred and what you plan to do."

"Will do, Jordan, and call me if you have any developments," Jim replied.

CAMPUS INTERVIEWS

When Fred came in for a day-and-a-half campus visit, Jim had hopes of selling him on Lawrence State on the spot. The interview schedule included a series of meetings with various faculty, college and university administrators, and graduate students. There was also to be a formal presentation on Fred's current research and informal gatherings at meals hosted by the departmental faculty. Jim was generally pleased with the interviews as the faculty, students, and administrators seemed to respond well to Fred.

As Jim drove Fred to the airport, he told Fred that he expected to be able to call him within a couple days with positive news. He stated that he felt the interviews had gone well and that he hoped Fred had retained his interest in the position. Fred replied that he was very much interested, and that he now hoped things would work out for him and Alice at Lawrence State.

The next day Jim talked with members of the faculty recruiting committee and the dean and reviewed the written evaluations by faculty, administrators, and students who had met with Fred or attended his seminar. These evaluations were uniformly favorable, affirming Jim's tentative decision to make Fred an offer. Jim wrote a hiring proposal, which specified the academic rank, salary, and the other major terms and conditions of the appointment. He went over it with the dean and got the necessary approval to make the offer.

Before calling Fred, he decided to give Jordan Allen a call to check on Alice's status and inform him of the imminent offer. When Jim asked about Alice's chances, Dr. Allen replied that it would be a few days before he would know any more, since their other candidate was due in to interview the next day and the department had high hopes of hiring her. Jim thanked Jordan for the information, and they agreed to keep in close contact. He then made the call to Fred offering him a faculty position (as described in the introduction to the case).

Early the next week, Jim received the call from Jordan Allen with the news that Alice Johnston was being invited for an interview. He was pleased to hear this and, only half kidding, said, "Now, be nice to her during her visit." Jordan replied that they would have to "see how it goes" and that he, too, hoped Alice Johnston would be well received by the faculty. Jordan agreed to call Jim following her interview.

As Jim had promised, he called Fred Johnston on Friday afternoon, one week after he had extended the job offer and following the Johnstons' interviews at Evergreen College in Wisconsin. "Hello, Fred," he said, "I'm calling to follow up on our last discussion about our offer to join the faculty here."

Fred responded: "Jim, I was expecting your call, and I do have some news. Evergreen offered us both contracts before we left the campus. But there are more problems than I thought with the school, at least from my standpoint. There is little summer teaching,[5] limited travel funds, a fifteen-hour teaching load,[6] and, frankly, not much support for research and publication. The salary offers were interesting. They offered me $3,500 less than you did, but promised Alice about $3,000 more than Dr. Allen indicated English could pay. I'm sure they know what they're doing, low balling me and loading up way above market rate on her. She's seen no schools paying quite that much in her field. She was pretty impressed."

"I suppose she would be," said Jim, "But isn't it the total package which should count, not just what one of you gets?"

Fred continued: "I am happy to say Lawrence State has finally scheduled an interview for Alice, next Wednesday. If English makes her a reasonable offer, we're on our way to Lawrence, even if the money package turns out a little less attractive. Timing is now of utmost importance. Evergreen wants our decision by Monday, but I think we can stall them until Friday, after Alice gets back from Lawrence. Alice has explained our situation to Dr. Allen, and he promised to act quickly after her interview."

Jim grimaced, but kept his voice pleasant, "Fred, thanks for the update. I'll call Jordan Allen so that he'll know of our department's continued strong interest in you. I really appreciate your candor in sharing this with me. Let's see, I'll call you back on Friday, or you call me before if there's anything new."

"I'll do it," replied Fred. "Goodbye now."

Jim was anxious to hear about Alice's interview with the English Department. His spirits were not lifted by a letter he got the following Wednesday from his back-up candidate for the business policy position. She had accepted another job, noting that she couldn't wait any longer for Lawrence State to act.

Early Thursday morning, Jordan Allen called. "Jim," he began, "Alice Johnston was in yesterday and, well, our feelings about her are rather mixed. She's a pleasant, congenial person. But several members of the recruiting committee think Alice is really more interested in teaching the works of Shakespeare than technical writing. We're a little concerned about the fit. We're not sure what we're going to do, but we have a meeting tomorrow to talk about it."

"Well, Jordan, this news concerns me," Jim replied. "But I will tell you that we can get them both if you offer her a job. I don't think there's any question about it. Then you and I could move on to working on something else! I guess you have to do what's best for you, but it is getting late in the year for us to hire. We'll be sitting here empty handed for the fall semester if we can't fill this position soon. And I'd guess you'll have to fill your slot in the near future if you're going to?"

"I do appreciate your situation, and we'll be mindful of it in our discussions. We want to cooperate with you as much as possible," said Jordan, "I'll give you a call."

"Thanks, Jordan, and I'll look forward to learning of your decision. Now, help us out if you can."

Jim leaned back in his chair and reflected on what had become a complex and frustrating recruitment and selection experience. Had he done everything he could to increase the chances that Fred would come to LSU? Had he used the right approach in promoting Alice's candidacy for the job in the English Department? He wondered what more he could do? Maybe he should call Alice to inform her of the concerns of the English Department about her teaching interests? Perhaps then she could better "sell" herself to them? Or could he possibly persuade Jordan to use his influence with the committee? Or should he ask the dean to involve the provost[7] who could better consider the university's interest in this matter? Maybe some leverage could be exercised by his office to help the Management Department fill the position? After all, from the university perspective, Fred would be an excellent hire and Alice would surely be an acceptable one, Jim reasoned. Or had he already gone too far in pressuring Jordan?

As Jim packed up his briefcase to leave for the day, he pondered how this situation he'd been wrestling with for six months would come out. Maybe LSU should develop a policy that would promote better cooperation among departments that were recruiting working couples? Jim had recalled a recent faculty position announcement from Oregon State University that had a tagline stating an institutional policy of "being responsive to the needs of dual-career couples." On the other hand, perhaps it would be better to simply avoid recruiting dual-career couples in the future and consider only individual candidates? He wondered.

STEP 2: Prepare the case for class discussion.

STEP 3: Answer each of the following questions, individually or in small groups, as directed by your instructor.

DESCRIPTION
1. Trace each person's career.

DIAGNOSIS
2. What is the major dilemma faced by Jim Franklin?
3. What are Alice Johnston's and Fred Johnston's priorities?
4. Using your knowledge of personal and career development, evaluate the situation.

5. What problems exist for the dual-career couple in the case?
6. What needs must the university meet?

PRESCRIPTION

7. What should Franklin do?
8. What provisions should the university make for this type of situation?

....

STEP 4: Discussion. In small groups or with the entire class, or in written form, share your answers to the questions above. Then answer the following questions:

1. What symptoms suggest a problem exists?
2. What problems exist in the case?
3. What theories and concepts help explain those problems?
4. How can the problems be corrected?
5. Are the actions likely to be effective?

....

NOTES

1. Names of institutions and persons in the case are disguised. The university is a comprehensive state institution with about 24,000 students in a southeastern city with a population of over 500,000.
2. Although the evaluation of qualifications in these areas is difficult and subjective, teaching may be judged by student evaluations, peer or administrative evaluations, quality of course syllabi, etc. Research is measured largely by the quality and quantity of one's scholarship reported in professional journals, books, or at professional conferences. Service may be gauged by one's performance in activities of professional associations, professional contributions to the community, and work on university committees or projects.
3. The Academy of Management is the leading academic association in management. It publishes a placement roster in the spring and another in the fall, listing job applicants as well as openings.
4. The typical Ph.D. program includes two or more years of course work beyond the master's degree, comprehensive written and oral examinations, and the dissertation. The dissertation is an advanced treatise, often exceeding 150 pages, based on independent research and demonstrating mastery of the candidate's own subject as well as of the scholarly method. Ph.D. candidates often accept teaching jobs after completing their examinations while working on the dissertation.
5. The usual contract is for nine months, and summer teaching offers a way for many faculty members to earn added income.
6. Nationally accredited business schools generally limit teaching loads to twelve semester hours, nine if a graduate course is included.
7. At LSU, the provost served the function of the academic vice president or vice president, academic affairs at many other universities. Jim and Jordan reported to their respective deans, who in turn reported to the provost with regard to academic matters.

This case was prepared by Thomas R. Miller of Memphis State University and Arthur Sharplin of McNeese State University as the basis for class discussion rather than to illustrate either effective or ineffective handling of a managerial situation. All proper names have been disguised. Distribution by the North American Case Research Association. © 1991.

Activity 3–4 **UNDERSTANDING RACE AND GENDER DIFFERENCES**

....

STEP 1: Draw a picture of yourself on a large piece of newsprint with colored markers making the following assumption:

Pretend you are to be reincarnated and you can choose how you will come back . . . as long as you choose a different race **and** gender.

STEP 2: On the left side of the paper, answer the following questions:

1. Why did you choose this persona?
2. What do you like about your choice?

On the right side of the paper, answer the following questions:

1. What do you dislike about your choice?
2. What are you concerned about as you face the future as this new persona?

STEP 3: Discussion. Your instructor will direct each student to present their picture in small groups or to the class as a whole. Share your answers to the questions above. Then answer the following questions:

1. What are the advantages and disadvantages of each choice?
2. What issues concern you in facing the future as your new persona?

Adapted and reprinted with permission of the authors, Bonita L. Betters-Reed and Lynda L. Moore.

Activity 3–5   ATTITUDES TOWARD PEOPLE WITH DISABILITIES

STEP 1: Read the following two passages.

Passage 1: People with disabilities are a burden on society. They place normally functioning people at risk. Grossly overgenerous disability payments and outrageously expensive disability programs have raised taxes and drained government funds that could have been put to better use elsewhere. Most people with disabilities are not capable of contributing to society. They should be kept out of sight and out of mind, where they belong.

Passage 2: People with disabilities can work and function as active participants in society. They have the right to be educated, the right to have an occupation or profession, the right to live independently, the right to safe and independent travel, and the right to live and die with dignity.

STEP 2: Using a scale of 0 to 70, where the attitude expressed in the first paragraph represents 0 and that expressed in the second paragraph represents 70, write a number along that scale that represents your own attitude toward people with disabilities. Label that score "A" for Attitude. Then, using the same scale, write the number you think represents other people's attitudes toward people with disabilities. Label that score "O" for Other.

STEP 3: Complete the Behavior Questionnaire below. Answer each question by putting a number between 0 and 7 as shown in the space beside the question.

_____ I have offered assistance to a person with a disability. (0 = never, 7 = often)

_____ When encountering a person with a disability, I have moved away to avoid a direct confrontation. (0 = often, 7 = never)

_____ I have engaged a person with a disability in friendly conversation. (0 = never, 7 = often)

_____ I have made a rude comment or snide remark to others about a person with a disability. (0 = often, 7 = never)

_____ I have tried to learn about at least one disabling condition. (0 = never, 7 = often)

_____ I have felt pity when observing a person with a disability. (0 = often, 7 = never)

_____ I was impressed by a person with a disability after seeing the person do something I didn't think he or she could do. (0 = never, 7 = often)

_____ I have used terms such as "crip," "tard," or "spaz," when referring to an "able-bodied" person. (0 = often, 7 = never)

_____ Upon hearing others use inappropriate language or terms about a person with a disability, I have interceded and corrected them. (0 = never, 7 = often)

_____ Upon reflection, I realize I have acted inappropriately when interacting with a person with a disability. (0 = often, 7 = never)

STEP 4: Score the Behavior Questionnaire. Then record your score on the same scale of 0 to 70 used in Step 2. Label that score "B" for Behavior.

STEP 5: In small groups of six to eight people, discuss your pattern of scores on the scale. As part of your discussion, answer the following questions:

1. Was there a typical pattern for the group?
2. What experiences that you have had might lead to this pattern?
3. How did the group's O (Other) scores compare to their A (Attitude) scores? How do you account for this pattern?

4. How did the group's A (Attitude) scores compare with their B (Behavior) scores? How do you account for this pattern?
5. If your A (Attitude) score was less than 60, how can you develop more positive attitudes toward people with disabilities?
6. If your A (Attitude) score was higher than your B (Behavior) score, how can you change your behavior to better reflect your attitudes?

Adapted and reprinted with permission from Albert S. King, Doing the right thing for employees with disabilities. © September 1993, Training & Development, American Society for Training and Development. Reprinted with permission. All rights reserved.

Activity 3–6   **TRAVELING TO FOREIGN CULTURES**

STEP 1: Your instructor will divide the class into two groups and provide each group with color-coded badges. Print your name in bold letters on the badge and wear it throughout the exercise.

STEP 2: Working with your group members, your first task is to invent your own cultural cues. You are to think about the kinds of behaviors and words that will signify to all members that they belong together in one culture. For each category provided below, identify and record at least one important attribute for your culture.

Facial expression

Eye contact

Handshake

Body language

Key words or phrases

STEP 3: Now that you have defined desirable cultural aspects for your group, practice them. It is best to stand with your group and to engage one another in conversations involving two or three people at a time. Your aim in talking with one another is to learn as much as possible about each other—hobbies, interests, where you live, what your family is like, courses being taken, and so on, all while practicing the behaviors and words identified in Step 2. It is not necessary for participants to answer questions of a personal nature truthfully. Invention is permissible because the conversation is only a means to the end of cultural observation. Your aim at this point is to become comfortable with the indicators of your particular culture. Practice until the indicators are second nature to you.

STEP 4: You now should assume that you work for a business organization that operates in the culture that you defined and practiced. This business has decided that it would like to explore the potential for doing business with companies in a foreign culture. Your awareness of the global marketplace tells you that to plan an effective approach to a foreign country's business leaders you must first understand the culture of that country.

You are to learn as much as possible about another culture. To do so, you will send from one to three representatives, when designated by your instructor, on a "business trip" to the other culture. These representatives must, as much as possible, behave in a manner that is consistent with your culture, as defined in Step 2. At the same time, each representative must endeavor to learn as much as possible about the people in the other culture, while keeping eyes and ears open to cultural attributes that will be useful in future negotiations with foreign businesses. (*Note:* At no time will it be considered ethical behavior for the representative to ask direct questions about the foreign culture's attributes. These cultural attibutes must be gleaned from firsthand experience.)

While your representatives are away you will receive one or more exchange visitors from the other culture who will be interested in learning more about your organizational culture. You must strictly adhere to the cultural aspects you defined in Step 1 and practiced in Step 3 as you respond to the visitor(s).

STEP 5: When told to do so by your instructor, all representatives return to their native cultures. Each group then discusses and records what it has learned about the foreign culture based on the exchange of visitors. The aim is to try to decipher the behaviors expected of members of the other culture. This information will be shared with all group members and will serve as the basis for orienting the next representatives who will make a business trip.

STEP 6: The instructor will select one to three different group members to make another trip to the other culture to check out the assumptions that your group has made about the other culture. This "checking out" process will consist of actually practicing the other culture's cues to see whether they work. Both groups will be standing and conducting their business of getting to know one another as in Steps 3 and 4.

STEP 7: The travelers return and report on findings to the home group, and the group then prepares to report what it learned about the other culture.

STEP 8: Discussion. With the entire class, answer the following questions:

1. What did you learn about the other culture?
2. How easily did you learn about the other culture?
3. What is the effect of having people from two different cultures interact?

By Susan R. Zacur and W. Alan Randolph, Traveling to foreign cultures: An exercise in developing awareness of cultural diversity, *Journal of Management Education* 17(4) (November 1993): 510–513. Reprinted by permission of Sage Publications, Inc.

$\mathcal{A}$ctivity 3–7   JOHN FRANKLIN CASE

STEP 1: Read the John Franklin case.

Late in the evening, John Franklin sat down to talk with the interviewer about the time he had spent in the Middle East and his current position with Major Construction Company, Inc. Franklin had recently returned to the United States after working in Saudi Arabia for three years, and said he felt as if his "defense mechanisms" were starting to return.

John Franklin was a black American; after growing up and working in the United States, the differences in cultures that he had seen in Saudi Arabia were dramatic. Life in Saudi Arabia had a tremendous effect on him. He had worked with a number of different people from a variety of nations, but he had not experienced the racial prejudices he had felt in America. Upon his return to the United States, Franklin noticed that he felt more cautiousness towards his white counterparts than he had in the Middle East and he recalled having had this same feeling prior to going to Saudi Arabia. Thinking about this feeling and reflecting on his experiences, he considered the question, "What was it like being a black American in Saudi Arabia and how was it different from being black in America?"

BACKGROUND

Franklin was currently a project manager with Major Construction Company in the United States. For the previous years, he had worked for SEI Engineering, a Saudi Arabian construction company. Franklin had traveled to Saudi Arabia after working for four years on various construction jobs in the Sunbelt region. He was born and raised in Tennessee, but had worked throughout the states and had traveled previously to Saudi Arabia while working for another U.S. company. He remembered his visits to the Middle East as very enjoyable. "Americans were well-respected for their ingenuity," he told the interviewer.

The move to the Middle East was prompted by the vast financial opportunities offered there. "The 1981 Reagan tax plan eliminated or reduced taxes for Americans working outside of the United States, making it much more attractive," Franklin commented. "This was the major incentive for most of the expatriates in Saudi Arabia—the money!" Highly regarded for their skills, Americans were also paid a premium to work in Saudi Arabia. Benefits paid by companies operating in Saudi Arabia included medical, housing, automobiles, and education and travel expenses.

Franklin's job with SEI Engineering had consisted of managing a variety of construction projects in and around the capital city of Riyadh. SEI, which was owned by an American-educated Saudi, built facilities for Saudi royalty and government ministries. Projects included sports complexes, hospitals, dormitories, and office buildings. Franklin went to SEI as a construction manager and was promoted to the position of director of construction management after a year and a half. His duties included the management and supervision of engineers from countries such as Korea, the Philippines, India, Denmark, England, Scotland, Sweden, and the United States. A variety of religious backgrounds was also represented, as Muslims, Hindus, Buddhists, and Christians were included among the workers. Construction projects progressed much more slowly in Saudi Arabia than in the United States, partly because of owner fickleness and partly because of logistical problems associated with obtaining building materials. Another key obstacle was communications; although English was the business language in Saudi Arabia, communicating with various laborers was a challenge: "You would quickly pick up certain words to communicate with the laborers. Showing emotion was important. We also used hand signals to a great extent," Franklin explained.

REFLECTION ON SAUDI ARABIA

Managing in a foreign country was a unique experience for Franklin. It was important for him always to try to see things from the laborer's perspective. Managing workers who were from so many diverse backgrounds exposed him to the vast differences among people. Although the cultural differences were clearly evident, there were few conflicts. All foreign workers in Saudi Arabia were "invited" to work there; you could not enter the country unless you had government authorization and were sponsored by a Saudi representative. Because of this climate, all expatriates were given equal treatment. Racial and religious factors seldom came into play. The government considered foreign workers to be in the country for a specific purpose and treated them accordingly. This environment suited John Franklin well: "I felt like I was free, or rather, equal . . . at least accepted as an equal for my abilities. If someone did not like you, it wasn't because of your race or religion."

In addition to respecting his educational background, the Saudis trusted Franklin, in part *because* of his being a black American. The black American was thought to be an underdog and the Saudis felt they related to the experiences of black Americans. White Americans were thought to be a part of the "system." Franklin recalled, the Saudis would often confide in Franklin regarding business proposals.

When putting a proposal together, or presenting a competing bid, often after the meeting the Saudis would ask what I really thought about the negotiations, even if I was involved in the bid. They would ask, "Is this guy giving me a fair shake, are they being honest with me?" They felt more comfortable with me. They felt they could trust me. This wouldn't happen in the States.

Franklin believed that the great variety of cultures found on the construction sites in Saudi Arabia made race/cultural relations easier than if only a few cultures had been represented. In addition, because so many of the workers were foreigners and were isolated, there was a comraderie that bound them together and made working together easier: "It was nice . . . it was nice not being a minority."

Franklin indicated that management problems that existed in the United States were also present in Saudi Arabia, but the preconceived notions that were common in the United States were not present there. He admitted that there were prejudices, but they were not related to racial differences. The prejudices that he had seen were related to social, cultural, and religious differences that existed primarily in the Middle East. Franklin felt that in Saudi Arabia he was allowed to manage based on his abilities, not the color of his skin. He believed that white Americans had more difficulty adapting to the Saudi culture: "The biggest difference you notice is in the dealings with a white American when he realizes that for the first time he is a minority. It's a big change for him. When he's sitting in a meeting and we're all black [Saudis or Americans]—that was interesting."

CONTRASTS

Franklin noted particular contrasts between how people were treated in the United States and in the Middle East. He had returned to the United States because he wanted to raise his daughter here. His job as a project manager with Major Construction Company had responsibilities that were very similar to those of his previous job in Saudi Arabia and he felt comfortable with the types of projects that Major Construction handled. The relaxed racial atmosphere that he had experienced in Saudi Arabia, however, did not exist in the States. Franklin felt that here he was always on guard around his coworkers, and he believed that they always second-guessed his judgment. He felt tension in social settings as if his peers were being especially careful not to tell offensive jokes or make derogatory comments around him. In Saudi Arabia there had been no pressure to conform and Franklin felt confident and self-assured about his abilities. He recalled:

> Here everything is based on color. Being used to that caught me off stride in Saudi Arabia. There, the race issue never crosses your mind. But it doesn't hit you all at once; it's gradual. You gradually go from one extreme to the other. Whereas in the States you're always on guard, in Saudi Arabia I relaxed and lost that guarded feeling—that "sixth sense" that all black Americans have. It was a good feeling.

The relaxed racial climate that Franklin experienced in Saudi Arabia made coming back to the United States difficult. He knew that the conditions in Saudi Arabia could be attributed to many different factors, but he wondered whether this climate could be duplicated here. At Major Construction Company, Franklin supervised workers that were both black and white. He wondered how his prejudices would affect his supervision and whether his "defensiveness" toward whites affected his performance. In considering what he could do about his prejudices, he decided to begin looking for answers in his experiences in Saudi Arabia.

STEP 2: Prepare the case for class discussion.

STEP 3: Answer each of the following questions, individually or in small groups, as directed by your instructor.

DESCRIPTION
1. Compare and contrast John Franklin's experience as an African-American in the United States and in Saudi Arabia.

DIAGNOSIS
2. What factors contribute to his two experiences?
3. How does race affect perceptions and attributions in the workplace in the United States and in Saudi Arabia?

PRESCRIPTION
4. How can John's company improve its management of diversity?

ACTION

   5. Are these actions likely to be effective?

....

STEP 4: Discussion. In small groups or with the entire class, or in written form, share your answers to the questions above. Then answer the following questions:

   1. What symptoms suggest that a problem exists?
   2. What problems exist in the case?

3. What theories and concepts help explain those problems?
4. How can the problems be corrected?
5. Are the actions likely to be effective?

Prepared by Bryan W. Smith under the supervision of James G. Clawson. Copyright © 1990 by the Darden Graduate Business School Foundation, Charlottesville, Virginia.

*A*ctivity 3–8   **"AGE AND ATTITUDES"**

....

STEP 1: View the ABC video entitled "Age & Attitudes."

....

STEP 2: Answer the following questions, individually or in small groups, as directed by your instructor:

   1. Why does age discrimination occur in the workplace?

2. What are the consequences for older workers and for other workers?
3. What are the advantages and disadvantages of employing older workers?
4. Why should an organization develop a diverse work force that includes older workers?
5. What legal responsibilities does a manager have regarding using age as a hiring or promotion criteria?

....

STEP 3: Assume you have been asked to advise the managers of the retail store in which you work about ways to ensure that age discrimination does not occur. In small groups, develop a set of guidelines for use by the managers.

Chapter 4

Chapter Outline

Motivating and Rewarding Individuals

Motivating Workers at Wal-Mart

I'm really fired up," Andy Wilson is telling the people in the blue smocks, his Alabama accent dripping Dixie. "This is going to be a great store, and I just want you to know how much we 'preciate the job you're doing. Give yourselves a hand." In just a few minutes Wal-Mart store No. 1,784, in Salem, Oregon, will officially open. But not before Wilson, a Wal-Mart regional vice president who has flown 2,000 miles across the country in a DeSoto of a prop-engine plane to get here, dusts these newcomers with the cultural pollen that has helped Wal-Mart flower.

"My job isn't important," he continues. "You're the people who make it happen." The session ends with a rousing Wal-Mart cheer—"Give me a W! Give me an A! Give me an L! Give me a squiggly! . . ."—and a solemn pledge by each associate, Wal-Martese for employee, to greet every customer within ten feet, "so help me, Sam."

The speech reminding these hourly workers that they are the very essence of the enterprise, or something like it, will probably be repeated, in all sincerity, by Wal-Mart executives in 100 stores every day. And if each speaker sounds as if he just stepped off a front porch in Tupelo or Arkadelphia, that's because they all did start the week in that metropolis of merchandising, Bentonville, Arkansas.

Wilson is one of 15 regional vice presidents who spend week after grueling week hopscotching their territories. Today it's Salem, which is about as far from Bentonville as any Wal-Mart store that has ever sold a swamp cooler. But Salem is not out of range of Air Wal-Mart, nor of one of the more unique modes of managing ever erected. The inventor was the late Sam Walton, who could never get enough information about what shoppers were buying and who could never talk to enough customers. He figured the best way to find both in quantity was to visit the stores. This he did as he piloted Wal-Mart to spectacular growth.[1]

All managers face a significant challenge—motivating employees to produce desired outcomes, including efficiency, quality, and innovation, as well as satisfaction and commitment. What motivates individuals to behave, think, or feel in certain ways? What factors make you or others more willing to work, to be creative, to achieve, to produce? Theory and research in the area of motivation provide a systematic way of diagnosing the degree of motivation and of prescribing ways of increasing it.

In the first part of this chapter we examine five major theoretical ways of thinking about motivation: (1) needs theories, (2) equity theory, (3) reinforcement theory, (4) expectancy theory, and (5) goal setting. We also consider their implications for diagnosing and implementing new ways of working together in organizations. Managers and other workers can apply these theories in motivating organizational members to increase their performance and work together more effectively. Although no one theory applies to every person in every situation, each can help you apply the diagnostic approach to specific work situations. After discussing the motivation theories, the chapter concludes with a discussion of the organization's reward system, which comprises the formal set of motivational approaches and rewards that managers use. The reward system is a powerful tool for encouraging specific worker outcomes and stimulating employees to work to accomplish organizational goals.

NEEDS THEORIES

Think again about the situation at the Salem Wal-Mart store. How does Andy Wilson motivate the workers? Early motivation theorists would explain such a situation by saying that managers should attempt to meet employees' needs—their basic requirements for living and working productively. As the work force in organizations becomes more diverse, recognizing the individuality of needs becomes paramount. Identifying and responding to them becomes a critical issue in effective management.

Can you identify the needs of the Wal-Mart associates? To do a good job of identifying them, you probably would need to spend a great deal of time talking with the employees and observing their behavior both in and out of the work situation. Some workers might have basic physiological and safety and security needs. Others might have needs for esteem or growth.

In this section we present four of the most popular needs theories: (1) Maslow's hierarchy of needs theory, (2) Alderfer's ERG theory, (3) McClelland's need for achievement theory, and (4) Herzberg's two-factor theory. Each of these theories describes a specific set of needs the researchers believe individuals have and each differs somewhat in the number and kinds of needs identified. The theories also differ as to how unfulfilled needs influence motivation, as discussed in the following sections. Table 4–1 shows the different identified needs. Diagnosing the needs and then finding ways to meet unsatisfied needs can increase motivation.

MASLOW'S HIERARCHY OF NEEDS

Abraham Maslow offered a simple scheme for thinking about an individual's needs.[2] The hierarchy of needs arranged needs from an individual's most basic, lowest level needs to a person's high-level needs, as shown in Figure 4–1: (1) phys-

TABLE 4–1

List of needs

MASLOW	ALDERFER	MCCLELLAND	HERZBERG
Physiological Safety and security	Existence		Hygiene
Belongingness and love	Relatedness	Need for affiliation	
Self-esteem Self-actualization	Growth	Need for achievement Need for power	Motivators

FIGURE 4–1   *Maslow's hierarchy of needs*

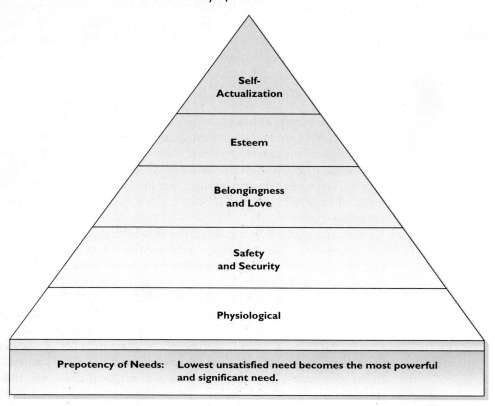

Self-
Actualization

Esteem

Belongingness
and Love

Safety
and Security

Physiological

**Prepotency of Needs: Lowest unsatisfied need becomes the most powerful
and significant need.**

iological, (2) safety, (3) belongingness and love, (4) esteem, and (5) self-actualization. Beginning with an emphasis on satisfying physiological needs, individuals
typically progressed over time to a concern with safety and security, belongingness,
esteem, and self-actualization needs.

Physiological needs refer to an individual's most basic needs for food, water,
shelter, and sex, or more broadly the ability to care for workers' children, and medical or dental coverage. Increasingly, benefits that meet such needs include extensive health-care coverage, as well as the provision of child-care and even elder-care
services and subsidies. Dependent-care offerings (see Chapter 3) may include referral services, subsidized care, on-site day care, temporary care, or efforts to increase the supply of day-care providers.

BROWN & ROOT. The Houston engineering and construction company Brown &
Root, Inc., hired Kinder-Care at Work to run an on-site day-care center for children
of its 2,500 headquarters employees.

AT&T. AT&T donated money to neighborhood childcare centers and received priority in placing its employees' children there.[3]

Safety and security needs describe a person's desire for security or protection.
While safety needs once focused on the handling of hazardous materials and problems with remote parking locations, the popular press has recently reported prob-

lems associated with the extensive use of video-display terminals and the effects of secondary smoke in the workplace. Some companies attempt to meet safety needs by instituting extensive safety programs that may involve watchdog committees and stringent corporate oversight of the use of hazardous materials. Other organizations have instituted no smoking policies and special security precautions for workers who must walk to remote parking areas.

In addition to avoiding on-the-job hazards, security needs focus on short-term and long-term job protection. Union contracts that include employment guarantees reflect workers' needs for security.

NATIONAL HEALTH AND HUMAN SERVICES EMPLOYEE UNION. Local 1199 of the National Health and Human Services Employees Union in New York exchanged a decrease in the rate of pay increases for job security.[4]

XEROX. Xerox workers in Webster, New York, agreed to exchange changes in the work structure for greater job security in a 7-year contract negotiated with the Amalgamated Clothing and Textile Workers Union.[5]

Belongingness and love needs focus on the social aspects of work and non-work situations. Almost all individuals value interpersonal relationships and seek social interactions with others. Building on these needs may facilitate the worker cooperation many organizations now try to create. Many organizations now use work teams for accomplishing organizational goals.

DANA COMPUTER SERVICES. Dana Computer Services, for example, used self-managing teams, where team members have complete responsibility for analyzing a problem and implementing solutions, to change the firm's billing structure and improve disaster recovery from computer failures and testing procedures.[6]

In addition to improving organizational performance, teams such as these meet the social needs of their members. Many organizations also conduct regular social activities, such as sports leagues or holiday parties.

Esteem needs encompass a person's concern for mastery, competence, and status. Some individuals who possess esteem needs desire recognition for their accomplishments. They may want the material symbols of success, such as a large office or an executive job title, public recognition, or other perks associated with success—special privileges or rewards that may include country club membership or a luxury car. Other individuals with esteem needs wish to master their work, demonstrate competence and accomplishments, or build a reputation as an outstanding performer. They strive to demonstrate *self-efficacy*, a judgment an individual makes about his or her competence and ability to perform a task or accomplish a goal. Self-efficacy has been shown to have a strong relationship to worker performance.[7]

Self-actualization needs reflect an individual's desire to grow and develop to his or her fullest potential. An individual often wants the opportunity to be creative on the job, or desires autonomy, responsibility, and challenges. Although Maslow believed that the needs for self-actualization may be difficult to meet, managers can provide individuals with the opportunity to learn on the job and grow as an individual through training or increased challenges.

Satisfying Prepotent Needs Maslow stated that the lowest, unsatisfied need became *prepotent*—an individual's primary or focal need. Consider a single mother who has just lost her job; she might be concerned with providing food for herself and her family. In this case her prepotent needs would be those that are physiological. If instead she has accumulated a large amount of savings or has inherited a large amount of money, then higher-level needs such as social or esteem needs may become prepotent. According to Maslow, motivating an individual requires satisfying his or her prepotent need. In the case of the single mother who provides the sole financial support for her family, an organization might motivate her by offering significant financial compensation to help meet her prepotent physiological needs. Managers of the more affluent single mother might use team membership or other social activities to meet higher-level needs.

Because individual workers likely differ in their needs, and an individual employee's needs vary at different times, managers begin by diagnosing their employees' needs. Next, they identify an array of ways to meet individual needs, as shown in Table 4–2.

TABLE 4–2   *Mechanisms for meeting needs*

NEED	ORGANIZATIONAL CONDITIONS
Physiological	Pay
	Subsidized breakfast or lunch programs
	Company housing
Safety	Company benefits plans
Security	Pensions
	Seniority
	Pay
	Child care
	Medical and dental benefits
Love	Coffee breaks
Belongingness	Sports teams
Relatedness	Company picnics and social events
Affiliation	Work teams
	Pay
Esteem	Autonomy
	Responsibility
	Pay (as symbol of status)
	Prestigious office location and furnishings
Achievement	Job challenges
Competence	Pay
Power	Leadership positions
	Authority
Self-actualization	Challenges
Growth	Autonomy

Consider again the situation faced by Andy Wilson. To motivate the Wal-Mart stores, Wilson can ask three questions:

■ Which needs have been satisfied?

■ Which unsatisfied needs are lowest in the hierarchy?

■ How can those needs be satisfied?

Satisfying most workers' physiological and safety needs will remain key, according to Maslow's theory. Wal-Mart typically will satisfy them through giving reasonable wages and job security. If the company can satisfy these basic needs, Wilson can then seek ways to satisfy higher-order needs, such as belongingness, esteem, or self-actualization.

Evaluation of the Theory Although Maslow emphasized the concept of prepotency, more recent research has questioned its validity.[8] In addition, workers may not have precisely five needs, the order may differ from that proposed by Maslow, or they may have multiple rather than a single prepotent need. Further, the theory does not generalize to workers in other countries.[9] For example, Japanese workers may value security over self-actualization.[10] Workers in Scandinavian countries, which emphasize the quality of work life, emphasize their social needs as the key influence on motivation.[11] The rank ordering of needs also varies in different cultures.[12]

ALDERFER'S ERG THEORY

Clayton Alderfer developed an alternative needs theory, known as ERG theory.[13] He collapsed Maslow's hierarchy into three types of needs—existence, relatedness, and growth—as shown in Figure 4–2. *Existence* or lower-order *needs* include physiological and security needs. *Relatedness needs* correspond to Maslow's belongingness and love needs. *Growth needs,* which correspond to Maslow's esteem and self-actualization needs, combine with relatedness needs to comprise the higher-order needs.

Alderfer's theory, like Maslow's, stated that unsatisfied needs motivate an individual. For example, individuals with unsatisfied security needs would be motivated if their job satisfied these needs. Individuals with unsatisfied esteem needs would be motivated if their job met these needs. The mechanism of need satisfaction differs, however, from Maslow's. Although both theorists agreed that individuals first satisfied lower-order and then higher-order needs, Alderfer felt that satisfying higher-order needs caused them to increase in importance. As an individual satisfied his or her relationship needs, for example, they became more intense, rather than dissipating. The person continued to seek ways to satisfy the relationship needs.[14]

Individual differences in various needs may be associated with differences in an individual's developmental level as well as differences in group experiences. For example, after a worker at a Wal-Mart store receives a high school diploma his or her existence needs might predominate. Attaining financial security might cause his or her needs to shift to primarily relationship ones. Later, added financial responsibilities, such as a family or aging parents, may cause existence needs to again become important.

FIGURE 4–2   *Needs according to ERG theory*

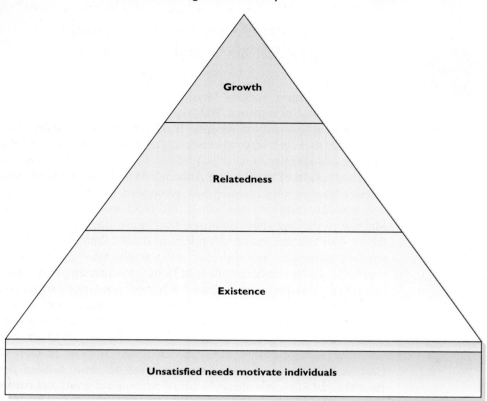

In some circumstances, an individual might experience *frustration* in satisfying a higher-level need, which would cause a return to a lower-order need. For example, if an individual failed to satisfy his or her social needs, that person might focus instead on meeting security needs as a substitute for the unsatisfied social needs. Consider also an employee who earns a good salary, has a reasonably high standard of living, and has made many friends at work. According to Maslow and Alderfer this person probably would be motivated to satisfy his or her growth needs.

What if, in trying to satisfy these needs, the individual finds that he or she is continually frustrated in attempts to get more autonomy and responsibility, features of a job that generally encourage individual growth? When asked, the employee now reports that having friends at work and getting together with them outside of work is most important. Frustration in satisfying a higher (growth) need has resulted in a regression to a lower (relatedness) need. A manager such as Andy Wilson recognizes this tendency and attends to his employees' needs for relationships and growth by encouraging open communication and continued pride in their work.

Managerial Responses In using Alderfer's theory to diagnose motivational challenges, such as motivating poorly performing employees to improve their productivity, we can ask questions similar to those we asked with Maslow, with the addition of three more:

- What needs are the individuals involved in the situation experiencing?

- What needs have been satisfied and how have they been met?

- Which unsatisfied need is the lowest in the hierarchy?

- Have some higher-order needs been frustrated?

- Has the person refocused on a lower-level need?

- How can the unsatisfied needs be satisfied?

Evaluation of the Theory Many of the same criticisms that apply to Maslow's theory also apply to Alderfer's. We can question, for example, the precise number and order of needs. Cultural variations likely exist requiring managers to carefully diagnose workers' needs before developing and implementing a motivational plan.

MCCLELLAND'S TRICHOTOMY OF NEEDS THEORY

David McClelland and his associates offer a different way of thinking about needs.[15] Instead of organizing needs into a hierarchy, their research originally sought explanations for the relative industrial success of various countries. For example, why did the United States have greater success than certain African countries? These researchers attributed the success to the predominance of a *need for achievement* among many of the managers in the industrialized countries.[16]

Their research subsequently has expanded to focus on three needs: need for achievement, need for affiliation, and need for power. *Need for achievement (nach)* reflects an individual's desire to accomplish goals and demonstrate competence or mastery. Individuals high in this need focus their energies on getting a job done quickly and well. *Need for affiliation (naff)* resembles Maslow's belongingness need and Alderfer's relatedness need. It describes the need for social interaction, love, and affection. *Need for power (npow)* reflects the need for control over a person's work or the work of others. Ruling monarchs, political leaders, and some executives in large corporations may have a need for power.

McClelland and his colleagues argue that they can teach individuals to increase their need for achievement and hence improve their performance. A person may demonstrate each need overtly or covertly; a worker at General Motors may seek a job with more autonomy or may work harder when a position with autonomy is given. He may enjoy social activities or complain about always working alone. Although each person has all three needs to some extent, only one of them tends to motivate an individual at any given time. More recently, these researchers have studied the need for power in greater detail. The results of one study indicated that sales managers high in the need for power run more productive departments than sales managers high in the need for affiliation.[17] A longitudinal study of individuals' career advancement in a utility company suggested that although their overall pattern of motives did not differ significantly, successful male and successful female managers used power differently in their work. Men used power to counteract specific behaviors they encountered in the workplace and women used it to gather resources necessary to perform their jobs better.[18]

Consider how Andy Wilson might act if he were high in the need for achievement, high in the need for affiliation, or high in the need for power. Now answer the same questions for a person with whom you have worked. Diagnosing the level of each of these needs should provide answers about how to motivate an individual. Providing clearly structured tasks whose accomplishment allows them to demonstrate mastery and competence helps motivate individuals high in the need for achievement. Giving workers the opportunity to work on teams or participate in recreational activities helps motivate those high in the need for affiliation. Providing an individual with autonomy and supervisory responsibility that allows him or her to exert control over his or her own and possibly others' work should help meet the need for power.

Figure 4–3 can help identify your own or another's predominant need at any given time. Take a few moments and answer the questions posed for yourself. Note that occasionally an individual may experience more than one of these needs equally strongly so you might have equally positive responses to two or more sets of items.

FIGURE 4–3   *Questions to identify need for achievement, need for affiliation, and need for power*

1. Do you like situations where you personally must find solutions to problems?

2. Do you tend to set moderate goals and take moderate, thought-out risks?

3. Do you want specific feedback about how well you are doing?

4. Do you spend time considering how to advance your career, how to do your job better, or how to accomplish something important?

If you responded yes to questions 1–4, then you probably have a high need for achievement.

5. Do you look for jobs or seek situations that provide an opportunity for social relationships?

6. Do you often think about the personal relationships you have?

7. Do you consider the feelings of others to be very important?

8. Do you try to restore disrupted relationships when they occur?

If you responded yes to questions 5–8, then you probably have a high need for affiliation.

9. Do you try to influence and control others?

10. Do you seek leadership positions in groups?

11. Do you enjoy persuading others?

12. Are you perceived by others as outspoken, forceful, and demanding?

If you responded yes to questions 9–12, then you probably have a high need for power.

SOURCE: Based on R.M. Steers and L.W. Porter, *Motivation and Work Behavior* (New York: McGraw-Hill, 1979), pp. 57–64. Copyright 1979 by McGraw-Hill, Inc. Reproduced with permission.

The projective **Thematic Apperception Test (TAT)** also measures these needs. The respondent describes what he or she sees occurring in a series of pictures. What do you see in Figure 4–4? The respondent **projects** his or her needs into the description of the picture. For example, if you viewed the picture as a problem-solving meeting, then you would receive a positive score on the need for achievement. If you viewed the picture as being a social gathering, then you would receive a positive score on the need for affiliation. If you viewed the picture as being a situation dominated by a single person, then you would receive a positive score on the need for power. Professional test administrators have detailed protocols for scoring the pictures included in the TAT and similar tests. Because of the time and skill required in the administration and scoring of the test, its cost is relatively high and only a trained professional can administer and score it.

Evaluation of the Theory McClelland and his associates continue to study the three needs and provide consultation about their effects. Yet the measurement

FIGURE 4–4   *Example of a TAT picture*

of needs using projective instruments is cumbersome and support for the theory is inconsistent.

HERZBERG'S TWO-FACTOR THEORY

Frederick Herzberg and his associates focused on ways of increasing job satisfaction, rather than explicitly motivating workers to perform.[19] They divided work into two types of components—motivators and hygiene factors—as shown in Figure 4–5.

Motivators are features of the job's *content,* including responsibility, self-esteem, autonomy, and growth. They satisfy higher-order needs and result in job satisfaction. Increasing motivators should ultimately motivate a person to exert more effort and perform better. Managers can increase the motivators in a job by changing the way the job should be done to allow individuals more opportunities for autonomy, responsibility, and creativity.

Hygiene factors are features of the job's *context,* including company policies and practices, wages, benefits, and working conditions. Improving the hygiene factors reduces a person's dissatisfaction with his or her work situation and ultimately allows the motivators to have an impact. Although hygiene factors *per se* do not encourage individuals to exert more effort, they must be at an acceptable level before motivators can have a positive effect. For example, offering autonomy and responsibility when working conditions and other contextual factors are not resolved results in worker dissatisfaction and limits the occurrence of motivation.

According to Herzberg's theory the manager attempts to increase overall satisfaction; this means simultaneously reducing dissatisfaction and increasing satisfaction. Improving job conditions alone will not increase worker motivation because it will merely reduce dissatisfaction, not increase satisfaction. Andy Wilson's ensuring that each Wal-Mart store remains freshly painted and in good condition will not by itself motivate workers. It will set the stage for increasing job motivators, such as greater worker involvement in decision making, which should result in increased job satisfaction.

Evaluation of the Theory How can managers use this theory to diagnose and improve performance? Although Herzberg and his associates have conducted nu-

FIGURE 4–5   *Herzberg's theory*

Hygiene Factors *The Environment*		Motivators *The Job*	
Job Dissatisfaction	**No Job Dissatisfaction**	**No Job Satisfaction**	**Job Satisfaction**
• Pay • Status • Security • Working conditions • Fringe benefits • Policies and administrative practices • Interpersonal relations		• Meaningful and challenging work • Recognition for accomplishment • Feeling of achievement • Increased responsibility • Opportunities for growth and advancement • The job itself	

merous empirical studies that support this theory, in general its research support is limited.[20] Problems exist in labeling work characteristics as either a hygiene factor or motivator. In addition, the same factor, particularly pay, has been linked to both satisfaction and dissatisfaction.

Recognizing that the theory has been subjected to significant criticism, we can simplify its conclusions to a single question: Does the situation have sufficient hygiene factors and motivators to result in overall satisfaction? Answering this question should allow a manager to diagnose deficiencies in the work situation and propose solutions. If, for example, work conditions, job security, pay, and benefits are below industry standards, then the manager can propose ways of improving them. If a job lacks responsibility, autonomy, or challenges, then changing the way the job is done should increase worker motivation.

EVALUATION OF NEEDS THEORIES

The extent to which current needs theories explain motivation in organizations has been questioned by some researchers who maintain that the concept is difficult to prove or disprove for several reasons.[21] First, needs are difficult to specify and measure. Second, relating the satisfaction of needs to various job or organizational characteristics, such as the institution of a benefits plan, can be problematic. For example, when lavish benefit programs become standard, employees take them for granted and they lose their motivational powers. Third, needs-satisfaction models fail to account for variances in individuals' behaviors and attitudes. Fourth, attributing needs to individuals may stem from a lack of awareness of external causes that influence behavior. Finally, applying needs may result in stereotyping individuals and ignoring the dynamic quality of individual behavior.

EQUITY THEORY

Motivating employees also means ensuring that equity or fairness exists in the workplace. *Equity theory,* a motivation theory that addresses this issue, has evolved from social psychological theory called *social comparison theory.* This theory suggests that individuals compare their own job performance to another, their *comparison other,* and make judgments about its comparability.

THE EQUITY EQUATION

Consider, for example, Sue Jones. She just received a 4 percent annual pay increase. How does her manager judge whether this increase will motivate Sue to continue her already excellent performance? Now consider Jessica Smith. She received a 3 percent pay increase from the same company. How motivating will such an increase be for her? Individuals assess their own and their comparison other's outcomes as a function of their inputs. Outcomes include wages, benefits, promotions, job titles, job content, and other relevant or irrelevant outcomes that a worker perceives he or she receives as a result of doing a particular job. Inputs include effort, age, education, experience, and other relevant or irrelevant factors that the person perceives to contribute to getting the job done. An individual then looks at the ratio of his or her outcomes to inputs and compares this to the *perceived* ratio of a comparison other person's outcomes to inputs, as shown in Figure 4–6.

For example, Wal-Mart employee Paul DuPre, may assess the ratio of the frequency of his promotions (outcomes) to his effort (inputs). According to equity theory, his motivation to perform would be a function of whether he perceived his ratio was the same, more, or less than the ratio of a coworker's frequency of promotions to her effort.

Equity theory further states that a person is motivated in proportion to the perceived fairness of the rewards received for a certain amount of effort.[22] You may have heard your colleague James say, "I'm going to stop working so hard—I work harder than Susan and she gets all the bonuses," or your classmate Sarah say, "Why should I bother studying? Alan never studies and still gets A's—and he's no smarter than I am." James and Sarah have compared their effort and the rewards they received to the effort exerted and rewards received by Susan and Alan. James and Sarah have *perceived* an inequity in the work and school situation. In fact, no actual inequity may exist, but the perception of inequity influences James's and Sarah's subsequent actions.

Specifically, James and Sarah compare their perceptions of two ratios, (1) the ratio of their outcomes to their inputs to (2) the ratio of another's outcomes to inputs. For example, James may feel that he receives $20 for each hour of effort he contributes to the job. In contrast, he may assess that Susan receives $40 for each hour of effort she contributes to the job. James perceives that his ratio of outcomes to inputs (20 to 1) is less than Susan's (40 to 1). In fact, Susan may only receive $10 for each hour of effort she contributes to the job. But, according to equity theory, the facts do not influence motivation; *perceptions* of the situation do. Recent research suggests, however, that equity calculations may be difficult because of cognitive differences in assessment and performance.[23] Instead, individuals look for

FIGURE 4–6   *Equity theory*

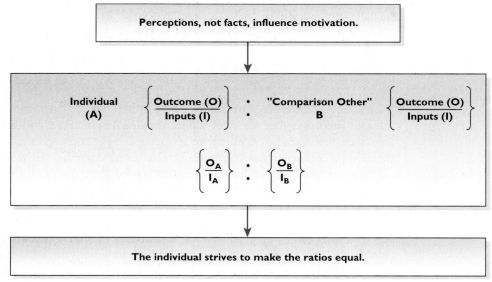

long-term rather than short-term parity in work situations. They compare their rank order on merit and rank order on a scale of reward outcomes, and see equity as a goal to work for over time.[24]

Note that the assessment of equity is based on perception, rather than objective equality. One of Andy Wilson's employees may perceive that the ratio of his outcomes to inputs differs from that of a coworker and thus be demotivated, whereas in reality, lack of information prevents him from **knowing** that the ratios are equal. Certainly, culture influences these perceptions. If the store were located in a Far Eastern or European country, the perception of inequity may have changed as a function of expectations associated with social class, job category, or educational status.

RESPONSES TO PERCEIVED INEQUITY

According to equity theory, the greatest motivation results when a person has ratios equal to those of his or her comparison other. That person strives to make the ratios of outcomes to inputs, O/I, equal.[25] Ratios that differ cause the perceiver, in this case Paul DuPre, to alter either his own inputs or outcomes, or his perception of his comparison other's inputs or outcomes. Table 4–3 shows some of the responses to perceived inequities. An individual may alter his or her own inputs or outcomes. He or she may exert less effort, work fewer hours, distract himself or herself while on the job, or refuse additional training. He or she may attempt to secure additional

TABLE 4–3   *Responses to inequitable conditions*

CONDITION	RESPONSES
$\dfrac{O_A}{I_A} > \dfrac{O_B}{I_B}$	A increases inputs
	A asks for reduced outputs
	B reduces inputs
	B asks for increased outputs
	A or B changes comparison person
	A or B rationalizes that equity exists
	A or B leaves the situation
$\dfrac{O_A}{I_A} < \dfrac{O_B}{I_B}$	B increases inputs
	B asks for reduced outputs
	A reduces inputs
	A asks for increased outputs
	A or B changes comparison person
	A or B rationalizes that equity exists
	A or B leaves the situation

pay or a job promotion, change his or her job title, or request increased or different job responsibilities.

In theory, the same adjustment process occurs when a person perceives he or she receives too much reward for the input or has too complex a job in comparison to others.[26] If the person perceives that he or she has received too much reward for the input rather than too little, that person may try to remedy this inequity by exerting more effort or changing the inputs and even the outputs to create equity. If you were overpaid, would you be motivated to increase your effort? Although such an *overjustification effect* has been documented, the empirical evidence about this phenomenon is inconsistent.[27]

Alternatively, an individual may adjust his or her perception of the comparison other's inputs or outputs. Paul DuPre may decide that his original perception of his coworkers' effort or frequency of promotions was inaccurate. He may choose instead to ignore the situation. Or he may change his comparison person. The reaction described here is based on research about workers in the United States. Differences may exist in reactions to inequities as a function of cultural differences.

Determining whether equity exists in the workplace often involves assessing organizational fairness, also known as *organizational justice.* For example, an individual may evaluate whether the rules for giving pay raises, the procedures for administering pay, the level of pay, the distribution of jobs, and the pace of work is equitable between himself and selected coworkers.[28] Judgments about fairness or justice can be made about an *outcome,* such as pay, the *procedures* that result in the outcome, such as the rules for distributing pay, and the *system* that generates the procedures and outcomes, such as the organizational reward system.[29] The goals of organizational justice include effective individual and group performance, creation and maintenance of a sense of community, and a focus on individual dignity and humaneness.[30]

EVALUATION OF EQUITY THEORY

While equity theory basically makes strong intuitive sense, the empirical evidence has been mixed.[31] The concept of *equity sensitivity* in part explains these findings by suggesting that individuals have different preferences for equity (e.g., a preference for higher, lower, or equal ratios) that cause them to react consistently but differently to perceived equity and inequity.[32] A time lag may also affect their reactions.[33] Some individuals may not react immediately to inequity but only perceive it if it exists over a long period of time. Differences in intelligence, social values, personality, and gender may also influence an individual's perception of inequity.[34] Women and minorities today may be particularly attuned to inequity because of the extensive and intense discrimination many of them have experienced.

In a sense, equity theory oversimplifies the motivational issues by not explicitly considering individual needs, values, or personalities. This oversimplification becomes particularly important as the work force becomes more diverse. Cross-cultural differences may also occur in preferences for equity, as well as the preferred responses to inequitable situations.

Nevertheless, diagnosing inequities in the workplace may reveal the cause of motivation problems. A manager can then act to reduce the inequities. He or she can ask questions such as the following to assess equity:

- What contributions or inputs does the person make to the situation?

- What is his or her level of education, effort, or experience?

- What benefits or outcomes does the person receive?

- What is the level of job complexity, pay, or status of that person?

- What is the ratio of inputs to outcomes?

Managers must check that reasonable comparability exists among individuals in terms of their outcome-to-input ratios. They must also ensure that individuals make equity judgments on the basis of accurate information. Recognizing that some information about performance and pay must remain confidential, managers should inform employees about reasons for particular wages, promotions, or job changes. Finally, they must ensure that outcomes are a function of and consistent with relevant inputs. Paying workers for their effort, not for their gender, for example, is essential, as is paying workers for their contribution to performance.

REINFORCEMENT THEORY

According to reinforcement theory, a manager motivates employees by encouraging desired behaviors and discouraging undesired behaviors. Managers must learn to reward productivity, quality performance, and commitment, for example, and discourage absenteeism, declining performance, and inefficiencies. ***Reinforcement theory*** prescribes ways of facilitating desired or target behaviors such as higher performance, increased creativity, or improved quality by applying ***reinforcers*** such as higher pay, praise, or challenging assignments when the desired behavior occurs.

Recall the situation at the Salem, Oregon, Wal-Mart store described in the introduction. How did Andy Wilson encourage workers to be productive? He used praise and thanks as one type of reward. He also told them that they were the key to the store's success.

EATON CORPORATION. At its Kearney plant, which manufactures valves and gears, workers benefit from improved plant performance. In a quarter when workers topped the previous year's profit and cost criteria by 7 percent, workers received a 7 percent quarterly bonus. Such rewards reinforce the behaviors that led to meeting the criteria. In addition, workers get a cumulative bonus of $25 a year for perfect attendance. For example, a worker with four years of perfect attendance receives a $100 bonus.[35]

TYPES OF REINFORCEMENT

Reinforcement techniques can either encourage or eliminate the desired behavior by applying or removing reinforcements.

Positive Reinforcement Positive reinforcement involves pairing a desired behavior or outcome with rewards or feedback. For example, a person who packs tea sets receives ten cents for each one packed; the desired behavior—packing the tea sets—is paired with the financial rewards. This feedback shapes behavior by encouraging the reinforced or rewarded behavior to recur. If the behavior is not precisely what is desired by a superior or client, repeated reinforcements that result in successive approximations to the desired behavior can move the actual behavior closer to the desired behavior. For example, if a travel agent increases the accuracy of his or her ticketing, the agent's boss might positively comment about the improvement. Additional praise might follow if that person makes fewer ticketing errors. Praise would continue until the best performance occurred. This behavior would then be reinforced with praise or even financial incentives until it became more or less permanent, but praise would be discontinued if any reversion to previous behaviors occurred.

MARY KAY COSMETICS. Women who sell Mary Kay Cosmetics receive recognition and rewards in proportion to their sales and the sales of those they supervise. Women receive color-coded suits, sashes, badges, cars, and other symbols of their sales performance. The level of their position rises and their salary increases as they recruit additional consultants. A woman who together with her saleswomen sells $1 million in a year receives a bracelet that reads "$1,000,000" with the numerals written in diamonds. Mary Kay Ash, the founder and president of the company, personally crowns four "Queens of Seminar" at each yearly meeting as recognition of their sales or recruiting excellence.[36]

Negative Reinforcement In negative reinforcement, an individual acts to stop an aversive stimulus. The term *negative* stems from the removal of the individual from a negative or undesirable situation when the desired behavior occurs. A consultant may try to complete an overdue project to stop unrequested overtime. Telephone salespeople are monitored until they consistently meet acceptable standards of speed, courtesy, and so on.

Extinction Extinction *passively eliminates* an undesired behavior by withholding positive reinforcement. Typically, the failure to apply positive reinforcements causes the desired behaviors to cease. A person who repeatedly works overtime but receives neither compensation, status, nor praise for this added effort likely will stop the overtime hours, depending on other motivating forces at work. By withholding reinforcement, a supervisor may also cause desired behaviors, such as productivity, creativity, or attendance, to stop.

Punishment Punishment eliminates an undesirable behavior by having a negative event follow the undesirable behavior. In this way it differs from negative reinforcement, when the subject acts to stop or avoid an aversive stimulus. Using punishment, a superior officer assigns kitchen patrol to a newly recruited army private who ignores a directive about the misuse of computers in his or her job.

How will the private react to the punishment? Most likely the recruit will feel bitterness or anger toward the superior or toward the misuse of computers. This attitude, which results from the use of punishment, may have long-term negative consequences on the private's performance. Punishment often creates secondary consequences of tension and stress and may result in unpredictable and unobservable outcomes and so should be used only as a last-resort motivator. Punishment may not permanently eliminate undesired behavior because it does not offer an alternative to the desired behavior. If a worker repeatedly misuses a piece of equipment and receives punishment each time he or she misuses the equipment, the behavior may not change because no correct way of using the equipment (an alternative to the desired behavior) is presented.

Punishment may also have consequences for observers. It may deter similar behavior in observers.[37] Or they may positively reinforce the behavior being punished.[38] The newly recruited army private's "speaking back" to a superior may be applauded by the other recruits.

SCHEDULES OF REINFORCEMENT

The timing of reinforcers or rewards has a significant effect on their impact. Compare the behavior of an employee who receives a weekly paycheck to one who is paid for each product he or she sells or produces. How would the behavior of workers under each of these systems change if they periodically and unexpectedly received a bonus for exceptional performance?

Reinforcement schedules have two components, as shown in Table 4–4: first, the *timing* of the reinforcement relative to the behavior being reinforced; second, the *frequency* of the reinforcement. Reinforcers given according to an *interval* schedule tie them to the elapsing of a specific amount of time. Weekly or monthly paychecks, yearly bonuses, or biyearly salary increases illustrate the use of an interval schedule. Reinforcers given according to a *ratio* schedule tie them to the performance of a certain number of behaviors. Receiving a certain wage for a set level of production or sales, known as *piecework* and *commission* systems, respectively, illustrate ratio schedules.

LINCOLN ELECTRIC COMPANY. Lincoln Electric Company in Cleveland, Ohio, used ratio schedules as the basis of their wage system and successfully fostered high worker performance.[39]

A ratio schedule applies best in situations where the proper responses can be clearly delineated. In implementing such a schedule, managers also need to pay attention to the means of accomplishing the desired outcomes, such as making equipment repairs, offering training, or experimenting with new processes.

Reinforcers can also be fixed or variable. *Fixed* reinforcers, such as the weekly paycheck, are scheduled to occur at a predetermined and hence expected time. *Vari-*

TABLE 4–4   *Schedules of reinforcement*

	FIXED	VARIABLE
Interval	Reinforcement or reward given after the first proper response following a specified period of time	Reinforcement or reward given after a certain amount of time with that amount changing before the next reinforcement
	Weekly or monthly paycheck	Supervisor who visits shop floor on different unannounced days each week
		Unexpected merit bonuses
Ratio	Reinforcement or reward given after a specified number of proper responses	Reinforcement or reward given after a number of responses with that number changing before the next reinforcement
	Pay for piecework	Praise

able reinforcers are applied at unpredictable and varied times. A manager may praise a worker once a day for a week and then not again for another three weeks.

In general, interval and fixed schedules encourage short-term repetition of a behavior. Ratio and variable schedules encourage long-term continuation. Assume that a manager wants a computer programmer to write error-free computer code. To establish the desired behavior, the manager should begin with a fixed-interval schedule of reinforcement. The manager might review the code daily and praise the programmer each day for error-free code. In the medium-run, the manager might switch to a variable-interval schedule, offering praise every three days for good performance. Sustaining the behavior in the long-term probably calls for a variable-ratio schedule, unexpectedly offering praise or even monetary bonuses after an unspecified amount of error-free code has been completed.

BEHAVIOR-MODIFICATION PROGRAMS

Managers can increase the power of wages and benefits by tying them directly to certain types of performance. As we discussed earlier, commission systems and piecework plans tie pay directly to sales and production. Managers can also offer bonuses or one-time payments to reward particularly creative or productive behavior. In investment banking, bonuses may comprise 50 percent or more of an executive's salary.

EMERY AIR FREIGHT. Some organizations integrate reinforcement techniques into a comprehensive behavior-modification program. In one of the earliest experiments, Emery Air Freight used positive rewards, goal setting, and praise to maximize the use of containers in shipping packages.[40] At Emery, profitability was a function of the percentage to which huge shipping containers were filled. Freight packers set goals and then compared their packing to the goals set. Meeting their goals provided feedback about the quality of their behavior and reinforced the behavior that led to goal accomplishment. Container utilization increased from 40 percent to 85 percent and resulted in significant financial savings.

More recently, similar programs have been implemented in a wide range of settings, and have addressed diverse outcomes.[41] In a furniture manufacturing plant, daily feedback about the quantity of output posted in the work area increased efficiency.[42] In one manufacturing plant, workers drew numbers for bingo cards each day they were on time and worked a complete day. Weekly winners spun a roulette wheel for cash prizes.[43] Providing observational feedback to supervisors about hazardous conditions in six factory departments as well as offering compliments for good practices and suggestions for improvements resulted in reduced hazard rates.[44] In a retail drugstore, cashier performance was posted on charts. Good performance was reinforced with movie tickets, soft drinks, and candy bars. It resulted in improvements in precision, punctuality, and proficiency in closing-out the registers.[45]

Some companies offer their employees the opportunity to participate in profit-sharing programs where they either receive a proportion of company profits or can buy certain amounts of company stock. These opportunities are designed to motivate workers to perform better since they have a specific stake in improved company performance. At the extreme, employees may own all of the stock in a company, as described in more detail later in this chapter.

To diagnose the behavior of workers at Wal-Mart or other companies using reinforcement theory, we can ask the following questions:

- What behaviors are desired?

- Are these behaviors observable and measurable?

- What reinforces these behaviors?

- When are the reinforcements applied?

- What are the consequences of these reinforcements?

- How can the reinforcement pattern be improved?

Reinforcement theory should be applied in conjunction with the principles of social learning presented in Chapter 2. In addition, rewards or reinforcements must meet an employee's specific needs and be applied equitably. Theorists believe that equitable behavior occurs as a result of attempts to maintain cognitive consistency and maximize outcomes.[46]

EVALUATION OF REINFORCEMENT THEORY

The basic formulation of reinforcement theory is simple, clear, has generated extensive research, and has considerable explanatory power; yet, its focus on the individual, its restriction to comparison of similarities, and methodological problems may limit its usefulness.[47]

Managers can encourage desired behavior in employees by applying a wide array of rewards and punishments. However, money, in the form of wages and benefits, remains the most common reinforcer used in organizations in the United States and other Western countries, but appears to have some but limited direct impact on behavior. Most workers assume that they will receive their regular wages unless they deviate significantly from acceptable performance. Similarly, workers expect to receive benefits such as medical insurance, vacation time, sick leave, and pensions, and so such benefits do not seem to motivate better performance.

Managers can also use praise to encourage desired behaviors. Although one of the least costly benefits, praise is not used as extensively as it could be. Managers can also redesign jobs in response to successful or unsuccessful behavior by an employee. However, if an employee does not desire additional responsibility, then this type of reinforcer would be ineffective.

Managers must ensure that they reinforce the behavior they desire.[48] Often, universities are perceived to reward research but hope that good teaching will follow. The "pay for performance" controversy emphasizes that managers should assign reinforcers for the desired behavior, not automatically give pay increases for seniority or effort.

EXPECTANCY THEORY

Motivating employees involves meeting their needs, ensuring equity in the workplace, reinforcing desired behaviors, and setting specific, challenging, and accepted goals. Expectancy theory provides a view of motivation that integrates these elements into a single theory. It has dominated research about motivation since the early 1970s, principally because it has strong empirical support, integrates diverse perspectives on motivation, and provides explicit ways to increase employee motivation.[49] Perhaps more than the preceding theories, expectancy theory offers a comprehensive view of motivation that integrates many of the elements of the needs, equity, and reinforcement theories.

THE ORIGINAL FORMULATION

Victor Vroom popularized this theory in the 1960s. His model stated that motivation was a function of expectancy, valence, and instrumentality.[50]

$$\text{Motivation} = E \times V \times I \text{ (Expectancy} \times \text{Valence} \times \text{Instrumentality)}$$

Consider the motivation of a train conductor using this formulation. First, motivation is a function of *expectancy,* which refers to an individual's perception that his or her effort will result in performance, such as high productivity, increased sales, or more innovations from the individual worker. A train conductor has high expectancy if his or her effort, such as working long hours, results in higher levels of performance, perhaps reflected by the number of fares processed or time spent loading and unloading passengers. The conductor's expectancy decreases when the links between effort and performance decline. For example, if he or she lacks the training to process fares and load the train quickly, then he or she may work extremely hard but still not produce at a high level. Alternatively, he or she may lack the proper equipment to allow hard work to pay off. An accounts payable clerk may spend hours working on accounts, but may make many errors. Adding computer equipment may increase the clerk's expectancy because it will reduce the computational errors, thereby increasing the likelihood that effort will lead to performance.

Instrumentality, according to Vroom, refers to the individual's perception that performance will result in certain positive or negative outcomes, such as promotion, increased wages, greater fatigue, or interpersonal isolation. High instrumentality would exist for the train conductor, for example, if reducing the time in the station results in a promotion or pay increase. High instrumentality would also occur if reducing the time results in resentment by his coworkers because he makes them look inefficient. Instrumentality declines when performance is not perceived to be linked to specific outcomes.

Valence describes the value the individual attaches to various outcomes that result from performing. For example, the conductor may value increased pay and promotion, but devalue resentment from his coworkers or fatigue.

Vroom's theory states that motivation is a function of the interaction (or multiplication) of expectancy, instrumentality, or valence. As each of the components increases, motivation also increases; as each component decreases, motivation also decreases. Because of the multiplicative effect, if any of the three components decreases, motivation decreases.

Think of the situation at the Wal-Mart store in terms of expectancy theory. The workers perceive that if they work hard, then they will sustain a high level of performance (a positive expectancy). They may also hope that if they produce, then they will receive praise, a pay raise, or a promotion (a positive instrumentality).

They likely value keeping these outcomes (positive valence). In this s[...]
itive motivation will occur. If, on the other hand, they perceive that there [...]
lihood that they will receive praise, a pay raise, or a promotion, their instru[...]
ity and ultimately their motivation will drop.

AN INTEGRATED VIEW OF MOTIVATION

A more recent formulation of expectancy theory reflects the role of unsatisfied needs, equity, reinforcements, and goal setting in motivation.[51]

$$\textbf{Motivation} = [E \rightarrow P] \times \Sigma\ [(P \rightarrow O)(V)]$$

Here, $E \rightarrow P$ is analogous to expectancy and refers to the worker's perception of the likelihood that effort leads to performance. Setting specific, difficult, and accepted goals can increase this expectancy. $P \rightarrow O$ refers to the employee's perception that performance results in certain outcomes. V refers to valence, or the value of the outcomes. The valence of a certain outcome is closely tied to an individual's needs. Managers must recognize that the individual who has unsatisfied physiological or esteem needs may value a pay increase more than an individual who has unsatisfied belongingness needs.

The manager must also attempt to ensure that performance results in desired outcomes, along the lines of reinforcement theory. He or she must ensure that perceived equity exists in the relationship between performance and outcomes. In this formulation, the performance-to-outcome links are combined with valence to reflect the multiple outcomes that result from performance. High levels of performance may result in promotions, but they may also result in fatigue. Managers must diagnose the situation to promote valued outcomes. To diagnose the work situation using expectancy theory, a manager can ask whether expectancies, instrumentalities, and valences are high. If not, he or she can then seek ways to increase them.

We can examine the case of Wal-Mart worker Mary Fountaine using this formulation of motivation. If Mary perceives that devoting more hours to work will result in her performing better, then $E \rightarrow P$ will be positive. If she perceives that she receives pay and praise if she performs her job well, then $P \rightarrow O$ will be positive. If Mary likes receiving money and praise, then V will be positive. If, instead, Mary receives no praise or pay raise for good performance, then $E \rightarrow P$ and V remain positive, but $P \rightarrow O$ is negative, reducing her motivation.

Because performance can lead to multiple outcomes, each with different valences or values, each performance-to-outcome expectancy is multiplied by the corresponding valence. For example, consider a construction worker who knows that if he or she produces, he or she will receive pay, resulting in a positive performance-to-outcome expectancy. But this worker may also know that if he or she produces too much, he or she will be ostracized by his or her coworkers for being a "rate-buster." This performance-to-outcome expectancy is much less positive. These expectancies are then summed before being multiplied by the effort-to-performance expectancy.

In some countries, however, strengthening the effort-to-performance links or performance-to-outcome links may be viewed as a function of uncontrollable change, rather than as a result of managerial or worker control.[52] Expectancy theory best explains motivation in cultures where workers believe that they can control their environment.[53] Managers must ensure that the reward structure fits the culture. Not all cultures value monetary rewards or promotions in the same way. Expectancy theory has methodological limitations.

EXTRINSIC
MOTIVATION
FORMULATION

A revised expectancy theory, which was developed in the late 1970s, incorporates the intrinsic and extrinsic outcomes of performing a task.[54] In this model, motivation is reduced if an individual does not value either intrinsic or extrinsic outcomes, or if the person perceives that either the intrinsic or extrinsic performance-to-outcome expectancies are low. For example, the construction worker's motivation will be reduced either if she does not like doing her tasks (intrinsic) or if she does not receive desired rewards (extrinsic) for performing them.

EVALUATION OF EXPECTANCY THEORY

Evidence for the validity of the expectancy model is mixed.[55] Although the expectancy equation may oversimplify the motivational process, managers can still use it to diagnose motivational problems or to evaluate effective motivation.

- Does the individual perceive that effort will lead to performance?

- Does the individual perceive that certain behaviors will lead to specified outcomes?

- What values do individuals attach to these outcomes?

Answers to these questions should help managers determine the level of an employee's work motivation, then identify any deficiencies in the job situation and prescribe remedies. The expectancy perspective implies the value of equity in the work situation as well as the importance of consistent rewards. In fact, both equity theory and reinforcement theory have been viewed as special cases of expectancy theory.[56] It also addresses the issue of individual differences and offers the opportunity for quantification of the various facets of motivation. Hence, expectancy theory, more than any other theory presented so far, offers a comprehensive diagnostic tool.

GOAL-SETTING THEORY

Just as expectancy theory can serve as an integrative view of motivation, so can goal setting. Goal-setting theory holds that the process of setting goals can focus behavior and motivate individuals. Further, motivation is increased if individuals receive ongoing feedback about their progress toward achieving their goals. This feedback acts as reinforcement that helps keep motivation high. Although extensive research has been conducted on the goal-setting process and its relationship to performance, in this section we highlight only a sample of the findings. One of the earliest goal-setting programs involved truck drivers setting goals in a logging operation.[57] The drivers loaded logs and shipped them to the processing mills. When they were assigned a goal of loading at 94 percent capacity, their performance rose from loading at approximately 60 percent capacity to 80 percent in the first month. After a decline to 70 percent in the second month, it was then sustained at 90 percent.

GRANITE ROCK COMPANY. One of the 1992 Malcolm Baldrige National Quality Award winners, Granite Rock Company, introduced a comprehensive goal-setting program for employees. The Individual Professional Development Plan requires all employees to set annual goals. Since introducing this program, company earnings per employee have been 30 percent higher than the industry average.[58]

....

GOAL CHARACTERISTICS

Goals, which any member of an organization can set, describe a desired future state, such as reduced costs, lower absenteeism, higher employee satisfaction, or specified performance levels. Once established, they can focus behavior and motivate individuals to achieve the the desired end state. For example, a salesperson may wish to sell 40 percent more than he did in the same month in the previous year. A branch manager in a bank might want to hire four new tellers in the current year, two of whom might be minorities. Goals such as these help focus an individual's or group's behavior and help them perform.

Goals can vary in at least three ways: (1) specificity, (2) difficulty, and (3) acceptance. The *specificity* or clarity of goals refers to the extent to which their accomplishment is observable and measurable. "Increasing sales by 50 percent" or "reducing absenteeism by 20 percent by June 15" are specific goals. We can measure and observe whether they have been accomplished. "Improving sales" or "reducing turnover" are still observable and measurable, but less specific. "Working hard" or "putting more effort into the job" are even less specific. Specific goals tend to motivate workers more effectively than less specific goals, in part because the target is easier to visualize.

Goal difficulty refers to how hard a person or group finds accomplishing the goal. Increasing sales by 5 percent may be easy, by 10 percent may be moderately difficult, and by 25 percent extremely difficult. How difficult do you think the goal of increasing productivity is at a plant scheduled for closing? Motivating employees requires setting goals of increasing difficulty up to a reasonable level of challenge, since recent research suggests that performance increases as the difficulty of goals increases until they are impossible to accomplish.[59] Individuals who feel that they can accomplish a goal likely will be more motivated than those who do not believe it is possible.[60]

NUTRASWEET. The company offered its managers bonuses of $100,000 if they could meet sales goals in Africa, the Middle East, and India. The managers attempted to meet the goals, but generating new business took longer than expected. In addition, the goals did not include establishing distribution agreements that could increase future sales. The goals were virtually impossible to attain because these unanticipated circumstances were not considered in setting the goal.[61]

Acceptance of the goal refers to whether those who must accomplish the goal accept it as their own; that is, whether they "buy into it." A variety of factors influence goal acceptance.[62] Generally, involving the individual who is expected to accomplish the goal in the goal setting increases its acceptance. Joint goal setting, where both a supervisor and subordinate participate in the goal setting, is more powerful in creating acceptance than simply telling a subordinate his or her goal. The involvement of the workers in decision making at Wal-Mart likely keeps them committed to accomplishing their own and the organization's goals. Of course, the authority of the person who sets the goal will influence motivation. Bosses with high-level positions typically have greater influence. Coworkers can also influence a worker's motivation to accept a goal.

EVALUATION OF GOAL-SETTING THEORY

Difficulties can arise in applying goal-setting theory if managers oversimplify the motivational issues so that they conform to the theory. Effective motivation may require establishing an array of goals at all levels of the organization. Early research indicated that goal-setting programs improve performance at both managerial and nonmanagerial levels over an extended period of time in a variety of organizations.[63] It also recognized the role of feedback as a necessary condition for goal setting. Individuals required information about their effectiveness in meeting their goals as part of continuing to work toward them.[64]

More recent research has suggested that performance was a function of employees' ability, acceptance of goals, level of the goals, and the interaction of the goal with their ability.[65] Characteristics of the participants in goal setting, such as their authority or education, may have an impact on its effectiveness. For example, workers are more likely to accept goals from individuals with legitimate authority.[66] Acceptance of the goals also has consequences for how difficult the goals can be. Workers are likely to perform a task if the goals are difficult **and** accepted, but not difficult and rejected.[67] When joined with attempts to raise expectancies that effort leads to performance, setting difficult goals can boost productivity.[68] But most research has looked at single goals.[69] Studies of setting multiple goals suggest that accomplishment of one results in some sacrifices of a second, reflecting the limited cognitive capacity of individuals.[70] In very complex jobs, however, goal setting may not be feasible because multiple goals may be necessary. Or goal setting may lead to bureaucratic behavior, where setting the goals becomes an end in itself. The effects of goal setting may also differ across cultures.[71]

Figure 4–7 offers a summary model of the factors that affect performance. Individuals set goals in response to work-related demands placed on them, which in turn leads to performance. The strength of the relationship between goals and performance is affected by the worker's ability, commitment to the task, receipt of feedback about performance, the complexity of the task, and other situational constraints. Further, performance increases when workers pay attention to a task, exert effort on it, and persist over time in doing it.

In diagnosing a situation where employees lack motivation to perform the job correctly and effectively, we can analyze the goal-setting behavior in terms of the research just described. We can evaluate each of the factors shown in Figure 4–7 and offer ways of improving them. In particular, we can focus on goals and make three assessments. First, we ask whether the individuals have goals. Second, we determine if the individuals accept their goals. Such acceptance depends on whether the individuals perceive the goals as reasonable, are themselves self-assured, and have previous successes in accomplishing goals. Third and finally, we assess whether feedback has been provided on route to goal accomplishment.

FIGURE 4–7   *Factors that affect performance*

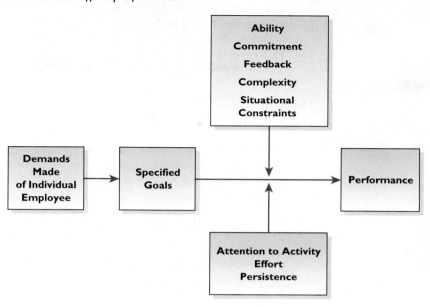

MOTIVATING A DIVERSE WORK FORCE

We have already seen that many theories of motivation do not explain motivation in every culture. This fact has special significance for the global manager who has to manage people from a variety of cultural backgrounds. Domestic managers also must effectively motivate a diverse work force that has a wide range of needs, values, expectancies, and aspirations.

Significant variations can exist across different cultures in workers' predominant needs.[72] The ordering of needs may vary in different countries. For example, workers in countries characterized as being high on uncertainty avoidance (e.g., Japan) value security over self-actualization.[73] Different cultures may also place relatively more value on lower rather than higher needs, or vice versa. In France, belongingness heavily influences motivation, whereas in Holland fairness and in the United States recognition are most influential. Differences in individuals' views of equity in a situation may also depend on their cultural background. We might predict, for example, that equity sensitivity would be greater among individuals from the United States and Canada, where power and status differences are less tolerated than among individuals from China, Japan, or South America, where power and status differences are more accepted. Different reinforcers may also be useful in different cultures. Praise may be valued over pay increases; job flexibility and autonomy over job titles. Managers need to be attuned to variations in attitudes and behaviors in different cultures regarding expectancies and goal setting as well.

MOTOROLA. Motorola implemented the "I Recommend" program in Malaysia, whereby employees are rewarded for offering cost-saving ideas. The "100 Club" includes workers who offer at least 100 cost-saving ideas and have at least 60 percent of them implemented. Motorola has had some, although not complete success in bringing this program to the United States. Workers in Plantation, Florida, participate in a similar program that identifies star employees and gives cash and non-monetary awards for good suggestions. But they lack the enthusiasm of their Malaysian counterparts.[74]

CREATING EFFECTIVE REWARD SYSTEMS IN ORGANIZATIONS

An organization's reward system incorporates the motivational principles described in this chapter into formal mechanisms for improving or reinforcing quality performance. It can also be used to support the organization's strategy.[75] A comprehensive reward system calls for a diagnosis of the organization, its members, and their individual work situations to best choose and allocate rewards.[76] It includes both compensation and nonpay components, such as promotions or praise.[77] It should respond to the organization's environment, help accomplish the organization's goals, and relate to the organization's culture. An effective reward system must create a high quality of work life, encourage organizational effectiveness by rewarding better performance, and pay attention to the needs of individuals. It must also avoid creating ethical dilemmas for those individuals it affects.[78] Twelve typical errors in the design of reward systems are shown in Table 4–5.

Organizations can offer two types of rewards. ***Intrinsic*** rewards include rewards associated with the job itself, such as challenging assignments, responsibil-

TABLE 4–5   *Errors in reward systems*

1. Failing to consider the state of the industry.
2. Confusing productivity and quality measures with financial performance.
3. Locking the firm into a rigid sharing formula.
4. Making rewards contingent on a single performance measure.
5. Failing to include all employees in the reward opportunity.
6. Failing to obtain middle-management commitment to the reward program.
7. Failing to build necessary management supervisory skills in allocating rewards.
8. Lacking organizational input into the design of the reward system.
9. Failing to convince employees that the opportunity to earn rewards is real.
10. Lacking performance feedback.
11. Offering cash awards as the only option.
12. Failing to grant rewards on a timely basis.

SOURCE: Based on M. J. Cissell, Designing effective reward systems, *Compensation and Benefits Review,* November–December 1987.

ity, autonomy, and opportunities for growth. ***Extrinsic*** rewards include all other rewards that are typically external to the job's content, such as higher pay, a promotion, a larger office, and a new job title. Effective reward systems combine both types of rewards and so include wages, benefits, and other incentives.

The growth of U.S. corporations abroad and of foreign-owned corporations in the United States has created challenges in designing effective and equitable multinational reward systems. Variations in the standard of living in different countries, the need to offer incentives to attract workers to certain locations throughout the world, and the desire to maintain a degree of consistency across work sites influence compensation and other nonmonetary rewards offered. Selecting rewards that motivate employees in these situations and determining appropriate wages and benefits becomes a major challenge for executives of such organizations.

BUILDING A FAIR AND MOTIVATING SYSTEM OF WAGES

According to the motivation theories, pay acts as a powerful reward and can motivate workers to perform better.[79] It can meet diverse needs and reinforce desired behaviors. However, because of the complexity and difficulty in applying pay correctly, organizations frequently misuse it as a reward. They may, for example, give all employees the same pay increase, regardless of their performance. Organizations may not satisfy the needs they intend to meet with pay.

In theory, wages should reflect the performance of an individual. In practice, organizations develop systematic wage systems that are tied to the nature of an individual's job and his or her longevity with the organization. Some workers may receive ***hourly*** wages, in which case their total pay is a function of the number of hours they work. Other workers earn ***salaries,*** which are fixed yearly rates, earned regardless of the precise number of hours they work. Usually, hourly workers hold lower-level jobs in the organization and salaried workers hold managerial or professional positions. Because of the status differences often inherent in the allocation of wages, some organizations have recently eliminated hourly employees and classified all employees as salaried employees.

GENERAL MOTORS. The Saturn division of General Motors classifies all employees as salaried workers. They also put 20 percent of their pay at risk if they do not meet prespecified performance goals.[80]

Moderate-to-large organizations frequently design a ***wage system*** that formalizes the pay structure in the organization. Each job is assigned to a wage grade; this grade determines the range of wages available to a particular job holder. Adjustments in the actual wage may occur according to the job holder's length of employment, level of education, level of performance, or entering salary. Two secretaries in a university may both be at wage level 5, but their actual salaries may differ by $3,000 because one secretary has just been promoted to level 5 and the second has held a level-5 job for 10 years. In general, managers should have some flexibility in administering the wage system to ensure that pay reinforces good performance.

Pay compression, where new job holders earn more than current job holders, is a major problem in organizations. Frequent adjustments in the wage scale may need to occur in some industries to ensure equity in the workplace. Top executives must also ensure that the wage scale remains competitive with other organizations in the same industry. Particularly in a tight labor market, offering competitive wages is essential for retaining a motivated and productive work force. An American Hospital Association survey reported that the salaries and benefits of staff nurses have exceeded those of nurse managers and administrators, who typically hold higher-level positions in the organization.[81]

Top management must decide whether it will assign pay on the basis of jobs held by the workers or the skills or competencies workers have.[82] ***Job-based pay*** rewards people for performing specific jobs and moving up the hierarchy, whereas ***skill-based*** pay rewards people for building more competencies and increasing their skills. Job-based pay reinforces the link between an individual's job and organizational outcomes. It supports a culture that emphasizes bottom-line performance. Skill-based programs support a culture that reflects a concern for individual development and learning and an environment that requires greater flexibility from a relatively permanent work force.[83]

XEL COMMUNICATIONS. At Xel Communications workers can earn an additional 50 cents per hour for each new task they can perform.[84]

POLAROID. Polaroid recently put all managers on skill-based pay.[85]

Wage systems must also consider the market position of the pay offered. If, for example, a company pays on average higher wages than its competitors, and learns that a major competitor pays on average lower wages, would the company's management continue to offer high pay levels? Some companies prefer to take a leadership position in compensation. Management of these organizations assumes that paying well will result in their attracting the best people. Others are willing to risk attracting somewhat less-qualified workers by offering lower financial rewards. The market position chosen certainly influences the organization's ability to cope with its environment. When a tight labor market exists, organizations with an aggressive "leader" strategy typically fare best in securing the workers they need. When, on the other hand, labor is very available, these compensation leaders may unnecessarily spend a premium. Even if there is widespread unemployment and competition for specific entry-level or even mid-level jobs, certain categories of workers, such as senior software engineers, may be in demand.

Top management must also determine which organizational members will make pay decisions. Responsibility can be decentralized throughout the organization to supervisors or can be centralized and systematized in a corporate compensation system. Communication of compensation decisions varies from very secretive to very open. The processes chosen frequently complement the organization's structure and reinforce its culture.

OFFERING BENEFITS

Organizations typically complement the wages they pay with an array of benefits, as shown in Table 4–6. Originally offered by organizations to increase worker motivation, more recently they affect the attraction and retention of employees. By law, all organizations must offer their workers time off for certain holidays, as well as worker's compensation insurance, in case they are injured on the job. In addition, almost all organizations offer a minimum of one week of vacation a year, which workers might accrue at a specified rate, such as one day for each two months worked. Larger organizations add medical insurance, pension plans, and other income protectors to the array of benefits. Reducing the cost of health-care benefits

TABLE 4–6   *Lists of benefits*

Health Protectors	**Income Supplements**
Medical insurance	Bonuses
Dental insurance	Profit-sharing plans
	Stock bonus plans
Income Protectors	Stock options
Accidental death insurance	
Disability insurance	**Other Benefits**
Life insurance	Business and professional memberships
Pensions	Club memberships
Retirement benefits	Company automobiles
Supplementary unemployment benefits	Credit unions
Workers' compensation	Day care
	Education costs
Time Off with Pay	Flexible work arrangements
Holidays	Recreational facilities
Personal days	Subsidized housing
Maternity or paternity leave	Subsidized meals
Sabbaticals	
Sick leave	
Vacations	

currently provides a major challenge for top executives. Managers must balance the cost of benefits with their value for attracting, motivating, and retaining employees.

Although most organizations use benefits to supplement wages, their value in motivating workers is somewhat controversial.[86] They are intended to motivate employees, improve employee morale, and reward loyalty. Benefits also increase job satisfaction, attract good employees, reduce turnover, and prevent unionization. They can enhance employee security, maintain a favorable competitive position, and enhance the organization's image among employees. While profit sharing and bonuses can be directly tied to performance, sick days and some health protectors are increasingly being viewed as essential and separate from the reward system.

In selecting benefits, managers must assess how well each benefit responds to workers' needs and its cost-effectiveness. Some organizations offer *flexible benefits plans,* where workers are given a fixed amount of dollars or points to allocate to various health, pension, vacation, child-care, or other benefits. Such a choice prevents the duplication of benefits and ensures that benefits better respond to worker needs. Or some employers create *flexible spending accounts,* which allow workers to pay for benefits with before-tax dollars, thereby creating tax benefits and reducing the "real" cost of the benefits.

USING INCENTIVES

Incentive programs are formalized reward programs that pay an individual or group of individuals for what they produce. They incorporate the motivational principles described earlier in the section on reinforcement theory. If a worker packs shipping containers, then he or she receives a certain amount of money for each container filled. Often, the more containers filled, the more pay the worker receives. Or a salesperson receives a fee for each container sold. Piecework systems, commission plans, and merit bonuses are the most common incentive systems. They directly link pay to performance.

Piecework systems tie compensation to individual performance by paying workers for each item produced. *Commissions* link pay to sales levels rather than production rates. Individuals may receive a certain percentage of total sales, or new sales, or they may receive compensation for reaching a sales quota. *Bonuses* are one-time lump-sum payments that are tied to exceptional performance. Increasingly, organizations use these instead of merit increases because their cost in the long run is less. Merit increases reward past performance, but become a cost of future performance regardless of its quality. A 6 percent merit increase changes the base pay rate and so applies for the rest of a worker's employment in an organization, even if subsequent performance does not merit such a pay level.

MONSANTO. Workers at the Monsanto chemical plant in Lulin, Louisiana, can receive a 5 percent to 10 percent performance bonus. Early plans that tied bonuses to plant safety and to the plant's overall success failed. Instead, Monsanto now links the bonuses to the results of the workers' individual work units of 50 to 60 employees. Monsanto has introduced more than 60 unique bonus programs worldwide that were similarly built to meet worker and organizational needs from the bottom up, rather than imposed on work units by corporate headquarters.[87]

Gain-sharing programs, such as the Scanlon Plan, Improshare, or Rucker Plan, allow workers to share in productivity improvements by earning bonuses based on group performance.[88] Workers typically get a portion of the financial gains on a formula basis. Such programs have been shown to result in increased coordination, teamwork, and knowledge sharing. They also contribute to better meeting of social needs, increased attention to cost savings, and increased acceptance of change due to technology and new methodologies. More calls for more efficient management and planning, successful reduction of overtime, increased creativity and sharing of new ideas, and more flexible labor management relations also occur.[89]

Incentives can reinforce organizational goals and their use supports an emphasis on "bottom-line" performance. Although they can increase productivity and lower production costs, they can also adversely affect the quality of the product, cause workers to trade off long-term for short-term gains, and ignore the means by which individuals attain results.[90]

AMERICAN EXPRESS. After a one-year pilot program, American Express introduced an incentive plan for 10,000 employees in the consumer-lending and consumer-card groups. During the pilot program, 98 percent of 1,500 employees received bonuses of 4 percent of their salary. The company refined the plan after the pilot program, however, to fit its goals more clearly with the corporate goals. American Express reduced the criteria for payouts to increasing customer satisfaction, employee productivity, and shareholder gains.[91]

EMPLOYEE OWNERSHIP

Perhaps the ultimate reward to workers is for them to own part of the organization. Employee stock ownership, often incorporated in an ESOP plan, as well as more direct ownership are two such options.[92]

UNITED AIRLINES. United Airlines gave employees 55 percent of its stock in exchange for wage and productivity concessions.[93]

Worker-owned cooperatives, such as the Mondragon Cooperatives in Spain, have served as a model for employee ownership of companies in the United States and abroad.[94] In these organizations workers sit on the corporate board and top-management teams and thus can exert control over the organization's direction and operation. While these efforts were initially not well received by top executives in the United States, recent opportunities for employee ownership have increased.

SCIENCE APPLICATIONS INTERNATIONAL. Employee ownership has boosted productivity at Science Applications International, a $1.3 billion high-technology research and engineering firm. Employees own 46 percent of the company's shares outright. The company's retirement plans hold another 41 percent in reserve. Only employees recommended by their managers for their performance can buy stock on trading days. The company motivates its professional staff by tying stock options to performance and offering a large percentage of the employees the option to buy stock. The company's stock price has increased at a 27 percent annual compound rate over the past 20 years.[95]

Worker representation on boards of directors has been viewed as a lesser form of worker ownership. Known as *codetermination,* this structure also gives workers a direct voice in the operation of their companies. Other worker participation ideas, such as work councils, have been incorporated into quality–of–working–life programs, as described in Chapter 12.

SUMMARY

An array of theories indicate what motivates individuals on the job. According to needs theories, managers can motivate individuals by meeting their needs. Managers can meet unsatisfied needs in a variety of ways that involve altering the job's responsibility, challenges, autonomy, level of pay, or title, among others. Maslow's hierarchy of needs theory identifies five needs; individuals are motivated to satisfy the lowest-level unsatisfied need. Alderfer's ERG theory collapses the five needs into three. McClelland and his associates' trichotomy of needs theory examines the need for achievement, need for affiliation, and need for power in the workplace. Herzberg's two-factor theory distinguishes between hygiene factors, which reduce dissatisfaction, and motivators, which increase satisfaction.

Equity theory suggests that individuals compare the ratio of their own outcomes, such as pay or promotions, to inputs, such as effort or experience, to another person's. Perceived differences result in behaviors to equalize the ratios. According to reinforcement theory, a manager motivates employees by encouraging desired behaviors and discouraging undesired behaviors. Expectancy theory looks at an individual's expectancy, instrumentality, and valence to determine their motivation. Goal-setting theory says that individuals are motivated by setting specific, moderately difficult, and accepted goals.

A comprehensive reward system motivates employees with wages, benefits, and incentives. An effective reward system ties rewards to performance. It also offers a sufficient number and diversity of rewards.

DIAGNOSTIC QUESTIONS

The following questions can help diagnose the reward system, as well as the degree of motivation in an organizational system.

- Do rewards satisfy individuals' needs?

- Are rewards applied equitably and consistently after desired behaviors?

- Do individuals value the rewards they receive?

- Are rewards consistently applied in proportion to performance?

- Do individuals perceive that their efforts correlate with performance?

- Do individuals set goals that are specific and challenging, yet accepted?

- Do individuals receive feedback about their goal accomplishment as part of the organization's reward system?

- How would you characterize the components of the organization's reward system?

- Does the reward system encourage desired outcomes such as innovation, productivity, or attendance?

- Are benefits and incentive systems effective in motivating desired outcomes?

Activity 4–1   EXPECTANCY QUESTIONNAIRE

STEP 1: Answer Questions 1, 2, and 3 by circling the answer that best describes your feelings.

Question 1: Here are some things that could happen to people if they do their jobs *especially well.* How likely is it that each of these things would happen if you performed your job *especially well?* (You may use your job as student.)

		Not at All Likely	Somewhat Likely	Quite Likely	Extremely Likely
a.	You will get a bonus or pay increase	(1) (2) (3)	(4) (5)	(6)	(7)
b.	You will feel better about yourself as a person	(1) (2) (3)	(4) (5)	(6)	(7)
c.	You will have an opportunity to develop your skills and abilities	(1) (2) (3)	(4) (5)	(6)	(7)
d.	You will have better job security	(1) (2) (3)	(4) (5)	(6)	(7)
e.	You will be given chances to learn new things	(1) (2) (3)	(4) (5)	(6)	(7)
f.	You will be promoted or get a better job	(1) (2) (3)	(4) (5)	(6)	(7)
g.	You will get a feeling that you've accomplished something worthwhile	(1) (2) (3)	(4) (5)	(6)	(7)
h.	You will have more freedom on your job	(1) (2) (3)	(4) (5)	(6)	(7)
i.	You will be respected by the people you work with	(1) (2) (3)	(4) (5)	(6)	(7)
j.	Your supervisor will praise you	(1) (2) (3)	(4) (5)	(6)	(7)
k.	The people you work with will be friendly with you	(1) (2) (3)	(4) (5)	(6)	(7)

Question 2: Different people want different things from their work. Here is a list of things a person could have on his or her job. How *important* is each of the following to you? (You may use your job as student.)

	Moderately Important or Less	Quite Important	Extremely Important

How important is . . . ?

a. The amount of pay you get — (1) (2) (3) (4) (5) (6) (7)

b. The chances you have to do something that makes you feel good about
yourself as a person — (1) (2) (3) (4) (5) (6) (7)

c. The opportunity to develop your skills and abilities — (1) (2) (3) (4) (5) (6) (7)

d. The amount of job security you have — (1) (2) (3) (4) (5) (6) (7)

How important is . . . ?

e. The chances you have to learn new things — (1) (2) (3) (4) (5) (6) (7)

f. Your chances for getting a promotion or getting a better job — (1) (2) (3) (4) (5) (6) (7)

g. The chances you have to accomplish something worthwhile — (1) (2) (3) (4) (5) (6) (7)

h. The amount of freedom you have on your job — (1) (2) (3) (4) (5) (6) (7)

How important is . . . ?

i. The respect you receive from the people you work with — (1) (2) (3) (4) (5) (6) (7)

j. The praise you get from your supervisor — (1) (2) (3) (4) (5) (6) (7)

k. The friendliness of the people you work with — (1) (2) (3) (4) (5) (6) (7)

Question 3: Below you will see a number of pairs of factors that look like this:

Warm weather $\rightarrow$ sweating (1) (2) (3) (4) (5) (6) (7)

You are to indicate by circling the appropriate number to the right of each pair how often it is true for you personally that the first factor leads to the second on your job (or your job as student). Remember, for each pair, indicate how often it is true by circling the number under the response that seems most accurate.

	Never	Sometimes	Often	Almost Always

a. Working hard $\rightarrow$ high productivity — (1) (2) (3) (4) (5) (6) (7)

b. Working hard $\rightarrow$ doing my job well — (1) (2) (3) (4) (5) (6) (7)

c. Working hard $\rightarrow$ good job performance — (1) (2) (3) (4) (5) (6) (7)

STEP 2: Using the questionnaire results.

The results from this questionnaire can be used to calculate a work-motivation score. A score can be calculated for each individual and scores can be combined for groups of individuals. The procedure for obtaining a work-motivation score is as follows:

a. For each of the possible positive outcomes listed in questions 1 and 2, multiply the score for the outcome on question 1 (P → O expectancies) by the corresponding score on question 2 (valences of outcomes). Thus, score 1a would be multiplied by score 2a, score 1b by score 2b, and so forth.

b. All of the 1-times-2 products would be added together to get a total of all expectancies-times-valences.

c. The total should be divided by the number of pairs (in this case, eleven) to get an average expectancy-times-valence score.

d. The scores from question 3 (E → P expectancies) should be added together and then divided by three to get an average effort-to-performance expectancy score.

e. Multiply the score obtained in step c (the average expectancy-times-valence) by the score obtained in step d (the average E → P expectancy score) to obtain a total work-motivation score.

STEP 3: Discussion. Answer the following questions in small groups or with the entire class:

DESCRIPTION

1. What score did you receive? Compare it with the scores of other class members.

DIAGNOSIS

2. How motivating is your job?
3. What factors influence your score?
4. How does the content of your job relate to your score?
5. Can you explain the score using expectancy theory?
6. Can you explain the motivation potential of your job using
   a. reinforcement theory?
   b. equity theory?
   c. needs theories?

PRESCRIPTION

7. How would you improve the motivating potential of your job?

Reprinted by permission from D. A. Nadler and E. E. Lawler III, *Motivation: A diagnostic approach*. In *Perspectives on Behavior in Organizations*, ed. J. R. Hackman, E. E. Lawler III, and L. W. Porter (New York: McGraw-Hill, 1977).

$\mathscr{A}$ctivity 4–2　GOAL SETTING EXERCISE

STEP 1: Think about a job you now hold or a job you have held in the past. If you have never been employed think about an "ideal" middle-management job.

STEP 2: Answer the following questions about that job:

1. How effective were (are) the methods used by your manager in generating maximum employee work performance? (Circle one)
   a. Highly effective
   b. Moderately effective
   c. Ineffective

2. How satisfied were (are) you with this job?
   a. Highly satisfied
   b. Moderately satisfied
   c. Unsatisfied

STEP 3: Complete the job objectives questionnaire.

As employees, each of us has certain objectives that are part of our work. Sometimes, these objectives are spelled out in detail; other times, the objectives are simply intuitively "understood." The following statements refer to your job, and to the objectives that are associated with your job. Read each statement, then circle the number indicating *how untrue* or *how true* you believe each statement to be. (If you prefer, you can think about a job you've had with some organization in the past.)

	Definitely Not True	Not True	Slightly Not True	Uncertain	Slightly True	True	Definitely True
1. Management encourages employees to define job objectives.	−3	−2	−1	0	1	2	3
2. If I achieve my objectives, I receive adequate recognition from my supervisor.	−3	−2	−1	0	1	2	3
3. My objectives are clearly stated with respect to the results expected.	−3	−2	−1	0	1	2	3
4. I have the support I need to accomplish my objectives.	−3	−2	−1	0	1	2	3
5. Achieving my objectives increases my chances for promotion.	−3	−2	−1	0	1	2	3
6. My supervisor dictates my job objectives to me.	−3	−2	−1	0	1	2	3
7. I need more feedback on whether I'm achieving my objectives or not.	−3	−2	−1	0	1	2	3
8. My supervisor will "get on my back" if I fail to achieve my objectives.	−3	−2	−1	0	1	2	3
9. My job objectives are very challenging.	−3	−2	−1	0	1	2	3
10. Management wants to know whether I set objectives for my job or not.	−3	−2	−1	0	1	2	3
11. My supervisor will compliment me if I achieve my job objectives.	−3	−2	−1	0	1	2	3
12. My objectives are very ambiguous and unclear.	−3	−2	−1	0	1	2	3
13. I lack the authority to accomplish my objectives.	−3	−2	−1	0	1	2	3
14. Achievement of objectives is rewarded with higher pay here.	−3	−2	−1	0	1	2	3
15. My supervisor encourages me to establish my own objectives.	−3	−2	−1	0	1	2	3
16. I always have knowledge of my progress toward my objectives.	−3	−2	−1	0	1	2	3
17. My supervisor will reprimand me if I'm not making progress toward my objectives.	−3	−2	−1	0	1	2	3
18. My objectives seldom require my full interest and effort.	−3	−2	−1	0	1	2	3
19. Management makes it clear that defining job objectives is favorably regarded.	−3	−2	−1	0	1	2	3
20. My supervisor gives me more recognition when I achieve my objectives.	−3	−2	−1	0	1	2	3
21. My objectives are very concrete.	−3	−2	−1	0	1	2	3
22. I have sufficient resources to achieve my objectives.	−3	−2	−1	0	1	2	3
23. My pay is more likely to be increased if I achieve my objectives.	−3	−2	−1	0	1	2	3
24. My supervisor has more influence than I do in setting my objectives.	−3	−2	−1	0	1	2	3
25. I wish I had better knowledge of whether I'm achieving my objectives.	−3	−2	−1	0	1	2	3
26. If I fail to meet my objectives, my supervisor will reprimand me.	−3	−2	−1	0	1	2	3
27. Attaining my objectives requires all my skill and know-how.	−3	−2	−1	0	1	2	3

STEP 4: For each of the nine "scales" (A through I), compute a total score by summing the answers to the appropriate questions. Be sure to subtract "minus" scores.

Question Number	Question Number	Question Number	Question Number
1. + ( )	3. + ( )	6. + ( )	4. + ( )
10. + ( )	12. + ( )	15. + ( )	13. + ( )
19. + ( )	21. + ( )	24. + ( )	22. + ( )
Total Score	Total Score	Total Score	Total Score
A	B	C	D

Question Number	Question Number	Question Number	Question Number	Question Number
7. + ( )	9. + ( )	5. + ( )	2. + ( )	8. + ( )
16. + ( )	18. + ( )	14. + ( )	11. + ( )	17. + ( )
25. + ( )	27. + ( )	23. + ( )	20. + ( )	26. + ( )
Total Score	Total Score	Total Score	Total Score	Total Score
E	F	G	H	I

STEP 5: Next, on the following graphs, write in a large "X" to indicate the total score for each scale. You can also name or describe each scale in the space provided.

A _____   −9 −7 −5 −3 −1 | 1 3 5 7 9

B _____   −9 −7 −5 −3 −1 | 1 3 5 7 9

C _____   −9 −7 −5 −3 −1 | 1 3 5 7 9

D _____   −9 −7 −5 −3 −1 | 1 3 5 7 9

E _____   −9 −7 −5 −3 −1 | 1 3 5 7 9

F _____   −9 −7 −5 −3 −1 | 1 3 5 7 9

G _____   −9 −7 −5 −3 −1 | 1 3 5 7 9

H _____   −9 −7 −5 −3 −1 | 1 3 5 7 9

I _____   −9 −7 −5 −3 −1 | 1 3 5 7 9

STEP 6: In small groups answer the following:

1. What common patterns exist in your questionnaire responses and graph?
2. Do the patterns that are highly effective, moderately effective, and ineffective differ? In what ways?
3. Do the patterns differ for jobs that are highly satisfying, moderately satisfying, and unsatisfying?

STEP 7: Discussion. In small groups, with the entire class, or in written form, as directed by your instructor, answer the following questions:

1. What characteristics of goals and goal setting contribute to effective organizational behavior and satisfying organizational experiences?
2. What characteristics contribute to ineffective behavior and unsatisfying experiences?

Based on Peter Lorenzi, Henry P. Sims, Jr., and E. Allen Slusher, Goal setting, performance and satisfaction: A behavioral demonstration. *Exchange: The Organizational Behavior Teaching Journal* 7 (1982):38–42.

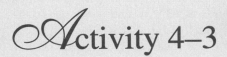 **Activity 4–3** MOTIVATING DIVERSITY IN MIDDLE AND TOP MANAGEMENT

STEP 1: Consider the following situation.

You have recently become the chief operating officer of a large high-technology company that specializes in telecommunications. You are very committed to increasing the diversity of your work force, but know that you must develop a master plan to help motivate other managers in the company to support this goal. To date, your organization has primarily included white males born in the United States. The previous COO was reluctant to promote women and minorities into top management because he felt that they would have difficulty fitting into the executive ranks. As a result, there are currently very few women and minorities who hold top-management positions, and about 20 percent who hold middle-management positions. The lower ranks of the organization have a significant number of women and minorities who have entered the organization in recent years.

STEP 2: Individually or in small groups, incorporating your knowledge of motivation theories, design a motivational plan for reaching this goal.

STEP 3: Discussion. In small groups or with the entire class, share the plans you developed. Then answer the following questions:

1. What motivation theories have you incorporated into your plans?
2. How do your plans reflect elements of an effective reward system?
3. How effective do you expect these plans to be? Why?

$\mathcal{A}$ctivity 4–4   TRAVELER IMPORT CARS, INC.

STEP 1:   Read the Traveler Import Cars, Inc., case.

BACKGROUND

Randy Traveler had been a partner in Capitol Imports, one of the most prosperous foreign car dealerships in greater Columbus, Ohio, selling expensive European automobiles. His wife, Beryl, a holder of an MBA degree from a respected private university, was a consultant specializing in automobile dealerships.

In 1979, Randy and Beryl decided to go into business for themselves. Since between the two of them they had four decades of automobile dealership experience, they elected to acquire their own dealership. With some luck, they obtained a dealership selling a brand of Japanese cars that had become known in the United States for its very high quality. Randy became president and Beryl executive vice-president.

EVOLUTION OF THE FIRM

Stage 1

After obtaining the Japanese dealership, Randy and Beryl decided to locate it approximately two miles from Capitol Imports. The decision was made on the basis of immediate availability of a suitable facility. This location, however, was several miles from a major shopping area of any kind, and the closest automobile dealership was Capitol Imports. Furthermore, the location was approximately three miles from the nearest interchange of a major interstate highway. Nonetheless, the dealership was located on a busy street within easy access to half a dozen upper-middle-class-to-affluent neighborhoods with residents predisposed to purchasing foreign automobiles with a high-quality image.

A number of key employees were enticed by Randy and Beryl to leave Capitol Imports and join Traveler Import Cars. Stuart Graham, who was in charge of Finance and Insurance at Capitol Imports, became general manager at Traveler Import Cars. Before specializing in finance and insurance, Graham was a car salesman. Several mechanics and car salesmen also left Capitol Imports to join Traveler Import Cars. As a rule, the poli-

cies and procedures that pertained to Capitol Imports were relied on at Traveler Import Cars, Inc., for the first five years of operations.

No one at Traveler Import Cars was unionized, but the mechanics were given everything that unionized mechanics received at other dealerships in order to remove the incentive to unionize. By everything, it is meant direct compensation, indirect compensation (fringe benefits), and work rules.

Randy and Beryl viewed their dealership as a family. This was in some measure due to the fact that the dealership was part of a Japanese corporation (which viewed its employees as family), and partly due to the beliefs that Randy and Beryl shared about organizations. Randy and Beryl made every effort to involve subordinates in day-to-day decision making. As tangible evidence of her commitment to democratic leadership, Beryl decided to introduce a quality circle into Traveler Import Cars, Incorporated. This was done by selecting five nonsupervisory employees (one from each part of the organization) to meet once a month with Beryl and Stuart Graham in order to discuss problems, possible solutions, and implementation strategies. No training whatsoever regarding quality circles was provided anyone involved with the so-called "quality circle," and this included Beryl and Stuart.

Stuart Graham, on the other hand, was a benevolent autocrat, although he tried to create the facade of a democratic leader because he understood well Randy and Beryl's leadership preferences. Most employees agreed with Randy and Beryl that Traveler Import Cars was a family. Furthermore, most employees felt free to voice an opinion on anything to Randy, Beryl, and Graham, or to any other supervisor or manager, for that matter.

Stage 2

As long as the dealership was small everything went well, largely because Randy and Beryl made all key decisions, provided daily direction to supervisors and managers (including the general manager—Stuart Graham, who should have been running the dealership on a day-to-day basis), and resolved problems through face-to-face communications with the involved individuals. As the dealership grew and prospered, it generated enough money for growth. Expanding the dealership rapidly was impractical because of the limited allotment of cars due in large measure to the so-called "voluntary" import quotas by the Japanese car manufacturers. The demand for these cars was so great that cars were even sold from the showroom floor, leaving at times few models for new customers to view.

The first acquisition that Randy and Beryl made was a car leasing company, which they located next to the dealership. Randy elected to spend most of his time building up the car leasing company, leaving the operations of the dealership to Beryl. The second acquisition consisted of another car dealership located approximately 10 miles from the original one. The new dealership sold another make of Japanese cars and an expensive European make. The newly acquired dealership was located in the midst of automobile dealerships on a main road, but was housed in inadequate facilities and beset by many problems. Beryl became the chief operating officer of the second dealership as well. Soon after acquiring the second dealership, Randy and Beryl decided to construct new facilities adjacent to the existing ones.

Stage 3

The newly acquired dealership created a great deal of additional work for Beryl, but she understood and accepted that reality because she and Randy knowingly acquired a business that had been plagued by problems prior to acquisition. What bewildered and frustrated Beryl was the fact that the operation of Traveler Import Cars, Inc., took so much of her time as well as physical and psychic energies. After all, it has been five years since she and Randy purchased that dealership. Many key supervisory and management personnel now had five years of experience with the dealership, yet the task of running Traveler Import Cars was just as consuming at this time as it was when the dealership was new. Frequently, Beryl would tell one of the managers to do something, but it wouldn't get done. Decisions were reached at management meetings, but they did not get implemented. Programs were initiated, but were frequently permitted to drift and disappear. Important deadlines were being missed with increasing frequency. Mechanics and salesmen were coming to work late and taking excessive lunch breaks with greater frequency. Beryl knew that these problems were not due to insubordination or lack of motivation. Yet, if she did not directly oversee implementation of an important decision, it did not get implemented.

In order to relieve herself of some of the work load, Beryl hired two experienced managers. In order to justify their salaries, however, they spent half of their time at Traveler Import Cars and the other half at the newly acquired dealership. The newly hired managers had good ideas, yet Beryl was working just as hard as ever, and the problems that motivated Beryl to hire two experienced managers remained practically unchanged. In spite of the problems, the dealership grew as rapidly as the increase in the quota of cars that was allotted to the dealership by the manufacturer permitted. In addition, Traveler Import Cars began wholesaling parts to service stations and car repair shops, and started to lease cars in direct competition with the leasing operation managed by Randy. Although an organizational chart did not exist, it would look like Figure 4–8, if Randy and Beryl bothered to construct one.

About this time, Randy and Beryl's marriage had come undone, and Randy remarried a lady considerably his junior. Even so, Beryl and Randy maintained their business relationship, and were able to work together professionally without visible acrimony. Beryl now had more money than she knew what to do with, and was about to make much more because the newly acquired dealership was being turned around rapidly, largely due to Beryl's considerable talents, the new facility, and the rapidly recovering economy. Yet Beryl no longer wanted to work as hard as she had in the past.

Beryl understood that Stuart Graham lacked the right stuff to be general manager of a car dealership in a metropolitan area, and she approached Randy on the matter. His response was: "Stuart Graham is too valuable of an asset because Traveler Import Cars, Inc., had generated a $500,000 after-tax profit last year. He must be doing something right."

Even though Beryl had been a consultant to automobile dealerships for 20 years, she decided nonetheless to retain a consultant. Beryl was fortunate to contact a particularly astute consultant by the name of J. P. Muzak. Her request was that Muzak straighten out the quality circle, which she felt wasn't living up to her expectations. Muzak, however, was reluctant to get involved unless he was permitted to conduct a thorough needs analysis before selecting any kind of intervention strategy. Beryl, after thinking the matter through, assented to Muzak's proposal. The organizational needs analysis relied on confidential structured interviews with all the managers, supervisors, and select nonsuper-

FIGURE 4–8

Organizational chart of Traveler Import Cars, Inc.

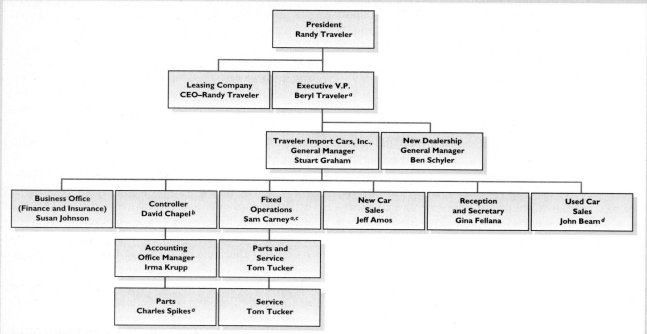

[a] These individuals spent approximately one-half of their time at Traveler Import Cars and one-half at the new dealership.

[b] David Chapel is the controller for Traveler Import Cars, the new dealership, and the leasing company. He spent about one-half of his time at Traveler Import Cars and one-half at the new dealership.

[c] Sam Carney owned and operated his own small business prior to joining Traveler Import Cars, Inc. Charles Spikes was a supervisor at a local office of a national automobile parts distributor before coming to work for Traveler Import Cars, Inc.

[d] John Beam frequently is asked by Randy Traveler to assist with matters pertaining to the leasing company.

visory personnel. The summary of Muzak's organization needs analysis follows.

POSSIBLE PROBLEM AREAS

Goals

Although general goals (such as providing the best customer service possible) exist at the organizational level, many individuals report that what is expected of them, in terms of specific and measurable objectives, isn't clearly defined. It is difficult to make a superior happy if the subordinate isn't sure just what it is that the boss wants.

Also, there does not appear to be a philosophy for setting goals. For example, should goals and objectives be imposed unilaterally by the superior on the subordinate, or should the goals and objectives be set jointly between the superior and subordinate?

Organizational Structure

The organizational structure in a number of instances appears to be confusing. Specifically, a number of individuals appear to be reporting to two or more superiors. Irma Krupp reports to David Chapel and Stuart Graham. Tom Tucker reports to Sam Carney and Stuart Graham. Charles Spikes reports to Tom Tucker, Sam Carney, and Stuart Graham. John Beam had Susan Johnson's job before he became manager of used cars. David Chapel believes that he reports to the two general managers, to Beryl, and to Randy. Gina Fellana appears to report to everyone.

There is the perception that few managers know what they can do on their own authority and what they must get approved and by whom.

Communications

There appear to be too many meetings and they do not seem to be as productive as they could be. On this point there is a consensus.

A paper flow problem exists in several areas. The Accounting Office at times does not receive properly filled out forms from the Business Office. It appears that Susan Johnson does not have the time to fill out carefully and on a timely basis all the forms and attend to her other finance and insurance duties. The Accounting Office at times does not receive the necessary paper work from New Car Sales. The Parts Department at times doesn't receive on a timely basis the necessary information from New Car Sales.

Some individuals complain that their superiors do not keep them informed. Everything is a secret.

Training and Development

A number of individuals have risen through the ranks into supervisory and managerial positions. Since these individuals have never received formal managerial training, the void must be filled by coaching. In a number of cases, the void has not been filled by coaching, and these persons are learning through trial and error—an expensive and time-consuming way of learning, indeed.

The consensus is that the computer equipment is adequate to the task, but the operators need additional training to realize the potential of the equipment. The mechanics receive the latest training from the manufacturer.

Performance Appraisal

Many people reported that they do not receive a periodic formal appraisal. Thus, their need for performance feedback is frustrated.

Wage and Salary Administration

Numerous individuals have reported that it is the subordinate who has to initiate a wage or salary increase. Most individuals report that they would like to see the superior initiate wage and salary action at least annually. Moreover, a number of individuals are not sure on what basis they are remunerated. The absence of a systematic periodic performance appraisal is responsible, in part, for this perception.

Discipline

In a number of instances, individuals arrive late, take extended lunch breaks, and violate rules with impunity. This creates a demoralizing effect on others.

Control System

The financial control system at the top of the organization appears to be satisfactory. The operational control systems in the rest of the organization are problematic.

Morale

While there is still the feeling that the organization is a family and the best place the employees have ever worked, the feeling is starting to diminish.

Sundry Problems

1. Quality circle may need restructuring along traditional lines.
2. The time it takes to make decisions should be shortened.
3. The organization has difficulty implementing decisions that have been made.
4. Lack of follow-up presents serious problems.
5. Policies and programs are permitted to drift and disappear (motivator board is an example).
6. Managers may not be delegating enough.
7. New car salesmen do not always turn customers over to the Business Office, resulting in loss of revenue to the dealership.
8. Service desk is crucial and it has been a revolving door.

At a meeting, Muzak presented the findings of his needs analysis to the management team of Traveler Import Cars, Inc., and a discussion ensued regarding each of the possible problem areas. Randy Traveler did not attend since he relegated the operation of the dealership to Beryl. At the end of the discussion, the management team agreed that all the problems uncovered by Muzak were real and, if anything, understated.

Muzak did not present at the meeting his assessment of the potential of the key managers. This he did in a private discussion with Beryl. In summary, Muzak concluded that Stuart Graham was too set in his ways to change. Moreover, he displayed too much emotion publicly, and lacked the respect of his subordinates. Jeff Amos was considered by his subordinates to be a nice guy, but was indecisive, lacked firmness, was manipulated by subordinates, and did not enjoy the respect of his subordinates. Tom Tucker was probably in over his head in his present position. He was only a high school graduate, he was not a mechanic, was unsure of himself, and lacked the confidence of his subordinates. Lastly, he was quite impulsive. His previous experience was as a service desk writer (the person to whom the customer explains the car problems and who writes the work order). All the other managers and supervisors were thought to possess the necessary potential that could be realized through training and experience.

STEP 2: Prepare the case for class discussion.

STEP 3: Individually, in small groups, or with the entire class, as directed by your instructor, answer the following questions.

DESCRIPTION
1. Describe the situation at Traveler Import Cars.
2. Describe Randy's, Beryl's, and Graham's performance during the case.

DIAGNOSIS
3. What problems existed at Traveler Import Cars?
4. How do (a) needs, (b) equity, (c) reinforcement, (d) expectancy, and (e) goal-setting theories explain the situation?
5. How effective is the reward system at Traveler Import Cars?
6. Using your knowledge of perception and attribution, evaluate the situation.

7. Using your knowledge of personality, personal development, and career development, evaluate the situation.

PRESCRIPTION
8. What changes should be made in this situation?

STEP 4: Discussion. In small groups, with the entire class, or in written form, share your answers to the questions above. Then answer the following questions:

1. What symptoms suggested that a problem existed?
2. What problems existed in the case?
3. What theories and concepts help explain the problems?
4. How can the problems be corrected?
5. Are the actions likely to be effective?

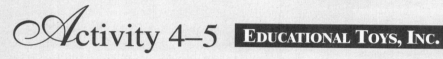

Activity 4–5   EDUCATIONAL TOYS, INC.

STEP 1: Read the following description of Educational Toys, Inc.

Educational Toys is a large toy distributor that relies on "Educational Toy Account Representatives" who sell the products door-to-door or during neighborhood parties rather than through retail outlets. Each account representative has a supervisor who oversees his or her performance. Regional managers supervise from ten to fifteen supervisors each.

To date, the only information used in assessing a regional manager's performance has been the percentage of goods sold by the salespeople in the region. Regional managers receive 5 percent of the worth of the goods the account representatives in their region sell. Recently many managers have complained that they are not rewarded on many of the important parts of their jobs, such as training and development of account representatives, supervision of the supervisors, and identification of the most appropriate products for their region, among other activities. The supervisors also receive rewards in the form of a 5 percent share of the worth of the goods sold by the account representatives.

Top management of Educational Toys, Inc., has agreed to revise the company's reward system for supervisors and regional managers. They want a system that is relatively easy to administer and consistent across the thirty sales regions of the country.

STEP 2: In groups of four to six, design a reward system for the regional managers and supervisors.

STEP 3: Discussion. In small groups or with the entire class, share your systems. Then answer the following questions:

1. What do these systems have in common?
2. How do they differ?
3. What are the strengths and weaknesses of each system?
4. What changes would you recommend?
5. What role do the regional managers and supervisors play in the determination of rewards?

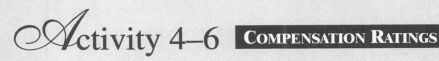

Activity 4–6   COMPENSATION RATINGS

STEP 1: You are the director of engineering at a rapidly growing firm in a fast-moving industry. Many of your engineers move into supervisory positions in your firm very quickly. Others, after two or three years, move into better positions in your competitors' companies. You want to be sure to keep those who work hard and make significant contributions to your firm. You must determine pay increases for the engineers described below. Beside each name, write the percentage increase you would give that person. Each currently earns between $35,000 and $63,000.

Herb Holliday Herb has been with your firm over three years. While his work was quite good during his first year on the job, it has gotten progressively worse, even though he works quite hard at it. His coworkers have complained to you that he doesn't do his share—that he tries to get by on his old accomplishments and by his occasional brilliant insights. Others say his rich bride takes all his time and attention.

Eliza Everready Eliza's rich husband can't understand why she works so hard. She's always the first in the office and the last to leave. During her three years with the firm she has become a leader among her peers because of her hard work. And you couldn't ask for better work from an employee. She uses her excellent skills to produce highly creative work in great quantities.

Stanley Snorr Everyone thinks Stanley is a goof-off except you. He certainly leads the irresponsible bachelor's life off the job, or so you've heard. His work is some of the best in his department, which surprises you since he never seems to work hard and you hired him a year ago, not for his skills, but because he is the boss's son.

Henry Hustle Henry always looks as if he is working so hard he'll drop. Even though his coworkers praise his work, when you review it, the quantity does not seem up to par. Maybe he hasn't had a chance to make up for the deficiencies in his skills you knew he had when you hired him a year ago. Still, he really needed a job then, and still does because of his mother's huge medical bills.

Carla Camphor Carla has worked for you for five years, the longest of any engineer. Recently, you have noticed that the quality of her work has declined significantly. She just doesn't seem to be trying. Her coworkers have started to refuse to work with her—they say she isn't up to date and doesn't try to improve her skills. You know she isn't desperate for money since she has no dependents and already earns a nice salary.

Hermione Higglebottom Hermione and her three fatherless children are struggling to make ends meet. She always works extra hours, generally taking piles of work home with her. She joined your firm a year ago; her strong recommendation as a hard worker from her previous employer got your attention even though you felt her academic background was outdated. You were right—the quality of her work has been below average. Even her coworkers have commented about it.

Michael Makeshift Mike is a hot-shot engineer who has been with your firm for two years. His impressive academic credentials called him to your attention originally—and he hasn't disappointed you yet. His work is of high quality, but he puts in a lot of overtime to make sure it's perfect. Everyone else says he does terrific work too. Mike married when he was in college; his salary barely makes ends meet for his wife and two children.

June James Even though June is easily distracted by her family's financial and health problems, her work is of high quality. Her coworkers don't seem to think too much of her, though, perhaps because she doesn't seem to work too hard—she's often late for work and leaves early. You're a bit surprised by the high quality of her work since she was not one of the stronger applicants when you hired her a year ago.

STEP 2: Now, in groups of four to six, reach a consensus about the percentage increase each person should receive. Be prepared to justify the increases.

STEP 3: Discussion. In small groups, or with the entire class,

1. Explain your reasons for each increase.

2. Use any relevant theory of motivation to justify your compensation plan.

3. Which factors influence pay decisions? Should these factors be influential?

This exercise is based on one written by Edward E. Lawler III, and is adapted with his permission.

$\mathcal{A}$ctivity 4–7 THE SALARY PROBLEM

STEP 1: Read the following scenario.

Sandy Sturgis had just met with the top-performing employee in the division. Tracy McLeish had worked for Applications Unlimited for three years. During that time Tracy had been promoted twice, initially into a first-level supervisory position and then, three months ago, into a middle-management position. Tracy had insisted on meeting with Sandy, saying she was furious about some salary information she had just obtained.

Tracy told Sandy that she had inadvertently learned that her salary was $5,000 less than a newly hired manager. The new manager did not have an MBA, which Tracy had, had approximately the same job history as Tracy, but had never worked for an organization precisely like Applications Unlimited. Tracy said that the new manager was also untried in turning around projects quickly and cost effectively. Tracy wanted an immediate pay increase of $10,000—$5,000 more than the other manager because of her advanced education and special experience at Applications Unlimited. She threatened to leave immediately—right in the middle of a critical project—if the increase was denied.

Sandy knew that top management had put a freeze on any pay raises for the rest of the year. Sandy promised Tracy to look into the situation and get back to her within the week.

STEP 2: Analyze and evaluate the situation. What problems exist in this situation?

STEP 3: You are Sandy. Prepare a response to Tracy. In preparing your response, consider at least three possible options and solutions.

STEP 4: Your instructor will select one or more students to deliver their response to Tracy. (Your instructor or another classmate will play the role of Tracy.)

STEP 5: In small groups, prepare a revised response to Tracy. What elements should the response include?

STEP 6: With the entire class, discuss the contents of a revised response. Then answer the following questions:

1. What factors should Sandy consider?
2. What options are available to Sandy?
3. How does motivation theory help you choose among these options?
4. Which solution or option do you recommend implementing? Why?
5. How can this situation be avoided in the future?

$\mathcal{A}$ctivity 4–8 JAMESTOWN ADVANCED PRODUCTS CASE

STEP 1: Read the Jamestown Advanced Products case.

I'm a tinkerer by nature and a turnaround manager by experience. I buy troubled businesses, get them op-

erating at a profit, and then sell them when the mundane details begin to outweigh the challenges. Over the past 16 years I've done that with three companies. But the company I currently own, Jamestown Advanced Products Inc., is different from the others. For one thing, there aren't many mundane details left for me to handle. My employees solve most of the problems by themselves.

Jamestown Advanced Products is a metal-fabricating business I started three years ago as the result of a telephone call from a friend. At the time, I was president and owner of another metal fabricator in Jamestown, New York, which I was about to sell. In fact, I had been looking forward to taking some time off, but the call forced me to reconsider my plans.

My friend had been doing subcontract work for a large building-products company that was importing industrial plumbing assemblies from Korea. Hoping to improve turnaround time and quality, it wanted to shift to a domestic supplier. The deal represented about $1 million of business a year, my friend said. We would be expected to produce fabrications in various sizes and models, and about 40 percent of the work would involve special orders to be turned around in less than two weeks. Custom work of that sort requires a manufacturing process significantly more flexible than the one my company had been using, so I would have to start a new company if I decided to accept the offer. But the business was mine, I was told, if I could commit to producing and delivering the specified quantity of metal products every week. And one other thing: I'd have to do it at the same price the Korean supplier was charging.

That was a challenge I could get interested in. To help me make my decision, the building-products company was willing to share all sorts of information, including the amount of product it intended to buy and the prices it would pay. From that, I was able to construct a projected income statement. The good news was that the numbers seemed to work, indicating a pretax profit margin of 12 percent. The bad news was that the numbers worked only as long as I could hold direct labor expenses to 11 percent of sales. And labor, I knew, would be difficult to control, particularly when so much product was being made to order.

Nevertheless, I went ahead and made a proposal to the company. I said I would start a business to fabricate the products it wanted, deliver them within the specified time frames, and charge the same price as the Koreans. But since the start-up required an investment of about $600,000 for machinery and working capital, I wanted a long-term contract. Otherwise, I might be forced to sell off the equipment at a loss if the relationship soured.

We settled on a three-year contract. The customer, for its part, made a commitment to buy a certain amount of goods each year and to provide regular projections of its delivery needs. We also came up with a formula for raising prices based on increases in the cost of raw materials. Finally, we agreed the customer could terminate the relationship only if I failed to meet its quality standards or deliver on time.

And so I had a new business.

In looking at my situation, I could see only one variable that could make or break the company, and that was labor. Not that my estimates of output per man-hour were unrealistic. But I knew they required a work force that wanted to meet and sustain a high level of productivity. And I do mean want. In my experience as both an employee and a manager, I've found that employee attitudes are a major factor in productivity. After all, every owner would like employees to strive for higher and higher levels of output, but they seldom do. The problem is that workers (even ours) are somewhat cynical about management. They quickly lose their motivation if they see their productivity increasing and they don't get the lion's share of the gain.

But with this company, I had an advantage. I could arrange things however I wanted. So I decided to set up a serious bonus program, one that would give employees as much incentive as I had to keep labor costs below 11 percent of sales.

The idea was simple: I would pay them decent base wages, totaling 11 percent of sales. If employees got the labor costs below 11 percent, I would pay them the difference in the form of a quarterly bonus. If labor costs went over 11 percent, of course, the difference would be coming out of the company coffers. I put all that in writing.

In addition, I agreed that at the end of every week, I would provide sales totals, gross payroll numbers, whatever employees thought they needed to check out the system. If they didn't trust me, they could (with a little effort) verify the numbers on their own. The feedback would be almost immediate, so they could study the results with an eye toward improvement. I thought it was feasible for them to produce at a labor rate of 9 percent, in which case they could be earning quarterly bonuses of up to $1,500 each.

We started gearing up in October 1987 with just four production people. All of them got $6 an hour, which was about the norm for similar jobs in our area, and I didn't promise to pay more until they earned more. Employees seemed to like the idea of being rewarded for efficiency. As far as I was concerned, that was most important. We could teach them how to operate equipment. It's much harder to persuade people to accept a completely different approach to compensation.

Employees spent the first few weeks getting used to the equipment and building prototypes. They knew what was expected of them in terms of output, and everybody thought it was doable. Then, in early December, we began building products according to our customer's production schedule. Immediately people saw how hard it was. For one thing, they were still learning their jobs. The engineer, for instance, would write programs with errors in them. The operators of our numeric-control turret presses would put clamps in the wrong position, then smash them. Or they would bend pieces of metal too far or not far enough, which would make it hard for welders to weld pieces efficiently. I knew it would take time to get production up to speed, and I had budgeted for it. But the employees were disappointed at our slow progress.

During the first two or three months our labor costs were almost 50 percent above the target. We were spending $16 per $100 of goods instead of $11. Since there were no supervisors, I played the role of foreman and cheerleader. When the employees had a good week, we analyzed why they had been more efficient; when they had a bad week, we looked for reasons.

As we went along, I shared as much information as I dared to. Every week I would tape a sheet of paper with three numbers on it to a metal post: the past week's production, our direct labor cost, and the percentage of labor to production. I avoided talking about profits—or the lack of them—for fear that employees would think the business was going to fail. Instead, I talked about cash flow and performance relative to plan, both of which, I explained, were right on target.

After we'd been at it for about four months, people could see signs of improvement. By then, we had 10 or 11 production employees, and labor costs had dropped to about 13 percent. There were still peaks and valleys, but employees, for the most part, were encouraged. I'd walk through the plant, and they would always have ideas for streamlining production. They would say, "What about moving these components from here to there?" or, "Why don't we produce parts in bigger batches?" My role as cheerleader and foreman began to diminish.

As we moved into the summer of 1988, however, we lost some of our momentum. In June we had a surge of about $300,000 in orders, representing more than 40 percent of the $700,000 in production we had planned for the entire year. Our people, who were working a lot of overtime already, couldn't keep up, so we had to bring in six new employees. They weren't trained, of course, so our efficiency suffered. That was a big psychological setback for the people who thought they were closing in on their bonuses. But we had no choice: we had to satisfy our customer.

For about three months we were running three shifts. We had 18 people working in production and 4 others (including myself) backing them up. I gave out small raises in an effort to encourage the employees who had been trying so hard, increasing their base pay from $6 an hour to $6.75. Ironically, the increases added to the payroll cost, which made it somewhat harder for people to qualify for the bonus. But since there hadn't been any bonuses yet, nobody cared.

It was a tough summer. Among other things, it was brutally hot, and the plant had no air-conditioning. Morale was low. Two of the original employees got called back by companies from which they had been laid off, and they left, taking jobs that paid about $10 an hour. They said they had lost confidence about hitting the bonus targets anytime soon. Frankly, so had a lot of other people. Whenever employees expressed their doubts to me, I would take them through the numbers again. We would look at the improvement in performance since the spring. Now that they were getting more efficient, I said, they had to learn how to think beyond the task at hand, to order materials in advance so they wouldn't run out.

In early fall the situation began to improve. We caught up on production and could eliminate our third shift. Because it was by far the least efficient one, we thereby lowered our labor costs significantly. That brought us down to 10 production people. By October they were working in the bonus zone. Week after week labor came in below the 11 percent target, running from 9 percent to 10.4 percent. I kept setting aside money to pay out at the end of the quarter. As people saw the total rising, they were thrilled, and so was I.

But after seven straight weeks in the bonus zone, something happened: we stopped shipping goods. In itself, that was not a problem. We had to have periods during which we could build up our inventory of standard goods so we could handle the special orders with a minimum of disruption. It was all part of the plan.

However, employees saw the inventory accumulating, and they got nervous. Talk of layoffs spread through the plant. I tried to address the employees' fears, explaining why we needed a reserve of finished products. Nobody, I told them, was going to be laid off. But no matter what I said, people were scared by the sight of growing inventory. In response, they started working less efficiently. By the end of the quarter the bonus was wiped out.

As you might expect, this turn of events deflated a lot of employees. They knew they had had the money in their hands and they had blown it. For my part, I really wanted them to earn a bonus. To the extent that the inventory had thrown them off, I felt partly responsible for their failure to get it. I also believed that when they finally saw a bonus check, it would motivate them tremendously.

So just before Christmas I called the employees together. I told them I would pay the bonus based on their performance in the first seven weeks of the quarter. I said we would never do this again, but I wanted them to know we were really serious about the system. Then I handed out the checks. Under the formula we'd worked out, the bonuses averaged $372 a person.

It worked. During 1989 we paid out a bonus check every quarter and the employees earned every cent. The bonus payments, which averaged $340 in the first quarter, grew to an average of $771 in the last quarter. Granted, our sales increased from $1 million to about $1.4 million, which played a role. But most of the increase was the result of rising productivity. We were doing more work with 11 people than we had done the previous year with as many as 18.

As time went on I could see the change in employees' attitudes. Before we were making bonus payments, workers didn't seem to care if we spent money on overtime because of a production snag. It was the company's nickel, not theirs. But once they crossed into bonus territory, they saw that production problems were costing them money, and they became very diligent about finding ways to improve.

Meanwhile, they were operating increasingly on their own. We would just give them a general overview of our production needs for the following week and they'd take it from there. They knew that the faster the work got done, the more they stood to make. To speed up the process, they began telling one another how many parts they needed, when, and in what order. Some would even come in early to lay out their parts on pallets. We tried to help them save time by putting phones at each workstation, so an employee could call a vendor directly if, say, a machine malfunctioned.

Along the way, the problems began to change. In the early days they had generally involved things or systems—faulty materials, for example, or poorly organized work flow. But now, more often than not, the bottlenecks were people. We had a brake-press operator, for instance, who was having trouble keeping up. One day I walked into the plant and found a shouting match going on between him and another employee, who had run out of things to do. We asked her to operate the machine for a while. After a little practice, she began processing the work a great deal faster than he could. Now when we get backed up on the brake press, we usually ask her to run it on overtime. In addition to the extra hours, she has since received a raise, which also increased her share of the quarterly bonus pool.

As the bonus system has evolved, so has the pay scale. I handle that myself, setting everyone's base wage, and the information is not public. In the beginning, I assumed employees would keep their wages secret. I was wrong. I've found that everybody knows about any changes in wages within minutes. In deciding on wages, I simply try to be equitable. Every so often, I sit down and list employees in descending order according to their value to the company. The list is never posted, but people are aware of it. They know that when they become more efficient or learn a new skill, I'll adjust their pay. As a matter of policy, I don't lower anyone's wages, but employees who don't get raises wind up with smaller percentages of the overall bonus distribution. Clearly, there's an incentive for people to improve.

The system isn't for everybody, however. Some people, I've found, can't handle the responsibility, and others don't like the pressure. Last November, for example, we moved to a new plant and added some people in the process. I thought we might become overstaffed, but—for reasons I still don't fully understand—we lost three employees in three months. One guy came in one morning, left a half hour later, and never came back. Another fellow, a product tester, fell behind and stopped checking for quality; people were furious with him (returns eat into the bonus) and pressured him to leave. The third person became a prankster. Among other things, he set a pile of rags on fire with a welding torch. Why anybody would do that is beyond me. I fired him.

We now have a total of eight people working in production, and we're producing more goods more efficiently every month. Production people earn from $6.50 to $8.75 an hour before bonuses, which have lately averaged more than $1,115 a quarter. At the beginning of 1990, moreover, I decided to sweeten the pot. Instead of allocating 11 percent for direct labor, I've set the figure at 12 percent, thereby paving the way for even bigger bonuses down the road.

Meanwhile, the system is still evolving. Recently we've had to deal with an issue of tardiness, which upset several employees. One person's late arrival, they said, disrupted everyone else's schedule and ultimately reduced the bonus pile. Under the old rules, a tardy employee lost some wages but still received a full bonus at the end of the quarter. The others thought that wasn't fair. We batted the issue around for several months. How much lateness or absenteeism could employees tolerate? How punitive should they be? Finally, last winter, we agreed on new rules. Employees could be tardy—defined as one minute late— or absent without notice no more than five times a quarter. Beyond that, they would lose the entire quarterly bonus, which would be divvied up among the other workers. The new policy went into effect during the second quarter. In June, just as the quarter was coming to an end, two employees went over the limit.

A couple of people felt bad about this development. They thought the penalty was too harsh. The arguments got kind of nasty, so I called a meeting. Someone proposed that the offenders be paid half the bonus they would otherwise be entitled to. I suggested we put it to a vote of all the employees who were eligible for the bonus under the new policy. It was a secret ballot. They unanimously agreed to give the two employees half of their shares.

In the wake of that incident, the employees decided to revise the policy. A person can still lose the quarterly bonus by being late or absent without notice more than five times, but from now on that share will be rolled over into the next quarter's pool, which will then be divvied up by everyone according to the formula. We'll see how that works.

Looking back over the past three years, I can see how my role has changed along with everyone else's. I no longer spend much time pumping up the organization and helping people make decisions. I don't set employment policies, either—the employees do. Yes, I sometimes serve as a kind of referee, but they come up with the options. We have a bookkeeper who han-

dles the payroll and the day-to-day financial matters. My daughter Wendi does the purchasing and production scheduling.

And me? I concentrate on the issues involving the company's long-term direction. I'm also responsible for finding more business. At the moment, I'm negotiating to add some new product lines, and I feel under considerable pressure. There are eight people out in the plant, getting better at their jobs all the time. Before too long they will be able to produce more than we can ship. At that point, it will be important for us to have additional work.

So that's my problem right now. I have to admit, its's a good problem to have.

....

STEP 2:   Prepare the case for class discussion.

....

STEP 3:   Individually, in small groups, or with the entire class, as directed by your instructor, answer the following questions.

DESCRIPTION

1. Why did the owner of Jamestown Advanced Products, Inc. institute a bonus program?
2. When did the owner grant the first bonus?
3. How did productivity change over time?

DIAGNOSIS

4. What are the advantages and disadvantages of a bonus system?
5. What prevented workers from earning bonuses early in the company's history?
6. How well did the bonus system motivate employees?
7. How do needs, equity, reinforcement, expectancy, and goal-setting theories of motivation explain the success of the bonus system?
8. How do perception, attribution, learning, and individual differences explain the success of the bonus program?

PRESCRIPTION

9. What refinements have been made in the system?
10. Are additional refinements necessary?

ACTION

11. What issues did the owner encounter in managing the system?

STEP 4: Discussion. In small groups, with the entire class, or in written form, share your answers to the questions above. Then answer the following questions:

1. What type of incentive system was offered?
2. How effective was the system?
3. What theories and concepts help explain the system's effectiveness?

4. What changes are still necessary in the incentive system?

From J. W. Wehrenberg, How my company learned to run itself, reprinted with permission, *Inc.,* magazine (January 1991):54–60. © 1991 by Goldhirsh Group, Inc., 38 Commercial Wharf, Boston, MA 02110.

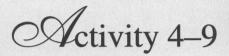 "WINNING—WINNING AND LOSING, COMPETITIVE SPIRIT"

STEP 1: View the ABC video entitled "Winning—Winning and Losing, Competitive Spirit."

STEP 2: In small groups or with the entire class, answer the following questions:

1. What motivates individuals to compete?
2. How does motivation theory explain the competitive spirit shown in the video?
3. What makes the difference between a winner and a loser?
4. How does motivation theory explain this difference?
5. Do organizations want all "winners?"
6. How can organizations motivate workers to be "winners?"

Chapter 5

Chapter Outline

Developing High-Performance Work Teams

LEARNING OBJECTIVES

After completing the reading and activities in Chapter 5, students will be able to

1. Discuss the reasons for the rise of the self-managed work team.

2. List five reasons why work groups form.

3. Differentiate between various types of work groups.

4. Cite the characteristics of effective work groups.

5. Diagnose a group's goals, norms, roles, and structural configuration.

6. Compare and contrast the progressive and noncontinuous models of group development.

7. Describe four major strategies for improving group performance.

Self-Managed Teams at W.L. Gore & Associates

W.L. Gore & Associates manufactures Gore-Tex, the waterproof fabric found in outdoor clothing and spacesuits, as well as other Teflon products for medical and industrial uses. William L. "Bill" Gore, the founder of W.L. Gore & Associates, created a company with a unique way of operating: Gore introduced the concepts of worker self-management, empowerment, and teams more than thirty years ago. No employee has a formal title—all are known as associates—and the company has no formal structure. To be hired, an individual must be sponsored by an existing employee, who must also find work for the "new" employee to do. The sponsor continues to advise the associate and even "market" his or her abilities to project teams in the company.

For example, an individual who acts as a product specialist takes charge of developing a new product. This person then creates a team to work on the product development. The team expands its membership as needed to perform various functions in developing and ultimately manufacturing the product. Team members decide how the team will operate and what staff and financial resources the team requires. They do not need to consult with individuals outside the team on budget or other decisions that mainly affect the team and its product. Team members would perform functions traditionally performed by managers, such as scheduling and assigning jobs, maintaining equipment, ordering supplies, and keeping business data about the team's performance.

Teams can grow to become a plant, but can have no more than 200 associates, so that members are familiar with all those in the group. In principle, an entire work operation can become a large self-managing team in which each member is self-managing. As the team grows it divides into multiple teams known as manufacturing cells. Each team member can perform most manufacturing processes, but agrees to assume certain ones as his or her personal responsibility. Once an associate makes a commitment, he or she is expected to follow it. Each team has a leader who emerges from within the team as a result of discussion and consensus.

The approach used at W.L. Gore & Associates is in marked contrast to that used in companies with a clearly established set of reporting relationships and formal titles for all employees. In traditionally functioning companies, leaders are appointed and teams are not self-managing, but are supervised by a manager. In thirty years, W.L. Gore & Associates has grown to a company with 5,600 associates, 35 plants worldwide, and revenues close to $1 billion.[1]

The self-managed work teams found at W.L. Gore & Associates are a prototype for the workplace of the future. Reengineering and the resultant long-term changes in the way work is done have contributed to the elimination of layers of management and an increased allocation of responsibility to nonmanagerial employees. As self-managed work teams become more common, they will change the way we and those in the field of organizational behavior think about work groups. Hence, this chapter will use both self-managed and traditionally managed work teams as examples as we discuss research about the way groups form and function in the workplace.

We begin this chapter with a discussion of the rise of self-managed work teams. Then we examine the nature of various types of work groups. We continue with a discussion of the underpinnings of effective group performance. Next we describe ways work groups develop. We conclude the chapter with strategies for improving group performance.

THE RISE OF THE SELF-MANAGED WORK TEAM

As the problems organizations face have become more complex, individual problem solving has been inadequate. Based in part on the success of the Japanese in manufacturing in the 1970s and 1980s, corporations in the United States and abroad have altered their cultures to encourage teamwork and collaboration. Executives in organizations authorize and legitimize teams to encourage creativity, facilitate the use of diverse intellectual resources, and inspire multifaceted problem solving.

Downsizing and reengineering have resulted in a significant decrease in the numbers and layers of management. At the same time, executives have wanted to give workers more autonomy and control over their work and thereby increase their work satisfaction. As a result, workers have been given more responsibility for managing their own jobs and the workplace culture has fostered self-managed teams. Although traditional management practices and the resulting mindset in traditionally managed organizations may hinder the development of self-managed teams, organizations are overcoming these barriers. Self-managed teams are proliferating and in the process are demonstrating positive outcomes. Companies realize the benefits of self-managed teams as increased productivity, streamlining of functions, flexibility, quality, commitment, and customer satisfaction.[2]

MARTIN MARIETTA. At Martin Marietta Corp.'s Government Electronic Systems plant an employee team reduced the manufacturing cycle from 253 to 126 days. Another team cut the physical space needed for production by 50 percent. Other teams reduced scrap by 57 percent and defects by 54 percent.[3]

To introduce self-managed teams requires managers to alter their views of power and control. In a case study of a warehouse operation, the early part of the transition was characterized by initial suspicion, uncertainty, and resistance. Gradually the managers realized the positive potential of the new work system. As they continued to wrestle with their new role of team facilitator, the managers eventually learned a new language and practiced new behaviors.[4]

COMMERCIAL FLIGHT SYSTEMS. Commercial Flight Systems, a division of Honeywell, Inc. in Minneapolis, addressed concerns about the credibility of self-directed teams among workers by creating a management team to complement worker teams at lower levels of the organization.[5] A staff of on-site performance management advisers provides consultation and support to both types of teams at CFS.

Successful self-management requires numerous conditions:[6]

■ ***Commitment from top management.*** Top management must provide sufficient time and resources for self-managed teams to develop and function.

- *Mutual trust between employees and managers.* A willingness to take risks and share information will flow from this trust.

- *A commitment to training.* Employees must be trained in technical skills and managerial skills such as budgeting and scheduling. Other types of external support such as group observers or facilitators may also be needed.

- *Selection of appropriate operations.* Not all jobs or activities fit well with the use of self-managed teams. They must allow autonomy of decision making and benefit from team performance.

- *Union participation.* Labor–management relations change in self-managed teams. Generally, the adversarial relationship is eliminated. New forms of compensation must often be negotiated.

EDY'S GRAND ICE CREAM. Edy's Grand Ice Cream experienced difficulties with their initial attempts at self-management. The early emphasis was primarily social and did not hold employees accountable for short-term, bottom-line results. In 1990, teams of employees began a complete overhaul of the organization, creating cross-functional teams aligned by business units, as well as some functional and coordinating teams. For example, teams of 4–5 business-unit people who make the ice cream are now responsible for quality checks, meeting business goals, internal scheduling, discipline, training, and career development. With 100 percent of employees now on self-directed teams, rework, cycle time, inventory, and costs have all declined significantly in the past five years; productivity and sales volume have increased.[7]

Self-managed teams are not restricted to the United States.[8]

INFOSYS. Infosys in Bangalore, India, forms teams to do the required work and then disbands them upon its completion.[9]

FIAT. Fiat's new $2.9 billion plant uses numerous independent, multiskilled teams to perform the work.[10]

SUN LIFE. Sun Life Assurance Society of Bristol, England, reorganized customer service representatives into teams that handle claims from start to finish. The use of teams cut the time required to settle claims by one-half and resulted in a 45 percent increase in new business.

Diagnosing the factors that influence group behavior helps managers and employees predict the ways these self-managed teams and other groups in the workplace will act, plan ways to support functional attitudes and behavior, and prepare to counteract dysfunctional actions and attitudes. In this chapter we examine the way effective groups develop and function to help us understand how self-managed teams evolve and perform effectively.

THE NATURE OF WORK GROUPS

How can managers help groups function at maximum effectiveness? What factors help a team become as productive as possible?

WHY WORK GROUPS FORM

Work groups form for a variety of reasons, as shown in Figure 5–1. Although individuals may have some choice in the groups to which they belong, particularly

FIGURE 5–1   *Reasons for team formation*

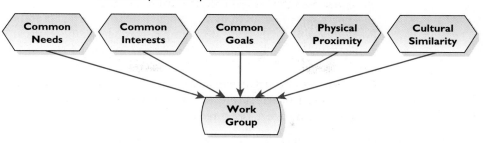

when first joining an organization, for the most part they have relatively little discretion in selecting group membership.

Some groups form because individuals have ***common needs.*** Members of a group may need similar challenges, such as members of a parasailing team. They may satisfy their basic needs for food, shelter, and security, such as members of an Israeli kibbutz. Or, they may satisfy their needs for variety, such as the members of W.L. Gore & Associates's work teams, where each member does a variety of tasks over the work year.

Groups also form because individuals have ***common interests.*** Nurses join professional associations to share their interests in practicing cardiac, intensive-care, or pediatric nursing, furthering their knowledge and enhancing the image of their profession. Employees from various departments in an insurance company may join a task force to work on improving the quality of working life.

Groups also form to attain ***common goals.*** Employees in the human resources department, for example, share the common goal of helping workers become productive and satisfied in their jobs, as well as meeting the legal requirements surrounding employment. The work units at W.L. Gore & Associates form to accomplish the company's product development and manufacturing goals.

Groups also form when individuals share ***physical proximity.*** Often employees who work in the same department or in the same type of job may share social activities. Bank tellers who work in one branch typically develop a group identity that affects their work reputation. Sometimes this physical proximity helps to reinforce dysfunctional group attitudes and assumptions. Members of a production department, for example, may unite in assuming the design engineers do not care about the practical problems of production. One way to fix this problem is to move the two departments into the same area, where the physical proximity can foster communication and common goals.

Finally, groups form because of ***cultural similarity.*** New immigrants often join organizations where others from their native country work. U.S. workers living abroad often join groups with other Americans both on and off the job.

TYPES OF WORK GROUPS

A ***work group*** involves two or more people in a work setting who collaborate in some way to accomplish their group's and the organizational goals and attain their desired outcomes. A work group may attack and resolve problems, creatively explore possibilities or alternatives, or execute well-developed plans, among other activities.[11]

Formal–Informal Individuals may belong to formal or informal work groups. *Formal groups,* such as an accounting department or the teams at W.L. Gore & Associates, are those officially sanctioned and organized by managerial or other authority to help accomplish the organization's goals. Two-thirds of large companies have formed senior management teams; in organizations such as AT&T, Eastman Kodak, and New York Life Insurance, these work groups operate autonomously and attempt to change the corporate hierarchy.[12]

Informal groups, in contrast, are those that arise spontaneously in an organization or within formal groups. These may form around friendships between coworkers or interests shared by employees in different formal groups. For example, several computer programmers may form an informal group because they spend social time together or because they are working on masters degrees at the same university. Individuals generally belong to informal groups voluntarily, whereas they often have little choice about membership in formal work groups.

Traditionally Managed–Self-Managed We can also consider work groups to be either *traditionally managed,* in which a designated individual serves as the official leader or manager, or *self-managed,* where workers share responsibility for managing the work group.

A self-managed or self-directed work team has full responsibility for completing a well-defined part of the work, generally the finished product or service or a significant component of it. They also have discretion over decisions.[13] While managers do not oversee the daily work activities of self-directed team members, they may continue to coach the team, develop an overall strategy for the teams in their area, champion innovation, and provide resources for the team. The managers also serve as a liaison to other parts of the organization, suppliers, and customers.

CHAPARRAL STEEL. A team of mill workers from Chaparral Steel traveled around the world to evaluate new production machinery. The machines they selected and installed helped make their mill one of the world's most efficient.[14]

TIMCREST STEEL. Timcrest Steel's Faircrest plant converted its entire work force of almost 500 employees to self-directed work teams, with a resulting 25 percent decrease in manufacturing costs and a 37 percent drop in maintenance costs during the last five years.[15]

Permanent–Temporary We can also classify work groups as *relatively permanent* or *temporary.* Relatively permanent groups work together for long periods of time, generally at least one year, on a repetitive set of tasks.

AT&T SUBMARINE SYSTEMS. The submarine systems plant of AT&T in Clark, New Jersey, has used the team approach to reduce the costs of its product by more than 30 percent. This approach likely prevented the plant from closing.[16]

Temporary work groups, such as task forces or committees, form for short, pre-specified amounts of time to complete a unique set of tasks or projects. For example, a bank may form a temporary team to develop a special promotion for a new type of account the bank introduces.

Single Function–Multiple Functions Groups can contain individuals from *single* or *multiple* disciplines or functions. Cross-functional work groups, groups composed of individuals from engineering, marketing, and production, for example, have become increasingly common in organizations because they bring diverse expertise to complex problems.

BOEING AIRCRAFT. Boeing created design/build teams to develop its new 777 aircraft. These teams combined designers, engineers, and production staff onto teams that worked on the new aircraft from its inception, rather than having each function work on the new aircraft sequentially. Because production employees participated in the design phase, they could alert the designers to features that would eventually cause production difficulties and look for solutions early in the development process. This collaboration saved Boeing both time and money.[17]

CINCINNATI MILACRON. Cincinnati Milacron, a manufacturer of plastics-molding machines, formed a team that included employees from purchasing, marketing, inventory, manufacturing, and engineering to build a world-class injection molding machine to compete with the Japanese. Their goals were to lower costs by 40 percent, increase speed and improve operating times by 40 percent, and cut the usual two-year developmental time to nine months. The team talked with customers and examined competitors' machines. Members recorded their work, met weekly, but made key decisions daily in response to problems that arose. They discussed team issues only with team members to ensure cross-functional communication. They learned that their Japanese competitors did not use cheaper parts but assembled parts more sensibly. "Tear down the walls" described the interactions among team members. In the first year of production of the new product, named Vista, the company sold 2.5 times as many machines as it had in the best year of sales of Vista's predecessor.[18]

CHRYSLER. A cross-functional team at Chrysler designed the new Neon, which was intended to compete with well-equipped, low-cost, small Japanese cars.[19] A core group of 150 employees at Chrysler mobilized 600 engineers, almost 300 suppliers, and assembly workers to deliver the new model in 42 weeks, rather than in several years, at a much lower cost than any recent small cars.

Quality Circle *Quality circle* describes a special type of work group composed of five to ten members. The earliest quality circles focused on enhancing the quality of production. In 1985, more than 90 percent of the Fortune 500 companies had some form of quality circles.[20] Today they recommend all types of improvements to the work process, such as cutting costs by changing purchasing practices, redesigning equipment to improve manufacturing efficiency, and reengineering entire sets of work activities.[21] Members of quality circles are typically trained to identify, analyze, and solve problems and may also monitor ongoing work processes or process improvements.[22]

Quality circles have resulted in improved employee satisfaction as well as increased profits through cost savings.[23] But quality circles have also resulted in dysfunctional outcomes, such as an overemphasis on profit rather than corporate growth, lack of effective communication, selection of inappropriate problems to solve, and overestimation of the benefits given the time spent.[24]

CHARACTERISTICS OF EFFECTIVE WORK GROUPS

What characteristics do work groups need to perform well? First, effective work groups typically form because they have common goals and interests. Teams that form merely because of common needs, physical proximity, or even cultural similarity may not be as effective.

Second, an effective group is attractive and cohesive. ***Attractiveness,*** the extent to which individuals want to belong to a group, increases as the group is viewed as more cooperative, has prestige, encourages interaction among group members, is relatively small, and is perceived as successful by others.[25] Group membership can lose its attractiveness if the new members of a work group feel that the group makes unreasonable demands on individuals, if some members dominate the group too often, or if competition exists between members. When a group no longer meets an individual's needs, membership becomes less attractive. As the attractiveness of group membership falls, individuals make less effort to perform well and reach the group's goals.

Cohesive groups, those with a strong interpersonal attraction among group members, demonstrate increased performance, satisfaction, quality of interaction, and goal attainment.[26] Cohesiveness develops most easily in small, homogeneous, and stable groups, although too many changes in membership in a short time hurts cohesion.[27] Workers are often attracted to highly cohesive groups because the groups are highly committed to the task and provide a strong identity for organizational members. As cohesive groups work together they become even more cohesive. While increased cohesiveness can have positive results, in some situations it may result in lowered productivity.

Third, an effective work group has a strong group process.[28] Group members have a shared goal and use the group's resources to accomplish it. The team has mechanisms for encouraging differences of opinion, but can deal with conflicts that might arise. The group treats mistakes as opportunities for learning and improvement and hence encourages creativity and risk taking.

Fourth and finally, high-performing groups increasingly give their workers responsibility for making decisions and managing the group's activities.[29] Group members create a climate of trust in which group members communicate openly and honestly. Effective teams regularly review and evaluate their performance to identify areas for improvement.

THE UNDERPINNINGS OF EFFECTIVE GROUP PERFORMANCE

A group's goals, norms, roles, and structural configuration significantly contribute to its performance. Diagnosing these characteristics of a group is a first step in ensuring that members develop a common focus for their activities, create shared expectations about appropriate behaviors, assume functional roles within the group, and communicate effectively.

WORK-GROUP GOALS

The members of high-performing work groups share goals that focus on performance and facilitate accomplishing the organization's goals. ***Formal goals,*** those that are specifically stated orally or in writing, typically relate directly to the organization's goals and mission or the purpose of its existence. ***Informal goals,*** those implied by the team member's actions but not explicitly stated, can either contribute to or impede organizational goal accomplishment. Agreement about group goals increases the group cohesiveness or bonding.

THERMOS. Team members of a new product development team at Thermos, the manufacturer of Thermos bottles and lunch boxes, included employees from various disciplines and suppliers. The group's goal was to conduct market research and then design a new grill. The team named itself the Lifestyle team, rather than the grill team, to reflect their broader charge; that is, to meet customers' lifestyle needs, not just design a grill.[30]

As noted in Chapter 4, the most effective goals are challenging, specific, measurable, and accepted by group members. For example, "writing 2,000 lines of computer code for a new software update for an accounts receivable module by January 13" is a more specific objective than "updating the product." The specific objective must be sufficiently difficult and accepted by group members to be useful as a focus of group activity. Numerous specific objectives then comprise the group's goal.

Lack of a clear, performance-related goal as the primary focus of the group is a major cause of team failures.[31] Unfortunately, groups frequently lack agreed-upon goals. Instead, the members' individual goals overshadow or make up the group's goal. What if one group member wants to use performance on the project as a springboard to a job in another company? What would happen if one of the team members wants to sabotage the project? Sometimes the goals of individuals do not mesh well with the team's goal. Individuals who want to complete a job quickly, without regard for quality, may sabotage a team goal of high quality.

These individual goals are often referred to as ***hidden agendas,*** goals that individuals hide from the group. These hidden agendas can impede team performance. For example, in the consensus mode at W.L. Gore & Associates, a team member might try to control the team by continuously disagreeing with suggestions counter to his or her own view. Revealing hidden agendas is vital to effective team performance. A well-developed group will develop mechanisms to accomplish this. Group members should realize, however, that in most circumstances they can best achieve their individual goals by helping the group attain its goals.

WORK-GROUP NORMS

Norms refer to the unwritten and informal expectations that guide the behavior of group and organizational members. At W.L. Gore & Associates, norms might include employees' accepting responsibility for making decisions and then following through on them or continuing to act as a sponsor for a person after they begin their first team activities. In other situations, the norms might include little or no worker participation in decision making, a formal work environment of formal dress and formal communications, and a reliance on managers' decision making.

Sometimes norms develop through the interaction of team members as they reinforce certain behaviors and discourage others. For example, if team members encourage participation in agenda setting and decision making from all team members, then involvement becomes a norm. If a first and then a second employee consistently comes to work late, and the team accepts tardiness from these workers, then tardiness may become a norm. Sometimes the initial pattern of behavior becomes a norm. At other times, supervisors or coworkers may explicitly state certain expectations.[32] In other situations, group members transfer behavior from other groups. This behavior then becomes the norm in their present group. For example, group members may bring a "work ethic" from previous jobs, which they then practice in their new job, causing other group members to practice it as well. Alternatively, critical events such as the appointment of a new leader may establish norms.

Types of Norms and their Impact on Performance One classification indicates that norms differ in their importance to organizational functioning.[33] *Pivotal* norms guide behavior essential to the core mission of the organization. Pivotal norms include expectations about attendance, production, involvement in decision making, and acceptance of leadership. *Peripheral* norms guide behaviors that are important but not essential to achieving the organization's goals or mission. Peripheral norms include expectations about dress or social interactions outside the workplace.

A second classification focuses on the amount of a behavior expected. An *unattainable-ideal norm* describes behavior where "more is better."[34] For example, the more sales a salesperson makes the better. A *preferred-value norm* describes behavior where either too much or too little of the behavior elicits disapproval from group members. The workers on a traditional assembly line may disapprove if one worker outshines the others in productivity or if that worker does not produce his or her share. An *attainable-ideal norm* describes behavior where approval occurs for increasing amounts of behavior until an attainable goal is reached; further goal-oriented behavior lacks value. An advertising executive will receive approval for each new campaign idea he or she generates until the client chooses one of the ideas.

Generally a work group's norms facilitate goal accomplishment. Pivotal norms of productivity, participation, and openness contribute to improved group performance. In contrast, violation by employees of peripheral norms, not pivotal norms, typically has fewer negative consequences for the worker and the organization.

Compliance with Norms A group reinforces norms that express its central values, facilitate its survival, help predict the behavior of group members, prevent embarrassing interpersonal problems from arising, and clarify the group's identity.[35] Groups can also apply *sanctions,* coercive measures adopted to encourage agreement and compliance with norms. Sanctions include verbal reprimands or ridicule, formal punishments such as fines or firings, or informal actions such as isolation from the group. Compliance with norms tends to increase as the group's size decreases or as its homogeneity, visibility, or stability increases.[36] Diagnosing a team's norms and its compliance with them helps to explain group performance.

WORK-GROUP ROLES

In effective teams, individuals assume an array of roles, the set of expected behaviors associated with particular work and nonwork functions or positions. We can think of roles in groups as generally falling into three categories: task, maintenance, and individual roles.[37]

1. **Task Roles.** *Task roles* focus on task or goal accomplishment. Think of the work teams at W.L. Gore & Associates. What tasks do they have to accomplish? Each team develops and then manufactures a product. What roles are required to accomplish this task? A worker may act as a coordinator of activities,

seeker or giver of information, evaluator of problem-solving strategies, or implementor of these strategies.

2. **Maintenance Roles.** Roles such as harmonizer, encourager, and gatekeeper help build and maintain group performance. These *maintenance roles* focus less on tasks and more on group processes. For example, these roles may alleviate tension among group members, support individual worker's learning, screen information that enters or leaves the group, or encourage individual contributions and creativity. The person fulfilling the maintenance role of group observer makes a major contribution to the group's effectiveness by monitoring group operations and providing feedback about the quality of team performance.[38]

3. **Individual Roles.** While both task and maintenance roles tend to be functional and constructive, *individual roles* tend to be dysfunctional or destructive to the group, simply because they place individual needs above those of the group. Think of a team or group to which you have belonged that was ineffective. Did one individual try to dominate the group? Did he or she interrupt others and attempt to gain attention? Other individual roles reflect recognition-seeking behavior, resisting group progress, or passively avoiding group activities.

A group member may perform more than one role or several members may perform the same role. Frequently a pattern of roles emerges for each group member. NORDSTROMS. Nordstroms Inc., a Seattle-based retailer, recently created a top-management team of four copresidents. Each copresident had responsibility for a different part of the business. John J. Whitacre focused on shoes, restaurants, and budgeting; Galen Jefferson was in charge of women's wear and merchandise systems; Darrel J. Hume oversaw men's apparel, finance, and store planning; and Raymond A. Johnson handled accessories, kids' clothing, lingerie, legal, and personnel. Although each fulfilled a somewhat different role, they spoke with a single voice about company matters.[39]

STRUCTURAL CONFIGURATION OF WORK GROUPS

The group's *structural configuration,* also called its *communication network,* describes the relatively permanent role interactions in groups. These arrangements reflect the nature of communication among role holders and can contribute to a group's cohesiveness. Figure 5–2 illustrates five such communication patterns or networks. The wheel network has a single person who alone communicates with all others in the work group. The Y (particularly if we invert it) and the chain networks resemble the chain of command in a group. Communication flows up and down a hierarchy, with little skipping of levels or communication outside the hierarchy. The circle resembles the chain except the communication loop is closed. For example, the lowest-level member of a group may have a top manager as a mentor and communicate with him or her. In the completely connected network, all group members regularly communicate with all other members. Additional configurations, such as a star or a barred circle (where two additional points are connected across the circle) represent variations of these.[40]

The structural configurations differ in the way information is exchanged and in the characteristics of the network members. Figure 5–2 summarizes the typical performance of various networks along these dimensions. How do the networks com-

FIGURE 5–2   *Communication networks and their characteristics*

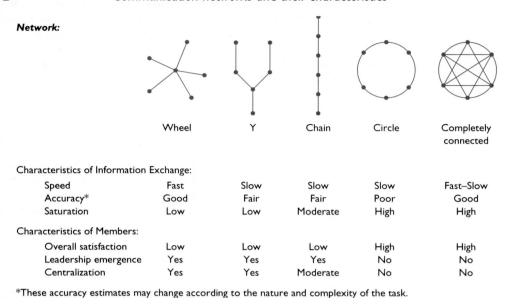

Network:

	Wheel	Y	Chain	Circle	Completely connected
Characteristics of Information Exchange:					
Speed	Fast	Slow	Slow	Slow	Fast–Slow
Accuracy*	Good	Fair	Fair	Poor	Good
Saturation	Low	Low	Moderate	High	High
Characteristics of Members:					
Overall satisfaction	Low	Low	Low	High	High
Leadership emergence	Yes	Yes	Yes	No	No
Centralization	Yes	Yes	Moderate	No	No

*These accuracy estimates may change according to the nature and complexity of the task.

SOURCE: Based on A. Bavelas, Communication patterns in task-oriented groups, *Journal of Accoustical Society of America* 22 (1950): 725–730.

pare in their *speed?* The speed of information exchange and ultimately of problem solving tends to be slowest in the Y, chain, and circle networks, somewhat faster in the completely connected, and fastest in the wheel. In the wheel configuration, for example, information exchange occurs relatively quickly between the center position and peripheral ones. It flows somewhat slower among the spoke positions because the center acts as an intermediary.

The *accuracy* of problem solving by the group, that is, the extent, frequency, and type of mistakes made, depends in part on the nature of the task. In which network is accuracy the greatest? Accuracy of a very complicated task may be greater in a completely connected network because information can be secured from all members of the group. The reverse may be true for a very simple task because the great exchange of information that occurs in the completely connected network may distort the information.

The *saturation* of the network refers to the amount of information passed along the network's segments. In which network is it lowest and highest? Saturation ranges from lowest in the wheel or Y to highest in the circle and completely connected networks. Networks with low saturation tend to have a single, relatively central node that acts as a focus of information and limits the amount of information passed along the rest of the segments. In the highly saturated networks, in contrast, information passes relatively equally through all segments.

Member satisfaction overall seems to be higher in the circle and completely connected networks than in the other three. Why? This satisfaction may be associated with the sharing of leadership responsibility and the decentralized decision making in groups with those structural configurations, as well as the difficulty in isolating group members.

Where in the configurations does *leadership* emerge? It emerges most naturally in central positions of the wheel, Y, and chain networks. Here individuals who hold positions that link with at least two other positions tend to collect more information and hence can exert greater influence over other group members. The existence of centralized decision making in the group, in which a single person has primary responsibility for decision making, resembles the emergence of leadership in the networks.

Of course, a single network cannot precisely describe communication in any group; more often a team uses variants of several networks. Identifying the predominant structural configuration, however, helps us explain or predict the performance and satisfaction of the group and its members and provides a useful diagnostic tool for identifying potential behavior problems. Effectiveness occurs when a fit exists between the network, group member, and task characteristics. Chapters 7 and 13 examine the network approach to interpersonal interactions in greater detail by discussing its application to communication and organizational design.

HOW WORK GROUPS DEVELOP

Work groups change over time, emphasizing different goals, norms, roles, and structural configurations as they develop. Group development has primarily considered only behaviors that occur within the group. More recently, however, an alternate view has looked at the significance of interactions between the group and its environment for group development. In this section we first examine the progressive model and the noncontinuous model, which both consider only interactions within the group. Then we describe a model that focuses primarily on external relationships in tracing group development. We conclude this section with a discussion of the development of self-managed teams.

THE PROGRESSIVE MODEL OF DEVELOPMENT

The traditional view of group development looks at development as a five-step process, as shown in Figure 5–3.[41] Each step involves activities directed both at performing the task *(task activity)* and dealing with the interpersonal interactions within the group *(group process)* needed to accomplish the task. The solid arrows represent typical developmental progression from one stage to the next and within stages. Creating an effective group requires a successful resolution of each stage.

Stage 1: Orientation In the first stage, also known as *forming, orientation to task* occurs. The work group looks at its task and determines the information it needs to perform it. During this stage, the group process of *testing and dependence* helps group members determine what interpersonal behaviors are required to accomplish the group's task. At W.L. Gore & Associates, for example, the orientation stage for a new team might include specifying the tasks to be performed by the team and identifying the roles various team members might play in performing these activities. During the first stage the leader provides structure by conducting regular

FIGURE 5–3

Stages of the progressive model of development

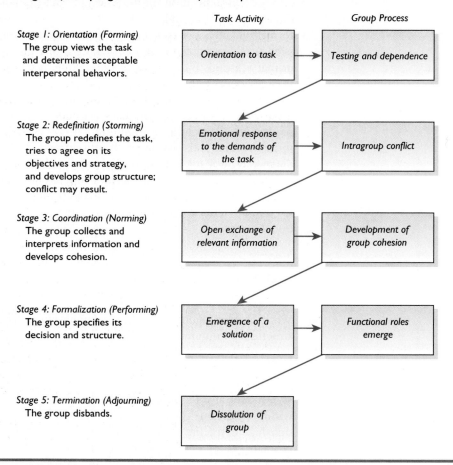

Task Activity   Group Process

Stage 1: Orientation (Forming)
The group views the task and determines acceptable interpersonal behaviors.

Orientation to task → Testing and dependence

Stage 2: Redefinition (Storming)
The group redefines the task, tries to agree on its objectives and strategy, and develops group structure; conflict may result.

Emotional response to the demands of the task → Intragroup conflict

Stage 3: Coordination (Norming)
The group collects and interprets information and develops cohesion.

Open exchange of relevant information → Development of group cohesion

Stage 4: Formalization (Performing)
The group specifies its decision and structure.

Emergence of a solution → Functional roles emerge

Stage 5: Termination (Adjourning)
The group disbands.

Dissolution of group

SOURCES: Based on A.C. Kowitz and T.J. Knutson, *Decision-Making in Small Groups: The Search for Alternatives* (Boston: Allyn and Bacon, 1980); B.W. Tuchman, Developmental sequences in small groups, *Psychological Bulletin* 63 (1965): 384–399; B.W. Tuchman and M.C. Jensen, Stages of small group development revisited, *Group and Organization Studies* 2(1977): 419–427.

meetings, encourages widespread participation of group members, shares relevant information, and encourages team members to ask questions. A group may not progress beyond the first stage if it lacks the skills to screen out irrelevant information and behavior.

Stage 2: Redefinition The group redefines its task in the ***storming*** stage. This redefinition is based on the information acquired during the orientation and the abilities and preferences of the group members. The task activities of this stage focus on team members offering ***emotional responses to the demands of the task.*** They determine whether they like the task as well as their degree of commitment to it.

Disagreements by members of the group in their reactions to the task demands often lead to the group process of ***intragroup conflict.*** Members may differ in the amount of time they will devote to a particular task, the priority they assign to the task, or the means by which they feel it will best be accomplished. The sharper these differences, the greater the intragroup conflict that results. A manager who anticipates differences such as these may be able to reduce the conflict or make it functional for the group.

Because group interaction typically increases, conflict over control among the group's members and with the group's leader may occur. Group members attempt to gain influence; they also test, judge, and evaluate each other. The effective leader at this stage also encourages team members to express their ideas and concerns. At W.L. Gore & Associates, for example, team members may differ in the time they want to devote to specific tasks, the scheduling of responsibilities, and the role of the advisors. Typically at this stage of development the group lacks good mechanisms for dealing with conflict.

GENERAL ELECTRIC. A team of machine operators at General Electric experienced disagreement and conflicts that prevented them from setting clear goals. They had failed to resolve the storming stage and needed to resolve the conflict before they could proceed to the next stage.[42]

Stage 3: Coordination An *open exchange of relevant information* occurs during the *norming* stage. Group members acknowledge that different emotional responses to the task are legitimate. Often this is the longest stage due to the time needed to collect and interpret information and to resolve frequent arguments about the meaning of the data, the nature of the task, and alternative tactics. Ideally, the members resolve their differences after an *open exchange of relevant information and opinions* and begin to act as a cohesive group. Group cohesion typically develops at this stage as the group once again becomes focused on task accomplishment. Members can now voice their disagreements. The leader encourages the team members to openly express their concerns. He or she also assigns challenging problems for the group to solve by consensus and begins to delegate significant amounts of responsibility to team members.

It should be noted that some groups do not complete this stage. Some disintegrate because they cannot resolve the intragroup conflict of the previous stage and group cohesion does not develop.

Stage 4: Formalization The group reaches closure on task performance at this *performing* stage. They may make a final decision or *a solution emerges.* At this stage the team must effectively resolve issues that arose at previous stages of group development, including their various emotional responses to the task, their differing interpretations of relevant information and opinions, and their specific proposals for action. In the group process component of this stage, *functional roles* emerge as a way of problem solving. At this time, the assignment of roles that match both the group's needs for leadership and expertise and the members' abilities and attitudes occurs. Productivity typically results from differentiation and performance of roles appropriate to the group's tasks.

Stage 5: Termination Some groups recycle through the stages of development, particularly as changes in the group's membership, task, or environment occur. For example, as a work team at W.L. Gore & Associates adds new members, the team begins its development anew and often moves more quickly through each stage. Some groups experience instead a fifth or *adjourning* stage. They dissolve because they have accomplished their goals or are unable to do so. Adjourning may mean the dissolution of the group or its reorientation to other tasks and responsibilities.

THE NONCONTINUOUS MODEL OF DEVELOPMENT

More recently, researchers have begun to think about group development differently.[43] Rather than viewing development as a continuous process, they use a noncontinuous model, also known as the ***punctuated equilibrium model,*** to describe it. During the first team meeting the group develops a unique approach to its task. These behaviors and attitudes dominate for half of the scheduled time. During the second half of the schedule, as the deadline looms, the group undergoes a major change. During this transition the group drops its old behavior patterns, adopts new ones, and makes immediate and significant progress toward accomplishing the goal. The image this approach conjures up is what happens to most people when they have a deadline. During the early part of the schedule they do some work, but do not intensely focus. As the deadline approaches, the intensity of their activities increases and they implement the behaviors that result in accomplishing the project.

Figure 5–4 illustrates the noncontinuous model of work-group development. For example, during the first meeting of a student team that was to prepare a detailed case analysis, one member proposed a concrete plan for accomplishing its task, which was opposed by other members of the group. During phase 1, team members continued to argue over the details of the plan. Halfway through the available time, during the transition period, the group chose goals and outlined the case analysis. During phase 2 they worked out the details of the outline and compiled them into a paper.

As part of their development, groups that focus on task-performance, such as special project groups, frequently develop ***habitual routines*** that affect group performance.[44] The routines begin at the start of the project and continue until it is halfway completed. Some routines may be focused on getting the job done or encouraging coordination of activities. Other routines may help maintain the team's energy and spirit. Still others may focus on evaluating and improving team performance. Such routines help groups save time and energy, develop a shared agreement about the situation, and develop a shared plan about proceeding. The routines also foster coordination, free members to focus on nonroutine challenges, contribute to members' confidence in performing their roles, and reduce the likelihood

FIGURE 5–4   *The noncontinuous model of development*

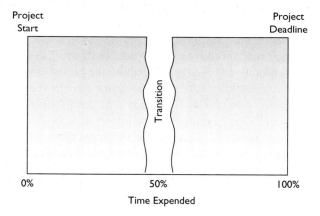

of their being perceived as deviant. Groups, like individuals, can develop bad habits, causing habitual routines to result in reduced performance, decreased innovation, or other undesirable outcomes.

Work teams may import, create, or develop such routines over time. As decision making occurs lower in the organization, workers may develop new routines for agenda setting, task performance, and job sequencing. Obviously, managers may want to encourage certain routines and discourage others to ensure high performance. Changing routines often requires significant attention and effort. The impetus for such a change may occur when groups encounter a novel or changed situation, experience failure, reach a milestone in group life, or cope with a change in the group's structure, task, or authority. Both the timing of the change and the tenacity of the routine will affect the ease with which it can be altered.

EXTERNAL RELATIONS AND GROUP DEVELOPMENT

Recent thinking suggests that models of group development and activities should include external as well as internal relationships.[45] A consideration of external relationships applies particularly well to understanding the development of groups such as product development teams, who interact frequently with individuals outside their work group. The first phase of this model, called the creation phase, involves extensive conversations between group members and people inside and outside the team. Next a transition from recognizing the potential feasibility of a product to committing to a single product idea occurs. Development, the next stage, includes extensive coordination, focusing first on dealing with technical groups internally and then shifting to efforts directed at building and maintaining relationships with other groups. Technology transfer, the second transition, describes the movement from team to organizational ownership of a product. Diffusion and ending, the final stage, sees a significant increase in external activities as the transfer of information and product ownership continues and concludes.

THE DEVELOPMENT OF SELF-MANAGED TEAMS

The transition from conventional to self-directed teams typically occurs in five stages, as shown in Figure 5–5. Each of these stages may incorporate some or all of the stages in the progressive or noncontinuous models, although they have not been explicitly studied in this context.

Start-up begins after initial planning by an executive team. It involves extensive training of all participants. A period of confusion typically follows. Teams may have difficulty adapting to their new roles and may resist the movement to self-directed teams. Managers also may obstruct the change because they perceive (correctly) that their role has been reduced. Persistence during the transition, how-

FIGURE 5–5   *Transition from conventional to self-directed team*

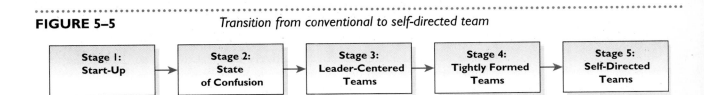

| Stage 1:
Start-Up | Stage 2:
State
of Confusion | Stage 3:
Leader-Centered
Teams | Stage 4:
Tightly Formed
Teams | Stage 5:
Self-Directed
Teams |

ever, typically will result in increasing numbers of converts. Teams often become functional by relying on an internal leader. These *leader-centered teams* usually experience less conflict with their managers and develop functional norms for conducting meetings and accomplishing assignments.

Tightly formed teams evolve from such leader-centered teams. In fact, teams that function effectively at this fourth stage may have difficulty assimilating new members and dealing productively with other teams. The eventual evolution in stage 5 to self-directed teams involves expanding organizational loyalties beyond the narrow team loyalties of stage 4, developing a commitment to both team and organizational goals. Team members continue to acquire new skills, perform new technical tasks, deal effectively with internal customers, improve their support systems, handle administrative responsibilities, and improve the way they do their work, such as the selection and sequencing of tasks to perform. At this stage team members exert significant control over individual performance. Such control can even exceed that provided by a more traditional manager.[46]

STRATEGIES FOR IMPROVING GROUP PERFORMANCE

Managers continually seek and implement strategies for improving work-group performance. Companies may form the wrong kinds of groups, use groups for the wrong purposes, or experience problems in motivating and rewarding groups.

US WEST VERSUS NYNEX. At US West in Duluth, Minnesota, a team of billing clerks offered significant strategies for streamlining the work and then lost their jobs as part of an organizational downsizing, completely negating any trust in top management's commitment to groups in the organization.[47] Faced with a similar situation, Nynex signed a contract that eliminates involuntary layoffs.[48]

Assuming that organizations form the right kinds of teams for the right purposes, strategies for improving group performance often include team building, improving group process, building on the strengths of a diverse work force, and reducing dysfunctional conflict.

IMPLEMENTING TEAM-BUILDING ACTIVITIES

Team-building activities typically begin by collecting data about team functioning using instruments such as the one shown in Figure 5–6. Team members or special observers, called *process observers,* may gather information about the team's communication, decision making, and leadership.[49] They may use specially constructed observation schedules or questionnaires to secure the necessary data or may obtain information about group functioning in less formal ways. For example, at W.L. Gore & Associates, individual team members can observe and document the nature and quality of group interactions.

The next step involves analyzing the data and presenting the results to team members. Often feedback by itself will improve team performance. Team members receive new insights about how effectively they act. Someone outside the team can also help the team develop an agenda for improving its performance. These objective outsiders may coach the group about ways to perform better. Team

FIGURE 5–6   *Team-effectiveness inventory*

Using the scale below, circle the number that corresponds with your assessment of the extent to which each statement is true about your team.

5 = strongly agree, **4** = agree, **3** = neutral, **2** = disagree, **1** = strongly disagree

1. Everyone on my team knows exactly why the team does what it does.	5 4 3 2 1
2. The team leader consistently lets the team members know how we're doing on meeting our customers' expectations.	5 4 3 2 1
3. Everyone on my team has a significant amount of say or influence on decisions that affect his or her job.	5 4 3 2 1
4. If outsiders were to describe the way we communicate within our team, they would use such words as "open," "honest," "timely," and "two-way."	5 4 3 2 1
5. Team members have the skills they need to accomplish their roles within the team.	5 4 3 2 1
6. Everyone on the team knows and understands the team's priorities.	5 4 3 2 1
7. As a team, we work together to set clear, achievable, and appropriate goals.	5 4 3 2 1
8. I would rather have the team decide how to do something rather than have the team leader give step-by-step instructions.	5 4 3 2 1
9. As a team, we are able to work together to solve destructive conflicts rather than ignoring conflicts.	5 4 3 2 1
10. The role each member of the team is expected to play makes sense to the whole team.	5 4 3 2 1
11. The team understands how it fits into the organization.	5 4 3 2 1
12. If my team doesn't reach a goal, I'm more interested in finding out why we have failed to meet the goal than I am in reprimanding the team members.	5 4 3 2 1
13. The team has so much ownership of the work that, if necessary, we would offer to stay late to finish a job.	5 4 3 2 1
14. The team leader encourages every person on the team to be open and honest, even if people have to share information that goes against what the team leader would like to hear.	5 4 3 2 1
15. There is a good match between the capabilities and responsibilities of each person on the team.	5 4 3 2 1
16. Everyone on the team is working toward accomplishing the same thing.	5 4 3 2 1
17. The team has the support and resources it needs to meet customer expectations.	5 4 3 2 1
18. The team knows as much about what's going on in the organization as the team leader does, because the team leader always keep everyone up-to-date.	5 4 3 2 1
19. The team leader believes that everyone on the team has something to contribute—such as knowledge, skills, abilities, and information—that is of value to all.	5 4 3 2 1
20. Team members clearly understand the team's unwritten rules of how to behave within the group.	5 4 3 2 1

(continued)

THE FIVE EFFECTIVENESS AREAS	RATINGS ON NUMBERED INVENTORY ITEMS				TEAM RATINGS
Team Mission	1	6	11	16	
Average of team members' ratings	— +	— +	— +	— =	_____
Team leader's ratings	— +	— +	— +	— =	
Goal Achievement	2	7	12	17	
Average of team members' ratings	— +	— +	— +	— =	_____
Team leader's ratings	— +	— +	— +	— =	
Empowerment	3	8	13	18	
Average of team members' ratings	— +	— +	— +	— =	_____
Team leader's ratings	— +	— +	— +	— =	
Open, Honest Communication	4	9	14	19	
Average of team members' ratings	— +	— +	— +	— =	_____
Team leader's ratings	— +	— +	— +	— =	
Positive Roles and Norms	5	10	15	20	
Average of team members' ratings	— +	— +	— +	— =	_____
Team leader's ratings	— +	— +	— +	— =	
	Total Team-Effectiveness Rating				_____

SOURCE: Reprinted with permission from V.A. Hoevemeyer, How effective is your team, *Training & Development* (September 1993): 68.

members also try to identify factors that facilitate or hinder their performance. Typically this means clarifying their expectations about their own and the team's functioning and focusing on what each person needs to do differently so as to accomplish the team's and organization's goals. This feedback and discussion of results is intended to help the team face their problems, evaluate their behaviors, and identify their challenges for future performance by answering questions such as the following:

What is it like to work here?

What helps or hinders working together?

What is our job and what are our responsibilities?

What are our expectations of our team and each other?

What changes could be made to improve performance?

What does each group member need to do differently?

What can this unit do to work more cooperatively?

How do other teams or work units perceive us and vice versa?

What commitment is each member willing to make to increase our effectiveness?[50]

Teaching team members to use structured decision-making techniques, such as brainstorming, the nominal group technique, the delphi technique, or creative problem solving (see Chapter 6), can improve group decision making. Team members may check perceptions, practice active listening, give feedback, and redesign jobs to increase trust, improve communication, and encourage confrontation of conflict.[51] They may also participate in training programs to learn to become more effective group members.

MICRON TECHNOLOGY. Micron Technology, a computer chip manufacturing company in Boise, Idaho, introduced a 15-hour training class titled "Reaching High Performance" to help orient new employees to the requirements of team activities. Units included joining the company team, participating in groups, gaining responsibility, planning employee development, resolving workplace issues, and dealing with change.[52]

For a group that needs outside resources, support, or information, such as consulting teams or product development teams, focusing only on internal processes may be insufficient or even counterproductive.[53] To be effective, a team must develop constructive ways of interacting with external constituencies. The team can use external strategies such as *informing* (identifying internal processes and then communicating them to others), *parading* (seeking visibility that emphasizes internal team building), and *probing* (interacting with others outside the team to learn about the environment).

Team functioning also improves when team members are empowered; that is, given the authority to make decisions or solve problems without managerial intervention. Creating a culture that supports collaboration is essential. Building trust, in particular, allows members to remain focused on the problem, encourages better communication and coordination, improves the quality of the results of collaboration, and encourages team members to pick up the slack for one another and consequently to improve overall team performance.[54] Finally, implementing a reward system that supports collaboration is critical. Through compensation, praise, or other reinforcers, organizational members must receive a clear message that collaboration is a priority.

IMPROVING GROUP PROCESS

How can team members improve their group's performance? Group members can contribute to better group performance by exerting more effort, bringing sufficient knowledge to the task, and using appropriate strategies for performing the task.[55] Table 5–1 identifies areas that can be altered to improve these conditions. For example, adjusting the group composition will help ensure that the group has sufficient knowledge and skills. Adjusting the organizational reward system should motivate ample effort.

Addressing the underpinnings of team performance—goals, norms, roles, and structural configuration—also improves team functioning. First, managers must try to focus all team members on a common goal. Identifying and dealing with hidden agendas is a first step. Working with group members to articulate specific but challenging goals encourages high performance.

Making sure that norms produce effective group performance is also key. Managers can play a particularly pivotal role in identifying and supporting appropriate

PROCESS CRITERIA OF EFFECTIVENESS	POINTS OF LEVERAGE		
	GROUP STRUCTURE	ORGANIZATIONAL CONTEXT	COACHING AND CONSULTATION
Ample effort	Motivational structure of group task	Organizational reward system	Remedying coordination problems and building group commitment
Sufficient knowledge and skill	Group composition	Organizational education system	Remedying inappropriate "weighting" of member inputs and fostering cross-training
Task-appropriate performance strategies	Group norms that regulate member behavior and foster scanning and planning	Organizational information system	Remedying implementation problems and fostering creativity in strategy development

SOURCE: Reprinted with permission from J.R. Hackman, ed., *Groups That Work (And Those That Don't)* (San Francisco: Jossey-Bass, 1989), p. 13.

norms. They can reward behavior that sets high standards, focuses on goal accomplishment, and supports collaboration. In addition, managers can identify leaders within the work groups who can help facilitate desirable norms.

Finally, managers must ensure that team members are functional in performing task and maintenance roles. The particular roles required may vary in different groups. Unlike traditional work groups, for example, self-managed teams may need more members who assume leadership roles. Using a checklist to tally the nature and frequency of role behaviors and individuals' interactions in a group, an observer can identify the roles played by group members. Figure 5–7 presents an example of such a checklist. Such a diagnosis should precede prescriptions for improving group functioning and effectiveness. After diagnosis, managers can fit the most appropriate individual to each role. Changing the roles of group members might require giving them special training or offering feedback about what roles they perform.

BUILDING ON THE STRENGTHS OF A DIVERSE AND CROSS-CULTURAL WORK FORCE

Diversity of group members with regard to age, sex, race, or ethnic origin can have consequences for group performance. Specifically, group members may have different needs, interests, and goals, as well as bring different experiences and perspectives to the situation. A multicultural team can pose special challenges, since differences in language and culture may exacerbate problems that interfere with high-quality performance. At the same time, diversity can also enrich their performance.

Table 5–2 summarizes the advantages and disadvantages of cultural diversity in groups. Multiculturalism brings diverse perspectives to the organization, resulting in multiple interpretations, greater openness to new ideas, increased flexibility, increased creativity, and improved problem solving skills.[56] Cultural diversity can foster increased creativity, better decisions, and ultimately, improved group effective-

FIGURE 5–7   *Role checklist*

For each team member, place a check beside a role each time he or she performs that role.

TASK-ORIENTED ROLES

_____   Agenda Setter

_____   Analyzer

_____   Coordinator

_____   Evaluator

_____   Information Giver

_____   Information Seeker

_____   Initiator

_____   Other:

MAINTENANCE ROLES

_____   Encourager

_____   Follower

_____   Gatekeeper

_____   Group Observer

_____   Harmonizer

_____   Standard Setter

_____   Other:

INDIVIDUAL ROLES

_____   Avoider

_____   Blocker

_____   Clown

_____   Dominator

_____   Recognition Seeker

_____   Other:

ness, but requires careful conversations to ensure all members are understood. A diverse work team facilitates dealing with a particular country or culture because the team likely has a member who understands the foreign environment and workers. At the same time, the diverse perspectives in a multicultural group may increase the ambiguity, complexity, or confusion in situations because the group may not be able to

Advantages

increased number of perspectives

multiple interpretations likely

greater openness to new ideas

increased flexibility

increased creativity

improved problem solving

improved understanding of foreign employees or customers

Disadvantages

increased ambiguity

increased complexity

increased confusion

increased mistrust

potential miscommunication

difficulty in reaching agreements

difficulty in reconciling diverse perspectives

difficulty in reaching a consensus

decreased group cohesion

reconcile different perspectives and use them constructively. Miscommunication and difficulty in reaching an agreement may result. Diversity can also cause decreased group cohesion due to miscommunication and mistrust, which results in decreased ability to reach decisions, and consequently, decreased effectiveness.

The society in which an organization operates provides a clue to the prevailing cultures that provide the context for team functioning.[57] Consider, for example, the differences between the cultures of the United States and Japan and the implications of these differences for corporate culture. Many U.S. companies reflect a cultural orientation of individualism. Japanese companies typically reflect their culture's collective orientation. Now compare the United States, which emphasizes capitalism, to the Scandinavian cultures, which emphasize socialism. Again, teamwork is more compatible with Scandinavian than U.S. culture. In Arab cultures, personal relationships and trust are primary and might provide yet another different context for team functioning.[58]

A culturally diverse work group's potential for effective or ineffective performance depends on the nature of the group's task, stage of development, and the leader's skill in managing diversity. One study of culturally homogeneous and diverse groups, for example, indicated that homogeneous groups initially scored higher on process and performance effectiveness, but over time both homogeneous and heterogeneous groups improved and eventually demonstrated no significant differences in process or overall performance.[59] We can diagnose the effectiveness of a culturally diverse work group by asking the following:

Do members work together with a common purpose?

Has the team developed a common language or procedure?

Does the team build on what works?

Does the team attempt to specify issues within the limits of the cultural differences involved?

Do the members recognize the impact of their own cultural background on individual and group behavior?

Does the team have fun?[60]

BRITISH PETROLEUM. Forty people representing 13 different nationalities at the European Finance Centre of British Petroleum participated in a two-day workshop to explore culture and cultural differences.[61] The workshop incorporated a variety of team-building exercises, including the development of "multiculture action points," which specified the ground rules for interacting in this cross-cultural environment.

GROUPE BULL. Taking a different approach, Groupe Bull sent 26 executives on a white water rafting trip on the River Spey in Scotland in 1990. The trip served as a metaphor for the way these managers from nine nations would need to collaborate to successfully navigate impending business challenges.[62]

The protocol for building an effective multicultural team often begins with diversity training. In addition, group members should acknowledge cultural differences, while minimizing cultural stereotypes. Managers can use quality feedback to reinforce desirable group behaviors and extinguish undesirable behaviors and attitudes. Using a third party to encourage interpersonal communication can also improve performance.

REDUCING DYSFUNCTIONAL CONFLICT

Some conflict can improve communication and lead to more effective problem solving. Although managers may want to encourage such conflict as a way of building a team, they simultaneously need to minimize the amount of conflict that results in undesirable outcomes. To do this, they can attempt to resolve the conflict directly or change the organization's structure to reduce conflict. Managers can also resolve conflict through negotiations. This formal process of trying to resolve differences can highlight the competitive differences between individuals and reach a solution acceptable to both parties.

ALLINA. Allina, a company that runs 17 nonprofit hospitals in Minnesota, failed to form functioning teams in the 1980s due to the hostile relationship between labor and management. The formation of a team of management and union officials provided the gateway to successful teamwork. The team created an employment center that helped place workers in other Allina hospitals or companies.

This program raised morale and saved the company $8 million in severance costs.[63]

SUMMARY

Self-managed work teams have become increasingly common in organizations and are becoming the prototype for work groups in the future. Work groups form because they have common needs, interests, goals, physical proximity, or cultural similarity. They may be formal or informal work groups, traditionally managed or self-managed, relatively permanent or temporary, and contain individuals from single or multiple disciplines. High-performing teams have a quality group process that results in desirable outcomes.

Effective work teams begin with a shared goal. The group develops norms that set expectations about acceptable behaviors and attitudes for the team. Members of effective teams assume either task or maintenance roles and avoid individual roles. The group's structural configuration describes the relatively permanent pattern of interactions in the group and reflects the exchange of information among members.

A work group's development has been characterized as either progressive or noncontinuous. Recent research has considered the relationship of the group to external constituencies as a key factor in its development. Self-managed teams move through a unique series of stages as they develop.

Managers use four primary strategies to improve group performance. They implement team-building activities, improve group process, build on the strengths of a diverse and cross-cultural work force, and reduce dysfunctional conflict.

DIAGNOSTIC QUESTIONS

We can diagnose the effectiveness of work teams by asking the following questions.

■ Do self-managing work teams exist and are they functional?

■ What other types of work groups exist?

■ How did each work group form?

■ What are the work group's goals and are they congruent with the organization's goals?

■ What are the work group's norms and are they functional?

■ What roles did the work group perform and are they functional?

■ Is the work group's structural configuration appropriate to the task, people, and information-processing needs of the group?

■ How effectively did the work group deal with all stages of development?

■ What strategies does the work group use to improve its effectiveness?

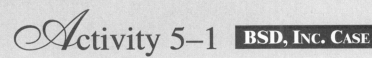

Activity 5–1 — BSD, Inc. Case

The President of BSD sat back in his chair and reflected on his "problem." Lots of his colleagues in the software business would love to have his "problem." It was mid-1988. He had been approached by the managing director of a large European port. The port had a problem. An average of six toxic spills a day were causing pollution concerns he could no longer ignore. The fire in the port last week, which was worsened by the use of inappropriate fire fighting materials, only graphically underlined the reality. "We have no idea what's stored where. We are completely out of control. You must help us."

BSD was a small (less than $20 million) firm with six offices. They developed and installed software for the inventory control of hazardous and toxic materials. The software ran primarily on mid-range computers, though there was a newly developed PC version. "How can we effectively do a job 7,000 miles from home?" the president wondered. "More importantly, did this represent a threat or an opportunity—or both?"

BSD was founded as a spinoff from PRC, a specialty chemical company. Originally, the inventory control software was developed to meet PRC's pollution control needs. Several enterprising individuals recognized the potential for the software in other settings. Initially, they set up a separate division (called the Business Systems Division) and set out to sell the system. The business grew rapidly. The shareholders in PRC, recognizing that capital needs to feed the rapid growth would overwhelm them, spun the division off, retaining a 20 percent equity interest.

Fire districts were the first customers, so BSD focused its efforts on that market exclusively. During the past two years the company had grown from 0 to almost $20 million in sales, with one of the best pretax margins in the industry. Now the opportunity presented itself to more than double in size (the president estimated that the port job was worth at least $25 million) and enter a new growth market. Furthermore, environmental concerns were just beginning to surface. A European national government had recently fallen over spending *too little* on environmental protection. George Bush, in his U.S. presidential campaign, was sounding very "green." It was

hard to pick up a paper and not read about some environmental issue on the front page. The market looked like it was about to take off. But, the downside risks were formidable. How BSD handled its decision to expand illustrates both how empowerment works as a strategic competitive weapon and a unique expansion strategy.

BEFORE THE PORT DECISION

BSD was a uniquely run organization. According to the president it was based upon four assumptions:

1. People want to be responsible for their own performance. They seek out opportunities to be autonomous and in control of their lives.
2. People want to learn and grow. They value opportunities to stretch their current capabilities and learn new ones.
3. People love to win. They will do almost anything to join a winning team—and avoid the losers like the plague.
4. People who are responsible and learning are highly motivated. They will produce results superior in every way—quality, service, quantity, and profitability.

To illustrate his assumptions, the president was fond of telling his favorite "golf" story. "Why," he'd ask, "Would people grouse and complain all week at work (where they get paid well and have the opportunity to do something of value) and then get up early on a Saturday morning, stand in line for several hours, and pay a great deal of money to hit a small white ball into a cup? The answer," he'd offer, "Is that they are responsible for their own performance, they keep learning how to hit the ball better, and they have a real chance to win (and get immediate feedback so they can judge whether they are winning or not). The more we can structure work so that it has the same characteristics as a golf game, the more successful both the enterprise and the people will be." The president set up BSD's systems to structure his company to meet his four assumptions.

Customer-Focused Multidisciplinary Teams

The entire company was organized into customer focused teams as shown in the chart. These teams were

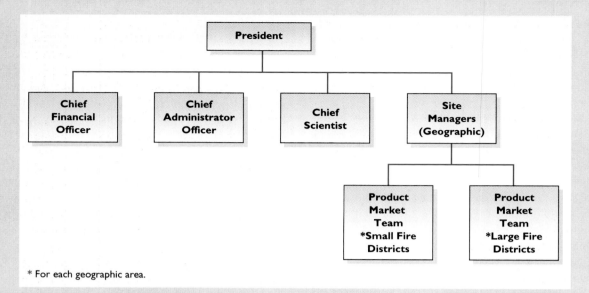

* For each geographic area.

responsible for selling, designing, installing, and supporting their type of customer in their geographic area.

This unique organization structure emerged originally as a historical accident. The first person in BSD was the programmer who designed the original program for PRC. He felt a distinct need to know more about fire districts and how they operated and how fire chiefs thought. So, he first hired a former fire chief. Out of necessity he taught the ex-chief how to program in the fourth-generation language in which the program was written. Much to his pleasant surprise, he found that it took the ex-chief only one month to become operational and three months to reach full capability with the language. After selling the first few systems they needed additional help. The ex-chief recruited several of his former employees and colleagues. They too learned programming skills quickly.

Initially, the team of the programmer and the ex-fire department personnel both sold and installed the system, since they were the only people in the company. The president assumed that that pattern would change as soon as the company grew sufficiently. It is standard in the industry to separate selling from installation on the assumption that salespeople are not good programmers and good programmers are not good salespeople. That assumption wasn't true in the beginning of BSD. Furthermore, it is common to separate downstream support from both selling and installation based on the assumption that it takes different skills to support a system than

it does to sell and install it. That also wasn't true during the start-up of BSD.

BSD began their selling campaign with large fire districts, figuring they had the money to afford the system. Many bought the system in their local geographic area. But, the inevitable happened—they ran out of large fire districts in their geographic area. To sell more they either had to seek out smaller districts within their geographic area, which meant changing their system somewhat, or they had to move into new geographic areas. When the time came to move on to new customers, the former fire department personnel balked. They liked dealing with their current customers (their former colleagues) and didn't want to turn them over to somebody else. They felt a proprietary and personal interest in their customers and wanted to personally assure them that they got the best support possible.

Sensing an opportunity for people to both assume increased responsibility and learn and grow, the president posed the following question to the group: "What can you do to assure that each customer gets the best service, from the best trained person (with all the skills necessary to provide that best service), at the same time assuring that you continue to learn and grow and don't stagnate?" Rather than deciding what to do, the president turned the decision over to the people who had to make the decision work. That one action set the tone for the entire management system in BSD.

The people decided to hire a whole new team to sell to smaller fire districts in their geographic area and hire new people from new geographic areas to sell there. They set up a rotation system within the teams to assure that individuals learned all the skills and set up an internal monitoring system to assure that the skills were current. They assumed responsibility for the training and monitoring themselves—and for assuring superior service to their customers. One of the team members offered to start the new team for the smaller districts and another offered to relocate temporarily to start up a new operation in a new geographic area. He said, "I know several chiefs there who could be our first customers, and I'd bet there are several retired folks up there who'd just love to come work for us."

The team members carried out their decision. New people were hired to seek new markets and each team equipped itself to perform all three activities—selling, installing and supporting—with the same superior level of competence. They set up training programs with local colleges to help in such areas as teamwork and basic programming skills. They took responsibility for their own learning.

By mid-1988, there were 42 people in the company, organized into 12 semiautonomous teams. These teams were responsible for hiring, training, and maintaining the level of service to customers. Most were former fire department officers.

Performance Management System

As the company grew, complaints began to arise about discrepancies in performance. One team servicing large fire districts would make twice the margins of another team servicing large fire districts in another area. Also, difficulties in one area would be relayed to chiefs in other areas and cause embarrassment to BSD employees in those areas.

The president tried several different tactics to deal with the discrepancies—all to no avail. Finally, one day, he realized that this was another opportunity to help people learn and become more responsible. At the next all-employee meeting he asked, "How can we assure consistent high performance across all teams? What can we do to be certain that we are all equally proud of the work of each person in the company?"

The 42 employees wrestled with the problem for a complete day. They felt strongly the need to do "something" without installing a Gestapo mentality and managing by fear. Finally they decided that each team would meet each week and set individual and team goals. The goals would expect responsible action from each member, be measurable, and be driven from the bottom up. These goals would then be entered on the e-mail system for every one to review and comment. Daily progress would be reported on the e-mail system and missed goals would be highlighted in red. Team members agreed to work cooperatively to help other team members (both in their own team and in other teams) to set realistic and stretching goals and then support them in attaining them. The first messages across the e-mail screen indicated that the help and support—as well as the challenge to stretch and grow—were there in great abundance. It was another example where the president used an issue to help people expand their areas of responsibility and learn new skills.

As a result, by mid-1988, each team member input his/her individual and team goals every week, reviewed and commented on others' goals, and reported daily progress. There was constantly a lively e-mail exchange about goals and performance among most people in the company. And, goal attainment averaged over 96 percent every week.

Real-Time Management Information System

The president believed that any effective information system had to meet the following four criteria:

1. Make behavior transparent for all people.
2. Provide real data—not accounting-massaged or sanitized data.
3. Occur in real time.
4. Include customer input.

To bolster the education system, the president guaranteed $200 for each person each year to spend as he or she saw fit on their personal growth and learning. The president guaranteed to match dollar for dollar any additional education expenditures incurred by the employee. Employees took scuba diving lessons, singing lessons, as well as teamwork seminars and advanced programming workshops. Many used their allowances to subscribe to magazines or buy books.

Many other port authorities approached BSD for help. BSD formed additional joint venture partnerships, patterned after their initial successful model. Today, BSD has 54 offices across the globe, 4 of the original offices, and 50 joint ventures stretching from Moscow to Singapore.

STEP 2: Prepare the case for class discussion.

STEP 3: Answer the following questions individually, in small groups, or with the class as a whole, as directed by your instructor.

DESCRIPTION

1. What types of teams existed at BSD?
2. Describe the use of self-managed work teams at BSD.

DIAGNOSIS

3. Were the self-managed work teams effective?
4. What problems existed in the teams' performance?
5. How were these problems addressed?
6. What factors influenced the functioning of the work teams?
7. How effective were the groups' process, considering, in particular, the groups' goals, norms, roles, and structural configurations?
8. How did the teams change over time?
9. Did the teams experience perceptual or attributional problems?
10. Did the groups' experience problems in motivation?
11. How did group process take into account individual differences?

PRESCRIPTION

12. What changes were made at BSD?
13. What was the impact of these changes?
14. What additional changes should be made?

ACTION

15. What issues were considered in implementing changes at BSD?
16. What issues should be considered in the future?

STEP 4: Discussion. In small groups, with the entire class, or in written form, share your answers to the questions above. Then answer the following questions:

1. Were the teams at BSD effective?
2. What symptoms suggested a problem existed?
3. What problems existed?
4. What theories and concepts help explain these problems?
5. How were the problems corrected?
6. What additional changes are necessary?

Reprinted with permission from James A. Belasco, Empowerment as a growth strategy, *Management International Review* 32 (1992): 181–188.

*A*ctivity 5–2   **PAPER TOWER EXERCISE**

STEP 1: Your instructor will organize the class into groups of five to eight people.

STEP 2: Each group will receive one 12-inch stack of newspapers and one roll of masking tape. The groups have twenty minutes to plan a paper tower that will be judged on the basis of three criteria: height, stability, and beauty. No physical work is allowed during the planning period.

STEP 3: Each group has thirty minutes for the actual construction of the paper tower.

STEP 4: Each group should sit near its tower. Your instructor will then direct you to individually examine all the paper towers. Your group must then come to a consensus as to which tower is the winner. A spokesperson from your group should report its decision and the criteria the group used in reaching it.

STEP 5: Discussion. In your small groups, answer the following questions:

1. What percent of the plan did each member of your group contribute?
2. Did your group have a leader? Who? How was he or she chosen?
3. Which of the following best describes your role in the planning session: dominator, facilitator, inventor, design engineer, questioner, clarifier, negativist, humorist, artist? Which describes your role in the building session?

4. How did the group generally respond to the ideas that were expressed?
5. List specific behaviors exhibited during the planning and building session that you felt were helpful to the group.
6. List specific behaviors exhibited during the planning and building session that you felt were dysfunctional to the group.

••

STEP 6: Discussion. With the entire class, answer the following questions:

1. How did the groups' behavior differ?
2. What characterized effective groups?

3. How does your knowledge of group dynamics, specifically norms, roles, goals, and structure, explain your own and other groups' behavior?
4. How could the behavior of the groups be improved?

_____

This exercise is based on The Paper Tower Exercise: Experiencing Leadership and Group Dynamics by Phillip L. Hunsaker and Johanna S. Hunsaker, unpublished manuscript. A brief description is included in *Exchange: The Organizational Behavior Teaching Journal* 4(2) (1979): 49. Reprinted by permission of the authors.

*A*ctivity 5–3   GROUP MEETING AT THE COMMUNITY AGENCY

ADVANCE PREPARATION

Gather role sheets for each character and instructions for observers. Set up a table in front of the room with five chairs around it, arranged in such a way that participants can talk comfortably and have their faces visible to observers. Read the following introduction and cast of characters.

INTRODUCTION

The Community Agency is a role-play exercise of a meeting between the chairman of the board of a social service agency and four of his subordinates. Each character's role is designed to recreate the reality of a business meeting. Each character comes to the meeting with a unique perspective on a major problem facing the agency as well as some personal impressions of the other characters developed over several years of business and social associations.

THE CAST OF CHARACTERS

John Cabot, the chairman, was the principal force behind the formation of the Community Agency, a multiservice agency. The agency employs 50 people, and during its nineteen years of operations has enjoyed better client relations, a better service record, and a better reputation than other local agencies because of a reputation for high-quality service at a moderate cost to funding agencies. Recently, however, competitors have begun to overtake the Community Agency, resulting in declining contracts. John Cabot is expending every possible effort to keep his agency comfortably at the top.

Ron Smith, director of the agency, reports directly to Cabot. He has held this position since he helped Cabot establish the agency nineteen years ago.

Joan Sweet, head of client services, reports to Smith. She has been with the Agency twelve years, having worked before that for HEW as a contracting officer.

Tom Lynch, head community liaison, reports to Joan Sweet. He came to the Community Agency at Sweet's request, having worked with Sweet previously at HEW.

Jane Cox, head case worker, also works for Joan Sweet. Cox was promoted to this position two years ago. Prior to that time, Jane had gone through a year's training program after receiving an MSW from a large urban university.

TODAY'S MEETING

John Cabot has called the meeting with these four managers in order to solve some problems that have developed in meeting service schedules and contract requirements. Cabot must catch a plane to Washington in half an hour; he has an appointment to negotiate a key contract that means a great deal to the future of the Community Agency. He has only 20 minutes to meet with his managers and still catch the plane. Cabot feels that getting the Washington contract is absolutely crucial to the future of the agency.

STEP 1:

1. Five members from the class are selected to roleplay one of the five characters.
2. All other members act as observers.
3. All participants read the introduction and cast of characters.
4. The participants study the roles. All should play their roles without referring to the role sheets.
5. The observers read the instructions for observers.

STEP 2:

1. When everyone is ready, John Cabot enters his office and joins the others at the table, and the scene begins.
2. Allow 20 minutes to complete the meeting. The

meeting is carried to the point of completion unless an argument develops and no progress is evident after 10 or 15 minutes of conflict.

STEP 3: Discussion. In small groups or with the class as a whole answer the following questions.

DESCRIPTION

1. Describe the group's behavior. What did each member say? What did each member do?

DIAGNOSIS

2. Evaluate the effectiveness of the group's performance.
3. What effects did such characteristics as group development, goals, roles, norms, and structural configuration have on its effectiveness?
4. Did any problems exist in leadership, power, motivation, communication, or perception?

PRESCRIPTION

5. How could the group's effectiveness be increased?

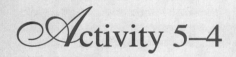

*A*ctivity 5–4 — PACIFIC MINES LIMITED: BRIAN BOYDELL'S LETTER CASE

STEP 1: Read the Pacific Mines Limited case.

As he left the office for the day, Brian Boydell felt pleased with himself. Everything seemed to be going well at last. The eight plant operators were back from Holland and Texas and were now writing training manuals. He felt proud of the way the operators were developing as a team. "I've done my best to be open and above board with them," he thought. "It's been hard work, but I think we finally have the relationship we need to make the team concept work."

PLANT BACKGROUND

As Brian recalled the past year, he remembered how apprehensive and excited he'd been when he accepted his new post in the fall. Pat Irving, project manager, had asked him to join a group of people who were devising a training program for the operators of Pacific Mines Limited's new plant in Carseland. He knew then that he

would be the management person working with the developing operations. Pacific Mines, specializing in ammonia–urea fertilizer production, was opening the new $135 million plant 40 kilometres east of Calgary in September of next year. It was to be highly automated, with a total operating group of eight workers on each of the five shifts, and 20 maintenance people on a day shift. Its capacity would be 430,000 tonnes of ammonia or 475,000 tonnes of urea per year. Initially, the consulting engineers would be responsible for the start-up of the operation, but the operating teams would take over the running of the plant after the plant had been checked out.

The new plant would use a well-known process to produce ammonia and urea. Natural gas fuelstock and nitrogen would be converted into ammonia in a high temperature, high pressure continuous flow process. Ammonia would then be combined with carbon dioxide to produce urea.

The competitive advantages of the new plant would result from the scale of the operation and the efficiency of production. The latter would depend primarily on fine tuning a complex set of interdependent processes and upon the elimination of "downtime"—the period of time when the plant computer was not functioning. Estimates of the cost of downtime were based on the cost of lost production. Contribution per tonne of ammonia was estimated at $150 per tonne. Refining the process would allow for an increase in production tonnage. There was generally no product differentiation and, consequently, the price for ammonia and urea was set as a commodity.

The eight operators would be expected to play an important role in diagnosing problems in the plant and eliminating downtime. In theory, the computer was supposed to run the plant. However, if something did go wrong, it would be up to the operators to take action—from manually adjusting valves and the production flows to shutting down the plant if the automatic controls failed. Plans had been made to have the operators periodically take over control of the plant from the computer in order to sharpen their skills. In a similar plant in Holland, virtually all problems were handled by the computer and operators did not get the chance to control the plant under normal conditions.

TEAM CONCEPT

The new plant was to be run on the basis of "team concept." There were to be no supervisors. Elected, unpaid team representatives would be responsible for voicing concerns, jobs would rotate on a periodic basis, salaries would be based on knowledge and training, not on job position, and there would be training provided in team building.

Pat Irving had really sold Brian on the concepts, saying that the traditional styles of management were passé in the 1980s. Pat was fond of reiterating four questions he'd picked up from some management course at an eastern business school:

1. What are we trying to do?
2. What is my part in it?
3. What is keeping me from doing better?
4. What am I doing about it?

Brian agreed that these questions seemed to keep everyone on track and he agreed with Pat that leaders in an organization should be "first among equals." The new "servant leadership" approach to management, as Pat described it, meant that while those with ability should lead, leadership should become service to others. Under such a system, traditional hierarchies would be eliminated.

The new plant was to be organized without supervisors and Brian sincerely felt that the team was making progress toward self-management. The team concept could only be beneficial to the employees, he mused. Pat had expressed the opinion that the employees had a claim on the business, along with the shareholders, the customers, and the community. If any group was short-changed, it would act to increase its share of return. The team concept was an attempt to give the employees a fair share of the pie.

So far, Brian had been pleased at how well the team building was going. He knew that the training team or "core" team (see Figure 5–8) hadn't met with the operators as often as he would have liked, but everyone was very busy working on the technical side of the new plant. Except for the last few weeks, he'd had frequent contact with the operators. It would be good when Bruce Floyd and the rest of the core team were together in one location. Bruce had been a central figure in the project for several years and frequently was away on technical matters. It would be the end of August before he moved to Calgary.

The first team building session held in Banff last May had produced the *Employee Relations Document* (see Figure 5–9 for excerpts). It had been developed by both the members of the operating team and the core team and expanded on Pat's ideas. "How many drafts did we work through?" Brian asked himself. "Was it four or five? We really put a lot of effort into that document. Thank heavens, the head office in Vancouver approved it." And the organization development people had put on a good program. Normally, he didn't trust those guys. They were too "touchy-feely" for him. The operators had liked the opportunity to work on the issues. During the week they had focused on Pat Irving's four questions as well as engaging in team building exercises. Brian had been worried when only a few of the core team could attend but that did not seem to matter now. The after-hours socializing that week seemed to strengthen the group and make everything more fun (see Figure 5–10 for the training schedule for operators).

One thing did bother Brian slightly. It was four months since they had hired the first eight operators and gone through the team building session and it would be difficult to start again. "The cost alone is scary," thought Brian. "I wish we had some guarantee that things would

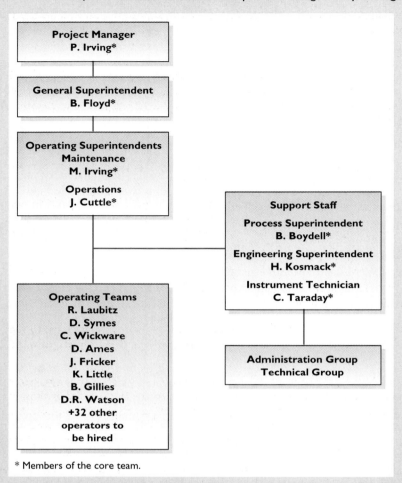

* Members of the core team.

work out. The training is my responsibility, so the $1.5 million program had better pay off. Not using the team concept would have saved us a lot of money and meant that we could have started training later" (see Figure 5–11 for a breakdown of the training costs developed in July of the previous year).

Brian also thought that the operators' trips to Holland and Texas had been a little unnerving. Four operators had traveled overseas for three weeks and four had visited the United States for four weeks to observe plants similar to the new Carseland operation. "I wonder how much they got out of the three weeks there?" Brian reflected. "Three weeks is a long time away from home and we had hoped they wouldn't party so much. It

was surprising that Jim Cuttle and Mike Irving, who also went, hadn't ensured that they work harder. The group doing the instructing didn't seem to help much either." Several of the operators had mentioned that the trip to the States could have been shortened since there was nothing to do at night in Borger, where the Texas plant was located. However, the Texas group had indicated they had learned a lot about ammonia production on the trip.

Brian congratulated himself and the core team on getting the operators involved—they seemed to be caught up in working out the technical details of the new plant. Brian had been pleased when Bill Gillies had asked Craig Taraday, the instrumentation expert, to

GENERAL

Objective

The basic objective of the employee relations system is to ensure safe, highly efficient, and uninterrupted operations with an integrated approach to the management of human resources. The system must respond to the needs, interests, and aspirations of people.

Management Philosophy

The following statement of management philosophy represents the type of environment and relationships for which we are striving:

> Company competitors differ from each other in the degree of creativity and initiative shown by their employees. Each person has an obligation to use all his or her capacities and those of his or her colleagues in contributing to the growth and betterment of the company's operations at Carseland.

Management has an obligation to provide an environment in which each person has freedom to develop and to use all his or her capacities.

Management Style

All levels of management will be expected to operate on a team basis and to support an integrated approach within and among teams, while encouraging personal initiative and responsibility.

A high value will be placed on obtaining sound creative decisions through understanding and agreement by team members. Decision making will take place by those who are close to the source of the problem and have the appropriate know-how. Ideas, opinions, and attitudes of people will be sought out in the continuing process of improving operating and administrative techniques. When conflict arises, every effort will be made to deal with it in an open manner, and to identify and resolve its underlying causes. Emphasis will be placed on developing talent and potential and encouraging, by example, a high degree of effort and participation. Openness, courtesy, and respect will be expected in all interpersonal relationships.

PERSONNEL POLICIES AND PROGRAMS

Organization

The organization will be designed in such a way as to establish a relationship among jobs that promotes flexible, intergrated work teams. This goal will be achieved in the Carseland organization by means of the following:

1. The number of authority levels will be kept at a minimum.

2. All employees will be encouraged to develop their job-related skills.

3. Versatility of operating and maintenance people is considered essential and will be encouraged by such innovations as block training, job rotation, and cross-trades training.

FIGURE 5–10   *Pacific Mines Ltd.: training schedule for operators*

April 1	Hire first eight operators	
April	Introduction to the company	1 week
	Training techniques	1 week
	Team building (Banff Springs Hotel)	1 week
	Ammonia familiarization	1 week
May	Urea familiarization	1 week
	Specialty training—ammonia or urea	
	(four operators for each specialty)	3 weeks
June	Visits to Geleen, Holland and Borger, Texas	3–4 weeks
July	Return home	
	Writing of training and operating manuals begins	
August–September	Writing of training and operating manuals	6–8 weeks
September–October	Begin training other operators	8 weeks

bring in the computer person from head office to talk to the operators. And the operators had liked being a part of the recent recruiting process to hire 18 more operators. They had provided a major source of information since 36 of the 42 applicants were personally known to them. In fact, many operators with steam certification in Alberta knew each other because there were so few in the province. Four of the eight operators hired had come from the same company and knew each other well (see Figure 5–12 for a brief description of the operators).

Brian also believed that the operators' role in decision making was expanding. Doug Ames, one of the eight, had suggested moving everyone from the team room where they had been working to the empty offices upstairs. (The group was sharing the building with the Calgary operators until the Carseland buildings were ready in December.) The team room led to a lot of group cooperation but it was crowded and those operators who were trying to write their manuals were easily disturbed by the others. Brian wondered if too much group interaction was dangerous. He knew that the operators had developed the habit of going drinking together on occasion and was concerned that the group might become socially rather than work oriented.

BRIAN BOYDELL'S PLANS

Brian was aware that he would have to get to work on the new salary schedules. The "pay for knowledge" concept was a good idea but it created difficulty in establishing rates, as there were no comparable jobs. Usually compensation was tied to a particular job. Estimates were of the job's difficulty, its skill and education requirements, and the working conditions involved. A salary would be determined accordingly. Under the "pay for knowledge" plan, an operator was paid for the amount of training and knowledge he or she had, regardless of the job performed. Thus a low-skill job would provide a high salary for a trained individual. This plan increased flexibility, as people could be switched quite easily from one job to another. At the same time, it allowed the operators to earn more money through their own efforts.

"It looks as if we will have to pay more money if we want to hire good people in September," Brian mused, "especially if we hope to get 18 more. Who knows what the pay will be when we hire the final 14 in December? Wages really seem to be getting out of hand. I'll be glad when the October 1 raise comes through. It will make my job of hiring easier. Setting the pay schedule for

January 28

Memorandum

To: Vice President, Pacific Region, Vancouver

From: Manager, Operations

Subject: Appropriation of Preproduction Expenses

This is a request for funds to carry on with preproduction training.

The amount requested is $1.5 million as outlined in my memo of July 24, attached. We are negotiating with the Alberta Department of Manpower and Labour to share this cost. We, therefore, request that $1.5 million be appropriated and $1.0 million be authorized at this time.

A budget is being prepared and monthly control statements will be issued.

P.W. Irving:mb
Enc.

c.c.   B. Floyd
          B. Boydell
          J. Homes
          P.W. Irving

July 24

Memorandum

Subject: Training Costs

It is important that those people who will be operating the new plants receive adequate training. Any operating errors will be extremely costly. The cost of this training should be carried as a separate cost centre to allow proper control.

The operators now involved—Irving, Floyd, Bilborn, Boydell, Hind, and Mintsberg—are not taken into account here. The cost of preproduction training at the plant is also not included in this estimate.

The estimated breakdown is:

For 24 months:

1 Supervisor @ $2400/month	$60,000
Expenses and travel $1500/month	36,000
	$96,000

(continued)

FIGURE 5–11   (continued)

For 21 months:
6 shift supervisors @ $28,000/year $300,000
3 maintenance supervisors @ $26,000/year   136,000
1 assistant supervisor @ $26,000/year   45,000
                                            $481,000

Expenses @ 52% $249,000 $730,000
Total staff $826,000
Air fares   25,000
                                                         $851,000

Purchase of two Carmody trainers (simulators) has been included in the capital estimates.

Programming of trainers $ 10,000

Labour of Murray Williams (trainer)
    4 months @ $2,000/month $ 8,000
Training films, tapes, etc.   10,000

    Total training equipment $28,000

4 junior engineers
    6 months @ $25,000/year $50,000

Operator Training:
10 operators
    1 year @ $20,000/year $200,000

20 operators
    6 months @ $20,000/year $200,000

Steam engineer training $ 30,000

Total operator training $ 430,000

    TOTAL $1,359,000

Unaccounted and contingency   141,000

                                                            $1,500,000

P.W. Irving:ft

c.c.   F.A. Moore, Vancouver
         B. Floyd, Head Office

these operators took from last December until April before we got approval from the head office. I wonder if the reorganization announced last week will speed up the process? Ron Holmes, the new VP, has a reputation of being a hard-nosed but fair and extremely competent manager. He must be, to be where he is at 44. I hope he knows what we're trying to do but I'll bet he doesn't, considering his background at General Coal Company, with its strong union. I guess I'll find out when I meet with him next week on the suggestion that we review salaries three times rather than twice a year."

As Brian left the building, he noticed a car coming toward him. It was one of the operators. Brian was surprised to see him, as most of the operators had been on

FIGURE 5–12   *Pacific Mines Ltd.: operator profiles*

Doug Ames
    Married, two children
    Third-Class Certificate
    District manager of distillery sales for two years
    Operator and shift supervisor of Calgary ammonia plant for seven years
    Plant operator for eleven years
    Hobbies: hockey, golf, curling, fastball
    Member of Fraternal Order of Eagles

Keith Little
    Married, two children
    Second-Class Certificate; St. John's First-Aid Certificate
    Plant operator for five years
    Previous supervisory experience
    Hobbies: ball, golf, curling, swimming

Joe Fricker
    Married, one child
    Second-Class Certificate, SAIT Power Engineering Diploma; one year university
    Operator of two different thermal power electrical generating stations for four
    years
    Hobbies: curling, badminton, mechanics

Dave Symes
    Married, two children
    Second-Class Certificate; one year university
    Operator of ammonia plant for four years, including gas and steam plants
    (Calgary)
    Worked as salesman for Western Canada Steel (summer job)
    Machine operator on railroad tie gang and signal helper for three summers
    Hobbies: tropical fish, astronomy, oil painting, case exploring
    Member of Moose Lodge

Rob Laubitz
    Married, two children
    Third-Class Certificate; Part A, Second Class; NAIT Gas Technology Diploma;
    St. John's First-Aid Certificate
    Operator in steam, and process of sulphur recovery and gas processing plant at
    Okotoks for three years
    Engineering technologist with oil company for three years
    Hobbies: woodworking

Chris Wickware
    Married, two children
    Operator for eight years
    Millwright at Edmonton Steel Mill for five years
    Hobbies: hunting, fishing
    Member of Royal Canadian Legion and Fraternal Order of Eagles
    Union steward for several years

(continued)

FIGURE 5–12   *(continued)*

Don R. Watson
      Married, three children
      Third-Class Certificate; two years university engineering
      Operator of fertilizer plants in Calgary for five years
      Hobbies: skiing, snowshoeing, motorcycling;
      Member of YMCA
      Union president in previous job

Bill Gillies
      Married, two children
      Second-Class Certificate
      Operator and relief shift supervisor in Calgary ammonia plant for ten years
      Operator in Fort Saskatchewan ammonia plant for three years
      Hobbies: hunting, football, carpentry, mechanics
      Member of Western Coop Social Club and Canton Meadows Community
      Association

a writing course at the Southern Alberta Institute of Technology (SAIT). The writing course was designed to help the operators develop the skills needed to write the training and operating manuals and was held at the other end of town. Pat and Brian believed that by having the operators write their own manuals, the final product would be intelligible to other operators and would encourage everyone to be more committed to the project.

When the car pulled up the operator handed Brian two envelopes saying, "I've been delegated to hand these to you." One envelope was addressed to him and the other to Pat Irving. As he read the letter (see Figure 5–13 for a copy of the letter), Brian's feeling of dismay turned to anger: "How could they do this to me? They aren't following the team concept at all! What are they trying to pull off anyway?"

STEP 2: Prepare the case for class discussion.

STEP 3: Answer the following questions individually, in small groups, or with the class as a whole, as directed by your instructor.

DESCRIPTION
  1. What steps occurred in creating the operating team?

  2. What steps did Brian Boydell take to get the team a pay raise?

DIAGNOSIS
  3. What symptoms suggest a problem exists at Pacific Mines Limited?
  4. What problems exist at Pacific Mines Limited?
  5. How do the concepts of goals, norms, roles, and structural configuration explain the team's functioning?
  6. How did the operating team change and develop over time?
  7. Did the team experience perceptual or attributional problems?
  8. Did the team experience problems in motivation?
  9. Was the reward system at Pacific Mines Limited effective?
10. Did group process take into account individual differences?

PRESCRIPTION
11. What changes are necessary at Pacific Mines Limited?
12. How should Brian Boydell solve the salary problem?

ACTION
15. What issues will affect the implementation of these changes?

FIGURE 5–13   *Pacific Mines Ltd.: Brian Boydell's letter*

July 21

Dear Mr. Irving:

During the latter part of June and early July, in response to our earlier request, Brian Boydell indicated the possibility of a July pay raise. However, this morning, Brian indicated that a raise in July would be impossible.

We, of the operator trainer team, respectfully submit this letter of discontent regarding the negative feedback to our requests.

The reasons for the raise are as follows:

1. All of us took wage cuts to come to the company.
2. The cost of living has escalated substantially.
3. We are receiving lower wages than competition staff for similar jobs.
4. We have a desire to maintain a *strong* and *loyal* team.

We also note that a 37.3 hour week has been adopted by numerous companies. We believe that Pacific Mines should not be among the exceptions.

We feel confident that you will give this letter your every consideration.

Sincerely,

The Operating Team
Doug Ames
Chris Wickware
Don R. Watson
Joe Fricker
Dave Symes
Keith Little
Rob Laubitz
Bill Gillies

c.c. Mr. Brian Boydell

STEP 4:   Discussion. In small groups, with the entire class, or in written form, share your answers to the questions above. Then answer the following questions:

1. What symptoms suggested a problem existed?
2. What problems existed?
3. What theories and concepts help explain the problems?
4. How can the problems be corrected?
5. Will the actions likely be effective?

Activity 5–5 · GENERAL WAINWRIGHT

STEP 1: Your instructor will divide the class into groups of six to eight students and assign each student one or two of the following roles: agenda setter, analyzer, evaluator, information giver, information seeker, encourager, gatekeeper, group observer, or harmonizer. During this activity you are to primarily play the role assigned to you by your instructor. Try not to play roles assigned to other group members.

STEP 2: It is 1941, and General "Hawk" Wainwright, Commander of the U.S. Air Force, needs fighter planes. Your team is to produce aircraft according to his top-secret plans (Figure 5–14).

You will be paid for each flight-certified aircraft, but fined for each crash and for each work-in-process plane at the end of the time period.

Production bids are in units of 5 (such as 5, 10, 15, etc.) planes that pass flight certification. A crash is defined as a plane that does not "hit" the wall area designated by the instructor. All crashed planes are unrecoverable.

STEP 3: Your team has five minutes to decide on and submit your aircraft production worksheet for the current production round (see Figure 5–15) or the team is ruled unsuitable for government production. The person assigned the observer role may not engage in production.

STEP 4: When the General says, "Up we go into the wild blue yonder," you have 15 minutes to complete production, including flight certification.

FIGURE 5–14

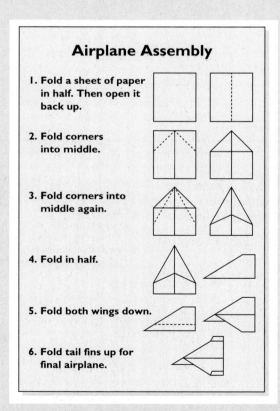

Airplane Assembly

1. **Fold a sheet of paper in half. Then open it back up.**

2. **Fold corners into middle.**

3. **Fold corners into middle again.**

4. **Fold in half.**

5. **Fold both wings down.**

6. **Fold tail fins up for final airplane.**

FIGURE 5–15

Aircraft Production Worksheet

Team #:	Team Observer:		
Team Leader:	Team Timekeeper:		
Categories/Figures	Round #1	Round #2	Round #3
"Bid" production units			
+ Flight certified @ $100 each			
– Work in Process	– $50 each	– $100 each	– $100 each
– Crashes	– $50 each	– $100 each	– $200 each
Profit			

STEP 5: When the General signals the end of the production run, you should calculate your team's profit as directed by your instructor. Your instructor will tell you how many rounds there will be.

STEP 6: Discussion. In small groups or with the entire class, answer the following questions:

1. How effectively did each person "stay in role"?
2. Did the group perform effectively?

3. What changes would have improved the group's performance?

This exercise was adapted and reprinted with permission from Peter Mears and Frank Voehl, *Team Building: A Structured Learning Approach* (Delray Beach, Fla.: St. Lucie Press, 1994.)

Activity 5–6 SUPER ED AND THE FOUR HORSEMEN

STEP 1: Read the following scenario.

Michelle Gray had been working with Ed, a structural engineer, on a graphics application project that involved both the computer department in the information technology division (which she represented) and the infrastructure department in the multicad division (represented by Ed and his four managers) of a large engineering firm whose fame had been built in the glory days of nuclear power. Although Michelle actually worked for the information technology division, she was temporarily assigned to the multicad division. Multicad was a new venture, and one which in her view seemed to have no clear goals, nor development plan. Ed and the four managers (known affectionately as "the Four Horsemen" or "the traveling team") spent more time attending conferences and trolling for new accounts than they did in the office.

Michelle had been frustrated by the lack of effective project management for quite some time, and Ed's decision that she should begin a translation task that she had specifically stated that she was not qualified for nor interested in was her breaking point.

"No!" she raged, "I will not work on that just because you say it is necessary. If you want the task to be a priority, you'll have to make that request through Vic" (her supervisor).

"But you are assigned to support this group and this is something we need done. Besides, if we have this translator, we'll bring in twice the business, so I don't understand what the problem is," came Ed's somewhat puzzled reply.

Twice nothing is still nothing, Michelle thought to herself. The truth was that she did not want to work on this project at all. She was tired of working on a project to which only sporadic attention was paid, and even less attention in terms of planning and management. Ed (known as Super-Ed to those in the department because of his somewhat irritating tendency to overuse one particular adjective!) seemed to think that if the team paid attention to this project once a month, an incredible (or to use Ed's word—super!) project would result. Michelle, on the other hand, felt that they should not continue to drag this project out. It was at the point where they should either commit themselves totally, or abandon the project entirely. Either way, an objective look at the entire project was necessary.

Part of the problem with this particular project was that it was done as a joint study with IBM, so the team was dealing primarily with "funny money," which had few limits placed on it. Whenever Ed's group needed a budget to which to charge time, this particular project received some attention. A meeting would be called, tasks assigned, and a timetable drawn up. Two weeks later, as Michelle diligently worked on her tasks, everyone else would have flitted off to the latest "hot project." This left her incredibly frustrated since many of her tasks depended upon the completion of others' tasks. Her own manager was in a different location, and she often did not see him for days at a time.

In the absence of official management, Ed decided that it was his duty to take charge. The classic "yes man," he constantly assured the team that they would "do well in spite of ourselves," an idea first presented by the first of the four horsemen. Michelle was tired of hearing this phrase, since she believed that they would not do well in spite of themselves, but only because of themselves. She was frustrated not only by this particular project, but by all of her projects with multicad. The story was always the same—a hit-and-run approach to project management. She was left with a list of tasks to complete and a disappearing project manager to help her complete them. To have Ed come in and drop more tasks on her because "they would bring in all kinds of business" frustrated her even more.

STEP 2: Diagnose the situation.

1. What symptoms exist?
2. What problems exist?
3. Is this an effective team?

STEP 3: Individually or in small groups, offer a strategy for building this work group into an effective team.

STEP 4: Discussion. Share your or your group's plan with the entire class. Decide which approach would be most effective and which would be least effective.

This situation is based on a case prepared by Teresa Marzolf as a student at Boston College and is used with her permission.

Activity 5–7   TEAM BEHAVIOR ANALYSIS

STEP 1: Select a team to observe. Justify that it qualifies as a team.

STEP 2: Spend at least five hours observing the team.

STEP 3: Describe the team's behavior. Keep a log of your observations.

STEP 4: Diagnose the team's behavior.

1. Describe its function.
2. Trace its formation and development.
3. Identify its goals, norms, roles, and structure and evaluate them.
4. Diagnose the team's overall effectiveness.

STEP 5: Prescribe a plan for improving the team's effectiveness.

STEP 6: Discussion. In small groups or with the class as a whole, or in writing, share your observations and analyses. Then consider the following questions:

1. What similarities are there among the teams? What differences? Can you develop profiles of types of teams?
2. What do effective teams look like? What do ineffective teams look like?

3. Trace the formation, development, and group dynamics of effective and ineffective teams. Compare and contrast the features of such teams.
4. Identify key elements in plans for increasing team effectiveness.

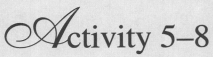 "ASSEMBLY LINE TEAMS ARE BETTER TRAINED AND MORE EFFICIENT"

STEP 1: View the ABC video entitled "Assembly Line Teams Are Better Trained and More Efficient."

STEP 2: You are the manager of a plant that manufactures inexpensive wristwatches. Currently the plant operates a traditional assembly line, in which each employee adds a single component to the product until it is packaged and ready for shipping. Recently, the number of defects in the wristwatches has been increasing. Employee morale also seems to be declining. Based on what you observed in the video and your knowledge of self-managing teams, offer a plan for creating self-managing teams in your plant. Be as specific as possible in your plan.

STEP 3: In small groups or with the entire class, share your plans. Then answer the following questions:

1. What elements do they have in common?
2. How do the teams in your plant compare to those in the video?
3. What would prevent them from being effective?

Chapter 6

Chapter Outline

- Selecting a New Plant Manager at Delta Manufacturing
- Criteria of Decision Effectiveness
    - **Quality**
    - **Timeliness**
    - **Acceptance**
    - **Ethical Appropriateness**
- Types of Managerial Decisions
    - **Programmed Decisions**
    - **Nonprogrammed Decisions**
- The Rational Decision-Making Process
    - **Analyze the Situation**
    - **Set Objectives**
    - **Search for Alternatives**
    - **Evaluate Alternatives**
    - **Make the Decision**
    - **Evaluate the Decision**
- Alternatives to Rational Decision Making
    - **Simon's Bounded Rationality**
    - **Intuitive Decision Making**
    - **Decision Making by Objection**
    - **The Garbage Can Model**
    - **Creative Problem Solving**
- Influences on Decision Making
    - **Individual Versus Group Decision Making**
    - **Decision-Making Skills**
    - **Decision-Making Style**
    - **Cognitive Biases**
    - **Groupthink**
    - **Culture**
- Techniques for Improving Decision Making
    - **Brainstorming**
    - **Nominal Group Technique**
    - **Delphi Technique**
    - **Consensus Mapping**
    - **Electronic Group Decision Making**
- Summary
- Diagnostic Questions
- Activities

Making Better Decisions

After completing the reading and activities in Chapter 6, students will be able to

1. Describe four criteria of an effective decision and evaluate whether a decision is effective.

2. Compare and contrast programmed and nonprogrammed decisions.

3. Identify the steps in a rational decision-making process.

4. Contrast the rational process to four alternative decision-making processes.

5. Compare and contrast individual and group decision making.

6. Show how decision-making skills and decision-making style influence the effectiveness of decisions.

7. Cite three cognitive biases and show how they influence decision making.

8. Define groupthink and describe how it hinders decision-making effectiveness.

9. Describe the challenges different cultures create in making decisions.

10. Offer five techniques for improving decision making.

Selecting a New Plant Manager at Delta Manufacturing

Margo Shaley, director of manufacturing operations, had to make a decision: Who would become general manager for the new manufacturing facility that her company was opening in Manila in three months? She was facing a real dilemma because she did not have the perfect candidate for the job. Should she try to transfer Ted Wofford to Indonesia, recognizing that his wife would also need a professional job placement in Indonesia? Should she promote an Indonesian national working in another Delta manufacturing facility to the general manager position? Should she hire the nephew of one of Delta's top executives, whose résumé had been sitting in her in-box for almost a month with a note to "find him a good job if at all possible"? Should she conduct a full-blown search for the best candidate outside Delta?

Delta, a manufacturer of sports clothing and equipment, had begun an aggressive overseas expansion of its manufacturing facilities in the mid-1980s as a way of cutting costs. Under the direction of Margo's predecessor, the company had opened four plants. Each had taken more than two years to perform at maximum efficiency. When she took her present job, Margo knew that the person she selected for this position would be critical both to the success of the new plant and to her own reputation in the company. Not only must the plant operate at or below budget, but the time required for it to function efficiently had to be cut from two years to less than six months. She believed that the person she hired as the general manager for the plant was critical to its success.

How should Margo Shaley manage the decision-making process? In a global environment managers face a barrage of such decisions every day. The nature of the decisions varies considerably among functional areas and for different levels of managers. Top executives, like Shaley's manager, tend to focus on long-term strategic decisions, such as moving production overseas. Middle-level executives, like Shaley, make decisions about ways to implement these strategies, delegating decisions that have shorter-term consequences to lower-level managers. Nevertheless, all decisions have a significant impact on the organization.

In this chapter we examine the nature of decisions and the decision-making process. We first look at the criteria for assessing the effectiveness of decisions. Next we consider the types of decisions managers and other organizational members make. We continue by tracing the steps in the rational decision-making process. Then we look at alternatives to rational decision making. We next investigate six major influences on decision making. The chapter concludes with a discussion of techniques for improving decision making.

CRITERIA OF DECISION EFFECTIVENESS

How does a manager know that he or she has made a good decision? Its quality, timeliness, acceptance, and ethical appropriateness determine its effectiveness, as illustrated in Figure 6–1.

QUALITY

How do we know that a scheduling decision is of high quality? How do we know that a new product decision is of high quality? A high-quality decision results in the desired outcomes while meeting relevant criteria and constraints. A scheduling decision is of high quality if the work gets done on time within budgetary constraints. The decision to launch a new product is of high quality if its introduction results in increased reputation, profits, or market share for the firm.

A high-quality decision helps an organization accomplish its strategic goals. It likely results in increased profits, service, or performance. A high-quality decision also meets the needs of the organization's stakeholders. It may, for example, improve the working conditions or performance of employees, increase the stock value for stockholders, or facilitate a manager's advancement in the organization.

High-quality decisions do not necessarily require optimizing. *Satisficing,* or selecting a satisfactory or acceptable decision, may be adequate given time, financial, and staffing constraints. An investment decision that ensures an eight-percent return may be as good as one that results in a ten-percent return, particularly if the time, personnel, or other resources required to select the satisfactory solution are less than the resources required to make the optimal decision.

What is the difference between satisficing and simply being lazy or negligent in gathering the information needed to make an effective decision? Researchers have found that managers tend to err in giving too much attention to information that is highly accessible, causes an emotional reaction, is specific to limited situations, or

FIGURE 6–1 *Criteria of effectiveness*

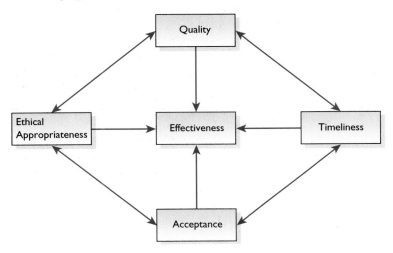

is received most recently.[1] To avoid these errors and make effective use of satisficing, managers need to collect reliable and relevant information and allow sufficient time to use the information once they collect it.

TIMELINESS

Managers should make decisions within an acceptable time frame. What would happen if a professor decided to offer a new course a week after the semester began? What would happen if a plant supervisor changed the vacation schedule after the workers had made their plans for the summer? What would happen if a new spreadsheet product missed its announced date of introduction by six months? Failures to make timely decisions in these situations would result in inefficient use of resources, decreased worker satisfaction, and inability to compete effectively in the marketplace. Even the best decision loses its value when made too late.

ACCEPTANCE

The third criteria of effectiveness focuses on whether those affected by the decision understand it, accept it, and can implement it. Consider the decision to retrain ten workers on new equipment. Worker resistance to this decision may devalue the training effort. In contrast, worker support for the retraining project may increase its impact. Top management increasingly recognizes that it must obtain the support of workers, particularly unions, when implementing significant decisions. German companies, for example, use worker councils to suggest and support changes. U.S. manufacturing plants have introduced cooperative efforts between union and management to implement production decisions. Japanese companies emphasize worker involvement in decision making because they have seen the links between inclusion and performance.[2] Japanese firms prepare workers for such participation by exposing their workers to a broad array of jobs, beginning with low-level positions in the organization and continuing their management development for a dozen years.

Margo Shaley should produce a decision that she and the rest of the company can accept and are willing to use as the basis of further action. For example, transferring an employee from the United States may be a high-quality decision, but the plant workers may oppose the hiring of a non-Philippino executive, crippling the work at the plant.

ETHICAL APPROPRIATENESS

Managers and other decision makers should also evaluate a decision according to how well it meets the criterion of *ethical justness.* Multiple and potentially conflicting stakeholders, interests, and values, as well as ambiguous laws, often give rise to ethical issues.[3]

JOHNSON & JOHNSON. In the mid-1980s, the United States was shocked when people died after taking Tylenol capsules, a popular over-the-counter painkiller. Someone had tampered with the capsules, mixing the painkiller with cyanide, but it was not clear whether the tampering had occurred at the factory or in the stores. Top managers at Johnson & Johnson, the maker of Tylenol, faced a difficult decision. Should they pull millions of dollars of inventory from store shelves and suffer an enormous loss or should they maintain the status quo while authorities investigated? Johnson & Johnson pulled the product in a variety of forms, stating that this was the only choice. The source of the tampering was never discovered, but Johnson & Johnson quickly introduced a number of antitampering measures that have become a standard for the pharmaceutical industry. These measures include tamper-resistant packaging and capsules, and the caplet, which combines the safety of tablets and the convenience of capsules.

CHRYSLER CORPORATION. During a test-drive training session, the washer on the suspension system of one car had broken. Should the company fix the defect, recall only a limited number of the cars, or recall all that had been produced? Lee Iacocca, Chrysler chairman at the time, chose to recall the first 4,000 cars in a new family of cars manufactured in the summer of 1992 because he wanted customers to know that Chrysler had a strong commitment to quality and customer service.[4]

Such ethical considerations should be *de rigeur* in organizations, but often they are not. Consider this dilemma.

> A former product manager for a competitor has just left that company. Now you are interviewing him. He is not the best applicant, but if you press him he would probably tell you about the competitor's plans for the coming year. Should you try to obtain this information? If the applicant gave you confidential information about a former employer, would you hire him?[5]

A person who makes a moral decision must first recognize the moral issue. Will the decision hurt or help others? Second, the decision maker must make a moral judgment. Third, the decision maker must decide to attach greatest priority to moral concerns. Finally he or she must act on the moral concerns of the situation by engaging in moral behavior.[6] Managers and nonmanagerial employees should decide whether their own and others' decisions meet ethical standards before implementing them.

Managers and employees can assess the ethics of their decisions by applying personal moral or societal codes of values, by applying philosophical views of ethical behavior, or by assessing the potential harmful consequences of behaviors to certain constituencies. They might ask questions such as "Would I repel customers by telling them about the decision?" or "Would I prefer to avoid the consequences of this decision?"[7]

The cultural context often affects whether a decision is considered ethical. The evaluation of a specific behavior, such as bribing officials, as ethical or nonethical may vary in different countries. How would you act if you believed that bribing an official was an unethical but common practice in the country in which you worked? In this situation the decision maker can either invoke his or her own personal beliefs or follow the norms of the culture present in the country in which the company is located.

TYPES OF MANAGERIAL DECISIONS

What types of decisions do managers make? They might determine who to hire or fire, where to place a new plant, when to advertise or launch a new product, or how much to budget for R&D. They might determine workers' schedules, identify new equipment to purchase, or specify pay increases for subordinates. Margo Shaley, for example, must decide who to hire as the general manager of the Manila plant. We can classify decisions in a variety of ways, including managerial–nonmanagerial, work–nonwork, formal–informal, routine–nonroutine, or policy–one time. Here we distinguish between programmed and nonprogrammed decisions.

PROGRAMMED DECISIONS

Which union workers will be granted overtime? Which employees will receive larger than average pay raises? Who is eligible for pension benefits? How much money should a recruiting department allocate to print versus nonprint media for advertising new positions? Answering these questions requires a ***programmed decision,*** one in which a specific problem has a relatively structured solution.

Programmed decisions are often based on standard operating procedures that have been tested through past experience. In such cases, programmed decisions involve ***rule following,*** that is, performing tasks by following a well-defined set of rules.[8] Once a decision maker identifies a decision as programmed, he or she next identifies and then applies the appropriate rules or procedures to result in a quality outcome. For example, a retail clerk will handle a product return as a programmed decision if the clerk can answer the following questions affirmatively: Does the customer have a receipt? Has the product been purchased within the time limits for returns? Are the store's price tags still on the product? Is the product price the same as when purchased? Is the original packaging intact?

As an alternative, employees can use ***rules of thumb*** or have ***heuristics*** to make programmed decisions whenever they have significant experience with similar decision-making situations. If, for example, the answer to any of the questions about the product return is "no," the clerk could then use a rule of thumb to handle what is still a programmed decision.

NONPROGRAMMED DECISIONS

Which new products should a high-technology company develop? Should the company introduce expanded family-related benefits? Which computer hardware and software should the company purchase to support the marketing function? How can the company change the corporate culture? Answering such questions requires making ***nonprogrammed decisions,*** decisions that cannot be handled by standard policies and rules. Margo Shaley's decision about whom to hire as general manager can be considered a nonprogrammed decision because there are no rules or policies to guide her decision.

Because nonprogrammed decisions are relatively unstructured and often unique, they require special treatment. They typically call for innovative solutions or unusual applications of existing rules of thumb or policies. These nonprogrammed decisions can pose significant challenges for managers, who must go beyond their repertoire of experience to find good solutions. Making nonprogrammed decisions often requires time, expertise, and creativity because the decision maker is breaking new ground. To further complicate matters, decisions that may be programmed in one situation may be nonprogrammed in others. For example, the budget for advertising job openings may be a programmed decision in a large company that has a historical record of successful recruiting for its open positions. When the company first embarks on recruitment advertising, has unusual difficulty filling positions, or markedly changes its recruitment strategy, the same problem may require a nonprogrammed decision. Nonprogrammed decisions call for a manager to verify first that the problem lacks both structure and a ready solution and then to apply a high-quality decision-making technique. One of the most popular decision-making techniques is the rational decision-making process.

THE RATIONAL DECISION-MAKING PROCESS

Using a systematic or *rational* process for making either programmed or nonprogrammed decisions should increase their effectiveness. In many situations this type of step-by-step decision-making process increases the likelihood that a high-quality, accepted, and ethical decision will result.[9] Consider the decision that Margo Shaley must make at Delta Products. She can proceed to a solution by performing the six steps shown in Figure 6–2. Analyze the situation, set objectives, search for alternatives, evaluate the alternatives, make the decision, and evaluate the decision.

ANALYZE THE SITUATION

The decision maker should begin by determining the key elements in the situation, including a recognition of a problem to be solved or decision to be made, followed by the exploration and classification of the decision situation.[10] Who are the important individuals and groups involved and affected? What organizational characteristics affect the decision? How does the environment influence the outcomes? How would Margo Shaley answer these questions? Clearly her selection decision involves the potential candidates as well as their eventual superiors, peers, and subordinates. The decision also depends on the relationship of the new plant to existing plants and to other organizational entities. The location of the plant in the Philippines also affects her decision. She must assess each aspect of the situation.

Next the decision maker identifies the situation's constraints and their effect on the decision. These constraints include the laws that affect employment both in the United States and the Philippines, the location of the new plant, characteristics of the general manager position, the nature of the available labor pool, and the time available for selecting the new manager.

Closely related to the constraints are the resources available. Margo Shaley should know the financial, time, staff, and material resources that affect the decision. While the available resources can act as a constraint, they can also be used, later on, to evaluate alternatives. For example, some alternatives may incur higher costs than others. From this situational analysis, the decision maker begins to formulate the issues to be addressed.

Ineffective decisions can result when decision makers fail to analyze the situation completely. They may not identify all the environmental influences, they may incorrectly assess the organizational resources required, or they may misconstrue individual preferences and abilities.

SET OBJECTIVES

In the rational process, the decision maker next identifies the goals and objectives that the decision must accomplish, as well as the criteria that will be used to assess its effectiveness. The way a decision maker frames the problem affects the ultimate

FIGURE 6–2   *The six-step decision-making process*

Analyze the Situation

What are the key elements of the situation?
What constraints affect the decision?
What resources are available?

Set Objectives

Is the problem stated clearly?
Do group members understand what they will work on?
By what criteria will decision making be judged?

Search for Alternatives

Are those individuals most involved in the problem also
   involved in the decision making?
Has complete information been sought? Are information
   holders involved in the decision making?
Is a diversity of means used to generate ideas?
Are all ideas encouraged, regardless of their content?

Evaluate the Alternatives

Do participants recognize that the process has switched to
   evaluation?
Are criteria for assessment clearly specified and understood
   by group members?
Are differences of opinion included in the evaluation?
Are some alternatives pilot tested?

Make the Decision

Are group members clear that selection is occurring?
Are they aware if they are satisficing or optimizing?
Are action plans made to fit with the decision?
Are the group members commited to the decision?

Evaluate the Decision

Are responsibilities for data collection, analysis, and reporting
   clearly assigned?
Does a comprehensive evaluation plan exist?
Does an evaluation schedule exist?

solution. Does a manager view a problem as cost cutting or revenue maximizing? Does he or she view it as a performance problem or a working condition problem?

Errors at this stage ultimately reduce the quality of the decision, yet identifying and correcting them may be difficult.[11] The decision maker needs to carefully identify the goals and objectives that the decision must accomplish and specify the criteria that will be used to assess its quality, timeliness, acceptance, and ethical appropriateness. Table 6–1 lists a set of such criteria. For example, Margo might focus on the goal of selecting a new general manager who can have the new plant functioning effectively within three months. A subobjective might be to identify only potential job holders who have previous experience in general management positions. A university president might set a goal of increasing student enrollment by ten percent. A marketing specialist might set a goal of reducing advertising costs by

TABLE 6–1 *Set of criteria for evaluating objectives*

1. *Relevance.* Are the objectives related to and supportive of the basic purposes of the organization?

2. *Practicality.* Do the objectives recognize obvious constraints?

3. *Challenge.* Do the objectives provide a challenge for managers at all levels in the organization?

4. *Measurability.* Can the objectives be quantified, if only in an order-of-importance ranking?

5. *Schedulability.* Can the objectives be scheduled and monitored at interim points to ensure progress toward their attainment?

6. *Balance.* Do the objectives provide for a proportional emphasis on all activities and keep the strengths and weaknesses of the organization in proper balance?

7. *Flexibility.* Are the objectives sufficiently flexible or is the organization likely to find itself locked into a particular course of action?

8. *Timeliness.* Given the environment within which the organization operates, is this the proper time to adopt these objectives?

9. *State of the art.* Do the objectives fall within the boundaries of current technological development?

10. *Growth.* Do the objectives point toward the growth of the organization, rather than toward mere survival?

11. *Cost effectiveness.* Are the objectives cost effective in that the anticipated benefits clearly exceed the expected costs?

12. *Accountability.* Are the assignments for the attainment of the objectives made in a way that permits the assessment of performance on the part of individual managers throughout the organization?

SOURCE: E. Frank Harrison, *The Managerial Decision Making Process,* 3rd ed. (Boston: Houghton Mifflin, 1987), p. 41. Copyright © 1987 by Houghton Mifflin Company. Reprinted with permission.

$10,000 without decreasing the advertising's effectiveness. The accomplishment of these and similarly set goals serves as one measure of the effectiveness of the decision and the decision-making process.

When possible, the objectives should state observable and measurable results. Some objectives, such as reducing absenteeism or increasing profits by a specified percentage or amount, are clearly observable and measurable. The goals of introducing new products or eliminating other product lines are also observable and measurable. Objectives related to employee attitudes such as satisfaction, commitment, or involvement, or the effectiveness of work processes are more difficult to observe and measure. In such cases, the decision maker will need to be skillful in crafting goals. For example, the decision maker might decide that absenteeism and turnover both reflect employee satisfaction. Thus, in setting a goal to *increase* employee satisfaction by a certain percent, the decision maker will set an objective to *reduce* absenteeism and turnover by the same percent.

Decision makers should not confuse objectives with the action steps needed to accomplish them. Setting goals should precede determining a plan and implementing it. For example, a plan to advertise in national newspapers is a means of accomplishing the goal of selecting a highly competent general manager.

SEARCH FOR ALTERNATIVES

The decision maker next identifies a set of realistic and potentially acceptable solutions to the problem or ways of accomplishing the stated objectives. These alternatives should achieve the decision objective without producing undesirable consequences. For example, Margo Shaley has at least four alternatives that likely will result in a satisfactory candidate—transferring Ted Wofford, promoting the Indonesian national, hiring the executive's nephew, or conducting a full-blown search.

Decision makers should use a variety of techniques to identify an array of alternatives. This stage should emphasize the generation of ideas, not their evaluation. (Techniques for improving the generation of alternatives are described later in this chapter.) Decision makers may err at this stage by not using information they have gathered, ignoring additional information they have requested, looking for information to support decisions after a decision has been made, and gathering irrelevant information.[12]

EVALUATE ALTERNATIVES

Now the decision maker evaluates each alternative in terms of whether it will result in a quality decision. The decision maker determines each alternative's feasibility, cost, and potential benefits, as well as the risks and potential consequences involved in implementing the alternative. For example, Margo should assess whether transferring Ted Wofford, hiring the executive's nephew, or reopening the search will result in a quality decision. Can you evaluate Margo's alternatives in terms of cost, feasibility, and possible adverse consequences? Table 6–2 provides such an assessment. We can see that the alternatives differ on these and probably other dimensions.

Managers need to use a systematic procedure for evaluating alternatives. One alternative is to use quantitative techniques such as linear programming or regression analysis. Quantifying the alternatives, even in less sophisticated ways, can sys-

TABLE 6–2 *Evaluation of alternatives open to Margo Shaley*

| | SELECTED DECISION CRITERIA | | | |
ALTERNATIVE	COST IN $	FEASIBILITY	LIKELIHOOD OF ADVERSE CONSEQUENCES	RELATIVE PROBABILITY OF SUCCESS IN SOLVING PROBLEM
Transfer Ted Wofford	moderate	moderate	low	high
Promote Indonesian national	low	high	moderate	moderate
Hire executive's nephew	low	moderate-high	moderate-high	low
Conduct a search	high	moderate	low	moderate-high

tematize their evaluation, dramatize differences among them, and even improve the quality of decision making. For example, Margo Shaley might score each of the four alternatives on their feasibility, cost, potentially adverse consequences, and probability of success. Summing the scores for each alternative would let her place them in rank order and ultimately select the highest ranked alternative. The process assumes that the criteria are equally weighted, that the numerical values are relatively exact, and that ranks alone are sufficient to provide the best choice. More commonly, however, decision makers use a qualitative rather than quantitative evaluation of alternatives.

MAKE THE DECISION

Ideally the decision maker chooses the alternative that best meets his or her objective within the constraints of the situation. Sometimes, as we noted earlier, the decision maker satisfices, that is, chooses a satisfactory decision because the costs involved in securing the optimal decision are too high. At other times, decision makers become committed to poor alternatives and cannot halt the course of action. Decision makers escalate their commitment to a decision when they feel responsible for their actions and the actions' consequences and these actions have consequences that cannot be changed. Also, commitment is increased when the decision makers believe poor performance reflects their own not the system's abilities and they act in public not private.[13]

WANG COMPUTERS. An Wang, the former CEO of Wang Computers became increasingly committed to remaining in the minicomputer market, rather than moving into the rapidly growing microcomputer market. His intense commitment to this decision eventually led to disastrous consequences for the company.[14]

EVALUATE THE DECISION

Too often, selecting an alternative and reaching a decision comprise the final step. However, before the decision is finalized the decision maker should review it as well as the decision-making process. This allows the decision maker a final opportunity to reassess the situation, adjust the objectives, and ensure that sufficient alternatives were examined. The decision maker can assess the likely outcomes of the decision and compare them to objectives set earlier. Once Margo Shaley decides whom to select for the general manager position, for example, she should review the steps that led to that decision, even verifying her approach with another person. Evaluation done *before* a decision is implemented is part of the decision-making process. Evaluation performed *after* implementation is part of management control and may call for corrective action and follow-up.

ALTERNATIVES TO RATIONAL DECISION MAKING

As the decisions managers make have become more complex, the rational approach to decision making has been viewed as less than adequate. For example, decision makers may be unable to completely analyze the situation. Or, they may have difficulty in generating a complete, high-quality set of alternatives. Assessing the quality of each alternative may be impossible. Finding the best alternative as required by the rational model may be unrealistic and inefficient given the realities of opposing stakeholders, limited information, time and cost constraints, communication failures, legal precedents, or perceptual limitations.[15] As a result, researchers have proposed a number of models to explain how decisions are made in these "real-world" circumstances.

SIMON'S BOUNDED RATIONALITY

Herbert Simon, a Nobel prize winner and early critic of the rational model, offered a decision-making model to address these criticisms.[16] Simon called his model "bounded rationality," because he felt the rational decision-making process was limited by such real-world considerations as a decision maker's inability to secure and process complete information relevant to the decision. In his model the decision maker first scans the environment for conditions that call for a decision. Margo Shaley operates at the *intelligence* stage when she learns that top management had agreed to build the Manila plant and has assigned her responsibility for staffing it. The decision maker next *designs* possible solutions to the problem by developing and analyzing possible courses of action. Finally, the decision maker *chooses* among the available alternatives. According to Simon, individuals *satisfice* because their attention, memory, comprehension, and communication are limited, which in turn limits their ability to process the information needed to reach an optimal solution.[17]

Simon's model emphasizes the generation of a reasonable number of alternatives that will produce a satisfactory decision, rather than the more exhaustive process of creating and evaluating a complete array of alternatives that will produce an optimal decision. In searching for a site for a new supermarket, the vice president for real estate acquisition of a large supermarket chain may evaluate only three or four satisfactory options. Seeking the perfect site, an optimal decision, may take too much time and too many staff resources and result in little or no added advantage.

MERCK PHARMACEUTICALS. Merck's finance department built a computerized economic model to analyze its proposed $6.6 billion acquisition of Medco, a mail-order pharmaceutical company.[18] This model examined various scenarios and could test the success of the merger under various conditions. The model could identify a set of reasonable alternatives for making a satisfactory decision, one that satisfied the constraints of the situation.

INTUITIVE DECISION MAKING

Some researchers argue that managers should completely replace the rational approach with *intuitive* decision making. Intuition has been conceptualized as a personality trait, an unconscious process, a set of observable behaviors, and as the distillation of years of experience making the same decision.[19]

In normal circumstances, intuitive decision making involves the use of a *compatibility test* to assess alternatives.[20] Using this test, which requires little control and cognitive processing, the decision maker compares each alternative to a set of standards, such as values, morals, beliefs, goals, and plans called *images.* Intuitive decision making results in decisions faster than rational decision making, uses the same or less information, but may not result in as high a quality decision.[21]

DECISION MAKING BY OBJECTION

This model assumes that decision makers seek a least-objectionable course of action, one that does not have a high probability of making matters worse.[22] In choosing between two reading programs, curriculum specialists in a public school system ideally would want a program that improves students' skills. Due to time constraints in making the decision, however, they might select the one that at least will not make students' performance worse.

According to this model, decision makers first produce a rough description of an acceptable resolution of the situation. Next they propose a course of action, accompanied by a description of the positive outcomes of the action. Objections to the action are raised, further delimiting the problem and defining an acceptable resolution. The decision makers repeat this process, creating a series of courses of action, each one having fewer objections than the previous one. Margo Shaley, for example, might choose to focus first on a single course of action, such as transferring Ted Wofford, decide whether it is objectionable, and if necessary offer other alternatives until she finds one that raises the least objections.

THE GARBAGE CAN MODEL

In an organization with unclear goals, uncertain means of achieving the goals, and changing participants in decision making, a diverse set of problems and solutions often present themselves simultaneously. Recognizing the complex and unsystematic quality of decision making that occurs in a variety of organizational circumstances, such as budget development and promotion decisions, the garbage can model uses the image of a garbage can to describe the serendipitous pairing of seemingly unrelated problems and solutions.[23]

Figure 6–3 illustrates this pictorially. If compatible problems and solutions arise at the time a decision is needed, a decision occurs. Otherwise, no decision re-

FIGURE 6–3 *Garbage can model of decision making*

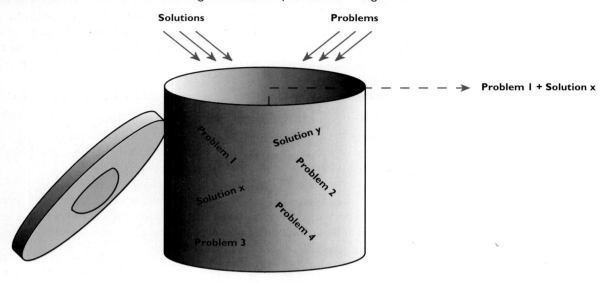

sults.[24] Quality decisions only occur when the stream of solutions coincides with the stream of problems and when the decision maker is alert to the opportunities for matching problems and solutions.[25] For example, Margo Shaley might interview a candidate who is **not** appropriate for the Manila position. However, this candidate **can** fill another vacant position in the company. Thus, the solution to one problem can be used to solve another problem, removing both a problem and a solution from the garbage can.

When individuals focus on a significant problem, they can often make a decision about a less significant problem. Margo Shaley may decide about allocating parking spaces in the new plant as she tries to choose the new plant manager. Conversely, solving a new problem may result in the solution of a previously unsolved problem. In making the selection decision, for example, Margo Shaley may need to rethink the way work will be done in the new plant and thereby, as an unintended consequence of the decision, improve the plant's functioning.

CREATIVE PROBLEM SOLVING

Rather than focusing on the rational decision-making process, decision makers can treat decision making as an exercise in creative problem solving. In this approach, decision makers focus almost exclusively on generating a wide array of creative alternatives, as well as restructuring the problem by viewing it in new ways. Creative problem solving attempts to change traditional patterns of thinking. Rather than thinking of a glass as half empty, the creative problem solver thinks of the glass as being half full.

HEWLETT-PACKARD. Hewlett-Packard allows engineers to spend one-tenth of their work time exploring projects outside their regular work requirements. They also can use the company's machine shop for personal projects during weekends. Both of these practices are designed to encourage creativity.[26]

In this model, individuals suspend judgment about an alternative. This typically results in more careful exploration of possibilities. Individuals can also delay judgment about the relevance of information to the decision being considered and the validity of an idea for themselves or others. Doing this allows ideas to survive longer and spawns other ideas. It also motivates other people to offer ideas they normally would reject and may result in the development of a new, more useful frame of reference for assessing them.[27] Brainstorming, described later in this chapter, is another related technique that results in more creative decision making.

Individuals can use a variety of techniques to encourage their creative thinking. First, they can use alternative thinking languages, such as expressing a problem in mathematical rather than verbal language or using visual models rather than verbal expressions of a problem. For example, we might suggest that Margo Shaley express her alternatives graphically, in the form of a decision tree. Decision makers might also make lists as a way of increasing their ability to process the information gained.

Creative decision makers can also develop a questioning attitude. Creative decision makers repeatedly challenge their assumptions. For example, Margo Shaley or any of her colleagues might repeatedly ask the question "why" about information gathered. Other individuals or group members might take a *devil's advocate approach,* in which they challenge assumptions and alternatives. Creating analogies, reversing situations, and breaking alternatives into their component parts also foster more creative decision making. These techniques reduce the perceptual, emotional, cultural, environmental, intellectual, and expressive blocks that hinder effective decision making.[28]

Failure to think of creative alternatives and solutions can result from a variety of circumstances.[29] Individuals may argue about, misunderstand, disagree with, or challenge new ideas. They may point out only the flaws in a different perspective. They may not listen well or they may fail to provide feedback about possibilities. They may act critically, disapprovingly, or judgmentally about new ideas.

INFLUENCES ON DECISION MAKING

Why do managers make bad decisions? In some situations we can attribute ineffective decision making to a poor decision-making process. In other situations the manager may lack the information, skills, or experience to make a quality decision. Managers who function in a global environment face great challenges in making effective decisions because of the complexity, uncertainty, and diversity they face. Diagnosing influences on decision making is a key step in improving its effectiveness. In this section we look at the following influences on decision making: an individual versus a group making the decision, the decision maker's skills, decision-making style, cognitive biases, groupthink, and culture.

INDIVIDUAL VERSUS GROUP DECISION MAKING

Managers often have to choose between using individuals or groups to make decisions. Both strategies have advantages and disadvantages. We will first discuss the advantages and disadvantages of group decision making. Then we will discuss some guidelines to use in choosing group decision making.

Advantages and Disadvantages The advantages of group decision making include the synergy created, the potential creativity that results, and the increased likelihood of acceptance of the decision. Disadvantages include the longer time frame required, the likelihood of more extreme decisions, and the ignoring of individual expertise.

Advantage: Synergy. Group decisions tend to create a synergy that combines and improves on the knowledge of the group members to make decisions of higher quality than the sum of individual decisions. This synergy results when each individual brings additional knowledge and skills to the decision.[30]

Advantage: Creativity. Increasing the group's attitudinal, behavioral, and cultural diversity helps it become innovative in dealing with difficult, discretionary tasks. The value of diversity decreases for groups that work on simple, repetitive, and routine tasks.[31]

Advantage: Acceptance. Because group decision making reflects a consensus, it more readily leads to acceptance of the decision than does individual decision making.

Disadvantage: A Longer Time Frame. Groups generally need more time to make decisions than individuals, since the group has to exchange information among many individuals and obtain a consensus. As a result, groups may try to save time or achieve consensus by satisficing, rather than by seeking an optimal solution.

Disadvantage: More Extreme Decisions. Early research suggested that groups tend to make riskier decisions than individuals.[32] Because no single person shoulders the consequences of a decision made by a group, individuals may feel less accountable and will accept more risky or extreme solutions. More recent research explains this phenomenon differently. It suggests that groups actually make decisions much closer to their initial predominant view, often a relatively extreme position; this may make the decisions appear risky because they are less likely to be a middle ground or compromise position.[33]

Disadvantage: Individual Expertise Ignored. Groups may ignore individual expertise, opting instead for group consensus. As a member of a group of peers, an individual may be particularly reluctant to discriminate among individuals on the basis of their expertise. Groups then may develop an inability to critically evaluate their decisions or decision-making process. When group members choose a colleague's solution that they consider to be good, however, the resulting decision equals the quality of a decision obtained by group decision making and is no riskier than a group decision.[34] But the effectiveness of such a **best-member strategy** depends on the probability that the group will select the real best member and on the potential for subjectivity in the solution.[35] Even then, recent research suggests that many groups can perform better than the most knowledgeable member acting alone.[36]

Circumstances Favoring Group Decision Making How should Margo Shaley decide whether to select the new general manager herself or convene a team of managers to make the selection? In deciding whether to use a group or individual decision-making process, decision makers should evaluate the type of problem, the importance of having the decision accepted, the desired solution quality, individual characteristics, the organizational culture, and the time available. Table 6–3 describes the circumstances that favor group or individual decision making.

TABLE 6–3   *Factors that favor group or individual decision making*

FACTOR	GROUP	INDIVIDUAL
Type of problem or task	When diverse knowledge and skills are required	When efficiency is desired
Acceptance of decision	When acceptance by group members is valued	When acceptance is not important
Quality of the solution	When the input of several group members can improve the solution	When a "best member" can be identified
Characteristics of individuals	When group members have experience working together	When individuals cannot collaborate
Organizational culture	When the culture supports group problem solving	When the culture is competitive
Amount of time available	When relatively more time is available	When relatively little time is available

■ *Type of Problem or Task.* Group decision making is superior when a task or problem requires a variety of expertise, when problems have multiple parts that can be addressed by a division of labor, and when problems require estimates because the diverse expertise and experience available results in improved information and better decisions. Individual decision making results in more efficiency in situations where policy dictates the correct solution. Individual decision making also tends to lead to more effective decisions for problems that require completion of a series of complex stages, so long as the individual receives input from many sources, which allows better coordination of the phases in solving the problem. In circumstances such as these, groups tend to prolong decision making, preventing a timely movement from stage to stage.[37]

■ *Acceptance of Decision.* Use of a group consensus also expedites the group's acceptance of the decision because individuals involved in making a decision generally become committed to that decision. At Delta, for example, the extent to which employees and managers accept the selection of a new manager likely will affect the new manager's effectiveness.

■ *Quality of the Solution.* Group decision making generally leads to higher-quality solutions, unless a best-member strategy can be identified in the beginning. Otherwise, finding a way to solicit a range of ideas would be appropriate. Thus, if Margo Shaley decides she lacks expertise, consulting with a team of executives or employees will probably produce a higher-quality decision.

■ *Characteristics of Individuals.* The personalities and capabilities of the people involved in the decision will help or hinder group decision making. Some individuals have difficulty collaborating in a group setting, whereas others are used to dealing with diverse viewpoints and attitudes. Also, individuals in groups can ignore individual expertise, creating tension, distrust, and resentment, which can hinder the identification of effective solutions.

- ***Organizational Culture.*** The organizational culture provides the context in which the decision-making process occurs. Supportive climates encourage group problem solving. Competitive climates stimulate individual responses. In countries outside the United States, where group-oriented behavior is more valued and rewarded, group decision making occurs more frequently than decision making by individuals.[38]

- ***Amount of Time Available.*** The amount of time available will determine whether group problem solving is feasible, since group decision making takes relatively more time than individual decision making. At Delta, Margo Shaley must have a new manager selected before the Manila plant opens. This time frame may limit the amount of group consultation possible.

DECISION-MAKING SKILLS

The quality of the decision depends in part on the level of the decision maker's skills. As shown in Figure 6–4, an individual's technical, interpersonal, and decision-making skills will influence the effectiveness of decision making. ***Technical or task skills*** refer to the individual's knowledge of the particular area in which the decision is being made—the technical aspects of the work operations. In the employee selection decision, Shaley's task skills refer to her knowledge of available job holders and the requirements of the position. ***Interpersonal or leadership skills*** relate to the way individuals lead, communicate with, motivate, and influence others. These skills particularly affect the acceptance of a decision. Margo Shaley must be able to marshal the support of executives and other employees at Delta for her decision. ***Decision-making skills*** refer to the basic abilities to perform the components of the rational decision-making process, including situational analysis and objective setting as well as the generation, evaluation, and selection of alternatives.

FIGURE 6–4   *Quality of decision making*

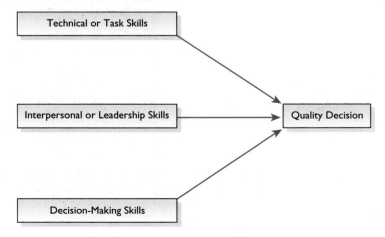

DECISION-MAKING STYLE

Individual personality characteristics influence the decision-making process. In most situations, the ability to understand an individual's decision-making style allows a manager to best match work assignments to this style, which in the long run has benefits for both the organization and the employee. Although there are many models of personality and personal style, Figure 6–5 presents one model that relates specifically to decision making.[39] It considers two dimensions, described as follows:

Cognitive complexity refers to an individual's ability to tolerate ambiguity. According to this model, leaders have a high tolerance of ambiguity (high cognitive complexity), but may focus either on generating ideas or implementing changes. Managers, in contrast, have a greater need for structure (lower cognitive complexity) and hence focus on doing rather than generating ideas or reacting rather than initiating changes.

Values orientation describes an individual's preference for or concern with technical/task issues or people/social issues. This dimension is linked to the predominant cerebral hemisphere in the individual's thinking. Those with

FIGURE 6–5   *Style of decision making*

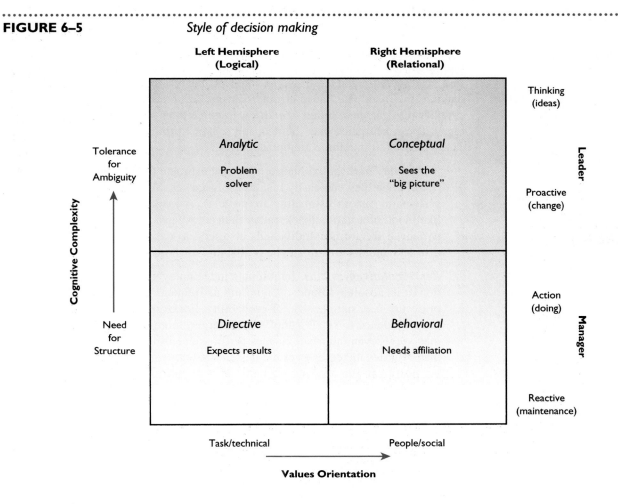

a predominant left hemisphere emphasize logical thought, which is accompanied by a focus on task and technical issues. Those with a predominant right hemisphere emphasize interpersonal relational thought, which is accompanied by a focus on people and social issues.

The resulting four styles—analytic, conceptual, directive, and behavioral—combine an individual's cognitive complexity with his or her values orientation (which also reflects the predominant cerebral hemisphere) and suggest the way a decision maker would approach the decision-making process. Individuals labeled leaders in this scheme tend to have either analytic or conceptual styles, depending on their values orientation, whereas individuals labeled managers have directive or behavioral styles. A decision maker with an analytic style, for example, has a high tolerance for ambiguity and focuses on solving particular problems, whereas a decision maker with a conceptual style also has a tolerance for ambiguity, but is concerned with relationships and hence "sees the big picture." Think of a manager you know. What type of style does he or she have? How does this style likely affect the decision-making process and outcomes? For example, the individual's style likely has significance for his or her comfort and ability to use the rational decision-making process. Style also affects the type and extent of information sought and used by the decision maker.

COGNITIVE BIASES

Individuals bring a diversity of cognitive skills, experience, and knowledge to decision making. Although these can provide valuable resources for improving decision making, they can also cause errors.[40] Errors occur because decision makers use simplifying strategies, called *heuristics,* to guide their judgments in decision making.[41] These heuristics bias the decision maker to think and act in certain ways. These biases fall into three major categories:[42]

- *Availability bias.* Individuals tend to overestimate the likelihood an event will occur when they can easily recall past instances. Such *availability* results in a systematic bias in estimating frequencies. A manager may overestimate the likelihood of a staff cutback, rather than an expansion, if he or she has only experienced the former. Individuals also tend to overestimate the likelihood of disasters and underestimate the probability of more common events.[43]

- *Representativeness bias.* Individuals judge an event in terms of their perception of its absolute frequency, ignoring its frequency relative to some base rate of occurrence, sample size, or probability. For example, they give as much or more credence to small samples as to larger, more representative, ones. They may view seven increases in sales performance in 10 months as more accurate than 70 sales increases over the past 100 months. In ignoring the base rate, or the historical rate at which certain events occur, individuals may assume, for example, that if no manager has been promoted in the last year, that management promotions are very rare, even though five have been promoted in each of the previous ten years.

- *Anchoring and adjustment bias.* Individuals make assessments by beginning with or *anchoring* onto an initial value and then *adjusting* it before making a final decision. Thus subsequent estimates are based on initial biases and may ignore whether events occur together or separately in estimating their frequency. Decision makers further err by demonstrating overconfidence in the infallibility of these judgments. Table 6–4 elaborates on these general categories of bias.

The way a decision maker *frames* a problem, that is, how he or she describes the situation, as a winning or losing situation, for example, has a significant impact on its outcome.[44] Individuals tend to take fewer risks regarding choices they frame in a positive fashion and tend to take more risks about choices they frame negatively.[45] For example, they avoid risks by choosing a sure gain of $250 over a 25 percent chance of winning $1,000 and a 75 percent chance of winning nothing. They take a greater risk by choosing a 75 percent chance of losing $1,000 and a 25 percent chance of losing nothing over a sure loss of $750. Individuals value a series of small gains more than a single gain of the same summed amount. For example, they would respond differently to a profitability situation framed as a gain of $1,000 a week for two months as opposed to a lump-sum profit of $9,000 at the end of two months.
COCA COLA. Coca Cola framed its introduction of a new formula of Coca-Cola as a choice between the certainty of continued loss of market share in the sugar cola market and experiencing a less probable but potentially greater loss in introducing a new formula. Because they framed the situation negatively they took the greater risk in abandoning a moderately successful product, which later they had to reintroduce as "Classic Coke."[46]

We also assume that we can estimate the likelihood of uncertain events, even though our estimates tend to be inaccurate. This assumption causes a decision maker to err in the evaluation of alternatives because he or she makes the assessment using inaccurate probabilities. Research has demonstrated, for example, that groups escalated their commitment to investment decisions in a failing course of action because they inaccurately assessed the probability of a turnaround and kept trying to recoup their losses, even if a realistic assessment of the situation would have caused them to cut their losses.[47]

GROUPTHINK

Groupthink occurs when members of a decision-making group avoid a critical evaluation of alternatives so that they can preserve a sense of group unity and consensus.[48] The attempt to reach a consensus at any cost causes members of such decision-making groups to avoid being too critical in their judgment of other group members' ideas.
NASA CHALLENGER. The Challenger spacecraft exploded and burned in space upon launch on February 3, 1986. A commission investigating the crash discovered that the decision process about launching the Challenger was flawed. The pressure to launch the Challenger resulted in NASA and Morton-Thiokol being willing to take inappropriate risks regarding safety. For example, the decision to launch the Challenger in temperatures significantly lower than those under which the O-ring, a critical component of the booster rocket's motor, had been previously tested was not challenged.[49]

The symptoms of groupthink are listed in Table 6–5. Victims of groupthink develop a sense of invulnerability and feel safe and protected from dangers and inef-

TABLE 6–4 *Summary of cognitive biases*

BIAS	DESCRIPTION

Biases Emanating from the Availability Heuristic

1. Ease of recall | Individuals judge events that are more easily recalled from memory, based upon vividness or recency, to be more numerous than events of equal frequency whose instances are less easily recalled. |

2. Retrievability | Individuals are biased in their assessments of the frequency of events based upon how their memory structures affect the search process. |

3. Presumed associations | Individuals tend to overestimate the probability of two events co-occurring based upon the number of similar associations that are easily recalled, whether from experience or social influence. |

Biases Emanating from the Representativeness Heuristic

4. Insensitivity to base rates | Individuals tend to ignore base rates in assessing the likelihood of events when any other descriptive information is provided—even if it is irrelevant. |

5. Insensitivity to sample size | Individuals frequently fail to appreciate the role of sample size in assessing the reliability of sample information. |

6. Misconceptions of chance | Individuals expect that a sequence of data generated by a random process will look "random," even when the sequence is too short for those expectations to be statistically valid. |

7. Regression to the mean | Individuals tend to ignore the fact that extreme events tend to regress to the mean on subsequent trials. |

8. The conjunction fallacy | Individuals falsely judge that conjunctions (two events co-occurring) are more probable than a more global set of occurrences of which the conjunction is a subset. |

Biases Emanating from Anchoring and Adjustment

9. Insufficient anchor adjustment | Individuals make estimates for values based upon an initial value (derived from past events, random assignment, or whatever information is available) and typically make insufficient adjustments from that anchor when establishing a final value. |

10. Conjunctive and disjunctive events bias | Individuals exhibit a bias toward overestimating the probability of conjunctive events and underestimating the probability of disjunctive events. |

11. Overconfidence | Individuals tend to be overconfident of the infallibility of their judgments when answering moderately to extremely difficult questions. |

Two More General Biases

12. The confirmation trap | Individuals tend to seek confirmatory information for what they think is true and neglect the search for disconfirmatory evidence. |

13. Hindsight and the curse of knowledge | After finding out whether or not an event occurred, individuals tend to overestimate the degree to which they would have predicted the correct outcome. Furthermore, individuals fail to ignore information they possess that others do not when predicting others' behavior. |

SYMPTOM	DESCRIPTION
Invulnerability	Members feel they are safe and protected from dangers, ostracism, or ineffective action.
Rationale	Members ignore warnings by rationalizing their own or others' behavior.
Morality	Members believe their actions are inherently moral and ethical.
Stereotypes	Members view opponents as truly evil or stupid and thus unworthy of or incompetent at negotiations around differences in beliefs or positions.
Pressure	Members pressure all individuals in the group to conform to the group's decision; they allow no questioning or arguing of alternatives.
Self-Censorship	Members do not express any questions about the group's decision.
Unanimity	Members perceive that everyone in the group has the same view.
Mindguards	Members may keep adverse information from other members that might ruin their perceptions of consensus and the effective decision.

SOURCE: Based on I. Janis, Groupthink, *Psychology Today* (June 1971).

fective action. They also ignore external criticism by rationalizing their own or others' behavior. Members tend to believe their actions are inherently moral and ethical. They also pressure all individuals in the group to conform to the group decision by allowing no debate about alternatives. When faced with threats, groups of executives likely procrastinate, "pass the buck," or support other members' rationalizations about the appropriate decision.[50]

Groupthink occurs most frequently in highly cohesive groups, particularly in stressful situations. Multicultural groups experience it less frequently because individual members have inherently different perspectives. Recent research posits, however, that groupthink alone does not explain decision-making fiascoes because it ignores a group's tendency to exaggerate the value, relevance, and perceived quality of the group's initial decision.[51]

To limit the likelihood of groupthink, groups and their leaders should

- ensure an open climate of discussion
- avoid overcontrolling the group's decisions
- implement a specific decision-making or problem-solving process
- actively seek dissenting voices
- do not mistake silence for consent

- get feedback from informed outsiders
- provide group members with enough time to study the problem and solutions.[52]

CULTURE

Margo Shaley functions as a global manager in a multinational environment. Based in the United States and working for a U.S. company, Shaley now must select a general manager for a manufacturing facility in Manila. She probably will first determine whether to hire a U.S. or Philippino national. She will make this decision within a broader cultural context, which includes her organization's goals and strategies, the nature of the labor force in Manila, and her experiences in managing in such situations.

Decision making occurs at individual, group, and organizational levels. Since many organizations now operate in a global environment, decision makers increasingly function in complicated and ambiguous situations. Intense competition and rapidly changing economic, social, political, and technological environments increase the complexity of the decision-making process and limit an organization's ability to control the outcomes of its decisions.[53] To be effective, managers need to develop effective tools for making decisions in a variety of cultures.

A culture's underlying values affect an individual's approach to decision making, particularly to problem recognition. U.S. managers, for example, see situations as a problem to be solved but Thai and Indonesian managers perceive that situations should be accepted as is, not changed.[54] Values may also affect the type of alternatives selected. In European countries, managers may rely more on historical patterns as the source of alternatives. In countries such as Israel, with more future-oriented cultures, managers may generate more new, untested alternatives.[55]

The speed of and responsibility for decision making is also culturally based.[56] The United States tends to be characterized by more rapid decision making, whereas many Middle Eastern cultures, such as Egypt, downplay time urgency. Responsibility for decisions may rest on the individual, as in the United States, or with a group, as in Japan. Factors considered irrelevant in the United States, such as saving face, can be crucial in the decision-making processes of Asian groups. Decisions can also be made at various levels in the hierarchy. For example, Swedish workers are more comfortable with decentralized decision making than are Indian or French employees. In Africa, middle managers rarely delegate authority.[57]

Cultural diversity poses both advantages and disadvantages for decision makers. Diverse groups must find effective ways to cope with differences in experience, customs, language, and other characteristics. Individual decision makers must reconcile their own views of a situation with potentially different perspectives offered in another culture. Cultural differences may pose unique constraints on the decision-making situation.

TECHNIQUES FOR IMPROVING DECISION MAKING

After completing a high-quality diagnosis of the decision-making process and factors that influence it, managers can improve decision making by selecting the appropriate individuals to participate in and implement quality decision making. Prescriptions for improving decision making might include one of five additional techniques: brainstorming, the nominal group technique, the delphi technique, consensus mapping, and electronic group decision making.

BRAINSTORMING

Brainstorming is a technique whereby individuals or groups generate large numbers of ideas or alternatives relating to a decision without evaluating their merits. For example, Shaley might list as many sources of general manager candidates as possible. Listing alternatives without evaluating them encourages group members to generate ideas rather than defend or eliminate existing ideas. Evaluation occurs after a large array of ideas has been generated.

Principles for brainstorming include:

- All ideas should be listed. No idea should be evaluated during the first part of brainstorming.

- Creativity should be encouraged. All ideas should be recorded, regardless of how frivolous or irrelevant they seem.

- Members should be encouraged to offer ideas related to those already on the list.

- Asking each participant to record and then offer five to ten ideas can help start the session.

- Setting a time limit for brainstorming, for example, five to ten minutes, can often stimulate the rapid generation of ideas.

Brainstorming typically helps decision makers think of unexpected and potentially useful possibilities for attacking a problem. It does not contribute significantly when specialized knowledge is required because it sacrifices the quality of an idea for ensuring quantity.[58] While brainstorming can result in many shallow and useless ideas, it can also push members to offer new ideas and typically increases the overall creativity of individuals and work groups.

NOMINAL GROUP TECHNIQUE

The *nominal group technique* (NGT) is a structured group meeting in which individuals brainstorm and then rank order a series of ideas as a way of resolving differences in group opinion.[59] A group of individuals is presented with a stated problem. Each person individually offers alternative solutions in writing. The group then shares the solutions and lists them on a blackboard or large piece of paper, as in brainstorming. The group discusses and clarifies the ideas. Group members then rank ideas and vote for their preference. If the group has not reached an agreement, they repeat the ranking and voting procedure until the group reaches some agreement. Table 6–6 presents a leader guide for NGT meetings.

An *improved nominal group technique* emphasizes anonymous input and voting, focuses on a single purpose in each group meeting, and delays evaluation until all inputs are displayed.[60] It also ensures that participants will have opportunities for discussing displayed items before voting, limits discussion to the pros and cons

TABLE 6–6   *Leader guide for NGT meetings*

Step 1. Silent Recording
  1. Present a written problem statement and a written outline of all process steps.
  2. Resist all but process clarifications.
  3. Maintain atmosphere by also writing in silence.
  4. Discourage members who attempt to talk to others.

Step 2. Round-Robin Recording
  1. Indicate the purpose of Step 2 (to create a record of the meeting).
  2. Ask members to present their problems briefly and clearly.
  3. Accept variations on a theme, but discourage duplicate items.
  4. Ask if an idea has been correctly recorded to gain approval before proceeding.
  5. Keep the list visible to all members by taping it on the wall.

Step 3. Interactive Discussion
  1. Indicate this step's purpose (to explain and consolidate).
  2. Skirt arguments, but accept both opinions when a difference arises.
  3. Give all items some consideration.
  4. Encourage elaborations from everyone without reference to who proposed them.
  5. Gain the group's agreement to merge similar ideas, keeping the ideas separate when the group objects.

Step 4. Prioritization
  1. Indicate the purpose of Step 4 (to set priorities).
  2. Explain the procedure.

SOURCE: Adapted from A.L. Delbecq, A. Van de Ven, and D.H. Gustafson, *Group Techniques for Program Planning* (Middleton, Wis.: Greenbrier, 1986). Reprinted with permission from P.C. Nutt, *Making Tough Decisions* (San Francisco: Jossey-Bass, 1989), p. 364.

of alternatives, and allows any individual to reword items. Computerized support for this approach exists.

The nominal group technique becomes more useful as a group increases in size and diversity of expertise. The technique encourages each group member to individually think about and offer ideas about the content of a proposal and then directs group discussion. It moves the group toward problem resolution by focusing on top-ranked ideas and eliminating less valued options systematically. The NGT also encourages continued exploration of the issues, provides a forum for the expression of minority viewpoints, gives individuals some time to think about the issues before offering solutions, and provides a mechanism for reaching a decision expediently through the ranking–voting procedure.[61] It fosters creativity by allowing extensive individual input into the process. Strong personality types will less often dominate the group because the NGT provides all group members an opportunity for systematic input. It encourages innovation, limits conflict, emphasizes equal participation by all members, helps generate a consensus, and incorporates the preferences of individuals in decision-making choices.[62]

DELPHI TECHNIQUE

The *delphi technique* is a structured group decision-making technique that uses repeated administration of rating scales to obtain opinions, first unfocused and then refocused, about a decision.[63]

Group members begin by exploring the subject individually. In the conventional delphi procedure a small group of these individuals then designs a questionnaire for use in polling a larger group of respondents. A larger respondent group completes the questionnaire. The results are then tabulated and used in developing a revised questionnaire, which is again completed by the larger group. Thus the results of the original polling are fed back to and discussed by the larger respondent group. This process continues until agreement is reached. Together, then, group members eventually reach an understanding of the group's view of the issues.[64]

Consider a university that is deciding whether to change its calendar from a semester to a trimester schedule. The delphi technique might assist administrators in making this decision. First, a small group of administrators, students, and faculty might be asked to consider the calendar change individually. Most likely they would have differing views about its value and feasibility. Then this group would convene to develop a questionnaire about the calendar change. They would administer this questionnaire to a larger group of administrators, students, and faculty. After tabulating the results, they would share them with the larger group. These results might uncover issues of agreement and disagreement. For example, the respondents might agree with the value of a calendar change, but have reservations because of unresolved issues regarding number of instructional hours, length of a reading period, and timing of final examinations. Administration of a revised questionnaire, which would focus particularly on these issues, might result in further clarification and agreement. Tabulation and feeding back of results, as well as construction and administration of revised questionnaires, would continue until all issues were considered and a consensus was reached. Computerized support is available for this technique. A computer summarizes the results and essentially replaces the small group.[65]

The delphi technique is very useful in a variety of circumstances.[66] It works well when face-to-face conversation is not possible and provides a systematic way for ensuring the input of many individuals, particularly when significant disagreements are likely. Especially when decision makers cannot apply precise analytical techniques to solving the problem, but prefer to use subjective judgments on a collective basis, delphi procedures can provide input from a large number of respondents. It can increase the effectiveness of group meetings when they do occur and reduce the likelihood of groupthink. Particularly if the individuals involved have failed to communicate effectively in the past, the delphi procedures offer a systematic method for ensuring that their opinions are presented. The delphi technique can overcome situations where individuals greatly disagree or where the anonymity of views must be maintained to protect group members. When time and cost prevent frequent group meetings or when additional premeeting communication between group members increases the efficiency of the meetings held, the delphi technique offers a significant value for decision making.

CONSENSUS MAPPING

Consensus mapping refers to a technique for structuring group problem solving that involves the clustering and categorizing of similar ideas to ultimately result in a solution.[67] Consensus mapping begins after a task group has developed, clarified, and evaluated a list of ideas. First, a facilitator encourages participants to search for clusters and categories of listed ideas. This search includes the listing and discussion of alternative clusters and categories by the entire group or subgroups and then production of a single classification scheme by group members working as a group or in pairs or trios. Next, by identifying common, overlapping, or redundant categories and clusters, the facilitator helps the group consolidate the different schemes developed by subgroups into a representative scheme, called a *strawman map,* for the entire group. Group members then make adjustments to this representative scheme until they reach a mutually acceptable solution. When there is more than one task group, a representative from each task group presents its revised map to members of other task groups. Finally, representatives from each task group produce a single, consolidated map or solution.

This technique works particularly well when groups must solve multidimensional, complex problems that have interconnected elements and many sequential steps. Its effectiveness depends on the quality of ideas generated by the task group and the ability of the facilitator to help the group refine the strawman map.

ELECTRONIC GROUP DECISION MAKING

Groupware, computer software that facilitates group decision making, has become available in the past several years. An extension of electronic mail, groupware lets workers share ideas and hold meetings on-line, even though they are in different locations.[68] Groupware includes electronic messaging, which facilitates communication among group members both sequentially and simultaneously, and teleconferencing systems, including video and audio conferencing, which support the concurrent exchange of ideas. Groupware supports the coordination of groups and the exchange of ideas, making it easier to reach a consensus on difficult problems. For example, groupware can help to coordinate participants concurrently making decisions that contribute to the making of a larger decision.[69]

SUMMARY

Decision making occurs at individual, group, and organizational levels. Managers and other organizational members can judge the effectiveness of the decisions in terms of their quality, timeliness, acceptance, and ethical appropriateness. Programmed decisions describe problems that have a relatively structured solution drawn from standard operating procedures or rules of thumb. Nonprogrammed decisions cannot be handled by standard rules and policies.

A rational decision-making process generally results in improved decision making. This process involves analyzing the situation, setting objectives, searching for alternatives, evaluating the alternatives, making the decision, and evaluating the decision. Alternatives to systematic decision making include Simon's bounded rationality, intuitive decision making, decision making by objection, the garbage can model, and creative problem solving.

Diagnosing influences on decision making is a key step in improving its effectiveness. These influences include the use of individual versus group decision making, the decision maker's skills, his or her decision-making style, cognitive biases, groupthink, and culture. Brainstorming, the nominal group technique, the delphi technique, consensus mapping, and electronic group decision making offer approaches for improving decision making.

DIAGNOSTIC QUESTIONS

The following questions should help managers and other organizational members increase the effectiveness of decision making.

■ Do decision makers make high-quality, timely, accepted, ethical decisions?

■ What type of decision is being made?

■ Do decision makers use the rational decision-making process?

■ Do ways of dealing with limitations in the process of decision making exist?

■ Do alternative models of decision making describe the process?

■ What factors influence decision making in the organization?

■ Do managers and other organizational members appropriately choose when individuals versus groups should make decisions?

■ Do individuals have appropriate skills and styles for making decisions?

■ Do decision makers recognize the cognitive biases in their decision making?

■ Does groupthink exist?

■ What techniques for improving decision making are used?

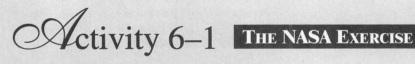

Activity 6–1 — THE NASA EXERCISE

STEP 1: Read the following instructions.

You are a member of a space crew originally scheduled to rendezvous with a mothership on the lighted surface of the moon. Due to mechanical difficulties, however, your ship was forced to land at a spot some 200 miles from the rendezvous point. During landing, much of the equipment aboard was damaged, and, since survival depends on reaching the mothership, the most critical items available must be chosen for the 200-mile trip. The 15 items left intact and undamaged after the landing include a box of matches, food concentrate, 50 feet of nylon rope, parachute silk, a portable heating unit, two .45 caliber pistols, one case of dehydrated Pet milk, two 100-lb. tanks of oxygen, stellar map (of the moon's constellations), life raft, magnetic compass, 5 gallons of water, signal flares, first aid kit containing injection needles, and a solar-powered FM receiver-transmitter.

Your task is to rank order them in terms of their importance to your crew in reaching the rendezvous point. Using a scoring sheet like the one in Table 6–7 place the number 1 by the most important item, the number 2 by the second most important, and so on, through number 15, the least important. You have 15 minutes to complete this phase of the exercise.

TABLE 6–7   *Scoring sheet*

ITEMS	INDIVIDUAL RANKING	GROUP RANKING	SURVIVAL EXPERT'S RANKING	INFLUENCE	INDIVIDUAL ACCURACY	GROUP ACCURACY
	Column 1	Column 2	Column 3	Column 4	Column 5	Column 6
Box of matches						
Food concentrate						
50 feet of nylon rope						
Parachute silk						
Portable heating unit						
Two .45 caliber pistols						
One case dehydrated milk						
Two 100-lb. tanks of oxygen						
Stellar map (of the moon's constellations)						
Life raft						
Magnetic compass						
5 gallons of water						
Signal flares						
First aid kit containing injection needles						
Solar-powered FM receiver-transmitter						
				Individual Influence Score	Individual Accuracy Score	Group Accuracy Score

STEP 2: After the individual rankings are completed, your instructor will direct you to form groups of four to seven members. Each group should then rank order the 15 items as a group. This group ranking should be a general consensus following a discussion of the issues, not just an averaging of each individual ranking. While it is unlikely that everyone will agree exactly on the group ranking, an effort should be made to at least reach a decision that everyone can live with. It is important to treat differences of opinion as a means of gathering more information, clarifying issues, and as an incentive to force the group to seek better alternatives. The group ranking should be listed in column 2.

STEP 3: The instructor will provide the expert's rankings. Enter them in column 3.

STEP 4: Each participant should compute the absolute difference between the individual ranking and the group ranking, and place the numbers in column 4; between the individual ranking and the expert's ranking and place the numbers in column 5; and between the group ranking and the expert's ranking and place the numbers in column 6. Then total the scores for columns 4, 5, and 6.

STEP 5: Discussion. In small groups or with the entire class, answer the following questions:

DESCRIPTION

1. Describe your group's operation.
2. Describe the decision-making process used by your group.

DIAGNOSIS

3. Which steps occurred in decision making? Which steps did you skip? Evaluate the effectiveness of the decision making.

PRESCRIPTION

4. How could your group have made a more effective decision?

Activity 6-2   ARCO COMPANY CASE

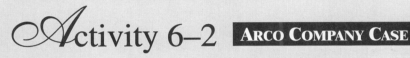

STEP 1: Read the Arco Company case.

In early February 1981, for reasons of declining profitability, the management of Arco Company, a Toronto-based producer of pumps and electrical controls, focussed their attention on the pumps division and the potential opportunities in the pumps market. Mounting problems in the division, opinions about which were numerous and various, prompted Max Chambers,

FIGURE 6–6   *Seating arrangement for special meeting, Arco Company*

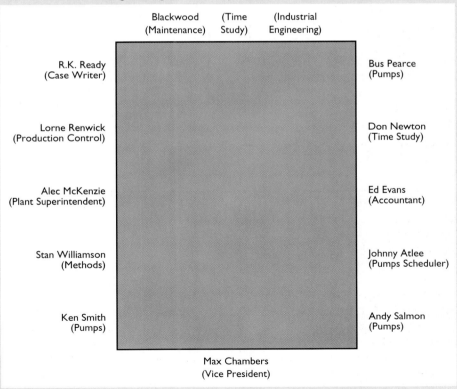

vice president of manufacturing, to call a special meeting of key management personnel to discuss possible action. Five men from pumps and eight men from other areas attended. Figure 6–6 shows the meeting's attendants. Figure 6–7 is a partial organizational chart of Arco.

Max began with a long, rambling talk in which he mentioned the main concerns in the pumps division's layout problems exacerbated by lack of floor space, and the high price of the pumps, which were manufactured in a job-shop format. The discussion, he said, should focus on "what changes, if any, we want to make in this pumps division." One change Max wanted discussed was the introduction of a mass-produced pump. To this end he introduced the name of a consultant, Jim Henderson, as someone who could assist in designing a new standard line. Or, he added, the pumps people could design the new line themselves. He closed his remarks by saying, "One thing I want is that you all contribute to the ultimate decision. I also want a full endorsement of whatever is decided."

The resulting discussion, in which everyone readily agreed that something had to be done about the pumps

FIGURE 6–7   *Arco Company, partial organizational chart, manufacturing division*

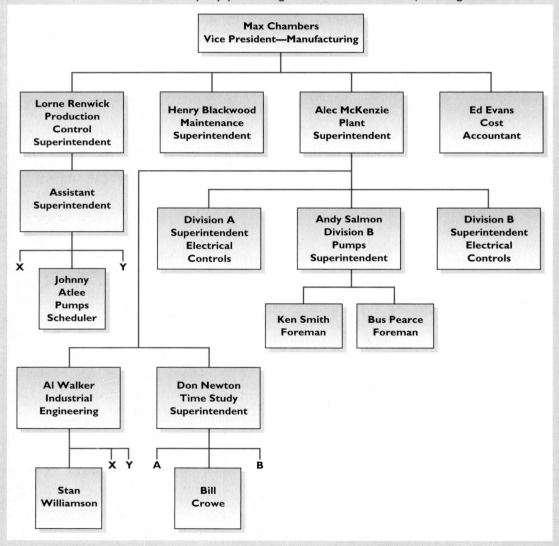

division, began with a discussion of Max's major proposal: having two lines, one to be streamlined, producing a standard pump, and one to continue the job-shop pump. Max elaborated on his concerns by saying that he wanted a new, cheaper pump to act as a catalyst to the sales people. He wanted the Sales department to develop a marketing plan to sell the new product.

Most of the discussion was among the electrical controls people, particularly Alec and Lorne. The pumps people, when pressed to contribute, indicated that they felt there were more urgent, immediate problems than developing a new pump. Max, Alec, and Lorne disregarded these remarks and continued to discuss the introduction of a new pump line. A few pointed and somewhat aggressive remarks were exchanged between Lorne and the pumps group. Further discussion centered on whether to hire Jim Henderson, the consultant, or do the survey themselves.

As the meeting closed, Max said, "I know that the President is ready to push the pumps business. If he is in this frame of mind, I think we should be prepared to assume the responsibility for organizing the manufacturing end of things. I shall be out of town until next Thursday. When I return, I would like your group decision about what to do in the pumps division. I shall go along with anything you decide."

BACKGROUND

The Arco Company, situated in a suburb of Toronto, was originally a producer of electrical controls. In 1976, the Company acquired the Delta Pump Company. Since that time, the ratio of electrical controls' sales to pumps' sales had increased from 2:1 to 4:1, while at the same time, the Company's profitability had been decreasing. Management felt that the high market share they enjoyed in electrical controls was as much as they would be able to get.

The pumps division currently had a book loss; however, the Company cost accountant attributed that to the unrealistically high overhead allocated to the pumps division. He believed that if Arco had discontinued producing and selling pumps without another product line, its profitability would have been lower.

PUMPS DIVISION

The pumps division operated independently of the other divisions, but it utilized common service facilities such as production control, accounting, maintenance, industrial engineering, and industrial relations. Three management people from Delta Pumps joined Arco after the merger: Ed Evans, Cost Accountant, Andy Salmon, Pumps Superintendent, and Stan Williamson, Methods Supervisor. In addition, the two foremen, Bus Pearce and Ken Smith, had come to Arco from Delta.

Two years after the merger, in an effort to centralize industrial engineering, the Company abolished the Pumps' Department of Time Study and Methods and moved Stan Williamson to the Industrial Engineering Department, reporting to Al Walker. The time study responsibilities were assumed by Don Newton's time study department. Both Newton and Walker had been brought into Arco by Alec McKenzie. Figure 6–8 indicates the office lay-out plan. Figure 6–9 shows both the on- and off-the-job interactions of these people.

PROFILES AND OPINIONS

(Table 6–8 gives more detailed background on some of the participants.)

Max Chambers, Vice-President of Manufacturing

Max had a degree in engineering, with some work towards a Master's degree at M.I.T. While there, he studied under Douglas McGregor, the author of "The Human Side of Enterprise." He believed that if Arco were to grow, it would have to be in the pumps division. To this end, he wanted to introduce a major change from job-shop pumps to mass-produced pumps. He had the agreement of the President of Arco to proceed in this direction, along with a promise of some financing to make the change. Regarding the issue of hiring a consultant to design the new layout, Max had hoped that the pumps division people would do the job themselves.

Lorne Renwick, Production Control Superintendent

Due to his long years of service with Arco, Lorne had a long-standing relationship with both the President of Arco and the President of the parent company. Most of the people in Arco felt that Lorne had a great deal of power. As Andy Salmon put it, "Lorne is the person you have to watch out for. Any time people do something different from the way he wants things done in his area,

FIGURE 6–8   *Office layout, Arco Company*

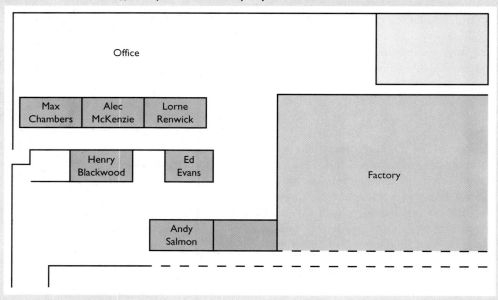

he stops you cold. There's no point in arguing with him once you find out that he is against you."

Lorne thought that having a new pump line was a good idea even though he disagreed with the idea of bringing in a consultant to design the layout. He had told Max so before the meeting. In Lorne's opinion, Max's idea was to increase pumps sales by introducing a new, profitable pump line, and the main purpose in calling the meeting was to get approval of the idea. He believed that Max wanted to use an outside consultant to design the new layout.

Lorne felt that the key men in the pumps division formed a "pumps clique" and he believed that the time had come to break it up. He felt the pumps people never shared their ideas with others and consciously tried to exclude others.

Lorne classified the executives in the company into two classes: one group that thought up ideas and one group that got them through. He considered himself as part of the latter group.

Alec McKenzie, Plant Superintendent

Alec's father-in-law was the president of the parent company, and his position in the company was seen by many as being a result of that relationship. He had very

little management experience. He was an electrical engineer and taught an evening course in engineering. Alec had high aspirations for the company.

He was strongly in favour of the consultant, although "at first I was opposed to the idea because I thought we could do it ourselves. As I thought about it, I began changing my mind."

Alec could not foresee pump sales increasing to the point where they could equal sales of electrical controls. He believed that the reorganization of the pumps division was a big job rather than a big decision, but that whatever was done would have to have the approval of Andy Salmon because Andy had the ideas. It would be the consultant's job to pull the ideas together in report form.

Andy Salmon, Pumps Superintendent

Andy and Stan Williamson were probably the most knowledgeable pumps people in Canada. Andy did not feel that the electrical people at Arco knew much about the pumps area. He felt that the pumps people were dominated by the electrical group through Lorne's scheduling. "There is a problem of electrical storage moving into the pumps area. If we had someone who could stand up to Lorne, then possibly, this problem

FIGURE 6–9   *Established patterns of interaction, Arco Company*

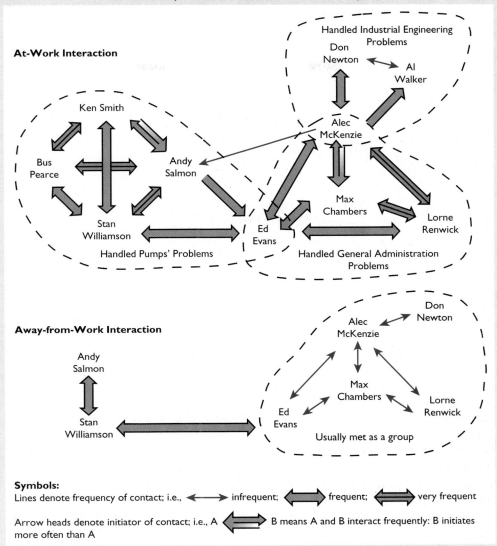

At-Work Interaction

Handled Industrial Engineering Problems

Handled Pumps' Problems

Handled General Administration Problems

Away-from-Work Interaction

Usually met as a group

Symbols:

Lines denote frequency of contact; i.e., ⟵⟶ infrequent; ⟸⟹ frequent; ⟸⟹ very frequent

Arrow heads denote initiator of contact; i.e., A ⟸⟹ B means A and B interact frequently: B initiates more often than A

could be solved internally. I guess that's one of our major problems: not having someone who can referee a battle between, let's say, Lorne and Pumps."

Andy was confused by the meeting, as he was not sure whether Max had wanted the group's opinions or had just wanted support for his idea of a new pumps line. Usually these decisions were made by top management and passed on, so Andy's expectations were unclear. In Andy's opinion, Max probably wanted to bring in an outsider to avoid the back-biting that would occur if the job were done internally.

Andy was in favour of expanding the pumps division, but would have preferred that he and Stan take on the responsibility for this expansion. He felt that he could make time to do the job and, if the consultant was only going to put ideas together, he and Stan could do it as well as the consultant. Andy and Alec McKenzie had discussed this idea, but Alec felt that the consultant would be the best alternative because the job could be done more quickly. Consequently, Andy agreed: "If that's the way they want it, that's the way we'll do it."

TABLE 6–8   *Personal information, manufacturing personnel, Arco Company*

	POSITION	AGE	SERVICE	EDUCATION	MARITAL STATUS	OUTSIDE INTEREST
Max Chambers	V.P. Manufacturing	48	19	Electrical Eng. U. of T. 1 yr. Post Grad. Bus. and Eng. Admin. at MIT	Married: one son	United Church—an executive President M.I.T. Club, Toronto
Stan Williamson	Methods Supervisor	59	31	2 yr. Tech. School 4 yr. Electrical course at night	Married: two sons and two daughters	Electronics and woodwork shop in basement—hobby
Bus Pearce	Foreman	49	32	2 yr. Tech. School 3 yr. night School: Mgmt. Training	Married: two daughters	
Lorne Renwick	Production Control Superintendent	59	42	1st yr. H.S.	Married: two sons	
Ken Smith	Foreman	47	23	Grade School	Married: one son and two daughters	Deacon, Baptist Church Treasurer, Leaside Foremen's Club Member, Chess Club President, Christian Men of Industry Bowling League
Andy Salmon	Pumps Division Superintendent	52	33	H.S. grad 1 yr. night classes: electricity	Married	
Alec McKenzie	Plant Superintendent	32	8	U. of T. Electrical Engineer	Married: one son and one daughter	Leaside Foreman's Club Member Professional Engineers Society Teaches course at U. of T. evening school, Gen. Mgmt.
Don Newton	Time Study Superintendent	34	1	H.S. Grad Night School, Ind. Supervisor	Married: one son and one daughter	Treasurer, Presbyterian Church Night Course at U. of T. in Administration Member, Ind. Engineering Assoc.
Ed Evans	Cost Accountant	53	25	U. of T. Comm. and Finance	Married	Member, Cost Accounting Group

Stan Williamson, Methods Supervisor

Stan thought the meeting was a mess with no definite purpose. Max had just sat back and tried to get people to do what he wanted them to do, but in this case, it was not clear what that was. Stan had talked to Max later and tried to pin him down, but with no results.

"The thing that really disturbs me is that Andy feels that the pressure is getting too great. On top of all his problems, he has to deal with untrained people such as Alec McKenzie and Don Newton, who have no experience in the pumps field at all. In the last 18 months or so, the carpet has really been pulled out from under the pumps people."

Ed Evans, Manufacturing Division Accountant

Ed felt that Max held the meeting to inform everyone at the same time about his plans for the pumps division. He believed that Max wanted to hire the consultant and that he would certainly be hired. He did not think the Sales department would change their approach to increase sales. In mentioning Lorne's contribution to the meeting, he said, "Lorne is a big talker. You can't believe much of anything he says. Anyway, he doesn't know anything about pumps—he is an electrical controls man."

Ken Smith, Pumps Assembly Foreman

Ken was disappointed that Max had been so indefinite about what should be done. He thought Max had been insincere in asking for opinions from the pumps people, since he had never done so before. Lorne had opposed pumps and blocked them at every turn in the past, so Ken did not believe that anything had changed. He also questioned the presence of such people as Henry, Lorne, John, Al Walker and others at a meeting which was supposed to deal with a pumps problem.

THE GROUP'S DECISION

When Max returned the following week, reports from the men ranged from Lorne Renwick's disapproval of hiring any consultant, to Stan Williamson's skepticism but willingness to cooperate, to the more widely held approval for hiring Jim Henderson. Max agreed to the decision. The consultant began work the following week.

THE CONSULTANT'S EFFORTS

A committee of six was formed to work with Jim Henderson, consisting of Andy Salmon (co-chairman) and Stan Williamson from pumps, and Don Newton, Bill Crowe, and Alec McKenzie (Chairman) from other areas. The consultant was introduced only to members of the committee.

During the next two months, opinions about Jim and the project polarized. Except for formal meetings, Jim had little contact with pumps people, and all reported information to Max came from nonpumps committee members. Pumps personnel complained to each other that Jim would not take suggestions or ask questions and were suspicious of the speediness and lack of consultation in arranging for the consultant.

Jim recommended an assembly line layout which utilized a conveyer. Only the nonpumps people were enthusiastic about the recommendation or project. Outwardly, Max Chambers remained neutral. Objecting to Jim and his proposal became the regular topic of discussion at the afternoon pumps division coffee break meetings.

ALEC'S BLOW-UP

On a Wednesday afternoon in April, 1981, Alec McKenzie was in a rage. He had just come from a pumps division coffee break meeting with Andy, Stan, and the two foremen. He had heard nothing but objections and criticisms about the consultant and the proposed conveyor setup for the pumps area. Alec was still enthusiastic about the plan, but very discouraged by the meeting's outcome. Figure 6–10 shows some of the objections that had been raised by the pumps people.

Alec discussed his feelings with the case writer who happened to see him just as he left the pumps meeting. Alec was "so god-damned mad" he could "hardly talk at all" as he discussed his feelings. The meeting was the first time he had heard Andy's views. He explained that he was not "getting any suggestions; not a bit of constructive criticism at all . . . nothing but opposition and objections." Alec continually returned to those phrases. He was enthusiastic about the plan and had "hoped other people wanted things to improve . . . wanted things done in a way that would be a credit to themselves and the organization." His anger turned to the pumps people: "They don't want

1. What will happen if there is a breakdown? Will the workers just stand around or will they be sent home?

2. What happens if you have trouble on a machine and need a new tool? A man would have to go to the tool shop and then run three quarters of the way through the plant to get the end plate he was working on.

3. There is not supposed to be any material or inventory on the floor, so if there is a material shortage, there is nothing to do but shut down the line.

4. It will have to be a standardized product—no changes can be made in a pump.*

5. Jim Henderson will not listen to suggestions, and will not ask questions.

*Stan did not think they should worry about the design because he believed that the plan would never get into operation.

anything–all they want is to have things stay as they are."

Alec's explanations of the suggested line flow and equipment usage revealed four possible benefits for pumps: direct and indirect labour savings; reduced process time (from seven weeks to one week); doubled production capacity in two-thirds of the present space; and a clean, organized shop. In Alec's opinion, a short delivery time was a necessity in the market.

Walking through the pumps plant area, Alec explained the plans he had for the available space. In reviewing the existing layout, he pointed out messy, untidy spots in the production, assembly, and test areas where materials and work in process lay on the floor, all the time referring to his embarrassment. "It's a discouraging, disgusting sight. You don't find this in other companies. It's an embarrassing, shameful, mess."

He spoke of the potential labour saving which could be realized with the new system, and of his own shame "to be associated with a company that looked like this." All he wanted, he emphasized, was "good, solid, constructive criticism, not just opposition and objections."

Although Alec recognized Arco's significant business opportunities, particularly in the pumps market, he was greatly distressed by the difficulty of getting ahead within the Company: "There's just no place to go, the Company's not providing anything."

Alec finally confided that until that afternoon's meeting, he had thought "sailing was clear." Now it appeared to him that everyone was sold on the plan except the four people who would have to make it work.

"We have the opportunity to do something really well, to do something we can be proud of, and all they want to do, as far as I can see, is just stay the same. I don't know what I'm going to do about it, but I've got to do something by tomorrow."

STEP 2:   Prepare the case for class discussion.

STEP 3:   Answer each of the following questions, individually or in small groups, as directed by your instructor.

DESCRIPTION
1. Briefly describe the decision to be made at Arco.
2. Describe the major individuals involved in the decision making.

DIAGNOSIS
3. What situation did the pumps division face?
4. What was Chambers's objective?
5. What alternatives were considered? Were the alternatives feasible?
6. How completely were the alternatives evaluated?
7. Was a quality decision reached?

PRESCRIPTION
8. How could more effective decisions be made?
9. What techniques could be used to improve decision making?

STEP 4: Discussion. In small groups, with the entire class, or in written form, share your answers to the questions above. Then answer the following questions:

1. What symptoms suggest a problem exists?
2. What problems exist in the case?
3. What theories and concepts help explain those problems?

4. How can the problems be corrected?
5. Are the actions likely to be effective?

This case was prepared by Al Milalchki of the Western Business School. Copyright (1982), The University of Western Ontario.

This material is not covered under authorization from CanCopy or any reproduction rights organization. Any form of reproduction, storage or transmittal of this material is prohibited without written permission from Western Business School, The University of Western Ontario, London, Canada N6A 3K7. Reprinted with permission, Western Business School.

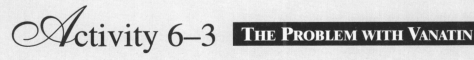

Activity 6–3 THE PROBLEM WITH VANATIN

STEP I: Read the following background information.

You are a member of the Booth Pharmaceutical Corporation board of directors. You have been called to a special board meeting to discuss what should be done with the product Vanatin.

Vanatin is a "fixed-ratio" antibiotic sold by prescription. That is, it contains a combination of drugs. On the market for more than 13 years, it has been highly successful. It now accounts for about $18 million per year, which is 12 percent of Booth Company's gross income in the United States (and a greater percentage of net profits). Profit from foreign markets, where Booth is marketed under a different name, is roughly comparable to that in the United States.

Over the past 20 years, numerous medical scientists (such as the AMA's Council on Drugs) have objected to the sale of most fixed-ratio drugs. The arguments have been that (1) there is no evidence that these fixed-ratio drugs have improved benefits over single drugs and (2) the possibility of detrimental side effects, including death, is at least double. For example, scientists have estimated that Vanatin is causing about 30 to 40 unnecessary deaths per year (that is, deaths that could be prevented if the patients had used a substitute made by a competitor of Booth). Despite recommendations to remove fixed-ratio drugs from the market, doctors have continued to use them. They offer a shotgun approach for doctors who are unsure of their diagnoses.

Recently, a National Academy of Science–National Research Council panel, a group of impartial scientists, carried out extensive research studies and recommended unanimously that the Food and Drug Administration (FDA) ban the sale of Vanatin. One of the members of the panel, Dr. Peterson of the University of Texas, was quoted by the press as saying, "There are few instances in medicine when so many experts have agreed unanimously and without reservation [about banning Vanatin]." This view was typical of comments made by other members of the panel. In fact, it was typical of comments that had been made about fixed-ratio drugs over the past 20 years. These impartial experts, then, believe that, while all drugs have some possibility of side effects, the costs associated with Vanatin far exceed the possible benefits.

The special board meeting has arisen out of an emergency situation. The FDA has told you that it plans to ban Vanatin in the United States and wants to give Booth time for a final appeal to them. Should the ban become effective, Booth would have to stop all sales of Vanatin and attempt to remove inventories from the market. Booth has no close substitutes for Vanatin, so that consumers will be switched to close substitutes currently marketed by rival firms. (Some of these substitutes apparently have no serious side effects.) It is extremely unlikely that bad publicity from this case would have any significant effect on the long-term profits of other products made by Booth.

The board is meeting to review and make decisions on two issues:

1. What should be done with Vanatin in the U.S. market (the immediate problem)?
2. Assuming that Vanatin is banned from the U.S. market. What should Booth do in the foreign

markets? (No government action is anticipated overseas.)

Decisions on each of these issues must be reached at today's meeting. The chairman of the board has sent out this background information, and he also wanted you to give some thought as to which of the following alternatives you would prefer for the domestic market:

1. Recall Vanatin immediately and destroy it.
2. Stop production of Vanatin immediately, but allow what has been made to be sold.
3. Stop all advertising and promotion of Vanatin, but provide it for doctors who request it.
4. Continue efforts to most effectively market Vanatin until its sale is actually banned.
5. Continue efforts to most effectively market Vanatin and take legal, political, and other necessary actions to prevent the authorities from banning Vanatin.

A similar decision must also be made for the foreign market *under the assumption that the sale is banned in the United States.*

STEP 2: Prepare your role.

STEP 3: The chairperson of the board will conduct the discussion of the Vanatin problem. By the end of 45 minutes, the group should reach a decision on what to do about both domestic and international distribution of Vanatin. At the end of the meeting, each chairperson should record the decisions of the group on the recording form.

STEP 4: The instructor will tabulate the types of decisions made by all the groups for the U.S. and foreign markets. You may record the decisions on the table below.

1. Record in columns 1 and 2 the actual decisions made by the discussion groups.
2. Privately note to yourself what you think Booth actually did in this case. The instructor will tally the predictions, and you may record these predictions in columns 3 and 4.
3. Record in columns 5 and 6 what Booth actually did.

Decision	DECISIONS MADE BY GROUPS*		WHAT DO YOU THINK HAPPENED?		WHAT ACTUALLY HAPPENED?	
	United States	Foreign	United States	Foreign	United States	Foreign
a. Recall immediately						
b. Stop production						
c. Stop advertising and promotion						
d. Continue to market						
e. Block FDA						
	(1)	(2)	(3)	(4)	(5)	(6)

*Record the letter designation of the group decision in the proper place.

STEP 5: Discussion. In small groups or with the entire class, answer the following questions:

1. What decisions did each group reach?
2. How ethical were the decisions reached?
3. What criteria did you use to evaluate the decisions?
4. How could you improve the decision making to make it more ethical?

This exercise was adapted by Roy J. Lewicki, Duke University, from an exercise developed by J. Scott Armstrong, University of Pennsylvania. It is reprinted from Douglas T. Hall, Donald D. Bowen, Roy J. Lewicki, and Francine S. Hall, *Experiences in Management and Organizational Behavior,* 2nd ed. (New York: John Wiley & Sons, 1982). For a report on research involving this exercise, see J. Scott Armstrong, "Social Irresponsibility in Marketing, Journal of Business Research, 5 (1977), 185–213.

Activity 6–4   ETHICAL DECISION MAKING

STEP 1: Read Cases 1–4. For each case, first decide what you would do and why. In doing this, consider what information you would use to investigate the question, what alternatives you would consider, and what criteria you would use in making your decision.

CASE 1: SALES REPRESENTATIVE IN THE MIDDLE EAST

You are the sales representative for your construction company in the Middle East. Your company has bid on a substantial project which it wants *very much* to get. Yesterday, the cousin of the minister who will award the contract suggested that he might be of help. You are reasonably sure that with his help the chances of getting the contract would increase. For his assistance, the minister expects $20,000. You would have to pay this in addition to the standard fees to your agent. If you do not make this payment to the minister, you are certain that he will go to your competition (who have won the last three contracts), and they *will* make the payment (and probably get this contract, too).

Your company has no code of conduct yet, although a committee was formed some time ago to consider one. The government of your country recently passed a Business Practices Act. The pertinent paragraph is somewhat vague, but implies that this kind of payment would probably be a violation of the act. The person to whom you report, and those above him, do not want to become involved. The decision is yours to make.

CASE 2: HAZARDOUS MATERIALS IN WEST AFRICA

For one year now, you have been international vice president of a multinational firm that produces and markets chemicals. The minister of agriculture in a small developing country in West Africa has requested a series of large shipments over the next five years of a special insecticide that only your firm prepares. The minister believes that this chemical is the only one that will rid one of his crops of a new infestation that threatens to destroy it. You know, however, that one other insecticide would probably be equally effective. It is produced in another country and has never been allowed in your own country.

Your insecticide, MIM, is highly toxic. After years of debate, your government has just passed a law forbidding its use in your country. There is evidence that dangerous amounts are easily ingested by humans through residue on vegetables, through animals that eat the crops, and through the water supply. After careful thought, you tell the minister about this evidence. He still insists on using it, arguing that it is necessary and it will be used "intelligently." You are quite sure that, ten years from now, it will begin to damage the health of some of his people.

Both the president and the executive vice president of your firm feel strongly that the order should be filled. They question the government's position, and they are very concerned about the large inventory of MIM on hand and the serious financial setback its prohibition will cause the company. They have made it clear, however, that the decision is up to you.

Note: While the company has a code of conduct and your government has a Business Practices Act, neither covers hazardous materials.

CASE 3: THE SOUTHEAST ASIAN ADVERTISING CAMPAIGN

You are the new marketing manager for a very large, profitable international firm that manufactures automobile tires. Your advertising agency has just presented for your approval elaborate plans for introducing a new tire into the Southeast Asian market. The promotional material clearly implies that your product is better than all local products. In fact it is better than some, but not as good as others. This material tries to attract potential buyers by explaining that for six months your product will be sold at a "reduced price." Actually, the price is reduced from a hypothetical amount that was established only so it could be "reduced." The ad claims that the tire has been tested under the "most adverse" conditions. In fact it has not been tested in the prolonged heat and humidity of the tropics. Finally, your company assures potential buyers that, riding on your tires, they will be safer in their car than ever before. The truth is, however, that they could have been equally safe on a competitor's tire that has been available for two years.

You know your product is good. You also know the proposed advertising is deceptive. Your superiors have never been concerned about such practices, believing they must present your products as distinctive in order to achieve and maintain a competitive edge. They are counting on a very favorable reception for this tire in Southeast Asia. They are counting on you to see that it gets this reception.

Whether you go with the proposed advertising or not is up to you. Your company has a code of conduct and your government has a Business Practices Act, but neither covers advertising practices.

CASE 4: CULTURAL CONFLICT IN THE MIDDLE EAST

You were quite upset last week when you read a strong editorial in the *New York Times,* written by a prominent journalist, that was highly critical of your company, especially its major project in a conservative Moslem country.

As the international vice president, you are responsible for this project, which is the building and running of a large steel plant. Based on the figures, this plant makes a lot of sense, both for your company and for the government of the country that approved the project. But as the journalist pointed out, it is to be built in a rural area and will have a very disruptive effect upon the values and customs of the people in the whole region. There will be many consequences. The young people from the other towns will move to work at the plant, thereby breaking up families and eliminating their primary source of financial and personal security. Working the second or third shift will further interfere with family responsibilities, as well as religious observances. Working year round will certainly mean that many people will be unable to return home to help with the harvest. As the young people will be paid more and more, they will gain more influence, thereby overturning century old patterns of authority. And, of course, the Westerners who will be brought in will probably not live up to the local moral standards and will not show due respect for local women.

The journalist ended by charging your company with "cultural imperialism" and claiming that your plant, if actually built and put into operation, would contribute to the disruption of the traditional values and relationships that have provided stability for the country through many generations.

You had known there would be some social changes, but you did not realize how profound they could be. You have now examined other evidence and discovered that a factory built several years ago by another foreign firm in a similar location is causing exactly these problems—and more. Widespread concern in the country over these problems is one reason for the increasing influence of traditionalists and nationalists in the country, who argue for getting rid of all foreign firms and their disruptive priorities and practices.

Your company has a code of conduct and your government has a Business Practices Act, but neither deals with the destruction of traditional values and relationships. You are on your own here. A lot is at stake for the company, and for the people of the region into which you had planned to move. The decision is yours.

STEP 2: In groups of four to six students, reach consensus about how to handle each situation.

DESCRIPTION

1. What decisions did each group reach?

DIAGNOSIS

2. How ethical were the decisions reached?
3. What criteria did you use to evaluate the decisions?

PRESCRIPTION

4. How could you improve your decision making to make it more ethical?

Activity 6–5   HOW BIASED IS YOUR DECISION MAKING?

STEP I: Answer each of the following problems.

1. A certain town is served by two hospitals. In the larger hospital about 45 babies are born each day, and in the smaller hospital about 15 babies are born each day. Although the overall proportion of boys is about 50 percent, the actual proportion at either hospital may be greater or less than 50 percent on any day. At the end of a year, which hospital will have the greater number of days on which more than 60 percent of the babies born were boys?
   a. The large hospital
   b. The small hospital
   c. Neither—the number of days will be about the same (within 5 percent of each other)

2. Linda is 31, single, outspoken, and very bright. She majored in philosophy in college. As a student, she was deeply concerned with discrimination and other social issues, and participated in antinuclear demonstrations. Which statement is more likely:
   a. Linda is a bank teller
   b. Linda is a bank teller and active in the feminist movement

3. A cab was involved in a hit-and-run accident. Two cab companies serve the city: the Green, which operates 85 percent of the cabs, and the Blue, which operates the remaining 15 percent. A witness identifies the hit-and-run cab as Blue. When the court tests the reliability of the witness under circumstances similar to those on the night of the accident, he correctly identifies the color of a cab 80 percent of the time and misidentifies it the other 20 percent. What is the probability that the cab involved in the accident was Blue, as the witness stated?

4. Imagine that you face this pair of concurrent decisions. Examine these decisions, then indicate which choices you prefer.

Decision I

Choose between:
   a. a sure gain of $240
   b. a 25 percent chance of winning $1,000 and a 75 percent chance of winning nothing

Decision II

Choose between:
   c. a sure loss of $750
   d. A 75 percent chance of losing $1,000 and a 25 percent chance of losing nothing

Decision III

Choose between:
   e. a sure loss of $3,000
   f. an 80 percent chance of losing $4,000 and a 20 percent chance of losing nothing

5. You have decided to see a Broadway play and have bought a $40 ticket. As you enter the theater, you realize you have lost your ticket. You cannot remember the seat number, so you cannot prove to the management that you bought a ticket. Would you spend $40 for a new ticket?

You have reserved a seat for a Broadway play for which the ticket price is $40. As you enter the theater to buy your ticket, you discover you have lost $40 from your pocket. Would you still buy the ticket? (Assume you have enough cash left to do so.)

6. Imagine you have operable lung cancer and must choose between two treatments—surgery and radiation therapy. Of 100 people having surgery, 10 die during the operation, 32 (including those original 10) are dead after one year, and 66 after five years. Of 100 people having radiation therapy, none dies during treatment, 23 are dead after one year, and 78 after five years. Which treatment would you prefer?

STEP 2: Your instructor will give you the correct answer to each problem.

STEP 3: Discussion. In small groups, with the entire class, or in written form, as directed by your instructor, answer the following questions.

DESCRIPTION
1. How accurate were the decisions you reached?

DIAGNOSIS
2. What biases were evident in the decisions you reached?

PRESCRIPTION
3. How could you improve your decision making to make it more accurate?

From D. Kahnemann and A. Tversky, Rational choice and the forming of decisions, *Journal of Business* 59 (4) (1986): 5251–5278; A. Tversky and D. Kahnemann, The framing of decisions and the psychology of choice, *Science* 211 (1981): 453–458; D. Kahnemann and A. Tversky, Extension needs intuitive reasoning, *Psychological Review* 90 (1983): 293–315; K. McKean, Decisions, decisions, *Discover Magazine* (June 1985).

Activity 6–6 — DAVE STEWART (S) CASE

STEP 1: Read the Dave Stewart (S) case.

Dave Stewart was a leasing agent for a major real estate development firm. A leasing agent sold office and warehouse space or locations for new construction to businesses and also negotiated with such clients over terms and conditions of contracts. Dave was his firm's primary contact in a business deal involving D.B. Snow, a company that had decided to lease or buy new facilities from Dave's firm. He ran into three troublesome situations over this one deal.

1. D.B. Snow wanted a ten-year lease term on the property and buildings, with an option to buy it all after five years, instead of leasing for a second five-year period. Snow and Dave agreed that the purchase price—should Snow decide to buy the leased facilities—would be equal to the expenses for certain property improvements that Dave's firm had incurred prior to its leasing arrangement with Snow. Dave knew that the actual amount his company had paid for improvements totaled $600,000, but his boss, Tom, instructed him to tell Snow

that the improvements had cost $900,000. Tom also told Dave that he should back down from the $900,000 bluff only if Snow questioned the figure.

2. Snow had signed a separate contract with Dave's firm that required the firm to reserve some land adjacent to Snow's leasing location for a future administrative building. Both Dave and Snow had thought there was enough land available for future construction, but Dave discovered later that a sewer easement and flood plain limited the available land and prohibited future construction of the administrative building. Snow had chosen Dave's building location over competing locations partly because it had been told that this land would be available. Tom told Dave to keep quiet about his discovery and to have architectural drawings prepared showing this adjacent building, which could not be built.

3. A local broker had represented Snow in its move to the new leasing location. This broker's standard commission was 4 percent of the gross lease amount over the whole lease term. Both Dave and his boss Tom knew that the broker expected to be paid according to the standard commission on the basis of the full ten-year

lease term ($240,000), even though Snow had the option to buy out after five years. Several weeks after Snow's lease was signed, Tom told Dave to tell the broker that, because Snow had the option to buy out after the fifth year, the arrangement represented the equivalent of a five-year lease. Consequently, Dave's firm would pay the broker only half the commission he expected—$120,000 instead of $240,000.

Dave had much to think about as he faced the decisions he had to make about how to handle the D.B. Snow deal. His boss expected him to carry out his orders without question. Dave knew that a fellow leasing agent in the same office would not even think twice before doing so. Dave was paid $50,000 annually by his firm and he needed the money badly. He still had school debts to pay off, he had almost no savings, and he and his wife had just had their first baby. If he followed his conscience, he would jeopardize his position with his employer and maybe face a personal financial crisis.

STEP 2: Prepare the case for class discussion.

STEP 3: Answer each of the following questions, individually or in small groups, as directed by your instructor.

DESCRIPTION
1. Describe the situation faced by Dave Stewart.

DIAGNOSIS
2. What decisions must Dave Stewart make?
3. What information is available for use in the decision making?
4. What ethical issues does he face?

PRESCRIPTION
5. What process should Dave use in making the decisions?
6. What advantages do individual and group decision making offer?
7. How can he ensure that he makes a high-quality, accepted, ethical decision?

ACTION
8. What outcomes are likely from each possible decision?

STEP 4: Discussion. In small groups, with the entire class, or in written form, share your answers to the questions above. Then answer the following questions:

1. What symptoms suggest that a problem exists?
2. What problems exist in the case?
3. What theories and concepts help explain those problems?
4. How should the situation be handled?

Activity 6–7 | BRAINSTORMING ACTIVITY

STEP 1: In groups of six to eight people, list as many possible answers to either of the following or to a question given to you by your instructor. "Think of as many uses as possible for a banana" or "What changes would make this course better?" Do not evaluate the answers or try to choose only good ones. Your instructor will tell you how much time you will have to develop your list of ideas.

STEP 2: Share your responses with the rest of the class.

STEP 3: Discussion. With the entire class, answer the following questions:

1. How effective was your group in generating ideas?
2. Did the group avoid evaluating the ideas?
3. How could your group improve its brainstorming?

Activity 6–8 DECISION MAKING IN GROUPS

STEP 1: Your instructor will organize the class into nominal groups of five to eight people and present the task to you.

STEP 2: Write your own ideas about the problem on a piece of paper.

STEP 3: In the small groups, each person should contribute one idea and list it on a flip chart. This type of sharing should continue until all ideas are publicly recorded.

STEP 4: Where necessary, briefly clarify each idea by means of examples and explanations, but do not debate for relative merits. Eliminate duplicate ideas and refine global ideas into two or more specific items.

STEP 5: As individuals, rank or classify all ideas in writing according to criteria specified by the instructor.

STEP 6: Tabulate and summarize all individual evaluations to produce a group decision.

STEP 7: With the entire class, share the decisions you reached.

STEP 8: The instructor will select a panel of experts (usually the entire class) who are informed about the task.

STEP 9: You will receive a question or questionnaire to complete in writing.

STEP 10: Your instructor or appointed members of the class will tabulate and summarize the data.

STEP 11: The instructor will feed back and discuss the summarized data with the class.

STEP 12: The instructor may repeat Steps 9, 10, and 11 until some consensus is reached about the task or problem.

STEP 13: With the entire class, share the decisions you reached.

STEP 14: Your instructor will organize you into small groups of five to eight individuals.

STEP 15: Each group will receive a problem or task.

STEP 16: As a group, you are to brainstorm possible solutions to the problem. List all ideas without discussion on a large piece of newsprint.

STEP 17: Using these ideas, reach consensus about a decision.

STEP 18: With the entire class, share the ideas you generated.

STEP 19: Discussion. In small groups, with the entire class, or in written form, as directed by your instructor compare and contrast the three approaches to decision making.

1. How did the approaches differ? How were they similar?
2. Which approach resulted in the most effective decisions?
3. Under what circumstances would each approach be effective? ineffective?
4. Offer ways of improving the effectiveness of the decision-making processes you used.

Based on Curtis W. Cook, Nominal group methods enrich classroom learning. *Exchange: The Organizational Behavior Teaching Journal* 5 (1980): 33–36.

$\mathscr{A}$ctivity 6–9   "THE JFK TAPES—CUBAN MISSILE CRISIS"

STEP 1: View the ABC video entitled "The JFK Tapes—Cuban Missile Crisis."

STEP 2: Individually or in small groups, trace the steps in the decision making about the Cuban Missile crisis. Then answer the following questions:

1. Did Kennedy and his advisors follow the steps in the rational decision-making process?
2. Do other models of decision making better describe the decision-making process?
3. Was the decision making effective?
4. Did groupthink exist?
5. What other factors affected the decision and the decision-making process?
6. How could the decision making about the Cuban Missile Crisis have been improved?

Chapter 7

Chapter Outline

- **Work-Out Programs at General Electric**
- **The Communication Process**
  - **Components of Communication**
  - **The Use of Language**
  - **Nonverbal Communication**
  - **Effective Listening**
  - **Communication Overload and Underload**
- **Directions of Communication**
  - **Downward Communication**
  - **Upward Communication**
  - **Lateral Communication**
- **Formal Versus Informal Communication**
  - **Media Used in Formal Communication**
  - **Communication Networks**
  - **The Grapevine**
- **Barriers to Communication**
  - **Perceptual and Attributional Biases**
  - **Interpersonal Relationships**
  - **Organization Structure**
  - **Physical Distance**
  - **Cultural Differences**
- **Overcoming Communication Barriers**
  - **Use Electronic Communication**
  - **Improve Interpersonal Interactions**
  - **Recognize Cultural Differences**
  - **Change the Organization's Structure**
- **Improving Communication in Special Situations**
  - **Conducting Productive Meetings**
  - **Conducting Effective Placement Interviews**
  - **Improving Performance Appraisals**
- **Summary**
- **Diagnostic Questions**
- **Activities**

Improving Communication

After completing the reading and activities in Chapter 7, students will be able to

1. Describe the two-way communication process and its components.

2. Comment about two ways language can facilitate and distort communication.

3. Describe typical deficiencies in listening and show how active listening addresses them.

4. Cite the five functions of nonverbal communication.

5. List the causes and outcomes of communication overload and underload.

6. Compare and contrast communication that occurs upward, downward, and laterally and offer strategies for communicating effectively in each direction.

7. Compare and contrast the advantages and disadvantages of formal and informal communication and their uses.

8. Identify five barriers to effective communication and cite at least one way to overcome each.

9. Discuss the nature and use of electronic communication in organizations.

10. Offer guidelines for increasing the effectiveness of meetings, placement interviews, and performance evaluations in organizations.

Work-Out Programs at General Electric

As the president of General Electric, John F. Welch, Jr., determined that one way to make his company more effective was to discard the traditional organizational hierarchy. Instead, he instituted a new team approach that emphasized employee involvement. Improving communication throughout the company became a key ingredient of this new management thrust.

Welch conceived of Work-Out to challenge individuals to think intensively and creatively, reassess the work needed to do their jobs, and jointly solve problems. Work-Out encourages communication among individuals' peers as well as with their bosses. Forty to 100 employees from all ranks and diverse functions attend a three-day session in a conference center.

A manager typically introduces the session and presents a tentative agenda. For the rest of the first day and continuing through the second day, teams of five or six people attack some or all of the items of the agenda. They attempt to identify problems, list complaints, discuss options, and propose solutions. They also prepare a presentation to be delivered to the boss on the third day. On the third day, the teams present a series of proposals. The boss may agree on the spot, disagree on the spot, or ask for more information from a team convened to provide it by a specific day. One boss reported:

" 'I was wringing wet within half an hour.'. . . His employees had set up the room so that Lauzon [the boss] had his back to his boss. 'They had 108 proposals, I had about a minute to say yes or no to each one, and I couldn't make eye contact with my boss without turning around, which would show everyone in the room that I was chicken. . . .' and Lauzon said yes to all but eight."[1]

Work-Out has opened communication. As one employee said, "When you've been told to shut up for 20 years, and someone tells you to speak up—you're going to let them have it."[2] Work-Out has also resulted in significant cost savings, as well as improved relations between labor and management. GE is now extending Work-Outs to include customers and suppliers.[3]

Communication involves the exchange of information between two or more parties. At General Electric, for example, participants in a Work-Out program exchange information with their peers on the team, as well as with their boss. Its primary function is the sharing of information including facts, assumptions, behaviors, attitudes, and feelings between individuals, groups, or even organizations. Communication also functions to build and reinforce interdependence between various parts of the organization. As a linking mechanism among the different organizational subsystems, communication is a central feature of the *structure* of groups and organizations. It helps coordinate tasks and activities within and between organizations.

We begin this chapter with an examination of the communication process. Next we discuss downward, upward, and lateral communication. Then we contrast formal and informal communication. We next identify barriers to communication and ways to overcome them. The chapter concludes with ways of improving communication in special situations.

THE COMMUNICATION PROCESS

Effective communication can be characterized as **two-way,** as shown in Figure 7–1. This model indicates that communication flows from one person or group to another and then, via feedback, back to the original person, making a closed loop or circle. The loop begins when a person, or sender, has a message he or she wants to communicate. The sender first **encodes** the message, meaning he or she expresses it in a way that he or she expects will be understood. The sender then **transmits** the message or conveys it through a **channel,** which is the formal or informal link between two parties, using a particular **medium,** such as face-to-face conversation, the telephone, a written memo, or electronic mail to convey the message.

A receiver then takes the message and tries to understand it by decoding what was received. Decoding may involve careful listening in the case of oral communication or careful reading in the case of written or electronic communication. The receiver then provides the sender with some feedback that shows what was received. In this and most communications **noise** interferes with communication and can limit its accuracy.

To get a better understanding of this process, we begin by looking at its components. Then we will look at other factors in the communication process: the use of language, nonverbal communication, effective listening, and communication overload and underload.

FIGURE 7–1 *The two-way communication process*

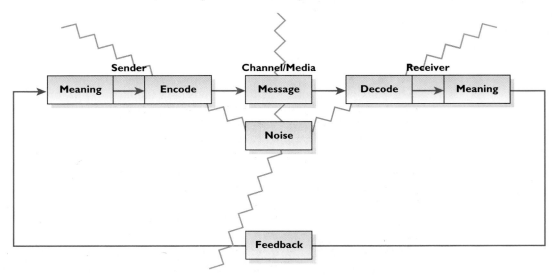

COMPONENTS OF COMMUNICATION

Looking again at the two-way model of communication, we can see that communication includes the following components: encoding, transmission, decoding, feedback, and noise.

Encoding A person with a meaning to convey first must determine how to express that meaning. As the background for encoding information, the sender uses his or her own *frame of reference.* It includes the individual's view of the organization or situation as a function of personal education, interpersonal relationships, attitudes, knowledge, and experience.

Consider an exchange between a female member of a Work-Out team, who we will identify as Jennifer Smith, and her boss at General Electric. Let us assume that Smith's team appointed her to present their ideas to their boss. Let us also assume that the first proposal she wishes to communicate describes a new way of scheduling jobs. Smith acts as a *sender* and begins with the information she wishes to communicate—the new approach to job scheduling. She then *encodes* this information in a way that she believes her boss will understand.

In encoding a message, the sender must evaluate the most effective way to convey the information. Think about an employee who wants to ask his supervisor for a pay raise. How should the employee word the question? Should he say "could I please have a pay raise?" or "I want to discuss my current salary with you" or "I want an increment in my financial status instantaneously." Obviously the language he uses will affect the message his boss ultimately hears. Most likely, he will use English unless he knows that his boss communicates better in another language. He might freely use special jargon that he knows his boss will understand. The nonverbal messages he encodes will also have an impact. Should he use a pleading tone, an arrogant one, an indifferent one, or some other tone? Should he stomp his feet and wave his hands, stand quietly, or sit in a relaxed position when asking? We will look at nonverbal communication in more detail later in this section.

Transmission After encoding, the sender transmits the message. Jennifer Smith transmitted the message about the schedule using a formal communication channel. She did not rely on the informal grapevine to send her message. She used the medium of face-to-face conversation. What other media alternatives are available? Smith could send a memorandum, send an electronic mail message, convene a meeting with her boss and his bosses, or submit a formal report. Table 7–1 lists a variety of transmission options as well as their advantages and disadvantages.

FORD MOTOR COMPANY. Linda M. Miller, who manages the Ford engine and fuel-tank plant in Dearborn, Michigan spends large amounts of time on the plant floor to ensure that workers communicate with her. She says that although managers may have an open door policy, many plant workers are reluctant to visit executives' offices. Her visibility in the plant encourages people to communicate face-to-face with her.[4]

NMR INSTRUMENTS. NMR, a manufacturer of scientific instruments, communicates with its customers using electronic mail. They distribute an electronic newsletter and encourage communication not only between the company and its customers but between customers.[5]

In determining the appropriateness of the media used, the employee should consider among other factors the media's richness, which refers to the amount of information it conveys and how well it facilitates understanding. Media richness is

TABLE 7–1 *Options for communication media*

	GENERALLY AVAILABLE	RELATIVELY LOW COST	HIGH SPEED	IMMEDIATE INTERACTION	HIGH IMPACT AND ATTENTION
Written					
Letters	X	X			
Memos and reports			X		X
Telegrams			X		X
Newspapers and magazines	X				
Handbooks and manuals	X	X			
Bulletins and posters	X	X			
Inserts and enclosures	X	X			X
Oral					
Telephone	X	X	X	X	X
Intercom and paging	X		X		X
Conferences and meetings	X			X	
Speeches	X			X	
Electronic					
Fax			X	X	X
Electronic mail			X	X	
Voice messaging			X		X
Computer conferencing			X		X
Audio conferencing				X	X
Video conferencing				X	X
Groupware				X	

Adapted with permission from Dale A. Level, Jr., and William P. Galle, Jr., *Business Communications: Theory and Practice* (Homewood, Ill.: Business Publications, Inc./Richard D. Irwin, Inc., 1988), pp. 91, 93.

determined by the speed the media provides feedback, the variety of communication channels on which it works, the extent of personal interactions allowed, and the richness of language it accommodates.[6] As tasks become more ambiguous, managers should increase the richness of the media they use. For example, they should send nonroutine and difficult communications through a rich medium, such as fact-to-face communication, and routine simple communications through a lean medium, such as a memo.[7] They should also use rich media to increase personal visibility and implement company strategies.[8]

LEVI STRAUSS. Tommye Jo Daves is responsible for the Valley River, North Carolina, plant that manufactures Levi's jeans, a significant advancement from her first position with Levi Strauss in 1959 as a stitcher. She received a personal invitation in the mail from the president of Levi Strauss to attend a Leadership Week. That experience emphasized the importance of having workers participate in decision making. She and her mostly female crew rely on communication from the plant's employees to make the plant run more smoothly and more profitably.

Decoding During the last part of the Work-Out conference, the boss has only a limited time to decode each proposal presented by the Work-Out team. For example, he must quickly determine what Jennifer Smith's proposal for a different job schedule means, and then agree, disagree, or send the proposal to a team for further study. He must also pay attention to nonverbal cues such as body language or tone of voice that accompany the transmission, because they may reveal a hidden meaning or explicit intent. Effective listening, which we discuss in greater detail later in this chapter, is a key component of effective decoding.

Both decoding and encoding occur within the communicators' frames of reference, that is, a view of the situation that results from the interaction of education, interpersonal relationships, attitudes, knowledge, and experience. A receiver who has a similar frame of reference as the sender will experience less difficulty in decoding than one whose frame of reference differs considerably. One of the major challenges of communicating globally is to develop common frames of reference or to find ways to bridge cultural differences.

Feedback *Feedback* refers to the receiver's acknowledgement that the message has been received. It provides the sender with information about the receiver's understanding of the message being sent. By agreeing or disagreeing to Jennifer Smith's job scheduling proposal, her manager will provide feedback that the communication was received. Of course, Smith does not know at that moment whether the precise message she sent was received. The actual implementation of the proposal will indicate the effectiveness of the communication. Quality feedback should indicate whether encoding or decoding errors occurred as well as signal problems or distortions during transmission. Thus, feedback limits the errors and inaccuracies that occur in transmission. Feedback may even call for a new transmission of the same or related message.

Without feedback, *one-way communication* occurs. This means there is no feedback between the receiver and sender. Too often, one-way communication occurs between managers and their employees. Faced with differences in their power, lack of time, and a desire to save face by not passing on negative information, employees may be discouraged from providing the necessary feedback to their managers.

INTEL. Andrew S. Grove, the CEO of Intel, sits in a cramped, open cubicle surrounded by books and stick-on notes. When he is in the office, Grove encourages any employee to stop and talk with him about any subject. This type of feedback, which he calls "constructive confrontation," encourages effective communication at Intel.[9]

Why do some managers fail to engage their employees in two-way communication? These managers often experience conflict between their roles as authorities and their desire to be liked by employees. Other managers rely too much on written memorandums as a way of communicating with employees. Memorandums are not a rich medium, since they involve a single channel of communication and provide limited opportunities for feedback. As such, memorandums limit the effectiveness of communication. Managers may also encourage one-way communication and hence discourage feedback because they lack the self-confidence needed to accept possible suggestions, criticisms, or new ideas from their employees.

Subordinates can also encourage one-way communication. Just as managers may attempt to protect their power positions, their employees may try to manipulate their boss's image of them. Frequently, for example, employees withhold negative information about themselves or their activities. Or they may not inform their manager about needs, interests, and values that contradict the organizational culture. For example, attorneys cannot tell their bosses that working overtime poses a hardship on their spouse or children because the organization values the accrual of billable hours and hence expects overtime from its employees. Other employees mistrust their managers and so withhold information from them.

Why do these situations arise? Some employees may assume that they and their bosses have different goals. Others mistrust their bosses. Still others lack the persistence needed to seek responses from their supervisors. Impression management, or trying to create a specific image for others in the organization, may also play a role in whether individuals seek feedback in that employees will assess how a request for feedback will be interpreted and how the resulting information will affect their public image.[10]

SCEcorp. John E. Bryson, CEO of SCEcorp and Southern California Edison Company, its main subsidiary, holds "town hall" meetings with 300 randomly chosen employees to discuss business. He also regularly holds "3C" (candor, challenge, and commitment) meetings with ad hoc teams and asks them to offer recommendations for business changes.[11]

Noise *Noise* refers to interference in the communication process. Fire engine sirens, building construction, and loud conversations on the side can interfere with accurate communication.

Noise can also be more subtle than physical noises. It can include the communicators' frames of reference, such as their education, values, and experiences, which distort the messages transmitted. Cultural differences can also create noise. Imagine the interference created when American-born managers in the United States and Japanese-born managers in Japan attempt to speak in English on the telephone. Can you list the potential sources of noise in that situation? Noise might include static or delays on the line, different experiences of the U.S. and Japanese managers, or cultural variations in tone of voice. Even the presence of a silent third party during a conversation may act as noise that distracts the receiver from hearing what the speaker said. Other sources of noise include differences in roles in the organization, biases in attributions, and various perceptual predispositions. Often, diagnosing these sources of noise is a first step in improving communication.

THE USE OF LANGUAGE

Often, we fail to recognize the impact of subtleties in language, ignoring the fact that shades of meaning can have significant consequences for communication. Yet, the words we use to encode a message influence its quality. In most languages, words have **denotations,** or literal meanings. Even so, many denotations are abstract or vague and thus leave room for interpretation.[12] As a result, different people may use the same word to mean different things. For example, managers and employees may assign very different absolute probabilities to words such as **very likely, probably,** and **reasonably likely.** Such bypassing, where individuals miss each other with their meanings, occurs most often in cross-cultural or stressful situations.[13]

The use of **jargon,** or technical terminology, can create distortions unless all parties understand it. Consider the conflict that might arise when a store manager asks the marketing department to put together a "marketing campaign" in a week. The store manager is using the term to denote a single newspaper advertisement. To the professionals in the marketing department, however, the term refers to a more elaborate, coordinated effort that might involve everything from advertisements to publicity and promotional contests.

Words also have **connotations,** or emotional messages that affect their meaning. Advertisers, for example, use "perfume-free" instead of "nonscented" because "free" has powerful, positive connotations. Managers who have to cut their staffs prefer to speak of "right-sizing" instead of "downsizing." Think about the experience of shopping for a personal computer. If the salesperson thinks the customer is a "power user," she may use very technical jargon to describe its speed, storage, and display. If, on the other hand, the customer seems to be a "technophobe" or novice, the salesperson may use very simple language.

Gender Differences in Communication Recent research suggests that men and women communicate differently.[14] A classic story illustrates a basic difference between male and female communication. A man and a woman were driving to a meeting at a location that they had never visited before. After fifty minutes of driving around in circles, the woman was visibly upset. When asked why, she responded that she was not upset about being lost, but she was furious that her male companion had repeatedly refused to stop and ask directions.

Women ask for information and men resist asking for it. Women tend to use *rapport-talk,* which focuses on building relationships and establishing connections, whereas men tend to use *report-talk,* which emphasizes demonstration of knowledge and skills and focusing attention on themselves.[15] On the job, women are more likely to use apologetic language, even if they do not mean to apologize, and say "thanks" ritualistically but for no apparent reason. They also give praise more frequently, and are more indirect in their comments.[16]

In one study women sounded more polite but also more uncertain, whereas men used more informal pronunciations, sounded more challenging, direct, and authoritative. The feminine style was more accommodating, intimate, collaborative, and facilitative, whereas the masculine style was more action-oriented, informational, and controlling.[17] Recognizing such differences should facilitate more accurate diagnosis of communication problems.

NONVERBAL COMMUNICATION

Nonverbal communication refers to the use of gestures, movements, material things, time, and space to clarify or confuse the meaning of verbal communication. For example, the kind of facial expressions that accompany a request for time off may indicate its importance or frivolity. If an interviewer arrives at an interview late, the interviewee may interpret any comments as less sincere than if the interviewer is prompt. Or a salesperson may use props to illustrate aspects of a sales pitch.

Nonverbal cues serve five functions.[18]

- *Repetition* of the message the individual is making verbally: An individual who nods after he or she answers affirmatively confirms the verbal message with the nonverbal gesture.

- *Contradiction* of the message the individual is trying to convey: An individual who pounds the table while stating that he or she does not care about the situation being discussed uses verbal and nonverbal communication that disagrees. The nonverbal communication may, in some cases, be more powerful or accurate than the verbal communication.

■ **Substitution** for a verbal message: An individual with "fire in his eyes" conveys information without using verbal messages.

■ **Complementing** a verbal message: A manager who beams while giving praise increases the impact of the compliment to the employee.

■ **Accenting** or underlining the verbal message: For example, speaking very softly or stamping your feet shows the importance an individual attaches to a message.

Senders can intentionally use nonverbal communication to increase the impact of their verbal communication. But nonverbal signals can also deliver unintended messages. English-speaking managers who supervise non-English-speaking workers often experience this problem.[19] For example, a gesture may have different meanings in different cultures. Consider the "A-OK" gesture with the thumb and forefinger circled. In the United States it means that things are fine, in Brazil it is an obscene gesture, and in Japan it means money.[20] Two Arabs discussing a business proposal will change the tone and volume of their voice dramatically depending on the subject matter because in Arab culture increased volume or pitch indicates a greater interest in the subject. An American interacting with them should follow the same approach to varying tone.[21] A Japanese manager may have a continuous smile on his face in a meeting. Does this mean he is pleased with the meeting's progress? Japanese people tend to communicate with minimal eye contact, facial expressions, or hand gestures. The smile may hide discomfort or embarrassment.[22]

EFFECTIVE LISTENING

Whereas language and nonverbal cues primarily influence the encoding of information by the sender, listening affects the quality of decoding by the receiver. As such, listening is vital to communication.

IBM. Lou Gerstner, the CEO of IBM chosen to rescue it in the early 1990s, began his tenure by spending extensive amounts of time listening to as many people as possible about the company. He believed that effective listening would help him identify the company's strengths, weaknesses, and problems.[23]

The bosses who participate in the Work-Out program must practice quality listening to ensure that they hear their subordinates' proposals correctly. Receivers can listen in directing, judgmental, probing, smoothing, or active ways, as described in Table 7–2.[24]

Deficiencies in listening can result when individuals do not pay careful attention to the message being transmitted, do not understand the language used to encode the message, do not spend enough time in decoding the message, or ignore the nonverbal cues that accompany the verbal message. Many of these deficiencies can be avoided by active listening.[25] **Active listening** means listening for what is said as well as the feelings behind the message. If an employee says, "I really think I will have trouble meeting this deadline," the manager must determine whether the employee means that there is no way he or she will meet the deadline, he or she is frus-

TABLE 7–2 *Types of listening*

TYPE	FUNCTION	EXAMPLE
Directing	Leads the speaker by guiding the limits and direction of conversation.	If I were you, I would just ignore it.
Judgmental	Introduces personal value judgments into the conversation. Injects personal values or opinions.	You are absolutely right. Tom is impossible to get along with.
Probing	Asks a lot of questions in an attempt to get to the heart of the matter.	When did all this start? What do you want me to do about it?
Smoothing	Pats the speaker on the head and makes light of his or her problems; urges conflict resolution.	You and Tom just had a bad day. Don't worry—tomorrow it will all be forgotten.
Empathic/Active	Tries to create an encouraging atmosphere for the speaker to use in expressing and solving the problem. Tends to feed back neutral summaries of what they have heard.	It seems that you are troubled by the fact that you and Tom don't get along.

SOURCE: From *Organizational Communication: A Managerial Perspective,* 2nd Edition by Jane Whitney Gibson and Richard M. Hodgetts, pp. 68–69. Copyright © 1991 by HarperCollins Publishers, Inc. Reprinted by permission.

trated with how the work is proceeding, he or she wants recognition, he or she lacks the skills to complete the job, or he or she has some other feeling.

A person who actively listens has to look for the ***total meaning*** of what the speaker says, not just the superficial or partial meaning. After an active listener has analyzed the feelings that accompany a communication, he or she must also acknowledge these feelings as part of the feedback. The boss might say to the employee who claims to be unable to meet a deadline, "I know this is hard work and sometimes you find it frustrating, but let's see if we can figure out a way to make it less frustrating for you."

Techniques for Active Listening To listen actively, you must pick up ***nonverbal*** as well as verbal cues. Try saying "I'd like to work on a different project" in a pleading tone of voice, then try a dogmatic tone of voice and then try a matter-of-fact tone of voice. How do the messages conveyed by the three different tones differ? The facial expressions an individual uses often provide more information about what he or she is thinking and feeling than the actual words the person says.

In active listening the receiver can provide feedback by ***paraphrasing*** the sender's message, restating it in his or her own way. For example, if the sender states, "I don't like the work you have been doing," the receiver (e.g., his employee) might paraphrase it as "you are saying that you are dissatisfied with my performance" or the receiver might paraphrase it as "you are saying that you want to assign me different types of work to do." Note that these ways of paraphrasing the original message suggest very different understandings of the original statement. The sender, upon receiving this feedback from the receiver, can then clarify his or her meaning.

Alternatively, the receiver may ***perception-check;*** that is, describe what he or she perceives is the sender's inner state at the time of communication to check his or her understanding of the message. For example, if the sender states, "I don't like the work you have been doing," the receiver might check his or her perception of the statement by asking, "are you dissatisfied with me as an employee?" or "are you dissatisfied with the quantity of my output?" Note that answers to these two questions will identify different feelings.

A third active listening technique is *behavior description.* Here the individual reports specific, observable actions of others without making accusations or generalizations about their motives, personality, or characteristics. Similarly, *description of feelings,* where the individual specifies or identifies another's feelings by name, analogy, or some other verbal representation, can increase active listening. Active listening techniques help ensure the communicator that he or she has accurate information. Ensuring a high quality of information is not the only challenge in communication. Both senders and receivers need to ensure that they have the appropriate quantity of information as well.

COMMUNICATION OVERLOAD AND UNDERLOAD

Often people send too much or too little information. Communication overload and underload may result for the person receiving the information. Has anyone ever given you such complicated directions that you have no idea where to begin to follow them? You may be experiencing *information overload.* It often occurs when a person experiences significant time constraints, the demands of a job are too great, or the job requires extensive coordination with other job holders.[26] Information overload can become particularly problematic when individuals use electronic mail and other electronic messaging systems extensively.

XEROX. A group of software developers at Xerox had so much information overload that they have structured *quiet times* into their days when they cannot interact with others inside or outside the organization.[27]

COMPUTER ASSOCIATES. The CEO of Computer Associates in New York limits employee access to electronic mail to several hours daily.[28]

In contrast, you may not have received enough information to perform a particular task or understand a situation you face. In this case, *information underload* has resulted. Underload often occurs when the sender has a low desire to communicate, such as when an individual functions in isolation from other organizational members or when great physical distance prevents frequent communication. The advent of electronic means of communication and decreased costs of telecommunications, as discussed later in this chapter, have decreased the frequency of information underload.

Figure 7–2 illustrates the personal and organizational factors that influence the amount of information transmitted. Job holders who require limited coordination with others, experience great physical distance from others, have highly routine jobs with few time constraints and few decisions to be made, and have a low ability and desire to communicate typically experience underload.[29] Job holders who require extensive coordination to do the job, experience close physical proximity to others, have unique job requirements with many time constraints and many decisions to be made, and have a high ability and desire to communicate often experience overload. Underload can result in alienation, lack of motivation, and apathy. Overload can cause high stress, confusion, and mistakes.

FIGURE 7–2

Communication load: a working model

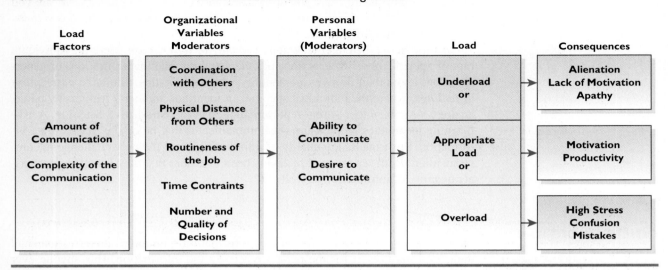

SOURCE: J.W. Gibson and R.M. Hodgetts, *Organizational Communication: A Managerial Perspective,* 2nd ed. (New York: HarperCollins, 1991), p. 283. Copyright © 1991 by Harper & Row, Publishers, Inc. Reprinted by permission of HarperCollins Publishers.

Cultural differences may cause overload or underload as well. Latin American cultures encourage verbal and nonverbal expression, whereas the Asian cultures support lower levels of communication. An individual's culture helps set expectations about the level of communication that is possible. Deviations from the level expected may result in overload or underload.

We can increase the efficiency of information use in a number of ways.[30]

■ Change the physical setting. Noise and distractions can be reduced or the physical layout altered to improve the flow of information.

■ Use filtering or screening devices that improve access to information. Changing the organization of bulletin boards, color coding information, or eliminating junk mail can improve access in this way.

■ Install technical devices such as software, videotapes, audio tapes, or improved phone systems.

■ Train the users to encode, transmit, and decode information more effectively. They can be encouraged to put information into a form that is more easily and efficiently disseminated.

DIRECTIONS OF COMMUNICATION

As shown in Figure 7–3, communication can follow a downward, upward, or lateral direction, which reflects the organization's structure. These structural factors can both facilitate and hinder communication.

FIGURE 7–3   *Directions of communication*

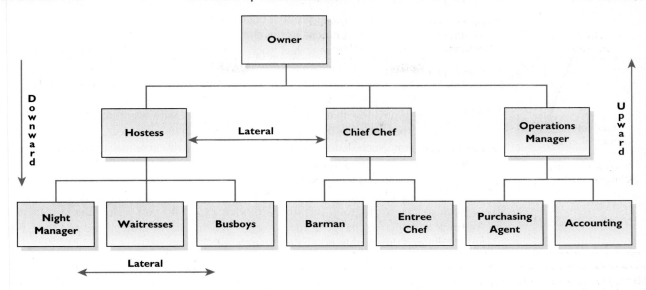

DOWNWARD COMMUNICATION

The president of a company communicates to the vice presidents. The middle managers disseminate information to their subordinates. Lower-level managers convey messages to staff members. Each of these managers communicates ***downward*** in the organization, that is, to individuals below them in the organizational hierarchy. Managers typically use downward communication to give information, orders, and directives to employees. John Welch at General Electric, for example, might have told his employees that he wanted them to design a program that would facilitate employee participation in decision making or in the development of new ideas.

Managers need to seek regular ways to share information, ideas, and both good and bad news with employees. All managers can encourage face-to-face communication with their direct reports by scheduling frequent staff meetings, making periodic contact by telephone, or using traditional or electronic mail to send information that does not require an immediate response. They can facilitate communication with other employees by regularly touring work sites, creating departmental, divisional, or company newsletters, organizing a communication hot-line in the organization, or using electronic mail to widely disseminate specific information.

ACTION INSTRUMENTS. Jim Pinto, the president of Action Instruments, which manufactures industrial computers for factory automation, regularly posts all current information about the company's operations and finances on a bulletin board in the lunch room. Because employees own 30 percent of the company's stock, Pinto insists on their having quality information to participate in decision making.[31] He believes that communication "must be continuous and consistent. It must not only be passive [open-door policy] but also positive, stimulating, pro-active, encouraging, rewarding."[32]

Although most managers intend to communicate accurately to their employees, some may consciously or unconsciously distort downward communication. They may pass on inaccurate, incomplete, or inconsistent information. Often managers withhold, screen, or manipulate information.[33] For example, they may fail to tell employees about potential product changes because they may be concerned about the employees' commitment to the changes. Or, they may delay news about staff cutbacks because they may feel such news would affect employee morale. The quality of downward communication is particularly important during a layoff. Giving full information and increasing managerial accessibility—even overcommunicating—are reasonable strategies.[34]

Sometimes downward communication begins with accurate and complete information but becomes distorted as the information moves through various levels of management. Such distortion may be the function of encoding, decoding, or transmission dysfunctions in the basic communication process, particularly if no feedback occurs. In one study, 923 managers and 4,708 subordinates in a large company in the communications industry gave significantly different answers to questions such as "In work-group meetings, to what extent do you make sure that there is frank and open exchange of ideas?" and "When tasks or projects are assigned, how clearly and thoroughly do you explain them?"[35]

At other times distortions may occur because managers lower in the hierarchy want to consciously or unconsciously change the message they pass down to the next level. For example, a middle manager may incorrectly feel that her employees will work harder if they do not receive top management's praise for their performance to date. Power differences, as discussed in Chapter 9, also can result in distortions.

Although most downward communication occurs within a single chain of command, sometimes managers send information to others lower in the organization but outside their own work unit. Distortions may be magnified in this situation because face-to-face contact is less common. Also, violations of the chain of command may further hinder accurate communication.

What happens when a manager frequently distorts information? Subordinates can become distrustful of their managers and begin to circumvent them to obtain more accurate information. If a plant manager feels that the vice president of operations is hiding plans for closing the plant, for example, he or she may seek other ways of verifying the information. Sometimes employees respond to distorted information over the long term by relying more on rumors or the informal network of contacts in the organization than on the formal chain of command.

Although open communication has been considered a panacea for many organizational problems, some researchers have argued that characteristics of the communicators, their relationships, and the organization and environment in which they function should influence how open communication should be.[36] Disclosure and directness can backfire if, for example, employees are not prepared to receive the information being sent, or managers are unwilling to deal with employees' reactions. Can you think of a situation where this might occur? Particularly in discussions about their performance, employees may not be prepared to hear about poor results and managers may be unprepared to deal with the employee's angry reaction.

UPWARD COMMUNICATION

Upward communication refers to messages employees send to their managers or to others who hold higher positions in the organization. The participants in the Work-Out programs at General Electric participate in upward communication on the final day of the program. They give their bosses a list of proposals, which the bosses must support or veto. Upward communication serves primarily as a feedback vehicle, closing the loop in downward communication to ensure that accurate encoding and decoding of information has occurred.

Upward communication can also occur outside an individual's work unit. The manager of training may communicate with the vice president of sales to determine the specific training requirements for his or her employees. An accounts receivable clerk may send information about a delinquent client with unique work specifications to the manufacturing manager. Increasingly, organizations are moving decision making to lower levels. Executives are empowering low-level managers and nonmanagerial employees to make significant decisions. This change makes quality upward communication imperative so that top executives have access to the decision outcomes.

An employee can create misunderstandings by distorting information upward: telling the boss only good news, paying the boss compliments whenever possible, always agreeing with the boss, avoiding offering personal opinions different from those of the boss, insulating the boss from detrimental information, covering up information potentially damaging to oneself, and selecting words that project only favorable impressions.[37]

Sometimes employees attempt to *save face* by delivering only positive information to their bosses. This commonly occurs when bosses do not receive negative news well. Either they blame subordinates for problems outside their control or they fail to develop joint solutions with employees. While this type of censorship may result in the employee being viewed positively by the boss in the short run, in the longer run it may backfire and cause the employee to be viewed as untrustworthy.

Managers must create a culture that encourages upward communication. Managers should encourage their employees to share information about their successes and failures, attitudes, work developments, and mistakes. For example, they might structure regular times for ensuring upward communication on a one-to-one basis, or from a work group, such as in the Work-Out program.

AVIS RENT-A-CAR COMPANY. Joseph Vittoria, CEO of Avis, blocks out several hours a day and sometimes entire days for unscheduled communication with subordinates and peers.[38] His office door is literally and figuratively open so that employees often stop by and can share what they are thinking with the CEO.

Employees must feel that they can trust their supervisors to receive whatever information they transmit to them, regardless of whether it is positive or negative. For example, an employee who has legitimate reasons for missing a deadline should know that his or her boss will carefully evaluate the reasons for the delay and help the employee meet his or her goals by offering constructive comments, not derogatory complaints. Such a culture promotes honest upward communication as a way of counteracting employees' tendencies to hide potentially damaging information. It encourages employee participation in decision making, rewards openness, and limits inflexible policies and arbitrary procedures. By acting constructively on upward communication, a manager reinforces it and limits executive isolation. Overemphasizing downward communication, remaining office-bound, and improperly delegating responsibilities can increase executive isolation.[39]

MANVILLE CORPORATION. When W. Thomas Stephens became the CEO of the Manville Corporation he toured several plants. He learned that the previous decade of crisis at Manville, which was in bankruptcy and facing lawsuits about asbestos use in the workplace, had created a "Why should I trust you?" attitude. He instituted a President's Council comprised of approximately fifteen Manville employees from different levels and functional areas to inform him about problems with communications from the top. The Council was to ensure that no communications were filtered out on their way up or down the hierarchy. Communication significantly improved after its inception. Council members use voice mail, informal conversations, and other ways of gathering data to identify issues to raise with the CEO. They successfully serve as a conduit between employees and top management.[40]

LATERAL COMMUNICATION

Not all communication occurs up and down the official organizational hierarchy. Often individuals send messages to individuals at the same organizational level, both in their own or other departments or divisions.

PACKARD-BELL COMPUTERS. At Packard-Bell, a manufacturer of personal computers, workers assembling different parts of a product may coordinate the use of inventories by lateral (or horizontal) communication. Sales representatives may discuss field problems with technical services personnel. The divisional marketing vice president may resolve sales problems by gathering information from other divisional marketing executives.

Communication directly between the subordinates typically has greater speed and accuracy. Although distortions can still occur in encoding, transmission, or decoding, lateral communication generally facilitates problem solving and coordination of work. It also encourages the development of a company-wide view of organizational goals and concerns.

Although lateral communication can occur through formal channels, more often it occurs informally because it occurs outside the hierarchy. Using the formal hierarchy slows down lateral communication. Still, in some cases, managers may insist that workers rely on the hierarchy for an exchange of information. Passing information from subordinate to manager to top manager to second manager to second subordinate is a way of checking decisions made, keeping managers informed, or reinforcing the chain of command.

Many organizations develop special roles to facilitate lateral communication. **Boundary spanners** exist where two groups or units interact. A product manager, for example, serves as the interface between marketing and production departments. A technical liaison may ease communication between engineering and marketing. The purchasing agent acts as the interface between a vendor and the manufacturing department. **Gatekeepers,** a special category of boundary spanners, screen information and access to a group or individual. They funnel information into the organization from outside.[41] The Chief of Staff of the President of the United States acts as a gatekeeper, determining who will and will not have access to the President. The executive secretary of the president of a company or the secretary of any manager may serve as a gatekeeper for that executive. Sometimes gatekeepers communicate with professionals inside and outside the organization, serving as the conduit for new technical information.

Although employees in different or distant departments may have problems communicating directly, the proliferation of electronic communication devices removes some obstacles. We discuss the use of electronic media to overcome organizational barriers later in this chapter.

FORMAL VERSUS INFORMAL COMMUNICATION

Managers and other organizational members can transmit messages formally or informally. *Formal communication* refers to transmission that uses formally established or regularly scheduled channels, such as from boss to employee. Formal communication typically is closely aligned to the organizational hierarchy and formal chains of authority and command. *Informal communication* refers to more spontaneous communication that occurs without regard for the formal channels of communication. The organization's grapevine is the prototypical vehicle of informal communication.

MEDIA USED IN FORMAL COMMUNICATION

Formal communication can use oral and written media. Staff meetings and written memorandums are media most commonly used in formal communication. Organizational leaders often look for new ways to formally promote communication throughout the organization, however. The Work-Out program described earlier in this chapter illustrates a new type of media, which brings together a diverse group of workers in a structured situation to facilitate their communication. Another example might be a speak-out program that includes suggestion boxes and rewards for cost-saving suggestions. The availability of electronic media has increased the opportunities for formal communication. Company newsletters or information bulletins are also useful for regularly disseminating information to large numbers of employees.

COMMUNICATION NETWORKS

Communication networks represent the patterns of formal or informal communication throughout an organization, as illustrated in Figure 7–4.[42] A *total systems network* describes the communication patterns throughout the entire organization, such as communication in a small company that distributes soft drinks. A *clique network* describes a group of individuals or departments who communicate exclusively with each other. An example might be the credit, billing, and service departments. A *personal network* represents individuals who communicate with specific individuals. Your personal network is the group of individuals with whom you communicate on a regular basis.

Networks vary in size, the extent to which they are interconnected, and how much an individual or clique dominates the total network.[43] Network analysis shows the pattern of interactions and allows the diagnosis of effective and ineffective patterns. It identifies groups or clusters that comprise the network, individuals that link the clusters, and other network members.[44] Network analysis helps to diagnose communication patterns and, consequently, communication effectiveness.

FIGURE 7–4   *Communication network of an organization*

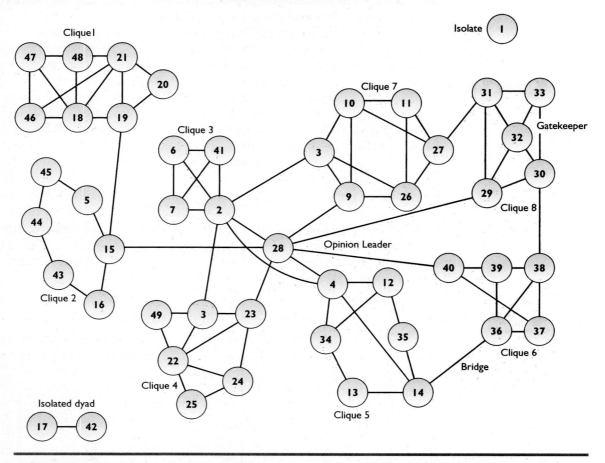

For example, network analysis can be used to represent the fabric of electronic interactions within an organization. Network analysis can then provide a template for the effective distribution of electronic messages, which in turn can facilitate interactions throughout the organization.

THE GRAPEVINE

The ***grapevine*** refers to the pattern of communication created outside the formal organization and official channels. It typically supplements or replaces the organizational hierarchy as the means for transmitting communication. The grapevine serves as an excellent source of information about employee attitudes as well as an emotional outlet for workers.[45]

Although managers frequently tap into the grapevine as a useful source of information, they must also recognize that the grapevine often distorts information. Just as in the game of telephone, individuals use the grapevine to pass information along, unchecked by official sources. Sometimes the grapevine replaces the formal communication media, removing management's ability to control the accuracy of information being disseminated in the organization.

Increasingly, managers are encouraged to use the grapevine to acquire more information about the problems, attitudes, and information gaps experienced by organizational members. In doing this, however, individuals should recognize that the grapevine typically carries an incomplete story, often presenting less than complete and inaccurate information. Similarly, managers can use the grapevine to reinforce information they convey to employees through formal channels. For example, a manager might comment about the effectiveness of individuals working on a new project both formally and informally.

BARRIERS TO COMMUNICATION

Although the basic communication process is relatively straight forward, deficiencies in communication are rampant in organizations. Perceptual and attributional biases, interpersonal relationships, organization structure, physical distance, and cultural differences can create barriers to communication.

PERCEPTUAL AND ATTRIBUTIONAL BIASES

As described in Chapter 2, perception refers to the ways individuals attend to stimuli in the environment and then organize them. Perceptual biases such as stereotyping, the halo effect, projection, and other self-fulfilling prophecies can distort communication. Stereotyping distorts communication by causing senders to assume that the receivers have certain characteristics based on the group to which they belong without validating that they in fact have these characteristics. For example, the workers at General Electric may stereotype their bosses as unresponsive until they participate in a Work-Out program where their bosses can counter these stereotypes by being receptive to new ideas. Like stereotyping, the halo effect can affect the accuracy of communication by causing managers and others to make inaccurate assumptions about their coworkers or subordinates. Because projection involves an emotional biasing of perceptions by fear, hatred, anger, uncertainty, love, deceit, or distrust, it colors the message sent and received. A worker who participates in the G.E. Work-Out program who expects his or her boss *not* to be receptive to new suggestions may only notice the ones the boss rejects. This would cause errors in subsequent communications.

Errors can also occur in attributing the *causes* of certain behaviors, events, or situations, as discussed in Chapter 2. Individuals who incorrectly attribute certain behaviors to individual versus situational causes may consequently err in communicating about these behaviors and their causes.

INTERPERSONAL TIONSHIPS

The nature and history of the interactions between individuals will influence their communication in at least four ways.[46] First, the extent to which they trust each other is a key factor. Trust tends to facilitate more accurate and open communication. When individuals or groups distrust each other, communication is more limited and reserved.

Second, a sender or receiver who has influence and power over the other may also inhibit communication. Rather than attempting to share information accurately or completely, the less powerful sender or receiver may try to protect himself or herself from the other's influence, and in so doing distort information. The effect of power differences is further exaggerated if the sender uses communication to promote his or her advancement in the organization.

Third, the groups to which the sender and receiver respectively belong may have different norms about the nature and quality of communication, which will influence its speed and accuracy. Some groups, for example, insist on using only written communications, whereas others prefer to rely on face-to-face conversations.

Fourth, each person's or group's attitudes toward collaboration and competition can also affect the quality of communication. Parties with competitive attitudes define conflict as win–lose, pursue only their own goals, understand and overemphasize their own needs, and emphasize only differences in positions and superiority of their own position.[47] Particularly when one or both individuals or groups takes a competitive attitude, communication between them can project this "we–they" or "win–lose" perspective. A we–they attitude can polarize the interacting groups and thus establish a communication barrier between them.

ORGANIZATION STRUCTURE

Structural factors can both facilitate and hinder communication. While the organizational hierarchy and chain of command provide direction for downward and upward communication, they may unnecessarily restrict the channels of transmission. Too often, organizational members feel that they cannot violate the hierarchy to communicate with the best or most appropriate person in the organization.

Centralization of authority restricts the dissemination of information because different members and groups in organizations have access to different information. The extent to which organizations have specialized work groups will also hinder communication, since departments or groups with different goals and expertise often experience difficulty in communicating effectively. Often they must seek ways of overcoming potential conflict to allow quality communication to occur.

PHYSICAL DISTANCE

Physical distance has an obvious effect on communication. Individuals near each other can more easily communicate face-to-face, check the accuracy of their communication by requesting feedback, and revise their communication. As the physical distance increases, noise also increases, creating greater communication distortions. Until recently, a global marketplace, for example, was difficult to achieve due to the physical distance between many countries and organizations.

Now, telecommunications and other electronic media bridge large distances and reduce the problems created by physical distance. Organizations with multiple sites can easily create complex communication networks that facilitate communication accuracy and speed. In addition, many executives spend large amounts of time touring company sites and speaking with employees.

WAL-MART. David Glass, the CEO of Wal-Mart, spends two or three days each week visiting stores and asking sales associates and customers questions like: How are sales? How is apparel selling? Should we be doing something different? Are you challenged enough by your work?[48]

CULTURAL DIFFERENCES

Cross-cultural issues may affect the quality of communication. Effective communication requires deciphering the basic values, motives, aspirations, and assumptions that operate geographical, occupational, functional, or social-class lines. It also means seeing our own culture as different, but not necessarily better.[49]

Consider the following example.

> You work in a Japanese company in the United States. You have noticed that the Japanese staff explains only the conclusion to Americans when they address a problem, rather than discussing the steps to the conclusion. Also, the Japanese staff sends reports directly to Japan without showing them to you.[50]

In this case the senders did not communicate in a way that the receivers understood or they sent messages that had a different meaning in the receivers' culture. Different languages pose an obvious barrier to communication, but differences in the meaning of nonverbal communications can have a particularly strong and unintended impact. For example, different cultures have very different norms for the appropriate amount of interpersonal space. Interpersonal distance is high among South Americans, Southern and Eastern Europeans, and Arabs, and low among Asians, Northern Europeans, and North Americans.[51]

Consider a study of 436 managers in the People's Republic of China, which found that formality dominated their daily exchanges.[52] What communication dysfunctions might result in their interactions with managers from the United States, who are often comfortable using first names and more informal interactions? Even American managers at Japanese-owned companies in the United States have experienced communication problems due to the language barrier.[53]

The compatibility or incompatibility of the verbal and nonverbal styles used to communicate can also influence the effectiveness of intercultural communication. The Japanese use an indirect style and hide the speaker's true intent. Arabs use very expressive and elaborate language. North American communication tends to be direct and succinct.[54]

OVERCOMING COMMUNICATION BARRIERS

Individuals can improve their formal and informal communication by overcoming the barriers we just described. In particular, using electronic communication, improving interpersonal interactions, and changing the organization's structure will have a significant impact.

USE ELECTRONIC COMMUNICATION

Electronic media for communication includes voice and electronic messaging; audio, video, and computer conferencing; and integrated systems.[55] Messaging systems allow an individual to leave and retrieve either voice or electronic messages.

Voice messaging supplements telephone communication and typically includes the ability to store, retrieve, edit, and forward messages, as well as distribute them to a prespecified list. Electronic messaging substitutes for telephone or face-to-face interactions by creating a formal document that conveys the desired information across the telephone lines or computer network. The user receives his or her messages in an electronic in-box, ready to be answered, filed, or discarded. Electronic messaging systems can create, edit, store, retrieve, forward, and distribute messages in a way similar to voice mail systems.

UNUM CORPORATION. James F. Orr III, CEO of UNUM Corp., a large insurance company, invites his 5,500 employees to communicate with him through the organization's electronic mail system. He replies to messages daily, often following up a message with a personal telephone call.[56]

Conferencing systems add an interactive component to messaging systems. Audio systems resemble a telephone conference call and so substitute for face-to-face communication. Video conferencing systems serve the same purpose as audio systems but add a visual component by transmitting voice and visual images of participants. Computer systems, in contrast, do not use either audio or video accoutrements. The conference is conducted purely on the computer screen, with participants responding to messages as they are delivered. Computer conferencing allows for private communication among participants. It also allows for polling of conference participants and hence can support nominal group decision making or the use of the delphi technique. Computer conferencing also provides a transcript of the proceedings, which can be used to prepare and edit shared documents.

Integrated systems, such as groupware, supplement traditional written communication with messaging, word processing, and data processing. They can retrieve shared documents, as well as develop electronic calendars and scheduling. Integrated systems also have the ability to create, edit, store, retrieve, and forward formal documents.

Electronic messaging and conferencing facilitates communication within organizations by increasing interactions among organizational members, speeding the ease and time of response, and disseminating information more widely in organizations. Because such systems allow for nearly instantaneous dissemination of information and rapid response across long distances, electronic media facilitate managing in a global environment. Use of the Internet, a global information network, by Japanese during 1993–1994 doubled to include two million Japanese electronic mail addresses.[57]

In these and other countries, information overload, where too much information is passed to individuals and they receive too much "junk mail" or unnecessary information to which they must respond, may eventually occur. Electronic "filters" have been written to sort mail and weed out junk.

Management information systems, computer systems that manage and analyze large quantities of information, also facilitate communication. Executive information systems and group decision support systems, both types of management information systems, expand communication beyond a single sender by gathering, filtering, and sharing information and by supporting decision making.[58] Some organizations have information specialists who make relevant computer-based information available to organization members.[59] Other organizations integrate the use of management information systems technologies into the regular performance of jobs at all levels in the organization.

IMPROVE INTERPERSONAL INTERACTIONS

Increasing the level of trust is a first step in improving interpersonal interactions, since increased trust should result in more accurate perceptions and attributions and ultimately in active listening. Improved interpersonal interactions should also facilitate communications between individuals in different cultures by encouraging the communicators to recognize, tolerate, and respond to differences.

Create a Supportive Communication Climate To improve communication, managers and employees generally need to create a trusting and supportive environment. Such a climate has the objective of using communication for problem solving, rather than evaluation, which makes employees feel defensive and threatened. A supportive climate also ensures that individuals do not disparage, or otherwise fail to affirm others' communications.[60] Phrases such as "that makes sense, but," "I've heard that before," "Be serious, will you," or "What makes you think that's true?" illustrate discounting.

Superiors, subordinates, and other communicators can create a supportive atmosphere in six specific ways.[61]

- They use descriptive rather than evaluative speech and hence give and ask for information rather than praise, blame, pass judgment, or imply the receiver should change.

- They take a problem-solving orientation, which implies collaborating in exploring a mutual problem, rather than trying to control the listener or persuade him or her by imposing the communicator's personal attitudes.

- They are spontaneous, honest, and reveal their goals, rather than appearing to use *strategy,* which involves manipulating others and having ambiguous and multiple motivations.

- They convey empathy for the feelings of their listener, rather than appearing unconcerned or neutral about the listener's welfare. They give reassurance that they are identifying with the listener's problems, rather than denying the legitimacy of the problems.

- They indicate that they feel equal rather than superior to the listener. They suggest that they will enter a shared relationship, not simply dominate the interaction.

- They communicate that they will experiment with their own behavior and ideas, rather than be dogmatic about them. They do not give the impression that they know all the answers and do not need help from anyone.

Supportive communication emphasizes a congruence between thoughts and feelings and communication.[62] An individual who feels unappreciated by a supervisor, for example, must communicate that to the supervisor, rather than deny it or communicate the feeling inaccurately. Communication must also validate an individual's importance, uniqueness, and worth.[63]

Use the Johari Window Model Interpersonal communication can also be improved by encouraging individuals to communicate using knowledge of themselves and others that is as complete as possible. The **Johari Window** provides an analytical tool that individuals can use to identify information that is available for use in communication.[64] Figure 7–5 illustrates this model of interpersonal knowledge. Note that information about an individual is represented along two dimensions: (1) information known and unknown by the individual and (2) information known and unknown by others.

Together these dimensions form a four-category representation of the individual.

■ *Open self:* Information known by the individual and known by others.

■ *Blind self:* Information unknown by the individual and known by others, such as others' perceptions of your behavior or attitudes.

■ *Concealed self:* Information known by the individual and unknown by others; secrets we keep from others about ourselves fall into this category.

■ *Unconscious self:* Information that is unknown to the individual and unknown to others.

To ensure quality communication, in most cases an individual should communicate from his or her open self to another person's open self and limit the amount of information concealed or in the blind self. Guarded communication may be appropriate, however, if one party has violated trust in the past, if the parties have an adversarial relationship, if power and status differentials characterize the culture, if the relationship is transitory, or if the corporate culture does not support openness.[65]

Use an Assertive Communication Style An **assertive** style, which is honest, direct, and firm, also improves communication. With this style a person expresses personal needs, opinions, and feelings in honest and direct ways and stands up for his or her rights without violating the other person's.[66] Assertive behavior is reflected in the content and the nonverbal style of the message.

Consider the situation of a boss whose subordinate has missed two important deadlines in the last month. How would the boss respond assertively? The boss might say to the worker: "I know you missed the last two deadlines. Is there an explanation I should know? I need you to meet the next two deadlines. I need to know as soon as possible when you are facing problems, so that I can understand the situation." Or, "I need to know how you plan to avoid this situation in the future."

FIGURE 7–5   *Johari window*

	Known by Self	Unknown by Self
Known by Others	Open Self	Blind Self
Unknown by Others	Concealed Self	Unknown Self

SOURCE: Based on a model developed by Drs. Joseph Luft and Harry Ingham and described in *The Personnel Relations Survey* by Jay Hall and Martha S. Williams, Teleometrics International, The Woodlands, Texas.

Note that an assertive response can include the expression of anger, frustration, or disappointment.

We can contrast this to nonassertive and aggressive styles. In **nonassertive communication,** the sender does not stand up for his or her personal rights and indicates that his or her feelings are unimportant. The person may be hesitant, apologetic, or fearful. In **aggressive communication,** the sender stands up for his or her rights without respecting the rights of the other person. Aggressive behavior attempts to dominate and control others by sounding accusing or superior. Men often mislabel assertive communication by women as aggressive because the honesty and directness does not fit with their preconceptions about feminine communication.

RECOGNIZE CULTURAL DIFFERENCES

To ensure quality communication in multicultural situations, communicators should first assume that cultural differences exist and try to view the situation from the perspective of their colleagues.[67] They can then adjust their encoding or decoding, use of language, nonverbal cues, or listening skills in response to likely differences. Knowing the characteristics of diverse cultures facilitates such an adjustment. A **cultural integrator**—a person who understands cultural differences and the ways the organization can adapt to them—can also reduce the barrier of inadequate cross-cultural sensitivity.[68] U.S. companies can select a cultural integrator, for example, from among U.S. citizens familiar with the foreign country or from foreign nationals who are familiar with U.S. customs. Consider, for example, how a cultural integrator might help a salesman trying to do business in Japan or India. Until all individuals have cross-cultural sensitivity, such special arrangements may be necessary for quality multicultural communication.

CHANGE THE ORGANIZATION'S STRUCTURE

Recent changes in the design of organizations have been made in an attempt to flatten the organizational hierarchy, thereby increasing lateral communication.

HERMAN MILLER COMPANY. Herman Miller Co., the furniture manufacturer, uses cross-functional teams with significant self-management responsibility as the basic structure for accomplishing work tasks.[69] CEO Kerm Campbell believes that a good manager's responsibility is to stay out of the way of employees, giving them much more autonomy and placing more emphasis on lateral instead of vertical communication.

As described in Chapters 13 and 14, such changes in organizational design increase interpersonal interactions, give more responsibility and autonomy to lower-level workers, and empower workers at all levels. These three outcomes also facilitate communication.

IMPROVING COMMUNICATION IN SPECIAL SITUATIONS

Effective communication is important in every business situation. Thus, you will want to be careful to diagnose the way you and others communicate. You will also want to be aware of communication issues in special situations, such as meetings, employment interviews, and performance appraisals.

CONDUCTING PRODUCTIVE MEETINGS

Most managers spend large amounts of time in meetings with their subordinates and bosses, as members of cross-functional work teams, or as participants in special task forces. Conducting productive meetings poses a major challenge to many managers. The first step in conducting quality meetings is to ensure that meetings are the appropriate vehicle for the type of communication required. Too often, meetings are used to share information that could better be disseminated by a short memorandum or a quick telephone call. Other times, meetings are scheduled to resolve complicated problems before basic fact-finding and research has been completed.

The following briefly describes the steps in conducting an effective meeting.

- ■ *Determine the goal or purpose of the meeting.* What should be accomplished by the end of the meeting? Is the meeting intended to share information, identify a problem, or reach a decision?

- ■ *Prepare for the meeting.* This includes finding and reserving the appropriate location, determining and allocating a reasonable time limit, identifying the individuals who should attend, developing an agenda, and distributing it with any other materials participants need to be prepared for the meeting. The *agenda* comprises the guidelines for the meeting. It specifies the topics to be covered, questions to be answered, or information to be shared. It includes a clear allocation of time to each item on the agenda. Often, preparing the agenda is an interactive task that requires sharing draft versions with participants.

- ■ *Conduct the meeting.* Convene the meeting on time and observe time limits specified in the agenda. Have you ever attended a meeting where one individual dominated the discussion, was never stopped by the convener of the meeting, and nothing was accomplished? The meeting leader should ensure that appropriate individuals participate in a controlled fashion.

- ■ *Conclude the meeting.* This step should involve a recap of what was accomplished, a specification of the next steps, and an assignment of responsibility. Often, minutes of the meeting are distributed to relevant individuals for their records, as well as for information about the next steps.

CONDUCTING EFFECTIVE PLACEMENT INTERVIEWS

In employment interviews the communicators transmit information that allows them to make decisions about the fit between a job applicant and an available position. The interviewer can ask open-ended questions or closed-ended questions. *Open-ended* questions, such as "Tell me about your experience in financial analysis," and "What do you consider your weaknesses as an employee?" allow the interviewee to structure the response to the question and present information that he or she feels is important. *Closed-ended* questions, such as "Tell me the first thing you would say to a potential customer," and "How many employees have you supervised during the past year?" allow the interviewer to focus a response more precisely. An interview can move from open-ended questions to closed-ended questions, alternate the two types of questions, or begin with closed-ended questions and end with open-ended ones. Figure 7–6 offers one example of the structure of an interview.

Conducting interviews effectively requires the manager to share facts about actual job-related behaviors. In a selection interview, for example, both parties might focus on information presented in the résumé or in work samples provided by the applicant.

FIGURE 7–6 *Sample interview guidelines for a selection interview*

OPENING

- Give a warm, friendly greeting—smile.

- Names are important—yours and the applicant's. Pronounce it correctly and use first and last names consistently. Tell the applicant what to call you and then ask the applicant for his or her preferred form of address.

- Talk briefly about yourself (your position in the company and then your personal background, hobbies, interests, etc.) to put the applicant at ease so that she or he might reciprocate with personal information.

- Ask the applicant about hobbies, activities, or some other topic that you believe will be of interest to "break the ice."

STRUCTURE THE INTERVIEW

- State the purpose of interview: "The purpose of this interview is to discuss your qualifications and to see whether they match the skills needed to work as a selection interviewer. First, let's talk about your work experience and next your education and training. Then I will give you a preview of what the interviewer's job is really like. Finally, there will be a chance to ask about anything you want. How's that?"

- Since you plan to take notes, mention this to the applicant: "By the way, I will be taking some notes during the interview so that I don't miss any pertinent information that may come from our discussion. Okay?"

WORK EXPERIENCE: MOST RELEVANT JOB

- Use this comprehensive opening question: "Let's talk about your work experience. How about starting with the job that you feel gave you the best preparation for working as a selection interviewer. Tell me all about the job: how you got it, why you chose it, your actual job duties, what you learned on the job, the hours and your at-

tendance record, the pay, why you left (or are leaving), and things like that."

- Probe and follow up to cover each of these items thoroughly: how the applicant got the job, reasons for choosing it, job duties, etc.

- Summarize the major facts and findings from the applicant's most relevant job. For example: "Let me summarize what we have covered to make sure that I've got it right. You worked as a _____ where most of your time was spent doing _____ and _____, and you used these skills, _____ and _____. You chose the job because of _____ and your reasons for leaving it are _____ and _____. Anything else to add?"

OTHER WORK EXPERIENCE

- If time is available, discuss other jobs the applicant has held that might be pertinent. Get a brief overview of each job the applicant has held. Emphasize jobs held in the last five years or less, since older experience is less likely to be relevant for your decision.

- Ask the work experience questions you specifically prepared for this applicant when you planned the interview.

- Summarize your major findings about all jobs. When the summary is satisfactory to the applicant, go on to discuss education and training.

AFTER THE INTERVIEW

- Take time to write summary notes immediately. Describe the applicant's behavior and the impressions he or she created. Cite facts and specific incidents from the interview or from the person's work or educational history.

- Wait a day and then complete the Evaluation Form.

SOURCE: From Rowland/Ferris, *Personnel Management.*, IE © 1982, pp. 148–149. Reprinted by permission of Prentice–Hall, Inc., NJ.

IMPROVING PERFORMANCE APPRAISALS

In a performance appraisal, the manager and employee share information about the employee's performance to date and his or her future development. Depending on how it is conducted, a performance appraisal can make an employee defensive or it can increase commitment and motivation. In a performance-appraisal meeting, the discussion should rely on direct observational data rather than hearsay reports. It should describe specific behavior rather than make evaluative statements or describe an individual's personality. Supervisors should describe both positive and negative behaviors and use the same basic form and level of detail for each subordinate.

RAYCHEM. The president of Raychem, a $1.5 billion electrical equipment and electronics company, learned from employees that they considered him a poor contingency planner. He agreed with their assessment but was surprised he had not done a better job of hiding this weakness from them.[70]

PERRIER. The CEO of Nestle's U.S. Perrier division learned that his managers feared him so much they had stopped bringing problems and ideas to him.[71]

What is your attitude toward giving feedback? You can assess it by completing the questionnaire shown in Figure 7–7. The lower your score, the more discomfort you feel in giving feedback. Recognizing a discomfort about giving or receiving feedback is a prerequisite for improving two-way communication in performance evaluation situations.

To increase the effectiveness of communication and the reliability of appraisals supervisors must obtain complete descriptions of subordinate behavior drawn from

FIGURE 7–7 *Attitude toward feedback: feedback questionnaire*

Indicate the degree of discomfort you would feel in each situation given below, by circling the appropriate number: 1—high discomfort; 2—some discomfort; 3—undecided; 4—very little discomfort; 5—no discomfort.

1 2 3 4 5	**1.** Telling an employee who is also a friend that he or she must stop coming to work late.
1 2 3 4 5	**2.** Talking to an employee about his or her performance on the job.
1 2 3 4 5	**3.** Asking an employee if he or she has any comments about your rating of his or her performance.
1 2 3 4 5	**4.** Telling an employee who has problems in dealing with other employees that he or she should do something about it.
1 2 3 4 5	**5.** Responding to an employee who is upset over your rating of his or her performance.
1 2 3 4 5	**6.** An employee's becoming emotional and defensive when you tell him or her about mistakes in the job.
1 2 3 4 5	**7.** Giving a rating that indicates improvement is needed to an employee who has failed to meet minimum requirements of the job.
1 2 3 4 5	**8.** Letting a subordinate talk during an appraisal interview.
1 2 3 4 5	**9.** An employee's challenging you to justify your evaluation in the middle of an appraisal interview.
1 2 3 4 5	**10.** Recommending that an employee be discharged.
1 2 3 4 5	**11.** Telling an employee that you are uncomfortable in the role of having to judge his or her performance.
1 2 3 4 5	**12.** Telling an employee that his or her performance can be improved.
1 2 3 4 5	**13.** Telling an employee that you will not tolerate his or her taking extended coffee breaks.
1 2 3 4 5	**14.** Telling an employee that you will not tolerate his or her making personal telephone calls on company time.

many sources. The notion of *360-degree feedback,* which refers to the involvement of multiple raters, including superiors, coworkers, and the individual himself or herself, in performance evaluations, highlights the importance of comprehensive, quality communication.[72] When organizational members rely on a single source of information, persistent biases occur. One study indicated that raters who felt positive emotions toward ratees were most lenient and those with negative emotions were least lenient.[73] Another study suggested that the raters who thought workers did well in one area, such as dependability, tended to think the employee did well in several areas.[74] Maintaining a daily or weekly record of employee performance helps reduce such biases.

Some question whether performance appraisal procedures typically used in the United States can be transferred to other countries.[75] One study indicated that performance appraisals in Thailand should reflect a high degree of formal control, focus on individual performance, and include high employee involvement in the appraisal process. In contrast, performance appraisal in Malaysia should *not* involve employees in the evaluation process. Performance appraisal in Indonesia, unlike in both Thailand and Malaysia, should measure performance on a group basis.

SUMMARY

Effective communication involves a two-way process. The sender encodes the message and transmits it through various channels using various media to the receiver who decodes it. Feedback from the receiver acknowledges what message he or she heard and provides the sender with information about whether additional transmission is required. Noise often interferes with the transmission and distorts the information sent and received. The sender can improve the communication process by carefully selecting the most appropriate language for encoding. Both sender and receiver should identify the meaning of nonverbal cues. The receiver should listen actively and effectively to improve the decoding process. Generally, transmission should attempt to avoid communication overload or underload.

Communication occurs in three directions in organizations. Downward communication emphasizes the dissemination of information from boss to subordinate. Upward communication provides feedback to supervisors about their subordinate's thoughts and performance. Lateral communication facilitates the interactions between coworkers, departments, or other work groups within an organization. Distortions that hinder communication can occur in each direction. Communication can occur formally through various media. Organizational members often build networks of associates or use the grapevine for informal communication.

Barriers to communication include perceptual and attributional biases, interpersonal relationships, organization structure, physical distance, and cultural differences. Managers and employees can use electronic media, improve interpersonal interactions, recognize cultural differences, and change the organization's structure to overcome these barriers. Meetings, placement interviews, and performance appraisals provide special situations in which effective communication is essential.

DIAGNOSTIC QUESTIONS

We can use the following diagnostic questions in assessing communication effectiveness.

- ■ What encoding and decoding errors occur in communication?
- ■ What media are the most appropriate for transmission?
- ■ What types of noise exist in the organization?
- ■ Does quality feedback occur?
- ■ Do senders use effective language?
- ■ What purposes does nonverbal communication serve?
- ■ Does effective listening occur?
- ■ Does communication overload or underload exist?
- ■ How effective are downward, upward, and lateral communication?
- ■ What vehicles facilitate formal and informal communication?
- ■ What barriers hinder communication?
- ■ How do the organization and its members overcome communication barriers?

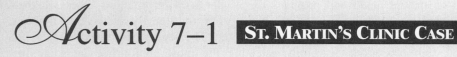

$\mathscr{A}$ctivity 7–1　ST. MARTIN'S CLINIC CASE

STEP 1: Read the St. Martin's Clinic Case.

Allen Binford, recently appointed human resources manager of St. Martin's Clinic, was looking at the view from his office window and considering how best to draft a presentation that he was due to give to the senior nursing staff the following Wednesday. He also wondered how he could help reestablish communication lines between individual staff members and management in the current combative situation.

The previous week, Mr. Cohen, St. Martin's administrator, had announced at a top-level management meeting that pressures in the health-care environment would be forcing the hospital to change some long-standing policies. These changes were necessary as the number of patients at the clinic was in a steady decline since the turmoil of the strike in 1985. As a result, the hospital authorities had entered into an agreement with a private industrial medical scheme. This scheme of-fered medical coverage for industrial workers mostly situated in the East Oakland area. However, one of the conditions of the agreement stipulated that the clinic would provide full medical services over an eighteen hour period: 6:00 to 24:00 hours. For the clinic staff, this meant the introduction of more shift work.

Cohen had outlined these changes to the management committee, which included the introduction of shifts for diagnostic staff members (X-ray, echocardiography, EKG, physical therapy, vascular lab, nuclear medicine, ultrasound), and a large increase in the amount of shift work for emergency nursing staff. This movement toward more shift work was needed to facilitate the workload in the out-patients' department at the times that were convenient to employers rather than the clinic itself. Staff would have to be persuaded that these changes were in everyone's best interests.

However, this was not the most difficult task facing Binford. The chief administrator, Mr. Cohen, stressed during his meeting with Allen Binford that the most urgent need at the clinic was to persuade staff to put their recent difficulties behind them and to show a more positive attitude toward both their patients and colleagues. Both Cohen and Binford accepted that this was a lot to ask for considering the bitterness that had developed during the recent strike. Nevertheless, Cohen had instructed Binford that the two issues had to be dealt with in the one presentation. Binford had objected to this policy as he thought Mr. Cohen wanted too much out of one individual presentation. Presentations, in Binford's view, should be restricted to one topic. Binford also realized that any long-term change could not be achieved through one presentation. Nevertheless, he was obliged to go along with Mr. Cohen's instructions.

The two administrators had discussed various alternatives of communicating with the staff, which included interviews with senior personnel, small group presentations to department heads by senior management, a formal memo from department heads, and departmental presentations. However, because these proposed changes could not be separated from the general air of unrest at the clinic, it was decided that the timing aspect of the communication was of utmost importance. It was imperative that the grapevine should not be the channel of communication and that staff should hear it from formal sources. This is why presentations to small groups over a period of one or two days was out of the question. Likewise, individual interviews were out of the question for the same reason.

Mr. Cohen and Mr. Binford had debated whether to write a long explanatory memo to all hospital staff instead. They had eventually decided against this as essential questions could not be answered immediately, which would encourage speculation among personnel. So they decided on a formal presentations format, which would be followed by a more informal question and answer session in working groups organized by department heads. They further decided to ask all department managers to attend a special meeting at eight on Wednesday morning to inform them of the proposed changes and to brief them on the question and answer session over which they had to preside. Position papers would have to be provided for department managers to help them with these sessions. These various activities would have to be carefully monitored and coordinated. What Mr. Cohen did not want was for time to elapse between the presentations, as this would

only result in the grapevine becoming more active than usual. With regard to the nursing staff, where morale was at an all-time low, it was agreed that Mr. Binford, as human resources manager, should speak to all of them.

As it had been decided that all the nurses (all three shifts) should be assembled at one time to hear Mr. Binford's presentation, contract nurses were to be employed to cover for the day and night shifts. This would give nurses the time to divide into their working units for the question and answer sessions. It was with the nurses that Mr. Cohen was most concerned because it was here that the strike had caused most damage and good working relationships had not yet been reestablished. He knew very well that any clinic depended on the professionalism, dedication, and caring attitude of its nursing staff above all else. So it was essential that Allen Binford's presentation be given every facility. The presentations were arranged for the following Wednesday afternoon in working hours.

Later, when Mr. Cohen and Allen Binford discussed the nurses' forthcoming presentation, three essential points were agreed on:

1. It was to be the occasion to announce the proposed increase in shift work at the clinic.
2. It was to be the occasion to begin educating the nurses to the reality of the marketplace in which the clinic operated.
3. It was the occasion to announce *"something new"* that would begin the process of recreating that old team spirit that had once existed in the clinic.

Mr. Cohen made it clear to Mr. Binford that it was up to him to come up with that *"something new"* that was to form part of his *Action Plan* in the presentation.

THE PRESENTATION

As Mr. Binford looked out the window, the problems seemed almost insurmountable. How could he open up the channels of broken communication? Should he start the hospital newsletter again? What about the changes administration wanted him to communicate? Binford knew that he had a difficult audience to persuade. He knew that Mr. Cohen wanted him to do too much in one presentation, and finally he knew that he needed a very good *"Action Plan,"* which would have to include that *"something new."*

Another issue that worried him was the need to create common ground with the nurses. Many of them had stayed at St. Martin's after the strike merely because it was easier or more convenient to stay than go through all the problems of looking for a new job. One thing he could not afford was further discontentment among the nurses. Whatever common ground he decided on, would have to be linked to the *"Action Plan."* It would have to be something positive. It would have to provide some degree of motivation, a clear indication of how each person in the audience could participate (personal involvement), and finally, an indication of the long-term gains (rewards) both individually and collectively for all personnel. On the negative side, cuts in costs in order to avoid redundancies would not impress the nurses, neither would the introduction of more shift work, which could be viewed as something convenient to management and the investors only. The presentation could be seen as a propaganda tool for management; an effort by management to manipulate personnel into forgetting the recent past. It could also be conceived as a form of coercion; a form of threat to jobs if the changes were not accepted.

With these ideas, Mr. Binford concluded that the only common point was the very existence of the clinic itself: care for its patients. This seemed an issue to develop as a possible meeting point. If he could succeed in creating common ground based on this point, the rest of the presentation would be relatively easy. These thoughts crowded through his mind as he began to prepare his presentation.

ST. MARTIN'S HISTORY

St. Martin's Hospital was located in Berkley, California, and had a reputation for providing quality health care. It was founded as a nonprofit making organization in 1950 by Dr. John Byrne and its growth was largely due to the positive and caring attitude of its personnel, public support, and a qualified internship program for physicians that had gained much prestige with the local medical faculties and medical association. By 1987, it offered extensive services for both in-patients and out-patients.

The founder had originally encouraged a family atmosphere among employees. There were yearly hospital picnics and staff members often spent free time together. Some departments had fielded sporting teams for local community events. Management had actively participated in these extracurricular activities. A biweekly newsletter kept employees informed of hospital events.

In 1985, a nursing strike, which affected the entire Bay Area and included both the public and private sectors, abruptly changed the work atmosphere at St. Martin's. The hospital unions demanded a substantial increase in salaries for hospital personnel. Rather than give in to union demands for higher wages, management decided to support other hospital management boards and curtail emergency services by routing special cases to other hospitals. A skeleton crew kept the hospital active for the three-month period of the strike. During this time some of the striking nurses returned to their positions, while others remained on the picket-line. Management eventually won the battle, but in the process, succeeded in creating considerable hostility in a once united nursing staff. Some of this tension could still be felt in April 1987.

During the strike, the personnel department stopped producing the biweekly newsletter as management focused all their efforts on resolving the situation. At the same time, the department lost two of its regular staff members to retirement. These individuals had been heavily involved in employee relations. Many in management felt that one, Bob Ward, had acted as a link between administration and staff. He had coordinated the annual barbecues and other special activities. Once the strikes had been resolved, human resources had not replaced these individuals, nor had the department resumed production of the biweekly newsletter.

New Human Resources Management

Mr. Binford had worked at St. Martin's for ten years. His experience as an X-ray technologist, and later as the radiology department manager led to his promotion to human resources manager in February 1987. Having worked in a nonnursing unit during the strike, he had experienced some of the nurses' hostility upon their return. Often, patients were sent to the department late for a study, which in turn disrupted X-ray's schedule for the whole day. Eventually the problem appeared to diminish. However, Mr. Binford knew that the hostility of some nurses had not disappeared entirely.

Changes in the Hospital Industry

By 1986, hospitals across the nation were facing a number of serious problems. Rising health-care costs

Patients

St. Martin's primary objective is to care for its patients. We also believe we have the moral responsibility to care for our patients in the best possible way.

People

St. Martin's people are instrumental in achieving the highest-quality service based on individual care of our patients, efficient use of modern medical technology and of sound administration. This constitutes our main asset.

The clinic consists of all members of the staff without exception. Consequently, staff members will be represented on all administrative and management committees.

We believe our people respond to the individual satisfaction obtained from the high degree of care that they show to their patients, their professionalism, the recognition they receive from their fellow collaborators, and their feeling of personal achievement and individual responsibility. St. Martin's people should have total dedication to their patients and the general interest of the clinic.

We believe our staff should take pride in their clinic as a public service.

We believe in building a team of experts to be able to provide extensive services. Senior hospital staff are responsible for the selection, education, and training of their juniors.

All St. Martin's people should have their job performance reviewed by their supervisors to ensure our service standards are kept.

We believe in providing programmes to support the St. Martin's style. We encourage professional and personal developments of all our personnel.

Earnings

St. Martin's is a nonprofit-making organization whose purpose is to provide high-quality service to its patients. We believe the best way to improve our service is to reinvest our profit in the continuous training and development of our personnel and in our facilities. Commitment is rewarded by a friendly work atmosphere, training, extracurricular activities as well as remuneration.

Through continuous service to our patients we will attain:

- Patients' belief that we are the best clinic for their needs.
- A staff who believe that their clinic is providing a good public service.
- A community that considers us a fine example of what a medical clinic should be.
- Suppliers and service people who respect our professionalism and enjoy contributing to our goals.

had forced insurance companies to limit their payments according to the type of operation performed. The average hospital stay for a patient had decreased from 7 to 3.5 days. At the same time, hospitals were facing increased competition among themselves. A recent surge of health consciousness in the United States was causing individuals to be more selective about their choice of hospital. Administrators were even utilizing marketing strategies to lure patients to their hospital.

Administration Decisions

With these factors in mind, administration at St. Martin's was facing a number of difficult decisions. Unfortunately the departments that would be affected were those where considerable tension had been created during the course of the strike.

Another change administration felt should be arranged would be for some of the diagnostic staff members to move to shift schedules. This would allow out-patients to come at their convenience rather than at the typical 8–5 department hours. This announcement would affect mostly those departments with two to three staff members. Medical technicians would be asked to work shifts for the first time: 6:00 to 14:00 hours and 14:00 to 22:00 hours. The last two hours would be covered by emergency staff.

One final factor had been brought to administration's attention. A recent patient survey had revealed ambivalence toward St. Martin's staff. Some patients had gone as far as stating, "I would never return to such an uncaring hospital." It was obvious that, were the hospital to maintain its competitive edge, the staff's attitude would need to be modified.

Recently, Binford had begun discussing with his colleagues the possibility of producing a mission statement and a general statement of policy for the clinic. These discussions had stopped when the present problems became urgent, which left Binford with two half-finished documents. "Perhaps these could be used in the presentation," he thought. "Perhaps the process of completing the documents could form part of an action plan, which would bring people more into contact with each other, and possibly foster the creation of a common identity."

STEP 2: Prepare the case for class discussion.

STEP 3: Answer each of the following questions, individually or in small groups, as directed by your instructor.

DESCRIPTION

1. Briefly describe the situation at St. Martin's Clinic.

DIAGNOSIS

2. What type of communication dysfunctions exist at St. Martin's Clinic?
3. Did two-way communication exist between the administration and the nurses?
4. What barriers to communication exist?
5. How do Mr. Cohen and Mr. Binford plan to reduce these barriers?
6. Given your knowledge of communication concepts, is this plan likely to be effective?
7. Using your knowledge of perception, attribution, individual differences, motivation, group process, and decision making, analyze the situation at St. Martin's Clinic.

PRESCRIPTION

8. What changes are necessary?

ACTION

9. What impact will these changes likely have?

STEP 4: Discussion. In small groups, with the entire class, or in written form, share your answers to the questions above. Then answer the following questions:

1. What symptoms suggest that a problem exists?
2. What problems exist in the case?
3. What theories and concepts help explain those problems?
4. How can the problems be corrected?
5. Are the actions likely to be effective?

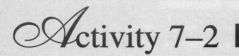

Activity 7–2 DIAGNOSING COMMUNICATION

STEP 1: Think about a work situation in which you have been or are currently involved.

STEP 2: Complete the questions on page 293 about that situation.

STEP 3: Score each question by adding the numbers for the responses you gave. If your total score for a question is 15–36, you have analyzed yourself as a very ineffective communicator; if your score is 37–58, you have analyzed yourself as an ineffective communicator; if your score is 59–80, you have analyzed yourself as an

1. I Think My Communication with My Subordinates:

	7	6	5	4	3	2	1	
Increases my credibility								Decreases my credibility
Is precise								Is imprecise
Is clear								Is unclear
Answers more questions than it raises								Raises more questions than it answers
Is effective								Is ineffective
Is competent								Is incompetent
Is productive								Is unproductive
Gets the results I want								Does not get the results I want
Is impressive								Is unimpressive
Creates a positive image of me								Creates a negative image of me
Is good								Is bad
Is skillful								Is unskillful
Is relaxed								Is strained
Is self-rewarding								Is not self-rewarding
Does not embarrass me								Does embarrass me

Total Score _____

2. I Think My Communication with My Supervisor:

	7	6	5	4	3	2	1	
Increases my credibility								Decreases my credibility
Is precise								Is imprecise
Is clear								Is unclear
Answers more questions than it raises								Raises more questions than it answers
Is effective								Is ineffective
Is competent								Is incompetent
Is productive								Is unproductive
Gets the results I want								Does not get the results I want
Is impressive								Is unimpressive
Creates a positive image of me								Creates a negative image of me
Is good								Is bad
Is skillful								Is unskillful
Is relaxed								Is strained
Is self-rewarding								Is not self-rewarding
Does not embarrass me								Does embarrass me

Total Score _____

3. I Think My Communication with My Peers:

	7	6	5	4	3	2	1	
Increases my credibility								Decreases my credibility
Is precise								Is imprecise
Is clear								Is unclear
Answers more questions than it raises								Raises more questions than it answers
Is effective								Is ineffective
Is competent								Is incompetent
Is productive								Is unproductive
Gets the results I want								Does not get the results I want
Is impressive								Is unimpressive
Creates a positive image of me								Creates a negative image of me
Is good								Is bad
Is skillful								Is unskillful
Is relaxed								Is strained
Is self-rewarding								Is not self-rewarding
Does not embarrass me								Does embarrass me

Total Score _____

effective communicator; if your score is 81 or above, you have analyzed yourself as a very effective communicator.

STEP 4: Discussion. In small groups, with the entire class, or in written form, as directed by your instructor, answer the following questions.

DESCRIPTION

1. In which type of communication are you most effective? least effective?

DIAGNOSIS

2. What are your deficiencies as a communicator?

PRESCRIPTION

3. How could you improve your communication?

Reprinted with permission from L. Sussman and P. D. Krivonos, *Communication for Supervisors and Managers*. Sherman Oaks, Calif.: Alfred Publishing, 1979.

Activity 7–3   ARE YOU REALLY LISTENING?

STEP 1: Below are some statements that were made by employees to their manager. Read each statement and select the response that best represents active listening by placing an X next to it.

1. Each day brings new problems. You solve one and here comes another. . . . What's the use?
   _____ a. I'm surprised to hear you say that.
   _____ b. That's the way it is. There's no use getting upset over it.
   _____ c. I know it's frustrating and sometimes discouraging to run into problem after problem.
   _____ d. Give me an example so I know what you're referring to.

2. At our meeting yesterday, I was counting on you for some support. All you did was sit there and you never said anything!
   _____ a. I was expecting you to ask for my opinion.
   _____ b. You're evidently upset with the way I handled things at the meeting.
   _____ c. Hey, I said some things on your behalf. You must not have heard me.
   _____ d. I had my reasons for being quiet.

3. I don't know when I'm going to get that report done. I'm already swamped with work.
   _____ a. See if you can get someone to help you.
   _____ b. All of us have been in that situation, believe me.
   _____ c. What do you mean swamped?
   _____ d. You sound concerned about your workload.

4. I've been scheduled to be out of town again on Friday. This is the third weekend in a row that's been messed up!
   _____ a. Why don't you talk with someone higher up and get it changed?
   _____ b. Going on the road must be a burden to you.
   _____ c. Everyone has to be on the road—it's part of the job.
   _____ d. I'm sure this is the last trip you'll have to make for a while.

5. It seems like other people are always getting the easy jobs. How come I always get the hard ones?
   _____ a. You feel I'm picking on you and that I'm being unfair in assigning work.
   _____ b. What evidence do you have for saying that?
   _____ c. If you'd look at the work schedule, you'd see that everyone has hard and easy jobs.
   _____ d. What about that job I gave you yesterday?

6. When I first joined this company, I thought there would be plenty of chances to move up. Here I am, four years later, still doing the same thing.
   _____ a. Let's talk about some of the things you could do to be promoted.
   _____ b. Maybe you just haven't worked hard enough.
   _____ c. Don't worry, I'm sure your chance will come soon.
   _____ d. Getting ahead must be important to you. You sound disappointed.

7. Performance evaluations are here again. I wish I could just give all my people good ratings—it sure would be easier.

_____ a. I know, but that's not possible.

_____ b. We all feel that way; don't get upset over it.

_____ c. Performance evaluations seem to bother you.

_____ d. Just do the best you can.

8. It's the same old thing day in and day out. Any child could do this job!

_____ a. Your work is evidently getting you down and making you feel useless.

_____ b. I always thought you liked your job.

_____ c. What good is complaining going to do?

_____ d. If you've got some ideas on improving your job, I'll be happy to listen.

9. I really appreciate getting the promotion. I just hope I can do the job.

_____ a. Don't worry. I'm sure you'll get better as you get more experience.

_____ b. What makes you think you can't do the job?

_____ c. Don't worry. Most people have those same feelings.

_____ d. I'm sure you can do it, or you would not have been promoted.

10. I'm tired. That last sale really wore me out. I don't think I can handle another customer.

_____ a. Sure you can. Just rest a few minutes and you'll be fine.

_____ b. What have you been doing that's gotten you so tired?

_____ c. You sound like you're exhausted.

_____ d. We all get feeling that way; don't worry about it.

STEP 2: Your instructor has information about the appropriate responses. You can verify your answers with these data.

STEP 3: Two volunteers are to be selected. These volunteers will be asked to role-play a common communications encounter. Everyone else is to act as observers.

STEP 4: As observers, be prepared to discuss the following issues:

1. Did the situation seem to be satisfactorily resolved?
2. How did active listening help resolve it? Why?
3. What barriers, if any, emerged during this activity?
4. How might you make use of this technique in interpersonal communication?

_____

Excerpted from *Organizational Behavior: Learning Guide/Experimental Exercises* by Bruce Kemelgor, copyright © 1988 by the Dryden Press, reprinted by permission of the publisher.

$\mathcal{A}$ctivity 7–4 NONVERBAL COMMUNICATION

STEP 1: Your instructor will organize you into groups of five or six people. Two groups will work together; one will act as a decision-making group and the other as observers.

STEP 2: The decision-making group should rank-order the importance of the eight leadership characteristics listed below. You have approximately ten minutes to complete the task. During the ranking procedure the decision-making group may communicate only verbally. You may not use gestures, facial movements, body movements, or any other nonverbal communication.

List of Leadership Traits

_____ extroverted personality

_____ sensitivity to others

_____ technical expertise

_____ strong ethical values

_____ task orientation or concern for production

_____ charisma

_____ internal locus of control

_____ power

STEP 3: After watching the decision making, observers should answer the following questions:

1. How effective was communication?
2. What barriers to communication existed?
3. What purpose does nonverbal communication serve?

STEP 4: Discussion. With the two groups (decision makers and observers) together or with the entire class, answer the following questions:

1. How effective was communication?
2. What happens when nonverbal communication is absent?
3. What purposes does nonverbal communication serve?

Based on "The Blind Decision-Makers" by Jeffrey Powers, *Exchange: The Organizational Behavior Teaching Journal* 1 (January 1975): 32–33.

$\mathscr{A}$ctivity 7–5   ONE-WAY VERSUS TWO-WAY COMMUNICATION

STEP 1: Your instructor will select one student to act as the communicator. He or she will be given two pictures to describe to you.

STEP 2: The communicator will describe a picture to you. You are to reproduce the picture he or she is describing. The communicator may neither ask if you have questions, request information from you, nor speak with you nonverbally. You may not communicate with the communicator either verbally or nonverbally.

STEP 3: The communicator will describe a second picture to you. Again, you are to reproduce the picture he or she is describing. This time you may ask the com-

municator any questions you wish, about his or her directions or anything else.

STEP 4: Your instructor will direct you to score the pictures.

STEP 5: Discussion. With the entire class, answer the following questions:

1. Which trial was more satisfying? Why?
2. Which trial yielded more accurate results? Why?
3. How can we translate our experience here into improving communication in organizational situations?

$\mathscr{A}$ctivity 7–6   COMMUNICATING ASSERTIVELY

STEP 1: The following questions will be helpful in assessing your assertiveness. Be honest in your responses. All you have to do is draw a circle around the number that describes you best.* For some questions the

assertive end of the scale is at zero, for others at four. Key: zero means no or never; one means somewhat or sometimes; two means average; three means usually or a good deal; and four means practically always or entirely.

1. When a person is highly unfair, do you call it to his or her attention? 0 1 2 3 4

2. Do you find it difficult to make decisions? 0 1 2 3 4

3. Are you openly critical of others' ideas, opinions, or behavior? 0 1 2 3 4

4. Do you speak out in protest when someone takes your place in line? 0 1 2 3 4

5. Do you often avoid people or situations for fear of embarrassment? 0 1 2 3 4

6. Do you usually have confidence in your own judgment? 0 1 2 3 4

7. Do you insist that your spouse or roommate take on a fair share of household chores? 0 1 2 3 4

8. Are you prone to "fly off the handle"? 0 1 2 3 4

9. When a salesman makes an effort, do you find it hard to say "No" even though the merchandise is not really what you want? 0 1 2 3 4

10. When a latecomer is waited on before you are, do you call attention to the situation? 0 1 2 3 4

11. Are you reluctant to speak up in a discussion or debate? 0 1 2 3 4

12. If a person has borrowed money (or a book, garment, thing of value) and is overdue in returning it, do you mention it? 0 1 2 3 4

13. Do you continue to pursue an argument after the other person has had enough? 0 1 2 3 4

14. Do you generally express what you feel? 0 1 2 3 4

15. Are you disturbed if someone watches you at work? 0 1 2 3 4

16. If someone keeps kicking your chair in a movie or a lecture, do you ask the person to stop? 0 1 2 3 4

17. Do you find it difficult to keep eye contact when talking to another person? 0 1 2 3 4

18. In a good restaurant, when your meal is improperly prepared or served, do you ask the waiter/waitress to correct the situation? 0 1 2 3 4

19. When you discover merchandise is faulty, do you return it for an adjustment? 0 1 2 3 4

20. Do you show your anger by name calling or obscenities? 0 1 2 3 4

21. Do you try to be a wallflower or a piece of the furniture in social situations? 0 1 2 3 4

22. Do you insist that your property manager (mechanic, repairman, etc.) make repairs, adjustments, or replacements that are his/her responsibility? 0 1 2 3 4

23. Do you often step in and make decisions for others? 0 1 2 3 4

24. Are you able openly to express love and affection? 0 1 2 3 4

25. Are you able to ask your friends for small favors or help? 0 1 2 3 4

26. Do you think you always have the right answer? 0 1 2 3 4

27. When you differ with a person you respect, are you able to speak up for your own viewpoint? 0 1 2 3 4

28. Are you able to refuse unreasonable requests made by friends? 0 1 2 3 4

29. Do you have difficulty complimenting or praising others? 0 1 2 3 4

30. If you are disturbed by someone smoking near you, can you say so? 0 1 2 3 4

31. Do you shout or use bullying tactics to get others to do as you wish? 0 1 2 3 4

32. Do you finish other people's sentences for them? 0 1 2 3 4

33. Do you get into physical fights with others, especially with strangers? 0 1 2 3 4

34. At family meals, do you control the conversation? 0 1 2 3 4

35. When you meet a stranger, are you the first to introduce yourself and begin a conversation? 0 1 2 3 4

STEP 2: Scoring. Look at your responses to questions 1, 2, 4, 5, 6, 7, 9, 10, 11, 12, 14, 15, 16, 17, 18, 19, 21, 22, 24, 25, 27, 28, 30, and 35. These questions are oriented toward *nonassertive* behavior. Do your answers to many of these items tell you that you are rarely speaking up for yourself? Or are there perhaps some specific situations that give you trouble?

Look at your responses to questions 3, 8, 13, 20, 23, 26, 29, 31, 32, 33, and 34. These questions are oriented toward *aggressive* behavior. Do your answers to many of these questions suggest you are pushing others around more than you realized?

You may examine your *assertive* responses by noting how often you answered 3 or 4 to the questions in the first paragraph and 0 or 1 to the questions in the second paragraph. In short, it is assertive to "usually" take the action described in the first group of items, and to rarely do those things described in the second set of items.

STEP 3: Check the statement indicating your most likely response to each situation below.[†]

1. When there's an unpleasant job that has to be done, I . . .
   a. do it myself.
   b. give it as punishment to someone who's been goofing off.
   c. hesitate to ask a subordinate to do it.
   d. ask someone to do it just the same.
2. When the boss criticizes me, I . . .
   a. feel bad.
   b. show her where she's wrong.
   c. try to learn from it.
   d. apologize for being stupid.
3. When an employee isn't working out, I . . .
   a. give him rope to hang himself.
   b. do everything I can to help him work out before I have to fire him.
   c. put off firing him as long as possible.
   d. get rid of him as quickly as possible if the guy is no good.
4. When my salary increase isn't as large as I think it should be, I . . .
   a. tell the boss in no uncertain terms what to do with it.
   b. keep quiet about it.

   c. say nothing, but take it out on the boss in other ways.
   d. feel bad.
5. When a subordinate continues to ignore instructions after I've explained something for the third time, I . . .
   a. try to give her something else to do.
   b. keep telling her until she does it.
   c. tell her that if she doesn't do it right this time, she's out the door.
   d. try to explain it in a different way.
6. When the boss rejects a good idea of mine, I . . .
   a. ask why.
   b. walk away and feel bad.
   c. try it again later.
   d. think about joining the competition.
7. When a co-worker criticizes me, I . . .
   a. give her back twice the dose she gave me.
   b. avoid her in the future.
   c. feel bad.
   d. worry that she doesn't like me.
8. When someone tells a joke I don't get, I . . .
   a. laugh with the rest of the group.
   b. say it was a lousy joke.
   c. say I didn't get it.
   d. feel stupid.
9. When someone points out a mistake I've made, I . . .
   a. sometimes deny it.
   b. feel guilty as hell.
   c. figure it's only human to make mistakes now and then.
   d. dislike the person.
10. When a subordinate fouls up a job, I . . .
    a. blow up.
    b. hate to tell him about it.
    c. hope that he'll do it right the next time.
    d. don't give him that job to do again.
11. When I have to talk to a top executive, I . . .
    a. can't look the person in the eye.
    b. feel uncomfortable.
    c. get a little nervous.
    d. enjoy the interchange.
12. When a subordinate asks me for a favor, I . . .
    a. sometimes grant it, sometimes not.
    b. feel uncomfortable if I don't grant it.

c. never grant any favors if I can help it. It sets a bad precedent.

d. always give in.

STEP 4: Scoring.

1. Nonassertive managers hate to ask people to do unpleasant work, and they often wind up doing it themselves (answers *a* and *c*). The aggressive manager might give such odious tasks as punishments (answer *b*). The assertive manager might hesitate to ask the subordinate, but would ask just the same (answer *d*).

2. The aggressive manager argues with the boss when criticized (answer *b*). Feeling bad or guilty, though a common reaction, is a nonassertive response (answer *a*). But apologizing for being stupid is the limit (answer *d*). The assertive response, assuming the criticism is valid, is to try to learn from the remark (answer *c*).

3. The hard-nosed authoritarian manager would get rid of a "bad" employee as quickly as possible (answer *d*). The nice-guy manager would put if off—forever, if possible (answer *c*)—and would give the poor performer rope to hang himself so the manager would feel justified in firing him (answer *a*). The assertive manager would try hard to help the employee work out, but would fire him in the end if necessary (answer *b*).

4. When people don't like a situation, but they say nothing about it, resentment builds up in them. This resentment often leads to forms of passive aggression; they "get back" in other, devious ways. Answers *b, c,* and *d* are compliant reactions. Choice *a* is an aggressive reaction. No assertive choice was given here.

5. Choices *b* and *d* are both assertive ones. Choice *a*—giving the employee something else to do—is evading responsibility and a compliant reaction. Threatening is the hard-guy approach (answer *c*).

6. Planning to join the competition is passive aggression: "I'll get even; they'll be sorry!" Choices *a* and *c* are assertive responses.

7. Choice *a*—"giving her back twice the dose she gave me"—is the aggressive response. Choices *b, c,* and *d* are all nonassertive. No assertive choice was given here.

8. Choices *a* and *d* are nonassertive responses. Assertive people are not afraid to say they didn't get the joke (answer *c*). The aggressive person blames the guy for telling a lousy joke (answer *b*).

9. A common reaction when someone points out a mistake we have made is to feel guilty, to dislike the person for telling us about it, and perhaps even to deny we did it. But assertive people know they have the right to make mistakes.

10. Blowing up at an employee is a tough-guy approach, showing no respect for the employee's rights and feelings (answer *a*). Choices *b, c,* and *d* are all nonassertive responses to this problem. No assertive response was given.

11. It's normal to be a little nervous when you have to talk to an executive, but feeling so uncomfortable that you can't even look the person in the eye is extreme nonassertiveness. If you enjoy the interchange, that's assertive (answer *d*). And that's great.

12. Managers who don't feel comfortable negotiating with subordinates sometimes make a policy of not granting any favors. Nice-guy managers just about always grant favors and feel uncomfortable if they don't. The assertive manager feels free to say yes or no, depending on the circumstances (answer *a*).

STEP 5: Discussion. Compare your responses to the questions in Steps 1 and 3. How assertive are you? In what situations do you act assertively? Nonassertively? Aggressively? How can you act more assertively? Individually, in small groups, or with the entire class, offer three to five strategies for acting more assertively.

STEP 6: The instructor will divide the class into groups of three and assign each group one of the following communication styles: assertive, nonassertive, or aggressive. Your group should prepare a short role play that illustrates how you would respond to the following situation in your assigned style. (The instructor or another member of the class will assume the role of your boss during the role play.)

Your boss has recently given you an assignment that you neither like nor feel you have the qualifications to perform. You will be meeting with the boss on another matter in ten minutes and must decide whether and how to express your reaction to the assignment.

....

STEP 7: Discussion. Compare the role plays. How was the communication the same? different? Which role plays illustrated effective communication? ineffective communication? Why?

_____

$\mathcal{A}$ctivity 7–7 | JANE COSTELLO CASE

....

STEP 1: Read the Jane Costello Case.

In November 1983, Jane Costello was the youngest executive on the corporate staff at Chase, Beacon and Company, a large New York publishing company. As director of the new investor relations department, she was responsible for designing and implementing a program for improving communications between the company and its current and potential stockholders. Although she was only 31 years old, she had been chosen for the job in May 1982 because she had had several years of experience in the investment community.

Eighteen months into the job, Jane felt she had made important headway toward meeting the original goals of her department, but she wondered what she could do to convince senior management to take advantage of her particular skills when shaping corporate policy. During the previous summer she had written a memorandum to the chairman of the board, Hamilton Chase III, concerning questions that major investors had recently been asking about the company, and had included her own recommendations for responding to the issues involved. The chairman's response had been immediate. Within 90 minutes of receiving her message, he had called a meeting. Present, in addition to Chase and Jane herself, were Russell Timm, the company's legal counsel; Rob Rittenhouse, the vice president of public affairs (to whom Jane reported); and Ted Page, the senior vice president for administration (to whom Rittenhouse reported).

Chase had questioned Jane closely about the exact wording of the investors' queries and had then spent the rest of the meeting talking with Timm and Page.

Several weeks later both Rittenhouse and Page told Jane that her memorandum to the chairman had been "more than a bit presumptuous," and that she "had overstepped her boundaries." It was not the first time they had criticized her style of communication with senior management.

....

BACKGROUND

Jane Costello radiated self-confidence and enthusiasm whenever she spoke. Energetic and articulate, she dressed with the same flair that characterized her manner of speaking. There was a sparkle about her, a sense of drive and purpose. Anyone who had known her only since her arrival at Chase Beacon might have been surprised to hear her description of herself at age 20 when she graduated from college.

> I was shy and frightened. I didn't think a whole lot about myself in those days. When I did, it wasn't with much satisfaction.

At 17, Jane had looked forward to attending Earlham College in Indiana as a way out of a "claustrophobic" situation at home. But once there,

> I finished college in three years because I hated it so much. I was totally unequipped for being on my own. At college I took only English courses—I had no intellectual curiosity.

Jane decided to be a teacher: she sent applications to most of the public school systems in the state and accepted the first offer she received. It was from a high school in a small rural town about 50 miles outside of Indianapolis. She recalled:

I didn't think of a job in terms of a career commitment. I didn't have any idea of what I had gotten myself into or what I planned to do with the rest of my life. I was there and I just did it, almost like a piece-worker in a factory.

To Jane's amazement, the school board found her teaching style objectionable and five months later, she was fired. Believing that her ability to type was all she could now rely on, she found a secretarial position in a state government office responsible for the state's pension funds. With the job came a salary that was $1,500 more than she had been earning as a teacher.

Despite the fact that her typing skills were really minimal, the professionals in her department responded to her enthusiasm.

This job was a big deal to me. I was an active part of a busy office. To me, the stimulation was incredible and I was energetic. I came across as a real go-getter. Of course, I started from scratch. I had to ask people what a bond was because I didn't have any idea and our office had responsibility for managing $200 million worth of bonds. But I had all this energy. I loved it there.

After six months she was spending about three-quarters of her time on nonsecretarial jobs. She talked with brokers. She was involved in decisions on stocks and bonds to be added or dropped from the pension fund. She met a number of Wall Street brokers when they came to Indianapolis on business.

As a result, she began to understand the complexities of the stock market. Three years later she decided to move again and to try for a job in New York City. She put her furniture in storage, sold her car, and moved to the Barbizon Hotel in Manhattan.

Once there, she called Wall Street brokers she had met in Indianapolis and after seven weeks she found a position as a research assistant with Houghton and Everett, investment bankers. Her salary was $21,000. She also enrolled in evening courses at New York University Graduate School of Business.

After about six months on her new job, Jane called a meeting of the four security analysts whom she assisted and suggested that they give her more work to do. She recalled:

They made some effort, but they were used to doing things themselves. Security analysts are independent individual performers. So I went to the head of the personnel department and asked some general questions about consulting, which I thought might be a good place for me. He arranged a meeting with Rich Gehrig, one of the whiz kids. He was a senior vice president in the corporate finance department. I had an hour-long talk with Rich and he called the personnel department and told them he wanted me on his staff.

Jane described Houghton and Everett as a company that emphasized excellence.

The company song is—you are the smartest people in the world. Their typical male associate is a Harvard MBA, from the top 10 percent of his class. He is groomed for two or three years, travels, meets clients all over the country, while still serving in a support role. By the end of his second or third year he becomes a vice president. Most of the men who are vice presidents are making $100,000 by the time they are 30 or 31.

Like most brokerage companies, H&E had several specialized divisions. The corporate finance department, in which Jane worked, was one of them.

I was taken on as an attachment to Rich Gehrig. He advised companies on how to handle their financial problems and I was his back-up person. Sometimes he would send me to the library for a week to learn everything I could about a whole industry. Then I would report back on what the key issues were so that he could pursue these with the client. I had a little office in the back and was still making $21,000, less than some of the secretaries.

A year after Jane started work, the corporate finance department was reorganized and this helped her gain more responsibility.

With a bigger corporate finance department, I had a lot more flexibility. I let the people in the group know what I was willing to do and capable of doing, though still in a support role.

That's usually the role of the associate: support. You're not going to go out much on your own to work with clients. But your days are your own and you are an individual performer. You work with one or two senior people at a time and over the course of a year you work with a number of different people. You feel pretty independent because you're not strongly supervised, you determine your own priorities, and you're playing on a team but it's not cohesive. Everyone fits into the organization in an individual sort of way.

Three years later Jane had earned her MBA. In spite of this she had begun to feel that she was in a rut, going nowhere with the company. Around her men with MBAs were being promoted to vice presidencies. She decided upon two courses of action: to send out résumés to other companies and to discuss the situation with Rich Gehrig.

> I had this incredible session with Gehrig. I told him I was sick and tired of being ripped off. "You guys are paying the new associates from Harvard $32,000 a year and I'm only getting $26,500. I have my MBA plus I've been with you for four years and I worked for several years before that. He said, "All right, I'll see what I can do." He went to the president of the company. He not only got me a raise to $35,000 but all the vice presidential privileges as well—use of the officers' dining room and the potential of earning 30–40 percent of my salary as a member of the officers' bonus pool.

Jane was not immediately named a vice president, however. She explained:

> It was the company's policy that the announcement of the new vice presidents was made after a board of directors meeting in June. Whether it was normal for people to get their privileges before the announcement, I didn't know. I wasn't actually told I would be made a vice president in June. I didn't know what to expect.

Before she could find out what would happen in June, Jane left the company. She had this to say about leaving Houghton and Everett:

> The implication that you are the best runs through the company so you have some very egotistical, high-powered people who think they are gods. I wasn't aware of that at the beginning but once I was it was a real challenge to try to compete because I'm a very competitive person. But I couldn't

win. If I was ever going to be vice president, I knew it would be a second-level sort of thing. That's when I started thinking there are places where corporations can use people like me.

> I realized I didn't know anything about good management because Houghton and Everett was not managed like a standard corporation. The whole scene just wasn't for me. I am a process person. I think in terms of organizing resources to meet objectives. Planning, implementing, evaluating—that's the way my mind works.

> Then, too, I had begun to realize my potential. Business school had a lot to do with making me realize that I am a bright, capable person.

In January 1982, even before she met with Gehrig, she had sent her résumé to all Fortune 500 companies with headquarters in New York. This happened to coincide with Chase Beacon's search for a director of investor relations and Rob Rittenhouse, vice president for public affairs, invited her for an interview. After several meetings with Jane, Rittenhouse recommended her to the chairman, Hamilton Chase III. At the time Chase felt strongly that the position should be filled by an older and more experienced person, preferably a company veteran. He told Rittenhouse to continue his search. More than 100 interviews later, Rittenhouse advised Chase that Jane was still the best candidate. She was offered the job and accepted it immediately.

CHASE, BEACON AND COMPANY

Chase Beacon was one of the oldest, largest, and most respected publishing houses in the United States. (Annual operating revenues in 1982 were $1.4 billion, a growth of 10.5 percent over 1981.) Founded in the 1890s by two magazine publishers, the company established its early reputation by publishing technical journals for scientists and engineers. By 1930, it was publishing fifteen magazines. In the 1940s, the company added works of fiction, nonfiction, and educational texts. During the 1950s, expansion continued with the addition of paperback books, a highly acclaimed scientific encyclopedia, and specialized periodicals in the fields of medicine, art, architecture, and the social sciences.

In the 1960s and early 1970s, Chase Beacon acquired two companies in the information systems industry, five radio and television stations, a number of special interest book clubs, and several established news, sports, and fashion magazines. Each acquisition was brought into one of the company's operating divisions. (In 1982, the company had eight divisions: domestic books; international books; specialized periodicals; general audience periodicals; educational texts and services; radio and television; information services; and book clubs.) Although corporate management set overall company policy, each division president was virtually autonomous. He ran his division as an independent profit center. Division presidents had considerable prestige and influence within the company.

Hamilton Chase III became chairman of the board, chief executive officer, and president of Chase Beacon in 1982. He was the fourth member of the Chase family to hold these positions and Chase Beacon was still considered a "family business" by some of its older executives, many of whom had been with the company for their entire careers. In 1982, seven of the eight division presidents had been with Chase Beacon since the 1950s. The company employed 12,000 people and was considered a leader among U.S. corporations in the area of social responsibility. It had begun a conscious effort to upgrade its women managers in the 1970s and by 1982, two women were corporate staff officers (a vice president and senior vice president) and others held important line positions.

THE INVESTOR RELATIONS DEPARTMENT

Investor relations was a new unit within the department of public affairs, which included internal communications (employee newspapers) and the contributions department. (See Figure 7–8 for a partial organizational chart.) In Jane's opinion there was a need to be met:

> I think the company finally realized that Wall Street people really do speak a different language. They think differently. It's not a whole new world for people like me. I don't make mistakes through ignorance of the language that a corporate person might make.

She believed that as a result her role had expanded.

> When I drew up my department plan, it included having the chairman make a number of speeches to bankers and large investors around the country. But he only wanted to do one or two speeches a year because he was concentrating on the internal affairs of the company. So although it wasn't part of my role as negotiated before I came here, I have become the company spokesman. My official job description doesn't reflect that. It's just something that happened.

> When they wrote my job description, they were hoping to hire somebody from inside the company, someone who would be a superb administrator, setting up meetings, knowing who was going to be there, what kind of people they were, what they were interested in, but not actually running the meetings as I do. It's a bit of an unusual situation, but I think my personal style has something to do with it. I'm an articulate person and I'm comfortable speaking to groups of 100 people or more.

Soon after Jane assumed her position, she was asked to make a speech at a lunch for the eight division controllers. This was her formal introduction to the organization. Rob Rittenhouse also introduced her to the eight division presidents, one by one. Beyond that it had been up to her to establish her own information network. She said:

> When an investor calls me up to get information, if I don't know the answer, I look in the company telephone directory to see who's in charge of that area and I make a call. Sometimes I call people up and introduce myself and ask them to lunch, but I don't have a lot of time for that because I'm also setting up lunches with potential investors. But I want to keep in touch with marketing, with finance, with legal people.

> I want to know everything that's happening in the divisions. In my field I have to know what our company's strengths are; its weaknesses; problems it's struggling with; opportunities for the future; management's ideas about what the company will look like in ten years and how they're going to get there.

> I know what kind of information I need because securities analysts and investment people always ask the same kinds of questions. I know what their concerns are, and how they think.

Jane explained how the environment at Chase Beacon differed from what she had experienced in other jobs.

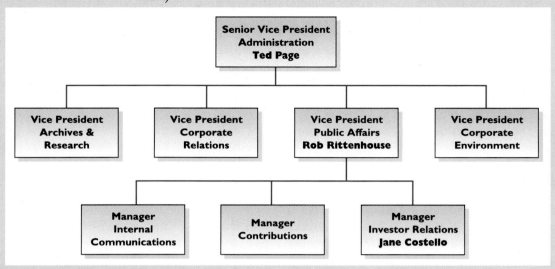

In the beginning I really didn't think I had to ask permission to do anything. In all my jobs I was an individual performer. Here they want team players. The corporate reality is that it's an authoritarian environment.

She described her working relationship with Rob Rittenhouse:

He's the kind of guy who lets the people reporting to him pretty much do their own thing. I don't think we understand each other on a personal level, however. He kids me about taking this job too seriously. During my first year, I worked 40 out of 52 Sundays. I only took 12 Sundays off. He wants me to care a little less.

When he hired Jane, Rittenhouse told her that the chairman would have preferred a man in his 40s or 50s for the job, had he been able to find such a person. Jane remarked:

So almost as soon as I came here I knew there had been resistance to hiring me. I was told *that* within 30 days so I would know what kind of resistance to overcome! The whole first year on the job, my boss spent a lot of time telling me to be less visible. I was told that I should "cool it" and not go too fast in the beginning, that I should try to "charm"

people. He told me to be more charming, less threatening, to calm down, not to come on too strong, not to give somebody six ideas in a meeting but just to slightly suggest one. So as I met senior executives, he gave me tips on how to deal with each one.

Jane had not been at Chase Beacon for very long before she recognized that Rob Rittenhouse had been "extraordinarily disturbed" by a number of the initiatives she had taken. She had written letters to potential investors to accompany mailings from her department. In addition, she had written to several division presidents and to senior vice presidents on the corporate staff, asking for information and also setting up meetings between senior management people and potential investors. Rittenhouse had learned of these contacts indirectly, from other managers. Jane described his response:

Rob is a man who avoids confrontations. He has a difficult time giving negative feedback, but finally he said to me, "Listen, I want to see everything that comes out of your secretary's typewriter, for approval. I want you to advise me about whatever you do before you do it."

Jane attributed these early problems at Chase Beacon to her "lack of sensitivity to the power of the written word." She said:

Rob has told me that I have been perceived by the company as arrogant. I think my reputation came from the way I wrote. My memos weren't couched in a gentle enough tone. I wrote, "I think you should . . ." or "I want you to . . ." instead of "You might consider . . ." or "I'd like to suggest . . ."

Jane said that another problem was her own youthfulness.

I have been told since the day I joined the company that it would be terrific if I had some gray hairs. My boss and his boss tell me that if I had some gray hairs, management would probably like me a lot better.

I don't mean to say that I don't have other problems. I had lunch with the number-three man in the company today and he still calls me "dear." I changed my hairstyle this summer. Everyone here talked to me about that for weeks. They talk a lot about my clothes.

Jane's biggest concern was that top management was not using her as a resource person.

I need to interact with the division heads, plus the top six or eight people in the company, so that if an investor or a reporter asks me a question about Chase Beacon, I can go to the right place for information. They are prompt in giving me answers but they aren't asking me questions to learn something useful for themselves. They don't involve me in long-range planning, where my knowledge of the financial community could be helpful. They don't ask me for advice on where the stock market is going—how they should manage their pension money. They don't use me as a consultant on the money market.

I've tried to send "alert" memos on what investors are asking about, but they feel that sort of thing is none of my business. It's probably a reflection of their perception of this department's role within the company. It may be a matter of my personal style.

At this point, I feel my best bet is still to keep testing the water, occasionally sending an "alert" memo, including—gently—a recommendation that might reflect that there is expertise here that might be called upon.

Jane said that she was learning how to communicate more effectively within the company by emulating Rob Rittenhouse.

I defer to his authority and make him aware that I defer to his authority. I see the way he defers to the chairman, just by things like always ending a conversation or a memo with a question: "What do you think?" "Would you like me to follow up on this?" I end all my memos to Rob in the same way now.

I've watched him very carefully. I see how he sits when he and the chairman and I are in a meeting, how he handles himself. I see how his personality changes, how he chooses his words. I feel his fear, his incredible fear—"What do you want?" "Do you mean this?"—Trying to pull out of the chairman what the chairman wants, making it clear with every sentence that he knows the chairman is the boss. I have watched that very carefully and picked up on it. It's not quite second nature to me yet but it's getting to be, in terms of the way I react to him.

All this is a super education. I have accepted that in order to be as extraordinarily effective in business and as successful as I plan to be, I have to be more sensitive. This is an important thing for me to learn, because it really does work. That's why it doesn't grate on me to do this. I accept the fact that I am in the learning phase. I realize that it compromises me, or forces me to change somewhat, but I have really accepted that this might make the difference between the people who are allowed to shoot up in the company without any resistance and those who aren't.

Jane discussed some of her goals for her department in the next year.

I want to send corporate information to hundreds of people to tell them who we are. I want to redesign the annual report and our quarterly reports so that they are more informative. So far my recommendations in that area have not been accepted.

Investor relations is very marketing oriented. I want to really sell the company image. I want to be more aggressive in getting our message out. I want to compete with every other company whose stock is sold in the market.

I want to be more aggressive on staffing. An investor relations department for a company this size needs at least five or six professionals. We are only three and a half now and we're being reduced to two and a half in 1984. Management doesn't feel we need that extra person.

Jane also discussed her personal long-term goals.

Wall Street people see corporate investor relations as a stepping-stone to a line position. In this company, I know the good divisions, who's good to work with and whom to avoid. I know where the company is expecting growth in the 1990s. In five years, I will be running a division. If it comes to the point where I can't move on a fast track here, I might go to law school. That probably is a good credential for a chief executive of the 1990s.

STEP 2:   Prepare the case for class discussion.

STEP 3:   Answer each of the following questions, individually or in small groups, as directed by your instructor.

DESCRIPTION

1. Briefly describe Jane's view of her performance.
2. How would you describe the relationship between Jane and the other employees at Chase, Beacon and Company?

DIAGNOSIS

3. How effective is communication at Chase, Beacon and Company? What dysfunctions exist?

4. How effective is Jane's communication style?
5. What barriers to communication exist in the company?
6. Using your knowledge of perception, attribution, and motivation, evaluate Jane's performance.

PRESCRIPTION

7. What techniques could Jane use to improve her communication?

ACTION

8. What resistances will she encounter in using these techniques?

STEP 4:   Discussion. In small groups, with the entire class, or in written form, share your answers to the questions above. Then answer the following questions:

1. What symptoms suggest that a problem exists?
2. What problems exist in the case?
3. What theories and concepts help explain those problems?
4. How can the problems be corrected?
5. Are the actions likely to be effective?

The Jane Costello Case was prepared for the Institute for Case Development and Research, Simmons Graduate School of Management, Boston, MA. Copyright © 1990 by the President and Trustees of Simmons College. Reprinted by permission.

Activity 7–8   PERFORMANCE FEEDBACK EXERCISE

STEP 1:   Read the following scenario.

Dr. Brilliant, a professor, and Pat, Dr. Brilliant's student research assistant, are meeting at Dr. Brilliant's request to discuss Pat's performance during the previous semester. The following are their perceptions of the last semester experience of working together.

Dr. Brilliant's Comments About Pat

Pat is a good research assistant. Projects are eventually completed, but only after repeated requests that they be finished. For example, I have asked Pat three times to give me an updated draft of the summaries of interviews that have been conducted for the Space Project. The project's documentation is also a mess; it's half in my office and half in Pat's cubicle. Pat's computer skills are excellent, and Pat's writing is exceptional for a student. But Pat's quantitative skills are not as strong as I need, particularly for my upcoming research project.

Pat's Comments About Dr. Brilliant

I learn an incredible amount from Dr. Brilliant, and that is very important to me. What I want most from this working relationship is to learn. It is frustrating because Dr. Brilliant is so busy that I feel as if I only get part of the directions or objectives at any one time. I wish Dr. Brilliant and I could schedule regular time together. I know Dr. Brilliant wants a better project system, but I am not sure about how to create one.

STEP 2: You are Dr. Brilliant. Based on the information above, prepare a brief performance feedback for Pat.

STEP 3: With a partner, give each other the performance feedback, alternating playing the roles of Dr. Brilliant and Pat.

STEP 4: Compare the way each person gave the performance feedback. Note what was most and least effective in each person's delivery.

STEP 5: Discussion. In small groups or with the entire class, answer the following questions:

DESCRIPTION
1. Briefly summarize the main events of the meetings.
2. Describe the perceptions and attributions Dr. Brilliant and Pat seem to have about each other. What effects do these have?

DIAGNOSIS
3. Evaluate the communication process during the interview.
4. What types of barriers to effective communication occurred?

PRESCRIPTION
5. Is it possible for most interviewers to avoid the pitfalls in this type of situation? How?
6. How can communication about performance feedback be improved?

This exercise was prepared by Ms. Karen S. Whelan, a doctoral student in the Organization Studies Department of the Carroll School of Management, Boston College, and is used with permission.

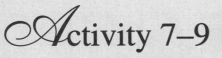

Activity 7–9 "Voice Mail Jail"

STEP 1: View the ABC video entitled "Voice Mail Jail."

STEP 2: In small groups or with the entire class, answer the following questions:

1. What is "voice mail jail"?
2. How does a person enter "voice mail jail"?
3. How does voice mail affect communication in organizations?
4. Does voice mail encourage two-way communication?
5. How can organizations effectively use voice mail?

Chapter 8

Chapter Outline

Leading Effectively

LEARNING OBJECTIVES

After completing the reading and activities in Chapter 8, students will be able to

1. Describe the way a manager's traits affect his or her leadership ability.

2. Specify the behavioral dimensions of leadership and show how they affect workers' attitudes and behavior.

3. Describe the ten managerial roles.

4. Describe five situational leadership theories and use each situational leadership theory to select the most effective leadership style in a given situation.

5. Describe four nonsituational theories and their implications for leadership effectiveness.

6. Offer a prescription for becoming a transformational leader.

7. Describe superleadership and show how it can increase leadership effectiveness.

8. Offer a protocol for leading a multicultural work force.

Linda Wachner Takes the Reins at Warnaco

In 1986, Linda Wachner faced a major challenge. She had just taken over the leadership of Warnaco, a manufacturer of women's lingerie, in a $486 million leveraged buyout. Her goal was to take the company public and ensure its profitability in a hostile and unimproving economic climate. Wachner knew she had to make radical changes to restore the company's competitiveness.

Since 1986, the company has gone public, the stock price has risen 75 percent from the initial offering, the debt has been cut by 40 percent, sales have increased by 30 percent, earnings before taxes has increased 140 percent, and the operating cash flow has almost doubled. Wachner has had an unrelenting focus on the company's performance. Her own financial situation is tied closely to the company's since she owns 10 percent of it: she purchased 1.3 million shares for about $15 less than the public stock offering price.

As the only female CEO of a Fortune 500 company, Wachner's leadership has been carefully scrutinized. Wachner combines energy, drive, and enthusiasm with hard-core fiscal management, a focus on the customer, and high demands from her workers. Viewed as a tough boss, her employees often feel that she expects too much. As part of her "Do it now" philosophy, which focuses on responding to consumer preferences in the short and long run, she has also reaped significant savings from cutting costs. For example, she reduced the corporate office staff from 200 to 7. Some say that Wachner does not do a good job of managing people because of her single-minded focus on company profitability. She is unrelenting in getting to the point and requiring her colleagues to do the same.

"Have I yelled at meetings? No question. Do I think I've ever hurt anybody? I hope not. Look, I just want people to be good, and I apply an enormous amount of pressure to get everybody moving this company in the right direction" she says. "I know I push very hard, but I don't push anyone harder than I push myself. Last year I traveled 200 days, visiting stores and plants and so on."[1]

At the same time, she motivates her workers with her praise of their work. She visits the stitchroom almost daily, picking up and examining the fabric, lace, and trim the seamstresses are working on: "These are to *die* for," Wachner declares as she holds up the garments with a supremely satisfied smile. "Beautiful. Just beautiful."[2] Maintaining the same grueling schedule may be difficult for employees, but Wachner emphasizes keeping their energy high and focusing on a common goal. This determination has created a "hard-as-nails" image, but a style that gets the job done.[3]

Is Linda Wachner an effective leader? Was she born to be an effective leader or did she learn how to be a leader? In this chapter, we will see how the field of organizational behavior has tried to answer these questions by analyzing the leader's personality, the behaviors of leaders and followers, and the situations in which leaders and followers interact. At the end of the chapter, we will see how each of these factors affects leadership in today's global economy.

TRAIT THEORY

Trait theory suggests that leaders have certain personality, social, and physical characteristics, known as *traits,* that influence whether the person acts as a leader.[4] First introduced in the 1940s and 1950s, trait theory originally proposed that individuals were born to be leaders. Supported by the development of psychological testing and an interest in what made the "great" leaders of the world, trait theory compared leaders and nonleaders.

More than 100 studies on leader traits conducted during the first half of the twentieth century supported the assertion that leaders were born by showing that leaders differed from nonleaders in their intelligence, initiative, persistence in dealing with problems, self-confidence, alertness to others' needs, understanding of the task, desire to accept responsibility, and preference for a position of control and dominance.[5]

More recent research assumed that leaders are not necessarily born, but can learn the requisite skills and traits shown in Table 8–1. Trait theory proposes that, like Linda Wachner, most leaders have the traits of energy, tenacity, and initiative. They generally demonstrate ambition and are achievement oriented. They show originality, enthusiasm, and persistence. Trait researchers further agree that leaders differ from nonleaders in their drive (achievement, ambition, energy, tenacity, and initiative), desire to lead, honesty and integrity, self-confidence, cognitive ability, and knowledge of business.[6]

Trait theory suggests that certain traits can increase the likelihood of a leader's effectiveness.[7] One study of senior management jobs showed that an effective leader requires a broad knowledge of and solid relations within the industry and the company, an excellent reputation, a strong track record, a keen mind, strong interpersonal skills, high integrity, high energy, and a strong drive to lead.[8]

TABLE 8–1   *Traits and skills found most frequently to be characteristic of successful leaders*

TRAITS	SKILLS
Adaptable to situations	Clever (intelligent)
Alert to social environment	Conceptually skilled
Ambitious and achievement oriented	Creative
Assertive	Diplomatic and tactful
Cooperative	Fluent in speaking
Decisive	Knowledgeable about group task
Dependable	Organized (administrative ability)
Dominant (desire to influence others)	Persuasive
Energetic (high activity level)	Socially skilled
Persistent	
Self-confident	
Tolerant of stress	
Willing to assume responsibility	

SOURCE: Reprinted with permission from Gary Yukl, *Leadership in Organizations,* 2nd ed. (Englewood Cliffs, N.J.: Prentice Hall, 1989), p. 176. Copyright © 1989 by Prentice Hall.

Another series of studies at the Center for Creative Leadership validated the basic premise that effective and ineffective leaders had different traits and skills. The studies compared successful managers and "derailed" managers, managers who advanced into middle or top management but failed to perform effectively.[9] The results indicated that successful managers had characteristics that derailed managers lacked. Successful managers demonstrated emotional stability and composure. They were calm and confident rather than moody or angry during crises. They admitted mistakes and then tried to correct problems rather than blaming others or hiding mistakes. They had strong interpersonal skills. They had diverse functional and technical experiences that gave them a broader perspective for solving problems.

EVALUATION OF TRAIT THEORY

The use of the trait approach has had more historical than practical interest to managers. Although some research suggests that traits can contribute to effective leadership, the research also suggests that they are not sufficient by themselves for ensuring effectiveness.[10] Some consideration of the effects of different leadership behaviors or situations must occur.

Research about leaders outside the United States also challenged trait theory. Traits judged necessary for top, middle, and low-level management differed among leaders of different countries. For example, United States and British managers valued resourcefulness, the Japanese intuition, and the Dutch imagination, but for lower and middle managers only.[11]

BEHAVIORAL THEORIES

Critics of trait theory suggested that leaders' **behaviors** determined their effectiveness. Path-breaking studies in the 1950s focused on two dimensions of leadership style—orientation to task and orientation to employees. Later work focused on the roles performed by managers.

TASK- AND EMPLOYEE- ORIENTED BEHAVIORS

Researchers at Ohio State University conducted a set of experiments to test the idea that leaders' behaviors influenced their effectiveness.[12] These experiments used two criteria to classify leadership behaviors.

- *Initiating structure* referred to the degree to which a leader structures his or her own role and subordinates' roles to help accomplish the group's goal. Behaviors characterized as initiating structure included scheduling the work of subordinates or coworkers, assigning employees to tasks, maintaining standards of performance, or delineating the specific tasks individuals will perform. A supervisor who told his or her subordinates that they should do everything they could to get the job done on time demonstrated initiating structure leadership, as did a manager who failed to involve workers in any aspect of decision making.

- *Consideration* referred to the degree to which the leader addressed individuals' needs. Consideration behaviors included two-way communication, respect for subordinates' ideas, considering subordinates' feelings, and demonstration of mutual trust between leader and subordinates. A boss who demonstrated great concern for his or her workers' satisfaction with their jobs and commitment to their work had an employee-oriented leadership style.

Table 8–2 shows some of the results of these studies. They measured the association between leadership behavior and leadership effectiveness, measured in the results reported here as task performance of the leader's work unit, subordinate turnover, and subordinate grievance rate. Note that leaders high on both initiating structure and consideration have subordinates who show high performance, low turnover, and low grievance rate. Those leaders low on both behaviors have subordinates with the opposite outcomes—low performance, high turnover, and high grievance rate. A combination of high initiating structure and low consideration resulted in high subordinate performance, but also high turnover and high grievance rate. A combination of low initiating structure and high consideration resulted in low subordinate performance, as well as low turnover and low grievance rate.

Studies at the University of Michigan in the 1950s complemented the studies done at Ohio State University.[13] They looked at *production orientation*—or focus on accomplishing the task—and *employee orientation*—or focus on supporting employees in doing their work. Supervisors of highly productive work groups tended to be both production and employee oriented. They spent more time in planning departmental work and supervising their employees and less time in performing the same tasks as subordinates. They also gave their subordinates greater freedom in accomplishing the task.[14]

Subsequent research by Rensis Likert added *participative* leadership to the styles studied.[15] Such leaders used group meetings to encourage worker participation in decision making, communication, cooperation, and conflict resolution. Participative leaders supported and guided group discussions and focused them on decision making and problem solving. Participative leadership, when combined with setting high goals, technical expertise, supportive behaviors, and leaders acting as a central information link, was associated with the outcomes of high productivity, high quality of work, and low absenteeism, low turnover, and low grievance rate.

TABLE 8–2   *Outcomes of the Ohio State University leadership studies' behavioral model*

| | | MANAGER'S INITIATING STRUCTURE | |
		HIGH	LOW
MANAGER'S CONSIDERATION	HIGH	High performance Low grievance rate Low turnover	Low performance Low grievance rate Low turnover
	LOW	High performance High grievance rate High turnover	Low performance High grievance rate High turnover

SOURCE: Based on R.H. Stogdill and A.E. Coons, eds., *Leader Behavior: Its Description and Measurement* (Columbus: Ohio State University Bureau of Business Research, 1957).

HARLEY-DAVIDSON. Richard Terlink, CEO of Harley-Davidson, Inc., the motorcycle manufacturer, encourages employee participation in improving product quality. Employees are encouraged to make decisions that will help exceed customers' expectations, as well as suggest ways to reduce waste, correct defects, and decrease product variability. The company does not make decisions by committee or consensus, but offers individuals the opportunity to make a difference by offering suggestions that influence decisions.[16]

What leadership behaviors did Linda Wachner demonstrate? Did she show effective leadership according to these models? At times she seemed to be high on both dimensions, emphasizing both consideration for her employees and structuring of tasks to ensure that the work was accomplished. At other times, she seemed to be more focused on the task, giving her employees little slack in getting the job done.

Evaluation of these Theories Ideally, according to the Ohio State and University of Michigan studies, leaders should demonstrate both high initiating structure and high consideration. Is this possible? Current thought indicates that a single pattern of leader behaviors is not always effective because of the complexity of organizational situations. In addition, the Ohio State researchers relied too heavily on data generated by questionnaires rather than observations.[17] The method of collecting data did not allow researchers to precisely determine whether leadership style caused the outcomes observed.

As for trait theory, the ability to generalize behavioral theories to multinational and multicultural situations is limited. One study of leadership behaviors in Japan, for example, showed that in most situations high task-oriented (called performance) and high employee-oriented (called maintenance) behaviors resulted in the best outcomes.[18] In some situations, particularly when leaders supervised short-term project groups, had subordinates prone to anxiety, or experienced situations that called for low effort, leaders high on performance behavior but low on maintenance behavior had better outcomes.

MANAGERIAL ROLES

Henry Mintzberg's study of chief executive officers offered a different way of looking at leadership behaviors. He listed the roles managers perform as a way of describing their behavior.[19] According to this research, managerial work encompasses ten roles, as shown in Table 8–3. Three roles focus on *interpersonal* contact—figurehead, leader, liaison. Three roles involve mainly *information processing*—monitor, disseminator, spokesman. Four roles relate to *decision making*—entrepreneur, disturbance handler, resource allocator, and negotiator. Although almost all roles include activities that could be construed as leadership, influencing others toward a particular goal, most roles can apply to both managerial and nonmanagerial positions.

Consider some managers you have observed. Now consider your own performance in managerial roles. Finally, consider Linda Wachner's performance. What roles did a manager perform in each of these situations? While not all managers will perform every role, some diversity of role performance must occur.

Managers can diagnose their own and others' role performance and then offer strategies for altering it. Table 8–4 shows the most frequent roles played by a variety of managers. The choice of roles will depend to some extent on the manager's

TABLE 8–3   *Mintzberg's Roles*

ROLE	DESCRIPTION
Figurehead	The manager, acting as a symbol or representative of the organization, performs diverse ceremonial duties. By attending Chamber of Commerce meetings, heading the local United Way drive, or representing the president of the firm at an awards banquet, a manager performs the figurehead role.
Leader	The manager, interacting with subordinates, motivates and develops them. The supervisor who conducts quarterly performance interviews or selects training opportunities for his or her subordinates performs the role of leader. This role emphasizes the socioemotional and people-oriented side of leadership and deemphasizes task activities, which are more often incorporated into the decisional roles.
Liaison	The manager establishes a network of contacts to gather information for the organization. Belonging to professional associations or meeting over lunch with peers in other organizations helps the manager perform the liaison role.
Monitor	The manager gathers information from the environment inside and outside the organization. He or she may attend meetings with subordinates, scan company publications, or participate in companywide committees as a way of performing this role.
Disseminator	The manager transmits both factual and value information to subordinates. Managers may conduct staff meetings, send memorandums to their staff, or meet informally with them on a one-to-one basis to discuss current and future projects.
Spokesperson	The manager gives information to people outside the organization about its performance and policies. He or she oversees preparation of the annual report, prepares advertising copy, or speaks at community and professional meetings.
Entrepreneur	The manager designs and initiates change in the organization. The supervisor who redesigns the jobs of subordinates, introduces flexible working hours, or brings new technology to the job performs this role.
Disturbance handler	The manager deals with problems that arise when organizational operations break down. A person who finds a new supplier on short notice for an out-of-stock part, who replaces unexpectedly absent employees, or who deals with machine breakdowns performs this role.
Resource allocator	The manager controls the allocation of people, money, materials, and time by scheduling his or her own time, programming subordinates' work effort, and authorizing all significant decisions. Preparation of the budget is a major aspect of this role.
Negotiator	The manager participates in negotiation activities. A manager who hires a new employee may negotiate work assignments or compensation with that person.

SOURCE: These roles are drawn from H. Mintzberg, *The Nature of Managerial Work* (Englewood Cliffs, N.J.: Prentice-Hall, 1979).

specific job description and the situation in question. For example, managing individual performance and instructing employees are less important for middle managers than for first-line supervisors, and less important for executives than for either lower level of manager.[20]

Evaluation of the Theory Mintzberg's theory describes only a limited aspect of leadership and management behavior. He studied only a small sample of chief executive officers. Hence the generalizations of his results is questionable.

TABLE 8–4   *Eight managerial job types*

MANAGERIAL JOB TYPE	KEY ROLES	EXAMPLES
Contact person	Liaison, figurehead	Sales manager Chief executive in service industry
Political manager	Spokesperson, negotiator	Top government, hospital, university manager
Entrepreneur	Entrepreneur, negotiator	Owner of small, young business CEO of rapidly changing, large organization
Insider	Resource allocator	Middle or senior production or operations manager Manager rebuilding after crisis
Real-time manager	Disturbance handler	Foreman Head of organization in crisis Head of small, one-manager business
Team manager	Leader	Hockey coach Head of R&D group
Expert manager	Monitor, spokesperson	Head of specialist group
New manager	Liaison, monitor	Manager in a new job

SOURCE: Adapted from H. Mintzberg, *The Nature of Managerial Work* (Englewood Cliffs, N.J.: Prentice-Hall, 1973).

SITUATIONAL THEORIES

Contingency or situational theories differ from the earlier trait and behavioral theories in asserting that no single way of leading works in all situations. Recent research suggests that managers should select a leadership style that ***best fits with the situation at a given time.*** Effective managers diagnose the situation, identify the leadership style that will be most effective, and then determine if they can implement the required style. Early situational research suggested that three general factors affect the appropriate leadership style in a given situation.

Subordinate Considerations reflect the leader's awareness of subordinates' expertise, experience, competence, job knowledge, hierarchical level, and psychological characteristics.

Supervisor Considerations reflect the leader's degree of upward influence, as well as his or her similarity of attitudes and behaviors to those in higher positions.

Task Considerations reflect the degree of time urgency, amount of physical danger, permissible error rate, presence of external stress, degree of autonomy, degree of job scope, importance and meaningfulness, and degree of ambiguity of the work being performed.

The precise aspects of each dimension that influence the most effective leadership style vary in different situations. Most situational theorists suggest that effective leaders develop a repertoire of leadership styles, which they adapt to different situations. At Warnaco, for example, Linda Wachner is results oriented but may use either a directive or a supportive style. In this section, we will examine five theories that tried to help managers select the right leadership style for various situations.

MCGREGOR'S THEORY X AND THEORY Y

One of the older situational theories, McGregor's Theory X–Theory Y formulation calls for a leadership style based on individuals' assumptions about other individuals, together with characteristics of the individual, the task, the organization, and the environment.[21] Although managers may have many styles, Theory X and Y have received the greatest attention.

- *Theory X* managers assume that people are lazy, extrinsically motivated, incapable of self-discipline or self-control, and want security and no responsibility in their jobs.

- *Theory Y* managers assume people do not inherently dislike work, are intrinsically motivated, exert self-control, and seek responsibility.

How can a manager use McGregor's theory to help him or her lead workers effectively? What *prescription* might McGregor offer for improving the situation? If a manager had Theory X assumptions, he or she would suggest that the manager verify them. If the individuals truly require extrinsic motivation, then an autocratic style might be appropriate. For some managers with Theory X assumptions, a management development program in which the manager would be introduced to the concept of Theory Y and taught some management tools for tapping into the worker's inherent pride in their work or desire for responsibility would be appropriate. If a manager had Theory Y assumptions, McGregor might advise a diagnosis of the situation to help the manager choose from a repertoire of available styles. Such a diagnosis should ensure that the selected style matched the manager's assumptions and action tendencies, as well as the internal and external influences on the situation.

SUNBEAM-OSTER. Paul B. Kazarian, the former chairman of Sunbeam-Oster, was hired to resurrect the bankrupt company, but instead alienated workers and members of the company's Board of Directors. He demonstrated a Theory X style. According to Sunbeam employees, he abused and humiliated employees and suppliers, used obscene and vulgar language, and shot BBs at empty chairs during meetings.[22]

CP INDUSTRIES. Jack Croushore is CEO of CP Industries, Inc., a company based near Pittsburgh, Pennsylvania, which manufactures pressure vessels for storing and transporting gases. He changed his assumptions from Theory X to Theory Y when he became the plant manager of Christy Park Works, a U.S. Steel plant that later became CP Industries. He continued to use Theory Y assumptions in his role as CEO.

Before moving to the Christy Park Works, he frequently gave workers disciplinary slips and suspended them without pay. Now, workers who fail to follow procedures are not reprimanded. Croushore decided that he would treat workers the way he would like to be treated. He trusts workers to act appropriately, encourages them to take responsibility, and wants them to make decisions. For example, teams of hourly workers hire and develop new employees. Although the plant has reduced its work force, productivity has increased.[23]

Evaluation of the Theory Although McGregor's theory has been viewed favorably because of its intuitive appeal, little empirical research has been conducted to support or refute it. Although the more recent reinterpretation of Theory X and Theory Y stated that internal and external factors influence the appropriate style, the theory does not specify which style should be used in given situations.

FIEDLER'S THEORIES

Fred Fiedler and his associates took a different approach. Instead of having a repertoire of styles, they argued, a leader's style is relatively fixed.[24] The leader prefers either a *task-oriented* or a *relations-oriented* style. (These are similar to the initiating structure and consideration factors identified in the Ohio State research.) Thus, leaders are most effective when they either choose situations that match their preferred style or when they change the situation to fit their preferred style.

Fiedler and his associates developed the Least-Preferred Coworker (LPC) scale to help identify managers' preferred styles. Figure 8–1 presents an excerpt from this scale. Those who score high on the LPC scale have a task-oriented, or controlling, active, and structuring style. Low-scoring leaders have a relationship-oriented, permissive, passive, considerate leadership style.

To create a fit between style and situation, a leader next analyzes three dimensions of the situation: (1) leader–member relations, (2) task structure, and (3) position power of the leader.

- **Leader–member relations** refers to the extent to which the group trusts the leader and willingly follows his or her directions. Does Linda Wachner of Warnaco have subordinates who readily follow instructions, set goals, and cooperate with her? If so, she has good leader–member relations. If not, her leader–member relations are poor.

- **Task structure** refers to the degree to which the task is clearly defined. A bank teller's job has relatively high task structure. The branch manager's job has less.

- **Position power** means the extent to which the leader has official power to influence others. Typically, a manager has position power whereas a nonmanagerial employee does not.

Table 8–5 shows the type of leadership style called for in situations with combinations of these three characteristics. An effective manager diagnoses the situation along these three dimensions and then determines whether his or her style fits with the assessment. Consider the president of a new start-up company where the ten employees are handpicked, the tasks are highly ambiguous, but the president's authority is clear. What type of style would best fit the situation? Now consider the situation of a well-established market research department, where the employees

FIGURE 8–1

Think of the person *with whom you can work least well*. Describe this person as he or she appears to you by marking the appropriate place on each scale.

	8	7	6	5	4	3	2	1	
Pleasant	8	7	6	5	4	3	2	1	Unpleasant
Friendly	8	7	6	5	4	3	2	1	Unfriendly
Rejecting	1	2	3	4	5	6	7	8	Accepting
Tense	1	2	3	4	5	6	7	8	Relaxed
Distant	1	2	3	4	5	6	7	8	Close
Cold	1	2	3	4	5	6	7	8	Warm
Supportive	8	7	6	5	4	3	2	1	Hostile
Boring	1	2	3	4	5	6	7	8	Interesting
Quarrelsome	1	2	3	4	5	6	7	8	Harmonious
Gloomy	1	2	3	4	5	6	7	8	Cheerful
Open	8	7	6	5	4	3	2	1	Guarded
Backbiting	1	2	3	4	5	6	7	8	Loyal
Untrustworthy	1	2	3	4	5	6	7	8	Trustworthy
Considerate	8	7	6	5	4	3	2	1	Inconsiderate
Nasty	1	2	3	4	5	6	7	8	Nice
Agreeable	8	7	6	5	4	3	2	1	Disagreeable
Insincere	1	2	3	4	5	6	7	8	Sincere
Kind	8	7	6	5	4	3	2	1	Unkind

SOURCE: Adapted from F.E. Fiedler, *A Theory of Leadership Effectiveness* (New York: McGraw-Hill, 1967). Reprinted with permission.

complain about their lack of autonomy, assert that their manager lacks respect from his superiors, and indicate that the task is clear and well structured. The first situation would call for a task-oriented style, the second for a relations-oriented style.

Fiedler's more recent ***cognitive resource theory*** focuses instead on predicting group performance from leader intelligence and experience.[25] He and his associates tested and found support for three propositions:

1. Leader ability contributes to group performance when the leader is directive.

2. In low-stress conditions high intelligence results in good decisions whereas no relationship or a negative one exists between intelligence and decision in high-stress conditions.

TABLE 8–5 *Fiedler's model of effective leadership*

DESCRIPTION OF THE SITUATION			EFFECTIVE LEADERSHIP STYLE
LEADER–MEMBER RELATIONS	TASK STRUCTURE	POSITION POWER	
Good	Structured	Strong	Task oriented
Good	Structured	Weak	Task oriented
Good	Unstructured	Strong	Task oriented
Good	Unstructured	Weak	Relations oriented
Poor	Structured	Strong	Relations oriented
Poor	Structured	Weak	Relations oriented
Poor	Unstructured	Strong	Either
Poor	Unstructured	Weak	Task oriented

3. Experience and quality of leadership decisions are positively related in conditions of high interpersonal stress, but no relationship exists in low-stress conditions.

Evaluation of the Theories Although Fiedler and his colleagues have performed large numbers of studies to validate the LPC model, research support remains mixed.[26] For example, their LPC theory suffers from significant measurement problems, particularly regarding the leader's style. Also, the research has generally ignored leaders who receive medium LPC scores.

Some studies have been conducted to validate the cognitive resource theory, but questions remain about the quality of the instruments used to measure the variables in the theory.[27] Also, systematic attempts to rule out alternative explanations of the results have been inadequate.[28]

PATH-GOAL THEORY

Unlike Fiedler's theory, which identifies only two dimensions of leadership style and three features of the situation, path-goal theory attempts to reflect better the complexity of organizational situations.[29] According to this theory, leaders attempt to influence their subordinates' perceptions of the payoffs for accomplishing their goals and show them ways to achieve the goals. The impact of a leader's behavior on follower satisfaction and effort depends on the nature of the situation, including characteristics of the task, subordinates, and environment.

Basically, the leader chooses from four styles:

- *Directive style:* The leader tells subordinates what is expected of them, gives them guidance about what should be done, and also shows them how to do it.

- *Supportive style:* The leader shows concern for the well-being and needs of his or her subordinates by being friendly and approachable.

- *Participative style:* The leader involves subordinates in decision making, consults with them about their views of the situation, asks for their suggestions, considers those suggestions in making a decision, and sometimes lets the subordinates make the decisions themselves.

- *Achievement-oriented style:* The leader helps subordinates set goals, rewards the accomplishment of these goals, and encourages subordinates to assume responsibility for their attainment.

ELECTRONIC DATA SYSTEMS. Ross Perot, a U.S. presidential candidate in 1992, built Electronic Data Systems into a billion dollar corporation. He has been described as one who expects subordinates to argue with him but then to present a unified position outside the corporation. He seemingly listens to others until he determines a course of action and then refuses to discuss the issue again.[30] Perot's style combines directive and consultative styles.

According to this theory, an effective leader will attempt to increase the subordinates' expectancies and valences (see Chapter 4 for discussion of expectancy theory). For example, the manager should ensure that a worker's effort results in performance. This might mean improving the tools, techniques, and skills of workers through the securing of new equipment, the introduction of special training programs, or the removal of other barriers to performing.

Applying Path-Goal Theory The leader will begin by choosing a leadership style that fits the situation. To do this, the leader has to assess five aspects of the situation and people involved:

1. *Assess the task.* Is the task structured or unstructured? Are the goals clear or unclear? Structured tasks and clear goals require less direction than less structured tasks and less clear goals. For example, the Perot Doctrine has been described as "See snake; kill snake."[31]

2. *Assess the leader's formal authority.* Managers tend to have more formal authority than nonmanagerial employees, and top executives have more than middle-or lower-level managers. Managers with formal authority typically should not use a directive style because it duplicates their authority, but they may use supportive, achievement-oriented, or participative styles.

3. *Assess the nature of the work group.* The leader should assess its cohesiveness as well as its experience in working together. The more cohesive the group, the less need for supportive leadership since this is redundant with the group's character. Similarly, the more experience the group has in collaborating, the less it requires directive, supportive, and participative leadership styles.

4. *Assess the organization's culture.* A culture that supports participation also supports a participative leadership style. A culture that encourages goal accomplishment or a results orientation reinforces an achievement-oriented style.

5. *Assess the subordinates' skills and needs.* Subordinates skilled in a task require less direction than those less skilled. Subordinates with high achievement needs require a style that helps meet these needs. Subordinates with social needs require a style that helps meet these needs.

Then the leader has to decide which style responds best to environmental contingencies and subordinates' characteristics. Table 8–6 illustrates such a matching. The right-hand columns indicate whether each of the four prototype leadership styles fits with the feature of the situation listed in the left-hand column when considered independently of other situational characteristics. For example, only directive leadership is inappropriate when the task is structured since directive leadership is redundant and does not complement either the subordinates' needs or characteristics of the situation. For subordinates with high achievement needs, in contrast, only an achievement style will satisfy their needs.

M/A-Com. Rick Hess, M/A Com's chief operating officer, tries to get his employees to challenge themselves. This achievement-oriented style fits with the organization's culture, which encourages them to reach their potential.[32]

Application of the path-goal theory, then, first requires an assessment of the situation, particularly its participants and environment, and second a determination of the most congruent leadership style.

Evaluation of the Theory Research to validate the path-goal theory has produced mixed results.[33] The measurement of leadership style focuses on very broad categories of behavior.[34] The research has primarily used questionnaires to measure both leadership and its outcomes, which may limit the accuracy of the results. The failure of the research to conclusively state what outcomes result from the use of

---

TABLE 8–6   *Effective leadership styles under different conditions*

SAMPLE SITUATIONAL CHARACTERISTICS	LEADERSHIP STYLES			
	DIRECTIVE	**SUPPORTIVE**	**ACHIEVEMENT**	**PARTICIPATIVE**
Task				
Structured	No	Yes	Yes	Yes
Unstructured	Yes	No	Yes	No
Clear goals	No	Yes	No	Yes
Ambiguous goals	Yes	No	Yes	No
Subordinates				
Skilled in task	No	Yes	Yes	Yes
Unskilled in task	Yes	No	Yes	No
High achievement needs	No	No	Yes	No
High social needs	No	Yes	No	Yes
Formal authority				
Extensive	No	Yes	Yes	Yes
Limited	Yes	Yes	Yes	Yes
Work group				
Strong social network	Yes	No	Yes	Yes
Experienced in collaboration	No	No	No	Yes
Organizational culture				
Supports participation	No	No	No	Yes
Achievement-oriented	No	No	Yes	No

---

particular styles in certain situations also limits the ability to generalize the results to different situations. Finally, path-goal theory's reliance on expectancy theory means that the validity of this leadership theory depends on the validity of expectancy theory.

A PARTICIPATION THEORY OF LEADERSHIP

Victor Vroom and Philip Yetton and later, Arthur Jago, also examined the issue of the appropriate leadership style, but focused instead on the process of *participation in decision making* because they viewed it as the process most responsible for an organization's success.[35] They assumed that leaders used four basic styles in making decisions: authoritative, consultative, group-based, and delegative. These styles led to different decision-making processes for solving both individual and group problems, which they labeled as A, C, G, or D to reflect the basic style, as shown in Table 8–7.

According to this theory, leaders should consider numerous factors in analyzing the situation, which are reflected in the eight questions in the decision tree, shown in Figure 8–2. Answers to these questions lead the manager down the appropriate branch of the decision tree, resulting in the identification of one or more decision-making processes appropriate for the situation.

TABLE 8–7   *Decision-making processes*

FOR INDIVIDUAL PROBLEMS	FOR GROUP PROBLEMS
AI You solve the problem or make the decision yourself, using information available to you at that time.	**AI** You solve the problem or make the decision yourself, using information available to you at the time.
AII You obtain any necessary information from the subordinate, then decide on the solution to the problem yourself.	**AII** You obtain any necessary information from subordinates, then decide on the solution to the problem yourself.
CI You share the problem with the relevant subordinate, getting his or her ideas and suggestions. Then you make the decision, which may or may not reflect your subordinate's influence.	**CI** You share the problem with the relevant subordinates individually, getting their ideas and suggestions without bringing them together. Then you make the decision, which may or may not reflect your subordinates' influence.
GI You share the problem with one of your subordinates, and together you analyze the problem and arrive at a mutually satisfactory solution in an atmosphere of free and open exchange of information and ideas.	**CII** You share the problem with your subordinates in a group meeting, in which you obtain their ideas and suggestions. Then you make the decision, which may or may not reflect their influence.
DI You delegate the problem to one of your subordinates, providing him or her with any relevant information that you possess, but giving him or her responsibility for making the decision and your support for any decision reached.	**GII** You share the problem with your subordinates as a group. Together you generate and evaluate alternatives and attempt to reach true consensus on a solution. Acting as a coordinator of the discussion, you are willing to accept and implement any solution that the entire group supports.

Adapted with permission from V.H. Vroom and A.G. Jago, Decision-making as a social process: Normative and descriptive models of leader behavior, *Decision Sciences* 5 (1974): 745.

FIGURE 8–2

A. Is there a quality requirement such that one solution is likely to be more rational than another?
B. Do I have sufficient information to make a high-quality decision?
C. Is the problem structured?
D. Is acceptance of decision by subordinates critical to effective implementation?
E. If I were to make the decision by myself, is it reasonably certain that it would be accepted by my subordinates?
F. Do subordinates share the organizational goals to be attained in solving this problem?
G. Is conflict among subordinates likely in preferred solutions? (This question is irrelevant to individual problems.)
H. Do subordinates have sufficient information to make a high-quality decision?

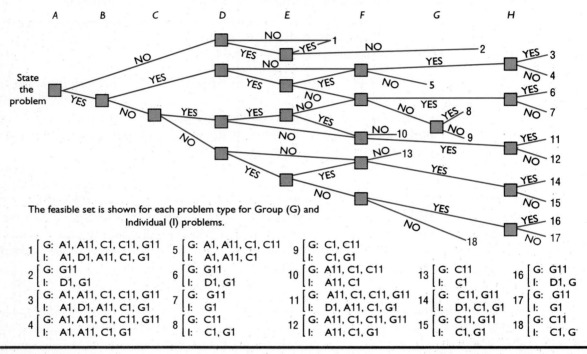

The feasible set is shown for each problem type for Group (G) and Individual (I) problems.

1	G: A1, A11, C1, C11, G11	5	G: A1, A11, C1, C11	9	G: C1, C11
	I: A1, D1, A11, C1, G1		I: A1, A11, C1		I: C1, G1
2	G: G11	6	G: G11	10	G: A11, C1, C11
	I: D1, G1		I: D1, G1		I: A11, C1
3	G: A1, A11, C1, C11, G11	7	G: G11	11	G: A11, C1, C11, G11
	I: A1, D1, A11, C1, G1		I: G1		I: D1, A11, C1, G1
4	G: A1, A11, C1, C11, G11	8	G: C11	12	G: A11, C1, C11, G11
	I: A1, A11, C1, G1		I: C1, G1		I: A11, C1, G1

13	G: C11	16	G: G11
	I: C1		I: D1, G
14	G: C11, G11	17	G: G11
	I: D1, C1, G1		I: G1
15	G: C11, G11	18	G: C11
	I: C1, G1		I: C1, G

SOURCE: Reprinted from V. H. Vroom and A. G. Jago, Decision making as a social process: Normative and descriptive models of leader behavior *Decision Sciences* 5 (1974): 748.

Applying the Model To see how this works, let us look at how Linda Wachner might use the decision tree to decide whether to introduce a new line of lingerie?

A. *Is there a quality requirement such that one solution is likely to be more rational than another?* Yes. The decision to introduce a new product line cannot be decided by flipping a coin. There are factors that determine whether it is a good decision.

B. *Do I have sufficient information to make a high-quality decision?* No. Linda probably requires special market and product development information that other members of her staff have.

C. *Is the problem structured?* No. Changing customer preferences, new production techniques, and an unpredictable economic situation influence the decision and prevent its solution by standard procedures.

D. *Is acceptance of the decision by subordinates critical to effective implementation.* No. Subordinates would accept a decision made by Linda Wachner.

E. *If I were to make the decision by myself, is it reasonably certain that it would be accepted by my subordinates?* (This question is skipped.)

F. *Do subordinates share the organizational goals to be attained in solving this problem?* Yes. They seem to be committed to Warnaco's goals.

G. *Is conflict among subordinates likely in preferred solutions?* (This question is skipped.)

H. *Do subordinates have sufficient information to make a high-quality decision?* No. They need information Linda Wachner has about the organization's goals, financial status, and so on.

The feasible set is Number 15 for group problems, which calls for extensive subordinate involvement in making the decision (CII or GII is a feasible approach).

Choice of the specific approach will depend on the time available for making the decision and the extent to which the leader wishes to develop the group by involving them in decision making.

Numerous revisions have occurred to this tree. The most recent version uses a computerized question–response format to generate the appropriate decision style. This reformulation uses the same decision processes—AI, AII, CI, CII, GII, GI, DI—as the original model, as well as the criteria of decision quality, decision commitment, time, and subordinate development.[36] Because it uses a computer to process the data, however, the range of possible responses includes probabilities, rather than "yes" or "no" answers to each diagnostic question.

Evaluation of the Theory Research has indicated that decisions made about a particular problem using the feasible processes identified by the decision tree result in more effective outcomes than those decisions that do not use feasible processes.[37] The theory provides a set of diagnostic questions for analyzing a problem but tends to oversimplify the process. The most recent formulation attempts to address limitations in the model but still does not capture the complexity of most decision-making and leadership situations. For example, it ignores time constraints and does not offer a complete range of style options. The theory also focuses too narrowly on the extent of subordinate involvement in decision making. The computerized model adds to the time required to use the model and may be more helpful in training than in actual managerial practice.

LIFE CYCLE THEORY

The life cycle theory, also called the situational theory by its authors, specifies that effective leadership results from the fit between a leader's style and the readiness of his or her followers—a different aspect of the situation than identified by other theorists.[38] A follower's readiness likely increases over the life cycle of his or her relationship with the leader, calling for a change in the leader's style over time.

In their theory, Paul Hersey and Ken Blanchard identify two dimensions of leadership style.

- **Task behavior** refers to behaviors in which the leader specifies an individual's or group's duties, activities, and responsibilities by goal setting, organizing, scheduling, directing, and controlling.

- **Relationship behavior** refers to the communication behaviors of the leaders, such as listening, giving support, facilitating interactions, providing feedback, and supporting individuals and groups.

As shown in Figure 8–3, combining these two dimensions results in four decision styles labeled S1 through S4, or 1 through 4, in various parts of the figure.[39]

Telling (1 or S1)—high task and low relationship. The leader guides, directs, establishes guidelines, provides specific instructions, and closely supervises performance. Ross Perot, for example, regularly engages in telling behavior. A dysfunctional telling-style leader dictates without really considering the subordinates at all.

Selling (2 or S2)—high task and high relationship. The leader explains decisions, clarifies them, and persuades subordinates to follow them as necessary. Sam Walton frequently used this style as he toured the Wal-Mart stores. Selling that is too intense, however, can result in badgering of subordinates with too much structure and consideration.

Participating (3 or S3)—low task and high relationship. The leader shifts significant responsibility to the followers, encourages subordinates to participate in decision making, and facilitates collaboration and commitment. In extreme cases the leader can bend too greatly to the will of his or her subordinates, rather than correctly judging the amount of participation that is appropriate.

Delegating (4 or S4)—low task and low relationship. The leader only observes and monitors subordinate performance, after giving them responsibility for decisions and implementation. Improper application of this style can result in the leader disengaging too much from the decision-making process.

TEXAS INSTRUMENTS. At Texas Instruments, CEO Jerry Junkins believes he has capable workers. He created 3,000 teams of workers who have control over scheduling, setting profit targets, ordering materials, and devising strategies. This delegative style fits with the workers' high maturity.[40]

According to the life cycle theory, selecting the appropriate style requires the leader to determine the *readiness* of his or her followers. Follower readiness includes two main components—ability and willingness. The *ability* of the subordinates describes whether they have the necessary knowledge, skills, and experience to perform the task. New hires, for example, may not have the ability to do the job unless they received specific job-related training prior to securing the job. *Willingness* describes whether the subordinates have the motivation, commitment, and confidence to do the task. Some salespeople, for example, have the skills, knowledge, and experience to double their sales from the previous year, but they may lack the motivation and commitment to attain such a goal.

CAPITAL CITIES/ABC. Tom Murphy delegates authority as a way of controlling costs. He believes that a manager who hires the best employees and

FIGURE 8–3 *Life cycle model of leadership*

Task Behavior
The extent to which the leader engages in defining roles telling what, how, when, where, and if more than one person, who is to do what in
• Goal-setting
• Organizing
• Establishing time lines
• Directing
• Controlling

Relationship Behavior
The extent to which a leader engages in two-way (multi-way) communication, listening, facilitating behaviors, socioemotional support
• Giving support
• Communicating
• Facilitating interactions
• Active listening
• Providing feedback

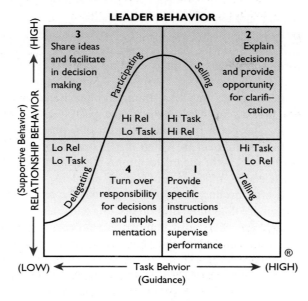

LEADER BEHAVIOR

3 Share ideas and facilitate in decision making	**2** Explain decisions and provide opportunity for clarification
Hi Rel / Lo Task	Hi Task / Hi Rel
Lo Rel / Lo Task	Hi Task / Lo Rel
4 Turn over responsibility for decisions and implementation	**1** Provide specific instructions and closely supervise performance

(LOW) ◄── Task Behvior ──► (HIGH)
(Guidance)

FOLLOWER READINESS

High		Moderate		Low
R4	R3	R2	R1
Able and willing or confident	Able but unwilling or insecure	Unable but willing or confident	Unable and unwilling or insecure

FOLLOWER DIRECTED   LEADER DIRECTED

Decision Styles

1
Leader-made decision

2
Leader-made decision with dialogue and/or explanation

3
Leader/follower-made decision or follower-made decision with encouragement from leader

4
Follower-made decision

Ability has the necessary knowledge, experience and skill

Willingness has the necessary confidence, commitment, motivation

When a Leader Behavior is used appropriately with its corresponding level of readiness, it is termed a High Probability Match. The following are descriptors that can be useful when using Situational Leadership for specific applications:

S1	S2	S3	S4
Telling	Selling	Participating	Delegating
Guiding	Explaining	Encouraging	Observing
Directing	Clarifying	Collaborating	Monitoring
Establishing	Persuading	Committing	Fulfilling

SOURCE: P.H. Hersey and K.H. Blanchard, *Utilizing Human Resources,* 5th ed. Copyrighted material from Leadership Studies, Inc. All rights reserved. Used by permission.

delegates responsibility to them will need fewer employees overall to complete the required work.[41]

    Applying the Theory A leader such as Linda Wachner can use this theory to select the best leadership style for managing her subordinates by assessing the readiness of her followers and then fitting her style to their ability and willingness to performance. Note in Figure 8–3 that follower readiness (in the middle of the figure) moves from low to high. The curve that represents leadership style over time (in the top of the figure) correspondingly moves (right to left) from telling to selling to participating to delegating. If Linda Wachner has subordinates who are unable and unwilling to perform (low readiness), she should use the telling style. If her workers are unable but willing to perform (moderate readiness), she should use the selling style. If the workers are able but unwilling to perform (moderate readiness), she should use the participating style. If her workers are able and willing to perform, she should use the delegating style.

BAMA PIE AND BAMA FOODS LTD. When Paula Marshall-Chapman became CEO of her family's business, Bama Pie and Bama Foods Ltd. of Tulsa, she replaced her father's ironclad style of the past twenty years with a more participative style. She put a management team into place and helped train them to create a team environment in which they listened to and adopted employee suggestions, particularly with regard to improving quality. Marshall-Chapman repeatedly emphasized the importance of finding problems early in the production process rather than after production of faulty goods. The company tripled its size and now supplies more than three million biscuits daily, as well as apple and cherry pies, to McDonald's.[42] Marshall-Chapman might have applied the life cycle model to select her leadership style. Workers with moderate-to-high readiness fit well with her participative style.

Evaluation of the Theory Some researchers have supported the utility of the theory, while others have questioned its conceptual clarity, validity, robustness, and utility.[43] Organizations frequently use training materials related to the life cycle theory for management development. Problems exist, however, with the instruments used to measure follower readiness and leader behaviors, particularly the Leadership Effectiveness and Description (LEAD), the instrument most commonly used to measure leadership style.

NONSITUATIONAL THEORIES

Not all contemporary theorists believe that effective leadership means fitting the appropriate style to characteristics of the situation. Instead, exchange theory, attribution theory, operant conditioning theory, and substitutes for leadership focus on social interactions without specifically looking at the leader–situation match.

EXCHANGE THEORY

Exchange theory does not focus on the leader's style *per se*, but discusses what he or she gives to followers and the results of such an exchange for both individual and organizational performance.[44] The leader gives subordinates resources, autonomy, or involvement in decision making in exchange for a higher commitment to organizational goals and operations, more effort, or increased performance. For example, exchange theory might predict that if Linda Wachner gave the women in the stitchroom more autonomy, she would receive greater effort from them. Or, she might offer them more challenging jobs in exchange for their willingness to work more hours.

This exchange works somewhat differently for two types of followers.[45] The leader allows a great deal of latitude to the *cadre* or ingroup of followers. This small group of individuals closest to the leader has his or her greatest trust, often as a result of the individuals' competence, dependability, or compatibility with the leader. These workers demonstrate higher performance, lower turnover, and greater satisfaction with supervision than other workers. The remaining employees, known as **hired hands,** or the outgroup, receive little latitude from the leader and tend to demonstrate lower performance, lower satisfaction, and higher turnover. Membership in the ingroup and outgroup, as well as the consequences of such membership, depend on the cultural context. Which employees constitute the ingroup and outgroup, for example, may vary in different countries, where customs, social status, and history influence relations among people.

Distinguishing among individual employees is somewhat natural and can be expected. Yet, managers must recognize that belonging to the ingroup versus the outgroup has different consequences. They may need to adjust their leadership behaviors to prevent these differences from becoming dysfunctional. Such distinctions may also have ethical implications. A conscious attempt to deviate from equal treatment of employees can have significant consequences.

Evaluation of the Theory The research on exchange theory has been criticized because it relies on a narrow data base, does not explain how individuals become part of the ingroup, does not sufficiently study the organizational outcomes associated with the exchange relationship, and operationalizes the nature of the leader–subordinate or leader–boss exchange in diverse and inconsistent ways.[46] Another limitation to exchange theory is the lack of study of the process by which the leader–member relations develop. For example, how does an individual become an ingroup member?[47] In addition, researchers must still study the impact of highly differentiated versus relatively undifferentiated ingroups.

Yet, exchange theory encourages managers and other organizational members to diagnose the **status** of followers vis-à-vis leaders in choosing a leadership style. It is important that the leader not develop such differentiated relationships that members of the outgroup question whether they really have an opportunity to advance in the organization. The leader must ensure that he or she develops trusting, supportive, respectful relations with both groups of subordinates.[48]

OPERANT CONDITIONING THEORY

We can use positive reinforcement theory (see Chapter 4) to offer a different perspective on leadership and ways organizational members can work together more effectively. We can identify two basic components to this model.[49]

1. The leader's behavior prompts responses by subordinates. The subordinates' responses then either reinforce, extinguish, or punish the leader's behavior. For example, a leader may give his subordinates more autonomy and responsibility. Their increased productivity will reinforce this behavior and cause the leader to continue to empower them in this way.

2. The subordinates' behavior causes responses in other parts of the organization. Responses to the subordinates' behaviors then reinforce, extinguish, or punish the behavior. If, for example, the subordinates exert autonomy by making too many requests of other departments, the complaints by these departments over time likely will extinguish the subordinates' autonomous behaviors.

Evaluation of the Theory Rewarding performance and punishing failures may not always create the desired outcomes because of the influence of other persons and situational factors.[50] Still, these simple interactions may combine over time to create a dynamic model of leader–follower behavior. The model, however, remains relatively untested, with little empirical research specifically directed at operant conditioning as an explanation of leadership effectiveness.

ATTRIBUTION THEORY

Attribution theory suggests that a leader's judgment about his or her followers is influenced by the leader's attribution of the causes of the followers' behaviors.[51] A leaders' attributions can be biased. These attributions affect the way he or she treats the staff. The fairness and accuracy of the attributions, in turn, affect the staff's perceptions of the leader and their willingness to follow, cooperate, and perform.[52]

The researchers focused on attributions because they believed that effective leaders must recognize biases in their attributions and consequent actions. The theory suggests that leaders make typical attributional biases (see Chapter 2): They link themselves with successes in the group and remove themselves from failures.[53] Thus, they might incorrectly take credit for the group's success by suggesting that it was due to the interpersonal support or skills of the leader. They might attribute the group's failure to outside influences, such as time constraints, lack of resources, or absence of member skills.

As shown in Figure 8–4, leadership begins with a particular situation, in this case, one of poor quality production. Leader behavior then involves attributing the cause of the behavior (linkage number 1) by determining whether the behavior is distinctive or unique to a particular task, consistent and frequent, and whether followers demonstrate the same behavior. Once the leader attributes a cause to the sit-

FIGURE 8–4 *An attributional leadership model*

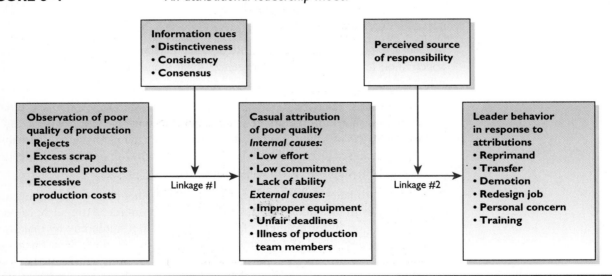

SOURCE: Adapted from Terence R. Mitchell and Robert E. Wood, An empirical test of an attributional model of leader's responses to poor performance. In *Academy of Management Proceedings,* ed. Richard C. Huseman, 1979, p. 94.

uation, he or she then responds after determining whether the leader or followers are responsible for the behavior (linkage number 2).

Evaluation of the Theory The attributional model of leadership poses some definitional and measurement problems.[54] No specific instruments have been developed or administered to measure leaders' or followers' behavior in this model. Little empirical data have been collected to validate the model.

SUBSTITUTES FOR LEADERSHIP

Some researchers hold that leadership is not always necessary. In fact, certain characteristics of subordinates, the tasks, or the organization, as shown in Table 8–8, may neutralize or eliminate the need for certain styles of leadership. An established team of skilled subordinates, for example, may not need the task-oriented directions of a new manager.[55] Indeed, they might resent the new manager. A study of a group of staff nurses showed, for example, that educated nurses could work autonomously and productively without leadership by the head nurse.[56] The organization, too, may have a culture that fosters worker autonomy and responsibility, again mitigating the need for leadership.

By extension, organizations can manipulate these characteristics to cope with ineffective leadership or eliminate it entirely.[57] Many organizations have laid off middle managers who once managed workers now working in self-managed teams.

TABLE 8–8   *Substitutes for leadership*

CHARACTERISTIC
Of the subordinate
1. ability, experience, training, knowledge
2. need for independence
3. "professional" orientation
4. indifference toward organizational rewards
Of the task
5. unambiguous and routine
6. methodologically invariant
7. provides its own feedback concerning accomplishment
8. intrinsically satisfying
Of the organization
9. formalization (explicit plans, goals, and areas of responsibility)
10. inflexibility (rigid, unbending rules and procedures)
11. highly specified and active advisory and staff functions
12. closely knit, cohesive work groups
13. organizational rewards not within the leader's control
14. spatial distance between superior and subordinates

SOURCE: From S. Kerr and J.M. Jermier, Substitutes for leadership: Their meaning and measurement, Organizational Behavior and Human Performance 26 (December 1978): 375–403. Copyright © 1978 by Academic Press, Inc. Reprinted with permission.

Instead, the teams handle coordination problems by goal setting and using other staff as back-up resources.

GENERAL MILLS. A General Mills cereal plant in Lodi, California, removed managers from the night shift because the workers could handle the manufacturing tasks themselves. The workers' skills served as substitutes for leadership.[58]

Evaluation of the Theory This theory looks at characteristics of the situation as influencing the type of leadership required. It expands the notion of leadership by removing it from a single individual. Although some testing of the theory has occurred, the results are limited. More extensive measurement of the ability of specific characteristics to fulfill specific leadership functions is necessary.

TRANSFORMATIONAL LEADERSHIP AND SUPERLEADERSHIP

Recent thinking about effective leadership has supplemented the situational approach with a revival of trait theory that emphasizes the importance of a leader's charisma and his or her ability to use personal influence to facilitate individual development.

TRANSFORMATIONAL LEADERSHIP

The managerial challenges of the 1980s gave rise to a new type of leader. A transformational or charismatic leader is a leader who uses charisma to inspire his or her followers and makes significant changes in organizational functioning. Charismatic leaders emerge more often when an organization experiences stress or transitions.[59] A charismatic leader uses self-confidence, dominance, moral conviction, and charisma to inspire his or her followers.[60] Followers' trust in the correctness of leaders' beliefs, similarity of leader's and followers' beliefs, and followers' unquestioning acceptance of affection for and obedience of the leader are among the indicators of charismatic leadership.[61] Charismatic leaders engage in managing others' impressions of their leadership so that others view them as competent and successful. They serve as role models to followers, often stating ideological goals for followers and setting high expectations for their behavior. Table 8–9 compares charismatic and noncharismatic leaders.

BURGER KING. Jeffrey Campbell, the CEO of Burger King from 1983 to 1987, led his managers in a religious-like experience shortly after taking over the top-management position.[62] Each manager was asked to personally and silently assess whether they could meet the challenge of turning the company around while the theme music from *Chariots of Fire* played in the background. He saw earnings increase substantially after creating an almost evangelical experience for top managers, only to see them pale for the next four years in comparison to McDonalds.

A transformational leader begins by developing a *vision* for what his or her organization, department, or work group ideally should be. This vision guides the manager in finding the best way to ensure desired outcomes such as quality, performance, and productivity. Transformational leaders attempt to motivate workers by focusing on higher ideals. This behavior contrasts with that of *transactional leaders,* leaders who instead focus on compliance with existing organizational rules,

TABLE 8–9   *Behavioral components of charismatic and noncharismatic leaders*

	NONCHARISMATIC LEADER	CHARISMATIC LEADER
Relation to Status Quo	Essentially agrees with status quo and strives to maintain it	Essentially opposed to status quo and strives to change it
Future Goal	Goal not too discrepant from status quo	Idealized vision that is highly discrepant from status quo
Likableness	Shared perspective makes him/her likable	Shared perspective and idealized vision makes him/her a likable and honorable hero worthy of identification and imitation
Trustworthiness	Disinterested advocacy in persuasion attempts	Disinterested advocacy by incurring great personal risk and cost
Expertise	Expert in using available means to achieve goals within the framework of the existing order	Expert in using unconventional means to transcend the existing order
Behavior	Conventional, conforming to existing norms	Unconventional or counternormative
Environmental Sensitivity	Low need for environmental sensitivity to maintain status quo	High need for environmental sensitivity for changing the status quo
Articulation	Weak articulation of goals and motivation to lead	Strong articulation of future vision and motivation to lead
Power Base	Position power and personal power (based on reward, expertise, and liking for a friend who is a similar other)	Personal power (based on expertise, respect, and admiration for a unique hero)
Leader–Follower Relationship	Egalitarian, consensus seeking, or directive Nudges or orders people to share his/her views	Elitist, entrepreneur, and exemplary Transforms people to share the radical changes advocated

SOURCE: Reprinted with permission from A. Conger and R.N. Kanungo, Toward a behavioral theory of charismatic leadership in organizational settings, *Academy of Management Review* 12 (1987): 641.

trade rewards for agreement with the leader's wishes, and even abdicate their leadership responsibility. Was Linda Wachner a transformational or transactional leader? She clearly had a vision, which guided her leadership at Warnaco. She wanted the company to have fashion flair, a customer orientation, and financial strength. She transformed it from a conservative, lifeless organization into an energetic, focused, competitive one.

APPLE COMPUTERS. Steve Jobs, the first CEO of Apple Computers, recognized the opportunity to create a user-friendly and technologically sophisticated computer. He hired talented professionals and convinced them that the vision was attainable. Early successes helped build trust in the vision. Finally, he achieved the vision by motivating and converting organizational members to the new vision. Even as Apple Computers grew and went public, its employees considered themselves members of a family, committed to Jobs's vision of the new technology.[63]

A transformational leader helps subordinates see a need to revitalize their organization. Real crises may create such a need. Employee visits to other organizations or calls to challenge the leader's assumptions may also assist in creating this perceived need. The leader involves subordinates in planning for and creating this new vision. The leader must help workers or other managers to reframe the way they think about the organization. For example, an accounting or law firm might reframe the company's major objective as providing top-quality client service rather than maximizing billable hours. Finally, institutionalizing the change calls for replacing the organization's old culture with a new one.

FORD MOTOR COMPANY. When the leadership at Ford Motor Company decided to create a "new company" to compete with the Japanese imports in the 1980s, the emphasis on quality called for substantial changes in the way work was done at Ford.[64] Individuals and work teams became more accountable for achieving the quality vision. Transforming the organization helped create a competitive advantage and humane workplace.

A boss who is a transformational leader motivates subordinates to do better than they expected in three ways.[65] First, the leader raises their consciousness about the importance of certain outcomes, such as high productivity or efficiency. Second, he or she shows the value of workers concentrating on what benefits their work team can generate rather than on their personal interests. Third, the leader raises the workers' need levels so that they value challenges, responsibility, and growth. Managers identified as top performers rated higher on transformational leadership than a group of ordinary managers.[66] CEOs of major business divisions of corporations who succeeded in developing new businesses differed from those who attempted new business development and failed.[67] They inspired pervasive commitment through the division by insisting that the entire division pursue new business development, making it part of the job and not the object of special rewards. They also demonstrated intense, undistracted, and long-term personal commitment to new business development and assigned the best people to it. They built confidence among their subordinates by helping them increase their competence and giving them the freedom to take initiative. They applied appropriate discipline to the process by carefully selecting the new venture, using the appropriate strategy, and managing failures. Because some research suggests that the charisma of a leader also cascades to his or her followers,[68] training higher-level managers in transformational skills should have a more widespread impact than training only lower-level managers.

Recent research suggests that some women leaders demonstrate an interactive leadership style that resembles transformational leadership because they encourage participation, share power and information, and energize others.[69] Some researchers even argue that women may be better suited to run the companies of the 1990s and beyond.[70] Others suggest that no consistent differences exist between male and female managers' behavior, although differences in the evaluation of the behaviors may occur.[71]

DEAN WITTER. Kathy Birk, manager of a Dean Witter office in Indianapolis, uses a distinctly nonmale style that emphasizes conciliation and support rather than confrontation and authority. Birk uses extra attention and sensitivity to nurture her staff. She doesn't chew people out, she says. She tells her staff what she prefers for them to do. She then tries to persuade, rather than confront them about how to act.[72] She essentially allows her brokers to determine the best way to do their work and encourages them to motivate themselves. This new way of working with subordinates may fit better with the flatter organizations of this decade and the next century.[73]

A "dark side" to charismatic leadership may exist if the leader overemphasizes devotion to himself or herself, makes personal needs paramount, or uses highly effective communication skills to mislead or manipulate others.[74] Charismatic leaders may be so driven to achieve a vision that they ignore the costly implications of their goals. Failed visions result when:

- The vision reflects the internal needs of the leaders rather than those of the market or constituents.

- The resources needed to achieve the vision have been seriously miscalculated.

- An unrealistic assessment or distorted perception of market and constituent needs exists.

- A failure to recognize environmental changes prevents redirection of the vision.[75]

CAMPEAU. Robert Campeau's blind ambition caused him to engage in major financial transactions that resulted in the demise of two major department store chains plus his own empire. He completed a leveraged buyout of the Allied and Federated Department Store chains, which involved obligating these companies to so much debt that they could not repay their loans and ultimately sought bankruptcy protection. The layoffs of thousands of workers followed.[76]

Evaluation of the Theory Although practitioners have widely embraced charismatic and transformational leadership, the ultimate impact of these theories remains unstudied. Reliance on interview, questionnaire, historical, and case-study methodology in the few studies done has not allowed a systematic study of whether this type of leadership causes particular outcomes.[77] While it seems possible that individuals can become transformational leaders, even if they have essentially non-charismatic personalities, this assumption needs to be tested. In addition, a more complete examination of the impact of transformational leadership in different cultures is essential. One study showed, for example, that charismatic leadership had a greater impact on North American than on Mexican workers.[78]

SUPERLEADERSHIP

The *superleader* goes one step beyond the transformational leader. He or she helps followers to discover, use, and maximize their abilities.[79] Similar to the transformational leader, the superleader empowers followers to contribute fully to organizations. The *superleader* attempts to make subordinates into *self-leaders* who take primary responsibility for motivating and directing their personal behaviors.[80]

A leader becomes a superleader by performing the following steps:

1. Becomes a self-leader. As a self-leader, an individual may use an array of behavior-focused and cognitive-focused strategies that include personal goal setting, practice, providing rewards or punishments to oneself, and making sure activities result in a sense of competence, purpose, and self-control.

2. Models self-leadership by displaying self-leadership behaviors and encouraging others to rehearse and then produce them.

3. Encourages employees to create self-set goals.

4. Creates positive thought patterns by continuously observing, evaluating, and improving assumptions, beliefs, mental images, and thinking in general.

5. Rewards self-leadership behaviors and constructively reprimands other behaviors. Rewards include natural rewards that stem from the task, such as a sense of competence and increased responsibility, and self-administered rewards, such as self-recognition, self-praise, and self-congratulations.

6. Uses teamwork to promote self-leadership.

7. Creates a culture of self-leadership.[81]

Employee self-leadership combined with self-leadership systems in the organization, such as a supportive culture, use of teams, and design of work result in increased employee commitment, motivation, capability, performance, and innovation.

Evaluation of the Theory Superleadership offers significant promise for identifying new ways for individuals to work together in organizations. However, little research exists yet to confirm or disconfirm its validity.

LEADING A MULTICULTURAL WORK FORCE

The theories we have examined so far were largely formulated in the United States, using U.S. managers and cultural assumptions. What happens once a manager moves into the global economy and is challenged to lead a multinational, multicultural work force? Can these same theories be used to diagnose these global management challenges? The answer is that it depends on a variety of factors.

Managing a multinational work force poses special challenges in selecting a leadership style. A global manager is a sensitive, innovative, and participative leader who can communicate interculturally, builds on cultural differences through international collaboration, and leads change in the organization to improve intercultural performance.[82] Such a manager continuously acquires current information about the culture in which he or she is functioning and adapts his or her leadership style to it.

MCKINSEY AND COMPANY. Rajat Gupta became the consulting firm's first non-Western leader in 1994. He describes himself as a "global citizen." He was born in India, educated in the United States, and worked in the United States and Europe. He has been described as being the smartest person in his Harvard Business School class, an egoless leader, an apolitical individual, and a person who will lead by consensus. His style is not Western. Once, when presenting a new program to a client, he waited in silence for more than a minute and allowed the client to reach his own decision, rather than taking the more Western approach of giving the client more facts and persuading him to agree with the consultant's conclusions.[83]

How do the key components of a situation change for a leader managing multiculturally and multinationally? Because most leadership research to date focuses on leaders in the United States, a definitive answer to this question is not possible. We can hypothesize, however, that leaders must adjust their style to the cultural norms of a particular work group. We know, for example, that a collectivist orientation characterizes the Japanese culture, whereas an individualistic orientation describes the U.S. culture.[84] The circumstances in which an achievement-oriented style would work likely differ in these two types of cultures. Similarly, cultures with a masculine orientation, such as in Latin America, may have a different attitude toward authoritarian leadership than those with a more feminine orientation. Managers must understand the cultural context, as well as cultural idiosyncrasies relating to the work to be done, the people who will do the work, and their own competencies before selecting a style.

GENERAL ELECTRIC. After General Electric's purchase of the Hungarian Tungsram Company, a state-owned manufacturer of light bulbs, GE management discovered bulb cartons filled with rocks. Tungsram workers had previously used this technique to collect bonuses for production volume.[85]

Participative management approaches may not be suitable to employees in cultures where significant power differences between managers and workers are expected and respected.[86] In multinational organizations, leaders can be parent-country nationals, home-country nationals, or third-country nationals. Although multinational firms act as a force behind a global convergence of styles, considerable differences remain among the different nationals working for the same company.[87] These leaders bring cultural biases to the organizational situations that influence both the style they choose and their ultimate effectiveness.

Leading in a multicultural environment requires similar cultural sensitivity, strong intercultural communication skills, and the ability to adapt to a changing cultural environment. Managers must understand and acknowledge their own leadership competence, as well as determine the particular cultural aspects that affect performance.

SUMMARY

An array of theories has attempted to identify a leader and explain leadership effectiveness. Trait theory stated that leaders had specific personal characteristics. Abilities, skills, and traits also distinguished effective from ineffective leaders. Behavioral theory said that effective leadership was associated with a concern for task and a concern for people. Behavioral theory also specified the roles of a manager.

Situational theories of leadership focused on the fit between a leader's style and characteristics of the situation. McGregor differentiated between leaders with Theory X and Theory Y assumptions. Fiedler and his associates said the effectiveness of a leader's style depended on leader–member relations, the task's structure, and the position power of the leader. Path-goal theory said that leadership effectiveness depended on the fit between the style and such situational characteristics as the task, subordinates, formal authority, work group, and organizational culture. Vroom and Yetton's decision-making model offered a procedure to help leaders decide the appropriate amount of employee participation in decision making. The life cycle model said that leadership effectiveness was a function of the fit between the leader's style and the maturity of his or her followers.

Nonsituational models included exchange theory, operant conditioning theory, attribution theory, and substitutes for leadership. Exchange theory emphasized the leader's interaction with subordinates and superiors. Operant conditioning theory examined the role of positive reinforcement in encouraging specific leadership behaviors. Attribution theory said that individuals' perceptions of the causes of followers' behavior influence their leadership effectiveness. Substitutes for leadership suggested that effective leadership often can occur without a leader.

Most recently, leadership theory has focused on the transformational leader and the superleader. An effective transformational leader recognizes the need to revitalize the organization, creates a vision of the new organization, and then implements and institutionalizes this vision. A superleader encourages his or her followers to act as self-leaders. The leadership theories to date have offered little explanation of the special leadership challenges posed by a multicultural work force.

DIAGNOSTIC QUESTIONS

Answering the following questions can assist in improving leadership in an organization.

- Do the managers have the traits necessary for effective leadership?

- Do the managers display the behaviors required for effective leadership?

- Do managers exhibit an array of appropriate managerial roles?

- Do the leaders have Theory Y assumptions about their followers?

- Does the leadership style fit with the nature of the task, leader–member relations, and the position power of the leader?

- Is leadership redundant to the situational features and the followers' needs?

- Do the leaders encourage the appropriate amount of participation in decision making?

- Does leadership style fit with the maturity of the followers?

- Do leaders give subordinates resources and autonomy in exchange for particular behaviors?

- Do leaders reward follower behavior and vice versa?

- Do followers attribute attitudes to the leaders accurately?

- Do substitutes for leadership exist?

- Do transformational leaders exist and are they effective?

- Do superleaders exist and are they effective?

- Are leaders able to lead a multicultural work force?

Activity 8–1   **LEADERSHIP STYLE INVENTORY**

STEP 1: Assume you are involved in each of the following situations. Read each item carefully and think about what you would do in each circumstance. Then circle the letter of the alternative that you think would most closely describe your behavior in the situations presented. Circle only one choice. For each situation, interpret key concepts in terms of the environment or situation in which you most often think of yourself as assuming a leadership role. Do not change your situational frame of reference from question to question.

SITUATION 1

The employees in your program appear to be having serious problems getting the job done. Their performance has been going downhill rapidly. They have not responded to your efforts to be friendly or to your expressions of concern for their welfare.

What Would You Do?

a. Reestablish the need for following program procedures and meeting the expectations for task accomplishment.

b. Be sure that staff members know you are available for discussion, but don't pressure them.

c. Talk with your employees and then set performance goals.

d. Wait and see what happens.

SITUATION 2

During the past few months, the quality of work done by staff members has been increasing. Recordkeeping is accurate and up to date. You have been careful to make sure that all staff members are aware of your performance expectations.

What Would You Do?

a. Stay uninvolved.

b. Continue to emphasize the importance of completing tasks and meeting deadlines.

c. Be supportive and provide clear feedback. Continue to make sure that staff members are aware of performance expectations.

d. Make every effort to let staff members feel important and involved in the decision-making process.

SITUATION 3

Performance and interpersonal relations among your staff have been good. You have normally left them alone. However, a new situation has developed, and it appears that the staff members are unable to solve the problem themselves.

What Would You Do?

a. Bring the group together and work as a team to solve the problem.

b. Continue to leave them alone to work it out.

c. Act quickly and firmly to identify the problem and establish procedures to correct it.

d. Encourage the staff to work on the problem, letting them know you are available as a resource and for discussion if they need you.

SITUATION 4

You are considering a major change in your program. Your staff has a fine record of accomplishment and a strong commitment to excellence. They are supportive of the need for change and have been involved in the planning.

What Would You Do?

a. Continue to involve the staff in the planning, but you direct the change.

b. Announce the changes and then implement them with close supervision.

c. Allow the group to be involved in developing the change, but don't push the process.

d. Let the staff manage the change process.

SITUATION 5

You are aware that staff performance has been going down during the last several months. They need continual reminding to get tasks done on time and seem unconcerned about meeting objectives. In the past, redefining procedures and role expectations has helped.

What Would You Do?

a. Allow your staff to set their own direction.

b. Get suggestions from the staff but see that the objectives are met.

c. Redefine goals and expectations and supervise carefully.

d. Allow the staff to be involved in setting goals, but don't pressure them.

SITUATION 6

You have just been appointed as the director of a new program that had been running smoothly under the previous director. She had the reputation for running a tight ship. You want to maintain the quality of the program and the service delivery, but you would like to begin humanizing the environment.

What Would You Do?

a. Do nothing at the present time.

b. Continue with the administrative pattern set by the previous director, monitoring the staff and emphasizing the importance of task accomplishment.

c. Get the staff involved in decision making and planning, but continue to see that objectives are met and quality is maintained.

d. Reach out to staff members to let them feel important and involved.

SITUATION 7

You are considering expanding your unit's responsibilities. Your staff members have made suggestions about the proposed change and are enthusiastic. They operate effectively on a day-to-day basis and have shown themselves willing to assume responsibility.

What Would You Do?

a. Outline the changes and monitor carefully.

b. Reach consensus with the staff on the proposed changes and allow the staff members to organize the implementation.

c. Solicit input from the staff on proposed changes, but maintain control of the implementation.

d. Let the staff handle it.

SITUATION 8

Staff members have been working well. Interpersonal relations and morale are good. The quality of service delivery is excellent. You are somewhat unsure of your apparent lack of direction of the group.

What Would You Do?

a. Be careful not to hurt your relationship with the staff by becoming too directive.

b. Take steps to assure that staff members are working in a well-defined manner.

c. Leave the staff alone to work as they have been.

d. Discuss the situation with the staff and then initiate the necessary changes.

SITUATION 9

You have been appointed to replace the chairman of a task force that is long overdue in making requested recommendations for certification requirements. The group is not clear on its goal. Attendance at meetings has been poor. Frequently, the meetings are more social than task oriented. Potentially, they have the knowledge and experience to complete the task.

What Would You Do?

a. Let the group members work out their problems.

b. Solicit recommendations from the group, but see that the objectives are met.

c. Redefine and clarify the goals, tasks, and expectations, and carefully supervise progress toward task completion.

d. Allow group involvement in setting goals, but don't push.

SITUATION 10

Your employees are usually able to take responsibility. However, they are not responding well to your recent redefinition of performance standards.

What Would You Do?

a. Supervise carefully to assure that standards are met.

b. Solicit input from the staff on performance standards. Incorporate their suggestions and

monitor their progress toward meeting the
standards.
c. Allow staff involvement in the redefinition of
performance standards, but don't push.
d. Avoid confrontation. Apply no pressure and see
what happens.

SITUATION 11

You have been promoted to the position of manager.
The previous manager appeared to be uninvolved in the
affairs of the staff. They have adequately handled their
tasks and responsibilities. Their morale is high.

What Would You Do?

a. Become active in directing the staff toward
working in a clearly defined manner.
b. Involve your staff in decision making and consistently reinforce good contributions.
c. Discuss past performance with your staff and
then examine the need for new procedures.
d. Continue to leave the staff alone.

SITUATION 12

You have recently become aware of some internal difficulties on your staff. They had been working well together for the past year. The staff has an excellent record
of accomplishment. Staff members have consistently
met their performance goals. All are well qualified for
their roles in the program.

What Would You Do?

a. Allow your staff members to deal with the new
problem themselves.
b. Tell the staff how you propose to deal with
the situation and discuss the necessity for
these procedures.
c. Make yourself available for discussion but
don't jeopardize your relationship with the staff
by forcing the issue.
d. Act quickly and firmly to nip the problem in
the bud.

STEP 2: Scoring.

1. Circle the letter you chose for each situation in
the areas below, labeled Flexibility and Effectiveness (page 344). For example, if you an-

swered alternative C for Situation 1, circle the
Cs in row 1 under Flexibility and Effectiveness.
2. Add the number of letters you circled in each
column under Flexibility and enter in the boxes
labeled S1, S2, S3, and S4.

			FLEXIBILITY			
		S1	S2	S3	S4	
	1	A	C	B	D	
	2	B	C	D	A	
	3	C	A	D	B	
	4	B	A	C	D	
SITUATION NUMBER	5	C	B	D	A	
	6	B	C	D	A	
	7	A	C	B	D	
	8	B	D	A	C	
	9	C	B	D	A	
	10	A	B	C	D	
	11	A	C	B	D	
	12	D	B	C	A	

S1	S2	S3	S4

3. Still focusing on Flexibility, place the total of
each column in the corresponding quadrant of
the style matrix. That is, the S1 score goes in the
Style 1 box (high task, low relationship), the S2
score goes in Style 2 (high task, high relationship), and so on.
4. Now add the number of letters you circled in
each column under Effectiveness and enter in
the boxes below each column.

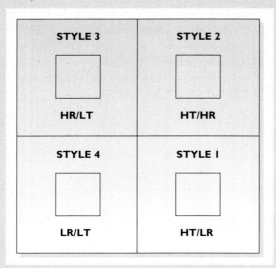

STYLE 3 □ HR/LT	**STYLE 2** □ HT/HR
STYLE 4 □ LR/LT	**STYLE 1** □ HT/LR

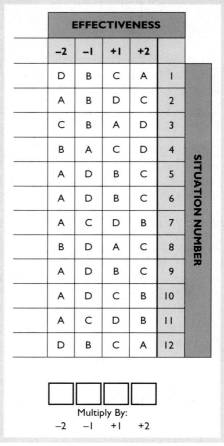

EFFECTIVENESS				SITUATION NUMBER
−2	**−1**	**+1**	**+2**	
D	B	C	A	1
A	B	D	C	2
C	B	A	D	3
B	A	C	D	4
A	D	B	C	5
A	D	B	C	6
A	C	D	B	7
B	D	A	C	8
A	D	B	C	9
A	D	C	B	10
A	C	D	B	11
D	B	C	A	12

5. Then multiply each number by the number directly under it. Be sure to indicate + or − as appropriate, and put the answer in the next box below that.

6. Now add the four numbers and enter in the box labeled Total. Again, be sure to include the + or − sign.

7. On the Effectiveness scale, find the number in the Total box and mark it with an arrow.

□ □ □ □
Multiply By:
−2 −1 +1 +2

□ + □ + □ + □ = □ TOTAL

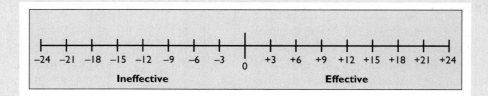

−24 −21 −18 −15 −12 −9 −6 −3 0 +3 +6 +9 +12 +15 +18 +21 +24

Ineffective   **Effective**

STEP 3: Discussion. In small groups or with the entire class, answer the following questions:

1. What does your style matrix tell you?
2. How balanced are your scores?
3. Do you have one predominant quadrant?

4. Do you have the potential flexibility to use all four leadership behaviors?
5. In terms of effectiveness, how well did you do?

———————

Excerpts from *Organization Behavior: Learning Guide/Experiential Exercises* by Bruce Kemelgor, copyright © 1988 by The Dryden Press, reprinted by permission of the publisher. This exercise is adapted from the Managerial Skills Profile. Federal Government Publication 79-141 P. It is based, in part, on Hersey and Blanchard's "Leader Effectiveness and adaptability description," San Diego: University Associates.

Activity 8–2   MANAGERIAL DIARY

STEP 1: Select a manager to observe.

STEP 2: Keep a diary of the manager's activities for as long as one day. Observe him or her as much as possible during that time.

STEP 3: For each activity list the work role performed, in the three columns below:

Activity   Duration   Role

STEP 4: Discussion. Answer the following questions in small groups or with the entire class:

DESCRIPTION
1. Which activities did the manager perform?

DIAGNOSIS
2. Which roles did the manager perform? Which roles did the manager omit?
3. Was the manager effective? Why or why not?
4. Was the manager an effective leader? Use appropriate leadership theories to explain your answer.

Activity 8–3   THE X-Y-Z OF MANAGERIAL ATTITUDE

STEP 1: Complete the following questionnaire.

Assign a weight of 0 to 10 to each statement. The firmer your belief in one statement rather than the statement it is paired with, the higher the score. The points assigned to each pair must total 10 (6-4, 2-8, 5-5, etc.). Be honest with yourself. Evaluate each statement based on how you actually feel, not how you think you should feel. Explanations of the assumptions underlying the three management philosophies follow the scoring key.

1. The average human being instinctively dislikes work and will avoid it if possible.   (a) _____
   The expenditure of physical and mental effort in work is as natural as play or rest.   (b) _____
   10

2. A worker is motivated by participating in setting goals.   (c) _____
   People who don't use much imagination and ingenuity on the job probably don't have much of either.   (d) _____
   10

3. Receiving recognition for one's accomplishments is motivating to a worker.   (e) _____
   If people are allowed to set their own goals and standards of performance, they tend to set them higher than the boss would.   (f) _____
   10

4. A worker is motivated by having additional duties delegated to him/her.   (g) _____
   If anything is going to get done, the manager has to make the decisions.   (h) _____
   10

5. The average person prefers to be directed and wishes to avoid responsibility.
    The average human being learns, under proper conditions, not only to accept but to seek responsibility.

    (i) _____
    (j) _____
    10

6. Most jobs do not allow for individual self-fulfillment.
    Work can be designed to allow workers more freedom and autonomy on the job.

    (k) _____
    (l) _____
    10

7. Most people are imaginative and creative, but they may not show it because of limitations imposed by supervision and the job.
    Having trust that both they and management share the same goals is motivating to workers.

    (m) _____
    (n) _____
    10

8. If employees receive more information than they need to perform their tasks, they will misuse it.
    If employees have access to inside information, they tend to have better attitudes and behave more responsibly.

    (o) _____
    (p) _____
    10

9. Group decision making helps determine goals and improves worker productivity, even without supervision.
    Asking employees for their ideas results in the development of useful suggestions.

    (q) _____
    (r) _____
    10

10. Providing opportunities for workers to utilize all their skills in performing their jobs will increase productivity.
    Rules and procedures are necessary to get workers to be productive.

    (s) _____
    (t) _____
    10

11. Minimizing management status symbols increases workers' respect of the manager.
    Managers are entitled to the privileges and perquisites of their positions.

    (u) _____
    (v) _____
    10

12. Pay increases are the best way to keep employees motivated.
    A trusting relationship among members of an organization is a good way to keep employees motivated.

    (w) _____
    (x) _____
    10

STEP 2: Score the questionnaire.

In the columns below, write the score you assigned to each statement next to the letter of that statement. Then write the sum of the scores at the bottom of each column.

Everyone uses some combination of styles, but the column with the highest score will identify your basic managerial attitude and philosophy. If all three scores are within a few points of one another, you probably adjust your style to fit particular situations. If this instrument indicates that your attitude is strongly X, Y, or Z, you need to consider if your style is appropriate for the people you are supervising.

THEORY X SCORE EQUALS THE SUM OF	THEORY Y SCORE EQUALS THE SUM OF	THEORY Z SCORE EQUALS THE SUM OF
(a) _____	(b) _____	(f) _____
(d) _____	(c) _____	(l) _____
(h) _____	(e) _____	(n) _____
(i) _____	(g) _____	(p) _____
(k) _____	(j) _____	(q) _____
(o) _____	(m) _____	(s) _____
(t) _____	(r) _____	(u) _____
(w) _____	(v) _____	(x) _____
Total _____	Total _____	Total _____

Theory X

The philosophy of Theory X management style is based on the view of human nature embodied in the following three statements:

1. People have a natural aversion to work.
2. People need to be coerced, controlled, and threatened with punishment to get them to put forth adequate effort toward the achievement of company goals.
3. The average person prefers to be directed, wishes to avoid responsibility, has little ambition, and wants security most.

Theorists now ask how much of the behavior described above is inherent human nature and how much is behavior learned from bosses who manage with those assumptions. Perhaps the assumptions become self-validating. Workers who are always treated by an authoritarian management as though they are lazy tend to behave that way.

Theory Y

Theory Y assumptions represent a much more positive assessment of human behavior. Following are the basic premises of Theory Y:

1. The expenditure of physical and mental effort in work is as natural as play or rest.
2. External control and threat of punishment are not the only means for bringing about effort toward corporate goals. People will exercise self-direction and self-control to achieve goals they find important.
3. Commitment to objectives is in proportion to the rewards associated with their achievement.
4. The average person learns, under proper conditions, not only to accept but to seek responsibility.
5. The capacity to exercise a relatively high degree of imagination, ingenuity, and creativity in solving work problems is widely, not narrowly, present in the population.
6. Under the conditions of modern industrial life, the brainpower of the average person is only partially utilized.

Theory Z

Theory Z, a contemporary perspective based in part on lessons learned from Japanese management practices, suggests that managers get more out of their employees because of mutual trust and cooperation. This management philosophy is based on the following assumptions:

1. Long-term, even lifetime, employment is expected by both managers and employees.
2. Employees need freedom and the opportunity to grow.
3. Decisions should be group decisions involving workers and managers.

4. Subordinates are whole people at work (in contrast to being thought of as titles or as units of production).
5. Management has a broad concern for subordinate welfare.
6. Open communication, both vertically and horizontally, is the norm.
7. There is complete trust among groups and individuals because they all have the same goals—the good of the organization.
8. Cooperation, not competition, is the basis for relationships within the company.

STEP 3: Discussion. In small groups or with the class as a whole, answer the following questions:

1. What does your profile look like?
2. What are the implications for managing subordinates?
3. What changes should you make in your assumptions?

Excerpts from *Organization Behavior: Learning Guide/Experiential Exercises* by Bruce Kemelgor, copyright © 1988 by The Dryden Press, reprinted by permission of the publisher.

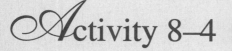 **Activity 8–4** THE NEWTOWN TOOLS AND TIMBER COMPANY CASE

STEP 1: Read the Newtown Tools and Timber Company Case.

The Newtown Tools and Timber Company was located in the center of Newtown, a medium-size town situated in northern England. With profits increasing by over 50 percent in the five years between 1981 and 1985, the company was beginning to make quite a name for itself in the local community (see Figure 8–5 for evolution of sales and after-tax profits). As a result, the company was thinking in terms of expanding operations into the Midlands and even the London area.

The initial rise in profits had coincided with the arrival of Brian Stevenson, son of the owner, Jack Stevenson. At the time, the business was being operated in an efficient but conservative manner, without much thought of growth, very much in the line of the relaxed approach to life displayed by the senior Stevenson. Being sixty years old, the latter had decided to retire to the peace and quiet of his garden, leaving the business in the hands of his younger son, Brian.

Brian was a recent graduate of the Manchester Business School, where he had studied, in particular, the management of small businesses. He was young, aggressive, and determined. Although fortunate to have moved into a family business, he had all the markings of a self-made man. He immediately put into practice the ideas he had learned in Manchester.

Brian's ideas about the managing of employees can be summed up in a viewpoint recently expressed to a colleague: "I never like to hire anyone brighter than I am. Only one person can run the show and make the decisions and that's me. I don't believe in fringe benefits and unnecessary coffee breaks. Work is really like a game. Employees try to get away with as much as they can, and employers try to get as much work out of employees as they can."

Before Brian had become manager, many old-time employees were carried on the payroll somewhat out of sympathy. Absenteeism and lateness tended to be overlooked as long as employees did a fair day's work. Wages paid were above average, and Jack Stevenson had ac-

FIGURE 8–5 *Newtown Tool and Timber Company*

	1981	1982	1983	1984	1985
Sales	450,000	493,200	575,100	624,600	699,300
After-tax Profits	41,220	44,730	52,020	55,800	62,370

quired a reputation as a generous employer to a number of immigrants from Asian and Caribbean countries. Jack Stevenson was a liberal thinker and believed strongly in merit rather than race as a pay criterion. The atmosphere was generally convivial and employees often adjourned to the local cricket club for a drink after work, where they would be joined from time to time by Jack Stevenson himself, whom they affectionately referred to as "the old man." Employees seemed to enjoy their work. This could be attributed more to the social environment than to the work itself, which offered little stimulation or opportunity for advancement within the company. As a result, work habits were usually sloppy and advantage was sometimes taken of the laxity in discipline.

Brian Stevenson's style of management altered the situation. Those older employees who were incapable of doing their jobs were asked to leave the company. Discipline was more strictly enforced and unnecessary socializing during working hours was frowned upon. Wage increases were not as high as previous years. After a period, wages fell back to the industry average. Brian was friendly with the staff, but always made it quite clear that there was a certain distance between them and himself that should not be bridged. Employee turnover was high at first, but settled down once employees attuned themselves properly to the new environment.

Brian had very definitive ideas about how business should relate to the community. His feelings were as follows: "Business is business. If a man pulls a fast one on me, it's my fault for being taken in. I expect everyone else to feel the same."

A local businessman once summed up the attitude of those in the area to Brian: "Brian's about as shrewd as they come. Maybe he wouldn't be the right man to run a big department store in a large city, but he really knows how to run his business and get every last penny out of it. His bills are lower than mine, and I'm half his size. I'd love to be in on a business deal with that bloke."

Brian's reputation for collecting overdue accounts was well known. He believed he had the highest collection rate for accounts receivable of anyone in the region. A hundred miles would not be too far to travel to collect a bad account. He prided himself on knowing all the tricks in the game when it came to collecting overdue debts.

Brian's business was his life. He did not regard it as a means to obtaining new luxuries or paying for foreign holidays, but as an intense game in which only the truly dedicated and competitive would come up winners.

Even when treating himself to rare pleasures, his thoughts were never far from the business environment.

Brian's brother Jeremy viewed the business methods employed by Brian with some distaste. He was the manager of the other branch of the family business, the Riverside Tool and Timber Company, located in the nearby town of Riverside. The philosophies of the two brothers concerning business and life in general were poles apart.

Jeremy, four years older than Brian, had an intensely strong social conscience. He had studied psychology and philosophy at a nearby university, but his lack of motivation prevented him from graduating. As a schoolboy he had suffered certain psychological problems. These he had managed to overcome, but as a result of the traumas he had gone through he had developed a personality that strongly empathized with the needs of others. He felt strongly that it was his duty to help change society so that it developed along lines fairer to all sectors of the population.

After being sent down from university, Jeremy involved himself in a number of social projects, allowing him to satisfy many of his deeper needs. With the arrival of a wife and child into his life, Jeremy found that he could not feed three mouths on his meager salary, so he accepted his father's offer to manage the Riverside branch. This was shortly after Jack Stevenson had relinquished control of the Newtown branch and coincided with the resignation of the Riverside manager.

Like his brother, Jeremy believed in the goal of profit maximization for the firm. However, he did not agree with Brian that this could only be achieved through an authoritarian attitude toward employees and ruthless competitiveness within the community. He believed that equal, if not better, profits than those of the Newtown operation could be attained by having happier employees and improving community relations.

As a result, under Jeremy's management the environment at the Riverside plant evolved along the same lines as at Newtown, when Jack Stevenson had been in charge. Employees felt relaxed by the informal working atmosphere. They were all on first-name terms with Jeremy, who encouraged them to communicate with him. "My door is always open," he would say, "no matter what time of day or night. Your problems are mine and that doesn't only refer to business problems."

Jeremy spent a lot of time consulting with employees. He tried to keep everything as open as possible, including potentially tricky questions such as employee's respective wages. Conflict was always brought into the open and thrashed out. The essential difference between Riverside and the way Jack Stevenson had run Newtown was that Jeremy attempted to enrich the job of each individual. This was a particularly difficult task, as the business was not a large, varied one, and the duties involved were quite similar and straightforward. Nevertheless, he decided to utilize whatever capacity there was for granting additional authority to an employee in his activities and increasing the accountability of individuals for their own work. At the same time all unnecessary controls were removed.

Jeremy continued to fulfill his social responsibilities. The business made larger than usual donations to local charities and once sponsored a marathon walk in aid of educational facilities for the mentally handicapped. Jeremy himself was active in a social work program for youths and took time off from the business once a week to counsel drug addicts at a rehabilitation center.

Business relations within the community were cordial. Jeremy was known as a warm, charming person by customers—one always keen to lend a helping hand when a problem arose. Customers were aware that they could take advantage of Jeremy when times were hard. Consequently, bad debts at the firm were far higher than normal. Competitors used Jeremy's open and frank attitude to outmaneuver him in negotiations with suppliers and to poach some of his sales.

Jeremy was aware of this situation. He felt things would iron themselves out in time, once people trusted him more. He had a desire to expand the business, but was not prepared to sacrifice his other obligations and interests, which he considered to be of equal importance.

Sales at Riverside had increased, but the net profit to sales ratio was not as high as in Newtown (see Figure 8–6). In Jeremy's opinion this was chiefly due to the higher wages and bad debts in Riverside. Jack Stevenson, being the largest shareholder in both branches, was concerned about the differing profits achieved and methods employed. He felt it important that a managerial policy consistent to both firms be employed. He was well aware of the differences in character and outlook between the brothers, but was sure that a combination of the two styles would produce higher overall efficiency. His major headache was in bringing the brothers together and deciding on the correct trade-off between styles.

STEP 2:   Prepare the case for class discussion.

STEP 3:   Answer the following questions, individually, in small groups, or with the class as a whole, as directed by your instructor.

DESCRIPTION
1. Describe Brian's and Jeremy's leadership styles.

DIAGNOSIS
2. Was Brian an effective leader?
3. Was Jeremy an effective leader?
4. Using the various theories of leadership, evaluate the effectiveness of each man's leadership style.
5. Did Brian and Jeremy motivate their employees effectively?
6. Evaluate the quality of communication in the case.

PRESCRIPTION
7. What changes should be made at Newtown and Riverside?

ACTION
8. What factors will influence whether these changes are successful?

FIGURE 8–6   *Riverside Tool and Timber Company*

	1981	1982	1983	1984	1985
Sales	459,000	508,500	552,600	603,000	642,600
After-Tax Profits	36,720	41,490	45,900	48,870	52,200

STEP 4: Discussion. In small groups, with the entire class, or in written form, share your answers to the questions above. Then answer the following questions:

1. What symptoms suggest that a problem exists?
2. What problems exist in the case?
3. What theories and concepts help explain the problems?

4. How can the problems be corrected?
5. Are these actions likely to be effective?

Activity 8–5   LEADERSHIP ROLE PLAY

STEP 1: Divide the class into groups of seven people. Read the general description of the situation below. The instructor will distribute seven roles to each group. Each person in the group should then prepare one role. In preparing for the role play, try to put yourself in the position of the person whose role you are playing.

GENERAL DESCRIPTION OF THE SITUATION

It is August 1, and you are about to have a meeting with the six people you are living with during the summer in an old Victorian house in the city of Medropolis. This city has exciting cultural and educational possibilities, a lovely beach area nearby, a large depressed inner-city area, and a rather conservative political atmosphere.

You are a national group who has come here this summer for various reasons:

Lee West is here for a summer rest after a very demanding work year.

Sandy Brown is a community organizer in the inner city.

Fran Miller is a counselor at an inner city mental health center.

Cam Jones is summer director of curriculum at School District 3 in Medropolis' inner city.

Jan Johnson is teaching summer courses at the medical school.

Brooks Baines is studying philosophy by taking summer courses at the university.

Sam Smith is a secretary in School District 3 for the summer.

You must all return to your homes by August 15. Sandy, Cam, and Fran lived here last year and will continue to live here next year.

You have an important decision to make at this meeting. Robert Stodge, the superintendent of School District 3, has asked a close friend of yours, Jane Goodenough, for seven people to help him with a census on the weekend of August 12–13. Mr. Stodge is an organization man who cares much about doing what the State Education Director asks of his superintendents. His assistant, David Guitar, loves his work with the people of the district, which he feels is slowly developing a community sense; he is responsible for the organization of the census. It is rumored that several inner-city schools may be consolidated within the next two years, and that School District 3's continued existence may be in question. Your friend has asked you to decide whether or not you will accept this two-day assignment *as a group.* You do not know whether your collection of data will be used responsibly or be a waste of time.

You are to call your friend in a half hour and report your decision. You all agreed when you set the meeting time that you could make your decision in half an hour. (If you don't call Jane within that time, she will call you.)

STEP 2: Each group of seven participants should convene the group meeting in part of the room. You have a half hour to make a decision about whether to conduct the census.

STEP 3: Report your group's decision to your instructor.

STEP 4: Discussion. Answer the following questions, in small groups or with the entire class.

DESCRIPTION

1. Characterize each participant. How are they similar? different?

DIAGNOSIS

2. What problems did you encounter in reaching agreement? Why?
3. Did a leader emerge?
4. Was the leader effective?
5. Using your knowledge of leadership theories, analyze the leadership you experienced.
6. Did you experience stress?
7. Did you experience issues of adult development?
8. Using motivation, communication, and perceptual theories, explain the outcomes of the meeting.

_____

Reprinted by permission of Sara Ann Rude, St. Louis, Missouri.

Activity 8–6 — DECISION-MAKING CASES

STEP 1: Read each case below.

STEP 2: For each case, apply the Vroom and Yetton model and indicate the most appropriate decision-making process. Be sure to list your answers to each diagnostic question and the resulting problem style.

CASE I

You are president of a small but growing Midwestern bank, with its head office in the state's capital and branches in several nearby market towns. The location and type of business are factors that contribute to the emphasis on traditional and conservative banking practices at all levels.

When you bought the bank five years ago, it was in poor financial shape. Under your leadership, much progress has been made. This progress has been achieved while the economy has moved into a mild recession, and, as a result, your prestige among your bank managers is very high. Your success, which you are inclined to attribute principally to good luck and to a few timely decisions on your part, has, in your judgment, one unfortunate by-product. It has caused your subordinates to look to you for leadership and guidance in decision making beyond what you consider necessary. You have no doubts about the fundamental capabilities of these men but wish that they were not quite so willing to accede to your judgment.

You have recently acquired funds to permit opening a new branch. Your problem is to decide on a suitable location. You believe that there is no "magic formula" by which it is possible to select an optimal site. The choice will be made by a combination of some simple common sense criteria and "what feels right." You have asked your managers to keep their eyes open for commercial real estate sites that might be suitable. Their knowledge about the communities in which they operate should be extremely useful in making a wise choice.

Their support is important because the success of the new branch will be highly dependent on your managers' willingness to supply staff and technical assistance during its early days. Your bank is small enough for everyone to feel like part of a team, and you feel that this has and will be critical to the bank's prosperity.

The success of this project will benefit everybody. Directly, they will benefit from the increased base of operations, and, indirectly, they will reap the personal and business advantages of being part of a successful and expanding business.

CASE II

You are regional manager of an international management consulting company. You have a staff of six consultants reporting to you, each of whom enjoys a considerable amount of autonomy with clients in the field.

Yesterday you received a complaint from one of your major clients to the effect that the consultant whom you assigned to work on the contract with them was not doing his job effectively. They were not very explicit as to the nature of the problem, but it was clear that they were dissatisfied and that something would have to be done if you were to restore the client's faith in your company.

The consultant assigned to work on that contract has been with the company for six years. He is a systems analyst and is one of the best in that profession. For the first four or five years his performance was superb, and he was a model for the other more junior consultants. However, recently he has seemed to have a "chip on his shoulder," and his previous identification with the company and its objectives has been replaced with indifference. His negative attitude has been noticed by other consultants, as well as by clients. This is not the first such complaint that you have had from a client this year about his performance. A previous client even reported to you that the consultant reported to work several times obviously suffering from a hangover and that he had been seen around town in the company of "fast" women.

It is important to get to the root of this problem quickly if that client is to be retained. The consultant obviously has the skill necessary to work with the clients effectively. If only he were willing to use it!

CASE III

You have recently been appointed manager of a new plant that is presently under construction. Your team of five department heads has been selected, and they are now working with you in selecting their own staffs, purchasing equipment, and generally anticipating the problems that are likely to arise when you move into the plant in three months.

Yesterday, you received from the architect a final set of plans for the building, and, for the first time, you examined the parking facilities that are available. There is a large lot across the road from the plant intended primarily for hourly workers and lower-level supervisory personnel. In addition, there are seven spaces immediately adjacent to the administrative offices, intended for visitor and reserved parking. Company policy requires that a minimum of three spaces be made available for visitor parking, leaving you only four spaces to allocate among yourself and your five department heads. There is no way of increasing the total number of such spaces without changing the structure of the building.

Up to now, there have been no obvious status differences among your team, who have worked together very well in the planning phase of the operation. To be sure, there are salary differences, with your administrative, manufacturing, and engineering managers receiving slightly more than the quality control and industrial relations managers. Each has recently been promoted to his new position, and expects reserved parking privileges as a consequence of his new status. From past ex-

perience, you know that people feel strongly about things that would be indicative of their status. So you and your subordinates have been working together as a team, and you are reluctant to do anything that might jeopardize the team relationship.

CASE IV

You are executive vice president for a small pharmaceutical manufacturer. You have the opportunity to bid on a contract for the U.S. Department of Defense pertaining to biological warfare. The contract is outside the mainstream of your business. However, it could make economic sense since you do have unused capacity in one of your plants, and the manufacturing processes are not dissimilar.

You have written the document to accompany the bid and now have the problem of determining the dollar value of the quotation that you think will win the job for your company. If the bid is too high, you will undoubtedly lose to one of your competitors. If it is too low, you would stand to lose money on the program.

There are many factors to be considered in making this decision, including the cost of the new raw materials and the additional administrative burden of relationships with a new client, not to speak of factors that are likely to influence the bids of your competitors, such as how much they *need* this particular contract. You have been busy assembling the necessary data to make this decision but there remain several "unknowns," one of which involves the manager of the plant in which the new products will be manufactured. Of all your subordinates, only he is in the position to estimate the costs of adapting the present equipment to their new purpose, and his cooperation and support will be necessary in ensuring that the specifications of the contract will be met. However, in an initial discussion with him when you first learned of the possibility of the contract, he seemed adamantly opposed to the idea. His previous experience has not particularly equipped him with the ability to evaluate projects like this one, so that you were not overly influenced by his opinions. From the nature of his arguments, you inferred that his opposition was ideological rather than economic. You recall that he was actively involved in a local "peace organization" and, within the company, was one of the most vocal opponents to the war in Vietnam.

STEP 3: Compare your responses to those given by Vroom and Yetton. Your instructor will distribute these.

STEP 4: Discussion. In small groups or with the class as a whole, answer the following questions:

1. In what situations would using the Vroom and Yetton model improve your decision making?

2. In what situations would the model be of little value?

Reprinted with permission from V.H. Vroom and A.G. Jago, Decision making as a social process: Normative & descriptive models of leader behavior, *Decision Sciences* 5 (1974): 750–753.

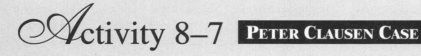

Activity 8–7 — PETER CLAUSEN CASE

STEP 1: Read the case of Peter Clausen.

THE ADVERTISING AGENCY

It was 8:30 on a Monday morning and Peter Clausen was going through his mail in his office located in a modern building in Bigtown in Indolandia. He had just returned from a lovely weekend spent with his wife and two children on a beach not too far from the city.

Peter was the managing director of McKintosh, the leading advertising agency in Indolandia, which was set up 10 years ago as a joint venture between a small local agency and McKintosh, New York. McKintosh had 70 subsidiaries and affiliated agencies in 56 countries and prided itself on being amongst the top 10 advertising agencies in the world.

Peter, who was born in Denmark, joined McKintosh in Copenhagen 11 years ago as an account executive in the client service department. On his own initiative he was transferred to New York from where he was sent to Indolandia two and a half years ago. At the age of 36 he was in charge of 55 members of staff, one being his British creative director, Dick White.

As the workload increased, he tried to have another expatriate brought in to act as head of the client service department. However, his request for a work permit from the government had been turned down. Since most of McKintosh's clients were multinational firms, with expatriate directors or marketing managers, they expected an expatriate on the agency side to be their main contact. It was for this reason that Peter had to spend a substantial amount of his time in meetings with clients, a task he felt was rather superfluous, since he had full trust in his local client service staff. Instead of discussing the conceptual and main creative work

with the agency's team before it was presented to the client's, he often found himself selling the material to them regardless of whether he liked the output or not. To overcome this problem, he brought in additional expatriates on tourist visas from offices in the neighboring countries for short periods whenever major advertising campaigns had to be developed.

BUSINESS PRINCIPLES OF MCKINTOSH

McKintosh's reputation in the market was that of an agency with good creative work, coupled with the best quality final products locally available, such as artwork, photography, typesetting, and films. The latter was due to the fact that the majority of the advertising material was brought in from the United States or Europe only to be adopted locally. McKintosh also had the image of a reliable and trustworthy partner—highly appreciated in a country like Indolandia, where media rates (prices for space in print media or time on air on radio and television) were practically never fixed and where it was possible to obtain agency commissions from so-called "official" rates of up to 70 percent. Most agencies in town charged their clients the full "official" rates or offered them a small discount, pocketing the rest for themselves. As this business was very profitable and the purchase of space and time in the media made up the bulk of advertising budgets of almost all clients, agencies were able to offer development work on advertising campaigns either very cheaply or free of charge.

Peter Clausen's predecessor had decided to implement a different system. He had asked his media buyers to bargain very hard to obtain the lowest rates of all agencies in the country, based on the fact that they placed more orders than anyone else. On the obtained rate he then slapped a standard agency commission of 20 percent and charged the total to the customers. As a result McKintosh could claim and prove that in terms of media buying they were the cheapest agency in Indolandia. To make up for the lost revenue, however, McKintosh's fees for creative services and artwork were higher than those of most of their competitors. Most of McKintosh's clients not only accepted, but appreciated, this more open pricing policy.

CONTROL MECHANISM

Peter Clausen happily went along with this system which had even enabled him to attract new clients into the agency. He did this by comparing the amount of money clients of other agencies spent for a given media plan with the proposal his own media buyers would give him. Peter also considered this a useful control mechanism for his own staff in the media department, which under the given rate system could find it rather easy to divert funds into their own pockets in the form of kickbacks from the media owners.

Another substantial part of McKintosh's business was the printing of advertising material such as brochures, labels, cartons, point-of-sale material, posters, etc. Almost each job was somewhat unique. Differences in paper quality, size, quantities, color scheme, delivery schedule, and so on, made it necessary to request quotations from printers for each new job. These differed substantially, even for similar work to be done, due to a variety of factors, one of them probably being the lack of knowledge on the printer's side of their own costs.

This situation necessitated quotations from at least three printers for each job, a time consuming, but, as Peter felt, worthwhile effort. It forced printers who knew that their prices would be compared with their competitors to quote realistically. Peter also assumed that it would reduce the opportunities for the print buyers to give out favors to certain suppliers, since all quotations had to be delivered to the office in closed envelopes and would be opened only in the presence of himself or his financial director. Over time, Peter Clausen had visited the most important printers in Bigtown to look at their facilities and at the same time to explain to them their purchasing procedures. He also got personally involved in negotiations with both printers and media from time to time. During those meetings, Peter tried to demonstrate to suppliers as well as to his own print and media buyers that it was he and not his staff who took the final decision. He hoped that this would reduce the temptation of suppliers to offer special incentives to his buyers in exchange for attractive orders.

AN UNEXPECTED VISITOR

Peter Clausen had gone through all of his mail and had just stepped out of his office when he met Mr. Chan, the representative of one of Indolandia's biggest printers, in the corridor. He knew him quite well and somehow liked him—probably because his company had always delivered on time and also produced good quality material. Mr. Chan was Chinese and probably part of the family who owned the company. He was a tough negotiator, knowledgeable and self-confident and his relationship with the buying department was apparently good.

That morning Mr. Chan seemed to be quite irritated. When Peter invited him into his office for a chat he gladly accepted, especially since the chief buyer he wanted to see was not around. Mr. Chan immediately started to talk about his business relationship with McKintosh. He stated that over time the volume of jobs he received from the agency had steadily diminished, despite the fact that he had never let his customers down and delivered the best quality in town. Peter admitted that he had been unaware of this and promised to look into the matter. Mr. Chan further explained that it was McKintosh's chief buyer who was pushing him out of business and who might gradually squeeze the whole agency out of business by making it uncompetitive.

It was at that moment that Peter realized that the discussion involved him in much more than exchanging pleasantries. Mr. Chan continued to accuse his chief buyer of having forced him not only to include in his quotations, "the usual 10 percent," but then 15 percent, and even 25 percent lately, to be paid to him as soon as the agency had paid the printer. Mr. Chan felt that the chief buyer had not asked the other printers to increase their percentages. As a result his quotations had probably become so high they were no longer considered.

After listening attentively to Mr. Chan's accusations, Peter Clausen asked Mr. Chan how to solve the problem. Mr. Chan shrugged his shoulders and advised him to get rid of his chief buyer. Then asked whether he would repeat his accusation in front of the chief buyer and other witnesses Mr. Chan smiled and said, "Do you think I want to kill my business? Do you think I want to kill myself? Even if you repeat what I have told you I shall always deny having made those statements. It is your problem, and my problem, but I can try to get orders from other sources while you might price yourself out of the market." With those last words he stood up and walked out of the door.

MR. TANI'S COMMENT

The nice weekend was soon forgotten. Peter realized that he had to do something. Probably the whole agency knew about "the usual 10 percent." His staff might even laugh about his control procedures, his closed envelopes, and visits to suppliers.

Would there be any way to confront his chief buyer with some hard facts? Was there any way of firing him? Peter suddenly remembered that his secretary had once told him that the chief buyer was closely related to somebody in the immigration department of the government and had even helped Peter to obtain the first extension of his work permit, which was very difficult to obtain without special connections, or a substantial amount of money.

Peter called in his financial director, Mr. Tani, a man who had worked for over 30 years for a European multinational, had an impeccable track record, and had joined the agency six years ago after he had reached the retirement age in his former firm.

To Peter this man was the only person in the agency he could trust and whose advice he highly appreciated, mainly because of Mr. Tani's maturity and fatherly attitude towards him and everybody else in the agency.

After having recounted the discussion with Mr. Chan, Peter asked him how the agency could stop fraudulent activities in the agency and how to get rid of the chief buyer and anybody else involved in "illegally taking money that did not belong to the company." The more Peter actually talked about it the more desperate, frustrated and at the same time, aggressive he became towards Mr. Tani who patiently sat listening to him. When Peter finally stopped talking and invited Mr. Tani to comment, he replied with a question. "Peter," he said, "How long have you been in this country?" And before

Peter could react, he added, "Have you never realized that you work in Indolandia?"

STEP 2: Prepare the case for class discussion.

STEP 3: Answer the following questions, individually, in small groups, or with the class as a whole, as directed by your instructor.

DESCRIPTION
1. Describe Peter Clausen's leadership style.
2. What complaint did Mr. Chan make to Clausen?

DIAGNOSIS
3. What problems did Clausen experience in exerting leadership?
4. Was Peter Clausen an effective leader?
5. Was Peter Clausen an effective manager?
6. What situational contingencies should Clausen have considered in selecting his leadership style?
7. How should working in Indolandia affect Clausen's leadership style?

PRESCRIPTION
8. What style should Clausen use?
9. How should he deal with Mr. Chan?

ACTION
10. What likely will result from these actions?

STEP 4: Discussion. In small groups, with the entire class, or in written form, share your answers to the questions above. Then answer the following questions:

1. What symptoms suggest a problem exists?
2. What problems exist in the case?
3. What theories and concepts help explain the problems?
4. How can the problems be corrected?
5. Are the actions likely to be effective?

This case was prepared by Hellmut Schütte, Affiliate Professor at IN-SEAD. Copyright 1985–1986 INSEAD, Fountainebleau, France. All rights reserved.

$\mathscr{A}$ctivity 8–8  "THE SHAKEUP AT THE WHITE HOUSE"

STEP 1: Using your knowledge of leadership theory, formulate a ten-point plan for effective leadership by the White House chief of staff.

STEP 2: View the ABC video entitled "The Shakeup at the White House."

STEP 3: In small groups, compare the leadership of Thomas F. "Mack" McLarty to your protocol. What deficiencies existed in his leadership?

STEP 4: Now consider the description of how Leon Panetta will perform the job of Chief of Staff. You can collect news clippings to gain additional information about his leadership. Is he likely to overcome the deficiencies in leadership demonstrated by McLarty? How well does Leon Panetta match your protocol of an effective leader?

Chapter 9

Chapter Outline

Using Power and Managing Conflict

LEARNING OBJECTIVES

After completing the reading and activities in Chapter 9, students will be able to

1. Offer a definition of power.

2. Outline five models of power.

3. Describe and illustrate four sources of power.

4. Describe the impact of organizational politics.

5. Identify the outcomes, levels, and stages of conflict.

6. Identify the causes of stress and propose ways for dealing with them.

7. Offer two primary strategies for managing conflict.

Conflict in the Computer Engineering Group

T he computer engineering group of Computer Designers, Inc. was composed of approximately fifteen members who were hardware or software engineers. Each group member belonged to a subgroup of three to five people who focused on a particular project. The senior person with the most technical experience acted as project leader for the subgroup and reported to the group manager, whose primary responsibilities included administrative activities, capital budgeting, long-term planning, and linking the group with upper management. Intergroup communication about specific technical issues was common, but there was no active collaboration on end products. Each group managed its own project and was fairly autonomous, with the project leaders providing the necessary technical direction.

For a nine-month period, the computer engineering group lacked a manager since the previous manager had left to pursue other opportunities within the company. In the interim, Gary Snaith, a project leader in one of the subgroups, acted as the group manager until one was hired. Because a formal group manager was not present, the group developed a feeling of independence. Productivity and morale were high, projects were completed on time, and customers were satisfied with the level of support and the products they received. The working environment was extremely stable and calm. Only the lack of a liaison between upper management and the group concerned the group members. With no one at the helm, the project leaders were worried that upper management might grow ignorant of the group's progress and make uninformed decisions regarding the group.

Then Lynda Smerling, the newly hired group manager, arrived. Within a few months of Smerling's arrival, the climate of the group began to change. Smerling began inquiring into the subgroups' activities and started to make decisions on the subgroups' behalf. Smerling required that the subgroups focus on specific goals and did not allow for group member interaction or feedback. Project leaders were required to submit design decisions for approval and Smerling would make changes without allowing the project leaders to respond. Soon the project plans reflected the preferences of Smerling instead of those of the subgroup.

The only instance in which Smerling did not become involved in subgroup decisions was with the Architecture Group (AG) project. This project lacked a supervisor and had only one person, Steven Jenkins, working on it. According to Smerling, she preferred letting Jenkins do as he wished so that she could keep the AG project alive. Jenkins was aware of her attitude and used the situation to his benefit. For example, he was overheard by a coworker to say, "I'll do anything to further my benefit and apologize later." Once Jenkins took the secretary's typewriter home without filing the necessary property removal paperwork. He also borrowed computer terminals and other equipment without authorization and only returned them after Snaith threatened to report a theft to security.

What the other group members found most distressing was not Jenkins's behavior *per se,* but that Smerling allowed him to behave as he did without reprimanding or penalizing him. This resulted in numerous hallway conversations about Smerling's ineffectiveness and feelings of depression among group members. Frequently, group members wondered aloud why their projects required so much direction from

Smerling, while they perceived that Jenkins's project required non
tent about being promoted to Principal Engineer. When Smerling ret
promotion, he threatened to quit.[1]

At Computer Designers, we can see the sorts of conflict that arise within groups when people with different amounts of power interact. Often, these conflicts are a major source of stress for employees. In this chapter, we take a closer look at power, conflict, and stress, focusing on the interactions within work groups. Then, in Chapter 10, we will look at the ways groups interact, with a focus on using negotiation and other strategies for managing intergroup relations.

A DEFINITION OF POWER

Power refers to the potential or actual ability to influence others in a desired direction. Who has power in the situation of the computer engineering group? Gary Snaith, Lynda Smerling, and Steven Jenkins have the most visible power, although other members of the computer engineering group, as well as workers outside the group, may also have power.

THE NATURE OF INFLUENCE

Different individuals and groups within and outside the organization can exert power. Individual employees, including top and middle management, technical analysts and specialists, support staff, and other nonmanagerial workers can influence the actions an organization takes to reach its goals. Formal groups of employees, such as various departments, work teams, management councils, task forces, or employee unions, as well as informal groups, such as those workers with offices near each other or those who see each other socially, can similarly exercise power. Non-employees may also try to influence the behavior of an organization and its members. Owners, suppliers, clients, competitors, employee associations (e.g., unions and professional associations), the general public, and directors of the organization may exert power that affects the organization.[2]

Individuals can exert influence in a variety of ways.[3] They may exert regular, ongoing influence, such as when managers demonstrate authority over subordinates. Or, they can exert influence periodically, when unique circumstances occur, such as the expiration of a labor contract or a change in the economic or technological environment. Lynda Smerling, for example, exerts influence to prevent Steven Jenkins from receiving the promotion he desires. Influence can also focus on specific individuals, groups, or even events, or occur more generally, with the entire work situation as a target.

We can begin our diagnosis of power by identifying those exerting influence. We can also assess the appropriateness of the power efforts. Do they result in accomplishing individual, group, and organizational goals? Do they lead to desired outcomes? Is power being used in ethical ways? To control abuses and ensure the rights of all organizational members, managers may need to establish informal norms or more formal guidelines for using power.

BRIDGESTONE/FIRESTONE. After an almost six-month strike by members of the United Rubber Workers, the tire manufacturer hired 2,300 permanent replacement workers. This action demonstrated the influence of the president of Bridgestone over union members. His intention not to rehire all striking workers, even if the two sides agreed to a contract, reflected his power with regard to Bridgestone employees.[4]

DIRECTIONS OF INFLUENCE

Influence can occur in the same three directions as communication, described in Chapter 7: downward, upward, and lateral. Most influence attempts are directed downward in the organization. Managers, for example, can give direct orders to subordinates, establish guidelines for their decision making, approve or reject subordinates' decisions, or allocate resources to them.

Individuals can also exert upward influence. To promote or protect their self-interests they can control the type of information passed to superiors or withhold information they feel is detrimental to themselves. Occasionally, workers will punish or reward their superiors, by withholding or providing a quality work effort, for example. Managing the boss effectively requires understanding and responding to his or her needs.[5]

Lateral influence can also occur. Sometimes the influence is positive, as when peers offer advice or provide service. At other times, influence attempts between entities at the same level, such as functional departments, line and staff groups, or labor and management, can result in competition.[6] The parties may resort to power struggles as they try to strengthen their power vis-à-vis the power of the other parties. As the parties' interdependence increases, however, they can less afford conflict. Thus, they may rely more on negotiation and cooperation rather than on power struggles to resolve their differences.

MODELS OF POWER

To understand power, we can look at various models of power. Theorists and practitioners have translated an early view of power, which considered it evil and as mainly stemming from coercion,[7] into models that acknowledge that power can be constructive as well as destructive.

POWER AND DEPENDENCE

This model holds that we can initially diagnose power by measuring the extent or force of the dependence inherent in a relationship that includes power behavior.[8] The power that person A has over person B is determined by the degree that B depends on A. For example, the power that Lynda Smerling has over Steven Jenkins is determined in part by Jenkins's dependence on her. He depends on her for his promotion, thereby increasing her power over him. At the same time, Smerling depends on Jenkins to complete the AG project, which gives him power over her. Subordinates like Jenkins often initiate an act of power, such as withholding information, to counteract job-related dependencies on their managers.

Nature of Dependence Dependence arises because a person, group, or organization relies on another person, group, or organization to accomplish his, her, or its tasks. In personal relationships, dependence may occur when one person comes to rely on another person for help or psychological support. In business settings, a subordinate depends on his or her boss for directions and resources. A manager in turn depends on his or her subordinates for assistance in accomplishing tasks and identifying obstacles to achieving a work group's goal. The person being relied or depended upon automatically has some power—the potential or actual ability to influence the other.

We have already looked at dependence in the computer engineering group at Computer Designers. Now consider a job that you have held. On whom did you depend in performing your work? Did you depend on your boss, your coworkers, customers, or maybe the owner of the company? A job holder's dependence is related to characteristics of the organization and its environment. As the organization's goals become more ambitious, managers become more dependent on those involved in coordinating the actions needed to accomplish these goals. Dependence also increases as the organization becomes larger, causing greater reliance on the specialties that result from the division of labor. Because technology increases specialization, it also increases managers' dependence on specialists who can help them perform their jobs. As the uncertainty of the environment increases, managers also become more dependent on others who can reduce the ambiguity in organizational situations for them. Finally, dependence is a function of the organization's formal structure, measurement systems, and reward systems. For example, diffusing authority throughout the organization to individuals other than managers creates greater dependencies.

Dealing with Dependence According to this model, individuals engage in power-oriented behavior to reduce their dependence on others. They also try to increase the dependence of others on them, thus increasing their own relative power. A technician who must rely on his or her boss for pay raises may reduce his or her dependence by becoming indispensable to the boss. By acquiring unique expertise or knowledge, the technician develops power. Or, the director of purchasing may attempt to reduce his or her dependence on a supplier by finding alternative sources of goods or services. To cope with dependence, managers draw from bases of power and establish trade relations and alliances, as described later in this chapter.

Diagnosing Dependence and Power We can use a power/dependence analysis in diagnosis. Managers and other organizational members who perform such an analysis should answer the following questions:

- On whom do you really depend and how important and appropriate is each dependency?

- What is the basis of each dependency?

- Does a pattern of dysfunctional dependence exist, what created it, and what consequences resulted?

- How much effective power-oriented behavior do you engage in and is it sufficient to cope with your job-related dependencies?[9]

Then we can diagram the relationships, as shown in Figure 9–1 for the introductory scenario. According to these diagrams, who has the greatest need to exert power on an ongoing basis? Lynda Smerling and Gary Snaith rely on constituencies other than Steven Jenkins. They probably use many sources of power to reduce their dependence. But Jenkins's dependence on Smerling has increased with his reliance on her for his promotion. Because he has increased his dependence, he also has increased his need to exert power over Smerling.

FIGURE 9–1   *Dependence diagrams for Computer Designers*

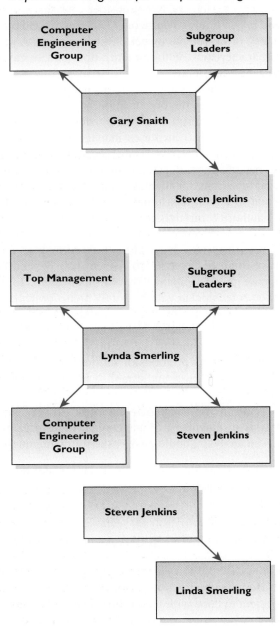

POWER AS EXCHANGE

A second model views power as a more general property of a social relationship, rather than merely a counteraction to dependence. Historically, power was viewed as an exchange process, in which a person who commands services needed by others exchanges them for compliance with his or her requests.[10] For example, a supervisor, such as Gary Snaith or Lynda Smerling, exchanges time off for high-quality performance by workers.

Sometimes individuals or groups will develop a social exchange network to help them negotiate the allocation of valued resources.[11] In such cases managers spend more time than usual making deals, interacting across departments, and even exchanging resources across organizational boundaries.[12]

AMERICAN EXPRESS. The CEO of American Express started the One Enterprise program, which encourages collaboration between different business lines. This program led to collaborative projects between divisions, such as cross-marketing and joint purchasing.[13]

POWER AS AN INDIVIDUAL NEED OR PERSONALITY TRAIT

Power can also be considered as an individual need, as described in Chapter 4. The *need for power* is an individual motivator that causes a person to seek and build power.[14] Have you worked with anyone who seems to have a high need for power? How would you characterize their behavior? You may recall that individuals with a high need for power try to influence and control others, seek leadership positions in groups, enjoy persuading others, and are perceived by others as outspoken, forceful, and demanding. Often politicians, top managers, or informal leaders are perceived as having a high need for power. Do any individuals in the opening case have a high need for power? Steven Jenkins, who openly voiced his ambition, flaunted procedures for borrowing equipment, and actively sought a promotion, seems to have a high need for power.

An individual's personality can also affect the person's exertion of power and influence. One recent study showed, for example, that personality explains the type of influence tactics used. People high on Machiavellianism more often used nonrational and indirect tactics (e.g., deceit, thought manipulation) and people low in Machiavellianism more often used rational and direct tactics (e.g., reason, persistence, assertion). Those high on need for approval used rational and indirect tactics (e.g., hinting, compromise, bargaining) while those low on need for approval used nonrational and direct tactics (e.g., threat, evasion, reward).[15]

EMPOWERMENT: POWER AS A RESOURCE TO BE SHARED

The models of power we have discussed so far view power as a limited resource, which can inspire power struggles and competition. **Empowerment,** a newer model, holds that individuals and organizations can actually increase their power by sharing it with others.[16] In a common scenario, managers give workers the training and authority they need to act with more autonomy. As a result, the empowered workers feel more involved, experience greater job satisfaction, and are more likely to support the manager's goals. Thus, the manager's influence increases both within the group and within the organization. Table 9–1 shows different activities leaders and managers can use to empower followers or subordinates.

TABLE 9–1 *Differences in the empowering process as a function of role: leaders compared with managers*

EMPOWERING PROCESS	LEADER ACTIVITIES	MANAGER ACTIVITIES
Providing direction for followers/subordinates	Via ideals, vision, a higher purpose, superordinate goals	Via involvement of subordinates in determining paths toward goal accomplishment
Stimulating followers/subordinates	With ideas	With action; things to accomplish
Rewarding followers/subordinates	Informal; personal recognition	Formal; incentive systems
Developing followers/subordinates	By inspiring them to do more than they thought they could do	By involving them in important decision-making activities and providing feedback for potential learning by giving them training
Appealing to follower/subordinate needs	Appeal to needs of followership and dependency	Appeal to needs for autonomy and independence

SOURCE: Adapted and reprinted with permission from W.W. Burke, Leadership as empowering others. In S. Srivastva and Associates, *Executive Power* (San Francisco: Jossey-Bass, 1986), p. 73.

JOHN DEERE. John Deere, a manufacturer of farm equipment, achieved a remarkable turnaround after a significant downsizing in the 1980s. They increased worker empowerment and made employee training and continuing education a top corporate priority. Training time in the Moline plant increased from 15 to 28 hours for each employee. As part of the worker empowerment, the Harvester Works' Seeding Division instituted a program in which line employees met with farmers to resolve their complaints about defective parts or machinery, rather than having sales or service personnel in corporate headquarters handle complaints over the telephone. This outreach program enhanced the company's customer service reputation. Programs such as this resulted in increased profits and a 35 percent increase in net income for the company between 1993 and 1994.[17]

The Hazards of Powerlessness The empowerment model stems, in part, from a recognition that powerlessness can have extremely negative consequences for organizations.

Powerlessness can stem from a number of sources.[18] These include

1. *Organizational culture.* Significant organizational changes, such as reorganizations or downsizings, an excessive emphasis on competition, an impersonal bureaucratic climate, or poor communication can make individual employees feel they have little control over their work lives.

2. *Management style.* An authoritative supervisor who emphasizes employee failures but fails to offer reasons for management decisions also promotes feelings of powerlessness.

3. *Job design.* Employees often feel powerless when their jobs involve little variety, unrealistic goals, too many rules, low opportunities for advancement, and a limited supply of the resources needed to perform the job.

4. ***Reward systems.*** Powerlessness also occurs when the organization does not reward competence or innovation or when the rewards are unappealing.

Together, these feelings of powerlessness can sap employee motivation and commitment, lowering the organization's chance of meeting its goals.

Women and minorities, in particular, can experience powerlessness in organizations. A combination of formal and informal practices may put them outside the mainstream of managerial activity. For example, they may receive too much supervision, focus extensively on routines, and fail to delegate to other organizational members.

As the work force becomes more diverse, managers are challenged to ensure that they do not contribute to the powerlessness of a job holder. By being patronizingly overprotective, failing to provide signs of managerial support, assuming that an employee does not know the ropes, ignoring the job holder in informal socializing, and failing to provide organizational supports, managers contribute to such powerlessness.[19] The likelihood of doing so seems to increase with minorities and women and must be carefully avoided. Individuals in powerless jobs, particularly women, use acquiescence as a response to feelings of powerlessness.[20] They fail to use the more powerful strategies of negotiation, coalition formation, and persuasion in these situations.

Empowerment and Self-Managing Teams A manager may empower workers by providing a positive emotional atmosphere, rewarding staff achievements in visible and personal ways, expressing confidence in subordinates' abilities, fostering initiative and responsibility, and building on success.[21] Many of these requirements can be met by creating self-managing teams, in which individual members perform and supervise all aspects of the job (see Chapter 6).

PICKER INTERNATIONAL. Workers in the Computed Tomography Division of Picker International, which makes systems that give two- and three-dimensional views of the human body, handled a wiring problem on a circuit board themselves, rather than referring it to their supervisors or other work groups. When a discrepancy between the plan and actual wiring surfaced in the test bays of the manufacturing and quality group, a test technician identified it, an engineer wrote a correction to the plan, and another technician volunteered to work overtime to repair existing boards. The problem was solved within 48 hours. The group's manager views himself as the team's ***coach,*** thereby empowering team members to make decisions. The group's production capacity doubled and its on-time record has remained at 100 percent since the teams were introduced in the late 1980s.[22]

This type of worker empowerment has changed the role of middle managers. They now oversee more workers, manage more diverse types of tasks, and may also perform more special projects.

CARBOLINE. A senior regional sales manager with Carboline, a manufacturer of corrosion-resistant coatings, now manages 27 rather than 12 employees. He has organized his sales force into leaderless teams of three to four employees. The teams are responsible for specific projects.[23]

Empowerment and Performance Empowering workers has had significant advantages for organizations. Not only do workers' attitudes improve, but some programs have financial benefits for individual employees.

L-S ELECTROGALVANIZING COMPANY. Employees who have participated in a worker–management initiative at L-S Electrogalvanizing Company run plant operations, do their own scheduling, set production goals, set pay scales based on skills, and staff the organization. An employee gain-sharing committee modifies the pay-for-skills program semiannually to focus on continuous improvement. Workers can receive a payout of as much as 25 percent of their salary from the component of the plan that reduces the cost of customer complaints and another 5 percent for increased productivity.[24]

PFIZER, INC. Worker empowerment has also improved profits and reduced development cycle time for corporations. The executive director of medical chemistry at Pfizer, Inc., the pharmaceutical firm, organized a 30-member team to study a potential cause of schizophrenia. He appointed a group leader and then allowed the group to work entirely without direction from him.[25] Pfizer has slashed its average development time for new compounds from 4.5 to 3 years or less.

CROSS-CULTURAL ISSUES

Power relations can have a significant effect on the functioning of an organization. This is especially true for multicultural and multinational organizations, where individuals may experience significant power differentials. Societies differ, for example, in their *power distance*—the extent to which a society accepts the fact that power in institutions and organizations is distributed unequally.[26] In high power distance countries, such as India, Mexico, and France, subordinates accept the unequal distribution of power. They frown on subordinates who bypass their bosses. In low power distance countries, such as Austria, Denmark, and Sweden, bypassing superiors is expected.

An American executive went to London to manage the company's British office. Although the initial few weeks were relatively uneventful, one thing that bothered the executive was that visitors were never sent directly to his office. A visitor first spoke with the receptionist, then the secretary, then the office manager, and finally was escorted by the office manager to see the American. The American was annoyed with this practice, which he considered a total waste of time. When he finally spoke with his British employees and urged them to be less formal, sending visitors directly to him, the employees were chagrined.

After a number of delicate conversations, the American executive began to understand the greater stress on formality and hierarchy in England. He slowly learned to ignore his feelings of impatience when the British used their proper channels for greeting guests. As a result, visitors continued to see the receptionist, secretary, and office manager before being sent in to meet the American.[27]

Other cross-cultural differences in power behavior may accompany variations in power distance. We know, for example, that individuals differ in their attitudes toward power and in their abilities to use it.[28] Most likely these differences are cross-culturally determined. The predominant or most useful sources of power may also be culturally linked. Those in the United States may favor charisma, while the Japanese may favor legitimacy. (We will discuss these sources of power in more detail in the next section.)

Power imbalances among culture groups may also have significant consequences.[29] These include intergroup conflict and, when the imbalance persists over a long time, reduced motivation when minority group members perceive their limited opportunities. For example, Mexican-American students in a school system with a substantial percentage of Mexican-American faculty and administrators had more positive educational experiences than those in schools with less minority representation in the staff.[30]

Effective action requires accurate diagnosis of the diverse attitudes toward power in different cultures and recognition of the way these attitudes affect the behavior of organizational members.

SOURCES OF POWER

How can individuals reduce their powerlessness and dependence and meet their need for power? They can draw on the sources shown in Figure 9–2: (1) the position they hold, (2) their personal characteristics, (3) the resources or information they can access and control, and (4) informal networks, trade relations, or alliances they form. Sources of power are ways of developing the power needed to influence behavior, change the course of events, overcome resistance, and convince people to do what they otherwise would not.[31]

POSITION POWER

Individuals frequently derive power from the position or job they hold in an organization. Authority, centrality, and control of rewards and punishments provide position power to individuals or groups.

Authority Managers can exert influence over others simply because of the authority associated with their job. This *legitimate power* results in subordinates obeying a manager's rules or orders. The orders are considered valid due to the po-

FIGURE 9–2   *Sources of power*

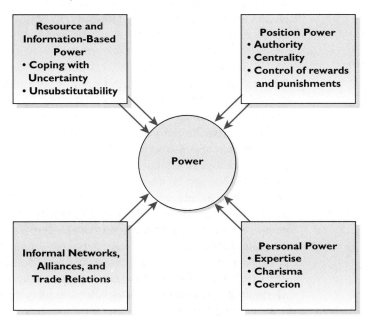

sition the manager holds. Such job holders have the authority to provide direction for and control over the work done by their subordinates simply because they hold a certain position in the hierarchy. One study showed that as a supervisor's legitimate power increased, a subordinate's compliance increased, but his or her satisfaction with supervision decreased.[32] Who has legitimate authority over the computer engineering group at Computer Designers? Gary Snaith, as acting group manager, and Lynda Smerling, as the official group manager, probably have such power over their subordinates, but not with regard to each other.

Centrality Other positions accrue power because of their centrality. The more a position's activities are linked and important to those of other individuals or subunits, the greater its *centrality*.[33] At a large consumer goods company, a product manager has greater centrality than a senior research scientist because the activities of more job holders are linked to the product manager than to the research scientist. Sometimes a job that lacks official authority can develop position power because it becomes central to other positions. The administrative assistant to the chief executive officer of a company can develop such centrality. Consider too the position power of the chief of staff to a U.S. senator or the president. The chief of staff accrues most of his or her power because he or she controls access to the official. The power that results from centrality has been shown to increase when used in conjunction with upward appeal, coalition formation, and exchange by the position holder.[34]

Control of Rewards and Punishments Individuals with position power frequently add to their authority because they control the delivery of rewards and punishments in the organization. An individual may use rewards such as pay raises, status, desirable work assignments, praise, recognition, or group sanctions to encourage compliance by others with desired behaviors or goals.

A manager might also force individuals to behave in certain ways by punishing them. He or she might demote or dismiss them, increase the supervision they receive, or withhold compensation or promotions. A manager effectively uses this power if his or her subordinates believe that obeying the manager will result in the receipt of extrinsic or intrinsic rewards.

PERSONAL POWER

Personal power stems from knowledge or personality traits that allow an individual to influence the behavior of others. Of these, expertise, charisma, and the ability to coerce others into action are especially noteworthy.

Expertise An individual who has unique or special knowledge, skills, and experience may use this expertise as a source of influence and as a way of building personal power. At Computer Designers, Steven Jenkins may exert expertise power because of his special knowledge of the AG project. A dentist can influence patients to act in certain ways because he or she has medical knowledge. A computer specialist can influence nontechnical staff because he or she has special knowledge of computers that is vital to the rest of the staff. As organizations have become increasingly technology oriented, technical support staffs have acquired increased power in organizations.

Charisma Some individuals influence others because they have *charisma,* a personal magnetism that causes others to identify with them and their aspirations.

Individuals with charisma often exert power because they influence others to follow their lead. A movie star, politician, or any organizational member with a charismatic personality may use this as a base of power. Employees may work long hours to meet difficult deadlines simply because their manager has the charisma needed to convince them the project is worth the extra effort.

CITY OF ATLANTA. The successive mayors of Atlanta for the past two decades, Andrew Young and Maynard Jackson, were charismatic African-American leaders who had emerged from the U.S. civil rights movement. Beginning with the November 1993 election, Atlanta voters could choose from a new generation of candidates who lacked the charisma and national stature of these leaders.[35]

Coercion A manager who exerts power by evoking fear has *coercive power.* The president of a company where workers are on strike could threaten to replace any striking workers or take the company into bankruptcy. Thus, the president has coercive power. The use of coercive power often has secondary, dysfunctional consequences. It can create ongoing stress and anxiety for workers. In extreme cases it can lead to increased absenteeism and turnover and may encourage sabotage in the workplace.

RESOURCE- AND INFORMATION-BASED POWER

Access to resources or information is a third major source of power. Resources include money, material, and staff. Individuals who formulate rules to regulate the control of resources, as well as those who actually possess, allocate, and use the resources will acquire power.[36] The person who determines or administers the budget, for example, controls resources and secures power. Workers who control the scheduling of prized machinery or allocation of computer equipment can also acquire resource-based power. In addition, a unit's centrality may interact with its ability to control internal resources in an organization.[37]

We can describe and diagnose the use of resources along three dimensions: (1) internal–external, (2) vertical–lateral, and (3) legitimate–illegitimate.[38] Along the *internal–external* dimension, people may rely on resources internal to the organization, such as exchanging favors or forming networks with other employees. When these sources fail or become inadequate, individuals may turn outside the organization for resources, joining professional organizations or forming alliances outside the organization. The *vertical–lateral* dimension refers to individuals who exert influence by relating to superiors or subordinates as opposed to peers. Mentor–protégé activities occur vertically in the organization. Coalition formation occurs laterally. The third dimension, *legitimate–illegitimate,* contrasts normal-to-extreme behavior. At Computer Designers, for example, Steven Jenkins's request for a promotion was a legitimate exercise of power but his unauthorized borrowing of equipment was not.

Information-based power can accompany the control of resources, but it can also occur independently in organizations. The first individuals in a company who can use the new computer software have information-based power. Such power differs from expert power in its greater transience—expertise is more permanent than information-based power. Information-based power increases when organizat subunits, including specific departments, individual managers, or ad hoc ⌐ of workers, can use information to cope with uncertainty and increas stitutability. Information-based power helps explain the importance of office gossip or the grapevine. People who get information first tend to have more power because they can better deal with uncertainty and are less replaceable.

Coping with Uncertainty Some organizational members can use information to help others reduce workplace uncertainty caused by unclear task demands, a rapidly changing environment, introduction of new technology, or an ambiguous organizational structure. As a result, these managers or nonmanagerial employees may acquire power. In a unionized plant, managers who know the provisions of the current contract may secure information-based power because they can help other managers cope with uncertainty in managing the union workers. So may managers who acquire information about pending layoffs, introduction of new technology, or budgetary shortfalls. Consider a division in a multinational company that experiences a 20 percent budget cutback. The manager who knows which if any workers will lose their jobs in the cutback can arrange for transfers or retraining that will help workers cope with uncertainty. Hence, the manager has power. Or consider the role an R&D department can play in bringing a new technology "on-line" in a company. Not only can the department's members educate workers about the technology, they can also modify it to meet product demands and organizational needs. This department would gain power from its ability to use both information and expertise to help other members respond effectively to environmental and organizational changes.

Boundary-spanner roles, roles associated with positions that interact with individuals or groups in other organizations, have significant power potential. Individuals in such roles as public relations director or purchasing agent deal with the outside environment for the benefit of the organization's members. Their ability to cope with uncertainty for others is one source of power. The ability to channel or control information going to the organization's members is another. Identifying boundary spanners and diagnosing their effectiveness in this role, then, are important means of assessing power in organizations. (See Chapters 7 and 13 for further discussion.)

Unsubstitutability In general, the fewer substitutes there are for the activities of an organizational entity—an individual or group—the more power it has. Consider an organization in which you have worked. Who or which group performed activities that no one else could readily perform? The president was probably less substitutable than a secretary. The chief financial officer may have been more substitutable than the chief information officer. A unit that can bring resources into the organization from the outside may also have low substitutability.

Who in the situation at Computer Designers has power because of their lack of substitutability? Only Steven Jenkins appears to have power because of his unique ability to perform the AG project. In contrast, Gary Snaith clearly is substitutable since Lynda Smerling replaces him. She, too, likely has high substitutability and hence limited power from this source.

INFORMAL NETWORKS, ALLIANCES, AND TRADE RELATIONS

Individuals and groups can acquire power by increasing their contacts with others because they share information and provide support for them. They can build informal networks, foster alliances, and create trade relations.

Informal Networks Informal networks play a significant role in the exercise of power. The operation of the informal network may result in transfer of legitimate authority from a supervisor to an influential subordinate. Managers can identify three types of informal networks.

1. The *advice network* describes the people to whom others turn to get work done.

2. The *trust network* includes the people who share confidential or delicate information.

3. The *communication network* refers to the people who talk to each other about work-related matters.[39]

The following questions help us identify the informal network:

- Who has relevant information?

- To whom does that person communicate the information?

- How many others have access to it?

- What potential sources of power exist in the team?

Developing an informal network of contacts requires spending scheduled and unscheduled time meeting with coworkers and other organizational members. The composition of and interactions in networks of women and minorities likely differ from those of their white male counterparts.[40] Dealing with and penetrating the *old-boys' network* in organizations has been a major challenge faced by upwardly mobile women and minority executives.

WOMEN'S NETWORKS. Women's groups, such as the 100-member Women's Business Network, a program sponsored by the Chamber of Commerce of a Boston suburb, New York's Financial Women's Association, Boston's New England Women in Real Estate, and the National Association for Female Executives, Inc., in New York, the largest program of its kind in the United States with 248,000 members, offer women the opportunity to network with other women in business.[41]

Trade Relations *Trade relationships,* reciprocal relationships and lateral exchanges between parties, contribute to the acquisition and exercise of power. For example, a trainer in the human resources department might exchange a reduction in training budget with the marketing department for subsequent assistance in promoting training programs. Managers participate in trade relationships with other managers by exchanging personnel or other resources to get their jobs done.[42] They can enhance their power by using their reputation for making things happen, forming alliances, holding a position with legitimate authority, and developing a favored status vis-à-vis other peers.

Alliances By forming alliances, special partnerships that attempt to exert concerted influence within or between organizations, managers and employees can influence others without having or using formal authority.[43] Alliances between two or more individuals form when they have resources or favors to exchange. They might exchange currencies such as resources, assistance, cooperation, recognition, visibility, personal support, and gratitude, among others. Such reciprocity can occur between peers, between supervisor and subordinate, or between members of different organizations. Managers then act as integrators or facilitators. They devote larger amounts of time to boundary-spanning activities.[44] A person making an exchange to use influence needs to view the other as a potential ally and understand his or her world. The influencer must also know how to use exchange, focus on effectiveness, and use a repertoire of influence approaches.

An alliance can be organized as a coalition, "an interacting group of individuals, deliberately constructed, independent of formal structure, lacking its own internal formal structure, consisting of mutually perceived membership, issue oriented, focused on a goal or goals external to the coalition, and requiring concerted member action."[45] Allies frequently form a coalition to support a mutual interest. They bring their larger pool of resources to the situation, including greater expertise and commitment. They often act politically to support or oppose an organizational program, policy, or change. Negotiations play a major role in their actions.

THE CHICAGO BOARD OF TRADE AND THE CHICAGO MERCANTILE EXCHANGE. A personality clash between Pat Arbor and Jack Sandner, the presidents of these two exchanges, has prevented them from attaining a larger share of the world's futures and options trading. Attempts to form alliances between the Board of Trade and the Mercantile Exchange through such joint ventures as the development of a computer network that allows 24-hour trading for customers around the world, negotiations for unified banking and clearing of trades, and the development of hand-held trading computers have faltered. Although Arbor and Sandner claim that they can now cooperate, unified action remains elusive.[46]

ORGANIZATIONAL POLITICS

Individuals may secure and exercise power from any of these sources for the sole purpose of advancing their personal goals, causes, ideas, or positions.[47] The resulting actions, which stem primarily from their self-motivations, which often are not directed at the organization's good, and which detract from a rational working of their organization, often are viewed as *organizational politics,* or self-serving power-oriented behavior.[48] Political behavior increases as resources become less available, uncertainty increases, and goals become more complex and difficult to attain. Individuals or groups may use a variety of political tactics, as shown in Figure 9–3.

As individuals attempt to exert power for their own purposes they may conflict with others' attempts, resulting in competing drives for control and power struggles. These struggles may be reflected in personnel selection, performance evaluations, and promotions.[49] In one study, for example, organizational members saw politics as contributing to declining morale, inferior organizational performance outcomes, and increased organizational control.[50] Another study concluded that organizational politics can particularly damage lower status employees, who react by demonstrating increasingly negative attitudes toward the organization.[51] Playing the political game may become so salient for employees that they lose sight of the real goals of the organization, resulting in dysfunctional organizational performance. Ethical concerns often arise about the use of political behavior in organizations. Occasionally, however, organizational politics may result in the airing and interplay of diverse opinions and agendas, resulting in more effective decision making.

FIGURE 9–3　　　　　　　　　*Tactics used to exert influence*

SCALE	DEFINITION
Pressure Tactics	The person uses demands, threats, or intimidation to convince you to comply with a request or to support a proposal.
Upward Appeals	The person seeks to persuade you that the request is approved by higher management, or appeals to higher management for assistance in gaining your compliance with the request.
Exchange Tactics	The person makes an explicit or implicit promise that you will receive rewards or tangible benefits if you comply with a request or support a proposal, or reminds you of a prior favor to be reciprocated.
Coalition Tactics	The person seeks the aid of others to persuade you to do something or uses the support of others as an argument for you to agree also.
Ingratiating Tactics	The person seeks to get you in a good mood or to think favorably of him or her before asking you to do something.
Rational Persuasion	The person uses logical arguments and factual evidence to persuade you that a proposal or request is viable and likely to result in the attainment of task objectives.
Inspirational Appeals	The person makes an emotional request or proposal that arouses enthusiasm by appealing to your values and ideals, or by increasing your confidence that you can do it.
Consultation Tactics	The person seeks your participation in making a decision or planning how to implement a proposed policy, strategy, or change.

SOURCE: Gary Yukl and Cecilia M. Falbe, Influence Tactics and Objectives in Upward, Downward, and Lateral Influence Attempts, *Journal of Applied Psychology* 75 (1990): 133. Used with permission.

SUMMING UP

Let us look at the introductory scenario again. What types of power do the people have? Figure 9–4 summarizes the sources of power each person or group probably uses. Note that the individuals and groups use multiple sources of power. Generally,

FIGURE 9–4　　　　　　　　　*Sources of power in the computer engineering group*

Gary Snaith (Acting Group Manager)
Centrality (limited)
Authority (limited)
Expertise
Access to Resources
Control of Information
Informal Network

Steven Jenkins (Project Leader, AG Project)
Expertise
Coping with Uncertainty
Unsubstitutability

Linda Smerling (Group Manager)
Centrality
Authority
Control of Rewards/Punishments
Coercion
Access to Resources
Control of Information

however, some sources are viewed as having a greater effect than others and as being more appropriate in certain situations. For example, structural (position) and prestige (personal) power as well as ownership power (managers acting as agents of shareholders) have been linked to strategic choices made by top executives.[52] Typically, the more bases of power an individual can draw on, the more powerful that person is.

THE NATURE OF CONFLICT

Conflict refers to a disagreement, opposition, or struggle between two or more individuals or groups. It results from incompatible influence attempts between and within individuals, groups, or organizations.[53] Lynda Smerling and her subordinates experience conflict over her handling of Steven Jenkins. Smerling and Jenkins experience conflict in their feelings about Jenkins's promotion. Conflict often accompanies differences in power among parties.

Conflict most commonly arises from four circumstances.[54] First, conflict can occur when individuals or groups perceive they have mutually exclusive goals or values. Second, behavior designed to defeat, reduce, or suppress an opponent may cause conflict. Third, groups that face each other with mutually opposing actions and counteractions cause conflict. Finally, if each group attempts to create a relatively favored position vis-à-vis the other, conflict may ensue. For example, conflict likely will occur at Computer Designers if Lynda Smerling and Steven Jenkins have different goals regarding the AG project, if she refuses to grant his promotion, if he decides to ignore or even sabotage the AG project, or if she repeatedly reminds him of her superior position.

Conflict can easily occur in multinational or multicultural situations, since basic differences in language, norms, personal styles, and other cultural characteristics hinder effective communication and set the stage for conflict. Cross-cultural sensitivity and understanding are key ingredients for minimizing dysfunctional conflict.

We can describe conflict along a number of dimensions. For example, conflict can be public (overt, visible, and authorized) or private (covert, hidden, and unauthorized), formal or informal, rational (premeditated or logical) or nonrational (spontaneous, impulsive, and emotional).[55] The likelihood of conflict increases when parties interact, view their differences as incompatible, and see conflict as a constructive way of resolving disagreements.[56]

Perceptions play a major role in conflicts. Individuals may frame or cognitively experience conflict along three dimensions.

■ *Relationship/Task.* Parties focus either on their ongoing relationship or the content of the conflict.

■ *Emotional/Intellectual.* Parties pay attention either to the emotional or the cognitive components of the conflict.

■ *Cooperate/Win.* Each party can either attempt to cooperate with the other party or try to win at the other party's expense.[57]

How individuals or groups handle the conflict often depends on the way they frame it along each dimension. For example, by focusing on relationships the parties are more likely to maintain respect for others. By focusing on task the parties may avoid the onus of reacting emotionally. Framing the conflict in one way rather than the other does not guarantee that the conflict will be either functional or dysfunctional. Rather, the outcomes of conflict depend on a variety of factors, described in the next section.

OUTCOMES OF CONFLICT

Conflict can have positive or negative outcomes.

Functional Outcomes Some conflict is beneficial. It can encourage organizational innovation, creativity, and adaptation. Conflict also can result in higher worker enthusiasm or better decisions. Can you think of a personal conflict where such positive outcomes occurred? If so, you may realize that you came to hold a different perspective on an issue or learned that your own perceptions or information had been inaccurate. By exchanging and clarifying thoughts you may have gained insight. Sometimes, conflict leads to a search for new approaches that will resolve disagreements or long-standing problems. The U.S. government, through the constitutional guarantees for free speech and the free press, relies on this type of conflict as a way of ensuring widespread involvement of citizens and sharing of ideas. Conflicting groups, for example, may form an alliance as a way of handling competition for limited resources. Conflict can also energize participants and result in greater productivity because it results in an intensity about task performance.

Dysfunctional Outcomes Conflict can also be dysfunctional for organizations, resulting in reduced productivity, lower morale, overwhelming dissatisfaction, and increased tension and stress. It can arouse anxiety in individuals, increase the tension in an organizational system and its subsystems, lower satisfaction, and decrease productivity. In addition, some people, often the losers in a competitive situation, feel defeated and demeaned. As the distance between people increases a climate of mistrust and suspicion may arise. Individuals or groups may focus more narrowly on their own interests, preventing the development of teamwork. Production and satisfaction may decline. Turnover and absenteeism may increase.

Factors that Influence the Outcomes of Conflict Whether the conflict is functional or dysfunctional depends on several factors.

1. *The sociocultural context.* Differences in sociocultural background between parties will exaggerate barriers and reduce the likelihood of functional conflict resolution.[58]

2. *The issues involved.* Highly significant, long-standing complex issues are more likely to cause dysfunctional outcomes than are trivial, simple, and recently created issues.

3. *Cognitive frame.* Those with cooperative attitudes are more likely to seek a functional outcome than those with competitive attitudes.

4. *Characteristics of the conflicting parties.* The knowledge, experiences, and personal styles of the parties may influence the outcomes of conflict. For example, different outcomes may result if both parties have significant expertise about the issues of the conflict than if neither party has relevant knowledge.

5. ***Misjudgments and misperceptions.*** Errors in perceptions and attributions may cause the parties to act on the basis of inaccurate information, often exaggerating existing conflict or creating new disagreements.

Effective managers learn how to create functional conflict and manage dysfunctional conflict. They develop and practice techniques for diagnosing the causes and nature of conflict and transforming it into a productive force in the organization. To do this, they need to understand the levels and stages of conflict.

LEVELS OF CONFLICT

To manage conflict effectively, managers must diagnose precisely where it exists so they can choose appropriate management strategies. Conflict can occur at the individual, group, and organizational levels.

Individual Level: Role Pressures At the individual level, an individual may experience ***cognitive conflict,*** an intellectual discomfort created by trying to achieve incompatible goals. A design engineer, for example, may be forced to sacrifice the quality of a proposed design change to meet an imposed deadline. ***Affective conflict*** occurs when ***competing emotions*** accompany the incompatible goals and result in increased stress, decreased productivity, or decreased satisfaction for the individual. The design engineer may experience both frustration and excitement in trying to reconcile the incompatible goals. These and other conflicts at an individual level can usually be traced to role conflict and role pressure.

Roles Each person has a prescribed set of activities or potential behavior that constitute a ***role*** that individual performs.[59] Roles can be both formal (vice president) and informal (office gossip). Roles are also found in both work and nonwork settings. Typically, an individual who holds a particular role relates to or interacts with others in comparable or related roles, known as the ***role set.*** A woman may hold the roles of manager, wife, mother, and community activist. As a manager she may even hold the roles of supervisor and subordinate simultaneously. Both role holders and others have ***expectations*** of how a role holder will think and behave.

Role Ambiguity Generally, an individual will operate ***in role;*** that is, according to expectations associated with the role. Occasionally, role holders operate out of role and perform activities typically not associated with their roles, however. In role, a factory worker assembles engines. Out of role, he or she makes heated political oratories during work hours. You might say, however, that such behaviors are not really out of role. People often have differing expectations about the activities that are appropriate to a role, particularly in a complex, global environment. These differing expectations are an example of ***role ambiguity.*** Role ambiguity also occurs when role expectations have not been adequately clarified. The new employee who receives no orientation to the job often experiences role ambiguity because he or she lacks complete information about job activities and responsibilities and the employing organization. One study of information center employees showed a strong link between lack of role ambiguity and job satisfaction.[60]

Role Conflict Differing expectations that pressure a role holder to perform in one way rather than another can result in ***role conflict,*** conflict created by incompatible role expectations of any type. Complying with one set of role-related pressures hinders or prevents compliance with a different set of role-related pressures. For example, top management may expect an accountant to be both detail oriented and accurate as well as fast, processing as many error-free accounts as possible each work day.

A study of senior auditors in a Big Eight (now Big Six) public accounting firm indicated that organizational stressors and personal stressors contributed to role conflict and role ambiguity.[61] Organizational stressors included conflicting objectives, formalized policies, excessive work time requirements and pressures, coordination deficiencies in performing activities, suppression of information, and insufficient decision-making authority. Personal stressors included unacceptable distance from relatives, dissatisfaction with available personal time, and family's attitude toward the accountant's employment. Role conflict and role ambiguity may lead to such dysfunctional work-related behaviors as tension, stress, job dissatisfaction, propensity to leave the organization, and lowered organizational commitment.[62]

Often the multiple roles a person plays create diverse, potentially conflicting expectations. For example, managers who are also spouses and parents might experience role conflict when they must deal with a sick child on the same day a mandatory meeting for all managers is scheduled. Each type of role conflict implicitly or explicitly pressures the role holder to conform to others' expectations. A "good parent" will tend to the sick child. A "good employee" will make the business meeting a top priority. Generally, the more extreme the pressure, the more intense the conflict. We can identify four types of role conflict:

■ *Intrasender*—when one person sends a role holder conflicting or inconsistent expectations. An accountant whose boss tells him or her, on the one hand, to audit as many clients as possible and, on the other hand, to perform accurate, highly detailed audits, may experience intrasender conflict.

■ *Intersender*—when different people with whom the role holder interacts have different expectations of him or her. A dental hygienist may receive different instructions about the nature and extent of tests he or she should provide from the supervising dentist and from patients requesting services.

■ *Interrole*—when the expectations associated with a person's different roles come into conflict. The working mother who has a sick child feels she is expected to be at work and perform her job as well as to be at home and to care for her sick child.

■ *Person-role*—when the activities expected of a role holder violate the individual's values and morals. The devout employee who is asked to work on a religious holiday falls into this category, as does the employee who is pressured to perform unethical acts, such as distorting data to represent the company in a favorable light.

Role Overload When the expectations sent to a role holder are compatible but their performance exceeds the amount of available time or knowledge, *role overload* occurs. A person who holds a full-time job and has too many tasks to complete in the available time likely experiences role overload. So too does a person who is asked to perform tasks that exceed his or her knowledge, skills, or abilities. Overload typifies top-management jobs, where the role holder often has more responsibilities than a single individual can handle.

Individual Level: Interpersonal Conflict When two individuals disagree about issues, actions, or goals and where joint outcomes become important, there is interpersonal conflict. Lynda Smerling and Steven Jenkins may experience interpersonal conflict about his promotion. Interpersonal conflict often arises from differences in individuals' status, perceptions, and orientations. Such conflict may motivate individuals to reveal additional relevant issues or it may prevent any further communication. To further complicate matters, some individuals are more likely to engage in conflict than others. In one study, for example, individuals with a Type A behavior pattern (see Chapter 3) had a higher frequency of conflict than those with a Type B pattern. Women reported a lower frequency of conflict than men.[63]

Group Level Like individuals, groups may also experience either cognitive or affective intragroup conflict. For example, members of a product design team may draw different conclusions about the nature of design specifications and hence experience cognitive or substantive conflict. The group members may even feel excited about different aspects of the design and thereby experience affective conflict, which results from their different emotional responses to the same situation.

Intergroup conflict exists between or among groups, such as marketing and technical services departments. Such conflicts can be traced to competing goals, competition for limited resources, cultural differences, power discrepancies, and attempts to preserve the groups' separate identities.[64] Intergroup conflict also can exist between groups responsible for different aspects of the same process. Design and manufacturing, for example, sometimes clash over the best way to create and bring a new product to market.

Organizational Level While in one sense encompassing all of the previous levels, intraorganizational conflict is diagnosed when conflict characterizes overall organizational functioning. Organizational conflict can be seen when widespread conflict exists within organizational units, such as competition within or between departments or between individual employees. This conflict can be vertical, horizontal, and diagonal.

- *Vertical conflict* occurs between supervisor and subordinates. Managers and subordinates, for example, may disagree about the best ways to accomplish their tasks or the organizational goals. Union representatives and plant managers may argue about work rules throughout the organization.

- *Horizontal conflict* exists between employees or departments at the same level. Marketing and manufacturing may disagree about product specifications or quality standards.

- *Diagonal conflict* often occurs over the allocation of resources throughout the organization—to product development or product sales, for example—or over the involvement of staff people in line decisions.

Some intraorganizational conflict can energize workers and inspire innovation because it reveals new ideas and perspectives. Uncontrolled and unmanaged it can demoralize workers and cause performance to deteriorate because the conflict saps their energy and distracts them from their jobs.

Conflict can also exist between organizations. The amount of conflict may depend on the extent the organizations create uncertain conditions for competitors, suppliers, or customers; attempt to access or control the same resources; encourage communication; attempt to balance power in the marketplace; and develop procedures for resolving existing conflict.[65] Recent attempts to manage such conflict and ensure that it has a positive impact on organizational performance have emphasized the formation of strategic alliances and partnerships.

SEMATECH. SEMATECH, a consortium of U.S. semiconductor manufacturers and the U.S. government was founded to engineer the recovery of the U.S. semiconductor industry. Founded in 1987 by 14 companies, including Digital Equipment, Hewlett-Packard, Intel, IBM, Motorola, and others, the consortium had an operating budget of $200 million annually, half contributed by member companies in proportion to their annual sales and the other half contributed by the U.S. government. Members of the consortium used their financial and personnel resources to recapture market share from the Japanese and to ensure that U.S. companies controlled computer resources essential for the military security of the United States. SEMATECH has focused on improving the technology of chip manufacture and transferring these improvements to member companies. For example, during its first five years the consortium reduced the size of lines etched on chips, causing their manufacturers to regain market share.[66]

Identifying the level of conflict is a prerequisite to selecting appropriate strategies for managing it. Accurate diagnosis also involves specifying the stage of conflict, as described in the next section, since not all conflict involves overt warfare.

STAGES OF CONFLICT

The nature of conflict changes over time. When a group cannot accomplish a goal or complete a task, they experience frustration. Then those involved may perceive that conflict exists and formulate ideas about the conflict issue. They gather information and consider multiple points of view to gain a better understanding of the conflict issue. Those affected respond, resolving the conflict or igniting more conflict.[67] Diagnosing the nature of conflict is aided by considering it as a sequence of conflict episodes. Regardless of the level of conflict, an historical but still useful view suggests that each conflict episode proceeds through one or more of five possible stages, as shown in Figure 9–5: (1) latent, (2) perceived, (3) felt, (4) manifest, and (5) conflict aftermath.[68] By specifying the stage of conflict a manager can determine its intensity and select the best strategies for managing it.

Latent Conflict Conflict may begin when the conditions for conflict exist. Individuals or groups may have power differences, compete for scarce resources,

FIGURE 9–5   *Stages of conflict*

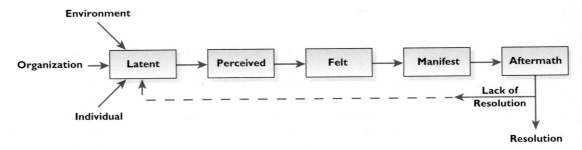

strive for autonomy, have different goals, or experience diverse role pressures. These differences provide the foundation for disagreement and ultimately conflict. Departments such as R&D and production frequently experience latent conflict because of inherent differences in perceptions and attitudes. Can you think of other situations where latent conflict exists or where you have experienced latent conflict? What types of latent conflict exist in the computer engineering group of Computer Designers?

Perceived Conflict When differences of opinion are voiced, when incompatible goals or values become apparent, when individuals demean others or try to enact opposing actions, the conflict moves to the next stage of *perceived conflict.* If Lynda Smerling feels threatened by Steven Jenkins's ambitions, then perceived conflict may exist.

Felt Conflict When one or more parties feels tense or anxious as a result of such disagreements or misunderstandings, conflict has moved beyond perceived to *felt conflict.* Typically there is a time lag between intellectually perceiving that conflict exists and then feeling it "in the pit of your stomach." Here the conflict becomes personalized to the individuals or groups involved. Have you experienced felt conflict? Do you think Lynda Smerling experiences felt rather than perceived conflict?

Manifest Conflict Observable behavior designed to frustrate another's attempts to pursue his or her goals is *manifest conflict,* the most overt form of conflict. Both open aggression and withdrawal of support illustrate manifest conflict. At this stage conflict must be used constructively or resolved if effective organizational performance is to occur. If a physician confronts a nurse about a patient's treatment, manifest conflict may ensue. If the doctor demonstrates anger or if the nurse refuses to support the physician's requests, the conflict would be dysfunctional. If, on the other hand, the doctor or nurse used the manifest conflict as an opportunity for improving problem solving, the conflict might be functional.

Conflict Aftermath The conflict episode ends with its *aftermath,* after the conflict has been managed and the resulting energy heightened, resolved, or suppressed. If the conflict is resolved, the parties may experience a new reality as they adjust their perceptions.[69] Unresolved conflict, which exists everywhere, simply sows the seeds for manifest conflict later. The process continues and is a normal part of organizational life.

STRESS IN ORGANIZATIONS

Stress refers to a psychological and physiological state that results when certain features of an individual's environment challenge that person, creating an actual or perceived imbalance between demand and capability to adjust that results in a nonspecific response.[70] In stressful situations individuals experience first alarm, then resistance, and finally, when their resources are consumed, exhaustion.[71] In the *alarm* stage individuals face a *stressor*—an aspect of the situation that causes a rise in adrenaline and increased anxiety. Stressors include physical challenges, such as heat or disease, as well as role conflict, role overload, task ambiguity, uncertainty, competition, and other aspects of a work or nonwork situation. If the stressor per-

FIGURE 9–6   *A stress episode*

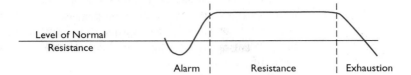

This diagram shows the course of the General Adaption Syndrome. Initially, an adjustive demand causes a stage of alarm and mobilization, and resistance drops below normal. Then, as we begin to adapt, our resistance rises well above normal until, eventually, in exhaustion, resistance falls below normal again.

SOURCE: From Hans Selye, *The Stress of Life.* Copyright © 1956, 1976 by Hans Selye. Used by permission of McGraw-Hill Book Company.

sists, individuals try to respond to it during the **resistance** stage. They may deal with the stressor directly or use it to energize them to greater productivity or creativity. If the stressors persist and create physiological or psychological damage, **exhaustion** has occurred. Figure 9–6 illustrates this progression.

Think about a situation in which you experienced stress. How did you feel? What contributed to the stress? What alleviated it? How did you perform when you experienced stress? You may have felt stress, for example, when you had too many tasks to complete in too short a time, when you failed to advance in an organization, or when you received a promotion and questioned your ability to fulfill your new responsibilities.

The responses to stress are quite varied.[72] Some respond to stress by becoming more productive and creative. Have you ever heard a friend or coworker say "I work best when I have a deadline in sight. I can't do anything productive unless I feel some pressure." This person likely uses the stress resulting from time pressure constructively—to increase his or her productivity. Others experience gastrointestinal, glandular, and cardiovascular disorders or respond to stress by overeating, drinking alcohol excessively, or taking drugs. Others become impatient, detached, or filled with despair.

Still others experience **burnout,** a particular and intense reaction that is represented by emotional exhaustion, the development of negative or impersonal responses to workers, and loss of self-esteem or low feelings of accomplishment.[73] Burnout results in a variety of physical, emotional, interpersonal, attitudinal, and behavioral consequences.[74] For example, the emotional exhaustion that accompanies burnout was associated with decreasing professional commitment and intention by the employees to leave the organization in which they worked.[75] A study of active trade union members indicated that they most often experienced the emotional exhaustion of burnout when intrasender role conflict and qualitative role overload were present.[76]

Physiological and psychological reactions to stress can decrease a person's satisfaction, creativity, and productivity. These behavior changes can in turn increase a person's level of stress, which in turn causes a further decrease in effectiveness.

CAUSES OF STRESS

Stress has become increasingly common in organizations, largely because individuals experience increased job complexity and increased economic pressures.[77] Personal health habits such as exercising, eating a quality diet, and getting enough sleep are negatively associated with stress. Lifestyle changes such as marriage, divorce, beginning a new job, or having a baby have shown a positive relationship to stress.[78] Personality traits have also been shown to contribute to stress.[79] For example, a study of women in public accounting indicated that having a Type A personality or working with someone with a different personality type was positively associated with stress.[80] Individual career characteristics such as occupational level, career stage, and stage of adult development may also cause stress. Individuals at the beginning of their career who are trying to establish themselves often experience stress. *Midcareer crisis* is virtually synonymous with stress. Even facing the changes of retirement creates significant stress for individuals. Table 9–2 lists the major life-stress events for individuals in the United States and also provides a way of calculating the probability that an individual will experience stress-related illness.

TABLE 9–2   *Stress events*

Complete the scale by circling the mean value figure to the right of each item if it has occurred to you during the past year. To figure your total score, add all the mean values circled (if an event occurred more than once, increase the value by the number of times). Life event stress totals of 150 or less indicate generally good health, scores of 150 to 300 indicate a 35–50 percent probability of stress-related illness, and scores of 300+ indicate an 80 percent probability.

LIFE EVENT	MEAN VALUE
1. Death of spouse	100
2. Divorce	73
3. Marital separation from mate	65
4. Detention in jail or other institution	63
5. Death of a close family member	63
6. Major personal injury or illness	53
7. Marriage	50
8. Being fired at work	47
9. Marital reconciliation with mate	45
10. Retirement from work	45
11. Major change in the health or behavior of a family member	44
12. Pregnancy	40
13. Sexual difficulties	39
14. Gaining a new family member	39
15. Major business readjustment	39

TABLE 9–2   *(continued)*

LIFE EVENT	MEAN VALUE
16. Major change in financial state	38
17. Death of a close friend	37
18. Changing to a different line of work	36
19. Major change in the number of arguments with spouse	35
20. Taking out a mortgage or loan for a major purchase	31
21. Foreclosure on a mortgage or loan	30
22. Major change in responsibilities at work	29
23. Son or daughter leaving home	29
24. In-law troubles	29
25. Outstanding personal achievement	28
26. Wife beginning or ceasing work outside the home	26
27. Beginning or ceasing formal schooling	26
28. Major change in living conditions	25
29. Revision of personal habits	24
30. Troubles with the boss	23
31. Major change in working hours or conditions	20
32. Change in residence	20
33. Changing to a new school	20
34. Major change in usual type and/or amount of recreation	19
35. Major change in church activities	19
36. Major change in social activities	18
37. Taking out a mortgage or loan for a lesser purchase	17
38. Major change in sleeping habits	16
39. Major change in number of family get-togethers	15
40. Major change in eating habits	15
41. Vacation	13
42. Christmas	12
43. Minor violations of the law	11

SOURCE: Reprinted with permission from *Journal of Psychosomatic Research,* 11, Thomas H. Holmes, Social Readjustment Rating Scale, Copyright 1967, Pergamon Press, Inc.

Predicting the level of stress in situations can be difficult, largely because stress is often person-specific and can also be culture-specific. Simple requests for overtime or revisions of completed work may cause stress, whereas managing an organization in a competitive environment may not.

DEALING WITH STRESS

Diagnosis of stress is obviously the first step in using or reducing it. A **stress audit,** as shown in Figure 9–7 is useful for such diagnosis and asks questions about the manifestations, causes, and consequences of stress. Effective organizational members must know how to manage stress—when to increase and decrease it by recognizing both its energizing and destructive effects.[81] Managers can encourage productive stress by helping employees build challenge into their work and assume incremental responsibility and autonomy over time. They can also help individuals cope with dysfunctional stress by supporting workers' attendance at stress management programs or eliminating stressors that cause the dysfunctional stress.[82]

McDonnell Douglas. The head of McDonnell Douglas's 2,000-person facilities management division used an Employee Assistance Team to help prepare managers for a major downsizing effort. The company planned to reduce 260 managers at five levels to 170 at three levels. Members of the Transitions team tried to reduce the stress associated with the downsizing by giving a two-hour presentation about alternative career options, ways of telling friends and family about a demotion, and ways of recognizing denial and coping with anger.[83]

Organizations can encourage individuals to secure treatment for symptoms of stress. Many organizations offer health protection, health promotion, and wellness programs.[84] Here are some of the ways leading corporations suggest that employees manage the unavoidable stress of living and working in a global economy.

■ *Get regular exercise.* Many corporations, such as Ameritech in Hoffman Estates, Illinois, provide on-site health clubs where their employees can exercise, relieving some of the physical tension associated with work-related stress.

FIGURE 9–7   *Sample questions in a stress audit*

1. Do any individuals demonstrate physiological symptoms?

2. Is job satisfaction low, or are job tension, turnover, absenteeism, strikes, and accident-proneness high?

3. Does the organization's design contribute to the symptoms?

4. Do interpersonal relations contribute to the symptoms?

5. Do career-development variables contribute to the symptoms?

6. What effects do personality, sociocultural influences, and the nonwork environment have on the relationship between the stressors and stress?

- **Eat well.** Most company cafeterias offer a wide variety of salads, fresh fruit, and other healthy foods, along with nutritional information concerning most offerings. Good nutrition can help the body withstand the rigors of ongoing stress.

- **Monitor personal health.** Many companies sponsor wellness programs that promote healthy lifestyles as well as programs that help employees stop smoking or using other ineffective techniques for coping with stress.

- **Learn to identify and reduce sources of stress.** In addition to courses on stress management, some companies sponsor retreats or seminars on conflict resolution and other personal skills that help employees identify and eliminate needless sources of stress.

Organizations can also redesign jobs or restructure organizations to reduce dysfunctional stress. Or they can change organizational policies and practices, such as by rewarding delegation of responsibilities, positive interpersonal interactions, and constructive conflict resolution.

MANAGING CONFLICT IN MULTINATIONAL AND MULTICULTURAL ORGANIZATIONS

The ease of managing conflict can vary greatly.[85] For example, conflict that involves a matter of principle, large stakes, and a single transaction tends to be more difficult to manage than conflict that involves minor issues, small stakes, and a long-term relationship. Conflict in which one party is viewed as gaining at the expense of the other, has weak leadership, feels harmed, and in which there is no neutral third party available as an intermediary, is difficult to resolve or manage productively.

STYLES OF CONFLICT RESOLUTION

Individuals can use at least five behaviors for dealing with conflict, as shown in Figure 9–8. Avoidance, accommodation, compromise, forcing, and collaborating differ in the extent to which they satisfy a party's own concerns and those of the other party.[86]

Competing Individuals who use the *competing* mode try to satisfy their own concerns. They are unwilling to satisfy others' concerns to even a minimal degree. This strategy works well in emergencies, on issues calling for unpopular actions, in cases where one party is correct in its position, or where one party has much greater power. To improve morale in the computer engineering group, Lynda Smerling might refuse to consider Steven Jenkins's promotion until he returns all equipment and completes the AG project.

Collaboration *Collaborating* emphasizes problem solving with a goal of maximizing satisfaction for both parties. Smerling and Jenkins, for example, might work together to find a way to meet the needs of both of them. Successful collaboration involves seeing conflict as natural, showing trust and honesty toward others,

FIGURE 9–8   *Styles of conflict resolution*

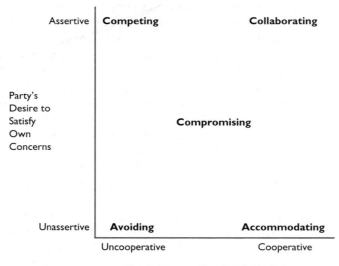

SOURCE: Adapted from K.W. Thomas, Conflict and conflict management. In M.D. Dunnette, ed., *Handbook of Industrial and Organizational Psychology* (New York: Rand McNally, 1976). Used by permission of Houghton Mifflin Company.

and encouraging the airing of every person's attitudes and feelings. Each party exerts both assertive and cooperative behavior. Parties can use it when their objective is to learn, use information from diverse sources, and find an integrative solution. The collaborative process includes three phases:[87]

Phase I—Problem Setting. The problem is defined, resources identified, and a commitment to collaboration by the stakeholders obtained.

Phase II—Direction Setting. Ground rules are established, an agenda set, and subgroups are organized. A joint information search, exploration of options, and reaching of agreement occurs.

Phase III—Implementation. Constituencies are dealt with and external support is built. Compliance with the agreement is monitored.

Compromise *Compromise* represents an intermediate behavior on both the assertiveness and cooperative dimensions. It can include sharing of positions, but not moving to the extremes of assertiveness or cooperation. Hence it often does not maximize satisfaction of both parties. In one study, compromisers had a different communication style from avoiders. They were more likely to focus on communicating information about the job, product, or plan than give messages about rules, regulations, or policies.[88] This style works well when goals are important, but not sufficiently important for the individual or group to be more assertive. It also works when the two parties have equal power or when significant time pressure exists.

Avoidance Individuals or groups may withdraw from or *avoid* the conflict situation. They act to satisfy neither their own nor the other party's concerns. This mode works best when individuals or groups face trivial or tangential issues, they have little chance of satisfying their personal concerns, conflict resolution will likely result in significant disruption, or others can resolve conflict more effectively. Lynda Smerling might handle her conflict with Steven Jenkins over his promotion by avoiding the issue. Of course, this approach might have dysfunctional consequences because the promotion is very important to Steven.

Accommodation Individuals or groups who *accommodate* demonstrate a willingness to cooperate in satisfying others' concerns, while at the same time they are unassertive in addressing their own needs. Accommodating individuals often smooth over conflict. This mode builds social credits for later issues, results in harmony and stability, and satisfies others. Smerling might accommodate herself to Jenkins's wishes by offering him the promotion, expecting that he would offer high-quality performance on the AG project in exchange.

Each style works best in different situations, as suggested in Table 9–3. The behavior an individual or group chooses depends on that party's experiences in dealing with conflict, his or her own personal dispositions in interpersonal relations, as well as the specific elements of a particular conflict episode.

These styles may have significantly different impacts in different cultural settings. When conflicts arise between American and Japanese business people, for example, each tends to use resolution methods successful in their country, which may only antagonize the other party.[89] Westerners operating in Asian cultures need to pay attention to the importance of maintaining face in conflict situations, be sensitive to the value of quiet observation, listen attentively and respect the other party's presence, and discard their own model of effective conflict resolution.[90] Asians, such as the Japanese, in turn, need to be conscious of the differences between their own and Western assumptions. For example, they need to pay attention to differences in problem-solving assumptions. They need to focus on resolving the substantive issues of the conflict, engage in an assertive style, and recognize individual responsibility for conflict resolution.[91]

FORMAL CONFLICT RESOLUTION PROCESSES

Three types of formal processes can address conflicts in organizations and attempt to resolve them: (1) grievance procedures, (2) mediation and arbitration, and (3) negotiation.[92] Diagnosing and then implementing acceptable conflict resolution processes is essential for effective management.

Grievance Procedures Grievance procedures provide a formal process by which workers can complain to management if they feel they have not been treated properly or if their rights have been violated. A formal grievance procedure helps management respond to a worker's complaints and clarifies a worker's contractual work requirements. It also provides a structure for hearing and resolving the complaint. Workers typically file grievances to protest unfair treatment or contractual

CONFLICT-HANDLING MODES	APPROPRIATE SITUATIONS
Competing	1. When quick, decisive action is vital, e.g., emergencies. 2. On important issues where unpopular actions need implementing, e.g., cost cutting, enforcing unpopular rules, discipline. 3. On issues vital to company welfare when you know you're right. 4. Against people who take advantage of noncompetitive behavior.
Collaborating	1. To find an integrative solution when both sets of concerns are too important to be compromised. 2. When your objective is to learn. 3. To merge insights from people with different perspectives. 4. To gain commitment by incorporating concerns into a consensus. 5. To work through feelings that have interfered with a relationship.
Compromising	1. When goals are important, but not worth the effort or potential disruption of more assertive modes. 2. When opponents with equal power are committed to mutually exclusive goals. 3. To achieve temporary settlements to complex issues. 4. To arrive at expedient solutions under time pressure. 5. As a backup when collaboration or competition is unsuccessful.
Avoiding	1. When an issue is trivial or more important issues are pressing. 2. When you perceive no chance of satisfying your concerns. 3. When potential disruption outweighs the benefits of resolution. 4. To let people cool down and regain perspective. 5. When gathering information supersedes immediate decision. 6. When others can resolve the conflict more effectively. 7. When issues seem tangential or symptomatic of other issues.
Accommodating	1. When you find you are wrong—to allow a better position to be heard, to learn, and to show your reasonableness. 2. When issues are more important to others than yourself—to satisfy others and maintain cooperation. 3. To build social credits for later issues. 4. To minimize loss when you are outmatched and losing. 5. When harmony and stability are especially important. 6. To allow subordinates to develop by learning from mistakes.

SOURCE: Kenneth W. Thomas, Toward multi-dimensional values in teaching: The example of conflict behaviors, *Academy of Management Review,* 1977, 2, Table 1, p. 487. Reprinted by permission.

violations, to draw attention to health or safety hazards, or to exercise their power as a test of worker prerogatives.

In a unionized situation, the aggrieved employee presents the complaint orally to the first-line supervisor and union steward. Unresolved grievances then can proceed through a series of appeals until they are satisfactorily resolved. In a nonunionized situation, the grievance procedure may be less formal. Some organizations appoint an ***ombudsperson*** who facilitates the grievance resolution process or represents the worker in dealing with management. The nature and use of grievance resolution procedures may vary in multinational or multicultural settings.

Mediation and Arbitration These third-party interventions use trained individuals to help resolve conflict in organizations in the United States. In *mediation* a neutral party tries to help disputing parties reach a settlement of the issues that divide them. The mediator focuses on bringing the parties to agreement by making procedural suggestions, keeping channels of communication open, helping parties establish priorities, and offering creative solutions. A good mediator tries to determine the true intentions of each party and communicate them to the other.

An *arbitrator,* in contrast to a mediator, acts as a judge in a dispute. Arbitration is a quasi-legal proceeding that resembles a formal judicial procedure but does not take place in a court of law. In arbitration each party presents its position on disputed matters to the arbitrator, who then judges the situation and decides on the disposition of each issue. For example, if a worker files a grievance against his or her employer that he or she was unfairly discharged, an arbitrator will listen to evidence about the matter from both sides and reach a judgment about the fairness and appropriateness of the discharge. The nature of mediation and arbitration may vary considerably outside the United States due to different laws, customs, and values.

Negotiation We examine this process in detail in Chapter 10. There we will show how negotiation can help resolve conflict between two groups.

SUMMARY

Power may be one of the least understood, but most important, areas of organizational behavior. Power refers to the potential or actual ability to influence others in a desired direction. Individuals may exert power upward, downward, or laterally in organizations. Individuals exert power to overcome job-related dependencies. Social exchanges may create power. Also, individuals may have a need for power. Empowerment results in individuals and organizations increasing their power by sharing it with others. Cross-cultural differences also affect the exertion of power.

Individuals and groups may accrue power from a variety of sources. Position power stems from authority, centrality, and control of rewards and punishments. Personal power derives from an individual's or group's expertise, charisma, or use of coercion. Resource- and information-based power accrues to individuals or groups that can cope with uncertainty for others or that are unsubstitutable. Informal networks, alliances, and trade relations also serve as sources of power. Organizational politics, generally considered to be the use of self-serving, power-oriented behavior obtained from any of these sources, typically results in power struggles and other dysfunctional organizational behavior.

Conflict frequently characterizes individuals and groups in organizations. Its consequences can be functional, such as increased creativity and exchange of ideas, or dysfunctional, such as increased stress, absenteeism, turnover, or decreased satisfaction and performance. It can exist within and between individuals, groups, and organizations. Conflict progresses from latent to perceived, felt, and manifest stages, and finally to a conflict aftermath.

Conflict by itself is neither good nor bad. It must be assessed in the context of the individuals, groups, and organizations involved. The effective organizational member may endure or consciously create conflict. Diagnosing its causes should aid in controlling its dysfunctions and encouraging functional ties. Stress experienced by individuals can have significant costs to organizations. Individuals and groups can manage conflict using competing, collaborating, compromising, avoiding, or accommodating styles. Grievance resolution processes, mediation and arbitration, and negotiation can also resolve conflict.

DIAGNOSTIC QUESTIONS

The following questions can help diagnose the nature of power and conflict in an organization.

- Who has power in the organization?

- What dependencies exist in the organization?

- What do individuals exchange for power in the organization?

- Do any individuals have a power-oriented personality?

- How is powerlessness overcome in the organization?

- How do cultural differences affect power in the organization?

- From what sources does power stem?

- Do organizational politics help or hinder the accomplishment of organizational goals?

- Is there conflict in the organization?

- Are the outcomes of conflict functional or dysfunctional?

- What level of conflict exists?

- What stage of conflict exists?

- Do individuals experience stress and what are the consequences?

- How is conflict managed in the organization?

$\mathscr{A}$ctivity 9–1   CATHERINE DEVEREAUX CASE

STEP 1:   Read the Catherine Devereaux Case.

Dr. Catherine Devereaux, a specialist in cross-cultural communication, was an associate director of the Center for American/Asian Relations at Stanford University. The Center (CAAR), a research and teaching project dedicated to improving the quality of communication between American and Asian business leaders, was administered and staffed by a consortium of faculty from several area universities. Although CAAR originally was funded by a grant from a major oil company, the Center also raised a portion of its income from fees paid by business executives who attended short training programs taught at Stanford by Center faculty.

In late 1987, the directors of CAAR began to consider other ways to generate more income for the Center. The original funding was running out and remaining research grants were not adequate to support the Center's activities. In addition to supporting research projects, CAAR offered numerous courses and workshops; published the bi-monthly *Journal of Cultural Communication;* and developed and distributed teaching materials. The total annual budget for CAAR was roughly $400,000.

CAAR had begun offering seminars for executives in 1987. Called "Cultural Communications," these seminars were generally two-day sessions for which participants from industry paid $1,100 each to attend. With the support of an outside marketing and conference firm, Conference Promotions (CP), CAAR ran five of these seminars a year. Under the agreement with Conference Promotions, CAAR was guaranteed $40,000 for each seminar. In 1988, these seminars generated approximately $200,000 in income—half the center's operating budget.

In early 1988, Dr. Devereaux became involved in discussions about future fundraising activities. She and another staff member, Dr. Walter Barnes, had developed two workshops which they believed could become new executive seminars. After a meeting with the Center's advisory board, it was agreed to add the new programs, again with Conference Promotions doing the marketing and organizing. As she proceeded to work up budgets and fees for the new seminars, Dr. Devereaux was mindful of the fact that she had not been very successful in generating research grants. Thus, she hoped to make the new ventures profitable for CAAR.

HISTORY OF CAAR AND THE CULTURAL COMMUNICATIONS SEMINARS

The Center for Asian/American Relations (CAAR) operated under the aegis of Stanford University, but was actually run by a consortium of faculty, graduate students, and staff from several area institutions: the University of California at Berkeley, San Francisco State College, and San Jose State University. The Center had evolved from a series of faculty seminars begun at Stanford in 1980. The seminars, which brought together faculty from a range of disciplines, were regarded as an opportunity for academics to investigate means to further the quality of communication between Asian and American business and government organizations. The Center was housed on the Stanford Business School Campus; faculty associated with CAAR administered their own research projects and taught in the various courses offered.

In 1983, an umbrella organization was formed for the purpose of providing an administrative infrastructure to support the various activities. A three-year grant was obtained from a major oil company, and subsequently renewed, that paid for support staff and services. At the time, CAAR had five separate research programs (later expanded to seven); published a bi-monthly journal; offered several graduate level courses; and distributed a range of printed and audio-visual teaching materials through the CAAR Case Institute.

Dr. Walter Barnes, an associate professor in the political science department at Berkeley, was the Center's first executive director. Under Dr. Barnes, the Center greatly expanded its educational and curriculum development activities and also fostered links with the local Asian business community. At the end of Dr. Barnes' three-year term, Dr. George Stewart, editor of the *Journal of Cultural Communication* and a professor of anthropology at San Francisco State, became executive director.

By this time, 1986, the scope of CAAR activity was such that grant money was not adequate to meet operating expenses. In 1987, the Center began to offer "Cultural Communication" seminars to American and Asian business executives.

When he became executive director in 1987, Dr. Stewart asked Dr. Catherine Devereaux to join CAAR as an associate director. She became the first woman to join the Center in an administrative capacity. (Of the fifteen faculty associated with the Center, two are women.) Dr. Barnes stayed on as an associate director but devoted only a fraction of his time to Center activities. Despite the reduction in time commitment, Barnes continued to have a large impact on the Center. He supervised several research projects and periodically organized multidisciplinary conferences, which in turn attracted additional support—usually in the form of corporate gifts to the Center.

Dr. Devereaux, who knew Dr. Barnes prior to joining the Center, characterized her colleague as follows:

> Walt is important to the organization. He is very committed to CAAR. He's got boundless energy and is a brilliant teacher. The Case Institute is filled with the cases and exercises that he has developed.
>
> When Walt was executive director, a lot of things happened. New programs were developed and new staff and faculty became involved. I think that it's been hard for him to make a transition to associate director. Sometimes he still thinks he runs the show.
>
> He's a real innovator but he also can exaggerate. Walt is a super salesman; he can convince you of almost anything. One of my colleagues says that when Walt walks by, he always checks to see that his wallet is in his pocket. I think that you have to be careful when you deal with him; he can be very persuasive. Generally, I try to stay on his good side.

Prior to joining CAAR, Dr. Devereaux knew Dr. Stewart only slightly. They had been on several panels together at academic conferences on the subject of cross-cultural communication. After working with him for several months, Dr. Devereaux described her impressions of Stewart in the following manner:

> George is a respected academic. He writes a lot and frequently presents papers at professional conferences around the world. Administration is not his strong suit. I don't think he's that interested. He rarely pays attention to the finances and has had only a fleeting interest in the new fund-raising activities under consideration. He teaches in the executive conference, and for awhile he tried to interest some multinational corporations in becoming associates. I guess I would characterize his style as "hands-off."

Devereaux explained that the Center was not hierarchically structured for the professional staff. It was an association of independent professionals who collaborated on certain research and teaching activities but were otherwise independent.

Catherine Devereaux was a professor in the Communications Department at San Francisco State. She was a graduate of Pomona College and received her Ph.D. from the Kellogg School of Management at Northwestern University. In addition to teaching, she was the author of a textbook on organizational behavior and was considered an authority on cross-cultural communication. Dr. Devereaux devoted approximately 50% of her time to research, teaching, and administration at the Center.

HISTORY OF THE EXECUTIVE SEMINARS

CAAR began offering executive seminars at about the time Dr. Devereaux joined the Center. These seminars dealt with aspects of culture and communications as they related to business dealings in the Far East. Early on CAAR had entered into a relationship with Sam Gallagher, the president of a for-profit firm called Conference Promotions. Conference Promotions (CP) both marketed and administered the executive seminars. Gallagher used direct mail as well as professional contacts to recruit participants; his firm also arranged for facilities to be used and managed all of the logistical aspects of the sessions, such as providing for participants' meals and writing materials. According to Dr. Devereaux, "All we do is come in and teach." Further,

> There is no limit on the number of persons who can attend the seminar, and usually between 160–180 pay the $1,100 for the one and one-half days of instruction and workshops. The arrangement between CAAR and CP for these seminars is that no matter what the enrollment, CP will pay CAAR a flat fee. The first year that fee was $25,000

but has been revised upward to $40,000. The advantage to CAAR from this arrangement is that the Center incurs no costs or risk.

The idea to add two new seminars originated with Dr. Barnes. During early discussions about how to increase funding, Barnes said, "We should do what we do well, which is running seminars." He had been working on a new workshop for a program at Berkeley called "U.S.-Japan Trade Relations," which was intended to bring leaders from Japan and the United States together to develop a framework for trade. His suggestion was that he try it out at Berkeley, and, if it proved successful, it could become the model for another executive seminar.

Simultaneously, Dr. Devereaux and he had developed a communications program for Spartan Laboratories, a corporate associate of the Center. Devereaux explained that this program, "Managing Diversity in the Workplace," also had potential as a seminar:

> We ran the Managing Diversity seminar last April at Spartan, and it was great. My idea was always that we would sell the cases and videos we developed for Spartan as a package, and generate funds for the Center that way. But I also saw that it could become an executive program aimed at helping managers deal with the diverse work force of the future.

The two new programs would be longer than the executive program. Barnes would oversee the U.S.-Japan program and Devereaux, the Managing Diversity seminar.

PLANNING THE SEMINARS

In June 1988, staff members from both CAAR and CP met to discuss the new executive programs. Present from CAAR were George Stewart, Walt Barnes, Catherine Devereaux and the administrative director of CAAR, Jane Stuart. CP personnel attending were Sam Gallagher and the vice president for marketing, Pete Larson. Catherine described the meeting as follows:

> It was a breakfast meeting, but it was not a formal planning session in any sense. Walt's U.S.-Japan course had just concluded and so people had a sense of what the program was like. We spent some time describing the "Managing Diversity" project, its translation into an executive program and the distribution of the training materials.

We all agreed that the "Managing Diversity" program would conform to the basic model of the "Cultural Communications" seminar. That is, CP would market and administer it and CAAR faculty would do the teaching. We agreed that in these programs, unlike the Cultural Communications seminars, faculty should be compensated. After all, we were asking for more commitment of time and effort in these programs than in Cultural Communications. Thus, in addition to negotiating about the relative shares of net revenue that would go to CP and CAAR, we would also have to consider how the faculty would be compensated. Would it be a fixed cost, or would it come out of CAAR's share of the revenues? We agreed that Sam Gallagher of CP and I would meet in a few weeks to discuss these issues.

Marketing and distributing the Managing Diversity curriculum materials put us into a new arena. We had developed the materials to be sold to the corporate market as a package. Our idea had been that the Case Institute at CAAR would distribute and sell the materials at a standard price based on the size of a training program a firm might run. For planning purposes, we estimated that the materials (three cases, two videos, hand-outs, and teaching notes) required for a class size of 10 should be priced at $1,800. In our discussions with CP, Sam felt (and we agreed) that he could probably do a better job marketing the package and producing it at a lower cost than our Case Institute. We would need to work out these terms and also some agreement on the copyright of the materials.

The final issue that came up at the meeting was a real surprise. We later called it the "talent agency concept." Walt introduced the issue by saying, "Sam has a problem: CP only makes money if people enroll in the Cultural Communications seminar on-site at Stanford. However, he often gets calls from potential attendees who would rather arrange for in-house training. Sam would like to accommodate them. That is, he would like to arrange for one of our faculty to go on-site and offer the Cultural Communications seminar to a corporate group. In return for finding the client and arranging the on-site Sam would like a share of the fee." I knew that currently when Sam gets these calls he frequently refers them to Walt and George and some of the other faculty.

After the meeting, it was agreed that Barnes and Devereaux would meet with Sam Gallagher separately to work out the arrangements for the U.S.-Japan and Managing Diversity programs respectively. The feeling was that there was no reason that the programs should have the same contract, since they were targeting two different markets and because of the materials component of Managing Diversity.

Catherine and Sam Gallagher met in mid-July. They discussed both the size and the length of the Managing Diversity program. Catherine told Gallagher that the curriculum warranted a three-day program and that the size needed to be limited. Pricing was Sam's expertise.

Gallagher proposed that CP pay CAAR a guaranteed rate based on the number of participants. This was a different structure from the Cultural Communications seminars where CAAR was guaranteed a fixed amount for each seminar. Gallagher explained that Managing Diversity was directed at human resource officers and trainers rather than operating managers. This was a new market, one with less discretionary power to spend company funds than the executive seminar market; therefore, the marketing effort to fill a class would be costly. He would have to do a big mailing with a probable yield of no more than two persons per thousand; he estimated that it would cost him $25,000 to market Managing Diversity. He proposed that CAAR price the program at $2,450 and that CAAR would receive the following share of the revenues:

At 50 attendees, CAAR's share would be $25,000. Above 50 attendees, CAAR and CP would split net revenue, 50/50.

Gallagher's proposal also included a provision for the "talent agency" concept: he proposed that CP get one-third of the fees. On the materials, CP proposed a 50/50 split on the net revenues from their sale. Gallagher ended his presentation by saying, "You realize that these are bargaining positions." (See Figure 9–9 for Gallagher's proposal.)

Because it was summer, Devereaux knew that no one would be around to discuss Gallagher's contract proposals. She was on her own in developing a counter proposal. She sent a memo to Barnes and Stewart outlining what she proposed to do. In it, she outlined some of her concerns:

1. The CAAR/CP split at 50 attendees (30% of the net revenues to CAAR) seemed very generous to CP especially since it would yield only $25,000 to CAAR for three days worth of faculty time investment.

2. CAAR would do better financially under Gallagher's plan as the number of attendees increased. There were two problems here: If Gallagher's marketing efforts faltered and we had only 50 attendees, the income to CAAR might not be worth the effort. Secondly, the structure of the deal was such that it was in both our interests financially to have a lot of people, but what about pedagogically? The attendees were going to be paying top dollar to attend, and would expect faculty attention. As the numbers of attendees increased, so might the time commitment of faculty and the number of faculty who would have to participate.

3. The "talent agency" concept is a problem. As Gallagher proposed it, the revenues from an in-house program would be allocated in the following way: the faculty would charge his/her per diem, CP would take 33%, and CAAR would get the balance to put into general funds. Devereaux wondered why the faculty would agree to such an arrangement.

4. The proposal on the materials seemed okay in its structure. However, given the up-front costs that CAAR incurred in their development, a more reasonable split seemed warranted.

5. There was no mention of faculty salaries in Gallagher's proposal, the presumption being that they would come out of CAAR's revenues.

After receiving her memo, Walt Barnes called Devereaux. He commented, "the split on the seminar is too good a deal for Sam." Barnes suggested that the proposal should be rewritten to make the remuneration very attractive to CAAR at 50 participants. Further, he felt that as part of the agreement, Gallagher should bear the cost of faculty compensation, estimated at $10,000, as a fixed cost. He also felt that the split on the materials should benefit CAAR, as it had undertaken the cost of development.

Devereaux continued to feel uncomfortable with the proposal, particularly since she was the one charged with negotiating the terms. She was not a member of the

FIGURE 9–9   *General contract revisions for discussion (draft 7/13/88)*

1. CP Responsibilities: Same as Cultural Communications Seminar (create, produce, mail, register, on-site preparation and administration).

2. CAAR Responsibilities: Prepare/select program materials on a timely basis. Submit masters to CP and all instructors. Teach program.

3. Financial Arrangements: See attached.

4. In-house: All requests for in-house presentations of this program will be routed through CP. CP will receive 35% and CAAR 65% of all revenues subsequently generated. Faculty consulting fees for in-house presentations will be paid from CAAR's share.

5. Marketing and Resale of Program and Related Instructional Materials: CP will develop a marketing plan for CAAR approval and then be responsible for marketing of program materials. This activity will be at CP's expense. CP will receive 50% of gross revenues and CAAR 50%. CP will either reimburse CAAR for materials at CAAR's cost or produce similar materials at its expense.

6. No complimentary guests.

7. If session is cancelled, no payments made to CAAR.

8. If participants less than 35, 75% gross operating profit to CAAR.

Program on Managing Diversity (Draft)

Assumptions Used for Business Plan

- Three-day program length

- 50 minimum and 100 maximum attendees

- Audience profile
  Human resource executives and trainers
  Teams desirable
  Medium to large organizations

- Price/registration Fee: $2,450

- Variable Cost per attendee: 200 (includes meals and materials)

- Session Expenses
Room rental	$1,000–2,000
Transportation	$1,000–1,750
Contract Labor	$500
Total	$2,500–4,250

- Promotion: Net 1.75–2.0 per 1,000

- Timing: 2–4 sessions per year

(continued)

FIGURE 9–9　　　　　　(continued)

Financial Estimates (Based on 50 Attendees)

Price	$ 2,450
Gross Revenue	122,500
Direct Expense	
Promotion	25,000
Variable	10,000
Session	4,000
CAAR Flat Rate at 50	25,000
Over 50, CAAR Rate is 50% of revenues:	
at 75 attendees	$ 43,375
at 100 attendees	$ 61,750

Stanford Business School faculty and knew that Stanford was sensitive about the use of its name for revenue-producing activities, especially if the instructors involved were not Stanford faculty. The "talent agency" concept, the compensation for program faculty, and joint sales of curricular materials were potentially sticky issues. She decided to consult Richard Warren, a member of CAAR's advisory committee and a well-respected member of the business school faculty.

Warren saw no problem with the materials agreement but suggested that the issues of faculty salaries and referral fees to CP be raised at the next advisory committee meeting. Devereaux described what happened when it was brought up at the meeting:

> Walt was amazing. Remember, he was the one who introduced the talent agency concept at our initial meeting with CP. When we started to discuss it, he diverted attention by linking it with other potentially sticky ethical issues such as the consulting business faculty got from the Cultural Communications conferences. Walt backed off from the talent agency idea when he saw the resistance. On the issue of compensation for teaching in the programs, Warren said that faculty could not be paid extra salary, but that they could be compensated in the form of research funds set aside for their use.

After the meeting, Devereaux prepared her counterproposal to Gallagher. She met with Stewart to review it.

> I told George that I was going to propose a 50/50 split on the program, with faculty salaries as a fixed cost, and based on attendance of 50. On the materials, I felt that a 65/35 split was fair, the larger share reflecting our development costs. I planned to reject the referral fee proposal based on the consensus of the advisory committee. George agreed with my plan. (See Figure 9–10 for the Devereaux's counterproposal.)

After reviewing the proposal with Stewart, Devereaux set up a breakfast meeting with Sam Gallagher. She described his reaction to her revisions:

> Sam didn't like it. He claimed that a 50/50 split would mean that he would have to provide us with a complete accounting of his expenses. I admit I hadn't thought about the need to monitor his costs for such an agreement. He also was not pleased about the rejection of the talent agency fees and our proposal for the materials. He claimed he required the larger share of the materials income because his costs would be higher. He wanted to back off his initial 50/50 split and change it to 65/35 in his favor. The discussion was quite tense.

Between the time Devereaux left Gallagher and returned to her office, Gallagher had telephoned George Stewart to discuss the meeting.

1. CP Responsibilities: Same as Cultural Communications Seminar (create, produce, mail, register, on-site preparation and administration).

2. CAAR Responsibilities: Prepare/select program materials on a timely basis. Submit masters to CP and all instructors. Teach program.

3. Financial Arrangements: See attached.*

4. In-house: This provision is not acceptable to CAAR in any form. Faculty members will continue to make their own arrangements for consulting and in-house training resulting from this program. This is the subject of a Task Force at CAAR.*

5. Marketing and Resale of Program and Related Instructional Materials: This provision is fine in concept, with the following conditions. (1) CAAR will receive 65% of gross revenues, reflecting the development of them, or (2) CAAR will receive a flat rate of $1,800 for each set of materials sold.*

6. CAAR and CP will work out an agreement for low fee attendees.

7. If session is cancelled, no payments made to CAAR.

8. If participants less than 35, 75% gross operating profit to CAAR.

Financial Arrangements

Estimated Budget with 50 Participants for a Three Day Program

Price	$ 2,450
Gross Revenue	122,500
Direct Expense	
Promotion	25,000
Variable	10,000
Session	4,000
	39,000
Faculty Salaries	10,000
	$ 49,000
Net Revenue	$ 73,500
50/50 Share to CAAR	$ 36,750
At 75 attendees with 50/50 split	$ 56,725

*Changes made by CAAR in these items.

George told me that Sam had called and that he was afraid that he had offended me. He wanted to arrange a meeting with the three of us. I said to George, "I can't believe that you took this phone call. If he had something to say about our meeting, he should have called me." George reassured me that Sam was not going behind my back. "Oh no,

Sam thinks the world of you. He wants to give you some consulting." I said, "Listen George, Sam has just done an end run." I was pissed.

George scheduled an informal meeting soon after that with Catherine and Walt. In the meantime, Catherine made an attempt to locate another vendor of the services Sam Gallagher offered. She was concerned that the marketing costs he was quoting were very high and that, without other bids, CAAR was in a weak bargaining position. When she discussed the idea of another vendor, Walt vetoed the idea, saying that they would not be able to obtain such a detailed proposal from another firm.

At the meeting, Barnes proposed that CAAR go with Gallagher's original proposal with the modification that faculty salary be part of the expenses and not taken out of CAAR's share of the revenues. "As usual Walt dominated the meeting," said Devereaux. "George was not that involved. I knew that Sam was getting a great deal from us, but didn't feel that I had support from George to challenge Walt. So I said, sure, go ahead, as long as the salary issue is treated as an expense. With 50 attendees, we would get the $25,000 plus the $10,000 for salaries. We discussed the materials and they went along with my proposal to sell them to CP and then CP could price in such a way that they realized a return on the marketing and production. We agreed that $700 was a reasonable price for CAAR to charge CP given our cost calculations."

A meeting was set with Gallagher for the following week to discuss contracts for the U.S.-Japan and Managing Diversity Programs. In the interim, Devereaux and Barnes had a brief conversation at the monthly Faculty Roundtable. She described their conversation and her reactions to it:

> Walt said, "I saw Sam on Sunday; he was over at our house for lunch. He's a good guy who wants to be a partner with us in these seminars and other ventures." I knew that Sam and Walt had other dealings. Sam refers consulting opportunities to Walt, and Walt has used Sam to organize other seminars conducted under private auspices.
>
> I responded to Walt, "Sam is a nice guy but he is in business, and we are a non-profit group. I just want to make sure that these seminars pay off for CAAR as well as for Sam." Walt said that Sam was interested in helping us raise money and in doing the fair thing.
>
> From my perspective, it was important that the Center get a substantial share of the funds. But it seemed that bringing in funds was secondary to some of the others. As I think about it, I think it was important to me personally because I saw it as a

way for me to bring money into the Center and compensate for my failure to raise substantial research funds.

In November, a breakfast meeting was held at the Hyatt Suburban. The purpose was to establish the contract terms for the two new programs. Present were George Stewart, Walter Barnes, Catherine Devereaux, Sam Gallagher and Pete Larson. Barnes led the discussion.

It soon became evident to Devereaux that "her" program–Managing Diversity–was going to be less profitable than the U.S.-Japan Program that Walt was coordinating. CAAR would be guaranteed $25,000 for U.S.-Japan at 40 participants; it would take 50 attendees before CAAR would receive this amount for Managing Diversity. "Why the discrepancy?" asked Catherine. Gallagher said that it "would be easier to market U.S.-Japan because the Cultural Communications seminar was a direct feeder into it. A special marketing effort would have to be mounted for Managing Diversity because it was a different target audience, thus expenses would be higher." Since we had no way to verify this argument, Catherine accepted it. No one else was interested.

On the sale of materials, CP's proposal was based on the principle of a guaranteed amount. There were problems with this principle in terms of copyrights and the relationship between production costs and price. Devereaux proposed that they agree on a price at which CAAR would sell the materials to CP. Without mentioning numbers, they agreed to meet later to work out a transfer price.

After some additional discussion about the two new programs, Walt produced the new contract proposal. It was supposed to be identical to Gallagher's original proposal with the addition of $10,000 for faculty time as a program expense. After all those present looked over the document, the following discussion took place:

Walt (to Catherine): Are these numbers OK with you?

Catherine: Yes, as far as they go. But I don't see an item for faculty compensation.

Walt: Sam, how do you think we should manage this, the $10,000 for faculty time?

Sam: Well, I could send CAAR's share of the revenues in two checks, and break out the $10,000 that way.

Walt: You mean one check for $15,000 which is our share of the revenues and $10,000 for the faculty salaries?

Sam: Yeah.

Devereaux was speechless at first. Then she said, "My understanding was that faculty compensation was to be regarded as an expense. I understood that this program would raise at least $25,000 for CAAR's general funds if we had 50 people enroll. Now you're telling me that only $15,000 will go into the general funds and CAAR will totally absorb the faculty salaries." Walt told Catherine that she had misunderstood; they had never agreed to treat faculty salaries as an expense. Stewart was silent: Devereaux later reflected on the meeting:

Clearly this had been intentional. It was a performance to coopt me. Basically what we ended up accepting from Sam was his opening offer, an offer that he had called a "bargaining position." We accepted it.

Later I said to George: "I can't believe we accepted his opening offer! All our estimates about the funds these programs could generate were inflated. We need to cut the estimates by at least a third in order to pay the faculty salaries." George told me that I get too excited.

The next day Sam called Catherine to report that he had gone over the numbers and found that his costs were not as high as he thought. Thus, at an enrollment of 40, CAAR would get $25,000 and $32,000 at 50 people and $1,000 per registrant over 50. This was certainly an improvement over his original proposal (Figure 9–9), and came close to my proposal with the exception of the faculty salaries (Figure 9–10).

STEP 2: Prepare the case for class discussion.

STEP 3: Individually, in small groups, or with the entire class, as directed by your instructor, answer the following questions:

DESCRIPTION
1. Describe the interactions between Catherine Devereaux, Walter Barnes, George Stewart, and Sam Gallagher.
2. What types of negotiations did they conduct?

DIAGNOSIS
3. What bases of power did Catherine use?
4. Did she use power effectively?
5. Did she build informal networks, alliances, or trade relations?
6. How effectively did she conduct negotiations inside and outside the organization?
7. What problems arose?

PRESCRIPTION
8. How should she have handled the negotiations more effectively?
9. What additional sources of power should she use?

ACTION
10. What likely would have been the consequences?

STEP 4: Discussion. In small groups, with the entire class, or in written form, share your answers to the questions above. Then answer the following questions:

1. What symptoms suggest a problem exists?
2. What problems exist in the case?
3. What theories and concepts help explain the problems?
4. What should have been done differently?
5. How effective would such actions likely be?

The Catherine Devereaux case was prepared by Jeanne Stanton and Deborah M. Kolb for the Institute for Case Development and Research, Simmons Graduate School of Management, Boston, MA. Copyright © 1989 by the President and Trustees of Simmons College. Reprinted by permission.

Activity 9–2 — DIAGNOSIS OF SOURCES OF POWER

STEP 1: Think of the three people who had the most influence over you in the last year. Choose one experience where each person influenced you. Describe each of these experiences in one paragraph.

STEP 2: In dyads, identify the sources of power used in each experience. Reach consensus with your partner.

STEP 3: With the class as a whole, the instructor will tally the frequency of each source of power used. Then the instructor will ask you to describe the outcomes or consequences (behaviors and attitudes) of each influence experience.

STEP 4: Discussion. In small groups or with the entire class, answer the following questions:

DESCRIPTION

1. Which sources of power were used most frequently? least frequently?

DIAGNOSIS

2. Under what circumstances was each type of power used? Does a pattern emerge?
3. Which types were most effective? least effective?

PRESCRIPTION

4. How could these people tap into additional sources of power?

Activity 9–3 — EMPOWERMENT PROFILE

STEP 1: Complete the following questionnaire. For each of the following items, select the alternative with which you feel more comfortable. While for some items you may feel that both a and b describe you or neither is ever applicable you should select the alternative that better describes you most of the time.

1. When I have to give a talk or write a paper, I . . .
   _____ a. Base the content of my talk or paper on my own ideas.
   _____ b. Do a lot of research, and present the findings of others in my paper or talk.

2. When I read something I disagree with, I . . .
   _____ a. Assume my position is correct.
   _____ b. Assume what's presented in the written word is correct.

3. When someone makes me extremely angry, I . . .
   _____ a. Ask the other person to stop the behavior that is offensive to me.
   _____ b. Say little, not quite knowing how to state my position.

4. When I do a good job, it is important to me that . . .
   _____ a. The job represents the best I can do.
   _____ b. Others take notice of the job I've done.

5. When I buy new clothes, I . . .
   _____ a. Buy what looks best on me.
   _____ b. Try to dress in accordance with the latest fashion.

6. When something goes wrong, I . . .
   _____ a. Try to solve the problem.
   _____ b. Try to find out who's at fault.

7. As I anticipate my future, I . . .
   _____ a. Am confident I will be able to lead the kind of life I want to lead.
   _____ b. Worry about being able to live up to my obligations.

8. When examining my own resources and capacities, I . . .
   _____ a. Like what I find.
   _____ b. Find all kinds of things I wish were different.

9. When someone treats me unfairly, I . . .
    _____ a. Put my energies into getting what I want.
    _____ b. Tell others about the injustice.

10. When someone criticizes my efforts, I . . .
    _____ a. Ask questions in order to understand the basis for the criticism.
    _____ b. Defend my actions or decisions, trying to make my critic understand why I did what I did.

11. When I engage in an activity, it is very important to me that . . .
    _____ a. I live up to my own expectations.
    _____ b. I live up to the expectations of others.

12. When I let someone else down or disappoint them, I . . .
    _____ a. Resolve to do things differently next time.
    _____ b. Feel guilty, and wish I had done things differently.

13. I try to surround myself with people . . .
    _____ a. Whom I respect.
    _____ b. Who respect me.

14. I try to develop friendships with people who . . .
    _____ a. Are challenging and exciting.
    _____ b. Can make me feel a little safer and a little more secure.

15. I make my best efforts when . . .
    _____ a. I do something I want to do when I want to do it.
    _____ b. Someone else gives me an assignment, a deadline, and a reward for performing.

16. When I love a person, I . . .
    _____ a. Encourage him or her to be free and choose for himself or herself.
    _____ b. Encourage him or her to do the same thing I do and to make choices similar to mine.

17. When I play a competitive game, it is important to me that I . . .
    _____ a. Do the best I can.
    _____ b. Win.

18. I really like being around people who . . .
    _____ a. Can broaden my horizons and teach me something.
    _____ b. Can and want to learn from me.

19. My best days are those that . . .
    _____ a. Present unexpected opportunities.
    _____ b. Go according to plan.

20. When I get behind in my work, I . . .
    _____ a. Do the best I can and don't worry.
    _____ b. Worry or push myself harder than I should.

STEP 2: Score your responses as follows:

Total your a responses: _____
Total your b responses: _____

(Your instructor will help you interpret these scores.)

STEP 3: Discussion. In small groups or with the entire class, answer the following questions:

DESCRIPTION

1. Look at the two totals. Which score is highest? Which is lowest?
2. Do your scores describe you well? Why or why not?

DIAGNOSIS

3. Think of some experiences you have had that confirm your score.
4. Think of some experiences you have had that disconfirm your score.
5. How does this information help you to act more effectively in organizations?

"The Empowerment Profile" from *The Power Handbook* by Pamela Cuming. Copyright © 1980 by CBI Publishing. Reprinted by permission of Van Nostrand Reinhold Co., Inc.

Activity 9–4 | FIGHT AT THE INVESTMENT CLUB CASE

STEP 1: Read the Fight at the Investment Club Case.

It started with a fight over Big Macs.

The members of the Golden Years Investment Club rarely disagreed with each other about where to put their money. In fact, most times they left the final decision to Lenn Width, the septuagenarian leader of the group, whose 34-year track record with Golden Years had led *Business Week* to call him "a dazzling role model" for individual investors in a cover story last May.

But on this crisp October evening in 1992, one of the newest members—David Korn, a young architect who had joined the 26-member club a year earlier—decided it was time to dump one of the group's longtime holdings.

"We should sell McDonald's," Korn announced. "It's a stagnant company."

Width was taken aback. He'd been a loyal McDonald's shareholder for years, and had no intention of bailing out now. "It's a growth company," he countered angrily.

"Brinker International and Buffets—those are growth companies," Korn shot back in a voice that now carried an unmistakable tone of condescension. "They're growing at 20, 30 percent a year."

The other members sat in shocked silence; no one ever talked to Width this way.

"They're too speculative," Width said, his voice rising.

Finally, Korn couldn't take it any longer. "I despise McDonald's," he practically shouted. "The bathrooms are filthy, and the food isn't that great."

This is not the sort of exchange that you normally read about in the press coverage of investment clubs, those glowing paeans to the virtues of togetherness. ("Who Needs Merrill Lynch When You Can Get Maxine and Helen?" said the *Chicago Tribune*. "Investment Clubs? They're Just Between Friends," raved the *Vancouver Sun*.) Nor is it something you'd hear them boasting about at the National Association of Investors Corp., an umbrella group for investment clubs. ("If you'd come to one of our national conventions, you'd find it is one of the friendliest places you'll ever visit," says NAIC Chairman Thomas O'Hara.)

But the truth is, once you get beyond the Norman Rockwell-like image of these clubs painted by much of the nation's press—one Illinois group's meetings are "joyously social affairs in which no little time is spent gossiping and catching up," says the *Chicago Tribune*—you'll see that they can deteriorate into snakepits of clashing egos, vindictive political maneuvers and nasty personal attacks. "Oh, yes," concedes the NAIC's O'Hara: "They can be real knock-down affairs."

Just ask David Korn.

To Korn, there seemed no better way to start dabbling in the market than to join an investment club. So when he spotted an ad for an investment-club seminar in the *Seattle Post-Intelligencer* back in May 1991, the budding investor hurried over to the Bellevue Public Library to be among the first in line.

Width, a featured speaker, didn't disappoint. For almost an hour, he regaled the audience with stories from his 35 years as an investor. He told them about how his club, made up entirely of amateurs, was managing a portfolio worth nearly $65,000. He explained how he personally collects thousands in dividends, including $1,000 a year from his largest holding, First Interstate Bank. And he bragged about how he escaped the bloody 1987 market crash, snaring enough profit beforehand to buy himself a brand-new Cadillac. "He gave a beautiful testimonial to the power of investing," Korn says. "I was inspired."

After Width's address, Korn raced to the back of the room, wading through a small cluster of people to shake the speaker's hand. Korn was eager to join an investment club, he explained. Did Width know of any? In fact, he did. Width's own club was looking for new members, and he asked Korn to visit their next meeting. Korn was elated. "Wow," he thought to himself. "I really hit pay dirt."

Who could blame him? The Golden Years Investment Club certainly seems a perfect model for groups of this kind. A collection of middle-age professionals, retirees and a few homemakers, the club meets on the third Thursday of every month in Margaret McManus's cozy Seattle living room to vote on stocks they want to buy and sell. It's all very democratic. Members invest a minimum of $30 every month, which buys them shares in the club. (As in a mutual fund, a share's value is determined by dividing the portfolio's value by the total number of shares.) The more shares the members own, the more votes they have when it comes time to pick stocks.

The club also has a strict investment philosophy, one largely crafted by Width. A stock must have been publicly traded for at least five years; its sales must be growing by 15 percent a year; and it's got to have a return on equity of 10 percent or better. Width also has a special fondness for companies with dividend-reinvestment plans, such as Quaker Oats and Colgate-Palmolive. Known as DRIPs, these plans allow investors to plow their dividends back into more shares without paying broker fees.

It's a conservative strategy that has largely paid off over the years, with steady, if sometimes unspectacular, growth. (That record has faltered in the past few years. The average rate of return since 1984 has been just under 7 percent, according to member Gary Ball, a 47-year-old engineering manager, eight points below what the S&P 500 delivered over that time.) But if other members have different notions of where their money should go, they quickly learn that it is hard to get Width to cede control. "Too expensive," he'll say of stocks that don't meet his criteria. "Too speculative." Alyce Goss, a former office manager, joined Golden Years in 1991 and left in frustration after just three months. "Lenn rules the roost," she says. "It was, 'Either you do it my way or we don't do it at all.'"

Betty Smith, a 62-year-old medical technologist, remembers proposing that the group buy Microsoft back in 1990, when it was trading at $56.50 a share. She had done her homework and knew it was a solid investment. But while other club members responded with interest, Width immediately dismissed the stock. "Too expensive," he said with a wave of his hand. (Microsoft, with two 3-for-2 stock splits, has climbed almost 240 percent since then.)

Even the club's reading materials have to pass muster with the founder. At one recent meeting, a member suggested they buy a $289 subscription to the biweekly *Red Chip Review,* which covers stocks in the Western states. When a sample copy made the rounds, Width flipped casually through it and then placed it firmly in his lap, refusing to pass it along. "We already have this information," he said, staring blankly around the room. End of discussion. Says Harry Hughes, a 64-year-old retired naval officer: "I think a lot of us are in awe of Lenn."

Width, 75, doesn't dispute that he's bossy. "I imagine some people think of this as my club," he says. "And in many ways it is."

Knowing little of the group's dynamics when he joined up, Korn was soon to get a quick education in the way things worked. "Let's sell Clearly Canadian," he suggested at his second meeting, not aware it was one of Width's favorite stocks. Briskly rebuffed, he kept trying. "Let's buy Boise Cascade." "How about Rollins Environmental Services?" "Chambers Development?" Each time the answer was a resounding

no. Too risky, said Width. Too expensive. Too speculative.

Looking back on that meeting, Korn, 35, acknowledges his first ideas weren't all that hot. Clearly Canadian climbed 12 percent in the three months after he wanted to sell it. Boise and Chambers went into a slump, while Rollins climbed some 20 percent before crashing the next year.

But he isn't the type to back down from a challenge. Every night after work and on the weekends, he would spend hours reading everything he could find about the market, from newspapers and magazines to research reports and stock charts. Every lunch hour, he could be found among a huddle of men in Rainier Square, punching up stock prices on a stock-quote machine. "When I'm pushed hard," he explains, "I'll push back."

Korn's hard work finally paid off in August 1992—more than a year after he'd joined the club. Based on its increasing profit margins and growth potential, Korn stood up and recommended buying Structural Dynamics Research, an engineering-software maker, at about $12 a share. Club President Gary Ball knew the company well and liked it, too. When Width weighed in with his yes vote, the deal was done. (The group sold the stock last year for a profit of $780, or about $4 a share.)

Emboldened by his success, that night Korn volunteered to take on a big project for the club: He and Betty Smith would review all the stocks in its portfolio and compare them with others in the same industries. Ball was all for the exercise. He'd been trying to make the club more democratic for some time, and this seemed like an excellent way to start.

For the next month, Korn and Smith went all out. Studying individually each night and meeting once a week after work, they thoroughly researched all 17 stocks in the club, plus 38 others that might be better alternatives. When they reported back to the members at the next meeting, their hour-long presentation made quite a splash. Ball was impressed, and he urged the other members to review the proposals carefully. "I asked myself, 'How did we pick these stocks in our portfolio? How did this happen?'" Ball says. "It did not make Lenn look good."

That message wasn't lost on Width. Though he wasn't at the meeting—it was the first one he'd missed in years—word got back to him fast. And he wasn't pleased. "My feeling was, here's this kid who's only been around 12 or 14 months and he's trying to change everything we've worked on for years," says Width. "I didn't like that. I wasn't going to let that happen."

It probably shouldn't have come as too much of a surprise that Width and Korn were on a collision course. The two could not be more different. Width, a heavyset former lumber-yard owner with a deep, booming voice, has a no-nonsense manner. Korn, a New Jersey native and a graduate of Manhattan's Cooper Union, could easily serve as a poster boy for the New Age generation. An avid student of the martial arts and a follower of a meticulously healthful diet, he traveled to Korea in 1984 and spent three months at a Zen temple, rising every morning at 3:15 to chant and pray and wash his clothes in a nearby stream. At times, he seems to revel in his idiosyncracies, and even conducted one interview for this article from a cordless phone in his bathtub. ("Uh oh," he said at one point, "I think I'm losing water here. Hold on a minute.") "David is unusual," says Betty Smith. "But he's smart."

Korn and Width's relationship, tempestuous from the start, soon went into a tailspin. The worst blow-up came in October, when they locked horns over McDonald's. (Members voted to hang on.) But that was only one of many battles. Though they sat at opposite ends of the room at club meetings, they bickered incessantly. "At every meeting Lenn would suggest that we buy more dividend-reinvestment stocks and David would say we shouldn't be throwing our money away," says John Kelly, a 42-year-old Boeing engineer who has belonged since 1983. "It was awful. It was so tense." Reiko Hurvitz, who had joined in 1992, says she felt like gulping a bottle of Maalox before every meeting. "It seemed like they spent so much time fighting, we barely talked about stocks anymore."

Soon the pair were no longer confining their battles to the group meetings. Noticing that Structural Dynamics had lost nearly five points since August, Width called Korn at work one day to hector him about it. "Did you see the price drop?" he demanded. "Yes, Lenn," Korn sighed. The phone went dead in his ear. Width had hung up.

Korn wasted little time returning fire. The next time he sent in his $30 monthly check, says club treasurer Width, Korn had scrawled a note on the bottom of the check: Structural Dynamics up two points, McDonald's down one. Width didn't find it very funny. "He knew I was the only person who was going to see that," Width complains. "He did it on purpose."

By then it was clear to Width that something would have to be done. Never in the club's history had he been forced to kick anybody out, but increasingly that looked like his only option. Not only was Korn challenging his authority, he seemed to be winning recruits. At the December meeting, Davin Dillon, a friend of Korn's, stood up and suggested buying Amgen, a biotech company that was considerably riskier than anything else in the group's portfolio. Though the stock had gone up almost 35 percent in the past six months and analysts were cheering it on, "I hated Amgen," Width recalls. "I told them it was pie in the sky." The group voted to buy 50 shares at around $76.

Korn was thrilled with the new direction the club seemed to be taking. But that night, as ballots were being passed out for club officers, several members recall Korn's making a crucial misstep.

"I'd like to nominate David as group secretary," Betty Smith proposed. "I think he'll be a good note taker."

"But what about Carol?" asked Ball.

"Hey, I can do a great job with this," Korn insisted.

"But Carol has been our secretary for years," Width said, defending his friend.

"Look, her notes aren't that good," Korn spat back. "I could do a better job than her."

The group sat stone-faced. Later, several members said that Korn had committed a faux pax that angered even some of his staunchest supporters. Korn knew he had overstepped his bounds as well. "I had an immediate feeling that I'd made a mistake," he remembers. "My intention was good, but the execution was poor."

Width sensed an opportunity that night, and he seized it. Soon after the meeting broke up, he drafted a petition calling for the club to disband and start anew—without Korn. "It's either him or me," Width vowed. "And it's not going to be me."

Width spent the next few weeks on the attack, collecting signatures for his petition. It was an awkward time for many members. They respected Width—most of them had joined because of him, after all—but then Korn was in many ways a breath of fresh air. "Personally, I liked David," says member Travis Smith, who signed the petition. "But the biggest part of every meeting was spent listening to them fight. We all realized something had to be done."

In early January, Width made his move. Calling all his supporters, he announced he was planning a secret meeting on Jan. 7 to discuss getting rid of Korn. "Look, David is disruptive," Smith remembers Width telling him. "He's ruining the club." Those who tended to side with Korn, including newly elected President John Kelly, were not invited.

The meeting took place at a conference room in the nearby Northshore Senior Center, where Width is a volunteer. Four tables had been shoved together to make a large conference table, and Width sat at one end, petition in hand, as roughly a dozen members filed silently in.

"You know why we're here," he said, eyeing the group. "I have enough signatures here to disband the club."

Ball, visibly displeased, tried to bluff him. "If you dissolve the club and we sell all the stocks, we'll have to pay taxes" on the profit, he argued. "I don't want to do that."

No problem, Width explained. They'd just pay off people they didn't want in the club with cash. The others would get stock, so they'd hold onto their old portfolio and not have to pay capital-gains tax.

The whole scenario made Grant Haller uncomfortable. The 49-year-old newspaper photographer knew that the conflict between Korn and Width had to be settled, but calling a secret meeting was no way to solve it. "I think there are problems with a club if it can disband and not tell people where they are going to meet the next week," he said. But Width persisted: "It's him or me," he repeated.

Finally, after two hours of debate, they decided to bring the matter up for a vote of the full membership at the club's regular meeting in two weeks.

Korn, who'd been tipped off about the secret meeting by another member, wasn't terribly concerned. He felt he had every right to be an active member of the club, and he wasn't about to back down. Still, his heart was racing as the meeting to decide his fate got under way.

Korn spoke first, breaking the awkward silence. "I have no quarrel with Lenn," he announced. "It's not personal." According to several people in the room, he then turned to Width and challenged him directly: "I know about the secret meeting. You know, the manly thing to do would have been to call me to resolve our disagreement." Width looked away as Korn went on. "How could such a young man as me threaten someone who knows as much as you do?"

Width turned toward his nemesis, blood rushing to his face. "The way I count it, you could be gone right here," he shouted. "There are a lot of people who don't want you here."

Korn couldn't believe that no one was coming to his defense. But he soldiered on. Reaching into a manila folder, he pulled out a list of 45 stocks separated by industry. Twelve were owned by the club. The others were easily outperforming the Golden Years picks. "This comparison explains my point," he said. "It's not about personalities."

Width trembled with anger at this last insult. "It's either him or me," he said, pointing at Korn.

Haller stepped in again. "I don't think this is the proper way to run an organization," he said. Instead, he suggested they rewrite their bylaws to allow the membership to vote on whether Korn could stay. It was agreed, and a committee was formed to handle the chore.

Defeated, Korn headed straight to his car and drove silently home, aware the end was at hand. "I felt sad, not because I was [getting] booted out of the club, but because people had been so inhumane," he says. "No one stood up and said, 'Hey, this is unfair to David.'"

The handwriting was on the wall: When the ballots went out in March, they carried only one line: "Do you favor having David Korn terminated from the club— yes or no?" The vote was 17 to 6 in favor of tossing Korn, with three abstentions.

Korn—who says he never received a ballot—felt a strange sense of relief when he heard the news. At last, it was over. "It wasn't like I was going to get on my hands and knees and beg for forgiveness," he says. "Lenn invited me into the club and he invited me out. That's that." Korn himself has found solace in his new career: He's now a stockbroker.

It's a balmy evening in late April, a year after Korn's ouster. Twelve members of the Golden Years club have gathered in Margaret McManus's tiny living room, sitting knee-to-knee on folding chairs, as plates of homemade chocolate-chip and sugar cookies are passed around. Width is back in control, and there hasn't been an argument in ages. Though members have been punished for buying Amgen—it has tumbled by nearly 50 percent since they bought in—they're certainly glad to have stuck with McDonald's. At $58.88, it's up some 38 percent since Korn dismissed it as "stagnant."

But not everyone is thrilled with the way things are going. Frustrated with the club's meager returns, Ball, who is once again president, has thought about quitting. Betty Smith shows up but has also joined another club. Kelly will come right out and say it: He misses Korn. "It's not the same with David gone," he says. "It will never be the same."

It certainly seems as though there will be few fireworks tonight. Width, decked out in a red sweater with an American flag pinned to his lapel, sits calmly at the far end of the room, while at its center, Edith Smith delivers a lecture on the merits of Aflac, an underwriter of supplemental cancer insurance. It is one of four presentations on Aflac that night, and attention is clearly beginning to flag. Jim Hirning yawns; Leonard Witonsky leafs casually through a flier advertising an upcoming investors' fair. The rest of the group shuffles through stacks of papers, staring blankly at a slide projector illustrating Smith's talk.

The group already owns and likes Aflac, and the consensus seems to be that it's time to load up on more. But Width advises caution, suggesting that further investment should be limited to just $100. "We've just had four presenters show it was a good stock," challenges Haller. "Why don't we buy more?"

Width dismisses the idea. "No. I have a regular method for investing. We don't want to get too excited about a company and start pouring money into it."

"But there were four positive reports," counters Haller. "We like this stock."

Smith and John Kelly huddle near the end of McManus's gold-and-black plaid couch. "I think the group should buy $1,000," Kelly whispers to Smith. "Should I say something?"

"If you do, I'll second it."

A moment later, Kelly clears his throat. "I'd like to motion to buy $1,000," he says.

"Yes, that's a good idea," Smith chimes in.

Width's temper begins to rise. "I don't care," he snaps. "Put $1,000 in the stock if you can. Take a vote. Whatever."

Haller seems taken aback by Width's response. "Why did we spend our time looking at these stocks if no one is going to buy them?" he says. "Why did we do all this work?"

Width throws up his hands and turns his back to the group. "We have this fight every single time and I'm tired of it."

Kelly and Smith sit mute. So do the others.

"Are we going to vote or what?" demands Width.

They do. The club elects to put only another $100 into Aflac.

Width has gotten his way. Again.

STEP 2: Prepare the case for class discussion.

STEP 3: Answer the following questions, individually, in small groups, or with the entire class, as directed by your instructor.

DESCRIPTION
1. Describe the interaction among members of the Golden Years Investment club, particularly between David Korn and Lenn Width.

DIAGNOSIS
2. Is there functional or dysfunctional conflict between the two men?
3. What level of conflict exists?
4. At what stage is the conflict?
5. What causes the conflict?
6. What results from the conflict?

PRESCRIPTION
7. What options are available to improve the situation?
8. What style of conflict resolution did Korn, Width, and other members of the club attempt to use? Was it effective?

ACTION
9. How effective will each option likely be?
10. What costs and benefits probably will result from implementing the prescription?

STEP 4: Discussion. In small groups, with the entire class, or in written form, share your answers to the questions above. Then answer the following questions:

1. What symptoms suggest that a problem exists?
2. What problems exist in the case?
3. What theories and concepts help explain the problems?
4. How can the problems be corrected?
5. Are the actions likely to be effective?

$\mathcal{A}$ctivity 9–5 KING ELECTRONICS

STEP 1: Divide the class into groups of four people. Read the following general description of the situation. The instructor will distribute four roles to each group. Each person in the group should then prepare one role. In preparing for the role play, try to put yourself in the position of the person whose role you are playing.

GENERAL BACKGROUND

King Electronics Company, located in the San Fernando Valley outside Los Angeles, manufactures special government orders on precision instruments. The company has no major product but applies its specialized skills to very complex projects and has done this successfully. Its flexibility in moving from project to project has built a reputation for high quality, for the ability to manufacture precise instruments, and for quick production and delivery.

Many jobs require that proposals with technical and cost information be hand carried to Washington, D.C., by a specific deadline. While management realizes that the nature of its business necessitates rigid time constraints and short time frames, it has been successful because of this opportunistic reaction time. As a result, King Electronics has been rewarded appropriately for its efforts in meeting its customers' demands. See the accompanying organizational chart of the Cost Proposal Section (Figure 9–11).

STEP 2: Each group of four participants should convene the group meeting in part of the room. Your instructor will tell you how much time you have to reach a solution.

STEP 3: Report your group's solution to your instructor.

STEP 4: Discussion. Answer the following questions, in small groups or with the entire class.

DESCRIPTION
1. Characterize each participant's behavior. What style did they use?

DIAGNOSIS
2. What problems did you encounter in reaching an agreement? Why?
3. Evaluate the effectiveness of conflict resolution in this situation.

Reprinted with permission from Conflict Management by Randolph Flynn and David Elloy, National Institute for Dispute Resolution (Washington, D.C.), Working Paper, 1987.

FIGURE 9–11   *Organizational chart for King Electronics*

Activity 9–6   DIAGNOSIS OF STRESS

STEP 1: Complete the following questionnaire by checking the appropriate column:

Do You Frequently   Yes   No

1. Neglect your diet?
2. Try to do everything yourself?
3. Blow up easily?
4. Seek unrealistic goals?
5. Fail to see the humor in situations others find funny?
6. Act rude?
7. Make a "big deal" of everything?
8. Look to other people to make things happen?
9. Have difficulty making decisions?
10. Complain you are disorganized?
11. Avoid people whose ideas are different from your own?
12. Keep everything inside?
13. Neglect exercise?
14. Have few supportive relationships?
15. Use psychoactive drugs, such as sleeping pills and tranquilizers, without physician approval?
16. Get too little rest?
17. Get angry when you are kept waiting?
18. Ignore stress symptoms?
19. Procrastinate?
20. Think there is only one right way to do something?
21. Fail to build in relaxation time?
22. Gossip?
23. Race through the day?
24. Spend a lot of time lamenting the past?
25. Fail to get a break from noise and crowds?

STEP 2: Score your responses by scoring 1 for each *yes* answer and 0 for each *no* answer. Total your score.

1–6: There are few hassles in your life. Make sure, though, that you aren't trying so hard to avoid problems that you shy away from challenges.

7–13: You've got your life in pretty good control. Work on the choices and habits that could still be causing some unnecessary stress in your life.

14–20: You're approaching the danger zone. You may well be suffering stress-related symptoms, and your relationships could be strained. Think carefully about choices you've made, and take relaxation breaks every day.

Above 20: Emergency! You must stop now, rethink how you are living, change your attitudes, and pay scrupulous attention to your diet, exercise, and relaxation programs.

STEP 3: Discussion. In small groups or with the class as a whole, answer the following questions:

DESCRIPTION

1. What was your score?
2. How much stress does this represent?
3. How does this compare to scores of others in the class?

STEP 4: Think about a stressful situation you have experienced.

1. Describe the situation.
2. What symptoms of stress did you experience at the time?
3. What caused the stress?
4. How did you reduce the stress?

STEP 5: Individually or in small groups, offer a plan for coping with or reducing stress.

Source: Adapted with permission from Stress Index by A.E. Slaby, M.D., Ph.D., M.P.H., *60 Ways to Make Stress Work for You* (Summit, N.J.: PIA Press, 1988).

Activity 9-7 — BEHAVIOR DESCRIPTION QUESTIONNAIRE

STEP 1: Complete the following questionnaire.

Consider situations in which you find that your wishes differ from the wishes of another person. How do you usually respond to such situations?

On the following pages are several pairs of statements describing possible behavior responses. For each pair, please circle the "A" or "B" statement, depending on which is most characteristic of your own behavior. That is, please indicate which of these two responses is more typical of your behavior in situations where you find that your wishes differ from someone else's wishes. In many cases, neither the "A" nor the "B" statement may be very typical of your behavior; but please select the response which you would be more likely to use.

1. **A.** There are times when I let others take responsibility for solving the problem.
   B. Rather than negotiate the things on which we disagree, I try to stress those things upon which we both agree.
2. **A.** I try to find a compromise solution.
   B. I attempt to deal with all of his and my concerns.
3. **A.** I am usually firm in pursuing my goals.
   B. I might try to soothe the other's feelings and preserve our relationship.
4. **A.** I try to find a compromise solution.
   B. I sometimes sacrifice my own wishes for the wishes of the other person.
5. **A.** I consistently seek the other's help in working out a solution.
   B. I try to do what is necessary to avoid useless tensions.
6. **A.** I try to avoid creating unpleasantness for myself.
   B. I try to win my position.
7. **A.** I try to postpone the issue until I have had some time to think it over.
   B. I give up some points in exchange for others.
8. **A.** I am usually firm in pursuing my goals.
   B. I attempt to get all concerns and issues immediately out in the open.

9. **A.** I feel that differences are not always worth worrying about.
   B. I make some effort to get my way.
10. **A.** I am firm in pursuing my goals.
    B. I try to find a compromise solution.
11. **A.** I attempt to get all concerns and issues immediately in the open.
    B. I might try to smooth the other's feelings and preserve our relationship.
12. **A.** I sometimes avoid taking positions that would create controversy.
    B. I will let him have some of his positions if he lets me have some of mine.
13. **A.** I propose a middle ground.
    B. I press to get my points made.
14. **A.** I tell him my ideas and ask him for his.
    B. I try to show him the logic and benefits of my position.
15. **A.** I might try to soothe the other's feelings and preserve our relationship.
    B. I try to do what is necessary to avoid tensions.
16. **A.** I try not to hurt the other's feelings.
    B. I try to convince the other person of the merits of my position.
17. **A.** I am usually firm in pursuing my goals.
    B. I try to do what is necessary to avoid useless tensions.
18. **A.** If it makes the other person happy, I might let him maintain his views.
    B. I will let him have some of his positions if he lets me have some of mine.
19. **A.** I attempt to get all concerns and issues immediately out in the open.
    B. I try to postpone the issue until I have had time to think it over.
20. **A.** I attempt to immediately work through our differences.
    B. I try to find a fair combination of gains and losses for both of us.
21. **A.** In approaching negotiations, I try to be considerate of the other person's wishes.
    B. I always lean toward a direct discussion of the problem.

22. **A.** I try to find a position that is intermediate between his and mine.
    B. I assert my wishes.
23. **A.** I am very often concerned with satisfying all our wishes.
    B. There are times when I let others take responsibility for solving the problem.
24. **A.** If the other's position seems very important to him, I would try to meet his wishes.
    B. I am concerned to work out the best agreed course of action.
25. **A.** I try to show him the logic and benefits of my position.
    B. In approaching negotiations, I try to be considerate of the other person's wishes.
26. **A.** I propose a middle ground.
    B. I am nearly always concerned with satisfying all our wishes.

27. **A.** I sometimes avoid taking positions which would create controversy.
    B. If it makes the other person happy, I might let him maintain his views.
28. **A.** I am usually firm in pursuing my goals.
    B. I feel that differences are not always worth worrying about.
29. **A.** I propose a middle ground.
    B. I feel that differences are not always worth worrying about.
30. **A.** I try not to hurt the other's feelings.
    B. I always share the problem with the other person so that we can work it out.

Scoring the "Behavior Description Questionnaire"

Circle the letters below (and on page 411) which you circled on each item of the questionnaire.

ITEM NO.	COMPETITION (FORCING)	COLLABORATION (PROBLEM SOLVING)	SHARING (COMPROMISE)	AVOIDING (WITHDRAWAL)	ACCOMMODATION (SMOOTHING)
1.				A	B
2.		B	A		
3.	A				B
4.			A		B
5.		A		B	
6.	B			A	
7.			B	A	
8.	A	B			
9.	B			A	
10.	A		B		
11.		A			B
12.			B	A	
13.	B		A		
14.	B	A			
15.				B	A
16.	B				A
17.	A			B	
18.			B		A
19.		A		B	
20.		A	B		
21.		B			A
22.	B		A		
23.		A		B	
24.			B		A
25.		A			B

ITEM NO.	COMPETITION (FORCING)	COLLABORATION (PROBLEM SOLVING)	SHARING (COMPROMISE)	AVOIDING (WITHDRAWAL)	ACCOMMODATION (SMOOTHING)
26.		B	A		
27.				A	B
28.	A	B			
29.			A	B	
30.		B			A

Total number of items circled in each column:

Competition	Collaboration	Sharing	Avoiding	Accommodation
_____	_____	_____	_____	_____

STEP 2: Discussion. In small groups or with the class as a whole, answer the following questions:

1. What did your score pattern look like?
2. Do any patterns emerge among groups in the class?
3. Which modes have you found to be most commonly used? least commonly used?
4. Which modes have you found to be most effective? least effective?
5. In what situations has each mode been most effective?

_____

Reprinted with permission from Conflict Management by Randolph Flynn and David Elloy, National Institute for Dispute Resolution (Washington, D.C.), Working Paper, 1987.

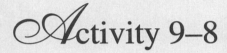

Activity 9–8   THE SUMMER INTERNS

STEP 1: The instructor will divide the class into subgroups of three or four (the latter if an observer is to be used). One person should play the role of Samantha (Sam) Pinder, who will mediate the dispute. The other two parties will play the roles of Brenda Bennett (director of personnel) and Harold Stokes (vice president—engineering), who are having a dispute over the hiring of summer interns.

STEP 2: Each party should read his or her role information and prepare to play the role. Remember to:

1. Empathize with the role. Try to see the world as your assigned character sees it and behave accordingly.
2. Do not add facts that are not in the case.
3. Stay in role. Do not jump out of the role to comment on the process.
4. Try to make it realistic.

The person playing the third party will try to defuse the conflict and seek a resolution. Do not make it unnecessarily difficult for this person; "play along" to observe how third party dispute resolution can work. On the other hand, you are not required to settle if you believe that your character's needs are truly not being met by the proposed agreement.

STEP 3: Sam Pinder will "lead" each small group in an effort to resolve the Summer Interns problem. When you have achieved a resolution, write it down so you can report it to the class later.

STEP 4: Discuss how the mediation session went in each of the small groups. If you had an observer assigned, the observer can comment on the strengths and weaknesses of the mediator's efforts.

STEP 5: Report to the class on the outcome of the mediation session; describe particular problems that may have occurred with the mediation session in your small group.

1. What were some of the different settlements arrived at by different groups?

2. How did your group's specific settlement emerge? How much influence did Pinder have in shaping the final settlement? How much influence did Stokes and Bennett have?

3. Was the mediation process fair? Was the outcome that was achieved fair? What made it fair or unfair?

4. What tactics did the mediator use that were most effective? Least effective?

5. When would it be most useful to use mediation in an organization? When would it be least useful to use mediation?

6. What are some of the major problems and obstacles to using mediation as a manager?

———————

Reprinted with permission of the National Institute for Dispute Resolution, 1726 M Street, NW, Suite 500, Washington, D.C., 20036. Call (202) 466-4764 for further information.

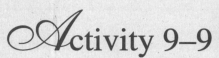 *Activity 9–9*

"MEN, WOMEN, & WORK—SEXUAL HARASSMENT IN THE WORKPLACE"

 ABCNEWS

STEP 1: View the ABC video entitled "Men, Women, & Work—Sexual Harassment in the Workplace."

STEP 2: Individually, in small groups, or with the entire class, answer the following questions:

1. Why is sexual harassment considered a *power* issue?
2. Why is sexual harassment illegal?
3. How common is sexual harassment in the workplace?

4. What constitutes sexual harassment in the workplace?
5. What responsibilities do employees have in cases of possible sexual harassment?
6. What responsibilities do employers have in cases of possible sexual harassment?
7. If you experienced sexual harassment, how would you handle the situation?
8. If you were the manager of a worker who complained of being sexually harassed, how would you handle the complaint?
9. If you were the manager of a worker accused of sexual harassment, how would you handle the complaint?
10. How can you conduct an audit of your organization's policies for dealing with a potential harassment situation?

Chapter 10

Chapter Outline

- Union and Management at Caterpillar
- The Importance of Group Interaction
- Types of Group Interdependence
    - Pooled Interdependence
    - Sequential Interdependence
    - Reciprocal Interdependence
    - Team Interdependence
- Factors that Affect Intergroup Interactions
    - Perceptual Differences
    - Power Differences
    - Task Relations
    - Cross-Cultural Differences
- Improving Intergroup Relations
    - Interpersonal Techniques
    - Structural Mechanisms
- The Process of Negotiation
    - Negotiating Paradigms
    - The Steps in Negotiation
- Negotiation Strategies and Tactics
    - Negotiation Strategies
    - Negotiation Tactics
    - Negotiator Types
    - Cross-Cultural Issues in Negotiations
- Summary
- Diagnostic Questions
- Activities

Managing Intergroup Behavior and Negotiating Effectively

LEARNING OBJECTIVES

After completing the reading and activities in Chapter 10, students will be able to

1. Describe four types of interdependent groups and their behavioral and attitudinal consequences.

2. Diagnose examples of perceptual differences, task relations, and power differences among groups and their influence on intergroup relations.

3. Describe a range of strategies for dealing with interactions between groups.

   Describe the use of negotiation in organizations.

5. Compare and contrast the distributive and integrative bargaining paradigms.

6. Outline the steps in an effective negotiating process.

7. Describe the role of strategies and tactics in negotiations.

8. Offer a protocol for negotiating with and managing relations between culturally diverse groups.

In June 1994, 14,500 workers stormed off the job at Caterpillar, Inc., the U.S.'s largest manufacturer of earth-moving equipment. Almost two years after management won a bitter 5½ month strike, management and the union had not found a compatible way to work together. The company had not returned to its prestrike emphasis on employee involvement, self-managing work teams, and labor–management cooperation, which had resulted in a 30 percent increase in productivity since 1986. Instead, they remained at odds with members of the United Automobile Workers (UAW) over a variety of issues, including reasonable contract provisions.

The strike began in 1992 as a limited strike by 2,400 workers represented by the UAW at plants in Decatur and Peoria, Illinois. Caterpillar management's decision to lock out workers at other plants in Peoria and Aurora resulted in the larger strike, which idled 12,600 workers. Top management refused to yield to the union's demands because they believed that meeting them would prevent Caterpillar from being competitive worldwide. The company won the strike by threatening to permanently replace the striking workers, who were all represented by the United Automobile Workers union.

After management broke the strike, grievances rose significantly. At the Aurora plant, for example, grievances at the last stage of the process before arbitration rose from 20 to more than 300. The union also conducted a work slowdown. Caterpillar has since repeatedly disciplined and fired workers for what the union perceives to be minor actions, including wearing T-shirts that criticize the company. According to the National Labor Relations Board regional director, workers feel indignant about the perceived unjust treatment by management. While management remains concerned about foreign competition, the union wants greater job security. Still, the union perceives management's plans to hire new permanent workers as a threat to their right to strike.[1]

The situation at Caterpillar describes an attempt to resolve a major challenge facing organizations: the problematic interactions of groups within an organization, in this case the union and management. What went wrong at Caterpillar? Why did the union and management experience difficulty in working together? Why has the conflict persisted? Why have negotiations continued to break down? In this chapter we answer these questions by considering the issues associated with intergroup relations. Then we discuss negotiation, a process for reconciling different and often incompatible interests of interdependent parties. We conclude the chapter by examining prescriptions for improving the relations between groups.

THE IMPORTANCE OF GROUP INTERACTION

No two groups in an organization can be truly independent. Typically, one group depends on another for resources, such as raw materials, information, or assistance in performing a task. Obviously, union workers depend on management for their jobs, wages, assignment of responsibilities, and supervision in performing their jobs. We can describe this interdependence in transactional terms, referring to the exchange of resources such as budgeted funds, support services, products, and information between two work units.[2] Work units become more interdependent in three circumstances:

1. Group interdependence increases as more resources are exchanged or more exchanges occur in a given amount of time.

2. Group interdependence increases as a greater variety of resources is exchanged.

3. Group interdependence increases with the extent that resources flow both ways between the groups.

Managers who assess the nature and extent of interdependence in an organization can better understand the potential for conflict. They can interview and observe key organizational members to learn about the exchange of resources. Data about the nature of the work flow, the people with whom group and organizational members interact most frequently, and the types of decisions made by various individuals or groups reflect the nature of interdependence experienced by various groups in the organization.

ALLIED-SIGNAL. The company's mastery of purchasing resulted in a 21 percent increase in profits. The purchasing department regularly interacts with the sales force of its major suppliers. Allied-Signal has insisted that suppliers agree to lower the cost of each component purchased by 6 percent each year.[3]

Intergroup relations also have significant consequences for individual behavior. The interplay of group interactions affects the way a person constructs his or her reality. For example, an individual's position in the organizational structure (upper, middle, or lower) will determine that person's perception of events.[4] These perceptions, in turn, will affect the individual's performance.

TYPES OF GROUP INTERDEPENDENCE

Interdependence occurs in one of four ways, as shown in Figure 10–1: (1) pooled, (2) sequential, (3) reciprocal, and (4) team.[5] The letters A through D in the figure refer to four separate groups. The arrows show whether the groups interact directly and the direction of the interaction. In pooled interdependence, for example, groups A, B, C, and D have no direct interactions. In sequential interdependence the interactions form a definite order: A's actions influence B's, B's in turn influence C's, and so on. In reciprocal interdependence, pairs of groups interact in both directions, in no prescribed order. In team interdependence groups all interact in both directions with every other group. In the next sections we examine each of these types in greater detail. Most groups demonstrate each type of interaction at various times, but often the relationships between groups form a more enduring pattern that can best be described by one of the four types.

FIGURE 10–1

Types of interdependence

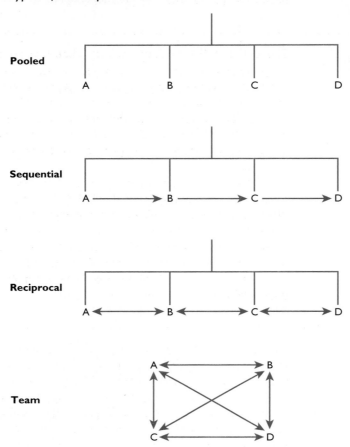

POOLED INTERDEPENDENCE

Groups that rely on each other only because they belong to the same parent organization show *pooled* interdependence. Two stores in a chain such as Home Depot or Wal-Mart show pooled interdependence because their reputations depend on their identification with the parent organization. Two subsidiaries within a conglomerate may show pooled interdependence because they share a common advertising agency or benefit from mass buying power. The maintenance workers and the cafeteria workers in a single organization are two departments that, for the most part, demonstrate pooled interdependence.

NUCOR. Nucor, a steel manufacturer, gives its 21 plant managers a large amount of independence in operating their facilities. Extensive communication between the headquarters and the plant, as well as careful measuring of performance in each plant, results in competition between plants.[6]

Groups with pooled interdependence may obtain their reputation, staff resources, financing, or other services from corporate headquarters. Such groups may sometimes compete for resources, but generally they operate relatively independently. Because these groups have limited interactions, pooled interdependence has few potentially dysfunctional consequences for groups until their representatives need to work together.

SEQUENTIAL INTERDEPENDENCE

Sequential interdependence occurs when one group's operations precede and act as prerequisites for the operations of the second group. In a manufacturing plant, the assembly group and the packing group exhibit sequential interdependence. In the U.S. Postal Service, the postal workers at a central post office demonstrate sequential interdependence with the letter carriers in the local post offices. In a hospital, the nurses have sequential interdependence with the purchasing department. The purchasing department buys supplies that the nurses then use.

Problems may arise in this type of interaction when the first group does not perform its job effectively. If, for example, purchasing does not order required supplies, the nurses may have difficulty meeting the medical needs of their patients. In cases such as this, members of the second group may resent the first group and try to limit their interactions with it, often by using alternative ways to meet their requirements. The nurses, for example, may order too many supplies and then store them until needed. In extreme cases where collaborative relations do not exist between these groups, sabotage may occur.

RECIPROCAL INTERDEPENDENCE

Two groups whose operations precede and act as prerequisites to the other's have reciprocal interdependence. At Caterpillar, union workers and management demonstrate reciprocal interdependence. The two groups must repeatedly interact to perform their jobs effectively. Sales and support staff typically have this type of interdependence. A salesperson selling computer software relies on technical support staff to handle problems users face. The technical support staff requires the sales staff's input in identifying ongoing customer problems.

HALLMARK CARDS. At this greeting card manufacturer, artists, designers, printers, and finance staff depend on each other in designing and producing a card. They work on cross-functional teams to encourage more effective interaction and reduce delays in moving the product among functions.[7]

As the extent of group interdependence increases, that is, as groups move from pooled to sequential to reciprocal interdependence, the potential for conflict and dysfunctional behavior increases correspondingly. Conflict is common when there is reciprocal interdependence.

TEAM INTERDEPENDENCE

Where multiple groups interact, reciprocal interdependences may multiply. In such cases we can characterize the interdependence as parallel to the completely connected communication network (described in Chapter 7). When their functioning is considered over time, each group's operations precede and act as prerequisites for every other group's operations. For example, the various departments supervised by a vice president of marketing—sales, support, advertising, and research—may exhibit this type of interdependence. Or we might characterize the overall interdependence of nurses, physicians, and hospital administration in this way. Groups with team interdependence have the greatest potential for conflict and the highest requirements for effective communication.

FACTORS THAT AFFECT INTERGROUP INTERACTIONS

What factors affect the relationship between the union and management at Caterpillar? In this section we examine perceptual differences, power differences, task relations, and cross-cultural differences as influencing intergroup behavior. Changes in these factors over time likely influenced the dynamics of the interactions between the two groups, as well as their interaction with other groups inside and outside the company.

PERCEPTUAL DIFFERENCES

Perceptual differences, as shown in Figure 10–2, influence group and intergroup interactions. A particular role an individual holds or a group to which he or she belongs influences perceptions.

AMERICAN EAGLE. In early December 1994, pilots of the commuter airline American Eagle refused to fly Avion de Transport Regional (ATR) aircraft. The U.S. Federal Aviation Administration suspected that icing caused the crash of an American Eagle airplane in Roselawn, Indiana, on October 31, 1994, as well as contributed to previous accidents. The airline suspended pilots who refused to fly. Subsequently, the FAA banned the use of the ATR turboprop aircraft in icing and potential icing situations. The Franco–Italian manufacturer of the plane objected to the ban as unnecessary. Differences in the perceptions of the pilots, American Eagle management, and ATR management about the aircraft's safety contributed to problematic interactions between the groups.[8]

The perceptions of group members combine to influence their attitude toward their own and other groups. Clearly, the perceptions of union members toward Caterpillar's management changed as a result of the first strike and management's

FIGURE 10–2   *Nature of perceptual differences*

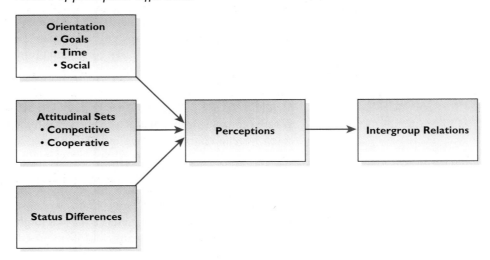

subsequent actions. Similarly, management's perceptions of the value of self-managing teams and employee responsibility were modified as a result of the strike.

Orientations Differences in focus or orientations influence the way one group views another's actions. Groups' goal, time, and social orientations may differ.

Different goals will provide different focuses for group activities. Marketing departments typically concern themselves with the attractiveness of a product to consumers. Research and development groups focus on the product's innovative characteristics and its value to the advancement of scientific knowledge. Production departments emphasize a product's ease of production. What goal differences exist between the union and management at Caterpillar? The union wanted higher wages and job security, whereas management wanted to keep costs low to ease competition with foreign equipment manufacturers. How might these goal differences create perceptual differences? These groups may differ in their perceptions of management's contract offers, discipline procedures, and design of jobs. They may also differ in their perceptions of the purpose of hiring new temporary workers. These differences contributed to the work stoppages at Caterpillar.

Groups also differ in their time orientation—the extent to which they focus on events now and in the future. An R&D department, for example, has a long-term orientation since new product formulation takes long periods of time. In contrast, a production department has a short-term orientation since it focuses on meeting immediate inventory needs. The marketing department may reflect a short-term orientation in its concern for selling the product now, whereas the technical services staff may have a different time orientation in its concern for keeping the product functional over the medium or long term.

How do the union and management at Caterpillar differ in time orientation? Management appears concerned about the long-term financial viability of the company, while the workers seem to focus more on their current economic situation. These differences again influence the nature of the interactions between the groups.

The social or extra-work orientations of the groups might also differ. Consider again the unionized workers at Caterpillar and the nonunionized managers. The professional allegiances and social interactions of groups such as these probably differ. The unionized workers might be more involved with union activities and may choose their friends from other union members. The managers would be oriented toward their professional group—other managers.

Attitudinal Sets The sets of attitudes different groups hold also contribute to their perceptual differences. Diagnosing the differences in attitudinal sets among groups can help managers and other group members plan for possible conflicts. For example, group attitudes may reflect competitive or cooperative feelings about other groups.[9]

■ *Competitive attitude*—a group encourages its members to have negative attitudes toward the task, distrust other group members, dislike other group members, and act without considering others.

■ *Cooperative attitude*—a group encourages trust, mutual influence, coordination of effort, and acceptance of differences between its members and those of other groups.

A second attitudinal set is the extent to which a group (because of its individual members) has a **cosmopolitan** versus **local** orientation.[10]

Cosmopolitans—individuals who have little loyalty to their employing organization, a high commitment to specialized role skills, and tend to orient toward their professional group.

Locals—individuals who have high loyalty to their employing organization, little commitment to specialized role skills, and tend to orient toward their employing organization.

Nurses might have a local orientation and physicians a cosmopolitan one. Production workers might have a local orientation and engineers a cosmopolitan one. If these differences exist for these groups, their perceptions would also differ, creating a major challenge for anyone who wants to meld the groups into a strong team.

Status Differences Individuals' perceptions frequently influence their view of their own *status,* that is, their rank and standing relative to others, in an organization. Often these perceptions lack clarity and validity. If a group of factory workers perceives they have relatively low status compared to a group of managers, they make few demands on the managers, allowing them to direct and organize the factory workers. Or, the workers might feel resentment or jealousy of employees with higher status. For effective performance, each interacting group must understand clearly what the organization and other groups expect of it. The group must then assess whether these expectations fit with its own perceptions of its members' jobs and its members' positions in the organization's hierarchy.

Differences in education, experience, or background may influence perceptions of status. Traditionally, union members and management are perceived to have a different status in organizations such as Caterpillar. Such differences may be reinforced by the rewards assigned in the organization. Differences in identity due to race, gender, ethnicity, and religion also affect perceptions of status. In managing a multicultural work force, managers must ensure that differences are confronted and that distinctions based on these factors do not play a dysfunctional role in intergroup interactions. The managers can use the conflict negotiation approaches described in Chapter 9 and the strategies for managing intergroup relations described later in this chapter for this purpose.

POWER DIFFERENCES

Interacting groups often experience performance difficulties when they differ in the power or the amount of influence and control they have over others. We have discussed power in Chapter 9, but this section highlights three ways power differences affect intergroup relations.

Perceptions of Substitutability If the activities of a group are viewed as replaceable or if another group can perform the same work, the group is considered substitutable. If a group of line managers can train other workers, then these managers may view the trainers in the human resources department as substitutable, diminishing their power. Management at Caterpillar perceives the union workers as substitutable, thereby diminishing their negotiating power.

Ability to Cope with Uncertainty How well a group can deal with and compensate for a rapidly changing environment also influences its power.[11] Typically, engineers can cope with uncertainty better than technicians because of their broader professional training and more diverse experiences. Hence, they have greater power from this source. In some organizations the marketing department can cope with uncertainty better than production because marketing employees can more easily make adjustments for the client. In other organizations the reverse is true. Any difference in the ability to cope with uncertainty would contribute to power differences between the two groups and potentially to dysfunctional intergroup relations.

Control of and Access to Resources The amount of money, people, and time a group controls also influences its power. The greater the amount of resources it controls the more power the group has. Managers who control budgets often have greater power than those who do not. Further, when two groups must divide resources, disagreements often arise about their optimal allocation, creating conflict between them. In hospitals, physicians typically have greater access to resources and more influence over their allocation than do nurses. This may further contribute to differences in power between the two groups.

KAISER PERMANENTE AND THE SERVICE EMPLOYEES INTERNATIONAL UNION. Union organizer Ingrid Nava attempted to increase the power of union workers vis-à-vis management by helping them pressure management from inside the organization. She spent 12-hour days in one of the Kaiser hospitals in California helping workers press for higher wages and a curtailment of staff and hours reductions, thereby exerting more control on resources required for the hospital to function. Nava met with workers in all offices in the hospital, urged them to attend rallies, asked for examples of management abuse, and encouraged workers to petition management about their grievances. Her actions have resulted in workers feeling increased power in dealing with management because they believe that they are not substitutable and help management cope with uncertainty in the workplace through performing their job responsibilities effectively.[12]

TASK RELATIONS

Task relations, the activities or processes that interdependent groups perform and the way these activities interrelate, play a significant role in intergroup relations. Both the interaction of task activities and their clarity or ambiguity have consequences for intergroup relations.

Task Interaction Tasks performed by group members can be independent, dependent, or interdependent of tasks performed by members of the same or different groups, as shown in Figure 10–3.

FIGURE 10–3   *Nature of task interdependence*

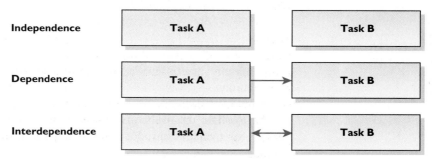

- *Independent*—where one group's task can be done without any relationship to another group's. A machine operator and an accountant can each perform his or her task without any assistance from the other.

- *Dependent*—where one group's task follows and has another's as a prerequisite. Company recruiters depend on line managers to identify the types of personnel required.

- *Interdependent*—where each group's task follows and is prerequisite, at some time, to the others. The copy editor of a publishing firm works on a manuscript provided by an author, who then checks the changes made by the editor.

The nature of task relations generally resembles the nature of interdependence among groups described earlier. Groups showing pooled interdependence most often have independent task relations. Groups showing sequential interdependence most often have dependent task relations. Groups showing reciprocal or team interdependence most frequently have interdependent task relations.

Because the independent task groups have less interaction, they have much less potential for problematic relations with other groups than do those with dependent or interdependent task relations. Interdependent tasks most frequently contribute to problematic relations between interacting groups.

Task Ambiguity The clarity or ambiguity of the task describes whether the interacting groups have clear, predetermined guidelines to follow. Task ambiguity often contributes to difficulty in the groups' interactions, since a particular group may not understand its responsibilities and the requirements of its task. For example, designers of a new product may not understand the boundaries of their job, often infringing on the domains of manufacturing and marketing. This situation also results in more task uncertainty.

CROSS-CULTURAL DIFFERENCES

Groups from different cultures often interact in multinational organizations or as part of interorganizational alliances. Differences in time and social orientations, language, and customs may become exaggerated as two or more groups try to work together. Acknowledging such differences often facilitates intergroup interaction.

IMPROVING INTERGROUP RELATIONS

Managers and employees can use interpersonal techniques and structural mechanisms to improve the relations between groups.

INTERPERSONAL TECHNIQUES

Three techniques can improve interactions between two or more groups: (1) confrontation meeting, (2) organizational mirror, and (3) other third-party interventions.

Confrontation Meeting This one-day meeting requires the two interacting groups to share the problems they face and offer solutions for resolving them.[13] First, a top manager introduces the issues and goals that are the focus of the confrontation. The manager may have identified these issues on the basis of prior discussions with group members. Then, in small subgroups drawn from the various interacting groups, the participants gather more detailed information about the problems they face. Next, representatives from each subgroup report on their findings to the entire group. In natural work groups, participants set priorities for the problems and determine early action steps. They set a concrete agenda about the steps they will take to resolve their problems. Implementation of the plan follows. A top-management team continues to plan and monitor follow-up action. Four to six weeks later the group reconvenes to report its progress.

The confrontation meeting is most effective in dealing with intergroup problems when the following conditions exist. First, there is a need for the total management group to examine its own workings. Second, very limited time is available for the activity and top management wishes to improve the conditions quickly. Third, there is enough cohesion in the top team to ensure follow-up. Fourth, there is real commitment to resolving the issues on the part of top management. Finally, the organization is experiencing or has recently experienced some major change.

Organizational Mirror This set of activities provides a host group with structured feedback about the way it is perceived by various organizational groups.[14] A consultant begins by conducting preliminary interviews with all groups' members. Then he or she reports data from these interviews to the invited and host groups. The groups next discuss the data presented. Small, heterogeneous groups with representatives from the diverse groups meet, discuss the data further (if appropriate), and develop action plans for the problems identified. Implementation of the action plans should follow. Like the confrontation meeting, the organizational mirror requires top management commitment and follow-up for effective action to result.

Third-Party Interventions This approach is frequently used to resolve intergroup conflict, such as the labor–management strife at Caterpillar. As described in Chapter 9, a third party can act as a mediator, arbitrator, or fact finder, as well as provide confrontational or procedural consultation.[15]

CHRYSLER CORPORATION. In 1987, in one of the early moves to self-management, Chrysler managers and UAW officials from the New Castle, Indiana, plant visited Adelaide, Australia, to see how Mitsubishi had converted formerly owned Chrysler plants into a team-management concept. Returning to the United States, both sides agreed that they wanted to keep the plant open. They also recognized that they would need a third party to help transform the plant from top-down management to a team concept. They invited the consultant Kepner-Tregoe to facilitate the change, to act as an objective party and umpire in helping reconcile differences.[16]

In a potentially risky strategy, a third party may *escalate* the conflict as a way of increasing creativity or revealing issues in a way that will ultimately defuse the conflict.[17] The third party may stimulate the conflict by teaching the parties to fight fairly or showing them effective ways to prove their point. Or they may change the conflict's antecedent conditions, such as leadership style or organizational structure. He or she may extend the conflict issues by stressing differences or introducing new facets of existing issues. Bringing in other parties, which may result in coalition formation, can also augment the conflict. Finally, he or she can identify consequences that encourage escalation, such as convincing the party it will lose face if it does not fight for its beliefs. Because of potential side effects and lack of qualified change agents, few individuals and groups request escalative interventions.

In carrying out the intervention, the third party can also assume one of two roles: an interpersonal facilitator or an interface conflict solver.[18] As an *interpersonal facilitator,* the third party assumes an active role of identifying areas of agreement and disagreement between the parties. Contact between parties occurs primarily through the facilitator, who acts as a go-between, message carrier, spokesperson for one or both groups, or a solution proposer. The facilitator deals with the leaders or key members of disputing parties who meet to exchange positions and formulate proposals or counterproposals. This model works best when two people are involved and personal chemistry prevents quality discussion.

As an *interface conflict solver,* the third party leads key members of opposing groups through a series of meetings and activities that identify and resolve differences. He or she sets expectations, establishes group rules, determines the sequence of speaking, ensures candor, curbs the expression of hostility, avoids evaluations, introduces procedures to reduce disagreements, ensures understanding of positions or statements, and checks implementation of agreed-upon changes.

Third parties can also assume peacemaking roles. Women may be particularly skilled and comfortable in performing such roles.[19] In these roles, third parties *provide support, reframe* people's understandings of a situation, *translate* people's perceptions of each other, or *orchestrate* occasions for revealing private conflicts.

STRUCTURAL MECHANISMS

Structural mechanisms such as redesigning formal reporting relationships, adding special managerial roles, or using standard operating procedures more extensively and effectively can improve intergroup relations.

Redesigning Reporting Relationships Interactions between two or more groups generally improve when a common superior is assigned to coordinate the work of the interacting groups. In this position the manager acts as a conduit for information, often setting priorities for interacting groups or individuals and resolving disputes as they occur.

Project, product, matrix, or other integrative structures, which group individuals who work on the same product or project, also facilitate work group interactions (see Chapter 13). In a hospital, for example, a medical team made up of nurses, physicians, social workers, and other support personnel may serve a small group of patients with similar illnesses in the same ward.

Introducing Special Roles or Groups Individuals may be temporarily or informally placed in positions that allow them to act as conduits between interacting groups. The benefit is that they expedite communication by resolving issues through peers, rather than by using a common supervisor to solve them.[20] The trade-off is that the employees who informally perform these linking roles can distort communication and even contribute to conflict if they inaccurately or inappropriately alter information passed between groups.

To prevent this, some organizations appoint a permanent coordinating individual or group of people to act as an interface between interacting groups. A project or product manager, for example, coordinates the decisions of such interdependent groups as sales representatives, R&D engineers, and the production line. A unit manager in a hospital, who may be either a medical or nonmedical person, may fulfill the role of coordinating all activities on a particular medical service such as outpatient, emergency, or obstetrics.

Special groups of representatives from all parties can be convened to work on problems faced by the interacting groups. An example is the *task force,* a temporary group that typically includes representatives from the different constituencies interested in addressing a particular problem. Task forces integrate by presenting the ideas of their group to the others' representatives.

Changing Organizational Procedures, Plans, and Goals A specification of rules and regulations that govern the activities of two groups might also improve their interaction. For example, disagreements between the wait staff and cooks in a restaurant over who managed whom could be resolved by changing the procedures for conveying orders between the two groups. The advantage of introducing clearly specified procedures is that they eliminate the ambiguity about who is responsible for particular tasks and how these tasks should be performed. This frees employees to concentrate their energies on the tasks rather than on interpersonal issues.

Organizations can also use clearly specified plans and goals to direct the activities of interacting groups while minimizing their interaction. By using plans, even the integration of groups geographically distant can be effective. The use of common or superordinate goals can have an influence similar to plans because they create a common focus for the groups' activities.

THE PROCESS OF NEGOTIATION

Negotiation is a process by which two or more interdependent parties use bargaining to reconcile their differences. Most people have had the experience of negotiating an increase in salary or the price of a car. Negotiations also played an important role in the relations between union and management at Caterpillar.

Negotiations typically have four key elements.[21]

- *A degree of interdependence between the parties:* The union and management at Caterpillar depended on each other to perform their jobs.

- *A perceived conflict between the parties:* The union and management disagreed about the provisions of the contract.

- *An opportunistic interaction between the parties:* In their various negotiations the union and management looked for opportunities to influence the other. Each cared about and pursued its own interests and tried to influence decisions to its advantage.

- *The possibility of agreement:* The union and management both hoped they would ultimately agree about the provisions of the contract.

In this section we examine these elements in more detail by looking first at the distributive and integrative paradigms. Then we trace the four stages of the negotiation process.

The negotiating process demonstrates a fundamental tension between the *claiming* and *creating* of value.[22] *Value claimers* view negotiations purely as an adversarial process. Each side tries to *claim* as much of a limited pie as possible by giving the other side as little as possible. Each party claims value through the use of manipulative tactics, forcible arguments, limited concessions, and hard bargaining.

Value creators, in contrast, call for a process that results in joint gains to each party. They try to *create* additional benefits for each side in the negotiations. They emphasize shared interests, developing a collaborative relationship, and negotiating in a pleasant, cooperative manner.

A negotiator incorporates these strategies singly or in combination in one of two basic paradigms. *Distributive bargaining* takes an adversarial or win–lose approach. *Integrative bargaining* takes a problem-solving or win–win approach.

Distributive Bargaining The classical view considers bargaining as a win–lose situation, where one party's gain is the other party's loss. Known also as a *zero-sum* type of negotiation (because one party's gain equals the other party's loss, for a net gain of zero), this approach characterizes the purchase of used cars, property, and other material goods in organizations. It has also been applied to salary negotiations and labor–management negotiations, such as the bargaining at Caterpillar.

Distributive bargaining emphasizes the claiming of value. The choice of opening offers, the ability to influence the opponent to view the situation in a way favorable to the negotiator, and the careful planning of offers and counteroffers can influence the ability to claim value and "win" the negotiation. Power plays a key role in successful distributive bargaining because it increases a party's leverage and ability to shape perceptions.

Integrative Bargaining Recent research encourages negotiators to transform the bargaining into a win–win situation.[23] Here, both parties gain as a result of the negotiations.

XEROX AND THE ACTWU. Three years before the 1992 talks were scheduled between Xerox and the Amalgamated Clothing & Textile Workers Union, Joseph Laymon, Xerox's director of corporate industrial relations, approached the ACTWU about conducting negotiations differently. He proposed that they use smaller negotiating teams, participate in training, identify the best negotiation practices, and end position bargaining. Both sides agreed. They visited selected plants to see the types of productivity gains possible from creating focused factories. They introduced them in 1991. The 1992 negotiations followed significant training in problem-solving, interpersonal, and negotiating skills, among others. The union brought only twelve demands to the table, in contrast to 150 to 200 previously. Management brought seven demands compared to 75 to 150 previously. A contract agreement was reached after a series of preliminary meetings and just one three-hour Saturday meeting.[24]

Known also as a *positive-sum* type of negotiation, because the gains of each party yield a positive sum, this approach has recently characterized international negotiations, labor–management negotiations, and specific job-related bargaining. Integrative bargaining will occur at Caterpillar if the union and management take a win–win approach and can reach a solution that is acceptable to both parties and results in mutual gains.

THE STEPS IN NEGOTIATION

We can identify four basic steps in an effective negotiation for either distributive or integrative bargaining. First, the parties *prepare* for the negotiations. Second, they determine their *best alternative* to a negotiated settlement. Third, they identify their own and the other party's *interests*. Fourth, they make *trade-offs* and in integrative bargaining attempt to create *joint gains* for the parties involved.

Preparation Preparation for negotiations should begin long before the formal negotiation begins. In a labor–management situation, such as the contract negotiation at Caterpillar, both sides should engage in ongoing preparations. Each party gathers information about the other side—its history, likely behavior, previous interactions, and previous agreements reached by the parties. Each party polls its members to determine their wishes, expectations, and preferences regarding a new agreement. Each party might also examine the situation in competitor organizations. Caterpillar management, for example, refused to agree to the same contract provisions that the UAW had reached with John Deere, a major competitor of Caterpillar.

Evaluation of Alternatives The two sides attempt to identify the *bargaining range,* that is, the range in which both parties would find an agreement acceptable. Consider the issue of wages at a unionized company. Assume that the employees represented by a union want an $8.00 per hour wage increase but will settle for $6.00. Figure 10–4(a) illustrates their target price ($8.00) and resistance price ($6.00). Now, assume management wants to pay $2.00 more per hour, but is willing to pay $4.00 more. Figure 10–4(b) illustrates the target price ($2.00) and resistance price ($4.00). The *bargaining range* includes the wages that would satisfy both sides. It is the overlap between the parties' resistance points. Figure 10–4(c) shows that, given the initial resistance points, no bargaining range exists for the employees and management. If, however, the employees' union convinces management's representatives that employee services are more valuable than management originally thought, management may raise its resistance point to $7.00, as shown in Figure 10–4(d). Then, a bargaining range exists between $6.00 and $7.00. In determining this range, each party asks questions such as the following, known as the min–max strategy:[25]

- What is the minimum I can accept to resolve the conflict?

- What is the maximum that I can ask for without appearing outrageous?

- What is the maximum I can give away?

- What is the least I can offer without appearing outrageous?

- What is the minimum the other party can accept to resolve the conflict?

- What is the maximum the other party can ask for without appearing outrageous?

- What is the maximum the other party can give away?

- What is the least the other party can offer without appearing outrageous?

The bargainers determine the alternatives acceptable to them and also identify their *best alternative* if a negotiated settlement is not reached. For some employees,

FIGURE 10–4

Hypothetical bargaining range for wage demands

A. Employees' Demands

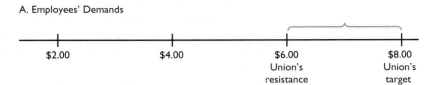

B. Management's Offer

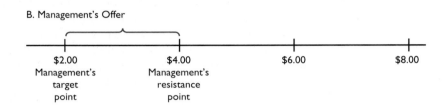

C. No Bargaining Range

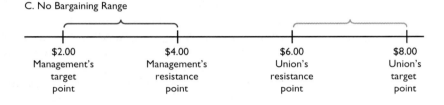

D. Bargaining Range Between $6.00 and $7.00

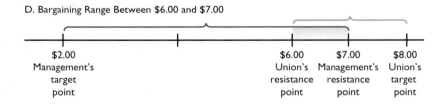

for example, striking might be their best alternative. For others, securing a position outside the company might be the best alternative. Identifying a set of alternatives, including the best one, helps individuals determine whether to continue the negotiation or seek another course of action.

AMERICAN AIRLINES. In 1993, when labor negotiations over a new contract for flight attendants broke down, Robert Crandall, the president of American Airlines, threatened to replace 21,000 flight attendants if they went on strike. He likely viewed this as his best alternative to a negotiated agreement because he viewed this as a way of showing labor that the airline required significant cost-savings. He also called for changes in work rules and the right to use subcontractors to perform jobs previously performed by union workers. His goal was to cut labor costs by as much as 20 percent. United States President Bill Clinton intervened, encouraged management and the flight attendants' union to agree to binding arbitration, and ended the strike. During the five-day strike, American lost between $15 million and $20 million each day, contributing to the company's fourth straight yearly loss. Some labor experts viewed Clinton's action as potentially buoying the power of union and reducing the ability of management to win cost-saving contracts with labor.[26]

The cognitive biases that affect decision making (see Chapter 6) also influence negotiations. The way a negotiator frames a situation (e.g., describing it as a gain or a loss), the nature of the initial anchoring or starting value, the frequency of the situation, and the negotiator's analysis of his or her own abilities to make judgments will also affect the assessment of alternatives and ultimately the progress of the negotiation.[27] Recent research suggests, for example, that bargainers who frame a situation as a possible loss for themselves generally have a better outcome than those negotiators who frame the situation as a possible gain. Viewing the outcome as a possible gain, however, results in more integrative settlements.[28]

Identifying Interests Negotiators act to satisfy their own interests, which may include substantive, relationship, personal, or organizational ones. Managers' or workers' interests can include their reputation, relationship with other parties, long-term organizational goals, various precedents, or even the bottom line. The interests of union and management at Caterpillar might converge on an improved standard of living, creating a positive working relationship with each other, or improving their status vis-à-vis the other party. In focusing on their own interests, a party often ignores or simplifies the interests of the other party, particularly when uncertain future events play a role in each party's interests.[29] The person or group must assess the other party's interests and then decide how to respond to those interests in their offers.

Even though negotiators try to reach agreements on a specific position or a specific issue, the underlying interests are generally broader and may be satisfied by various alternatives. For example, either increasing wages or offering more flexible hours may improve the quality of life for employees. Effective negotiations call for satisfying interests by identifying and exploring a range of possible positions on specific issues.

In assessing what interests are at stake, managers can use the following advice:[30]

- Consider both tangible interests and subtler interests, such as reputation, fairness, and precedent.

- Separate interests from issues and positions. Meeting esteem needs differs, for example, from insisting on a ten percent pay increase.

- Recognize that interests may have either intrinsic or instrumental value. Increased autonomy may have value by itself or may be viewed as a means to accomplish other personal goals.

- Understand that interests depend on perceptions, which are subjective.

- Note that interests and issues can change intentionally or accidentally.

Making Trade-Offs and Creating Joint Gains Bargainers use trade-offs to satisfy their own and others' interests. Recent labor–management negotiations have traded wage increases for job security provisions. Either position (increased wages or better job security) would meet the interests of maintaining a certain standard of living. One way to assess trade-offs is to begin by identifying the best and worst possible outcomes. Next, specify what impact trade-offs will have on these outcomes. Finally, consider whether the changed outcomes will better meet the parties' interests.

In addition to making trade-offs as a way of reaching a satisfactory negotiating outcome, integrative bargaining attempts to create gains for both parties. A party may offer something relatively less valuable to it but more valuable to the other party. Or, the parties may build on shared interests. They may also use economies of scale to create joint gains. Negotiators need to overcome the idea that a fixed pie of outcomes exists, avoid nonrational escalation of conflict, pay attention to others' cognitions, and avoid devaluing the others' concessions while overvaluing their own.[31] Unions that cooperate with management typically reach agreements that benefit both sides and have five key elements:

- gradual loosening of union work rules;

- more union flexibility regarding compensation;

- increased union participation in teams directed at improving quality and increasing production;

- increased availability of corporate cost and profit data to unions;

- retention of collective bargaining rights regarding compensation and work rules.[32]

SCOTT PAPER COMPANY. Unlike its competitor International Paper Company, which attempted to reduce costs by directly attacking the United Paperworkers Union, Scott Paper formed a partnership with union officials beginning in 1990. Together they formed a committee of ten top officials from labor and management. Their intention was to collaboratively work to meet the needs of their various stakeholders—employees, customers, the union, and the community. They significantly reduced costs and increased quality by establishing teams in which workers had more decision-making authority.[33]

The following describes ways of creating joint gains in a variety of circumstances:

- Differences in *relative valuation* can lead to exchanges, directly or by "unbundling" (considering separately) differently valued interests.

- Differences in *forecasts* can lead to contingent agreements when (1) the items under negotiation are uncertain and themselves subject to different probability estimates, or when (2) each party feels that it will fare well under (and perhaps can influence) a proposed contingent resolution procedure.

- Differences in *risk aversion* suggest insurance-like risk-sharing arrangements.

- Differences in *time preference* can lead to altered patterns of payments or actions over time.

- Different *capabilities* of the parties can be combined into a solution that creates value for both sides.

- Other differences (evaluation criteria, precedence and substance, constituencies, organizational situation, conceptions of fairness, and so on) can be fashioned into joint gains.

- *Mutually preferred positions* on single issues can create common value.

- *Shared interests* on a range of settlements can be made salient or linked to create common value.

- *Economies of scale* can lead to the creation of private and common value.[34]

Satisfactory agreements can be either explicit or implicit, as shown in Figure 10–5.[35] An explicit written agreement covers all contingencies and binds the parties by an external enforcement mechanism. An implicit oral agreement offers flexibility for responding to unforeseen circumstances and binds the parties by the nature of their personal relationship.

FIGURE 10–5　　　　　*Continuum of agreements*

Explicit ⟵⟶ Implicit

Relationship of parties
is not dependent on identity,
limited to substance,
and transferable to other
situations.

Communication
is limited, verbal,
and formal.

Exchange of promises
involves specific terms,
with carefully stated
obligations, that are detailed
and measurable.

Performance
involves a clear beginning
and ending to the contract,
inclusion of the future in
the contract, and no requirement
for future cooperation.

Duties
are to self, sharply
divide the costs and
benefits, accept
conflict of interest,
and deal with problems
individually.

Relationship of parties
is dependent on identity,
unlimited in content,
and nontransferable to other
situations.

Communication
is extensive, verbal
and nonverbal, and formal
and informal.

Exchange of promises
involves vague terms,
with ill-defined obligations
that are diffuse
and unmeasurable.

Performance
involves no clear beginning
and ending to the contract,
no inclusion of the future
in the contract,
and a requirement
for future cooperation.

Duties
are to both parties,
with joint costs
and benefits, muted
conflict of interest,
and deal with problems
jointly.

SOURCE: Adapted from R. T. Moran and W. G. Stripp, *Dynamics of Successful International Business Negotiations.* (Houston: Gulf, 1991): 111-112.

NEGOTIATION STRATEGIES AND TACTICS

In effective bargaining situations the negotiators attack the problem, not the people, and treat negotiation as joint problem solving. They remain open to persuasion and explore interests rather than take a position, create multiple options, and try to improve their alternatives in case they do not reach an agreement.[36] In addition, successful negotiators draw upon a variety of negotiation strategies, tactics, and styles, keeping cross-cultural issues in mind.

NEGOTIATION STRATEGIES

Three common negotiation strategies exist: (1) competition, (2) collaboration, and (3) subordination, as described in detail in Table 10–1.

■ A *competitive* strategy, which frequently accompanies distributive bargaining, focuses on achieving a party's goals at the expense of the other party's goals. The group (or individual) may use secrecy, threats, or bluffs as a way of hiding its own goals and uncovering the goals of the other party.

■ A *collaborative* strategy, typically used with integrative bargaining, emphasizes pursuing common goals held by the two parties. This strategy calls on each party to accurately communicate its needs to the other, take a problem-solving approach, and look for solutions that satisfy both parties.

■ A *subordinating* strategy has one party put its goals after the other party's to avoid conflict. This individual or group becomes overly concerned with the other's goals rather than its own or both parties'.

Choosing a strategy may depend on the desired relationship between the negotiating parties and the importance of substantive (content) outcomes to the manager.[37] Figure 10–6 illustrates the way these two dimensions can influence the strategy chosen by one party. In Situation 1, for example, both the relationship outcome and substantive outcome are important to the manager. This calls for **trusting collaboration,** in which both parties demonstrate openness and seek win–win outcomes. Situation 2 calls for **open subordination,** since establishing a relationship overshadows the sub-

FIGURE 10–6   *Considering a unilateral negotiation strategy*

| | | **Is the Substantive Outcome Very Important to the Manager?** | |
		Yes	No
Is the Relationship Outcome Very Important to the Manager?	Yes	**Trustingly Collaborate** when both types of outcomes are very important *Situation 1*	**Openly Subordinate** when the priority is on relationship outcomes *Situation 2*
	No	**Firmly Compete** when the priority is on substantive outcomes *Situation 3*	**Actively Avoid Negotiating** when neither type of outcome is very important *Situation 4*

SOURCE: Reprinted with permission from G. T. Savage, J. D. Blair, and R. L. Sorenson, consider both relationships and substance when negotiating strategically, *Academy of Management Executive* 3(1) (1989):40.

TABLE 10–1 · *Characteristics of negotiation strategies*

COMPETITIVE	COLLABORATIVE	SUBORDINATIVE
1. Behavior is purposeful in pursuing own goals at the expense of the other party.	Behavior is purposeful in pursuing goals held in common with others.	One party consciously subordinates own goals to avoid conflict with other party.
2. Strategy involves secrecy and keeping one's cards close to the vest. It is characterized by high trust in one's self and low trust in the other party.	Strategy calls for trust and openness in expressing one's thoughts and feelings, actively listening to others, and actively exploring alternatives together.	Strategy means that one party is totally open to the extreme of exposing his or her vulnerabilities and weaknesses to the other.
3. Parties have accurate personal understanding of own needs, but publicly disguise or misrepresent them. Neither party lets the other know what it really wants most, so that the other won't know how much it is really willing to give up to attain the goal.	Parties have accurate personal understanding of own needs, and represent them accurately to the other party. Each party has empathy and cares about the needs of the other party.	One party is so concerned with the other's needs that his or her needs are buried or repressed.
4. Parties are unpredictable, mix strategies and the element of surprise to outfox the other party.	Parties' actions are predictable. While flexible behavior is appropriate, it is not designed to take the other party by surprise.	One party's actions are totally predictable. His or her position is always one that caters to the other party.
5. Parties use threats and bluffs and put each other on the defensive. Each always tries to keep the upper hand.	Parties share information and are honest with each other. They treat each other with mutual understanding and integrity.	One party gives up own position to mollify the other.
6. Search behavior is devoted to finding ways of appearing committed to a position. Logical and irrational arguments alike may serve this purpose. Each party engages in destructive manipulation of the other's position.	Search behavior is devoted to finding mutually satisfying solutions to problems utilizing logical, creative and innovative processes and developing constructive relationships with each other.	Search behavior is devoted to finding ways to accommodate to position of other party.
7. Success is often enhanced (when teams or organizations are involved on each side) by creating a bad image or stereotype of the other, by ignoring the other's logic, and by increasing the level of hostility. These tend to strengthen in-group loyalty and convince competitors that one means business.	Success demands that bad stereotypes be dropped, that ideas be given consideration on their merit (regardless of sources), and that hostility not be induced deliberately. In fact, healthy positive feelings about others are both a cause and an effect of other aspects of collaborative negotiations.	Success is determined by minimizing or avoiding all conflict and soothing any hostility. Own feelings are ignored in the interest of harmony.

(continued)

TABLE 10–1   (continued)

COMPETITIVE	COLLABORATIVE	SUBORDINATIVE
8. Unhealthy extreme is reached when one party assumes that everything that prevents the other from attaining its goal facilitates movement toward one's own goal; thus each party feels that an integral part of its goal is to stop the other from attaining its goal.	Unhealthy extreme is reached when one party assumes that whatever is good for others and the group is necessarily good for one's own self, when one cannot distinguish one's identity from that of the group or the other party, or when one party will not take responsibility for itself.	Unhealthy extreme is characterized by complete acquiescence to the other's goal at the expense of personal or organizational goals. Concern with harmony results in total avoidance of conflict. The subordinate party becomes a doormat for the other party.
9. Key attitude/behavior is "I win, you lose."	Key attitude/behavior is "What is the best way to meet the goals of both parties?"	Key attitude/behavior is "You win, I lose."
10. If impasse occurs, a mediator or arbitrator may be required.	If difficulties arise, a facilitator skilled in group dynamics may be used.	If behavior becomes chronic, assertiveness training or a psychotherapist may be used.

SOURCE: Reprinted, by permission from R. W. Johnston, Negotiating strategies: Different strokes for different folks, *Personnel* (March–April 1982.)

stantive outcome. Situation 3 demands **_firm competition_** to attain the desired substantive results at the expense of the relationship. Situation 4 calls for **_active avoidance_** of negotiation, since the negotiator values neither outcome.

NEGOTIATION TACTICS

Negotiators use a variety of **_tactics,_** short-term focused maneuvers, to accomplish their objectives.[38] For example, the negotiator can choose to wait out the other party or, conversely, take a unilateral action and thus treat the negotiation outcome as a **_fait accompli._** Or, the negotiator can suddenly shift his or her approach or do the reverse of what is expected, thereby catching the other party unprepared. He or she can also withdraw from the negotiation or impose time, dollar, or deadline limits. Finally, the negotiator can grant or withhold favors or show anger, intimidating the other party.

THE KOSS CORPORATION. When Michael Koss, the current CEO, and his father John Koss, founder of the company, were attempting to prevent their company from entering bankruptcy, they negotiated an innovative agreement with their bank. The team from the bank who signed the agreement soon disappeared and was replaced by a new team that set an array of new conditions. In addition, one of the bankers tried to intimidate Michael Koss by querying him about his father's personal financial and banking situation during the negotiations. The corporation could not work with the new team and was forced into bankruptcy three months later.[39]

NEGOTIATOR TYPES

Table 10–2 describes seven types of negotiators who deliberately choose a style that supports negotiation tactics. Often the ethical appropriateness of such tactics is questionable.

TABLE 10–2　　　　　*Type of negotiators*

TYPE	METHOD
The aggressive-opener negotiator	Discomfort the other side by making cutting remarks about their previous performance, their numbers, their unreasonableness, or anything that can be used to insinuate that the opposition is hardly worth speaking to.
The long-pause negotiator	Listen to the other side but do not answer immediately their propositions but rather appear to give them considerable thought with the result that long silences ensue for the purpose of getting the other to reveal as much of their case as possible without revealing your own.
The mocking negotiator	Mock and sneer at your opposition's proposals to get the other side so "uptight" that they say something that they will regret later.
The interrogator	Meet all proposals with searching, prodding questions that are couched in such a way that the opposition feels that they have not thoroughly done their homework. Challenge any answers in a confronting manner and ask the opposition to explain further what they mean.
The cloak-of-reasonableness negotiator	Appear to be agreeable and helpful while making impossible demands for the purpose of winning the friendship and confidence of the opposition.
Divide-and-conquer negotiator	Produce dissension among the opposition so that they have to pay more attention to their own internal disagreements rather than the disagreements with the opposition. Ally with one member of the team and try to play him or her off against the other members of the team.
Billy Bunter negotiator	Pretend to be particularly dense and by so doing exasperate the opposition in hopes that at least one member of the opposing team will reveal information as he tries to find increasingly simple ways to describe proposals, with each proposal being elaborated and amplified so that Billy Bunter can understand it.

SOURCE: Based on R. Gourlay, Negotiations and bargaining, *Management Decision* 25(3) (1987): 19–20.

CROSS-CULTURAL ISSUES IN NEGOTIATIONS

The assumptions that underlie effective negotiations differ significantly in various parts of the world. Consider the following situation.

> Your company has just received confirmation that a high-level delegation from the People's Republic of China will visit your office. Since the Chinese have already received a sample of your products, the purpose of their visit is probably to
>
> (a) sign an agreement to act as your local distributor in China.
>
> (b) establish a firm relationship with the company management.
>
> (c) learn more about your company's technological advancements.
>
> (d) visit your country as a reward for their hard work at home.[40]

In this situation the answer is (b), since most Chinese begin by establishing rapport and acquiring commitment. Technical details are handled by lower-level managers.

To begin, individual characteristics of negotiators vary in different cultures, as shown in Table 10–3. Their general approach also differs. In Asia, the general approach to negotiations focuses on saving face for all parties.[41] Being too frank,

TABLE 10–3   *Key individual characteristics of negotiators*

AMERICAN MANAGERS	JAPANESE MANAGERS	CHINESE MANAGERS (TAIWAN)	BRAZILIAN MANAGERS
Preparation and planning skill	Dedication to job	Persistence and determination	Preparation and planning skill
Thinking under pressure	Perceive and exploit power	Win respect and confidence	Thinking under pressure
Judgment and intelligence	Win respect and confidence	Preparation and planning skill	Judgment and intelligence
Verbal expressiveness	Integrity	Product knowledge	Verbal expressiveness
Product knowledge	Listening skill	Interesting	Product knowledge
Perceive and exploit power	Broad perspective	Judgement and intelligence	Perceive and exploit power
Integrity	Verbal expressiveness		Competiveness

SOURCE: Professor John Graham, School of Business Administration, University of Southern California, 1983. Reprinted in N.J. Adler, *International Dimensions of Organizational Behavior,* 2nd ed. (Boston: PWS-Kent, 1991), p. 187.

critical, insincere, impatient, and unadaptable will result in ineffective negotiations. Questions are asked indirectly, not directly: "I've developed a shortcut for manufacturing these garments at a lower cost but ensuring higher quality and would appreciate any suggestions you have for improving it," not "Can you make this garment cheaper but improve its quality?"

Negotiating with Russians, in contrast, has historically posed different challenges.[42] The Russians emphasize building arguments on asserted ideals and deemphasize building relationships. They appeal to ideals and make few concessions. An opponent's concessions are viewed as weaknesses and are almost never reciprocated. They have been described as making no effort to build continuing relationships, often offering an extreme initial position and ignoring any deadlines.

Arabs, on the other hand, use primarily an emotional rather than an ideological or factual negotiating style.[43] They request and make concessions throughout the negotiating process and almost always reciprocate an opponent's concessions. Initial positions are extreme, but deadlines are casual. They focus on building a long-term relationship. The business climate and personal relationship are critical.[44]

North Americans, in contrast, appeal to logic and counter opponents' arguments with objective facts rather than with subjective feelings or asserted ideals.[45] They may make small concessions early and then usually reciprocate an opponent's concessions. But they take a moderate initial position, build only a short-term relationship, and value deadlines greatly. In sum, American negotiators involved in cross-cultural negotiations should be aware of differences in negotiators' styles and the way negotiators view the process itself.

SUMMARY

Effective intergroup relations require managers and other organizational members to diagnose the extent and causes of their interdependence. Groups can demonstrate pooled, sequential, reciprocal, or team interdependence. Groups experiencing reciprocal or team interdependence more often experience dysfunctional conflict and other problems than those showing pooled or sequential interdependence.

Perceptual differences, including time, goal, and social orientations, attitudinal set, and status differences create differences between groups. Task relations reflect the nature of group interdependence and can reinforce problematic interactions. Power differences, including the extent of a group's substitutability, its ability to cope with uncertainty, and its access to resources influence the effectiveness of its interactions with other individuals or groups. Cross-cultural differences can also exaggerate problems of interacting groups. Prescriptions for improving intergroup relations include the use of interpersonal interventions and introduction of structural mechanisms.

Negotiation describes a process in which two or more parties attempt to reach an agreement. In distributive bargaining, one party's gain is the other's loss. In integrative bargaining, mutual gains for both parties occurs.

Effective negotiation includes preparation, evaluation of alternatives, identifying interests, and making trade-offs and creating joint gains. Negotiators may pursue competitive, collaborative, or subordinative strategies. Negotiators use an array of tactics to supplement these strategies.

DIAGNOSTIC QUESTIONS

The following questions can help diagnose and improve intergroup relations and negotiations in the organization.

■ What is the nature of the relationships between groups in the organization?

■ What factors contribute to these relationships?

■ How effective are the intergroup relations?

■ What types of negotiations occur in the organization?

■ Do the negotiations tend to be distributive or integrative?

■ What types of preparations for negotiations occur?

■ Are interests identified?

■ Is the best alternative to a negotiated agreement determined?

■ Is the bargaining range specified?

■ How effective are intercultural negotiations?

■ What mechanisms exist for managing the relationships between groups?

Activity 10–1 · GENERAL DYNAMICS IN THE NAVAJO NATION CASE

STEP 1: Read the General Dynamics in the Navajo Nation Case.

Mike Enfield sat at his desk and looked out across the 21,440-square-foot plant floor of the General Dynamics assembly and test facility in the Navajo Nation. As plant manager, he knew that the company was in the middle of negotiations with the Navajo Tribe to extend the company's lease for another 20 years. Given his experience with the facility, he wondered if it was worth it. "I'd describe us as a 'schoolbus'—a 1952 school bus! We continually put new engines in so that we don't have to buy a new body. We just never break down," said Enfield, when asked to describe his operation. "Around here everybody wears more than one hat. This is a utility vehicle. Maybe you can afford a new motor, but you can't afford the whole thing very often. I'm not a Masarati and I wouldn't want to be. That's for the snobs from somewhere else."

It was late in 1984 and lease negotiations with the Navajo Tribal Council had been underway for over a year. General Dynamics wanted to expand the building by 15,000 square feet and to extend the existing long-term lease. Enfield continued: "I think business can operate here very well—if people running the business are willing to go into the Navajo culture and learn rather than trying to force the Navajo into our culture when they don't want to come in." He believed his Navajo employees, all 320 of them, could meet any trial.

BACKGROUND

In the mid-1960s General Dynamics needed to expand its electronic assembly capability to handle excess work at the Pomona Division Plant in California. New contracts with the Department of the Navy, the Department of the Air Force, and the U.S. Missile Command would require additional floor space and an expanded work force. Several sites were considered. For example, there were possiblities in Asia. Atari was moving a plant from California to the Far East to be more profitable, resulting in the loss of 1,700 jobs in California. Mexico had a large available labor force. Canada seemed a possibility, but there were some problems with transportation.

After preliminary discussions with the Navajo Tribe and the Bureau of Indian Affairs in 1967, General Dynamics decided to pursue the possibility of locating near Window Rock, Arizona. It appeared to be an attractive business opportunity and a chance to play a positive role in Navajo economic development. The Navajo Nation is located in the four corners area of the Southwestern United States where the borders of Utah, Colorado, New Mexico, and Arizona meet. (See Figure 10–7.)

Two factors seemed basic. First, General Dynamics believed that a socially responsive company would have to be committed to a positive role in Navajo economic development, reservation life, and the well-being of the people living in the area. Second, the company would have to operate more profitably in the Navajo Nation environment than at another location. This second factor would be a primary factor in the decision to open a plant in any location.

INITIAL CONCERNS

William H. Govette, Pomona's Vice President of Fabrication and Assembly, who was responsible for the operation of the Navajo Facility in 1984,

FIGURE 10–7 *The Navajo Nation in the Four Corners region*

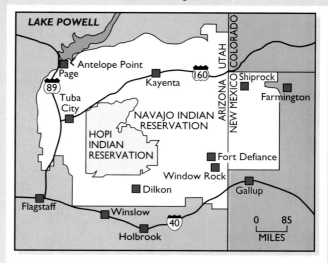

recalls that General Dynamics had four initial concerns.[1]

1. Was there a plant site that offered sufficient available labor, ample housing, and adequate transportation service?
2. What type of building would be required to manufacture the product? Was the required building available or would the tribe be willing to build a facility that suited the company needs?
3. Was the Tribe willing to purchase the equipment necessary for production?
4. How would the training of employees be provided?

BEGINNING OPERATION OF THE NAVAJO FACILITY

In 1968, Navajo medicine men performed the traditional blessing ceremony at the dedication of the new General Dynamics Navajo Facility at Fort Defiance, Arizona. The blessing chants referred to beauty and harmony in an indefinite, intangible, time and space.

> May it be delightful my house;
> From my head may it be delightful;
> To my feet may it be delightful;
> Where I lie may it be delightful;
> All above me may it be delightful;
> All around me may it be delightful.[2]

Enfield and the first 50 Navajo employees could now pass beyond the neat split rail fence and enter the new air-conditioned steel and concrete electronic assembly plant.

The Navajo Tribe had constructed a modern building to General Dynamics specifications. The lease agreement had a 15-year term, with a guarantee that 75 percent of the construction cost would be paid back in 5 years and the remaining 25 percent over the next 10 years. The tribe had also agreed that major repairs and modifications would be negotiated. To equip the plant, the tribe agreed to purchase all required equipment. General Dynamics then leased the equipment and agreed to repay the cost of the items over a 10-year period.

The site was 5 miles from tribal headquarters at Window Rock and 35 miles from Gallup, New Mexico, on interstate highway I-40. Major truck, bus, and scheduled airline routes pass through Gallup. Window Rock has a 6,700-foot paved, lighted private landing strip.

The partnership between General Dynamics and the Navajo Nation was the result of fortunate timing. In 1968, the Bureau of Indian Affairs was encouraging industry to locate on Indian land, and Pomona needed to expand its electronic assembly capability to provide missile components for Navy and Air Force contracts. By 1984, the population of the Navajo Nation was rapidly approaching 200,000; 33.9 percent were unemployed, and about 18,000 Navajo people were actively seeking work.[3]

STATE OF AFFAIRS IN 1984

The Labor Pool

Dennis Hardy, the Navajo superintendent of Standard Missile, talked about the early days of training the Navajo employees. "General Dynamics originally entered into an agreement with the Manpower Development and Training Act Federal Funding Program to train employees in electronic assembly through a 6-week course. Later we moved to a 40-hour concentrated course. Did all our own screening and training." Hardy had his white shirt sleeves turned up at the cuffs. The coat to his gray suit was draped over a chair and his vest was open. Outside the window of the Navajo facility a dog howled and an answering yowling seemed to come from nearby. Hardy stopped to listen. Then he talked for a while about the full-grown German shepherd he recently brought back from Flagstaff Animal shelter for his 4-year-old son.

After a detailed description of the Flagstaff trip, Hardy straightened his tie and returned to the discussion of training:

> Employees are now given detailed training at the time of hiring—usually in basic soldering, welding, and assembly. On-the-job training lasts from a few weeks to several months, depending on the job complexity. Anyway, under the old Manpower Development courses we were producing 40 percent rejects. That had to change. With our own training program, rejects are now less than 10 percent.

By 1984 the facility was involved in assembly work all the way from insertion of electronic components into circuit boards to final assembly of the Standard Missile and Phalanx Missile lines.

Art Stockdale, who conducted professional development activities both on-site at Fort Defiance and at the Pomona division headquarters, reported on the Navajo facility trainees:

> I have not found a more attentive and appreciative group. . . . Each participant is willing to relate both work and cultural experiences to the concepts that are presented. I found that as a group they are dedicated employees. The mutual respect that they have for one another is something all organizations would do well to emulate.

"I was QA manager for years," said Enfield, "We're on a par with anybody. I'm a great believer in the Navajo people. I'm betting my butt on them. They have something going that doesn't go anywhere else. That is, this isn't simply General Dynamics, this is **The Navajo Facility!**"

Over the years, the Fort Defiance, Arizona plant generally met or exceeded established cost, quantity, and quality requirements for each product. The on-site managers consistently reported that quality control simply wasn't needed. This cut expenditures and made the product both high quality and low cost.

AFFIRMATIVE ACTION AND LABOR COSTS

General Dynamics realized a definite affirmative action advantage through the employment of native Americans, who were underrepresented in the general work force. This gave the company an advantage in bids on U.S. government contract work. Additionally, with the high unemployment rate on the Navajo Nation, most of the company's new employees began work at federal minimum wage pay rates or only slightly higher than current rates, Job progression in the Navajo facility began with basic assembly and moved on to more advanced assembly techniques with increases in pay at each progression. In spite of minimum wage rates, Enfield believed the employees were the best in the aerospace industry. "I have never heard one person who works for me tell me 'you can't do it that way.' You give them the work, and they do it—they are superproductive. Our high productivity is related to the 90 percent acceptance rates."

Enfield reported that turnover rates were about the same as in the surrounding states, but he said he didn't count statistics. "If they fail school, that's not job-related turnover." By 1984, nine of the employees had 15 years of service, 30 had 10 years, and 33 had more than 5 years. Turnover rates had averaged about 10 percent per year. Enfield insisted that the average to low turnover rates were evidence of Navajo employees' satisfaction with both their wages and their jobs.

Mattie Singer, a Navajo production supervisor for Standard Missile, said that there was always the need to learn to operate new equipment. Singer started work at the Navajo facility about the same time as Hardy. "I like it when there's a lot of challenge," confided Singer. "In the 16 years I've been here, I've enjoyed every minute. There are so many things I have benefited from. Dineh (the Navajo people) have a skilled crafts tradition. We take what someone shows us, and then we make it better." Mattie Singer's picture is in the entryway next to the perfect attendance chart. Her team recently won a trophy in the bowling tournament.

CULTURAL AND TRADITIONAL CONSIDERATIONS

Because the Navajo Nation is located within U.S. borders, the temptation was to adopt a business and management model appropriate to California, or Michigan, or Georgia. It was difficult to think of the Navajo Nation as a foreign country. Shouldn't companies here be able to operate as they would in any domestic location? General Dynamics said "no," and the General Dynamics management team adjusted to the customs of the host culture as in an international setting.

A smile appeared across Mike Enfield's suntanned features when he talked about cross-cultural considerations.

> Corporate life for most means that if you're not in the intensive care ward, you're not a success. You've got to be able to scream and intimidate. The Navajo will simply refuse to do it if you order them around. I get just bristling mad cause I can't force my will upon them. Pretty soon when you get beat up as much as I have you say, "maybe if I just ask them to do it, they'll do it."
>
> We're going for a twenty-year lease right now and expanding the building, but none of those things would have happened if we didn't produce **our** way, the Navajo way. Our philosophical way. I lean toward the Navajo peacefulness not toward the corporate grind, not toward traditional U.S. business practices.

Enfield believed that without knowledge of and respect for the Navajo culture the General Dynamics operation would have collapsed. To avoid this, General Dynamics took great care to ensure that the culture was respected.

First, before making the decision to locate in the Navajo Nation, the company made extensive studies of Navajo culture and traditions. Figure 10–8 contains a Navajo adaptation of Edward T. Hall's cultural primary message systems researched by Bill Strasen at General Dynamics in the mid-1960s and made available to General Dynamics staff.

The company's Industrial Relations Educational Services produced a 30-page monograph to assist personnel who visited or worked in the Navajo Nation. The monograph, with an extensive bibliography, contained information on geography, history, economy, religion, social structure, belief system, and education.

Second, the company took pains to assure respect and acceptance of Navajo traditions by careful screen-

FIGURE 10–8   *The Navajo*

PRIMARY MESSAGE SYSTEM	NAVAJO TRAITS
1. Interaction	Very precise language in description and meaning. All communication is face-to-face, verbal, with unanimous agreement of everyone a vital requirement.
2. Association	No formal "tribe." Family organization based on "clan" of wife's relatives. Richer men may have more than one wife (in separate hogans).
3. Subsistence	Primarily an agrarian culture. Sheep are very important to the Navajo.
4. Gender status	Women are equal of men, and often are the key decision makers.
5. Territoriality	Within hogan women sit only on south side, men only on north side. Grazing land and "sacred" salt areas are shared by all.
6. Temporality	Time is measured by the season or task to be accomplished, not by white man's minutes and hours.
7. Learning	All teaching is verbal; learning is by mimic and rote. Instructors are the oldest, hence wisest, members of the clan. Until 1960 there were no Navajo writings from which to learn.
8. Play	Navajo enjoy humor. Recreation is geared to non-competitive games.
9. Relationships	The "medicine man" is the supreme authority. The entire "clan" is responsible for a wrong doing by one of its members.
10. Resource exploitation	Hogans constructed of mud, grass, and logs. Adapts to environment.

SOURCE: Adapted from a framework of Edward T. Hall by Bill Strassen, General Dynamics Corporation, Pomona, CA, 1976.

ing and briefing of non-Indian employees before visits to the Navajo facility. Candidates for positions had to show a willingness to relocate to a totally different type of environment.

Third, non-Indian candidates for managerial positions spent several days in the Fort Defiance area with their families. They met members of the Navajo tribe with whom they would work on a regular basis. Housing, schools, and employment of the entire family were discussed. Frequently, non-Indian candidates decided they might not enjoy, or even tolerate, being a visible, white European-American minority person within the dominant native American culture.

Fourth, General Dynamics continued the screening process until suitable non-Indian candidates were found. In the Navajo culture, family and religious responsibilities truly predominated and were respected by the organization even when those customs were at odds with traditional U.S. business practice. A balance had to be achieved between the company's production needs and a unique tribal culture.

ABSENTEEISM

"In California or Arizona you would discipline someone who was gone nine days, but here we put them on leave of absence. You've got to recognize their right to go to the nine-day Yeibichai healing ceremony, and you've got to recognize that their job is second to that—not first," said Enfield when asked about absenteeism. The Yeibichai healing rite is only one of many ceremonials.

Dennis Hardy agreed. "You know, we have no separate word for 'religion.' The white man turns his religion on and off. With us, each and every daily act is influenced by the supernatural."

In such circumstances, absenteeism can easily become a problem. Enfield said he planned for absenteeism by overstaffing. There were then enough people on hand to perform day-to-day tasks, and there were no large fluctuations in the work force. Nevertheless, a major concern was a work force unaccustomed to coming to work every scheduled workday.

ABILITY OF NAVAJOS TO ACCEPT LEADERSHIP RESPONSIBILITY

The long-range goal of General Dynamics was to adequately train Navajos to take over the operation of the facility. Navajos identified as having management po-

tential were brought to the Pomona, California plant for management and technical training. Management training was also carried on at Fort Defiance. The Navajo Nation facility opened with a management team of 26 non-Indians. By 1984 the facility had over 300 employees, and 14 of the 22-member management team were Navajos. Enfield said:

Amy Allen is a Navajo in production control being trained by Carl Gentry, Edna Yazzie, Donald Young, Ernest Tso—they're all being trained for various disciplines. All we've got to do is be smart enough to put them to work. That's what I'm doing. We now have two production superintendents, and both are Navajos. The personnel and cost person is a Navajo being trained for all the finance administration. . . . What do you do with a guy like me who's been here 15 years? My wife's a Navajo. Throw me out? You've got three of us like that. I think we consider ourselves Navajos. We're probably closer to that than our own society. But, we have a neat thing in that we recognize both. We prefer one over the other, but we know how to deal with both.

ALCOHOL-RELATED PROBLEMS

While alcohol-related problems exist in industry located in all areas, such problems have been extensive and acute on American Indian reservations, where high unemployment has exacerbated an already serious alcoholism rate. General Dynamics needed to be informed in detail in order to cope with the situation adequately. With tribal agency cooperation, plant management worked with families to reduce or correct alcohol-related difficulties. General Dynamics looked upon their relationship with the tribe as a partnership. They were partners, working together to solve mutual problems and improve local economic and social conditions.

CONTINUING-EDUCATION FACILITIES

An industrial environment demands that all employees, regardless of position, keep current with the "state of the art" in their occupations. In 1984, continuing-education facilities in the Navajo Nation were minimal or nonexistent. The Navajo Tribe was considering this factor and moving toward consensus to create the necessary educational facilities so that their employees could advance and ultimately move into management. However, to date nothing concrete has been done.

HOUSING AND MEDICAL FACILITIES FOR NON-INDIANS

Because all land belongs to the tribe, neither Navajo nor non-Indian employees could simply go out and buy a lot and build a house. There were no apartment complexes, townhouses, or condos until you reached Gallup, New Mexico, 35 miles to the southeast. Housing for Navajo employees was not readily available, especially if the employee was from another part of the reservation. Navajo Indians were accustomed to waiting 6 years to get a home site lease. The limited housing provided for Indians was not available to non-Indian personnel.

Medical help for non-Indians on the Navajo Nation was almost nonexistent. The large Indian Health Service hospital at Fort Defiance was for Indians only, since Indian hospitals are operated as part of Indian treaty agreements with the federal government. For non-Indians, the closest medical facilities were in Gallup. General Dynamics managers felt this was a serious problem, especially for non-Indian families with children. (In 1984, only eight non-Indian families with children remained on the Navajo Facility staff.)

NEGOTIATING WITH THE TRIBAL GOVERNMENT

The Navajo Tribe was governed by a Tribal Council composed of seventy-four elected members and presided over by a chairman and vice chairman. The seventy-four delegates represented the number of districts, called "chapters," spread across the Navajo Nation. Meetings were held every 3 months, and unanimous decisions were preferred. Consensus building took time. Everyone had to approve or disapprove, so things moved slowly. Fourteen different committees with from 3 to 18 members advised the Tribal Council on matters such as health, education, alcohol, resources, and welfare. Chapter officers and grazing committees also advised the Tribal Council as did the judiciary.

Tribal officers had an "official" vested interest in encouraging business investment and development. However, nonofficial people, both Indian and non-Indian government bureaucrats, displayed a greater diversity of opinions about such investment. Corporate representatives needed to seek out a variety of people to gain a fuller comprehension of the total environment. Bureau of Indian Affairs officials, local business persons, teachers, editors of local newspapers, and other members of the Indian population needed to be consulted.

Lease negotiations were frustrating and time-consuming because tribal officials sometimes could not reconcile the needs of industry with tribal needs. "If it's a question of Janie Tso's sheep grazing on a particular corner lot versus an electronic assembly facility employing a hundred people, those sheep are probably going to have first priority," said Dennis Hardy. "And, maybe they *should* have priority. The dineh have been here a long time. We'll still be here when the industries are gone."

Building improvements and modifications were extremely complex because many tribal and governmental committees had to give approval. Both the Navajo Tribal Council and the Bureau of Indian Affairs must approve all lease agreements. In the years between the mid-1960s, when General Dynamics began operations at the Navajo Facility, and the mid-1980s new layers were added to both of these bureaucratic structures. Each of these new offices had to supply its approval, and what little centralization had existed in the past became nonexistent. Lease agreements requiring 10 years of negotiation were not infrequent. Enfield estimated that lease agreements necessitated that a company representative be at tribal headquarters in Window Rock almost daily to complete the 67-step site lease process and receive archaeological clearance and environmental assessment under seven separate federal laws.[4]

Additionally, tribal elections, which were conducted every 4 years, could bring lease negotiations to a standstill. In the past, negotiations that had been under way for as long as 3 years and were nearing completion had been scrapped when the election of a new tribal chair put things back to square one. Historically, a new tribal chair changed tribal government personnel completely. Everyone was replaced—from top administrators, to clerical staff, to janitorial services. Long-standing animosities frequently developed among tribal political factions, preventing implementation of planned development.

In 1972, the Navajo 10-Year Plan for industrial development on the Navajo Nation was promulgated by Tribal Chairman Peter MacDonald. The following were the objectives of the plan.

1. What is rightfully ours, we must protect; what is rightfully due us, we must claim.
2. What we depend on from others, we must replace with the labor of our own hands and the skills of our own people.

3. What we do not have, we must bring into being. We must create for ourselves.[5]

The original General Dynamics lease negotiated in 1967 required a year for initial approval under Tribal Chairman Raymond Nakai. However, as the original 15-year lease neared completion in the early 1980s, the corporation, seeking a new 20-year lease and expanded plant, found itself dealing with officials who could not reconcile the corporation's and the tribe's needs. Unrealistic demands were made and time was lost. In addition to renegotiating the original lease, the General Dynamics Pomona Division was seeking to expand to a second off-site assembly facility in the Navajo Nation.

The Navajo Tribe had land, a highly stable, dedicated work force, and a proud heritage of craftsmanship, productivity, and quality. However, the tribe also had a multilayered bureaucracy that was slow to respond to private industry.

The federal government's Overseas Private Investment Corporation encouraged economic development programs in foreign countries through direct loans, loan guarantees, and insurance against political risk, but these programs were unavailable to private industry seeking to locate on sovereign American Indian nations.

SUMMARY

Back in the Navajo facility at Fort Defiance, Arizona, Mike Enfield wondered how the tribe could achieve government centralization and stability to facilitate economic development. He wondered whether or not General Dynamics should continue with negotiations for the second facility in the Navajo Nation. Even the needed approval for lease extension and expansion of the present plant was still circulating through layers of Navajo bureaucracy. He sat down to list both the advantages and the disadvantages of operating on the Navajo Indian Reservation. How long could he keep the old 1952 school bus going? How should General Dynamics react to the objectives in Peter MacDonald's 10-Year Plan? Certainly there were some concessions General Dynamics might try to get from the tribe after 16 years of successful operation. A mutually beneficial partnership forged from respect and understanding now existed. Enfield wanted to keep that partnership alive and growing, but it was an ethical dilemma. Were employee pride and favorable public image enough? Should a company seek to establish a viable business operation for purely ethical reasons?

[1]William H. Govette. Address at the American Indian National Bank Enterprise and Resource Development Seminar, Albuquerque, New Mexico, March 22, 1983.

[2]Edward T. Hall. *The Silent Language* (Greenwich, Conn.: Fawcett Publications, 1959).

[3]Navajo Economic Development Program 1988 Annual Progress Report, *The Navajo Tribe,* Window Rock, 1988.

[4]"Business site lease procedures," Navajo Reservation and Tribal Trust Land, final draft, August 23, 1991.

[5]*A Study to Identify Potentially Feasible Small Business of The Navajo Nation,* vol 2 (Provo, Utah: Center for Business and Economic Research, Brigham Young University, 1975).

STEP 2: Prepare the case for class discussion.

STEP 3: Answer the following questions, individually, in small groups, or with the entire class, as directed by your instructor.

DESCRIPTION

1. Describe the negotiation currently undertaken by General Dynamics and the Navajo nation.

DIAGNOSIS

2. How effective is the negotiation?

3. How does the ongoing relationship between the parties influence the negotiation?

4. Does each party successfully prepare, identify interests, propose alternatives, and recommend trade-offs?

5. To what extent does Mike Enfield consider cross-cultural issues?

6. What problems have arisen?

PRESCRIPTION

7. What should be done to reach a quality agreement?

ACTION

8. Will the outcomes likely be positive?

STEP 4: Discussion. In small groups, with the entire class, or in written form, share your answers to the questions above. Then answer the following questions:

1. What symptoms suggest that a problem exists?

2. What problems exist in the case?

3. What theories and concepts help explain the problems?
4. What should have been done differently?
5. How effective would such actions likely be?

Prepared by Fairlee E. Winfield, Northern Arizona University. Originally presented at a meeting of the Southwest Case Research Association, March 1992. Management cooperated in the field research for this case, which was written solely for the purpose of stimulating student discussion. All events and individuals are real. Copyright © 1993 by the *Case Research Journal* and Fairlee E. Winfield.

$\mathcal{A}$ctivity 10–2 — WORLD BANK: AN INTERGROUP NEGOTIATION

This is an intergroup activity. You and your team are going to engage in a task in which money will be won or lost. ***The objective is to win as much as you can.*** There are two teams involved in this activity, and both teams receive identical instructions. After reading these instructions, your team has 15 minutes to organize itself and to plan its strategy.

STEP 1: The class is divided into two groups. The size of each of the groups should be no more than ten. Those not in one of the two groups are designated as observers. However, groups should not have less than six members each. The instructor will play the role of the referee/banker for the World Bank.

STEP 2: Read the World Bank Instruction Sheet that follows:

WORLD BANK GENERAL INSTRUCTION SHEET

Each team represents a country. Each country has financial dealings with the World Bank. Initially, each country contributed $100 million to the World Bank. Countries may have to pay further monies or may receive money from the World Bank in accordance with regulations and procedures described below under sections headed Finance and Payoffs.

Each team is given twenty cards. These are your ***weapons.*** Each card has a marked side *(X)* and an unmarked side. The marked side of the card signifies that the weapon is armed. Conversely, the blank side shows the weapon to be unarmed.

At the beginning, each team will place ten of its twenty weapons in their armed positions (marked side up) and the remaining ten in their unarmed positions (marked side down). These weapons will remain in your possession and out of sight of the other team at all times.

There will be ***rounds*** and ***moves.*** Each round consists of seven moves by each team. There will be two or more rounds in this simulation. The number of rounds depends on the time available. Payoffs are determined and recorded after each round.

1. A move consists of turning two, one, or none of the team's weapons from armed to unarmed status, or vice versa.
2. Each team has 2 minutes for each move. There are 30-second periods between moves. At the end of 2 minutes, the team must have turned two, one, or none of its weapons from armed to unarmed status, or from unarmed to armed status. If the team fails to move in the allotted time, no change can be made in weapon status until the next move.
3. The length of the 2½-minute periods between the beginning of one move and the beginning of the next is fixed and unalterable.

Each new round of the experiment begins with all weapons returned to their original positions, ten armed and ten unarmed.

Finances

The funds you have contributed to the World Bank are to be allocated in the following manner:

Sixty million dollars will be returned to each team to be used as your team's treasury during the course of the decision-making activities.

Eighty million dollars will be retained for the operation of the World Bank.

Payoffs

1. If there is an attack:
   a. Each team may announce an attack on the other team by notifying the referee/banker during the 30 seconds following *any* 2-

minute period used to decide upon the move (including the seventh, or final, decision period in any round). The choice of each team during the decision period just ended counts as a move. An attack may not be made during negotiations.

b. If there is an attack (by one or both teams), two things happen: (1) the round ends and (2) the World Bank levies a penalty of $5 million for each team.

c. The team with the greater number of armed weapons wins $3 million for each armed weapon it has over and above the number of armed weapons of the other team. These funds are paid directly from the treasury of the losing team to the treasury of the winning team. The referee/bankers will manage this transfer of funds.

2. If there is no attack: At the end of each round (seven moves), each team's treasury receives from the World Bank $2 million for each of its weapons that is at that point unarmed, and each team's treasury pays to the World Bank $2 million for each of its weapons remaining armed.

NEGOTIATIONS

Between moves each team has the opportunity to communicate with the other team through its negotiators.

Either team may call for negotiations by notifying the referee/bankers during any of the 30-second periods between decisions. A team is free to accept or reject any invitations to negotiate.

Negotiators from both teams are **required** to meet after the third and sixth moves (after the 30-second period following that move, if there is no attack).

Negotiations can last no longer than 3 minutes. When the two negotiators return to their teams, the 2-minute decision period for the next move begins once again.

Negotiators are bound only by: (a) the 3-minute time limit for negotiations and (b) their required appearance after the third and sixth moves. They are otherwise free to say whatever is necessary to benefit themselves or their teams. The teams similarly are not bound by agreements made by their negotiators, even when those agreements are made in good faith.

Special Roles

Each team has 15 minutes to organize itself to plan team strategy. During this period before the first round begins, each team must choose persons to fill the following roles. (Each team must have each of the following roles, which can be changed at any time by a decision of the team.)

- *Negotiators*—activities stated above.
- A *representative*—to communicate team decisions to the referee/bankers.
- A *recorder*—to record the moves of the team and to keep a running balance of the team's treasury.
- A *treasurer*—to execute all financial transactions with the referee/bankers.

STEP 3: Each group or team will have 15 minutes to organize itself and plan strategy before beginning. Before the first round each team must choose (a) two negotiators, (b) a representative, (c) a team recorder, (d) a treasurer.

STEP 4: The referee/banker will signal the beginning of round one and each following round and also end the exercise in about one hour.

STEP 5: Discussion. In small groups or with the entire class, answer the following questions.

DESCRIPTION
1. What occurred during the exercise?

DIAGNOSIS
2. Was there conflict? What type, level, or stage?
3. What contributed to the relationships among groups?
4. Evaluate the power, leadership, motivation, and communication among groups.

PRESCRIPTION
5. How could the relationships have been more effective?

Adapted from *The 1975 Annual Handbook for Group Facilitators* by J.E. Jones & J.W. Pfeiffer (Eds.). Copyright © 1975 by Pfeiffer & Company, San Diego, CA. Used with permission.

$\mathscr{A}$ctivity 10–3 | FAIRFIELD FLYER WAGONS

STEP 1: Students will manufacture wagon parts (wheels, long sides, short sides, bottoms, and handles). These parts will be used during Step 2.

1. Your instructor will pass out the necessary materials.
   Rulers
   Quarters
   Scissors
   Paper
   Pencils
   "Pooled Interdependence Template" IN/OUT labels (3 "OUT" for manufacturing departments; 1 "IN," 1 "OUT PASSED," and 1 "OUT REJECTED" for Quality Control). Pieces of paper with the above legends are sufficient.

2. Your instructor will arrange the room. Use extra chairs or desks for IN/OUT stations and attach IN/OUT labels with tape.

3. Your instructor will divide the class into the following four departments. Each will be provided with the materials specified below.

   a. Wheel Department: "Wheel Department Template", quarters, scissors, paper, pencils

   b. Sides Department: "Sides Department Template", rulers, scissors, paper, pencils

   c. Bottom and Handle Department: "Bottoms and Handle Department Template", rulers, scissors, paper, pencils

   d. Quality Control: All department templates, rulers

4. Appoint or have each department select a manager.

5. Review the following manufacturing procedures.

Wheel Department

Your job is to produce as many wheels as possible. Make sure that they are the right size (the diameter of a quarter) and do not waste materials. The department manager will distribute raw materials, collect the finished wheels, and deliver them to the "OUTPUT" table where they will be collected by the instructor for delivery to Quality Control.

Sides Department

Your job is to produce as many long and short sides as possible. Make sure that they are the right size (see your template) and do not waste materials. You should produce the same number of long and short sides. The department manager will collect the finished sides, separate them into long and short batches, and deliver them to the "OUTPUT" table, where they will be collected by the instructor for delivery to Quality Control.

Bottom and Handle Department

Your job is to produce as many bottoms and handles as possible. Make sure that they are the right size (see your template) and do not waste materials. You should produce the same number of handles and bottoms. The department manager will collect the finished wheels and deliver them to the "OUTPUT" table where they will be collected by the instructor for delivery to Quality Control.

Quality Control

Check each part against the template. Put those that pass inspection on the "OUT PASSED" table and those that fail inspection on the "OUT REJECTED" table.

Communication **between** any of the departments is prohibited. Managers may communicate only with the people within their departments.

6. Have a 15-minute production run.

7. Participate in a brief discussion?

   a. Was there a need for communication between the manufacturing departments? If so, what kind? If not, why not?

   b. Was there a need for communication between the manufacturing departments and the Quality Control department? Why or why not?

   c. Did your physical/spatial relationship to any other department influence your ability to do your job? Why or why not?

....

STEP 2: Students will assemble wagons from the parts manufactured during Part I. The groups will be sequentially interdependent.

1. Your instructor will pass out the necessary materials.
   Assembly Instructions
   Rulers
   Tape
   Pencils
   Wagon parts manufactured during Part I
   Sample finished wagon
   "IN/OUT" labels (as indicated on Suggested Room Layout)

2. Your instructor will rearrange the room according to the Suggested Room Layout.

3. Your instructor will divide the class into the following six departments and provide each with the materials specified below.

   a. Attach handle to bottom: Step 1 Assembly Instructions, rulers, tape, pencils, handles, and bottoms from Part I.

   b. Attach long sides to bottom: Step 2 Assembly Instructions, rulers, tape, pencils, long sides from Part I.

   c. Attach short sides: Step 3 Assembly Instructions, rulers, tape, pencils, short sides from Part I.

   d. Fold and tape sides together: Step 4 Assembly Instructions, tape.

   e. Attach wheels: Step 5 Assembly Instructions, rulers, tape, pencils, wheels from Part I.

   f. Quality control: All Assembly Instructions, sample finished wagon, rulers, "Quality Control Guidelines".

4. Appoint or have each department select a manager.

5. Go over production procedure. Each department should follow the Assembly Instructions provided.

6. Have a 15-minute production run.

7. Participate in a brief discussion.

   a. What difficulties did you have?

   b. Would your task have been easier or would you have been more productive if you could have communicated with the other departments? If so, which departments? What type of communication would have been the most effective? Would memos have helped?

   c. Did the spatial relationship between the departments help or hinder your ability to get your work done? How? How would it have affected your ability to get your work done if the departments with which you interacted were in different rooms? In a different order?

....

STEP 3: Students will manufacture wagons under two conditions of reciprocal interdependence.

1. Your instructor will provide the necessary materials.
   Assembly Instructions
   Rulers
   Tape
   Pencils
   Sample finished wagon
   Paper clips
   Paper cut into $11'' \times 3\frac{5}{8}''$ rectangles
   "Reciprocal Drawing Template"
   Scissors
   Copies of "Interdepartmental Memos"

Quality Control Guidelines (attached)
"IN/OUT" labels (4 "IN," 4 "OUT")

2. Your instructor will rearrange the room according to Suggested Room Layout.

3. Your instructor will divide the class into the following departments and provide each with the materials specified below.

   a. Drawing: Paper cut into 11″ × 3⅝″ rectangles, pencils, rulers, quarters, "Reciprocal Drawing Template", copies of Interdepartmental Memo #1, paper clips

   b. Cutting: Scissors, pencils, copies of Interdepartmental Memo #2, paper clips

   c. Assembly: Tape, pencils, rulers, Step 1 through 5 Assembly Instructions, copies of Interdepartmental Memo #3, paper clips

   d. Quality control: Rulers, sample completed wagon, pencils, Quality Control Guidelines, copies of Interdepartmental Memos #4, #5, and #6, paper clips

Start assembly off with one handle and bottom per person and cutting with one set of long sides drawn per person.

4. Appoint or have each department appoint a manager.

5. Review the following manufacturing procedure.

   Condition 1: You must follow all directions exactly. You are only permitted to communicate with other departments using the memos provided. Managers may only communicate with the workers within their own department. There is to be no discussion between departments. Your instructor will deliver any necessary memos, which should be placed on your "OUT" table for pick-up.

Drawing Department

Parts must be drawn according to the drawing template.

   Step 1: Draw long sides on paper.
   Step 2: Send to Cutting Department (put on "OUT" table).

Step 3: When paper returns from the Cutting Department (on "IN" table) draw handle and send back to Cutting Department.

Step 4: Repeat above for short sides, wheels, and bottom (in that order), sending the paper to the Cutting Department after each part is drawn (that is, after both short sides are drawn, after four wheels are drawn, after bottom is drawn).

You may work on several sheets of paper simultaneously, but you must follow the steps above in order. For example, from one sheet of raw material: draw two long sides, send to Cutting Department; draw one handle, send to Cutting Department; draw two short sides, send to Cutting Department; draw four wheels, send to Cutting Department; draw one bottom, send to Cutting Department.

If you receive requests from the Quality Control Department,

   a. Get more raw material (paper).
   b. Redraw the part specified on the "Redraw" memo.
   c. Send redrawn part to Cutting Department with a "Recut" memo completed and attached (attach memos with paper clips).
   d. Put remaining raw material aside for other rejected parts.

Cutting Department

Step 1: When you receive drawing from the Drawing Department cut out long sides.
Step 2: Send long sides to Assembly Department and paper back to Drawing Department.
Step 3: Repeat above for handle, short sides, wheels, and bottom, each time sending cut parts to Assembly and paper to Drawing.

You may work on different sheets simultaneously, but you must follow the steps above in order for each.

If you receive a "Recut" memo from the drawing department.

   a. Recut part

   b. Send recut part to Assembly Department with "Reassembly" memo completed and attached (attach memos with paper clips)

Assembly Department

Follow Assembly Instructions in the following order:

   Step 1: Attach handle to bottom.
   Step 2: Attach long sides to bottom.
   Step 3: Attach short sides to bottom.
   Step 4: Fold sides up and tape.
   Step 5: Attach wheels to long sides.
   Step 6: Send to Quality Control.

If you receive a rejected wagon from Quality Control,

   a. Follow the directions on the attached memo. You will either have to reassemble the wagon or hold it until you receive a new part from the Cutting Department.

   b. Send the reassembled wagon back to Quality Control with a "Reassembly" memo completed and attached (attach memos with paper clips).

Quality Control

   Step 1: Check each wagon against the "Quality Control Guidelines" (attached).

   Step 2: If the wagon meets specifications, send to shipping.

   Step 3: If the wagon is assembled wrong return to Assembly Department with a "Reassemble" memo completed and attached (attach memos with paper clips).

   Step 4: If wagon contains a part that is the wrong size,

   a. Remove faulty part from wagon.

   b. Send faulty part to Drawing Department with a "Redraw" memo completed and paper clipped to the faulty part.

   c. Send remainder of wagon to Assembly Department with a "Hold" memo completed and paper clipped to wagon.

6. Have a 15-minute production run.

7. Participate in a brief discussion.

   a. What difficulties did you have?

   b. Would your task have been easier or would you have been more productive if you could have communicated with the other departments? If so, which departments? What type of communication would have been most effective?

   c. Did the spatial relationship between departments help or hinder your ability to get your work done? What changes would you suggest?

   Condition 2: Appoint a single "Plant Manager." Other managers become members of their department.

8. Take the next 20 minutes to decide what changes you would like to make. Use the previous discussion to guide your decisions. You may make changes within the following constraints:

   a. You must remain in the same functions—that is, you cannot change jobs.

   b. You must follow the same manufacturing procedure in the same order.

9. Participate in a 15-minute production run.

STEP 4: Discussion. In small groups or with the entire class, answer the following questions:

   a. Did the changes you made during Condition 2 improve your ability to do your job? How?

   b. How did the need for interdepartmental coordination and communication change as they became more interdependent?

   c. Did the spatial/physical relationship between departments become more important as technology became more interdependent? Why?

This exercise was developed by Cheryl L. Tromley. It was presented at the Eastern Academy of Management, Buffalo, NY, 1990, and appeared in Lisa A. Mainiero and Cheryl L. Tromley, *Developing Managerial Skills In Organizational Behavior,* 2nd ed. (Englewood Cliffs, NJ: Prentice-Hall, 1994). It is adapted and reprinted with permission.

Activity 10–4 — WINDSOCK, INC.

STEP 1: The class is divided into four groups: Central Office, Product Design, Marketing/Sales, and Production. Central Office is a slightly smaller group. If groups are large enough, assign observers to each one. Central Office is given 500 straws and 750 pins. Each person reads only the role description relevant to his or her group.

STEP 2: Groups perform functions and prepare a two-minute report for stockholders.

STEP 3: Each group gives a two-minute presentation to stockholders.

STEP 4: Observers share insights with sub-groups.

STEP 5: Discussion. In small groups or with the entire class, answer the following questions:

DESCRIPTION
1. What occurred during the exercise?

DIAGNOSIS
2. Was there conflict?
3. What contributed to the relationships among groups?
4. Evaluate communication and leadership in the groups.

PRESCRIPTION
5. How could the relationships have been more effective?

Christopher Taylor and Saundra Taylor Teaching Organizational Building through Simulation, *Organizational Behavior Teaching Review* 11(3) pp. 136–138, © 1986–1987. Reprinted by permission of Sage Publications, Inc.

Activity 10–5 — HENRY BIRKS & SONS CASE

STEP 1: Read the Henry Birks & Sons Case.

As she left the training session she had helped to lead, Anne Haley felt frustrated. It was 6:30 P.M. on Tuesday, April 12, 1988, when she headed home from the all-day program. Only three months ago she had been appointed Merchandise Manager for Henry Birks & Sons, in charge of buyers, called Department Managers, for the 16 stores in the Toronto Area. Last week she had agreed to help lead a discussion with store managers on how to make buyers' visits to stores more productive. "I wanted to improve relations between buyers and store managers," she reflected, "but it was one-sided. They just unloaded on me."

THE BIRKS TRADITION

A national jewelry and gift store, Birks formerly catered to the carriage trade, but now appealed to a wider cross section of the community. The branch stores, which represented over two-thirds of Birks' sales, played a major role in the expanded market penetration. Nowhere in the company was this penetration better developed than Toronto.

Founded by Henry Birks in 1879, Birks in 1988 had 5,000 employees in stores from coast to coast. With its Head Office in Montreal, it remained a family controlled firm. Birks' well-known blue boxes, a packaging tradition with the company for decades, were a distinctive part of the high-quality image. Well regarded by the trade both in Canada and the United States, Birks had become the largest jeweler in Canada by a significant margin.

In 1987–1988 the large downtown Toronto Store, located in the Eaton Centre, generated 30 percent of sales in the Toronto Area. Ontario, as the major sales region, generated 45 percent of national sales, and had a sales increase of 13 percent over the previous year. The Toronto Area alone represented 26 percent of national sales.

While the buoyant Ontario economy made it difficult to get new staff at an entry level, many employees had been with the company for years. Birks had a history of promoting from within.

ANNE HALEY'S ROLE

Eleven years ago Anne Haley had started with the company as a sales clerk, when she was still at the University of New Brunswick. Her talent was recognized early, and by 1982 she had been promoted to buyer—officially Department Manager for Fashion Jewelry—in New Brunswick. Her management training consisted of spending several days with the retiring Department Manager. Yet in the recession of the early 1980's, when other departments in the New Brunswick Area had poor sales, her departments were doing well. In 1984, she was appointed manager of the Fredericton Store, and in the two years she was in charge, sales and profits made significant advances.

In 1986, Anne moved to Toronto as a Department Manager for Giftware. In late 1987, the President of Henry Birks (Ontario), Edward Ballon, who was also Toronto Area Manager, appointed her to her present position of Merchandise Manager, with responsibility for half of the Toronto Area volume. Reporting to her were buyers for such departments as fashion jewelry, hand-bags, silver, china, crystal, and giftware. The buyers for fine jewelry and watches, two very large departments, were exceptions. They reported directly to Ed Ballon. (See Figure 10–9: Organizational Chart.)

One of Anne's responsibilities was to make sure, through her buyers, that stores were properly stocked with fast-moving items. Recently there had been some slip ups in this area. In one instance, a store had been out of Royal Doulton figurines, one of the china department's big sellers. Anne was anxious that such mistakes weren't repeated. Yet, as she had told Ed Ballon, "a common problem is we don't get enough feedback from the stores."

THE DIVISION OF RESPONSIBILITY AT BIRKS

Buyers had responsibility for buying and stocking in each store. They received monthly figures about sales of every item. The system of monthly stock control required sales staff to count stock.

In addition, each month Anne's Department Manager visited each store to check on what was selling, to notify store sales staff about upcoming promotions, and to remove some slow-moving items from the shelves for

FIGURE 10–9   *Henry Birks & Sons, Toronto-area organizational chart*

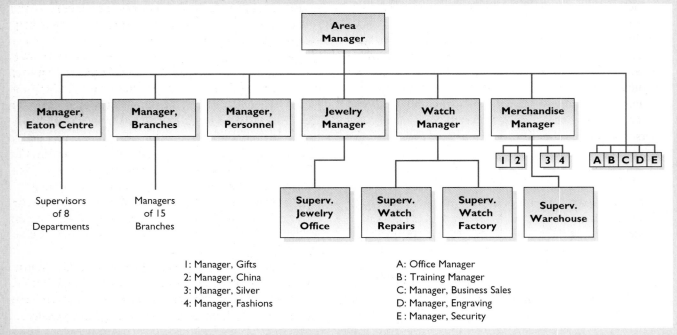

salespeople to ship back to the warehouse. These visits were brief, since buyers covered three to four stores in a day. In between these visits, the sales staff were supposed to report to buyers when stock was getting low, since there was usually a one-and-a-half-week lead time needed to get new stock from a supplier.

Branch managers, by comparison, were responsible for the profitability of their individual stores. They received monthly figures on their store's overall sales and on departmental totals. They were supposed to pass on departmental data to sales supervisors in each department.

For sales information about individual items, branch managers and supervisors had statistical data, but tended to rely on personal knowledge and that of their sales staff.

Up until three years previously, buyers had the complete say on all aspects of merchandising. Now, they were urged to give advice on displaying merchandise, but the final say was with branch managers. Buyers still had the final say on merchandise assortment, and although sales personnel were free to suggest what should be bought, buyers often did not encourage such suggestions. Some intimidated the sales staff. On the other hand, according to Anne, sales staff sometimes frustrated buyers by not displaying properly an item that a buyer wanted to push.

Buyers tended to stay in their jobs a long time. Most, especially the recent ones, had previously been branch managers, and saw themselves as having more expertise than branch managers. In their performance evaluations, they were judged by the turnover rate of merchandise in their department—by improvement in gross profit and by inventory control. Their buying choices were crucial. Yet, as Anne said to her boss, "We cannot buy effectively, unless we know what's selling." Anne knew that buyers needed the cooperation of sales personnel in reporting low stock in the stores.

THE HISTORY OF CONFLICT

For years before Anne's appointment, there had been friction between buyers and branch managers. Anne's predecessor didn't get on well with the former Manager of Toronto Area Branch Stores. This friction was reflected down the line, when buyers went into individual stores.

The sense of hostility had decreased recently. Two of the more abrasive buyers had left. The new manager of Toronto Area Branch Stores, Gary Heaney, got on well with Anne and they talked nearly every day.

Like Anne, Gary was young, personable, and had a strong track record. His original interest in joining Birks was diamonds, and he had worked at the company as a Registered Jeweler before becoming Manager of the Sherway Store—one of the largest and most effective branches in the Birks organization. Like most of the 15 branch managers who now reported to him (the Eaton Centre Store reported directly to Ed Ballon), his experience did not include buying. Both Gary and Anne wanted to increase cooperation between their two areas.

Still, the friction remained. Buyers reported to Anne that a lot of sales staff were not communicating with them? "We go in to make sure the store is looking good, but they won't be open with us." Anne heard that a few branch managers had to be "coaxed" even to come out of their offices during a visit.

Although branch managers were supposed to notify supervisors of the buyer's schedule for visiting, the buyer sometimes arrived to find that the supervisor was not there. Buyers complained that on these occasions "there was no thought of letting us know."

Anne's buyers generally felt that the hardest branch managers to deal with were those that "were diamond-oriented" and had little interest in other merchandise. Anne sensed, however, that some of the older buyers had the worst relations. As one senior buyer said about a branch manager who seemed not interested in the buyer's area, "There's no point wasting my time talking to him. I just go in and do my job."

Anne thought that the branch managers were often unduly impatient with delays in getting merchandise; they often wanted things "now" and didn't realize "our problems in getting things through." They didn't seem to appreciate the need for prompt reporting when stock was getting low, and why items they needed took so long to appear. They didn't understand all the steps in the process of getting stock on the shelves, and why it often took one and a half weeks to get items from a supplier.

Anne had talked about the situation informally with Gary and some of the branch managers, but wished that "something concrete would be set down, saying, 'These are the rules.'"

Her boss, Ed Ballon, was aware of the difficulties in the relationship between branch personnel and buyers, but felt that overall the process was effective, since the Toronto Area had made spectacular increases in sales.

THE TRAINING SESSION

In an effort to improve relations between buyers and branch managers, Gary Heaney asked Anne to take part in a training program he was organizing for branch managers, to be held on four consecutive Tuesdays in April. On the first day, along with participating in other sessions on merchandise and promotions, Anne was to help lead a session entitled, "Productive Store Visits: A Discussion about Maximizing Benefits to the Department and Branch Managers." It was scheduled for 5 o'clock on the first day of the program. (See Figure 10–10: Agenda.) Anne readily agreed.

The session was held away from Head Office in a building Birks regularly used for group meetings. After being introduced by Gary, Anne began by explaining what the buyers wanted when going to the stores—"what we hoped to accomplish."

From her perspective the meeting soon turned into a gripe session: "Everyone was tired and they wanted to go home, so they just criticized. I got hit with everything the department managers—buyers—weren't doing." Among the things she heard were that:

- buyers' attitudes were arrogant;
- buyers didn't take any time to speak to people;
- buyers didn't spend much time in the store;
- jewelry and watch buyers didn't visit regularly;
- buyers didn't think the stores had qualified managers and supervisors;

FIGURE 10–10   *Agenda: Tuesday Division, Management Training Program—Session I. Tuesday, April 12—Yonge & Temperance*

MERCHANDISE MANAGEMENT		
9:00 A.M.	Store Results & Store Objectives	E.M. Ballon
10:00 A.M.	Coffee	
10:30 A.M.	Basic Stock for 1988	Anne Haley Joe Van
	(i) Jewelry—Roger Smith (ii) Watches—Burkhard von Oppeln (iii) Gifts—Anne Haley Never Out Stock of Basic Items!	
12:30 P.M.	Lunch	
1:30 P.M.	Organizing for Promotions—A Case Study	Gary Heaney Jane Campbell
	(i) Major Promotions (ii) Minor Promotions (iii) Unadvertised Promotions	
3:30 P.M.	Tea	
4:00 P.M.	Promoting & Administering Large Sales— A Discussion (i) Group A—Roger Smith (ii) Group B—Gary Heaney	Roger Smith
5:00 P.M.	Productive Store Visits—A Discussion Maximizing Benefits to the Department and Branch Managers	Anne Haley Gary Heaney
5:30 P.M.	Adjourn	

- branch managers wanted more attention from buyers;
- buyers often just removed slow-moving merchandise from the shelves—"threw it on the floor"—for the supervisors to invoice and ship to the warehouse. On a busy day this interfered with selling.
- supervisors often didn't know exactly when the buyers were coming.

The meeting ended inconclusively according to Anne, with just a statement that "we'd work on things." Although Gary seemed pleased with the way the session had gone, she was not. She sensed personal hostility and thought that the stores were complaining about some things that weren't valid.

STEP 2: Prepare the case for class discussion.

STEP 3: Answer the following questions, individually, in small groups, or with the entire class, as directed by your instructor.

DESCRIPTION
1. Describe the relationship between buyers and store managers.

DIAGNOSIS
2. What type of interdependence do the groups demonstrate?
3. What factors affect the interactions between these groups?

4. Does conflict exist? If so, at what level and stage does it exist?

PRESCRIPTION
5. Why was the training session not successful?
6. How could the interactions between the groups be improved?

ACTION
7. What are the costs and benefits of other options for improving the relations between the buyers and store managers?

STEP 4: Discussion. In small groups, with the entire class, or in written form, share your answers to the questions above. Then answer the following questions:

1. What symptoms suggest that a problem exists?
2. What problems exist in the case?
3. What theories and concepts help explain the problems?
4. How can the problems be corrected?
5. Are the actions likely to be effective?

This case was prepared by Professor Margo Northey of the Western Business School. Copyright © 1988, The University of Western Ontario. This material is not covered under authorization from CanCopy or any reproduction rights organization. Any form of reproduction, storage or transmittal of this material is prohibited without written permission from Western Business School, The University of Western Ontario, London, Canada N6A 3K7. Reprinted with permission, Western Business School.

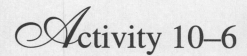 **Activity 10–6**

NEGOTIATION SKILLS: A SELF-ASSESSMENT EXERCISE

STEP 1: Complete the following questionnaire.

> Please respond to this list of questions in terms of what you believe you do **when interacting with others.** Base your answers on your typical day-to-day activities. Be as frank as you can.
>
> For each statement, please enter on the Score Sheet the number corresponding to your choice of the five possible responses given below:
>
> 1. If you have **never (or very rarely)** observed yourself doing what is described in the statement.
> 2. If you have observed yourself doing what is described in the statement **occasionally, but infrequently:** that is, less often than most other people who are involved in similar situations.

3. If you have observed yourself doing what is described in the statement about **an average amount:** that is, about as often as most other people who are involved in similar situations.

4. If you have observed yourself doing what is described in the statement **fairly frequently:** that is, somewhat more often than most other people who are involved in similar situations.

5. If you have observed yourself doing what is described in the statement **very frequently:** that is, considerably more than most other people who are involved in similar situations.

Please answer each question.

1. I focus on the entire situation or problem.
2. I evaluate the facts according to a set of personal values.
3. I am relatively unemotional.
4. I think that the facts speak for themselves in most situations.
5. I enjoy working on new problems.
6. I focus on what is going on between people when interacting.
7. I tend to analyze things very carefully.
8. I am neutral when arguing.
9. I work in bursts of energy with slack periods in between.
10. I am sensitive to other people's needs and feelings.
11. I hurt people's feelings without knowing it.
12. I am good at keeping track of what has been said in a discussion.
13. I put two and two together quickly.
14. I look for common ground and compromise.
15. I use logic to solve problems.
16. I know most of the details when discussing an issue.
17. I follow my inspirations of the moment.
18. I take strong stands on matters of principle.
19. I am good at using a step-by-step approach.
20. I clarify information for others.
21. I get my facts a bit wrong.
22. I try to please people.
23. I am very systematic when making a point.
24. I relate facts to experience.
25. I am good at pinpointing essentials.
26. I enjoy harmony.
27. I weigh the pros and cons.
28. I am patient.
29. I project myself into the future.
30. I let my decisions be influenced by my personal likes and wishes.
31. I look for cause and effect.
32. I focus on what needs attention now.
33. When others become uncertain or discouraged, my enthusiasm carries them along.
34. I am sensitive to praise.

35. I make logical statements.
36. I rely on well tested ways to solve problems.
37. I keep switching from one idea to another.
38. I offer bargains.
39. I have my ideas very well thought out.
40. I am precise in my arguments.
41. I bring others to see the exciting possibilities in a situation.
42. I appeal to emotions and feelings to reach a "fair" deal.
43. I present well articulated arguments for the proposals I favor.
44. I do not trust inspiration.
45. I speak in a way which conveys a sense of excitement to others.
46. I communicate what I am willing to give in return for what I get.
47. I put forward proposals or suggestions which make sense even if they are unpopular.
48. I am pragmatic.
49. I am imaginative and creative in analyzing a situation.
50. I put together very well-reasoned arguments.
51. I actively solicit others' opinions and suggestions.
52. I document my statements.
53. My enthusiasm is contagious.
54. I build upon others' ideas.
55. My proposals command the attention of others.
56. I like to use the inductive method (from facts to theories).
57. I can be emotional at times.
58. I use veiled or open threats to get others to comply.
59. When I disagree with someone, I skillfully point out the flaws in the others' arguments.
60. I am low-key in my reactions.
61. In trying to persuade others, I appeal to their need for sensations and novelty.
62. I make other people feel that they have something of value to contribute.
63. I put forth ideas which are incisive.
64. I face difficulties with realism.
65. I point out the positive potential in discouraging or difficult situations.
66. I show tolerance and understanding of others' feelings.
67. I use arguments relevant to the problem at hand.
68. I am perceived as a down-to-earth person.
69. I go beyond the facts.
70. I give people credit for their ideas and contributions.
71. I like to organize and plan.
72. I am skillful at bringing up pertinent facts.
73. I have a charismatic tone.
74. When disputes arise, I search for the areas of agreement.
75. I am consistent in my reactions.
76. I quickly notice what needs attention.
77. I withdraw when the excitement is over.
78. I appeal for harmony and cooperation.
79. I am cool when negotiating.
80. I work all the way through to reach a conclusion.

STEP 2: Score the completed questionnaire.

> Enter the score you assign each question (1, 2, 3, 4, or 5) in the space provided. *Please note:* The item numbers progress across the page from left to right. When you have all your scores, add them up *vertically* to attain four totals. Insert a "3" in any number space left blank.
>
> 1. _____ 2. _____ 3. _____ 4. _____
> 5. _____ 6. _____ 7. _____ 8. _____
> 9. _____ 10. _____ 11. _____ 12. _____
> 13. _____ 14. _____ 15. _____ 16. _____
> 17. _____ 18. _____ 19. _____ 20. _____
> 21. _____ 22. _____ 23. _____ 24. _____
> 25. _____ 26. _____ 27. _____ 28. _____
> 29. _____ 30. _____ 31. _____ 32. _____
> 33. _____ 34. _____ 35. _____ 36. _____
> 37. _____ 38. _____ 39. _____ 40. _____
> 41. _____ 42. _____ 43. _____ 44. _____
> 45. _____ 46. _____ 47. _____ 48. _____
> 49. _____ 50. _____ 51. _____ 52. _____
> 53. _____ 54. _____ 55. _____ 56. _____
> 57. _____ 58. _____ 59. _____ 60. _____
> 61. _____ 62. _____ 63. _____ 64. _____
> 65. _____ 66. _____ 67. _____ 68. _____
> 69. _____ 70. _____ 71. _____ 72. _____
> 73. _____ 74. _____ 75. _____ 76. _____
> 77. _____ 78. _____ 79. _____ 80. _____
> IN: _____ NR: _____ AN: _____ FA: _____

NEGOTIATION STYLE PROFILE

Enter now your four scores on the bar and chart below. Construct your profile by connecting the four data points.

DESCRIPTION OF STYLES

Factual

Basic Assumption "The facts speak for themselves."

Behavior Pointing out facts in a neutral way, keeping track of what has been said, reminding people of their

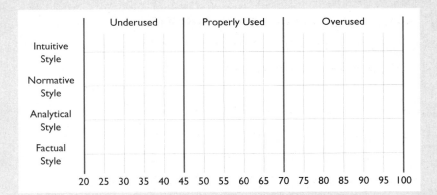

statements, knowing most of the details of the discussed issue and sharing them with others, clarifying, relating facts to experience, being low-key in their reactions, looking for proof, documenting their statements.

Key Words Meaning, define, explain, clarify, facts.

Intuitive

Basic Assumption "Imagination can solve any problem."

Behavior Making warm and enthusiastic statements, focusing on the entire situation or problem, pinpointing essentials, making projections into the future, being imaginative and creative in analyzing the situation, keep switching from one subject to another, going beyond the facts, coming up with new ideas all the time, pushing and withdrawing from time to time, putting two and two together quickly, getting their facts a bit wrong sometimes, being deductive.

Key Words Principles, essential, tomorrow, creative, idea.

Normative

Basic Assumption "Negotiating is bargaining."

Behavior Judging, assessing, and evaluating the facts according to a set of personal values, approving and disapproving, agreeing and disagreeing, using loaded works, offering bargains, proposing rewards, incentives, appealing to feelings and emotions to reach a "fair" deal, demanding, requiring, threatening, involving power, using status, authority, correlating, looking for compromise, making effective statements, focusing on people, their reactions, judging, attention to communication and group processes.

Key Words Wrong, right, good, bad, like.

Analytical

Basic Assumption "Logic leads to the right conclusions."

Behavior Forming reasons, drawing conclusions and applying them to the case in negotiation, arguing in favor or against one's own or others' position, directing, breaking down, dividing, analyzing each situation for cause and effect, identifying relationships of the parts, putting things into logical order, organizing, weighing the pros and cons thoroughly, making identical statements, using linear reckoning.

Key Words Because, then, consequently, therefore, in order to.

GUIDELINES FOR NEGOTIATING WITH PEOPLE HAVING DIFFERENT STYLES

1. Negotiating with someone having a *factual* style—
   - Be *precise* in presenting your facts.
   - Refer to the *past* (what has already been tried out, what has worked, what has been shown from past experiences. . .).
   - Be *indicative* (go from the facts to the principles).
   - Know your dossier (including the details).
   - Document what you say.
2. Negotiating with someone having an *intuitive* style—
   - Focus on the situation as a whole.
   - Project yourself into the future (look for opportunities).
   - Tap the imagination and creativity of your partner.
   - Be quick in reacting (jump from one idea to another).
   - Build upon the reaction of the other person.
3. Negotiating with someone having an *analytical* style—
   - Use logic when arguing.
   - Look for causes and effects.
   - Analyze the relationships between the various elements of the situation or problem at stake.
   - Be patient.
   - Analyze various options with their respective pros and cons.
4. Negotiating with someone having a *normative* style—
   - Establish a sound relationship right at the outset of the negotiation.
   - Show your interest in what the other person is saying.
   - Identify his or her values and adjust to them accordingly.
   - Be ready to compromise.
   - Appeal to your partner's feelings.

STEP 3: Discussion. In small groups or with the class as a whole, answer the following questions:

1. What did your score pattern look like?
2. What are the implications of your score for negotiating cross culturally?

Casse, Pierre. *Training for the Cross-Cultural Mind* 2d ed. Washington DC: Society for Intercultural Education, Training and Research, 1981. Out of print.

$\mathscr{A}$ctivity 10–7 UGLI ORANGE ROLE PLAY

STEP 1: The instructor will divide the class into groups of three—in each group one person will play Dr. Roland, one will play Dr. Jones, and one will be an observer. The instructor will then distribute the roles to each group. After assigning one role for each group member, read the role descriptions. Then spend five minutes "getting into your role."

STEP 2: The group leader will read—

I am Mr(s). Cardoza, the owner of the remaining Ugli oranges. My fruit-exporting firm is based in South America. My country does not have diplomatic relations with your country, although we do have strong trade relations.

After you have read about your roles, you may negotiate with the other firm's representative. Spend about ten minutes meeting with the other firm's representative and decide on a course of action. Be prepared to answer the following questions:

1. What do you plan to do?
2. If you want to buy the oranges, what price will you offer?
3. To whom and how will the oranges be delivered?

STEP 3: The observers will report the solutions reached. Then they will describe the process used in their negotiating team.

STEP 4: Discussion. Answer the following questions with the entire class.

DESCRIPTION
1. What solution did each group reach?

DIAGNOSIS
2. What are some key features of a bargaining situation?
3. What influences the effectiveness of negotiations?

PRESCRIPTION
4. How can the effectiveness of negotiations be improved?

Reprinted by permission of the author, Robert J. House, University of Toronto.

$\mathscr{A}$ctivity 10–8 SALARY NEGOTIATIONS

INTRODUCTION

In this simulation, you will play the role of either a manager or subordinate in a negotiation over salary. Both in securing employment as well as promotions, we frequently are in a position to negotiate with our superiors over salary; and, once we achieve managerial rank, we do the same with subordinates. This is one of the most common and, at the same time, most personal forms of negotiation. For many people, it is also the most difficult. Since salary can be a means of satisfying many needs—economic, recognition, status, or competitive success measure—it leads to complex negotiations.

STEP 1: **(5 Minutes)** The class will be divided into groups of three; two will be assigned the roles of manager and subordinate, the other as an observer. Role-players will be assigned either an "A" or a "B" role in one of the Salary Simulations. Assemble with your trio in the place specified by the instructor.

STEP 2: **(5 Minutes)** Read your assigned role and prepare a strategy. If you are an observer, review the Observer Reporting Sheet and make sure you understand what to look for.

STEP 3: **(10 Minutes)** Carry out your discussion with your counterpart. If you finish before the allotted time is up, review the sequence of events with the other party and tell the other what he or she did that was productive or unproductive to the negotiations.

If you are an observer, make brief notes during the roleplay on your Observer Reporting Sheet. When the roleplay is over, review the sheet and add further details where necessary.

STEP 4: **(10 Minutes)** In your trio, discuss the outcome of the negotiation. The observer should report what he or she saw each party doing. Review what steps or positions seemed most and least useful.

At the end of the time for Step 4, the observer should hand his Observer Reporting Sheet to the instructor.

Observer Reporting Sheet

Round _____ .

How did A open meeting? _____

_____

_____

How did B respond to the way A opened the meeting? _____

_____

_____

Was an agreement reached? Yes _____ , no _____ .

What was the salary agreed to, if there was an agreement? _____

Were there any other added features in the settlement achieved? _____

_____

Will future relations between A and B be better (+), worse (−), or the same (=) as a result of this meeting? List the opinions of A, B, and the observer.

A _____ , B _____ , Observer _____ .

STEP 5: **(5 Minutes)** In your trio, change role assignments so that the person filling an A role now fills a B role, the person filling the B role now becomes observer, and the previous observer now fills an A role.

STEP 6: **(5 Minutes)** Repeat step 2.

STEP 7: **(10 Minutes)** Repeat step 3.

STEP 8: **(10 Minutes)** Repeat step 4.

STEPS 9, 10, 11, 12: **(30 Minutes)** Repeat steps 5, 6, 7, 8.

STEP 13: **(30 Minutes)** The instructor will post the results from the three sets of roleplays. Examine the different outcomes and explore reasons why they occurred and their consequences.

STEP 14: Discussion Questions

1. Were there any differences in the way negotiations were handled when:
   a. Both parties in a roleplay were satisfied?
   b. One was satisfied?
   c. Both were dissatisfied?
2. Were some people playing the same role dissatisfied with an outcome that others in the same role found satisfying? Why? How do you account for this?
3. Poll quickly those who were satisfied with the outcome. Ask why they were satisfied.
4. Poll quickly those who were dissatisfied with the outcome. Ask why they were dissatisfied.
5. What was the effect observing another's negotiation on how you negotiated? Did what you see as an observer affect how satisfied you felt with your own outcome?

Developed by Roy J. Lewicki and published in Lewicki and Litterer. *Negotiations: Readings, Exercises, and Cases,* Richard D. Irwin, Homewood, Il. 1985. Used with permission.

*A*ctivity 10–9   PELICAN LANDING NEGOTIATION

STEP 1: Read the following background information:

HISTORIC OLD TOWN

Old Town was the historic district, along the east bank of the Green River, that had formed the core of the original Springfield settlement. As the community flourished over the years following its founding, almost all the new growth had taken place just across the river in what was now identified in everyone's mind, and on most maps, as Springfield. Downtown Springfield bordered the Green River, with the rest of Springfield spreading west beyond it. This divergence of growth was probably as much a result of a feud between two of the families that had settled Springfield as it was the topography east of Old Town.

Although still linked to downtown Springfield by two old bridges, Old Town had been largely ignored as a commercial area. For decades, in fact, Old Town had

been characterized as "light industrial" or "the warehouse district." Eventually, however, even those uses had been discontinued, and Old Town now contained little more than old vacant buildings and empty lots littered with broken glass, weeds, and abandoned vehicles. The City of Springfield owned much of the property in Old Town.

PELICAN LANDING AND THE BENDER CORPORATION

The Bender Corporation, a real estate development and property management company based 20 miles upstream from Springfield in Kentwood, also owned a lot of the property in Old Town, and it was now interested in turning Old Town into a residential community containing a combination of condominiums and rental units. Pelican Landing, as the project was to be called, was designed to include a small marina also. The proposed development had been tentatively endorsed by The Downtown Springfield Merchants Association and the local media.

The Bender Corporation had recently completed a similar development, called Miraloma Pointe, in Kentwood. After a shaky beginning, Miraloma Pointe now seemed to be doing well. Corbett thought that Pelican Landing was just the type of development that could stimulate the Bender Corporation and generate much needed new business. The past decade had not been kind to the company. Corbett leaned back and briefly reflected upon the events that had contributed to Bender's present financial plight.

When Corbett first became Vice President, the Bender Corporation was relatively small but very dynamic. The corporation had earned its reputation by specializing in urban residential development projects—condominiums, apartment buildings, or a combination of the two. After completion, the property management division would take care of selling or renting the units. Even if the entire development had been built for or sold to a third party, the property management division would often be retained to manage the project.

Interest in the Bender Corporation was high, as were the profits. A lot of growth was taking place in Kentwood and the cities nearby, and Bender could boast of a dozen medium- or large-scale projects in various stages of planning or construction at any one time—developments such as the Divisadero Center, or the award winning Latimer Towers. Not only were the buildings full (thus generating large rents or management fees for the Bender Corporation), but the demand for more construction was high. It seemed that everyone wanted to live in "a Bender building."

Unfortunately, and suddenly (as it appeared to Corbett in retrospect), everything came to a standstill. Not only did new urban construction slow down, but people and companies started leaving the cities for other states or the less expensive suburbs. The opening of the interstate highway west of Kentwood, instead of bringing people to the city, seemed to have the opposite effect. Bedroom communities sprang up overnight along the interstate corridor.

Not only did Corbett find suburban tract houses and shopping malls aesthetically displeasing, Corbett knew they represented a loss of the company's income. As demand for urban living had dropped, so had rents, sales, and new construction. Corbett had been severely criticized for failing to anticipate and to capitalize on urban flight by building in the suburbs, but that was water over the dam.

What was important now was that cities once again represented opportunities for growth, and workers were again looking for homes near the city center. The Bender Corporation, after surviving some lean years, was now poised to take advantage of the young professionals' renewed interest in living and working in the city. That was why Corbett was excited about Pelican Landing.

Many cities, although welcoming new projects in their area, were also eager to seek concessions from a developer before agreeing to pursue a project.

STEP 2: Your instructor will divide the class into groups of two. Your instructor will then distribute the roles to each person. After assigning the roles of Lee Lawson and Chris Corbett, read the role description. Then spend five minutes "getting into your role" and preparing for the negotiation.

STEP 3: After you have read about and prepared your roles, negotiate with the other party. Spend about fifteen to twenty-five minutes meeting with the other person and decide on a course of action.

STEP 4: The instructor will ask each pair to report its agreement. Then describe the process used in your negotiation.

STEP 5: Discussion. Answer the following questions with the entire class:

DESCRIPTION
1. What solution did each group reach?
2. Which group reached the best solution?
3. Which person reached the best solution?

DIAGNOSIS
4. What are some key features of the negotiating situation?
5. What influenced the effectiveness of negotiations?
6. Were any creative alternatives offered?

PRESCRIPTION
7. How could the effectiveness of the negotiations be improved?

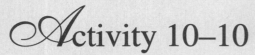

Activity 10–10

"OVERWORKED GM EMPLOYEES STRIKE AT FLINT PLANT"

STEP 1: View the ABC video entitled "Overworked GM Employees Strike at Flint Plant."

STEP 2: Your instructor will divide the class into small groups. Each group will be assigned the role of either the union leader who represents the strikes depicted in the video or the human resources vice president who represents General Motors.

STEP 3: After you have read about and prepared your roles, negotiate with the other party, as directed by your instructor. Spend about 15 to 25 minutes trying to identify the key issues impeding agreement and then reaching an agreement.

STEP 4: The instructor will ask each pair of groups to report its agreement. Then describe the process used in your negotiation.

STEP 5: Answer the following questions with the entire class.

DESCRIPTION
1. What solution did each group reach?

DIAGNOSIS
2. What were the key issues impeding settlement?
3. What process did the parties use to reach an agreement?
4. What hindered reaching an agreement between parties?
5. What effect did each party's interests and best alternative to a negotiated agreement have on the negotiations?

PRESCRIPTION
6. How could a strike have been avoided?
7. How could the effectiveness of the negotiations have been improved?

Chapter 11

Chapter Outline

- **The Changed Culture at UPS**
- **The Functions of Organizational Culture**
- **Revealing an Organization's Culture**
  - **Mission Statements**
  - **Heroes and Heroines**
  - **Myths and Stories**
  - **Rituals and Ceremonies**
  - **Physical Arrangements**
- **Creating a Culture of Total Quality**
  - **Customer Satisfaction**
  - **Continuous Improvement**
  - **Worker Empowerment**
  - **Leadership**
- **Learning Organizations**
- **Creating and Changing the Organization's Culture**
  - **Implementing Total Quality Programs**
  - **Creating a Learning Organization**
- **Summary**
- **Diagnostic Questions**
- **Activities**

Building an Organizational Culture

After completing the reading and activities in Chapter 11, students will be able to

1. Define organizational culture and list the functions it can serve.

2. Describe and give an example of five components of an organization's culture.

3. Illustrate an organization that has changed its culture.

4. Describe the four pillars of total quality management.

5. List the characteristics of a learning organization.

6. Offer three strategies for changing an organization's culture.

7. Discuss the steps to implementing total quality management in an organization.

8. Offer a plan for creating a learning organization.

The Changed Culture at UPS

I n the early 1990s, United Parcel Service was losing significant business to competitors such as Federal Express and Roadway Package System. In response, the company launched an ambitious, long-term effort to change its culture and operating procedures to focus on customer service. Now the company has a "can do" corporate culture that offers flexible pricing, instant tracking information about packages, and increased employee stock ownership.

UPS has shifted its focus from residential to business deliveries and now offers discounts, flexible pickup and delivery times, and specially designed shipping plans for its corporate customers. All customers can now choose between one-, two-, and three-day arrivals at prices competitive to Federal Express.

The company has also undergone a dramatic transformation in its use of information technology. A $2 billion infusion in the early 1990s and plans for an additional $3.2 billion investment have allowed the company to develop a mobile communications system that provides up-to-date information about the status of each shipment. Delivery drivers carry computerized clipboards and have on-truck computers to provide instantaneous tracking information. Managers have received significant training to support the new customer-oriented culture.

UPS's emphasis on customer service has paid off. For example, Eastman Kodak Company threatened to remove UPS from its accepted shipper's list, citing the shipper's lack of responsiveness. Now UPS has a full-time service representative on-site at Kodak. Representatives such as these suggest ways corporate clients can reduce shipping costs and improve delivery. UPS has found that meeting customer requests for next-day service led in turn to earlier pickups, new sorting procedures, earlier delivery times, and more uniform work flows. The company has saved money while delivering faster service.[1]

Like UPS, many companies are changing their culture to increase their competitiveness. An increased focus on customer service, quality, and employee involvement are just a few of the features that characterize these efforts to change organizational culture for the better. In this chapter we first examine the nature of organizational culture in general. We discuss its functions and the ways of revealing the culture in an organization. The second part of this chapter discusses *total quality management,* a comprehensive effort to improve both organizational effectiveness and efficiency. We examine the relationship of TQM to an organization's culture and learn about the four pillars of total quality management. The next part of this chapter looks at the nature of a learning organization—its purpose, characteristics, and effectiveness. We conclude the chapter by discussing ways of changing an organization's culture.

THE FUNCTIONS OF ORGANIZATIONAL CULTURE

An organization's *culture* describes the part of its internal environment that incorporates a set of assumptions, beliefs, and values that organizational members share and use to guide their functioning.[2] Strong, strategically appropriate, and adaptive organizational cultures have a positive effect on an organization's long-term economic performance.[3]

IBM. Lou Gerstner faced the task of altering IBM's old culture to allow the company to respond more quickly and more effectively to a dynamic environment. The old culture was risk-averse, slow to change, and arrogant. Little cooperation existed between different divisions. Gerstner has focused on supporting innovative employees and their ideas, downsizing the company, and focusing on achieving bottom-line results.[4]

The culture can affect the way individuals make sense of events, even influencing their schemas for organizing and retaining information (see Chapter 2).[5] At UPS, for example, the culture focuses on the belief that customer service should underlie all activities. Culture also refers to shared meanings or interpretations that are largely tacit and unique to group or organizational members, and that focus their actions.[6]

Managers use culture in a variety of ways:[7]

- *Support the organization's business strategy.* At UPS, the new customer-service culture reinforced the business strategy of offering more flexible and responsive package pricing, pickup, and delivery to corporate customers.

- *Prescribe acceptable ways for managers to interact with external constituencies* such as shareholders, the government, or customers. The UPS culture directed managers to take a "can do" attitude with regard to their corporate customers, which led to putting service representatives on site.

- *Make staffing decisions.* Workers who are reluctant to use new technology or managers who lack a customer-service orientation likely will experience employment problems at UPS.

- *Set performance criteria.* Managers and other employees can be evaluated on the basis of their ability to meet standards consistent with the culture. At UPS, these standards reflect the new dedication to customer service.

- *Guide the nature of acceptable interpersonal relationships in the company.* UPS's corporate culture encourages managers and workers to jointly find creative solutions to customers' problems.

- *Select appropriate management styles.* The customer-service culture combined with the increased availability of information technology at UPS probably increased worker empowerment and fostered a change in management style that supported decentralized decision making.

Generally, culture is considered to provide consistency to an organization by integrating diverse elements into a coherent set of beliefs, values, assumptions, and consequent behaviors. In fact, some researchers hold that the strength and consistency of an organization's culture, the clarity of its mission, its emphasis on involving employees in decision making, and its ability to foster a positive response to organizational change can predict organizational effectiveness.[8]

Recent research, however, suggests two other possibilities.[9] An organization's culture may be a "mosaic of inconsistencies," with meaning shared only within subcultures, such as departments, divisions, or even work teams, rather than across the entire organization. Alternatively, no shared meanings or understandings exist. Instead, culture refers to the amalgamation of what individual organizational members experience. In this book, we consider the first and second possibilities only—that culture can exist either organization-wide or within subunits of an organization.

REVEALING AN ORGANIZATION'S CULTURE

An early model examined organizational culture at three levels, known as artifacts (level 1), values (level 2), and assumptions (level 3), as shown in Figure 11–1.[10] To reveal the culture, you can begin with the artifacts, audible and visible patterns of behavior, technology, and art, at level 1. Then you search deeper, in levels 2 and 3 in turn, for the underlying values and assumptions and the more subtle, less apparent reflections of the culture. To create culture, you can begin at the deepest level by formulating the assumptions of level 3, which then become values of level 2, and ultimately are reflected in artifacts, such as mission statements, of level 1.

HANNA ANDERSON. This Portland, Oregon, company sells children's clothing by mail. Their corporate values include "social action," specified as "We will research specific opportunities for Hanna to contribute to the community." The company introduced a program called Hannadowns. Customers received a 20 percent credit for returning to the company clothes their infants had outgrown. Hanna Anderson then laundered the clothing and gave it to needy families or women's shelters. This program illustrates a cultural artifact that reflects the organization's values of contributions to the community and high product quality. The Hannadowns program indicates that the clothing's quality is so good the company buys it back from customers.[11]

A more recent model describes organizational culture as dynamic because assumptions, values, artifacts, and symbols interact in four cultural processes:[12]

- ■ *Manifestation.* Cultural assumptions are revealed in the perceptions, cognitions, and emotions of organizational members. At UPS, assumptions about the "can do" attitude are changed into perceptions that customer service has top priority.

- ■ *Realization.* Perceptions, cognitions, and emotions are transformed into tangible artifacts. Artifacts can include rites, rituals, myths, and stories. The top priority given to the value of customer service at UPS is reflected in such stories as the turnaround at Kodak.

- ■ *Symbolization.* Particular artifacts take on a specific symbolic significance. On-site service representatives who try to secure the best deals for customers now symbolize the way UPS does business.

FIGURE 11–1   *A model of the levels of culture*

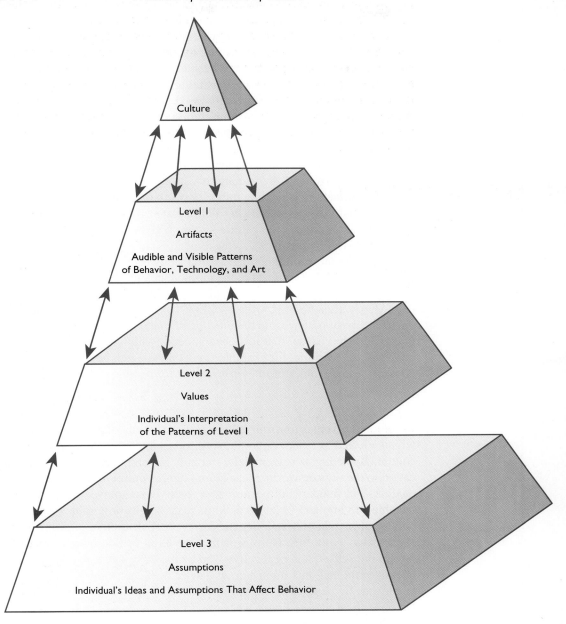

- ■ *Interpretation.* The meaning of symbolization processes is determined by people inside and outside the organization. Kodak executives see the on-site representative as a symbol of the "new" UPS.

  We most often look at culture, however, by observing its artifacts, shown at level 1 in Figure 11–1. At this level, the components of an organization's culture include its mission statement, heroes and heroines, myths and stories, rituals and ceremonies, and physical arrangements, as discussed in the next sections.

MISSION STATEMENTS

A company's culture reflects the basic organizational philosophy of its leaders. This philosophy as well as the most basic values, beliefs, and assumptions underlying the organization's culture is often expressed in the company's mission.

BEN & JERRY'S ICE CREAM. As one of the top producers of super-premium ice cream in the country, Ben & Jerry's Ice Cream built its corporate culture around a mission of social good and responsibility. Despite the challenge of maintaining these ideals in the face of extremely rapid growth, company founders Ben Cohen and Jerry Greenfield refused to compromise their social goals. The company's management style, which focuses on people, fun, and egalitarian economic goals, complemented their 1960s-rooted social consciousness. The appointment of a new CEO, the first who was not a company founder, continued the tradition of social activism. Robert Holland, Jr., brought his strong managerial skills as well as a long-time commitment to educating minority youth to his new leadership role.[13]

A formal *mission statement,* as illustrated by Johnson & Johnson's credo in Figure 11–2, expresses the culture's basic beliefs, defines success for employees, and establishes standards of achievement. The requirements of the industry in which the organization functions as well as its national culture may exert an influence on the beliefs expressed in the mission statement.[14]

ALCOA. Paul O'Neill instituted dramatic changes at Aluminum Company of America (Alcoa) after he took over as CEO. His goal was to close the gap between Alcoa's current practice and the practice of market leaders by at least 80 percent in two years. He insisted that this change occur within Alcoa's value structure. Risk taking and innovation, for example, were encouraged, but within the bounds of the company's core values of integrity, respect for people, and safety.[15]

HEROES AND HEROINES

Heroes and heroines transmit culture by personifying its corporate values. A leader who is viewed as a hero or heroine reinforces the basic values of an organization's culture. By acting as role models, symbolizing and hence representing the organization to the outside world, these heroic figures preserve the organization's special qualities, set standards of performance, motivate employees, and make success attainable and human.[16] Managers who create heroes or heroines foster a set of corporate values that may stabilize the current organization or expedite change.

SOUTHWEST AIRLINES. Herb Kelleher, the CEO of Southwest Airlines, is a flamboyant but self-effacing executive who by the early 1990s had built Southwest Airlines into the nation's ninth-largest carrier. Kelleher knows many of Southwest's employees by name. They in turn call him the familiar "Uncle Herb" or "Herbie." He once dressed as Klinger from the TV show "Mash" and visited maintenance hangers at two o'clock in the morning. He even got hit on the head by a cargo-bay door when working as a baggage handler, one of his many attempts to learn how being an employee at Southwest felt.[17]

MYTHS AND STORIES

Myths are stories about corporate heroes and heroines that facilitate the transmission and embedding of culture. What does the repeated telling of a story about the spectacular rise of a copy editor to the presidency of a major advertising firm sug-

FIGURE 11–2   *Corporate mission statement*

JOHNSON & JOHNSON

Our Credo

We believe our first responsibility is to the doctors, nurses, and patients,
to mothers and fathers and all others who use our products and services.
In meeting their needs everything we do must be of high quality.
We must constantly strive to reduce our costs
in order to maintain reasonable prices.
Customers' orders must be serviced promptly and accurately.
Our suppliers and distributors must have an opportunity
to make a fair profit.
We are responsible to our employees,
the men and women who work with us throughout the world.
Everyone must be considered as an individual.
We must respect their dignity and recognize their merit.
They must have a sense of security in their jobs.
Compensation must be fair and adequate,
and working conditions clean, orderly and safe.
We must be mindful of ways to help our employees fulfill
their family responsibilities.
Employees must feel free to make suggestions and complaints.
There must be equal opportunity for employment, development
and advancement for those qualified.
We must provide competent management,
and their actions must be just and ethical.
We are responsible to the communities in which we live and work
and to the world community as well.
We must be good citizens—support good works and charities
and bear our fair share of taxes.
We must encourage civic improvements and better health and education.
We must maintain in good order
the property we are privileged to use,
protecting the environment and natural resources.
Our final responsibility is to our stockholders.
Business must make a sound profit.
We must experiment with new ideas.
Research must be carried on, innovative programs developed
and mistakes paid for.
New equipment must be purchased, new facilities provided
and new products launched.
Reserves must be created to provide for adverse times.
When we operate according to these principles,
the stockholders should realize a fair return.

SOURCE: Courtesy of Johnson & Johnson.

gest about a company's values? Does a story about the heir to the family fortune being the designated company president give the same impression? Clearly, the themes of such stories provide clues to an organization's culture. Consider the following, which reflects a culture in which employees take responsibility for meeting customer needs.

STEW LEONARD'S. The president of Stew Leonard's told the following story. "I unwrap one of our tuna sandwiches and this package of mayonnaise rolls out. I figure, the sandwich has enough mayo already. So I call Bill Hollis, my deli manager, and tell him, get rid of the extra mayo, it's expensive. "So next week, I open a sandwich, the Hellman's pops out again. I call Bill again, and he says, you gotta talk to Mary Ekstrand, she makes the sandwiches. I call Mary, who says, 'Sorry Stew, the customers want the extra mayo, so I'm packing it again.' You know my reaction? Bravo, Mary!"[18]

RITUALS AND CEREMONIES

Rituals, such as posting team accomplishments or year-end results, and ceremonies, such as retirement dinners or employee-of-the-month awards, contribute to corporate culture by dramatizing the organization's basic values. The award of a pin for twenty-five years of service, for example, reflects a company that values loyalty. Often linked with a corresponding organizational story about the value of long-term company service, such events can provide an explanation of new behavior patterns or reinforce existing ones.[19]

Rituals or ceremonies can also act as rites of passage, delineating entry into an organization's inner circle or expediting transitions in leadership. For example, a "new team" breakfast or dinner demarcates the change from the former to current team composition. In addition to celebrating passage into new social roles, rites can also enhance or dissolve social identities, renew or refurbish social structures, reduce conflict, and encourage common feelings among group members.[20]

PHYSICAL ARRANGEMENTS

The selection and arrangement of offices and furnishings often reveal significant insights into corporate culture and its underlying values. Compare the culture of an investment firm that provides only a desk and telephone for its brokers to the culture of a competitor that provides its brokers private offices. How might the cultures of these two firms differ? Often the physical arrangements can be used to support cultural values. By arranging desks in a bullpen area or providing many conference rooms, for example, an organization can encourage teamwork. E-mail and video-conferencing are another way to encourage communication and teamwork between workers at remote locations.

CREATING A CULTURE OF TOTAL QUALITY

At one time, the term quality conjured up images of the quality control inspector who identified faulty products after they came off the production line. Today, however, the term is associated with a long-term organization-wide effort to create a culture that facilitates the production of quality goods and services.[21] Such efforts are called *total quality management (TQM)* or *continuous quality improvement (CQI)*. The movement dates back to the 1950s, when W. Edwards Deming, an American academician and consultant, helped the Japanese rebuild their industry after World War II.[22] To remain competitive, companies around the world were forced to follow the Japanese example. The culture of TQM is characterized by the key value of customer satisfaction, which leads to efforts directed at continuous improvement.[23] These efforts are most likely to occur when workers are empowered by their leaders, who often demonstrate a special style of leadership. We look at each of these elements in turn in this section.

CUSTOMER SATISFACTION

The customer is at the center of all TQM activities. The underlying assumption is that customer satisfaction is the best indication of a quality good or service. Efforts to improve quality begin by listening to customers to identify their needs, preferences, and expectations. This information is collected and then disseminated throughout the organization. This information is then translated into specifications for the product or service that should have high utility.[24] UPS, for example, has dropped its policy of prompt delivery at any cost, giving drivers free time to talk with customers.

ZEBRA TECHNOLOGIES. Zebra Technologies introduced a new low-end printer in response to its customers' demands.[25]

KINDERCARE. KinderCare, a national child care organization, opened a center at an Illinois train station to specifically address the needs of commuters.[26]

Concern for the customer also extends to new policies toward suppliers. These include making purchasing decisions in terms of cost and quality, reducing the number of suppliers, establishing long-term contracts with suppliers, and developing cooperative relationships.[27] Each of these changes encourages suppliers to provide components with required specifications faster, more reliably, and at the lowest possible cost.

MARRIOTT. A team from numerous Marriott departments asked hotel guests what they valued. Its goal was to develop new standards for customer service and identify and correct any impediments to excellent service. The team found, for example, that guests disliked waiting to check in and repeating information at the hotel after they had made reservations by telephone. The team measured front-desk activity, studied the characteristics of cruise ship arrival procedures, which had the reputation for being fast and meeting customer needs, and reevaluated job classifications. They proposed ways to reduce check-in speed from almost three minutes in 1990 to one minute and 35 seconds in 1994.[28]

CONTINUOUS IMPROVEMENT

TQM programs foster continuous improvement in both an organization's product and the processes for creating it. The assumption underlying continuous improvement is the Japanese concept of *kaizen,* that every employee will seek gradual, continuous improvement in performance. Statistical control including control charts, Pareto analyses, and cause-and-effect diagrams are among the tools that support this underlying assumption and are used to diagnose, control, and improve the process.

Continuous improvement attempts to reduce the cost of quality by instituting measures to prevent poor quality. These measures guard against internal failures such as the need for rework or downtime and external failures such as customer complaints or returns.[29] Companies often try to create a *zero-defect* product, which means in theory that no exceptions or defects are tolerated. A manufacturer, for example, attempts to eliminate the need for reworking parts by performing jobs right the first time. A railroad can measure on-time delivery of cargo. As described earlier, TQM also puts demands on suppliers and subcontractors to provide high-quality defect-free components.

To identify truly excellent processes, companies may also **benchmark** selected processes at competitors or other industry leaders to identify truly excellent processes. Benchmarking involves gathering data about how well a company does in comparison to an "excellent" company in specific areas. The results help to create strategies for improvement. Usually, small teams conduct research and field trips to learn about excellent processes in another organization. Companies such as Ford Motor Company, IBM, Milliken, and Motorola, among others, use benchmarking as a standard improvement tool.[30]

XEROX. After learning that their competitors were selling copier machines at what the machines cost Xerox to make, Xerox became one of the first companies to introduce total quality management. Xerox benchmarked every function and task. For example, they benchmarked distribution at L.L. Bean, the Freeport, Maine, catalog-sales merchandiser. As a result of benchmarking, Xerox reduced suppliers from 5,000 to 300, increased the use of common parts among various machines from 20 to 70 percent, and reduced quality problems by two-thirds, manufacturing costs by one-half, development time by two-thirds, and direct labor by one-half.[31]

WORKER EMPOWERMENT

TQM places great emphasis on including all employees in its culture because of their role in continuous improvement. They organize employees for involvement by creating self-managing work teams, cross-functional teams, and task teams.[32] Human resource systems including selection, training, performance evaluation, and compensation support worker empowerment, giving workers responsibility for decision making and accountability for its outcomes. In their empowered role, employees are expected to call attention to specific quality problems in their normal work, look for ways to perform their jobs better, and identify ways to improve organizational functioning to create continuous improvement in organizational processes.[33]

CHRYSLER. Dennis K. Pawley, executive vice president for manufacturing, described true empowerment in this way: "True empowerment is, 'O.K., I trust you in this group of ten people so much that I'm going to pull the supervisor out and you will be self-directed. Here's the work that has to get done. You folks understand what the quality levels are and make sure you continuously improve it. Understand that we have to continuously improve productivity. You're responsible for that. Develop your own reward systems and how you are going to recognize each other's performance, control absenteeism, and schedule vacations.' These are the things the foreman used to do." This philosophy has resulted in a significant reduction of salaried management and increased production.[34]

EASTMAN CHEMICAL COMPANY. Eastman Chemical Company integrated quality improvement into the fabric of the company rather than keeping it apart from the company's culture. Information flows upward and downward in the organization. Top management involvement includes weekly all-day meetings of an interlocking team, a steering committee composed of senior managers who also lead teams of workers. The company has thousands of teams that include a large percentage of the employees. Workers with special expertise are chosen to participate on teams and excused only under unusual circumstances. Teams have initiated a major corporate reorganization, developed expert manufacturing systems, and improved plant maintenance. In addition, Eastman employees maintain ongoing contact with their counterparts in customers' organizations.[35]

LEADERSHIP

Quality depends on top management having a vision of excellence that they translate into organizational practices. Such practices include:

- communicate the importance of each employee's contribution to total quality;

- stress the quality-related synergies available through cooperation and teamwork;

- empower employees to "make a difference"; and

- reinforce individual and team commitment to quality with a wide range of rewards and reinforcements.[36]

IBM. IBM, in Rochester, Minnesota, has a "Speak Up" program that requires top management to acknowledge employees' comments and suggestions within ten days. Other quality leaders use employee attitude surveys to assess employee satisfaction and identify potential problems.[37]

Although TQM is usually a top-down effort, top management's support and relinquishing of some power is a prerequisite for effective TQM.[38] At UPS, for example, the effort to improve customer service originated with CEO Kent "Oz" Nelson. But it then involved large numbers of workers in making continuous improvements and ensuring customer satisfaction.

LEARNING ORGANIZATIONS

Creating a *learning organization* is useful for implementing total quality management. The idea of a learning organization originated with the idea of single-loop versus double-loop organization.[39] A *single-loop* or *adaptive* organization uses routine learning to accomplish its objectives, without significant changes in its basic assumptions. In contrast, a *double-loop* or *generative* organization uses experience to reevaluate its objectives and basic values and modify its culture.

A learning organization has the ability to fundamentally revitalize itself.[40] It can be characterized as a double-loop organization. It goes through a continuous cycle of experience, examination of experience, formulation of hypotheses about the experience, experimentation to test the hypotheses, and experience once again (see Figure 11–3).[41] Hence, the learning organization collects data to help individuals examine their experiences in the organization. The learning organi-

FIGURE 11–3 *Double loop learning process*

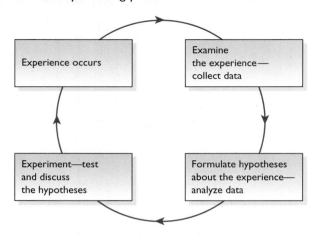

zation will also analyze the data to help individuals develop hypotheses about the experience and ways of improving it. They conduct open dialogue, which includes both constructive dissent and acknowledgement of failures as part of experimenting with the new learnings and applying them to organizational situations.[42] Organizational members learn from both past experiences as well as the best practices of other organizations and transfer knowledge rapidly and efficiently through the organization.[43] The learning organization has specific mechanisms for renewal, such as periodic reviews, strategic planning efforts, or system-wide training programs.[44]

A learning organization is characterized as follows:[45]

- Continuous learning by individuals, teams, and the organization provides a competitive advantage. Managers complete skill inventories and audits of the learning capacity of individuals and groups. They create systems for sharing learning and using it in business each day.

- Individuals have a shared vision, which reflects both its underlying assumptions and values, which emerges from many places in the organization. Organizational leaders help create and nurture the vision as well as inspire commitment from workers, who contribute their ideas and are empowered to implement them.

- The entire organizational system including its strategy, structure and information flow, work processes, performance goals, training, individual and team development, and rewards and recognition is involved.

- Executives value learning as a continuous process and believe that intentional activities can increase its quantity and quality and that shared learning is easiest to maintain. They model calculated risk taking and experimentation. They create a culture that rewards employee initiative and encourages feedback by employees to higher level managers.

■ Managers support decentralized decision making and employee empowerment. Frequent use of cross-functional work teams is encouraged.

GS TECHNOLOGIES. In the early 1990s, GS Technologies, a steel manufacturer, had experienced significant downsizing and had large numbers of outstanding worker grievances. In addition, its market share was eroding and its CEO had begun to receive hate mail. Top executives decided that their only hope was to change their culture and become a learning organization. They began by using a dialogue tool that helps to expose conflict in the group. After a particularly stormy meeting, union and management participants began to discuss their anger and cleared the air. They then began to solve some critical productivity problems. After participating in a series of activities to help them become a learning organization, GST saw their sales and profits increase. However, the company's failure to involve large numbers of workers in the learning organization and a change in union leadership have significantly hindered its attempts.[46]

THE U.S. ARMY. The U.S. Army has continued to reexamine and renew itself since the Operation Desert Storm victory. Prompted by problems with inventory control, outdated technologies, and an inadequate communication system during Operation Desert Storm, the Army has sought to become a more adaptive and flexible learning organization. The Army now subjects everyone to highly stressful maneuvers that bring soldiers close to the breaking point. Then they participate in an After Action Review, a public performance appraisal. Colonels, lieutenants, and even more junior officers together discuss where each has erred, ideally learning from each other and creating a shared vision as a way of becoming a high-performance organization.[47]

COOPERS & LYBRAND. As a way of increasing its employees' ability to act effectively, Coopers & Lybrand created a culture of continuous learning. They identified critical success factors and barriers to learning and then developed a strategy for increasing learning that involved providing workers training opportunities and assignments that supported their personal development.[48]

CREATING AND CHANGING THE ORGANIZATION'S CULTURE

We can diagnose an organization's culture to determine whether it supports organizational goals, encourages continuous quality improvement, or creates a learning organization. If not, we can change it. That is the strategy of an increasing number of top executives, who believe a changed culture will enhance performance. To carry out the change, though, the executives have to win over the other managers and employees who may be very comfortable with the existing culture.

CHASE MANHATTAN BANK. CEO Thomas G. Labrecque changed the bank's culture to increase teamwork and flexibility. By selling peripheral units, he reduced the number of autonomous business units, which tended to create competition rather than collaboration among executives. He also encouraged managers of different units to develop joint strategies so the bank could expand its client relationships. Unfortunately, his desires had limited impact until top executives participated in Vision-Quest, an intervention designed to reinvigorate companies by helping executives define a common vision and then work as a team to accomplish it. Now Chase is moving to implement the five core values they identified: customer focus, respect for each other, teamwork, quality, and professionalism. For example, the company's reward system includes an assessment of how well employees adhere to the new values.[49]

Every prescription for change recommends that managers and other organizational members conduct a careful diagnosis of the current culture. Beyond that, researchers disagree about the **best** way to change culture. One model suggests we follow five guidelines for instituting changes in culture.[50]

1. Develop a clear vision of the organization's future direction and the culture required to meet it.

2. Ensure top management's support.

3. Have top managers model the new culture for subordinates by having their behavior represent the desired values, expectations, and behaviors.

4. Make changes in an organization's structure, human resource systems, and management styles and practices to support the shift in culture. If an organization assumes an egalitarian, people-oriented culture, managers must encourage, measure, and reward worker participation in decision making. If an organization assumes a more authoritarian, production-oriented culture, managers must encourage, measure, and reward worker obedience to authority and "bottom-line" performance.

5. Select and socialize newcomers to fit with the new culture. Retrain or terminate existing employees who do not fit. The merger of two organizations or a radical cultural change in a single organization is likely to result in some employee casualties.

Another model, shown in Figure 11–4, illustrates how change can occur as cultures attempt to perpetuate themselves.[51] After a behavior occurs (1), managers and employees justify the existing culture (2). They then communicate its characteristics to individuals inside and outside the organization (3). Managers make sure to hire and socialize members who "fit in" with the culture (4) and remove members who do not (5). Changing the culture can occur by intervening at any of the numbered points. For example, the inability to justify existing behavior may contribute to changing it and the resulting culture. Failure to communicate the nature of the current culture, but to instead discuss a preferred culture, can also lead to change. Finally, cultural change can occur as a result of the hiring and firing processes. Managers can hire individuals who do not fit with the culture and retain employees who deviate from it.

Some researchers have suggested that different processes may be required to change different cultures, depending on a given organization's stage of development, orientation, ability to change, experience with alternate cultural frameworks, and history.[52] Some trial-and-error is to be expected.

SAMSUNG. Samsung Chairman Lee Kun-Hee has made a dramatic effort to change the once stodgy, conservative company with hierarchical, inward-looking management. He wants senior managers to delegate more authority and become more actively involved in setting priorities, refocusing product development, and im-

FIGURE 11–4   *How culture tends to perpetuate itself*

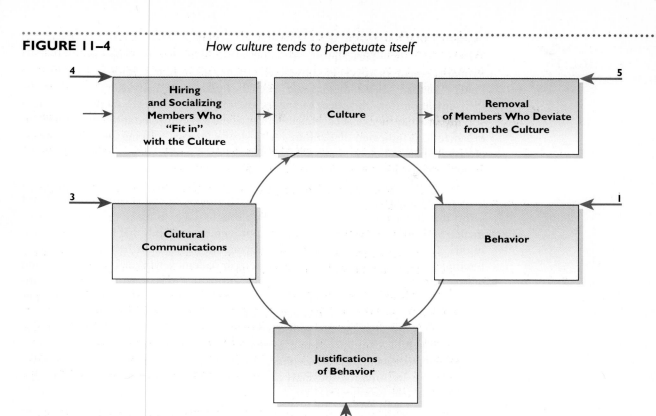

Managers seeking to create cultural *change* must intervene at these points, Conversely, managers seeking to *maintain* the prevailing culture must counteract any such intervention by others and prevent any weakening of these processes.

SOURCE: Reprinted with permission from V. Sathe, How to decipher and change culture. In R.H. Kilmann, M.J. Saxton, R. Serpa, and associates, eds., *Gaining Control of Corporate Culture* (San Francisco: Jossey-Bass, 1985), p. 245.

proving quality. Early attempts to institute change failed. One consultant was just ignored by all the top managers. Lee responded by issuing the "Frankfurt Declaration," which called for "Quality first, no matter what." Over a period of two months, he met with all 850 senior executives in cities around the world. In round-the-clock meetings with groups of twenty to forty executives, Lee showed them how poorly Samsung products were positioned. All 850 Samsung executives also spent six months in Samsung's CEO School training programs being reeducated. In addition, the company sent 400 men abroad for 12 months with a huge expense account to do whatever they wanted, as long as they returned with an excellent knowledge of the culture and language of the country visited. Finally, Lee has insisted that all employees work from 7 A.M. to 4 P.M. in a country where the normal workday is 9 A.M. to 8 P.M. Although too early to show results, experts predict that these culture changes will produce results for Samsung.[53]

Implementing total quality management programs and creating learning organizations are two additional ways of changing an organization's culture.

IMPLEMENTING TOTAL QUALITY PROGRAMS

There are countless prescriptions for implementing a culture that supports total quality management. Figure 11–5 shows one. Organizations first develop an image of the kind of company they want to create. Then they gather and analyze data to determine their deviation from this idea. Members learn new techniques to facilitate problem solving and may then take courses to reinforce the learning. One study of 34 different organizations indicated that cultures with strong internal training and development efforts helped initiate and sustain TQM efforts.[54] Finally, they institutionalize the systems necessary to make total quality a permanent part of the organization.[55]

E.I. DuPont. At E.I. DuPont, a survey conducted in 1991 indicated failure cost approximated $400 million annually. To reduce these costs managers instituted a TQM effort that involved three steps. First, they sought ways to make process improvements. Second, they offered training in improvement methods that included increasing the customer focus, upgrading all networks of interactions between customers, internal DuPont departments, and suppliers, broadening worker involvement, and upgrading the quality of employee thinking. Third, they executed projects for continuous improvement that included training sales personnel about how to secure better information from customers or conducting periodic customer surveys.[56]

The U.S. government has introduced a national award, the Malcolm Baldrige National Quality Award, to recognize and reward manufacturing and service companies that meet standards of excellence. An organization is judged on the categories of leadership, information and analysis, strategic quality planning, human resources, quality assurance products and services, quality results, and customer satisfaction.[57] Table 11–1 lists sample questions in each area from the Self-Assessment Questionnaire. Winners include the Ritz-Carlton Hotel Company, AT&T Universal Card Services, General Motors Cadillac Division, among others.

FIGURE 11–5 *Implementing total quality*

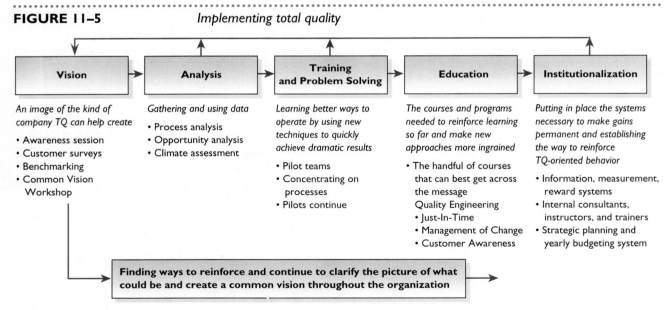

SOURCE: From Dan Ciampa, *Total Quality: A User's Guide to Implementation* (Reading, Mass.: Addison-Wesley, 1992), p. 107. Copyright © 1992 by Addison-Wesley Publishing Company. Reprinted with permission of the publisher.

TABLE 11–1
Sample questions from the Malcolm Baldrige National Quality Award Self-Assessment Questionnaire

LEADERSHIP

Have all of the executives in your organization received adequate training on quality concepts and tools?

Are all of the executives visibly involved in the development of an effective quality culture?

INFORMATION AND ANALYSIS

Does the organization collect quantifiable data on all important dimensions of quality of the products and services that are produced?

Are quality data collected and reported on in all functions and departments in the organization, including support functions such as accounting, marketing, et cetera?

STRATEGIC QUALITY PLANNING

Does your company collect thorough and appropriate quality-related competitive comparison data and use world-class benchmarks to develop plans?

Are employees, customers, and suppliers involved in the planning process?

HUMAN RESOURCE UTILIZATION

Do you have a corporate plan for the utilization of employees in relation to the quality improvement process?

Does your organization have a structured curriculum for training all levels of employees in quality improvement concepts and tools?

QUALITY ASSURANCE OF PRODUCTS AND SERVICES

Does your organization use a systematic process such as Quality Function Deployment to define customer requirements and expectations?

Is there an auditing process that is used to periodically evaluate the effectiveness of the quality management system?

QUALITY RESULTS

Is your organization among the top 20 percent in customer satisfaction with your products and services?

Are the data on your level of customer satisfaction collected in a thorough and objective manner?

CUSTOMER SATISFACTION

Has the trend in customer satisfaction data over the last three years been improving for your organization?

Does your organization have an effective process for handling customer service and complaints?

SOURCE: Reprinted with permission from the Association for Quality and Participation: M.G. Brown, How to determine your quality quotient, *Journal for Quality and Participation* (June 1990): 76–80.

Advice to organizational leaders implementing total quality programs would include the following:[58]

- Define quality.

- Pay attention to customer satisfaction.

- Focus on continuous improvement.

- Modify the work process.

- Emphasize prevention and an error-free attitude.

- Manage by facts.

- Encourage employee participation and involvement in quality.

- Build partnerships with customers and suppliers.

However, quality improvement programs can fail. Companies may see TQM as a quick-fix solution rather than a long-term commitment. For example, a project manager reduced lead time in his manufacturing area by 40 percent, but failed to realize that more than 90 percent of the lead time came from waiting outside the manufacturing area. Hence, more widespread participation in the organization was necessary.[59] Careful analysis and planning is also essential to TQM effectiveness to ensure that the program's design results in desired outcomes.[60]

NORTHERN TELECOM. At Northern Telecom, employees were confused by multiple quality improvement efforts and a corresponding array of goals. There was no shared definition of quality. When asked, employees said *quality* meant, among other things, "no functional defects," "customer satisfaction," "error-free software," and "100 percent on-time delivery." This lack of agreement led to conflicting goals between different departments, as well as between departments and the larger organization.[61]

CREATING A LEARNING ORGANIZATION

Companies can create a learning organization by supporting the learning of individuals and teams in the organization. The key here is developing and offering employees a comprehensive training program that meets their individual needs.

MANULIFE FINANCIAL. Manulife Financial, one of the top fifteen life insurers in North America, created the Continuous Learning Centre to foster its employees' learning. The Centre offers formal training programs, financial support for external training, on-the-job development opportunities, self-study programs, internal and external networks, and mentors and coaches to support individual learning.[62]

Learning involves reducing anxiety in organizations.[63] One way to do this is to create a group that leads and supports the change throughout the organization.[64] This steering committee begins by going through its own learning process and then designing the organizational learning process. The steering committee can create numerous working groups to help develop and implement plans for particular areas of the organization.

Building an organization that can learn involves recognizing and then creating or improving five component technologies:[65]

- *Systems thinking.* Recognizing that business involves a series of interrelated and interdependent actions (see Chapter 1 for more discussion).

- ■ *Personal mastery.* Continually clarifying and deepening individuals' personal visions, focusing their energies, developing patience, and viewing reality objectively.

- ■ *Mental models.* The assumptions and generalizations that influence the way individuals perceive and interpret events and then take action based on their perceptions and attributions.

- ■ *Shared vision.* The capacity of organizational members to have a common view of the future state of the organization.

- ■ *Team learning.* Extensive dialogue among team members followed by recognition and analysis of patterns of interaction of group members.

To create a learning organization requires a special type of leadership, where leaders are responsible for learning.[66] This type of leader assumes three roles. The first role is as the designer of the organization, including its vision and core values. Second is the role of teacher, who helps organizational members gain insight into the organization's current reality. Third is the role of steward, where the leader shepherds the organization and its members in changing the way it operates.

SUMMARY

An organization's culture describes part of an organization's internal environment that incorporates a set of assumptions, beliefs, and values that are shared by organizational members and help guide their functioning. A culture has three levels: assumptions, values, and artifacts. We can uncover a culture by examining an organization's mission, heroes and heroines, myths and stories, rituals and ceremonies, and physical arrangements.

Organizations that create a culture around improving quality focus on meeting customer needs to achieve customer satisfaction. Often known as total quality management or continuous quality improvement, this organization-wide effort attempts to achieve continuous improvement in the quality of goods and services. Continuous improvement, worker empowerment, customer satisfaction, and leadership constitute the four pillars of total quality management.

A learning organization obtains a competitive advantage from continuous learning by individuals, teams, and the organization. A learning organization conducts systematic problem solving, experiments with new procedures, learns from both past experiences and the best practices of others, and transfers knowledge rapidly and efficiently through the organization.

We can diagnose an organization's culture to determine its fit with organizational goals, its encouragement of continuous quality improvement, and its contribution to creating a learning organization. Although executives may want to retain their current organizational culture, increasingly top management believes that a culture change will enhance performance. Changing the culture involves developing a clear vision about the organization's future and ensuring top management's support. It also involves having management model the new culture for subordinates and changing the organization's structure, human resource systems, and management styles and practices to support the new culture, as well as selecting, training, evaluating, and rewarding employees to help them fit with the new culture.

Companies can also implement a series of diagnostic and action steps to create either a total quality management or a learning organization.

DIAGNOSTIC QUESTIONS

Answering the questions listed here can help diagnose and change an organization's culture.

- What type of culture exists in the organization?
- What comprises the culture and do these components reinforce or contradict it?
- Does a concern for quality exist in the organization?
- Does the organization strive to satisfy the customers, continually improve, empower workers, and have a vision of excellence?
- Is the organization a learning organization?
- What characteristics of a learning organization are present and lacking?
- How should the culture be changed?
- What changes are necessary to increase the emphasis on quality?
- What changes are necessary to create a learning organization?

*A*ctivity 11–1 · ORGANIZATION CULTURE QUESTIONNAIRE

STEP 1: Select an organization with which you are very familiar. You can choose your college or university or an organization in which you were employed.

STEP 2: Complete the Organizational Culture Questionnaire on page 489.

STEP 3: Individually or in small groups compare your organizations by answering the following questions for each one:

1. What are the dominant values of the organization?
2. What assumptions underlie these values?
3. What artifacts represent these values?
4. What are some of the behavioral norms of the organization that an outsider or a newcomer would quickly notice?

5. How do the leaders of the organization reinforce these values and norms?
6. How are newcomers socialized in this organization?

STEP 4: Discussion. In small groups or with the entire class, answer the following questions:

1. What are the key components of the organizations' cultures?
2. Compare where the organizational culture actually is to where it ideally should be for each organization. How extensive is this discrepancy for the organizations analyzed?
3. What individual and organizational outcomes does organizational culture affect?

From Kolb, Osland, Rubin, *Organizational Behavior: An Experiential Approach*, 6/E. © 1995, pp. 34, 346–347, 363. Reprinted by permission of Prentice–Hall, Inc. Englewood Cliffs, N.J.

For each of the seven organizational culture dimensions described, place an (a) above the number that indicates your assessment of the organization's *actual* position on that dimension and an (i) above the number that indicates your choice of where the organization should *ideally* be on this dimension.

1. **Conformity.** The feeling that there are many externally imposed constraints in the organization; the degree to which members feel that there are many rules, procedures, policies, and practices to which they have to conform rather than being able to do their work as they see fit.

| Conformity is not characteristic of this organization. | 1 2 3 4 5 6 7 8 9 10 | Conformity is very characteristic of this organization. |

2. **Responsibility.** Members of the organization are given personal responsibility to achieve their part of the organization's goals; the degree to which members feel that they can make decisions and solve problems without checking with superiors each step of the way.

| No responsibility is given in the organization. | 1 2 3 4 5 6 7 8 9 10 | There is a great emphasis on personal responsibility in the organization. |

3. **Standards.** The emphasis the organization places on quality performance and outstanding production, including the degree to which the member feels the organization is setting challenging goals for itself and communicating these goal commitments to members.

| Standards are very low or nonexistent in the organization. | 1 2 3 4 5 6 7 8 9 10 | High challenging standards are set in the organization. |

4. **Rewards.** The degree to which members feel that they are being recognized and rewarded for good work rather than being ignored, criticized, or punished when something goes wrong.

| Members are ignored, punished, or criticized. | 1 2 3 4 5 6 7 8 9 10 | Members are recognized and rewarded positively. |

5. **Organizational clarity.** The feeling among members that things are well organized and that goals are clearly defined rather than being disorderly, confused, or chaotic.

| The organization is disorderly, confused, and chaotic. | 1 2 3 4 5 6 7 8 9 10 | The organization is well organized with clearly defined goals. |

6. **Warmth and support.** The feeling that friendliness is a valued norm in the organization, that members trust one another and offer support to one another. The feeling that good relationships prevail in the work environment.

| There is no warmth and support in the organization. | 1 2 3 4 5 6 7 8 9 10 | Warmth and support are very characteristic of the organization. |

7. **Leadership.** The willingness of organization members to accept leadership and direction from qualified others. As needs for leadership arise, members feel free to take leadership roles and are rewarded for successful leadership. Leadership is based on expertise. The organization is not dominated by, or dependent on, one or two individuals.

| Leadership is not rewarded. Members are dominated or dependent and resist leadership attempts. | 1 2 3 4 5 6 7 8 9 10 | Members accept and reward leadership based on expertise. |

Activity 11–2 GE FANUC NORTH AMERICA (A) CASE

STEP 1: Read the GE Fanuc North America (A) Case.

Marybeth Sullivan-Rose sat in her office just off the production floor at GE Fanuc Corporation's world headquarters in Charlottesville, Virginia. As human resources manager, she was responsible for the company's High Involvement Work Force (HIWF) programs. This responsibility included managing the training of and relationships with the 42 HIWF teams that were on their way to becoming highly efficient and highly productive contributors to GE Fanuc's bottom line.

The progress that had been made was formally recognized in October 1992 when *Industry Week* magazine named GE Fanuc one of America's top ten plants. According to *Industry Week,* the award represented "what can be accomplished when managers and employees take up the quest for continuous improvement and world-class manufacturing."

In a month, Sullivan-Rose would be taking maternity leave. When she returned, she would be in a different role at the plant. Her successor, Cheryl Platte, who had been transferred from finance, had been working with Sullivan-Rose for the past several weeks, "learning the ropes." Sullivan-Rose was straddling a fine line: "I want Cheryl to have a clear sense of what is going on here. There are a number of reasons for HIWF. All of us in management have our own theories about this program, (see Figure 11–6), yet I want her to draw her own conclusions about where we are."

GENERAL ELECTRIC CORPORATION (GE)

Thomas Edison's General Electric Lighting Company, which had started in Schenectady, New York, in 1868, had grown into one of the largest businesses in the world.

> Few corporations are bigger (298,000 employees); none is as complex. GE makes 65-cent light bulbs, 400-thousand-pound locomotives, and billion-dollar power plants. It manages more credit cards than American Express and owns more commercial aircraft than American Airlines. Of the seven billion pounds of hamburger Americans tote home each year, 36 percent keeps fresh in GE refrigerators, and after dinner, one out of five couch potatoes tunes into GE's network, NBC.[1]

GE had always been an innovator: it was on the leading edge of management organization (Strategic Business Units [SBU'S] were a GE idea); it constantly created new ways of assessing its profitability and its markets (Activity Based Costing was born at GE and market research was another GE initiative); and its products were new and bold (lighting, turbines, aircraft engines). Nevertheless, by the late 1970s the company had grown into an unwieldy behemoth whose brains were isolated from its muscles by as many as nine layers of management.

In 1981, Jack Welch became GE's chief executive officer (CEO). His strategy for the increasingly global arena of the 1980s was simple and straightforward. GE would only be in businesses that were number one or two in their markets and that could win in an increasingly competitive global environment. Those that could not succeed would be fixed, closed, or sold. As a result, Welch led the divestiture of $10 billion in assets and acquired $19 billion in new, world-class businesses. GE consolidated 350 product lines and business units into 13 key business areas (Aerospace, Aircraft Engines, Appliances, Financial Services, Industrial and Power Systems, Lighting, Medical Systems, NBC, Plastics, Communications and Services, Electrical Distribution and Control, Motors, and Transportation Systems.) Twenty-nine pay levels were compressed into five broad bands, and 100,000 jobs were eliminated. The results were impressive. Market capitalization increased by 450 percent and, by 1990, sales had reached $58 billion with a net profit of $4.3 billion.

THE FACTORY-AUTOMATION PRODUCTS DIVISION

A key aspect of Welch's strategic vision during the early 1980s was a future in which factories would be heavily automated. As part of a campaign to grow GE's "high-tech" reputation, Welch assembled the company's best resources and people and invested $500 million to start a new division in Charlottesville, Virginia. Welch viewed the Factory-Automation Products division as a

FIGURE 11–6 *GE Fanuc North America (A): management perspectives*

Bob Collins, CEO, GE Fanuc North America

We used to have a "traditional" management here. We would put people into boxes and say "this is your job." In essence, we were also saying "this is not your job." As we became more global and found competitors we never knew we had, we had to manage differently. The rules of competition changed; we could no longer compete on just quality or delivery time. Those became given; we had to compete on price too. That meant that productivity was key. We are careful to have everything driven by the market, so people perceive these changes as a viable reason and way to sell HIWF. HIWF is a way to cut costs. We're inventing this on the fly, but the process is inherently correct; we've done so little wrong that the process must be correct. It has been hard to link some shop-floor jobs directly to profit, but it is profit that is the bloodstream of the business, it is profit that generates cash.

Bob Wayand, Senior Vice President, Manufacturing

We got into HIWF for three reasons. First, we needed something to sustain the six percent productivity growth we had been realizing. Second, we were just running out of time. We couldn't micromanage any longer and we needed to get those resources out there, those people, to pick up more responsibility. Third, there is nobody that knows their job better than the one who is doing it. With thirty-five years at GE, HIWF was a tough idea for me. Some would say I held it up for six months, but I wanted to be absolutely sure that we did this thing right.

Tim Smith, Plant Manager

I enjoy seeing changes. It is easy to ask someone a question and stand there and wait for an answer. They don't always like it, but I am trying to get people to think. We are really trying to empower people here. For example, I am not aware of a single request for tools or process improvement that has been turned down. It is so rewarding to see people having excellent conversations; they are focusing on positive things and getting them done. And I just walk away from those conversations feeling really good.

Donald C. Borwhat, Senior Vice President, Human Resources

From a performance standpoint, GE Fanuc was strengthened by our efforts to empower our work force through HIWF. The process was designed to maximize inputs from our production associates and to put management in the role of enablers—counseling teams, eliminating barriers, and encouraging them to win and be successful in their intellectual efforts. HIWF is designed to draw our production associates into the decision process via problem solving. Continual improvement of our manufacturing processes is our main focus. HIWF's goal is to continue to improve GE Fanuc's productivity and allow us to compete in a new, ever-changing world economy.

Marybeth Sullivan-Rose, Manager, Human Resources

When I present the process to customers, I use HIWF as a selling tool. I tell them that what is in it for them is less cost. Why do we do HIWF? It is the right thing to do for people, but let's also be realistic, we do this to make ourselves better and we do it to make the customer better.

complete source for the robots, controllers, software, motors, sensors, and other machinery that would drive the "factory of the future." This division aimed to overtake Fanuc, the Japanese company that dominated the world ($1 billion in sales) in industrial robotics and machine-tool controllers.

For a variety of reasons, Welch's ambitious goals did not pan out. Robots proved to be more difficult to incorporate into existing plants than anyone had thought. Even the simplest robot had to be custom fitted for each client's needs. In addition, the recession of the early 1980s had depressed capital expenditures. By 1985, GE had lost $200 million in Charlottesville and had gained little, if any, ground on Fanuc. The Charlottesville plant was in disarray; morale was low, and a constant parade of executives had failed to turn the business around. The global market for robotic production never materialized and American machine-tool manufacturers were rapidly losing ground to Japan, where more efficient, flexible, and price-competitive machines were being made. In 1987, Welch chose a new strategy.

GE FANUC JOINT VENTURE

Today the factory of the future looks different than Welch's 1981 vision of it. Robots have not replaced humans, but automated technology is a critical component of every manufacturing process. The machine tools, lathes, and presses used to punch, drill, cut, mill, and form raw materials into salable products are now directed by combinations of small computers and software programs that drastically reduce variability and increase efficiency. The "brain and nervous system" of the tool is a Programmable Logic Controller (PLC) or a Custom Numerical Controller (CNC). General Electric and Fanuc have made both. In 1987, the leading-edge work on CNCs was being done by Fanuc in Japan; the leading-edge work on PLCs was being done by GE in the United States.

In January 1987, Jack Welch of GE and Dr. Seiuemon Inaba, CEO of Fanuc, which had formerly been GE's chief competitor, announced the creation of a joint venture known as GE Fanuc. The two parties agreed to capitalize on their individual strengths; GE gave up CNCs, Fanuc gave up PLCs, and the firms agreed to share their markets. Ownership of the GE Fanuc holding company was split evenly; there were three divisions, GE Fanuc North America, GE Fanuc Europe, and Fanuc-GE Asia. Operating control and size of the three divisions varied (see Figure 11–7).

GE Fanuc North America's new CEO, Robert P. Collins, enthusiastically predicted 1987 annual sales of $250 million, a 20 percent increase over the combined product-line performance of each party in the venture. The joint venture was an exciting development that coincided with a radical new strategic initiative that Welch had launched at GE.

WORK-OUT

Welch conceived Work-Out, on an airplane in September, 1988, and it was initiated corporatewide in January 1989. Designed to get useless and unnecessary work out of the system (hence the name "Work-Out") and encourage people to work more closely together, Work-Out represented a radical assault on traditional canons of management. According to Welch's view of the 1990's, "a corporate Gulliver is doomed without the Lilliputian virtues [of] speed, simplicity, and self-confidence." Aided by outside consultants and academics, GE began to change the way business and management were conducted at its many locations,

FIGURE 11–7 GE FANUC North America (A)—GE FANUC worldwide organization: structure, ownership, and size of GE FANUC joint venture

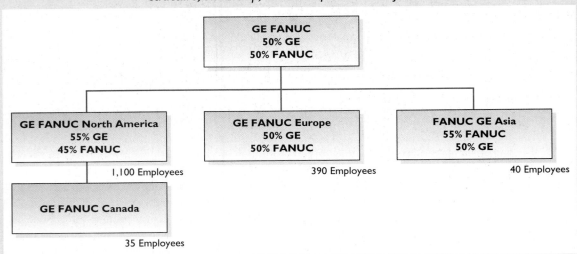

including GE Fanuc's. The 1989 GE Annual Report summed up Welch's vision:

> Work-Out is a fluid and adaptable concept, not a "program." It generally starts as a series of regularly scheduled "town meetings" that bring together large cross sections of a business—people from manufacturing, engineering, customer service, hourly, salaried, high and lower levels—people who in their normal routines work within the boxes on their organizational charts and have few dealings with one another.
>
> The initial purpose of these meetings is simple—to remove the more egregious manifestations of bureaucracy: multiple approvals, unnecessary paperwork, excessive reports, routines, rituals. Ideas and opinions are often; at first, voiced hesitantly by people who never before had a forum—other than the water cooler—to express them. We have found that, after a short time, those ideas begin to come in a torrent—especially when people see action taken on the ones already advanced.
>
> With the desk largely cleared of bureaucratic impediments and distractions, the Work-Out sessions then begin to focus on the more challenging tasks: examining the myriad processes that make up every business, identifying the crucial ones, discarding the rest, and then finding a faster, simpler, better way of doing things. Next, the teams raise the bar of excellence by testing their improved processes against the very best from around the company and from the best companies around the world.
>
> The individual is the fountainhead of creativity and innovation, and we are struggling to get all our people to accept the countercultural way. Only by releasing the energy and fire of our employees can we achieve the decisive, continuous productivity advantages that will give us the freedom to compete and win in any business anywhere on the globe.
>
> We have seen, with the demolition of the control superstructure we once imposed on our business, and we are beginning to see even more clearly, as Work-Out starts to blossom, that controlling people doesn't motivate them. It stifles them. We've found that people perform better, even heroically, when they see that what they do every day makes a difference.

WORK-OUT AND HIWF

GE Fanuc was, in many ways, a microcosm of the efforts Welch was making across the entire corporation. In Charlottesville, sharp distinctions existed between management and workers, and this situation led to an atmosphere of mistrust and suspicion. Mounds of paperwork and Byzantine mazes of approval processes were necessary to get things done and were overseen by a bloated middle-management layer. The initial reaction to Work-Out at GE Fanuc was less than enthusiastic. Many viewed it as just another management initiative that would run its course and go away.

At the end of the initial Work-Out process, the workforce had identified more than 200 projects that, when completed, would reduce unnecessary work and contribute to the corporate goals of speed, simplicity, and self-confidence. By 1990, Work-Out was finished, and by 1991, most of the projects were completed.

Donald C. Borwhat, senior vice president of Human Resources at GE Fanuc, recalls,

> We had built up tremendous momentum with Work-Out. We had gained a new level of trust with the work force. The real challenge was what to do with all of it. We had already been thinking about some kind of work-team idea—self-directed, high involvement, and so on—but we didn't know how to do it. We kicked the idea around for several months and then decided to move on it.

The momentum was sustained through a new initiative known as the High Involvement Work Force (HIWF).

THE HIWF PHILOSOPHY

The HIWF goal was to create a facility that was the most efficient and productive possible and that enjoyed the best-possible quality of work life. The basic premises of HIWF were: everyone is a potential contributor; those closest to the work influence decisions; and employees are empowered to influence results. These premises inverted the traditional organizational pyramid, where communication and decision making flowed down from the top and where upper management formulated strategies and handed them to middle managers, who in turn worked through supervisors who oversaw the workers who actually did the work.

HIWF envisioned a new workplace where employees had significant impact on their jobs, where planning was as important as production and thinking was a key part of the job, where people were treated as professionals and were recognized, appreciated, and proud of a job well done. As a symbol of this new vision, senior management elected to extend "dress-down Fridays" throughout the work week. CEO Bob Collins recalls, "Suits and ties implied a class distinction. We wanted to break this barrier down, because it was a real impediment to what we were trying to do."

The new HIWF culture meant a flatter organization with management as a shared function (see Figure 11–8). Everyone was empowered and *expected* to contribute, and the role of the manager/supervisor was one of leader and developer. Finally, the entire initiative was built on the concept of goal-directed, highly communicative, involved, and consensus-oriented teamwork.

THE HIWF ROLL OUT

GE Fanuc hired a consultant to assess the company's readiness for a work-team structure. The consultant spent two days in Charlottesville during January 1991 interviewing key management personnel and a random cross section of hourly workers. He also spent a great deal of time surveying the work-flow process and the physical plant. A week later, he submitted a report outlining his observations and conclusions, which cited a number of factors as either conducive or detrimental to the HIWF effort (see Figure 11–9). Overall, however, he suggested that GE Fanuc was ready. Borwhat and his team now had to design an implementation strategy.

From Borwhat's perspective, it was critical that HIWF roll out right the first time. He sent Larry Jones, a human resources manager and a key team member, on a tour of several production facilities that were using work teams. Jones benchmarked the best practices at these plants and brought them back to Charlottesville. Realizing that the pace of unfolding such a significant change, which would alter the entire culture, would be hard to predict, Jones outlined an ambitious timeline for implementation of HIWF (see Figure 11–10, pages 496–497). Jones remembers, "We were really shooting from the hip on this; Collins thought it would take six months, Borwhat said a year and I thought several [years]."

By early 1991, a steering committee composed of key personnel had been formed to oversee HIWF's implementation. HIWF soon faced its first test when business conditions required layoffs at the factory. In order to allay fears that HIWF was a rubric for cost cutting, management had promised that no one would be laid off as a result of HIWF. Recognizing the critical nature of this promise, GE Fanuc made a new decision. For the first time, the layoffs were made at the salary level, rather than at the hourly level. This action proved to be a key factor in gaining the employees' trust and commit-

FIGURE 11–8　　　　*GE FANUC merger organizational chart: inverted pyramid*

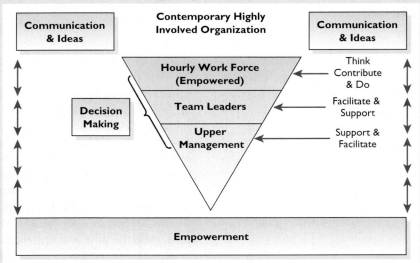

FIGURE 11–9 *GE Fanuc North America (A): consultant's findings*

FACTORS THAT MAY HELP HIWF ROLLOUT

- Top-management support
- Steady projected business growth
- Work force size and physical layout conducive to team interactions
- Attractive wage-and-benefits package
- Well-regarded plant manager
- Flexibility in labor costs
- Work force desirous of greater responsibility and autonomy
- Work force generally satisfied with employment at GE Fanuc
- Excellent training facilities

FACTORS THAT MAY HINDER HIWF ROLLOUT

- Previous top-management turnover
- Mixed perceptions of the history of and motivation for the joint venture
- Uncertainty about financial-measurement status (cost center or profit center)
- Discrepancy in educational achievement
- Past history of layoffs at Charlottesville plant
- Differences among supervisory styles and uses of rewards and punishments
- Extraordinary division between technicians and "pool-grade" levels
- Strong desire to see immediate impact
- Shift in strategic focus from product to customer
- Perceived favoritism and inconsistent application of policies and procedures, especially in hiring processes
- Past negative experiences with "open communication"
- Inordinate amount of "turf building"
- Virtual absence of goals and measures
- High level of anxiety about and potential resistance to change, especially at the middle- and low-management ranks
- Concern that employee-generated process improvements could cost jobs

---

ment to the HIWF goals and philosophy. The momentum was gathering.

November and December 1991 were significant months in the HIWF roll out. The human resource function was reconceptualized (see Figure 11–11, page 498). A full-time HIWF coordinator was hired to be a champion on the factory floor who could solidify and represent the process and offer real-time support to the teams. The governing structure of the HIWF teams was established and an orientation program to explain the new systems was held for the entire work force. Training programs were begun to acquaint the team developers (formerly supervisors) with new skills, such as meeting facilitation and group goal setting. Finally, the hourly work force was organized into 42 teams of 10 to 12 people (see Figure 11–12, page 499). Each team consisted of "Normal Work Units," people who now worked together in the same general area. According to Borwhat, "None of us got a whole lot of sleep those months!"

The work force strategy was to provide a series of incremental training opportunities that would offer specific skills roughly in the sequence and time in which the groups needed them. In January 1992, to coincide with the first HIWF meetings, formal training in team-meeting skills was provided for all of manufacturing. In February, management-skills training began. Over the period of March through September 1992, workshops in goal setting, conflict management, and problem solving were conducted. HIWF at GE Fanuc was underway.

FIGURE 11-10

GE FANUC merger organizational chart, GE FANUC automation N.A., Inc.: implementation timetable

Team Responsibilities
Time-Phased Objectives

Teams fully responsible for

6 Months	12 Months	18 Months	24 Months	Longer

• Establish teams
• Everyone on a team
• Effective meetings
• Communications across the organization
• Receive training for:
  • Meeting skills
  • Facilitation
  • Goal setting
  • Problem management
	• Establish and maintain team goals
	• Measure work performance
	• Setting/scheduling work priorities
	• Identify, analyze, and solve problems effectively
	• Operate in cooperation/ conjunction with other teams
	• Scheduling personnel
		• Scheduling overtime, vacation, etc.
		• Interview and hire team members
		• Resource allocation (people)
		• Selecting leadership roles (team leaders)
			• Area cost responsibility
			• Administer approval authority
			• Anticipate and compensate for peak work loads
				• Peer appraisals
				• Salary allocation
				• Budget achievement
				• Multiskilled cross-trained

Teams participate in (making a significant contribution)

• Formulation of internal policies/ procedures • Implement work, improvements, and changes—workout	• Meeting operating goals of the business • Formal communications programs	• Handling discipline • Developing/conducting training • Staff evaluations	• Team design/redesign • Investment decisions • Research new/improved work concepts (work simplification) • Evaluate other teams	• Managing the manufacturing process • Administer work force fluctuations • Pay delivery redesign

HIWF

1991

Names	Dates	Sept.				Oct.				Nov.				Dec.			
		3	10	17	24	1	8	15	22	29	5	12	19	26	3	10	17	24
Create Steering Committee	9/3/91–9/3/91																	
Get coordinator on board	9/3/91–11/4/91																	
Orient Steering Committee	9/3/91–9/3/91																	
Steering Committee site visits	9/3/91–10/14/91																	
Draft Charlottesville Factbook	10/1/91–10/1/91																	
Draft comm. plan for change	9/11/91–9/11/91																	
ID equipment needs meeting places	10/4/91–10/4/91																	
Train the trainers	11/11/91–11/12/91																	
Preliminary new org. chart	11/13/91–11/13/91																	
Review org. chart—strong comm.	11/13/91–11/13/91																	
Review org. chart—outside group	11/13/91–11/26/91																	
Complete comm. plan for change	11/15/91–11/15/91																	
Complete orientation nonmfg.	12/4/91–12/4/91																	
Complete orientation mfg.	12/5/91–12/5/91																	
Reexamine supervisor roles/titles	12/11/91–12/11/91																	
Final new org. chart	12/13/91–12/13/91																	
Define measurement areas	11/27/91–11/27/91																	
Create team rosters/leadership role	12/13/91–12/13/91																	
Create team meeting place/time	12/20/91–12/20/91																	
Quantify measurement areas	12/27/91–12/27/91																	

FIGURE 11–10   *(continued)*

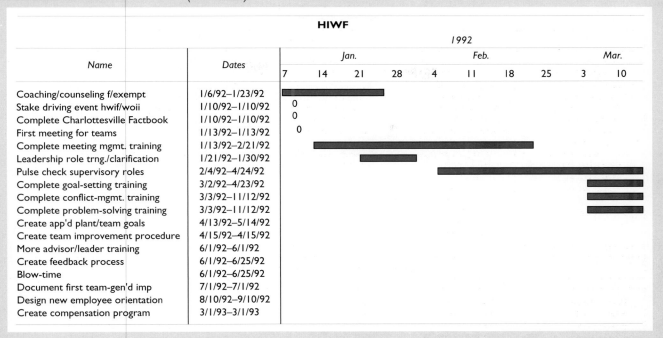

Name	Dates	HIWF 1992

HIWF

1992

Name	Dates	Jan. 7	14	21	28	Feb. 4	11	18	25	Mar. 3	10
Coaching/counseling f/exempt	1/6/92–1/23/92	▬	▬	▬	▬						
Stake driving event hwif/woii	1/10/92–1/10/92	0									
Complete Charlottesville Factbook	1/10/92–1/10/92	0									
First meeting for teams	1/13/92–1/13/92		0								
Complete meeting mgmt. training	1/13/92–2/21/92		▬	▬	▬	▬	▬	▬			
Leadership role trng./clarification	1/21/92–1/30/92			▬							
Pulse check supervisory roles	2/4/92–4/24/92					▬	▬	▬	▬	▬	▬
Complete goal-setting training	3/2/92–4/23/92									▬	
Complete conflict-mgmt. training	3/3/92–11/12/92									▬	
Complete problem-solving training	3/3/92–11/12/92									▬	
Create app'd plant/team goals	4/13/92–5/14/92										
Create team improvement procedure	4/15/92–4/15/92										
More advisor/leader training	6/1/92–6/1/92										
Create feedback process	6/1/92–6/25/92										
Blow-time	6/1/92–6/25/92										
Document first team-gen'd imp	7/1/92–7/1/92										
Design new employee orientation	8/10/92–9/10/92										
Create compensation program	3/1/93–3/1/93										

HIWF IN ACTION

Each HIWF team met once a week for an hour. Most meetings were held in one of the many conference rooms in the HIWF area, an entire floor in a building allotted exclusively for team meetings and HIWF activities. Three roles were important to team functioning. Each team chose a team facilitator (responsible for orchestrating the meeting's agenda and facilitating the discussion), a production communicator (responsible for overseeing actual production responsibilities), and an administrative coordinator (responsible for keeping meeting notes and minutes).

In addition to these internal roles, each team was overseen by a team developer. The developers, formerly supervisors, were responsible for ensuring that the teams were evolving in an effective and efficient manner. Developers were themselves members of a team that met on a weekly basis to provide support and advice to one another.

At first, HIWF was difficult for everyone involved. The team developers were specifically instructed not to interfere with the team process. People struggled with the idea of unlearning well-established work routines and replacing them with new ones. In the ensuing months, some teams picked up the process quickly, while others floundered. Sullivan-Rose became concerned that the effort was in jeopardy: "I felt like things were hitting the wall. We started off with a hands-off approach, but it became clear that we were going to have to get more involved. We had teams coming to us begging for help."

In the summer of 1992, GE Fanuc instituted the "support-a-team" concept. Various employees from the salaried ranks volunteered to serve as external-support resources for all teams. Support-a-team members attended meetings and offered in-meeting and out-of-meeting advice and counsel. Moreover, the team developers were asked to take a more active role in facilitating the growth and learning of their teams.

By the spring of 1993, the process was running more smoothly and Sullivan-Rose was due to leave in April. Some teams were performing in an exemplary fashion and were even asked to make presentations to the entire work force at the monthly operations meetings. Nevertheless, some teams were still struggling with issues that had nagged them from the start. With her maternity leave coming in just a few weeks, Sullivan-Rose felt pressed to get

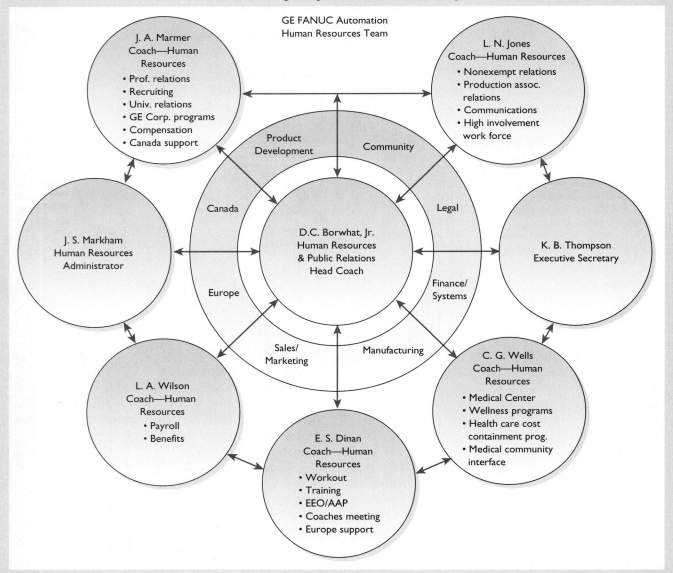

GE FANUC Automation
Human Resources Team

J. A. Marmer
Coach—Human
Resources
• Prof. relations
• Recruiting
• Univ. relations
• GE Corp. programs
• Compensation
• Canada support

L. N. Jones
Coach—Human Resources
• Nonexempt relations
• Production assoc.
  relations
• Communications
• High involvement
  work force

Product
Development

Community

Canada

Legal

J. S. Markham
Human Resources
Administrator

D.C. Borwhat, Jr.
Human Resources
& Public Relations
Head Coach

K. B. Thompson
Executive Secretary

Europe

Finance/
Systems

Sales/
Marketing

Manufacturing

L. A. Wilson
Coach—Human
Resources
• Payroll
• Benefits

C. G. Wells
Coach—Human
Resources
• Medical Center
• Wellness programs
• Health care cost
  containment prog.
• Medical community
  interface

E. S. Dinan
Coach—Human
Resources
• Workout
• Training
• EEO/AAP
• Coaches meeting
• Europe support

Cheryl Platte ready for the challenges she would soon face. Clearly, the disparity of performance among the teams was a perplexing issue. Sullivan-Rose had some ideas about what made a team perform well or poorly, but she reflected, "I think it is critical to Cheryl's success in this process for her to make her own deductions."

STEP 2: Prepare the case for class discussion.

STEP 3: Answer the following questions individually, in small groups, or with the class as a whole, as directed by your instructor.

DESCRIPTION
1. How did the GE Fanuc plant react to the Work-Out process?
2. Why was the High Involvement Work Force created?

FIGURE 11-12   GE FANUC merger organizational chart: HIWF teams

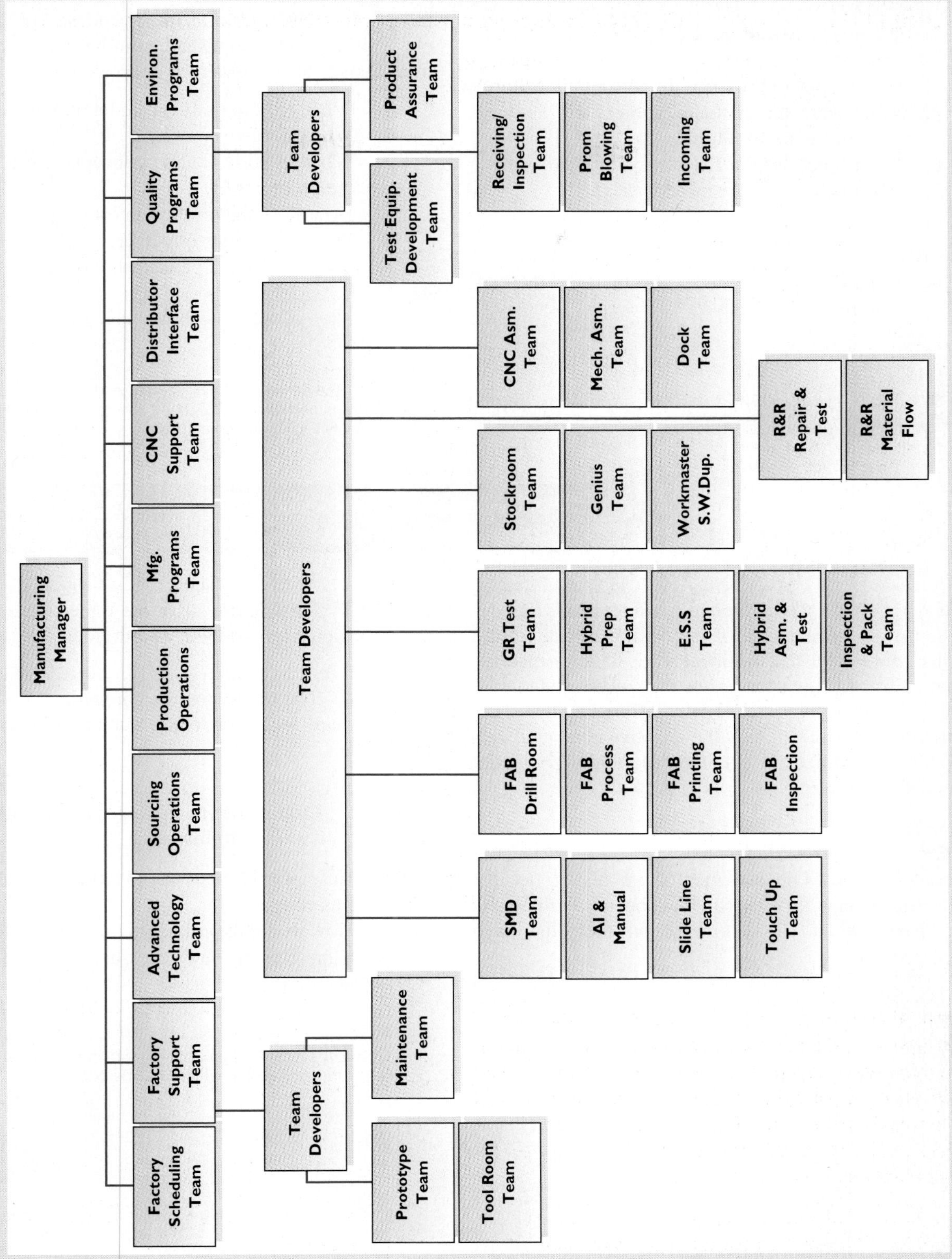

Manufacturing Manager

Factory Scheduling Team

Factory Support Team

Advanced Technology Team

Sourcing Operations Team

Production Operations

Mfg. Programs Team

CNC Support Team

Distributor Interface Team

Quality Programs Team

Environ. Programs Team

Team Developers

Prototype Team

Tool Room Team

Maintenance Team

Team Developers

SMD Team

AI & Manual

Slide Line Team

Touch Up Team

FAB Drill Room

FAB Process Team

FAB Printing Team

FAB Inspection

GR Test Team

Hybrid Prep Team

E.S.S Team

Hybrid Asm. & Test

Inspection & Pack Team

Stockroom Team

Genius Team

Workmaster S.W.Dup.

R&R Repair & Test

R&R Material Flow

CNC Asm. Team

Mech. Asm. Team

Dock Team

Team Developers

Test Equip. Development Team

Product Assurance Team

Receiving/ Inspection Team

Prom Blowing Team

Incoming Team

DIAGNOSIS

3. What type of culture did the GE FANUC plant have before the new initiative was introduced?
4. How would you describe the new HIWF culture?
5. What were the artifacts, values, and assumptions of the new culture?
6. What functions did the new culture perform?
7. Was the new culture effective?

PRESCRIPTION

8. What changes are necessary to make the new culture more effective?

ACTION

9. What issues should be considered in implementing this prescription?

STEP 4: Discussion. In small groups, with the entire class, or in written form, share your answers to the questions above. Then answer the following questions:

1. What symptoms suggested a problem existed?
2. What problems existed?
3. What theories and concepts help explain the problems?
4. How were the problems corrected?
5. Were the actions effective?
6. What additional changes are necessary?

[1]Thomas A. Stewart, "GE keeps those ideas coming," *Fortune,* August 12, 1991.

Prepared by Ted Forbes and Lynn Isabella, Associate Professor of Business Administration, copyright © 1993, the University of Virginia Darden School Foundation, Charlottesville, VA.

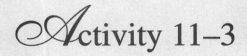 **11–3** **ASSESSING THE ORGANIZATIONAL CULTURE OF THE CLASSROOM**

STEP 1: Write down three to five statements that describe (a) the current state of the organizational culture in this course and (b) the ideal state of the organizational culture in this course. For the current state try to think of both positives and negatives. For the ideal state, do not limit yourself to only the negative characteristics you have identified in (a). Consider other potential facets of the culture.

STEP 2: The instructor will ask each participant to read out loud one statement from his or her list and write it on a flipchart or blackboard. Participants can "pass" when all statements on their list have been recorded.

STEP 3: The class will examine the statements to see if all are comprehensible and that there are no duplicates. Some statements may need to be combined.

STEP 4: Participants mark the three statements that are most significant to them as individuals.

STEP 5: The marks will be counted, identifying the major issues regarding the organizational culture in the course.

STEP 6: Discussion. In small groups or with the entire class, answer the following:

1. How would you characterize the culture of this course?
2. How would the culture of this course ideally be?
3. What changes are necessary to create the ideal culture?

From Kolb, Osland, Rubin, *Organizational Behavior: An Experiential Approach,* 6/E. © 1995 pp. 34, 346–347, 363. Reprinted by permission of Prentice–Hall, Englewood Cliffs, N.J.

$\mathscr{A}$ctivity 11–4　AFFINITY DIAGRAM EXERCISE

An affinity diagram is a problem analysis technique for collecting ideas and analyzing their similarities and relationships. You can use an affinity diagram to brainstorm ideas, promote teamwork, break down communication barriers, facilitate understanding in a group, and gain consensus among people with different viewpoints.

Team members should follow four general rules in constructing an affinity diagram:

1. Team members have complete freedom to express their ideas.
2. Criticism is not allowed.
3. Team members list as many ideas a possible within the specified time period.
4. Team members can combine and improve on the ideas of other team members.

STEP 1: Select a theme for the affinity diagram. The theme should be capable of being addressed by the people and in the time available. The theme is a brief statement that presents the question or problem of concern. Weakness-based themes are frequently easier to work with.

STEP 2: Write the theme or problem on the top corner of a large sheet of newsprint or poster board.

STEP 3: Each team member should write a series of succinct sentences that address or answer the theme or problem statement. Each sentence should include a single idea. Print each sentence on a separate self-stick note using black ink. Often the number of sentences (and notes) will be limited due to time or space constraints. A typical affinity diagram might result in 40–60, but as many as 100, items.

STEP 4: Put all notes in random order on the newsprint so that everyone on the team can read them.

STEP 5: Team members should read and review all notes to ensure that the meaning of the ideas expressed is clear. Where clarification is necessary, rewrite the note.

STEP 6: Team members should group the notes into similar ideas. Generally place no more than three notes in a group. This number may be increased to four or five in a grouping if team members generate a large number of sentences in Step 2. All team members should do the grouping simultaneously, without discussion. A team member may move or regroup ideas during this period. The grouping process should continue until all team members are satisfied with the groupings. The team should strive to have between 5 and 10 groupings. Groupings can contain one note. The team should check that no important ideas have been omitted and add them to the groupings as necessary.

STEP 7: The team should write a sentence that describes the essential idea of each grouping in blue ink, stack the notes that compose the group, and place the new sentence on top of that grouping. You do not have to write a new title for a grouping that contains a single note.

STEP 8: Rearrange the groupings so that those with the greatest similarity are near each other so that interrelationships can be indicated. Draw arrows to represent causality or contradictions: → for causality and >< for contradiction.

STEP 9: Indicate the importance of each grouping by voting. Each individual has three votes. To vote, place a red dot next to the grouping with the highest priority, a blue dot next to the grouping with the second highest priority, and a green dot next to the grouping with the third highest priority. Each person should put one red, one blue, and one green dot on the affinity diagram.

STEP 10: Write a one paragraph summary about the results and place it in the lower corner of the newsprint.

Activity 11-5 — THE MEDICINE CABINET CASE

STEP 1:   Read the Medicine Cabinet Case.

Jessica and Jeffrey Smith decided to do some redecorating in their house. The bathroom medicine cabinets were one of the items they decided to replace. They were about twenty years old, were dirty and rusty, and didn't provide enough storage space. After shopping in a number of discount and specialty stores, the Smiths found exactly the cabinets they wanted at a reasonable price in The House Store. They arranged to purchase the mirrors and have an electrician install them.

Three weeks after the mirrors were installed, Jessica noticed a large crack near the lights in the mirror. Because she believed that no one in her family had done anything unusual to cause the crack, she called The House Store to ask them how to replace the broken part of the mirror. After ten rings, the automatic voice mail answered. After listening to the recording, which seemed to last forever, Jessica pressed "5" because she did not know the extension of her party and was connected to the store operator, who then transferred her call to the customer service department. The person at customer service did not know how to handle her problem and transferred her call to the kitchen department. After ten rings, a salesman in the kitchen department answered and told Jessica that she needed to speak with someone in household appliances and that he would transfer her call. Jessica waited patiently and after a minute realized that she had been disconnected. She called The House Store again, listened to the same voice mail recording, and asked the operator to transfer her to the home appliance department. A salesman answered the telephone after only three rings, and told Jessica that his department did not handle bathroom cabinets and that Jessica should speak to someone in customer service. Although the salesman also tried to transfer her call, Jessica was once again disconnected. She called The House Store again, listened to the voice mail, was connected to customer service and told them that she was getting very annoyed with the way her problem was being handled. The customer service representative asked his supervisor how to handle this problem. He then connected her to someone in plumbing, who told Jessica to bring in the defective part and they would replace it.

Jeffrey Smith delivered the defective part to the store the next day. He went directly to the customer service desk. A service representative called someone from plumbing who met Jeffrey and immediately exchanged the part.

STEP 2:   In groups of four to six students, identify the quality problems described in the situation. Next hypothesize the causes of these problems. Finally, offer a plan for improving quality in the store.

STEP 3:   Discussion. Share your plans with the entire class. Then answer the following questions:

1. What types of quality problems exist?
2. What typically causes these problems?
3. How can the problems be corrected?

Activity 11-6 — ROVER LEARNING BUSINESS CASE

STEP 1:   Read the Rover Learning Business Case.

BACKGROUND

The Rover Learning Business (RLB) is an individual business within the Rover Group. It was set up in 1990 with the objective of providing a continuous learning environment for Rover Group associates, and later for the supplier and the franchised dealer network. It has a Board of Governors consisting of external members, mostly senior academics, and internal members, mostly Board members and senior executives from the Rover Group. The President is Sir Graham Day and the Chairman is George Simpson. The Deputy Chairman is Professor Bhattacharyya, Professor of Manufacturing Systems at Warwick University.

RLB was established partly as a result of a learning and development survey of the work force conducted by the Electoral Reform Society and partly out of a need to reduce the cost of high labour turnover, leading to interruptions in effective task teams. The survey, using a stratified random sample, found, amongst other things, that 78 percent of the work force were prepared to use their own time to increase their knowledge and skills base. Senior Managers wished to respond to this and felt that the typical approach of asking people to "talk to their Training Managers" would not be successful. RLB was set up as a company-wide initiative to facilitate learning. It had a Senior Executive Committee made up of senior people from the Business Units. The Committee worked closely with Personnel. The Managing Director reports directly to the Personnel Director of Rover Group and, indirectly, to the Managing Director of the Rover Group.

THE ROLE OF ROVER LEARNING BUSINESS

Success Through People is the all-embracing goal, for Rover's policy of "success through people" is fundamental to the continuing success of the Group and investment is seen to be necessary at all levels.

Within this goal, RLB has identified a number of objectives and key activities:

(a) *Long-Term Investment in People:* The staff of sixty specialists are dedicated to providing a continuous learning and development environment for the Rover Group associates, suppliers, and the franchised dealers. The business works within the context of an "extended enterprise," treating suppliers and dealers very much as business partners.

(b) *Motivating and Enabling the Work Force:* RLB aims to motivate and enable individuals to make the most of the opportunities Rover has available for their personal achievement. This supports the continued growth and vision of the Group, its key suppliers and dealer network.

(c) *Change Management:* RLB contributes to the people aspects of change management by supporting the key thrusts of business, customer satisfaction, reduction in breakdown, growth in Europe and movement upmarket. It is involved in implementing the Group quality strategy and aims to ensure total quality throughout every area of the enterprise.

(d) *Keeping Ahead in Technical Innovation:* RLB is involved in new model and other technical programmes to ensure that Rover is at the leading edge of technical and quality achievements. It helps to share innovations amongst different areas of the Group.

(e) *Preparing for the Future:* The links which Rover Learning Business have made with a number of external bodies is done to ensure adaptability for the future.

These objectives are derived from a statement made by George Simpson, Chairman and Chief Executive of the Rover Group, which can be summed up under the phrase "companies which learn quickest will be the winners."

INITIAL WORK

The initial work concentrated on the first three objectives and so was concerned with motivation and developing people. The first issue addressed was how to get people back into the "learning mode" after being out of education for years. The first instrument, offered in 1990, was the Rover Employee Assisted Learning Incentive. Everyone was offered £100 to undertake a course which need have nothing to do with work, but must be offered by an accredited organisation. Take up was 5 percent of employees in the first year. This low take up was put down to a lack of trust and a general feeling of "what's the catch?"

The second instrument, devised in July 1991, was called Personal Learning Pays, which consisted of an audio cassette and book aimed at helping people to understand their preferred learning style. However, this was not very user-friendly and was too complex for some associates. By Year 3, the take up of Personal Learning Pays was 25 percent. The scheme was suspended for two months in 1992, when all pay increases were stopped and executive pay was pegged for three years and administrative increases delayed for six months. When the scheme was relaunched, the environment had changed in mid-1992. The Company had made a commitment to lifetime employment. This did not necessarily mean in Rover, but it did mean that there was a commitment to facilitate the enhancement of skills so associates could stay in employment, in Rover if possible but, if not, with a supplier or dealer, or elsewhere in industry and commerce.

ENVIRONMENTAL ISSUES

Threats

The world car market was changing because of the Japanese success. The U.K. and European car markets were facing one million vehicles produced by transplants and needed to respond to that threat. Rover had to manage the business differently to cope with more competition and needed to make a step increase in productivity. Quality would no longer be sufficient to provide a competitive edge. There was a need to "work smarter."

Responses

There was considerable reduction in managerial layers from eight or nine levels to four or five levels between the Managing Director and the line workers.

In 1987, a total quality management programme, initiated with the help of P.A. Management Consultants, endeavoured to change the culture within the organisation and embed a new way of working into it. So the Total Quality Leadership Programme was developed, with the help of Price Waterhouse and two smaller consultants, to provide lateral thinking. Frameworks were designed which varied to suit the needs of different Business Units. The operating units can vary considerably, from ten people manufacturing cells at Swindon Body and Pressing Plant to thirty people cells at Longbridge.

A separate, but closely allied initiative was the Personal Development File. This aimed at encouraging people to take responsibility for their own learning and development and involved each individual having a Personal Development File. This could be a single sheet of paper or box file—whatever was appropriate. It could be personally confidential or used with the Manager. Its use was voluntary, but 78 percent requested it, although only 60 percent have active boxes. It recorded past experiences and academic qualifications and required individuals to analyse their strengths and weaknesses. In order for the Personal Development File to work in the best possible way, there was a need to develop the Manager as coach.

The Employee Assisted Learning Incentive £100 has been pooled by teams to enable them to satisfy their own learning needs. For example, team building skills which some cells identified as being needed have drawn on this source of funds. This has further developed the use of Personal Development Files. Thus, the learning schemes have aimed at creating an environment for learning and enhancing the skills of everyone in the business. They have encouraged Business Units to take responsibility for their learning and have facilitated the management of change.

CHANGE MANAGEMENT

Another strand to RLB's activities, associated with the second three objectives, has been its involvement in the people side of change management. This involves a process which is shown in Figure 11–13, "The Change Management Process." A business need is identified and then a Champion to deal with this problem is found. The Change Champion's function is to enroll Change Agents into the process. It is the Change Agent's role to work with the key players or expert group, in order to develop a specification and design a change process and plan. They then have to prepare the Change Agents, create change material and prepare a change environment before actually implementing the change. Once the implementation process has begun, then it is a matter of measuring what is happening by recording and comparing with best practice and benchmarking where possible. This then leads to the development of new best practice and an improvement of the change material used. These new best practices are then recorded on the corporate learning database.

An example of some of the sorts of issues that are looked at: there was a warranty problem which seemed impossible for the Rover engineers to solve. However, once they were brought together with the suppliers, they could work together on the problem, create their joint objectives, and were able to solve the problem in two weeks.

The learning database attempts to record what individual Business Units have learned, so this information can be shared. The information is recorded using the change management process diagram as a template. Figure 11–14 (page 506) shows how the findings from a training session concerned with added value and elimination of waste were recorded. This example of the model in practice demonstrates the advantage of having a clear process for participants to follow. The session involved ten people initially, but this process has subsequently been used in all business units and functions within the Company. The ten participants spent a day identifying objectives, processes, and people to facili-

FIGURE 11–13 *Change management process*

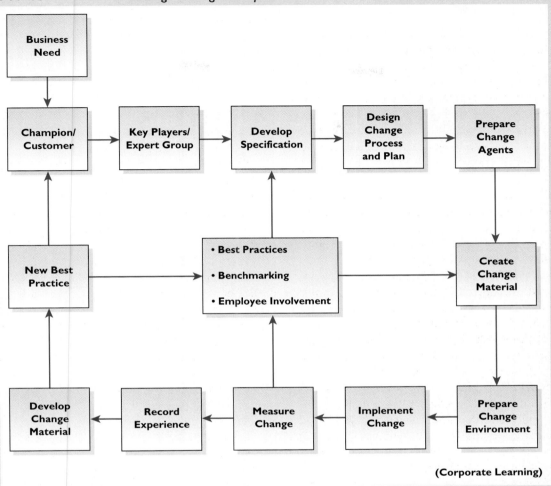

(Corporate Learning)

tate change. This can be shared, via the database, with other Business Units and evaluated in the light of the customer experience and bottom line performance.

The idea behind creating a central database or a corporate learning database is that it becomes possible to record best practice and to develop benchmarking. The approach taken is one of "copy plus," that is the idea of continuous improvement so that anyone can interrogate the database using three fields—first of all, best practices, secondly, learning processes and thirdly, grant aid given. Not anyone can log on as input is restricted to Line Managers who are linked to the network. However, interrogation of the database is now fairly widespread and since August 1993, has been based on personal computers and available on the fac-

tory information system. So, when anybody has a work problem, they can look up and see if another area within Rover has had a similar problem. They can then copy the solution on the database and perhaps add to that solution. Hence the term "copy plus." By adding to the solution, they are, in fact, enhancing learning and recording their best practice back onto the database.

RLB feel that they have learned considerably from their links with Honda and have run two Rover Learning events entitled "Learning From Honda" (see Figure 11–15, pages 507 and 508) to encapsulate the lessons learned from the relationship between the two Companies. However, the learning is not only one way. Honda has learned from the operation of Hitachi presses in Swindon, where the output from these presses is higher

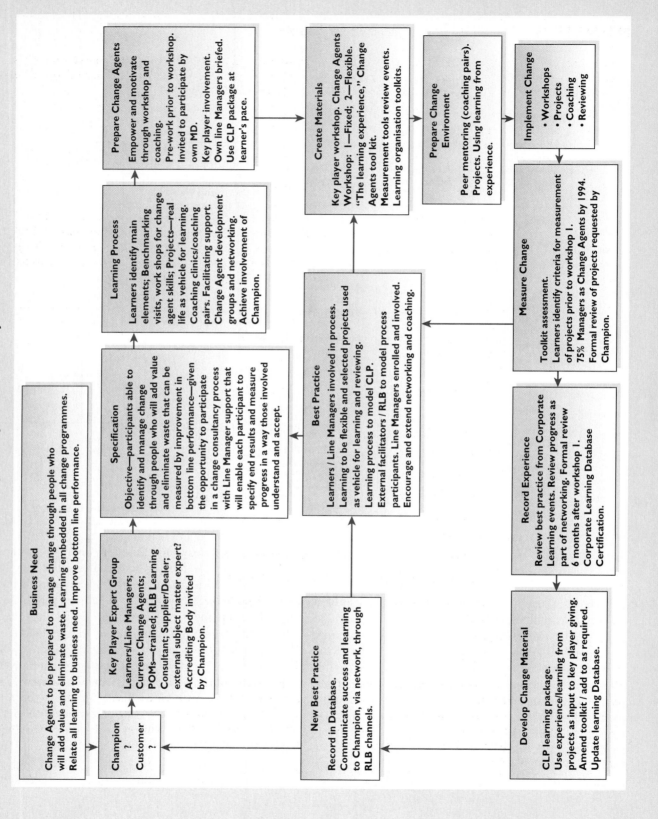

Business Need

Change Agents to be prepared to manage change through people who will add value and eliminate waste. Learning embedded in all change programmes. Relate all learning to business need. Improve bottom line performance.

Champion ? Customer ?

Key Player Expert Group

Learners/Line Managers; Current Change Agents; POMs—trained; RLB Learning Consultant; Supplier/Dealer; external subject matter expert? Accrediting Body invited by Champion.

Specification

Objective—participants able to identify and manage change through people who will add value and eliminate waste that can be measured by improvement in bottom line performance—given the opportunity to participate in a change consultancy process with Line Manager support that will enable each participant to specify end results and measure progress in a way those involved understand and accept.

Learning Process

Learners identify main elements; Benchmarking visits, work shops for change agent skills; Projects—real life as vehicle for learning. Coaching clinics/coaching pairs. Facilitating support. Change Agent development groups and networking. Achieve involvement of Champion.

Prepare Change Agents

Empower and motivate through workshop and coaching. Pre-work prior to workshop. Invited to participate by own MD. Key player involvement. Own line Managers briefed. Use CLP package at learner's pace.

Create Materials

Key player workshop. Change Agents Workshop: 1—Fixed; 2—Flexible. "The learning experience," Change Agents tool kit. Measurement tools review events. Learning organisation toolkits.

Prepare Change Enviroment

Peer mentoring (coaching pairs). Projects. Using learning from experience.

Implement Change

• Workshops
• Projects
• Coaching
• Reviewing

Best Practice

Learners / Line Managers involved in process. Learning to be flexible and selected projects used as vehicle for learning and reviewing. Learning process to model CLP. External facilitators / RLB to model process participants. Line Managers enrolled and involved. Encourage and extend networking and coaching.

Measure Change

Toolkit assessment. Learners identify criteria for measurement of projects prior to workshop 1. 75% Managers as Change Agents by 1994. Formal review of projects requested by Champion.

Record Experience

Review best practice from Corporate Learning events. Review progress as part of networking. Formal review 6 months after workshop 1. Corporate Learning Database Certification.

Develop Change Material

CLP learning package. Use experience/learning from projects as input to key player giving. Amend toolkit / add to as required. Update learning Database.

New Best Practice

Record in Database. Communicate success and learning to Champion, via network, through RLB channels.

FIGURE 11–15   *Learning from Honda America*

The business need was identified as "introduce manufacturing best practices into all Rover Group Business Units." Two people were identified as the champions of the exercise. The key players and expert group involved were the programme co-ordinators and trainers who had visited Honda America. Six objectives were identified:

- To demonstrate the "Honda way" of working.
- Implement best practice.
- Share best practice and involve other teams.
- Participate in Honda America Rover network.
- Participate in cultural exchanges.
- Identify future needs to continuously improve "tomorrow's jobs."

In designing the change process and plan, a fact gathering visit to Honda America for two weeks was arranged. To ensure that the best use was made of the visit, there were pre-visit orientation programmes and post-visit reviews were held. Preparation of change agents was a lengthy stage in the whole exercise. It identified what was wanted from the change agents in terms of changes initiated. This list was completed by an identification of essentials, or musts, and also by a list of wants.

WANTS	MUSTS
Interested, flexible, energetic participants capable of working on line.	Clearly defined programme co-ordinator.
Derning philosophy.	Key contacts in each business unit.
Charting techniques.	Participants from all Business Units.
Problem solving.	Participant profiles.
Process questioning.	Local itinerary briefings.
Continuous improvement.	Pre-visit orientation trainings.
People empowerment and involvement.	Visit to Honda in Swindon.
Process flow charting.	Understand Rover Tomorrow—The New Deal.
Presentation skills.	Committed to Rover Tomorrow.
Note taking and report writing.	Respect for confidentiality.
Capable of sharing learning.	

The key points at this stage were seen as the importance of on the spot experience. To really learn what is going on, participants need to work with all associate levels in the partner area, so that they effectively become a member of the team. Participants need to understand and experience the Honda way, philosophies, policies, and practices. Participants from Business Units should be encouraged to share learning with other members and groups and there is a need for periodic review of improvements implemented. Participants need to be involved in the pre- and post-visit programmes, as well as the review of group work.

(continued)

FIGURE 11–15   (continued)

The creation of change material to facilitate the change involved producing a document "Rover Tomorrow–The New Deal." This change involved relating the event to Rover Tomorrow–The New Deal, which describes what the Company commits to do in its relationship with all associates and what associates commit to do in return. The personal profile sheet was also used and material was created for the pre-visit orientation programme. Preparing the change environment and implementing change involved local briefings and pre-visit orientation training, as well as an itinerary of visits over six months.

Measurements of change were made three weeks after the visit and six months after the visit. The three week visit aimed to review the original visit and invite Managers' input and identify modifications to the improved future programmes. This can lead to a modification of change material. At the six month visit, there was a review and sharing of changes and an invitation to Managers to input their considerations. Their report was then issued to all Business Units. These visits were logged, so experience was recorded and those closely involved kept a personal log. The six month report follows up and identifies good practice and considers what is necessary to implement new best practice.

SOURCE: Process developed by Small and Medium Cars, RLB, Canley.

than that achieved by Honda in Japan. They came to see why the productivity was higher and believe that they can learn something from it. The incentive for the Swindon operation to produce a very high output from these presses was based on the fact that they wanted to be less dependent on Rover as the prime customer. They also wanted to quote for competitive contracts in the worldwide pressings market. They needed to increase their output in order to be able to meet the needs of these other contracts, alongside existing Rover, Honda, and Rolls Royce business.

RLB BUSINESS PLAN 1993

RLB plan to continue their extended enterprise scheme and to support all individuals involved in that network. They have the objective to create a total awareness of the learning opportunities available to people and wish to enhance the life planning of workers to include retirement planning, pensions, wills, and making a career plan. They are going to produce a themed diary to encourage further bonding between associates and learning. They intend to produce for associates a handout on why learning is important to them and the Company. They are also going to research into existing programmes, particularly the Personal Development Files, to see how they can improve the level of involvement.

Central to all of these is the concept of empowerment, creating the space and time to provide people with education, development, authority, tools, facilities

and support to take control of their work and maximise their contribution. RLB also intend to improve Line Manager support to enable them to become agents for change and to provide them with a comprehensive toolkit to enable them to progressively introduce change and to provide help on coaching, monitoring, and meeting skills. They intend to do further work on the sharing of corporate learning through workshops and conferences and to make more people aware of the corporate learning database, so that it can actually become operational at a factory level. They hope to have one hundred and fifty trained experts in the use of this database by the end of 1993.

The change management process is likely to include further work on distribution efficiency and further development on the Total Quality Leader Programme. This will involve extending the present network of Change Agents and supporting them with a Total Quality Leader's toolkit of skills. The overall aim is to achieve change management performance that is world class in any environment.

The implementation of the RLB and its effects on quality, performance, and profitability was hailed an unqualified success by early 1994.

A significant loss, when Rover was bought by BAC, had been turned round into a £56 million pretax profit for the fiscal year ended 1993. Industrial analysts called Rover "the manufacturing company which leads Britain out of the recession." As a successful company, however, Rover became a valuable asset for BAC and, therefore, offered considerable attraction to other car manufacturers who had not learned to manage change so successfully. BMW made a bid for BAC's 80 percent stake in Rover PLC in February 1994.

STEP 2: Prepare the case for class discussion.

STEP 3: Answer the following questions individually, in small groups, or with the class as a whole, as directed by your instructor.

DESCRIPTION
1. Why was Rover Learning Business started?
2. What were the objectives of RLB?

DIAGNOSIS
3. How effective was RLB in meeting its objectives?
4. Did RLB have the characteristics of an effective learning organization?
5. What culture did RLB create within itself and within the Rover group?

PRESCRIPTION
6. What changes are necessary to improve the Rover Group as a learning organization?

7. How can RLB contribute better to making the Rover Group a learning organization?

ACTION
8. What issues should be considered in making further changes in these organizations?

STEP 4: Discussion. In small groups, with the entire class, or in written form, share your answers to the questions above. Then answer the following questions:

1. What symptoms suggested a problem existed?
2. What problems existed?
3. What theories and concepts help explain the problems?
4. How were the problems corrected?

This case was prepared by Kate Murray and Hildegard Wiesehöfer, University of Derby, as a basis for class discussion rather than to illustrate either effective or ineffective handling of a business situation. The material has been compiled from fieldwork and with the cooperation of Rover Learning Company. Copyright © 1994, K. Murray and H. Wiesehöfer, University of Derby.

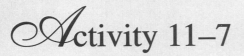

Activity 11–7 "EMPLOYERS SPYING ON EMPLOYEES"

STEP 1: View the ABC video entitled "Employers Spying on Employees."

STEP 2: Individually, in small groups, or with the entire class, answer the following questions:

1. What types of cultures did Sheraton and K-Mart create?
2. How did the secret videotaping of employees and visits to their homes contribute to the respective cultures?
3. What were the components of the cultures in these organizations?
4. What outcomes resulted from these cultures?
5. Do employers have a right to spy on employees?
6. What recourse do employees have in these situations?

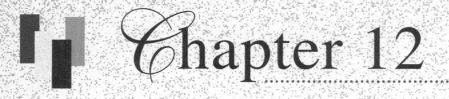

Chapter 12

Chapter Outline

Work Design, Technology, and Innovation

LEARNING OBJECTIVES

After completing the reading and activities in Chapter 12, students will be able to

1. Highlight the challenge of job design for organizations.

2. Compare and contrast work simplification, job enlargement, job enrichment, and sociotechnical redesign.

3. Cite the advantages and disadvantages of three alternative work arrangements.

4. Describe the evolution and content of quality-of-work-life programs.

5. Describe the impact of information technology on organizations.

6. Describe the basic issues in reengineering work.

7. Describe the process of innovation.

8. Offer three strategies for increasing innovation in organizations.

Connecticut Mutual Life Insurance Redesigns the Way It Works

I n the early 1990s, Connecticut Mutual Life Insurance Company radically changed the way it did business. The insurer introduced a comprehensive program called "One Image," named after the extensive use of optical disks to store records. This program gave workers an array of information technologies to improve performance and changed the flow of work across departments. In a key move, the company replaced its paper files with computerized files, which streamlined the way employees handled claims and questions. Previously, customer representatives had to recall a paper file from the company's football field-sized warehouse. Now, storing customer records on optical disks lets workers instantly call up all necessary forms and correspondence on their desktop computers. Paperwork changes that took six days now take seconds using the new information technology.

The way employees do work has also changed to take advantage of the new automation. Connecticut Mutual introduced cross-functional work teams made up of employees who have the skills needed to service an account from beginning to end. Because the cross-functional teams foster individual responsibility and facilitate the coordination of work, fewer levels of management are needed. At the same time, the insurer instituted a major reorganization, which even required employees to reapply for their jobs. Called the "Transformation Project," this restructuring has already reduced twelve business units to four and redefined numerous functions as a way of better delivering service to customers.[1]

The changes at Connecticut Mutual echo changes occurring at thousands of companies around the world. In this chapter we explore the interplay between work and technology and the way it affects job design. At the end of the chapter we see how the same interplay can lead to innovation throughout an organization.

THE CHALLENGE OF JOB DESIGN

Changes such as those at Connecticut Mutual attempt to increase worker productivity and organizational effectiveness. They reflect a search for both organizational efficiency and effectiveness as well as worker satisfaction and productivity.

The search for efficiency in job design began as early as the eighteenth century, with theorists such as Adam Smith, who believed that the division of labor lead to greater productivity. The emphasis on specialization, reducing a job to its component parts, dominated the first part of the twentieth century with the emergence of scientific management (see Chapter 1). Work simplification, as described later in this chapter, has continued this approach to job design.

Technology became an important component of job design with the introduction of the mechanically paced assembly line. Later, technology helped organizations use labor, generally the most significant expense in organizations, more efficiently. Technology also contributes to more efficient work flows and supports job designs that increase efficiency. The risk of introducing new technology, however, is that it mechanizes job activities without considering the workers involved, particularly their needs, skills, and expectations. Thus, more recent approaches to job design, such as job enrichment, quality-of-working-life approaches, and alternative work schedules, described later in this chapter, explicitly incorporated elements that increase worker satisfaction.

Human factors play a major role in job performance and hence are critical in designing jobs. The sociotechnical school (see later in this chapter) explicitly recognized the importance of both technology and the human element in job design. Jobs with too narrow a scope, while potentially very efficient, can be boring and dehumanizing. Jobs with too broad a scope can be frustrating and demoralizing. Because both extremes are ultimately wasteful, organizational leaders must carefully design jobs to meet both technological options and human factors. In particular, worker satisfaction becomes important in assessing job redesign options.

Although organizations face an ongoing cycle of adopting new technology and revamping job design to better use this technology for producing and delivering products and services, organizations must also ensure that technology does not dehumanize the job. The challenge of job design then becomes finding ways to successfully marry technology and human factors in job design. Managers have to strike the right balance of efficiency and worker satisfaction. The next section describes an array of work design options that managers can use to design work.

WORK DESIGN OPTIONS

The design of work or jobs (used interchangeably in this book) refers to determining the content of tasks, their sequencing and other interrelationships, and the context in which they are performed. Redesigning work or changing the way jobs are performed can increase worker performance and satisfaction. It can reinforce the benefits of new organizational designs (see Chapters 13 and 14) by fitting job design to the new structure, introducing new ways of coordinating work, or modifying the chain of command to allow a more rapid response to environmental changes. In this section we examine six options for designing work: work simplification, job enlargement, job enrichment, the sociotechnical approach, alternative work arrangements, and quality-of-work-life programs.

WORK SIMPLIFICATION

Work simplification refers to a process of reducing a job to its component parts and then reassembling these parts into an optimally efficient work process. In the manufacture of lacquer bookcases and storage units, for example, the manufacturing process might be divided into many discrete tasks, each performed by a separate individual. One worker might always cut the backs of the bookcases. Another might insert the shelf pegs into the frames. Still another might attach the doors for the storage units. This type of simplified manufacturing process would have the following characteristics (we could identify a similar set of characteristics for the equivalent "white-collar" positions in a bureaucracy):

- mechanical pacing, or the use of an automated assembly line;

- repetitive work;

- concentration on a fraction of the product;

- specification of the tools and techniques used in production;

- limited social interaction among workers to ensure they pay close attention to the task;

- sufficient training to ensure workers have appropriate skills.[2]

Industrial engineers, staff members who evaluate and improve work processes, study the exact series of motions in a job, using detailed observation records and drawing extensive diagrams of the work process. Next, they monitor the time required for each part of the job. Then they identify and attempt to eliminate all false, slow, and useless movements. Finally, they redesign the job by collecting into one series the quickest and best movements. To accomplish the last step, work simplification typically involves extensive use of machines or office equipment, optimum spacing of rest periods, high specialization of work activities, and matching of workers to jobs best suited to their abilities, experience, and aptitudes. Engineers must design any equipment to fit the mental and physical characteristics of the operators.[3]

An effective work simplification design finds ways of ensuring that the process operates smoothly and cost-effectively. Managers attempt to efficiently move and reposition items between operations, assemble separate tasks into a more efficient total process, balance the line to reduce downtime in less time-consuming tasks and encourage effective work pacing, and provide sufficient external supervision.[4] Some Total Quality Management programs (see Chapter 11) have redesigned jobs in this way to reduce the number of defects in manufactured products.

Jobs that have become overly complex typically benefit from work simplification. So do jobs that require a precise design of tasks and their interrelationships to increase productivity. Work simplification can also create significant dysfunctions. Workers may become bored or have limited opportunities for individual growth if top management automates and mechanizes production for its own sake rather than for improving worker performance.

JOB ENLARGEMENT

In ***job enlargement,*** the scope of the job is expanded horizontally, increasing the number of different but related processes it involves. Job enlargement offers the opposite solution to work simplification for designing work. Rather than encouraging an individual to concentrate on a fraction of the product or service, job enlargement requires workers to perform numerous, often unrelated, job tasks.

In a recent experiment, a job redesigned via job enlargement combined clerical jobs, such as coder and keyer of data, increased employee satisfaction, reduced mental boredom, increased chances of catching errors, and provided better customer service in the short run.[5] In the longer run, however, after two years the redesigned job with more tasks alone resulted in decreased satisfaction, efficiency, and customer service and increased mental overload and errors.[6] When workers gained more knowledge as a result of job enlargement, rather than just performing more related tasks, increased customer satisfaction, improved customer service, decreased overload, and fewer errors resulted.[7]

The earliest job enlargement programs involved *job extension,*[8] in which workers did more of the same job. Now *job rotation* is a more common form of job enlargement. The worker performs two or more tasks, but alternates among them in a predefined way over a period of time. For example, a worker might attach the wheel assembly one week, inspect it the next, and organize the parts for assembly during the third. Job rotation provides a hedge against absenteeism since workers can perform more than a single function. It also contributes to training workers in numerous jobs or tasks as a way of supporting their career advancement. While used extensively in Japan by companies such as Toyota, U.S. companies have shown less interest in adopting it, relegating job rotation to hourly workers in factories because they do not consider it the best approach to developing and employing skilled workers.[9]

JOB ENRICHMENT

Job enrichment involves changing a job both *horizontally* by adding tasks and *vertically* by adding responsibility. The widespread use of self-managed teams in organizations, as described in Chapter 5, has resulted in significant job enrichment. In these teams specialization of tasks is significantly reduced, workers have the responsibility of performing large sequences of tasks in their entirety, and workers receive training on an array of jobs so that they can exchange jobs with other workers as necessary. Frederick Herzberg's motivation-hygiene model (see Chapter 4) provided the roots for job enrichment programs. He enriched jobs by increasing motivators such as challenge, autonomy, and responsibility in the job.[10]

Declining work motivation, dissatisfaction with growth opportunities and the job in general, and lack of work effectiveness may signal a need for job enrichment. Enriched jobs often meet the needs of the increasingly educated work force many companies employ.

MARRIOTT HOTELS. Guest service associates (GSAs) check guests into the hotel, secure the required paperwork from a lobby rack, and escort the guests to their rooms. The GSAs combine the jobs of doorman, bellman, and reception desk clerk into a single position, thereby enriching the job. The GSA also handles guest requests previously made to other departments, such as housekeeping or room service.[11]

The Job Characteristics Model The *job characteristics model* of enrichment specifies five core characteristics of the job that significantly influence the behaviors and attitudes of workers.[12]

- *Skill variety.* The degree to which a job requires the worker to perform activities that challenge his or her skills and use diverse abilities. A state police trooper's job has more skill variety than a crossing guard's job.

- *Task identity.* The degree to which a job requires completion of a "whole" and identifiable piece of work, that is, doing a job from beginning to end with a visible outcome. Assembly-line workers in a furniture factory who assemble an entire chair or bookcase have jobs with high task identity.

- *Task significance.* The degree to which the job is perceived to have a substantial impact on the lives of other people. Classroom teaching has greater task significance than lunchroom monitoring.

- *Autonomy.* The degree to which the job gives the worker freedom, independence, and discretion in scheduling work and determining how he or she will carry it out. Self-managed teams have high autonomy.

- *Feedback.* The degree to which a worker, in carrying out the work activities required by the job, gets information about the effectiveness of his or her efforts. A clerk who receives a list of transcription errors each day receives feedback.

Three critical psychological states—*experienced meaningfulness, experienced responsibility,* and *knowledge of results*—affect personal and work outcomes. These include internal work motivation, "growth" satisfaction, general job satisfaction, and work effectiveness. Skill variety, task identity, and task significance influence the extent to which an individual job holder experiences the job as meaningful. As workers use their diverse abilities, complete entire tasks, and view their work as having an impact on others' lives, they more likely will experience the jobs as meaningful. Autonomy in the job influences the extent to which an individual believes he or she is responsible for outcomes of the job. A manager likely feels more responsible for his or her job outcomes than does a person the manager supervises. Feedback in the job increases the individual's knowledge of the actual results of the work activities. Increasing the amount of information available to a job holder increases the individual's ability to know and evaluate his or her effectiveness.

The individual's knowledge and skill, strength of his or her growth needs (needs for learning, personal accomplishment, and development), and satisfaction with the work context moderate the links between the core job characteristics and critical psychological states and between the critical psychological states and outcomes.[13] For example, individuals who have the skills and knowledge to perform enriched jobs will be more satisfied than those who are less competent. Individuals with high growth needs typically respond more positively to enriched jobs than those with low growth needs because the latter individuals may not value such opportunities or may be negatively stressed by them. Individuals satisfied with the work context may be more able to take advantage of the opportunities provided by enriched jobs than those dissatisfied with the work context because they are too preoccupied with that aspect of the work. Figure 12–1 summarizes the relationships of the job characteristics model.

Strategies of Enrichment The job characteristics approach calls for enriching a job by increasing one or more of the core dimensions.[14]

Combining tasks increases skill variety and task identity—for example, having a single customer service representative in an insurance company handle all issues relating to a specific account.

Forming natural work units that distribute work in a natural and logical way increases task identity and task significance—for example, giving a nurse the job of doing all skilled nursing tasks for a given patient.

FIGURE 12–1

The job characteristics model

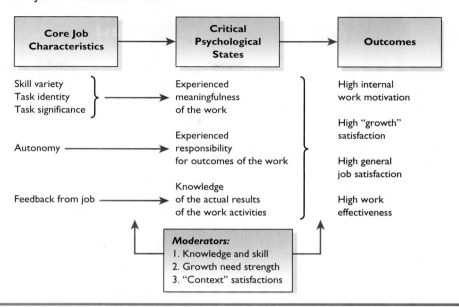

SOURCE: From J.R. Hackman and G.R. Oldham, *Work Redesign,* Copyright © 1980, Addison-Wesley Publishing Co., Inc. Reprinted with permission of the publisher.

Establishing client relationships increases skill variety, autonomy, and feedback—for example, having groups of bank loan officers always deal with the same clients.

Loading a job vertically to combine implementation and control increases autonomy—for example, giving production workers responsibility for quality control or meeting schedules.

Opening feedback channels increases knowledge of results—for example, letting an assembly-line worker know the number and type of defects in products produced.

Job enrichment programs work better for less complex jobs than for inherently richer jobs. Managers can expect enrichment to succeed only if workers want and seek fulfillment in their work and value jobs requiring greater skill and effort. Differences in employer and employee goals may hinder the effectiveness of work enrichment programs. Some managers may want their workers to demonstrate more initiative and autonomy, but the workers want less involvement and learning; or the opposite may be true.

Figure 12–2 presents a checklist for evaluating the factors that may affect job enrichment. Complete this checklist for a job that might be enriched. The lower the total score (1 or 2), the more conducive the job is to being enriched. The higher the score (4 or 5), the less effective job enrichment efforts likely will be. Managers can use data such as these to help diagnose the nature of the job, technology,

FIGURE 12–2   *Job enrichment evaluation form*

THE JOB ITSELF

1. Quality is important and attributable to the worker.	/1/2/3/4/5/	Quality is not too important and/or is not controllable by the worker.
2. Flexibility is a major contributor to job efficiency.	/1/2/3/4/5/	Flexibility is not a major consideration.
3. The job requires the coordination of tasks or activities among several workers.	/1/2/3/4/5/	The job is performed by one worker acting independently of others.
4. The benefits of job enrichment will compensate for the efficiencies of task specialization.	/1/2/3/4/5/	Job enrichment will eliminate substantial efficiencies realized from specialization.
5. The conversion and one-time setup costs involved in job enrichment can be recovered in a reasonable period of time.	/1/2/3/4/5/	Training and other costs associated with job enrichment are estimated to be much greater than expected results.
6. The wage payment plan is not based solely on output.	/1/2/3/4/5/	Workers are under a straight piecework wage plan.
7. Due to the workers' ability to affect output, an increase in job satisfaction can be expected to increase prductivity.	/1/2/3/4/5/	Due to the dominance of technology, an increase in job satisfaction is unlikely to significantly affect productivity.

TECHNOLOGY

8. Changes in job content would not necessitate a large investment in equipment and technology.	/1/2/3/4/5/	The huge investment in equipment and technology overrides all other consideration.

THE WORKERS

9. Employees are accustomed to change and respond favorably to it.	/1/2/3/4/5/	Employees are set in their ways and prefer the status quo.
10. Employees feel secure in the jobs. Employment has been stable.	/1/2/3/4/5/	Layoffs are frequent. Many employees are concerned about the permanency of employment.
11. Employees are dissatisfied with their jobs and would welcome changes in job content and work relationships.	/1/2/3/4/5/	Employees are satisfied with their present jobs and general work situation.
12. Employees are highly skilled blue- and white-collar workers, professionals, and supervisors.	/1/2/3/4/5	Employees are semi- and unskilled blue- and white-collar workers.
13. Employees are well educated with most having college degrees.	/1/2/3/4/5/	The average employee has less than a high school education.
14. Employees are from a small town and rural environment.	/1/2/3/4/5/	The company is located in a large, highly industrialized metropolitan area.
15. The history of union–management (if no union, worker–management) relations has been one of cooperation and mutual support.	/1/2/3/4/5/	Union–management (worker–management) relations are strained, and the two parties are antagonistic to one another.

FIGURE 12-2   *(continued)*

MANAGEMENT		
16. Managers are committed to job enrichment and are anxious to participate in its implementation.	/1/2/3/4/5/	Managers show little interest in job enrichment and even less interest in having it implemented in their department.
17. Managers have attended seminars, workshops, and so forth, are quite knowledgeable of the concept, and have had experience in implementing it.	/1/2/3/4/5/	Managers lack the training and experience necessary to develop and implement job enrichment projects.
18. Management realizes that substantial payoffs from job enrichment usually take one to three years to materialize.	/1/2/3/4/5/	Management expects immediate results (within six months) from job enrichment projects.
Total score _____	÷ 18 = _____	Job Enrichment Rating

SOURCE: William E. Reif and Ronald C. Tinnell, A diagnostic approach to job enrichment, *MSU Business Topics* (Autumn 1973): 29–37. Reprinted by permission of the publisher, Division of Research, Graduate School of Business Administration, Michigan State University.

workers, and management to predict the likely impact and appropriateness of work enrichment.

SOCIOTECHNICAL APPROACH

Building on job enrichment, the sociotechnical approach to design emphasized both the use of teams, such as the cross-functional teams at Connecticut Mutual, to motivate employees and the introduction of appropriate technologies to improve task performance.

In the 1950s and 1960s, researchers at the Tavistock Institute in England were the first to note the importance of work groups in handling new technology.[15] The sociotechnical approach was used mainly when introducing new technology to offset the potentially dehumanizing effects of increased automation. In the 1970s, Scandinavian automobile manufacturers introduced the concept of *autonomous work groups* as a way of meeting workers' social needs while introducing technological innovation into work.[16] In these self-regulating groups, employees who performed interdependent tasks worked in a common unit, controlled their own task assignments, and performed many roles traditionally assigned to management. According to this sociotechnical paradigm, autonomous work groups integrated and optimized social and technical systems.[17] Sociotechnical design reduces management to a few layers, encouraging a collaborative relationship.

CHEVRON CHEMICAL COMPANY. Chevron used a sociotechnical systems approach to redesign its Rock Springs, Wyoming, phosphate fertilizer plant. A group of employees drawn from diverse levels and functions conducted an organizational analysis, including interviews of all employees. They analyzed both the workers' satisfaction and the plant's technical system. The team proposed ways of redesigning the plant and obtained and responded to employees' reactions to the recommendations before implementing them. The Chevron plant experienced a 98 percent improvement in productivity over a five-year period.[18]

The introduction of autonomous or self-regulating work groups alleviated the isolation and boredom traditionally felt by the manufacturing workers, particularly with increasing automation. One study of semiautonomous work groups in Australia indicated that they experienced different perceptions, emotions, and behaviors. Even weekly meetings of employees and supervisors resulted in positive improvements in worker satisfaction, productivity, and attendance.[19] Yet, two recent studies suggested that such positive results might not continue in the long term. The use of autonomous work groups resulted in increased personal stress, lower job satisfaction, decreased organizational commitment, and less trust in management than in comparable, traditionally functioning groups.[20] If the positive outcomes of autonomous work groups are in fact transient, then more frequent redesign may be needed to offset negative consequences. Today, the emphasis on self-managing teams has supplanted explicit applications of the sociotechnical approach.

VOLVO. Volvo pioneered the team-assembly approach. At the Kalmar plant, a team of workers spent 20 or 25 minutes working on a car before it passed to the next team. At the Udevalla plant, a team of workers assembled an entire car. Yet, Volvo announced the closing of both plants by 1994 because of declining demand. These innovative attempts to humanize the assembly line had higher costs and lower productivity and thus were sacrificed to requirements of cost-cutting and deteriorating market conditions.[21]

ALTERNATIVE WORK ARRANGEMENTS

In contrast to work simplification, job enlargement, and job enrichment, which focus primarily on a job's *content,* alternative work arrangements concentrate on a job's *context.* Flexible hours, telecommuting, and part-time employment attempt to help workers balance the demands of work and family.

Flexible Hours Programs that offer workers flexible hours give employees some discretion in creating their work schedules. Such programs take two basic forms: discretionary systems and compressed work weeks.

Discretionary systems, in which the worker chooses the precise days or hours worked, include flexible working hours and staggered starts. *Flextime,* probably the most common discretionary system, offers workers the choice of starting and ending times so long as they work certain specific hours daily (such as 10:00 A.M. to 3:00 P.M.) and meet the hour requirements of a normal work week (usually 35 to 40). For example, one office clerk might work from 7:00 A.M. to 3:00 P.M., whereas another clerk might work from 10:00 A.M. to 6:00 P.M. In a *staggered* week, another form of flextime, workers alternate between working a four-day 32-hour week and a six-day 48-hour week.

The *compressed work week* allows employees to work the number of hours in a traditional five-day week (usually between 35 and 40) in four or even three days. This alternative has arisen from attempts to reduce commuting time, costs, and congestion, as well as give workers more concentrated time for family or other nonwork activities, thereby increasing their satisfaction. Although a four-day work week may result in greater employee satisfaction, some believe that this improved attitude may occur at the expense of employee efficiency because of fatigue from the long working hours.

CHEVRON. Chevron Corporation adopted a variety of flexible work schedules. These included flextime, different summer schedules, and compressed work weeks. Chevron discovered a low correlation between hours worked and productivity, contradicting the hypothesis that compressed weeks decrease worker efficiency. In addition, in one Chevron unit studied, productivity improved with no cost to customer satisfaction when workers could set their own hours.[22]

Scheduling work in two-week rather than one-week blocks enhances the attractiveness of this option. For example, an employee may work four days, have a four day-break, then work four more days, followed by a normal two-day weekend break. Such a schedule is often followed by firefighters or police officers to help alleviate the intensity of their jobs.

A MIDWESTERN POLICE DEPARTMENT. One study of police officers who switched from an 8-hour rotating schedule to a 12-hour shift with four days on and four days off showed that the schedule change reduced interference with personal activities, improved the police officers' attitudes toward their schedule, improved their general attitude toward their work environment, reduced their stress and fatigue, and increased the overall organizational effectiveness. General attitudes about work such as commitment, involvement, and motivation did not change.[23]

In Germany and Austria, several companies experienced so much success with flexible work hours that they proposed a *flexyear,* as the next logical step in flexible scheduling.[24] In this arrangement workers would agree to the number of hours they will work in the following year, but have the freedom to allocate them as desired. They would receive equal amounts of pay each month, but might work two or three times as many hours in one month as in another.

Telecommuting Increasingly workers are using information technology to perform their jobs at a site away from the organization's physical plant. Most often, these employees already use computers for large parts of their job and can be connected to their corporate location by a modem. Salespeople who spend large amounts of time out of the office may also base their operations at home. Some workers prefer the option of a flexible location as a way of reducing commuting time and allowing them more flexibility in meeting family responsibilities. A major drawback to this type of work arrangement is the more limited social interaction experienced by remote workers, which may cause feelings of isolation and alienation from the organization and its employees.[25] Often, however, these workers spend at least one or two workdays at the work site, thereby alleviating these feelings.

AT&T. AT&T has 8,000 salespeople who work from virtual offices, that is, from their cars or client's location using laptops and modems. Twenty thousand white-collar employees work at home at least part of the week. In addition to providing workers more flexibility, AT&T saved two dollars in occupancy and real estate costs for every one dollar spent on virtual offices and telecommuting.[26]

Part-Time Employment *Part-time employment* includes jobs done by permanent employees who work less than whole weeks with predictable or unpredictable hours. Employers like using part-time workers because they typically save the costs of benefits. Two variations of part-time work became more popular during the 1980s: job sharing and job splitting.

In *job sharing* a whole job is divided into two parts according to time and day of the week and is performed by two individuals. Together the job holders are responsible for completing the work. Each typically performs all the tasks of the job, although limited specialization of job responsibilities occasionally occurs because of individual skills or preferences. One job sharer might work mornings and the second afternoons. Or, one might work the first 2½ days of a five-day week, while the second works the last 2½ days.

In *job splitting* the jobs are divided according to tasks or skills rather than schedule. In splitting a secretarial job, for example, one person might take all dictation, while the second might do all the manuscript typing.

Contingent Workers *Contingent workers* are hired and paid to complete specific projects or tasks. They may be free-lance employees who wish to retain their personal flexibility and autonomy by having the discretion to develop their own work schedules so long as they complete the project by the specified deadline. Or they may be contract workers, employed by outsourcing firms who have contracted to provide certain noncore services to a company, such as managing the mail room or the office complex's physical plant, or working on special medium-term projects. Software development or distribution companies often hire this type of employee because it provides them with maximum flexibility. This type of employment can also create difficulties in the workplace, particularly if workers become frustrated about pay or benefits differentials.

KOLMAR LABORATORIES. The company began to employ temporary workers as a way of reducing labor costs. Temporary workers earned $5.60 per hour compared to $9.00 plus benefits for full-time workers. Temporary and permanent employees worked on the same teams, and often fought because the temporary workers lacked the incentive to work faster. The company began to pay the permanent employees for skills acquisition rather than output. It also began to offer temporary employees full-time positions as openings occurred. Kolmar reduced its temporary work force from approximately one-half of its 600 assembly-line workers in 1992 to none of its 400 workers in 1994.[27]

Effectiveness of Alternative Work Arrangements To manage alternative work options, managers need to screen candidates carefully, set appropriate goals, and then develop a viable work plan. Managers need to identify the personal characteristics and job design considerations that fit best with alternative work arrangements. For example, an organization may find that only highly mature and highly experienced employees make good candidates for telecommuting. Similarly, jobs with little dependence on other jobs make better candidates for flexible hours than those that are intricately entwined with other positions. Managers must find ways to monitor the number of hours worked and to ensure that the organization's needs are met. They must maintain open communication, provide ongoing support, and remain flexible in dealing with employees who take advantage of alternative work options.[28]

A number of studies have documented the benefits of alternative work schedules, including reduced payroll costs, greater corporate flexibility, and successful response to employee needs.[29] Responses to the redesign of the job context have also included an increase in productivity, since workers use less sick leave to handle personal needs. Other responses have included decreased turnover, absenteeism, and overtime, increased employee satisfaction and morale, and decreased transportation demand during peak hours.[30]

Flextime is less successful when a company has multiple continuous shifts, machine-paced assembly work, few employees, or highly interdependent operations.[31] The major resistance to atypical work schedules stems from the perception that work must be done at the same time by all workers because their tasks are interdependent. To overcome this constraint, carefully scheduling tasks and, in manufacturing settings, building a small inventory of different product components might be required.

QUALITY–OF–WORK–LIFE PROGRAMS

Quality-of-work-life (QWL) programs incorporated many principles of job enrichment and sociotechnical redesign into comprehensive efforts to improve the quality of the working situation. Such programs began in the 1970s as a way of ensuring the following: adequate and fair compensation, a safe and healthy working environment, personal growth and development, satisfaction of social needs in the workplace, personal rights, compatibility between work and nonwork activities, and the social relevance of work life.[32] Quality-of-work-life programs typically included participative problem solving, job enrichment, innovative reward systems, and work environment improvements. Today, the elements of quality-of-work-life programs are generally included in total quality management, worker empowerment, or even family-friendly organizations.

AMERICAN AIRLINES. American introduced a QWL program in the late 1980s designed to create an environment that treated each employee with respect. The QWL program included a variety of employee involvement programs, including QWL groups that met to discuss barriers to efficiency and morale. "IdeAAs in Action" was a suggestion program to use employee ideas to generate profits, promote feelings of involvement, develop entrepreneurial attitudes, and support the corporate QWL program. A flight attendant's idea to purchase larger bottles of water served on flights saved American almost $55,000 annually. The IdeAAs program saved American $83 million in its first 2½ years.[33]

QWL programs have encouraged workers to participate with management in making decisions about problems and opportunities in the workplace, as a way to increase organizational effectiveness and improve worker satisfaction, commitment, and performance.[34] Besides participative problem solving, QWL programs have restructured the basic nature of jobs and work systems, fitted rewards to the desired work processes and outcomes, and improved the work environment.

Table 12–1 compares and contrasts three generations of QWL programs—in the 1970s (first generation), early 1980s (second generation), and late 1980s (third generation). Often these three generations existed sequentially in a single organization as it became more experienced in the use of QWL principles.

GENERAL MOTORS. An early and well-known QWL program was initiated at the General Motors assembly plant in Tarrytown, New York, in 1970, at a time when the plant had one of the poorest production and labor records at GM. The plant manager invited workers to participate in the planning and implementation of changes in plant operations and many of the workers' suggestions were adopted.

TABLE 12–1 *Three generations of quality–of–work–life programs*

	FIRST GENERATION	SECOND GENERATION	THIRD GENERATION
Structure			
Integration	QWL outside of/parallel to regular organizational structure. Perceived as a program	Some integration of QWL with regular organizational structure	QWL inseparable from regular organizational structure. Organizational structure becomes flatter
Adaptation	QWL structure externally imposed by centralized experts/authority	QWL structure shows some adaptations and local variations	Each local QWL structure unique to the particular working environment
Centralization	QWL structure centralized	QWL structure partly centralized, partly decentralized	QWL structure decentralized
Involvement	QWL structure involves only selected employees	QWL structure involves many or most employees	QWL structure involves all employees
Process			
Decision Making	Decision making is management prerogative. QWL provides input to management decisions	Ranges from QWL responsibility for some decisions at discretion of managers to managers being removed from day-to-day work decisions	Roles of management, non-management, and union redefined. Decisions now made by those closest to impact. Organization managed jointly at all levels
Facilitation	Facilitation provided by centralized external resources	Facilitation moved under decentralized local control	Each employee acquires skills of facilitator and takes on role as needed
Training and Education	Need for training and education determined and provided by centralized external sources. Focus on orientation for all and skills for facilitators	Groups identify own training needs and arrange as needed. Focus on skills needed for QWL process for all participants	Training locally determined and expands to include any process or work-related skill needed. All acquire skills in QWL process and organization management including financial, etc.
Union-Management Relationship	Formal union–management relationship adversarial. Much time spent building up informal communication, respect, and trust	Union–management relationship takes on more collaborative, cooperative tone. Both sides move back and forth between collaborative and adversarial roles as needed	Collaborative union–management relationship formalized or roles redefined as traditional distinctions between management and nonmanagement become blurred
Content			
Issues	Issues peripheral to the business and tend to focus on the environmental	Expanded range of issues moves beyond environmental to encompass employee, union, planning, policy, business, and day-to-day work issues. Constraints are contract and company policy	No distinction between "QWL issues" and other issues. All ideas considered. Contract and company policy built on QWL foundation

SOURCE: M. London, *Change Agents: New Roles and Innovation Strategies for Human Resources Professionals.* San Francisco: Jossey-Bass, 1988, pp. 142–143. Used with permission.

The plant management followed this by conducting voluntary joint training of workers and supervisors in problem solving. Ninety-five percent of the work force volunteered to participate in the three-day paid training program. Subsequent evaluations showed that the quality of performance increased, absenteeism dropped, and the number of grievances fell from 2,000 in 1971 to 32 in 1978.[35]

Quality-of-work-life programs after that became more comprehensive. In the early 1980s, ten GM plants introduced an operating team system in which a team of ten to fifteen workers received all work assignments and allocated them during regular team meetings.[36] Later in the decade the Saturn plant of General Motors extended this concept further. Union representatives joined planning groups, work teams were self-managing, team members were responsible for cost and quality control as well as innovative changes, and status differences were deemphasized in pay and job title.[37]

Other aspects of QWL projects include union support and involvement in the process, voluntary participation by employees, guarantee of job security, training programs in team problem solving, initiation of job redesign efforts, availability of skill training, involvement of workers in planning and forecasting, periodic meetings between workers and management to discuss plant production and operations, and responsiveness to employee concerns.[38] In all unionized organizations, union–management cooperation is key to many QWL efforts.[39]

The research about quality-of-work-life programs offers substantial evidence of their effectiveness.[40] Worker participation in QWL programs has been linked to low grievance rates, low absentee rates, fewer disciplinary actions, more positive worker attitudes, and greater participation in suggestion programs.[41] Although the elements of quality-of-work-life programs persist, programs labeled QWL have virtually disappeared from organizations today, replaced by more comprehensive programs, such as TQM or corporate reengineering.

THE IMPACT OF INFORMATION TECHNOLOGY

Managers are learning how to harness the power of computers and other new technologies to automate work processes, redesign jobs, and hence improve performance. Connecticut Mutual Life Insurance Company uses computers to replace large amounts of manual work and paper files. Whereas different clerks once sent bills, entered payments, reported claims, and handled customer questions, a computerized system now allows immediate viewing and updating of any part of a client's record. Manufacturing also has used computers to introduce greater flexibility. Robots can perform some of the dirty or hazardous jobs, such as painting cars, previously performed by workers. Agile manufacturing, in which modular manufacturing facilities and computer controls allow rapid retooling and shifting of the manufacturing sequence to accommodate new products, has become popular. These uses allow organizations to enrich individual jobs by making information more accessible to workers and supporting increased autonomy and responsibility. Developing and implementing strategies for using information technology now receives high priority in many organizations.

Information technology refers to computer hardware, software, and communication devices. An *information system* combines information technology with data, procedures for processing these data, and people who collect and use the data. Individuals use information systems to collect, store, process, retrieve, and communicate information. Information systems help managers handle information efficiently and effectively and make large quantities of information available to employees relatively quickly and at a relatively low cost. As at Connecticut Mutual, information technology can streamline complicated or awkward processes and can perform them more quickly and reliably.

NISSAN MOTOR COMPANY. Nissan replaced the conveyor belt in its assembly plant in Kyushu, Japan, with an information system that includes intelligent motor-driven dollies and platforms that carry cars at variable speeds on the assembly line. The platforms emit computer-controlled signals to help direct the activities of robots and employees involved in the production process. This system is designed to allow the simultaneous production of as many as six different Nissan car models by automatically adjusting the equipment to perform the specialized functions required for each automobile.[42]

THE USE OF INFORMATION SYSTEMS

Executives use information systems strategically to enhance decision making, improve their sales and marketing capability, and foster adaptability to change.[43] Information technology's real power lies in its ability to process data to produce information, which can be stored and retrieved.

- Information technology is enabling fundamental changes in the way work is done, often resulting in reengineering work processes, as described later. For example, robotics has changed physical production, data processing computers have altered clerical tasks, and CAD/CAM tools have affected new product design.

- Information technology is enabling the integration of business functions at all levels within and between organizations. For example, just-in-time inventory control places goods on the plant floor near where they are used and in quantities that can be consumed within one to three days instead of stockpiling large quantities of goods in a central location for use sometime in the future.

- Information technology is causing shifts in the competitive climate in many industries. For example, some large supermarkets use information systems to request that suppliers restock their shelves immediately only with needed products, thereby keeping their costs low.

- Information technology presents new strategic opportunities for organizations that reassess their missions and operations. Automation can provide new products for organizations to sell. For example, several airlines developed and marketed reservations systems that they sold to travel agents for booking flights. Information systems gave the airlines a competitive advantage by reducing labor costs, providing additional information for competition, and helping transform organizations to more effectively face a turbulent environment.

- Successful application of information technology will require changes in management and organizational structures.

■ A major challenge for management will be to lead their organizations through the transformation necessary to prosper in a globally competitive environment.[44]

BOSTON CHICKEN. Managers in this national chain of franchises, now renamed Boston Market, that sell roasted chicken and side dishes use information systems as a key component of their growth strategy. These systems facilitate communication, eliminate duplication of effort, and provide useful product information. Thirty-two regional partners, who will open about 300 stores a year, collaborate by computer on menus, distribution problems, and expansion plans. Customer complaints are recorded in a database and can be sorted by region or type. Patterns are identified and reported electronically to each regional headquarters and to each store. Managers can develop solutions to a problem, test them, and then report the results by computer to other store managers. Boston Chicken's initial stock offering began at $20 and closed at $48.50 the first day. Although it fell back to $37 by late 1994, it still sold at 62 times estimated earnings.[45]

But managers cannot just add information technology and expect significant improvements in work processes. They need to carefully think about ways to use information technology to improve the delivery of services and the manufacturing of products. Recently, many organizations have used information technology to streamline or reengineer the way work is done, as described in the next section.

REENGINEERING WORK

Reengineering refers to rethinking, reinventing, and redesigning one or more of an organization's business systems, such as accounts receivable, purchasing, or product development, and its related jobs.[46] Reengineering goes beyond the typical refining of existing processes to identify the core processes and reorganize work to eliminate unnecessary processes and steps. Generally, this type of basic redesign uses information technology extensively and reduces the time required to perform the work, the number of employees involved, and ultimately, the costs of the process. Reengineering also gives control over tasks to those on the "front line," particularly those who interact with customers.

BELL ATLANTIC. The regional telephone company reduced its order processing time in one-half by having one team handle the entire process. Information systems made all the information required to handle the order available to team members so they could handle all phases of the processing without sending the order outside the team. Previously, processing an order involved 28 handoffs of tasks.[47]

Reengineering attempts to attain dramatic improvements in corporate performance, reflected in cost, quality, service, and speed. Executives considering reengineering would ask how the company would look if they were recreating it today and had contemporary technology available to use in performing the organization's activities.

GTE. GTE determined that customers wanted to deal with a single person with all of their problems and questions, such as correcting a faulty bill or ordering new services. GTE established a "customer care center" in Garland, Texas, to pilot reengineered jobs that took advantage of information technology. They first changed the jobs of repair clerks, renaming them "front-end technicians." Next, testing and switching equipment was moved to their desks, so they could test the lines and switches while the customer was still on the telephone. GTE started assessing clerks on how often they handled a problem themselves without passing it to someone else in the company, rather than evaluating them on how fast they terminated the telephone call. Next they incorporated sales and billing. Customers' calls are received by a voice mail system, "a push-button telephone menu," that eventually connects customers to an operator who, using a database of information about solutions to problems incurred by customers, can handle a wide range of problems.[48]

Reengineered processes have the following characteristics:

- Several jobs are combined into a single job, similar to job enlargement and job enrichment. At Connecticut Mutual, for example, workers perform all aspects of servicing an account. Information systems make the information required for servicing directly available to the workers.

- Workers make decisions. As in job enrichment, individuals are empowered to solve problems and take action. At Connecticut Mutual, this might mean giving workers the discretion to settle most claims without seeking authorization from higher management.

- The steps in the process are performed in a logical order. Some steps can be performed simultaneously with others, in part because information systems often hold much of the information relevant to the tasks. For the same reasons, subsequent steps can begin while the present steps are underway.

- Processes have multiple versions so they can fit the situation. Reengineering eliminates standardization of processes by giving employees more options for performing a task. The use of information systems to make large quantities of information available to employees supports this flexible approach. For example, claims processing at Connecticut Mutual may vary depending on the customer or type of claim.

- Work is performed where it makes the most sense. Insurance representatives at Connecticut Mutual can call up and complete all forms required to do their job, rather than passing some to other workers.

- Checks and controls are reduced. Checking the accuracy of processes often occurs at the end of a sequence of steps rather than at each step. Individuals are judged on results rather than on how well they followed the process.

- Contact with external groups is limited to that essential to the process. The claims department would have minimal contact with groups outside the department.

- A single manager provides a single point of contact. Information systems provide that person with all necessary information. For example, one individual at Connecticut Mutual would handle all accounts of a client.

- Companies have both centralized and decentralized structures (see Chapter 13), placing decision making at the most appropriate level and position in the organization. The company uses technology to facilitate the sharing of information.[49]

ITT SHERATON. Sheraton invited Michael Hammer, one of the original developers of the concept of reengineering, to talk with senior management and sent 22 executives to his three-day seminar. The result was the invention of a new hotel. ITT eliminated any processes that did not add value to running the hotel. For example, the company eliminated paperwork that did not directly affect customer service. The company reduced the 40 managers and 200 employees required to run an average-sized hotel to 14 managers and 140 employees.[50]

Information technology plays a major role in reengineering work processes. Technology removes limits to the way employees perform their work, allowing companies to redefine the way work is done and ultimately achieve a competitive advantage.[51] For example, shared databases of information allow multiple workers simultaneous access to the same information. Expert systems allow generalists access to specialized expertise. Telecommunications technology allows both the centralization and decentralization of decision making. Decision support tools allow managers and employees to make better informed, more analytical decisions. Because of the extensive use of information technology, organizations can often reduce the number of managers, thereby flattening the structure and giving workers more control over their jobs. Such restructuring, however, may require workers to develop a broader range of skills or seek out additional training to perform the new work processes. Ensuring top management's support for the reengineering effort is critical and lack of support often explains the failure of some reengineering efforts.[52]

Reengineering efforts are not limited to the United States. Both Japanese and European companies have shown interest in business process reengineering.[53] For example, more than one-fifth of the United Kingdom's largest 100 companies have instituted business process reengineering.[54]

KAO CORPORATION. This Japanese company has instituted reengineering to simplify, reduce, and replace its business processes. This approach was introduced to allow management to reduce costs by more than the 15 percent believed to be the limit if restructuring of processes from the start did not occur.[55]

Reengineering has had mixed results to date. One study of 100 companies indicated that successful projects must define the process to be redesigned broadly in terms of cost or customer value, but it must also change the organization's roles and responsibilities, measurement and incentives, organizational structure, information technology, values, and skills.[56] Effective reengineering requires that executives clearly understand its applications and limitations, that managers with the authority to make changes lead the process and create a sense of urgency about change, and that they begin with customers' needs and determine how to meet them.[57] The reengineering effort also should empower workers, encourage continuous improvement, and carefully manage consultants, if used. Increasingly, reengineering has become one of the components of a Total Quality Management program.

Some researchers argue that reengineering fails to look to the future. Rather, it mainly involves catching up with competitors.[58] The widespread adoption of reengineering by consultants and software vendors has diluted its impact, often resulting in only incremental improvements in productivity.[59] In addition, the management literature has offered little methodology or research about the use and impact of reengineering.[60]

For reengineering to succeed, managers must address four broad issues:[61]

Purpose. Managers must clearly know the purpose of the organization and the reengineering. They can ask questions such as: What is this process for? What is the purpose of the reengineering? What is the company in business for?

Culture. Successful reengineering requires a change in a company's culture. Top management must generate a culture of willingness and mutual confidence in the reengineering effort.

Process and Performance. Managers must set significantly different objectives about the type of process and performance desired. They can ask questions such as: How do we get the kind of processes we want? How do we get the performances we need from workers? How do we set norms and standards and measure results for performance?

People. Reengineering must ask hard questions about who should be involved in the process. These questions include: Whom does management want to work with? How can managers find good people both inside and outside the company? How do we get them to work here? How do we know whether they are the kind of people we want?

All people and all processes change in reengineering. All managers and workers need to question the old ways of managing and working. This includes a recognition that the traditional approach to management, through using a hierarchical control approach, does not work. Managers must overcome the fears of letting go, losing control, misplaced trust, losing popularity, and failure.[62] They need to develop an innovative approach to work, as described in the next section.

INNOVATION IN THE WORKPLACE

Reengineering illustrates one type of innovation organizations have undertaken to become more competitive. In addition to the way work is performed, other innovations in the United States have focused on updating technology and developing and offering new products and services. In this section we look at the process of innovation as it applies to changes in technology, products, services, and work processes.

We can characterize innovation along three dimensions, as shown in Figure 12–3. Although this typology originally referred only to technological innovation, it can be applied more broadly, to most types of innovations in organizations:[63]

■ ***Primary–Derivative.*** Primary innovation results from primary research, which focuses on testing theoretical relationships. Derivative innovation evolves from the application of primary research to real-world situations.

■ ***Low–High Level of Diffusion.*** Diffusion, or the integration of the innovation into the organization or society, ranges from low to high.

■ ***Incremental–Radical.*** Incremental innovation describes the introduction of new technology, processes, or products that closely resemble existing

FIGURE 12–3   *Types of innovation*

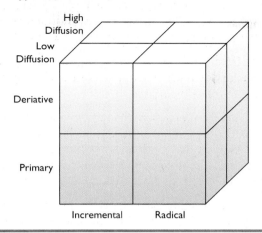

SOURCE: Adapted with permission from U.E Gattiker, *Technology Management In Organizations* (Newbury Park, Calif.: Sage, 1990), p. 22.

technology, products, or processes. Radical innovation refers to technology, products, or processes that differ dramatically from what previously existed.

NEC. Scientists employed by NEC Research Institute Inc. in Princeton, New Jersey, follow a process that emphasizes primary research. The Japanese electronics manufacturer pays American scientists merely to think. For example, one scientist is trying to understand everything he can about flies. Japanese industrial leaders believe that allowing scientists to explore fundamental scientific questions will eventually pay off by identifying totally new directions for research and eventually product development.[64]

THE INNOVATION PROCESS

How does innovation occur? Figure 12–4 shows a classic model of innovation.[65] It begins with the recognition that a demand exists for the new product, service, or process. Next, the basic idea is formulated, integrating the technical and market issues into a design concept. The problem-solving stage follows. Here, the design is elaborated on and resource and technical problems are addressed. False starts may consume time at this stage.[66] A solution, often a technological invention, moves the design into the prototype of a new product or process. In the development stage, the innovator faces and attempts to solve problems associated with the production process, sometimes resulting in job design changes. Finally, the solution is used and diffused in the workplace.

JOHNSON CONTROLS. Johnson Controls, a manufacturer of climate control systems for office buildings, decided to change the way it competed with industry leader Honeywell. In a two-year needs assessment, a team of engineers discovered that the cost of maintaining the system was as important to customers as the initial purchase price. In response, the company designed Metasys, a system that costs less to install *and* maintain than its predecessors and its competitors' systems. Metasys resulted in $500 million of revenues in its first year.[67]

FIGURE 12–4

The innovation process

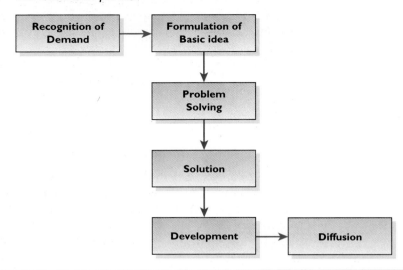

SOURCE: Based on D.G. Marguis, The anatomy of successful innovations (November 1969), *Managing Advanced Technology* I (1972): 35–48.

RYDER INTERNATIONAL. This $25 million company approaches innovation somewhat differently because it develops products for other companies. It focuses on medical and health-care markets for companies such as Textron, Bausch & Lomb, and Ciba Geigy, and emphasizes the design and development of plastic and electronics products. Ryder can develop a prototype for a new product, typically requested by a corporate sales manager, in one to two weeks. Ryder manufactures the products it designs, but its clients market and distribute them. Ryder's designers often sketch their ideas onto napkins at lunch and then rush them to the company's model building department. This example illustrates the way the company has eliminated rigid procedures for its designers to give them the freedom they need to innovate new products rapidly.[68]

In Japan the process of innovation occurs at three levels simultaneously.[69] At the first level the Japanese look for incremental improvements for existing products, services, or processes. At the second level they try to make a significant jump between existing and new products, services, or processes by offering modifications to existing ones and then extending these further to new ones. At the third level they attempt true innovation via a focus on primary research. The Japanese hope that a success at one of these three levels will result in either a new or improved product to replace the existing one. In addition, companies that successfully innovate, such as Sony, create a culture of innovation and a vision for the company's future twenty or thirty years from now.[70]

SONY CORPORATION. Sony's engineers release an average of 1,000 new products a year: 800 are improvements on previous products and 200 are new products designed to create new markets. Product ideas either come from top management or from the engineers themselves. Engineers are given great latitude in developing products. For example, the only instructions to engineers developing the videocassette for Sony were to make it the size of a book. Tomoshi Hirayam spent the flight from Great Britain to Tokyo sketching and writing the ideas for a device he called the "auxiliary brain," which eventually became the Sony Palm-Top™, a pocket-sized notepad computer. Sony hires university graduates who prefer not to specialize, but rather like moving among product groups, remain open-minded, and have broad interests. The company encourages employees to obtain exposure to large numbers of projects and products, as well as their problems and customers' needs. Sometimes Sony hires unconventional talent, such as Michael MacKay, who not only built recording studios, but also made rock videos, filmed documentaries, designed computers, and created videogames.[71]

ROLES AND FUNCTIONS

Three major patterns of work on new products, services, and processes are possible. First, the work may be centralized in a single research and development facility with sole responsibility for innovation in all areas. Second, the work may be decentralized into different units or operating divisions. Here, individual groups work on innovations relating to specific products, services, or work processes of the organization. Third, a combination of corporate and divisional labs or other sites for product, service, or process development may exist.[72] These laboratories may approach innovation by creating multidisciplinary teams, but still require talented individuals for innovation to result.[73]

Table 12–2 describes the functions critical to the innovation process. Individuals generate ideas, champion them, lead projects, serve as gatekeepers, and sponsor the innovations. Connecticut Mutual Life Insurance Company, for example, needed managers or employees to perform each of these functions as they automated their key systems.

The general management of the organization or division plays a significant role in developing new technology. So do R&D specialists, sometimes under the leadership of the chief technical officer or chief information officer. Organizations must also have individuals who champion new technology because organizational members and leaders may differ significantly in their commitment to new work products and processes. Two roles are particularly critical: the innovation champion and the innovation manager.

An *innovation champion,* a person who takes personal responsibility for introducing the innovation and marshalling the resources required to produce it, plays an essential role in diffusing innovation throughout an organization. One study of innovation champions in 43 organizations showed that champions built cross-functional ties, established autonomy, circumvented the organizational hierarchy, used informal means of persuasion, and involved all organization members in decision making.[74]

An *innovation manager* has the responsibility for creating conditions in which creativity can occur, as well as overseeing the more practical aspects of product or system development. This type of management differs from the traditional management of daily operations. Instead, the innovation manager supports the team in visualizing the innovation, that is, identifying the likely users and uses of the product or service. In addition, the innovation manager uses informal rather than formal control and communication systems and does not interrupt the team's momentum to conduct progress reviews. Instead, the innovation manager collects and evaluates

CRITICAL FUNCTION	PERSONAL CHARACTERISTICS	ORGANIZATIONAL ACTIVITIES
Idea Generating	Expert in one or two fields. Enjoys conceptualization. Comfortable with abstractions. Enjoys doing innovative work. Usually is an individual contributor. Often will work alone.	Generates new ideas and tests their feasibility. Good at problem solving. Sees new and different ways of doing things. Searches for breakthroughs.
Entrepreneuring or Championing	Strong application interests. Possesses a wide range of interests. Less propensity to contribute to the basic knowledge of a field. Energetic and determined. Puts self on the line.	Sells new ideas to others in the organization. Gets resources. Aggressive in championing his or her "cause." Takes risks.
Project Leading	Focus for decision making, information, and questions. Sensitive to the needs of others. Recognizes how to use the organizational structure to get things done. Interested in a broad range of disciplines and in how they fit together (e.g., marketing, finance).	Provides the team leadership and motivation. Plans and organizes the project. Ensures that administrative requirements are met. Provides necessary coordination among team members. Sees that the project moves forward effectively. Balances the project goals with organizational needs.
Gatekeeping	Possesses a high level of technical competence. Is approachable and personable. Enjoys the face-to-face contact of helping others.	Keeps informed of related developments that occur outside the organization through journals, conferences, colleagues, other companies. Passes information on to others. Finds it easy to talk to colleagues. Serves as an information resource for others in the organization (i.e., authority on who to see or on what has been done). Provides informal coordination among personnel.
Sponsoring or Coaching	Possesses experience in developing new ideas. Is a good listener and helper. Can be relatively objective. Often is a more senior person who knows the organizational ropes.	Helps develop people's talents. Provides encouragement, guidance, and acts as a sounding board for the project leader and others. Provides access to a power base within the organization—a senior person. Buffers the project team from unnecessary organizational constraints. Helps the project team to get what it needs from the other parts of the organization. Provides legitimacy and organizational confidence in the project.

SOURCE: Reprinted from Staffing the innovative technology-based organization, by E.B. Roberts and A.R. Fusfeld, *Sloan Management Review* (Spring 1981): 19–34, by permission of the publisher. Copyright © 1981 by the Sloan Management Review Association. All rights reserved.

ongoing information about project planning and implementation.[75] Principles of innovation management include

- develop responsibility and commitment;

- develop extreme clarity between all team members about the task at hand;

- enrich the team's jobs by giving members whole tasks (tell them what to do or what to achieve, but do not tell them how to do their work);

- make sure that creative ways of working are used;

- provide the team optimal conditions needed to ensure success in working on the task they have accepted;

- be prepared to give support and encouragement when problems arise.[76]

3M. Over a period of at least five years, division managers at 3M act as innovation managers and are expected to develop new products that will account for at least one-fourth of their division's revenue. Scientists and other technical people are expected to spend as much as 15 percent of their time on new projects. As innovation champions, they are free to peddle their new ideas to any part of the company for support in further developing and producing it. Managers are discouraged from merely "killing" a project. Instead, employees are expected to find ways to further develop and eventually produce it.[77]

An organization's ability to innovate also depends on its resources, its managers' understanding of the technological environment, and innovative strategies used by competitors.[78] Managers and employees must adopt a mind-set that encourages the development and presentation of new ideas. They also must willingly expend resources for innovative activities. Flexible organizational designs (see Chapter 13) as well as collaboration within and between organizations also facilitate innovation.[79] Adopters of innovations who have a broad and influential social network can influence the diffusion of innovation in organizations.[80]

UNION CARBIDE. Some teams of scientists do much of their own initial laboratory work at Union Carbide so that they can take advantage of serendipitous moments, such as when experimental results go in unexpected directions. One research team discovered a new generation of materials for oil refining and chemical processing because the scientists, rather than their technicians, did much of their own lab work.[81]

SUMMARY

The early search for efficiency in performing work contributed to a role for technology in facilitating better work flows and job design, as well as worker satisfaction. Work simplification, which reduces a job to its component parts and then optimally reassembles them, continued the emphasis on efficiency. Subsequent approaches to job design focused more on worker satisfaction. Job enlargement increases the scope of a job through job extension or job rotation. Job enrichment changes a job horizontally by adding tasks and vertically by adding responsibility. Sociotechnical redesign emphasizes the use of autonomous work groups for handling new technology. Alternative work arrangements involve the use of flexible work hours, telecommuting, or part-time employment to the workplace. Quality–of–work–life (QWL) programs incorporated many principles of job enrichment and sociotechnical redesign into comprehensive efforts to improve the quality of the working situation.

Information technology plays a significant role in job redesign. Information technology refers to computer hardware, software, and communication devices. An information system combines information technology with data, procedures for processing these data, and people who collect and use the data. Individuals use information systems to collect, store, process, retrieve, and communicate information. Information systems help managers handle information efficiently and effectively and make large quantities of information available to employees relatively quickly and at a relatively low cost.

Information systems have allowed the reengineering of work. Reengineering work refers to starting over and rethinking the way companies do business. It means identifying the core processes and reorganizing around them, eliminating unnecessary processes and steps. Generally, this type of redesign results in reducing the time required to perform the work, the number of employees involved, and ultimately the costs of the process.

Job redesign and reengineering illustrate process innovations. Innovations in technology, products, services, and processes describe new ways of thinking and acting in organizations. Innovation can be characterized along three dimensions: primary–derivative, low–high level of diffusion, and incremental–radical. Idea champions and idea managers play significant roles in the innovation process.

DIAGNOSTIC QUESTIONS

The following questions can help diagnose issues related to work design, use of technology, and innovation in organizations.

- ■ Are the jobs appropriately simplified?
- ■ Are the jobs appropriately enriched?
- ■ Do autonomous work groups exist and are they effective?
- ■ Do alternate work arrangements exist and are they effective?
- ■ Do quality-of-work-life programs exist and are they effective?
- ■ Are there mechanisms for the effective development and deployment of information technology?
- ■ Do opportunities exist for reengineering work?
- ■ What types of innovation occur in the organization?
- ■ Is the innovation process effective?

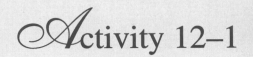

Activity 12–1

STEP 1:   Read the American Optical Co. Case.

It is the spring of 1976. Floyd Sundue, director of the fledgling Soft Contact Lens Division of the American Optical Corporation, is faced with a fundamental decision regarding the design of a new production facility. The conventional approach is to design such a facility as a single-flow shop. The specific manufacturing process provides him with a unique opportunity to implement a new concept—autonomous work groups. His past experience with organizations indicates the new facility could benefit from the approach.

As Floyd mulls over his notes, he knows a decision must be made quickly. The market for soft contact lenses has been growing rapidly. It has been dominated by Bausch & Lomb—the first company to obtain FDA approval for their product. Now, five years later, FDA approval for American Optical is imminent. The slow approval process has given Bausch & Lomb a virtual monopoly of the market. However, the market has continued to grow at a rapid pace. Floyd knows he needs to get his product on the market quickly if he wants to be a major producer of soft contact lenses.

HISTORY OF THE SOFT CONTACT LENS

The hydrophilic (water absorbing) material from which the lenses are produced was first developed by the Czechoslovakians. It was intended for the treatment of eye diseases such as glaucoma or to place drugs under the skin. In theory, the material would absorb the drug to be administered. Then, once in place, it would be gradually released over an extended period of time. The purpose was to administer drugs to a patient.

In 1965, the Czechoslovak Academy licensed Flexible Lenses (a subsidiary of National Patent Corporation) to sell the material in Europe and the Americas. The licensee approached American Optical with the material, but no agreement could be reached. Bausch & Lomb was then approached. They recognized the vast potential in using the material for the manufacture of a soft contact lens. Agreement was reached, and, in 1971, Bausch & Lomb placed the first soft contact lens on the market. They were the undisputed market leader in soft contact lenses.

In the late 1960s, there was another development with far-reaching implications for the industry. The Federal Food and Drug Administration (FDA) reviewed the material and classified it as a drug. This classification means that a prospective manufacturer must meet stringent requirements before receiving FDA approval for marketing the product. Specifically:

1. Intensive clinical studies of the lens material and the procedure for regular cleaning suggested to the user.
2. Implementing procedures for recalling lenses distributed through various marketing channels.
3. The process, facilities, and controls must conform to good manufacturing practices as interpreted by the FDA.

Approval of a New Drug Application or any significant alteration of approved materials or processes required three to four years. The earliest a company could enter the market was 1974, even if it had a new material patented and a manufacturing process developed. Bausch & Lomb had a significant time advantage over their competition. Until 1974, they monopolized the market.

HISTORY OF AMERICAN OPTICAL

American Optical, located in Southbridge, Massachusetts, was founded about 1833 and went public about 1869. In 1967, Warner-Lambert purchased American Optical. At the time, American Optical revenues were about $148 million and net income was about $10 million.

In the early 1970s, Warner-Lambert decided to market the soft lens and, in 1973, purchased it from Griffin Laboratory of Buffalo and Toronto. Griffin Laboratory, a subsidiary of Frigitronics, had patent approval and appeared likely to receive FDA approval soon. Griffin's present production was being sold primarily to the

Canadian market. American Optical dubbed it the SOFTCON lens.

Approval came in 1974. However, the approval only covered sales to the smaller therapeutic lens segment of the market. Patients requiring protection for an irritated eye could use the lens under close supervision. Examples are irritation due to an infected eyelid or as a "bandage" after eye surgery.

This was a disappointment. The major market segment was for corrective usage. These users would insert the lens in their eyes and be responsible for cleansing it daily without any supervision. The FDA had withheld approval because the daily cleaning and sterilization process was considered inadequate. Patents and the physical characteristics of the Griffin lens material prevented the company from adopting a similar heat-based process.

Dave Inman, president of the Optical Division of Warner-Lambert, initiated a search for another contact lens manufacturer while efforts to improve the SOFT-CON cleaning process continued. He located Union Optical Company, which appeared likely to receive FDA approval for corrective use soon. American Optical bought the right to market the lens for corrective use in early 1975. They called this lens AOSOFT.

This purchase reflected the importance that the AO management attached to quickly entering the soft contact lens market. The market had expanded from $8 million sales in 1971 to more than $55 million by 1974. Bausch & Lomb continued to dominate the market. A new competitor, Continuous Curve, was making lenses. The urgency of entering the market seemed evident, especially if AO was to have any significant share.

The responsibility for both manufacturing and marketing was assigned to Floyd Sundue. Floyd had wide exposure to numerous facets of business both as a consultant and as assistant to Inman. He was also experienced in implementing the concept of autonomous work groups.

DESCRIPTION OF THE PHYSICAL PROCESS

The American Optical process for producing soft lenses was based on the following steps (see Figure 12–5). First, raw material was pulled from inventory. The chemicals were mixed and formed into rods. The rods were labeled and held until the Quality Assurance De-

FIGURE 12–5 *Soft contact lens cutting and polishing*

"Buttons" or hard disks about 1/4-inch thick with face and diameter trimmed are sent to processing.

The button is lathed on one side to the shape of the eye's cornea (base curve) and the edge is beveled. Then, edge and base curve are both polished.

The front side is mounted and lathed to a specific curvature and thickness to fill the prescription of the patient. The original button now has a center thickness of 1/10 millimeter.

The front side is polished for an optically clear prescription lens.

The lens is hydrated in a saline solution to make it soft, and given a final inspection by the module.

The lens is placed in a vial, labeled, and is sent to Quality Assurance for audit.

partment had taken samples and had given approval. Then small (approximately ½ inch long) buttons were cut and grouped into lots of approximately 50. The buttons were placed in jars. The buttons in each jar were cut to the same prescription specifications. Typically, two jars formed an order.

The initial step in cutting the lens was performed by a Base Curve Cutter. Here, the button was held securely in a chuck and the lathe cut the concave side of the lens which would be in direct contact with the eyeball. This was a critical operation, and the lathe needed to be set up exactly to the engineering specifications.

The second step was Bevel Grinding. Here the edge of the base curve was beveled. Succeeding stations buffed the edge and polished the bevel. These operations contributed to a better fit on the eye. Then the base curve was polished for optical clarity.

After the beveling and polishing operations, the button was mounted on a chuck. The chuck was a round tube with a convex end. Hot wax was used to fix the concave base curve to this end. The chuck held the base curve while the front curve was out on the lathe.

The Front Curve Cutter cut the button to a specific curvature and thickness. At its thickest, the lens was about one-tenth of a millimeter. With such tight tolerances, the lathe had to be set up and operated to precisely engineered specifications.

The convex surface was then polished to get an optically clear lens. The lens then went through an ultrasonic vapor degreaser to remove it from the chuck and clean the wax off it. At this point, all the cutting and polishing operations required to make a prescription lens were completed. It was now necessary to soften the hard plastic lens.

Before being sent for softening, all lenses were thoroughly inspected at the Dry Inspection Station. Under a microscope the inspector could spot defects like pits, gouges, and scratches.

Next, the lenses were softened by placing them in a saline solution. The lenses absorbed the moisture until they were completely soft. The hydration process took between ten to twelve days.

During hydration the lens grew larger. Certain material and process defects only became apparent then. So, another inspection of all lenses was done under a microscope. Defective lenses were discarded.

The remaining lenses were free of any physical defects. However, even though they were all cut to the same prescriptive specifications, the margin of error was so small that a small percentage often differed from the required specifications. A significant fraction of the buttons in an order met the derived specifications. The remaining nondefective lenses were usable but met different prescriptive standards. Each lens had to be correctly labeled for physical characteristics. This labeling required another inspection of all lenses, which was done on a magnified projector. The lenses were each placed in a separate vial and labeled.

The final step was to sterilize the lens. This was done in an autoclave over a one-day period. The lens was then moved to a quarantine area to ensure that the sterilization was effective. After a couple of days in quarantine, it was moved to the finished good inventory racks and was ready for shipping.

PRESENT FACILITIES

American Optical had been waiting for FDA approval for some years. SOFTCON had therapeutic approval since 1974. Now it appeared that AOSOFT would receive approval for corrective use. As yet the demands on manufacturing had been light. While they waited for approval, the emphasis had been on improving productivity.

Processing was presently being done in leased facilities in Framingham, Massachusetts. Three experimental modules had been set up. The module layout is shown in Figure 12–6. Each module could make either AOSOFT or SOFTCON lenses with some changes to the equipment. Switching over required approximately two days.

Each module would operate for two shifts. Each of the six teams had eleven people with tasks broken down as shown below:

OPERATOR FUNCTION	TASK BREAKDOWN
A	Base Curve Cutting
B	Bevel Grinding, Edge Buffing, Bevel Polishing, Base Curve Polishing
C	Measure, Mount, and Inspect for Optical Clarity
D	Front Curve Cutting
E	Front Curve Polishing, Deblocking, and Cleaning
F	Dry Inspection
G	Hydrating and Wet Inspection
H	Label Making, Vial Filling, and Capping

The Rod Casting and Button Making operations were highly automated. Presently, one person was responsible for making all the buttons required. The small teams and their separate physical facilities were dictated by the experimental nature of the work. Floyd had seen an opportunity to implement the autonomous work group concept. He felt the experience gained would help in designing the larger facility which

FIGURE 12–6   *Module floor plan*

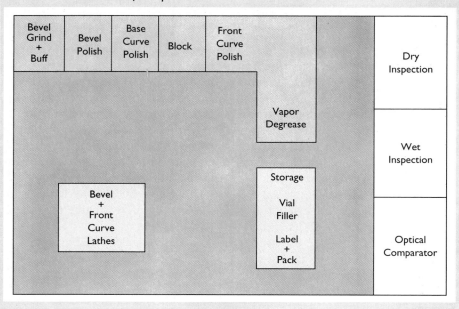

would be required when the corrective lens approval was received.

He organized each work group so it would have the full responsibility for decisions directly affecting their own work—including when to take breaks (e.g., lunch hours); hiring and firing personnel; planning the day's production; and assignment of tasks. Each team was responsible for the work they produced. Furthermore, each team was responsible for checking the work of team members before them in the process sequence. This checking was in addition to the 100 percent inspections done as part of the process.

Teams were carefully selected to have a blend of experienced and entry-level operators who were compatible with each other. Some operators were interviewed on three separate occasions. Each member of the team went through a fourteen-week training period. Benefits of the product to society were demonstrated, and they were given a great deal of technical information about the process.

The results had been very gratifying. Paul Rivens, his Personnel Manager, had summarized them in a memorandum (Figure 12–7). Floyd placed a lot of emphasis on these results as he thought of the design of the new facility.

Floyd had also obtained estimates of process time and equipment capacity (Figure 12–8, page 542). These estimates were based on performance of the six experimental teams. He noted that manufacturing now assumed a 150 percent increase in standard yield versus the old Griffin Laboratory standard. Although lower than the yields claimed by Rivens in his memorandum, productivity was clearly up.

Floyd had further reason to trust the increased productivity figures. He had organized a Quality Assurance function with one objective. They were to ensure that American Optical complied with every FDA requirement. This meant that in addition to sampling for product quality, adequate documentation was required on each batch as it went through the production process. If the FDA suspected the process was not properly followed, adequate documentation was necessary to convince them it was. If the documentation was unavailable, the FDA could shut down the entire facility. These records also provided an independent check on productivity. They corroborated the figures in Rivens' memorandum.

Another piece of data Floyd had collected was the cost of equipment (Table 12–3, page 542). The equipment cost represented about half the total cost of installing a module. The other half was primarily the labor cost of installation.

FIGURE 12–7   *Memorandum from Rivens to Sundue*

```
TO:      Floyd Sundue
FROM:    Paul Rivens
DATE:    February 1976
RE:      Autonomous Work Groups
```

As you requested at our last staff meeting, these are my comments on the viability of the autonomous work group concept for the large-scale production of lenses. I am convinced that (a) this concept will work based on the results achieved with the test groups and (b) it must be implemented if we are to attract a stable well-motivated labor force in the Framingham area.

Test Group Results:

A pilot team with 11 members was formed in Framingham in 1974. Since then, five other teams have been hired and trained. The operating results have been good. After a fourteen-week training period, productivity has tripled and yield almost doubled when compared to the rates achieved at Griffin Labs.

The modules were set up as an easily distinguishable physical facility to reinforce the team's feelings of independence. Work locations were positioned so operators faced each other and could communicate and socialize easily. All efforts were made to provide a well-lighted and pleasant work space.

We found the proximity of the equipment encourages the operators to switch jobs. This reinforces their training. It also helps the team cover for absentees and to work with other operators in order to reach the production targets they set. It also provides the operators with an opportunity to break the routine of a repetitive, boring job.

Detractors at corporate offices say the socializing between team members and the job switching can be counterproductive. The productivity and yield performance figures indicate that this is simply not true. The teams also show a willingness to impose and police standards of behavior. For example, the second shift supervisor asked operators to formulate such standards. They have compiled a code covering clothes, language, break times, etc. Morale and productivity continue to be high.

The tests have also given us greater insight into the functioning of work groups. This experience will enable us to form effective teams on an ongoing basis. For example, we asked our first test teams to select their own team leader. Three teams tried, this and in each case the leader appeared incapable of leading, perhaps because the teams had chosen leaders they could manipulate. Subsequently, we selected the team leader, trained him in recruiting and supervisory skills, and built the team around him. This has proven to be an effective strategy.

Evidence of high morale is our low rates of absenteeism (5 percent) and turnover (10 percent). These rates are particularly significant as our labor is primarily entry-level and unemployment in the Framingham area is only 2.8 percent. As you know, when both factors are present, we would typically have high rates of turnover and absenteeism. This did not happen. Perhaps the pay structure (a base salary 10 percent above the area average with merit increases in the third, sixth, and ninth months) has contributed to this. I believe, however, that the main reason is the autonomous work group. The team members develop strong relationships as they work in the same module day after day trying to achieve common goals. They are reluctant to leave what has become an enjoyable and stimulating work environment.

The results support the high morale evident in the teams. The teams have identified with, and feel accountable for, the finished lens. So, they evidence considerable pride and satisfaction in meeting production targets with a quality product.

The motivation and stability of the teams must be of prime concern in an era of labor confrontation. The experience of the American industry confirms that conventional organizations cause employee alienation and low morale. The effects are high absenteeism, turnover, and sometimes acts of sabotage, and the election of an unfriendly union. Griffin Labs had set up a conventional flow shop. They had a union. They also had low productivity and yields.

The results of our test groups are extremely encouraging. Productivity is high and the work force appears well satisfied. I feel the concept has proven itself. Our new facility should be designed to house more such modules.

THE COMPETITION

Other than Bausch & Lomb, there are two major competitors to American Optical for the soft contact lens market. These are Continuous Curve Contact Lenses, Inc., and the Milton Roy Corporation. Continuous Curve succeeded in obtaining the necessary approval in 1974. Milton Roy is due to get approval shortly. Other manufacturers are primarily small laboratories spread around the country. They make special lenses for therapeutic use and are a negligible factor in the corrective lens market.

Table 12–4 (page 543) shows dollar sales over the past five years, with the 1976, 1977, and 1980 forecast. The present market of $94 million is expected to more than double by 1980. American Optical's target for 1980 is a 20 percent market share.

Bausch & Lomb has the timing advantage and consumer recognition. Their manufacturing process differs from American Optical's. It is a highly automated technique. They spin-cast the liquid monomer (hydrophilic material) in a revolving mold. The amount of plastic injected into the mold, the rotation speed, and the mold's design determine the shape of the lens. The result is a lens with an aspherical base curve. The lens is polished for optical clarity and hydrated to make it soft.

The American Optical management feels it has a superior product on several counts:

■ It knows the hydrophilic material it uses has a higher moisture content than Bausch & Lomb's. Bausch & Lomb has a 38.6 percent moisture

---

FIGURE 12–8 *Equipment capacity*

Base Curve Lathe: 95–105 lenses per day

Base Curve Polish: 175 lenses per day

Measure and Mount: 100–110 lenses per day

Front Curve Cut: 35–45 lenses per day

Front Curve Polish; Deblock and Clean: 100–110 lenses/day for all 3 lathes

Dry Inspection: 70 lenses per hour

Wet Inspection (Vertexometer): 2 orders* per day

Wet Inspection (J&L): 2 orders per day

*An order is 100 lenses at the first workstation. As it is processed, defective lenses are discarded. Figures for wet inspection and for packing represent capacity assuming yield standards are met.

TABLE 12–3 *Equipment costs/module*

ITEM DESCRIPTION	QUANTITY	COST/ITEM
Lathes	4	$5,500.00
Polishers	4	950.00
Bevel Grinder	1	800.00
Vapor Degreaser	1	3,500.00
Ultrasonic Cleaners	4	1,200.00
Radius Gauges and Tools	1	800.00
Microscopes	3	1,100.00
Vertexometer	2	1,500.00
Optical Comparator	1	2,500.00
Oven for hydrating solution	1	1,000.00
Laminar Flow Booth for Packaging	1*	800.00
Vial Filler for Saline Solution	1	7,000.00

*The Laminar Flow Booth can package 1,200 lenses/day.

TABLE 12–4 *Sales ($ millions)*

YEAR	BAUSCH & LOMB	CONTINUOUS CURVE	MILTON ROY CORPORATION	AMERICAN OPTICAL	
				AOSOFT	SOFTCON
1971	8				
1972	18				
1973	33				
1974	54	3.5			0.5
1975	70	5			1
1976*	85	6	1		2
1977*	100	11	3	7	2
1980*	130			50	10

*Forecasted years

content compared to 42.5 percent for AOSOFT and 55 percent for SOFTCON. The higher moisture content is more gentle to the cornea. American Optical expects this will help obtain better physician and customer acceptance.

■ American Optical cuts a spherical base curve on their lens versus the Bausch & Lomb aspherical base curve. The spherical curve conforms more closely to the spherical contours of the human eye. The AO lens would prove easier to fit.

■ American Optical bevels the edge of the lens to provide a less ragged edge than the Bausch & Lomb lens. This would make it easier to wear, increasing customer acceptance.

Management is also encouraged by results in countries where soft contact lenses are already being sold. Lenses manufactured by both techniques are sold in Canada, France, Germany, and the United Kingdom. Doctors have expressed a definite preference for the lathe-cut lens over the spin-cast lens.

American Optical intends to take an aggressive marketing stance. A program to increase consumer recognition has been developed. The company will offer about 200 different types of AOSOFT lens. A large finished goods inventory will be maintained to satisfy customer orders expeditiously.

Floyd has devoted considerable time to developing the marketing strategy. He now feels he should concentrate on manufacturing. If manufacturing cannot produce enough lenses, the company's growth will be constrained.

EVALUATION OF ALTERNATIVES

The current facilities (three modules for six teams) could produce about $6 million worth of lenses. The leased space provided no room for expansion. It was evident that new facilities would have to be built. With this in mind, American Optical had purchased a tract of land close to the leased facilities. They planned on the new facility starting production in 1977.

The conventional design of such facilities was the approach used by Griffin Laboratory. There would be a Base Curve Cutting Department, followed by a Bevel and Polish Department and so on. Each operation would be done in a specialized area. The present modular facility could continue primarily as a developmental group with the capability to supplement production if necessary.

The approach Floyd was leaning toward was to continue with the autonomous work group concept. Results, so far, had been excellent. True, they had been with experimental teams, but other firms—Volvo, General Foods, etc.—had reported equally good results. If he selected this alternative, a large building could be constructed with separate modules within it. As increasing sales required increased production, more modules could be added.

There were, he recognized, some very tangible benefits associated with the conventional flow shop. First, the capacity of each department could be better balanced. The equipment would be more fully utilized and capital cost would be lower. A rough calculation (Table 12–5) showed that better utilization could be achieved in the modules. But, he knew that two additional people were required to perform certain management tasks, minor maintenance, set up equipment, and handle material.

Second, less training time is required when an operator needs to know only one job. One of the strengths of a module was the variety of jobs it offered. The experimental groups had been trained on each job. Training over the 14-week period also showed workers how an autonomous work group operated.

Third, setup time would increase with the modular approach. Each team would set up its work at the beginning of a shift and clean up at the end. This meant an hour of lost production. In a conventional flow shop, the new shift would continue with the work left by the last shift. There would be less setup and cleanup time. Floyd also recognized some very substantial intangible benefits to be obtained by using autonomous work groups.

Results of the experiment had shown, he felt, that the teams identified with and felt accountable for the end product. This was evident by their high morale. Absenteeism and turnover were low. The effects of low morale and employee alienation could be acts of sabotage or unionization with the intent to strike. He was well aware of the present atmosphere of labor confrontations as in the recent bitter strike at General Motors in Lordstown. This attitude could be expected to be widespread amongst the entry-level work force which American Optical was planning to hire. Yet, these workers had been making a quality product and appeared to derive satisfaction and pride from meeting their productivity targets. What is more, these targets were much higher than those achieved by the conventional flow shop of Griffin Laboratory. Though some of the increased productivity could be attributed to process improvements, he felt that the operator's attitude was the biggest contributor.

Another important feature that the work groups provided was manufacturing control. Since the operators were entry-level, they had little prior experience. The module concept made it easy to sequence jobs with each team. Further, if defects appeared on inspection, it would be relatively easy to trace it to a specific machine or operator. A conventional flow shop would require each job to carry considerable documentation to perform the same function. The rapid identification and accurate tracing of process problems would increase yield substantially.

The modular design would also make it easier to alter manufacturing capacity. Forecasts of the soft contact lens market size had been notoriously inaccurate. For example, in 1974 the total industry sales were expected to peak at $100 million. Sales were already approaching that figure (see Table 12–4) in 1976. A peak of $300

TABLE 12–5 *Utilization percentages*

TASK	CAPACITY	UTILIZATION (PERCENT)
Base Curve	100 lenses/day	100
Base Curve Polish*	175 lenses/day	57
Measure and Mount	105 lenses/day	95
Front Curve	120 lenses/day	83
Front Curve Polish	105 lenses/day	95
Dry Inspection*	70 lenses/hour	18
Vertexometer†	2 orders/day	50
J&L†	2 orders/day	50
Label and Pack	1 order/day	100

*One person can perform Base Curve Polish and Dry Inspection.
†One person can perform the Vertexometer and J&L functions.

million, sometime in the early 1980s, was now projected. Floyd felt this was very optimistic. He felt the $200 million sales in 1980 would be the peak. Given this wide range of potential sales, he felt the modular design offered the most flexibility.

Finally, the modular design made it easier for Quality Assurance because it generated data per the FDA requirements. It would be possible to meet FDA requirements with a conventional flow shop as well. However, a new reporting system would have to be devised and possibly more data collected.

CONCLUSION

As Floyd reviewed the alternatives open to him, he tended to favor the autonomous work group approach. But, he wondered, had he considered all the pros and cons? Was there some way he could quantify the intangible benefits? The experimental work groups had performed well. Would the results continue to be as good? He knew the Executive Committee would favor the conventional flow shop approach. Should he supplement his efforts to convince them that the new concept was a preferable alternative with additional data?

STEP 2: Prepare the case for class discussion.

STEP 3: Answer the following questions, individually, in small groups, or with the entire class, as directed by your instructor.

DESCRIPTION
1. Describe the process for producing soft lenses.

DIAGNOSIS
2. Why is American Optical considering the introduction of autonomous work groups?
3. Further explain the advantages and disadvantages of this work redesign using theories or concepts from the following areas: perception, motivation, communication, decision making, group dynamics, intergroup relations, leadership, power, and organization structure.

PRESCRIPTION
4. Should management institute the new work design?

ACTION
5. What secondary consequences would the redesign have?
6. Should they renegotiate the contract?

STEP 4: Discussion. Share your answers to the above questions, in small groups, with the entire class, or in written form. Then answer the following questions:

1. What symptoms suggest that a problem exists?
2. What problems exist in the case?
3. What theories and concepts help explain the problems?
4. How can the problems be corrected?
5. Are the actions likely to be effective?

Case prepared by Associate Professor Ashok Rao based on research done by Professors Ashok Rao and Herb Graetz. Copyright © by Ashok Rao.

*A*ctivity 12–2   JOB DESIGN EXERCISE

STEP 1: Your instructor will describe his or her job as a college professor.

STEP 2: Ask your instructor the questions on page 546 about his or her job with a view to rating the job of college professor on each of the five core job dimensions as follows (7 = very high, 6 = high, 5 = some-

what high, 4 = moderate, 3 = somewhat low, 2 = low, 1 = very low). Your instructor will take a quick poll of the class for each dimension.

STEP 3: Divide into trios and take turns presenting a job you have held for analysis. First, briefly explain the job, then answer questions as if you were being interviewed by a newspaper reporter about it. The two trio members doing the analysis will briefly confer after asking a few questions on each of the five core job dimensions and assess a score from 1 to 7 for each.

●●●

STEP 4: Compare the scores on the various jobs analyzed. For each job, indicate which dimensions received a low score. How could you change the job to increase the score?

_____

Excerpted and adapted from Maneiro, Tromley, *Developing Managerial Skills in Organizational Behavior,* 2/E (Englewood Cliffs, N.J.: 1994) pp. 110–111.

Skills Variety: Describe the different identifiable skills required to do your job. What is the nature of the oral, written, and/or quantitative skills needed? Physical skills? Do you get the opportunity to use all your skills?

Task Identity: What is your product? Are you involved in its production from beginning to end (including delivery)? If not, are you involved in a particular phase of its production from beginning to end?

Task Significance: How important is your product? How important is your role in producing it? How important is your job to the people you work with? If your job were eliminated, how inferior would your product be? Where does your product fit in the spectrum from "high end" to "low end"?

Autonomy: How much independence do you have on your job? Do you have to follow a strict schedule? If so, how much can you control it? Are you subject to the call of a beeper or a boss or a customer during your off hours? How much of your work is delegated to you to decide how to do it yourself? How closely are you supervised? To what degree are you held accountable?

Feedback: What feedback *systems* are in place concerning your job? Do you get regular feedback *from your job itself* on how you are doing? From your customers? From other stakeholders? From your peers and/or subordinates? From your supervisor?

*A*ctivity 12–3   LONG-LIFE INSURANCE COMPANY

●●●

STEP 1: Read the following scenario.

The group life insurance department of the Long-Life Insurance Company employs 100 people: 30 actuaries, 30 analysts, and 40 clerks. Together these employees set insurance rates, design and run computer programs to provide them with information required to set rates, answer questions from other departments about existing policies, and maintain records about the purchase of life insurance by customers. All members of the department work from 9 to 6 with one hour for lunch between 12 and 1.

Recently, the department has been experiencing increasing absenteeism among its workers. In addition, many complain that the mandatory lunch period often interrupts their train of thought. Other departments in the company complain that they frequently cannot obtain answers to questions since they do not necessarily work the same hours as those in the group department.

The computer programmers have repeatedly stated that they could do more productive work if they spent several days a week at home where there are fewer interruptions and distractions.

STEP 2: Individually or in small groups, design alternate work arrangements for the group life insurance department.

STEP 3: Discussion. In small groups or with the entire class, share the plans you developed. Then answer the following questions:

1. What elements do these plans have in common?
2. What are the strengths and weaknesses of each plan?
3. What types of alternate work arrangements are feasible for the group life insurance department?
4. What problems might arise as a result of the implementation of these plans?

Activity 12–4 SOCIOTECHNICAL REDESIGN EXERCISE

STEP 1: Your instructor will organize the class into teams. You will be a member of one of these teams whose job it will be to accomplish a simple production task. This will entail gathering, stapling, and folding three-page packets of paper, then stuffing them into envelopes and sealing them. You will determine the layout and production process you will use. Teams will compete with each other to complete the production task in the shortest time.

STEP 2: Read the following directions, and ask your instructor about any points that need clarification.

Four members of your team will be performing a "production" task. Your team's first assignment is to select those four individuals. Remaining team members will participate in the planning process, but once production begins, they will act as observers, filling the roles specified by your instructor.

Your team will receive the following materials: stapler(s), staples, rubber bands, three stacks of colored paper, and envelopes.

Use all of the paper at your workstation to form as many three-page packets as you can. The colors must be in the same sequence for every packet that you complete. Staple each packet of three pages in the upper left-hand corner, then fold the packet to fit an envelope. Stuff each packet into an envelope. Seal each envelope. Count envelopes into stacks of five and put a rubber band around each stack. You will be competing with the other teams to see who can complete the entire task in the shortest time.

The work may be structured in any way your team decides. You will have five to ten minutes to discuss the technique you will employ. Do not begin setting up your process until you have been instructed to do so.

STEP 3: Design you team's process using at most four members of your team.

STEP 4: Your instructor will indicate when production can begin. Your team's goal is to be the first team to complete the task. Team members who are not participating in the manufacturing process may be assigned special roles by the instructor.

STEP 5: Discussion. In small groups or with the entire class, discuss the way individual groups performed by answering the following questions:

1. Which team finished the task first? Why?
2. What did you observe about productivity rates at the beginning of the operation compared with the end?
3. Did the team's initial estimates of subtask times (e.g., stapling, folding) differ from actual task times? If so, how did the teams respond?
4. How did the team members feel as they performed the production task?

This exercise is adapted with permission from K. Brown, Integrating sociotechnical systems into the organizational behavior curriculum: Discussion and class exercise, *Organizational Behavior Teaching Review,* 12(1) (1987–1988): 35–48.

$\mathscr{A}$ctivity 12–5 | TRW—OILWELL CABLE DIVISION CASE

STEP 1: Read the TRW—Oilwell Cable Division Case below.

It was July 5, 1983 and Bill Russell had been expecting the phone call naming him general manager he had just received from the corporate office of TRW in Cleveland. Bill had been the acting general manager of the Oilwell Cable Division in Lawrence, Kansas, since January when Gino Strippoli left the division for another assignment. He had expected to be named general manager but the second part of the call informing him that he must lay off twenty people or achieve an equivalent reduction in labor costs was greatly disturbing to him. It was now 8:00 A.M. and at 8:15 A.M. Bill had called a meeting of all plant personnel to announce his appointment and, now, to also announce the impending layoffs. He was wondering in his own mind how to handle the tough decisions that lay before him.

TRW

TRW is a diversified, multinational manufacturing firm that in 1983 had sales approaching $5.5 billion (see Table 12–6). Its roots can be found in the Cleveland Cap Screw Company, which was founded in 1901 with a total investment of $2,500 and employment of 29. Today, through a growth strategy of acquisition and diversification, the company employs 88,000 employees at over 300 locations in 17 countries. The original shareholders investment of $2,500 in 1901 has grown to over $1.6 billion in 1983. As quoted from the company's 1983 Data Book, "This growth reflects the company's ability to anticipate promising new fields and to pioneer in their development—automotive, industrial, aircraft, aerospace, systems, electronics, and energy. We grew with these markets and helped create them."[1]

The organizational chart depicting TRW as it exists in 1983 is contained in Figure 12–9.

OILWELL CABLE DIVISION, LAWRENCE, KANSAS

The Oilwell Cable Division is part of the Industrial and Energy Segment of TRW. In 1983, this segment of TRW's business represented 24 percent of its sales and 23 percent of its operating profits. The pumps, valves, and energy services group, of which the Oilwell Cable Division is a part, accounted for 30 percent of the Industrial and Energy Segments net sales. The financial data for TRW by industry segment are contained in Tables 12–7 and 12–8.

The Oilwell Cable Division had its beginning as the Crescent Wire and Cable Company of Trenton, New Jersey. When TRW acquired Crescent, the company was losing money, occupied an outmoded plant, and had significant labor problems. In order to improve the profitability of the Crescent division, TRW decided to move its operations out of Trenton. The first decision was to move oilwell cable production to Lawrence, Kansas, in 1976. The line was moved into a new building and all new equipment was purchased. Only Gino Strippoli, the plant manager, and three other employees made the move from Trenton to Lawrence.

The reason for choosing Lawrence as the new site for Crescent division was fourfold. Most importantly, Lawrence was considerably closer to the customer base of the division which was in northeast Oklahoma. Second, Kansas was a right-to-work state and, given the labor problems of the Trenton plant, TRW was looking for a more supportive labor environment for its new operations. Third, the wage rates for the Lawrence area were very reasonable compared to Trenton. Finally, there was an already existing building that could house the oilwell cable production line in an industrial park in North Lawrence. In addition to the building, there was considerable acreage next to the building that would allow for future expansion.

By just moving the oilwell cable line to Lawrence, TRW hoped to be able to focus in on this product and make it more profitable before moving the other products from the Crescent plant in Trenton. By 1978, when the Oilwell Cable plant had reached division status, no further consideration was given to moving the rest of the Trenton plant. The remaining operations in Trenton were sold.

TABLE 12–6   *TRW financial data for 1979–1983*

STATEMENT OF CONSOLIDATED EARNINGS
($ MILLIONS EXCEPT PER SHARE DATA)

	1983	1982	1981	1980	1979
Net sales	$5,493.0	$5,131.9	$5,285.1	$4,983.9	$4,560.3
Other income	64.6	69.1	52.9	42.4	45.3
	5,557.6	5,201.0	5,338.0	5,026.3	4,605.6
Cost of sales	4,285.1	4,011.0	4,116.4	3,876.3	3,534.6
Administrative and selling expenses	840.6	791.0	734.9	693.1	631.6
Interest expense	29.7	51.2	65.9	66.5	52.3
Other expenses	37.3	7.8	34.8	27.0	32.2
	5,192.7	4,861.0	4,952.0	4,662.9	4,250.7
Earnings before income taxes	364.9	340.0	386.0	363.4	354.9
Income taxes	159.7	143.7	157.2	158.9	166.4
Net earnings	205.2	196.3	228.8	204.5	188.5
Preference dividends	3.5	5.7	8.5	11.6	15.9
Earnings applicable to common stock	$ 201.7	$ 190.6	$ 220.3	$ 192.9	$ 172.6
Fully diluted earnings per share	$ 5.36	$ 5.20	$ 6.13	$ 5.49	$ 5.11
Primary earnings per share	5.53	5.49	6.60	6.15	5.86
Cash dividends paid per share	2.65	2.55	2.35	2.15	1.95
Fully diluted shares (millions)	38.3	37.8	37.3	37.3	36.9
Primary shares (millions)	36.5	34.7	33.4	31.4	29.5
Percent of sales					
Net sales	100.0%	100.0%	100.0%	100.0%	100.0%
Other income	1.2	1.3	1.0	0.8	1.0
	101.2	101.3	101.0	100.8	101.0
Cost of sales	78.0	78.2	77.9	77.8	77.5
Administrative and selling expenses	15.3	15.4	13.9	13.9	13.9
Interest expenses	0.6	1.0	1.2	1.3	1.1
Other expenses	0.7	0.1	0.7	0.5	0.7
	94.6	94.7	93.7	93.5	93.2
Earnings before income taxes	6.6	6.6	7.3	7.3	7.8
Income taxes	2.9	2.8	3.0	3.2	3.7
Net earnings	3.7	3.8	4.3	4.1	4.1
Preference dividends	0.0	0.1	0.1	0.2	0.3
Earnings applicable to common stock	3.7%	3.7%	4.2%	3.9%	3.8%

SOURCE: Reprinted from *1983 TRW Inc. Data Book* with permission of TRW Inc.

FIGURE 12–9   *Organizational structure at TRW*

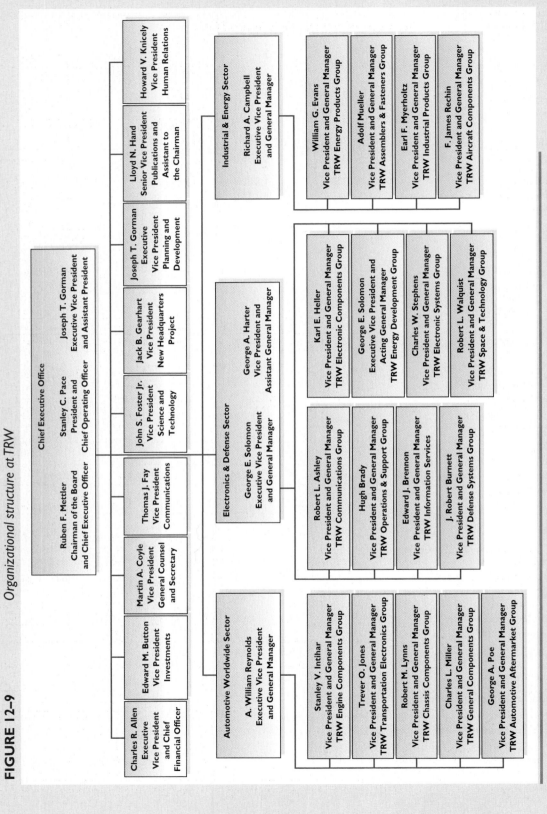

SOURCE: Reprinted from 1983 TRW Inc. Data Book with permission of TRW Inc.

TABLE 12–7   *Segments of business by industry—TRW*

	1983		1982		1981		1980		1979	
Net Sales										
Car & Truck										
Original equipment	$1,123		$1,052		$1,200		$1,291		$1,367	
Replacement equipment	472		483		490		461		432	
	1,595	29%	1,535	30%	1,690	32%	1,752	35%	1,799	39%
Electronics & Space Systems										
Electronic components	396		406		437		419		363	
Computer-based and analytical services	729		546		393		377		284	
Electronic systems, equipment, and services	951		767		772		648		552	
Spacecraft	628		486		430		355		302	
	2,604	47%	2,205	43%	2,032	38%	1,799	36%	1,501	33%
Industrial & Energy										
Fasteners, tools, bearings	486		496		596		562		558	
Pumps, valves and energy services	394		471		506		436		380	
Aircraft components	414		425		461		435		322	
	1,294	24%	1,392	27%	1,563	30%	1,433	29%	1,260	28%
Net Sales	$5,493	100%	$5,132	100%	$5,285	100%	$4,984	100%	$4,560	100%
Operating Profits										
Car & Truck	$ 116.8	27%	$ 129.2	30%	$ 146.0	30%	$ 149.4	31%	$ 192.7	44%
Electronics & Space Systems	214.2	50	170.0	40	123.3	25	133.3	28	88.9	20
Industrial & Energy	98.2	23	126.9	30	219.9	45	193.9	41	156.8	36
Operating Profit	429.2	100%	426.1	100%	489.2	100%	476.6	100%	438.4	100%
Company staff expense	(56.0)		(53.9)		(48.5)		(49.4)		(43.3)	
Interest income	15.1		15.4		12.6		1.4		3.1	
Interest expense	(29.7)		(51.2)		(65.9)		(66.5)		(52.3)	
Equity in affiliates	6.3		(14.0)		(1.4)		1.3		9.0	
Gain on debt exchange	—		17.6		—		—		—	
Earnings Before Income Taxes	$ 364.9		$ 340.0		$ 386.0		$ 363.4		$ 354.9	
Segment Assets										
Car & Truck	$ 968.6	33%	$1,029.7	35%	$1,101.3	38%	$1,148.1	40%	$1,157.2	43%
Electronics & Space Systems	1,113.7	37	1,000.6	34	888.3	31	865.1	31	779.9	29
Industrial & Energy	886.2	30	921.6	31	915.0	31	808.2	29	752.4	28
Segment Assets	2,968.5	100%	2,951.9	100%	2,904.6	100%	2,821.4	100%	2,689.5	100%
Eliminations	(102.0)		(83.2)		(61.7)		(77.9)		(72.2)	
Company staff assets	381.3		176.3		211.9		68.0		79.6	
Investment in affiliates	73.6		79.8		71.8		74.3		52.2	
Total Assets	$3,321.4		$3,124.8		$3,126.6		$2,885.8		$2,749.1	
Operating Margin										
Car & Truck	7.3%		8.4%		8.6%		8.5%		10.7%	
Electronics & Space Systems	8.2		7.7		6.1		7.4		5.9	
Industrial & Energy	7.6		9.1		14.1		13.5		12.4	
TRW segments	7.8		8.3		9.3		9.6		9.6	
Operating Return on Segment Assets										
Car & Truck	12.1%		12.5%		13.3%		13.0%		16.7%	
Electronics & Space Systems	19.2		17.0		13.9		15.4		11.4	
Industrial & Energy	11.1		13.8		24.0		24.0		20.8	
TRW segments	14.5		14.4		16.8		16.9		16.3	

Dollar amounts in millions
SOURCE: Reprinted from *1983 TRW Inc. Data Book* with permission of TRW Inc.

TABLE 12–8

Quarterly financial data—TRW

	1983				1982			
	Q4	Q3	Q2	Q1	Q4	Q3	Q2	Q1
Net Sales								
Car & Truck								
Original equipment	$ 288.9	$ 256.9	$ 298.4	$ 278.7	$ 226.5	$ 226.8	$ 300.0	$ 299.0
Replacement equipment	110.1	119.5	127.2	115.5	110.2	116.8	132.5	123.3
	399.0	376.4	425.6	394.2	336.7	343.6	432.5	422.3
Electronics & Space Systems								
Electronic components	104.2	102.5	98.2	90.9	84.4	101.7	112.3	107.0
Computer-based and analytical services	187.3	184.0	190.1	167.6	178.8	158.1	110.0	98.7
Electronic systems, equipment and services	213.8	195.9	201.9	239.7	205.5	193.3	187.7	180.8
Spacecraft	143.9	148.2	162.2	173.8	93.6	123.8	149.8	119.1
	649.2	630.6	652.4	672.0	562.3	576.9	559.8	505.6
Industrial & Energy								
Fasteners, tools, and bearings	127.1	117.9	122.5	118.4	104.9	113.1	132.8	145.2
Pumps, valves, and energy services	106.9	93.6	96.1	97.0	106.3	114.0	118.3	132.0
Aircraft components	99.2	100.4	108.7	105.8	97.9	94.6	113.1	120.0
	333.2	311.9	327.3	321.2	309.1	321.7	364.2	397.2
Net Sales	$1,381.4	$1,318.9	$1,405.3	$1,387.4	$1,208.1	$1,242.2	$1,356.5	$1,325.1
Operating Profits								
Car & Truck	$ 27.2	$ 30.2	$ 34.2	$ 25.2	$ 20.7	$ 28.4	$ 49.4	$ 30.7
Electronics & Space Systems	50.1	56.5	54.2	53.4	46.1	47.4	44.3	32.2
Industrial & Energy	30.2	24.4	25.7	17.9	24.9	22.7	34.6	44.7
Operating Profit	107.5	111.1	114.1	96.5	91.7	98.5	128.3	107.6
Company staff expense	(15.0)	(13.5)	(14.2)	(13.3)	(12.2)	(14.5)	(13.7)	(13.5)
Interest income	5.5	3.9	3.5	2.3	3.2	4.5	3.8	3.9
Interest expense	(5.0)	(7.3)	(8.4)	(9.0)	(17.1)	(10.0)	(10.7)	(13.4)
Equity in affiliates	.4	3.3	4.1	(1.5)	(1.9)	(5.7)	(.3)	(6.1)
Gain on debt exchange	—	—	—	—		17.6		
Earnings Before Income Taxes	93.4	97.5	99.1	74.9	63.7	90.4	107.4	78.5
Income taxes	40.8	38.7	45.9	34.3	32.2	31.4	45.7	34.4
Net Earnings	$ 52.6	$ 58.8	$ 53.2	$ 40.6	$ 31.5	$ 59.0	$ 61.7	$ 44.1
Earnings Per Common Share								
Fully diluted	$ 1.37	$ 1.54	$ 1.39	$ 1.06	$ .81	$ 1.55	$ 1.66	$ 1.18
Primary	1.41	1.59	1.44	1.09	.83	1.65	1.76	1.25
Common dividends paid	.70	.65	.65	.65	.65	.65	.65	.60
Operating Margin								
Car & Truck	6.8%	8.0%	8.0%	6.4%	6.1%	8.3%	11.4%	7.3%
Electronics & Space Systems	7.7	9.0	8.3	7.9	8.2	8.2	7.9	6.4
Industrial & Energy	9.1	7.8	7.9	5.6	8.1	7.1	9.5	11.3
TRW segments	7.8	8.4	8.1	7.0	7.6	7.9	9.5	8.1
Effective income tax rate	43.7	39.7	46.3	45.6	50.6	34.7	42.6	43.8

Dollar amounts in millions except per share data
SOURCE: Reprinted from *1983 TRW Inc. Data Book* with permission of TRW Inc.

TABLE 12–8　　　　　　　　*(continued)*

	1981				1980				1979		
Q4	Q3	Q2	Q1	Q4	Q3	Q2	Q1	Q4	Q3	Q2	Q1
$ 275.6	$ 273.3	$ 321.7	$ 328.7	$ 337.0	$ 279.4	$ 329.2	$ 345.7	$ 341.1	$ 315.9	$ 356.9	$ 362.?
108.5	123.8	130.4	127.6	115.2	110.4	125.4	109.7	108.5	112.2	118.9	92.?
384.1	397.1	452.1	456.3	452.2	389.8	454.6	455.4	449.6	428.1	475.8	445.?
107.5	113.2	107.3	108.8	99.9	106.2	105.7	107.1	94.9	91.7	97.1	79.?
104.3	85.0	98.5	105.4	99.5	101.5	97.0	78.8	79.4	72.3	71.9	60.?
185.5	203.0	201.3	182.7	178.0	156.2	162.5	151.3	155.9	131.6	143.2	121.?
109.7	110.7	103.6	105.8	100.4	88.8	83.6	82.0	83.9	78.4	72.9	67.?
507.0	511.9	510.7	502.7	477.8	452.7	448.8	419.2	414.1	374.0	385.1	328.?
139.4	143.9	156.6	156.0	137.9	131.4	146.3	146.3	142.3	135.4	144.3	136.?
122.9	127.6	132.2	123.0	114.8	116.0	106.6	98.6	101.5	95.9	100.5	82.?
118.4	110.2	113.5	119.5	117.6	103.6	110.4	104.0	87.6	78.2	83.2	72.?
380.7	381.7	402.3	398.5	370.3	351.0	363.3	348.9	331.4	309.5	328.0	291.?
$1,271.8	$1,290.7	$1,365.1	$1,357.5	$1,300.3	$1,193.5	$1,266.7	$1,223.5	$1,195.1	$1,111.6	$1,186.9	$1,064.?
$ 29.9	$ 34.8	$ 44.6	$ 36.7	$ 34.1	$ 33.6	$ 41.0	$ 40.7	$ 40.2	$ 42.2	$ 56.5	$ 53.?
(21.4)	73.1	38.4	33.2	33.5	33.7	35.5	30.6	24.9	22.5	25.3	16.?
45.6	54.6	62.8	56.9	50.0	50.4	50.1	43.4	41.7	38.4	46.4	30.?
54.1	162.5	145.8	126.8	117.6	117.7	126.6	114.7	106.8	103.1	128.2	100.?
(10.5)	(12.8)	(12.5)	(12.7)	(12.8)	(13.8)	(11.5)	(11.3)	(11.4)	(12.5)	(10.9)	(8.?)
5.6	5.4	1.2	.4	.6	.3	.2	.3	1.2	.2	.2	1.?
(14.0)	(16.3)	(18.4)	(17.2)	(17.7)	(17.3)	(17.3)	(14.2)	(14.4)	(13.4)	(12.6)	(11.?)
(1.9)	(1.9)	1.1	1.3	(3.0)	1.1	2.0	1.2	3.0	2.3	1.1	2.?
33.3	136.9	117.2	98.6	84.7	88.0	100.0	90.7	85.2	79.7	106.0	84.?
6.4	53.9	53.3	43.6	34.9	39.1	42.1	42.8	41.0	33.4	51.8	40.?
$ 26.9	$ 83.0	$ 63.9	$ 55.0	$ 49.8	$ 48.9	$ 57.9	$ 47.9	$ 44.2	$ 46.3	$ 54.2	$ 43.?
$ .72	$ 2.22	$ 1.72	$ 1.47	$ 1.32	$ 1.30	$ 1.57	$ 1.30	$ 1.20	$ 1.25	$ 1.47	$ 1.1?
.72	2.42	1.86	1.60	1.45	1.45	1.78	1.47	1.36	1.44	1.71	1.3?
.60	.60	.60	.55	.55	.56	.55	.50	.50	.50	.50	.4?
7.8%	8.8%	9.9%	8.0%	7.5%	8.6%	9.0%	8.9%	8.9%	9.9%	11.9%	12.1%
(4.2)	14.3	7.5	6.6	7.0	7.4	7.9	7.3	6.0	6.0	6.6	4.9
12.0	14.3	15.6	14.3	13.5	14.4	13.8	12.4	12.6	12.4	14.1	10.4
4.3	12.6	10.7	9.3	9.0	9.9	10.0	9.4	8.9	9.3	10.8	9.4
19.2	39.4	45.5	44.2	41.2	44.5	42.1	47.2	48.1	41.9	48.9	47.8

TEAM MANAGEMENT AT LAWRENCE

When Gino Strippoli was given the task of starting up operations in Lawrence, he saw a great opportunity to establish a new management system. With a new plant, new equipment, and almost all new employees, the time seemed perfect to test the value of team management. Gino had long been a supporter of team involvement and now a golden opportunity was being presented to him to set up an experiment to test his ideas.

Team management is a form of worker participation whereby team members are responsible for task related decisions concerning their areas of responsibility. Teams are formed along functional lines. In the case of the TRW-Lawrence plant, eleven teams exist ranging in membership from four to seventeen. The titles of the teams and brief descriptions of their make-up are shown in Table 12–9. Figure 12–10 depicts the current organization of the Oilwell Cable Division.

The five production teams listed in Table 12–9 are formed around the production process in use at TRW-Lawrence. Each of the teams meets on a weekly basis or as needed with exception of the resource team, which meets every two weeks. The typical meeting lasts an hour and a half to two hours. There is no formal structure for the team meeting but most meetings would adhere to an agenda similar to the one described below:

1. Scheduling manhours and overtime
2. Round-robin discussion/reporting from various plant committees (e.g., safety, gainsharing, etc.)
3. Area manager's comments regarding scrap, labor efficiency, and any new information since the last meeting.

Other decisions made by the team are listed in Figure 12–11, which illustrates the roles of the various levels of management at the Oilwell Cable Division. The figure also shows the relationships between levels. For instance, management has the responsibility for setting overall divisional goals and objectives and providing the resources necessary to the teams in order that these targets are attained.

The role of the area managers is one of being an intermediary. They are present at most teams to act as facilitators and to provide the teams information necessary to carry out their scheduling functions. In addition, the area managers fill a coordination function by meeting twice a week to discuss mutual problems and to discuss other items that should be presented at the weekly team meetings.

As can be seen in the figure, the teams are filling managerial roles and the decisions they make are more typical of those made by supervisory levels in more traditional plants. In essence, they, the team members, are given control over their work areas.

For decisions that affect the entire plant, a task force or a division-wide committee is established that includes representatives from all of the teams. Examples of some of these division-wide committees include safety, gainsharing, and benefits.

RESULTS FROM TEAM MANAGEMENT

After some initial start-up problems with the team management concept, the experiment started by Gino Strippoli in 1976 seems to now be a success. In a 1981 article in *Fortune* titled, "What Happens When Workers Manage Themselves?" Gino is quoted as saying: "In the beginning we considered it (team management) an experiment, but somewhere along the way we said, 'This is no longer an experiment; this is how we operate.' "[2]

The success of the experiment was not only written up in *Fortune* but also was the subject of several case studies.[3] But this success was not achieved easily. In the beginning, there was a good deal of mistrust among employees regarding management's motives. Also, when first starting up the Lawrence facility, there was only one union employee brought from Trenton. The rest of the people hired had little experience with the production process involved in making wire cable. As a result, there was a lot of frustration with a high level of turnover. The turnover rate of 12 percent in the first two years of operation compared to a national average of 3.8 percent at this time.[4]

But Gino was not to be deterred from seeing his experiment succeed. He realized that he was concentrating too heavily on team involvement concepts and not paying enough attention to technical concerns. A compensation scheme was developed that encouraged employees to master the various pieces of equipment in the plant. This action seemed to have the desired effect for the division became profitable for the first time in January 1978.

TABLE 12–9　　　　　*Team structure–TRW*

TEAM	NUMBER OF TEAMS	COMPOSITION
Management	1	Members of management
Resource	1	Management information systems, Design engineering, Process engineering, Employment, Accounting, Chemists, etc.
Technical	1	Nonexempt laboratory personnel
Administration	1	
Maintenance	1	Boiler, Electrical, Mechanical
Shipping and Receiving	1	
Production	5	Extruding, Armoring, Braiding

FIGURE 12–10　　　　*Organizational structure at the Oilwell Cable Division*

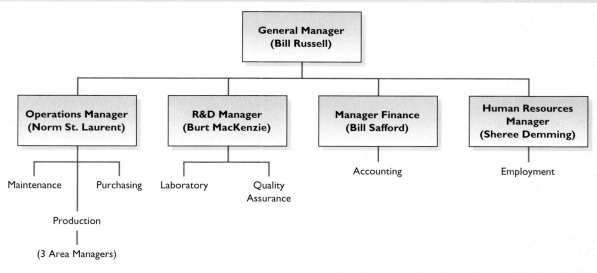

An organizational chart for the Oilwell Cable Division does not exist and the chart presented here represents the casewriters' depiction of the structure existing at TWR-Lawrence based on discussions with division personnel.

FIGURE 12–11

Roles of various levels of management at the Oilwell Cable Division.

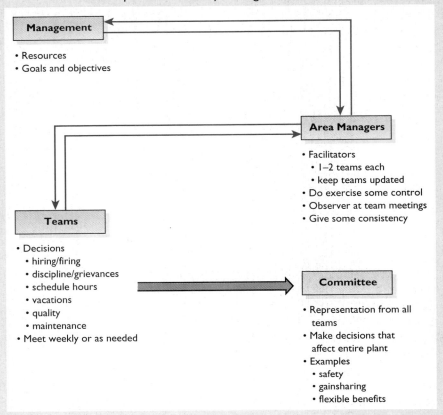

In 1978, employment had dropped from a high of 132 to what seemed to be a more optimal level of 125. Turnover dropped from an excess of 12 percent to a range of 2–4 percent, which was more in line with the national average for manufacturing firms. More impressive was the absentee rate which hovered in the range of 2½–3 percent during the period 1978–82. The national average during this period was closer to 6.5 percent.[5] Productivity was improving steadily as well. The Oilwell Cable Division now enjoyed the highest productivity of any plant in the oilwell cable industry.

It was not only the objective data that indicated that team management was succeeding but comments from employees at the Oilwell Cable Division seemed to confirm this as well. By and large, all employees rated TRW-Lawrence as a good company and preferred the team management concept to more traditional methods of management.

Some sample comments from the various levels of "management" verify this conclusion.

Team Members ". . . an excellent place to work." "Team management gives employees a good deal of responsibility." "Now at least we have some control over scheduling." "The company gains as much as the employee because of the flexibility. Now there is little idle time." "Team management gives the employee a feeling of equality." "System allows for the maximum contribution of each member of the team."

Area Managers "The plant is not a Utopia but I do feel better at the end of the day." "Decision making is more difficult but team management results in easier implementation and better understanding by team members."

Management "System allows for crossing over lines of responsibility. There is not the turf issue that exists in traditionally structured plants." "Team management concept has resulted in an excellent labor climate. TRW-Lawrence is a good place to work and the workers here are receptive to change." "The major benefit of the team management concept is flexibility while maintaining goal orientation."

This last statement is one of the real keys to team management—flexibility. Under such a management system idle time is greatly reduced as is the involvement of the plant manager in day-to-day operating problems. As noted by Strippoli, "I really feel for the first time that I am managing rather than putting out fires. The teams are putting out the fires way down in the organization."[6]

From the worker's point of view, the major benefit of team management is their ability to control their job. This control has resulted in a high level of commitment by the employees as evidenced by the numerous suggestions made by the teams that have resulted in significant improvements in quality and productivity.

Of course, the team management concept is not without its difficulties. As noted earlier, there are numerous problems with start up. It takes awhile for participants to become comfortable with the system and to accept the responsibility of managing themselves. In this case, this was a period of two years. However, after the settling-in period, productivity improved dramatically and has been maintained at that level

through 1982. This achievement is illustrated in Figure 12–12.

In addition to start-up problems, the people who filled middle-management positions had great difficulty in adjusting to their new roles as facilitators as opposed to being bosses in the traditional sense. This is an area that is often overlooked in implementing participation schemes in factories. In the case of Oilwell Cable Division, this inability to adapt to a new system resulted in four area managers leaving their positions. Plant management tried to deal with this problem by providing facilitator training for area managers. While the current area managers still express some frustration at not being able to simply "tell" workers what to do, they do feel the team management concept is a much more effective system than traditional supervisory systems and they would not want to go back to a traditional system.

All in all, Gino was very pleased with the experiment. At the end of 1982, he left the Lawrence facility for another assignment and Bill Russell, who had been Gino's operations manager, replaced him as the acting general manager.

THE OILWELL CABLE DIVISION'S MARKET

The basic product produced by the Oilwell Cable Division is wire that provides power to submersible pumps used in oil drilling. As a result, the demand for its prod-

FIGURE 12–12   *Productivity at TRW-Lawrence (1978–1983)*

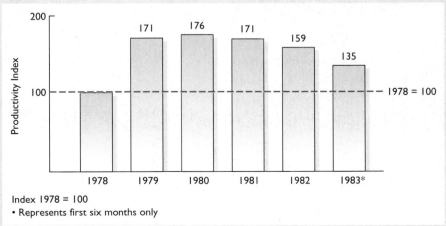

Index 1978 = 100
• Represents first six months only

uct is directly dependent on the demand for submersible pumps, a demand which is a function of the price of crude oil. As the price of oil increases, the demand for pumps increases as it became economically feasible to drill deeper wells.

Drilling deeper wells also produces a need for cables that are able to withstand the harsher environments found in such wells. For example, these wells often require the use of lead jackets to protect the cables from the corrosive effect of hydrogen sulfide.

With the Iranian oil crisis of 1979 and the resultant increase in oil prices, cable producers were able to sell pretty much all they were able to produce. Prices were determined on the basis of quality and delivery. Now, however, with the advent of an oil glut, demand for submersible pumps was dropping and the competitive factors in the market were determined more on the basis of price.

In all, TRW had ten competitors in the cable market. TRW was the market leader with a significant share of the market but, in 1982 and 1983, it was facing strong competition from both domestic and foreign producers. Foreign competition was becoming stronger because of the strength of the U.S. dollar.

Location was also a competitive factor that foreign competitors enjoyed especially with regard to oil and gas drilling in Southeast Asia and the Middle East. As the production of cable was basically a semicontinuous process, economics of scale were important. With this in mind, it was infeasible to build smaller plants nearer to a customer base that was widely dispersed. As noted earlier, one of the reasons for moving to Lawrence was so that TRW could be closer to its primary customers in Oklahoma.

By the end of June, 1983, the market for cable had fallen off dramatically. As Bill Russell reviewed the quarterly financial data (see Table 12–8) and he observed the idle equipment and employees in the plant, he knew he had to do something soon if he were to maintain market share and profitability.

THE LAYOFF DECISION

As Bill Russell prepared to meet with all personnel at the Lawrence facility, he wondered how he would handle the process of laying off 16 percent of the current work force of 125. Two things particularly troubled him. First, his predecessor, Gino Strippoli,

had implied that there would never be a layoff at the Oilwell Cable Division. Second, and perhaps more importantly, he had to decide whether the decision as to how to reduce labor costs was a decision he should make alone or one that the teams should undertake as their responsibility.

It was now 8:15 A.M. and Bill headed out to meet his employees.

ENDNOTES

[1]*TRW 1983 Data Book*, TRW Inc., 23555 Euclid Avenue, Cleveland, Ohio 44117.

[2]Charles G. Burck, What happens when workers manage themselves, *Fortune* (July 27, 1981): 62–69.

[3]See for instance, Anil Verma Electrical cable plant. In Thomas A. Kochan and Thomas A. Barocci, ed., *Human Resource Management and Industrial Relations* (Boston: Little, Brown and Company, 1985), pp. 425–435 and Cal W. Downs and Mary Lee Hummert *Case History of TRW Oilwell Cable Division Team Management* (unpublished manuscript, University of Kansas, Lawrence, Kansas, 1984).

[4]*Handbook of Labor Statistics*, U.S. Department of Labor, Bureau of Labor Statistics, December 1983, p. 180.

[5]*Handbook of Labor Statistics*, p. 136.

[6]Burck, What happens, p. 69.

STEP 2: Prepare the case for class discussion.

STEP 3: Answer the following questions, individually, in small groups, or with the entire class, as directed by your instructor.

DESCRIPTION

1. Describe the manufacturing process in Lawrence.

DIAGNOSIS

2. Why is the Oilwell Cable Division considering introducing work redesign?

3. Further explain the advantages and disadvantages of the work redesign using theories or concepts from the following areas: perception, motivation, communication, decision making, group dynamics, intergroup relations, leadership, power, and organizational structure.

PRESCRIPTION

4. How should the team's responsibilities be changed?
5. Should the work be redesigned?

ACTION

6. What consequences would the redesign have?

STEP 4: Discussion. Share your answers to the above questions, in small groups, with the entire class, or in written form. Then answer the following questions:

1. What symptoms suggest a problem exists?
2. What problems exist in the case?
3. What theories and concepts help explain the problems?
4. How can the problems be corrected?
5. Are the actions likely to be effective?

Reprinted by permission of the publisher from TRW-Oilwell Cable Division, by T.J. Hyclak and S. Demming, *Journal of Management Case Studies*, vol. 3, pp. 170–181. Copyright © 1987 by Elsevier Science Publishing Co., Inc.

$\mathscr{A}$ctivity 12–6   REENGINEERING THE ADMISSIONS PROCESS

STEP 1: Read the following description of an admissions process.

Admissions to the doctoral program in the School of Management at State University is highly selective. Members of the admissions staff perform the following steps:

1. Return each telephone call received about the program by answering any questions and mailing a brochure that includes a postcard request for an application.
2. Log each telephone call into a database of potential applicants.
3. Reply to each letter requesting information about the program by mailing a brochure that includes a postcard request for an application.
4. Log each letter request into a database of potential applicants.
5. Process each postcard request for an application received by mailing the applicant a complete admissions packet.
6. Log each complete admissions packet mailed into database of potential applicants.
7. Create a folder for each individual for whom any of the following is received: application form, letter of recommendation, GMAT or GRE scores, transcript, other information.
8. Log each application form received into an applicant database.
9. Record on checklist attached to the folder when each part of the application (appli-

cation form, three letters of recommendation, GMAT or GRE scores for tests taken within the past five years, transcripts from all colleges or universities attended) is received.
10. Contact individuals by telephone if parts are missing (e.g., recommendations, test scores, etc.) two weeks before March 1 due date.
11. Collect all applications folders into a single pile. Verify that all materials are completed and included within the packet.
12. Circulate the folders to the faculty who serve on the admissions committee.
13. Record each faculty member's rating (accept, marginal accept, marginal reject, reject) of each candidate on a master form.
14. Summarize the ratings and distribute to the admissions committee of the faculty for final decisions.

STEP 2: In groups of three to five students, offer a plan for reengineering the admissions process. Be as specific as possible.

STEP 3: Share your plans with the entire class. What are the essential components of a reengineering plan for the admissions process? Combine these components into a master reengineering plan. How effective will this plan likely be?

$\mathcal{A}$ctivity 12–7 — PLANNING FOR INNOVATION

STEP 1: Read the following scenario.

Mason, Inc., is a Fortune 500 company that designs, develops, and manufactures personal grooming products. From 1950 to 1985 it was a leader in introducing new, profitable products into the marketplace. Its Research and Development Division grew from 20 to 150 professionals during that time. Since 1985, however, the company has relied on its past successes and has failed to introduce any significant innovative product into the marketplace. Top management wants to reestablish Mason's reputation as the number-one innovator in the industry.

STEP 2: Individually or in small groups, offer a plan for encouraging innovation at Mason, Inc. Discuss staffing, rewards, organizational structure, work design, and any other facets of organizational behavior that apply.

STEP 3: Discussion. In small groups or with the entire class, share the plans you developed. Then answer the following questions:

1. What elements do these plans have in common?
2. How well do the plans follow the innovation process?
3. Do the plans incorporate provisions for fulfilling the various roles required for innovation?
4. What are the strengths and weaknesses of each plan?
5. What should be the components of an effective plan?

$\mathcal{A}$ctivity 12–8 — "ENHANCED IMAGING TECHNOLOGY"

STEP 1: View the ABC entitled "Enhanced Imaging Technology."

STEP 2: Individually, in small groups, or with the entire class, answer the following questions:

1. How has information technology affected the practice of medicine?
2. How has information technology changed the performance of jobs at Brigham and Women's Hospital?
3. What consequences does improved information technology have for physicians? For patients? For hospitals?
4. How can physicians contribute to the further development of information technology for assisting surgery?
5. How can hospitals or other medical organizations encourage such innovation?

Chapter 13

Chapter Outline

Structuring Adaptable and Responsive Organizations

LEARNING OBJECTIVES

After completing the reading and activities in Chapter 13, students will be able to

1. Define the basic building blocks of an organization's structure.

2. Identify four types of division of labor.

3. Compare and contrast five coordinating mechanisms.

4. Illustrate organizations with high and low information-processing capacity.

5. Distinguish mechanistic from organic structures.

6. Compare and contrast the formal and informal organization.

7. Compare and contrast functional, market-oriented, and integrated structures.

8. Describe four new organizational forms and show how they respond to a changing environment.

9. Summarize the key issues in using structure to attain a competitive advantage.

U nilever, a Dutch–British consumer-goods company founded in 1930, has become a model of transnational companies: it thinks globally and acts locally. It remains in touch with local markets while creating economies of scale in certain functions. To appreciate the magnitude of this accomplishment, consider the fact that its production facilities are located in more than 75 countries and run by more than 17,000 managers and 277,000 employees. How does Unilever face the challenge of dealing with a dynamic global environment? A great deal of the answer lies in its structure. The company structure emphasizes both flexibility and adherence to corporate policy.

Unilever has approximately 500 operating companies, each of which has a unique identity. Brands such as Lipton Tea are known even in countries without a Unilever operation. Decision making is decentralized to the individual companies, which are organized by product category in North America and Europe and by geography in the rest of the world. This structure has allowed Unilever to reshape its businesses to respond to new market trends. For example, three directors now collectively manage Unilever's food businesses and sustain a flat structure and work-force diversity that creates a nimble organization. Food products are organized into five strategic (not product) groups—edible fats, ice cream, beverages, meals and meal components, and professional markets such as bakeries. Ultimately, however, further reorganization will be necessary to respond to market trends that differentiate global fast foods, international foods, and national foods.

Despite the decentralized decision making, managers share a common vision and understanding of corporate strategy. Unilever's strategy focuses on retaining and developing "back-to-core" businesses, such as food, health products, consumer goods, and specialty chemical operations, which capitalize on the company's technological and management competencies. This emphasis led the company to divest itself of many peripheral businesses, such as wallpaper, floor coverings, and turkey breeding. The strategy has paid off. In Asia, for example, Unilever has grown dramatically in sales of detergents and personal products. Sales of food products lag there but are expected to grow significantly. Still, companies such as Unilever must adapt to local conditions. Hindustan Lever, for example, uses mobile shops to sell shampoo and detergent to farmers in rural India. In Indonesia, Unilever packages detergent in small packets that sell for about seven cents each.[1]

How does Unilever's structure help it act competitively? What are the components of its structure? How are these components organized into a coherent structure? In this chapter we consider the options available for structuring companies. The chapter first examines the building blocks of organization structure. Then we compare and contrast an organization's formal and informal structure. Next we look at a variety of structural prototypes and consider their significance for organizational performance. We also review some new, flexible, and responsive structural models.

The chapter concludes with comments about designing organization structures to attain a global competitive advantage. Chapter 14 then discusses the criteria for choosing among structural options.

BASIC BUILDING BLOCKS OF STRUCTURE

Structure refers to the delineation of jobs and reporting relationships in an organization. Its principal function is to influence and coordinate the work behavior of the organization's members in accomplishing the organization's goals. The *organizational chart* shows the grouping of individuals into departments, the formal reporting relationships, and the way the activities of various organizational members are coordinated. In this section we discuss the basic building blocks that comprise organizational structures: centralized versus decentralized decision making, chain of command, span of control, division of labor, coordinating mechanisms, and information processing. We conclude the section with an integrative way of thinking about these building blocks.

CENTRALIZATION VERSUS DECENTRALIZATION

Organizations differ in the location and nature of decision making. In the local ice cream parlor, only the top manager may make decisions about the flavors to sell or the hours of service. In a small consulting firm, in contrast, individual consultants may decide which projects to accept and what to charge various clients. The same differences can exist in large companies. In many banks, top executives retain control of decision making. At Unilever, in contrast, decision making is decentralized to individual companies and likely even lower in these organizations, giving middle- and lower-level managers more responsibility and autonomy.

Centralization refers to limiting the responsibility for making decisions to those at the top of the organization's hierarchy. The manager of the ice cream parlor centralizes decision making by allowing no other employees to make major decisions.

Decentralization refers to extending the responsibility for decision making to others in the organization. Typically, decentralization means giving individuals below top management, and even at the bottom levels of the organization, some control of decisions. Decentralization assumes that the individuals who are closest to the problem likely have the most knowledge about it and are thus best suited to make decisions about the best way to handle it. Thus, decentralizing decision making allows organizations to respond more quickly to changing conditions. It also speeds decision making because decisions do not hit the bottleneck that often exists when all problems must be handled by a limited number of top executives.

OWENS-CORNING FIBERGLAS. This company has created stand-alone units to pursue business in Asia. In China, in particular, Owens-Corning gives their managers significant autonomy and control over decision making. The president of the Asia Pacific region believes that having to check with a boss about decision making compromises the credibility of senior-level local managers.[2]

CHAIN OF COMMAND

Every organization can be described in terms of its reporting relationships. The accounts receivable clerk, for example, reports to the accounts receivable manager, who in turn reports to the assistant controller, who reports to the controller. This *chain of command* describes the supervisory relationships in an organization. The organizational chart presents all chains of command in a given organization and hence portrays the reporting pattern in that organization.

In most organizations, each individual reports to one and only one supervisor. This results in clear lines of authority: each person knows to whom to communicate problems or questions. Occasionally, in the matrix organization (described below), an individual may have more than one supervisor. While this may facilitate communication in an organization, it can also create confusion.

SPAN OF CONTROL

Although each individual typically reports to a single person, many organizational members have more than one subordinate. Known as the *span of control,* the number of people reporting to a single manager can range from one to hundreds, although generally it varies from one to ten. Research has repeatedly sought an optimal span of control, but the appropriate span of control generally depends on characteristics of the supervisor, subordinates, task, and organization.

DIVISION OF LABOR

Organizations allocate responsibilities in a variety of ways. Some workers focus on just a small aspect of the overall task. At one time, for example, an assembly-line worker in an automobile plant only attached the hub caps to the tire assembly. More recently, automobile workers have responsibility for performing a wider array of jobs. They might assemble the entire wheel or even the entire car.[3]

The extent of *specialization,* or the degree to which individual jobs focus on a specific and limited set of activities, varies for different positions and at different levels in the hierarchy. Positions lower in the organizational hierarchy typically call for greater specialization than those higher in the organization. Certain functions also require more extensive specialization. The advertising director might perform a more limited array of activities than the night supervisor of a manufacturing plant. The division of labor typically occurs in four ways: horizontal, vertical, personal, and spatial.[4]

Horizontal Differentiation The grouping of jobs at the same level in the hierarchy according to their function, customer, product, process, or geographical area refers to *horizontal differentiation.* At Unilever, horizontal differentiation is reflected in its 500 operating companies, which are organized by product category or by geography. This structure allows Unilever to reshape its businesses to respond to new market trends. Within each functional area, additional differentiation would occur: in the marketing department, for example, in customer service, sales, market research, and advertising. Look at Figure 13–1, which illustrates two types of horizontal differentiation. In the chart on the left, horizontal differentiation is relatively high, with many divisions at the level shown. In the right-hand chart, the horizontal division of labor is relatively low.

The extent of horizontal differentiation can vary extensively, depending on such factors as the manager's preference and the organization's size, age, goals, and product or service. As horizontal differentiation increases, potential barriers to communication are increased. Because communication occurs more easily within a unit than across units, horizontal differentiation may limit the expertise used in making decisions unless there is extensive coordination and communication between groups.

US WEST. The International Chief of US West complained that the group in charge of cellular-telephone projects in Eastern Europe does not work closely enough with a team investigating potential investments in Spain and Latin America. The hori-

FIGURE 13–1   *Types and degrees of differentiation*

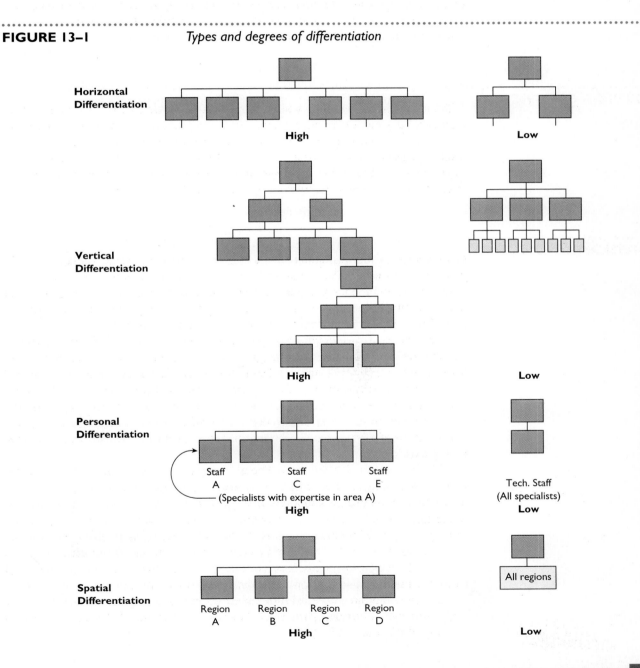

zontal differentiation of the organization into groups such as these hinders effective communication.[5]

Vertical Differentiation *Vertical differentiation* describes the allocation of responsibilities to jobs according to their level in the hierarchy. Tall organizations, as shown in the left-hand column of Figure 13–1, have many levels in the hierarchy for their size. Flat organizations, as shown in the right-hand column, have relatively few. Compare the organization of a medium-sized bank, which may have seven or eight levels in its hierarchy, to that of a large law firm, which often has only three levels in its hierarchy.

As vertical differentiation increases, so do the checks and balances that limit the number of mistakes made in action. Where there is an extensive hierarchy, decisions made by lower-level employees are more often checked by higher-level employees than in flatter organizations. Tall structures offer the second advantage of providing more avenues for advancement within the organization. This may explain the taller hierarchies found in Japanese plants. The diversity of available positions also supports a closer fitting of individuals' personal needs and abilities to jobs.

But tall structures often slow decision making if multiple levels of the hierarchy are involved in the process. If centralization of decision making accompanies vertical differentiation, workers low in the hierarchy may experience decreased motivation as a result of a lack of autonomy and involvement. In contrast, flatter structures have the potential for faster communication and greater adaptability. Of course, even in a tall structure, decentralization of decision making is possible.

MITSUKOSHI DEPARTMENT STORES. Japan's oldest department store had five levels of management in every store to help meet the expectations of its employees for high-level titles and promotions. In 1992, the company reduced the hierarchy to two levels as a way of improving productivity.[6]

Personal Differentiation Division of labor according to the worker's individual expertise or training is known as *personal differentiation.* Professional organizations often emphasize personal division of labor. For example, a hospital organizes around the specialties of its physicians, with special groups for gerontology, pediatrics, and cardiology. In large hospitals, the groupings occur around increased specializations, such as pediatric cardiology, neonatology, lymphoma oncology, and so on. Various departments within an organization can also vary in their degree of personal differentiation. A large university, for example, may also organize groups within departments around individuals' expertise, such as international finance, British literature, or econometrics.

The more extensive the personal differentiation, the more likely the organization is taking advantage of individual expertise. This type of organization becomes increasingly valuable in situations that call for special expertise, such as high-technology manufacturing or marketing.

Spatial Differentiation Finally, organizations may group jobs or workers according to their geographical location. Known as *spatial differentiation,* this type of division of labor responds best to differences in customers, suppliers, or even regulations in different locations. Certainly, most transnational corporations such as Unilever consider geographical differences when organizing. So do large national corporations that service diverse regions of a single country.

COORDINATING MECHANISMS

Once an organization has created positions and departments or other groupings of workers, some means of coordinating the disparate groups must occur. *Coordination* refers to the extent and means by which an organization integrates or holds together its various parts and facilitates their working together to accomplish a common goal or activity. It can occur in five ways: mutual adjustment, direct supervision, standardization of work processes, standardization of outputs, and standardization of skills.[7]

Mutual Adjustment Informal but direct communication between individuals, also known as *mutual adjustment,* is the most common way of coordinating. Two programmers working on a software product who speak regularly to coordinate their activities rely on mutual adjustment. The members of top management of Unilever, who regularly attend meetings to discuss strategy and human resources management, use mutual adjustment for coordination. Increasingly, mutual adjustment occurs through the use of electronic media. Individuals can have immediate access to coworkers around the world through e-mail or telephone communication. Very simple organizations generally rely heavily on mutual adjustment to coordinate the work. Very complex organizations use it to reduce ambiguity in communication and task performance.

Direct Supervision More formalized control occurs when an individual directly supervises or has responsibility for the work of one or more other workers. The team leader of a market research project may coordinate the work of her subordinates by using direct supervision. She then provides guidance, timetables, and feedback to her subordinates about their performance. Direct supervision coordinates activities through the chain of command to ensure that the work is performed in the desired way. It often occurs simultaneously with other coordinating mechanisms, such as mutual adjustment or standardization of work processes.

The increased emphasis in organizations on empowering and using teams of workers has changed the roles of managers and reduced the amount of direct supervision used for coordination. Many organizations have substituted mutual adjustment for direct supervision of employees.

Standardization of Work Processes Managers frequently specify the actual steps employees should follow in performing the work for their employees and hence *standardize the work processes.* Production that uses assembly-line technology, such as the manufacturing of some automobiles or the preparation of hamburgers at McDonalds, typically involves standardization of work processes, where each step in the process is defined. The procedures may be structured by equipment, computer programs, or in writing. Specifying the procedures in this way reduces the need for other forms of coordination. Traditionally, standardization of work processes was useful for coordinating highly specialized or relatively unskilled jobs, for specifying repetitive tasks, or for simplifying parts of very complex jobs. Today, however, many of these activities are performed by empowered work teams with the autonomy to adjust work processes as required to meet customer needs.

Standardization of Outputs Instead of specifying the process, coordination can also occur by specifying the nature of the outputs, known as *standardization of outputs.* For example, managers judged on their group's productivity or profitability have their work coordinated by standardization of outputs. Salespersons who must meet a certain quota, regardless of how they accomplish their goal, also have their work coordinated in this way. Historically, top managers have had their work coordinated by standardization of outputs, allowing them discretion to devise the best processes to get the job done. Increasingly, standardization of outputs is being used at lower levels of the organization, allowing more workers to respond creatively to changing conditions.

Standardization of Skills Teachers, lawyers, medical personnel, and other professionals rely on their training and expertise to coordinate their work. Licenses, certification programs, and training offer ways of standardizing skills. For example, CPAs and board-certified surgeons participate in these types of programs directed at creating and maintaining skills standards. Nurses know how to interact with physicians and other medical personnel as a result of the training they receive in school and on the job. Lawyers know their courtroom responsibilities vis-à-vis other courtroom personnel as a result of their legal training. Often, professionals such as these also use mutual adjustment to complement the standardization of skills.

INFORMATION PROCESSING

Organizational structures can also be characterized in terms of the extent to which their structures facilitate the collection and processing of information.[8] Some structures have a low capacity for processing information. They tend to rely on the hierarchy for communication and problem solving and hence deal with information slowly and deliberately. Structures with high horizontal differentiation or high vertical differentiation and structures that rely on direct supervision or standardization of work processes typically have a relatively low information-processing capacity.

Other structures, such those with more limited horizontal and vertical differentiation or those that use mutual adjustment or standardization of skills or outputs, have a high capacity for processing information. They can readily identify and respond to important information. High-capacity structures increase the adaptability and responsiveness of organizations. Using electronic media and other information technologies to facilitate communication between departments, divisions, and subsidiaries can increase the capacity for information processing.

MECHANISTIC VERSUS ORGANIC STRUCTURES

We can combine the building blocks described so far into two general patterns of organizational structuring: mechanistic and organic structures. The *mechanistic structure* describes a structure with relative stability and inflexibility in its organization of activities and workers. The *organic structure,* in contrast, emphasizes flexibility and the ability to adjust rapidly to change.

Mechanistic Structures Mechanistic structures typically have extensive centralization of decision making accompanied by a unitary chain of command. They rely on extensive horizontal and vertical division of labor to encourage specialization of activities throughout the organization. Although this specialization can be advantageous in relatively predictable situations, it tends to slow decision making and impede effective communication. Mechanistic structures rely on coordination by standardization of work processes and direct supervision, two approaches that limit the discretion of most workers in the organization to make and implement decisions. Such structures typically have a low capacity for processing information, again suggesting their value in relatively stable situations.

NESTLE. Chairman Helmut Maucher inherited a sluggish, centralized bureaucracy that disliked making hostile bids for other companies and was the subject of numerous boycotts about its sale of baby formula in Third-World countries. He changed the structure by pushing decision making into seven strategic business units, significantly reducing the power of headquarters' bureaucrats and giving responsibility to a group of globally minded executives. Nestle now operates more effectively, developing and introducing new products more readily.[9]

Organic Structures The organic structure deemphasizes job descriptions and specializations and encourages individuals throughout the organization to assume responsibility for making important organizational decisions. Unilever's creation of so many operating units reflects a relatively organic structure at the top of the organization. Characterized by decentralization of decision making, an organic structure typically relies on a unitary chain of command, but may occasionally shift to multiple lines of authority. Horizontal and vertical differentiation tend to be less extensive, while personal and spatial differentiation may be greater. The organic structure relies on mutual adjustment and standardization of outputs, giving individuals great discretion in how they attain organizational goals. Finally, organic structures have a high capacity for information processing. Thus, organic structures offer a much greater ability to respond to unexpected changes than do mechanistic structures.

THE INFORMAL ORGANIZATION

So far we have focused our discussion on the formal organization, which describes the prescribed lines of communication, authority, and reporting relationships. The informal organization, in contrast, describes the behavior that underlies or accompanies the formal structure in an organization. Sometimes these operating relationships and patterned interactions differ from those shown in the organizational chart. For example, a quality-control manager may formally report to the chief engineer, but to do the job effectively, the quality-control manager has to develop an informal but effective relationship with the plant general manager.

Differences between the informal and formal charts can indicate that the formal reporting relationships may be cumbersome or dysfunctional. Diagnosing these differences provides insight into what would constitute a more effective structure. These differences occur for four major reasons.

1. ***Employees may lack knowledge about the official channels of communication so use others.*** Some lower-level employees, for example, may rely on former supervisors for information, rather than going to their current superiors with questions and problems. Technical employees with a problem may go directly to the person they feel has greatest expertise in a particular area, rather than referring it to their boss.

2. ***Interpersonal obstacles may prevent workers from using the formal reporting channels.*** Some workers may experience personality clashes with their

bosses and seek assistance from other managers. The head of MIS may work more effectively with the executive vice president than with the vice president of finance/MIS. Other workers may have difficulty communicating with managers because of different personal styles, experiences, or perceptions of job requirements.

3. *Workers may be able to obtain a faster response if they bypass certain channels.* If a worker has difficulty obtaining needed supplies, he or she may request them directly from the purchasing agent, rather than relying on his or her boss to obtain them or waiting for the required paperwork to be processed through channels. The worker may use the grapevine rather than formal channels to secure information.

4. *In some organizations nonofficial relationships become legitimized and substitute for the formal ones.* Top management may redesign the official reporting relationships to reflect the informal ones that facilitate employee performance and the accomplishment of organizational goals.

Diagnosis of an organization's structure should include an assessment of the causes of any discrepancies between the informal and formal structures. *Social network analysis,* or evaluation of the pattern of interactions between organizational members, can facilitate such an evaluation.[10] Network analysis identifies the nature of the links between individuals or positions, the roles individuals play, and the characteristics of positions in the network, as well as other properties of the network, such as connectedness, reachability, and openness to the outside.[11] This network structure can complement or circumvent the formal structure. In one study of patient complaints in a hospital, for example, employees sent complaints to managers, who kept passing them to other managers until they were resolved. Use of this network superseded the formal procedure for dealing with problems.[12] In the next sections we examine the formal prototypes of organizations that the informal structure may accompany.

FUNCTIONAL STRUCTURE

A functional structure groups employees according to the major category of organizational work activity. One of the subsidiaries of Unilever, for example, might group employees into marketing, manufacturing, accounting, R & D, and human resources functions. Within each of these broad groupings, further groupings by functional area may have occurred. In the marketing function, for example, separate groups for marketing research, advertising, sales, and sales support may exist.

CHARACTERISTICS AND USES

Figure 13–2 shows an excerpt from an organizational chart for a functional structure. Note the relatively high horizontal and vertical differentiation that characterizes such a structure. The functional structure works best under these circumstances:

■ when the roles or jobs in the organization group well into functional areas;

■ when a relatively small amount of communication outside the groupings is required;

FIGURE 13–2   *Functional structure*

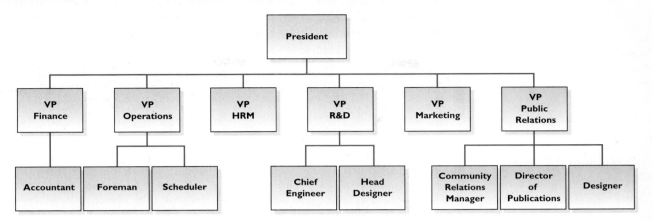

- when the organization has a well-developed product or service;

- when few exceptions occur and therefore rapid communication is less necessary;

- when the environmental conditions are relatively benign, such as a stable and predictable market demand;

- when the organization is small to medium-sized, making face-to-face communication feasible.

TYPES OF FUNCTIONAL STRUCTURES

Functional structures can be further characterized as one of three types: simple structure, machine bureaucracy, or professional bureaucracy.

Simple Structure This type of functional structure describes relatively small and young organizations that primarily use mutual dependence and direct supervision as coordinating mechanisms.[13] A men's clothing store, a family restaurant, and a small consulting firm probably have this structure. In the simple structure, the top manager has significant control. Thus, entrepreneurs frequently organize their firms along these lines. As the organization grows, the simple structure will frequently departmentalize further by function. As it becomes increasingly large and develops additional products or services, the organization will develop a more complex structural form that relies on other means of coordination.

Machine Bureaucracy As organizations increase in size, horizontal and vertical differentiation tend to increase, leading to the standardization and formalization of behavior characteristic of a ***machine bureaucracy.***[14] Direct supervision and standardization of work processes provide the key coordinating mechanisms. Because relatively large operating units prevail in the machine bureaucracy, many large-scale manufacturing organizations, such as some automobile, steel, equipment, and consumer goods manufacturers, organize in this way. Although the machine bureaucracy originated with mass-production firms that relied on machinery to facilitate the process, this functional structure has characterized such service organizations as the airlines and the U.S. Postal Service.

Professional Bureaucracy This structure shares some of the formalization inherent in the machine bureaucracy, but it emphasizes standardization of skills rather than standardization of work processes for coordination.[15] Rather than originating with mass-production firms that used machinery, the professional bureaucracy originated with knowledge-based organizations that relied on skilled professionals to perform the work. A professional bureaucracy, such as a university or hospital, typically has little vertical or horizontal differentiation, but extensive personal differentiation. It uses training to ensure that workers have the required skills for effective organizational functioning.

ADVANTAGES AND DISADVANTAGES

The functional structure encourages individuals with jobs in the same area of specialization to work together. This type of interaction builds a strong loyalty to the functional group. It also offers a strong cadre of individuals experienced in specific areas who can contribute significantly to organizational performance. The relatively high vertical division of labor that often accompanies this structure provides employees many opportunities for advancement within a functional discipline for employees. This structure also avoids duplication of effort in different parts of the organization since only a single human resources department, operations division, or accounting group services the entire company.

The high horizontal and vertical differentiation can also cause problems. In particular, communication between functional areas can be limited, resulting in dysfunctional performance and even competition. At the same time, communication up the hierarchy may be necessary for dealing with problems and exceptions, making response time extremely slow.

MARKET-ORIENTED STRUCTURES

Unlike the functional structure, which groups employees according to functional area, the market-oriented structures group workers according to the market they serve, such as product, project, client, or geographical area. NASA relied on a project structure in organizing workers to focus on the Apollo, Saturn, and Space Shuttle projects. A consulting firm might organize its workers into projects for particular industry sectors, such as health care, government, and high technology.

JOHNSON & JOHNSON. Johnson & Johnson has 166 separately chartered companies that each sells its own products. They develop their own strategies, build relationships with customers and suppliers, and conduct all aspects of business independent of the parent corporation.[16]

CHARACTERISTICS AND USES

In any of these market-oriented structures, the organization is structured at one or more levels of the hierarchy by product, project, client, or geographical area, as shown in Figure 13–3. Unilever, for example, has geographical structures in some locations to respond to local needs.

XEROX. Xerox reorganized to create nine independent business divisions, organized around specific markets and products. Each has profit and loss responsibility.

The company also organized its sales and service staff into three geographic customer-operations divisions.[17]

At other levels, different structural configurations may exist. For example, in a product structure, a product manager supervises various functional groups. Often the top level of a geographical structure emphasizes location, while a more typical functional structure exists within each geographical division. Product, project, customer, and geographical groupings can occur at the department, division, or even

FIGURE 13–3 *Examples of market-oriented structures*

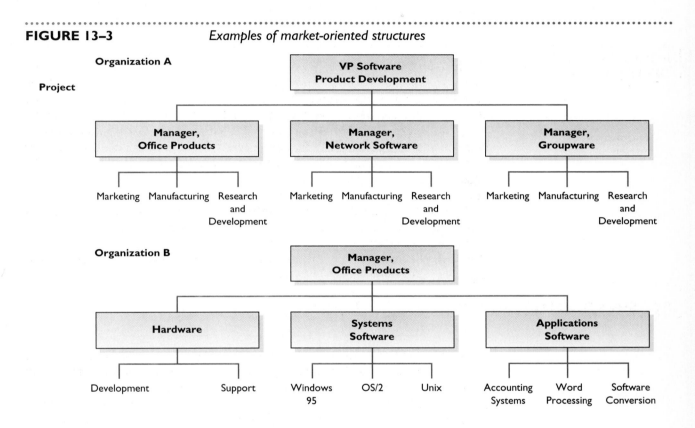

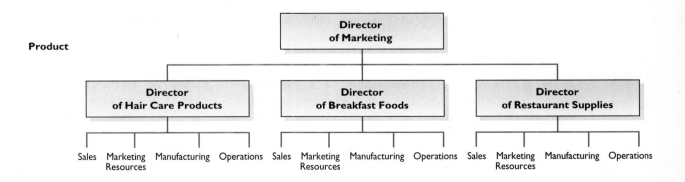

FIGURE 13–3   *(continued)*

Client

Geographical Location

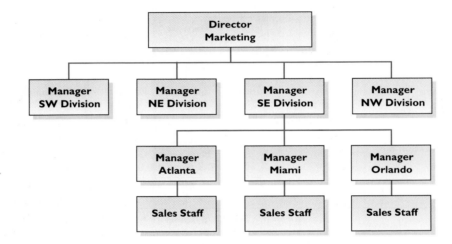

subsidiary level. The scope of coordination required within groupings may vary depending on the unit's size.

IBM. The manager in charge of the IBM Enterprise Group has a marketing, human resources, and R&D staff reporting to him or her. Similar staff will report to the manager of the Office Products Group and of the Mainframe Group.

The market-oriented structure responds effectively

■ when the company faces a relatively dynamic and unpredictable market situation;

■ when rapid communication is essential;

■ when responding to rapidly changing conditions is important;

■ when the organization has abundant resources for meeting customer needs.

THE DIVISIONALIZED FORM

Larger organizations that implement a market-oriented structure are often characterized as **divisionalized.** Companies such as Unilever that deal with diversified products create major units or divisions for each market or product. Unilever has approximately 500 operating companies, each of which has a unique product identity, such as Lipton Tea. Alternatively, the structure may incorporate a collection of relatively autonomous companies owned by a single parent, known as a **conglomerate.**

The divisionalized organization emphasizes standardization by outputs: each manager has bottom-line responsibility. Both the manager's and the organization's performance are judged by these outputs. This divisionalized structure allows organizations to respond to a heterogeneous environment, particularly to diverse cultures. The organization can set up mini-organizations that meet the unique needs of various countries and cultures. This structure also allows increased control in large organizations. By breaking the organization into profit-oriented units, managers are held more accountable. Finally, this structure takes advantage of and reduces the liabilities of a diverse product mix by emphasizing rather than ignoring it.

ADVANTAGES AND DISADVANTAGES

The market-oriented structure focuses on the unique needs of particular products, projects, customers, or geographical areas. This focus tends to create teams with the common goal of meeting market demands, an advantage when changing market needs require rapid response. Thus, this structure offers the ability to respond quickly to a changing market situation and provides rapid communication in these situations. When accompanied by decentralized decision making, this structure speeds problem solving and adaptation by the organization. The market-oriented structure also brings the diverse expertise of various functional specialists to bear on problems associated with the particular product, project, or client.

On the downside, this structure creates significant duplication of knowledge throughout the organization. Human resources professionals with similar experience and skills may be required to service two separate product groups. In this situation, the benefits of economy of scale that occur in the functional structure are unavailable. Not only are redundant services costly, but the focus on market requirements may prevent workers from developing a wider functional expertise that would let them move from market group to market group as needed.

INTEGRATED STRUCTURE

The **integrated structure** is a hybrid structure that can incorporate both functional and market-oriented structures. Sometimes called an **adhocracy,**[18] it responds to the needs of a changing and complex environment.

CHARACTERISTICS AND USES

This form uses a variety of *ad hoc* or temporary liaison devices (task forces, integrating roles, project teams, and matrix structures) to encourage mutual adjustment among organizational members. An adhocracy or integrated structure creates a flexible structure that can respond to a complex changing environment. In such an environment it tends to operate best with sophisticated information technologies, such as e-mail and video conferencing, which can facilitate teamwork and the sharing of information. Most integrated structures can be classified as forms of adhocracy.

The integrated structure has four major characteristics.

1. *Flexible groupings of individuals that change as organizational needs change.* These groupings allow the organization to take a functional, product, project, geographical, or client orientation. For example, task forces or project teams may be organized or disbanded as the organization introduces new products or withdraws obsolete ones.

2. *Groupings of individuals that emphasize a market focus.* A bank may organize temporary or permanent work teams to service small business, institutional, or other special interest group accounts.

3. *Decentralized decision making.* Increasing the autonomy, responsibility, and accountability of middle managers and professional staff allows the structure to respond more quickly to changing or unpredictable conditions.

4. *Groupings of employees that combine functional specialties.* A project team, for example, might include a marketing, engineering, and manufacturing specialist.

THE MATRIX

In the 1970s, some organizations created a structure that combined the best aspects of the functional and product structures. Known as the *matrix,* it was characterized by a duality of command: workers reported to two (or more) supervisors, one from their original functional area and the second from the product or project on which they worked. Figure 13–4 illustrates a matrix structure. Although this figure shows each worker reporting in two directions, some matrix structures have more than two dimensions. The assignment of workers to functional groupings remains relatively permanent, while the assignment to product, project, client, or geographical area changes as necessary.

L.M. ERICSSON. After first centralizing the sales of all products into a single unit in each country, the CEO introduced a matrix system that had unit managers report to product divisions and corporate headquarters. This encouraged sharing of information among 40 R&D laboratories worldwide and expedited the introduction of new products into the market. It also required executives to spend more time reaching a consensus.[19]

ADVANTAGES AND DISADVANTAGES

Because they group workers on a nonfunctional basis, the matrix and other integrated structures tend to be flexible in responding to a changing environment. Organizations can add or delete product or project groups as necessary in response to changing conditions. Organizations also seem to adopt matrix organizations when

FIGURE 13–4   *Matrix structure*

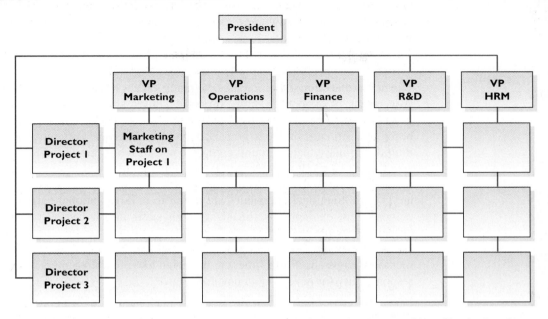

Each cell represents one or many employees who serve on the project listed for that row and are part of the staff listed in that column.

they have high information-processing requirements.[20] Because project groups share functional resources, some cost economies as well as better functional integration across projects can result. At the same time, because there is a functional dimension, workers retain a strong functional identity that helps them bring special expertise to the unique needs of various products or projects.

The matrix, in particular, is not without costs, however. The duality of command automatically doubles the overhead costs for managers. At the same time, workers may experience conflict and stress when they must report to at least two bosses with potentially different standards, expectations, and work priorities. Competition between these managers can lead to power struggles as well as difficulty in controlling work. Although some of these problems can be alleviated by clarifying responsibilities and devising procedures for identifying problems quickly, the potential downside has made the matrix a less popular organization in the past decade. DIGITAL EQUIPMENT CORPORATION. Shortly after Robert Palmer became CEO, he attributed the company's delay in shifting from minicomputers to personal computers to the use of the matrix. Groups within Digital such as engineering, manufacturing, and marketing spent too much time discussing the move and attempting to reach a consensus among the executives heading different branches of the matrix, rather than implementing the move.[21]

NEW ORGANIZATIONAL FORMS

The structures described so far vary in their ability to respond quickly, flexibly, and adaptively to the changing demands of the global marketplace. As a result, forward-thinking executives have devised new structures to respond to the continuing challenges of this arena. In this section we consider four such structures: (1) the horizontal organization; (2) alliances, partnerships, joint ventures, and other arrangements; (3) the dynamic network model or modular organizations; and (4) virtual organizations.

THE HORIZONTAL ORGANIZATION

The horizontal structure eliminates the management hierarchy and emphasizes empowerment of workers. These structures break the organization into its key processes and create cross-functional teams to manage and run the processes.[22] The horizontal structure reduces both horizontal and vertical differentiation, creating multidisciplinary teams around core processes, such as new product development (see Figure 13–5). It also focuses extensively on customer requirements and satisfaction, similar to the organization practicing total quality management (see Chapter 11). Multinational companies are trying to remove national barriers within the company, for example, by organizing their staffs into industrial rather than geographical groups.[23]

FORD MOTOR COMPANY. Ford merged manufacturing, sales, and product development in Europe and North America. It created five program centers with worldwide responsibility for new product development.[24]

GENERAL ELECTRIC. This manufacturing company replaced its hierarchy with more than 100 processes and programs. Jack Welch, its president, has described the company as having boundaryless management, where functions are seamless across groups of employees. This change was accompanied by changes in reward systems, performance appraisals, and training.[25]

Horizontal organizations have seven key elements:[26]

- Organize around process, not task.

- Flatten the hierarchy.

- Use teams to manage everything.

- Let customer satisfaction drive performance.

- Reward team performance.

- Maximize contact with suppliers and customers.

- Inform and train all employees.

ALLIANCES, PARTNERSHIPS, JOINT VENTURES, AND OTHER ARRANGEMENTS

We tend to think of individual organizations acquiring and developing their own resources to help them compete, but it is sometimes faster and cheaper to form a mutually beneficial alliance with another organization. Table 13–1 lists the types of strategic alliances, as well as their prototypical design, benefits, costs, success factors, and human resources issues. Management issues revolve around the need to blend different cultures and management styles, reconcile variations in job design, develop compatible staffing, training, performance evaluation, and compensation strategies, as well as address career issues such as promotions, and ensure congruent industrial relations systems in the allied organization.[27] The interorganizational linkages in these structures help protect organizations from failure because they bring additional resources to solving organizational problems and competing in the marketplace.[28]

FIGURE 13–5 *The horizontal organization*

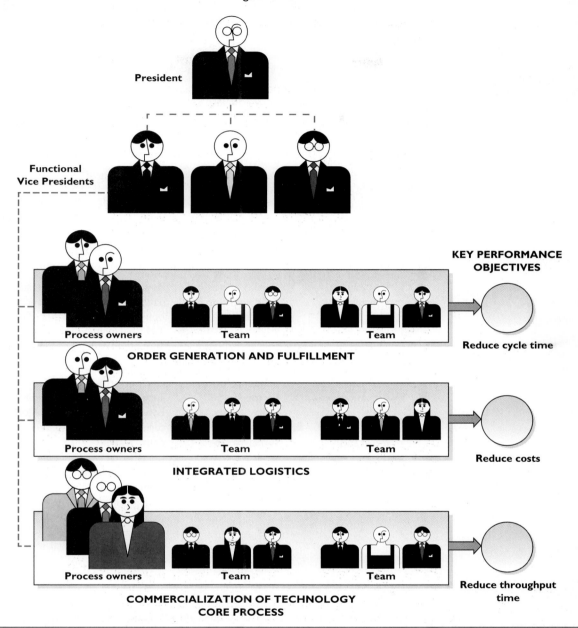

President

Functional
Vice Presidents

KEY PERFORMANCE
OBJECTIVES

Process owners   Team   Team

ORDER GENERATION AND FULFILLMENT

Reduce cycle time

Process owners   Team   Team

INTEGRATED LOGISTICS

Reduce costs

Process owners   Team   Team

COMMERCIALIZATION OF TECHNOLOGY
CORE PROCESS

Reduce throughput
time

SOURCE: Reprinted with permission from T.A. Stewart, The search for the organization of tomorrow, *Fortune* (May 18, 1992): 92–98.

CORNING. Corning has 19 partnerships that accounted for nearly 13 percent of its earnings in 1992. These alliances allow Corning to develop and sell new products more quickly.[29]

Even small businesses can use a variety of strategic alliances to develop and sustain technological leadership. These include joint ventures, equity investment in the small company, client-sponsored research contracts, marketing–distribution

TABLE 13–1   *Types of global strategic alliances*

STRATEGY	ORGANIZATION DESIGN	BENEFITS	COSTS	CRITICAL SUCCESS FACTORS	STRATEGIC HUMAN RESOURCES MANAGEMENT
Licensing— Manufacturing Industries	Technologies	■ Early standardization of design ■ Ability to capitalize on innovations ■ Access to new technologies ■ Ability to control pace of industry evolution	■ New competitors created ■ Possible eventual exit from industry ■ Possible dependence on licensee	■ Selection of licensee that is unlikely to become competitor ■ Enforcement of patents and licensing agreements	■ Technical knowledge ■ Training of local managers on-site
Licensing— Servicing and Franchises	Geography	■ Fast market entry ■ Low capital cost	■ Quality control ■ Trademark protection	■ Partners compatible in philosophies/values ■ Tight performance standards	■ Socialization of franchisees and licensees with core values
Joint Ventures— Specialization Across Partners	Function	■ Learning a partner's skills ■ Economies of scale ■ Quasi-vertical integration ■ Faster learning	■ Excessive dependence on partner for skills ■ Deterrent to internal investment	■ Tight and specific performance criteria ■ Entering a venture as "student" rather than "teacher" to learn skills from partner ■ Recognizing that collaboration is another form of competition to learn new skills	■ Management development and training ■ Negotiation skills ■ Managerial rotation

agreements, manufacturing agreements, agreements with universities or research institutes, limited R & D partnerships, and licensing of its technology to another company.[30] Small companies can use **contract manufacturers,** companies that produce goods that other companies sell, as a way of transforming a small amount of capital into large amounts of sales.[31]

GENERAL MILLS' YOPLAIT. General Mills introduced two new brands of Yoplait Yogurt, both linked to General Mills's cereal products (Trix and Cap'n Crunch). They contracted the production of both products to outside companies because Yoplait's plants were functioning at capacity. Both the Trix- and Crunch-related

TABLE 13–1 (continued)

STRATEGY	ORGANIZATION DESIGN	BENEFITS	COSTS	CRITICAL SUCCESS FACTORS	STRATEGIC HUMAN RESOURCES MANAGEMENT
Joint Ventures— Shared Value Adding	Product or line of business	■ Strengths of both partners pooled ■ Faster learning along value chain ■ Fast upgrading of technological skills	■ High switching costs ■ Inability to limit partner's access to information	■ Decentralization and autonomy from corporate parents ■ Long "courtship" period ■ Harmonization of management styles	■ Team building ■ Acculturation ■ Flexible skills for implicit communication
Consortia, Keiretsus, and Chaebols	Firm and industry	■ Shared risks and costs ■ Building a critical mass in process technologies ■ Fast resource flows and skill transfers	■ Skills and technologies that have no real market worth ■ Bureaucracy ■ Hierachy	■ Government encouragement ■ Shared values among managers ■ Personal relationships to ensure coordination and priorities ■ Close monitoring of member-company performance	■ "Clan" cultures ■ Fraternal relationships ■ Extensive mentoring to provide a common vision and mission across member companies

brands reached market more quickly and using less capital than they would have using traditional in-house production.[32]

Multinational partnerships offer another way to deal with global competition.

DRUG COMPANIES. Merck, Eli Lilly, Fujisawa, and Bayer shared the license on new drugs as a way of reducing development and distribution costs for the individual companies.[33]

TOSHIBA. The Japanese electronics giant uses strategic alliances as a key component of its corporate strategy. It has used partnerships, technology licensing agreements, and joint ventures as one way to becoming one of the world's leading makers of electronic equipment. Its joint venture with Motorola helped make Toshiba the leading maker of large-scale memory chips. Its partnership with IBM has allowed it to become a major supplier of color displays for portable computers.[34]

KEIRETSU. One interesting alliance is Japan's **keiretsu,** a family of companies joined under various financial agreements, with interlocking directorates, or based on informal social relationships.[35] Ranging in size from ten to hundreds of companies, the keiretsu can be either supplier oriented or bank centered. In a supplier-oriented alliance, companies such as Sony or Honda integrate vertically. In a bank-centered keiretsu, companies such as Mitsubishi integrate vertically and horizontally and have 20 to 40 percent of their stock owned by other members of the alliance. Figure 13–6 shows the Mitsubishi keiretsu and the percentage of each company owned by other members of the alliance. The keiretsu tends to have long-term financial stability because other members can help sustain it. This stability allows them to focus on long-term development and profitability.

THE DYNAMIC NETWORK MODEL: MODULAR ORGANIZATIONS

The *dynamic network* form of organizational structure extends beyond the boundaries of a single organization, as shown in Figure 13–7.[36] In its simplest form, the dynamic network model has a small staff that develops strategy, subcontracts the work to others, and then monitors the interface with the various subcontractors.[37] The core firm may "sell" personal computers but parcel out their design, manufacturing, sales, and distribution to subcontractors. Also known as *modular organizations,* this structural form demonstrates the epitome of flexibility.[38] It adds or subtracts parts as needed to function more competitively in the marketplace.

FIGURE 13–6   *The Mitsubishi keiretsu*

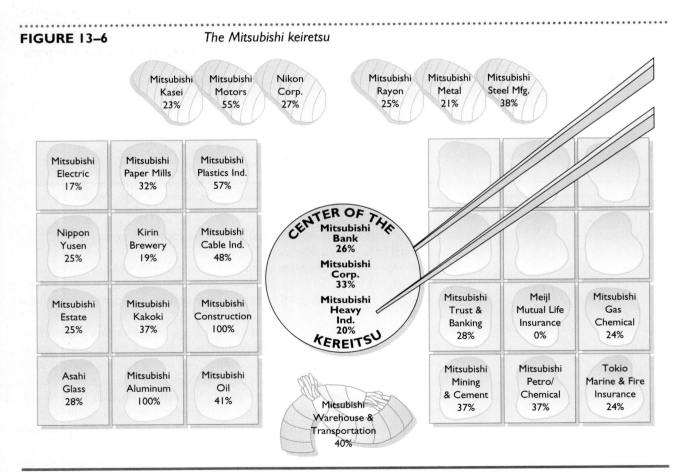

SOURCE: The mighty keiretsu, *Industry Week* (January 20, 1992): 52. Reprinted by permission of Eliot Bergman.

DELL COMPUTERS. Dell concentrates on marketing and service. It offers customers computers that are assembled to their individual specifications. Dell has extremely low manufacturing costs. The company leases two small factories where it assembles computers from parts purchased from suppliers. Instead, Dell spends extensively on training salespeople and service technicians. This arrangement has allowed Dell to compete successfully on both quality and price.[39]

The dynamic network takes a variety of forms.[40] For example, individual firms may join together in a partnership to work on international projects. In construction, the general contractor and its subcontractors may form a stable and continuous network over time. In the German textile industry, associations of specialists are formed, each with unique expertise. Strategic partnering in high-technology firms also illustrates such network organizations.

Dynamic networks have four characteristics.[41]

1. Independent organizations within the network perform the business functions. Such *vertical disaggregation* occurs for product design, marketing, manufacturing, and other functions.

2. *Brokers* assemble the business groups by subcontracting for required services, creating linkages among partners, or locating such functions as design, supply, production, and distribution.

3. *Market mechanisms* such as contracts or payment for results, rather than plans, controls, or supervision hold the functions together.

FIGURE 13–7   *Example of a dynamic network*

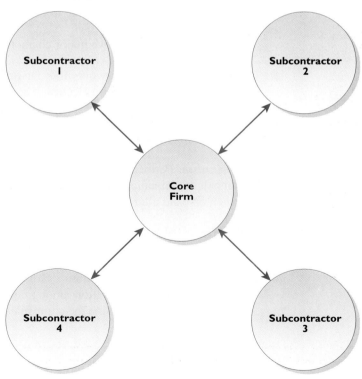

4. *Full-disclosure information systems* link the various network components.

Because the organizations pursue different strategies yet complement each other as part of the network, the dynamic network structure meets the need for innovation and efficiency. An internal network can also exist. Here the organization creates separate entrepreneurial and market components as separate divisions or profit centers with bottom-line responsibility and hence does not use companies outside the organization to perform these functions.[42]

THE VIRTUAL CORPORATION

The *virtual corporation* is a network of independent suppliers, customers, and even competitors, typically tied together by computer technology.[43] Information technology links the components of the network and allows them to share skills, costs, and access to markets.[44] In a sense, it is the epitome of a company with partnerships and alliances. Each participating organization contributes only its core competencies. The frequent regrouping of companies into virtual corporations creates the flexibility required to seize new opportunities.

SUN MICROSYSTEMS. This computer company is attempting to become a virtual corporation as a way of filling customer orders within 24 hours after their receipt. The goal is to compress time, increase quality, and lower costs. The company uses information technology to coordinate work at a network of suppliers, distributors, and manufacturing sites. The company now outsources distribution to three partners who guarantee that they will perform Sun's work quickly and at a low cost. Sun has also reduced its suppliers to a few companies, thereby allowing Sun to better control the quality and cost of components. Partnering has allowed the leadtime for workstations to decrease from three months to less than ten days.[45]

Virtual corporations have five major characteristics:[46]

- ■ *Technology.* Computer networks link far-flung companies with entrepreneurs and partnerships are based on electronic contracts.

- ■ *Excellence.* Each partner brings its core competencies to the corporation, allowing the creation of a "best-of-everything" organization.

- ■ *Opportunism.* Partnerships will be less permanent, less formal, and more opportunistic. Companies band together to meet a specific market opportunity and then disband after meeting the need.

- ■ *Trust.* The relationships in a virtual corporation require mutual trust because the participating companies are more reliant on each other than previously.

- ■ *No Borders.* The virtual corporation redefines the traditional boundaries of the company. Increased cooperation among competitors, supplies, and customers makes it difficult to determine the companies' borders.

DESIGNING ORGANIZATIONS FOR GLOBAL COMPETITIVENESS

Unilever meets the challenge of achieving global competitiveness by having created a structure in which its operating companies have autonomy. By decentralizing decision making, Unilever allows each company to respond flexibly to organizational demands.

This structure is well suited to meet the challenges Unilever faces as a transnational firm, one that operates in many different countries with different cultures and markets. It has enabled Unilever to diversify and expand its market. It has allowed Unilever to compete effectively by choosing locations that take advantage of low-cost production opportunities and high-technology research and development centers in particular countries. The structure has also allowed the company to respond to variations in values and attitudes in the different countries it inhabits. Finally, it has facilitated addressing issues of communication and control, which are key in multinational firms. Keeping subsidiaries in line with each other and with headquarters' personnel poses another challenge. Ensuring that each part of the organization receives complete, necessary, and relevant information also requires significant coordination. In Chapter 14 we will discuss in more detail the diagnostic process of analyzing business challenges and designing a structure to meet those needs.

SUMMARY

An organization's structure refers to the delineation of jobs and reporting relationships in an organization as a way of influencing and coordinating work behavior. Organizations with centralized decision making place control of decision making in the hands of a few, whereas decentralized decision making disperses decision making throughout the organization. Each worker usually reports to a single supervisor and hence demonstrates unity of command. Together, these reporting relationships define the chain of command. Structures also vary in their division of labor and the mechanisms for coordinating various parts of the organization. They may process information quickly or slowly. Combining these building blocks in various configurations results in mechanistic or organic structures.

A functional structure groups employees according to major functions, or categories of work activities. Market-oriented structures group employees according to the particular product, project, client, or geographical area on which they focus. Integrated structures combine both forms of grouping to create more flexible, market-driven organizations.

New forms of organizations respond to a dynamic environment and the demands of globalization. Horizontal structures, various types of alliances, the dynamic network model, and virtual corporations illustrate these new forms. Competing in a global environment poses special challenges and opportunities for organizations.

DIAGNOSTIC QUESTIONS

The following questions help diagnose an organization's structure.

- ■ Is decision making centralized or decentralized?

- ■ How large is the span of control of each manager?

- ■ What chain of command exists in the organization?

- ■ What division of labor is there?

- ■ What coordinating mechanisms are there?

- ■ How would you describe information processing in the organization?

- ■ Does the informal organization reinforce or contradict the formal organization structure?

- ■ What structural configuration describes the organization?

- ■ Does the organization use any new structural forms?

- ■ How does the organization's structure respond to the requirements of global competitiveness?

$\mathcal{A}$ctivity 13–1 ANALYSIS OF ORGANIZATION CHARTS

STEP 1: Study the organizational chart of three organizations presented in Figures 13–8 through 13–10. Compare and contrast them.

STEP 2: Answer the following questions individually, in small groups, or with the entire class, as directed by your instructor.

DESCRIPTION

1. Describe the division of labor and coordinating mechanisms for each.

DIAGNOSIS

2. Analyze the formal prototype for each organization.
3. Compare and contrast these designs.
4. What kind of informal organization might each organization have?
5. What employee attitudes and performance probably occur in each organization?

PRESCRIPTION

6. What structural changes, if any, might benefit each organization?

FIGURE 13–8   *Organizational chart of a library*

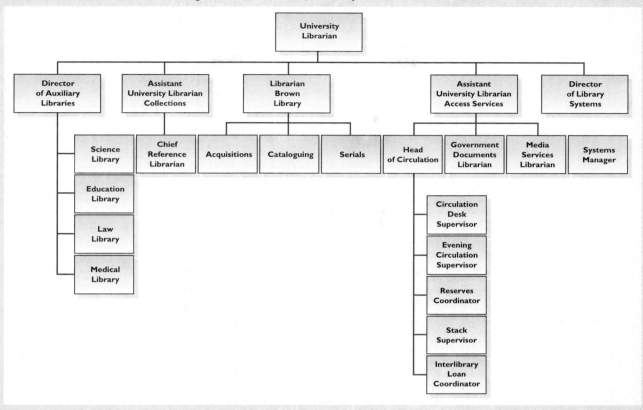

FIGURE 13–9   *Organizational chart of a computer software company*

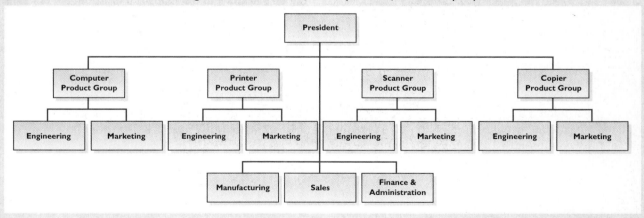

FIGURE 13–10   *Organizational chart of a medical products company*

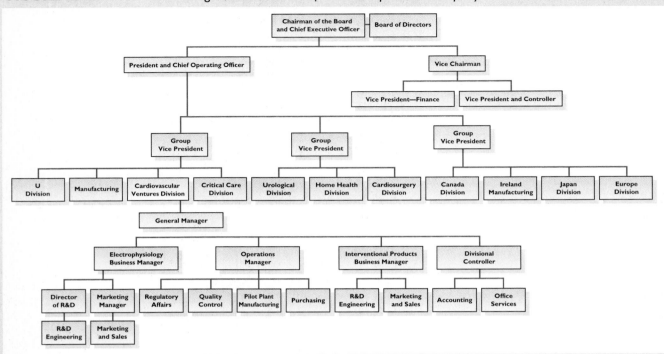

Activity 13–2   THE BLACK BOX COMPANY

STEP 1:   Read The Black Box Company Case.

The Black Box Company manufactured and distributed lead acid batteries for use in motor vehicles as well as motive power batteries used in a wide range of industrial applications. Before September 1988, the company sold both product lines through its branch sales forces, which were situated in all major cities and towns in the country. A gradual decline in market share and increased distribution costs of automobile batteries had led to a drastic change in policy.

In October 1988, the company's four major brands of automobile batteries were to be marketed only through distributors. This policy change had two immediate effects as motor accessory wholesalers would carry buffer stocks and use their own sales representatives to sell to service stations and other individual retailers. They would also be responsible for creditors. The company's 64 auto battery salesmen became redundant, leaving 40 salesmen in the industrial division. All but 11 senior salesmen were laid off in the auto division. These 11 were promoted to the position of special accounts managers, each of whom managed one area of the country; their job was to coordinate the automobile battery distributors' activities in each area, sort out their problems and perform PR duties when necessary. The industrial section to a large extent operated as it had. The other immediate effect was that each branch office lost its marketing function, at least where automobile batteries were concerned, and were thus considerably reduced in size and scope. Two of the smaller branches, which lacked the technical expertise necessary for handling industrial batteries, were closed down entirely and their areas split up between other branches. The branch managers would no longer report to the marketing vice president directly (see Figure 13–11); with their much greater industrial orientation they now reported directly to the national sales managers for industrial products. The national sales

FIGURE 13–11   *The Black Box Company*

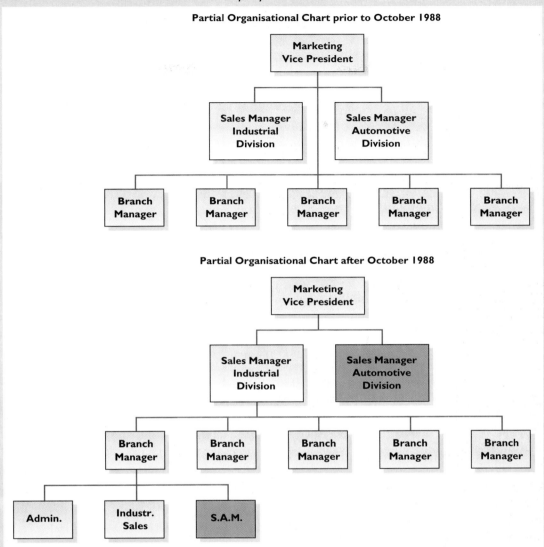

Partial Organisational Chart prior to October 1988

Partial Organisational Chart after October 1988

manager (auto) had what was known as "dotted line authority" over the special accounts managers, but had no authority over the branch managers who were their immediate superiors.

Company's Immediate History 1985–1988

There had been other changes in the company before 1988, some of which had been more fundamental. In early 1985, Black Box and another battery manufacturer, AEP Company, had merged, creating a situation of total functional duplication, during and after which a lot of employees had been made redundant or had left. In December 1985, a president had been appointed from outside both organizations with a brief from the board to trim staff levels. For a year, his presence overshadowed the company and the period had gone down in company folklore as being a progression "from merger to murder." The downturn in the economy had followed shortly afterwards, which had lead to further cost cutting programs. Although it left a more efficient company in its wake, times were hard for the company and its employees while it lasted.

REACTION TO THE OCTOBER 1988 CHANGES

Black Box branch managers, who generally tended to be technically oriented and fairly conservative individuals, viewed with concern the change that took place in automobile battery marketing. At first it was widely felt among themselves that they could market batteries just as well as the distributors despite head office explanations about why the changes were necessary. Gradually, however, as the new strategy proved to be working well, most branch managers realized its benefits and gave it their support.

"I have to admit that I was sceptical but it's starting to show results and that's proof enough for me" commented one manager.

Another said "I think that we were very defensive about having distributors doing what we had done for so long. Some of us, and that includes myself, spent a long time waiting to see what would happen and maybe secretly hoping that it would fail. It didn't, so we've learned to live with it."

PETER EKSTEIN

One person who could not reconcile himself to the change was the manager of an important east coast branch, Peter Ekstein. Six months after the change Ekstein made no secret of his doubts to his subordinates and at times could be heard protesting loudly about "this head office stupidity."

> Give us our due—we know the product and we know the customers. The distributors carry a very broad range of products of which ours is only one. There's little incentive for them to learn about our product in depth nor to understand the specific needs of our customers. That's where we add value that a distributor can't.

Jack Semper, the national sales manager (automobile) on one of his monthly visits to the branch, spent four hours with Ekstein trying to put across the reasons for the new policy. Semper left the branch with the impression that he had been successful; however the moment he had left Ekstein stormed into the general office and started upbraiding his staff. Speaking in a loud voice that could be heard all over the office he said that somebody was carrying tales about him to the head

office and if he ever found out who it was he would fire them.

> Disloyalty in the branch is unforgivable, we can't have our people here reporting every moan and groan to the head office. It creates a sense of unease; you can't speak freely because someone's spying on you. Spying is the lowest form of company life and I'll root it out in this branch if it's the last thing I do.

CARTER: THE SPECIAL ACCOUNTS MANAGER

Among Ekstein's staff was John Carter, 31, who held the position of special accounts manager for the area. Carter had been a strong supporter of the new policy and had often argued with Ekstein about it. "We seemed to go round and round in circles, arguing about what I could or couldn't do. The basis of the argument seemed quite simple to me, Peter didn't want to acknowledge my promotion to S.A.M. and wasn't willing to part with any authority. He fought like a tiger to hold on to everything. It was really affecting my ability to do the job I had been given." Carter had been in the office during Semper's visit and he said nothing during Ekstein's tirade.

Two months after the now famous four-hour meeting, reports began filtering through the head office about more and more complaints from distributors in John Carter's sales area. The distributors claimed that they would receive their stocks days after they were expected; or they found that the branch had sold batteries directly to retailers and the public in direct contravention of their agreement with the distributors. Jack Semper called Carter to the telephone about these problems. Carter said that his branch office was giving him little or no support or even cooperation. For example, his expense account was only approved after a week's delay; and when he should have been on the road seeing clients he was told by Ekstein to do three hours of stocktaking at the warehouse. On his next visit to the branch, Semper confronted Ekstein, who simply shrugged his shoulders, put the blame for the first distributor complaint on the freight department and for the second on the fact that very good industrial customers sometimes needed batteries very urgently "and we were just helping them out." Of the complaints of Carter, Ekstein hesitated then said they were nonsense; everyone had to do their share at stocktaking time.

> To be honest with you Jack, John Carter hasn't been too cooperative recently and it's been making the branch very unhappy. He often acts as if he's now the branch manager and I'm some kind of underling. It makes everyone uncomfortable having these confrontations all the time.

On this occasion Jack Semper had been accompanied to the branch by James Dewey, the national sales manager for industrial products. In the past Dewey had been a golf buddy of Peter Ekstein's before the latter had been transferred to the east coast. On the second day of their visit, Dewey set out to visit some important industrial clients with Ekstein, and Jack Semper took the opportunity to walk around the branch office and chat with the staff. The office staff told him how unhappy they were working for Ekstein. "He treats us like dirt," one typist said. "He never has a good word for anyone," a records clerk told Semper. "He thinks that because the branch is a long way from the head office he can do what he likes and to hell with the rules," said one of the technical support staff.

Semper took some of the sales staff to lunch and what he heard made him increasingly concerned. To him it appeared that Ekstein had always been insensitive to staff; however, with the slowdown in business, pay raises had become smaller and fewer staff had to shoulder a greater burden of work; together with the change in marketing policy, Ekstein had appeared to become even less sensitive to his subordinates' needs.

HEAD OFFICE ACTION

Semper felt that this problem was serious enough to discuss with the personnel vice president, Keith Kenny, in the head office. After discussing it, they agreed that the situation warranted Kenny's personal involvement. Peter Ekstein had a good track record and knew his job thoroughly, as well as having a reputation for very successful customer relations. To lose him would be bad for the company in the area, yet Semper felt decisive action was needed. The next week Kenny flew down to the branch with the marketing vice president, Dewey not being available at the time. Before their arrival they had asked Ekstein if they could interview each member of the branch office staff personally and spent the day do-

ing this. Each staff member was invited into an office where Kenny and the marketing VP sat. During the interviews all of them said that they were quite happy and contented working under Peter Ekstein. They denied any suggestion of Ekstein being autocratic or insensitive. The marketing VP and Kenny decided to do nothing after this visit.

On his next monthly visit, Jack Semper spoke to various staff members while Ekstein was seeing a client; he asked them the reason for telling the two vice presidents quite different views from those they had expressed so forcibly to him. The answer was unanimous; they were all in fear of their jobs and each felt that if he or she alone spoke out about Ekstein, the vice presidents would be bound to quote that person, whose job from then on would be in jeopardy. No one was prepared to take that risk.

Two days after returning to the head office, Semper had a call from John Carter to say that he wanted to hand in his resignation because he couldn't work with Ekstein any longer. It was only a matter of time, Semper felt as he put the telephone down, before more resignations would start to come in from Ekstein's branch.

STEP 2: Prepare the case for class discussion.

STEP 3: Answer the following questions, individually, in small groups, or with the entire class, as directed by your instructor.

DESCRIPTION
1. Describe the organization's structure prior to 1988 in terms of centralization versus decentralization, chain of command, span of control, division of labor, and coordinating mechanisms.
2. Classify the organization as functional, market-oriented, integrated, or other form.
3. Describe the organization's structure after 1988 in terms of centralization versus decentralization, chain of command, span of control, division of labor, and coordinating mechanisms.
4. Classify the new organization as functional, market-oriented, integrated, or other form.

DIAGNOSIS
5. Evaluate the appropriateness of both the old and new structures.

6. How does the new structure respond to information-processing needs?
7. Do you think the reorganization was justified? Why or why not?
8. Why did the new structure cause a problem for John Carter?

PRESCRIPTION
9. What additional changes are required?

ACTION
10. Was the process used to redesign the organization and then implement the changes effective? What costs and benefits resulted?

STEP 4: Discussion. Answer the following questions, individually, in small groups, or with the entire class, as directed by your instructor:

1. Describe the changes instituted at the Black Box Company.
2. To what problems did the reorganization respond?
3. Did the reorganization help solve these problems? Why or why not?
4. What problems did the reorganization create?
5. What changes are still needed?

This case of the Research Department at IESE was prepared by Professor Patrick A. Miller. It is intended to be used as a basis for class discussion rather than to illustrate either effective or ineffective handling of an administrative situation. Copyright © 1989, IESE.

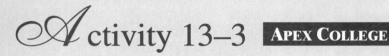

$\mathscr{A}$ctivity 13–3   APEX COLLEGE

STEP 1: Read the following information about Apex College.

Apex College clears its students for promotion or graduation each term. Currently it has the organizational structure shown in Figure 13–12. The student-record clerks record all grades received. The transcript-approval clerks compare student transcripts to course and credit requirements for each grade. Billing clerks check the arithmetic on the students' bills and enter correct charges and credits on the students' accounts. Loan clerks check to ensure that all loan requirements are met. Cashier clerks examine the students' financial status to authorize promotion.

STEP 2: Answer the following questions, individually, in small groups, or with the entire class, as directed by your instructor.

DESCRIPTION
1. Describe the division of labor.
2. Describe the coordinating mechanisms used.
3. What method of organizing is used?

DIAGNOSIS
4. What kinds of problems does this type of organization solve? create?
5. Is this the most effective kind of organization?

PRESCRIPTION
6. What changes would you recommend?

STEP 3: Discussion. In small groups or with the class as a whole, share your answers to the above questions. Then answer the following:

1. What symptoms suggest a problem exists?
2. What problems exist in the case?
3. What theories and concepts help explain the problems?
4. How can the problems be corrected?
5. Are the actions likely to be effective?

FIGURE 13–12   *Organizational chart for Apex College*

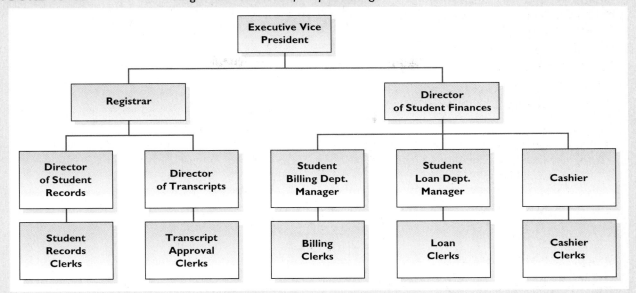

Activity 13–4   MAGNACOMP, INC.

STEP 1:   Read the following description of Magnacomp, Inc.

In this exercise you are operating as members of a work team producing Magnaunits. These are assembled from subassemblies and these subassemblies have to be built from smaller units.

The job of your team is to work together to assemble the final product "Z" at the lowest cost and with acceptable quality. Product cost is measured by the total employee-minutes required to produce the product. The following labor cost schedule is the basis for computing

NUMBER OF MEMBERS	COST IN $/ EMPLOYEE/MINUTE
3	100
4	125
5	150
6	175
7	200
8	225
9	265
10	305

the total cost for a team completing the exercise with an acceptable quality answer.

Thus, a team completing the task successfully in 15 minutes with five members would have a total cost of $150 \times 5 \times 15 = \$11,250$.

Quality is determined by the accuracy of the answer. Deviations greater than ± 10 percent will not be acceptable, and a new answer must be computed.

The assembly process is straightforward and there are no tricks in the method.

A deck of cards corresponding to individual parts will be distributed to each company by the instructor. They are identical for each company. These cards, representing raw materials coming into the plant, are in a random order. Operation cards also accompany the individual parts cards. Each part is coded by a letter–number combination. Before the parts can be assembled, various indicated computations must be performed. The parts can then be assembled into subassemblies by performing the appropriate operations.

Work flow is indicated by flowcharts, Figures 13–13 and 13–14, which show how assemblies are formed. They do not show the combining of operations. The operations necessary to combine subassemblies are

FIGURE 13–13   *Magnacomp, Inc., project 1, flow chart for manufacturing*

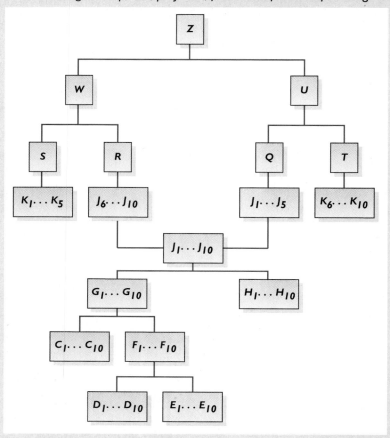

indicated on the operations cards included with the parts, and in the description of operations in the tables for Project 1 and Project 2.

The team determining the value of "Z" within ± 10 percent at the lowest cost will be declared the winner. If ties in cost occur, the team with the most accurate answer will win.

Two trials will be run: Project 1 and Project 2.

STEP 2: Team leaders will be selected. There will be three to five teams depending on class size. Each leader in turn will select two assistants from the class. Each team will then have 10 minutes for a private preliminary planning session. During this time decisions should be made as to an initial organizational structure and an operations plan should be formulated. At this time each team should estimate its manpower needs for the simu-

Magnacomp, Inc., Project 1

OPERATIONS

1. $Z = W + U$
2. $U = Q \div T$
3. $W = S \div R$
4. $S = K_1 + \ldots + K_5$
5. $R = J_6 + \ldots + J_{10}$
6. $Q = J_1 + \ldots + J_5$
7. $T = K_6 + \ldots + K_{10}$
8. $J_1 \ldots J_{10} = G_1 - H_1, G_2 - H_2, \ldots G_{10} - H_{10}$
9. $G_1 \ldots G_{10} = F_1 \times C_1, F_2 \times C_2, \ldots F_{10} \times C_{10}$
10. $F_1 \ldots F_{10} = D_1 - E_1, D_2 - E_2, \ldots D_{10} - E_{10}$
11. Where $C_1 \ldots C_{10}; E_1 \ldots E_{10}, D_1 \ldots D_{10}; H_1 \ldots H_{10}$ and $K_1 \ldots K_{10}$ are numerical values.

FIGURE 13–14   *Magnacomp, Inc., project 2, flow chart for manufacturing*

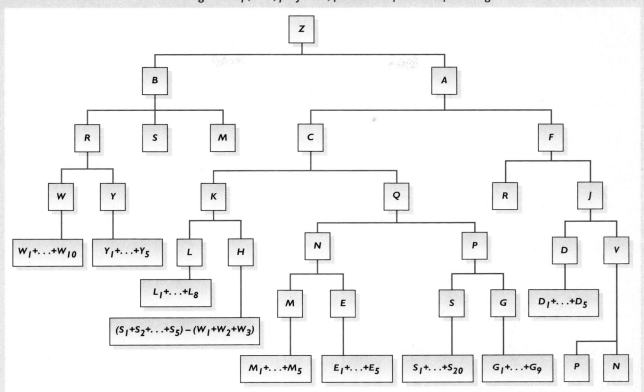

Magnacomp, Inc., Project 2

OPERATIONS

1. $Z = A + B$
2. $B = R - S + M$
3. $R = W \times Y$
4. $W = W_1 + \ldots + W_{10}$
5. $Y = Y_1 + \ldots + Y_5$
6. $A = C \div F$
7. $C = Q \times K$
8. $K = L \div H$
9. $L = L_1 + \ldots + L_8$
10. $H = (S_1 + \ldots + S_5) - (W_1 + W_2 + W_3)$
11. $Q = P \div N$
12. $N = M - E$
13. $P = S + G$
14. $M = M_1 + \ldots + M_5$
15. $E = E_1 + \ldots + E_5$
16. $S = S_1 + \ldots + S_{20}$
17. $G = G_1 + \ldots + G_9$
18. $F = R \div J$
19. $J = D - V$
20. $D = D_1 + \ldots + D_5$
21. $V = P - N$
22. Where $G_1 \ldots G_9; S_1 \ldots S_{20};$ $M_1 \ldots M_5; E_1; \ldots E_5; L_1 \ldots L_8;$ $W_1 \ldots W_{10}; Y_1 \ldots Y_5;$ and $D_1 \ldots D_5$ are numerical values.

lation. Each team will be allowed to select additional persons for the simulation, and they will be selected at the end of this planning period. Care should be taken in selecting additional personnel, since the evaluation of performance of the group will be affected by the size of the team. If the team is understaffed it may not be competitive with the other teams in the exercise, and if it is overstaffed the cost of additional personnel will reduce the efficiency measure of the team.

STEP 3: The selection of additional team personnel will occur. Those class members not selected will act as observers and report to the class during the discussion period.

STEP 4: A second planning session will now be conducted with the complete team. You will have ten minutes.

STEP 5: Begin the exercise. Complete the Project 1 phase of the Magnacomp, Inc., simulation. You will have twenty minutes.

STEP 6: At the conclusion of Project 1 a ten-minute period will be provided to allow each team to analyze its mode of operations and make changes if necessary.

STEP 7: Complete the Project 2 phase of the exercise. You will have twenty minutes.

STEP 8: Discussion. After the exercise each team should analyze its mode of operation, its effectiveness, the organizational structure developed, the communication channels, and the advantages and disadvantages of the system employed.

DESCRIPTION

1. Prepare an organizational chart of your company.
2. Is this the initial form of organization you used? If you modified your initial structure, when, how, and why?
3. How did each member feel about his or her role in the simulation? Why?
4. Do differences exist between the various teams in the exercise with respect to these questions?
5. How was the team's performance? How does it compare with the other teams?

DIAGNOSIS

6. Can differences be explained in terms of organizational structure?
7. How was the division of labor, coordination, and communication handled in the organization?

PRESCRIPTION

8. What changes would have improved the organization's functioning?

Reprinted by permission from *Managing for Organizational Effectiveness: An Experimental Approach*, by F.E. Finch, H.R. Jones, and J.A. Letterer (New York: McGraw-Hill, 1976), pp. 82–84.

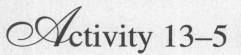

Activity 13–5 — HOSPITAL DEPARTMENTAL CONSOLIDATION

STEP 1: Read the following description.

Janet Johns is the administrator of Suburban Memorial Hospital, a 275-bed hospital in an upper class suburb located in the western states.

Mrs. Johns recently asked the new assistant administrator, Sam Donalds, to investigate whether a consolidation of the EKG, Pulmonary Function, and Cardio-Pulmonary Rehabilitation Departments would result in a significant savings to the hospital.

BACKGROUND

The three departments do basically the same types of patient tests. As medicine has progressed, there has been a movement away from static (at rest) testing to dynamic (in-motion) testing. Dynamic testing is used in the EKG Department for tests on the heart, in the Pulmonary Function Department for lung tests, and in the Cardio-Pulmonary Rehabilitation Department for both heart and lung.

At present there is a duplication of services and equipment among the three departments at Suburban Memorial. In addition, three separate technicians are employed as well as three different part-time physicians who work on a percentage basis, according to the volume of work.

The EKG and Pulmonary Function Departments make a significant contribution to Suburban's revenue. The contribution margin of Pulmonary Function has been 80 percent (for every $100 earned, the hospital spends only $20 to earn it) and that of EKG has been 60 percent.

Revenues for each department have been as follows:

DEPARTMENT	ANNUAL REVENUE	CONTRIBUTION MARGIN
EKG	$360,000	60%
Pulmonary Function	$520,000	80%
Cardio-Pulmonary (new department, less than one year)	$80,000	unknown

The total annual revenue of Suburban Memorial is $16.1 million and the net income is $1.3 million. Mr. Donalds had calculated that a departmental consolidation could initially save the hospital $100,000 by selling duplicated equipment. In addition, the annual savings would amount to the following:

$44,000	personnel costs (fewer technicians needed, etc.)
$15,000	ordering and supplies reduction (no duplication, less ordering)
$125,000	reduced physician fees (only one physician would be needed)
$16,000	plant and facilities (can lease out space not needed after consolidation)
$200,000	Total

Therefore, the annual savings, in essence additional revenue, would be $200,000 in addition to the initial $100,000 for the selling of equipment.

PHYSICIANS

Dr. Bartl, head of Pulmonary Function, is responsible for 80 percent of the pulmonary admissions to the hospital and about 4.7 percent of the total admissions. He is an extremely popular physician, attracting respiratory cases from well outside the normal service area of Suburban Memorial.

Dr. Neuman, head of EKG, controls 20 percent of the hospital's cardiac/internal medicine cases. She admits about 30 percent of the hospital's patients.

Finally, the head of the new Cardio-Pulmonary Rehabilitation Department, Dr. Hermann, controls 100 percent of those cases that at this point represent a negligible percentage of the hospital's patient revenue.

All three physicians have more or less equal support from the medical staff.

Ms. Johns is wondering what to do about the physicians if she decides to go through with the consolidation. One of the three physicians would have to be chosen (with a new reimbursement contract) to head this new department, or perhaps a new, salaried physician could be brought in. The combined workload would still be less than full time.

However, Ms. Johns sees several problems with either of those two alternatives. First of all, the physicians who would be "excluded" from this new department might become resentful and start admitting their out-of-service-area patients to other hospitals. Ms. Johns and Mr. Donalds have estimated a 25 per-cent probability that the three physicians would do so, which would mean a possible loss to the hospital of 15 percent of these physicians' admissions.

Ms. Johns has asked Mr. Donalds to prepare a report of the situation, including his recommendations, which will be discussed at the next management council meeting.

STEP 2: Assume you are Mr. Donalds, what would you recommend? Prepare the type of report Ms. Johns has asked for as if it were going to be presented to the management council.

STEP 3: Assuming the council votes for consolidation, prepare another report outlining your recommended strategy, which would result in the least amount of alienation and maximum cooperation.

STEP 4: Discussion. Share the designs. What are the advantages and disadvantages of each one. What key elements should be included in the design?

From D. Marcic, *Organizational Behavior: Experiences and Cases,* 3rd ed. (St. Paul: West, 1992).

Activity 13-6 — THE JOB-GETTER ENTERPRISE

STEP I: Read the following description of the Job-Getter Enterprise.

The Job-Getter Enterprise is a start-up publishing firm. The publication produced by the firm, the **JOB GETTER,** is a weekly magazine that publishes listings of available jobs in the area. The magazine is sold in local convenience stores, campus bookstores, and through vending machine newsracks, and it is distributed throughout northern California.

The business has been operating for three years and shows great promise. But the firm has yet to generate a regular profit. The founder, Martin Manicot, is convinced that his firm has grown to the point where he needs some help in redesigning his firm. He has asked you to serve as a team of consultants to help him redesign his organization. Here are some of the issues he wants you to consider.

THE ISSUES

Three key issues plague this entrepreneurial start-up:

1. Obtaining a variety of timely job listings is difficult. Job listings are advertised jobs that appear in the publication. If job listings are not timely, repeat sales for the magazine decline. Customers are unwilling to purchase the publication unless the job listings meet their needs, are timely, and are local.

2. Circulation and distribution remain a problem. Local distributors are not willing to carry an untested publication on their newsracks. Circulation has been low because the number of locations in which the new publication was sold were few. This is a problem because circulation is traditionally a key factor in attracting advertising for the publication.

3. The success of the publication depends on the number of advertisements sold. Full- and half-page advertisements account for the bulk of revenue. Advertisers include companies such as the local retail stores, employment placement agencies, food-service firms, manufacturing firms, and others who have continuous needs for employment. However, advertisers are reluctant to purchase advertising space unless circulation is sufficiently widespread.

4. Turnover of sales personnel plagues the business. Manicot has continually hired salespeople to sell advertising space. Once they realize the task is difficult, they leave for other jobs posted in the magazine. He has hired a number of college students part time as salespeople; the continual drain of personnel out the door has taken considerable time away from Manicot's other duties as he spends most of his time training new salespeople and less of his time on increasing circulation.

It is the task of the new publication to identify and publish timely job listings, while simultaneously increasing circulation and distribution to attract competitive advertising space.

THE DEPARTMENTS AND FUNCTIONS

The key functions of the new enterprise are summarized as follows:

1. *Sales:* Selling job listings and advertising space.
2. *Circulation and distribution:* Making the publication available in as many locations as possible; picking up and delivering the publication on a weekly basis.
3. *Production:* Putting together the weekly job listings, advertising space, formatting and proofreading, and printing the magazines.

Sales encompasses two categories: (1) job listings, listed for free in the publication and (2) advertising space, for companies who wish to advertise particular positions or continual employment needs. Job listings are gathered by telemarketing (calling local companies to determine if they want to list a job opening). Advertising space is sold through telemarketing and on-site visits. Typically, a company is contacted to determine if they would like to list available jobs for free. After the company receives a response from the publication (for example, twenty applicants say they saw the job listed in the magazine), that company is approached to see if they might like to purchase advertising space.

Circulation and distribution involve making the publication as widely available as possible. Currently approximately 700 outlets carry the magazine. There is potential for as many as 1,500 outlets or more. Owners of local convenience stores, college bookstores, grocery stores, and other likely locations must be visited regularly to obtain permission to distribute the magazine. Store owners receive a small percentage (10 percent) of every issue sold as an incentive. In addition, the publication is distributed through newsracks in urban areas. The magazine must be picked up and delivered to all these locations on a weekly basis so that timely information is distributed.

Production involves printing the magazine—typing the job listings, designing advertisements, and proofreading each issue. The issue is compiled by use of a graphics computer and then sent to a local print shop for presswork and binding.

THE JOBS AND THE PEOPLE

Currently, seven people are employed in sales jobs. Salespeople have been hired on a part-time basis, with only the sales manager, Jennifer, and one other salesperson hired full-time. Full-time salespeople concentrate on on-site visitations for advertising sales; they are paid part salary ($100 per week) and part commission (25 percent of the advertising space sold). Part-time salespeople concentrate primarily on telemarketing sales; they are paid minimum wage on an hourly basis ($4.25 an hour) and receive a 10 percent commission. One employee, Greg, serves as the circulation manager. He is responsible for increasing circulation by improving the number of outlets that carry the publication. The circulation manager is a salaried position, paid $325 per week with no commission. Another employee has been hired on a full-time basis to supervise the drivers who distribute and pick up the publication. This individual is paid a single sum for the distribution and collection of each issue during the month. The drivers who distribute the publication are hired part-time; currently there are five drivers, paid on a hourly basis.

Two part-time secretaries are responsible for the production of the magazine. Their duties involve inputting the job listings, designing advertising space, and proofreading each issue. The production secretaries are paid on an hourly basis and are offered flextime hours to complete their job tasks.

THE PROBLEMS

Manicot has found that his current organization design is not working. The salespeople concentrate on telemarketing (which can be done easily from home) more than on-site visitations to sell advertising space. Advertising sales are much lower than projected. For those salespeople who have attempted on-site visits to sell advertising space, much of their activity has centered around locations close to their homes, rather than larger targeted sales areas. The geographic span includes a territory of over 200 miles, with the Monterey Bay area as one location, Sacramento and points east as another area, and San Francisco and the Silicon Valley–San Jose basin as a third (see Figure 13–15). Manicot would like to expand into the Napa Valley area north of San Francisco as well, but he can't seem to get his salespeople to concentrate on that area.

The sales manager, Jennifer, complains that she cannot concentrate on sales, telemarketing, training new salespeople, and promotion all at the same time. She recognizes that in a small business it is often necessary to perform more than one task, but the combination of all four tasks is simply too much. As a result, her job performance suffers. Because her pay is directly tied to her sales, she spends most of her time selling rather than training or working on promotional activities.

The circulation manager, Greg, complains that his territory is too large for one individual. This is complicated by his other responsibilities, such as supervising Alfred, who oversees the truck drivers who distribute the publication. He says there is enough stress in his job battling major distributors who sell publications en masse to local stores. The geographic area for circulation is as dispersed as the sales territory. Additionally, he maintains he cannot sell the publication to new vendors until it is proven via circulation. Circulation will not be boosted until customers get to know the product, and are willing to purchase it on a repeat sales basis.

The distribution manager, Alfred, reports in only once every two weeks. He seems to want to do more than simple distribution and coordination of the drivers, but Manicot is unclear what that could be. Alfred is motivated, interested in earning more money, and a good

FIGURE 13–15   *San Francisco Bay area*

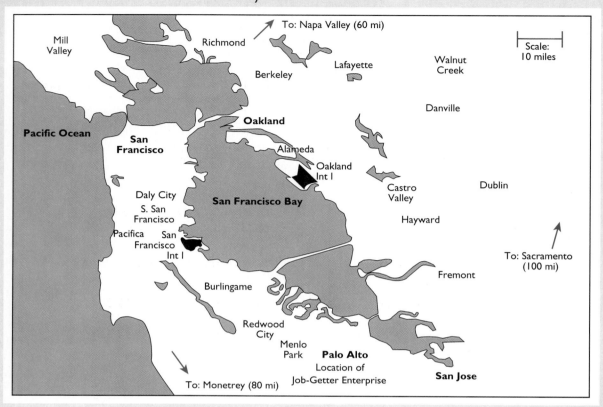

coworker. He has mentioned an interest in developing circulation or helping with sales from time to time, but as a part-time worker, it is unclear how much he really could contribute.

The production staff works primarily at home, and Manicot is displeased with the quality of their proofreading. Some of the listings were actually omitted in the last issue by mistake, causing delays in the timeliness of the information. Occasionally, new advertisers have been omitted from the publication, causing delays in revenue.

Turnover has plagued the sales ranks. Four part-timers and one full-timer have left the company during the past three months. Over the past three years, Manicot has lost a circulation manager and two other members of his production staff. Although turnover is to be expected in a small business, each time someone leaves, a new person must be trained properly. New employees cannot work to full capacity until they have been on the

job at least two full months. As a result, Manicot always seems to be running behind on his sales and circulation objectives.

Furthermore, Manicot is doing virtually everything himself—training new salespeople, performing on-site visits, proofreading the magazine, manning the phones, and obtaining new vendors for distribution. He feels he needs to create clear-cut jobs that specify the functions and responsibilities so that he can do what he really needs to do for the business—strategic planning and obtaining financing to capitalize the business. If he could get additional financing, he could afford to pay his personnel more competitively, hire more salespeople full-time, and reduce turnover.

STEP 2: Examine the current organizational chart for the Job-Getter Enterprise (Figure 13–16). Then, in groups of three to six people, design an organizational

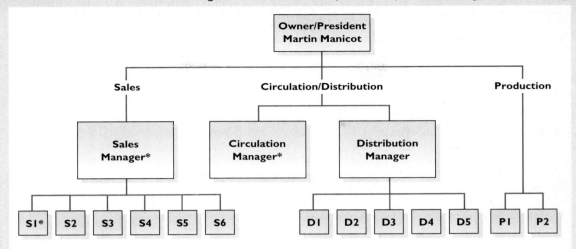

Financial Information: The Job–Getter Enterprise

Revenue per month:

Approximately 4,000 issues sold at $1 per issue: @ .70 return*	$2,800
Approximately 10 full pages of advertising space sold per month at $350 per page (after commissions paid)	$3,500
Total Revenue	$6,300

Expenses per month:

Office expenses (including office rental, five telephone lines, supplies)	$2,000
Production costs per issue for printing (20,000 issues printed)	$1,400

Compensation Costs:

Sales: $100 per week plus 20% commission	$ 400
Telemarketing: Minimum wage ($4.25 per hour) plus 10% commission. Total $2,600 per month	$2,600
Circulation: $325 per week, no commission/ $1,400 per month	$1,400
Production: Minimum wage ($4.25 per hour)/ $200 per month	$ 200
Delivery: Minimum wage ($4.25 per hour)/ $1,100 per month	$1,110
Total month expenses:	$9,800

Net loss	($3,500)

Number of current locations: 800

*.30 cents goes to vendors

chart that you feel is most appropriate to solve the problems of the Job-Getter Enterprise. Then draw the chart, complete with reporting relationships and functions that describe how you feel that Job-Getter Enterprise should be organized. Be certain that your chart includes spaces for individual position responsibilities, similar to the one drawn for the current Job-Getter Enterprise organization.

STEP 3: Discussion. In small groups or with the entire class, answer the following questions:

1. Which organizational design did you choose?
2. What are the advantages and disadvantages of this design?

Excerpted and reprinted with permission from L.A. Mainiero and C.L. Tromley, *Developing Managerial Skills in Organizational Behavior,* 2nd ed. (Englewood Cliffs, N.J.: Prentice-Hall, 1994).

Activity 13–7   LOGITECH INTERNATIONAL SA (B) CASE

STEP 1: Read the Logitech International SA (B) case.

"Structure is there to support the growth of the company; moreover, a company is not really something that you can put on a piece of paper; it is something which breathes, which lives," stated Daniel Borel, chairman of Logitech International SA.

The people who founded Logitech in 1981 really had two aims—to participate in the fast-growing personal computer industry by providing software and hardware products; and to create an organization that would span the world imbued with their own sense of excitement, aggressive opportunity seeking, and flexibility. The word "flexible," in fact, pervaded every aspect of the company. Words such as "flat structure," "open-door policy," "team work," "employee participation," "networks of small groups" became building blocks of the organization.

However, when the business and international strategy of the company was being reviewed in preparation for the 1990s, the question had come up: Was Logitech's organizational structure still appropriate? This question was debated with characteristic informality, with the result that there was no consensus on whether or not any change was even needed.

Among the founders, Giacomo Marini was the only person who had previously worked for large international companies (IBM and Olivetti). Being the chief operating officer, he felt the need for a more formal structure and had been instrumental in designing whatever structure the company did have in 1989–1990. Neither Borel nor Zappacosta felt any urgency in this re-

gard. "Zappacosta is our visionary, our long-term thinker who wants to make sure the business is on the right track," Borel explained. In turn, one of his colleagues described Borel with a different compliment: "Borel is for action yesterday, he is a doer."

HOW THE ORGANIZATION EVOLVED

The fact that Logitech virtually started as a multinational company influenced the way its organization evolved.

In 1982, the company had two sites—Switzerland and the United States. For personal reasons, Daniel Borel (chairman) lived in Switzerland, while Zappacosta (chief executive) and Marini (head of operations) were located in the United States. Mutual empathy, frequent travel, and an electronic mail system linked the two sites.

When the mouse business started in 1983, the Swiss group became the principal development unit. Since the main, if not only, market for the device was California, all the marketing effort was concentrated there. Borel, who was engaged in all aspects of the business, often traveled to the United States for extended periods of time between 1983 and 1987 and had a formal role in the United States as head of marketing and sales. (Figure 13–17 shows the organization of the U.S. company in September 1983.)

Meanwhile, Jean-Luc Mazzone, one of the earliest collaborators, started assembling a European team in Switzerland. With Borel absent in the United States and later in Taiwan, Mazzone was actually the chief operating officer for Europe. He looked after manufacturing and sales, as well as finance. The latter function—

team was also created to assist this "office in planning, control, and communication activities.

With Daniel Borel as chairman, taking care of special projects and acting as group coordinator, the office of the president consisted of Zappacosta, president and CEO of the group, and Marini, executive vice president and chief operating officer. All geographical areas and worldwide functions would report to this "office," with direct reporting to Marini. Moreover, this "office," in addition to group-level management responsibility, had direct management responsibility for the U.S. site and its corresponding geographic area. (Figure 13–19 provides an organization chart of the new structure.)

In terms of their respective roles, Zappacosta would "concentrate on the activities of setting directions, making the synthesis of strategies, identifying and setting corporate goals." Marini would "concentrate on translating corporate directions and goals into operating plans, initiating and controlling their execution, and exercising the day-to-day management process with the

TABLE 13–2   *Logitech International SA*

GROWTH IN HEADCOUNT (PERMANENT AND TEMPORARY) BY LOCATION (MARCH 31 OF EACH YEAR)						
	1982	1984	1986	1988	1990	1991
Switzerland[1]	2	10	40	82	110[2]	123
United States[1]	5	20	87	228	378	456
Ireland					75	153
Taiwan[1]				141	400	712
Sales Offices	3	3		12	17	26
	10	33	127	463	980	1470

[1]Includes country sales offices.
[2]Closed production in Switzerland, moved to Ireland.

Logitech Companies

HEADCOUNT BY FUNCTIONAL AREA (FOR PERIOD ENDING MARCH 31, 1991)				
FUNCTIONAL AREA	FAR EAST	NORTH AMERICA	EUROPE	TOTAL
	PERMANENT	PERMANENT	PERMANENT	PERMANENT
Administration	32	61	47	140
Sales	10	60	50	120
Marketing	4	47	29	80
R&D/Engineering	42	83	45	170
Manufacturing—Direct	487	126	80	693
■ Indirect	58	30	23	111
■ Staff	82	49	25	156
Total	715	456	299	1,470

TABLE 13–2 *(continued)*   *Logitech International SA*

DISTRIBUTION OF R&D AND ENGINEERING PERSONNEL BY LOCATION AND DISCIPLINE (MARCH 31, 1991)

Discipline	Europe	North America	Far East	
1. Software	11	21	9	
2. Electronics Engineering	13	17	11	
3. Optics	1	1	0	
4. Mechanical Engineering	2	14	7	
5. Other (Manufacturing, Engineering, Quality Assurance, product management)	8	30	15	
Totals	45	83	42	170

operating managers." To symbolize their joint role, Zappacosta and Marini moved their offices (in the United States) next to each other, whereas previously they had been at opposite ends of the building.

To assist and complement the chairman and the office of the president in top-level management activities of the group, the executive management committee (formed in 1989) was expanded in April 1990 to include—apart from the three founders—Morgan (chief operating officer, Europe), Fu (senior vice president and general manager, Far East), and Mazzone (vice president, strategic marketing for the group, but based in Europe).

The main organizational units, however, continued to be the areas. Logitech retained its traditional policy of giving local management at each site full profit and loss responsibility.

For cohesiveness at a global level, some executives were, however, given worldwide mandates for certain functions. The worldwide functional manager was not really expected to direct operations; rather, he would coordinate and provide team leadership for the particular function, working closely with site managers responsible for their function at the local level. The latter had a dotted line reporting to the worldwide functional manager and direct reporting to the site chief executive or general manager. In most cases, the worldwide func-

tional manager resided in the United States, but this was not a requirement.

Functional managers with worldwide responsibility and their locations were: Morgan (finance and administration, Switzerland); D'Ettore (human resources, U.S.); Righi (sales, U.S.); Van Natta (corporate communications, U.S.); Mills (quality, U.S.); Marini (engineering, U.S.); and Zappacosta (marketing, U.S.). Both Marini and Zappacosta were "acting" heads of their functions, until someone else was appointed.[1] (Figure 13–20 shows the allocation of worldwide functional responsibility and Figure 13–21 the structure of the U.S. company.)

LOGITECH'S VALUES AND CULTURE

"We work in one place, the globe." This simple phrase stated the business spirit and the cosmopolitan attitude at Logitech—the basis of its founders' beliefs from the beginning. The composition of the executive management committee—Borel (Swiss), Fu (Chinese), Marini (Italian), Mazzone (Swiss), Morgan (American), and Zappacosta (Italian)—not only tangibly expressed the company's philosophy, but guaranteed that different ge-

---

[1] Recently, a vice president for engineering, Rick Money, was appointed, and Fabio Righi took on the marketing role as vice president, sales and marketing.

FIGURE 13–19 *Logitech, Inc. (USA): organizational structure (April 1990)*

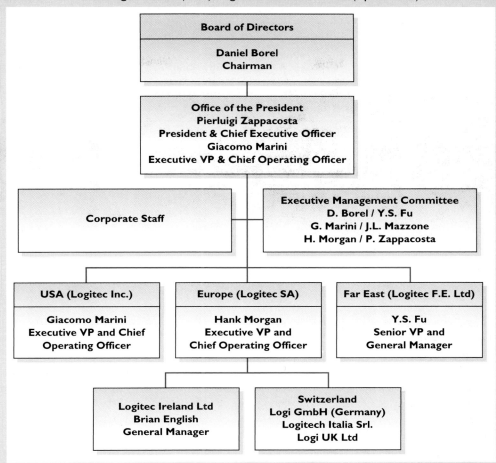

Board of Directors
Daniel Borel
Chairman

Office of the President
Pierluigi Zappacosta
President & Chief Executive Officer
Giacomo Marini
Executive VP & Chief Operating Officer

Corporate Staff

Executive Management Committee
D. Borel / Y.S. Fu
G. Marini / J.L. Mazzone
H. Morgan / P. Zappacosta

USA (Logitec Inc.)
Giacomo Marini
Executive VP and Chief
Operating Officer

Europe (Logitec SA)
Hank Morgan
Executive VP and
Chief Operating Officer

Far East (Logitec F.E. Ltd)
Y.S. Fu
Senior VP and
General Manager

Logitec Ireland Ltd
Brian English
General Manager

Switzerland
Logi GmbH (Germany)
Logitech Italia Srl.
Logi UK Ltd

ographic and cultural perspectives would inevitably be advocated within Logitech.

Coupled with its cosmopolitan make-up, Logitech's management reflected youthfulness, daring, and a spirit of adventure, a combination frequently found in high-tech start-ups with excellent results. At Logitech in 1991, the emphasis was on small groups that met "horizontally" for particular issues and projects; direct contact between senior management and employees was promoted; employees were urged to be more involved in running Logitech; and, the one thing to be abhorred was formal policies. As the head of administration, Bavaud stated, "We don't want a police state at Logitech."

Logitech's basic values consisted of a belief in people, trust, caring for the feelings of others, and the ability of everyone to do what is right. The metaphor often used to describe the organization was "a family that has bridged national differences."

Although at the time this case was written, no formal mission statement existed, it was felt that if one were ever created, it should reflect the fun, the creativity, and the responsibility experienced by each member of Logitech. Since Logitech's key descriptors and the usual format of a mission statement did not seem compatible, the question was raised: Should Logitech's statement be a written document? Or perhaps a cartoon or even a videotape?

The evolution of the Logitech logo also illustrated the company's self-image. Until 1988, Logitech's logo was a square surrounding a circle divided into four equal parts; the "framing" square represented Logitech's engineering background, the circle indicated its

FIGURE 13–20 *Logitech, International: group level functions (April 1990)*

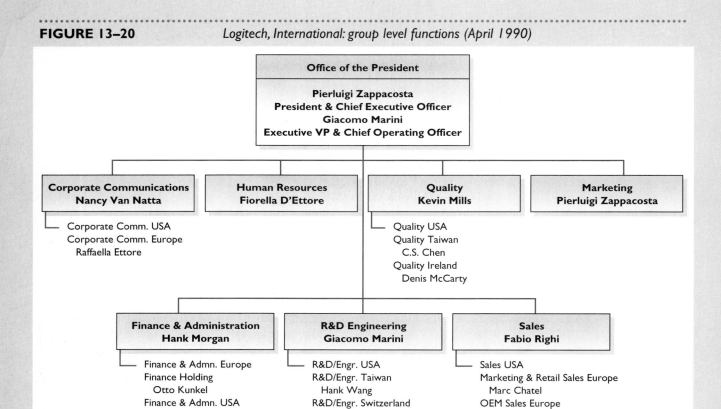

flexibility, and the darkened square represented the letter "L" in Logitech.

After the company went into the consumer market, the logo was redesigned to reflect the company's values and its vision of humanizing the computer: the irregular green shape represented the company structure, present yet enabling Logitech to "break away," to look toward the future and be innovative; the eye in the center represented the human aspect of the company, both in terms of its attitude toward employees as well as humanizing computer use; the red arrow pointing top right symbolized Logitech's moving forward, leading the change, while the three black lines represented the company's flexibility, coordination, and equilibrium.

ORGANIZATIONAL PROCESSES

Despite giving freedom to individuals and groups to pursue their tasks in a creative and responsible manner, no effort was spared to establish links throughout the company.

Communication was one of the important tools used. The electronic mail system, installed in 1982, the same day that Logitech had two locations, was continuously expanded. As Morgan put it, "We send and receive messages or copies of messages from all over the world every day. So we tend to know very quickly what is going on." *Logi News,* an internal newsletter, and formal meetings were other ways of keeping people involved.

Setting overall direction took place at two levels—the executive committee and the functions. The executive committee met every two months, with the discussions going on for a long time, sometimes over two days. A lot of things would be talked about. Decisions were not always made, but direction nevertheless evolved at these meetings. The decisions that were taken then were communicated and discussed throughout the organization via monthly company meetings at each site.

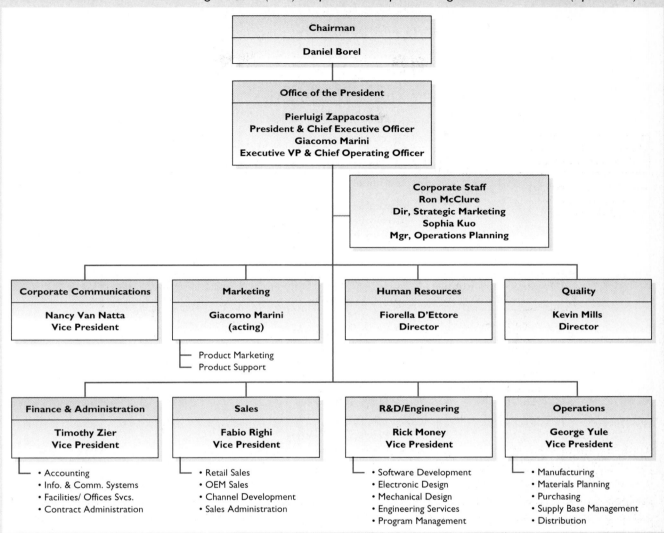

At the operational level, functional heads from each site met approximately once a year in order to coordinate policies and practices worldwide. Depending on the function, there would be frequent telephone and electronic mail exchanges as well.

In addition to these functional meetings and exchanges, a number of cross-functional, intersite teams were created. The main ones were **project teams** built around the introduction of new products, taking projects from initial development to mass production. (Figure 13–22 reproduces the membership of a recently consti-tuted project led by the U.S. organization.) In 1991, there were some 20 **project teams** with about half led by the U.S. and the remainder by other sites. Marini had coordinated the work done by these teams in the past, but they became the responsibility of the head of engineering, Rick Money, with the organizational restructuring.

The other main area where multifunctional, multisite teams were used was in **product management.** These teams worked to launch new products on the market that also included making competitor assessments, preparing translations and manuals, and designing and

1. United States
   Product Marketing (3)
   Mechanical Engineering (2)
   Cost & Reliability Engineering(3)

   Electrical Engineering
   Software Engineering
   Product QA
   Technical Publications (3)

   Technical Support
   Supply Base Management
   Quality Assurance
   Materials Planning
   Production Engineer
   Test Engineer

2. Logitech Switzerland
   Product Marketing
   Product Management
   Project Planning

3. Logitech Taiwan
   Product Engineering
   Project Planning

4. Logitech Ireland
   Product Engineering
   Project Planning

placing advertisements. In 1991, *product management* teams were being coordinated by Fabio Righi, vice president, sales and marketing.

POLICIES

In June 1988, Logitech went public in Switzerland. Previously, there had been occasional attempts to consolidate the operations worldwide, but they had resembled "exercises" to ascertain what the total entity might look like. A worldwide budget was, in fact, put together for the first time in 1988, enabling Logitech finally to compare "actual" with "budgeted."

It was still not entirely clear where Logitech's HQ was located, although the U.S. unit gradually started to assume that role mainly because, according to Marini, the Silicon Valley played an important role as a lead market, as well as providing Logitech with credibility. In any case, management believed that "headquarters" should provide a "service" rather than a "control" function and should not have the power that most companies normally would give to headquarters.

Each site also had its own policies with no formal "central" coordination. One policy area shared by all the company's locations was human resource management. Although acknowledging local practices and legal requirements, Logitech tended to hire people who would fit into its culture. Potential employees were expected to be flexible, internationally minded, and good team workers. Due to this careful selection process, Logitech had a very low turnover rate, a particularly remarkable achievement given its location in the Silicon Valley.

The company also encouraged transfers between sites. It hoped, thereby, to increase intercultural awareness within the company, decrease friction between sites and increase employee identification with Logitech International, rather than with a particular unit.

THE STRATEGY FOR THE 1990S

The strategy for the 1990s was framed to build on Logitech's evolving competence as a first-rate manufacturer of small electronic devices sold to a wide cross section of computer users. Fulfilling this strategy meant constantly introducing new products, all nevertheless aimed at facilitating access to personal computers. "Our goal," explained Zappacosta, "is to have one or more Logitech products on the desk of every personal computer user." As for the mouse itself, he wanted to transform what had become a commodity product into a fashion statement. "We want people to look at the mouse sitting next to their computer and say, "I like it, it's cool!"

Logitech's expanded business scope was evolving towards the *"senses of the computer."* Whereas the mouse represented the hand and the scanner the eyes—by perceiving 256 shades of grey and eventually color—it was expected that 3D and sound too would provide new avenues for product extension. The company's long-term strategy and outlook was to heighten brand awareness in the mass market, be the volume and share leader in the retail market, fuel growth through continuous product line extensions and innovations, and acquire or partner for competitive advantage.

As for geographical ambitions, Logitech wanted to strengthen its presence and reach into all world markets and be close to its customers. As Borel put it, "Unless you go out on the street, see what your competition is doing, see what is changing every day, you are lost. And it can happen very quickly." Also, compared to the present geographic distribution of sales—North America, 65 percent; Europe, 28 percent; and the Far East, 7 percent—Logitech expected the following distribution over the next few years—North America, 40 percent; Europe, 45 percent (including Eastern Europe); and the Far East, 14 percent.

THE DEBATE ON ORGANIZATION STRUCTURE

The starting point for the debate on organization was at the time of the April 1990 structure. While some managers were satisfied, others wanted to see greater clarity in the reporting relationships. Who, for example, should functional heads really report to, especially when they carried global responsibilities for their function? They would also like to see more effective team *processes* without, however, creating a bureaucratic organization. The engineering function had already set up a seven-man "Engineering Services Group" to oversee quality assurance, alpha and beta testing, cost and reliability, and documentation control. Working in matrix, their role was to make sure the 20 or so project teams maintained adequate standards, especially since that was what OEMs wanted. Similarly, Marini had previously coordinated procurement and operations through inter-site teams, but then in 1991 the company decided to create two new posts—director for strategic procurement and operations planning manager. (Figure 13–23 summarizes their job descriptions.)

Regarding the *project* and *product management* teams, there were two issues: how to make them smaller and less cumbersome; and how to maintain accountability and responsibility at the functional manager level for the tasks being accomplished.

Some people at Logitech felt undisguised nostalgia for the informal networking character of the company's earlier organization. With all the information technology at Logitech's command, they asked: "Why not simply continue as a modern distributed network structure, especially since so many management experts write about its virtues?" Even Borel admitted, "Why can't we operate as fast as we did when we were 20 employees?"

A more general issue was how to preserve Logitech's ability to act as a global company. Although the three founders were the main locus for a global view, they also realized that the company had become too large and complex for them to play this role exclusively. If changing Logitech's organization structure could be a way to meet this challenge, what sort of configuration would be most appropriate?

If Logitech stayed with its present *area* organization—with separate structures for Europe, the Far East, and the United States—it would still be able to focus on different segments (e.g., Taiwan could handle all OEM business), but would lose important synergies in product development and production planning. How, moreover, would business functions be governed and on what basis would competitors be identified?

Another option was to organize by *product technology*—mice and trackman (both sharing pointing device technology), scanning devices, application software, etc. Alternatively, it could organize along *product/market*

FIGURE 13-23   *Logitech Inc.*

Job Descriptions for New Appointments in Operations

Director, Strategic Procurement

As Strategic Procurement Director, you will work closely with the chief operating officer in the formulation and implementation of procurement strategies for LOGITECH manufacturing worldwide. Your major responsibilities will include: establishing, communicating, and maintaining the international procurement policies, working with a global team to implement strategies, providing directives and recommendations to the worldwide procurement groups, identifying areas where multiple sources will be needed, defining strategic commodities and project needs, maintaining a database of strategic commodities, vendors and relevant data, and preparing reports and analyses.

Operations Planning Manager

Reporting directly to the COO, you will be involved in the formulation and implementation of worldwide operations planning and strategy for new products, manufacturing, and distribution. Your job responsibilities will include: developing global manufacturing strategies, allocating manufacturing tasks to worldwide facilities, establishing performance measurements and monitoring the results, analyzing worldwide shipments and forecasts, reviewing operation reports, and preparing site reviews.

segments, such as pointing devices and application software for scanning devices. The latter approach would, at least, maintain the link between hardware and software which groupings along "products" might lose.

Making a choice was not expected to be easy. As Y.S. Fu, the general manager of Logitech Taiwan, explained, "We try to be locally present, this is both our strategy and our strength; we deal with local customers as local people; when IBM's Taiwanese International Procurement Office (IPO) talks to us, they feel they are talking to an independent company; we can make all the decisions, provide all the support; we don't have limitations from Switzerland or the United States, which is different from other foreign companies." A counter argument was found, however, in Borel's example of the way the company worked: "When Logitech Europe launched its Pilot Mouse (for first-time users) in order to combat the Taiwanese, the U.S. did not think an introduction was warranted in that region since there was already a strong presence at the low end. Eventually, the product was introduced at a later date."

Attention also needed to be focused on some *functions.* One such area was procurement. Compared to the current practice of letting each site procure on its own behalf, the idea was to centralize purchasing in order to gain better overall terms for Logitech. By creating several international procurement offices (IPOs)—like at IBM, where staff would be paid a commission on what they could source locally, the hope was to diminish the present dependence on the Far East for components. This would also introduce some competition in the procurement function itself. What would the effect of these IPOs be on Logitech's structure? "You have an IPO in Taiwan—does he report to the local manufacturing site or does he report to a worldwide sourcing organization?" Borel asked.

Finally, another question relating to organizational dimension was whether, and to what extent, the company should begin to set up divisions. Its initial software engineering business had been spun off into a new company—MULTISCOPE, Inc., but so far, Logitech had gone no further toward creating *divisions.*

STEP 2: Prepare the case for class discussion.

STEP 3: Answer the following questions, individually, in small groups, or with the entire class, as directed by your instructor.

DESCRIPTION

1. Describe the organization's structure in 1983, 1986, and 1990 in terms of centralization versus decentralization, chain of command, span of control, division of labor, and coordinating mechanisms.
2. Classify the organization at each of these times as functional, market-oriented, integrated, or other form.

DIAGNOSIS

3. Evaluate the appropriateness of each structure.
4. How does the 1990 structure respond to information-processing needs?
5. Do you think the reorganization in April 1990 was justified? Why or why not?
6. What were the key issues for reorganization after April 1990?

7. What structural prototype best meets the company's needs?

PRESCRIPTION

8. What additional changes should be made?

ACTION

9. What issues must Logitech's management consider in implementing these changes?

STEP 4: Discussion. Answer the following questions, individually, in small groups, or with the entire class, as directed by your instructor:

1. Describe the evolution of the structure of Logitech.
2. To what problems did each reorganization respond?
3. Did the reorganization help solve these problems? Why or why not?
4. What problems did each reorganization create?
5. What changes are still needed?

Activity 13–8 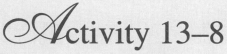 "FORD'S GLOBAL AUTOMOBILE STRATEGY"

STEP 1: View the ABC video entitled "Ford's Global Automobile Strategy."

STEP 2: In small groups, prepare two possible ways of organizing the manufacture and sales of Ford Motor Company's "car for the world." Be sure to consider that the car will differ slightly in North America, Central America, Europe, and Asia. If possible, draw two possible organizational charts for Ford.

STEP 3: Individually, in small groups, or with the entire class, answer the following questions:

1. What division of labor and coordination issues must Ford consider in designing this organization?
2. Should the organization be mechanistic or organic?
3. What structural prototypes are feasible?
4. Which structural prototypes did your group recommend? Why?
5. What are the advantages and disadvantages of each prototype?

Chapter 14

Chapter Outline

Creating Effective Organizational Designs

LEARNING OBJECTIVES

After completing the reading and activities in Chapter 14, students will be able to

1. Identify the components and dimensions of the environment.

2. Discuss the ways an organization's structure should respond to its environment.

3. Discuss the implications of technology for organizational design.

4. Describe the work-force issues organizations should consider in designing their structures.

5. Show the impact of an organization's strategy on its structures.

6. Comment about ways to fit an organization's structure to its goals.

7. Trace the stages in an organization's growth and describe their significance for the organization's structure.

8. Comment about the impact of downsizing on organizational design.

The Redesign of Oticon

Lars Kolind, the president of Oticon Holding A/S, a Danish hearing-aid manufacturer, transformed an ultratraditional organization into the "ultimate flexible organization." He viewed himself as the "naval architect who designs a ship" rather than the "captain who steers the ship." His goal was to change Oticon from an inflexible, machine-like structure to a flexible, organic structure that could readily transform knowledge into new product solutions. He believed that such a structure would respond to the highly competitive, rapidly changing environment his company faced, where competitors quickly matched new technological solutions offered by Oticon at an even lower cost. He also thought a different structure would help Oticon compete against its larger, more nimble competitors.

The company's focus changed from using improved technology to build smaller hearing aids to a market focus of offering improved solutions to hearing problems. Kolind's whimsical concept of "1,000 birch trees on wheels" that could be moved to demarcate continuously changing project clusters evolved into "the spaghetti organization." These images reflected the flexible, dynamic, even chaotic set of relationships and interactions that could change as needed and that Kolind envisioned as necessary for responding quickly, efficiently, and innovatively to the changing environment. The relationships included in this extremely organic structure consisted of project leaders and project owners, comprised of individuals interested in supporting a project's success. These included professional specialists who coordinated the diverse professions involved in hearing care and all individuals leading and participating in projects.

The hierarchy of the previous traditional structure was dismantled. A "network of experts" in special areas such as audiology, acoustics, psychology, chip design, marketing, and finance replaced it.

- Departments and titles disappeared. All activities became projects that informal groups of interested individuals pursued.

- Jobs were reconfigured into unique and fluid combinations of functions to fit each employee's capabilities and needs.

- All vestiges of the office were eliminated and replaced by open spaces filled with uniform workstations, each consisting of a drawer-less desk and computer, to encourage individuals to mingle and communicate with a large number of coworkers.

- Informal dialogue replaced memos as the accepted mode of communication. Electronic mail was discouraged because it hinders oral communication. All incoming mail was scanned into a computer system and then shredded.

Employees regularly engage in cross-functional collaboration. They also perform at least one activity outside their speciality and even their qualifications. Projects emerge chaotically. Project leaders do not have to secure permission to obtain resources. Kolind believes: "If you're in doubt, do it. If it works, fine. If not, we forgive you."

Each individual has access to all corporate strategic information through the computer system. This access resulted in the immediate discovery of a product developed in the 1980s, which had been buried because of lack of communication. Focusing on the first fully automatic hearing aid resulted in a powerful and highly profitable new product line.

The ability of individuals to act quickly and flexibly resulted in a significant competitive advantage. In the first two years after the redesign, profits, productivity, and innovation increased substantially. In 1993, for example, the company grew 23 percent in a declining market and increased its gross profit by 25 percent.[1]

What factors determine whether a structure is appropriate and effective for an organization? In Chapter 13, we examined the many options available for designing a structure. In this chapter, we focus on how to choose the right options for various circumstances. In particular, we diagnose the impact of an organization's (1) environment, (2) technology, (3) work force, (4) strategy, and (5) development on its structure.

RESPONDING TO THE ENVIRONMENT

Because most organizations face a demanding, intrusive, and somewhat uncontrollable *environment,* those factors *outside* the organization that influence its functioning, managers can use organizational design as one way of increasing the effectiveness of interactions with the environment.

COMPONENTS OF THE ENVIRONMENT

Economic and market circumstances, technological innovations, as well as federal, state, and local legislation and political, social, and cultural conditions external to the organization comprise its environment and influence an organization's functioning.

Economic Environment Organizations typically confront an unpredictable economic environment. In a few years inflation can move from double to single digits and back again. The prime rate—which influences an organization's ability to borrow more and hence to function in the marketplace—can also fluctuate widely. As businesses deal more globally, the stability of a variety of monetary currencies becomes significant for an organization's functioning. Organizations must be able to respond efficiently and adaptively to the changing economic situation in several countries at once. They must be able to reduce costs as necessary or use the ability to borrow money at a low rate as an opportunity for innovation or expansion.

MATSUSHITA ELECTRIC INDUSTRIAL COMPANY. Matsushita significantly reduced its headquarters staff in response to the downturn in Japanese exports caused by the rising value of the yen. The company planned to transfer 6,000 corporate staff members to jobs in marketing, sales, and production. The company also offered five-year contracts to scientists rather than lifetime employment. This change was intended to increase productivity by requiring the scientists to make important breakthroughs in order for their contracts to be renewed.[2]

National and international competitors as well as suppliers and customers make up the market aspect of the economic environment. For example, Oticon's redesign was prompted, in large part, by its need to compete with larger, more nimble organizations. The flexible structure was intended to allow Oticon to rapidly identify potential markets and develop new products for them.

Technological Environment Companies like Oticon face a constantly changing technological environment in which frequent advances in technology require a continued emphasis on research and development. Here we refer to the general technological context in which organizations function, rather than the specific technology or technical systems they use, which we consider later in this chapter. While many manufacturing companies share Oticon's need for basic research, both manufacturing and service organizations require automation and computerization that can speed the dissemination of information and hence increase productivity. The organizational structure thus must facilitate the acquisition, development, and introduction of new technology.

AT&T AND DELTA. AT&T and Delta announced a joint venture to provide computer services to the tourism and transportation industries. AT&T will provide computer services to Delta. Together they will develop and market new technology.[3]

Political/Legal Environment Increased government regulations have constrained management's actions in its production and employment practices. In the United States, occupational safety and health guidelines, equal employment opportunity regulations, and foreign trade tariffs and policies influence the way organizations can do business. Outside the United States, laws unique to countries such as Denmark, in which Oticon functions, create similar constraints on organizational functioning. In addition, the current political climate, which may support or hinder business initiatives, influences an organization's ability to compete.

Sociocultural Environment The sociocultural environment takes in a complex web of cultural considerations such as attitudes toward family life and social attributes such as demographics, or the makeup of the general population. Demographic changes include the population shifting geographically, the relative age distribution of workers and customers changing, and the educational level and expectations of organizational members increasing. In the United States many workers have moved from the industrial northeast and midwest to the south and west, reducing the pool of skilled workers available to companies in some locations. Large numbers of immigrants in the United States and other industrialized countries have altered the available labor pool. As the general population has aged and mandatory retirement has been eliminated, companies have used early retirement incentives to reduce the number of older workers. And, as a company extends its reach into international markets, it must deal with new sets of sociocultural considerations.

The Multinational/Multicultural Environment Organizations that function in a global environment face two major environmental pressures in addition to the environmental pressures faced by any organization.[4] First, they must be responsive to the local country and culture. Multinational organizations face very different challenges in the United States than in Eastern Europe, Japan, or other parts of Asia. Second, they must react to the forces pushing toward globalization. These include the elimination of economic borders between countries, the increasing similarity of consumer demands and hence products across countries, and the impact of improved communication technologies.[5]

ABB. Percy Barnevik, the CEO of Asea Brown Boveri (Holding) Ltd. sees a future with no national boundaries. He has acquired 60 companies on five continents to establish a constellation of factories worldwide that can serve customers around the world. The company attempts to capitalize on local differences by eliminating bureaucracy and allowing local executives almost complete decision-making responsibility. For example, executives in Atlanta can introduce new products without interference from corporate headquarters. This structure will allow the company to sell power equipment to everyone everywhere.[6]

Cultural differences often exist in the structures managers prefer and implement. For example, one study suggested that U.S. managers held an instrumental conception of structure, where structure was viewed as a means for accomplishing organizational goals, whereas French managers held a social one, where structure was viewed as a means for creating interpersonal interactions.[7] The organization's structure must obviously consider these cultural differences for maximum effectiveness. In addition, the structure must reflect the legal and regulatory constraints of the country in which a subsidiary is located.[8] These constraints may require the inclusion or positioning of certain groups in the structure. For example, German law creates worker councils as a formal component of the structure of unionized organizations.

MATCHING STRUCTURE TO ENVIRONMENTAL DIMENSIONS

Different types of structures will be more effective in different types of environments. An effective organizational structure must reflect three specific dimensions of the environment: its complexity, dynamism, and hostility/munificence.[9]

Complexity The number and variety of environmental elements that affect an organization vary considerably. A bank must deal with all environmental components described in the previous section, while a small sandwich shop must respond primarily to the economic environment and secondarily to the sociocultural environment. Hence, the branch bank has a more complex environment than does the pizza parlor. An organization that serves retail and wholesale markets faces a more complex environment than a comparable organization that only markets its product through retail outlets. Moving up the scale of complexity, a multinational firm, which must deal with the unique characteristics of numerous cultures and countries, experiences even greater environmental complexity.

As the complexity of the environment increases, organizations generally experience greater success if they decentralize decision making. Decentralizing decision making places expertise and authority in direct contact with the essential information in the environment. Oticon has decentralized decision making, giving managers and employees total control over project management and the use of resources, including their own time. This structure facilitates a faster response to new market trends and increased demand for new products. The ability to effectively decentralize assumes that qualified and dedicated people exist in sufficient numbers at the lower levels.

Although an organization can deal with new or sophisticated information more quickly, directly, and effectively as a result of decentralization, it can also fail to coordinate activities of its various parts and in an extreme case even send conflicting messages into the marketplace. Decentralization must be done only to the extent that adequate control can be maintained. As the environment becomes increasingly complex, organizations may divisionalize as one way of dealing with an extensive array of environmental elements. The divisionalized structure works best in larger, relatively older companies with complex economic, technological, political/legal, and sociocultural environments.

Dynamism The degree to which environmental elements change predictably over time also influences the choice of organizational structure. Changes in the prime rate, for example, affect the availability of funds to organizations. The Federal Reserve Bank raised the prime rate three percent from 1994 to 1995 to slow industrial expansion and maintain progress in reducing the jobless rate. Ongoing technological advancements also demand reactions from organizations. Technological change can occur so rapidly and unpredictably that it may make products obsolete within six to twelve months of their introduction.

The more frequently and unpredictably the environment changes, the more flexible and adaptable the organization's structure should be. Market-oriented and integrated structures (see Chapter 13) offer flexibility by emphasizing lateral relationships, decentralizing decision making, and deemphasizing status and rank differences. At Oticon, for example, flexibility increased when the company eliminated layers of management. Organizations can also create additional lateral linkages to improve the flow of information in the organization or between the organization and its environment. Divisionalized firms facing instability can also reduce uncertainty by divesting themselves of noncore businesses so that they can better understand the remaining markets.[10]

Hostility/Munificence The degree to which the environment creates conflict, threat, or unexpected or overwhelming competition for an organization reflects its *hostility* or *munificence.* Hostile environments occur when the following conditions exist:

- extensive competition, including price undercutting;

- threatened obsolescence;

- a government investigation;

- new or unexpected government regulations;

- threatened takeover;

- potential bankruptcy;

- lack of social responsibility.

Organizations with highly hostile environments require high centralization of decision making. Centralization allows the most controlled means of responding to competition or other threatening events. Organizations typically use this design strategy in the short run and it takes priority over other strategies for only a brief period of time. Organizations that must cope with a hostile environment over a prolonged period experience real threats to their survival because operating in a crisis mode tends to sap energy and resources. In a munificent environment, organizations that experience unexpected environmental pressures respond by increasing their specialization and the deployment of professionals to specialized areas so they can bring their special knowledge to efforts aimed at immediately addressing the problem.[11]

Design dilemmas can arise when an organization's environment has competing forces, ones that call for opposite strategies. How, for example, does management reconcile a decentralized structure required for a complex environment with the centralization required to deal effectively with a hostile environment? Alternatively, the proposed structure may not fit with internal characteristics of the organization, such as differing goals or different types of workers in different parts of the organization, creating the possibility of inconsistency in structures.[12] Resolving these dilemmas generally occurs in one of three ways:

- creating diverse structures within the same organization: the marketing and research and development departments may have one structure and manufacturing a different one;

- redesigning the structure within each work unit as its task and environmental demands change;[13]

- creating temporary structures in times of crisis, for example, convening a management council only in response to hostile environmental events.

IMPACT OF TECHNOLOGY

Technology is the process that converts raw materials into a product or service. Thus, technology can refer to the machinery used to alter raw materials to produce a finished product or the intellectual or analytical processes used to transform information into a product idea or service. The technical system used by an organization in producing and delivering its product or service significantly influences the nature of effective organizational structures. In this section we examine the fit between the technical system and its structure, rather than the general technological context in which the organization operates described earlier.

TECHNOLOGY TYPOLOGIES

Historically, three researchers—Joan Woodward, James Thompson, and Charles Perrow—have laid the foundation for the diagnosis and analysis of technology and its impact on organizational structure.

Production Processes Joan Woodward classified technology in three ways. A *unit* technology describes craft processes that produce custom-made products such as housewares, clothing, or art work, or even legal and medical services. *Mass production,* such as automobile or heavy equipment manufacturing, refers to assembly-line operations to produce standardized consumer goods. *Continuous flow* technology, such as chemical or oil refiners, describes an unsegmented, ongoing production process.[14]

A recent reformulation proposed the addition of a fourth type: *technical batch (or unit) processing,* such as aircraft production or check processing. Like the traditional unit processing, this technology has a small scale of operations. Unlike the traditional batch processing, the required knowledge complexity is high.

How would you classify the manufacture of hearing products at Oticon? Is the technology for product manufacture the same as for product design and development? Manufacturing typically uses a mass-production technology, whereas design and development rely more on a unit process.

Task Performance James Thompson describes technology in terms of the tasks performed by an organizational unit.[15] A *long-linked* technology involves the repetitive application of one technology to a standardized raw material. Mass-production assembly lines, such as post offices or steel manufacturing, use this technology. A *mediating* technology repeatedly applies a standardized method to unique raw materials. A social services agency imparts standardized counseling techniques to diverse clients to allow them to act functionally. *Intensive* technology applies diverse techniques and knowledge to various raw materials. The particular techniques used vary according to the problem or situation. Hospital patients receive different treatments depending on their symptoms and diagnosed problems.

Consider the technology used by Oticon. Long-linked, mass-production, and intensive technologies are used by different units in the organization. Manufacturing uses a long-linked technology. Human resources management uses a mediating technology. Technical support uses an intensive technology.

Knowledge Technology In a third classification scheme, Charles Perrow focuses specifically on knowledge technology.[16] *Task variability* refers to the number of exceptions that a job holder encounters. An assembly-line worker encounters relatively low task variability, whereas a physician in family medicine encounters high task variability. *Problem analyzability* addresses the extent to which the technology is well understood by those who use it. A salesperson's job has relatively low problem analyzability, whereas a quality-control engineer's job is high on this dimension.

Combining these two dimensions results in four types of technology, as shown in Figure 14–1. *Routine* technology, such as that used by many government agencies or manufacturing companies, involves few exceptions and is well defined, understood, and analyzable. A *craft* technology, such as that used by a potter, also has few exceptions but is ill defined and unanalyzable. Organizations such as bridge builders have an *engineering* technology, which has many exceptions but is well

FIGURE 14–1   *Perrow's classification of technology*

PROBLEM ANALYZABILITY		TASK VARIABILITY	
		ROUTINE WITH FEW EXCEPTIONS	HIGH VARIETY WITH MANY EXCEPTIONS
	WELL DEFINED AND ANALYZABLE	Routine	Engineering
	ILL DEFINED AND UNANALYZABLE	Craft	Nonroutine

SOURCE: Based on C. Perrow, A framework for the comparative analysis of organizations, *American Sociological Review* 32 (April 1967): 194–208.

understood. A nonroutine technology, such as that used by a psychiatrist, has many exceptions and is not well understood.

THE DESIGN RESPONSE

Henry Mintzberg integrates these three typologies and identifies two dimensions on which effective structure depends—regulation and sophistication.[17]

Regulation *Regulation* refers to the extent to which machinery and equipment control the employee's work. A regulating technology includes Woodward's mass production and continuous flow technologies, Thompson's long-linked and mediating technologies, and Perrow's routine and engineering technologies. Mintzberg suggests that a more regulating technology calls for a more mechanistic structure. The more routine the technology, the less the need for flexibility since responses to technology can be predetermined and nonvariant.

FLEET BANK. Fleet Services Company is the division of Fleet Financial Group responsible for data processing and check clearing. The president of the division created an assembly line to deal with the division's products: checks. His goal was to create a fast and accurate assembly line that was the lowest-cost producer in its class. He introduced a more bureaucratic structure to respond to the routinization of the check-processing technology. The reorganization reduced the number of employees from 7,000 to 4,000.[18]

A nonregulating technology includes Woodward's unit technology, Thompson's intensive technology, and Perrow's craft and nonroutine technologies. Nonregulating systems such as these call for an organic structure.[19] The less routine the technology, the greater the need for flexibility.

Sophistication *Sophistication* describes the complexity or intricacy of the technology. As the technical system increases in sophistication, the organization requires an increasingly elaborate administrative structure, more support staff who have decision-making responsibilities, and more integrating and linking devices. Decreasing sophistication calls for no specific structural provision.

Effective organizational structures buffer or protect the technology from environmental influences or disturbances.[20] The more specific the technology, such as that of a mechanized bottle capper, the less tolerance the process has for disturbances, and the more the organization must elaborate its structure and administration to protect the operation from disturbances by the environment. As organizations become more automated they require increasing rules and regulations, centralized control, and support staff as a way of buffering the technology. New technologies also change how the job is done and ultimately affect the division of labor, issues of control and coordination, and the organization–environment fit.[21] Organizational design must respond to the complexities created by new technologies.

THE WORK FORCE: DESIGN CONSIDERATIONS

As we have seen in Chapter 12, managers must consider many factors in job design. In addition to these factors, managers must realize that different structures will be more effective in supporting different types of workers as they perform different types of jobs. A highly creative designer, for example, would chafe at the restraints of a bureaucratic structure. An organization's structure must accommodate the different types of employees in various positions and locations. Considerations here include the employees' professionalism, expertise, and group memberships (such as union affiliation).

HITACHI. The Japanese high-technology company responds to the skills of its engineers by creating an egalitarian structure for its engineers in R&D rather than creating an administrative hierarchy.[22]

The structure might also consider workers' education, work experience, and demographic characteristics such as age, work values, life and career stages, commitment and other attitudes, as well as their personality variables (described in Chapter 3).

DIGITAL EQUIPMENT CORPORATION. Less than two years after a major restructuring created autonomous minicompanies organized by customer type, Digital reorganized again. This time the company organized the work force into units built around product groups, such as software or servers. In the first restructuring, the company found that many managers lacked knowledge about the industries in which they were now in charge. In addition, the first project organization combined low-margin products with high-margin services, which hindered the sales of both the products and services and was accompanied by a $72 million loss.[23]

Organizations that function in numerous countries likely have employees with different cultural backgrounds and the accompanying experiences, values, and educational differences. In addition, within a given country, an organization's members may come from both its home country and host country. Reconciling differences in perspectives as well as taking advantage of the different views becomes a major challenge in designing organizations. Establishing structures that allow for the fluid exchange of employees at various sites across the world also may be important for some companies. The transfer of skills and the translation of knowledge among locations occurs more easily in product or project structures, where individuals are used to working with diverse groups, than in functional structures, which tend to perpetuate a more holistic viewpoint. Network structures provide the greatest opportunity for taking advantage of synergy from diverse countries and using it to make the parent organization more competitive.

GOALS, STRATEGY, AND DESIGN

An organization's goals and strategy also influence the choice of an effective structure. Executives must first identify the organization's goals and strategy and then select an appropriate design.

ORGANIZATIONAL GOALS

Goals are the desired outcomes of individual or organizational activities and behaviors. They focus attention, provide a rationale for organizing activities, offer a standard for assessing performance, legitimize individual and organizational behavior, and provide an identity for the individual.[24] They communicate higher management's philosophy and intentions, and motivate people to achieve.

Early discussion of goal formation said it occurred in three steps.[25] First, as coalitions bargain about goals, competing groups provide other groups with inducements so that their own goals will predominate. Second, the coalition leaders attempt to strengthen and clarify the goal by trying to satisfy, at least minimally, the goals of all coalition members. Third, the group leaders and members adjust the goal or goals to reflect experience.

Other organizational theorists have historically viewed the process of goal formation as a two-step process of identifying constraints on an organization's operation,[26] such as specifying the resource pool or research expertise available and then determining what the organization can and should accomplish given these limitations. The amount of revenues desired, for example, may evolve from the available human resource pool or current market share. Neither goal formation process is straightforward. Organizations continually experience difficulty in specifying clear, responsive, and responsible goals.

Diversity of Goals Organizations such as Opticon, a large department store chain, a law office, or a hospital have different and varying goals that might relate to market share, profitability, product innovation, or quality of work life. Consider other organizations you have observed: a small retail store, your local government, a library, an elementary school, or a brokerage house. Can you identify the goals of these organizations? How do they change over time? Managers must identify the goals of all parts of the organization first and then choose the structure most likely to facilitate their accomplishments.

Table 14–1 reflects the diversity of goals organizations might have. It shows three typologies, each of which spans a range of possible goals. Not surprisingly, some similarities exist between them: output goals and management goals, for example. Together, these typologies list most of the types of goals organizations choose.

Goal Incompatibility Because organizations frequently have multiple goals, goals may conflict. For example, goals in the area of public responsibility may incur costs that detract from profitability. A goal of providing the highest quality service may conflict with a goal of minimizing costs. These conflicts frequently arise from an incongruence between different goal types, such as innovation and productivity goals or societal and output goals. Or, a conflict between the goals of influential individuals, groups, or departments in the organization may prevent diverse constituencies from agreeing on the organization's goals. At some companies, return on investment for stockholders may seemingly conflict with improved compensation and quality-of-work-life for employees. At others, a refocusing on new product development may interfere with a goal of manufacturing efficiency. Thus, defining an organization's goals requires significant and complex action to reconcile conflicting and incompatible goals. Otherwise, dysfunctional *goal displacement*—where individuals or groups divert their energies from the organization's original goals to different ones—may occur.

Organizational structures should facilitate goal accomplishment. The restructuring at Opticon, for example, is intended to increase the company's competitiveness by encouraging the development of new products. Typically, the more extensive and heterogeneous the goals, the more complex the structure needed to respond to them.[27]

TABLE 14–1   *Three typologies of organizational goals and examples*

PERROW'S CLASSIFICATION

TYPE OF GOAL	DEFINITION	EXAMPLE
Societal	Creation and maintenance of cultural values through production of goods or services	To increase the number of managers on boards of charitable organizations
Output	Kinds and quantities of outputs produced	To increase production by 15%
System	The functioning of an organization's system independent of its production of goods or services	To introduce a project structure
Product	Specific characteristics of goods or services	To develop a line of men's cologne
Derived	Organization's use of power in areas apart from production of goods and services	To introduce a mentoring program

DRUCKER'S CLASSIFICATION

TYPE OF GOAL	DEFINITION	EXAMPLE
Market standing	The organization's position in the market. Quality and share of the market	To become the sales leader in portable typewriters
Innovation	The value of new product development	To develop two new products
Productivity	The level of output organization-wide	To increase production of shoes by 35%
Physical and financial resources	The nature and extent of resources used in product development and production	To reduce the cost of raw materials by 10%
Profitability	Profit and return on investment	To increase profit by 5%
Manager performance and development	Managerial output, growth, activities, and style	To send all managers to at least one training course
Worker performance and attitudes	Individual output, turnover, absenteeism, satisfaction, and morale	To reduce turnover to less than 10% a year
Public responsibility	The organization's use of natural resources and contribution to the public good	To seek alternative sources of raw materials

GROSS'S CLASSIFICATION

TYPE OF GOAL	DEFINITION	EXAMPLE
Output	Kinds and levels of output	To add three products to the product line
Adaptation	Those that contribute to the ability to respond to environmental changes. For example, emphasis on R&D	To double the R&D staff
Management	Managerial output, activities, and style	To increase the amount of time managers spend in planning activities
Motivation	Encouraging employee motivation	To introduce an incentive program
Position	Those associated with each job in the organization	To increase the autonomy associated with each job

SOURCES: Adapted from C. Perrow, *Organizational Analysis: A Sociological View* (Belmont, Calif.: Wadsworth, 1970); P. Drucker, *The Practice of Management* (New York: Harper, 1954); E. Gross, The definition of organizational goals, *British Journal of Sociology* 20 (1969): 277–294.

ORGANIZATIONAL STRATEGY

The organization's *strategy,* which includes its basic mission, purpose, and goals, as well as the means for accomplishing them, also influences its structure. One schema classifies organizations into four strategic types.[28]

- *Defenders* are organizations that have a major share of the market and attempt to retain that share, such as Toys "R" Us. Companies like this emphasize planning and cost control rather than a search for new products. The resulting structure tends to be relatively bureaucratic, emphasizing high horizontal differentiation, centralized control, an elaborate hierarchy, and extensive formalization.

- *Prospectors* find and develop new products and markets. They emphasize innovation and rapid introduction of new products. Minnesota Mining and Manufacturing Company (3M) likely has this strategy. These organizations call for a more organic structure, with less division of labor, greater flexibility, and more decentralized decision making and control. 3M frequently purchases small companies and incorporates them intact into their organization.

- *Analyzers* combine characteristics of defenders and prospectors. They enter new markets or introduce new products after the prospectors. They also maintain efficiency like the defenders. This strategy calls for a hybrid structure, one that has moderately centralized control and encourages both flexibility and stability. Many banks combine elements of product and functional structures.

- *Reactors* design their strategies based on what others in the market have done. These companies may pursue one of the other three strategies incidentally, but often do so improperly and hence perform ineffectively. The IBM PC-clone makers, for example, do not focus on R&D but use more efficient manufacturing to undercut the more innovative pioneers. No specific structure fits with this strategy.

Managers of multinational organizations may choose from among these strategies or more typically choose one of four special strategic approaches.[29]

- *Global management,* typical of many oil companies, tends to have similar products in all regional markets. These organizations compete worldwide by creating few or no distinctions between markets and by developing global economics of scale in manufacturing, distribution, and sales.

- *Multinational management,* used by consumer-product companies in the food or electronics industries, emphasizes differences in its products and services for each country. These companies design marketing, sales, and even the product itself to meet specific country or regional requirements.

- *International management,* used by pharmaceutical companies, describes an organization between global and multinational management. These organizations sell similar products in all countries but tailor them somewhat to meet local regulations.

- *Transnational management,* used by companies such as Unilever (see Chapter 13), combines elements of each of these approaches. Beginning with either global, multinational, or international management, transnational management adds elements from the others to meet special market needs, a changing environment, or cost-reduction pressures.

IBM EUROPE. IBM Europe has historically served European countries individually. Managers are now encouraged to take a pan-European perspective and assume responsibilities for a single product line across national boundaries.[30]

How would you characterize Opticon's strategy? It can be viewed as a prospector, since it wishes to emphasize innovation and new products. Its introduction of a highly flexible structure with decentralized decision making fits with this strategy. Executives in organizations such as Opticon must identify the organization's strategy and then select the design that best responds to it.

ORGANIZATIONAL LIFE CYCLE

Most organizations evolve through a *life cycle,* a series of developmental stages, akin to those described for individuals in Chapter 3.

ORGANIZATIONAL SIZE AND AGE

The growth and aging of an organization influence the characteristics of the most effective structure.

Size As organizations increase in size they typically become more heterogeneous in their orientations as well as in the products and services they provide. This change necessitates increased differentiation in structure. Depending on the environment and the technology faced by the organization, this differentiation may result in a move from a simpler functional structure to any of the more complex ones. Figure 14–2 illustrates a typical progression as a typical organization, a restaurant, increases in size.

The results of some early research on organizational structure suggest the importance of knowing an organization's size in diagnosing the structure's effectiveness. Researchers in Aston, England, who studied organizations believe that size dictates certain structural dimensions, specifically the structuring of activities, specialization, standardization, formalization, span of control, and centralization.[31] Other researchers who studied the same organizations found that organizational size also modifies the influence of technology on structure, with larger organizations having a more bureaucratic structure regardless of their technology.[32] These results also suggest that the impact of size should not preclude the consideration of other contingencies.

ROADWAY SERVICES. Roadway Services, a $3.7 billion transportation giant, counteracts the stereotype of a large, lumbering company with a highly bureaucratic structure. Roadway recently created Global Air, a start-up that moves the company into small-package delivery. The company is known for its nimbleness and innovativeness.[33]

DANA CORPORATION. An auto-parts manufacturer that supplies major U.S. and foreign automobile manufacturers, Dana Corporation holds employment at its plants to less than 200 workers. When a division of the company grows too large, Dana

FIGURE 14–2   *Changes in organizational structure with increases in size*

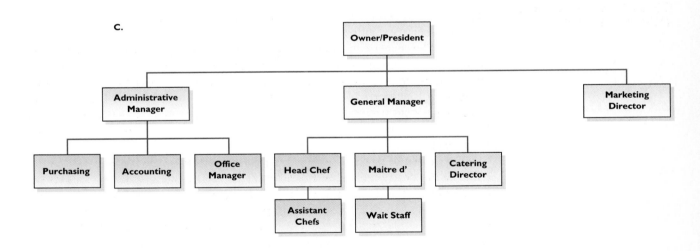

splits it in half because they believe that growing larger removes the flexibility they need to compete.[34]

Age The age of an organization, not surprisingly, often correlates with its size. As an organization ages, its behavior tends to become more standardized and formalized. The aging of the U. S. government illustrates this relationship quite well. Early communication occurred primarily through mutual adjustment. As the government got older, more procedures became standardized, and its structure became more mechanized and bureaucratic. Because age and size often correlate, separating the influences of each contingency on organizational structure poses difficulties for organizational analysts. In redesigning organizations, managers must consider the implications of both contingencies.

LIFE-CYCLE STAGES

Researchers have noted that an organization's movement through its life cycle occurs in a predictable sequence of stages that is not easily reversed.[35] Organizational growth can be described as progressing through four stages, as summarized in Table 14–2: entrepreneurial, collectivity, formalization, and elaboration.[36]

Entrepreneur Stage Organizational creation begins with the development of first ideas about the organization, moves to the making of commitments and initial planning, and then continues with implementation or making the new organization operational.[37] For small businesses, this stage incorporates two substages of small-business growth.[38]

■ *Existence* concerns the development of a customer base, the reliable delivery of the product, and the building of a sufficient cash flow to support the company's activities.

■ *Survival* describes the company becoming concerned with generating a profit. There is little formal planning and few formal systems. Growth occurs through supervision provided by the leader to a growing number of employees.

Collectivity Stage Organizations typically experience rapid growth at this stage. While innovation and expansion continue, some attempts to stabilize and routinize the organization begin.[39] Also known as the *success* stage, the owner decides whether to stabilize the company at its present size or strive for more growth.[40] The owner can consolidate the company, professionalize its functional management, and remove himself or herself from an active management role. Or, the owner can reinvest the profits in growth and retain control. Although the founding and early members of the organization remain committed to it, their involvement increasingly becomes a function of the incentives offered. Tasks must offer

....

TABLE 14–2 *Summary model of the organizational life cycle*

ENTREPRENEURIAL STAGE	COLLECTIVITY STAGE	FORMALIZATION AND CONTROL STAGE	ELABORATION OF STRUCTURE STAGE
Marshaling of resources	Informal communication and structure	Formalization of rules	Elaboration of structure
Lots of ideas		Stable structure	Decentralization
Entrepreneurial activities	Sense of collectivity	Emphasis on efficiency and maintenance	Domain expansion
Little planning and coordination	Long hours spent		Adaptation
Formation of a "niche"	Sense of mission	Conservatism	Renewal
"Prime mover" has power	Innovation continues	Institutional procedures	
	High commitment		

SOURCE: Reprinted by permission of R.E. Quinn and K. Cameron, Organizational life cycles and shifting criteria of effectiveness: Some preliminary evidence, *Management Science* 29 (January 1983), Copyright © 1983. The Institute of Management Sciences.

challenge and variety. The organization must provide growth opportunities. Employees require frequent, quality communication.[41]

Formalization The maturation of the company at this stage signals its movement from entrepreneurial to professional.[42] In this *take-off* stage the owner must address such issues as delegating responsibility and acquiring sufficient cash to finance growth.[43] As the company matures, ownership and management diverge, although the owner maintains stock control. The transition from owner–manager to a hired manager frequently signals the beginning of this stage in small businesses. In larger organizations, the emphasis on the structural elaboration through functional specialization, the development of systematic reward and evaluation systems, and the emphasis on formal planning and goal setting reflect this stage. This change in focus may motivate the more entrepreneurial, innovative workers to leave the organization to seek new outlets for their creativity. Individuals whose goals and orientations are more compatible with the stabilization and formalization processes replace them.

Elaboration Stage The mature organization strives to adapt to changing conditions, renew itself, and seek continued growth opportunities. Developing resource maturity, the company must consolidate its growth, expand its management staff and capabilities, elaborate into line and staff positions, and ensure a return on investment.[44]

HOME DEPOT. Home Depot plans to increase its outlets by 25 percent a year until it will have 800 stores by 1998. The company attacks new areas by first putting in three or four stores on the outskirts of a designated city. After these stores reach combined sales of about $50 million, the company opens enough new outlets to fill the territory and make the company dominant within three to five years. Finally, when a store's sales surpass the chain's average or when growth lags behind the rate of inflation, Home Depot replaces the store with two smaller ones.[45]

Some organizations will diversify their product markets as a way of ensuring their continued growth or they will search for new products and growth opportunities. They either emphasize decentralization of decision making and team efforts as ways of adapting or institutionalize formal controls and procedures. Companies that thrive

- accept change by continually reviewing and revising goals and procedures;

- listen to customers and involve them in new product development;

- decentralize authority to encourage rapid decision making;

- hire skilled workers who are versatile and responsive;

- teach and train employees continuously;

- control costs.[46]

When the mature organization fails to adapt, decline may result.[47] They deal with internal or external pressures that then threaten their long-term survival.[48] For some organizations, downsizing provides an early signal of organizational decline. BORDEN. Between 1986 and 1992, Borden made more than 90 acquisitions, including numerous small regional food companies. Borden transferred managers from its successful chemical businesses to the newly acquired food businesses. These executives lacked knowledge about how to market the food businesses and how to take them national. Sales fell for 15 quarters.[49]

A declining organization often has the characteristics shown in Table 14–3. It generally passes through a series of stages during which the organization is potentially salvageable.[50] First, it is blind to early warning signs. Receiving and using good information could halt the decline at this time.

CROSS PEN. The pen maker failed to realize that the market had changed. The company continued to produce skinny pens and pencils and lost a large share of the market to their competitor Montblanc's more fashionable, chunky writing instruments.[51]

Second, management recognizes the need to change but takes no action. Prompt action at this stage would stem the decline. In the third stage, it takes action, but selects an inappropriate one. Correct action here, determined by the par-

---

TABLE 14–3 *Negative attributes associated with organizational decline*

ATTRIBUTE	EXPLANATION
Centralization	Decision making is pulled toward the top of the organization. Less power is shared.
Short-term, crisis mentality	Long-term planning is neglected. The focus is on immediacy.
Loss of innovativeness	Trial and error learning is curtailed. There is less tolerance for risk and failure associated with creative activity.
Resistance to change	Conservatism and the threat-rigidity response lead to "hunkering down" and a protectionist stance.
Decreasing morale	Infighting and a "mean mood" permeates the organization.
Politicized special-interest groups	Special-interest groups organize and become more vocal. The climate becomes politicized.
Nonprioritized cutbacks	Across-the-board cutbacks are used to ameliorate conflict. Priorities are not obvious.
Loss of trust	Leaders lose the confidence of subordinates, and distrust among organization members increases.
Increasing conflict	Fewer resources result in internal competition and fighting for a smaller pie.
Restricted communication	Only good news is passed upward. Information is not widely shared because of fear and distrust.
Lack of teamwork	Individualism and disconnectedness make teamwork difficult. Individuals are not inclined to form teams.
Lack of leadership	Leadership anemia occurs as leaders are scapegoated, priorities are unclear, and a siege mentality prevails.

SOURCE: Reprinted with permission from B.A. Macy and H. Izumi, Organizational change, design, and work innovation: A meta-analysis of 131 North American field studies—1961–1991, *Research in Organizational Behavior* 7 (1993): 235–313.

ticular situation, would reverse the decline. In the fourth stage the organization reaches the point of crisis and faces the last chance for reversing the decline. In some cases an effective reorganization (often after declaring legal bankruptcy) can facilitate this reversal. If the organization reaches the fifth and final stage, it will be forced to dissolve. The speed of its dissolution will depend on how forgiving an environment it faces.

DOWNSIZING

Some organizations find that they must reduce or **downsize** their work force as a way of responding to environmental or technological changes. Declining economic conditions or shifts in demand for a product or service may mandate downsizing. Downsizing can also accompany increasing automation if it reduces the total number of employees previously necessary to do the same job. Companies can also use downsizing as a way of renewing the organization, by stripping away excess jobs and staff and reclaiming some of the vigor associated with younger, smaller organizations. Restructuring to increase efficiencies or economies of scale often occurs.

Downsizing has both positive and negative consequences. It can reduce costs, redirect strategy, and increase efficiency, but it can also destroy employee morale, injure sales, reduce quality, and result in little improvement in profits.[52] If downsizing is done as a short-term panic-stricken response to a hostile environment, then downsizing is doomed to failure. If, on the other hand, downsizing is part of a long-term strategy for performance and competitiveness, it likely will be more effective.

NYNEX. Nynex, the regional Baby Bell telecommunications company that serves New York and New England, reduced its labor force of 95,400 by 19,200 between 1990 and 1994 as a way of becoming more competitive. In 1994, the company cut 16,800 additional employees, or 22 percent of its work force. The company believed it could deliver the same or even improved services with fewer employees. Charges for the most recent cutbacks were estimated at $1.6 billion. These cutbacks have taxed the remaining members, significantly reducing morale but significantly improving the bottom line.[53]

DESIGN RESPONSES

Diagnosing an organization's position in its life cycle provides managers with data to use in designing an effective structure. Unique structural solutions exist for each stage of growth.[54] Young organizations require a flexible structure that can accommodate innovation and respond to uncertainty. As the organization moves into the collective or success stage, some formal procedures and policies can be introduced, but overall the organization likely has relatively informal communication and structure. As the organization formalizes, top management typically introduces formal planning, evaluation, and reward systems. Functional structures with centralized decision making often fit with the control, specialization of tasks, authority, and stability required at this stage. An organization's ultimate survival, however, increasingly depends on it having an adaptable and flexible structure.

REDESIGNING THE ORGANIZATION

A misfit between an organization's environment, technology, work force, goals, strategy, development, and its structure calls for redesigning the organization. The president of Opticon, for example, redesigned the organization in response to changes in its environment. Table 14–4 summarizes the changing characteristics of organizations, by contrasting the old and new approaches to organizational structure.

The process of redesigning an organization may look like the one shown in Table 14–5. It involves periodically and repeatedly fitting the pieces of the organizational chart together in a new way. This rearrangement must follow an assessment of the nature of the task, the people, and the existing organizational structure for compatibility and changeability. The process of redesign must also explicitly consider managers' and other employees' abilities to function effectively in the new structure and deal with resistances they likely will create.

Such an assessment should address a series of questions:

■ What environmental technological, work-force, strategic, and life-cycle factors have changed?

■ How should the organization's design respond to the changes?

■ Do dysfunctions exist in the present structure?

■ How can the dysfunctions be corrected?

■ What impact will the changes have on other aspects of organizational functioning such as motivation, communication, leadership, group dynamics, and individual development?

TABLE 14–4   *Changing organizational features*

OLD APPROACH	NEW APPROACH
Centralization of decision making	Decentralization of decision making
Focus on individual job holders	Focus on team performance of work
Emphasis on vertical communication	Emphasis on lateral communication
Reliance on functional departments	Reliance on cross-functional groupings
Minimal training of employees	Extensive training of employees
Work teams with managerial supervision	Self-managing work teams
Vertical integration	Use of alliances, partnerships, and joint ventures
Focus on product	Focus on market and customer
Creation of mega-organizations	Creation of network organizations

TABLE 14–5   *An eclectic design process*

STEP 1. PRELIMINARY PROJECT PLANNING

- Determine client's hopes and goals for program.
- Establish program scope.
- Assess special needs of target population.
- Choose design model.
- Select top-down versus bottom-up process.
- Determine appropriate depth of investigation.
- Consider resource/budget factors.

STEP 2. PROJECT START-UP

- Create parallel organization/steering committee/task force.
- Present leadership with rationale for program.
- Establish program parameters.
- Establish program goals, phases, time frames.
- Agree on steering-group processes.
- Decide on outward and upward communication channels during project.

STEP 3. PROJECT STUDY/ANALYSIS

- Review/update general organization diagnosis.
- Scan and collect data in line with design model.
- Determine alternative tasks and task processes.

- Test task processes against company mission and operative goals.
- Involve affected employees in review of work context and task processes.
- Project outcomes.
- Critique optimal design using design-model principles, standards, project goals, and organization experience.

STEP 4. IMPLEMENTATION PLANNING

- Develop and test prototypes.
- Determine implementation process.
- Match task processes and people.
- Create support systems.

STEP 5. IMPLEMENTATION

- Foster climate conducive to change.
- Form work groups.
- Begin team building/training/management development.
- Institutionalize changes.

STEP 6. IMPLEMENTATION MONITORING

- Hold status-review meetings, fine-tune design.
- Conduct independent program evaluation.
- Establish ongoing organization learning mechanism.

SOURCE: Reprinted by permission of publisher, from M.W. Stebbins and A.B. Shani, Organization design: Beyond the "Mafia" model, *Organizational Dynamics* 17(3) Copyright © 1989. American Management Association, New York. All rights reserved.

SUMMARY

Organizational redesign includes a regular, systematic diagnosis of current organizational structure, the factors that affect it, and the fit between the structure and these factors. Many organizations face changing economic, technological, political/legal, and sociocultural environments. In addition, the environment's complexity, dynamism, and hostility influence the selection of a design.

Typologies of technology describe production processes, task performance, and knowledge. A regulating technology calls for a bureaucratic structure. A nonregulating technology calls for a more flexible structure. A sophisticated technology calls for increasing an organization's administrative structure.

The organization's work force also influences its structure. A diverse work force calls for varying structural features to respond to differences among employees. The diversity of an organization's goals as well as incompatibilities between them result in different structural forms in different parts of an organization. Pursuit of a particular organizational strategy, for example, as a defender, prospector, analyzer, or reactor has design implications. Organizational structure also responds to the unique needs and characteristics of organizations at particular stages or those that are downsizing. The process of redesigning the organization involves periodically reviewing the organizational chart and reassembling the parts in more responsive and effective ways.

DIAGNOSTIC QUESTIONS

Answering the following questions helps determine the most appropriate and effective structure for organization.

- How are jobs grouped in the organization?

- Have groupings considered the impact of the organization's environment—its complexity, stability, and hostility?

- Have groupings considered the impact of the organization's technology—its regulation and sophistication?

- Have groupings been designed to meet the needs and abilities of the work force?

- Have groupings been designed to accomplish the organization's goals and implement its strategy?

- Does the structure make sense for the organization's stage of development?

- Does the structure make sense for the organization's size and age?

Activity 14–1 — CAMPION & BERGERAC CASE

STEP 1: Read the Campion & Bergerac Case.

In August 1992, Bryan Conan, managing partner of a major local Canadian office of one of the "Big Six" international public accounting firms, was trying to determine where his plan to restructure the office had gone wrong. The reorganization was motivated by a need to make the office more market driven. This need was particularly evident in the audit and accounting department where the market for these services had become very much a buyers' market. This situation was further exacerbated by increased competition among public accounting firms; this competition included such tactics as price cutting and, in some cases, treating these services as loss leaders. Bryan thought he had managed the change process well; however, recent events raised considerable doubt about its success.

CAMPION & BERGERAC

Campion & Bergerac was one of the "Big Six" international public accounting firms in Canada. Like other large public accounting firms, it had grown substantially during the 1980s but was feeling the impact of the recession of the early 1990s. In response to this environment, Campion & Bergerac was trying to consolidate a strong marketing and service approach that started in the 1980s. At that time marketing was somewhat foreign to accounting firms. For example, prior to the 1980s, direct advertising by chartered accountants was prohibited by their governing professional body. Consequently, some accountants still believed that technical excellence was a sufficient strategy for generating business and that overt marketing tactics were "unprofessional."

As with other public accounting firms, Campion & Bergerac was evolving from the role of traditional auditor to that of business advisor, providing an increased range of services and products to meet changing client needs. A strong client service and a marketing orientation were considered key elements of long-term success. While great strides had been made, marketing had yet to become a way of life within the firm. As a result, instilling a client service and marketing orientation across the firm, and particularly at the partner level, was a key goal of the firm for the 1990s.

Local Office

The Brampton, Ontario office of Campion & Bergerac was opened in the 1950s. Since then it had enjoyed considerable growth, through both market demand and mergers, and employed 160 staff in 1991. It was one of the two largest public accounting offices in the city. The office personnel profile is presented in Table 14–6. The

TABLE 14–6 *Campion & Bergerac office personnel profile, 1991*

	AUDIT & ACCOUNTS	TAX	MANAGEMENT SERVICES	TOTAL
Partners	15	3	4	22
Managers	11	5	7	23
Staff accountants	69	5	11	85
	95	13	22	130
Secretarial & clerical staff				30
Total				160

firm offered services in the areas of auditing and accounting, tax, and management advisory services.

In the audit and accounting area, staff members below partner level were organized largely on a pool system, whereby staff were assigned from the pool to client engagements as available and as required. Some exceptions to this rule operated where staff had built up particular ties with either clients or partners. Each of the areas of tax and management advisory services operated more on the staff system, whereby staff below partner level were organized in separate groups to handle the specialist functions of and within each area.

The Brampton office had a broad and diverse clientele, both in size and type. Over 80 percent of its clients were based in Canada and ranged in size from multinational giants to small local businesses. The firm provided services to virtually all types of industrial, commercial, governmental, recreational, financial, and social services organizations. While many clients were small growing businesses whose needs for professional services would grow with their business, many were also large complex organizations which required the resources that only a large firm could muster.

The office was generally organized around two broad activities: client services and office support services. Client services focused on the efficient and effective delivery of professional services to the firm's clients on a timely basis. The three main client service areas, with a designated partner in charge (PIC) of each area, were audit and accounting, taxation, and management advisory services. Practice office support services involved those internal activities necessary for the efficient and effective operation of the office. There were three main office support service areas: administration, human resources, and marketing. Each of these support service areas had a designated partner responsible for the area.

A management committee coordinated the activities of the PICs of the various client services and the partners responsible for the office support services. Membership of this committee included the office managing partner (OMP), the PICs of the three client service areas, and the three partners responsible for office support services. However, as the PIC of the audit and accounting client service area was also the partner responsible for human resources, the resulting management committee consisted of only six people (see Figure 14–3—Organizational Chart).

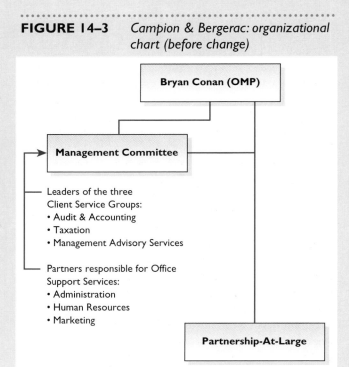

FIGURE 14–3 *Campion & Bergerac: organizational chart (before change)*

Bryan Conan—Brampton Office Managing Partner (OMP)

Bryan commenced his five-year term as office managing partner in July 1990. Previously, he was managing partner of a smaller local office (25 staff) of the firm. His appointment as OMP originated in the firm's national head office.

As office managing partner, Bryan had a number of managerial responsibilities including responsibility for the day-to-day management of the office, development of the office business plan, budgets and operating statements, the development of partners, office expansion, and representation of the firm in the local community. Bryan, in his position as managing partner of the office, was considered "first among equals."

Bryan was considered an "atypical CA" by his new fellow partners because of his apparently greater interest in new management practices as opposed to interest in his role as a public accounting professional. He considered himself a democratic leader, whereas his predecessor had been considered a "benevolent dictator." He espoused the practice of "management by walking about" and a participative decision-making style based on using discussions and meetings to build consensus before deciding upon any change proposals.

Local offices and local office managing partners had considerable autonomy within this national firm. Consequently, it was expected that as a new local office managing partner, Bryan would effect some changes to fit his personal style. A key difference in management style between Bryan and his predecessor was Bryan's desire to delegate. Bryan felt that delegation was necessary in order to manage an office with such a large number of partners. Indeed, while a management committee existed at the time of his appointment, it met only on an ad hoc basis mainly because of the management style of Bryan's predecessor. Bryan promptly instituted regular monthly meetings of this committee.

Another key difference between Bryan and his predecessor was Bryan's drive to create a heightened sense of working together by creating small groups. This, he believed, would produce an enthusiasm and integration of activities which, in turn, would result in a better service for clients. He also believed that the creation of small groups would allow him more time to concentrate on marketing the firm's services. Further, he believed that the main priorities of a local office managing partner were those of marketing and managing the firm, and if these tasks were to be performed effectively, he believed that the managing partner should have no client responsibilities.

PROPOSED CHANGE

Shortly after arriving, Bryan proposed a restructuring of the office organization. He suggested that the small group structure or modules of partners that effectively operated in the tax and management advisory services departments should be applied to the audit and accounting department. The audit and accounting department of the firm provided a wide range of services to clients such as audit examinations, non-audit reviews and preparation of financial statements, preparation of corporate and personal income tax returns, tax planning (both corporate and individual), advice to clients on general business practices, bookkeeping and accounting services including computerized accounting systems, preparation of cash flow projections and profit forecasts, preparation of presentations to banks in connection with bank financing, and business and security valuations.

The proposed restructuring meant that the 15 partners, 11 managers, and 69 staff accountants in the audit and accounting department would be reorganized into three modules. Each module would contain five partners, three or four managers and 21 to 24 staff and student accountants. Also, each module would have a designated module leader.

A second feature of the reorganization was to split the old management committee into two committees: a new management committee responsible for client services and an administrative committee responsible for office support services. Bryan felt that this division would better reflect the differences between these two broad activities.

The new management committee comprised the OMP and the five module leaders, that is, the three audit and accounting module leaders and the leaders of the tax and management advisory services modules. Bryan also added the director of human resources to the management committee. The director of human resources was the only management committee member who was not a partner. The administrative committee comprised the OMP and the three partners responsible for the office support service areas of administration, human resources, and marketing (see Figure 14–4 — Organizational Chart, after change).

Rationale for Change

In Bryan's view, the reorganization was intended to make the office more market oriented through heightened interaction among the partners, managers, and staff within the smaller modules. He anticipated that the module leaders would be better able to coordinate the smaller groups, enabling them to present a stronger marketing thrust. This represented a radical change in strategy. Historically, the firm and the local office had emphasized partner autonomy, seeking to enhance its reputation through audit and accounting technical excellence.

Three main precipitating conditions had led Bryan to propose this change:

1. The conditions associated with the market for the firm's services and the general economic climate were deteriorating. The local and national economies were in recession. The audit and accounting market was shrinking and becoming highly competitive. To compound the situation, clients were becoming very price

FIGURE 14–4   *Campion & Bergerac: organizational chart (after change)*

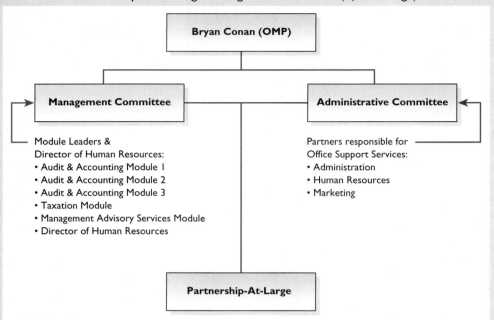

sensitive and were questioning the value of their audits. Some clients were requesting only the minimum amount of work to be performed in order to allow the auditors to opine their financial statements. For example, those with wholly owned subsidiaries were statutorily entitled to request a limited review audit.

2. A new mission statement had recently been issued by the managing partner at national headquarters that identified the need for all local offices to become more market-driven. Consequently, Bryan had identified the need for a stronger marketing thrust on the part of all staff. He felt that, compared to the previous loose organization of the audit and accounting department, the three new leaders with their smaller groups would be able to provide this stronger thrust.

3. The office had slid from earning above average net income per partner (NIPP) on a firm-wide basis to earning below average NIPP. As the new OMP, Bryan was expected by national head office to turn this situation around. Indeed, national headquarters viewed the office as "over-partnered."

Development of Change Proposal

In January 1991, Bryan formed a steering committee to assist him in developing a response to the precipitating conditions. He chose the director of human resources (an MBA) and the PIC of the management advisory services department (an engineer) to be the other members of the steering committee. Neither the director of human resources nor the PIC of management advisory services was an accountant. This committee quickly fine-tuned Bryan's ideas for a five-module structure for managing the client services side of the firm. While the creation of the position of module leader in the audit and accounting department would create a new level in the hierarchy of the firm, overall it was felt that the new structure would enhance the firm's ability to provide a marketing thrust that had not previously been available. In particular, it was felt that the module structure would help to:

- retain existing clients by delivering superior services;
- meet the expanding range of clients' service needs;
- enhance the firm's ability to cross-sell; and
- instill a sense of common purpose.

Indeed, the overall objective of this new structure was to improve the firm's ability to listen to clients in order to ensure that the firm's response was geared to clients' needs rather than the firm's (or partners') wants. Historically, Bryan felt that the firm had suffered from too many people doing their own thing.

The introduction of the module structure would largely affect the audit and accounting department, as the tax department and the management advisory services department were already organized in a module structure. By March 1991, having refined his plan with the steering committee, Bryan set about its implementation.

CHANGE IMPLEMENTATION PROCESS

In March 1991, Bryan presented his plan to a meeting of the managing committee, where it was generally supported. At that meeting they decided to hold an off-site half-day retreat of all partners, where the proposed change would be communicated to the partnership-at-large and where it could be discussed at length.

This meeting was held in April 1991. At the meeting Bryan outlined the purpose of and need for the change, and explained how it would lead to improved service delivery through increased interaction as a result of the smallness of the new modules. As Bryan put it, "it is fundamental that to have 'turned-on' and 'challenged' people you need rapport within groups; modules would give this." In general, this meeting resulted in few, if any, changes from the initial proposal.

Bryan had decided that there would be three modules in the audit and accounting department, based upon the idea that given about 15 partners, a grouping of five per module "seemed" right. Also, this size was in line with what was in operation in the management advisory service and tax departments. Bryan also chose the module leaders from among the partners, based on his assessment of who was the best person for the job. The leader of module 1 was the previous PIC of the audit and accounting client service area and the partner responsible for the support services of human resources. The leader of module 2 was previously the partner responsible for marketing and the leader of module 3 was the partner responsible for administration. These three partners continued to be responsible for their respective support service areas. No changes were made in the positions of PIC of taxation and PIC of management advisory services.

Bryan further explained that the position of module leader represented a new level in the hierarchy of the firm, a position he referred to as a "power position." Also, the new management committee would be made up of himself, the five module leaders, and the director of human resources. Previously, only partners were members of the management committee and their appointment for a fixed term allowed a high degree of rotation of partners through the management committee. Finally, Bryan explained that he would no longer carry a client load so that he could have sufficient time available to deal with strategic planning and external relations.

At the meeting it was decided that the three modules should be homogeneous with no status distinctions between them. To allocate individual partners to modules a number of external criteria were first considered, including:

1. type of industry, for example, construction, insurance, etc.
2. size of client—large versus small.

However, these standards proved unsuitable as neither of them produced homogeneous modules. Consequently, the criterion of previous personal ties between module leaders and other partners was finally chosen as the best one for creating approximately equal modules.

In May 1991, an in-house meeting involving all managers and all partners in the firm was held where the module structure was described and explained. The input or viewpoint of the managers was not requested. The allocation of managers to modules was done partly to continue previous work patterns and partly to maintain past partner/manager ties. The result was imperfect because many managers worked, and continued to work, across more than one module.

After these two meetings, the individual module leaders and the module members were left to carry out the implementation in day-to-day operations. Part of this process included a single meeting held by each module leader to explain the change to all their module members at a rank below that of manager. The new module structure necessitated a physical move within the office for many staff at all levels. These moves were required in order to ensure that people in each module would be located in the same general office area. These moves took place at the end of June 1991 and represented the effective beginning of operations under the new modular structure.

Regular module meetings were held in order to develop a common focus within each unit. Each of the modules held a biweekly meeting involving partners and managers. In two cases, within the audit and accounting modules, all partners and managers were included, while the third alternated between a full membership meeting and a partners-only meeting. The issues discussed were similar across modules and dealt with the basic functions of a public accounting practice, for example, personnel, marketing, personal development, computers, and billings and collections.

The question of allocating staff, below manager level, to a particular audit and accounting module was an unresolved issue. At a formal but superficial level, all staff were allocated to a module, although not all were aware of it. At a practical and operational level, staff worked across all three modules. The staff did not seem unduly concerned about this arrangement, but the result was little or no attachment to any one module.

SOME RESULTS

Between December 1991 and March 1992, all partners and managers were surveyed to determine what they believed were the reasons for the reorganization. Presented in Tables 14–7 and 14–8 are the resulting range of reasons for the reorganization and the effect of the reorganization on their work, as perceived by partners and managers.

1. Interaction

One reason for the shift to modules was a desire for more interaction, especially between people at different

TABLE 14–7 *Agreement on the reasons for reorganization*

	PARTNERS % AGREED	MANAGERS % AGREED
Too many partners	73	70
Increased interaction: partners & managers	55	70
Economic recession	45	0
Integrated service for the client	36	0
Producing "turned-on" people	27	0
Interaction between different services	27	17
Managing partner's lack of experience	18	17

TABLE 14–8 *Effects of the reorganization*

	PARTNERS	MANAGERS
	(% REPORTING NO EFFECT)	
Altered career development	91	87
Altered pattern of work allocation	73	39
Altered the way work is carried out	73	70
Altered allocation of responsibilities	55	13
Altered performance appraisal	45	52

levels within the firm. Many said that the reorganization, along with the physical move to new office areas, resulted in more interaction among certain levels. Partners and managers within a module definitely saw more of each other than under the previous system. However, interaction patterns were confined more often to people within a module. Managers had less interaction with other managers outside their module and also had much less interaction than previously with staff.

2. Work Activities and Allocation

To the question of whether the change had affected how people performed their jobs, the response was a unanimous "no effect." However, there were some small attempts to move responsibilities for billings and collections and personnel development from partners to managers.

With respect to allocation of work, a key concern was to maintain past ties with clients and to ensure continued contact with key staff. Consequently, the home module of staff was considered irrelevant or of much lower priority in the allocation process than prior ties with client.

3. Personnel Development

Largely because of biweekly meetings there was an increased interaction between managers and partners. Managers expressed a greater appreciation and understanding of the role and responsibilities of a partner and what was involved at the more senior levels of the firm.

4. Separate Practices

Each of the three modules exhibited the beginnings of a separate identity and culture as they struggled with the practicalities of implementation. Each module developed an individual style, significantly influenced by its leader and the leader's view of the module concept. The leader of Module 1 strongly supported the module concept but was uncertain how the position of module leader should fit into the hierarchy of the firm. The leader of Module 2 accepted, at least initially, the position of module leader as a new level of power in the hierarchy but encountered difficulties with its implementation. And the leader of Module 3 was against the module concept from the start and continued to operate in his previous collegial style, viewing his role as that of coordinator, not manager.

Consequently, Module 1 had a more "laid back" image and was seen as adopting a more cautious approach before taking action. Module 2 was definitely seen as taking a more directive stance with attempts to establish clear plans, direction, and follow-up. Module 3 tried to operate in a collegial fashion, relying upon close and established bonds to achieve agreement and common direction. "Ready Aim Aim, Ready Fire Aim, and Ready Aim Fire" was how the leader of Module 3 named them, respectively. Each module essentially became a separate division, coordinated by the management committee.

5. Committees

The revised management committee met at least monthly and on occasions biweekly. However, as the three leaders of the audit and accounting modules were also the partners responsible for the three office support service areas, the administrative committee rarely met.

POST-CHANGE VIEWS

Partners

A problem for many people, including the module leaders, was ambiguity about the role of the module leader. Initially, it had been left up to each leader and his (all leaders were male) colleagues to interpret the role. Partners tended to see it as a facilitator type of position that provided help and general direction but without any great power. Some partners did think that a power position was intended but denied the possibility of such a change. For most, though, it was certainly not a position that would replace any of the main tasks usually performed by the managing partner. A common example offered was the need for the managing partner to maintain an open-door policy and to continue to do all partner performance appraisals.

However, partners saw themselves as having less access to the office managing partner, a situation that did not please them. Module leaders had to resolve issues with partners, but felt they had no authority over their fellow partners, a feeling that was reciprocated. Consequently, module leaders saw their role as that of coordinator rather than a manager. For example, partners still went to the OMP, over "big issues." A further problem was that, due to the recession, there was considerable pressure on partners to generate work and fees. This led to a situation where little or no time was given to management and administrative issues. The partners' attention was very much focused on the bottom-line, to the neglect of all else.

Managers and Staff Accountants

From the perspective of the managers and staff accountants, the module leader was seen as having a definite place in the hierarchy, with authority and responsibility to go along with the job.

SOME SPECIFIC COMMENTS

Between December 1991 and March 1992, 75 staff members representing all levels of staff within the firm, from partners to secretaries, were asked whether or not the move to the module system was worthwhile for the firm. Of the responses, only 23 percent saw it as a positive move, 36 percent saw it as a negative move, and the remaining 41 percent were indifferent. The following are some of their comments.

STEERING COMMITTEE MEMBERS

OMP

"A more team-oriented approach will make those partners committed to a 'client-for life' approach feel very uncomfortable."

PIC Management Advisory Services

"In the past the managing partner has always been 'Big Daddy.' That has now been removed in this office and it has left people at a loss."

Director of Human Resources

"I'm not from an accounting background so I questioned the 'traditional wisdom.' I was not convinced that the organization was structured for the market."

MODULE LEADERS

Module 1

"The module system was introduced to get more cooperation and interaction from partners and managers. There was a problem of too many people doing their own thing."

"Promoting teamwork means we can bring more resources to clients."

"There was a lot of negative feedback from partners (over the module leaders) as it was seen as a 'caste' system."

"The allocation of managers was essentially a compromise."

Module 2

"The module leader introduces a new level of power."

"There was a lack of communication between the management committee and the other partners and managers generally."

"The module leader has no authority over the other partners; he can only suggest."

Module 3

"I was against the idea and the process. You don't need wholesale change to build rapport. I don't need the staff alongside me to get on with them."

"He (the OMP) tried to make the module leaders power positions; I'm against that and anyway it caused a lot of hassle with the partners."

"I see myself as a coordinator, not a manager. I initially turned down the request to be a module leader."

"My module has worked out well. The other two have conflicts and problems which derive from the power position idea. The other two tried to force their partners to do things. Partners do not accept the additional level. I work on an all-equal basis."

PARTNERS

Module 1

"I don't regard myself as having a boss; I am accountable to my clients. I don't actually need a managing partner to do my job."

"The module idea came from the OMP. It doesn't affect day-to-day work. The disappearance of the modules wouldn't matter at all."

"The module leaders are not a new level in the hierarchy. I would be very upset if our module leader tried to do my appraisal. That's the job of the managing partner."

"The reorganization was done by the management committee. I don't really know the reasons and it hasn't changed my life."

Module 2

"I never attended any of the meetings (about the module system) as they were called at short notice and I am one of the busier partners."

"From my personal point of view I didn't see the need for any change and I haven't noticed much change."

"The general consensus on the change was negative."

Module 3

"The module system doesn't affect me and anyway I'm not a supporter."

"Nothing on the reorganization comes up at partner meetings; there is no monitoring or review in the general partnership."

MANAGERS

"There is much more contact with the partners, and managers now know much more."

"The module meetings have produced a much better dialogue."

"The potential effect of the modules is diluted because organizationally they don't mean a hell of a lot to anyone."

"The staff don't feel part of the module system and this is a problem."

By August 1992, Bryan Conan was concerned about whether the new module structure was producing any of the results he had set out to achieve. He was aware of several of the negative comments that had been made concerning the changes. While considering what further actions he might take, he mused on whether the new module concept was really appropriate or whether the negative comments simply represented resistance to change.

STEP 2: Prepare the case for class discussion.

STEP 3: Answer the following questions, individually, in small groups, or with the entire class, as directed by your instructor.

DESCRIPTION

1. Describe the original organization at Campion & Bergerac in terms of division of labor and coordinating mechanisms.
2. Classify the original organization as functional, market oriented, integrated, or other form.
3. Describe the new organization at Campion & Bergerac in terms of division of labor and coordinating mechanisms.

4. Classify the new organization as functional, market oriented, integrated, or other form.

DIAGNOSIS

5. Compare and contrast the old and new structures.
6. What problems does each structure solve? create?
7. How well does the new structure respond to the environment?
8. How well does the new structure consider technology?
9. How well does the new structure respond to the organization's work force?
10. How well does the new structure respond to the organization's goals and strategy?
11. How well does the new structure respond to the organization's stage in the life cycle?

PRESCRIPTION

12. What changes are still required?

ACTION

13. What process was used to redesign the organization and implement the changes?
14. Was the process effective?
15. What were the costs and benefits associated with the change?

STEP 4: Discussion. In small groups or with the entire class, share your answers to the questions above. Then answer the following questions:

1. What symptoms suggested the problems existed?
2. What problems existed?
3. What theories and concepts help explain the problems?
4. How were the problems corrected?
5. Will the proposed changes likely be effective?

This case was prepared by John O'Dwyer under the supervision of Professor John Howard of the Western Business School. Copyright © 1992, The University of Western Ontario.

This material is not covered under authorization from CanCopy or any reproduction rights organization. Any form of reproduction, storage or transmittal of this material is prohibited without written permission from Western Business School, The University of Western Ontario, London, Canada N6A 3K7. Reprinted with permission, Western Business School.

Activity 14–2

WORDS IN SENTENCES COMPANY

STEP 1: Form companies and assign work places. Each group should include between seven and twelve people and should consider itself a company. In this exercise you will form a "miniorganization" with several other people. You will be competing with other companies in your industry. The success of your company will depend on (a) your objectives, (b) planning, (c) organizational structure, and (d) quality control. It is important, therefore, that you spend some time thinking about the best design for your organization.

STEP 2: Read the following directions and ask your instructor about any points that need clarification.

DIRECTIONS

You are a small company that manufactures words and then packages them in meaningful English-language sentences. Market research has established that sentences of at least three words but not more than six words are in demand. Therefore, packaging, distribution, and sales should be set up for three- to six-word sentences.

The words-in-sentences industry is highly competitive. Several new firms have recently entered what appears to be an expanding market. Since raw materials, technology, and pricing are all standard for the industry, your ability to compete depends on two factors: (1) volume and (2) quality.

GROUP TASK

Your group must design and participate in running a WIS company. You should design your organization to be as efficient as possible during each ten-minute production run. After the first production run, you will have an opportunity to reorganize your company if you want.

RAW MATERIALS

For each production run you will be given a "raw material word or phrase." The letters found in the word or phrase serve as the raw materials available to produce new words in sentences. For example, if the raw material word is "organization," you could produce the words and sentence: "Nat ran to a zoo."

PRODUCTION STANDARDS

There are several rules that have to be followed in producing "words in sentences." If these rules are not followed, your output will not meet production specifications and will not pass quality-control inspection.

1. The same letter may appear only as often in a manufactured word as it appears in the raw material word or phrase; for example, "organization" has two o's. Thus "zoo" is legitimate, but not "zoonosis." It has too many o's and s's.
2. Raw material letters can be used again in different manufactured words.
3. A manufactured word may be used only once in a sentence and in only one sentence during a production run; if a word—for example, "a"—is used once in a sentence, it is out of stock.
4. A new word may not be made by adding "s" to form the plural of an already used manufactured word.
5. A word is defined by its spelling, not its meaning.
6. Nonsense words or nonsense sentences are unacceptable.
7. All words must be in the English language.
8. Names and places are acceptable.
9. Slang is not acceptable.

MEASURING PERFORMANCE

The output of your WIS company is measured by the total number of acceptable words that are packaged in sentences. The sentences must be legible, listed on no more than two sheets of paper, and handed to the Quality Control Review Board at the completion of each production run.

DELIVERY

Delivery must be made to the Quality Control Review Board thirty seconds after the end of each production run.

QUALITY CONTROL

If any word in a sentence does not meet the standards set forth above, all the words in the sentence will be rejected.

The Quality Control Review Board (composed of one member from each company) is the final arbiter of acceptability. In the event of a tie vote on the Review Board, a coin toss will determine the outcome.

STEP 3: Design your organization using as many group members as you see fit to produce your words in sentences.

STEP 4: Production Run 1. The group leader will hand each WIS company a sheet with a raw material word or phrase. When the instructor announces "Begin production," you are to manufacture as many words as possible and package them in sentences for delivery to the Quality Control Review Board. You will have ten minutes. When the instructor announces "Stop production," you will have thirty seconds to deliver your output to the Quality Control Review Board. Output received after thirty seconds does not meet the delivery schedule and will not be counted.

STEP 5: While the output is being evaluated, you may reorganize for the second production run.

STEP 6: Production Run 2.

STEP 7: The results are presented.

STEP 8: Discussion. In small groups, and then with the entire class, answer the following questions.

DESCRIPTION

1. Draw the organizational chart for your WIS company.

DIAGNOSIS

2. Analyze its structure: describe (a) division of labor, (b) mechanisms of coordination, and (c) structural configurations.
3. Using your knowledge of organizational design and the contingencies that influence it, evaluate your WIS company's structure.

PRESCRIPTION

4. How could you have designed a more effective organizational structure?

The origin of this exercise is unknown.

Activity 14–3   GLOBAL FOOD REDESIGN PROBLEM

STEP 1: Read the description of the Global Food Corporation.

We have come a long way in building this business over the last several decades, including diversification into detergents and toiletries, and geographical expansion beyond the United States into Europe, South America, and Asia. But we face an even stronger challenge in the future, as well-focused large competitors like Proctor & Gamble move in on our detergent market. Similarly, General Foods is active in our fundamental business and British, Dutch, and German multinationals are increasingly competing with all of our product lines. Also, local domestic competitors, encouraged by their governments, are beginning to attack our market share.

Ted Adams, President of Global Foods, was challenging his colleagues to think creatively about the future of their business.

You're as familiar with the indicators as I am. Profit performance for each of our product lines varies widely by country, although no product line is losing money now. Overall our market share, even though it varies from country to country and from product to product, seems to be declining, and our profits are not improving. No two subsidiaries for a given business product line seem to be taking advantage of common expertise, such as buying raw materials, marketing, distribution, packaging, or research and development.

Global, established in 1927 as a New York-based small foods corporation, grew into one of the larger multinationals through diversification into processed food, toiletries, and detergents. Figure 14–5 shows its current organization structure. The multibillion dollar consumer goods company has well over one hundred thousand employees and operates in 20 countries. One of its best assets is worldwide recognition of its major brand names. While the three product line groups serve essentially the same consumers, they do require, in many markets, different marketing policies and distribution channels.

Operations in each country are autonomous, however the key executives in each country periodically meet to discuss marketing techniques. All three product lines depend on the common R&D group for new manufacturing process innovations, by infrequently communicating information from consumers back to R&D. Each country makes its own product modifications. However, a significant proportion of raw materials, and sometimes manufacturing process innovations, cut across at least two of the three product line groups, e.g., foods, detergents, toiletries. For example, the use of edible oils and fatty acids in manufacturing, and certain packaging techniques, are common to both food and detergents. Because of these manufacturing techniques, it is not uncommon that within a given country one plant may depend on the output of another plant from a different product line group.

Adams became Chief Executive Officer three years ago after a very successful career in two of the four major countries outlined in this case. He is very knowledgeable in foods and detergents. He had admired the existing structure when he was vice president of the India operation. As soon as he moved into the new position, however, he began to realize that the company was going to need more cash than it could generate internally because of inflation. At cabinet meetings, the vice presidents from each country make frequent capital investment proposals. These range from modernizing manufacturing facilities to meet local pollution and safety related investments to increasing outlays for business expansion. In the president's view, there simply isn't enough cash in the till to meet all the proposals. He wonders whether it

FIGURE 14–5   *Global food corporation (A): partial organizational chart*

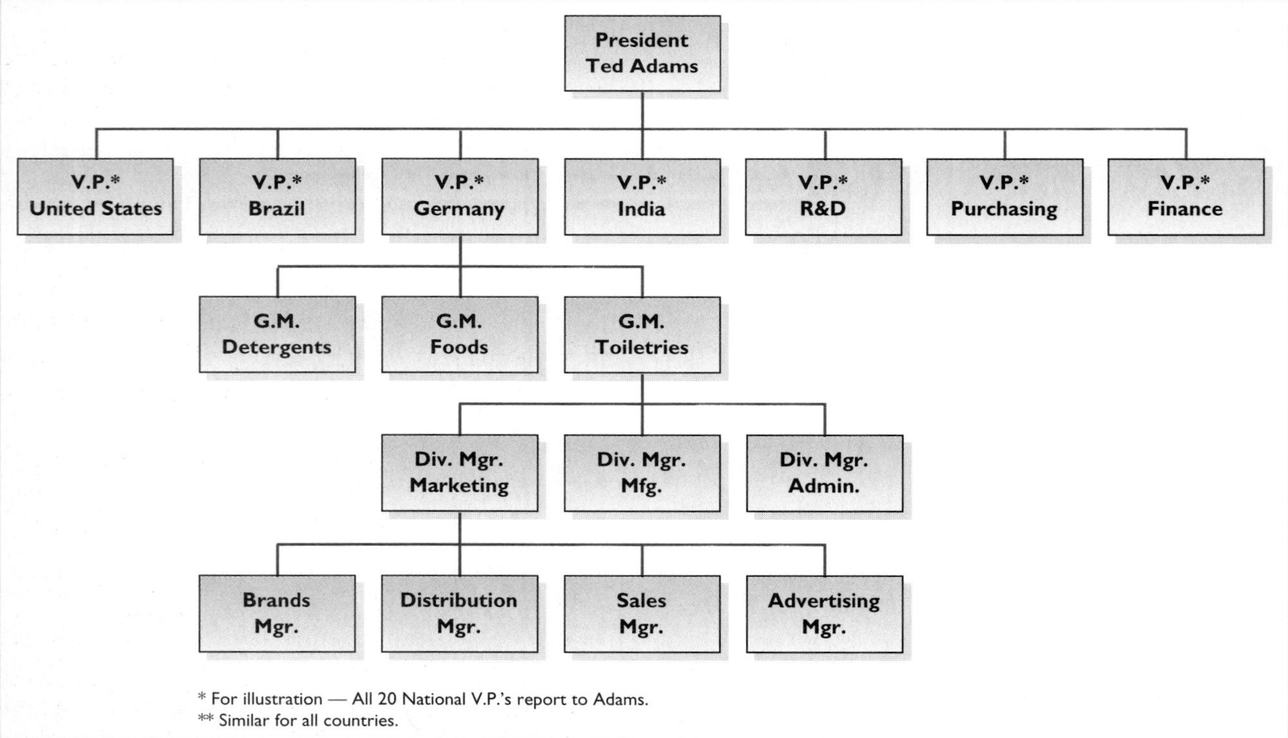

* For illustration — All 20 National V.P.'s report to Adams.
** Similar for all countries.

would be wise to allow expansion from each country as presented. Even if the company had all of the necessary funds, many of the proposals contain elements of risk that Adams does not believe represents any effective overall corporate strategy.

Global maintains a policy of appointing national citizens to run the businesses in their own countries. This frequently places them in a position of ambivalence when company and national interests are at odds. At lower levels people move frequently from country to country, and from product line to product line.

An important factor in decisions of where to deploy assets is the desire not to become overcommitted in high politically and economically volatile areas. For example, Brazil is experiencing a 40 percent inflation rate and some are predicting extreme labor unrest. While the Company wants to maintain current production levels, it does not want all of its eggs in one basket, particularly a fragile one.

When Ted Adams asked others at the meeting to comment on the key issues he got these reactions:

- Our net after taxes is only 3 percent of sales, and fluctuations in currencies and an error in raw materials purchasing could wipe out all the profit.

- 50 percent of our cost is in raw material and yet very few countries are self sufficient in raw materials.

- No one is looking specifically to discover substitutions for raw materials.

- Competitors are selectively attacking our markets.

- We are not fighting back cohesively.

- Let's not forget our advantage in understanding local government operations, personalities, and foibles.

- The corporate staffs (R&D, purchasing, and finance) participate only peripherally in policy decision making. We manage the critical flow of international currencies, but are viewed by others primarily as publishers of internal auditing and administrative reports.

- Consumerists are attacking us both for the aerosol propellants used in some of our toiletries and the heavy sugar content in some food products.

Adams and his vice presidents agree that their focus has been inward, without enough consideration to the external changes impacting on current decisions. Their objectives seem clear:

1. Regain aggressive leadership in each product line.
2. Prevent the erosion of market share and profit.
3. Have the flexibility to respond to external pressures peculiar to each market.

Adams asked each member of the committee to develop at least two alternatives for organizing the Company to prepare itself for further profitable growth and to withstand highly focused/concentrated competition. This assignment was given to stimulate each member to be not only creative, but also flexible and realistic in judging the pros and cons of each alternative.

For keeping the problem tractable the Executive Committee decided to limit the discussion to four countries and the three major product lines. Here is how they sized up the situation (see page 652):

Adams added as an afterthought that to develop alternative structures one must clearly define one's assumptions about the future environment.

· ·

STEP 2: In groups of two or three students, prepare answers to Adams' charge as if you were a member of Global's executive committee.

· ·

STEP 3: Share your responses with other small groups or the entire class.

· ·

STEP 4: Discussion. In small groups or with the entire class, answer the following questions:

1. How would you describe Global's current structure?
2. What changes should be made in the structure?
3. What would be the elements of a new structure?
4. Offer a redesign of Global Food Corporation.

	UNITED STATES	BRAZIL	INDIA	GERMANY
Inflation	10%	40%	15%	4%
Product demand	Maturing	High growth	High growth	Maturing except foods high
Competition	Open	Highly restricted	Highly controlled	Relatively open
Governmental regulation through price controls, etc.	None	Can happen without notice	Can happen without notice	None
Import of raw materials and equipment	No governmental permission required	Governmental permission required	Governmental permission required	No governmental permission required
Governmental support to native industry	None	High priority	High priority	Possible
Technology in marketing, manufacturing, and product development	High and locally available	Normally imported	Normally imported	High and locally available

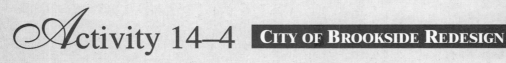

Activity 14–4   CITY OF BROOKSIDE REDESIGN

STEP 1: Review the organizational structure of the City of Brookside shown in Figure 14–6.

STEP 2: Answer the following questions, individually, in small groups, or with the entire class.

DESCRIPTION

1. Describe the organization's structure: its division of labor and coordinating mechanisms.
2. What structural paradigms best describe the organization?

DIAGNOSIS

3. Describe the nature of the following contingencies: (a) goals, (b) environment, (c) technology, (d) work force, (e) size, and (f) age.
4. How does the organization's structure fit with these contingencies?
5. Is the current design appropriate? effective?

PRESCRIPTION

6. What changes should be made?

FIGURE 14–6   *City of Brookside, existing organization*

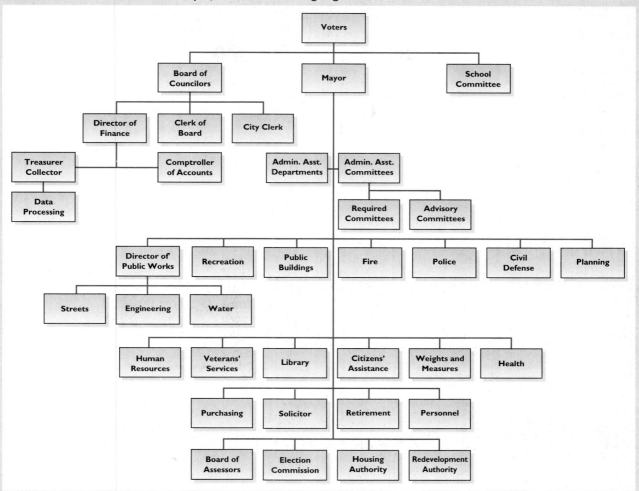

Activity 14–5   CENTURY SUPERMARKET REDESIGN

STEP 1: Review the organizational structure of the regional operations and sales divisions of Century Supermarket shown in Figure 14–7 (page 654).

STEP 2: Answer the following questions, individually, in small groups, or with the entire class.

DESCRIPTION

1. Describe the organization's structure: its division of labor and coordinating mechanisms.
2. What structural paradigms best describe the organization?

DIAGNOSIS

3. Describe the nature of the following contingencies: (a) goals, (b) strategy, (c) environment, (d) technology, (e) work force, (f) size, and (g) age.
4. How does the organization's structure fit with these contingencies?
5. Is the current design appropriate? effective?

PRESCRIPTION

6. What changes should be made?

FIGURE 14–7

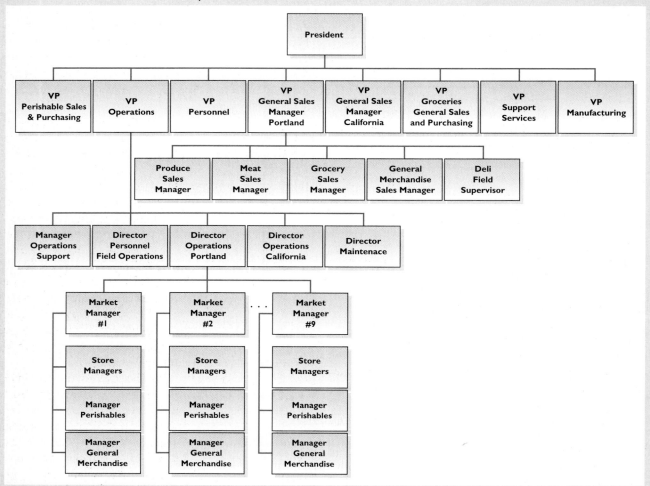

$\mathscr{A}$ctivity 14–6 — ORGANIZATIONAL LIFE-CYCLE EXERCISE

STEP 1: Choose two organizations.

STEP 2: Collect written documents that trace the history of each organization. Interview organization members who are familiar with the development of the organization. Gather any additional data available about the organization's growth and development.

STEP 3: In dyads or triads, share the data you have collected. Trace the stages in each organization's development. What issues did the organization face at each stage? What problems did the organization encounter in its development? Compare and contrast the development of the two organizations. How were they similar? different?

STEP 4: Discussion. In small groups or with the entire class, identify the stages in development you have identified. Which stages do these organizations have in common? How did the development of these organizations differ? How do effective organizations differ from ineffective organizations in their development?

$\mathcal{A}$ctivity 14–7 — FERGUSONCHEMICAL EUROPE CASE

STEP I: Read the Fergusonchemical Europe Case.

On a gray day in February 1985, Ian Robertson, Land Transportation Manager for Fergusonchemical Europe, sat in his office reviewing a recent organization survey. The results confirmed his worst fears. The survey, which had used scientific sampling procedures, showed the Fergusonchemical Europe's customers were receiving their products when promised only 75 percent of the time. The table on pages 656 and 657 presents a summary of the survey findings.

These recent findings alone gave management adequate grounds for concern and, combined with information acquired from previous reports, it was clear that Fergusonchemical Europe's customer service was unsatisfactory. The earlier surveys, two in particular, had disturbed the regional distribution management team and had motivated Regional Distribution Manager Philippe Magistretti, Marine Manager Peter Gordon, and Ian Robertson to initiate the recently completed survey.

In 1983, a survey of sales personnel showed that the sales personnel of Fergusonchemical Europe did not consider their organization competitive in areas important to customers. In addition, a 1984 survey of plastics users in the United Kingdom found that Fergusonchemical was not viewed as competitive as British Petroleum, Shell, or DSM in significant areas of customer service. The same two issues were cited repeatedly by Fergusonchemical customers as sources of frustration. First, Fergusonchemical frequently did not deliver on time. Second, when deliveries were delayed, Fergusonchemical often failed to inform the customers. Given the environment facing the chemical industry in Europe in general, and strategic decisions recently made by Fergusonchemical Europe in particular, distribution management realized, as did senior management, that the existing level of customer service had to be considerably improved.

FERGUSONCHEMICAL EUROPE AND THE INDUSTRY

Fergusonchemical Europe, a wholly owned subsidiary of Ferguson Corporation, was the ninth largest chemical company in Europe with revenues in 1984 of approximately 2.5 billion dollars. Fergusonchemical's products were classified into seven different chemical product lines. These product lines included: elastomers, plastics, solvents, plasticizers and intermediates, specialties, paramins, and olefins. Each product line was managed by a vice president based at company headquarters in Munich.

In addition to seven product segments, Fergusonchemical Europe was also divided into nine wholly-owned subsidiaries, each one serving one or more Western European countries: the United Kingdom, France, Belgium, West Germany, Netherlands, Italy, Spain, Portugal, and Sweden. Each affiliate had a managing director as well as marketing manager who coordinated sales within each product line. Salespeople reported to their respective marketing managers who, in turn, reported to both the affiliate managing director and a product vice president located in Munich. Because of this dual reporting relationship, Fergusonchemical Europe had a matrix organization design. Figure 14–8 presents an organization chart for Fergusonchemical Europe. Figure 14–9 presents a partial organizational chart which includes regional distribution personnel.

During the 1980's, a number of factors contributed to an increasingly competitive environment for European chemical companies. A key development was the creation of overcapacity, especially in the area of commodity chemicals. In response to strong demand and high earnings during the 1970's, a number of chemical companies expanded their production facilities. Favorable market opportunities during the 1970's also attracted a number of new competitors, primarily from the Gulf oil countries. Their access to large inexpensive oil reserves and relatively low labor costs posed a significant challenge to existing European chemical companies. Projections indicated that chemical companies based in the Middle East would continue to offer increasing competition in the future.

In addition to excess capacity and growing competition, European chemical companies in 1985 were still recovering from the devastating effects of the economic recession of the early 1980's. A number of European chemical companies, including German-based BASF and Hoechst and Dutch-based DSM, initiated strategic diversification programs in response to an increasingly competitive business environment.

Statistical check, last week of January 1985, customer delivery reliability

	SWEDEN			U.K.			NETHERLANDS		
	BEFORE	ON DAY	AFTER	BEFORE	ON DAY	AFTER	BEFORE	ON DAY	AFTER
P&I		3			8			1	
Specialties		2			2	3		2	
Elastomers		4		1	12	1		1	
Paramins		2		1	12	2		2	
Plastics		3			9	4		2	
Solvents		2	1		13			3	
Total		16	1	2	67	10		11	
Total %*		94	6	2	85	13		100	

	RAW DATA (TOTAL)			TOTAL	WEIGHTED PERCENTAGES (TOTAL %)		
	BEFORE	ON DAY	AFTER		BEFORE	ON DAY	AFTER
P&I	3	40	1	44	7	91	2
Specialties	3	22	11	36	8	61	31
Elastomers	4	33	12	49	8	67	25
Paramins	6	28	14	48	13	58	29
Plastics	2	30	18	50	4	60	36
Solvents	—	52	5	57	—	91	9
Total	18	205	61	284			
Total %	6	72	22		5	Weighted 75	20

*Raw data numbers of deliveries checked. Not statistically weighted.

Weather: The last week of January 1985 was affected by the thaw restrictions of truck movement in France. This particularly affected resins and elastomers.

FIGURE 14–8   *Structure of Fergusonchemical Europe*

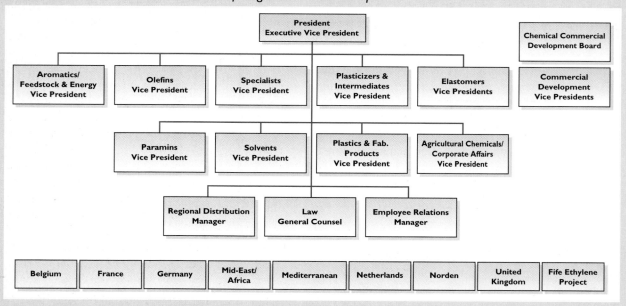

	GERMANY			FRANCE			ITALY			BELGIUM	
BEFORE	ON DAY	AFTER	BEFORE	ON DAY	AFTER	BEFORE	ON DAY	AFTER	BEFORE	ON DAY	AFTER
2	13			12	1		No Deliveries		1	3	
1	5	3	1	8	1	1	3	3			1
3	4	3		5	5		2	3		4	
1	2	6		6	2	4	3	3		1	1
1	9	5		2	2	1	3	3		2	4
	10	1		6	1		6	2		2	
8	43	18	1	39	12	6	17	14	1	12	14
12	62	26	2	75	23	16	46	38	4	44	52

WEIGHING CALCULATION

REGION WEIGHT	BEFORE	ON DAY	AFTER	
0.06	0.42	5.46	0.12	
0.07	0.56	4.27	2.17	
0.12	0.96	8.04	3.00	
0.15	1.95	8.70	4.35	
0.20	0.80	12.00	7.20	
0.40	—	36.40	3.60	
1	4.69	74.87	20.44	100

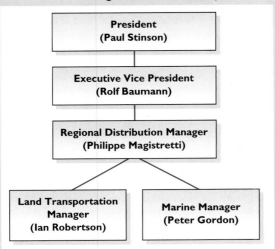

FIGURE 14–9 *Partial organizational chart, Fergusonchemical Europe*

President
(Paul Stinson)

Executive Vice President
(Rolf Baumann)

Regional Distribution Manager
(Philippe Magistretti)

Land Transportation Manager
(Ian Robertson)

Marine Manager
(Peter Gordon)

Fergusonchemical Europe, however, opted not to concentrate on diversification. Instead, the organization adopted what it termed a "value-added strategy," which influenced product decisions as well as customer relationships. With the existing industry overcapacity in commodity chemicals, Fergusonchemical Europe decided to focus on the production and sale of specialty chemicals. As specialty chemicals require a more lengthy complex production process, they can command higher prices and therefore offer greater profit potential. Fergusonchemical Europe believed that its technical expertise, production facilities, and resource base gave it a competitive advantage in this market segment.

In addition, the organization made a commitment to value-added customer service, using technical expertise, product knowledge, resource availability, and dedicated effort. Fergusonchemical Europe promised to provide a level of customer service superior to that offered by the competition. Executives described this new strategy as a change from production orientation to market orientation. The need for increased sensitivity to customer requirements was stressed throughout the organization.

Paul Stinson, President of Fergusonchemical Europe, was responsible for the development, articulation and selling of the new value-added strategy to both internal and external constituencies. This strategy was summarized by Paul Stinson in a document entitled *Our Future Vision,* which was published and widely distributed to company personnel.

SALES, DISTRIBUTION, AND CUSTOMER SERVICE OPERATIONS

In order to implement Fergusonchemical's goal of providing superior customer service, the existing structure needed reassessment. Each affiliate marketing manager served as the link between salespeople, the affiliate managing director, and the relevant product vice president at headquarters.

Affiliate marketing managers were assisted with their responsibilities by a secretary and a customer service coordinator. Customer service coordinators were responsible for ensuring that orders generated by sales personnel were smoothly executed. Activities frequently performed by customer service coordinators included processing orders, securing warehouse space, arranging for transportation needs, and answering customers' questions. Customer service coordinators usually reported to a single marketing manager and were considered members of the product team within each affiliate. In cases where product lines were small, a customer service coordinator would work with several marketing managers. In addition to expediting customers' orders, customer service coordinators occasionally assisted marketing managers with other administrative responsibilities. Fergusonchemical Europe employed approximately 120 customer service coordinators within their nine affiliate organizations. Figure 14–10 presents a demographic profile of customer service coordinators.

It was apparent from the findings of the recent corporate surveys that the existing organization of the distribution function was unsatisfactory. The regional distribution team (Philippe Magistretti, Ian Robertson, and Peter Gordon) was seriously concerned and began a reappraisal of Fergusonchemical Europe's distribution system.

The team felt strongly that distribution activities must be able to meet the dual objective of performing value-added customer service in a cost effective man-

ner. In their discussions, regional distribution management personnel frequently referred to recent management books that stressed the importance of quality in all business activities.

Regional distribution management was particularly concerned about the assignment of customer service coordinators to individual product groups within affiliate organizations. The team was convinced that this structure was both inefficient and ineffective. In most cases, a single customer service coordinator worked within a product group. Therefore, when this person was unavailable because of illness, vacation, or other job responsibilities, customer inquiries frequently went unanswered. Philippe Magistretti and his colleagues maintained that the existing arrangement put customer service "at risk."

Although regional distribution management was willing to acknowledge differences among productive groups, there were many similarities in the activities performed by customer service coordinators. With the current structure, it was difficult for customer service coordinators to assist or learn from one another. Opportunities for career growth and advancement were also restricted because customer service coordinators were isolated within individual product groups. The regional distribution team realized that the present system was inhibiting economies of scale with respect to customer service operations.

Studies indicated that optimum economies of scale could be reached only if a minimum of five customer service coordinators were centrally situated. A recent phone survey supported the team's case for reorganization. The survey showed that customer service coordinators took an average of 70 seconds to answer an inquiry. Regional distribution management believed that all customer inquiries should be answered within 30 seconds. Figure 14–11 presents the results of the telephone survey.

PROPOSED REORGANIZATION

The recent survey on delivery time delays convinced the regional distribution management team that it must prepare and implement a reorganization plan. The proposed reorganization would remove customer service coordinators from the individual product groups and consolidate them in a central location within each affiliate organization. Instead of each customer service coordinator reporting to an individual affiliate marketing manager,

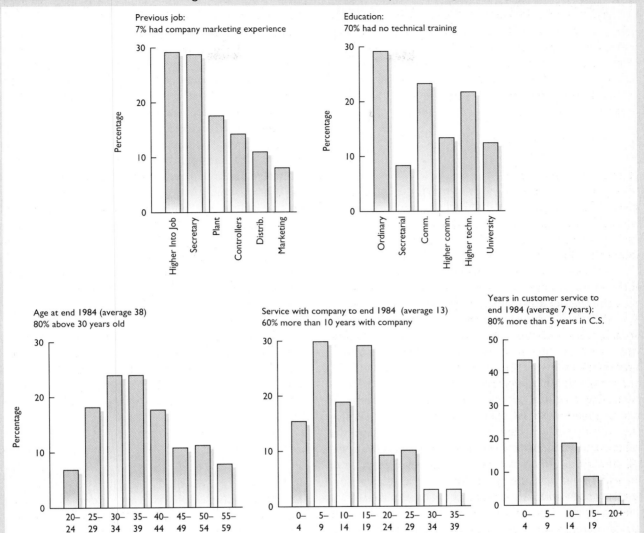

all customer service coordinators would report to an affiliate distribution manager.

The regional distribution team realized that the reorganization plan alone could not rectify the problem of late deliveries. Recent studies had shown that delivery times being quoted to customers were clearly unrealistic for some products. In addition, certain job descriptions needed rewriting in order to give better customer service. However, their analysis showed that a majority of late deliveries were attributable to an inappropriately organized customer service function.

Philippe Magistretti, Ian Robertson, and Peter Gordon were aware that their proposed reorganization would encounter stiff opposition. Affiliate marketing managers in particular would strongly resist the proposed reorganization. On numerous occasions affiliate marketing managers had stressed that the customer service coordinator was the cornerstone of the product team, serving as a vital communications link to the market. Placing the customer service coordinators on the product teams also enhanced their accessibility and commitment to product team mem-

FIGURE 14–11

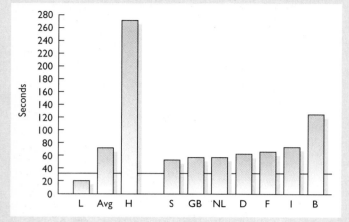

and cost. As members of a product team, customer service coordinators generally tried to maximize customer service even if it meant costs would be higher. Would a central affiliate distribution center sacrifice customer service in order to reduce costs?

In addition to the above obstacles, the regional distribution management team realized that it operated within a matrix organization of product lines, affiliates, and functions. However, Philippe Magistretti, Ian Robertson, and Peter Gordon felt no doubt that the reorganization was necessary. Furthermore, the executive vice president of Fergusonchemical Europe, Rolf Baumann, had publicly stated that he supported the establishment of centralized customer service groups within the affiliate organizations. Failure to improve the current level of customer service might well endanger Fergusonchemical Europe's recently adopted business strategy. The question now facing regional distribution management was how to achieve acceptance and implement the proposed reorganization plan.

STEP 2: Prepare the case for class discussion.

STEP 3: Answer the following questions, individually, in small groups, or with the entire class, as directed by your instructor.

DESCRIPTION

1. Describe the original organization at Fergusonchemical Europe in terms of division of labor and coordinating mechanisms.
2. Classify the original organization using (a) form of departmentation, (b) means of coordination, (c) organic versus mechanistic classifications, and (d) information-processing capacity.
3. Describe the proposed reorganization in terms of division of labor and coordinating mechanisms.
4. Classify the proposed reorganization using (a) form of departmentation, (b) means of coordination, (c) organic versus mechanistic classifications, and (d) information-processing capacity.

DIAGNOSIS

5. Compare and contrast the original and proposed organizations.

bers. Marketing managers feared that these benefits would be lost after the reorganization. Finally, affiliate marketing managers questioned whether customer service coordinators were qualified to assume the new responsibilities that the proposed reorganization would entail.

Customer service coordinators also expressed concern regarding the reorganization. Fergusonchemical Europe was described by numerous customer service coordinators as a product driven company, where the jobs considered most attractive were associated with the product lines. Functional jobs, on the other hand, were viewed by many as "a necessary evil," a concept fostered by some affiliate marketing managers. Customer service coordinators therefore feared loss of both status and identification with a product team with the proposed reorganization.

Richard Elsner, customer service coordinator for the United Kingdom affiliate, voiced the concern of many customer service coordinators. "My biggest source of job satisfaction is helping the customer, particularly when it requires a little bit extra. To help your customers you need rapport and influence within the product team. My fear is that if I am isolated from my product team, I will lose the rapport and influence necessary to help my customers."

Customer service coordinators also worried about possible conflicts of interest between customer service

6. How do the structures respond to changing information-processing needs?

7. How do the structures respond to the employees' needs?

8. Comment on differences in communication, span of control, unity of command, and decentralization in the structures.

9. What problems does each structure solve? create?

PRESCRIPTION

10. What changes were required in the original structure?

11. Does the reorganization provide the needed changes?

ACTION

12. Was the process used to redesign the organization and then implement the changes effective? What costs and benefits resulted?

STEP 4: Discussion. In small groups or with the entire class, share your answers to the questions above. Then answer the following questions:

1. What symptoms suggested that problems existed?

2. What problems exist in the case?

3. What theories and concepts help explain the problems?

4. How were the problems corrected? How should they have been corrected?

5. Will the proposed changes likely be effective?

Activity 14–8   "New Jobs Being Created"

STEP 1: View the ABC video entitled "New Jobs Being Created."

STEP 2: Individually, in small groups, or with the entire class, answer the following questions:

1. What impact will the increase in minimum wage likely have on the labor force?

2. Think of three different organizations. How will job growth affect these organizations?

3. Assume that these organizations will increase in size by 20 percent. What will be the impact of the increased size on their organizational design?

4. Draw the current organizational charts for these organizations and show how they should change if the number of employees increases by 20 percent.

Chapter 15

Chapter Outline

Changing Organizations for Increased Performance and Competitiveness

LEARNING OBJECTIVES

After completing the reading and activities in Chapter 15, students will be able to

1. Outline the four points on the continuum of planned change.

2. Diagnose the forces for and against change in a situation.

3. Describe the key issues and options in selecting a change agent.

4. Build an action plan for changing a situation.

5. Identify the major concerns in selecting interventions and implementing change.

6. Offer an approach to evaluating change.

7. Present a protocol for institutionalizing change.

8. Summarize the issues of managing for performance and competitiveness in a global environment.

The Turnaround at Allied-Signal

As it entered the 1990s, Allied-Signal, a manufacturer of aerospace equipment, automobile parts, and engineered materials such as fluorocarbons, specialty chemicals, and fabrics, had poor profit margins, large debts, a negative cash flow, and no clear mission or strategy. When Lawrence Bossidy became CEO in 1991, he decided to dramatically change the organization to make it more competitive.

Bossidy transformed the corporation, one of the aerospace industry's largest suppliers, by both cutting costs and preparing the company to expand and add jobs. In his first year he introduced a major restructuring plan that included selling small divisions, dramatically reducing the number of business units, and eliminating 6,200 salaried jobs. In addition, ten data-processing centers were combined into two.

The change program included establishing clear but ambitious goals such as an 8 percent annual revenue growth, creating a corporate vision, instituting a comprehensive total quality management program, reducing the number of suppliers while improving their quality and productivity, and changing human resources management throughout the organization. For example, the company reduced the time line for training the 90,000 employees in TQM tools from five to two years. Classroom training was primarily conducted by Allied-Signal managers and used real problems, such as reducing idle machine time or reducing the amount or cost of outsourcing. Bossidy himself spearheaded efforts to improve the caliber of top executives. These included improved college recruiting, hiring, career development, and training. The company also developed databases of employees' skills, altered employee evaluations to include provisions for improving weaknesses, and made career planning an explicit part of the appraisal process.

The changes met with little resistance, in part because employees knew that success would mean job security and advancement opportunities. In fact, the employees themselves pressed for more rapid change to ensure competitiveness. The company emphasized the use of cross-functional work teams and rewarded teamwork rather than individual contributions. Employees were encouraged to celebrate meeting goals. Workers were encouraged to examine the way they worked and to eliminate activities that did not add value.

In Bossidy's first two years as CEO, the company's earnings per share increased by 74 percent and in his first three years the company's stock moved from 30 to 76.[1]

How did Lawrence Bossidy change Allied-Signal Company? In this chapter we focus on organizational change, the *action* step of the diagnostic approach. We begin by looking at some general approaches to change. Then we examine in turn each step in organizational change, including identifying the forces for and against change, selecting a change agent, implementing change, evaluating change, and institutionalizing it. The chapter concludes with some summary comments about ensuring organizational performance and competitiveness.

THE NATURE OF CHANGE

As we have seen earlier in this book, companies are constantly trying to reinvent themselves. *Planned change* describes the systematic process of introducing new behaviors, structures, and technologies for addressing problems and challenges the organization faces. The behavioral focus deals with changes in member knowledge, skills, interactions, and attitudes. Often known as organizational development (OD), the behavioral focus can also involve improving communication, group behavior, intergroup behavior, leadership skills, and power relations, as well as changing the organizational culture.[2] The structural approach calls for redesigning organizations and jobs or work situations. The technological approach requires changing equipment, methods, materials, or techniques, such as by redesigning or reengineering the job and automating work processes.

Planned change usually involves a *change agent,* a person responsible for overseeing the change effort. This individual can work for the organization or for an outside firm. Regardless of his or her position, the change agent generally works extensively with managers and employees to diagnose problems and implement the changes (prescriptions) required to address them.

THE CONTINUUM OF PLANNED CHANGE

Researchers have classified organizational change as falling into one of four categories:[3]

- ■ *Tuning:* Incremental change in anticipation of changes in the environment or attempts to improve efficiency and effectiveness. Tuning can include improving policies and procedures, introducing new technologies, and developing employees, among other activities.

- ■ *Adaptation:* Incremental change in response to changes in the environment. For example, organizations may introduce new products or add features to existing products to respond to products offered by their competitors.

- ■ *Reorientation:* Discontinuous change that anticipates a change in the industry, often involving a fundamental redefinition of the organization, such as a significant change in identity, vision, strategy, or values. This type of change generally requires a visionary leader who can anticipate changes in the environment. It can include organizational redesign and reengineering. In some cases, when time allows, even discontinuous change can appear incremental because it can be introduced somewhat gradually.

- ■ *Re-creation:* Discontinuous change in response to crises or other unexpected changes in the environment. These changes tend to be abrupt and severe. This type of change may also challenge the organization's core values.

AT&T. Jerre Stead, head of the Global Information Solutions division, has led a reorientation change in the organization by changing the things the company does. He focused sales on five selected industries and cut staff by 20 percent, reorganized the division, and formed several hundred cross-functional teams to sell, service, and support customers. He also changed the reward system to support the results he desired: customer satisfaction, shareholder satisfaction, and profitable growth. Sales per employee almost doubled, from $130,000 to $220,000, just short of competitor Hewlett-Packard's $235,000 per employee, in about a year. 1994 orders were 20 percent greater than those in 1993 and customer satisfaction scores increased by more than 30 percent.[4]

The last two types of change have been described together as ***transformational change*** and have received extensive attention as organizations have sought to reinvent themselves.[5]

The transformational process has been described in two different ways. The first model of the transformational process suggests that it is a function of a reframing of the situation by individuals involved.[6] It begins with a challenge to the original ***frame*** or understanding of the situation. Typically, a crisis motivates such a need for a new understanding. Preparation for reframing occurs next. Here, different information about the problems lead to new understandings of the situation. Then participants develop new and different frames. The transformation concludes with members adopting and accepting the new view or understanding. This model applies to all stages of an organization's life cycle. Transformation can also apply to emerging organizations whose survival may depend on their ability to deal with critical issues at a single point in time. Internal conditions such as a surplus of resources, system readiness, sufficient information linkages within the organization, and a change agent with leadership and power are needed to permit transitions of the organization.

TENNECO. Michael Walsh began a dramatic turnaround at this conglomerate, which included gas pipelines and agricultural equipment, before he died from brain cancer. When he began the job as CEO, he learned that management had not recognized what a desperate situation the company faced. One subsidiary alone reported losses at least $300 million more than the company's board or Wall Street had anticipated. He and his top executives developed an action plan within 72 hours. Tenneco's six operating division presidents and a small corporate staff led the transformation. They helped key job holders visualize themselves as mini-CEOs. In the two years since the large-scale change efforts began, the company's debt-to-capital ratio decreased significantly and operating earnings increased significantly.[7]

A second model of transformational change, the ***punctuated equilibrium paradigm*** describes organizational change as an alternation of long periods of stability and short periods of revolutionary change.[8] During the stable or ***equilibrium*** periods ***deep structures*** comprise its operating and performance choices. These basic parts and activity patterns of a system make incremental adjustments to adapt to external changes. At times, however, ***revolutionary*** changes dismantle the deep structure. The organizations or other systems may outgrow their deep structures, lack sufficient resources for dealing with the environment, or face a traumatic external environment. Emotions of participants intensify and outsiders may play more critical roles during the revolutionary period. Ultimately, chaos becomes clarity and new deep structures develop.

EASTMAN KODAK. Eastman Kodak Company found itself stagnant and overly bureaucratic in the early 1980s. Its leadership responded to the resulting organizational ineffectiveness by changing the organizational structure, creating new alliances with customers, and facilitating new ideas and ventures in the middle 1980s.[9] Top management diversified the company extensively through acquisitions, joint ventures, and new start-ups. They integrated the organization by thinking about issues laterally—across departments and functions. They developed synergies between worldwide R&D and global manufacturing, made quality a key ingredient of the corporate culture, and changed the reward system to tie pay to performance.

What type of change has Allied-Signal experienced under Lawrence Bossidy's leadership? His introduction of a comprehensive change program reflects more than incremental change. Instead, his focus on changing the organization's goals, vision, and human resources management to make it more competitive suggests a discontinuous change to meet both anticipated and previous changes in the environment. Because discontinuous change is more intense than incremental change and Allied-Signal is a very complex organization, senior management's involvement was critical to the success of the planned change effort.[10]

THE CHANGE PROCESS

What process do individuals responsible for changing organizations use to ensure successful outcomes? Kurt Lewin offered one of the earliest ways of thinking about change. He described the change process as having three stages.

1. *Unfreezing.* Creating an awareness of a need for change and removing any resistances to change.

2. *Change.* Altering the organizational situation.

3. *Refreezing.* Stabilizing the organization after the change has occurred.

In the 1960s and 1970s, as employee involvement in change became more valued, the *action research* model became popular. In action research, as shown in Figure 15–1, the change agent collaborates extensively with the client in gathering and feeding back data. Together they collect and discuss the data and then use the data for planning.[11]

The model we present in this chapter incorporates some of the elements of these models but offers a more flexible, analytical approach to change. It begins with diagnosing the forces that affect change, followed by selecting a change agent, building an action plan, implementing the change, evaluating it, and institutionalizing it.

DIAGNOSING THE FORCES THAT AFFECT CHANGE

Change begins when the person responsible for making the changes or for ensuring that they occur obtains preliminary information about the situation and those involved. Often this is accompanied by an attempt to negotiate a preliminary agreement with key organizational leaders about the nature of the planned change and who will participate in its implementation. The change agent then attempts to understand the forces that affect the change. We can use an analytical technique called *force field analysis,* which views a problem as a product of forces

FIGURE 15–1 *Action research model*

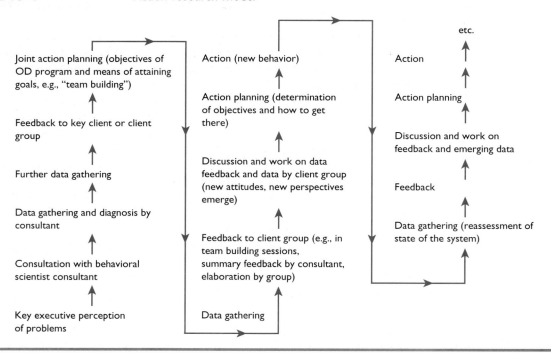

Source: W. French, Organization Development: Objectives, Assumptions and Strategies. © 1969 by the Regents of University of California. Reprinted from *California Management Review* 12 (2): 26, by permisson of the Regents.

working in different, often opposite directions.[12] An organization, or any of its subsystems, will maintain the status quo when the sum of opposing forces is zero. When forces in one direction exceed forces in the opposite one, the organization or subsystem will move in the direction of the greater forces. For example, if the forces for change exceed the forces against change, then change likely will occur.

To move an organization toward a different desired state requires either increasing the forces for change in that direction, decreasing the forces against change in that direction, or both. Generally, reducing resistance creates less tension in the system and fewer unanticipated consequences than increasing forces for change. At Allied-Signal, Lawrence Bossidy reduced the forces against change by showing employees its importance in maintaining their jobs. A complete analysis looks at ways to alter all forces—for and against change.

IDENTIFYING FORCES FOR CHANGE

Let us consider again the situation at Allied-Signal. What forces for change, also known as ***driving forces,*** existed? Increased environmental pressures for improved performance, huge levels of debt, and a negative cash flow are among the forces that spurred the change.

FLEET FINANCIAL GROUP. The purchase of the Shawmut Bank by Fleet Financial Group will result in a combined bank that is among the ten largest in the United States. The acquisition was motivated by the changing financial environment, increasing competition from other types of financial services firms, and the need to offer more services. The environmental pressures for increased competitiveness have resulted and will continue to result in work-force reductions.[13]

Changes in the organization's environment, such as new laws or regulations, rapidly increasing competition, or an unpredictable rate of inflation may require the organization to implement new structures or reward systems. New product development or product selection due to the availability of improved technology, changes in competition in the industry, or the unusual requirements of a new client may also affect the organization. Similarly, changes in the work force, such as better educated workers, more women, or better technically trained management may call for new forms of decision making or communication. Crises in organizations, such as a hostile takeover, potential bankruptcy, industrial accidents, product defects or tampering, major computer breakdowns, or a myriad of other causes, as shown in Table 15–1, can motivate change. Finally, reduced productivity, product quality, satisfaction, commitment, or increased turnover or absenteeism may call for changes in relations inside or between departments.

Careful description of the organizational system should pinpoint the forces for change. Can you make a complete list of forces for change at Allied-Signal Company? Or think about a situation you have faced that calls for change. What forces for change existed in that situation?

IDENTIFYING FORCES AGAINST CHANGE

This is a two-step process. First, the change agent must identify behaviors that signal resistance. These behaviors can range from lowered productivity, increased absenteeism, and poor morale to slowdowns, strikes, or unionization. Next, the

TABLE 15–1 *Types of organizational crises*

INTERNAL	EXTERNAL
Major industrial accidents	Widespread environmental destruction
Product injuries	Natural disasters
Computer breakdown	Hostile takeover
Defective, undisclosed information	Societal crises (civil or political)
Failure to adapt/change	Large scale systems failure
Sabotage by insiders	Sabotage by outsiders
Organizational breakdown	Terrorism
Communication breakdown	Executive kidnapping
On-site product tampering	Off-site product tampering
Illegal activities	Counterfeiting
Occupational health diseases	

SOURCE: P. Shrivastva and I.I. Mitroff, Strategic management of corporate crises, *Columbia Journal of World Business* 22 (Spring 1987).

change agent needs to identify the underlying forces for resistance. Often these resistance forces result from the following:

- *Ignoring the needs, attitudes, and beliefs of organizational members.* If workers have high security needs, for example, they may feel threatened by the increasing automation of the workplace.

- *Lacking specific information about the change.* Workers may not know when, how, or why it is occurring.

- *Failing to perceive a need for change.* Employees may feel that their organization is presently operating effectively and profitably. In these cases change often is neither voluntary nor requested by organizational members.

- *Demonstrating a "we–they" attitude and so viewing the change agent as their enemy.* Organizational members may feel inconsequential to the change, particularly when change is imposed by representatives of a distant corporate headquarters or of an outside consulting firm.

- *Viewing change as a threat to the prestige and security of their supervisor.* They may perceive the change in procedures or policies as a commentary that their supervisor's performance is inadequate.

- *Perceiving the change as a threat to managers' and employees' expertise, status, or security.* The introduction of a new computer system, for example, may cause employees to feel that they lack sufficient knowledge to perform their jobs. The revision of an organization's structure may challenge their relative status in the organization. The introduction of a new reward system may threaten their feelings of job security. Employees may fear change, desire to maintain power, or act complacent toward the change.

- *Having rigid organizational structures and employees with rigid thinking.* Conflicts between individual and organizational goals and organizational inertia against changing the status quo can also contribute to resistance to change. Lack of resources to support the change can also cause resistance.

Can you think of other forces against change in the situation at Allied-Signal? Employees' fears of the unknown and union opposition to the change could be considered possible forces against change. Think about another situation that calls for changes. What forces against change exist in that situation? How does the organization deal with these forces? After identifying the forces both for and against change, organizational leaders next select the appropriate change agent, who then develops an action plan, as described in the next sections.

SELECTING A CHANGE AGENT

Who could make the changes required for Allied-Signal to become a competitive and high-performing organization? Should the company rely on internal change agents? The CEO, Lawrence Bossidy, could be solely responsible for the change, other managers might play a lead role, or internal consultants might perform special facilitative roles. Should Allied-Signal instead use outside consultants to make the required changes? The company might hire experts with extensive experience in turning around troubled companies or the company might hire specialists in introducing TQM programs. The use of internal versus external change agents offers both advantages and disadvantages, as shown in Table 15–2.

Table 15–3 offers another way of thinking about change agents. Change agents can be characterized as *change generators,* who demonstrate the need for change to the organization, *change implementors,* who carry out the change activities specified by top management, and *change adopters,* lower-level managers and employees who practice the changes as part of their daily work.

INTERNAL CHANGE AGENTS

All managers and employees at Allied-Signal have first-hand knowledge of the organization, are known and immediately available to organizational members, and require almost no additional expenditures in fees or additional salary. However, because of their investment in the organization, insiders can be too close to and not objective in looking at the problem or they can be viewed as part of the problem. Their services can be costly if measured in time unavailable for other projects.

Historically, top managers have assumed significant responsibility for motivating and supporting change. As noted earlier, their support is particularly important

TABLE 15–2
Advantages and disadvantages of internal change agents and external agents

	INTERNAL AGENTS	EXTERNAL AGENTS
Advantages	Possess better knowledge of the organization	Have more objective views of the organization
	Are more quickly available	Have more experience in dealing with diverse problems
	Require lower out-of-pocket costs	Can call on more individuals with diverse expertise
	Are a known quantity	Have more technical knowledge, competence, and skills available
	Have more control and authority	
Disadvantages	May be too close to the problem	Have less knowledge of the organization
	May hold biased views	Require higher out-of-pocket costs
	May create additional resistance if viewed as part of the problem	Are an unknown quantity
	Must be reassigned; not available for other work	Have longer start-up time
		Reflect unfavorably on the image of management

TABLE 15–3   *Types of change agents*

CHANGE GENERATORS

1. *Key change agents.* Those who convert an issue into a felt need. This is usually the role of a charismatic leader. An example is Lee Iacocca, whose methods, style, and values dominated the change process at Chrysler. Iacocca eventually became a symbol of U.S. pride and rebirth.

2. *Demonstrators.* These change agents demonstrate support for the change conceptualized by the key change agent. They are first in the line of confrontation to face those who prefer the status quo. The demonstrator's role is to provide visible, vocal support for the change.

3. *Patrons.* These individuals support the change process, financially or psychologically. For instance, a patron of change may provide the key change agent with a budget, a prestigious title, a promotion, or other symbols of support.

4. *Defenders.* This role entails defending the change at the grass roots—the lower levels of the organization. The manager–defender is caught up by the charisma of the key change agent, by becoming an adherent, and by spreading the word among the troops. Defenders may see how they can benefit from the change, or they may be pushed into defending the change by resisters.

CHANGE IMPLEMENTORS

5. *External change implementors.* These individuals are invited from outside the organization to implement change. They may be consultants for organizational development efforts hired to articulate and implement the key change agent's vision. External change agents have the advantage of a fresh perspective and no vested interest in keeping things the way they are.

6. *External/Internal change implementors.* These individuals develop internal implementors. Staff managers from headquarters, who are alien to the field organizations, may have the task of carrying the word from on high to the masses. They are external in the sense that they appear to come from outside. Yet they are long-standing members of the organization with the traditional supports.

7. *Internal change implementors.* These are managers who assume the responsibility to implement the change in their own organizations. Convinced of the need for change, they model other change agents to move their units in the desired direction, often translating or redefining the change to meet their own needs.

CHANGE ADOPTERS

8. *Early adopters.* These managers practice the new change. The first adopters show the highest commitment and become the prototypes for the change. Going beyond implementation, they maintain the change, making it the norm in their organization.

9. *Maintainers.* These managers are primarily concerned with meeting current business needs, doing their jobs to keep the organization going. However, they are willing to adopt the change in the process, because they see how it contributes to their own work. Their objective is to sustain the organization and they realize that the change is one of the things that you have to do now and then to assure the organization's survival. An example is how managers readily take on new or added responsibilities in the wake of a reorganization of functions and reporting relationships.

10. *Users.* Managers become users when they make a habit of the change. Initially, they have the least commitment to the change, and they are probably the last adopters. Yet they are likely to benefit the most from the change. Without them, the change would never be successful.

SOURCE: M. London, *Change Agents: New Roles and Innovation Strategies for Human Resource Professionals* (San Francisco: Jossey-Bass, 1988), pp. 58–59. Used with permission of the publisher.

for discontinuous change, where special vision and leadership skills are required. Because top managers have access to the resources required to implement change, they often can mobilize the change effort more quickly than lower-level managers. AMERITECH. The vice president for sales and service at this midwestern Baby Bell was instrumental in helping employees accept the new corporate culture. He oversaw a work force that needed to respond to customer needs. They did so by participating in teams that have the autonomy to deliver what the customer wants and the accountability to be judged on how well they deliver. Employees were no longer guaranteed life-long employment. Rather, their jobs depended on Ameritech's success in competing in the dynamic telecommunications environment and on their personal ability to hone the skills needed by the company to compete.[14]

The manager of the group involved in a change often becomes the implementor of the changes. This selection occurs informally, primarily because he or she is closest to the situation, has greatest knowledge of it, and has control over it. Further, the manager is already on board, which can reduce the time required to begin the change. In addition, other organizational members already know the manager and have clear expectations about actions he or she might take.

Other organizational members can be used as internal consultants, likely reducing resistance to change from coworkers. They can focus on organizational processes and the nature of interactions between managers and subordinates, especially focusing on teaching managers how to develop others and help them conduct problem solving activities.[15]

UNION ELECTRIC. The utility company used internal consultants to help introduce and then win acceptance of a quality improvement process. The goals of the change included increased job satisfaction, improved operational results, a more innovative culture, more skilled employees, and improved communication through teamwork.[16]

EXTERNAL CHANGE AGENTS

External consultants are employed by other organizations than the one experiencing the change. Examples include consulting firms, accounting firms, or professional organizations. These external consultants tend to have more technical knowledge, diverse competencies, and objectivity in instituting change. On the downside, they may lack information about the particular situation, take longer to start implementing the change, and add large out-of pocket costs.

One study of the personality of change agents compared effective and ineffective organizational development consultants.[17] The results indicated that the most effective consultants could be described as empathetic, sensitive, open, tolerant, flexible, patient, friendly, cooperative, and imaginative. They developed and used information to understand situations and identify behavioral patterns. They acted in a self-reliant fashion, were bold, risk-taking, and initiating. In contrast, the least effective consultants were suspicious, tense, directive, and impersonal. They stayed within the bounds of known facts, focused on the practical, secured minimal information, and were more concerned with the "how" than the "why" of situations. They also were shy and aversive to risk.

MAKING THE SELECTION

To select the most appropriate change agent, an organization should follow these steps:

1. Determine the objective of the change.

2. Consider the extent of help and involvement desired.

3. Consider the extent of help and involvement available in the organization.

4. Identify individuals with expertise congruent with objectives.

5. Identify and specify relevant constraints: time, cost, effort, involvement, and other resources.

6. Communicate expectations including needs, constraints, and personal biases to the change agent.

7. Establish criteria for evaluating the change plan (e.g., cost, time, technical feasibility).

8. Determine the trade-offs in selecting various change agents (e.g., cost versus experience).

9. Assess which change agents fit the organization's needs.

FERRO CORPORATION. Ferro relied on McKinsey & Company, external consultants, to support a major corporate reorganization because Ferro lacked the internal expertise for the change effort. Ferro continues to use consultants to support projects in human resources, marketing, finance, and other areas. The company prefers to use consultants whom they have used successfully before to ensure quality performance.[18]

BUILDING AN ACTION PLAN

Following the identification of the forces for and against change, the person responsible for implementing the change must identify alternative actions for changing each force and then organize them into an action plan. The analytical approach we are describing here must be supplemented with a consideration of individuals' psychological reactions to change and the development of appropriate strategies for dealing with them.

Consider the situation at Allied-Signal again. What actions might be required to overcome resistance to the introduction of a comprehensive TQM program? Bossidy could implement the change slowly—an option he considered infeasible. He could test an experimental version of the new system—an option he considered too slow. He could increase employee participation in the change—a feasible option with low costs. By choosing the last option, Bossidy could overcome resistance to change, a key action issue for managers or external change agents.

Because employees can sabotage change efforts, increasing their cost and decreasing their effectiveness, managers must develop strategies for overcoming resistance to change. General approaches include the following:

■ *Extensive communication with employees.* The person responsible for change might schedule regular informational meetings for all employees affected by the change to highlight deficiencies in the existing situation and to keep employees informed about changes.

■ *Educational and training programs.* These activities prepare workers for their job and organizational requirements after the change.

■ *Employee involvement in decision making and other new programs or ways of doing business.* The change agent should also consider and respond to the needs of individual employees when possible since this helps individuals develop a vested interest in and ultimately support for the change.

- ■ **New organizational structures.** Steering committees, task forces, or other temporary structures can help establish a climate of innovation. Experimentation can reduce the organization's tendency to maintain a status quo.

- ■ **Staff changes.** Hiring or transferring staff can help ensure that employees have both the skills and attitudes required for the altered organization.

- ■ **New policies and procedures.** Particularly when change is rewarded, individuals will feel more comfortable in changing.

- ■ **Evolutionary rather than revolutionary changes.** Where possible, the person overseeing the changes should encourage workers to voluntarily alter their work situations and job performance.

HEWLETT-PACKARD. The general manager of the Santa Rosa, California, plant filled his schedule with "coffee talks." During these informal conversations, he attempted to keep workers informed about corporate goals and the plant's progress toward accomplishing them. Employees expressed their complaints and fears. At one session, for example, the general managers shared the results of a downsizing that reduced the regional operation of 3,300 employees by 10 percent. Employees asked questions about reported mergers of two plants and rumors that layoffs would continue. The general manager tried to address their concerns without committing himself to actions he could not deliver. He continued to emphasize Hewlett-Packard's focus on customer solutions rather than hardware production.[19]

SELECTING A CHANGE STRATEGY

The choice of a specific intervention strategy depends on several criteria: (1) the target system, (2) the target group, (3) the depth of intervention desired, (4) the nature of the prescribed change mechanisms, and (5) the expertise of the change agent. In this chapter we offer an overview of these options, rather than an in-depth analysis of particular intervention strategies. Managers and consultants require extensive specialized training to become expert in implementing specific interventions.

The Target System Intervention strategies can focus on the technical, social, administrative, or strategic systems.[20] Low productivity may signal problems with the technical system, which can be solved by providing capital improvements and offering workers additional training.

Inadequate quality of work life may suggest problems with the organization's social system. To address these problems, interventions should alter the reward system, integrate organizational values into change efforts, confront organizational power and politics, and improve communication.

An organization that responds slowly in receiving and distributing information may have an ineffective administrative or communication system. Ensuring that a logical organizational structure exists, communicating the structure to organizational members, clarifying policies, procedures, and standards, and maintaining a strong system for collecting and disseminating information can improve the effectiveness of the administrative system.

Management strength and competence reflects the health of the strategic system, which includes top management, planning, and management-information systems. Choosing appropriate management styles, systematically evaluating the environment, adapting to changing conditions, building executive-succession systems, and encouraging innovation are interventions that strengthen the strategic system.

OLIN POOL PRODUCTS. Doug Cahill, general manager, decided to deal with loss of market share, low customer satisfaction, late order shipping, and pressure on profit margins by restructuring the organization. After several attempts to find someone to blame for the poor performance, Cahill sketched "an organization so flat you could stick it under a door." He eliminated titles and converted fourteen departments into eight process teams, including fulfillment, new products, and resources. These teams formed a ring around the customer, who was viewed as the central core of the structure. Cahill's job was no longer shown on the chart. He based rewards on divisional profit and customer satisfaction. The new structure, with total autonomy given to teams, successfully handled an inventory crisis caused by a plant fire. Customers have responded positively to Olin's openness in sharing their problems with them. Sales and profits rose significantly.[21]

The Target Group Selecting the appropriate target for change depends on the nature of the diagnosed problem. Interventions can focus on a person, role, dyad or triad, team or group, intergroup interaction, or the entire organization.[22] The analysis of the forces for and against change also helps pinpoint the appropriate target. If, for example, one supervisor refuses to adopt a new policy, the target of change should be the individual. If, on the other hand, the organization lacks effective policies for dealing with unions, then the organization should be the target.

Too often, change agents misfocus interventions by addressing the wrong target. Consider the situation where some employees report late to work. Some organizations try to resolve this problem by instituting earlier official starting times. What is the target of this change? The organization tries to change the behavior of both good and poor-performing employees, often resulting in widespread dissatisfaction and no improvement in the tardiness problem. In this situation, the change should focus on the tardy individuals, rather than on the entire organization.

Depth of Intervention Similar assessment of the appropriate *depth* of intervention must occur. One historical view looked at strategies that ranged from deep—they touched the more private and central aspects of an individual and his or her relationship with others—to surface—they deal with issues outside the individual, such as their more formal and public role behavior.[23] The deepest level of interventions, which should only be used when more surface strategies cannot produce enduring change, try to increase the individual's knowledge of his or her own attitudes, values, and conflicts. Somewhat less deep processes attempt to alter individual work style by focusing on feelings, attitudes, and perceptions. Surface strategies include modifying reward systems, which interface with individual performance and motivation.

A second way of looking at the depth of intervention considers the level of the change attempt.[24] First-order changes reinforce present understandings of situations. They include adjustments in the structure, reward system, or other organizational behaviors. Second-order changes modify the present understanding in a particular direction. They involve a change in the schemata used to view the situation and may be a response to major environmental shifts or an experience of crisis.[25] A decline in productivity, once viewed as a technical problem, can now be handled as a quality-of-work-life issue. Third-order changes give organizational members the capacity to change their understanding of the situation. The introduction of the TQM programs at Allied-Signal is potentially a third-order change, since it requires employees and managers to think about the organization in a totally new way, with a strong focus on quality, team performance and accountability, and customer satisfaction. Training organizational members to view a situation through new lenses offers more long-term possibilities for change.

Nature of the Change Mechanisms The nature of the change mechanisms chosen depends on the problem diagnosis and the forces for and against change that must be altered. The following are a sample of change mechanisms.

Survey Feedback. Use of surveys as a way of gathering and providing feedback to organizational members about their or others' attitudes and behaviors.

Team Building. A variety of activities that help team members work together more collaboratively and productively.

Sensitivity Training. A structured experience in which individuals learn ways to handle conflict by confronting and resolving differences, as well as creating an awareness of new norms that emphasize teamwork.

Process Consultation. The use of an observer to provide feedback to a group about its decision making, leadership, and communication processes.

Confrontation Meeting. A structured interaction between two groups that experience conflict in which they air and attempt to resolve their differences.

Management Development. The training and education of managers to increase their knowledge and improve their skills.

Structural Change. Organizational redesign to improve interaction, coordination, and communication.

While some change mechanisms respond best to specific types of problems, use of multiple change mechanisms strengthens the action and resulting change.

The change strategies preferred vary in different countries. In Italy, for example, where managers' and consultants' values do not support dealing with emotionally charged issues in a group context, team building and third-party interventions are common, whereas sensitivity training, confrontation meetings, and process consultation are not.[26]

Expertise of the Change Agent Of course, the precise change mechanism used depends to some extent on the expertise of the change agent. Organizational members, as well as external consultants, often have training or experience in performing certain types of interventions. Thus selection of the strategy should complement selection of the change agent.

Development of an action plan concludes with a specification of each action in the order it will be performed. The action plan, which may be presented as a formal, written plan, should address the following elements:

■ actions to enhance forces for change;

■ actions to reduce forces against change;

- the feasibility of each action specified;
- a prioritization of actions;
- a timetable and budget.

IMPLEMENTING CHANGE

The change agent, together with other organizational members, implements the best change strategy. Lawrence Bossidy, for example, involved a large number of managers and employees in instituting the comprehensive TQM program at Allied-Signal.

The use of a broad-based steering committee to oversee the change may increase its likelihood of success.[27] Such a group, composed of representatives of top management, first-line supervisors, and rank-and-file employees, can advise on issues related to program budget as well as on organizational policies and priorities.

SONY. Executives at the San Diego Manufacturing Center introduced a program to change the site into a high-performance work system that used participatory management. A support team of employee volunteers was formed to support the change. Their role was to observe the changes and help internalize them. Team members visited other companies experiencing change. They performed skits for the work force to show the effects of participatory decision making. This team helped convince workers of the benefits of participatory management. After embracing participatory management practices, the San Diego site became the most profitable and cost-competitive producer of Trinitron tubes, a major component of the Trinitron television set.[28]

ETHICAL ISSUES IN IMPLEMENTATION

In their interactions with organizations, change agents often confront issues of integrity. Five types of ethical dilemmas include misrepresentation and collusion, misuse of data in change efforts, manipulation and coercion, value and goal conflict, and technical ineptness.[29] Some managers may implement their personal change agenda at the expense of a solid diagnosis of the organization's needs. Still others may promise more than they can deliver. Some consultants fail to build ways of institutionalizing the change into their process so the organization can continue to rely on (and pay) them. Table 15–4 presents the danger signs of unethical behavior.

Organizational leaders, as well as internal and external consultants, should ensure that the selection and implementation of change strategies respond to well-documented organizational and individual needs. They must also ensure that the change process respects the rights of individuals in the workplace.

HANDLING CRISES

Although crises typically cause unplanned change, managers need to be prepared to deal with them as part of implementing any changes. This may involve establishing a multifaceted portfolio of technology, conducting periodic crisis audits to identify the potential for a catastrophe, and building crisis-management teams or units that

TABLE 15–4 *Danger signs of unethical behavior*

1. Emphasis on short-term revenues over long-term considerations.

2. Routinely ignoring or violating internal or professional codes of ethics.

3. Looking for simple solutions to ethical problems, being satisfied with quick fixes.

4. Unwillingness to take an ethical stand if there is a financial cost.

5. Creation of an internal environment that discourages ethical behavior or encourages unethical behavior.

6. Dispatch of ethical problems to the legal department.

7. View of ethics solely as a public relations tool.

8. Treatment of employees that differs from treatment of customers.

9. Unfair or arbitrary performance appraisal standards.

10. Lack of procedures or policies for handling ethical problems.

11. Lack of mechanisms for internal whistle-blowing.

12. Lack of clear lines of communication.

13. Sensitivity only to shareholder needs and demands.

14. Encouragement of employees to ignore their personal ethical values.

SOURCE: Based on R.A. Cooke, Danger signs of unethical behavior: How to determine if your firm is at ethical risk, *Journal of Business Ethics* 10 (1991): 249–253.

can practice their coping skills far in advance of a disaster.[30] The effectiveness of an organization's response to a crisis depends on several factors.[31]

■ The organization's members must have or be able to secure adequate information and resources to cope with the emergency.

■ They must define emergency work, distinguish it from regular work, but maintain functional roles while doing it.

■ The organization must demonstrate flexibility in operations and decision making so managers can deal readily with uncertainty and loss of autonomy and control.

■ Organizational members must think creatively and avoid groupthink (see Chapter 5) in a crisis.

EVALUATING CHANGE

Follow-up evaluation—both informal and formal—is critical to the success of any organizational change and should occur regularly. The change agent collects data about the nature and effectiveness of the change as it occurs. Often the evaluation will compare the actual outcomes to anticipated or expected outcomes reflected in goals or effectiveness criteria. The results of the evaluation indicate whether the change process is complete, whether the desired outcomes resulted, and thus whether a return to an earlier stage, for example, assessing the forces for and against change, should occur.

THE FOUR LEVELS OF CHANGE

Affective change refers to participants' attitudes toward the intervention. Change agents or top management frequently use questionnaires or interviews to assess whether organizational members found the intervention useful or effective.

Learning refers to the participants' knowledge of new ways of acting and their acquisition of new skills as a result of an intervention. Did participants learn how to conduct quality circles or manage autonomous work groups? Did they acquire additional information about other cultures or international business as a result of training programs? Change agents can evaluate learning by analyzing the differences between scores on pre- and post-tests, follow-up interviews, or open-ended survey responses.

Behavioral changes include the participants' actions on the job. Do they interact differently with peers and subordinates? Do they use new or different techniques to accomplish their job activities?

Performance changes are reflected in objective organizational measures, such as productivity and quality rates, sales volume, profit, absenteeism, and turnover, as well as more subjective performance-appraisal ratings. We can assess, for example, whether the introduction of a new reward system increases worker output or whether a new quality-control system improves product quality.

MEASURING EFFECTIVENESS

The same tools used to diagnose the need for change—interviews, questionnaires, observation, or company records—can be used to measure the effectiveness of change efforts. In general, evaluation is most accurate when it uses multiple methods to measure the impact of the change. It should use the most appropriate methods to compare actual performance or outcomes to objectives, standards, policies, or other plans and then draw a summary conclusion about action effectiveness.

INSTITUTIONALIZING CHANGE

Action must extend beyond short-run changes if real organizational improvement is to result. Getting the change to "stick" must be a significant goal of the change effort. How, for example, do the changes made by Lawrence Bossidy at Allied-Signal become a permanent part of the organization's culture and way of doing business? Certainly, this will be influenced by the way the activities are performed as the organization moves from *prescription* to *action* in the diagnostic approach. Accurate targeting of forces influencing change, followed by careful selection of change agents and intervention strategies, and concluding with effective action contribute to long-range improvement. Unsuccessful outcomes may terminate the change process or may signal a need for additional or different changes.

Mechanisms for continually monitoring the changes must be developed and instituted. These monitoring mechanisms can include permanent committees or task forces to observe ongoing implementation and outcomes of the change, which can be further supported by the formulation of new organizational policies. Most of all, commitment to the change by all organizational members will expedite its institutionalization. Managers must build **_learning organizations,_** as described in Chapter 11, which emphasize ongoing adaptability and generativity.[32]

ENSURING ORGANIZATIONAL PERFORMANCE AND COMPETITIVENESS

Organizational effectiveness has been defined and assessed in four major ways:

1. the organization's ability to accomplish its goals;

2. its ability to acquire needed resources from its external environment, and thus achieve a competitive advantage;

3. the organization's ability to at least minimally satisfy all of its strategic constituencies, including suppliers, consumers, members, and so on; and

4. the relative emphasis the organization's key constituencies place on people over organization, flexibility over control, and means versus ends.

In this book we have looked at the issues related to managing in a wide range of organizations, including those that deal nationally and internationally. We have examined the unique challenges of leading and managing a multicultural work force. Managers and other organizational members have significant responsibility for ensuring organizational performance. The leadership style they choose, their ability to communicate with peers, subordinates, and superiors, the quality of their decision making, and their skill in group work, for example, contribute to organizational functioning. Understanding and choosing the appropriate individual and group behaviors are essential for employee productivity, satisfaction, adaptability, and other outcomes. Using the diagnostic approach should help managers and other organizational members improve personal and organizational behavior.

As good diagnosticians, managers must quickly recognize threats to organizational competitiveness. If profits and performance drop dramatically, a major alteration of the organization's culture, structure, and management style may be required. Remaking the organization, for example, through downsizing, reengineering, or organizational redesign, is another option. Managers must develop new and creative strategies for responding to increasing environmental pressures. The emphasis on teamwork, the movement to a more collaborative culture, and the call for visionary leadership are some of the factors that ultimately will stimulate the development of new organizational forms. The creation of new strategic partnerships, mega-organizations in the service sector due to mergers and acquisitions, and departments within existing organizations that focus on new product and service development and innovation should contribute to increased organizational competitiveness and performance.

AETNA. CEO Ronald E. Compton led the insurance company to rethink its product, market, and sales approach. The resulting changes are directed at positioning Aetna to be a more competitive and high-performing organization in the future. The company stopped selling automobile insurance in 28 states, even at a significant short-term cost, sold its individual health insurance unit, and initiated layoffs to reduce the work force. Aetna also introduced a direct claim line for customers, reducing the use of agents as intermediaries between customers and the company. He converted the company's three main divisions in 15 stand-alone businesses. Savings from reorganization are projected to be $100 million a year, but these must offset considerable property losses from a real-estate portfolio that includes many troubled properties.[33]

The manager's challenge to increase and preserve organizational effectiveness never stops. Apparently effective, high-performing organizations can experience unanticipated problems and even decline. Introducing change in multinational and multicultural organizations may be more difficult than in organizations that operate solely in the United States. Thus managers must be vigilant and use analytical tools such as the diagnostic approach to help ensure organizational effectiveness. They must understand the complexities of managing in a global economy and successfully develop and implement new competitive strategies, as well as manage an increasingly diverse work force. Improving individual, group, and organizational behavior and attitudes plays a major role in building effective organizations.

SUMMARY

Organizational change is the final step of the diagnostic approach, following description, diagnosis, and prescription. Action begins by identifying the forces for and against change. Next, selection of change agents—internal or external—occurs.

Action planning follows. This includes choosing the appropriate intervention strategy. Change agents must consider the target system, target group, depth of intervention, prescribed change mechanisms, and expertise of the change agent in selecting the appropriate strategy. Implementing action means ensuring that mechanisms for overseeing change are instituted, as well as that ethical issues are addressed.

Evaluation and institutionalization of changes conclude the process of planned change. Managers and employees can use the diagnostic approach to help ensure their organization's competitiveness and performance.

DIAGNOSTIC QUESTIONS

The following questions highlight the key issues in the action step of the diagnostic approach.

- ■ Are the steps of the change model implemented?
- ■ Are forces for and against change identified?
- ■ Are appropriate change agents selected?
- ■ Has an appropriate action plan been developed?
- ■ Do mechanisms exist for evaluating the change?
- ■ Do mechanisms exist for institutionalizing the change?
- ■ What mechanisms exist for ensuring organizational performance and competitiveness?

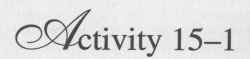

JIM COOPER AND THE EDUCATION SCHOOL: A CASE OF CULTURAL CHANGE

STEP I: Read the case of Jim Cooper and the Education School.

Jim Cooper faced a dilemma. Appointed the new dean of the University of Virginia School of Education in the spring of 1984, he had achieved a position and status of which many academics dream (especially in a university like University of Virginia, where the deans have very broad authority.) However, he was taking over a school that was under the gun, to say the least. University committees had been formed to examine the role and performance of the Education School. Faculty morale was very low. There was a sense of isolation, from the rest of the University and from other faculty and students. Cooper found a faculty eager for change, but divided as to what direction was needed. The School's reputation had declined, as had student enrollment, and there was even a rumor that the provost was considering phasing the School out.

The Education School's decline was typical of the problems confronting schools of education across the country. The late 1960s and early 1970s were the "go-go" years for education, times of record enrollments reflecting the high value students placed on the teaching profession. All that changed during the next decade. Business, computer science, and engineering schools were on the rise, many liberal arts fields suffered, and education seemed to be hit the hardest. Education schools that had added many new faculty (University of Virginia's faculty doubled) now faced embarrassing questions from provosts and state legislatures. Those schools that didn't provide convincing answers got hurt, some losing one third or more of their funding.

FIRST STEPS

Cooper made some initial decisions that proved very valuable. He received a commitment from the provost that the School would not lose any faculty slots for the next three years. He obtained funding from the University to hold a two-day faculty retreat at the start of the school year. Within his first month on the job he also reorganized his administrative team, replacing two of the three associate deans. The word got out to the faculty very quickly: Cooper is a mover.

To call Jim Cooper a "mover" is accurate (by his own account he has a very low tolerance for inaction); it is only partially correct, however. Cooper moves quickly, but he also studies the situation closely. During his initial interviews and in subsequent visits to the University before he took over he met with the other academic deans, the president, faculty, and grad students, and the secretary of education for Virginia. He asked people to identify the Education School's informal leaders, and he spent time learning about their views and forming relationships. Through all of these meetings he began to determine where his potential support lay, and what was on the agendas of other key people.

After he announced the selection of his new associate deans, he began planning the faculty retreat. He had taken part in a similar effort at another university, and knew that such a session could help him set his themes and gain active faculty involvement. He received help from others on the grounds who were experienced in helping organizations change, and the retreat idea took form. All 101 Education School faculty were asked to spend two days at Graves Mountain Lodge, to look at the School, at its future prospects, and to begin planning for needed changes. Jim found five experienced group facilitators to lead the faculty discussion, and all but five of the school's faculty attended.

Many faculty were skeptical about the retreat idea. Some years earlier similar (though less ambitious) efforts had been made, with little follow through. Jim knew this but he felt that a major statement was needed to let people know that this was not to be business as usual.

Most faculty felt that the retreat was a success, but they maintained their skepticism concerning long-term results. Jim had already decided that two days would be only a start, and at the retreat he announced that the faculty was to continue meeting in its small groups throughout the fall, in order to come up with written proposals concerning the changes needed in the school. The outside facilitators had agreed to continue in their role, and Jim and his associate deans deliberately stayed out of the sessions.

The retreat was successful for many reasons. Simply getting away together was a positive experience. The fact that the School had come up with the money was a statement about where Jim was coming from, about his values and priorities. The opportunity to relax and play together as well as work on School issues contributed to the positive climate.

These good feelings would not have been satisfying had Jim not made a personal statement about his aspirations for the School. He did so, and gave most faculty their first glimpse into his approach. In his talk he made reference to winning teams, and what it takes to create winning teams. The 12 points he listed are shown in Figure 15–2. These points, he was saying, were what he wanted and expected from all faculty and administrators in the School. Someone asked him for a copy of his points, and they were passed out to the faculty the following week.

In the speech Jim gave several examples to bring his points to life. One example was especially effective: he announced that the School would soon begin issuing "teacher warranties" on all of its graduates who go on and teach in Virginia schools. The School would offer to send a faculty member to work with any of its graduates who had difficulties in their first teaching year. This warranty caught the eye of the press, and it was picked up by the wire services as well as national news networks. While some faculty had concerns as to whether they could really help a poor teacher, there was agreement that the approach was creative and brought good publicity for the School.

FOLLOW THROUGH: LIFE AFTER THE RETREAT

The "retreat groups" continued meeting. Twice during the semester representatives from each group met with Jim and his staff to discuss the directions they were taking. Some focused on morale issues, others on a reorganization plan, physical plants needs, public relations problems, decision-making procedures, and communications issues.

While the retreat groups were meeting, Jim continued announcing new initiatives. One was Project Excellence, a joint effort of the School and the Charlottesville

FIGURE 15–2   *Jim Cooper's aspirations for the School of Education*

Characteristics of a Team (School of Education) that I would like to belong to:

1. Sense of confidence and security in ourselves and in the School. Think of ourselves as winners.

2. Sense of pride in the importance of what we do and how we do it. A willingness to tell the world that we're good. (New teacher warranty.)

3. Sense of pride, not envy, in the accomplishments of our colleagues. Not a zero sum game.

4. A sense of trust in each other and the belief that no one, especially our colleagues, is out to get us.

5. Commitment to having fun. People rarely succeed at anything unless they enjoy it.

6. Increased communication among ourselves, especially across departments. Good news swapping. MIT study indicates that if people are more than 10 meters apart, the probability of communicating at least once a week is only 8 or 9 percent. Must make special effort, especially since our building does not encourage communication.

7. An instructionally effective and physically attractive environment. School beautification plan.

8. Support for each other's ideas. "It is inherently easier to develop a negative argument than to advance a constructive one." Don't warn people, instead bolster them.

9. A willingness to take risks without guarantees, if the goal is a worthwhile one. "When in doubt, try it out." Demonstrate a bias toward action rather than sitting around waiting for someone else to take the necessary steps. Get your arms around almost any practical problem and knock it off. Don't just stand there, do something.

10. A willingness to give up some protected turf and privileges if in doing so the School will benefit. In the analogy for today, this means being willing to throw the block that will spring someone else into the clear.

11. A renewed commitment to meeting students' needs first, and professors' comforts second.

12. Strive to be "the best" at something. It doesn't much matter what it is as long as it helps the Redskins win.

and Albermarle public schools. Through this program the Education School provided funds to both school systems, which in turn awarded grants to teachers who proposed creative classroom approaches that couldn't be funded by regular school budgets. Innovations would be supported by grants of $50 to $500, and the city schools decided to add a matching grant to broaden their pool (see Figure 15–3).

That wasn't all. Jim decided that the public school teachers who supervised student teachers from the Education School needed more support and recognition, and closer ties with the School. He began the Clinical Instructor Project, which provided training and increased financial support for cooperating teachers. It also made them adjunct faculty members of the School, and gave them increased visibility and prestige. The General Assembly provided $98,000 to support and study the results of the project. In addition, Jim announced a warranty on the computer literacy of the school's graduates, similar in concept to the teacher warranty.

Jim wanted to make a statement early in his tenure about his directions. He also wanted to give faculty morale a quick boost. He knew that the retreat, successful as it was, soon would be only a pleasant memory if he

- -

FIGURE 15–3 *University of Virginia grant aids teacher projects*

By Julie Young of the Progress Staff

Teachers in the Charlottesville and Albermarle County schools will have a chance to try some special class projects this year with grant money being offered by the University of Virginia's School of Education.

Project Excellence, a joint project of the education school and the two local school systems, will provide money for creative classroom ventures that tight school budgets seldom allow, officials said Wednesday.

The project follows last week's proposal by new education dean James Cooper to place a warranty on U. Va. teaching graduates during their first year in school systems. Teachers with problems will be tutored on-site by their former U. Va. instructors under Cooper's proposal.

Project Excellence "is designed to support teachers in effecting a creative or stimulating classroom environment and help them carry out some ideas that promise to promote excellence in classroom instruction," said Mary P. Reese, assistant superintendent for personnel in the city schools.

Teachers have until next Wednesday to submit proposals on projects they would like to attempt this year, she said. Teachers might, for example, develop special prototype units in their subjects and use the grant money to have them copied, she said.

Innovative ideas ranging from $50 to $500 will be financed under the $3,000 grant—$1,500 from the University and a matching grant from the city school system's staff development budget, according to Mrs. Reese.

The University also will award $1,500 of the seed money to Albermarle County, but those funds will not be matched from the school budget, officials said.

Harold Burbach, associate dean of external relations and faculty affairs at the education school, said Wednesday the idea for the joint venture came from Robert F. McNergney, U. Va.'s director of teacher education, who administered such a project successfully in another state.

"We want to attempt through ideas and involvement to build a stronger link with the public schools," Burbach said. The project "will enable us to work in a direct way with teachers through the school systems."

Literature on effective teaching indicates it is important for teachers to be given occasional bureaucratic loopholes, he said. The University has been a little negligent in the past in "translating that (literature) into effective practices in the classroom," he said.

The funds will "empower teachers directly, with no bureaucratic maze" standing between them and creative exploration, Burbach said.

"Teachers have got to be given the authority to do what they're expected to do," he said.

School officials said they hope the projects also will boost teacher morale, and will be refined and shared with other teachers once they have been carried out.

The University is attempting through such projects this year to promote a positive image for its education school in the second year of the nation's excellence movement.

"Educators typically have been on the defensive" as their practices have come under fire in recent years," Burbach said. "We've got to assert ourselves."

didn't keep up the momentum. He worked to get media coverage of the School's initiatives, aware that the faculty (indeed, the whole University) was used to reading primarily negative statements about the Education School. The approach began working. Only the most cynical continued to say that this would be a process of all talk and not action.

By the second week of December each of the five retreat groups submitted its report, detailing the changes needed in the School. The faculty knew that the provost was expecting the School to come up with a new, simpler organization; he wasn't happy with the eight departments and 24 programs offered. Thus, Jim and his staff focused first on the new organization plan for the school, and on January 24, 1985 Jim sent his Proposed Reorganization Plan to the faculty.

The proposal, a 45-page document with careful references to the suggestions from each retreat group (as well as a rationale, statement of principles, extensive documentation, and explanation of new roles) suggested a simpler, leaner plan with just four departments. Aspects of the plan came directly from the retreat groups' proposals, and many faculty said they thought that Jim's proposal was as good as anything they would have offered. At the next faculty meeting, the new plan was endorsed by the faculty, unanimously.

INITIAL RESULTS, FUTURE DIRECTIONS

In the spring of 1985, it is much too early to determine the long-term effects that all of these changes will have on the U.Va. School of Education. Jim Cooper is actively recruiting some "heavyweights" in the education field to join the Education School faculty (he sees this as the best way to upgrade certain departments needing assistance). He is working on a national committee that is studying the state of the art in the teaching profession. He and his staff have submitted a grant proposal to develop an educational policy analysis center. They also expect to continue acting on other aspects of the retreat groups' proposals. The possibilities are great, as are Jim's energies and imagination.

What can be said concerning the *initial* results is that Jim Cooper and his staff have turned the School of Education around, in terms of morale, in terms of its previous lack of direction, in terms of its hopes for the future. A school that was fearing for its very life now has a renewed sense of life. Changes inevitably bring resistance and anger, and some of that has occurred. The primary feeling given off by the faculty, however, is one of optimism and a sense of direction. They aren't talking about phasing out the School of Education anymore.

STEP 2: Prepare the case for class discussion.

STEP 3: Answer the following questions, individually, in small groups, or with the entire class, as directed by your instructor.

DESCRIPTION
1. What conditions existed at the School of Education before the change?
2. What changes were implemented?

DIAGNOSIS
3. Were the changes effective?
4. What problems remain or will occur as a result of the changes?

PRESCRIPTION
5. What course of action or additional programs would you propose now?
6. Should other changes have been implemented?

ACTION
7. How does your plan of action compare to that actually implemented?
8. Which intervention strategies would have been more effective?
9. Were the changes evaluated?
10. Were the changes institutionalized?

STEP 4: Discussion. In small groups, with the entire class, or in written form, share your answers to the above questions. Then answer the following questions:

1. What symptoms suggested a problem existed?
2. What problems existed in the case?
3. What theories and concepts help explain the problems?
4. How were the problems corrected?
5. Analyze the change process.
6. Was the change effective?

Activity 15–2   ASSESSING READINESS FOR CHANGE

STEP 1: Choose an organization you know as a member or an employee.

STEP 2: Complete the following questionnaire about that organization.

The left-hand column lists 17 key elements of change readiness. Rate your organization on each item.

Give three points for a high ranking ("We're good at this; I'm confident of our skills here"); two for medium score ("We're spotty here; we could use improvement or more experience"); and one point for a low score ("We've had problems with this; this is new to our organization"). Be honest.

CATEGORY	SCORE
Sponsorship The sponsor of change is not necessarily its day-to-day leader; he or she is the visionary, chief cheerleader, and bill payer—the person with the power to help the team change when it meets resistance. Give three points—change will be easier—if sponsorship comes at a senior level; for example, CEO, COO, or the head of an autonomous business unit. Weakest sponsors: mid-level executives or staff officers.	
Leadership This means the day-to-day leadership—the people who call the meetings, set the goals, work till midnight. Successful change is more likely if leadership is high level, has "ownership" (that is, direct responsibility for what's to be changed) and has clear business results in mind. Low-level leadership, or leadership that is not well connected throughout the organization (across departments) or that comes from the staff, is less likely to succeed and should be scored low.	
Motivation High points for a strong sense of urgency from senior management, which is shared by the rest of the company, and for a corporate culture that already emphasizes continuous improvement. Negative: tradition-bound managers and workers, many of whom have been in their jobs for more than 15 years; a conservative culture that discourages risk taking.	
Direction Does senior management strongly believe that the future should look different from the present? How clear is management's picture of the future? Can management mobilize all relevant parties—employees, the board, customers, etc.—for action? High points for positive answers to those questions. If senior management thinks only minor change is needed, the likely outcome is no change at all; score yourself low.	
Measurements Or in consultant-speak, "metrics." Three points if you already use performance measures of the sort encouraged by total quality management (defect rates, time to market, etc.) and if these express the economics of the business. Two points if some measures exist but compensation and reward systems do not explicitly reinforce them. If you don't have measures in place or don't know what we're talking about, one point.	
Organizational Context How does the change effort connect to other major goings-on in the organization? (For example: Does it dovetail with a continuing Total Quality Management process? Does it fit with strategic actions such as acquisitions or new product lines?) Trouble lies ahead for a change effort that is isolated or if there are multiple change efforts whose relationships are not linked strategically.	

CATEGORY	SCORE

Processes/Functions

Major changes almost invariably require redesigning business processes that cut across functions such as purchasing, accounts payable, or marketing. If functional executives are rigidly turf conscious, change will be difficult. Give yourself more points the more willing they—and the organization as a whole—are to change critical processes and sacrifice perks or power for the good of the group.

Competitor Benchmarking

Whether you are a leader in your industry or a laggard, give yourself points for a continuing program that objectively compares your company's performance with that of competitors and systematically examines changes in your market. Give yourself one point if knowledge of competitors' abilities is primarily anecdotal—what salesmen say at the bar.

Customer Focus

The more everyone in the company is imbued with knowledge of customers, the more likely that the organization can agree to change to serve them better. Three points if everyone in the work force knows who his or her customers are, knows their needs, and has had direct contact with them. Take away points if that knowledge is confined to pockets of the organization (sales and marketing, senior executives).

Rewards

Change is easier if managers and employees are rewarded for taking risks, being innovative, and looking for new solutions. Team-based rewards are better than rewards based solely on individual achievement. Reduce points if your company, like most, rewards continuity over change. If managers become heroes for making budget, they won't take risks even if you say you want them to. Also: If employees believe failure will be punished, reduce points.

Organizational Structure

The best situation is a flexible organization with little churn—that is, reorganizations are rare and well received. Score yourself lower if you have a rigid structure that has been unchanged for more than five years or has undergone frequent reorganization with little success; that may signal a cynical company culture that fights change by waiting it out.

Communication

A company will adapt to change most readily if it has many means of two-way communication that reach all levels of the organization and that all employees use and understand. If communications media are few, often trashed unread, and almost exclusively one-way and top-down, change will be more difficult

Organizational Hierarchy

The fewer levels of hierarchy and the fewer employee grade levels, the more likely an effort to change will succeed. A thick impasto of middle management and staff not only slows decision making but also creates large numbers of people with the power to block change.

Prior Experience with Change

Score three if the organization has successfully implemented major changes in the recent past. Score one if there is no prior experience with major change or if change efforts failed or left a legacy of anger or resentment. Most companies will score two, acknowledging equivocal success in previous attempts to change.

Morale

Change is easier if employees enjoy working in the organization and the level of individual responsibility is high. Signs of unreadiness to change: low team spirit, little voluntary extra effort, and mistrust. Look for two types of mistrust: between management and employees, and between or among departments.

Innovation
Best situation: The company is always experimenting; new ideas are implemented with seemingly little effort; employees work across internal boundaries without much trouble. Bad signs: lots of red tape, multiple sign-offs required before new ideas are tried; employees must go through channels and are discouraged from working with colleagues from other departments or divisions.

Decision Making
Rate yourself high if decisions are made quickly, taking into account a wide variety of suggestions; it is clear where decisions are made. Give yourself a low grade if decisions come slowly and are made by a mysterious "them"; there is a lot of conflict during the process, and confusion and finger pointing after decisions are announced.

STEP 3: Score your responses. Assign scores as follows: High=3, Medium=2, Low=1. Total your scores on each item to obtain Total Score.

IF YOUR SCORE IS

TOTAL
SCORE

41–51: Implementing change is most likely to succeed. Focus resources on lagging factors (your ones and twos) to accelerate the process.

28–40: Change is possible but may be difficult, especially if you have low scores in the first seven readiness dimensions. Bring those up to speed before attempting to implement large-scale change.

17–27: Implementing change will be virtually impossible without a precipitating catastrophe. Focus instead on (1) building change readiness in the dimensions above and (2) effecting change through skunkworks or pilot programs separate from the organization at large.

STEP 4: Discussion. In small groups or with the entire class, compare your results. Which organizations are most ready for change? Which organizations are least ready for change? What can be done to increase the organizations' readiness for change?

Reprinted with permission from T.A. Stewart, Rate your readiness to change, *Fortune* (February 7, 1994): 108, 110.

$\mathcal{A}$ctivity 15–3   BRIDGETON TEMPORARY SERVICES

STEP 1: Your instructor will divide you into groups of four to six people; one group will represent management, and the rest, competing consulting groups.

STEP 2: Read the following description.

The Bridgeton Temporary Services provides bookkeeping and accounting services on a contract basis. Employees act as accounts payable clerks, accounts receivable clerks, general bookkeepers, computer programmers, and accountants. The seventy-five employees are each assigned to a supervisor who decides where each person will work. The supervisor also checks with the client for an evaluation of Bridgeton's employees. Employees report each day to the client, but must notify their supervisor at Bridgeton that they have arrived.

Employees have a variety of education, from high school diplomas to master's degrees. The firm also employs a number of working mothers with CPAs who do not want full-time employment. Employees generally stay with Bridgeton ten to twelve months. Then they secure full-time employment elsewhere, decide they do not wish to be employed at all, or obtain part-time employment with one of Bridgeton's clients. In addition to relatively high turnover, Bridgeton also suffers from high absenteeism. When questioned, the employees indicate that no one cares about them, that their pay is low, that their work frequently is uninteresting and below their capabilities, that they are moved among jobs too frequently, and that they frequently are not notified about their work assignment until thirty minutes before they are expected to be at the workplace. Many add that they feel someone is always looking over their shoulder. The company itself has more requests for temporary help than it can fill, yet is has been unable to secure enough workers. Some clients have complained about poor-quality work from some of the bookkeepers. Also, although revenues are increasing, profits have not kept pace.

....

STEP 3: *The Management Group.* Assume that you are the top management of Bridgeton Temporary Services. You are concerned with the high rate of turnover and absenteeism in your company. You want to hire a group of consultants to diagnose your company's problem and to recommend a plan for solving it. Shortly they will ask for a preliminary meeting to gather information to use in formulating their consulting proposal. You should be prepared to provide them with your requirements and timetables, as well as with any constraints, financial or otherwise, that you see as relevant to their task. You must then develop guidelines for judging the

various proposals presented. You expect, at a minimum, that each will include a diagnosis, change strategy, and plans for implementation, as well as the rationales on which these are based.

The Consulting Groups. Your group is interested in being hired as consultants to Bridgeton Temporary Services. The company's president is concerned with the high rate of turnover and absenteeism. The president has asked you to diagnose the company's problems and to recommend a plan for solving them. Specifically, the president wants you to answer the following questions:

1. What do you think the real problem is and why?
2. What solution(s) would you propose and why?
3. How would you implement your plan?
4. What reasons would you give for doing it this way?

You will have the opportunity to meet briefly with the top management of the firm in a short while to get answers to preliminary questions you have about the company. Then, on the date given by your instructor, you will offer your plan. The plan should include diagnosis, change strategy, and implementation.

....

STEP 4: The management and consulting groups meet, independently and then together.

....

STEP 5: The consulting teams present their proposals one at a time.

....

STEP 6: The management team selects the consulting team they would like to hire and then describes its criteria for selection.

....

STEP 7: Discussion. With the entire class, answer the following questions:

1. What group was hired? Why?
2. What symptoms existed?
3. What problems were identified?
4. What intervention strategies were proposed? Would they be effective?
5. What makes an effective consulting proposal?

Activity 15–4 | MANAGING AN ORGANIZATIONAL CRISIS

STEP 1: Read the following scenario.

You are the vice president of marketing of a small manufacturing firm that processes baby food from local produce. Your firm sells the food to mothers who wish only the freshest products for their infants. Your products are stored in the refrigerator section of the grocery store and have a relatively short shelf life. Because of the concern about preservatives and healthful living, your company has grown significantly in the past five years.

Yesterday the local newspaper revealed that they had done a chemical analysis of a batch of your food and found traces of a compound that is known to cause cancer in mice. They warned the public to stop buying your product. You know that if you cannot reassure the public about the integrity of your product, the loss of sales will threaten your company's survival.

STEP 2: Individually or in small groups, offer a plan for dealing with this crisis.

STEP 3: Discussion. In small groups or with the entire class, share the plans you have developed. Then answer the following questions:

1. What were the key elements of the plans?
2. How did the plans differ?
3. How could these differences be reconciled?
4. What are the strengths and weaknesses of each plan?
5. What problems might arise in their implementation?
6. What are the components of an effective plan for dealing with the crisis?

Activity 15–5 | MANAGERIAL SYSTEMS LTD.

STEP 1: Read the Managerial Systems Ltd. case.

INTRODUCTION

It had been a rough week for Managerial Systems Ltd. By Thursday, MSL's president, Ken Long, had received upsetting phone calls from consultants Phil Mercer, Ray Terrell, and Fred Sargent concerning client difficulties. He had also talked at length with Karen Webster about conflicts between her personal and professional lives. Crises always seemed to come in avalanches. Tomorrow's staff meeting promised to last the entire spring day, ruining any plans Ken had for sailing.

MANAGERIAL SYSTEMS LTD.

Managerial Systems Ltd. was a behaviorally based consulting organization focused on helping client companies improve the effectiveness of managerial systems through the application of sophisticated behavioral science technologies. (Figure 15–4 briefly explains the basics of behavioral consulting.) MSL consultants worked with client organizations to help define needs and then

identify the proper methods for satisfying those needs. (Figure 15–5 lists the types of services provided in the past.) All MSL consultants had at least a master's degree in the behavioral sciences and most had obtained a doctorate in a related field. Many had worked in the behavioral area in either private practice or with institutions prior to joining MSL. (Figure 15–6 is a selected biography of representative consultants' backgrounds.)

MSL incorporated in 1977 when Ken Long, the president, resigned his professorship at a prominent southern business school in order to devote his full time to the company. In the past four years MSL had expanded to ten consultants, two research assistants, and five support staffers. MSL's primary clients had been in the petrochemical industry. However, attempts to implement a strategy of diversification had begun this year.

The diversification into other industries presented something of a problem for MSL. MSL's consulting expertise had been developed and proven in the petrochemical field. But potential clients questioned how well that expertise would translate to their specific types of problems. To help overcome these questions, Ken had decided to concentrate in three areas related to the

FIGURE 15–4   *Description of Organizational Development (OD)*

Organizational Development (OD) is a process by which behavioral science principles and practices are used in an ongoing organization in a planned and systematic way. It is utilized to attain such goals as developing greater organizational competence while improving the quality of work life and the organization's effectiveness. (Effectiveness refers to setting and attaining appropriate goals in a changing environment.) OD differs from other planned change efforts such as the purchases of new equipment or floating a bond issue to build a new plant, in that the focus includes the motivation, utilization, and integration of human resources within the organization and is focused on total system change.

OD is a vehicle for helping organizations adjust to accelerated technological enrichment, group team building, or management by objectives. OD may use specific techniques, but only after the relevance and utility of a special technique has been clearly demonstrated by careful diagnosis.

Interventions or techniques can be grouped in ten basic classifications:

- Individual consultation (counseling—coaching) usually involving a change agent in a one-on-one helping interaction with a single client.
- Unstructured group training involving individuals in a group lacking specific task purpose except that of understanding individual or group dynamics.
- Structured group training including management and group development courses structured to change participant attitudes, convey knowledge, or develop skills.
- Process consultation involving small groups or work teams identifying and solving common problems.
- Survey-guided development, involving collection of data about client work-group or organizational functioning and feeding back data to work groups to use in problem solving.
- Job redesign involving altering the tasks, responsibilities, interactions patterns, or the technical and physical environment intrinsic to the work itself.
- Personnel systems involving implementation through traditional personnel functions.
- Management information and financial control systems involving tracking and evaluating employee or work-group performance.
- Organizational design involving a structural change in organizational authority and reporting relationships.
- Integrated approaches including more than one of the methods described above.

SOURCE: Edgar F. Huse, *Organization Development and Change* (St. Paul, Minn.: West, 1980).

prior experience of MSL. These included flow process plants, e.g., petrochemical, energy services and equipment companies, and banking. Ken anticipated no major problems transferring techniques from one industry to the others. This was because MSL tailors its behavioral intervention to a client's particular set of needs.

Ken wanted each consultant to bring in at least one new client by the end of the year. Each consultant was asked to make contacts in new companies and arrange a presentation of MSL's array of services to management. Several of the consultants expressed their feelings of uneasiness in taking on a sales role. They felt they lacked sufficient experience to decide which companies and executives to approach as potential clients. Once they managed to make contact, the consultants were worried about how to make an effective presentation. To alleviate these concerns, Ken had begun training the consultants in sales techniques. The consultants were taught basic sales techniques tailored to MSL's particular marketing needs.

Long felt it was important for MSL's consultants to have divergent backgrounds both academically and professionally. However, he insisted that potential consultants have a fundamental belief in the benefits of a capitalistic society. When hiring consultants he discussed at length how the individual felt about working for major oil companies. If there was a wide gap in the beliefs of MSL and the consultant, Ken would refuse to hire them. He felt the strains of working to improve a system one did not believe in would be detrimental to the consultant's working abilities and effectiveness. Ken encouraged the consultants to come to him to talk about any problems they were having on the job. He felt this minimized the chances of a consultant working him/herself into a corner over an issue.

FIGURE 15–5   *Consulting services rendered to clients—1980*

Organizational Development initiation, planning, and execution

Managerial effectiveness training

Supervisory skills training

Organizational team building

Organizational diagnostic climate
- Organizational climate
- Employee attitude assessment
- Specific areas of concern

Managerial expectations clarification
- Goal setting
- Organizational dissemination
- Individual superior–subordinate clarifications

Performance feedback enhancement
- Establishing organizational systems
- Expectations setting/feedback skills training

Development of organizational systems
- Progressive discipline
- Managerial communications
- Work system redesign
- Managerial succession system

Employee Assistance Programs
- Individual managerial counseling
- Employee psychological services
- Alcoholic/drug abuse program
- Assisting terminated and retiring employees

Effective planning and implementation of organizational changes

EEO Audit simulation

EEO Assimilation Programs

Research Studies
- Attrition problems
- Employee acceptance/rejection of anticipated change
- EEO-related employee attitudes
- Organization-wide training systems

Workshops on special topics
- Management of stress situations
- Assimilation of new managers
- Problems faced by temporary supervisors
- Successful specific conflict resolution

Facilitating development of overall top management goals

FIGURE 15–6   *Selected biographies of MSL consultants*

Karen Webster	30, MBA from Tulane University, BA, psychology, had been with MSL for four years. Prior to joining MSL, Karen worked in a managerial capacity in private business. Her consulting expertise was primarily in management and supervisory development.
Fred Sargent	55, had been with the firm for three years, joining MSL upon completion of a doctorate in adult education. He spent twenty-five years in the U.S. Army and rose to the rank of Colonel. During his military career, Fred held many managerial positions, planning and implementing numerous training programs. He also earned an MBA from Syracuse University while in the Army. His Army experiences carried over easily in behavioral consulting where Fred focused on development and execution of organizational needs analysis and management training programs.
Ray Terrell	32, received his Ph.D. in clinical psychology following a master's degree in counseling. He had joined MSL on a part-time basis one and a half years ago while continuing to teach at a local university. Small group facilitation had been Ray's specialty within MSL.
Phil Mercer	36, had been with MSL on a part-time basis for a year. He continued to teach in the social work department at a local university. His academic credentials included an MSW, an MPH, and a Ph.D. in human ecology, a discipline that works against exploitation of the environment. This degree strongly reflects Phil's personal values. He spent many years "throwing rocks at big business from the outside" but had never been a part of that world. He went into consulting to learn more about how big business works and to help improve conditions for people working in the system.

Ken emphasized the importance of doing a thorough job with a client company. Many times a client company would bring in MSL to solve a specific problem that management had isolated. MSL wanted to gather their own data in order to determine the validity of management's point of view and to find out if there were any additional problems related to the ones indicated. MSL was prepared to walk away from a contract if management refused to allow them to do the necessary research or if management wanted their services for any reason other than to improve working conditions.

THE DILEMMAS

Phil Mercer

Phil had just completed a large project on the reasons for the engineer attrition rate for a major oil company. The report and final recommendations would be ready the following week. Phil was quite pleased with the results. He attributed the success of the project to the agreement of management to release the report and the final recommendations to the engineers. The engineers took this as a sign that management was making a serious effort to correct many of the problems they faced at work. Therefore, they cooperated fully and candidly with Phil in the interviewing process.

Phil called Mr. Spencer, the vice-president of personnel, engineering, to inform him of the date the report would be ready. He also inquired about distributing the report to the engineers. Mr. Spencer said the report would not be released as planned. A two-page summary of it would be made available. The recommendations would be omitted.

This upset Phil. He had given his word to the engineers that they would receive copies of the report and the recommendations. He reminded Mr. Spencer of management's promise to release it. All the positive effects of the promised release would be negated and the engineers' attitudes would sour. Phil questioned the wisdom of such a move. Mr. Spencer blamed the change in plans on MSL's failure to stay within the contracted budget. He said there were insufficient funds available to copy the report. Phil was at a loss on what to reply, so he terminated the conversation, promising to call again in the next few days.

Phil reviewed his alternatives. He could try again to convince Mr. Spencer to release the results regardless of the costs involved. He thought this would be fruitless based on the previous conversation. Phil considered going directly to the engineers and giving them the report and the recommendations without management's approval. After all, they had been promised a copy of the report and he could provide it verbally anyway. He also thought about going to someone higher in the company who could countermand Spencer's decision.

Phil called Ken to talk about the situation. Ken suggested that Phil bring up the issue at tomorrow's staff meeting. Before hanging up Ken mentioned that the company had contacted him about another consulting job. He wanted Phil to think about whether MSL should accept the job in light of the situation with Mr. Spencer.

Fred Sargent

Hugh Cavanaugh was the operations manager of a medium-sized petrochemical refinery located on the Louisiana coast. The refinery was part of a large, well-known energy concern. Cavanaugh was from the traditional school of management ("seat of the pants" or "we've always done it this way"). At sixty-two, his physical condition was excellent, considering his recovery from open-heart surgery two years earlier. Although every other member of the management committee supported the plant manager's initiation of MSL's organizational development (OD) efforts within the refinery (which included supervisory training, team building, and EEO development work), Cavanaugh thought OD was a waste of time. He reportedly said, "Young Turks come in and try to change the organization when they don't even understand its history . . . besides, the refinery was maximizing production capacity way before all this new OD rubbish came up." Cavanaugh constantly refuted the OD effort along with other organizational changes. He was against the massive computerization then under way, and blatantly expressed his feelings throughout the refinery. As operations manager with thirty-seven years of experience, Hugh was in a potentially powerful position on the management committee. As a result, his negative attitude hindered the effectiveness of the management committee in the change process.

Dennis Kline, the refinery's young, aggressive plant manager, was a strong supporter of OD and realized its potential for improving the refinery's productivity. He had been in his present position for one year, and one of his first actions had been to initiate the OD effort with MSL's assistance. This was a good way to revitalize the work force while improving the bottom line. The OD effort would help him gain the respect of the refinery employees by demonstrating his concern for their working environment. Hugh had been his only obstacle to implementing the OD effort. He had tried to energize Hugh by utilizing him as a leader to work decisions and assume responsibility for part of the OD effort. Kline figured that if Cavanaugh felt ownership of the ideas and participated in them from their inception, he would realize their value and be won over. However, Cavanaugh refused to get involved in any way and stonewalled all of Kline's efforts over the entire year. Kline had tried everything short of firing Hugh.

Fred Sargent, MSL's senior consultant working with the management committee, knew that the members of the committee recognized Hugh's biases against OD, but they really did not have the professional insight and objectivity to see that he had no capability for change. Some of the committee members had blinders on due to their longtime friendship and respect for Hugh. As a result, the whole management committee was having a difficult time accepting the realities of the situation. But it was quite obvious to Sargent, based on his past consulting experience, that as long as Cavanaugh was a forceful member of the management committee, MSL's OD efforts could never reach their full potential.

Should Fred work with the management committee to accept the fact that Hugh would never change, he would be the catalyst for Hugh's encouraged early retirement. This would then allow Sargent to facilitate the OD process. But, if Fred was linked to Hugh's encouraged retirement, he might be labeled as a "hit man," which could inhibit his ability to work with the management committee and other members of the refinery organization. They might see Fred's actions as part of a conspiracy to do some housecleaning and thus find working through behavioral dilemmas with him quite threatening. In addition, the loss of Cavanaugh could be detrimental to the refinery's operations. His position as operations manager was a subtle link in labor negotiations currently under way as a result of a recent wildcat strike. Cavanaugh was well respected by his subordinates, and quite effective in the technical aspects of his job, which gave him influence on the union negotiations. It was Fred's feeling that Cavanaugh's work was his life and crucial to his survival, both psychologically and financially.

Feeling extremely frustrated, Fred approached George Davenport, process division manager, management committee member, and a longtime friend of Hugh Cavanaugh. George was in his early sixties, but, unlike Hugh, had been able to adjust to organizational changes quite well. He was able to see the potential benefits of OD and could look at the situation from a broad perspective.

Fred: George, I'm really concerned about the slow progress of the management committee in this recent OD effort concerning EEO and team building. What do you see as the barrier?

George: I seem to be having the same feelings that things are moving rather slowly. If only we could get Hugh on board . . . I think things would take off. I've tried to talk to him about the value of the OD efforts, but I can understand his objections. After all, our past experience with consultants billing themselves as OD experts has not been too good. They cost an arm and a leg and talk in generalities, never touching on our specific problems. However, your company has tailored its efforts to our specific needs. Also, Hugh's knowledge and understanding of company history can't be matched—even by the plant manager! He really feels outside consultants aren't qualified to facilitate changes in the organization.

Fred: But, George everyone else on the committee seems able and ready to accept the OD efforts. Hugh is living in the past. He's dug in his heels and won't budge.

George: Well, I do know he's too valuable not to have on the Management Committee at this point.

Fred Sargent was in a bind and didn't know what to do. If he didn't take any immediate action and chose to buy time, hoping to either change Hugh Cavanaugh or wait for his scheduled retirement, the entire OD effort might be doomed. Cavanaugh would do everything in his power to stop the effort, if not through the Management Committee, then verbally throughout the refinery. Another option for Sargent was to take on the biggest challenge of his career and spend all his time trying to change Hugh Cavanaugh. If he could somehow work it so Cavanaugh received full credit for part of the OD effort and was recognized by corporate headquarters for this accomplishment, he'd have no choice but to go along with the continuation of the effort.

Other options open to Fred include convincing Dennis Kline to "force" Hugh's early retirement with all the usual fanfare; going to the human resources vice president at corporate headquarters or the vice president of refining (who were both strong OD supporters) and explaining the situation; going to Hugh directly and asking him to retire; slowly showing the management committee in a calculated way that Hugh was damaging the refinery's effectiveness; or creating a scandal in order to get Hugh fired if he refused to retire.

Fred decided that the next step would be to bring his dilemma to MSL's monthly staff meeting for discussion.

Karen Webster

Karen had several problems at work to think about that night. She usually discussed things with her husband, Jack, in order to put things into a better perspective. The weekly staff meeting was coming up and she wanted to be prepared to present her dilemmas as clearly and concisely as possible to the other consultants to get their opinions.

Karen joined MSL at its inception and had been very active in helping the company to reach its current size and in building its good reputation. She was the only woman consultant for several years. MSL did most of its consulting in flow processing plants, and many of the plant managers were products of the "Good Ole Boy" syndrome. They had grown up in the back country and had been taught that women stayed at home. There were few, if any, women working in the plants because of the rough nature of the work. Karen found that it was difficult to get the managers to accept her as a professional, knowledgeable consultant. She had to prove herself time and again. She found that she couldn't allow her clients to think of her as a woman first and a consultant second. Her professional reputation had been built with these men through much hard work and continuing efforts to educate them.

After working for MSL for five years, Karen and Jack had decided to begin a family. A lot of thought had gone into this decision. Karen had no plans to stop working after the baby was born. This opened several areas of potential conflict between raising the baby and

Karen's career. However, after carefully evaluating the situation, she began planning her projects so any traveling would be completed by the end of her seventh month of pregnancy. Back in December she had confirmed plans for an eight-day team-building session at a plant seventy-five miles away. She planned to commute every other day. This session would be the culmination of almost a year of hard work.

Several days ago the client company had contacted Karen and stated that the session would have to be pushed back. The new dates coincided with the end of the eighth month of her pregnancy. She was very concerned about this change. The thought of having to drive to and from the plant every other day was not pleasant. She also disliked the idea of staying at the plant for the entire week. She knew Jack would be upset if she were gone from home so late in her pregnancy. She would tire more easily and would not be as effective as usual. However, she had made a commitment to the client to complete the team-building process. Karen felt very strongly about fulfilling her obligations to MSL and to her career.

Karen considered her options. On some projects it would be possible to bring in another consultant to complete the training. However, this was not the case with team building. Team building's purpose was to improve the effectiveness and performance of people who work together closely on a regular basis. Because of the difficulty and time necessary to build a close, trusting relationship between the consultant and the group, it would be impossible for another consultant to take over. She could also go back to the client company and try to convince management to allow the original dates to stand. She could refuse to do the training now and try to complete it after she returned to work.

As Karen talked with Jack she voiced these possibilities and wondered how the other consultants would react to her situation. She was worried about the impact cancellation would have on her career and professional reputation. There was even a possibility that MSL would lose the client if she canceled. How would her decision affect Ken's decision to hire other women consultants? Karen wanted to get some feedback from the other consultants at the staff meeting before making her decision.

Ray Terrell

Back at MSL's New Orleans office on the morning of the monthly staff meeting, Ray Terrell's mind began to wander. Only twenty-four hours ago he had been in Dallas, Texas, in the midst of a tension-filled management committee meeting and a potentially explosive discussion with Bill Matthews, vice president of refining of the southwest region for a major energy concern. Ray had decided that this was an issue to be discussed by the entire MSL professional staff, as it had serious implications for MSL's future. He began to jot down notes in preparation for the meeting.

During the first quarter of this year, Ray had become involved in an OD effort at one of the company's southwest region refineries located in Corpus Christi, Texas. Terrell, representing MSL, spent approximately three weeks in the data-gathering phase of the OD process, which included employee-consultant interviews in all refinery divisions. According to MSL's standard practice, prior to conducting the employee interviews, Ray had assured the employees that any information obtained during the interviews would be kept confidential. The management committee was aware of this practice but had no explicit confidentiality agreement with MSL. MSL had no formalized written statement on the subject of confidentiality in their signed contracts due to their philosophy of tailoring each OD effort to the particular client. It was strongly believed by all MSL consultants that their current practice was in the best interest of the client organization, the individual, and the consulting firm. This was based on the premise that a consulting organization's ability to connect accurate data about individuals and corporations was critical to successful performance. Effective data gathering depended on trust that the information would not be used to the possible detriment of the individual unless clearly indicated up front.

Upon completion of the data-gathering phase, Ray compiled his results into a written document and presented it to the refinery's management committee, which included Bill Matthews as an ex officio member. The report emphasized a heavy concern for race relations as expressed by black wage earners in particular. Ray had stated, in a broad general sense, that blacks felt mistreated given their seniority and the jobs they got in relation to other refinery workers with similar seniority. He supported this racial concern by stating that blacks felt they were not receiving as adequate career counseling and development as white workers were (both in technical areas and otherwise) so that blacks could compete for higher level positions. Ray's report concluded

with recommended action steps which specify supervisory training in EEO awareness and counseling skills as the first steps. In addition, Ray would undertake an intensive study and revamping of the company's employee training program and practices.

Following Ray's presentation, Plant Manager Ron Gallagher called for a discussion. The EEO issue was of great concern to the entire committee, given an impending Department of Labor audit within a few months. Negative audit results could cause significant delay in the expected promotions of Ron (to a headquarters divisional VP position) and Bill Matthews (to president of the corporation's small chemical division) at the end of the year. It was obvious to Ray the he had hit one of the company's most vulnerable spots. This meant that chances for successful implementation of his recommendations were even greater than he had expected. As a result, MSL could probably count on at least six months of steady billing. This would definitely please Ken.

The management committee discussion did not seem to be accomplishing anything. It was apparent the members were quite uncomfortable with the topic of EEO in addition to being defensive of their own subdivisions' nondiscriminatory posture. Finally Bill Matthews spoke. He congratulated Ray on his effective presentation, reiterated his deep concern for the findings, and stated that he was all for immediate action. However, it would be essential for the management committee to find out exactly who had expressed these concerns so that steps could be taken to rectify their situation right away. After all, Ray and MSL were working for management. Of course, his major concern was for the employees, but there was the upcoming audit to consider, since EEO charges or possible lawsuits could easily result in a prolonged audit and bad publicity. Once the situation was under control, the problem as a whole could be tackled.

When Matthews finished there was an awkward silence in the room. Ron Gallagher made an attempt to neutralize the situation by acknowledging the refinery's potential racial problem and admitting that blacks never came to any of the refinery's social gatherings.

Terrell could not believe that Matthews had the nerve to ask for identification of his information sources in front of the entire management committee! He was even more enraged that no one objected to the request. Terrell did not know how to respond. As a management consultant he did have a responsibility to management, but had Matthews overstepped the professional boundary? This company was currently MSL's largest client, having produced the majority of projects and billing days throughout MSL's short history. If this situation got out of control, there was the possibility that the relationship would be severed. This could be devastating to MSL, since their diversification strategy targets for this quarter had not been realized. At this point MSL was relying heavily on its current clients to produce further projects in other areas of their organizations. This vertical penetration marketing strategy had worked very well with almost no specific sales effort on the part of MSL consultants and now seemed crucial to the firm's immediate survival.

Since all refinery divisions were represented on the management committee would Ray be putting MSL's immediate financial future on the line if he did not divulge his information sources? Additionally, if Gallagher and Matthews did get those promotions into the upper echelons of the company, would he be jeopardizing MSL's future with the entire corporation and MSL's reputation in the industry? Finally, one of his goals as an MSL consultant was to improve organizational effectiveness. If he gave the management committee the information Matthews wanted, he could be the catalyst needed for the refinery to address the racial concerns affecting the organization's effectiveness.

Ray's mind raced through his confused thoughts. Matthews would be expecting an answer. Ray decided to hold his tongue for the moment and told the Management Committee he'd be in touch with them at their meeting next week.

THE STAFF MEETING

Ken opened the staff meeting with a brief discussion of the various projects in progress. He then asked the consultants if they had any problems they wanted to discuss. Four hands shot up and Karen, Phil, Ray, and Fred then presented the problems confronting them. Once the initial recitals had been made, Ken recommended a fifteen-minute coffee break so everyone could digest the problems they had just heard about. He asked the group to think about possible courses of action for each situation, the pros and cons of each, and what their final recommendations would be.

STEP 2: Prepare the case for class discussion.

STEP 3: Answer the following questions, individually, in small groups, or with the entire class, as directed by your instructor.

DESCRIPTION
1. Describe the situation. What symptoms of problems exist?

DIAGNOSIS
2. Diagnose the situation. What problems exist? What theories and concepts help explain the problems?

PRESCRIPTION
3. Prescribe ways of improving the situation.

ACTION
4. Devise an action plan.

STEP 4: Discussion. In small groups, with the entire class, or in written form, share your answers to the above questions.

This case was written by Molly Batson and Nancy Sherman under the supervision of Associate Professor Jeffrey A. Barach, A.B. Freeman School of Business. This case has been prepared as a basis for class discussion rather than to illustrate effective or ineffective administrative practices. Copyright © 1982 by the School of Business, Tulane University. Reproduced with permission.

Activity 15–6 CASE ANALYSIS

STEP 1: Choose a problematic situation you encountered in an organization of which you were a member.

STEP 2: Describe the situation.

STEP 3: Diagnose the situation.

STEP 4: Prescribe ways of improving the situation.

STEP 5: Devise an action plan.

STEP 6: Discussion. Share your analysis with the rest of the class, in small groups, with the entire class, or in written form.

Activity 15–7 ORGANIZATIONAL ANALYSIS

STEP 1: Choose an organization of which you were a member.

STEP 2: Describe the interpersonal processes, organizational structure, and work design that characterized the organization.

STEP 3: Diagnose any problems that existed in the organization.

STEP 4: Prescribe ways of improving the situation.

STEP 5: Devise an action plan.

STEP 6: Discussion. Share your analysis with the rest of the class, in small groups, with the entire class, or in written form.

Activity 15–8 "LABOR SECRETARY REICH PROPOSES SMOKING BAN IN THE WORKPLACE"

STEP 1: View the ABC video entitled "Labor Secretary Reich Proposes Smoking Ban in the Workplace."

STEP 2: In small groups discuss the feasibility of making your college or university a smoke-free workplace.

1. Identify the forces for and against change.
2. Indicate the ways to increase the forces for change and decrease the forces against change.
3. Select a change agent and justify your choice.
4. Develop an action plan.
5. Identify possible barriers to implementing the plan.
6. Develop a plan for evaluating whether the workplace has successfully become smoke free.
7. Offer ways of institutionalizing the change once it occurs.

Endnotes

CHAPTER 1

[1] General Motors: No excuses, *Economist* 329 (November 20, 1993): 75–76; D. Woodruff, Maybe GM didn't get such a bad deal, *Business Week* (November 8, 1993): 35; D. Woodruff, Dodging a collision course in Detroit, *Business Week* (June 21, 1993): 146–148; M. Oneal, 25 executives to watch, *The 1993 Business Week 1000* (1993): 53–103; B.S. Moskal, Smith freshens GM's stale air, *Industry Week* (October 4, 1993): 19–22; K. Kerwin, Can Jack Smith fix GM? *Business Week* (November 1, 1993): 126–135.

[2] Extensive writings exist regarding research methodology. Some good examples include A. Strauss, *Qualitative Analysis for Social Scientists* (New York: Cambridge University Press, 1987); W.B. Shaffir and R.A. Stebbins, eds., *Experiencing Fieldwork: An Inside View of Qualitative Research* (Newbury Park, Calif.: Sage, 1991); K.D. Broota, *Experimental Design in Behavioral Research* (New York: Wiley, 1989).

[3] T.R. Mitchell, An evaluation of the validity of correlation research conducted in organizations, *Academy of Management Review* 10 (1985): 192–205, discusses some of the drawbacks of correlational research as compared to experimental research; K.M. Borman, M.D. LeCompte, and J.P. Goetz, Ethnographic and qualitative research design and why it doesn't work, *American Behavioral Scientist* 30 (1986): 42–57, suggests ways of overcoming the limitations of qualitative research.

[4] A. Smith, *An Inquiry into the Nature and Cause of the Wealth of Nations,* 1776.

[5] F.W. Taylor, *The Principles of Scientific Management* (New York: Harper and Brothers, 1911), pp. 36–37.

[6] E.A. Locke, The ideas of Frederick Taylor: An evaluation, *Academy of Management Review* 7 (1982): 14–24.

[7] H. Fayol, *General and Industrial Management,* trans. C. Storrs (London: Pitman, 1949).

[8] L. Gulick and L. Urwick, eds., *Papers on the Science of Administration* (New York: Columbia University Institute of Public Administration, 1937); and J.D. Mooney and A.C. Reiley, *Onward Industry* (New York: Harper, 1931) offered complementary views of management. F.B. Gilbreth and L.M. Gilbreth, *Applied Motion Study* (New York: Sturgis and Walton, 1917) earlier offered a similar view.

[9] M. Weber, *The Theory of Social and Economic Organization,* trans. and ed. A.M. Henderson and T. Parsons (New York: Oxford University Press, 1947); M. Weber, *Essays on Sociology,* trans. and ed. H.H. Gerth and C.W. Mills (New York: Oxford University Press, 1946), pp. 196–198.

[10] R.M. Weiss, Weber on bureaucracy: Management consultant or political theorist? *Academy of Management Review* 8 (1983): 242–248, argues that Weber was not concerned with prescribing the characteristics of an efficient organization but rather was solely offering political theory.

[11] C.E. Snow, A discussion of the relation of illumination intensity to productive efficiency, *The Tech Engineering News,* November 1927. Cited in E.J. Roethlisberger and W.J. Dickson, *Management and the Worker* (Cambridge, Mass.: Harvard University Press, 1939).

[12] Roethlisberger and Dickson, *Management and the Worker.*

[13]K. Lewin, Forces behind food habits and methods of change, *Bulletin of the National Research Council* 108 (1943): 35–65.

[14]M. Radke and D. Klisurich, Experiments in changing food habits, *Journal of the American Dietetics Association* 23 (1947): 403–409.

[15]L. Coch and J.R.P. French, Jr., Overcoming resistance to change, *Human Relations* 1 (1948): 512–533.

[16]See C.S. Bartlem and E.A. Locke, The Coch and French study: A critique and reinterpretation, *Human Relations* 34 (1981): 555–566, for another view of the significance of research on participation.

[17]H. Simon, *Administrative Behavior,* 2nd ed. (New York: Macmillan, 1957); and J.G. March and H.A. Simon, *Organizations* (New York: Wiley, 1958).

[18]R.F. Bales, Task roles and social roles in problem-solving groups. In *Readings in Social Psychology,* 3rd ed., ed. E. Maccoby, T.M. Newcomb, and E.L. Hartley (New York: Holt, Rinehart and Winston, 1958), pp. 437–447; D. McGregor, *The Human Side of Enterprise* (New York: McGraw-Hill, 1960).

[19]McGregor, *The Human Side of Enterprise,* E.H. Schein, The Hawthorne group studies revisited: A defense of Theory Y (Cambridge, Mass.: M.I.T. Sloan School of Management Working Paper 756–74, December 1974).

[20]E.K. Trist and K.W. Bamforth, Some social and psychological consequences of the long-wall method of coal getting, *Human Relations* 4 (1951): 3–38.

[21]D. Katz and R.L. Kahn, *The Social Psychology of Organizations,* 2nd ed. (New York: Wiley, 1978).

[22]T. Burns and G.M. Stalker, *The Management of Innovation* (London: Tavistock, 1961).

[23]J. Woodward, *Industrial Organization: Theory and Practice* (London: Oxford University Press, 1965); P. Lawrence and J. Lorsch, *Organization and Environment* (Boston: Harvard Business School Division of Research, 1967).

[24]H. Mintzberg, *Structure in Fives: Designing Effective Organizations* (Englewood Cliffs, N.J.: Prentice-Hall, 1983).

[25]D.E. Lewis, Delicate balance, *The Boston Globe* (February 23, 1993): 35.

[26]B. Dumaine, The new non-manager managers, *Fortune* (February 22, 1993): 80–84.

[27]See *Profiles in Quality: Blueprints for Action from 50 Leading Companies* (Boston: Allyn and Bacon, 1991).

[28]B.J. Feder, At Motorola, quality is a team sport, *The New York Times* (January 21, 1993): D1, D7.

[29]J. Panepinto, Special delivery, *Computerworld* (March 7, 1994): 79–81.

[30]M. Moore, The second disaster in Bhopal, *Business & Society Review* 88 (1994): 26–28; J. Sarkar, A new chapter, *Far Eastern Economic Review* 157 (September 29, 1994): 70; M. Coeyman, Union Carbide: A survivor reinvests for growth, *Chemical Week* 154 (May 25, 1994): 29–30.

[31]A. Rogers, Where the Valdez players are now, five years later, *Fortune* (April 4, 1994): 13; A. Zipser, Exxon—Not quite slick enough, it's on the hook for billions, *Barron's* (June 20, 1994): 12; R. Gehani, Will oil spills sink Exxon's bottom line? *Business and Society Review* 75 (Fall 1990): 80–83; J.R. Harrald, H.S. Marcus, and W.A. Wallace, The Exxon Valdez: An assessment of crisis prevention and management systems, *Interfaces* 20(5) (1990): 14–30.

[32]See, for example, C.J. Loomis, How Drexel rigged a stock, *Fortune* (November 19, 1990): 83–91; J.W. Michaels and P. Berlin, My story—Michael Milken, *Forbes* (March 16, 1992): 78–100.

[33]W.H. Wagel and H.Z. Levine, HR '90: Challenges and opportunities, *Personnel* (June 1990): 18–42.

[34]R.R. Thomas, Jr., From affirmative action to affirming diversity, *Harvard Business Review* (March–April, 1990): 107.

[35]S. Overman, Managing the diverse workforce, *HR Magazine* 36(4) (April 1991): 32–36.

[36]Thomas, From affirmative action.

[1]E.J. Gibson, Development of perceiving, acting, and acquiring of knowledge. In *An Odyssey in Learning and Perception,* E.J. Gibson, ed. (Cambridge, Mass.: MIT Press, 1991).

[2]B.Dumaine, America's toughest bosses, *Fortune* (October 18, 1993): 41.

[3]R. Layne, Teachers avert clash, *The Newton Tab* (October 11, 1994): 1, 16.

[4]M.B. Howes, *The Psychology of Human Cognition* (New York: Pergamom, 1990); D.J. Schneider, Social cognition, *Annual Review of Psychology,* M.R. Rosenzweig and L.W. Porter, eds. 4(2) (1991): 527–561; H.P. Sims, Jr., and P. Lorenzi, *The New Leadership Paradigm: Social Learning and Cognition in Organizations* (Newbury Park, Calif.: Sage, 1992).

[5]Howes, *The Psychology of Human Cognition.*

[6]R.L. Solso, Prototypes, schemata and the form of human knowledge: The cognition of abstraction. In *Current Issues in Cognitive Processes,* C. Izawa, ed. (Hillsdale, N.J.: Erlbaum, 1989): 345–368.

[7]Sims and Lorenzi, *The New Leadership Paradigm.*

[8]Schneider, Social cognition.

[9]D.A. Gioia and P.P. Poole, Scripts in organizational behavior, *Academy of Management Review* 9 (1984): 449–459; D.A. Gioia and C.C. Manz, Linking cognition and behavior: A script processing interpretation of vicarious learning, *Academy of Management Review* 10 (1985): 527–529.

[10]D.A. Gioia, A. Donnellon, and H.P. Sims, Jr., Communication and cognition in appraisal: A tale of two paradigms, *Organizational Studies* 10 (1989): 503–530.

[11]D.A. Gioia, Pinto files and personal ethics: A script analysis of missed opportunities, *Journal of Business Ethics* 11 (May, 1992): 379–389.

[12]E.P. Kelly, A.O. Young, and L.S. Clark, Sex stereotyping in the workplace: A manager's guide, *Business Horizons* 36(2) (1993): 23–29.

[13]J. Flynn, Julia Stasch raises the roof for feminism, *Business Week* (January 25, 1993): 102.

[14]V.E. Schein and R. Mueller, Sex role stereotyping and requisite management characteristics: A cross cultural look, *Journal of Organizational Behavior* 13 (1992): 439–447.

[15]M.E. Heilman and M.H. Stopeck, Being attractive, advantage or disadvantage? Performance evaluations and recommended personnel actions as a function of appearance, sex, and job type, *Organizational Behavior and Human Decision Processes* 35 (1985): 202–215.

[16]D. Hatherly, J. Innes, and T. Brown, The expanded audit report—An empirical investigation, *Accounting & Business Research* 21 (Autumn 1991): 311–319.

[17]G. Haight, Managing diversity, *Across the Board* (March 1990): 22–29; L. Copeland, Learning to manage a multicultural work force, *Training* (May 1988): 49–56.

[18]J.H. Greenhaus and S. Parasuraman, Job performance attributions and career advancement prospects: An examination of gender and race effects, *Organizational Behavior and Human Decision Processes* 55 (1993): 273–297.

[19]E.E. Jones, *Interpersonal Perception* (New York: W.H. Freeman, 1990); E.K. Shaver, *An Introduction to Attribution Processes* (Cambridge, Mass.: Winthrop, 1975).

[20]H.H. Kelley, Attribution theory in social psychology, *Nebraska Symposium on Motivation* 14 (1967): 192–241.

[21]E.E. Jones and R.E. Nisbett, *The Actor and The Observer, Divergent Perceptions of the Causes of Behavior* (Morristown, N.J.: General Learning Press, 1971).

[22]E. Lesly, Who played dress-up with the books? *Business Week* (March 15, 1993): 34.

[23]J. Barry, *Moral Issues in Business* (Belmont, Calif.: Wadsworth, 1983).

[24]S.L. Payne and R.A. Giacalone, Social psychological approaches to the perception of ethical dilemmas, *Human Relations* 43 (1991): 649–665.

[25]J. Bartunek, Why did you do that? Attribution theory in organizations, *Business Horizons* 24 (1981): 66–71.

[26]H.H. Kelley and J.L. Michela, Attribution theory and research, *Annual Review of Psychology* 31 (1980): 457–501.

[27]D. Foust, They're bean counters, not gumshoes, *Business Week* (September 14, 1992): 92.

[28]A.K. Wiswell and H.V. Lawrence, Intercepting managers' attributional bias through feedback-skills training, *Human Resource Development Quarterly* 5(1) (1994): 41–53.

[29] W.B. Swann, Jr., Identity negotiation when two roads meet, *Journal of Personality and Social Psychology* 53 (1987): 1038–1051; Jones and Nisbett, *The Actor and the Observer.*

[30] R.G. Lord and J.E. Smith, Theoretical, information processing, and situational factors affecting attribution theory models of organizational behavior, *Academy of Management Review* 8 (1983): 50–60.

[31] I. Pavlov, *Conditioned Reflexes: An Investigation of the Physiological Activity of the Cerebral Cortex,* trans. and ed. G.V. Anrep (London: Oxford University Press, 1927). Comparable work was done in the United States by J.B. Watson and is described in *Behaviorism* (New York: Norton, 1924).

[32] B.F. Skinner, *About Behaviorism* (New York: Knopf, 1974); B.F. Skinner, *The Behavior of Organisms* (New York: Appleton-Century-Crofts, 1938).

[33] E.C. Tolman, *Purposive Behavior in Animals and Men* (New York: Appleton-Century-Crofts, 1932).

[34] Otis Port, Lev Landa's worker miracles, *Business Week* (September 21, 1992): 72, 74.

[35] F. Luthans, *Organizational Behavior,* 4th ed. (New York: McGraw-Hill, 1985); C.C. Manz and H.P. Sims, Vicarious learning: The influence of modeling on organizational behavior, *Academy of Management Review* 6 (1981): 105–113.

[36] A. Bandura, *Social Learning Theory* (Englewood Cliffs, N.J.: Prentice-Hall, 1978).

[37] Krystal Miller, At GM, the three R's are the Big Three, *Wall Street Journal* (July 2, 1992): B1, B4.

[38] S.G. Redding, Cognition as an aspect of culture and in relation to management processes: An exploratory view of the Chinese case, *Journal of Management Studies* (1980) 17(2): 127–148; J.B. Shaw, A cognitive categorization model for the study of intercultural management, *Academy of Management Review* 15(4) (1990): 626–645.

[39] N.J. Adler, *International Dimensions of Organizational Behavior,* 2d ed. (Boston: Kent, 1991).

[40] Adler, *International Dimensions.*

[41] S. Kumon, Some principles governing the thought and behavior of Japanists (contextuals), *Journal of Japanese Studies* 8 (1984): 5–28.

[42] J.S. Black and M. Mendenhall, Cross-cultural training effectiveness: A review and a theoretical framework for future research, *Academy of Management Review* 15 (1990): 113–136.

CHAPTER 3

[1] L. Copeland, Valuing workplace diversity, *Personnel Administrator;* T.H. Cox and S. Blake, Managing cultural diversity: Implications for organizational competiveness, *Academy of Management Executive* 5(3) (1991): 45–56.

[2] R. Mitchell, Managing by values, *Business Week* (August 1, 1994): 46–52.

[3] J.B. Rotter, Generalized expectancies for internal versus external control of reinforcement, *Psychological Monographs* 1(609) (1966): 80.

[4] M. Friedman and R. Roseman, *Type A Behavior and Your Heart* (New York: Knopf, 1974); M.T. Matteson and C. Preston, Occupational stress, Type A behavior and physical well-being, *Academy of Management Journal* 25 (1982): 373–391; D.C. Glass, *Behavior Patterns, Stress, and Coronary Disease* (Hillsdale, N.J.: Erlbaum, 1977).

[5] See, for example, J. Schaubroeck, G.C. Ganster, and B.E. Kemmerer, Job complexity, 'Type A' behavior, and cardiovascular disorder: A prospective study, *Academy of Management Journal* 37 (1994): 426–439; and P.E. Spector and B.J. O'Connell, the contribution of personality traits, negative affectivity, locus of control and Type A to the subsequent reports of job stressors and job strains, *Journal of Occupational and Organizational Psychology* 67(1) (1994): 1–12.

[6] M. Jamal and V.V. Baba, Type A behavior: Its prevalence and consequences among women nurses: An empirical examination, *Human Relations* 44 (1991): 1213–1228.

[7] R. Zemke, Second thoughts about the MBTI, *Training* 29(4) (April 1992): 43–47.

[8] C.G. Jung, *Collected Works,* ed. H. Read, M. Fordham, and G. Adler (Princeton, N.J.: Princeton University Press, 1953).

[9] S.D. Gladis, Are you the write type? *Training & Development* (July 1993): 32–36.

[10]J.A. Davey, B.H. Schell, and K. Morrison, The Myers–Briggs personality indicator and its usefulness for problem solving by mining industry personnel, *Group & Organization Management* 18(1) (March 1993): 50–65.

[11]M.F.R. Kets de Vries and D. Miller, Personality, culture, and organization, *Academy of Management Review* 11 (1986): 262–279.

[12]D. Shackleton, L. Pitt, and A.S. Marks, Managerial decision styles and machiavellianism: A comparative study, *Journal of Managerial Psychology* 5(1) (1990): 10–16.

[13]R. Christie and L.G. Geis, eds., *Studies in Machiavellianism* (New York: Academic Press, 1970).

[14]Christie and Geis, *Studies in Machiavellianism;* J.E. Durkin, Encountering: What low Machs do, in Christie and Geis, *Studies.*

[15]M. Gable and M.T. Topol, Machiavellianism and the department store executive, *Journal of Retailing* 64(1) (1988): 68–84.

[16]K.M. Kacmar and G.R. Ferris, Politics at work: Sharpening the focus of political behavior in organizations, *Business Horizons* 36(4) (July/August 1993): 70–74.

[17]E.A. Locke, E. Frederick, C. Lee, and P. Bobko, Effect of self-efficacy, goals, and task strategies on task performance, *Journal of Applied Psychology* 69 (1984): 241–25l; R.W. Lent, S.D. Brown, and K.C. Larkin, Comparison of three theoretically derived variables in predicting career and academic behavior: Self-efficacy, interest congruence, and consequence thinking, *Journal of Counseling Psychology* 34 (1987): 293–298; S.A. Stumpf, A.P. Brief, and K. Hartman, Self-efficacy expectations and coping with career-related events, *Journal of Vocational Behavior* 31 (1987): 91–108.

[18]M.E. Gist and T.R. Mitchell, Self-efficacy: A theoretical analysis of its determinants and malleability, *Academy of Management Review* 17(2) (1992): 183–211.

[19]Gist and Mitchell, Self-efficacy.

[20]R. Lachman, Factors influencing workers' orientation: A secondary analysis of Israeli data, *Organization Studies* 9 (1988): 497–510.

[21]B. Burlingham, This woman has changed business forever, *Inc.* (June 1990): 34–44.

[22]G. Greenwald, Why are attitudes important? In *Attitude, Structure, and Function,* ed. A.R. Pratkanis, S.J. Breckler, and A.G. Greenwald (Hillsdale, N.J.: Erlbaum, 1989), pp. 1–10.

[23]S. Oskamp, *Attitudes and Opinions,* 2nd ed. (Englewood Cliffs, N.J.: Prentice-Hall, 1991) offers a good overview of the measurement of attitudes.

[24]Summarized in Oskamp, *Attitudes and Opinions.*

[25]See M. Fishbein and I. Ajzen, *Beliefs, Attitude, Intention, and Behavior: An Introduction to Theory and Research* (Reading, Mass.: Addison-Wesley, 1975); I. Ajzen, *Attitudes, Personality, and Behavior* (Chicago: Dorsey, 1988).

[26]R.H. Fazio, How do attitudes guide behavior? In *Handbook of Motivation and Cognition* R.M. Sorrentino and E.T. Higgins, eds., (New York: Guilford, 1986): 204–243.

[27]A.R. Pratkanis, The cognitive representation of attitudes. In Pratkanis *et al., Attitudes,* pp. 71–98.

[28]Fazio, How do attitudes guide behavior?

[29]D.L. Ronis, J.F. Yates, and J.P. Kirscht, Attitudes, decisions, and habits as determinants of repeated behavior. In Pratkanis *et al., Attitudes,* pp. 213–239.

[30]Originally conceived by L. Festinger, *A Theory of Cognitive Dissonance* (Stanford, Calif.: Stanford University, 1957); and more recently discussed by H. Marcus and R.B. Zajonc, The cognitive perspective in social psychology. In *The Handbook of Social Psychology,* 3rd ed., Vol 1, ed. G. Lindzey and E. Aronson (New York: Random House, 1985), among others.

[31]E.A. Locke and G.P. Latham, *A Theory of Goal Setting & Task Performance* (Englewood Cliffs, N.J.: Prentice-Hall, 1990).

[32]L.M. Shore and H.J. Martin, Job satisfaction and organizational commitment in relation to work performance and turnover intentions, *Human Relations* 42(7) (1989): 625–638; M.T. Iaffaldano and P.M. Muchinsky, Job satisfaction and job performance: A meta-analysis, *Psychological Bulletin* 97 (1985): 251–273; C. Ostroff, The relationship between satisfaction, attitudes, and performance: An organizational level analysis, *Journal of Applied Psychology* 77 (December 1992): 963–974.

[33]J.A. Wagner III, Participation's effects on performance and satisfaction: A reconsideration of research evidence, *Academy of Management Review* 19 (1994): 312–330.

[34]R. Zeffane, Correlates of job satisfaction and their implications for work redesign: A focus on the Australian telecommunications industry, *Public Personnel Management* 23 (Spring 1994): 61–76.

[35]See, for example, Feldman, Careers in organizations: Recent trends and future directions, *Journal of Management* 15 (1989): 135–156. D.T. Hall, Breaking career routines: Midcareer choice and identity development. In *Career Development in Organizations,* ed. D.T. Hall and associates, (San Francisco: Jossey-Bass, 1986).

[36]See W. Kiechel III, How to manage older workers, *Fortune* (November 5, 1990): 183–186, for a list of stereotypes about older workers that must be dispelled.

[37]D.C. Feldman, Careers in organizations.

[38]E.W. Morrison, Newcomer information seeking: Exploring types, modes, sources, and outcomes, *Academy of Management Journal* 36(3) (1993): 557–589.

[39]E.W. Morrison, Longitudinal study of the effects of information seeking on newcomer socialization, *Journal of Applied Psychology* 78(2) (1993): 173–183.

[40]J.P. Meyer and N.J. Allen, Links between work experiences and organizational commitment during the first year of employment: A longitudinal analysis, *Journal of Occupational Psychology* 61 (1988): 195–209; D.M. Hunt and C. Michael, Mentorship: A career training and development tool, *Academy of Management Review* 8 (1983): 475–485; K.E. Kram, Phases of the mentor relationship, *Academy of Management Journal* 26 (1983): 608–625.

[41]P. Oster, The fast track leads overseas, *Business Week* (November 1, 1993): 64–68.

[42]W. Kiechel III, A manager's career in the new economy, *Fortune* (April 4, 1994): 68–72.

[43]K. Kram, Mentoring in the workplace. In *Career Development,* ed. Hall and associates, p. 162.

[44]See K.E. Kram, *Mentoring at Work: Developmental Relationships in Organizational Life* (Glenview, Ill.: Scott, Foresman, 1985); R. Rubow and S. Jansen, A corporate survival guide for the baby bust, *Management Review* (July 1990): 50–52; E.A. Fagenson, The mentor advantage: Perceived career/job experiences of proteges versus non-proteges, *Journal of Organizational Behavior* 10 (1989): 309–320; Kram, Mentoring in the workplace.

[45]R. Ragins, Barriers to mentoring: The female manager's dilemma, *Academy of Management Review* 42 (1989): 1–22.

[46]R.A. Noe, Women and mentoring: A review and research agenda, *Academy of Management Review* 13 (1988): 65–78 lists the six barriers; C.A. McKeen and R.J. Burke, Mentor relationships in organisations: Issues, strategies, and prospects for women, *Journal of Management Development* 8(6): 33–42; and R.J. Burke and C.A. McKeen, Mentoring in organizations: Implications for women, *Journal of Business Ethics* 9 (1990): 317–332 also discuss mentoring issues for women.

[47]D.A. Thomas, Racial dynamics in cross-race developmental relationships, *Administrative Science Quarterly* 38 (1993): 169–194.

[48]G.F. Dreker and R.A. Ash, A comparative study of mentoring among men and women in managerial, professional, and technical positions, *Journal of Applied Psychology* 75(5) (1990): 539–546; W. Whiteley, T.W. Dougherty, and G.F. Dreker, Relationship of career mentoring and socioeconomic origin to managers' and professionals' early career progress, *Academy of Management Journal* 34(2) (1991): 331–351.

[49]J.A. Wilson and N.S. Elman, Organizational benefits of mentoring, *Academy of Management Executive* 4(4) (1990): 88–94.

[50]Kram, Mentoring in the workplace.

[51]H. Keets, Avon calling—on its troops, *Business Week* (July 8, 1991): 53.

[52]R.A. Webber, Career problems of young managers, *California Management Review* 18 (1976): 19–33.

[53]L.S. Richman, How to get ahead in America, *Fortune* (May 16, 1994): 46–54.

[54]See K. Little, The baby boom generation: Confronting reduced opportunities, *Employment Relations Today* (Spring 1989): 57–63; and D.C. Feldman and B.A. Weitz, Career plateaus reconsidered, *Journal of Management* 14 (1988): 69–80; B.S. Moskal, Plateaued executives, *Industry Week* (September 20, 1993): 34–36; for current thinking about this issue.

[55]J.A. Raelin, An anatomy of autonomy: Managing professionals, *Academy of Management Executive* 3 (August 1989): 216–228; J.A. Raelin, C.K. Sholl, and D. Leonard, Why professionals turn sour and what to do, *Personnel* 62 (October 1985): 29–41.

[56]R. Henkoff, Companies that train best, *Fortune* (March 22, 1993): 62–75.

[57]See J. Raelin, *Professional Careers* (New York: Praeger, 1983); T.J. Allen and R. Katz, The dual ladder: Motivational solution or managerial delusion? *Research and Development Management* 16 (1986): 185–197; R. Katz, M.L. Tushman, and T.J. Allen, Exploring the dynamics of dual ladders: A longitudinal study (Cambridge, Mass.: MIT Sloan School of Management Working Paper 11–90, August 1990).

[58]T.J. Allen and R. Katz, The treble ladder revisited: Why do engineers lose interest in the dual ladder as they get older? (Cambridge, Mass.: MIT Sloan School of Management Working Paper 7–90, July 1990).

[59]D.T. Hall and Associates, Breaking career routines. In *Career Development,* p. 133.

[60]A. Howard and D.W. Bray, *Managerial Lives in Transition: Advancing Age and Changing Times* (New York: Guilford, 1988); J.R. Gordon, The midlife transition of professional women, International Federation of University Women Frennial Conference, San Francisco, August 1992; J.R. Gordon, Adding diversity to the work force 2000: Meeting the needs of working mothers at midlife, Women and Work Conference, Arlington Tx., May 1992.

[61]F.W. Dalton, P.H. Thompson, and R.L. Price, The four stages of professional careers: A new look at performance by professionals, *Organizational Dynamics* 6 (1977): 19–42.

[62]J.E. Piercy and J.B. Forbes, The phases of the chief executive's career, *Business Horizons* (May–June 1991): 22.

[63]L. Larwood and B.A. Gutek, Working toward a theory of women's career development. In *Women's Career Development,* ed. B.A. Gutek and L. Larwood (Newbury Park, Calif.: Sage, 1987), pp. 170–183.

[64]B. Leibowitz, C. Farren, and B.L. Kaye, *Designing Career Development Systems* (San Francisco: Jossey-Bass, 1986).

[65]J.M. Brett, L.K. Stroh, and A.H. Reilly, Pulling up roots in the 1990s: Who's willing to relocate? *Journal of Organizational Behavior* 14 (1993): 49–60.

[66]H. Cosell, *Women on a Seesaw* (New York: Putnam and Sons, 1985).

[67]M. Galen, Work & family, *Business Week* (June 28, 1993): 88.

[68]J. C. Mason, Working in the family way, *Management Review* 82(7) (July 1993): 25–28.

[69]This discussion is drawn from Race in the workplace: Is affirmative action working? *Business Week* (July 8, 1991): 50–63.

[70]B.L. Betters-Reed and L.L. Moore, The technicolor workplace, *Ms.* 3(3) (1992): 84–85.

[71]D.B. Henriques, Piercing Wall Street's 'lucite ceiling,' *The New York Times* (August 11, 1991): section 3, pp. 1, 6.

[72]E. Lesly and M. Mallory, Inside the Black business network, *Business Week* (November 29, 1993): 70–82.

[73]E. Lesly, Sticking it out at Xerox by sticking together, *Business Week* (November 29, 1993): 77.

[74]M. Janofsky, Race and the American workplace, *The New York Times* (June 20, 1993): section 3, p. 1, 6.

[75]S.M. Nkomo, The emperor has no clothes: Rewriting "race in organizations," *Academy of Management Review* 17(3) (1992): 487–513.

[76]K.G. Salwen, Why Ms. Brickman of Sarah Lawrence now rallies workers, *The Wall Street Journal* (May 24, 1991): A1, A4.

[77]S. Kintner, Older is better, *Women and Therapy* 2(4) (1983): 61–67.

[78]C. Gilligan, *In a Different Voice* (Cambridge, Mass.: Harvard University, 1982).

[79]Up against the glass ceiling, *Management Review* (April 1987): 6; A. Morrison, R. White, and E. Van Velsor, *Breaking the Glass Ceiling* (Reading, Mass.: Addison-Wesley, 1987); S. Caudron, The concrete ceiling, *Industry Week* 243 (July 4, 1994): 31–36.

[80]Five magic words: 'give me a bigger challenge,' *Fortune* (September 21, 1992): 56; E. Schine, Barbie is her friend, *Business Week* (June 8, 1992): 80.

[81]N.J. Adler, Women managers in a global economy, *HR Magazine* (September, 1993): 52–55.

[82]Adler, Women managers in a global economy.

[83]This discussion is drawn in part from W. Kiechel III, How to manage older workers, *Fortune* (November 5, 1990): 183–186.

[84]Presentation made by D.L. Baker, Director of Employment to the Textbook Authors Conference sponsored by the American Association for Retired Persons, Washington, D.C., October 14, 1994.

[85]Costs and benefits of hiring older workers: A case study of B&Q, reported in the commonwealth fund. In *The Untapped Resource: The Final Report of the Americans Over 55 at Work Program* (New York: The Commonwealth Fund, November 1993).

[86]E. Schonfeld, Women on the move—with husbands in tow, *Fortune,* (October 17, 1994): 20.

[87]A.B. Fisher, Japanese working women strike back, *Fortune* (May 3, 1993).

[88]Corporate America is still no place for kids, *Business Week* (November 25, 1991): 234–236; S. Shellenbarger, More job seekers put family need first, *The Wall Street Journal* (November 15, 1991): B1, B12.

[89]R.L. Rose, Small steps, *The Wall Street Journal* (June 21, 1993): R10.

[90]N. Stone, Building corporate character: An interview with Stride Rite Chairman Arnold Hiatt, *Harvard Business Review* (March/April 1992): 95–104.

[91]L. Jenner, Work-family programs: Looking beyond written policies, *HR Focus* 71 (January 1994): 19–20.

[92]C.H. Deutsch, Mastering the language of disability, *The New York Times* (February 10, 1991): 25.

[93]M.J. Mandel and C. Farrell, The immigrants, *Business Week* (July 13, 1992): 114–122.

[94]J.H. Sheridan, Dividends from diversity, *Industry Week* (September 19, 1994): 23–26.

[95]C.M. Solomon, The corporate response to work force diversity, *Personnel Journal* (August 1989): 49.

[96]J. Castelli, Education forms common bond, *HR Magazine* (June 1990): 46–49.

[97]R.T. Jones, B. Jerich, L. Copeland, and M. Boyles, How do you manage a diverse workforce? *Training and Development Journal* (February 1989).

[98]Are Older Workers "Good Buys"?—A Case Study of Days Inns of America, Reported in The Commonwealth Fund. In *The Untapped Resource.*

[99]J.J. Laabs, How Gilette grooms global talent, *Personnel Journal* (August 1993): 64–76.

[100]How do you manage a diverse workforce? *Training and Development Journal* (February 1989): 13–21.

[101]B.G. Foster, G. Jackson, W.E. Cross, B. Jackson, and R. Hardiman, Workforce diversity and business, *Training and Development Journal* (April 1988): 40.

CHAPTER 4

[1]Excerpted from and reprinted with permission from B. Saporito, A week aboard the Wal-Mart Express, *Fortune* (August 24, 1992): 77–84.

[2]A.H. Maslow, *Motivation and Personality,* 3rd ed. (New York: Harper & Row, 1987).

[3]T. Sega, Family care: Tips for companies that are trying to help, *Business Week* (September 28, 1992).

[4]K. Pallarito, N.Y. union deal saves jobs but cuts costs, *Modern Healthcare* 24 (September 26, 1994): 36.

[5]M.H. Cimini and C.J. Muhl, Job security in Xerox contract, *Monthly Labor Review* 117 (September 1994): 61.

[6]P. Weis, Achieving zero-defect service through self-directed teams, *Journal of Systems Management* 43(2) (February 1992): 27–29, 36.

[7]M.E. Gist and T.R. Mitchell, Self-efficacy: A theoretical analysis of its determinants and malleability, *Academy of Management Review* 17 (1992): 183–211.

[8]See M.A. Wahba and L.G. Bridwell, Maslow reconsidered: A review of research on the need hierarchy theory, *Organizational Behavior and Human Performance* 15 (1976): 212–240; V.F. Mitchell and P. Moudgill, Measurement of Maslow's need hierarchy, *Organizational Behavior and Human Performance* 16 (1976): 334–349; E.E. Lawler III, *Motivation in Work Organizations* (Monterey, Calif.: Brooks/Cole, 1973).

[9]G. Hofstede, Motivation, leadership, and organization: Do American theories apply abroad? *Organizational Dynamics* (Summer 1980): 42–63.

[10]Hofstede, Motivation, leadership, and organization.

[11]N. J. Adler, *International Dimensions of Organizational Behavior,* 2nd ed. (Boston: PWS-Kent, 1991).

[12]See, for example, B. Jaggi, Need importance of Indian managers, *Management International Review* 19(1) (1979): 107–113; M.K. Badawy, Styles of mideastern managers, *California Management Review* 22 (Spring 1980): 51–59.

[13]C.P. Alderfer, *Existence, Relatedness, and Growth: Human Needs in Organizational Settings* (New York: Free Press, 1972).

[14]F.J. Landy, *The Psychology of Work Behavior,* 3rd ed. (Homewood, Ill.: Dorsey, 1985) compares Maslow's and Alderfer's mechanisms of needs satisfaction.

[15]D. McClelland, *The Achieving Society* (Princeton, N.J.: D. Van Nostrand, 1961); D.C. McClelland, *Motives, Personality, and Society: Selected Papers* (New York: Praeger, 1984); F.J. Landy, *The Psychology of Work Behavior,* 3rd ed. (Homewood, Ill.: Dorsey, 1985); S.R. Jenkins, Need for achievement and women's careers over 14 years: Evidence for occupational structure effects, *Journal of Personality and Social Psychology* 53 (1987): 922–932.

[16]McClelland, *The Achieving Society;* McClelland, *Motives, Personality and Society.* S.R. Jenkins, Need for achievement.

[17]D. McClelland and D.H. Burnham, Power drive managers: Good guys make bum bosses, *Psychology Today* 7 (1985): 69–71.

[18]R.L. Jacobs and D.C. McClelland, Moving up the corporate ladder: A longitudinal study of the leadership motive pattern and managerial success in women and men, *Consulting Psychology Journal of Practice and Research* 46 (Winter 1994): 32–41.

[19]F. Herzberg, B. Mausner, and B.B. Snyderman, *The Motivation to Work* (New York: Wiley, 1959); F. Herzberg, *The Managerial Choice: To Be Efficient and To Be Human* (Salt Lake City: Olympus, 1982).

[20]See B.L. Hinton, An empirical investigation of the Herzberg methodology and two-factor theory, *Organizational Behavior and Human Performance* 3 (1968): 286–309; R. House and L. Wigdor, Herzberg's dual-factor theory of job satisfaction and motivation: A review of the evidence and criticism, *Personnel Psychology* 20 (1968): 369–389; J. Schneider and E. Locke, A critique of Herzberg's classification system and a suggested revision, *Organizational Behavior and Human Performance* 14 (1971): 441–458.

[21]G.R. Salancik and J. Pfeffer, An examination of need-satisfaction models of job attitudes, *Administrative Science Quarterly* 22 (1977): 427–456.

[22]J.S. Adams, Inequity in social exchange, *Advances in Experimental and Social Psychology,* ed. L. Berkowitz, 2 (1965): 267–300; see also E. Walster, W. Walster, and E. Berscheid, *Equity: Theory and Research* (Boston: Allyn and Bacon, 1978).

[23]F.J. Landy and W.S. Becker, Motivation theory reconsidered, *Research in Organizational Behavior* 9 (1987): 1–38.

[24]B.A. Mellers, Equity judgment, A revision of Aristotelian views, *Journal of Experimental Psychology: General* 111 (1982): 242–270; M.H. Birnbaum, Perceived equity in salary policies, *Journal of Applied Psychology* 68 (1983): 49–59.

[25]R.P. Vecchio, Predicting worker performance in inequitable settings, *Academy of Management Review* 7 (1982): 103–110, presents four mathematical models of equity theory.

[26]G.R. Oldham and H.E. Miller, The effect of significant other's job complexity on employee reactions to work, *Human Relations* 32 (1979): 247–260; J. Greenbert and G.S. Leventhal, Equity and the use of overreward to motivate performance, *Journal of Personality and Social Psychology* 34 (1976): 179–190.

[27]D. Schwab, Construct validity in organizational behavior. In *Research in Organizational Behavior,* vol. 2, ed. B. Staw (Greenwich, Conn.: JAI Press, 1980); M.R. Carrell and J.E. Dittrich, Equity theory: The recent literature, methodological considerations, and new directions, *Academy of Management Review* 3 (1978): 202–210.

[28]J.E. Dittrich constructed the Organizational Fairness Questionnaire to measure these and other dimensions; see J. Gordon, *A Diagnostic Approach to Organizational Behavior,* 4th ed. (Boston: Allyn and Bacon, 1993), p. 135 for an excerpt.

[29]B.H. Sheppard, R.J. Lewicki, and J.W. Minton, *Organizational Justice: The Search for Fairness in the Workplace* (New York: Lexington, 1992).

[30]Sheppard *et al., Organizational Justice.*

[31]R.E. Kopelman, Psychological stages of careers in engineering: An expectancy theory taxonomy, *Journal of Vocational Behavior* 10 (1977): 270–286; M.R. Carrell and J.E. Dittrich, Employee perceptions of fair treatment, *Personnel Journal* 55 (1976): 523–524; R.A. Cosier and D.R. Dalton, Equity theory and time: A reformulation, *Academy of Management Review* 8 (1983): 311–319.

[32]R.C. Huseman, J.D. Hatfield, and E.W. Miles, A new perspective on equity theory: The equity sensitivity construct, *Academy of Management Review* 12 (1987): 232–234.

[33]R.A. Cosier and D.R. Dalton, Equity theory and time: A reformulation, *Academy of Management Review* 8 (1983): 311–319.

[34]M.R. Carrell and J.E. Dittrich, Employee perceptions of fair treatment, *Personnel Journal* 55 (1976): 523–524.

[35]T.F. O'Boyle, A manufacturer grows efficient by soliciting ideas from employees, *The Wall Street Journal* (June 5, 1992): A1, A4.

[36]A. Farnham, Mary Kay's lessons in leadership, *Fortune* (September 20, 1993): 68–77.

[37]L.K. Trevino, The social effects of punishment in organizations: A justice perspective, *Academy of Management Review* 17(4) (1992): 647–676.

[38]S.F. Jablonsky and D.L. DeVries, Operant conditioning principles extrapolated to the theory of management, *Organizational Behavior and Human Performance* 7 (1972): 340–358.

[39]K. Chilton, Lincoln Electric's incentive system: Can it be transferred overseas? *Compensation and Benefits Review* 25 (November/December 1993): 21–30; C. Wiley, Incentive plan pushes production, *Personnel Journal* 72 (August 1993): 86–87; C. Wiley, The history of Lincoln Electric Company and its incentive plan, *Personnel Journal* 72 (August 1993): 88.

[40]H.W. Babb and D.G. Kopp, Applications of behavior modification in organizations: A review and critique, *Academy of Management Review* 3 (1978): 281–292.

[41]K. O'Hara, C.M. Johnson, and T.A. Beehr, Organizational behavior management in the private sector: A review of empirical research and recommendations for further investigations, *Academy of Management Review* 10 (1985): 848–864.

[42]M. Wickoff, P.C. Anderson, and C.R. Crowell, Behavior management in a factory setting: Increasing work efficiency, *Journal of Organizational Behavior Management* 4 (1982): 97–127.

[43]J.G. Carlson and K.D. Hill, The effect of gaming on attendance and attitude, *Personnel Psychology* 35 (1982): 63–73.

[44]B. Sulzer-Azaroff and M.C. De Santamaria, Industrial safety hazard reduction through performance feedback, *Journal of Applied Behavior Analysis* 13 (1980): 287–295.

[45]T.J. Newby and P.W. Robinson, Effects of grouped and individual feedback and reinforcement on retail employee performances, *Journal of Organizational Behavior Management* 5 (1983): 51–68.

[46]H. Wilke, Equity: Information and effect dependency. In *Equity Theory: Psychological and Sociological Perspectives,* ed. D.M. Messick and K.S. Cook (New York: Praeger, 1983).

[47]J. Martin and A. Murray, Distributive justice and unfair exchange. In Messick and Cook, *Equity Theory.*

[48]See S. Kerr, On the folly of rewarding A while hoping for B, *Academy of Management Journal,* 18 (1975): 769–783.

[49]M.G. Evans, Organizational behavior: The central role of motivation, *1986 Yearly Review of Management of the Journal of Management,* ed. J.G. Hunt and J.D. Blair (1986): 203–222; counters the overwhelming evidence in support of this theory by suggesting that the identification and assessment of an individual's valences over time remains a problem.

[50]V.H. Vroom, *Work and Motivation* (New York: Wiley, 1964).

[51]D.A. Nadler and E.E. Lawler III, Motivation: A diagnostic approach. In *Perspectives on Behavior in Organizations,* ed. J.R. Hackman, E.E. Lawler III, and L.W. Porter (New York: McGraw-Hill, 1977), pp. 26–38.

[52]B.M. Staw, Organizational behavior: A review and reformulation of the field's outcome variables, *Annual Review of Psychology* 35 (1984): 627–666.

[53]Adler, *International Dimensions.*

[54]B.M. Staw, *Intrinsic and Extrinsic Motivation* (Morristown, N.J.: General Learning Press, 1976) presents an early view; W.E. Scott Jr., J. Farh, and P.M. Podsakoff, The effects of "intrinsic" and "extrinsic" reinforcement contingencies on task behavior, *Organizational Behavior and Human Decision Processes* 41 (1988): 405–425; and P.C. Jordan, Effects of an extrinsic reward on intrinsic motivation: A field experiment, *Academy of Management Journal* 29 (1986): 405–412, present more recent examples.

[55]See L.E. Miller and J.E. Grush, Improving predictions in expectancy theory research: Effects of personality, expectancies, and norms, *Academy of Management Journal* 31 (1988): 107–122; T.R. Mitchell, Expectancy-value models in organizational psychology. In *Expectation and Actions: Expectancy-value Models in Psychology,* ed. N.T. Feather (Hillsdale, N.J.: Erlbaum), pp. 293–312.

[56]See J.P. Campbell and R.D. Pritchard, Motivation theory in industrial and organizational psychology. In *Handbook of Industrial and Organizational Psychology,* ed. M.D. Dunnette (Chicago: Rand McNally, 1976).

[57]G. Latham and J.J. Baldes, The practical significance of Locke's theory of goal setting, *Journal of Applied Psychology* 59 (1975): 122–124.

[58]C. Steinberg, Taking training for granite, *Training & Development* 47(2) (February 1993): 7–8.

[59]E.A. Locke, D.O. Chah, S. Harrison, and N. Lustgarten, Separating the effects of goal specificity from goal level, *Organizational Behavior and Human Decision Processes* 43 (1989): 270–297.

[60]E.A. Locke and G.P. Latham, *A Theory of Goal-Setting and Task Performance* (Englewood Cliffs, N.J.: Prentice-Hall, 1990).

[61]S. Tully, Your paycheck gets exciting, *Fortune* (November 1, 1993): 83–98.

[62]E.A. Locke, G.P. Latham, and M. Erez, The determinants of goal commitment, *Academy of Management Review* 13 (1988): 23–39.

[63]G.P. Latham and G.A. Yukl, A review of research on the application of goal setting in organizations, *Academy of Management Journal* 18 (1975): 824–845.

[64]See B.D. Bannister and D.B. Balkin, Performance evaluation and compensation feedback messages: An integrated model, *Journal of Occupational Psychology* 63 (1990): 97–111, for a model of intervening variables between feedback and motivation; see also J.R. Larson, The performance feedback process: A preliminary model, *Organizational Behavior and Human Performance* 33 (1984): 42–76; R.C. Liden and T.R. Mitchell, Reactions to feedback: The role of attributions, *Academy of Management Journal* 28 (1985): 291–308.

[65]E.A. Locke, E. Frederick, E. Buckner, and P. Bobko, Effect of previously assigned goals on self-set goals and performance, *Journal of Applied Psychology* 69 (1984): 694–699.

[66]M. Erez, P.C. Earley, and C.L. Hulin, The impact of participation on goal acceptance and performance: a two-step model, *Academy of Management Journal* 28 (1985): 50–66; Evans, Organizational behavior.

[67]M. Erez and I. Zidon, Effect of goal acceptance on the relationship of goal difficulty to performance, *Journal of Applied Psychology* 69 (1984): 69–78.

[68]D. Eden, Pygmalion, goal setting, and expectancy: Compatible ways to boost productivity, *Academy of Management Review* 13 (1988): 639–652.

[69]Locke and Latham, *A Theory of Goal Setting.*

[70]For example, see K.H. Schmidt, U. Kleinbeck, and W. Brockmann, Motivational control of motor performance by goal-setting in a dual-task situation, *Psychological Research* 4 (1984): 129–141.

[71] See, for example, M. Erez and P.C. Earley, Comparative analysis of goal-setting strategies across cultures, *Journal of Applied Psychology* 72 (1987): 658–665.

[72] Such differences do not always exist, as suggested by a comparable level of growth needs among computer programmers in the United States and Singapore, as described by J.D. Conger, Effect of cultural differences on motivation of analysts and programmers: Singapore vs. the United States, *MIS Quarterly* (June 1986): 189–196.

[73] Hofstede, Motivation, leadership, and organization.

[74] P. Engardio and G. DeGeorge, Importing enthusiasm, *Business Week* 1993 (21st Century Capitalism Issue): 122–123.

[75] See, for example, D. Lei, J.W. Slocum, Jr., and R.W. Slater, Global strategy and reward systems: The key roles of management development and corporate culture, *Organizational Dynamics* (1991): 27–41.

[76] D.B. Balkin and L.R. Gomez-Mejia, Toward a contingency theory of compensation strategy, *Strategic Management* 58 (1987): 169–182, calls for a contingency approach to determining compensation.

[77] R.M. Kanter, Holiday gifts: Celebrating employee achievements, *Management Review* (December 1986): 19–20, distinguishes between compensation and rewards and offers a list of ways of recognizing employees' accomplishments apart from pay.

[78] See E. Jansen and M. Von Glinow, Ethical ambivalence and organizational reward systems, *Academy of Management Review* 19 (1985): 814–822, for a discussion of possible misfits between individual ethical positions and those maintained by the organizational reward system.

[79] See E.E. Lawler III, *Strategic Pay: Aligning Organizational Strategies and Pay Systems* (San Francisco: Jossey-Bass, 1990) for extensive discussion of the role of pay.

[80] R.G. LeFauve and A.C. Hax, Managerial and technological innovations at Saturn Corporation, *MIT Management* (Spring 1992): 8–19.

[81] M.V.B. Brennan, Salary compression of nursing managers, *Nursing Management* 24 (April 1993): 46–49.

[82] G.E. Ledford, Jr., Three cases on skill-based pay: An overview, *Compensation and Benefits Review* 23(2) (1991): 11–23; G.E. Ledford, Jr. and G. Bergel, Skill-based pay case number 1: General Mills, *Compensation and Benefits Review* 23(2) (1991): 24–38; P.V. LeBlanc, Skill-based pay case number 2: Northern Telecom, *Compensation and Benefits Review* 23(2) (1991): 39–56; G.E. Ledford, Jr., W.R. Tyler, and W.B. Dixey, Skill-based pay case number 3: Honeywell Ammunition Assembly Plant, *Compensation and Benefits Review* 23(2) (1991): 57–77.

[83] See E.E. Lawler III, reward systems in organizations. In *Handbook of Organizational Behavior*, ed. J. Lorsch (Englewood Cliffs, N.J.: Prentice-Hall, 1983).

[84] H. Gleckman, Bonus pay: Buzzword or bonanza? *Business Week* (November 14, 1994): 62–64.

[85] M.A. Verespej, New responsibilities? New pay! *Industry Week* (August 15, 1994): 11–22.

[86] D.E. Bowen and C.A. Wadley, Designing a strategic benefits program, *Compensation and Benefits Review* 21(5) (1989): 44–56.

[87] Gleckman, Bonus pay.

[88] E.E. Lawler III, Gainsharing theory and research: Findings and future directions. In *Research in Organizational Change and Development*, vol. 2, ed. W.A. Pasmore and R. Woodman, (Greenwich, Conn.: JAI Press, 1988).

[89] Lawler, Gainsharing theory.

[90] T. Rollins, Productivity-based group incentive plans: Powerful, but use with caution, *Compensation and Benefits Review* 21(3) (1989): 39–50.

[91] Gleckman, Bonus pay.

[92] J.L. Pierce and C.A. Furo, Employee ownership: Implications for management, *Organizational Dynamics* (Winter 1990): 32–45.

[93] K. Labich, Will United fly? *Fortune* (August 22, 1994): 70–78.

[94] C. Rosen, Employee stock ownership plans: A new way to look at work, *Business Horizons* 26 (September–October 1983): 48–56, describes a variety of these plans.

[95] N.J. Perry, Talk about pay for performance! *Fortune* (1992).

CHAPTER 5

[1]J. Huey, The new post-heroic leadership, *Fortune* (February 21, 1994); T. Lester, The Gores' happy family, *Management Today* (February 1993): 66–68; F. Shipper and C.C. Manz, Employee self-management without formally designated teams: An alternative road to empowerment, *Organizational Dynamics* 20 (Winter 1992): 58–61.

[2]J.D. Orsburn, L. Moran, E. Musselwhite, and J.H. Zenger, *Self-directed Work Teams: The New American Challenge* (Homewood, Ill.: Business One Irwin, 1990).

[3]W.H. Miller, Martin Marietta, *Industry Week* (October 17, 1984): 227–228.

[4]C.C. Manz, D.E. Keating, and A. Donnellon, Preparing for an organizational change to employee self-management: The managerial transition, *Organizational Dynamics* (Autumn 1990): 15–26.

[5]T.E. Benson, A braver new world, *Industry Week* (August 3, 1992): 48–54.

[6]Orsburn et al., *Self-directed Work Teams.*

[7]T.B. Kirker, Edy's Grand Ice Cream, *Industry Week* (October 18, 1993): 31–32.

[8]J.A. Sasseen, The winds of change blow everywhere, *Business Week* (October 17, 1994): 92–93.

[9]Sasseen, The winds of change blow everywhere.

[10]Sasseen, The winds of change blow everywhere.

[11]C.E. Larson and F.M.J. LaFasto, *Team Work: What Must Go Right/What Can Go Wrong* (Newbury Park, Calif.: Sage, 1989).

[12]J.S. Lublin, Companies form teams to expedite decisions, *The Wall Street Journal,* December 20, 1991, p. B1.

[13]Orsburn et al., *Self-directed Work Teams:* A.G. Dobbelaere and K.H. Goeppinger, *The right and the wrong way to set up a self-directed work team, Human Resources Professional* 5(3) (Winter 1993): 31–35.

[14]B. Dumaine, Who needs a boss? *Fortune* (May 7, 1990): 52–53.

[15]D. Bottoms, Timkin, *Industry Week* (October 17, 1994): 31–32.

[16]B.P. Noble, An approach with staying power, *The New York Times* (March 8, 1992).

[17]J. Main, betting on the 21st century jet, *Fortune* (April 20, 1992): 102–117; D.J. Yang, When the going gets tough, Boeing gets touchy-feely, *Business Week* (January 17, 1994): 65–68.

[18]P. Nulty, The soul of an old machine, *Fortune* (May 21, 1990): 67–72.

[19]D. Woodruff, Chrysler's Neon, *Business Week* (May 3, 1993):116–126.

[20]T.R. Miller, The quality circle phenomenon: A review and appraisal, *SAM Advanced Management Journal* 54(1) (1989): 4–7, 12; E.E. Lawler III and S. Mohrman, Quality circles after the fad, *Harvard Business Review* (January–February 1985): 65–71.

[21]See S.D. Goldstein, Organizational dualism and quality circles, *Academy of Management Review* 10 (1985): 509–526; G.W. Meyers and R.G. Scott, Quality circles, Panacea or Pandora's Box? *Organizational Dynamics* 13 (Spring 1985): 34–50; L.R. Smeltzer and B.L. Kedia, Knowing the ropes: Organizational requirements for quality circles, *Business Horizons* 28 (July–August 1985): 30–34; G.P. Shea, Quality circles: The danger of bottled change, *Sloan Management Review* 27 (Spring 1986): 33–46; R.P. Steel and R.F. Lloyd, Cognitive, affective, and behavioral outcomes of participation in quality circles: Conceptual and empirical findings, *Journal of Applied Behavioral Science* 24 (1988): 1–17.

[22]K.D. Hutchins, *Quality Circles Handbook* (New York: Nichols, 1985).

[23]E.R. Ruffner and L.P. Ettkin, When a circle is not a circle, *SAM Advanced Management Journal* 52 (Spring 1987): 9–15.

[24]Ruffner and Ettkin, When a circle is not a circle.

[25]R.W. Napier and M.K. Gershenfeld, *Groups: Theory and Experience,* 4th ed. (Boston: Houghton Mifflin, 1989).

[26]D. Norris and R. Niebuhr, Group variables and gaming success, *Simulation and Games* 11 (1980): 301–312; L. Wheeless, V. Wheeless, and F. Dickson-Markham, A research note: The relations among social and task perceptions in small groups, *Small Group Behavior* 13 (1982): 373–384.

[27]N. Rosen, *Teamwork and the Bottom Line* (Hillsdale, N.J.: Erlbaum, 1989).

[28]P.G. Hanson and B. Lubin, Team building as group development. In W.B. Reddy and K. Jamison, *Team Building: Blueprints for Productivity and Satisfaction* (Alexandria, Va.: NTL Institute for Applied Behavioral Science, 1988).

²⁹L. Hirschhorn, *Managing the New Team Environment: Skills, Tools, and Methods* (Reading, Mass.: Addison-Wesley, 1991).

³⁰B. Dumaine, Payoff from the new management, *Fortune* (December 13, 1993): 103–110.

³¹Larson and LeFasto, *Team Work.*

³²D.C. Feldman, The development and enforcement of group norms, *Academy of Management Review* 9 (1984): 47–53.

³³E.F. Huse and J.L. Bowditch, *Behavior in Organizations: A Systems Approach,* 2nd ed. (Reading, Mass.: Addison-Wesley, 1977).

³⁴J. Jackson, A conceptual and measurement model for norms and values, *Pacific Sociological Review* 9 (1966): 35–47.

³⁵Jackson, *A conceptual and measurement model.*

³⁶Napier and Gershenfeld, *Groups.*

³⁷K.D. Benne and P. Sheats, Functional roles of group members, *Journal of Social Issues* 4 (1948) first introduced this classification.

³⁸E.H. Schein, *Process Consultation,* 2nd ed. (Reading, Mass.: Addison-Wesley, 1988).

³⁹L. Touby, Nordstrom's gang of four, *Business Week* (June 15, 1992): 122–126.

⁴⁰See R.S. Ross, *Small Groups in Organizations* (Englewood Cliffs, N.J.: Prentice-Hall, 1989); R.R. Ross and M.G. Ross, *Relating and Interacting* (Englewood Cliffs, N.J.: Prentice-Hall, 1982); M.E. Shaw, Communication networks fourteen years later. In *Group Processes,* ed. L. Berkowitz (New York: Academic Press, 1978).

⁴¹This discussion is based on J. Moosbruker, Developing a productive team: Making groups at work work. In W.B. Reddy and K. Jamison, *Team Building;* B.W. Tuchman, Developmental sequences in small groups, *Psychological Bulletin* 63 (1965): 384–399; F.L. Strodtbeck, Phases in group problem solving, *Journal of Abnormal and Social Psychology* 46 (1951): 485–495; B.W. Tuchman and M.C. Jensen, Stages of small group development revisited, *Group and Organization Studies* 2 (1977): 419–427.

⁴²P.E. Brauchle and D.W. Wright, Training work teams, *Training & Development* (March 1993): 65–68.

⁴³Discussion of this model is based on C.J.G. Gersick, Time and transition in work teams: Toward a new model of group development, *Academy of Management Journal* 31 (1988): 9–41.

⁴⁴C.J.G. Gersick and J.R. Hackman, Habitual routines in task-performing groups, *Organizational Behavior and Human Decision Processes* 47 (1990): 65–97.

⁴⁵D.G. Ancona and D.F. Caldwell, Bridging the boundary: External activity and performance in organizational teams, *Administrative Science Quarterly* 37 (1992): 634–665; Information technology and work groups: The case of new product teams. In J. Galegher, R.E. Kraut, and C. Egido, *Intellectual Teamwork: Social and Technological Foundations of Cooperative Work* (Hillsdale, N.J.: Erlbaum, 1990).

⁴⁶J.R. Barker, Tightening the iron cage: Concertive control in self-managing teams, *Administrative Science Quarterly* 38 (1993): 408–437.

⁴⁷B. Dumaine, The trouble with teams, *Fortune* (September 5, 1994): 86–92.

⁴⁸Dumaine, The trouble with teams.

⁴⁹E.H. Schein, *Process Consultation,* 2nd ed. (Reading, Mass.: Addison-Wesley, 1988).

⁵⁰P.R. Harris and R.T. Moran, *Managing Cultural Differences,* 2nd ed. (Houston: Gulf, 1987), pp. 174–175.

⁵¹U. Merry and M.E. Allerhand, Developing Teams and Organizations: *A Practical Handbook for Managers and Consultants* (Reading, Mass.: Addison-Wesley, 1977).

⁵²K. Bridges, G. Hawkins, and K. Elledge, From new recruit to team member, *Training & Development* (August 1993).

⁵³D.G. Ancona, Outward bound: Strategies for team survival in an organization, *Academy of Management Journal* 33 (1990): 334–365.

⁵⁴Larson and LeFasto, *Team Work.*

⁵⁵J.R. Hackman, ed., *Groups That Work (And Those That Don't):* (San Francisco: Jossey-Bass, 1989).

⁵⁶N.J. Adler, *International Dimensions of Organizational Behavior,* 2nd ed. (Boston: PWS-Kent, 1991).

57C.J. Fombrun, Corporate culture and competitive strategy. *Strategic Human Resource Management,* ed. C.J. Fombrun, N.M. Tichy, and M. Devanna, (New York: Wiley, 1984).

58P.R. Harris and R.T. Moran, *Managing Cultural Differences,* 3rd ed. (Houston: Gulf, 1991).

59W.E. Watson, K. Kumar, and L.K. Michaelsen, Cultural diversity's impact on interaction process and performance: Comparing homogeneous and diverse task groups, *Academy of Management Journal* 36 (1993): 590–602.

60*International Consulting News,* April 1987, Cited in Harris and Moran, *Managing Cultural Differences.*

61R. Neale and R. Mindel, Rigging up multicultural teamworking, *Personnel Management* 24(10) (January 1992): 36–39.

62R.T. Moran, P.R. Harris, and W.G. Stripp, *Developing the Global Organization* (Houston: Gulf, 1993).

63Dumaine, The trouble with teams.

CHAPTER 6

1C.A. O'Reilly III, Variations in decision makers' use of information sources: The impact of quality and accessibility of information, *Academy of Management Journal* 25 (1982): 756–771; M. Bazerman, *Judgment in Managerial Decision-Making,* 3rd ed. (New York: Wiley, 1994).

2J.S. McClenahen, People (still) the competitive advantage, *Industry Week* (May 6, 1991): 55–57.

3L.K. Trevino, Ethical decision making in organizations: A person–situation interactionist model, *Academy of Management Review* 11 (1986): 601–617.

4M.A. Verespej, Lee Iacocca's *Legacy, Industry Week* (February 15, 1993): 22.

5G.M. McDonald and R.A. Zepp, What should be done? A practical approach to business ethics, *Management Decisions* 28(1) (1990): 9–14.

6J.R. Rest, *Moral Development: Advances in Research and Theory* (New York: Praeger, 1986); T.M. Jones, Ethical decision making by individuals in organizations: An issue-contingent model, *Academy of Management Review* 16(2) (1991): 366–395.

7M.R. Hyman, R. Skipper, and R. Tansey, Ethical codes are not enough, *Business Horizons* (March–April, 1990): 17.

8J.G. March, *A Primer on Decision Making: How Decisions Happen.* (New York: Free Press, 1994).

9See J. Bulhart, *Effective Group Discussion* (Dubuque, Iowa: William C. Brown, 1986); J.T. Wood, G.M. Phillips, and D.J. Pedersen, *Group Discussion: A Practical Guide to Participation and Leadership* (New York: Harper & Row, 1986) for examples.

10J.S. Carroll and E.J. Johnson, *Decision Research: A Field Guide* (Newbury Park, Calif.: Sage, 1990).

11P.C. Nutt, Types of organizational decision process, *Administrative Science Quarterly* 29 (1984): 414–450.

12G.R. Ungson and D.N. Braunstein, eds., *Decision Making: An Interdisciplinary Inquiry* (Boston: Kent, 1982).

13D. Dodd-McCue, J.K. Matejka, and D.N. Ashworth, Deep waders in muddy waters: Rescuing organizational decision makers, *Business Horizons* (September–October, 1987): 54–57.

14J.S. Gold, Against All Odds, *Financial World* (June 23, 1992): 28–29.

15The last five reasons are drawn from R.C. Snyder, A decision-making approach to the study of political phenomena. In *Approaches to the Study of Politics,* ed. R. Young, (Evanston: Northwestern University, 1985).

16H.A. Simon, *The New Science of Management Decision* (New York: Harper, 1960).

17March, *A Primer on Decision Making.*

18R. Norton, A new tool to help managers, *Fortune* (May 30, 1994): 135–140.

19O. Behling and N.L. Eckel, Making sense out of intuition, *Academy of Management Executive* 5(1) (1991): 46–54.

20T.R. Mitchell and L.R. Beach, ". . . Do I love thee? Let me count. . . " Toward an understanding of intuitive and automatic decision making, *Organizational Behavior and Human Decision Processes* 47 (1990): 1–20.

[21]Behling and Eckel, Making sense.

[22]P.A. Anderson, Decision making by objection and the Cuban Missile Crisis, *Administrative Science Quarterly* 28 (1983): 201–222.

[23]J.G. March and J.P. Olsen, Garbage can models of decision making in organizations. In *Ambiguity and Command,* ed. J.G. March and R. Weissinger-Balon, (Marshfield, Mass.: Pitman, 1986), pp. 11–53; M.D. Cohen, J.G. March, and J.P. Olsen, A garbage can model of organizational choice, *Administrative Science Quarterly* 17 (1972): 1–25.

[24]M. Masuch and P. LaPotin, Beyond garbage cans: An AI model of organizational choice, *Administrative Science Quarterly* 34 (1989): 38–67.

[25]Masuch and LaPotin, Beyond garbage cans.

[26]J. Braham, Creativity: Eureka! *Machine Design* 64 (February 6, 1992): 32–36.

[27]E. DeBono, *Lateral Thinking: Creativity Step by Step* (New York: Perennial Library, 1990).

[28]J.L. Adams, *Conceptual Blockbusting: A Guide to Better Ideas,* 2nd ed. (New York: W.W. Norton, 1979).

[29]J.L. Adams, *The Care and Feeding of Ideas: A Guide to Encouraging Creativity* (Reading, Mass.: Addison-Wesley, 1986).

[30]J.P. Wanous and M.A. Youtz, Solution diversity and the quality of group decisions, *Academy of Management Journal* 29 (1986): 149–159.

[31]N.J. Adler, *International Dimensions of Organizational Behavior,* 1st ed. (Boston: Kent, 1986), p. 113.

[32]K. Dion, R. Baron, and N. Miller, Why do groups make riskier decisions than individuals? In *Advances in Experimental Social Psychology,* vol. 5, ed. L. Berkowitz (New York: Academic, 1970) presents some of the earliest work in this area; see Bazerman, *Judgement in Managerial Decision-Making,* for recent discussion of this phenomenon.

[33]H. Lamm and D.G. Myers, Group-induced polarization of attitudes and behaviors. In *Advances in Experimental Social Psychology,* vol, 11, ed. L. Berkowitz (New York: Academic, 1978).

[34]P.W. Yetton and P.C. Bottinger, Individual versus group problem solving: An empirical test of a best-member strategy, *Organizational Behavior and Human Performance* 29 (1982): 307–321.

[35]H.J. Einhorn, R.M. Hogarth, and E. Klempner, Quality of group judgment, *Psychological Bulletin* 84 (1977): 158–172.

[36]L.K. Michaelsen, W.E. Watson, and R.H. Black, A realistic test of individual versus group consensus decision making, *Journal of Applied Psychology* 74(5) (1989): 834–839.

[37]L.N. Jewell and H.J. Reitz, *Group Effectiveness in Organizations* (Glenview, Ill.: Scott, Foresman, 1981).

[38]See, for example, R.T. Pascale, Communication and decision making across cultures: Japanese and American comparisons, *Administrative Science Quarterly* 23 (1978): 91–110.

[39]A.J. Rose, R.O. Mason, and K.E. Dicken, *Strategic Management: A Methodological Approach* (Reading, Mass.: Addison-Wesley, 1987).

[40]J.D. Mullen and B.M. Roth, *Decision-Making: Its Logic and Practice* (Savage, Md.: Rowman and Littlefield, 1991).

[41]Bazerman, *Judgement in Managerial Decision-Making.*

[42]Bazerman, *Judgement in Managerial Decision-Making.*

[43]P. Slovic, B. Fischhoff, and S. Lichtenstein, Behavioral decision theory, *Annual Review of Psychology* 28 (1977): 1–39.

[44]Bazerman, *Judgement in Managerial Decision-Making;* March, *A Primer on Decision Making.*

[45]D. Kahnemann and A. Tversky, Rational choice and the forming of decisions, *Journal of Business* 59(4) (1986): 5251–5278; A. Tversky and D. Kahnemann, The framing of decisions and the psychology of choice, *Science* 211 (1981): 453–458.

[46]G. Whyte, Decision failures: Why they occur and how to prevent them, *Academy of Management Executive* 5(3) (1991): 23–31.

[47]G. Whyte, Escalating commitment in individual and group decision making: A prospect theory approach, *Organizational Behavior and Human Decision Processes* 54(3) (1993): 430–450.

[48]I. Janis, Groupthink, *Psychology Today,* June 1971.

[49]T.E. Bell and K. Esch, Anatomy of a Tragedy, *IEEE Spectrum* 24(2) (February 1987): 44–51.

[50]I.L. Janis and L. Mann, *Decision Making* (New York: Free Press, 1977).

[51]G. Whyte, Groupthink reconsidered, *Academy of Management Review* 14 (1989): 40–56; Lamm and Myers, Group induced polarization.

[52]V. Johnson, The groupthink trap, *Successful Meetings* 41(10) (1992): 145–146.

[53]E.F. Harrison, *The Managerial Decision Making Process,* 3rd ed. (Boston: Houghton Mifflin, 1987).

[54]N.J. Adler, *International Dimensions of Organizational Behavior,* 2nd ed. (Boston: PWS-Kent, 1991).

[55]Adler, *International Dimensions.*

[56]Adler, *International Dimensions.*

[57]P.R. Harris and G.T. Moran, *Managing Cultural Differences,* 3rd ed. (Houston: Gulf, 1991).

[58]Adams, *The Care and Feeding of Ideas.*

[59]J.B. Thomas, R.R. McDaniel, Jr., and M.J. Dooris, Strategic issue analysis: NGT + decision analysis for resolving strategic issues, *Journal of Applied Behavioral Sciences* 25(2) (1989): 189–200; G.P. Huber, *Managerial Decision Making* (Glenview, Ill.: Scott, Foresman, 1980).

[60]W.M. Fox, The improved nominal group technique (INGT), *Journal of Management Development* 8(1) (1989): 20–27.

[61]A. Van de Ven and A.L. Delbecq, Nominal versus interacting group process for committee decision-making effectiveness, *Academy of Management Journal* 14 (1971): 203–212.

[62]J.G. Mahler, Structured decision making in public organizations, *Public Administration Review* (July/August 1987): 336–342.

[63]H.A. Linstone and M. Turoff, ed. *The Delphi Method: Techniques and Applications* (Reading, Mass.: Addison-Wesley, 1975).

[64]A.L. Delbecq, A. Van de Ven, and D.H. Gustafson, *Group Techniques for Program Planning* (Middleton, Wis.: Greenbrief, 1986).

[65]K.L. Kraemer and A. Pinsonneault, Technology and groups: Assessment of the empirical research. In *Intellectual Teamwork,* ed. J. Galegher, R.E. Kraut, and C. Egido, (Hillsdale, N.J.: Erlbaum, 1990), pp. 375–405.

[66]Linstone and Turoff, ed., *The Delphi Method.*

[67]S. Hart, M. Boroush, G. Enk, and W. Hornick, Managing complexity through consensus mapping: Technology for the structuring of group decisions, *Academy of Management Review* 10 (1985): 587–600.

[68]C.A. Ellis, S.J. Gibb, and G.L. Rein, Groupware: Some issues and experiences, *Communications of the ACM* 34(1) (January 1991): 38–58.

[69]C. Ching, C.W. Holsapple, and A.B. Whinston, Reputation, learning, and coordination in distributed decision-making contexts, *Organization Science* 3(2) (1992): 275–297.

CHAPTER 7

[1]T.A. Stewart, GE keeps those ideas coming, *Fortune* (August 12, 1991): 41–49.

[2]Stewart, GE keeps those ideas coming.

[3]Stewart, GE keeps those ideas coming; J.P. Cosco, General Electric works it all out, *Journal of Business Strategy* 15(3) (May–June 1994): 48–50; J.D. O'Brian, GE's 'work-outs' change role of management, *Supervisory Management* 39(1) (January 1994): 6; D.K. Denton, Open communication, *Business Horizons* 36(5) (September–October, 1993): 64–69.

[4]B.S. Moskal, Glass ceiling, beware, *Industry Week* (April 18, 1994): 13–15.

[5]J.H. Sheridan, Varian, *Industry Week* (October 17, 1994): 47–49.

[6]R.L. Daft and R.H. Lengel, Organizational information requirements, media richness and structural design, *Management Science* 32 (1986): 554–571.

[7]R.H. Lengel and R.L. Daft, The selection of communication media as an executive skill, *Academy of Management Executive* 2 (1988): 225–232.

[8]Lengel and Daft, The selection of communication media.

[9]R.D. Hof, The education of Andrew Grove, *Business Week* (January 16, 1995): 60–62.

[10]E.W. Morrison and R.J. Bies, Impression management in the feedback-seeking process: A literature review and research agenda, *Academy of Management Review* 16(3) (1991): 522–541.

[11]W.H. Miller and J. Bryson: Fresh breath in a once-stale industry, *Industry Week* (November 15, 1993): 35–38.

[12]W.V. Haney, *Communication and Organizational Behavior* (Homewood, Ill.: Irwin, 1979) discusses this and other language distortions.

[13]J. Sullivan, N. Kameda, and T. Nobu, Bypassing in managerial communication, *Business Horizons* 34(1) (1991): 71–80.

[14]See, for example, D. Tannen, *You Just Don't Understand: Women and Men in Conversation* (New York: William Morrow, 1990); D. Tannen, *Talking from 9 to 5: How Women's and Men's Conversational Styles Affect Who Gets Heard, Who Gets Credit, and What Gets Done at Work* (New York: William Morrow, 1994).

[15]Tannen, *You Just Don't Understand.*

[16]Tannen, *Talking from 9 to 5.*

[17]S.S. Case, Cultural differences, not deficiencies: An analysis of managerial women's language. In *Women's Careers: Pathways and Pitfalls,* ed. S. Rose and L. Larwood (New York: Praeger, 1988).

[18]See M.L. Knapp, *Nonverbal Communication in Human Interaction* (New York: Holt, Rinehart and Winston, 1972); P. Ekman, Communication through nonverbal behavior, in *Affect, Cognition, and Personality,* ed. S.S. Tomkins and C. E. Izard (New York: Springer, 1965).

[19]C.L. McKenzie and C.J. Qazi, Communication barriers in the workplace, *Business Horizons* 26 (March–April 1983): 70–72.

[20]P.R. Harris and R.T. Moran, *Managing Cultural Differences,* 3rd ed. (Houston: Gulf, 1991).

[21]F. Elashmawi and P.R. Harris, *Multicultural Management: New Skills for Global Success* (Houston: Gulf, 1993).

[22]F. Elashmawi and P.R. Harris, *Multicultural Management.*

[23]J.H. Dobrzynski, 'I'm going to let the problems come to me,' *Business Week* (April 12, 1994): 32–33.

[24]J.W. Gibson and R.M. Hodgetts, *Organizational Communication: A Managerial Perspective,* 2nd ed. (New York: HarperCollins, 1991).

[25]C.B. Rogers and R.E. Farson, Active listening. In *Organizational Psychology: Readings on Human Behavior in Organizations,* ed. D. Kolb, I. Rubin, and J. McIntire (Englewood Cliffs, N.J.: Prentice-Hall, 1984): pp. 255–267.

[26]Gibson and Hodgetts, *Organizational Communication.*

[27]R. Tetzeli, Surviving information overload, *Fortune* (July 11, 1994): 60–66.

[28]Tetzeli, Surviving.

[29]The discussion of load is primarily based on Gibson and Hodgetts, *Organizational Communication.*

[30]P.G. Clampitt, *Communicating for Managerial Effectiveness* (Newbury Park, Calif.: Sage, 1991).

[31]G.A. Weimer, A manager for all seasons, *Industry Week* (June 1, 1992): 30–33.

[32]Weimer, A manager for all seasons, p. 33.

[33]P.V. Lewis, *Organizational Communication: The Essence of Effective Management,* 3rd ed. (New York: Wiley, 1987).

[34]J. Brockner, Managing the effects of layoffs on survivors, *California Management Review* (Winter 1992): 9–27.

[35]M.E. Schnake, M.P. Dumler, D.S. Cochran, and T.R. Barnett, Effects of differences in superior and subordinate perceptions of superiors' communication practices, *Journal of Business Communication* 27(1) (1990): 37–50.

[36]E.M. Eisenberg and M.G. Witten, Reconsidering openness in organizational communication, *Academy of Management Review* 12 (1987): 418–426.

[37]D. Fisher, *Communication in Organizations,* 2nd ed. (St. Paul, Minn.: West, 1993).

[38]A. Deutschman, The CEO's secret of managing time, *Fortune* (June 1, 1992): 135–146.

[39]Lewis, *Organizational Communication.*

[40]C.H. Deutsch, Call it 'C.E.O. disease,' then listen, *The New York Times* (December 15, 1991).

[41]R.A. Friedman and J. Podolny, Differentiation of boundary spanning roles: Labor negotiations and implications for role conflict, *Administrative Science Quarterly* 37 (1992): 28–47; and S. MacDonald and C. Williams, the survival of the gatekeeper, *Research Policy* 23(2) (March 1994): 123–132, offer examples of this role.

[42]E. Rogers and R. Agarwala-Rogers, *Communication in Organizations* (New York: Free Press, 1976).

[43]P.R. Monge, J.M. Brismier, A.L. Cook, P.D. Day, J.A. Edwards, and K.K. Kriste, Determinants of communication structure in large organizations. Paper presented at the meeting of the International Communication Association, Portland, Oreg., May, 1976. Cited in G.L. Kreps, *Organizational Communication,* 2nd ed. (New York: Longman, 1990).

[44]P.R. Monge and E.M. Eisenberg, Emergent communication networks. In *Handbook of Organizational Communication: An Interdisciplinary Perspective,* ed. F. Jablin, L. Putnam, K. Roberts, and L. Porter (Newbury Park, Calif.: Sage, 1991.)

[45]Lewis, *Organizational Communication.*

[46]This discussion is drawn largely from C.A. O'Reilly III and L.R. Pondy, Organizational communication. In *Organizational Behavior,* ed. S. Kerr (Columbus, Ohio: Grid, 1979).

[47]D.W. Johnson and F.P. Johnson, *Joining Together: Group Theory and Group Skills* (Englewood Cliffs, N.J.: Prentice-Hall, 1975).

[48]B. Saporito, David Glass won't crack under fire, *Fortune* (February 8, 1993): 75–80.

[49]E.H. Schein, Improving fact-to-face relationships, *Sloan Management Review* (Winter 1981): 43–52.

[50]J.H. Simon, U.S.–Japanese management enters a new generation, *Management Review* (February 1991): 42–45.

[51]N. Sussman and H. Rosenfeld, Influence of culture, language, and sex on conversational distance, *Journal of Personality and Social Psychology* 42 (1982): 66–74.

[52]W.W. Hildebrandt, A Chinese managerial view of business communication, *Management Communication Quarterly* 2 (November 1988): 217–234.

[53]Simon, U.S.–Japanese management.

[54]W.B. Gudykunst and S. Ting-Toomey, *Culture and Interpersonal Communication* (Newbury Park, Calif.: Sage, 1988).

[55]This discussion is based on M. Culnan and M.L. Markus, Information technologies. In *Handbook of Organizational Communication,* ed. Jablin et al.

[56]F. Rice, Champions of communication, *Fortune* (June 3, 1991): 111–120.

[57]Japan logs on to the internet, *Fortune* (September 5, 1994): 14–15.

[58]R.C. Huseman and E.W. Miles, Organizational communication in the information age, *Journal of Management* 14(2) (1988): 181–204.

[59]Kreps, *Organizational Communication.*

[60]W.T. Weaver, When discounting gets in the way, *Training & Development* (July 1993): 55–61.

[61]J.R. Gibb, Defensive communication, *ETC: A Review of General Semantics* 22 (1965).

[62]W.G. Dyer, *The Sensitive Manipulator* (Provo, Utah: Brigham Young University Press, 1980).

[63]D.A Whetton and K.W. Cameron, *Developing Management Skills* (Glenview, Ill.: Scott, Foresman, 1984), p. 209.

[64]J. Hall, Communication revised, *California Management Review* 15 (1973); J. Luft, *Group Processes: An Introduction to Group Dynamics* (Palo Alto, Calif.: Mayfield Publishing, 1970).

[65]L. Sussman, Managers: On the defensive, *Business Horizons* 34(1) (1991): 81–87.

[66]R.E. Alberti and M.L. Emmons, *Your Perfect Right* (San Luis Obispo, Calif.: Impact, 1982).

[67]N.J. Adler, *International Dimensions of Organizational Behavior,* 2nd. ed. (Boston: PWS-Kent, 1991).

[68]R.C. Maddox and D. Short, The cultural integrator, *Business Horizons* 31 (November–December 1988): 57–59.

69C.R. Day, Jr., One-on-one: Kerm Campbell, *Industry Week* (November 7, 1994): 36–40.

70B. O'Reilly, 360 feedback can change your life, *Fortune* (October 17, 1994): 93–100.

71O'Reilly, 360 feedback.

72W.W. Tornow, Editor's note: Introduction to special issue on 360-degree feedback, *Human Resource Management* (Summer/Fall, 1993) 32 (2&3): 211–219.

73A.S. Tsui and B. Barry, Interpersonal affect and rating errors, *Academy of Management Journal* 29 (1986): 586–599.

74See, for example, R. Jacobs and S.W.J. Kozlowski, A closer look at halo error in performance ratings, *Academy of Management Journal* 28 (1985): 201–212.

75C.M. Vance, S.R. McClaine, D.M. Boje, and H.D. Stage, An examination of the transferability of traditional performance appraisal principles across cultural boundaries, *Management International Review* 32 (1992): 313–326.

CHAPTER 8

1S. Caminiti, America's most successful businesswoman, *Fortune* (June 15, 1992): 103.

2Caminiti, America's most successful, 102.

3Caminiti, America's most successful, 102–106; Leaders of corporate change, *Fortune* (December 14, 1992): 104–113; Warnaco CEO eyes the landscape, *Fortune* (October 21, 1991): 193; L. Zinn, She had to be an owner, *Business Week* (June 8, 1992): 81; S. Strom, Fashion avenue's $100 million woman, *New York Times* (May 17, 1992): Section 3, 1, 6.

4B.M. Bass, *Handbook of Leadership: A Survey of Theory and Research* (New York: Praeger, 1981); S.A. Kirkpatrick and E.A. Locke, Leadership: Do traits matter? *Academy of Management Executive* 5(2) (1991): 48–60.

5R.M. Stogdill, Personal factors associated with leadership: A survey of the literature, *Journal of Psychology* 25 (1948): 35–71.

6Kirkpatrick and Locke, Leadership: Do traits matter? 49.

7G.A. Yukl, *Leadership in Organizations,* 2nd ed. (Englewood Cliffs, N.J.: Prentice-Hall, 1989).

8J.P. Kotter, *The Leadership Factor* (New York: Free Press, 1988), p. 30.

9M.W. McCall, Jr., and M.M. Lombardo, *Off the Track: Why and How Successful Executives Get Derailed* (Greensboro, N.C.: Center for Creative Leadership, 1983).

10B.M. Bass, *Bass & Stogdill's Handbook of Leadership: Theory, Research, and Managerial Applications,* 3rd ed. (New York: Free Press, 1991).

11B.M. Bass, P.C. Burger, R. Doktor, and G.V. Barrett, *Assessment of Managers: An International Comparison* (New York: Free Press, 1979).

12R.M. Stogdill and A.E. Coons, ed., *Leader Behavior: Its Description and Measurement* (Columbus: Ohio State University Bureau of Business Research, 1957).

13E. Fleishman, E.F. Harris, and R.D. Burtt, *Leadership and Supervision in Industry* (Columbus: Ohio State University Press, 1955); E. Fleishman and E.F. Harris, Patterns of leadership behavior related to employee grievances and turnover, *Personnel Psychology* 1 (1959): 45–53.

14R.L. Kahn and D. Katz, Leadership practices in relation to productivity and morale. In *Group Dynamics,* ed. D. Cartwright and A. Zander (Evanston, Ill.: Row, Peterson, 1953), pp. 585–611.

15R. Likert, *New Patterns of Management* (New York: McGraw-Hill, 1961).

16B.S. Moskal, Born to be real, *Industry Week* (August 2, 1993): 14–18.

17C.A. Schreisheim and S. Kerr, Theories and measures of leadership: A critical appraisal. In *Leadership: The Cutting Edge,* ed. J.G. Hunt and L.L. Larson (Carbondale, Ill.: Southern Illinois University, 1977); F. Luthans and D.L. Lockwood, Toward and observation system for measuring leader behavior in natural settings. In *Leaders and Managers: International Perspectives on Managerial Behavior and Leadership,* ed. J.G. Hunt, D. Hosking, C.A. Schriesheim, and R. Stewart (New York: Pergamon, 1984).

18J. Misumi and M.F. Peterson, The performance-maintenance (PM) theory of leadership: Review of a Japanese research program, *Administrative Science Quarterly* 30 (1985): 198–223; B.M. Bass, *Bass & Stogdill's Handbook;* J. Misumi, Research on leadership and group decisions in Japanese organizations, *Applied Psychology: An International Review* 38(4) (1989): 321–336.

[19]H. Mintzberg, *The Nature of Managerial Work,* 2nd ed. (Englewood Cliffs, N.J.: Prentice-Hall, 1979).

[20]A.I. Kraut, P.R. Pedigo, D.D. McKenna, and M.D. Dunnette, The role of the manager: What's really important in different management jobs, *Academy of Management Executive* 3(4) (1989): 286–293.

[21]D. McGregor, *The Human Side of Enterprise* (New York: McGraw-Hill, 1961; E.H. Schein, The Hawthorne studies revisited: A defense of Theory Y (Cambridge, Mass.: MIT Sloan School of Management Working Paper #756-74, 1974).

[22]R. Suskind and S. Alexander, Out of control: Fired Sunbeam chief harangued and hazed employees, they say, *The Wall Street Journal* (January 14, 1993): A-1, A-6; G. Smith, How to lose friends and influence no one, *Business Week* (January 25, 1993): 42–43.

[23]J.H. Sheridan and Jack Croushore, From tough guy to 'cream puff,' *Industry Week* (December 6, 1993): 11–16.

[24]F.E. Fiedler, Engineer the job to fit the manager, *Harvard Business Review* 43 (1965): 115–122; and F.E. Fiedler and M.M. Chemers, *Leadership and Effective Management* (Glenview, Ill.: Scott, Foresman, 1974) offered the earliest descriptions of this theory; F.E. Fiedler and J.E. Garcia, *New Approaches to Effective Leadership* (New York: Wiley, 1987) offers one of the most recent revisions.

[25]F.E. Fiedler, The contribution of cognitive resources to leadership performance, *Journal of Applied Social Psychology* 16 (1986): 532–548; F.E. Fiedler and J.E. Garcia, *New Approaches to Leadership: Cognitive Resources and Organizational Performance* (New York: Wiley, 1987).

[26]L.H. Peters, D.D. Hartke, and J.T. Pohlman, Fiedler's contingency theory of leadership: An application of the meta-analysis procedures of Schmidt and Hunter, *Psychological Bulletin* 97 (1985): 274–285; J.K. Kennedy, Jr., Middle LPC leaders and the contingency model of leadership effectiveness, *Organizational Behavior and Human Performance* 30 (1982): 1–14; Schreisheim and Kerr, Theories and measurement; S. Kerr and A. Harlan, Predicting the effects of leadership training and experience from the contingency model: Some remaining problems, *Journal of Applied Psychology* 57 (1973): 114–117.

[27]Yukl, *Leadership in Organizations.*

[28]Yukl, *Leadership in Organizations.*

[29]R.J. House, A path-goal theory of leader effectiveness, *Administrative Science Quarterly* 16 (1971): 321–338; R.J. House and T.R. Mitchell, Path-goal theory of leadership, *Journal of Contemporary Business* (Autumn 1974): 81–97; J. Indvik, Path-goal theory of leadership: A meta-analysis, *Proceedings of the Academy of Management* (1986): 189–192; J. Fulk and E.R. Wendler, Dimensionality of leader-subordinate interactions: A path-goal investigation, *Organizational Behavior and Human Performance* 30 (1983): 241–263; G.A. Yukl and J. Clemence, A test of path-goal theory of leadership using questionnaire and diary measures of behavior, *Proceedings of the Twenty-First Annual Meeting of the Eastern Academy of Management* (1984): 174–177.

[30]A. Farnham, And now here's the man himself, *Fortune,* June 15, 1992.

[31]Farnham, And now here's.

[32]B. Dumaine, The new non-manager managers, *Fortune* (February 22, 1993): 80–84.

[33]Yukl, *Leadership in Organizations.*

[34]G.A. Yukl and J. Clemence, A test of path-goal theory of leadership using questionnaire and diary measures of behavior, *Proceedings of the Twenty-First Annual Meeting of the Eastern Academy of Management* (1974): 174–177.

[35]V.H. Vroom and P.W. Yetton, *Leadership and Decision Making* (Pittsburgh: University of Pittsburgh Press, 1973) presents the original version of the theory; V.H. Vroom and A.G. Jago, *The New Leadership: Managing Participation in Organizations* (Englewood Cliffs, N.J.: Prentice-Hall, 1988) offers the most recent formulation.

[36]Vroom and Jago, *The New Leadership.*

[37]A. Crouch and P. Yetton, Manager behavior, leadership style, and subordinate performance: An empirical extension of the Vroom–Yetton conflict rule, *Organizational Behavior and Hu-*

man *Performance* 39 (1987): 384–396; J.T. Ettling and A.G. Jago, Participation under conditions of conflict: More on the validity of the Vroom–Yetton model, *Journal of Management Studies* 25(1) (1988): 73–83; D. Tjosvold, W.C. Wedley, and R.H.G. Field, Constructive controversy: The Vroom–Yetton model and managerial decision making, *Journal of Occupational Behavior* 7 (1986): 125–138; illustrate some of the supportive results.

[38]P. Hersey and K.H. Blanchard, *Management of Organizational Behavior,* 5th ed. (Englewood Cliffs, N.J.: Prentice-Hall, 1988).

[39]D.C. Lueder, Don't be misled by LEAD, *Journal of Applied Behavioral Science* 21 (1985): 143–151; P. Hersey, A letter to the author of "Don't be misled by LEAD," *Journal of Applied Behavioral Science* 21 (1985): 152-153; D.C. Lueder, A rejoinder to Hersey, *Journal of Applied Behavioral Science* 21 (1985): 154.

[40]B. Dumaine, Who needs a boss? *Fortune* (May 7, 1990).

[41]The national business Hall of Fame, *Fortune* (April 5, 1993): 108–114.

[42]M.A. Verespej, Pies, biscuits, and people, *Industry Week* (August 3, 1992): 55–59; J.F. McKenna, America's most admired CEOs, *Industry Week* (December 6, 1993); 22–32.

[43]R.P. Vecchio, Situational leadership theory: An examination of a prescriptive theory, *Journal of Applied Psychology* 72 (1987): 444–451; C.L. Graeff, The situational leadership theory: A critical view, *Academy of Management Review* 8 (1983): 285–291; Lueder, Don't be misled by LEAD; Lueder, A rejoinder to Dr. Hersey; Hersey, A letter to the author of "Don't be misled by LEAD";

[44]J. Cashman, F. Dansereau Jr., G. Graen, and W.J. Haga, Organizational understructure and leadership: A longitudinal investigation of the managerial role-making process, *Organizational Behavior and Human Performance* 15 (1976): 278–296; T.B. Scandura and G.B. Graen, Moderating effects of initial leader-member exchange status on the effects of a leadership intervention, *Journal of Applied Psychology* 69 (1984): 428–436.

[45]D. Duchon, S.G. Graen, T.D. Table, Vertical dyad linkage: A longitudinal assessment of antecedents, measures, and consequences, *Journal of Applied Psychology* 71 (1986): 56–60.

[46]R.M. Dienesch and R.C. Liden, Leader–member exchange model of leadership: A critique and future development, *Academy of Management Review* 11 (1986): 618–634; R.P. Vecchio and B.C. Gobdel, The vertical dyad linkage model of leadership: Problems and prospects, *Organizational Behavior and Human Performance* 34 (1984): 5–20.

[47]Yukl, *Leadership in Organizations.*

[48]Yukl, *Leadership in Organizations.*

[49]T.R.V. Davis and F. Luthans, Leadership reexamined: A behavioral approach, *Academy of Management Review* 4 (1979): 237–248.

[50]Bass, *Bass & Stogdill's Handbook.*

[51]J.C. McElroy, A typology of attribution leadership research, *Academy of Management Review* 7 (1982): 413–417.

[52]M. Martinko and W.L. Gardner, The leader/member attribution process, *Academy of Management Review* 12 (1987): 235–240.

[53]B. Calder, An attribution theory of leadership. In *New Directions in Organizational Behavior,* ed. B.H. Staw and G.R. Salancik (Chicago: St. Clair Press, 1977).

[54]J.C. McElroy and C.B. Shrader, Attribution theories of leadership and network analysis, *Journal of Management* 12 (1986): 351–362.

[55]J.P. Howell, D.E. Bowen, P.W. Dorfman, S. Kerr, and P.M. Podsakoff, Substitutes for leadership: Effective alternatives to ineffective leadership, *Organizational Dynamics* (Summer 1990): 21–38.

[56]J.E. Sheridan, D.J. Vredenburgh, and M.A. Abelson, Contextual model of leadership influence in hospital units, *Academy of Management Journal* 27 (1984): 57–78.

[57]J.P. Howell, D.E. Bowen, P.W. Dorfman, S. Kerr, P.M. Podsakoff, Substitutes for leadership: Effective alternatives to ineffective leadership, *Organizational Dynamics* (Summer 1990): 21–38.

[58]Dumaine, Who needs a boss?

[59]B.M. Bass, *Leadership and Performance Beyond Expectations* (New York: Free Press, 1985).

[60]R.J. House, A 1976 theory of charismatic leadership. In *Leadership: The Cutting Edge,* ed. J.G. Hunt and Larson (Carbondale, Ill.: Southern Illinois University Press, 1977); J. Conger, *The Charismatic Leader* (San Francisco: Jossey-Bass, 1989); J. Conger and R.N. Kanungo, Toward a behavioral theory of charismatic leadership in organizational settings, *Academy of Management Review* 12 (1987): 637–647.

[61]R.J. House, A 1976 theory of charismatic leadership. In Hunt and Larson, *Leadership.*

[62]D. Machan, The charisma merchants, *Forbes* (January 23, 1989): 100–101.

[63]G. Gendron and B. Bulingham, The entrepreneur of the decade: An interview with Steve Jobs, *Inc.* 14(4) (April 1989): 114–128; G. Rifkin, J. Connolly, N. Margolis, P. Keefe, and J. Daly, Twenty-five people who changed the world, *Computerworld* 26(25) (June 22, 1992): 52–59; J.S. Young, *Steve Jobs: The Journey Is the Reward* (Glenview, Ill.: Scott, Foresman, 1988).

[64]T. Englander, Ford: Quality driven, *Incentive* 163 (1) (January 1989): 23–24.

[65]B.M. Bass, Leadership, good, better, best, *Organizational Dynamics* 12 (Winter 1985): 26–40.

[66]J.J. Hater and B.M. Bass, Superiors' evaluations and subordinates' perceptions of transformational and transactional leadership, *Journal of Applied Psychology* 73 (1988): 695–702.

[67]I.C. MacMillan, New business development: A challenge to transformational leadership, *Human Resource Management* 26 (1987): 439–454.

[68]B.M. Bass, D.A. Waldman, B.J. Avolio, and M. Bebb, Transformational leadership and the falling dominoes effect, *Group and Organization Studies* 12 (March 1987): 73–87.

[69]J.B. Rosener, Ways women lead, *Harvard Business Review* 68 (November–December, 1990): 119–125.

[70]J. Fierman, Do women manage differently? *Fortune* (December 17, 1990): 115–118.

[71]See, for example, J. Adams and J.D. Hoder, *Effective Leadership for Women and Men* (Norwood, N.J.: Ablex, 1985); C.M. Seifert, Reactions to leaders: Effects of sex of leader, sex of subordinate, method of leader selection, and task outcome. *Dissertation Abstracts International* 45 (12B) (1986): 3999.

[72]S. Faison, Trying to play by the rules, *New York Times,* (December 22, 1991): 51.

[73]J. Fierman, Do women manage differently? *Fortune* (December, 17, 1990): 115–118.

[74]Conger, *The Charismatic Leader;* J.A. Conger, The dark side of leadership, *Organizational Dynamics* (Autumn 1990): 44–55.

[75]Conger, 1990, The darker side.

[76]H. Rosenberg, Wall Street: Life among the ruins, *Institutional Investor* 24(7) (June 1990): 92–102; C.J. Loomis, The biggest looniest deal ever, *Fortune* 121(14) (June 18, 1990): 48–72.

[77]Bass, *Leadership and Performance Beyond Expectations;* B.M. Bass, D.A. Waldman, B.J. Avolio, and M. Bebb, Transformational leadership and the falling dominoes effect, *Group and Organization Studies* 12 (1987): 73–87; N.M. Tichy and M.A. Devanna, *The Transformational Leader,* 2nd ed. (New York: Wiley, 1990); W.G. Bennis and B. Nanus, *Leaders: The Strategies for Taking Charge* (New York: Harper & Row, 1985).

[78]J.P. Howell and P.W. Dorfman, A comparative study of leadership and its substitutes in a mixed cultural work setting, Unpublished manuscript. Cited in B.M. Bass, From transactional to transformational leadership: learning to share the vision, *Organizational Dynamics* (Winter 1990): 19–31.

[79]C.C. Manz and H.P. Sims Jr., Superleadership: Beyond the myth of heroic leadership, *Organizational Dynamics* (Spring 1991): 18–35; C.C. Manz and H.P. Sims, Jr., *Superleadership: Leading Others to Lead Themselves* (Englewood Cliffs, N.J.: Prentice-Hall, 1989).

[80]C.C. Manz and H.P. Sims, Jr., *Superleadership;* C.C. Manz and H.P. Sims, Jr., Superleadership: Beyond the myth of heroic leadership, *Organizational Dynamics* (Spring 1991): 18–35.

[81]Manz and Sims, Superleadership: Beyond the myth.

[82]P.R. Harris and R.T. Moran, *Managing Cultural Differences,* 3rd ed. (Houston: Gulf, 1991).

[83]J.A. Byrne, A 'global citizen' for a global McKinsey, *Business Week* (April 11, 1994): 36.

[84]G. Hofstede, Motivation, leadership, and organization: Do American theories apply abroad? *Organizational Dynamics* (Summer 1980): 42–63.

[85]M.A. Verespej, Gutsy decisions of 1990, *Industry Week* (February 18, 1991): 23–34.

[86]Hofstede, Motivation.

[87]Bass, *Bass & Stogdill's Handbook.*

CHAPTER 9

[1]This case was adapted from one written by Nitin Y. Karkhanis for an Organizational Behavior class at Rivier College, April 1992 and is reproduced with permission.

[2]H. Mintzberg, *Power In and Around Organizations* (Englewood Cliffs, N.J.: Prentice-Hall, 1983).

[3]Mintzberg, *Power.*

[4]Z. Schiller, Blowup at Bridgestone, *Business Week* (January 30, 1995): 30–32.

[5]J. Gabarro and J. Kotter, Managing your boss, *Harvard Business Review* 58 (1980): 92–100.

[6]W.F.G. Mastenbroek, *Conflict Management and Organization Development* (Chichester, England: Wiley, 1987).

[7]A. Kaplan, Power in perspective. In *Power and Conflict in Organizations,* ed. R.L. Kahn and E. Boulding (London: Tavistock, 1964); M. Weber, *The Theory of Social and Economic Organization* (Glencoe, Ill.: Free Press, 1947).

[8]This discussion of dependence is based in large part on J.P. Kotter, Power, dependence, and effective management, *Harvard Business Review* 55 (1977): 125–136; and J.P. Kotter, Power, success, and organizational effectiveness, *Organizational Dynamics* 6 (1978): 27–40.

[9]J.P. Kotter, Power, success, and organizational effectiveness, 27–40.

[10]P.M. Blau, *Exchange and Power in Social Life* (New York: Wiley, 1964); R.M. Emerson, Power-dependence relations, *American Sociological Review* 27 (1962): 31–41.

[11]B. Markovsky, D. Weller, and T. Patton, Power relations in exchange networks, *American Sociological Review* 53 (1988): 220–236.

[12]R.M. Kanter, The new managerial work, *Harvard Business Review* (November–December 1989): 85–92.

[13]Kanter, The new managerial work.

[14]D. McClelland and D.H. Burnham, Power driven managers: Good guys make bum bosses, *Psychology Today* (December 1975): 69–71; D. McClelland, *Power: The Inner Experience* (New York: Irvington, 1975).

[15]W.C. Grams and R.W. Rogers, Power and personality: Effects of Machiavellianism, need for approval, and motivation on use of tactics, *Journal of General Psychology* (1990): 71–82.

[16]See, for example, R.M. Kanter, *The Change Masters* (New York: Simon & Schuster, 1983); and W.W. Burke, Leadership as empowering others. In S. Srivastva and Associates, Executive Power (San Francisco: Jossey-Bass, 1986); J.A. Conger and R.N. Kanungo, The empowerment process: Integrating theory and practice, *Academy of Management Review* 13 (1988): 471–482.

[17]M. Boyd, John Deere, *Incentive* 168 (May 1994): 52–53; K. Kelly, The new soul of John Deere, *Business Week* (January 31, 1994): 64–66.

[18]Conger and Kanungo, The empowerment process.

[19]R.E. Spekman, Influence and information: An exploratory investigation of the boundary person's bases of power, *Academy of Management Journal* 22 (1979): 104–117.

[20]L.A. Mainiero, Coping with powerlessness: The relationship of gender and job dependency to empowerment-strategy usage, *Administrative Science Quarterly* 31 (1986): 633–653.

[21]J.A. Conger, Leadership: The art of empowering others, *Academy of Management Executive* 3(1) (1989): 17–24.

[22]J.F. McKenna, Coach lets his team play the game, *Industry Week* (May 4, 1992): 12, 16.

[23]J.R. Brandt, Middle management: Where the action will be, *Industry Week* (May 2, 1994): 30–36.

[24]M.A. Verespej, Worker-managers, *Industry Week* (May 16, 1994): 30.

[25]Brandt, Middle management.

[26]G. Hofstede, Motivation, leadership, and organization: Do American theories apply abroad? *Organizational Dynamics* (Summer 1980): 42–63; G. Hofstede, *Culture's Consequences: International Differences in Work-Related Values* (Beverly Hills, Calif.: Sage, 1980).

[27]J. Oakes, MBA McGill University, 1984. In N.J. Adler, *International Dimensions of Organizational Behavior,* 2nd ed. (Boston: PWS-Kent, 1991), p. 51.

[28]D.E. Frost, A test of situational engineering for training leaders, *Psychological Reports* 59 (1986): 771–782.

[29]T. Cox, Jr., *Cultural Diversity in Organizations: Theory, Research & Practice* (San Francisco: Berrett-Koehler, 1993).

[30]A. Ramirez, Racism toward Hispanics: The culturally monolithic society. In *Eliminating Racism,* ed. P.A. Katz & D.A. Taylor (New York: Plenum, 1988), pp. 137–153.

[31]J. Pfeffer, Understanding power in organizations, *California Management Review* 34(2) (1992): 29–50.

[32]M.A. Rahim, Relationship of leader power to compliance and satisfaction with supervision: Evidence from a national sample of managers, *Journal of Management* 15(4) (1989): 545–556.

[33]See W.G. Astley and P.S. Sachdeva, Structural sources of intraorganizational power: A theoretical synthesis, *Academy of Management Review* 9 (1984): 104–113; I. Cohen and R. Lachman, The generosity of the strategic contingencies approach to sub-unit power within top management teams, *Organization Studies* 9(3) (1988): 371–391 provide recent empirical support for the strategic contingencies theory of organizational behavior originally described in D.J. Hickson, C.R. Hinings, C.A. Lee, R.E. Schneck, and J.M. Pennings, A strategic contingencies' theory of intraorganizational power, *Administrative Science Quarterly* 16 (1971): 216–227.

[34]D.J. Brass and M.E. Burkhardt, Potential power and power use: An investigation of structure and behavior, *Academy of Management Journal* 36 (1993): 441–470.

[35]Cities: Old orders changing, *Economist* (October 30, 1993): 26–27.

[36]S.J. Pfeffer and G.R. Salancik, *The External Control of Organizations* (New York: Harper & Row, 1978).

[37]J.D. Hackman, Power and centrality in the allocation of resources in colleges and universities, *Administrative Science Quarterly* 20 (1985): 61–77.

[38]D. Farrell and J.C. Petersen, Patterns of political behavior in organizations, *Academy of Management Review* 7 (1982): 403–412.

[39]D. Krackhardt and J. R. Hanson, Informal networks: The company behind the chart, *Harvard Business Review* 71 (July/August 1993): 104–111.

[40]H. Ibarra, Personal networks for women and minorities in management: A conceptual framework, *Academy of Management Review* 18 (1993): 56–87.

[41]L.R. Gallese, A new focus for women's groups, *The New York Times* (January 12, 1992): 23.

[42]R. E. Kaplan, Trade routes: The manager's network of relationships, *Organizational Dynamics* (Spring 1984).

[43]A.R. Cohen and D.L. Bradford, Influence without authority: The use of alliances, reciprocity, and exchange to accomplish work, *Organizational Dynamics* (1988): 5–16.

[44]Kanter, Power failures in management circuits, *Harvard Business Review* 57 (1979): 65–75.

[45]W.B. Stevenson, J.L. Pearce, and L.W. Porter, The concept of "coalition" in organization theory and research, *Academy of Management Review* 10 (1985): 256–268.

[46]G. Burns, A windy city squabble that's really the pits, *Business Week* (February 13, 1950): 62–63.

[47]D.K. Banner and T.E. Gagné, *Designing Effective Organizations: Traditional & Transformational Views.* (Thousand Oaks, Calif.: Sage, 1995).

[48]G.R. Ferris and T.R. King, Politics in human resources decisions: A walk on the dark side, *Organizational Dynamics* 20(2) (1991): 59–70.

[49]Ferris and King, Politics.

[50]J.J. Voyer, Coercive organizational politics and organizational outcomes: An interpretive study, *Organization Science* 5(1) (1994): 72–85.

[51]A. Drory, Perceived political climate and job attitudes, *Organization Studies* 14(1) (1993): 59–71.

[52]S. Finkelstein, Power in top management teams: Dimensions, measurement, and validation, *Academy of Management Journal* 35 (1992): 505–538.

[53]B. Kabanoff, Potential influence structures as sources of interpersonal conflict in groups and organizations, *Organizational Behavior and Human Decision Processes* 36 (1985): 115.

[54]A.C. Filley, *Interpersonal Conflict Resolution* (Glenview, Ill.: Scott, Foresman, 1975).

[55]D.M. Kolb and L.L. Putnam, The dialectics of disputing. In *Hidden Conflict in Organizations,* ed. D.M. Kolb and J.M. Bartunek (Newbury Park, Calif.: Sage, 1992), p. 18; D.M. Kolb and L.L. Putnam, The multiple faces of conflict in organizations, *Journal of Organizational Behavior* 13 (May 1992): 311–324.

[56]M. Deutsch, Subjective features of conflict resolution: Psychological, social, and cultural influences. In R. Vayrynen, *New Directions in Conflict Theory: Conflict Resolution and Conflict Transformation* (London: Sage, 1991).

[57]R.L. Pinkley and G.B. Northcraft, Conflict frames of reference: Implications for dispute processes and outcomes, *Academy of Management Journal* 37 (1994): 193–205; R.L. Pinkley, Dimensions of conflict frame: Disputant interpretations of conflict, *Journal of Applied Psychology* 75 (1990): 117–126.

[58]This discussion is drawn from Deutsch, Subjective features.

[59]See R.L. Kahn, D.M. Wolfe, R.P. Quinn, and J.D. Snoek, *Organizational Stress: Studies in Role Conflict and Ambiguity* (New York: Wiley, 1964) for the classic discussion, and M. Van Sell, A.P. Brief, and R.S. Schuler, Role conflict and role ambiguity: Integration of the literature and directions for future research, *Human Relations* 34 (1981): 43–71; S.E. Jackson and R.S. Schuler, A meta-analysis and conceptual critique of research on role ambiguity and role conflict in work settings, *Organizational Behavior and Human Decision Processes* 36 (1985): 16–78; K. Klenke-Hamel and J.E. Mathieu, Role strains, tension, and job satisfaction influences on employees' propensity to leave: A multi-sample replication and extension, *Human Relations* 43 (1990): 791–807; E. Kemery, A.G. Bedeian, K.W. Mossholder, and J. Touliatos, Outcomes of role stress: A multisample constructive replication, *Academy of Management Journal* 28 (1985): 363–375; J. Schaubroeck, J.L. Cotten, and K.R. Jennings, Antecedents and consequences of roll stress: A covariance structure analysis, *Journal of Organizational Behavior* 10 (1989): 35–58 for a more recent discussion.

[60]M. Igbaria and T. Guimaraes, Antecedents and consequences of job satisfaction among information center employees, *Journal of Management Information Systems* 9 (Spring 1993): 145–174.

[61]P. Senatra, What are the sources and consequences of stress? Do men and women differ in their perceptions? *The Woman CPA* (July 1988): 13–16.

[62]C.D. Fisher and R. Gitelson, A meta-analysis of the correlates of role conflict and ambiguity, *Journal of Applied Psychology* 68 (1983): 320–333; A.G. Bedeian and A.A. Armenakis, A path-analytic study of the consequences of role conflict and ambiguity, *Academy of Management Journal* 24 (1981): 417–424.

[63]R.A. Baron, Personality and organizational conflict: Effects of the Type A behavior pattern and self-monitoring, *Organizational Behavior and Human Decision Processes* 44 (1989): 281–296.

[64]Cox, *Cultural Diversity.*

[65]J. Pfeffer, Beyond management and the workers: The institutional function of management, *Academy of Management Review* 1 (1976): 26–46; H. Assael, Constructive roles of interorganizational conflict, *Administrative Science Quarterly* 14 (1968): 573–581.

[66]L.D. Browning, J.M. Beyer, and J.C. Shetler, Building cooperation in a competitive industry: SEMATECH and the semiconductor industry, *Academy of Management Journal* 38(1) (1995): 113–151.

[67]K.W. Thomas, Organizational conflict. In *Organizational Behavior,* ed. S. Kerr (Columbus, Ohio: Grid, 1979).

[68]L.R. Pondy, Organizational conflict: Concepts and models, *Administrative Science Quarterly* 12 (1967): 296–320.

[69]M. Egbers and J. Van der Vurst, Interpersonal conflict resolution: The unconscious ally, *Leadership and Organization Development Journal* 7(5) (1986): iii.

[70]A. Mikhail, Stress: A psychophysiological conception, *Journal of Human Stress* (June 1981): 9–15.

[71]H. Selye, *The Stress of Life,* 2nd ed. (New York: McGraw-Hill, 1976).

[72]See K. Karaseh and T. Theorell, *Healthy Work: Stress, Productivity, and the Reconstruction of Working Life* (New York: Basic Books, 1990); J. Eckenrode and S. Gore, ed., *Stress Between Work and Family* (New York: Plenum, 1990) for a wide ranging discussion of stress and its effects.

[73]C.L. Cordes and T.W. Dougherty, A review and an integration of research on job burnout, *Academy of Management Review* 18 (1993): 621–656; D. Friesen and J.C. Sarros, Sources of burnout among educators, *Journal of Organizational Behavior* 10 (1989): 179–188; W.D. Paine, ed., *Job Stress and Burnout: Research, Theory, and Intervention Perspectives* (Beverly Hills, Calif.: Sage, 1982); R. Golembiewski and R.F. Munzenrider, *Phases of Burnout: Developments in Concepts and Applications* (New York: Praeger, 1988).

[74]Cordes and Dougherty, A review and integration of research.

[75]R.T. Lee and B.E. Ashforth, A further examination of managerial burnout: Toward an integrated model, *Journal of Organizational Behavior* 14 (1993): 3–20.

[76]S.S. Nandram and B. Klandermans, Stress experienced by active members of trade unions, *Journal of Organizational Behavior* 14 (1993): 415–431.

[77]D.R. Frew and N.W. Burning, Perceived organizational characteristics and personality measures as predictors of stress/strain in the workplace, *Journal of Management* 13 (1987): 633–646.

[78]B.D. Steffy, J.W. Jones, and A.W. Noe, The impact of health habits and life-style on the stress-strain relationship: An evaluation of three industries, *Journal of Occupational Psychology* 63 (1990): 217–229.

[79]P.E. Spector and B.J. O'Connell, The contribution of personality traits, negative affectivity, locus of control and Type A to the subsequent reports of job stressors and job strains, *Journal of Occupational and Organizational Psychology* 67 (March 1994): 1–12, illustrates this relationship.

[80]L. Piccoli, J.M. Emig, and K.M. Hiltebeitel, Why is public accounting stressful? Is it especially stressful for women? *The Woman CPA* (July 1988): 8–12.

[81]B. Schneider, Organizational behavior, *Annual Review of Psychology* (Washington, D.C.: American Psychological Association, 1985).

[82]T.D. Jick and R. Payne, Stress at work, *Exchange: The Organizational Behavior Teaching Journal* 5 (1980): 50–56.

[83]A. Farnham, Who beats stress best—and how, *Fortune* (October 7, 1991): 71–85.

[84]J.R. Terborg, Health promotion at the worksite: A research challenge for personnel and human resources management. In K.H. Rowland and G.R. Ferris, ed., *Researching Personnel and Human Resource Management, Vol. 4* (Greenwich, Conn.: JAI Press), pp. 225–267; Steffy, Jones, and Noe, The impact of health habits and life-style.

[85]L. Greenhalgh, Managing conflict, *Sloan Management Review* (Summer 1986): 45–51.

[86]Thomas, Conflict and conflict management. In M.D. Dunnette ed., *Handbook of Industrial and Organizational Psychology* (Chicago: Rand McNally, 1976).

[87]B. Gray, *Collaborating: Finding Common Ground for Multiparty Problems* (San Francisco: Jossey-Bass, 1989).

[88]D.D. Morley and P. Shockley-Zalabak, Conflict avoiders and compromisers: Toward an understanding of their organizational communication style, *Group and Organization Studies* 11 (December 1986): 387–402.

[89]J.S. Black and M. Mendenhall, Resolving conflicts with the Japanese: Mission impossible?, *Sloan Management Review* 34 (Spring 1993): 49–59; A. Goldman, A briefing on cultural and communicative sources of Western-Japanese interorganizational conflict, *Journal of Managerial Psychology* 9(1) (1994): 7–12.

[90]S. Ting-Toomey, Managing intercultural conflict effectively. In *Intercultural Communication: A Reader,* 7th ed., ed. L.A. Samovar and R.E. Porter (Belmont, Calif.: Wadsworth, 1994), pp. 360–372.

[91]Ting-Toomey, Managing.

[92]This grouping with the exception of arbitration is presented by J. Stockard and D. Lach, Conflict resolution: Sex and gender roles. In J.B. Gittler, *The Annual Review of Conflict Knowledge and Conflict Resolution, Vol. 1* (New York: Garland, 1989), pp. 69–91.

CHAPTER 10

[1]K. Kelly, Much ado about pettiness, *Business Week* (July 4, 1994): 34–36; M.A. Verespej, Bulldozing labor peace at Caterpillar, *Industry Week* (February 15, 1993): 19; K. Kelly, Caterpillar's Don Fites: Why he didn't blink, *Business Week* (August 10, 1992): 56–57.

[2]J.E. McCann and D.L. Ferry, An approach for assessing and managing interunit interdependence, *Academy of Management Review* 4 (1979): 113–119.

[3]S. Tully, Purchasing's new muscle, *Fortune* (February 20, 1995): 75–83.

[4]K.K. Smith, An intergroup perspective on individual behavior. In *Readings in Managerial Psychology*, 4th ed., ed. H.J. Leavitt, L.R. Pondy, and D.M. Boje (Chicago: University of Chicago Press, 1989).

[5]J.D. Thompson, *Organizations in Action* (New York: McGraw-Hill, 1967); A.H. Van de Ven, A.L. Delbecq, and R. Koenig, Jr., Determinants of coordination modes within organizations, *American Sociological Review* 41 (1976): 322–338.

[6]S. Baker, Nucor, *Business Week* (February 13, 1995): 70.

[7]T.A. Stewart, The search for the organization of tomorrow, *Fortune* (May 18, 1992): 92–98.

[8]R.E. Schmid, Planes banned in icy weather, *The Boston Globe,* (December 10, 1994); European manufacturer protests US ban on ATR commuter planes, *The Boston Globe* (December 11, 1994): 18.

[9]D.W. Johnson and F.P. Johnson, *Cooperation and Competition: Theory and Research* (Edina, Minn.: Interaction, 1989).

[10]A.W. Gouldner, Cosmopolitans and locals: Toward an analysis of latent social roles, *Administrative Science Quarterly 2* (1958): 290.

[11]D. Hickson, C. Hinings, C. Lee, R. Schneck, and J.A. Pennings, A strategic contingencies theory of intraorganizational power, *Administrative Science Quarterly* 23 (1978): 65–90.

[12]P.T. Kilborn, Young organizers lead labor's push, *The New York Times* (June 3, 1993): D22.

[13]R. Beckhard, The confrontation meeting, *Harvard Business Review* 45 (1967): 154, presents an early description of this intervention.

[14]W.L. French and C.H. Bell, Jr. *Organization Development: Behavioral Science Interventions for Organization Improvement,* 2nd ed. (Englewood Cliffs, N.J.: Prentice-Hall, 1978).

[15]H. Prien, Strategies for third-party intervention, *Human Relations* 40 (1987): 699–720.

[16]D.J. McConville, The artful negotiator, *Industry Week* (August 15, 1994): 34–40.

[17]E. Van de Vliert, Escalative intervention in small-group conflicts, *Journal of Applied Behavioral Science* 21 (1985); 19–36.

[18]R.R. Blake and J.S. Mouton, Overcoming group warfare, *Harvard Business Review* 62(6) (1984): 98–108.

[19]See D. Kolb, Women's work: Peacemaking in organizations. In D. M. Kolb and J.M. Bartunek, ed. *Hidden Conflict in Organizations* (Newbury Park, Calif.: Sage, 1992).

[20]R. Likert and J. Likert, *New Ways of Managing Conflict* (New York: McGraw-Hill, 1976).

[21]D.A. Lax and J.K. Sebenius, *The Manager as Negotiator* (New York: Free Press, 1986).

[22]Lax and Sebenius, *The Manager.*

[23]R. Fisher and W. Ury, *Getting to Yes: Negotiating without Giving In* (Boston: Houghton-Mifflin, 1981) was an early call for this approach.

[24]Bargaining in Laymon's terms, *Industry Week* (February 15, 1993): 18.

[25]R. Gourlay, Negotiations and bargaining, *Management Decision* 25(3) (1987): 23.

[26]K. Kelly and W. Zellner, The airlines to labor: Buy in—Or get bashed, *Business Week* (November 1, 1993): 40; W. Zellner, Did Clinton scramble American's profit picture? *Business Week* (December 6, 1993): 44; J.T. McKenna, Clinton strike action may open a new era, *Aviation Week & Space Technology* (November 29, 1993): 27–28; B. Dumaine, Indian summer for big labor, *Fortune* (December 27, 1993): 18.

[27]M.A. Neale and M.H. Bazerman, *Cognition and Rationality in Negotiation* (New York: Free Press, 1991).

[28]W.P. Bottom and A. Studt, Framing effects and the distributive aspect of integrative bargaining, *Organizational Behavior and Human Decision Processes* 56(3) (1993): 459–474.

[29]J.S. Carroll and M.H. Bazerman, Negotiator cognitions: A descriptive approach to negotiators' understanding of their opponents, *Organizational Behavior and Human Decision Processes* 41 (1988): 352–370.

[30]Lax and Sebenius, *The Manager.*

[31]Neale and Bazerman, *Cognition.*

[32]P. Nulty, Look what the unions want now, *Fortune* (February 8, 1993): 128–135.

[33]A. Bernstein, Why America needs unions but not the kind it has now, *Business Week* (May 23, 1994): 70–82.

[34]Lax and Sebenius, *The manager.*

[35]R.T. Moran and W.G. Stripp, *Dynamics of Successful International Business Negotiations* (Houston: Gulf, 1991).

[36]R. Fisher and S. Brown, *Getting Together* (Boston: Houghton-Mifflin, 1988).

[37]G.T. Savage, J.D. Blair, and R.L. Sorenson, Consider both relationships and substance when negotiating strategically, *Academy of Management Executive* 3(1) (1989): 37–48.

[38]J. Nierenberg and I.S. Ross, *Women and the Art of Negotiating* (New York: Simon and Schuster, 1985).

[39]D.J. McConville, The artful negotiator, *Industry Week* (August 15, 1994): 34–40.

[40]F. Elashmawi and P.R. Harris, *Multicultural Management: New Skills for Global Success* (Houston: Gulf, 1993), p. 162.

[41]J.A. Reeder, When West meets East: Cultural aspects of doing business in Asia, *Business Horizons* 30 (1) (1987): 263–275.

[42]N.J. Adler, *International Dimensions of Organizational Behavior,* 2nd ed. (Boston: PWS-Kent, 1991).

[43]E.S. Glenn, D. Witmeyer, and K.A. Stevenson, Cultural styles of persuasion, *International Journal of Intercultural Relations,* vol. 1 (New York: Pergamon, 1984).

[44]S. Frank, Global negotiating: Vive les differences! *Sales & Marketing Management* 144(5) (1992): 64–69.

[45]Glenn, Witmeyer, and Stevenson, Cultural styles.

CHAPTER 11

[1]C.R. Day, Jr., Shape up and ship out, *Industry Week* (February 6, 1995): 14–20; C. Hawkins, After a u-turn, UPS really delivers, *Business Week* (May 31, 1993): 92–93; Package delivery, *Fortune* (May 31, 1993): 88; S. Kindel, When elephants dance, *Financial World* (June 9, 1992): 76–78.

[2]R.H. Kilmann, M.J. Saxton, and R. Serpa, Issues in understanding and changing culture, *California Management Review* 28 (1986): 87–94; E.H. Schein, *Organizational Culture and Leadership* (San Francisco: Jossey-Bass, 1985); E.H. Schein, Organizational culture, *American Psychologist* 45 (2) (1990): 109–119.

[3]J.P. Kotter and J.C. Heskett, *Corporate Culture and Performance* (New York: Free Press, 1992).

[4]P. Sellers, Can this man save IBM? *Fortune* (April 19, 1993): 63–67.

[5]S.G. Harris, Organizational culture and individual sensemaking: A schemabased perspective, *Organization Science* 5(3) (1994): 309–321.

[6]N.C. Morey and F. Luthans, Refining the displacement of culture and the uses of scenes and themes in organizational studies, *Academy of Management Review* 10 (1985): 219–229; M.R. Louis, Organizations as culture-bearing milieux. In *Organizational Symbolism,* ed. L.R. Pondy et al. (Greenwich, Conn.: JAI, 1980); G. Morgan, *Images of Organizations* (Beverly Hills, Calif.: Sage, 1986).

[7]L. Schein, *A Manager's Guide to Corporate Culture* (New York: The Conference Board, 1989).

[8]See D.L. Denison, *Corporate Culture and Organizational Effectiveness* (New York: Wiley, 1990).

9J. Martin and D. Myerson, Organizational culture and the denial, channeling, and acknowledge-ment of ambiguity. In *Managing Ambiguity and Change,* ed. L.R. Pondy, R.J. Boland Jr., and H. Thomas (New York: Wiley, 1988); and D. Meyerson and J. Martin, Cultural change: An integration of three different views, *Journal of Management Studies* 24 (1987): 623–647 provide the original categorization of perspectives; P.J. Frost, L.F. Moore, M.R. Louis, C.C. Sundberg, and J. Martin, ed., *Reframing Organizational Culture* (Newbury Park, Calif.: Sage, 1991) offer additional discussion and examples.

10V. Sathe, *Culture and Related Corporate Realities* (Homewood, Ill.: Irwin, 1985); Schein, *Organizational Culture and Leadership.*

11A. Farnham, State your values, hold the hot air, *Fortune* (April 19, 1993): 117–124.

12M.J. Hatch, The dynamics of organizational culture, *Academy of Management Review* 18 (1993): 657–693.

13M. Shao, A scoopful of credentials, *The Boston Globe* (March 1, 1995): 1, 15; R. Peo, 'Can we talk?' *Across the Board* 31(5) (May 1994): 16–23; J. Castelli, Finding the right fit, *HR Magazine* (September 1990): 38–41.

14G.G. Gordon, Industry determinants of organizational culture, *Academy of Management Review* 16(2) (1991): 396–415.

15T.E. Benson, Paul O'Neill: True innovation, true values, true leadership, *Industry Week* (April 19, 1993): 25–28; P.J. Kolesar, Vision, values, milestones: Paul O'Neill starts total quality at Alcoa, *California Management Review* 35(3) (Spring 1993): 133–165.

16T.E. Deal and A.A. Kennedy, *Corporate Cultures* (Reading, Mass.: Addison-Wesley, 1982).

17K. Labis, Is Herb Kelleher America's best CEO? *Fortune* (May 2, 1994): 44–52; W.G. Lee, A conversation with Herb Kelleher, *Organizational Dynamics* 23(2) (Autumn 1994): 64–74; C.A. Jaffe, Moving fast by standing still, *Nation's Business,* 79(10) (October 1991): 57–59; S.N. Chakravarty, Hit 'em hardest with the mostest, *Forbes* (September 16, 1991): 48–50.

18C.H. Deutsch, The parables of corporate culture, *The New York Times* (October 13, 1991): 25.

19S.L. Solberg, Changing culture through ceremony: An example from GM, *Human Resources Management* 24 (Fall 1985): 329–340.

20H.M. Trice and J.M. Beyer, *The Cultures of Work Organizations* (Englewood Cliffs, N.J.: Prentice-Hall, 1993).

21J. Stitt, *Managing for Excellence* (Milwaukee, Wis.: Quality Press, 1990); V.K. Omachonu and J.E. Ross, *Principles of Total Quality* (Delray Beach, Fla.: St. Lucie Press, 1994).

22W.E. Deming, *Quality, Productivity, and Competitive Position* (Cambridge, Mass.: MIT Center for Advanced Engineering Study, 1982); W.E. Deming, *Out of the Crisis* (Cambridge, Mass.: MIT Center for Advanced Engineering Study, 1984).

23P.N. Brody, Introduction to total quality management. In *Total Quality Management: A Report of Proceedings from the Xerox Quality Forum II, August, 1990.* Cited in R. Blackburn and B. Rosen, Total quality and human resources management: Lessons learned from Baldrige Award-winning companies, *Academy of Management Executive* 7(3) (1993): 49–66.

24J.W. Dean, Jr., and J.R. Evans, *Total Quality: Management, Organization, and Strategy* (St. Paul, Minn.: West, 1994).

25D. Greising, Quality: How to make it pay, *Business Week* (August 8, 1994): 54–59.

26S. Caminiti, New lessons in customer service, *Fortune* (September 20, 1993): 79–80.

27Dean and Evans, *Total Quality Management.*

28M.A. Verespej, How the best got better, *Industry Week* (March 7, 1994): 27–28.

29J.M. Juran, *Quality Control Handbook* (New York: McGraw-Hill, 1989).

30J. Main, How to steal the best ideas around, *Fortune* (October 19, 1992): 102–106.

31V.K. Omachonu and J.E. Ross, *Principles of Total Quality* (Delray Beach, Fla.: St. Lucie, 1994).

32Omachonu and Ross, *Principles.*

33E.E. Lawler, III, Total quality management and employee involvement: Are they compatible?, *Academy of Management Executive* 8(1) (1994): 68–76.

34B.S. Moskal, Pawley's quest for the elusive Grail, *Industry Week* (March 21, 1994): 26–38.

35T.M. Rohan, Culture change wins the Baldrige, *Industry Week* (January 3, 1994): 41–42.

[36]Blackburn and Rosen, Total quality.

[37]Blackburn and Rosen, Total quality.

[38]R.M. Grant, R. Shani, and R. Krishnan, TQM's challenge to management theory and practice, *Sloan Management Review* (Winter 1994): 25–34.

[39]C. Argyris and D. Schon, *Organizational Learning* (Reading, Mass.: Addison-Wesley, 1978); C. Argyris, *Overcoming Organizational Defenses* (Boston: Allyn & Bacon, 1990); P.M. Senge, *The Fifth Discipline: The Art and Practice of the Learning Organization* (New York: Doubleday, 1990).

[40]E. C. Nevis, A.J. DiBella, and J.M. Gould, Understanding organizations as learning systems, *Sloan Management Review* (Winter 1995): 73–85.

[41]Senge, *The Fifth Discipline*. M.E. McGill and J.W. Slocum, Jr., Unlearning the organization, *Organizational Dynamics* (Autumn 1993).

[42]Senge, *The Fifth Discipline*. P.M. Senge, The leader's new work: Building learning organizations, *Sloan Management Review*, (Fall 1990): 7–23; McGill and Slocum, Unlearning.

[43]D.A. Garvin, Building a learning organization, *Harvard Business Review* 71(4) (July/August 1993): 78–91.

[44]D.Q. Mills and B. Friesen, The learning organization, *European Management Journal* 10(2) (June 1992): 146–156.

[45]P.M. Senge, *The Fifth Discipline*. P.M. Senge, Transforming the practice of management, *Human Resource Development Quarterly* (Spring 1993); J.K. Bennett and M.J. O'Brien, The building blocks of the learning organization, *Training* 31(6) (June 1994): 41–49; K.E. Watkins and V.J. Marsick, *Sculpting the Learning Organization: Lessons in the Art and Science of Systemic Change* (San Francisco: Jossey-Bass, 1993) p. 8; P. West, The concept of the learning organization, *Journal of European Industrial Training* 18(1) (1994): 15–20.

[46]B. Dumaine, Mr. learning organization, *Fortune* (October 17, 1994): 147–157.

[47]L. Smith, New ideas from the Army (really), *Fortune* (September 19, 1994): 203–212.

[48]J. Rosenblum and R.A. Keller, Building a learning organization at Coopers & Lybrand, *Planning Review* 22(5) (1994): 28–29.

[49]K. Holland, A chastened Chase, *Business Week* (September 26, 1994): 106–109; J.W. Milligan, Can Chase become a high performance bank? *United States Banker* 103(10) (1993): 28–37.

[50]H. Schwartz and S. Davis, Matching corporate culture and business strategy, *Organizational Dynamics* (Summer 1981): 30–48.

[51]V. Sathe, How to decipher and change culture. In R.H. Kilmann, M.J. Saxton, R. Serpa, and associates, ed., *Gaining Control of Corporate Culture* (San Francisco: Jossey-Bass, 1985).

[52]A.L. Wilkins and W.G. Dyer, Jr., Toward culturally sensitive theories of cultural change, *Academy of Management Review* 13 (1988): 522–533; E.H. Schein, *Organizational Culture and Leadership*.

[53]L. Nakarmi and R. Neff, Samsung's radical shakeup, *Business Week* (February 28, 1994): 74–76; L. Kraar, Korea goes for quality, *Fortune* (April 18, 1994): 153–159.

[54]L. Morris, Organizational culture and TQM implementation, *Training & Development* 48(4) (1994): 69–71.

[55]D. Ciampa, *Total Quality: A User's Guide to Implementation* (Reading, Mass.: Addison-Wesley, 1992).

[56]Woodruff.

[57]M.G. Brown, How to determine your quality quotient, *The Journal for Quality and Participation* (June 1990): 76–80.

[58]T.E. Benson, The gestalt of total quality management, *Industry Week* (July 1, 1991): 30–31.

[59]A. Nordhaus-Bike, TQM, quick fix or long-term solution? *Business Loyola* (Fall 1993): 2–7.

[60]S. Caudron, Keys to starting a TQM program, *Personnel Journal* (February 1993): 28–35.

[61]R. Krishnan, A.B. Shani, R.M. Grant, and R. Baer, In search of quality improvement: Problems of design and implementation, *Academy of Management Executive* 7(4) (1993): 7–20.

[62]Watkins and Marsick, *Sculpting the Learning Organization*.

[63]E.H. Schein, How can organizations learn faster? The challenge of entering the Green Room, *Sloan Management Review* (Winter 1993): 85–92.

[64]Schein, How can organizations learn faster.

⁶⁵Senge, *The Fifth Discipline.*

⁶⁶Senge, The leader's new work.

CHAPTER 12

¹W. Symonds, Getting rid of paper is just the beginning, *Business Week* (December 21, 1992): 88–89; B. Rabkin, Winners will deliver real-time customer service, *National Underwriter* 98 (October 3, 1994): 51–52; M.P. Schwartz, Connecticut Mutual puts new spin on reengineering, *National Underwriter* 98 (April 25, 1994): 33, 40; M.P. Schwartz, Everyone at Connecticut Mutual reapplying for their job, *National Underwriter* 98 (April 18, 1994): 3, 38; K. Burger, Redefining customer service, *Insurance & Technology* 19 (February, 1994): 25; J. King, Re-engineering repercussions: Connecticut Mutual, *Computerworld* 27 (June 28, 1993): 149–150.

²F.W. Taylor, *The Principles of Scientific Management* (New York: Harper, 1911).

³C. Perrow, The organizational context of human factors engineering, *Administrative Science Quarterly* 28 (1983): 521–541.

⁴F.E. Emery, The assembly line—Its logic and our future, *National Labour Institute Bulletin* 1 (1975): 1–19.

⁵M.A. Campion and C.L. McClelland, Interdisciplinary examination of the costs and benefits of enlarged jobs: A job design quasi-experiment, *Journal of Applied Psychology* 76(2) (1991): 186–198.

⁶M.A. Campion and C.L. McClelland, Follow-up and extension of the interdisciplinary costs and benefits of enlarged jobs, *Journal of Applied Psychology* 78 (1993): 339–351.

⁷Campion and McClelland, Follow-up.

⁸J.D. Kilbridge, Reduced costs through job enlargement: A case, *Journal of Business* 33 (1960): 357–362.

⁹Few employers give job rotation a whirl, *The Wall Street Journal* (July 22, 1992): B1.

¹⁰F. Herzberg and A. Zautra, Orthodox job enrichment: Measuring true quality in job satisfaction, *Personnel* (September–October 1976).

¹¹R. Henkoff, Finding, training, & keeping the best service workers, *Fortune* (October 3, 1994): 110–122.

¹²J.R. Hackman and G. Oldham, *Work Design* (Reading, Mass.: Addison-Wesley, 1980).

¹³Hackman and Oldham, *Work Design.*

¹⁴Hackman and Oldham, *Work Design.*

¹⁵J. Woodward, *Industrial Organization: Theory and Practice* (London: Oxford University Press, 1965); E. Trist and K.W. Bamforth, Some social and psychological consequences of the long-wall method of coal getting, *Human Relations* 4 (1951): 3–38; A.K. Rice, *Productivity and Social Organization: The Ahmedabad Experiments* (London: Tavistock, 1958).

¹⁶T.G. Cummings, Self-regulating work groups: A sociotechnical synthesis, *Academy of Management Review* 3 (1978): 625–634.

¹⁷M.R. Weisbord, Participative work design: A personal odyssey, *Organizational Dynamics* 13 (Spring 1985).

¹⁸T. Christensen, A high-involvement redesign, *Quality Progress* 26 (May, 1993): 105–108.

¹⁹C.A.L. Pearson, Autonomous workgroups: An evaluation at an industrial site, *Human Relations* 45 (September, 1992): 905–936.

²⁰T.D. Wall, N.J. Kemp, P.R. Jackson, and C.W. Clegg, Outcomes of autonomous workgroups: A long-term field experiment, *Academy of Management Journal* 29 (1986): 280–304; J.L. Cordery, W.S. Mueller, and L.M. Smith, Attitudinal and behavioral effects of autonomous group working: A longitudinal field study, *Academy of Management Journal* 34(2) (1991): 464–476.

²¹Volvo to close 2 plants and cut 4,500 workers, *The New York Times* (November 5, 1992); S.D. Moore, Volvo planning 2 plant closings at Swedish sites, *The Wall Street Journal* (November 5, 1992).

²²M.A. Verespej, Face time's importance is fading away, *Industry Week* (June 15, 1992): 12–18.

²³J.L. Pierce and R.B. Dunham, The 12-hour day: A 48-hour, eight-day week, *Academy of Management Journal* 35 (1992): 1086–1098.

[24]J. Pontusson, The politics of new technology and job redesign: A comparison of Volvo and British Leyland, *Economic and Industrial Democracy* 11 (1990): 311–336; H.A. Hollingsworth and F.A. Wiebe, Flextime: An international innovation with limited U.S. acceptance, *Industrial Management* 31(2) (1989): 22–26.

[25]B. Shamir and I. Salomon, Work-at-home and the quality of working life, *Academy of Management Review* 10 (1985): 455–464.

[26]R.D. Hylton, The revolution in real estate, *Fortune* (September 5, 1994): 94–98.

[27]J. Fierman, The contingency work force, *Fortune* (January 24, 1994): 30–36.

[28]S.G. Schroeder, Alternate workstyles: A solution to productivity problems? *Supervisory Management* 28 (July 1983): 24–30; W. Olsten, Effectively managing alternative work options, *Supervisory Management* 29 (April 1984): 10–15.

[29]B. Olmsted, (Flex)time is money, *Management Review* (November 1987): 47–51; C. Scordato and J. Harris, Workplace flexibility, *HR Magazine* (January 1990): 75–78.

[30]J.W. Newstrom and J.L. Pierce, Alternative work schedules: The state of the art, *Personnel Administrator* (1979): 19–23.

[31]J.A. Hollingsworth and F.A. Wrebe, Flextime.

[32]R.E. Walton, Quality of working life: What is it? *Sloan Management Review* 15 (1973): 11–21.

[33]S.S. Brooks, Noncash ways to compensate employees, *HR Magazine* 39(4) (April 1994): 38–43; S.E. Groffman, American Airlines' employee suggestion program takes off, *Human Resources Professional* 4(4) (1992): 13–17; K. Doyle, When ideas take flight, *Incentive* (January 1992): 29–31, 76; P. Stuart, Fresh ideas energize reward programs, *Personnel Journal* 71(10) (1992): 102–103.

[34]D.A. Nadler and E.E. Lawler III, Quality of work life: Perspectives and directions, *Organizational Dynamics* (Winter, 1983).

[35]R.H. Guest, Quality of work life—Learning from Tarrytown, *Harvard Business Review* 57 (1979): 76–87.

[36]H.C. Katz, *Shifting Gears: Changing Relations in the U.S. Automobile Industry* (Cambridge, Mass.: MIT Press, 1985).

[37]M. Edid, How power will be balanced on Saturn's shop floor, *Business Week* (August 5, 1985).

[38]See I. Bluestone, How quality-of-worklife projects work for the United Auto Workers, *Monthly Labor Review* (July 1980); S.H. Fuller, How quality-of-worklife projects work for General Motors, *Monthly Labor Review* (July 1980): 39–41.

[39]J.W. Thacker and M.W. Fields, Union involvement in quality-of-work-life efforts: A longitudinal investigation, *Personnel Psychology* 40 (1987): 97–111.

[40]J. Simmons and W. Mares, *Working Together* (New York: Knopf, 1983); J.A. Pearce II and E.C. Ravlin, The design and activation of self-regulating work groups, *Human Relations* 40 (1987): 751–782.

[41]H.C. Katz, T.A. Kochan, and M.R. Weber, Assessing the effects of industrial relations systems and efforts to improve the quality of working life on organizational effectiveness, *Academy of Management Journal* 28 (1985): 509–526.

[42]C. Chandler and J.B. White, It's hello dollies at Nissan's new 'dream factory,' *The Wall Street Journal* (July 6, 1992): 13, 20.

[43]P.S. DeLisi, Lessons from the steel axe: Culture, technology, and organizational change, *Sloan Management Review* (Fall 1990): 83–93.

[44]M.S. Scott-Morton, *The Corporation of the 1990s: Informational Technology and Organizational Transformation* (New York: Oxford University Press, 1991).

[45]A.E. Serwer, Lessons from America's fastest growing companies, *Fortune* (August 8, 1994): 42–60.

[46]This discussion is drawn largely from M. Hammer and J. Champy, *Reengineering the Corporation: A Manifesto for Business Revolution* (New York: Harper Business, 1993).

[47]R. Jacob, Thriving in a lame economy, *Fortune* (October 5, 1992): 44–54.

[48]T.A. Stewart, Reengineering: The hot new managing tool, *Fortune* (August 23, 1993): 41–48.

[49]Hammer and Champy, *Reengineering the Corporation.*

[50]J.A. Byrne, Management's new gurus, *Business Week* (August 31, 1992): 44–52.

[51]Hammer and Champy, *Reengineering the Corporation.*

[52]R.E. Yates, Re-engineering guru retools idea, *Chicago Tribune* (February 3, 1995): 1, 2.

[53]J. Teresko, Japan: Reengineering vs tradition, *Industry Week* (September 5, 1994): 63–70; Re-engineering Europe, *Economist* 330 (February 2, 1994): 63–64.

[54]J. Woudhuysen, Engineers of a fresh approach, *Marketing* (June 3, 1994): 10.

[55]A.E. Alter, Japan, Inc. embraces change, *Computerworld* 28 (March 7, 1994): 24–25.

[56]G. Hall, J. Rosenthal, and J. Wade, How to make reengineering really work, *Harvard Business Review* 71 (November/December 1993): 119–131.

[57]Stewart, Reengineering.

[58]G. Hamel and C.K. Prahalad, Competing for the future, *Harvard Business Review* 72 (July/August, 1994): 122–128.

[59]D. Patching, Business process reengineering, *Management Services* 38 (June 1994): 10–13.

[60]T.H. Davenport and D.B. Stoddard, Reengineering: Business change of mythic proportions? *MIS Quarterly* 18 (June 1994): 121–127.

[61]J. Champy, Reengineering management: The mandate for new leadership, *Industry Week* (February 20, 1995): 33–42.

[62]Champy, Reengineering management.

[63]U.E. Gattiker, *Technology Management in Organizations* (Newbury Park, Calif.: Sage, 1990).

[64]J. Weber, Pure research, compliments of Japan, *Business Week* (July 13, 1992): 136–137.

[65]See D.G. Marquis, The anatomy of successful innovations (November 1969), Technology Communications, Inc. Reprinted in *Managing Advanced Technology,* vol. 1 (New York: American Management Association, 1972), pp. 35–48.

[66]A. Rubenstein, *Managing Technology in the Decentralized Firm* (New York: Wiley, 1989).

[67]B. Dumaine, Closing the innovation gap, *Fortune* (December 2, 1991): 56–62.

[68]D.R. Altany, Frank Ryder: Inventor, entrepreneur, dreamer, *Industry Week* (May 3, 1993): 31–36.

[69]Dumaine, Closing.

[70]Dumaine, Closing.

[71]B.R. Schlender, How Sony keeps the magic going, *Fortune* (February 24, 1992): 84.

[72]Rubenstein, *Managing Technology.*

[73]R. Buderi, American inventors are reinventing themselves, *Business Week* (January 18, 1993): 78–82.

[74]S.A. Shane, Are champions different from non-champions?, *Journal of Business Venturing* 9 (September 1994): 397–421.

[75]J.H. Arleth, New product development projects and the role of the innovation manager. In A. Cozijnsen and W. Vrakking, ed., *Handbook of Innovation Management* (Oxford: Blackwell Business, 1993), p. 125.

[76]Arleth, New product development.

[77]M. Schrage, Few try to imitate 3M's successes, *Boston Sunday Globe* (October 11, 1992): 76.

[78]R.A. Burgelman, T.J. Kosnik, and M. Van den Poel, Toward an innovative capabilities audit framework. In R.A. Burgelman and M.A. Maidique, *Strategic Management of Technology and Innovation* (Homewood, Ill.: Irwin, 1988).

[79]J.E. McCann, Design principles for an innovating company, *Academy of Management Executive* 5(2) (1991): 76–93.

[80]R.A. Wolfe, Organizational innovation: Review, critique and suggested research directions, *Journal of Management Studies* 31 (May 1994): 405–431.

[81]Buderi, American inventors.

CHAPTER 13

[1]F.A. Maljers, Inside Unilever: The evolving transnational company, *Harvard Business Review* 70(5) (September–October, 1992): 46–51; C.A. Bartlett and S. Ghoshal, Matrix management: Not a structure, a frame of mind, *Harvard Business Review* (July–August, 1990): 138–145; F.A. Maljers, Strategic planning and intuition in Unilever, *Long Range Planning* 23(2) (April 1990): 63–68; Unilever in Asia: Poor countries rich in wealthy people, *The*

Economist (August 15, 1992): 56–57; T. Lester, Balancing act, *International Management* 49(7) (1994): 30–31; P. Dwyer, Unilever's struggle for growth, *Business Week* (July 4, 1994): 54–56.

[2]P. Dwyer, Tearing up today's organization chart, *Business Week* (21st Century Capitalism edition, 1994): 80–90.

[3]Volvo's radical new plant: "The death of the assembly line?" *Business Week* (August 28, 1989).

[4]P.R. Lawrence and J.W. Lorsch, Differentiation and integration in complex organizations, *Administrative Science Quarterly* 12 (1967): 1–47, offers an early discussion of division of labor.

[5]Dwyer, Tearing up.

[6]E. Thornton, Japan's struggle to restructure, *Fortune* (June 29, 1993): 84–88.

[7]H. Mintzberg, *Structure in Fives: Designing Effective Organizations.* (Englewood Cliffs, N.J.: Prentice-Hall, 1983).

[8]M.L. Tushman and D.A. Nadler, Information processing as an integrating concept in organizational design, *Academy of Management Review* 3 (1978): 613–625.

[9]J. Templeman, Nestle: A giant in a hurry, *Business Week* (March 22, 1993): 50–54.

[10]W.B. Stevenson, Organization design. In R. Golembiewski, ed., *The Handbook of Organizational Behavior* (New York: Marcel Dekker, 1993).

[11]J. Fulk and B. Boyd, Emerging theories of communication in organizations, *Journal of Management* 17 (1991): 407–446.

[12]W.B. Stevenson and M.C. Gilly, Information processing and problem solving: The migration of problems through formal positions and networks of ties, *Academy of Management Journal* 34 (1991): 918–928.

[13]Mintzberg, *Structure in Fives.*

[14]Mintzberg, *Structure in Fives.*

[15]Mintzberg, *Structure in Fives.*

[16]W.E. Halal, A. Geranmayeh, and J. Pourdehnad, *Internal Markets: Bringing the Power of Free Enterprise INSIDE Your Organization* (New York: Wiley, 1993).

[17]R. Howard, The CEO as organizational architect: An interview with Xerox's Paul Allaire, *Harvard Business Review* 70(5) (September–October, 1992): 106–121.

[18]Mintzberg, *Structure in Fives.*

[19]J. Flynn, An ever-quicker trip from R&D to customer, *Business Week* (21st Century Capitalism Issue 1994): 88.

[20]L.W. Burns and D.R. Wholey, Adoption and abandonment of matrix management programs: Effects of organizational characteristics and interorganizational networks, *Academy of Management Journal* 36 (1993): 106–138.

[21]Dwyer, Tearing up.

[22]J.A. Byrne, The horizontal corporation, *Business Week* (December 20, 1993): 76–82; T.A. Stewart, The search for the organization of tomorrow, *Fortune* (May 18, 1992): 92–98; T. Brown, Future organizations, *Industry Week* (November 1, 1993): 20–28.

[23]K.L. Alexander and S. Baker, Borderless management, *Business Week* (May 23, 1994): 24–26.

[24]Alexander and Baker, Borderless management.

[25]Byrne, The horizontal corporation.

[26]Byrne, The horizontal corporation.

[27]W.F. Cascio and M.G. Serapio, Jr., Human resources systems in an international alliance: The undoing of a done deal, *Organizational Dynamics* 19(3) (1991): 63–74.

[28]A.S. Miner, T.L. Amburgey, and T.M. Stearns, Interorganizational linkages and population dynamics: Buffering and transformational shields, *Administrative Science Quarterly* 35 (1990): 689–713.

[29]J.A. Byrne, The virtual corporation, *Business Week* (February 8, 1993): 98–99.

[30]J.E. Forrest, Strategic alliances and the small technology-based firm, *Journal of Small Business Management* 28 (3) (1990): 37.

[31]S. Tully, You'll never guess who really makes. . . , *Fortune* (October 3, 1994): 124–128.

[32]Tully, You'll never guess.

[33] D. Lei and J.W. Slocum, Jr. Global strategic alliances: Payoffs and pitfalls, *Organizational Dynamics* (Winter 1991): 44–62.

[34] B.R. Schlender, How Toshiba makes alliances work, *Fortune* (October 4, 1993): 116–120.

[35] The discussion here is based on the mighty keiretsu, *Industry Week* (January 20, 1992): 52–54; C. Rapoport, Why Japan keeps on winning, *Fortune* (July 15, 1991): 76–85.

[36] R.E. Miles and C.C. Snow, Organizations: New concepts for new forms, *California Management Review* 28 (Spring 1986): 62–73.

[37] G. Morgan, *Creative Organization Theory: A Resourcebook* (Newbury Park, Calif.: Sage, 1989).

[38] S. Tully, The modular corporation, *Fortune* (February 8, 1993): 106–115.

[39] Tully, The modular corporation.

[40] W.W. Powell, Hybrid organizational arrangements: New form or transitional development? *California Management Review* 30 (Fall 1987): 67–87; see also W.W. Powell, Neither market nor hierarchy: Network forms of organization. In B.M. Staw and L.L. Cummings, *Research in Organizational Behavior* 12 (1990): 295–336.

[41] Miles and Snow, Organizations.

[42] C.C. Snow, R.E. Miles, and H.J. Coleman, Jr., Managing 21st century network organizations, *Organizational Dynamics* (Winter, 1992): 5–19.

[43] D. Bottoms, Back to the future, *Industry Week* (October 3, 1994): 61–64; Byrne, The virtual corporation.

[44] T.A. Stewart, Managing in a wired company, *Fortune* (July 11, 1994): 44–56.

[45] Sun's rise in the virtual world, *Industry Week* (October 3, 1994): 63.

[46] Byrne, The virtual corporation. pp. 98–99.

CHAPTER 14

[1] Adapted with permission from P. LaBarre, The disorganization of Oticon, *Industry Week* (July 18, 1994): 23–28.

[2] R. Neff, Tradition be damned, *Business Week* (October 31, 1994): 108–110.

[3] R. Sidel, AT&T, Delta ink $2.8b computer services venture, *The Boston Globe* (August 24, 1994): 43.

[4] H.W. Lane and J.D. DiStefano, *International Management Behavior: From Policy to Practice* (Boston: PWS-Kent, 1992).

[5] H. Crookell, Organization structure for global operations. In P.W. Blanush, J.P. Killing, D.J. Lecraw, and H. Crookell, *International Management: Text and Cases* (Homewood, Ill.: Irwin, 1991).

[6] G.E. Schares, Percy Barnevik's global crusade, *Business Week* (Enterprise 1993): 204–211.

[7] G. Inzerilli and A. Laurent, Managerial views of the organization structure in France and the U.S.A., *International Studies of Management and Organization* 13(1–2) (1983): 97–118.

[8] P.M. Rosenzweig and J.V. Singh, Organizational environments and the multinational enterprise, *Academy of Management Review* 16(2) (1991): 340–361.

[9] See G.G. Dess and D.W. Beard, Objective measurement of organizational environments, *Academy of Management Proceedings* (1982): 345–349 and D.D. Dess and D.W. Beard, Dimensions of organizational task environments, *Administrative Science Quarterly* 29 (1984): 52–73. See also S.M. Shortell, The role of environment in a configurational theory of organizations, *Human Relations* 30 (1977): 275–302; and R.B. Duncan, Characteristics of organizational environments and perceived environmental uncertainty, *Administrative Science Quarterly* 17 (1972): 313–327. H. Mintzberg, *The Structuring of Organizations*. Englewood Cliffs, N.J.: Prentice-Hall, 1979; H. Mintzberg, *Structure in Fives: Designing Effective Organizations* (Englewood Cliffs, N.J.: Prentice-Hall, 1983) specifies five dimensions: complexity, diversity, change, hostility, and uncertainty.

[10] B.W. Keats and M.A. Hitt, A causal model of linkages among environmental dimensions, macro-organizational characteristics, and performance, *Academy of Management Journal* 31 (1988): 570–598.

[11]See the study by M. Yasai-Ardekani, Effects of environmental scarcity and munificence on the relationship of context to organizational structure, *Academy of Management Journal* 32 (1989): 131–156.

[12]D. Miller, Environmental fit versus internal fit, *Organization Science* 3(2) (1992): 159.

[13]R.B. Duncan, Multiple decision-making structures in adapting to environmental uncertainty, *Human Relations* 26 (1973): 273–291; H.R. Johnson, Interactions between individual predispositions, environmental factors, and organizational design. In R.H. Kilmann, L.R. Pondy, and D.P. Slevin, eds., *The Management of Organizational Design, Vol. 2* (New York: North-Holland, 1976), pp. 31–58.

[14]J. Woodward, *Industrial Organizations: Theory and Practice* (London: Oxford University Press, 1965).

[15]J. Thompson, *Organizations in Action* (New York: McGraw-Hill, 1967).

[16]C. Perrow, A framework for comparative analysis of organizations, *American Sociological Review* 32 (April 1967): 196.

[17]Mintzberg, *Structuring of Organizations.*

[18]C. Stein, A master of the tight ship, *The Boston Globe* (November 22, 1992): 85.

[19]J.D. Ford and J.W. Slocum, Jr., Size, technology, environment, and the structure of organizations, *Academy of Management Review* 2 (1977): 561–575; L.W. Fry, Technology structure research: Three critical issues, *Academy of Management Journal* 25 (1982): 532–552.

[20]M. Jelinek, Technology, organizations, and contingency, *Academy of Management Review* 2 (1977): 17–26.

[21]M. Liu, H. Denis, H. Kolodny, and B. Stymne, Organization design for technological change. In R.R. Sims, D.D. White, and D.A. Bednar, eds., *Readings in Organizational Behavior* (Boston: Allyn and Bacon, 1992).

[22]N. Gross, Inside Hitachi, *Business Week* (September 28, 1992): 92–100.

[23]G. McWilliams, How DEC's 'minicompanies' led to major losses, *Business Week* (February 7, 1994): 32.

[24]R.M. Steers, *Organizational Effectiveness: A Behavioral View* (Santa Monica, Calif.: Goodyear, 1977), p. 21.

[25]R.M. Cyert and J.G. March, *A Behavioral Theory of the Firm* (Englewood Cliffs, N.J.: Prentice-Hall, 1963).

[26]H. Simon, *The New Science of Management Decision* (New York: Harper & Row, 1960).

[27]P.E. Connor, *Organizations: Theory and Design* (Chicago: Science Research Associates, 1980).

[28]R.E. Miles and C.C. Snow, *Organizational Strategy, Structure, and Process* (New York: McGraw-Hill, 1978).

[29]C.A. Bartlett and S. Ghoshal, *Managing Across Borders: The Transnational Solution* (Boston: Harvard Business School Press, 1989); C.A. Bartlett, Y. Doz, and G. Hedlund, *Managing the Global Firm* (London: Routledge & Kegan Paul, 1990).

[30]J.B. Levine, IBM Europe starts swinging back, *Business Week* (May 6, 1991): 52–53.

[31]See J. Child, Organizational structure, environment and performance: The role of strategic choice, *Sociology* 6 (1972): 1–22; D.S. Pugh, D.J. Hickson, C.R. Hinings, and C. Turner, The context of organizational structures, *Administrative Science Quarterly* 14 (1969): 91–114.

[32]D.J. Hickson, D.S. Pugh, and D. Pheysey, Operations technology and organization structure: An empirical reappraisal, *Administrative Science Quarterly* 14 (1969): 378–398.

[33]W. Zellner and R.D. Hof, How Goliaths can act like Davids, *Business Week* (Enterprise 1993): 192–201.

[34]Zellner and Hof, How Goliaths can act.

[35]See, for example, D. Lavoie and S.A. Culbert, Stages in organization and development, *Human Relations* 31 (1978): 417–438; I. Adizes, Organizational passages: Diagnosing and treating life cycle problems in organizations, *Organizational Dynamics* (Summer 1979): 3–24; L. Greiner, Evolution and revolution as organizations grow, *Harvard Business Review* (July–August 1972): 37–46.

[36]These steps parallel the four-stage business cycle: Startup, growth, maturity, and decline.

[37]J.M. Bartunek and B.M. Betters-Reed, The stages of organizational creation, *Journal of Community Psychology* 15(3) (1987): 287–303.

[38]N.C. Churchill and V.L. Lewis, The five stages of small business growth, *Harvard Business Review* (May–June, 1983).

[39]Greiner, Evolution and revolution; Adizes, Organizational passages.

[40]Churchill and Lewis, The five stages.

[41]R. Walton, Establishing and maintaining high commitment work systems. In J.R. Kimberly and R.H. Miles, eds, *The Organizational Life Cycle* (San Francisco: Jossey-Bass, 1980), pp. 208–291.

[42]D. Miller and P. Friesen, Archetypes of organizational transition, *Administrative Science Quarterly* 25 (1980): 269–299; D. Miller and P. Friesen, The longitudinal analysis of organizations: A methodological perspective, *Management Science* 28 (1982): 1013–1034; E.H. Schein, The role of the founder in creating organizational culture, *Organizational Dynamics* 12 (1983): 1–12.

[43]Churchill and Lewis, The five stages.

[44]Churchill and Lewis, The five stages.

[45]D. Greising, Home Depot, *Business Week* (February 13, 1995): 65.

[46]W. Zellner, Go-go goliaths, *Business Week* (February 13, 1995): 64–70.

[47]See D.A. Whetten, Sources, responses, and effects of organizational decline. In Kimberly and Miles, *The Organizational Life Cycle,* pp. 342–372.

[48]W. Weitzel and E. Johnson, Decline in organizations: A literature integration and extension, *Administrative Science Quarterly* 34 (1989): 91–109.

[49]K. Labich, Why companies fail, *Fortune* (November 14, 1994): 52–68.

[50]Weitzel and Johnson, Decline in organizations.

[51]Labich, Why companies fail.

[52]D.J. McConville, The upside of downsizing, *Industry Week* (May 17, 1993): 12–16.

[53]J.A. Byrne, The pain of downsizing, *Business Week* (May 9, 1994): 60–69.

[54]See R.K. Kazanjian, Relation of dominant problems to stages of growth in technology-based new ventures, *Academy of Management Journal* 31 (1988): 257–279.

CHAPTER 15

[1]S. Sherman, A master class in radical change, *Fortune* (December 13, 1993): 82–90; T.A. Stewart, Allied-Signal's turnaround blitz, *Fortune* (November 30, 1992): 72–76; A.L. Velocci, Jr., Turnaround earns Allied new credibility, *Aviation Week & Space Technology* (August 15, 1994): 38–41; S.F. Bovet, CEO serves as chief communicator of TQM program, *Public Relations Journal* 50(6) (June/July 1994): 16–17; N. Gilbert, CEO of the year: Larry Bossidy of Allied-Signal, *Financial World* (March 29, 1994): 44–52.

[2]W.L. French and C.H. Bell, Jr., *Organization Development: Behavioral Science Interventions for Organization Improvement,* 3rd ed. (Englewood Cliffs, N.J.: Prentice-Hall, 1984).

[3]D.A. Nadler and M.L. Tushman, Types of organizational change: From incremental improvement to discontinuous transformation. In D.A. Nadler, R.B. Shaw, A.E. Walton and Associates, *Discontinuous Change: Leading Organizational Transformation* (San Francisco: Jossey-Bass, 1995).

[4]T.A. Stewart, How to lead a revolution, *Fortune* (November 28, 1994); 48–61.

[5]M.L. Tushman, W.H. Newman, and E. Romanelli, Convergence and upheaval: Managing the unsteady pace of organizational evolution. In K.S. Cameron, R.E. Sutton, and D.A. Whetton, ed., *Readings in Organizational Decline: Framework, Research, and Prescriptions* (Cambridge, Mass.: Ballinger, 1988).

[6]See J.M. Bartunek and M.R. Louis, The interplay of organization development and organizational transformation. In W.A. Pasmore and R.W. Woodman, ed., *Research in Organizational Change and Development,* vol. 2 (Greenwich, Conn.: JAI, 1988); J.M. Bartunek, The dynamics of personal and organizational reframing. In R. Quinn and K. Cameron, ed., *Paradox and Transformation: Towards a Theory of Change in Organizations and Management* (Cambridge, Mass.: Ballinger, 1989).

[7]A master class in radical change, *Fortune* (December 13, 1993): 82–90.

[8]See C.J.G. Gersick, Revolutionary change theories: A multilevel exploration of the punctuated equilibrium paradigm, *Academy of Management Review* 16(1) (1991): 10–36; E. Romanelli and M.L. Tushman, Organizational transformation as punctuated equilibrium: An empirical test, *Academy of Management Journal* 37(5) (1994): 1141–1166.

[9]R.M. Kanter, *When Giants Learn to Dance* (New York: Simon & Schuster, 1989).

[10]Nadler and Tushman, Types of organizational change.

[11]W. French, Organization development—Objectives, assumptions, and strategies, *California Management Review* 12 (1969): 23–34.

[12]This technique is based on an early work in the field, K. Lewin, *Field Theory in Social Science* (New York: Harper & Row, 1951).

[13]K. Blanton, Giant Fleet-Shawmut deal will boost region, take toll, *The Boston Globe* (February 22, 1995): 1, 66; D.E. Lewis, Employees brace themselves for layoffs, *The Boston Globe* (February 22, 1995): 61, 66; Partners cite need to expand services, *The Boston Globe* (February 22, 1995): 61, 67.

[14]J. Huey, Managing in the midst of chaos, *Fortune* (April 15, 1993): 38–48.

[15]W.H. Wagel and H.Z. Levine, HR '90: Challenges and opportunities, *Personnel* (June 1990): 18–42.

[16]Wagel and Levine, HR '90.

[17]E.F. Hamilton, An empirical study of factors predicting change agents' effectiveness, *Journal of Applied Behavioral Science* 24(1) (1988): 37–59.

[18]B.S. Moskal, Don't shoot the consultants, *Industry Week* (October 19, 1992): 11–18.

[19]J. Huey, Managing in the midst of chaos.

[20]K. Albrecht, *Organization Development: A Total Systems Approach to Positive Change in Any Business Organization* (Englewood Cliffs, N.J.: Prentice-Hall, 1983).

[21]T.A. Stewart, How to lead a revolution.

[22]M.B. Miles and R.A. Schmuck, The nature of organization development. In *Organization Development in Schools,* ed. R.A. Schmuck and M.B. Miles (La Jolla, Calif.: University Associates, 1976).

[23]Miles and Schmuck, The nature of organization development.

[24]J.M. Bartunek and M. Moch, First-order, second-order, and third-order change and organizational development interventions, *Journal of Applied Behavioral Science* 23(4) (1987): 483–500; see also J.M. Bartunek, The multiple cognitions and conflicts associated with second order organizational change. In J.K. Murnigham, ed., *Social Psychology in Organizations: Advances in Theory and Research* (Englewood Cliffs, N.J.: Prentice-Hall, 1993), pp. 322–349.

[25]Bartunek, The multiple cognitions and conflicts.

[26]R.W. Bass and M.V. Mariono, Organization development in Italy, *Group and Organization Studies* 12(3) (1987): 245–256.

[27]W.L. French, A checklist for organizing and implementing an OD effort. In *Organization Development: Theory, Practice, and Research,* ed. W.L. French, C.H. Bell, Jr., and R.A. Zawacki (Dallas: Business Publications, 1978).

[28]T. Stevens, Sony, San Diego, *Industry Week* (October 17, 1994): 45–46.

[29]L.P. White and K.C. Wooten, Ethical dilemmas in various stages of organizational development, *Academy of Management Review* 8(2) (1983): 690–697.

[30]P. Srivastava and I.I. Mitroff, Strategic management of corporate crises, *Columbia Journal of World Business* 22 (Spring 1987): 5–12.

[31]D.S. Mileti and J.H. Sorenson, Determinants of organizational effectiveness in responding to low-probability catastrophic events, *Columbia Journal of World Business* 22(1) (1987): 13–21.

[32]P.M. Senge, The leader's new work: Building learning organizations, *Sloan Management Review* (Fall 1990): 7–23.

[33]K. Johnson, The new marching orders at Aetna, *The New York Times* (March 1, 1992): Sect. 3, 1, 6.

Recommended Readings

CHAPTER 1

Benveniste, G. *The Twenty-First Century Organization.* San Francisco: Jossey-Bass, 1994.

Denzin, N.K., and **Y.S. Lincoln,** ed. *Handbook of Qualitative Research.* Thousand Oaks, Calif.: Sage, 1994.

Leary, M.R. *Introduction to Behavioral Research Methods,* 2nd ed. Pacific Grove, Calif.: Brooks/Cole, 1995.

Pfeffer, J. *Competitive Advantage Through People: Unleashing the Power of the Work Force.* Boston: Harvard Business School, 1994.

Rosnow, R.L., and **R. Rosenthal.** *Beginning Behavioral Research: A Conceptual Primer.* New York: MacMillan, 1993.

CHAPTER 2

Ballesteros, S., ed. *Cognitive Approaches to Human Perception.* Hillsdale, N.J.: Erlbaum, 1994.

Jones, E.E. *Interpersonal Perception.* New York: W.H. Freeman, 1990.

Martinko, M., ed. *Attribution Theory: An Organizational Perspective.* Delray Beach, Fla: St. Lucie Press, 1994.

Masin, S.C., ed. *Foundations of Perceptual Theory.* New York: North-Holland, 1993.

Rachlin, H. *Introduction to Modern Behaviorism.* New York: W.H. Freeman, 1991.

Sims, H.P., Jr., and **Lorenzi, P.** *The New Leadership Paradigm: Social Learning and Cognition in Organizations.* Newbury Park, Calif.: Sage, 1992.

CHAPTER 3

Cox, T. *Cultural Diversity in Organizations: Theory, Research, and Practice.* San Francisco: Barrett-Koehler, 1993.

Cross, E.Y., Katz, J., Miller, F. and **Seashore, E.,** ed. *The Promise of Diversity.* Burr Ridge, Ill.: Irwin, 1994.

Fagenson, E.A. *Women in Management: Trends, Issues, and Challenges in Managerial Diversity.* Newbury Park, Calif.: Sage, 1993.

Hall, D.T., ed. *Career Development.* Brookfield, VT: Dartmouth, 1994.

Lerner, J.V. *Working Women and Their Families.* Thousand Oaks, Calif.: Sage, 1994.

Montross, D.H. and **Shinkman, C.J.,** ed. *Career Development: Theory and Practice.* Springfield, Ill.: C.C. Thomas, 1992.

Wrightsman, L.S. *Adult Personality Development: Theories and Concepts.* Thousand Oaks, Calif.: Sage, 1994.

CHAPTER 4

Kanungo, R.N. and **Mendonca, M.** *Work Motivation: Models for Developing Countries.* Thousand Oaks, Calif.: Sage, 1994.

Lawler, E.E. III. *Strategic Pay: Aligning Organizational Strategies and Pay Systems.* San Francisco: Jossey-Bass, 1990.

Locke, E.A. and **Latham, G.P.** *A Theory of Goal Setting and Task Performance.* Englewood Cliffs, N.J.: Prentice-Hall, 1990.

O'Neil, H.F. Jr. and **Drillings, M.** *Motivation: Theory and Research.* Hillsdale, N.J.: Erlbaum, 1994.

Weiner, B. *Human Motivation: Metaphors, Theories, and Research.* Newbury Park, Calif.: Sage, 1992.

Fisher, K. *Leading Self-Directed Work Teams.* New York: McGraw-Hill, 1993.

Katzenbach, J.R. *The Wisdom of Teams: Creating the High Performance Organization.* Boston: Harvard Business School Press, 1993.

Parker, G.M. *Cross-Functional Teams: Working with Allies, Enemies, and Other Strangers.* San Francisco: Jossey-Bass, 1994.

Tjosvold, D. and **Tjosvold, M.M.** *The Emerging Leader: Ways to a Stronger Team.* New York: Lexington Books, 1993.

Worchel, S., Wood, W., and **Simpson, J.A.** *Group Process and Productivity.* Newbury Park, Calif.: Sage, 1992.

Baron, R.S., Kerr, N.L., and **Miller, N.** *Group Process, Group Decision, Group Action.* Buckingham: Open University, 1992.

Bazerman, M. *Judgment in Managerial Decision-Making,* 3rd ed. New York: Wiley, 1994.

Klein, G.A. *Decision Making in Action: Models and Methods.* Norwood, N.J.: Ablex, 1993.

March, J.G. *A Primer on Decision Making: How Decisions Happen.* New York: Free Press, 1994.

Sims, R.R. *Ethics and Organizational Decision Making: A Call for Renewal.* Westport, Conn.: Quorum, 1994.

Zey, M. *Decision Making: Alternatives to Rational Choice Models.* Newbury Park, Calif.: Sage, 1992.

Fisher, D. *Communication in Organizations,* 2nd ed. Minneapolis: West, 1993.

Harris, T.E. *Applied Organizational Communication: Perspectives, Principles, and Pragmatics.* Hillsdale, N.J.: Erlbaum, 1993.

Heath, R.L. *Management of Corporate Communication: From Interpersonal Contacts to External Affairs.* Hillsdale, N.J.: Erlbaum, 1994.

Kovacic, B., ed. *New Approaches to Organizational Communication.* Albany: State University of New York, 1994.

Samovar, L.A. and **Porter, R.E.,** ed. *Intercultural Communication: A Reader.* Belmont, Calif.: Wadsworth, 1994.

Tannen, D. *Talking from 9 to 5: How Women's and Men's Conversational Styles Affect Who Gets Heard, Who Gets Credit, and What Gets Done at Work* (New York: William Morrow, 1994).

Bass, B.M. *Bass & Stogdill's Handbook of Leadership: Theory, Research, and Managerial Applications,* 3rd ed. New York: Free Press, 1990.

Chemers, M. and **Ayman, R.,** ed. *Leadership Theory and Research: Perspectives and Directions.* San Diego: Academic Press, 1993.

Rosenbach, W.E. and **Taylor, R.L.,** ed. *Contemporary Issues in Leadership,* 3rd ed. Boulder: Westview, 1993.

Sims, H.P., Jr., and **Lorenzi, P.** *The New Leadership Paradigm: Social Learning and Cognition in Organizations.* Newbury Park, Calif.: Sage, 1992.

Tjosvold, D. *The Emerging Leader: Ways to a Stronger Team.* New York: Lexington, 1993.

Fairholm, G.W. *Organizational Power Politics: Tactics in Organizational Leadership.* Westport, Conn: Praeger, 1993.

Frohman, A.L. *The Middle Management Challenge: Moving From Crises to Empowerment.* New York: McGraw-Hill, 1993.

Greenberg, J.S. *Comprehensive Stress Management,* 4th ed. Dubuque, Iowa: Brown & Benchmark, 1993.

Kolb, D.M. and Bartunek, J.M., ed. *Hidden Conflict in Organizations.* Newbury Park, Calif.: Sage, 1992.

Rahim, A., and Blum, A.A., ed. *Global Perspectives on Organizational Conflict.* Westport, Conn: Praeger, 1994.

CHAPTER 10

Bazerman, M.H., and Neale, M.A. *Negotiating Rationally.* New York: Free Press, 1992.

Fisher, R., and Ury, W. *Getting to Yes: Negotiating Agreement without Giving In,* 2nd ed. Boston: Houghton-Mifflin, 1991.

Foster, D.A. *Bargaining across Borders: How to Negotiate Business Successfully Anywhere in the World.* New York: McGraw-Hill, 1992.

Gudykunst, W.B. *Bridging Differences: Effective Intergroup Communication,* 2nd ed. Thousand Oaks, Calif.: Sage, 1994.

Johnson, R.A. *Negotiation Basics.* Newbury Park, Calif.: Sage, 1993.

Mead, R. *Cross-Cultural Management Communication.* New York: Wiley, 1990.

Taylor, D.M. *Theories of Intergroup Relations.* Westport, Conn.: Praeger, 1994.

CHAPTER 11

Creech, B. *The Five Pillars of TQM: How to Make Total Quality Management Work for You.* New York: Dutton, 1994.

Hodgetts, R.M. *Blueprints for Continuous Improvement: Lessons from the Baldrige Winners.* New York: American Management Association, 1993.

Kotter, J.P., and Heskett, J.C. *Corporate Culture and Performance.* New York: Free Press, 1992.

Martin, J. *Cultures in Organizations: Three Perspectives.* New York: Oxford University Press, 1992.

Schein, E.H. *Organizational Culture and Leadership,* 2nd ed. San Francisco: Jossey-Bass, 1992.

Trice, H.M., and Beyer, J.M. *The Cultures of Work Organizations.* Englewood Cliffs, N.J.: Prentice-Hall, 1993.

CHAPTER 12

Cozijnsen, A, and Vrakking, W., ed., *Handbook of Innovation Management.* Oxford: Blackwell Business, 1993.

Hammer, M., and Champy, J. *Reengineering the Corporation: A Manifesto for Business Revolution.* New York: Harper Business, 1993.

Herbig, P.A. *The Innovation Matrix: Culture and Structure Prerequisites to Innovation.* Westport, Conn.: Quorum, 1994.

Martin, M.J.C. *Managing Innovation and Entrepreneurship in Technology-Based Firms.* New York: Wiley, 1994.

Petrozzo, D.P., and Stepper, J.C. *Successful Reengineering.* New York: Van Nostrand Reinhold, 1994.

CHAPTER 13

Banner, D.K., and Gagné, T.E. *Designing Effective Organizations: Traditional & Transformational Views.* Thousand Oaks, Calif.: Sage, 1995.

Goldman, S.L., Nagel, R.N., and Preiss, R. *Agile Competitors and Vertical Organizations: Strategies for Enriching the Customer.* New York: Van Nostrand Reinhold, 1994.

Kilmann, R.H., Kilmann, I., and Associates. *Making Organizations Competitive: Enhancing Networks and Relationships Across Traditional Boundaries.* San Francisco: Jossey-Bass, 1991.

Kramer, R.J. *Organizing for Global Competitiveness: The Product Design.* New York: Conference Board, 1994.

Kramer, R.J. *Organizing for Global Competitiveness: The Geographic Design.* New York: Conference Board, 1993.

Worthy, J.C. *Lean But Not Mean: Studies in Organization Structure.* Urbana, Ill: University of Illinois, 1994.

CHAPTER 14

Cash, J.E., Jr. *Building the Information-Age Organization: Structure, Control, and Information Technologies.* Burr Ridge, Ill.: Irwin, 1994.

Galbraith, J. *Competing with Flexible Lateral Organizations.* Reading, Mass.: Addison-Wesley, 1994.

Huber, G.P., and Glick, W.H., ed. *Organizational Change and Redesign: Ideas and Insights for Improving Performance.* New York: Oxford University, 1993.

Rock, M.L., and Rock, R.H., ed. *Corporate Restructuring: A Guide to Creating the Premium Valued Company.* New York: McGraw-Hill, 1990.

Singh, J.V., ed. *Organizational Evolution: New Directions.* Newbury Park, Calif.: Sage, 1990.

CHAPTER 15

French, W.L., Bell, C.H., Jr., and Zawacki, R.A. *Organization Development and Transformation,* 4th ed. Burr Ridge, Ill.: Irwin, 1994.

Harrison, M.I. *Diagnosing Organizations: Methods, Models, and Processes,* 2nd ed. Thousand Oaks, Calif.: Sage, 1994.

Heckscher, C. and Donnellon, A., eds. *The Post-bureaucratic Organization: New Perspectives on Organization Change.* Thousand Oaks, Calif.: Sage, 1994.

Kanter, R.M., Stein, B.A., and Jick, T.D., ed. *The Challenge of Organizational Change: How Companies Experience It and Leaders Guide It.* New York: Free Press, 1992.

Nadler, D.A., Shaw, R.B., Walton, A.E., and Associates, ed. *Discontinuous Change: Leading Organizational Transformation.* San Francisco: Jossey-Bass, 1995.

Name Index

Knapp, M.L., 266*n*18
Knutson, T.J., 178
Kochan, T.A., 525*n*41
Koenig, R., Jr., 417*n*5
Kolb, D.M., 374*n*55, 426*n*19
Kolesar, P.J., 474*n*15
Kolind, Lars, 618
Kolodny, H., 625*n*21
Kopelman, R.E., 128*n*31
Kopp, D.G., 132*n*40
Kosnik, T.J., 535*n*78
Koss, Michael, 436
Kotter, J., 311*n*8, 360*nn*5, 8, 361*n*9, 471*n*3
Kowitz, A.C., 178
Kozlowski, 287*n*74
Krackhardt, D., 371*n*39
Kraemer, K.L., 237*n*65
Kram, K.E., 84*nn*43, 44, 85*n*50
Kraut, A.I., 315*n*20
Kreps, Gary L., 276, 281*n*59
Krishnan, R., 479*n*38, 486*n*61
Kriste, K.K., 275*n*43
Kumar, K., 189*n*59
Kun-Hee, Lee, 482–83

L

Laabs, J.J., 95*n*99
LaBarre, P., 619*n*1
Labich, K., 145*n*93, 634*nn*49, 51
Labis, K., 474*n*17
Labrecque, Thomas G., 481–82
Lach, D., 387*n*92
Lachman, R., 78*n*20, 368*n*33
LaFasto, F.M.J., 170*n*11, 173*n*31, 185*n*54
Lamm, H., 226*n*33
Landa, L., 44*n*34
Landy, F.J., 119*n*14, 121*n*15, 126*n*23
Lane, H.W., 620*n*4
LaPotin, P., 224*nn*24, 25
Larkin, K.C., 78*n*17
Larson, C.E., 170*n*11, 173*n*31, 185*n*54
Larson, J.R., 138*n*64
Larwood, L., 87*n*63
Latham, G.P., 80*n*31, 136*n*57, 137*nn*60, 62, 138*nn*63, 69
Laurent, A., 621*n*7
Lauzon, 260
Lavoie, D., 632*n*35
Lawler, E.E., III, 119*n*8, 135*n*51, 141*n*79, 142*n*83, 144*nn*88, 89, 171*n*20, 478*n*33, 523*n*34
Lawrence, H.V., 40*n*28
Lawrence, P., 14*n*23, 566*n*4
Lax, D.A., 427*n*21, 428*n*22, 431*n*30, 433*n*34
Laymon, Joseph, 428
Layne, R., 30*n*3
LeBlanc, P.V., 142*n*82
Ledford, G.E., Jr., 142*n*82

Lee, C., 78*n*17, 422*n*11
Lee, C.A., 368*n*33
Lee, R.T., 381*n*75
Lee, W.G., 474*n*17
LeFauve, R.G., 141*n*80
Lei, D., 140*n*75, 583*n*33
Leibowitz, B., 87*n*64
Lengel, R.H., 263*nn*6, 7, 8
Lent, R.W., 78*n*17
Leonard, D., 86*n*55
Lesly, E., 40*n*22, 90*nn*72, 73
Lester, T., 166*n*1, 564*n*1
Level, Dale A., Jr., 263
Leventhal, G.S., 128*n*26
Levine, H.Z., 17*n*33, 673*nn*15, 16
Levine, J.B., 630*n*30
Lewicki, R.J., 128*n*29
Lewin, K., 10–11, 667, 668*n*12
Lewis, D.E., 15*n*25, 669*n*13
Lewis, P.V., 272*n*33, 273*n*39, 276*n*45
Lewis, V.L., 632*nn*38, 40, 633*nn*43, 44
Lichtensetin, S., 230*n*43
Liden, R.C., 138*n*64, 329*n*46
Likert, J., 426*n*20
Likert, R., 313*n*15, 426*n*20
Linstone, H.A., 237*nn*63, 66
Little, K., 85*n*54
Liu, M., 625*n*21
Lloyd, R.F., 171*n*21
Locke, E.A., 8*n*6, 11*n*16, 78*n*17, 80*n*31, 125*n*20, 137*nn*59, 60, 62, 138*nn*65, 69, 311*nn*4, 6
Lockwood, D.L., 314*n*17
Lombardo, M.M., 312*n*9
London, M., 524, 672
Loomis, C.J., 16*n*32, 335*n*76
Lord, R.G., 41*n*30
Lorelli, Michael K., 85
Lorenzi, P., 30*n*4, 33*n*7
Lorsch, J., 14*n*23, 566*n*4
Louis, M.R., 471*n*6, 472*n*9, 666*n*6
Lubin, B., 172*n*28
Lublin, J.S., 170*n*12
Lueder, D.C., 326*n*39, 328*n*43
Luft, Joseph, 282
Lustgarten, N., 137*n*59
Luthans, F., 44*n*35, 314*n*17, 329*n*49, 471*n*6
Lwein, K., 11*n*13

M

McCall, M.W., Jr., 312*n*9
McCann, J.E., 417*n*2, 535*n*79
McClaine, 287*n*75
McClelland, C.L., 514*n*5, 515*nn*6, 7
McClelland, D.C., 115, 121–24, 363*n*14
McClenahen, J.S., 214*n*2
McConville, D.J., 425*n*16, 436*n*39, 635*n*52
McDaniel, R.R., Jr., 235*n*59
McDonald, G.M., 215*n*5

MacDonald, S., 274*n*41
McElroy, J.C., 330*n*51, 331*n*54
McGill, M.E., 479*n*41, 480*n*42
McGregor, D., 11*nn*18, 19, 317*n*21, 337
Machan, D., 332*n*62
Machiavelli, Niccolo di Bernardo, 77
MacKay, Michael, 533
McKeen, C.A., 84*n*46
McKenna, D.D., 315*n*20
McKenna, J.F., 328*n*42, 365*n*22
McKenna, J.T., 431*n*26
McKenzie, C.L., 267*n*19
MacMillan, I.C., 334*n*67
McWilliams, G., 626*n*23
Macy, B.A., 634
Maddox, R.C., 283*n*68
Mahler, J.G., 236*n*62
Main, J., 171*n*17, 478*n*30
Mainiero, L.A., 365*n*20
Maljers, F.A., 564*n*1
Mallory, M., 90*n*72
Mandel, M.J., 93*n*93
Mann, L., 233*n*50
Manz, C.C., 33*n*9, 166*n*1, 167*n*4, 335*nn*79, 80, 336*n*81
March, J.G., 11, 216*n*8, 222*n*17, 223*n*23, 627*n*25
Marcus, H.S., 16*n*31, 80*n*30
Mares, W., 525*n*40
Margolis, N., 333*n*63
Marguis, D.G., 532
Mariono, M.V., 677*n*26
Markovsky, B., 363*n*11
Marks, A.S., 77*n*12
Markus, M.L., 279*n*55
Marquis, D.G., 531*n*65
Marshall-Chapman, Paula, 328
Marsick, V.J., 480*n*45, 486*n*62
Martin, H.J., 80*n*32
Martin, J., 133*n*47, 472*n*9
Martinko, M., 330*n*52
Maslow, A.H., 115*n*2, 121, 145
Mason, J.C., 89*n*68
Mason, R.O., 229*n*39
Mastenbroek, W.F.G., 360*n*6
Masuch, M., 224*nn*24, 25
Matejka, J.K., 221*n*13
Mathieu, J.E., 376*n*59
Maucher, Helmut, 571
Mausner, B., 124*n*19
Mellers, B.A., 127*n*24
Mendenhall, M., 387*n*89
Merry, U., 185*n*51
Meyer, J.P., 83*n*40
Meyers, G.W., 171*n*21
Michael, C., 83*n*40
Michaels, J.W., 16*n*32
Michaelsen, L.K., 189*n*59, 226*n*36
Michela, J.L., 40*n*26
Mikhail, A., 380*n*70

Witten, M.G., 272*n*36
Wofford, Ted, 212
Wolfe, D.M., 376*n*59
Wolfe, R.A., 535*n*80
Wolsapple, C.W., 238*n*69
Wood, Robert E., 217*n*9, 330
Woodruff, D., 2*n*1, 171*n*19, 484*n*56
Woodward, J., 14*n*23, 519*n*15, 623*n*14
Wooten, K.C., 678*n*29
Woudhuysen, J., 529*n*54
Wrebe, F.A., 523*n*31
Wright, D.W., 179*n*42

Y

Yang, D.J., 171*n*17
Yasai-Ardekani, M., 623*n*11

Yates, J.F., 80*n*29
Yates, R.E., 529*n*52
Yetton, P.W., 226*n*34, 323*n*35, 324, 325*n*37
Yokich, Steve, 2
Young, A.O., 34*n*12
Young, Andrew, 369
Young, J.S., 333*n*63
Youtz, M.A., 226*n*30
Yukl, G.A., 138*n*63, 311*n*7, 320*nn*27, 28, 29, 322*nn*33, 34, 329*nn*47, 48, 373

Z

Zajonc, R.B., 80*n*30
Zautra, A., 515*n*10
Zeffane, R., 80*n*34

Zellner, W., 431*n*26, 630*n*33, 631*n*34, 633*n*46
Zemke, R., 76*n*7
Zenger, J.H., 167*nn*2, 6, 170*n*13
Zepp, R.A., 215*n*5
Zidon, I., 138*n*67
Zinn, L., 310*n*3
Zipser, A., 16*n*31

Subject Index

Decoding of message, 263–64
Deep structures, 666
Defenders, 629, 672
Delegating style of leadership, 326, 327
Dell Computers, 585
Delphi technique, 237
Delta Airlines, 620
Delta Manufacturing, 212
Demographics, workplace, 89–92
    gender, 90–91
    older workers, 91
    physically-challenged employees, 92
    race, 89–90
    two-career families, 91–92
Demonstrators, 672
Denotations, 265
Dependence, power and, 360–62
Dependent variable, 4–5
Depth of intervention, 676–77
Derivative innovation, 530
Description of feelings, 269
Description phase, 18–19
Design. See Organizational designs; Work
    design
Devil's advocate approach, 225
Diagnostic approach, 18–22
    action phase of, 19, 22
    description phase of, 18–19
    diagnosis phase of, 19–21
    prescription phase of, 19, 21–22
Diagonal conflict, 378
Diet, stress and, 385
Differentiation, types and degrees of,
    566–68
Diffusion of innovation, 530
Digital Equipment Corporation, 579, 626
Directive style, 229–30, 320
Direct observation, 4
Direct supervision, 569
Disaggregation, vertical, 585
Discretionary systems, 520
Disseminator role, 315
Dissonance, cognitive, 80
Distinctiveness, attribution and, 39
Distortions
    in downward communication, 272
    in perception, 34–38
        dealing with, 36–37
        halo effect, 35
        projection, 35–36
        self-fulfilling prophecy, 36
        stereotyping, 34–35
Distributive bargaining, 428
Disturbance handler role, 315
Diverse workforce. See Work-force
    diversity
Divide-and-conquer negotiator, 437
Divisionalized structure, 577
Division of labor, 566–68
Doc-It, 15

Documents, data collection from, 4
Double-loop (generative) organizations,
    479–80
Downsizing, 87, 167, 635
Downward communication, 271–72
Drexel, 16
Driving forces, 668
Drug companies, 583
Dual-career families, 91–92
Dual ladders, 86
Dynamic networks, 584–86
Dysfunctional outcomes of conflicts, 375

E

E.I. DuPont, 484
Early career, 83
    full membership in, 85
Eastman Chemical Company, 479
Eastman Kodak, 666–67
Eaton Corporation, 129
Economic environment, 619
Economies of scale, 433
Educational programs, change and, 674
Educational Toys, Inc., 156
Edy's Grand Ice Cream, 168
Elaboration stage, 632, 633
Electronic communication, 279–81
Electronic Data Systems, 321
Elegant Interiors, 28
Emery Air Freight, 132
Emotional responses to demands of task,
    178
Employee(s)
    ingroup and outgroup, 329
    involvement in decision making, 674–75
    older, 91
    ownership by, 144–45
    physically challenged, 92
    self-leadership by, 335–36
    trust between managers and, 168
Employment, part-time, 521–22
Empowerment, 363–66
    performance and, 365–66
    self-management teams and, 365
    TQM and, 478–79
Empty nest, career and, 88–89
Encoding of message, 261, 262, 264
Engineering technology, 624–25
Engineers, industrial, 514
Enrichment, job, 515–19
Entrepreneuring, 534
Entrepreneurs, 315, 316, 573
Entrepreneur stage, 632
Entry stage of career, 83
Environment, 619–23
    components of, 619–21
    global, 46–47
    matching structure to, 621–23
Equal employment laws, 17

Equifinality, 13
Equilibrium, 13, 666
Equity sensitivity, 128
Equity theory, 125–29
    equity equation, 125–27
    evaluation of, 128–29
    responses to perceived inequity,
        127–28
ERG theory, 119–21
Esteem needs, 117, 118
Ethical action, 16
Ethical issues
    in decisions, 214–15
    in implementation of change, 678, 679
Ethical justness, 214
Ethnocentrism, cultural, 73
Exchange, power as, 363
Exchange tactics, 373
Exchange theory, 328–29
Exemplars, 33
Exercise, to reduce stress, 384
Exhaustion, from stress, 381
Existence, organizational, 632
Existence needs, 119, 120
Expectancy theory, 133–36
    evaluation of, 136
    integrated formulation of, 135–36
    intrinsic-extrinsic motivation formulation
        of, 136
    original formulation of, 134–35
Experiments, laboratory, 5
Expertise, 368
    group decision making and, 226
Expert manager, 316
Expert systems, 529
Exposure by mentor, 84
Externalizers, 74–75
Extinction, 130
Extrinsic rewards, 141
Extrovert, 76
Exxon, 16
Exxon Chemical, 93

F

Facilitator, interpersonal, 426
Fait accompli, 436
Families, dual-career, 91–92
Family-friendly organizations, 92
Family issues, 87–89
Family Leave Act, 91
Federal Express, 86
Feedback, 264–65
    job enrichment through, 516
    opening channels for, 517
    survey, 677
    systems model of, 13
    360-degree, 287
Feedback questionnaire, 286
Feeling personality, 76

Feelings, 79
  description of, 269
Felt conflict, 380
Ferro Corporation, 674
Fiat, 168
Field studies, 5
Figure-ground, 32
Figurehead, 315
Fixed reinforcers, 131
Fleet Bank, 625
Fleet Financial Group, 668–69
Flexible benefits plans, 143
Flexible hours, 520–21
Flexible spending accounts, 143
Flextime, 520
Flexyear, 521
Focus, differences in, 421
Force field analysis, 667–68
Ford Motor Company
  communication at, 262
  horizontal organization, 580
  learning programs at, 46
  Pinto troubles, 34
  race issues at, 90
  transformational leadership at, 334
Forecasts, joint gains from, 432
Formal communication, 275–77
Formal goals, 172
Formal groups, 170
Formalization stage, 632, 633
Forming, 177–78
Frames, 231, 666
  of reference, 262
Frankfurt Declaration, 483
Frequency of reinforcement, 131
Friendship with mentor, 84
Frustration, 120
Full-disclosure information systems, 586
Full membership in early career, 85
Functional outcomes of conflicts, 375
Functional roles, 179
Functional structures, 572–74

G

Gain-sharing programs, 144
Garbage can model of decision making, 223–24
Gatekeepers, 274
Gatekeeping, 534
Gender, 90–91
  communication and, 266
General Electric, 179, 260, 337, 580
General Mills, 332, 582–83
General Motors, 2, 19–20, 46, 141, 523–24
Generative (double-loop) organizations, 479–80
Generators of change, 671, 672
Gerber Products, 83
Gestalt, 45

Gillette, 95
Glass ceiling, 90
Global competitiveness
  in automobile industry, 15
  organizational structures designed for, 587
Global environment, 46–47
Global management, 629
Goal displacement, 627
Goals
  defined, 626
  diversity of, 627
  formal, 172
  incompatibility of, 627
  informal, 172–73
  organizational design and, 626–28
  specificity or clarity of, 137
  work group formation and, 169
  of work groups, 172–73
Goal-setting theory, 136–39
  evaluation of, 138–39
  goal characteristics, 137–38
Granite Roc Company, 137
Grapevine, 276–77
Grievance procedures, 387
Group decision making, 225–28
Group dynamics, 10–11
Groupe Bull, 189
Group process, 177
Groups. See also Work groups
  communication and, 260
  conflicts in, 378
  informal, 170
  special, 426–27
  target, 676
Groupthink, 231–34
Groupware, 238, 280
Growth needs, 118, 119, 120
GS Technologies, 481
GTE, 527–28

H

Habitual routines, 180
Hallmark Cards, 419
Halo effect, 35
Harley-Davidson, 314
Hawthorne effect, 10
Health protectors, 143
Herman Miller Co., 283
Heroes and heroines, organizational, 474
Heuristics, 216, 230
Hewlett-Packard, 224–25, 675
Hidden agendas, 173
Hierarchy of needs, 115–19
Hindsight, 232
Hired hands, 329
Hitachi, 626
Home Depot, 633
Home Shopping Network, 91

Honeywell, 94
Horizontal conflict, 378
Horizontal differentiation, 566–68
Horizontal organizations, 580, 581
Hourly wages, 141
Human relations school, 10
Hygiene factors, 124
Hypothesis, 4

I

IBM, 92, 267, 471, 479, 576
IBM Europe, 630
Idea generating, 534
Illegitimate-legitimate dimension of power, 367, 369
Images, 223
Implementors of change, 671, 672
Improshare, 144
Incentives, 143–44
Income protectors, 143
Income supplements, 143
Incremental innovation, 530–31
Independent variable, 5
Individual decision making, 225–28
Individual roles, 175
Industrial engineers, 514
Influence
  directions of, 360
  nature of, 359–60
  tactics used to exert, 373
Informal communication, 275–77
Informal goals, 172–73
Informal groups, 170
Informal networks, 370–72
Informal organizations, 571–72
Information-based power, 369–70
Information overload, 269
Information processing, 314, 570
Information technology, 16
  work design and, 525–30
    information systems, 525, 526–27
    reengineering work, 527–30
Information underload, 269
Informing strategy, 185
Infosys, 168
Ingratiating tactics, 373
Ingroup, 329
Initiating structure, 312
Innovation, 530–35
  process of, 531–32
  roles and functions in, 533–35
Inputs, system, 12
Inquiry into the Nature and Cause of the Wealth of Nations, An (Smith), 6
Insider, 316
Inspirational appeals, 373
Institutional change, 680–81
Instrumentality, 134
Integrated structures, 577–79

Integration of innovation, 530
Integrative bargaining, 428
Integrative perspective, 7, 11–14
Integrator, cultural, 283
Intel, 264
Intensive technology, 624
Interdependence, group, 417–20
    pooled, 418–19
    reciprocal, 418, 419
    sequential, 418, 419
    team, 418, 419–20
Interests, work group formation and, 169
Interface conflict solver, 426
Intergroup relations, 414–67
    factors affecting, 420–24
        cross-cultural differences, 424
        perceptual differences, 420–22
        power differences, 422–23
        task relations, 423–24
    importance of, 416–17
    improving, 424–27
        interpersonal techniques, 424–26
        structural mechanisms, 426–27
    negotiation, 427–38
        cross-cultural issues in, 437–38
        defined, 427
        negotiator types, 436–37
        paradigms of, 428
        steps in, 429–33
        strategies, 434–36
        tactics, 436
    types of interdependence, 417–20
        pooled interdependence, 418–19
        reciprocal interdependence, 418, 419
        sequential interdependence, 418, 419
        team interdependence, 418, 419–20
Internal-external dimension of power, 369
Internalizers, 74–75
Internal states, attending to sensations
        according to, 21
International management, 629
International Paper Company, 432
International Trainee Program, 95
Interpersonal conflict, 378
Interpersonal contact, 314
Interpersonal effectiveness, 18
Interpersonal facilitator, 426
Interpersonal interactions
    as communication barrier, 277–78
    improving, 281–83
    organizational culture and, 471
Interpersonal skills, 228
Interpersonal techniques, intergroup
        relations and, 424–26
Interrogator (negotiator type), 437
Interrole conflict, 377
Intersender role conflict, 377
Intervention, depth of, 676–77
Interviews, 4
    placement, 284–85

Intragroup conflict, 178–79
Intrasender role conflict, 377
Intrinsic rewards, 140–41
Introvert, 76
Intuitive decision making, 223
Intuitive personality, 76
Inventories, 73
"I Recommend" program, 139–40
ITT Sheraton, 529

J

Japan, innovation process in, 532
Jargon, 265–66
Job-based pay, 142
Job characteristics model of enrichment,
    515–16, 517
Job design. *See* Work design
Job enlargement, 514–15
Job enrichment, 515–19
Job extension, 515
Job loading, vertical, 517
Job rotation, 515
Job satisfaction, 80
Job sharing, 522
Job splitting, 522
Job types, managerial, 316
Johari Window, 282
John Deere, 364
Johnson Controls, 531
Johnson & Johnson, 89, 92, 214–15, 475,
    574
Joint gains in negotiations, 429, 431–32
Joint ventures, 580–84
Judgment personality, 76
Justice, organizational, 128
Justness, ethical, 214

K

Kaiser Permanente, 423
Kaizen, 477
Kao Corporation, 529
Keiretsu, 583–84
Kepner-Tregoe, 425
KinderCare, 477
Knowledge technology, 624–25
Kolmar Laboratories, 522
Koss Corporation, 436

L

L.L. Bean, 478
L.M. Ericsson, 578
Labor, division of, 566–68
Laboratory experiments, 5
Labor-management relations, self-managed
        work teams and, 168
Landamatics, 43–44
Language, 265–66

Latent conflict, 379–80
Lateral communication, 274–75
Leader-centered teams, 182
Leader-member relations, 318, 320
Leader role, 315
Leadership, 11, 308–55
    behavioral theories of, 312–16
        managerial roles, 314–16
        task- and employee-oriented
            behaviors, 312–14
    of communication network, 177
    of multicultural work force, 336–37
    nonsituational theories of, 328–32
        attributional theory, 330–31
        exchange theory, 328–29
        operant conditioning theory, 329–30
    participative, 313
    situational theories of, 316–28
        cognitive resource theory, 319–20
        Least-Preferred Coworker (LPC)
            scale, 318–19, 320
        life cycle theory, 325–28
        participation theory, 323–25
        path-goal theory, 320–23
        Theory X and Theory Y, 317–18
    skills, 228, 311
    substitutes for, 331–32
    superleadership, 335–36
    TQM and, 479
    trait theory of, 311–12, 314
    transactional, 332–33
    transformational, 332–35
Leadership Effectiveness and Description
    (LEAD), 328
Learning, 42–47
    behaviorist approach to, 42–43
    change and, 680
    cognitive approach to, 43–44
    defined, 29, 42
    in global environment, 46–47
    managerial implications of, 45–46
    social learning approach to, 44–45
    team, 487
Learning organizations, 479–81
    creating, 486–87
Least-Preferred Coworker (LPC) scale,
    318–19, 320
Legal/political environment, 620
Legitimate-illegitimate dimension of
    power, 367, 369
Leslie Fay Companies, 40
Levi Strauss, 73, 263
Liaison devices, ad hoc or temporary, 578
Liaison role, 315
Licensing, 582
Life cycle, organizational, 630–35
    design responses, 635
    downsizing, 635
    organizational size and age, 630–31
    stages, 632–35